Biblical HERMEN-EUTICS

*A Treatise on the Interpretation
of the Old and New Testaments*

Milton S. Terry

ZONDERVAN
PUBLISHING HOUSE
OF THE ZONDERVAN CORPORATION
GRAND RAPIDS, MICHIGAN 49506

First printing of flexible edition   1974
Seventh printing   1979
ISBN 0-310-36831-6

Printed in the United States of America

PREFACE TO THE SECOND EDITION.

THE cordial welcome with which the first edition of this work has been received is evidence that a treatise of its character and scope is needed in our theological literature. The plan of the volume was largely suggested by what appear to be the practical wants of most theological students. Specialists in exegetical learning will push their way through all difficulties, and find delight in testing principles; but the ordinary student, if led at all into long-continued and successful searching of the Scriptures, must become interested in the practical work of exposition. The bare enunciation of principles, with brief references to texts in which they are exemplified, is too dry and taxing to the mind to develop a taste for exegetical study; it has a tendency rather to repel. In arranging the plan of the present treatise, it was accordingly designed from the outset to make it to a noticeable extent a *thesaurus of interpretation*. The statement of principles is introduced gradually, and abundantly illustrated and verified by means of those difficult parts of Scripture in the real meaning of which most readers of the Bible are supposed to be interested. It cannot be expected that all our interpretations will command unqualified approval, but our choice of the more difficult Scriptures for examples of exposition will enhance the value of the work, and save it from the danger, too common in such treatises, of running into lifeless platitudes. With ample illustrations of this kind before him, the student comes by a natural process to grasp hermeneutical principles, and learns by practice and example rather than by abstract precept.

In order to make the work a complete manual for exegetical study, we have in Part First, under the head of INTRODUCTION TO BIBLICAL HERMENEUTICS, a comparative estimate of other sacred books, an outline of the character and structure of the biblical languages, and two brief chapters on Textual Criticism and Inspiration. These topics are so connected with biblical interpretation, and some of them, especially a knowledge of the sacred tongues, lie so essentially at its basis, that our plan called for some such treatment as we have given them. The latest movements in the Higher Criticism approach the study of the Scriptures with the assumption that our sacred books and also the religion of Israel are nothing more than the sacred books and religions of other nations (Kuenen, Religion of Israel, Eng. trans., vol. i, p. 5). The chapter on the sacred books of the nations exhibits the fallacy of such assumptions, and furnishes information which, being stored in many costly volumes, it is difficult to acquire.

It should be observed, further, that Part Third is not a history of *Hermeneutics*, but of *Interpretation*. It is designed to be supplementary in its character, and somewhat of the nature of a bibliography of exegetics. The different methods of interpretation which have obtained currency or note are presented under the head of Principles (Part Second, chap. ii), but we have attempted no genetic history of Hermeneutics. In fact, no extended genetic development of hermeneutical principles is traceable in history. We find excellent examples of exegesis in the early Church, and execrable specimens of mystical and allegorical exposition put forth in modern times. History shows no succession of schools of interpretation, except in recent controversies, and these appear in connection with the varying methods of rationalistic assault, narrated in our chapters on the exegesis of the eighteenth and nineteenth centuries.

CONTENTS

AND

ANALYTICAL OUTLINE.

PART FIRST.

INTRODUCTION TO BIBLICAL HERMENEUTICS.

CONTENTS AND ANALYTICAL OUTLINE.

PART SECOND.

PRINCIPLES OF BIBLICAL HERMENEUTICS.

10   CONTENTS AND ANALYTICAL OUTLINE.

PART THIRD.

HISTORY OF BIBLICAL INTERPRETATION.

PART FIRST.

INTRODUCTION TO BIBLICAL HERMENEUTICS.

It were indeed meet for us not at all to require the aid of the written Word, but to exhibit a life so pure that the grace of the Spirit should be instead of books to our souls, and that as these are inscribed with ink, even so should our hearts be with the Spirit. But, since we have utterly put away from us this grace, come, let us at any rate embrace the second-best course. For if it be a blame to stand in need of written words, and not to have brought down on ourselves the grace of the Spirit, consider how heavy the charge of not choosing to profit even after this assistance, but rather treating what is written with neglect, as if it were cast forth without purpose, and at random, and so bringing down upon ourselves our punishment with increase. But that no such effect may ensue, let us give strict heed unto the things that are written; and let us learn how the Old Law was given on the one hand, and how, on the other, the New Covenant.— CHRYSOSTOM.

INTRODUCTION

TO

BIBLICAL HERMENEUTICS.

CHAPTER I.

PRELIMINARY.

HERMENEUTICS is the science of interpretation. The word is usually applied to the explanation of written documents, and may therefore be more specifically defined as the science of interpreting an author's language.[1] This science assumes that there are divers modes of thought and ambiguities of expression among men, and, accordingly, it aims to remove the supposable differences between a writer and his readers, so that the meaning of the one may be truly and accurately apprehended by the others.

Hermeneutics defined.

It is common to distinguish between General and Special Hermeneutics. General Hermeneutics is devoted to the general principles which are applicable to the interpretation of all languages and writing. It may appropriately take cognizance of the logical operations of the human mind, and the philosophy of human speech. Special Hermeneutics is devoted rather to the explanation of particular books and classes of writings. Thus, historical, poetical, philosophical, and prophetical writings differ from each other in numerous particulars, and each class requires for its proper exposition the application of principles and methods adapted to its own peculiar character and style. Special Hermeneutics, according to Cellérier, is a science practical and almost empirical, and searches after rules and solutions; while General Hermeneutics is methodical and philosophical, and searches for principles and methods.[2]

General and Special Hermeneutics.

---

[1] The word *hermeneutics* is of Greek origin, from ἑρμηνεύω, to *interpret*, to *explain*; thence the adjective ἡ ἑρμηνευτική (sc. τέχνη), that is, the *hermeneutical art*, and thence our word *hermeneutics*, the science or art of interpretation. Closely kindred is also the name Ἑρμῆς, Hermes, or Mercury, who, bearing a golden rod of magic power, figures in Grecian mythology as the messenger of the gods, the tutelary deity of speech, of writing, of arts and sciences, and of all skill and accomplishments.

[2] Manuel d'Herméneutique Biblique, p. 5. Geneva, 1852.

Biblical or Sacred Hermeneutics is the science of interpreting
the Holy Scriptures of the Old and New Testaments.
Inasmuch as these two Testaments differ in form, language, and historical conditions, many writers have
deemed it preferable to treat the hermeneutics of each Testament
separately. And as the New Testament is the later and fuller revelation, its interpretation has received the fuller and more frequent
attention.[1] But it may be questioned whether such a separate
treatment of the Old and New Testaments is the better course. It
is of the first importance to observe that, from a Christian point of view, the Old Testament cannot be fully
apprehended without the help of the New. The mystery of Christ, which in other generations was not made
known unto men, was revealed unto the apostles and prophets of
the New Testament (Eph. iii, 5), and that revelation sheds a flood
of light upon numerous portions of the Hebrew Scriptures. On the
other hand, it is equally true that a scientific interpretation of the
New Testament is impossible without a thorough knowledge of the
older Scriptures. The very language of the New Testament, though
belonging to another family of human tongues, is notably Hebraic.
The style, diction, and spirit of many parts of the Greek Testament
cannot be properly appreciated without acquaintance with the style
and spirit of the Hebrew prophets. The Old Testament also abounds
in testimony of the Christ (Luke xxiv, 27, 44; John v, 39; Acts
x, 43), the illustration and fulfillment of which can be seen only in
the light of the Christian revelation. In short, the whole Bible is
a divinely constructed unity, and there is danger that, in studying
one part to the comparative neglect of the other, we may fall into
one-sided and erroneous methods of exposition. The Holy Scrip-

Marginal notes:
Biblical or Sacred Hermeneutics.

Old and New Test. Hermeneutics should not be separated.

[1] Among the more important modern works on the hermeneutics of the New Testament are: Ernesti, Institutio Interpretis Novi Testamenti (Lips., 1761), translated into
English by M. Stuart (Andover, 1827), and Terrot (Edin., 1843); Klausen, Hermeneutik des neuen Testamentes (Lpz., 1841); Wilke, Die Hermeneutik des neuen Tes-
lamentes systematisch dargestellt (Lpz., 1843); Doedes, Manual of Hermeneutics for
the Writings of the New Testament, translated from the Dutch by Stegmann (Edin.,
1867); Fairbairn, Hermeneutical Manual of the New Testament (Phila., 1859); Immer, Hermeneutics of the New Testament, translated from the German by A. H. Newman (Andover, 1877). The principal treatises on Old Testament hermeneutics are:
Meyer, Versuch einer Hermeneutik des alten Testaments (1799); Pareau, Institutic
Interpretis Veteris Testamenti (1822), translated by Forbes for the Edinburgh Biblical
Cabinet. The hermeneutics of both Testaments is treated by Seiler, Biblical Hermeneutics, or the Art of Scripture Interpretation, translated from the German by
Wright (Lond., 1835); Davidson, Sacred Hermeneutics (Edin., 1843), Cellérier's Manual, mentioned above, recently translated into English by Elliott and Harsha (N. Y.,
1881), and Lange, Grundriss der biblischen Hermeneutik (Heidelb., 1878).

tures should be studied as a whole, for their several parts were given in manifold portions and modes (πολυμερῶς καὶ πολυτρόπως, Heb. i, 1), and, taken all together, they constitute a remarkably self-interpreting volume.

Biblical Hermeneutics, having a specific field of its own, should be carefully distinguished from other branches of theo- Distinguished logical science with which it is often and quite naturally from Introduction, Criticism, associated. It is to be distinguished from Biblical In- and Exegesis. troduction, Textual Criticism, and Exegesis. Biblical Introduction, or Isagogics, is devoted to the historico-critical examination of the different books of the Bible. It inquires after their age, authorship, genuineness, and canonical authority, tracing at the same time their origin, preservation, and integrity, and exhibiting their contents, relative rank, and general character and value. The scientific treatment of these several subjects is often called the "Higher Criticism." Textual Criticism has for its special object Textual Criticism. the ascertaining of the exact words of the original texts of the sacred books. Its method of procedure is to collate and compare ancient manuscripts, ancient versions, and ancient scripture quotations, and, by careful and discriminating judgment, sift conflicting testimony, weigh the evidences of all kinds, and thus endeavour to determine the true reading of every doubtful text. This science is often called the "Lower Criticism." Where such criticism ends, Hermeneutics properly begins, and aims to establish the principles, methods, and rules which are needful to unfold the sense of what is written. Its object is to elucidate whatever may be obscure or ill-defined, so that every reader may be able, by an intelligent process, to obtain the exact ideas intended by the author. Exegesis is the application of these principles and laws, Exegesis and Exposition. the actual bringing out into formal statement, and by other terms, the meaning of the author's words. Exegesis is related to hermeneutics as preaching is to homiletics, or, in general, as practice is to theory. Exposition is another word often used synonymously with exegesis, and has essentially the same signification; and yet, perhaps, in common usage, exposition denotes a more extended development and illustration of the sense, dealing more largely with other scriptures by comparison and contrast. We observe, accordingly, that the writer on Biblical Introduction examines the historical foundations and canonical authority of the books of Scripture. The textual critic detects interpolations, emends false readings, and aims to give us the very words which the sacred writers used. The exegete takes up these words, and by means of the principles of hermeneutics, defines their meaning, elucidates the scope and plan of each writer, and brings forth the grammatico-historical sense of what each book contains. The expositor builds upon the labours both of critics and exegetes, and sets forth in fuller form, and by ample illustration, the ideas, doctrines, and moral lessons of the Scripture.[1]

But while we are careful to distinguish hermeneutics from these kindred branches of exegetical theology, we should not fail to note that a science of interpretation must essentially depend on exegesis for the maintenance and illustration of its principles and rules. As the full grammar of a language establishes its principles by sufficient examples and by formal praxis, so a science of hermeneutics must needs verify and illustrate its principles by examples of their practical application. Its province is not merely to define principles and methods, but also to exemplify and illustrate them. Herme-

Hermeneutics both a Science and an Art. neutics, therefore, is both a science and an art. As a science, it enunciates principles, investigates the laws of thought and language, and classifies its facts and results. As an art, it teaches what application these principles should have, and establishes their soundness by showing their practical value in the elucidation of the more difficult scriptures. The hermeneutical art thus cultivates and establishes a valid exegetical procedure.

Necessity of Hermeneutics. The necessity of a science of interpretation is apparent from the diversities of mind and culture among men. Personal intercourse between individuals of the same nation and language is often difficult and embarrassing by reason of their different styles of thought and expression. Even the Apostle Peter found in Paul's epistles things which were difficult to understand (δυσνόητα, 2 Pet. iii, 16). The man of broad and liberal culture lives and moves in a different world from the unlettered peasant, so much so that sometimes the ordinary conversation of the one is scarcely intelligible to the other. Different schools of metaphysics and opposing systems of theology have often led their several advocates into strange misunderstandings. The speculative philosopher, who ponders long on abstract themes, and by deep study

[1] Doedes thus discriminates between explaining and interpreting: "To explain, properly signifies the unfolding of what is contained in the words, and to interpret, the making clear of what is not clear by casting light on that which is obscure. Very often one interprets by means of explaining, namely, when, by unfolding the sense of the words, light is reflected on what is said or written; but it cannot be said that one explains by interpreting. While explaining generally is interpreting, interpreting, properly speaking, is not explaining. But we do not usually observe this distinction in making use of these terms, and may without harm use them promiscuously." Manual of Hermeneutics, p. 4.

constructs a doctrine or system clear to his own mind, may find it difficult to set forth his views to others so as to prevent all misconception. His whole subject matter lies beyond the range of common thought. The hearers or readers, in such a case, must, like the philosopher himself, dwell long upon the subject. They must have terms defined, and ideas illustrated, until, step by step, they come to imbibe the genius and spirit of the new philosophy. But especially great and manifold are the difficulties of understanding the writings of those who differ from us in language and nationality. The learned themselves become divided in their essays to decipher and interpret the records of the past. Volumes and libraries have been written to elucidate the obscurities of the Greek and Roman classics. The foremost scholars and linguists of the present generation are busied in the study and exposition of the sacred books of the Chinese, the Hindus, the Parsees, and the Egyptians, and, after all their learned labours, they disagree in the translation and solution of many a passage. How much more might we expect great differences of opinion in the interpretation of a book like the Bible, composed at sundry times and in many parts and modes, and ranging through many departments of literature! What obstacles might reasonably be expected in the interpretation of a record of divine revelation, in which heavenly thoughts, unknown to men before, were made to express themselves in the imperfect formulas of human speech! The most contradictory rules of interpretation have been propounded, and expositions have been made to suit the peculiar tastes and prejudices of writers or to maintain preconceived opinions, until all scientific method has been set at nought, and each interpreter became a law unto himself. Hence the necessity of well-defined and self-consistent principles of Scripture interpretation. Only as exegetes come to adopt common principles and methods of procedure, will the interpretation of the Bible attain the dignity and certainty of an established science.

The rank and importance of Biblical Hermeneutics among the various studies embraced in Theological Encyclopedia and Methodology is apparent from the fundamental relation which it sustains to them all. For the Scripture revelation is itself essentially the centre and substance of all theological science. It contains the clearest and fullest exhibition of the person and character of God, and of the spiritual needs and possibilities of man. A sound and trustworthy interpretation of the scripture records, therefore, is the root and basis of all revealed theology. Without it Systematic Theology, or Dogmatics, could not be legitimately constructed, and would, in fact, be essentially

Rank and importance of Hermeneutics in Theological Science.

impossible. For the doctrines of revelation can only be learned from a correct understanding of the oracles of God. Historical Theology, also, tracing as it does the thought and life of the Church, must needs take cognizance of the principles and methods of scripture interpretation which have so largely controlled in the development of that thought and life. The creeds of Christendom assume to rest upon the teachings of the inspired Scriptures. Apologetics, polemics, ethics, and all that is embraced in Practical Theology, are ever making appeal to the authoritative records of the Christian faith. The great work of the Christian ministry is to preach the word ; and that most important labour cannot be effectually done without a thorough knowledge of the Scriptures and skill in the interpretation and application of the same. Personal piety and practical godliness are nourished by the study of this written word The psalmist sings (Psa. cxix, 105, 111) :

> A lamp to my foot is thy word,
> And a light to my pathway.
> I have taken possession of thy testimonies forever,
> For the joy of my heart are they.[1]

The Apostle Paul admonished Timothy that the Holy Scriptures were able to make him wise unto salvation through faith in Jesus Christ (2 Tim. iii, 15). And Jesus himself, interceding for his own chosen followers, prayed, "Sanctify them in the truth; thy word is truth" (John xvii, 17). Accordingly, the Lord's ambassador must not adulterate (2 Cor. ii, 17), but rightly divide, the word of the truth (2 Tim. ii, 15). For if ever the divinely appointed ministry of reconciliation accomplish the perfecting of the saints, and the building up of the body of Christ, so as to bring all to the attainment of the unity of the faith and of the knowledge of the Son of God (Eph. iv, 12, 13), it must be done by a correct interpretation and efficient use of the word of God. The interpretation and application of that word must rest upon a sound and self-evidencing science of hermeneutics.

[1] All scripture quotations in the present work have been made by translating directly from the Hebrew, Chaldee, and Greek originals. To have followed the Authorized Version would have necessitated a large amount of circumlocution. In many instances the citation of a text is designed to illustrate a process as well as a principle of hermeneutics. It is often desirable to bring out, either incidentally or prominently, some noticeable emphasis, and this can be done best by giving the exact order of the words of the original. The observance of such order in translation may sometimes violate the usage and idiom of the best English, but, in many cases, it yields the best possible translation.

CHAPTER II.

THE BIBLE AND OTHER SACRED BOOKS.

IT is no inconsiderable preparation for the hermeneutical study of the Bible to be able to appreciate its rank and value as compared with other sacred books. During the last half century Other religious the learned research and diligent labour of scholars have literatures a valuable preparation for hermeneutical study. made accessible to us whole literatures of nations that were comparatively unknown before. It is discovered that the ancient Egyptians, the Persians, the Hindus, the Chinese, and other nations, have had their sacred writings, some of which claim an antiquity greater than the books of Moses. There are not wanting, in Christian lands, men disposed to argue that these sacred books of the nations possess a value as great as the scriptures of the Christian faith, and are entitled to the same veneration. Such claims are not to be ignored or treated with contempt. There have been, doubtless, savage islanders who imagined that the sun rose and set for their sole benefit, and who never dreamed that the sounding waters about their island home were at the same time washing beautiful corals and precious pearls on other shores. Among civilized peoples, also, there are those who have no appreciation of lands, nations, literatures, and religions which differ from their own. This, however, is a narrowness unworthy of the Christian scholar. The truly catholic Christian will not refuse to acknowledge the manifest excellences of races or religions that differ from his own. He will be governed in his judgments by the precept of the apostle (Phil. iv, 8) : "Whatever things are true, whatever things are worthy of honour ($\sigma\epsilon\mu\nu\acute{a}$), whatever things are just, whatever things are pure, whatever things are lovely, whatever things are of good report, if there be any virtue and if there be any praise, think upon ($\lambda o\gamma\acute{\iota}\zeta\epsilon\sigma\vartheta\epsilon$, *exercise reason upon*) these things." The study and comparison of other scriptures will serve, among other things, to show how preeminently the Christian's Bible is adapted to the spiritual nature and religious culture of all mankind.[1]

---

[1] "This volume," says Professor Phelps, "has never yet numbered among its religious believers a fourth part of the human race, yet it has swayed a greater amount of mind than any other volume the world has known. It has the singular faculty of attracting to itself the thinkers of the world, either as friends or as foes, always and everywhere." Men and Books, p. 239. New York, 1882.

LITERATURE OF THE CHRISTIAN CANON.

The scriptures of the Old and New Testaments are the gradual accretion of a literature that covers about sixteen centuries. The *Outline of Biblical Literature as contained in the Christian Canon.* different parts were contributed at different times, and by many different hands. According to the order of books in the Christian Canon, we have, first, the five Books of Moses, which embody the Ten Commandments, with their various accessory statutes, moral, civil, and ceremonial, all set in a historical background of singular simplicity and grandeur. Then follow twelve Historical Books, recording the history of the Israelitish nation from the death of Moses to the restoration from Babylonian exile, and covering a period of a thousand years. Next follow five Poetical Books—a drama, a psalter, two books of proverbial philosophy, and a song of love ; and after these are seventeen Prophetical Books, among which are some of the most magnificent monuments of all literature. In the New Testament we have, first, the four Gospels, which record the life and words of Jesus Christ; then the Acts of the Apostles, a history of the origin of the Christian Church; then the thirteen Epistles of Paul, followed by the Epistle to the Hebrews, and the seven General Epistles; and, finally, the Apocalypse of John. Here, at a rapid glance, we see an ancient library of history, law, theology, philosophy, poetry, prophecy, epistles, and biography. Most of these books still bear their author's names, some of whom we find to have been kings, some prophets, some shepherds, some fishermen. One was a taxgatherer, another a tentmaker, another a physician, but all were deeply versed in sacred things. There could have been no collusion among them, for they lived and wrote in different ages, centuries apart, and their places of residence were far separate, as Arabia, Palestine, Babylon, Persia, Asia Minor, Greece, and Rome.[1] The antiquities and varying civilizations of these different nations and countries are imaged in these sacred books, and, where the name of an author is not known, it is not difficult to ascertain approximately, from his statements or allusions, the time and circumstances of his writing. The nation with whom these books originated, and the lands that nation occupied first and last, are so well known, and so accurately identified, as to give a living freshness and reality to

[1] Geike says: "Scripture proves throughout to be only so many notes in a divine harmony which culminates in the angel song over Bethlehem. What less than Divine inspiration could have evolved such unity of purpose and spirit in the long series of sacred writers, no one of whom could possibly be conscious of the part he was being made to take in the development of God's ways to our race?" Hours with the Bible, vol. i, p. 5.

these records; and the rich and varied contents of the several books are such as to make them of priceless value to all men and all ages. "I am of opinion," wrote Sir William Jones—a most, competent judge on such a subject—"that this volume, independently of its divine origin, contains more true sublimity, more exquisite beauty, more pure morality, more important history, and finer strains of poetry and eloquence, than can be collected from all other books, in whatever age or language they may have been written." [1] Let us now compare and contrast these scriptures with the sacred books of other nations.

THE AVESTA.

No body of sacred literature except the Christian Canon can be of much greater interest to the student of history than the scriptures of the Parsees, which are commonly called the Zend-Avesta. They contain the traditions and ceremonies of the old Iranian faith, the religion of Zoroaster, or (more properly) Zarathustra. *Antiquity and general character.* They have sadly suffered by time and the revolutions of empire, and come to us greatly mutilated and corrupted, but since they were first brought to the knowledge of the western world by the enthusiastic Frenchman, Anquetil-Duperron, [2] whose adventures in the East read like a romance from the Arabian Nights, the studies of European scholars have put us in possession of their general scope and subject matter. [3] They consist of four distinct sections, the Yasna, the Vispered, the Vendidad, and a sort of separate hagiographa, commonly called Khordah-Avesta.

The main principles of the Avesta religion are thus summed up by Darmesteter: "The world, such as it is now, is twofold, being the work of two hostile beings, Ahura-Mazda, the good principle, and Angra-Mainyu, the evil principle; all that is good in the world comes from the former, all *Doctrinal system of the Avesta.*

---

[1] Written on a blank leaf of his Bible.

[2] In his work entitled, Zend-Avesta, ouvrage de Zoroastre, contenant les Idées Théologiques, Physiques et Morales de ce Législateur, 3 vols., Par., 1771.

[3] Especially deserving of mention are Eugéne Burnouf, Commentaire sur le Yaçna, 3 vols., Par., 1833; Westergaard, Zendavesta, Copenh., 1852–54; Spiegel, who has published the original text, with a full critical apparatus, and also a German translation, with a commentary on both the text and translation, Lpz., 1853–1868; Haug, Essays on the Sacred Language, Writings, and Religion of the Parsees, Bombay, 1862; also Die Gathas des Zarathustra, Lpz., 1858; Windischmann, Zoroastrische Studien, Berl., 1863. An English version of the Avesta from Spiegel's German version, by A. H. Bleek, was published in London, in 1864, and a better one from the original text, by J. Darmesteter, (Part I, The Vendidad, Oxf., 1880), as Vol. IV, of The Sacred Books of the East, edited by Max Müller.

that is bad in it comes from the latter. The history of the world is the history of their conflict, how Angra-Mainyu invaded the world of Ahura-Mazda and marred it, and how he shall be expelled from it at last. Man is active in the conflict, his duty in it being laid before him in the law revealed by Ahura-Mazda to Zarathustra. When the appointed time is come, a son of the lawgiver, still unborn, named Saoshyant, will appear, Angra-Mainyu and Hell will be destroyed, men will rise from the dead, and everlasting happiness will reign over the world."[1]

The oldest portion of the Avesta is called the Yasna, which, along with the Vispered, constitutes the Parsee Liturgy, and consists of praises of Ahura-Mazda, and all the lords of purity, and of invocations for them to be present at the ceremonial worship. Many of these prayers contain little more than the names and attributes of the several objects or patrons of the Zoroastrian worship, and the perusal of them soon becomes tedious. The following constitutes the whole of the twelfth chapter, and is one of the finest passages, and a favourite:

The Yasna.

I praise the well-thought, well-spoken, well-performed thoughts, words, and works. I lay hold on all good thoughts, words, and works. I abandon all evil thoughts, words, and works. I bring to you, O Amesha-Spentas,[2] praise and adoration, with thoughts, words, and works, with heavenly mind, the vital strength of my own body.

The following, from the beginning of the thirteenth chapter, is another favourite:

I drive away the dævas (demons), I profess myself a Zarathustrian, an expeller of dævas, a follower of Ahura, a hymn-singer of the Amesha-Spentas, a praiser of the Amesha-Spentas. To Ahura-Mazda, the Good, endued with good wisdom, I offer all good. To the Pure, Rich, Majestic; whatever are the best goods to him, to whom the cow, to whom purity belongs; from whom arises the light, the brightness which is inseparable from the lights. Spenta-Armaiti, the good, choose I; may she belong to me! By my praise will I save the cattle from theft and robbery.

The latter part of the Yasna contains the religious hymns known as the Gathas. They are believed to be the oldest portion of the Avesta, and are written in a more ancient dialect. But a considerable part of them is scarcely intelligible, all the learning and labour of scholars having thus far failed to clear up

The Gathas.

[1] Darmesteter, Translation of the Avesta, Introduction, p. lvi.

[2] The Amesha-Spentas, six in number, were at first mere personifications of virtues and moral or liturgical powers; but as Ahura-Mazda, their lord and father, ruled over the whole of the world, they took by and by each a part of the world under their care. Comp. Darmesteter, p. lxxi.

the difficulties of the ancient text. The general drift of thought, however, is apparent. Praises are continually addressed to the holy powers, especially to the Holy Spirit Ahura-Mazda (Ormuzd), the Creator, the Rejoicer, the Pure, the Fair, the Heavenly, the Ruler over all, the Most Profitable, the Friend for both worlds. Many a noble sentiment is uttered in these ancient hymns, but, at the same time, a much larger amount of frivolous matter.

The Vispered is but a liturgical addition to the Yasna, and of similar character. It contains twenty-seven chapters, of   The Vispered. which the following, from the eighth chapter, is a specimen:

> The right-spoken words praise we.
> The holy Sraosha praise we.
> The good purity praise we.
> Nairo-Sanha praise we.
> The victorious peaces praise we.
> The undaunted, who do not come to shame, praise we.
> The Fravashis (souls) of the pure praise we.
> The bridge Chinvat[1] praise we.
> The dwelling of Ahura-Mazda praise we.
> The best place of the pure praise we,
>   The shining, wholly brilliant.
> The best-arriving at Paradise praise we.

The Vendidad, consisting of twenty-two chapters, or fargards, is of a different character. It is a minute code of Zoro-   The Vendidad. astrian laws, most of which, however, refer to matters of purification. The first fargard enumerates the countries which were created by Ahura-Mazda, and afterward corrupted by the evil principle, Angra-Mainyu, who is full of death and opposition to the good. The second introduces us to Yima, the fair, who refused to be the teacher, recorder, or bearer of the law, but became the protector and overseer of the world. Chapter third enumerates things which are most acceptable and most displeasing to the world, and chapter fourth describes breaches of contracts and other sins, and prescribes the different degrees of punishment for each, declaring, among other things, that a man's nearest relatives may become involved in his punishment, even to a thousandfold. Chapters fifth to twelfth treat uncleanness occasioned by contact with dead bodies, and the means of purification. Chapters thirteenth and fourteenth praise the dog, and heavy punishments are enjoined for those who injure the animal so important and valuable to a pastoral people. Fargards fifteenth and sixteenth give laws for the treatment of

[1] Over which the good are supposed to pass into Paradise.

women, and condemn seduction and attempts to procure abortion. Fargard seventeenth gives directions concerning paring the nails and cutting the hair. The remaining five chapters contain numerous conversations between Ahura-Mazda and Zoroaster, and appear to be fragmentary additions to the original Vendidad.

The rest of the Parsee scriptures are comprehended under what The Khordah- is commonly called the Khordah-Avesta, that is, the Avesta. small Avesta. This part contains the Yashts and Nyayis, prayers and praises addressed to the various deities of the Zoroastrian faith; also the Aferin and Afrigan, praises and thanksgivings; the Sirozah, praises to the deities of the thirty days of the month; the Gahs, prayers to the different subdivisions of the day; and the Patets, or formularies of confession.

These praises and prayers of the small Avesta are intended for the use of the people, as those of the Yasna and Vispered are principally for the priests. Taken altogether, these Parsee scriptures are a prayer-book, or ritual, rather than a bible. But though they are associated with the venerable name of Zoroaster, and tradition has it that he composed two million verses, yet nothing in this volume can with certainty be ascribed to him, and he himself is a dim and mythical personage. In all these writings there is a vagueness and uncertainty about subject matter, date, and authorship. Darmesteter says: "As the Parsees are the ruins of a people, so are their sacred books the ruins of a religion. There has been no other great belief in the world that ever left such poor and meagre monuments of its past splendor."[1]

ASSYRIAN SACRED RECORDS.

The cuneiform inscriptions on the monuments of the Assyrian, Vast range of Babylonian, and Persian empires have been found to literature in embody a vast literature, embracing history, law, science, poetry, and religion. To the interpretation of these monumental records a number of eminent orientalists,[2] chiefly English and French, have been, within the last half century, devoting unwearied study, and many of the most interesting inscriptions have been deciphered and translated into the languages of modern Europe. At the date of the earliest monumental records, two different races appear to have settled upon the plains of the Euphrates and Tigris, one using a Semitic, the other a Scythian or Turanian

[1] Translation of the Zend-Avesta; Introduction, p. xii.
[2] Among the most distinguished Assyriologists are Rawlinson, Hincks, Norris, George Smith, Talbot, Sayce. Botta, De Saulcy, Oppert, Lenormant, Menant, and Schrader.

language. They are designated by the names Sumir and Akkad, but what particular sections of the country each inhabited, or which particular language each spoke, does not appear.[1] They were, probably, much intermixed, as many of their cities bear both Semitic and Scythian names. "The Accadians," says Sayce, "were the inventors of the cuneiform system of writing, and the earliest population of Babylonia of whom we know. They spoke an agglutinative language, allied to Finnic or Tartar, and had originally come from the mountainous country to the southwest of the Caspian. The name *Accada* signifies 'highlander,' and the name of Accad is met with in the tenth chapter of Genesis."[2] The successive Assyrian, Babylonian, and Persian conquerors adopted the Accadian system of writing, and it became variously modified by each.

The inscriptions thus far deciphered are mostly fragmentary, and the study of them has not yet been carried far enough to furnish a full account of all the tribes and languages they represent. But enough has already been placed within the reach of English readers to show that those ancient peoples had an extensive sacred literature. Their prayers and hymns and laws were graven on monumental tablets, often on the high rocks, and they are worthy to be compared with the sacred books of other lands and nations.[3]

Inscriptions deciphered mostly fragmentary.

The royal inscriptions on these monuments are noticeable for their religious character. Though full of most pompous self assertion they abound with devout acknowledgments, showing that those ancient monarchs never hesitated to confess their dependence on the powers above. Witness the following inscription of Khammurabi, who ruled in Babylonia some centuries before the time of Moses:

Religious tone of the royal inscriptions.

Khammurabi the exalted king, the king of Babylon, the king renowned throughout the world; conqueror of the enemies of Marduk; the king beloved by his heart am I.

[1] "The Turanian people," says George Smith, "who appear to have been the original inhabitants of the country, invented the cuneiform mode of writing; all the earliest inscriptions are in that language, but the proper names of most of the kings and principal persons are written in Semitic, in direct contrast to the body of the inscriptions. The Semites appear to have conquered the Turanians, although they had not yet imposed their language on the country." Records of the Past, vol. iii, p. 3.

[2] Preface to his translation of a Tablet of Ancient Accadian Laws, Records of the Past, vol. iii, p. 21.

[3] A very convenient and valuable collection of these inscriptions, translated into English by leading oriental scholars, is published by Bagster & Sons, of London, under the title of Records of the Past (12 volumes, 1875–1881). Every alternate volume of the series contains translations from the Egyptian monuments.

The favour of god and Bel the people of Sumir and Accad gave unto my government.   Their celestial weapons unto my hand they gave.

The canal Khammurabi, the joy of men, a stream of abundant waters, for the people of Sumir and Accad, I excavated.   Its banks, all of them, I restored to newness; new supporting walls I heaped up; perennial waters for the people of Sumir and Accad I provided.

The people of Sumir and Accad, all of them, in general assemblies I assembled.   A review and inspection of them I ordained every year.   In joy and abundance I watched over them, and in peaceful dwellings I caused them to dwell.

By the divine favour I am Khammurabi the exalted king, the worshipper of the Supreme deity.

With the prosperous power which Marduk gave me I built a lofty citadel, on a high mound of earth, whose summits rose up like mountains, on the banks of Khammurabi river, the joy of men.

To that citadel I gave the name of the mother who bore me and the father who begat me.   In the holy name of Ri, the mother who bore me, and of the father who begat me, during long ages may it last![1]

Similar devout acknowledgments are found in nearly all the royal annals. Sargon's great inscription on the palace of Khorsabad declares :

The gods Assur, Nebo, and Merodach have conferred on me the royalty of the nations, and they have propagated the memory of my fortunate name to the ends of the earth. . . . The great gods have made me happy by the constancy of their affection, they have granted me the exercise of my sovereignty over all kings.[2]

Other tablets contain a great variety of compositions. There are mythological stories, fables, proverbs, laws, contracts, and deeds of sale, lists of omens and charms, legends of deities and spirits, and speculations in astrology. Not the least interesting among these records are the old Accadian and Assyrian hymns. Some of these remind us of the hymns of the Rig-Veda. Some have the tone of penitential psalms. The following is one of the best examples :

Specimens of psalms and prayers.

O my Lord! my sins are many, my trespasses are great;
And the wrath of the gods has plagued me with disease,
And with sickness and sorrow.
I fainted, but no one stretched forth his hand;
I groaned, but no one drew nigh ;
I cried aloud, but no one heard.

[1] Translation by H. F. Talbot, Records of the Past, vol. i, pp. 7, 8.
[2] Records of the Past, vol. ix, p. 3.

O Lord ! do not abandon thy servant.
In the waters of the great storm seize his hand.
The sins which he has committed, turn thou to righteousness.[1]

The following prayer for a king is interesting both as an example of Assyrian sacred poetry, and as evidence of a belief in immortality:

> Length of days,
> Long-lasting years,
> A strong sword,
> A long life,
> Extended years of glory,
> Pre-eminence among kings,
> Grant ye to the king, my lord,
> Who has given such gifts to his gods!
> The bounds vast and wide
> Of his empire and of his rule
> May he enlarge and may he complete.
> Holding over all kings supremacy,
> And royalty and empire,
> May he attain to gray hairs and old age;
> And after the life of these days,
> In the feasts of the silver mountain,[2]
> The heavenly courts,
> The abode of blessedness,
> And in the light of the Happy Fields,
> May he dwell a life eternal, holy,
> In the presence of the gods
> Who inhabit Assyria.[3]

The following Chaldean account of the Creation is a translation, by H. F. Talbot, of the first and fifth Creation Tablets, which are preserved, though in a mutilated condition, in the British Museum:

Chaldean accounts of Creation, etc.

From the First Tablet.

When the upper region was not yet called heaven,
And the lower region was not yet called earth,
And the abyss of Hades had not yet opened its arms,
Then the chaos of waters gave birth to all of them,
And the waters were gathered into one place.
No men yet dwelt together; no animals yet wandered about;

---

[1] Records of the Past, vol. iii, p. 136.
[2] The Assyrian Olympus. The epithet *silver* was doubtless suggested by some snowy inaccessible peak, the supposed dwelling-place of the gods.
[3] Translated by Talbot, Records of the Past, vol. iii, pp. 133, 134.

None of the gods had yet been born,
Their names were not spoken; their attributes were not known.
Then the eldest of the gods,
Lakhmu and Lakhamu were born,
And grew up. . . .[1]
Assur and Kissur were born next,
And lived through long periods.
Anu. . . .[2]

From the Fifth Tablet.

He constructed dwellings for the great gods.
He fixed up constellations, whose figures were like animals.
He made the year. Into four quarters he divided it.
Twelve months he established, with their constellations, three by
    three.
And for days of the year he appointed festivals.
He made dwellings for the planets; for their rising and setting.
And that nothing should go amiss, and that the course of none should
    be retarded,
He placed with them the dwellings of Bel and Hea.
He opened great gates on every side;
He made strong the portals, on the left hand and on the right.
In the centre he placed luminaries.
The moon he appointed to rule the night,
And to wander through the night, until the dawn of day.
Every month without fail he made holy assembly days.
In the beginning of the month, at the rising of the night,
It shot forth its horns to illuminate the heavens.
On the seventh day he appointed a holy day,
And to cease from all business he commanded.
Then arose the sun in the horizon of heaven in (glory).[3]

The mention here made of the seventh day as a holy day is important to the biblical theologian. "It has been known for some
time," says Talbot, "that the Babylonians observed the Sabbath
with considerable strictness. On that day the king was not allowed
to take a drive in his chariot; various meats were forbidden to be
eaten, and there were a number of other minute restrictions. But
it was not known that they believed the Sabbath to have been ordained at the Creation. I have found, however, since this translation of the fifth tablet was completed, that Mr. Sayce has recently
published a similar opinion."

---

[1] Lacunæ.   [2] The rest of this tablet is lost.
[3] Records of the Past, vol. ix, pp. 117, 118. Compare the translation and comments
of George Smith, Chaldæan Account of Genesis. New York, 1876. New Edition,
revised, 1880.

The following Accadian poem is supposed to be an ancient tradition of the overthrow of Sodom and Gomorrah. Mr. Sayce, whose translation is here given, observes that Accadian legend of Sodom and Gomorrah. "it seems merely a fragment of a legend, in which the names of the cities were probably given, and an explanation afforded of the mysterious personage, who, like Lot, appears to have escaped destruction. It must not be forgotten that the campaign of Chedorlaomer and his allies was directed against Sodom and the other cities of the plain, so that the existence of the legend among the Accadians is not so surprising as might appear at first sight."

An overthrow from the midst of the deep there came.
The fated punishment from the midst of heaven descended.
A storm like a plummet the earth (overwhelmed).
To the four winds the destroying flood like fire did burn.
The inhabitants of the cities it had caused to be tormented; their bodies it consumed.
In city and country it spread death, and the flames as they rose overthrew.
Freeman and slave were equal, and the high places it filled.
In heaven and earth like a thunder-storm it had rained; a prey it made.
A place of refuge the gods hastened to, and in a throng collected.
Its mighty (onset) they fled from, and like a garment it concealed (mankind).
They (feared), and death (overtook them).
(Their) feet and hands (it embraced).
Their body it consumed.
    . . . [1] the city, its foundation, it defiled.
    . . . [1] in breath, his mouth he filled.
As for this man, a loud voice was raised; the mighty lightning flash descended.
During the day it flashed; grievously (it fell). [2]

Similar to the above in general tone and character are the cuneiform accounts of the Deluge and the Tower of Babel. They are especially valuable in showing how the traditions of most ancient events were preserved among the scattered nations, and became modified in the course of ages. Notably inferior are these poetic legends to the calm and stately narratives of the book of Genesis, but they are, nevertheless, to be greatly prized. Were Assyriologists to gather up, classify, and arrange in proper order the religious records of ancient Assyria and Babylonia, it would be seen that these hoary annals and hymns of departed nations furnish a sacred literature second in interest and value to none of the bibles of the Gentiles.

[1] Lacunæ.   [2] Records of the Past, vol. xi, pp. 115–118.

The Veda.

The word Veda means knowledge, and is the Sanskrit equivalent of the Greek οἶδα, *I know*. It is often used to denote the entire body of Hindu sacred literature, which, according to the Brahmans, contains pre-eminently the knowledge which is important and worthy to be known. But the Vedas proper exist chiefly in the form of lyrical poetry, and consist of four distinct collections known as the Rig-Veda, the Sama-Veda, the Yajur-Veda, and the Atharva-Veda. These hymns are called Mantras, as distinguished from the prose annotations and disquisitions (Brahmanas), which were subsequently added to them. They are written in a dialect much older than the classical Sanskrit, and are allowed on all hands to be among the most ancient and important monuments of literature extant in any nation or language. The four collections differ much, however, in age and value. The Rig-Veda is the oldest and most important, and consists of one thousand and twenty-eight hymns. Nearly half the hymns are addressed to either Indra, the god of light, or Agni, the god of fire. According to Professor Whitney, it "is doubtless a historical collection, prompted by a desire to treasure up complete, and preserve from further corruption, those ancient and inspired songs which the Indian nation had brought with them, as their most precious possession, from the earlier seats of the race."[1] The Sama-Veda is a liturgical collection, consisting largely of hymns from the Rig-Veda, but arranged for ritual purposes. The Yajur-Veda is of a similar character, and consists of various formulas in prose and verse arranged for use at sacrificial services. The Atharva-Veda is the work of a later period, and never attained in India a rank equal to that of the other Vedas. In fact, says Max Müller, "for tracing the earliest growth of religious ideas in India, the only important, the only real Veda, is the Rig-Veda. The other so-called Vedas, which deserve the name of Veda no more than the Talmud deserves the name of Bible, contain chiefly extracts from the Rig-Veda, together with sacrificial formulas, charms, and incantations, many of them, no doubt, extremely curious, but never likely to interest any one except the Sanskrit scholar by profession."[2]

The same distinguished scholar elsewhere observes: "The Veda has a twofold interest; it belongs to the history of the world and

General character of the Vedas.

Max Müller's views of the Rig-Veda.

---

[1] Oriental and Linguistic Studies, p. 13. New York, 1873.
[2] Chips from a German Workshop, vol. i, p. 8.

to the history of India. In the history of the world the Veda fills a gap which no literary work in any other language could fill. It carries us back to times of which we have no records anywhere, and gives us the very words of a generation of men of whom otherwise we could form but the vaguest estimate by means of conjectures and inferences. As long as man continues to take an interest in the history of his race, and as long as we collect in libraries and museums the relics of former ages, the first place in that long row of books which contains the records of the Aryan branch of mankind will belong forever to the Rig-Veda." [1]

Confining our observations, therefore, to the Rig-Veda, we note that it is in substance a vast book of psalms. Its one thousand and twenty-eight lyrics (*suktas*), of various length, are divided into ten books (*mandalas*, circles), and together constitute a work about eight times larger than the one hundred and fifty Psalms of the Old Testament. The first book is composed of one hundred and ninety-one hymns, which are ascribed to some fifteen different authors (*rishis*). The second book contains forty-three hymns, all of which are attributed to Gritsamada and his family. The next five books are also ascribed each to a single author or his family, and vary in the number of their hymns from sixty-two to one hundred and four. The eighth book has ninety-two hymns, attributed to a great number of different authors, a majority of whom are of the race of Kanva. The ninth book is also ascribed to various authors, and has one hundred and fourteen hymns, all of which are addressed to Soma as a god. "The name Soma," says Grassmann, "is derived from a root, *su*, which originally meant 'to beget,' 'to produce,' but in the Rig-Veda is applied altogether to the extracting and pressing of the plant used for the preparation of soma, and the soma itself therefore meant originally the juice obtained by this procedure." [2] The tenth book, like the first, contains one hundred and ninety-one hymns; but they wear a different style, breathe a different spirit, and appear to belong to a much later period. "We find," says Grassmann, "in this, as in the first book, songs belonging to the springtime of vedic poesy, but also songs belonging to a time not very remote, as the time of the most recent period of vedic lyrics, such as presents itself to us in the Atharva-Veda." [3]

The Rig-Veda a vast book of Psalms.

Variety of authors.

[1] History of Ancient Sanskrit Literature. Second Edition, p. 63. Lond., 1860.

[2] Grassmann's Rig-Veda. Metrical Version in German, with Critical and Explanatory Annotations (2 vols. Lpz., 1876, 1877). Preface to Ninth Book, vol. ii, p. 183.

[3] Rig-Veda. Preface to Tenth Book, vol. ii, p. 288.

Our limits will allow us to present only a few specimens, but
Specimens of these will suffice to show the general character and
Vedic Hymns. style of the best Rig-Veda hymns. The following is
Max Müller's translation of the fifty-third hymn of the first book,
and is addressed to Indra:

1. Keep silence well! we offer praises to the great Indra in the house of
the sacrificer. Does he find treasure for those who are like sleepers?
Mean praise is not valued among the munificent.

2. Thou art the giver of horses, Indra, thou art the giver of cows, the
giver of corn, the strong lord of wealth; the old guide of man, disappoint-
ing no desires, a friend to friends:—to him we address this song.

3. O powerful Indra, achiever of many works, most brilliant god—all
this wealth around here is known to be thine alone: take from it, conqueror,
bring it hither! do not stint the desire of the worshipper who longs for
thee!

4. On these days thou art gracious, and on these nights, keeping off the
enemy from our cows and from our stud. Tearing the fiend night after
night with the help of Indra, let us rejoice in food, freed from haters.

5. Let us rejoice, Indra, in treasure and food, in wealth of manifold delight and splendor. Let us rejoice in the blessing of the gods, which gives
us the strength of offspring, gives us cows first and horses.

6. These draughts inspired thee, O lord of the brave! these were vigour,
these libations, in battles, when for the sake of the poet, the sacrificer,
thou struckest down irresistibly ten thousands of enemies.

7. From battle to battle thou advancest bravely, from town to town thou
destroyest all this with might, when thou, Indra, with Nami as thy friend,
struckest down from afar the deceiver Namuki.

8. Thou hast slain Karnaga and Parnaya with the brightest spear of
Atithigva. Without a helper thou didst demolish the hundred cities of
Vangrida, which were besieged by Rigisvan.

9. Thou hast felled down with the chariot-wheel these twenty kings of
men, who had attacked the friendless Susravas, and gloriously the sixty
thousand and ninety-nine forts.

10. Thou, Indra, hast succoured Susravas with thy succours, Turvayana
with thy protections. Thou hast made Kutsa, Atithigva, and Ayu subject
to this mighty youthful king.

11. We who in future, protected by the gods, wish to be thy most
blessed friends, we shall praise thee, blessed by thee with offspring, and
enjoying henceforth a longer life.[1]

The following is a translation, by W. D. Whitney, of the eighteenth hymn of the tenth book. It furnishes a vivid portraiture of
the proceedings of an ancient Hindu burial, and holds even at the
present day an important place among the funeral ceremonies of the
Hindus. The officiating priest thus speaks:

[1] Chips from a German Workshop, vol. i, pp. 30–33.

1. Go forth, O Death, upon a distant pathway,
    one that's thine own, not that the gods do travel;
I speak to thee who eyes and ears possessest;
    harm not our children, harm thou not our heroes.

2. Ye who death's foot have clogged[1] ere ye came hither,
    your life and vigour longer yet retaining,
Sating yourselves with progeny and riches,
    clean be ye now, and purified, ye offerers!

3. These have come here, not of the dead, but living;
    our worship of the gods hath been propitious;
We've onward gone to dancing and to laughter,
    our life and vigour longer yet retaining.[2]

4. This fix I as protection for the living;[3]
    may none of them depart on that same errand;
Long may they live, a hundred numerous autumns,
    'twixt death and them a mountain interposing.

5. As day succeeds to day in endless series,
    as seasons happily move on with seasons,
As each that passes lacks not its successor,
    so do thou make their lives move on, Creator!

6. Ascend to life, old age your portion making,
    each after each, advancing in due order;[4]
May Twashter, skilful fashioner, propitious,
    cause that you here enjoy a long existence.

7. These women here, not widows, blessed with husbands,
    may deck themselves with ointment and with perfume;
Unstained by tears, adorned, untouched with sorrow,
    the wives may first ascend unto the altar.

8. Go up unto the world of life, O woman!
    thou liest by one whose soul is fled; come hither!
To him who grasps thy hand,[5] a second husband,
    thou art as wife to spouse become related.

[1] Allusion to the custom of attaching a clog to the foot of the corpse, as if thereby to secure the attendants at the burial from harm.

[2] The friends of the deceased seem to have no idea of soon sharing his fate; they desire to banish the thought of death.

[3] The officiating priest drew a circle and set a stone between it and the grave, to symbolize the barrier which he would fain establish between the living and the dead.

[4] Addressed to the attendants, who hereupon left their places about the bier, and went up into the circle marked off for the living. First the men went up, then the wives, and finally the widow.

[5] The person who led the widow away was usually a brother-in-law, or a foster child.

9. The bow from out the dead man's hand now taking,[1]
        that ours may be the glory, honour, prowess—
Mayest thou there, we here, rich in retainers,
        vanquish our foes and them that plot against us.

10. Approach thou now the lap of earth, thy mother,
        the wide-extending earth, the ever-kindly;
A maiden soft as wool to him who comes with gifts,
        she shall protect thee from destruction's bosom.

11. Open thyself, O earth, and press not heavily;
        be easy of access and of approach to him;
As mother with her robe her child,
        so do thou cover him, O earth!

12. May earth maintain herself thus opened wide for him;
        a thousand props shall give support about him;
And may those mansions ever drip with fatness;
        may they be there for evermore his refuge.

13. Forth from about thee thus I build away the ground;
        as I lay down this clod may I receive no harm;
This pillar may the Fathers here maintain for thee;
        may Yama there provide for thee a dwelling.

We add a single specimen more, a metrical version of the one hundred and twenty-ninth hymn of the tenth book, which is especially interesting as being full of profound speculation. "In judging it," says Max Müller, "we should bear in mind that it was not written by a gnostic or by a pantheistic philosopher, but by a poet who felt all these doubts and problems as his own, without any wish to convince or to startle, only uttering what had been weighing on his mind, just as later poets would sing the doubts and sorrows of their heart."

        Nor Aught nor Naught existed; yon bright sky
        Was not, nor heaven's broad woof outstretched above.
        What covered all? what sheltered? what concealed?
        Was it the water's fathomless abyss?
        There was not death—yet was there naught immortal,
        There was no confine betwixt day and night;

---

[1] Up to the moment of interment a bow was carried in the hand of the deceased. This was at last taken away to signify that his life-work was now done, and to others remained the glory of conquests. The body was then tenderly committed to the earth. Compare Whitney's annotations on this hymn, and his essay on the Vedic Doctrine of a Future Life in the Bibliotheca Sacra for April, 1859, and also in his Oriental and Linguistic Studies, pp. 46–63. New York, 1873.

The only One breathed breathless by itself,
Other than It there nothing since has been.
Darkness there was, and all at first was veiled
In gloom profound—an ocean without light—
The germ that still lay covered in the husk
Burst forth, one nature, from the fervent heat.
Then first came love upon it, the new spring
Of mind—yea, poets in their hearts discerned,
Pondering, this bond between created things
And uncreated. Comes this spark from earth
Piercing and all-pervading, or from heaven?
Then seeds were sown, and mighty powers arose—
Nature below, and power and will above—
Who knows the secret? who proclaimed it here,
Whence, whence this manifold creation sprang?
The gods themselves came later into being—
Who knows from whence this great creation sprang?
He from whom all this great creation came,
Whether his will created or was mute,
The Most High Seer that is in highest heaven,
He knows it—or perchance even He knows not.[1]

Every discerning reader must note the polytheistic teachings of the Veda. Mr. Hardwick calls attention to this in the following remarks: "If we lay aside expressions in the vedic hymns which have occasionally transferred the attributes of power and omnipresence to some one elemental deity, as In- dra, for example, and by so doing intimated that, even in the depths of nature-worship, intuitions pointing to one great and all-embracing Spirit could not be extinguished, there are scarcely a dozen 'mantras' in the whole collection where the unity of God is stated with an adequate amount of firmness and consistency. The great mass of those productions either invoke the aid, or deprecate the wrath of multitudinous deities, who elsewhere are regarded as no more than finite emanations from the 'lord of the creatures;' and therefore in the sacred books themselves polytheism was the feature ever prominent, and, what is more remarkable, was never openly repudiated."[2]

The Vedas are mainly polytheistic.

[1] Chips from a German Workshop, vol. i, pp. 76, 77.

[2] Christ and other Masters, p. 184. Compare Introduction to the several volumes of Wilson's Translation of the Rig-Veda, and Colebrook's Essay on the Vedas, first published in the Asiatic Researches, and later in his collected works. Lond., 1873. On the translation and interpretation of the Veda, see Muir, in Journal of the Royal Asiatic Society (Lond., 1866), and Whitney, in the North American Review (1868); also in his Oriental and Linguistic Studies, pp. 100–132.

The Buddhist Canon.

Buddhism in India was a revolt from Brahmanism. Its founder
was Sakya-muni, sometimes called Gautama, being of
the family of the Sakyas, and the clan of the Gautamas,
and belonging by birth to the warrior class (Kshatriya).
Stripping the story of his life of the numerous fables and superstitious legends of later times, it would appear that this distinguished
child of the Sakyas grew up a beautiful and accomplished youth,
but took no interest in the common amusements of the young, and
gave himself much to solitude and meditation. The problems of
life and death and human suffering absorbed his inmost being. He
at length forsook parents and wife and home, and, after years of
study, penances, and austere self-denial, attained the conviction
that he must go forth among men as an Enlightener and Reformer.
Max Müller says: "After long meditations and ecstatic visions, he
at last imagined that he had arrived at that true knowledge which
discloses the cause and thereby destroys the fear of all the changes
inherent in life. It was from the moment when he arrived at this
knowledge that he claimed the name of Buddha, the Enlightened.
At that moment we may truly say that the fate of millions of millions of human beings trembled in the balance. Buddha hesitated
for a time whether he should keep his knowledge to himself, or
communicate it to the world. Compassion for the sufferings of
man prevailed, and the young prince became the founder of a
religion which, after more than 2000 years, is still professed by
455,000,000 of human beings."[1]

Sakya-muni's life, according to the best authorities, extended
over the latter part of the sixth and the first half of the
fifth century before Christ. He broke with Brahmanism from the first, and pronounced himself against the Vedas, the
system of caste, and sacrifices. How far Kapila's system of the
Sankhya philosophy may have been a preparation for Buddhism is a
question,[2] but that Buddha became a mighty reformer, and that his
system almost succeeded for a time in overthrowing Brahmanism in
India, are matters of history. "The human mind in Asia," observes
J. F. Clarke, "went through the same course of experience afterward repeated in Europe. It protested, in the interest of humanity,
against the oppression of a priestly caste. Brahmanism, like the
Church of Rome, established a system of sacramental salvation in

Life and influence of Sakya-muni, or Buddha.

Buddha a Reformer.

---

[1] Essay on Buddhism, in Chips from a German Workshop, vol. i, p. 211.
[2] Comp. Hardwick, Christ and other Masters, pp. 147–169; and Müller's Chips from a German Workshop, vol. i, pp. 222–226.

the hands of a sacred order. Buddhism, like Protestantism, revolted, and established a doctrine of individual salvation based on personal character. Brahmanism, like the Church of Rome, teaches an exclusive spiritualism, glorifying penances and martyrdom, and considers the body the enemy of the soul. But Buddhism and Protestantism accept nature and its laws, and make a religion of humanity as well as of devotion. To such broad statements numerous exceptions may doubtless be always found, but these are the large lines of distinction."[1]

The sacred scriptures of Buddhism are commonly called the Tripitaka, which means the "three baskets," or three Compilation of collections of religious documents. Buddha, like Jesus, the Tripitaka. left no written statement of his teachings; but very soon after his death, according to tradition, a great council was called (about B. C. 477), at which the sayings of the great master were written down with care. A hundred years later another council assembled, to consider and correct certain deviations from the original faith. But it was probably not until a third council, convened by King Asoka about B. C. 242, that the Buddhist canon in its present form was completed.[2] At that great council King Asoka, "the Indian Constantine," admonished the members of the assembly "that what had been said by Buddha, that alone was well said;" and at the same time he provided for the propagation of Buddhism by missionary enterprise. And it is worthy of note that, as Christianity originated among the Jews, but has had its chief triumphs among the Gentiles, so Buddhism originated among the Hindus, but has won most of its adherents among other tribes and nations.

The Tripitaka, as we now possess it, consists of the Vinaya-Pitaka, devoted to ethics and discipline; the Sutra- Contents and Pitaka, containing the Sutras, or discourses of Buddha; magnitude of the Tripitaka. and the Abhidharma-Pitaka, which treats of dogmatical philosophy and metaphysics.[3] The entire collection constitutes an immense body of literature, rivaling in magnitude all that was ever included under the title of Veda. It is said to contain 29,368,000 letters, or more than seven times the number contained in our English Bible. The Tibetan edition of the Tripitaka fills about three hundred and twenty-five folio volumes. The mere titles of the divisions, sub-divisions, and chapters of this Buddhist canon would cover several pages. The greater portion of this immense literatura

[1] Ten Great Religions, pp. 142, 143. Boston, 1871.
[2] See Oldenberg's Introduction to the Vinaya-Pitaka, and Müller's Introduction to the Dhammapada, in vol. x, of Sacred Books of the East.
[3] Comp. Chapter xviii, of Spence Hardy, Eastern Monachism. Lond., 1850.

ture, in its most ancient texts, exists as yet only in manuscript. But as Buddhism spread and triumphed mightily in southern and eastern Asia, its sacred books have been translated into Pali, Burmese, Siamese, Tibetan, Chinese, and other Asiatic tongues. In fact, every important nation or tribe, which has adopted Buddhism, appears to have a more or less complete Buddhist literature of its own, and the names of the different books and treatises vary according to the languages in which they are extant.[1] Amid the multiplicity of texts and versions it is impossible now to point with confidence to any authoritative original; but the form of the canon as it exists among the Southern Buddhists, and especially in the Pali texts, is esteemed most highly by scholars.

The fundamental doctrines of Buddhism are few and simple, and, *Principal, doctrines of Buddhism.* in substance, may be briefly stated as consisting of the Four Verities, the Eightfold Path, and the Five Commandments. The Four sublime Verities are, (1) All existence, being subject to change and decay, is evil. (2) The source of all this evil and consequent sorrow is desire. (3) Desire and the evil which follows it may be made to cease. (4) There is a fixed and certain way by which to attain exemption from all evil. The Eightfold Path consists of (1) Right Belief, (2) Right Judgment, (3) Right Utterance, (4) Right Motives, (5) Right Occupation, (6) Right Obedience, (7) Right Memory, and (8) Right Meditation. The Five Commandments are, (1) Do not kill; (2) Do not steal; (3) Do not lie; (4) Do not become intoxicated; (5) Do not commit adultery. There are also five other well-known precepts, which have not, however, the grade of the commandments, namely, (1) Do not take solid food after noon; (2) Do not visit scenes of amusement; (3) Do not use ornaments or perfumery in dress; (4) Do not use luxurious beds; (5) Do not accept gold or silver.[2]

Specimens of Buddha's discourses. The following passage from the first chapter of the Maha-Parinibbana-Sutta, one of the subdivisions of the Sutra-Pitaka, is a specimen of the discourses of Buddha:

And the Blessed One arose, and went to the Service Hall; and when he was seated, he addressed the brethren, and said:

"I will teach you, O mendicants, seven conditions of the welfare of a community. Listen well and attend, and I will speak."

---

[1] Thus the Sanskrit name Tripitaka becomes Tipitaka and Pitakattaya in Pali, and Tunpitaka in Singhalese. Buddhism itself becomes Foism in China, and Lamaism in Thibet.

[2] For an extensive presentation of the doctrines and usages of Buddhism, see Spence Hardy, Eastern Monachism; also his Manual of Buddhism, New Edition, Lond., 1880. Edwin Arnold has beautifully expressed in poetical form the leading doctrines of Buddha, in the eighth book of his Light of Asia.

"Even so, Lord," said the Brethren, in assent, to the Blessed One; and he spake as follows:

"So long, O mendicants, as the brethren meet together in full and frequent assemblies—so long as they meet together in concord, and rise in concord, and carry out in concord the duties of the order—so long as the brethren shall establish nothing that has not been already prescribed, and abrogate nothing that has been already established, and act in accordance with the rules of the order as now laid down—so long as the brethren honour and esteem and revere and support the elders of experience and long standing, the fathers and leaders of the order, and hold it a point of duty to hearken to their words—so long as the brethren fall not under the influence of that craving which, springing up within them, would give rise to renewed existence—so long as the brethren delight in a life of solitude—so long as the brethren so train their minds that good and holy men shall come to them, and those who have come shall dwell at ease—so long may the brethren be expected not to decline, but to prosper.

"So long as these seven conditions shall continue to exist among the brethren, so long as they are well instructed in these conditions, so long may the brethren be expected not to decline, but to prosper."

"Other seven conditions of welfare will I teach you, O brethren. Listen well, and attend, and I will speak."

And on their expressing their assent, he spake as follows:

"So long as the brethren shall not engage in, or be fond of, or be connected with business—so long as the brethren shall not be in the habit of, or be fond of, or be partakers in idle talk—so long as the brethren shall not be addicted to, or be fond of, or indulge in slothfulness—so long as the brethren shall not frequent, or be fond of, or indulge in society—so long as the brethren shall neither have, nor fall under the influence of, sinful desires—so long as the brethren shall not become the friends, companions, or intimates of sinners—so long as the brethren shall not come to a stop on their way [to Nirvana] because they have attained to any lesser thing—so long may the brethren be expected not to decline, but to prosper.

"So long as these conditions shall continue to exist among the brethren, so long as they are instructed in these conditions, so long may the brethren be expected not to decline, but to prosper."

"Other seven conditions of welfare will I teach you, O brethren. Listen well, and attend, and I will speak."

And on their expressing their assent, he spake as follows:

"So long as the brethren shall be full of faith, modest in heart, afraid of sin, full of learning, strong in energy, active in mind, and full of wisdom, so long may the brethren be expected not to decline, but to prosper.

"So long as these conditions shall continue to exist among the brethren, so long as they are instructed in these conditions, so long may the brethren be expected not to decline, but to prosper."

"Other seven conditions of welfare will I teach you, O brethren. Listen well, and attend, and I will speak."

And on their expressing their assent, he spake as follows:

"So long as the brethren shall exercise themselves in the sevenfold higher wisdom, that is to say, in mental activity, search after truth, energy, joy, peace, earnest contemplation, and equanimity of mind, so long may the brethren be expected not to decline, but to prosper.

" So long as these conditions shall continue to exist among the brethren, so long as they are instructed in these conditions, so long may the brethren be expected not to decline, but to prosper."

" Other seven conditions of welfare will I teach you, O brethren. Listen well, and attend, and I will speak."

And on their expressing their assent, he spake as follows:

"So long as the brethren shall exercise themselves in the sevenfold perception due to earnest thought, that is to say, the perception of impermanency, of non-individuality, of corruption, of the danger of sin, of sanctification, of purity of heart, of Nirvana, so long may the brethren be expected not to decline, but to prosper.

" So long as these conditions shall continue to exist among the brethren, so long as they are instructed in these conditions, so long may the brethren be expected not to decline, but to prosper."

" Six conditions of welfare will I teach you, O brethren. Listen well, and attend, and I will speak."

And on their expressing their assent, he spake as follows:

" So long as the brethren shall persevere in kindness of action, speech, and thought among the saints, both in public and in private—so long as they shall divide without partiality, and share in common with the upright and the holy, all such things as they receive in accordance with the just provisions of the order, down even to the mere contents of a begging bowl—so long as the brethren shall live among the saints in the practice, both in public and in private, of those virtues which (unbroken, intact, unspotted, unblemished) are productive of freedom, and praised by the wise; which are untarnished by the desire of future life, or by the belief in the efficacy of outward acts; and which are conducive to high and holy thoughts—so long as the brethren shall live among the saints, cherishing, both in public and in private, that noble and saving faith which leads to the complete destruction of the sorrow of him who acts according to it—so long may the brethren be expected not to decline, but to prosper.

"So long as these six conditions shall continue to exist among the brethren, so long as they are instructed in these six conditions, so long may the brethren be expected not to decline, but to prosper."

And while the Blessed One stayed there at Ragagaha on the Vulture's Peak he held that comprehensive religious talk with the brethren on the nature of upright conduct, and of earnest contemplation, and of intelligence. "Great is the fruit, great the advantage of earnest contemplation when set round with upright conduct. Great is the fruit, great the advantage of intellect when set round with earnest contemplation. The mind set round with intelligence is freed from the great evils, that is to say, from sensuality, from individuality, from delusion, and from ignorance." [1]

[1] Buddhist Suttas, translated from Pali, by T. W. Rhys Davids, pp. 6–11, vol. xi, of Sacred Books of the East. Oxford, 1881.

The following is the twentieth chapter of the Dhammapada, another subdivision of the Sutra-Pitaka:

The best of ways is the eightfold; the best of truths the four words; tho best of virtues passionlessness; the best of men he who has eyes to see.

This is the way, there is no other that leads to the purifying of intelligence. Go on this way! Everything else is the deceit of Mara (the tempter).

If you go on this way, you will make an end of pain! The way was preached by me, when I had understood the removal of the thorns (in the flesh).

You yourself must make an effort. The Tathagatas (Buddhas) are only preachers. The thoughtful who enter the way are freed from the bondage of Mara.

"All created things perish," he who knows and sees this becomes passive in pain; this is the way to purity.

"All created things are grief and pain," he who knows and sees this becomes passive in pain; this is the way that leads to purity.

"All forms are unreal," he who knows and sees this becomes passive in pain; this is the way that leads to purity.

He who does not rouse himself when it is time to rise, who, though young and strong, is full of sloth, whose will and thought are weak, that lazy and idle man will never find the way to knowledge.

Watching his speech, well restrained in mind, let a man never commit any wrong with his body! Let a man keep these three roads of action clear, and he will achieve the way which is taught by the wise.

Through zeal knowledge is gotten, through lack of zeal knowledge is lost; let a man who knows this double path of gain and loss thus place himself that knowledge may grow.

Cut down the whole forest (of lust). not a tree only! Danger comes out of the forest (of lust). When you have cut down both the forest (of lust) and its undergrowth, then, Bhikshus, you will be rid of the forest and free!

So long as the love of man toward women, even the smallest, is not destroyed, so long is his mind in bondage, as the calf that drinks milk is to its mother.

Cut out the love of self, like an autumn lotus, with thy hand! Cherish the road of peace. Nirvana has been shown by Sugata (Buddha).

"Here I shall dwell in the rain, here in winter and summer," thus the fool meditates, and does not think of his death.

Death comes and carries off that man, praised for his children and flocks, his mind distracted, as a flood carries off a sleeping village.

Sons are no help, nor a father, nor relations; there is no help from kinsfolk for one whom death has seized.

A wise and good man who knows the meaning of this, should quickly clear the way that leads to Nirvana.[1]

[1] The Dhammapada, translated by F. Max Müller, pp. 67–69, vol. x, of Sacred Books of the East. Oxford, 1881. Published also along with Rogers' translation of Buddhaghosha's Parables (Lond., 1870), and Müller's Lectures on the Science of Religion. New York, 1872.

Chinese Sacred Books.

Three diverse religious systems prevail in China—Buddhism,
Three religions Taoism, and Confucianism, each of which has a vast
of China. multitude of adherents. The sacred books of the first
named consist of translations of the Buddhist canon from various
languages of India, principally, however, from the Sanskrit, and
need no separate notice here.[1] The great book of Taoism is the
Tao-teh-King, a production of the celebrated philosopher Laotsze,
who was born about six hundred years before the Christian era.
The sacred books of Confucianism are commonly known as the five
King and the four Shu.

The Tao-teh-King is scarcely entitled to the name of a sacred
The Tao-teh- book. It is rather a philosophical treatise, by an acute
King. speculative mind, and resembles some of the subtle portions of Plato's dialogues. It is about the length of the book of
Ecclesiastes, to which it also bears some resemblance. But it is denied, on high authority, that there is any real connexion between
Taoism as a religion now prevalent in China and this book of
Laotsze.[2] The Tao-teh-King has been divided into eighty-one
short chapters, and is devoted to the inculcation and praise of what
the author calls his *Tao*. What all this word is designed to represent is very difficult, if not impossible, to determine. In the Introduction to his translation of the work, Chalmers says: "I have
thought it better to leave the word *Tao* untranslated, both because
The meaning it has given the name to the sect (the Taoists), and be-
of Tao. cause no English word is its exact equivalent. Three
terms suggest themselves—the Way, Reason, and the Word; but
they are all liable to objection. Were we guided by etymology,
'the Way,' would come nearest to the original, and in one or two
passages the idea of a *way* seems to be in the term; but this is too
materialistic to serve the purpose of a translation. 'Reason,' again,
seems to be more like a quality or attribute of some conscious being
than *Tao* is. I would translate it by 'the Word,' in the sense of
the Logos, but this would be like settling the question which I wish
to leave open, viz., what amount of resemblance there is between
the Logos of the New Testament and this *Tao*, which is its nearest
representative in Chinese. In our version of the New Testament

---

[1] The extent of this literature may be seen in Beal's Catena of Buddhist Scriptures
from the Chinese. Lond., 1871.

[2] See Legge, Lectures on the Religions of China. Lecture 3d, on Taoism as a Religion and a Philosophy. New York, 1881.

in Chinese we have in the first chapter of John, 'In the beginning was *Tao*,' etc."[1]

Others have sought by other terms to express the idea of Tao. It has been called the Supreme Reason, the Universal Soul, the Eternal Idea, the Nameless Void, Mother of being, and Essence of things. The following is from Laotsze himself, and one of the best specimens of his book, being the whole of chapter twenty-fifth, as translated by Chalmers: {Laotsze's account of Tao.}

There was something chaotic in nature which existed before heaven and earth. It was still. It was void. It stood alone and was not changed. It pervaded everywhere and was not endangered. It may be regarded as the mother of the universe. I know not its name, but give it the title of *Tao*. If I am forced to make a name for it, I say it is Great; being great, I say that it passes away; passing away, I say that it is far off; being far off, I say that it returns. Now Tao is great; heaven is great; earth is great; a king is great. In the universe there are four greatnesses, and a king is one of them. Man takes his law from the earth; the earth takes its law from heaven; heaven takes its law from Tao; and Tao takes its law from what it is in itself.

The moral teachings of the book may be seen in chapters sixty-third and sixty-seventh, which are thus translated by Legge:

(It is the way of Tao) not to act from any personal motive; to conduct affairs without feeling the trouble of them; to taste without being aware of the flavour: to account the great as small and the small as great; to recompense injury with kindness.

(The follower of Tao) anticipates things that would become difficult while they are easy, and does things that would become great while they are little. The difficult things in the world arise from what are easy, and the great things from what are small. Thus it is that the sage never does what is great, and therefore can accomplish the greatest things.

He who assents lightly will be found to keep but little faith. He who takes many things easily is sure to meet with many difficulties. Hence the sage sees difficulty in (what seem) easy things, and therefore never has any difficulties.

All in the world say that my Tao is great, but that I seem to be inferior to others. Now it is just this greatness which makes me seem inferior to others. Those who are deemed equal to others have long been—small men.

But there are three precious things which I prize and hold fast. The first is gentle compassion; the second is economy; the third is (humility), not presuming to take precedence in the world. With gentle compassion I can be brave. With economy I can be liberal. Not presuming to claim

[1] The Speculations on Metaphysics, Polity, and Morality, of "the Old Philosopher," Laotsze; translated from the Chinese, with an Introduction by John Chalmers, A.M., pp. xi, xii. Lond., 1868.

precedence in the world, I can make myself a vessel fit for the most distinguished services. Now-a-days they give up gentle compassion, and cultivate (mere physical) courage; they give up economy, and (try to be) lavish
(without it); they give up being last, and seek to be first:—of all which
the end is death. Gentle compassion is sure to overcome in fight, and to
be firm in maintaining its own. Heaven will save its possessor, protecting
him by his gentleness.[1]

It has been disputed whether the Tao-teh-King acknowledges
Leaves the per- the existence of a personal God. Professor Douglas
sonal existence declares that Laotsze knew nothing of such a being,
of God doubt-
ful.   and that the whole tenor of his philosophy antagonizes
such a belief. Legge, on the other hand, affirms that the Tao-teh-
King does recognize the existence of God, but contains no direct
religious teaching. Laotsze's Taoism, he observes, is the exhibition
of a way or method of living which men should cultivate as the
highest and purest development of their nature. It has served as
a discipline of mind and life for multitudes, leading some to with-
draw entirely from the busy world, and others to struggle earnestly
to keep themselves from the follies and passions of reckless and
ambitious men. The highest moral teaching of Laotsze is found in
the chapter sixty-third, quoted above, in which he says that Tao
prompts "to recompense injury with kindness." In this particular
he surpassed Confucius, whose great glory it was to enunciate, in
negative form, the golden rule, "What you do not want done to
yourself, do not do to others." Confucius confessed that he did
not always keep his own rule, much less could he adopt the loftier
precept of Laotsze, but said rather, "Recompense injury with justice, and return good for good."[2]

Far more extensive and important, however, taken as a whole,
Confucius and are the sacred books of Confucianism, which is *par ex-
the   ancient cellence* the religion of the Chinese Empire. But Con-
Chinese script-
ures.   fucius was not the founder of the religion which has
become attached to his name. He claimed merely to have studied
deeply into antiquity, and to be a transmitter and teacher of the
records and worship of the past. "It is an error," says Legge,
"to suppose that he compiled the historical documents, poems, and
other ancient books from various works existing in his time. Portions of the oldest works had already perished. His study of those
that remained, and his exhortations to his disciples also to study
them, contributed to their preservation. What he wrote or said
about their meaning should be received by us with reverence; but

[1] Lectures on the Religions of China, pp. 222–224.
[2] Comp. Legge, Ibid., pp. 143 and passim.

if all the works which he handled had come down to us entire, we should have been, so far as it is possible for foreigners to be, in the same position as he was for learning the ancient religion of his country. Our text-books would be the same as his. Unfortunately most of the ancient books suffered loss and injury after Confucius had passed from the stage of life. We have reason, however, to be thankful that we possess so many and so much of them. No other literature, comparable to them for antiquity, has come down to us in such a state of preservation."[1]

The five King are known respectively as the Shu, the Shih, the Yi, the Li Ki, and the Khun Khiu.[2] The name *King*, Names of the five King. which means a web of cloth, or the warp which keeps the threads in place, came into use in the time of the Han dynasty, about B. C. 200, and was applied by the scholars of this period to the most valuable ancient books, which were regarded as having a sort of canonical authority.

The Shu King is a book of historical documents, somewhat resembling the various historical portions of the Old Testament, and is believed to be the oldest of all the The Shu King. Chinese books. Its contents relate to a period extending over seventeen centuries, from about B. C. 2357 to B. C. 627. It commences with an account of Yao, the most venerable of the ancient kings, of whom it is written: "He was reverential, intelligent, accomplished, and thoughtful,—naturally and without effort. He was sincerely courteous, and capable of all complaisance. The bright influence of these qualities was felt through the four quarters of the land, and reached to heaven above and earth beneath. He made the able and virtuous distinguished, and thence proceeded to the love of all in the nine classes of his kindred, who thus became harmonious. He also regulated and polished the people of his domain, who all became brightly intelligent. Finally, he united and harmonized the myriad states; and so the black-haired people were transformed. The result was universal concord."

The Shu King is about equal in extent to the two books of Chronicles, and is divided into five parts, which are designated respectively, the books of Thang, Yu. Hsia, Shang, and Kau. These are the names of so many different ancient dynasties which ruled in China, and the several books consist of the annals, speeches, counsels, and proclamations of the great kings and ministers of the ancients.

[1] Preface to his translation of the Shu King in vol. iii of the Sacred Books of the East, as edited by Max Müller..

[2] We here adopt the orthography followed by Legge in his translations for the Sacred Books of the East.

The following passage is one of the most favourable specimens, and illustrates the tone and character of Chinese morality, and their most popular conceptions of virtue. It is from the third book of Part II, which is entitled "The Counsels of Kao-yao." Kao-yao was the minister of crime under the reign of the great Emperor Shun (about 2300 B. C.), and is celebrated as a model administrator of justice ·

Kao-yao said, " O! there are in all nine virtues to be discovered in conduct, and when we say that a man possesses (any) virtue, that is as much as to say he does such and such things." Yu asked, "What (are the nine virtues)?" Kao-yao replied, "Affability combined with dignity; mildness combined with firmness; bluntness combined with respectfulness; aptness for government combined with reverent caution; docility combined with boldness; straightforwardness combined with gentleness; an easy negligence combined with discrimination; boldness combined with sincerity; and valour combined with righteousness. (When these qualities are) displayed, and that continuously, have we not the good (officer)? When there is a daily display of three (of these) virtues, their possessor could early and late regulate and brighten the clan (of which he was made chief). When there is a daily severe and reverent cultivation of six of them, their possessor could brilliantly conduct the affairs of the state (with which he was invested). When (such men) are all received and advanced, the possessors of those nine virtues will be employed in (the public) service. The men of a thousand and men of a hundred will be in their offices; the various ministers will emulate one another; all the officers will accomplish their duties at the proper times, observant of the five seasons (as the several elements predominate in them),—and thus their various duties will be fully accomplished. Let not (the Son of Heaven) set to the holders of states the example of indolence or dissoluteness. Let him be wary and fearful (remembering that) in one day or two days there may occur ten thousand springs of things. Let him not have his various officers cumberers of their places. The work is Heaven's; men must act for it! "

A passage in Part V, Book 4, thus enumerates the five sources of happiness, and the six extreme evils:

The first is long life; the second, riches; the third, soundness of body and serenity of mind; the fourth, the love of virtue; and the fifth, fulfilling to the end the will of Heaven. Of the six extreme evils, the first is misfortune shortening life; the second, sickness; the third, distress of mind; the fourth, poverty; the fifth, wickedness; the sixth, weakness.

The Shih King is a book of poetry, and contains three hundred and five pieces, commonly called odes. It is the psalter of the Chinese bible, and consists of ballads relating to customs and events of Chinese antiquity, and songs and hymns to

The Shih King.

be sung on great state occasions and in connexion with sacrificial services.[1] The following is a fair example of the odes used in connexion with the worship of ancestors. A young king, feeling his responsibilities, would fain follow the example of his father, and prays to him for help:

> I take counsel, at the beginning of my rule,
> How I can follow the example of my shrined father.
> Ah! far-reaching were his plans,
> And I am not yet able to carry them out.
> However, I endeavour to reach to them,
> My continuation of them will still be all-deflected.
> I am a little child,
> Unequal to the many difficulties of the state.
> Having taken his place, I will look for him to go up
> and come down in the court,
> To ascend and descend in the house.
> Admirable art thou, O great Father;
> Condescend to preserve and enlighten me.[2]

The Yi King is commonly called "the Book of Changes," from its supposed illustrations of the onward course of nature and the changing customs of the world.[3] It contains eight trigrams, ascribed to Fuhsi, the mythical founder of the Chinese nation, and hence some have believed it to be the oldest of all the Chinese scriptures. But according to Legge, "not a single character in the Yi is older than the twelfth century B. C. The text of it, not taking in the appendices of Confucius, consists of two portions—from king Wan, and from his son, the duke of Chau. The composition of Wan's portion is referred to the year B. C. 1143. As an authority for the ancient religion of China, therefore, the Yi is by no means equal to the Shu and the Shih. It is based on diagrams, or lineal figures, ascribed to Fuhsi, and made up of whole and divided lines (—— and — —). What their framer intended by these figures we do not know. No doubt there was a tradition about it, and I am willing to believe that it found a home in the existing Yi. . . . The character called Yi is the symbol for the idea of change. The fashion of the world is continually being altered. We have action and re-action, flux and reflux—now one condition, and immediately its opposite. The

The Yi King.

---

[1] See The Shih King; or the Book of Ancient Poetry, translated into English Verse, with Essays and Notes, by James Legge. Lond., 1876.

[2] Decade III, Ode 2, p. 329, Sacred Books of the East, vol. iii. Oxford, 1879.

[3] The Yi King is translated and annotated by Legge in vol. xvi of the Sacred Books of the East. Oxford, 1882.

vicissitudes in the worlds of sense and society have their correspondencies in the changes that take place in the lines of the diagrams.
Again, certain relations and conditions of men and things lead to
good, are fortunate; and certain others lead to evil, are unfortunate;
and these results are indicated by the relative position of the lines.
Those lines were systematically changed by manipulating with a
fixed number of the stalks of a certain plant. In this way the Yi
served the purpose of divination; and since such is the nature of
the book, a reader must be prepared for much in it that is tantaliz-
ing, fantastic, and perplexing." [1]

The two remaining classics are of less interest and importance.
The Li Ki and The Li Ki King is a record of rites, consisting of three
the Khun Khiu. collections, called "the Three Rituals," and is the most
bulky of the Five King. It contains regulations for the administration of the government, describes the various officers and their
duties, and the rules of etiquette by which scholars and officers
should order their conduct on social and state occasions. The
Khun Khiu King is of the nature of a supplement to the historical
annals of the Shu King. It was compiled by Confucius from the
annals of his native state of Lu, and extends from the year B. C. 722
to B. C. 481.

The Chinese classics known as "the Four Shu" have not the
rank and authority of the Five King. They are the works of disciples of Confucius, and consist (1) of the Lun Yu, or Discourses
of Confucius and conversations between him and his followers;
(2) the works of Mencius, next to Confucius the greatest sage and
teacher of Confucianism; (3) the Ta Hsio, or Great Learning,
ascribed to Tszang-tsze, a disciple of Confucius; and (4) the Kung
Yung, or Doctrine of the Mean, a production of Tszesze, the grandson of Confucius. [2] There is also the Hsiao King, or Classic of
Filial Piety, which holds a high place in Chinese literature. [3]

In the preface to his translation of the Sacred Books of China,
Legge observes, "that the ancient books of China do not profess to
have been inspired, or to contain what we should call a Revelation.
Historians, poets, and others wrote them as they were moved in
their own minds. An old poem may occasionally contain what it
says was spoken by God, but we can only understand that language
as calling attention emphatically to the statement to which it is

---

[1] The Religions of China, pp. 37, 38.

[2] See The Chinese Classics, with a Translation, Critical and Exegetical Notes, Prolegomena, and copious Indexes. Hong Kong, 1861–1865.

[3] The Hsiao King is translated and annotated by Legge in vol. iii of Sacred Books
of the East.

prefixed. We also read of Heaven's raising up the great ancient sovereigns and teachers, and variously assisting them to accomplish their undertakings; but all this need not be more than what a religious man of any country might affirm at the present day of direction, help, and guidance given to himself and others from above."

Whatever the true solution of the questions may be, the facts that distinguished Chinese scholars dispute as to whether the Confucian Sacred Books recognize the existence of a personal God, and that missionaries, in translating the Christian Scriptures into Chinese, scruple over a word that will properly represent the Christian idea of God, show the comparative vagueness and obscurity of the religion of the Chinese scriptures.

THE EGYPTIAN BOOK OF THE DEAD.

A most mysterious and interesting work is the Sacred Book of the ancient Egyptians, commonly known as the Book of the Dead. Some Egyptologists prefer the title "Funeral Ritual," inasmuch as it contains many prescriptions and prayers to be used *Its different* in funeral services, and the vignettes which appear on *names.* many copies represent funeral processions, and priests reading the formularies out of a book. But as the prayers are, for the most part, the language to be used by the departed in their progress through the under world, the title "Book of the Dead" has been generally adopted.

The Egyptian title of the work is, Book of the *Peri em hru*, three simple words, but by no means easy of explanation when taken together without a context.[1] *Peri* signifies "coming forth," *hru* is "day," and *em* is the preposition signifying "from," susceptible, like the same preposition in other languages, of a variety of uses. The probable meaning of *Peri em hru* is "coming forth by day," and is to be understood mainly of the immortality and resurrection of the dead. The book exists in a great number of manuscripts recovered from Egyptian tombs, and the text is very corrupt; for as the writing was not intended for mortal eyes, but to be buried with the dead, copyists would not be likely to be very scrupulous in their work. But the book exists not only on papyrus rolls that were deposited in the tombs, but many of the chapters are inscribed upon coffins, mummies, sepulchral wrappings, statues, and the walls of tombs. Some tombs may be said to contain entire recensions of

---

[1] The Religion of Ancient Egypt, by P. Le Page Renouf. Hibbert Lectures for 1879, p. 181. New York, 1880. Our account of the Book of the Dead is condensed mainly from Renouf's fifth Lecture.

the book. But no two copies contain exactly the same chapters, or
Corrupt and follow the same arrangement. The papyrus of Turin,
confused con- published by Lepsius, contains one hundred and sixty-
dition of the
text.   five chapters, and is the longest known. But a considerable number of chapters found in other manuscripts are not included
in it. None of the copies contain the entire collection of chapters,
but the more ancient manuscripts have fewer chapters than the
more recent. There is a great uniformity of style and of grammatical forms, as compared with other productions of Egyptian literature, and nothing can exceed the simplicity and brevity of the
sentences. A critical collation of a sufficient number of copies of
each chapter will, in time, restore the text to as accurate a standard
as could be attained in the most flourishing days of the old Egyptian monarchy.

The book is mythological throughout,[1] and assumes the reader's
Its obscurity familiarity with its myths and legends. The difficulty
in the subject of its exposition is not in literally translating the text,
matter.   but in understanding the meaning concealed beneath
familiar words. The English translation by Samuel Birch, published in the fifth volume of Bunsen's Egypt's Place in Universal
History, is an exact rendering of the text of the Turin manuscript,
and to an Englishman gives nearly as correct an impression of the
original as the text itself would do to an Egyptian who had not
been carefully taught the mysteries of his religion.

The foundation of Egyptian mythology is the legend of Osiris.[2]
The Osiris le- Having long ruled in Egypt, he was at last slain by the
gend the basis evil Typhon, enclosed in a mummy case, and cast into
of Egyptian
mythology.   the river Nile. Isis, his sister and spouse, sought long
for his body, and at length found it at Byblus, on the Phœnician
coast, where it had been tossed by the waves. She brought it back
to Egypt, and buried it; and when Horus, their son, grew up, he
slew the evil Typhon, and so avenged his father. Osiris, however,
was not dead. He had, in fact, descended to the under world, and
established his dominion there, and at the same time revived in the
person of his son Horus, and renewed his dominion over the living.

[1] "The Ritual," says Birch, "is, according to Egyptian notions, essentially an inspired work; and the term Hermetic, so often applied by profane writers to these
books, in reality means inspired. It is Thoth himself who speaks and reveals the
will of the gods and the mysterious nature of divine things to man. . . . Portions of
them are expressly stated to have been written by the very finger of Thoth himself,
and to have been the composition of a great God." Introduction to his translation of
the Funeral Ritual, in Bunsen's Egypt's Place in Universal History, vol. v, p. 133.

[2] On this Egyptian legend comp. Bunsen, Egypt's Place in Universal History, vol. i,
pp. 423–439, and George Rawlinson, History of Ancient Egypt, vol. i, pp. 365–371.

The usual explanation of this legend makes it a mythical portraiture of the annual dying and reviving of the powers **The probable** of nature under the peculiar conditions of the valley of **meaning of the** the Nile. Osiris represents the fertilizing river; Isis **myth.** the fruit-bearing land; Typhon the evil spirit of the parched deserts and the salt sea, the demon of drought and barrenness. Horus is the sun, appearing in the vernal equinox, and heralding the rising of the Nile. Accordingly, when the Nile sinks before the scorching winds of the Libyan desert, Osiris is slain by Typhon. Isis, the land, then sighs and yearns for her lost brother and spouse. But when the Nile again overflows, it is a resurrection of Osiris, and the vernal sun destroys the demon of drought and renews the face of nature. Other slightly varying explanations of the legend have been given, but whatever particular view we adopt, it will be easy to see how the drapery of these legends might, in course of time, come to be used of the death and resurrection of man. Hence we find that the names of mythical personages are constantly recurring in the Book of the Dead.

The beatification of the dead is the main subject of the book. The blessed dead are represented as enjoying an existence **Beatification of** similar to that which they had led on earth. They **the dead the** have the use of all their limbs, eat and drink, and satisfy **main subject.** all their physical wants as in their earthly life. But they are not confined to any one locality, or to any one form or mode of existence. They have the range of the entire universe, in every shape and form which they desire. Twelve chapters of the Book of the Dead consist of formulas to be used in effecting certain transformations. The forms assumed, according to these chapters, are the turtledove, the serpent Sata, the bird Bennu, the crocodile Sebek, the god Ptah, a golden hawk, the chief of the principal gods, a soul, a lotusflower, and a heron. The transformations to which these chapters refer, however, are far from exhausting the list of possible ones. No limit is imposed on the will of the departed, and in this respect the Egyptian doctrine of transmigration differs widely from the Pythagorean.

Throughout the Book of the Dead, the identification of the deceased with Osiris, or assimilation to him, is taken for **Identification** granted, and all the deities of the family of Osiris are **with Osiris.** supposed to perform for the deceased whatever the legend records as having been done for Osiris himself. Thus, in the eighteenth chapter, the deceased is brought before a series of divinities in succession, the gods of Heliopolis, Abydos, and other localities, and at each station the litany begins:

O Tehuti [or Thoth], who causest Osiris to triumph against his opponents, cause the Osiris (such a one) to triumph against his opponents, even
as thou hast made Osiris to triumph against his opponents.

In the next chapter, which is another recension of the eighteenth,
and is entitled the "Crown of Triumph," the deceased is declared
triumphant forever, and all the gods in heaven and earth repeat
this, and the chapter ends with the following:

Horus has repeated this declaration four times, and all his enemies fall
prostrate before him annihilated. Horus, the son of Isis, repeats it millions
of times, and all his enemies fall annihilated. They are carried off to the
place of execution in the East; their heads are cut off, their necks are brok-
en; their thighs are severed, and delivered up to the great destroyer who
dwells in Aati; they shall not come forth from the custody of Seb forever.

But not to Osiris only is the deceased assimilated. In the forty-
second chapter every limb is assimilated to a different
deity; the hair to Nu, the face to Ra, the eyes to
Hathor, the ears to Apuat, the nose to the god of Sechem, the lips
to Anubis, the teeth to Selket, and so on, the catalogue ending with
the words: "There is not a limb in him without a god, and Tehuti
is a safeguard to all his members." Further on it is said:

*Other assimi-
lations.*

Not men, nor gods, nor the ghosts of the departed, nor the damned,
past, present, or future, whoever they be, can do him hurt. He it is who
cometh forth in safety. "Whom men know not" is his name. The "Yesterday which sees endless years" is his name, passing in triumph by the
roads of heaven. The deceased is the Lord of eternity; he is reckoned even
as Chepera; he is the master of the kingly crown.

The one hundred and forty-ninth chapter gives an account of the
terrible nature of certain divinities and localities which
the deceased must encounter—gigantic and venomous
serpents, gods with names significant of death and destruction,
waters and atmospheres of flames. But none of these prevail over
the Osiris; he passes through all things without harm, and lives in
peace with the fearful gods who preside over these abodes. Some
of these gods remind one of the demons in Dante's Inferno. But
though ministers of divine justice, their nature is not evil. The
following are invocations, from the seventeenth chapter, to be used
of one passing through these dangers:

*Dangers of the
deceased.*

O Ra, in thine egg, radiant in thy disk shining forth from the horizon,
swimming over the steel firmament, sailing over the pillars of Shu; thou
who hast no second among the gods, who producest the winds by the
flames of thy mouth, and who enlightenest the worlds with thy splendours,

save the departed from that god whose nature is a mystery, and whose eyebrows are as the arms of the balance on the night when Aauit was weighed. . . . O Scarabæus god in thy bark, whose substance is self-originated, save the Osiris from those watchers to whom the Lord of spirits has entrusted the observation of his enemies, and from whose observations none can escape. Let me not fall under their swords, nor go to their blocks of execution; let me not remain in their abodes; let me not rest upon their beds [of torment]; let me not fall into their nets. Let naught befall me which the gods abhor.

We have not space for further illustrations of this most interesting work. It will be seen how this Funeral Ritual, or Book of the Dead, embodies the Egyptian doctrines of a future state, and the rewards and punishments of that after life.[1] But it will also be observed how thoroughly its theology is blended with all that is superstitious and degrading in a polytheistic mythology.

The Koran.

The Mohammedan Bible is a comparatively modern book, and easily accessible to English readers.[2] It is about half the size of the Old Testament, and contains one hundred and four- General charteen chapters, called Suras. It is doubtful whether acter. Mohammed ever learned to read or write. He dictated his revelations to his disciples, and they wrote them on date leaves, bits of parchment, tablets of white stone, and shoulder-blades of sheep. These were written during the last twenty years of the prophet's life, and a year after his death the different fragments were collected by his followers, and arranged according to the length of the chapters, beginning with the longest and ending with the shortest. So the book, as regards its contents, presents a strange medley, having no real beginning, middle, or end. And yet it is probably a faithful transcript of Mohammed's mind and heart as exhibited during the latter portion of his life. In some passages he seems to have been inspired with a holy zeal, and eloquently proclaims the glory of Almighty God, the merciful and compassionate. Other

[1] See J. P. Thompson's Article on the Egyptian Doctrine of a Future State, in the Bibliotheca Sacra, January, 1868, in which a fair analysis of the teachings of the Book of the Dead is given.

[2] Sale's English version of the Koran has been published in many forms, and his Preliminary Discourse is invaluable for the study of Islam. The translation of Rev. I. M. Rodwell (Lond., 1861) has the Suras arranged in chronological order. But the recent translation by E. H. Palmer (vols. vi and ix of Müller's Sacred Books of the East) is undoubtedly the best English version.

passages have the form and spirit of a bulletin of war.[1] In another he seems to make an apology for taking to himself an additional wife.[2] Another suggests a political manœuvre. But, on the whole, the Koran is a most tedious book to read. It is full of repetitions, and seems incapable of happy translation into any other language. Its crowning glory is its glowing Arabic diction. "Regarding it," says Palmer, "from a perfectly impartial and unbiassed standpoint, we find that it expresses the thoughts and ideas of a Bedawi Arab in Bedawi language and metaphor. The language is noble and forcible, but it is not elegant in the sense of literary refinement. To Mohammed's hearers it must have been startling from the manner in which it brought great truths home to them in the language of their everyday life."[3] Mohammed was wont to urge that the marvellous excellence of his book was a standing proof of its divine and superhuman origin. "If men and genii," says he, "united themselves together to bring the like of this Koran, they could not bring the like, though they should back each other up!"[4]

The founder of Islam appears to have been from early life a Life and claims contemplative soul. In the course of his travels as a of Mohammed. merchant he probably often met and talked with Jews and Christians. The Koran contains on almost every page some allusion to Jewish history or Christian doctrine; but Mohammed's acquaintance with both Judaism and Christianity appears to have been formed from oral sources, and was confused with many vague and silly traditions. It should be observed, too, that at that period an earnest seeker after truth, under circumstances like those which tended chiefly to fashion Mohammed's mind and character, might very easily have become bewildered by the various traditions of the Jews and the foolish controversies of the Christians. The Church was then distracted with controversy over the Trinity and the use of images in worship. To Mohammed, a religion which filled its churches with images of saints was no better than a gross idolatry. His knowledge of Jesus was gathered largely from the apocryphal gospels and through Jewish channels. Hence we may understand the reason of the perverted form in which so many Christian ideas are treated in the Koran.

Mohammed claimed to be the last of six great apostles who had been sent upon divine missions into the world. Those six are

[1] Sura iii, 135-145; viii, xl. Comp. Muir, Life of Mahomet, vol. iii, p. 224.
[2] Sura xxxiii, 35-40; lxvi.
[3] The Qur'an. Translated by E. H. Palmer. Introduction, p. lxxvii.
[4] Koran, Sura xvii, 90.

Adam, Noah, Abraham, Moses, Jesus, and Mohammed. Nothing specially new or original is to be found in the Moslem bible. It has been maintained that "Islam was little else than a republication of Judaism, with such modifications as suited it to Arabian soil, plus the important addition of the prophetic mission of Mohammed." [1] The following passage from the fifth Sura well illustrates the general style of the Koran:

[20] God's is the kingdom of the heavens and the earth and what is between the two; he created what he will, for God is mighty over all! But the Jews and the Christians say, "We are the sons of God and his beloved." Say, "Why then does he punish you for your sins?" nay, ye are mortals of those whom he has created! He pardons whom he pleases, and punishes whom he pleases; for God's is the kingdom of the heavens and the earth, and what is between the two, and unto him the journey is. O people of the book! our apostle has come to you, explaining to you the interval of apostles; lest ye say, "There came not to us a herald of glad tidings nor a warner." But there has come to you now a herald of glad tidings and a warner, and God is mighty over all! When Moses said to his people, "O my people! remember the favour of God toward you when he made among you prophets, and made for you kings, and brought you what never was brought to any body in the worlds. O my people! enter the holy land which God has prescribed for you; and be ye not thrust back upon your hinder parts and retreat losers." [25] They said, "O Moses! verily, therein is a people, giants; and we will surely not enter therein until they go out from thence; but if they go out then we will enter in." Then said two men of those who fear,—God had been gracious to them both,—"Enter ye upon them by the door, and when ye have entered it, verily, ye shall be victorious; and upon God do ye rely if ye be believers." They said, "O Moses! we shall never enter it so long as they are therein; so, go thou and thy Lord and fight ye twain; verily, we will sit down here." Said he, "My Lord, verily, I can control only myself and my brother; therefore part us from these sinful people." He said, "Then, verily, it is forbidden them; for forty years shall they wander about in the earth; so vex not thyself for the sinful people."

[30] Recite to them the story of the two sons of Adam; truly when they offered an offering and it was accepted from one of them, and was not accepted from the other, that one said, "I will surely kill thee;" he said, "God only accepts from those who fear. If thou dost stretch forth to me thine hand to kill me, I will not stretch forth mine hand to kill thee; verily, I fear God the Lord of the worlds; verily, I wish that thou mayest draw upon thee my sin and thy sin, and be of the fellows of the fire, for that is the reward of the unjust." But his soul allowed him to slay his brother, and he slew him, and in the morning he was of those who lose. And God sent a crow to scratch in the earth and show him how he might

---

[1] Mohammed and Mohammedanism. Lectures by R. Bosworth Smith, p. 143. New York, 1875.

hide his brother's shame, he said, "Alas, for me! Am I too helpless to become like this crow and hide my brother's shame?" and in the morning he was of those who did repent.

[35] For this cause have we prescribed to the children of Israel that whoso kills a soul, unless it be for another soul or for violence in the land, it is as though he had killed men altogether; but whoso saves one, it is as though he saved men altogether.[1]

The one hundred and twelfth Sura is held in special veneration among the Mohammedans, and is popularly accounted equal in value to a third part of the entire Koran. It is said to have been revealed in answer to one who wished to know the distinguishing attributes of Mohammed's God. The following is Palmer's version:

> In the name of the merciful and compassionate God
> Say, He is God alone!
> God the Eternal!
> He begets not, and is not begotten!
> Nor is there like unto him any one!

The following passage, from the beginning of the second Sura, is to be understood as the words of the Angel Gabriel to Mohammed, and showing him the character and importance of the Koran:

That is the book! there is no doubt therein; a guide to the pious, who believe in the unseen, and are steadfast in prayer, and of what we have given them expend in alms; who believe in what is revealed to thee, and what was revealed before thee, and of the hereafter they are sure. These are in guidance from their Lord, and these are the prosperous. Verily, those who misbelieve, it is the same to them if ye warn them or if ye warn them not, they will not believe. God has set a seal upon their hearts and on their hearing; and on their eyes is dimness, and for them is grievous woe. And there are those among men who say, "We believe in God and in the last day;" but they do not believe. They would deceive God and those who do believe; but they deceive only themselves and they do not perceive. In their hearts is a sickness, and God has made them still more sick, and for them is grievous woe because they lied. And when it is said to them, "Do not evil in the earth," they say, "We do but what is right." Are not they the evil doers? and yet they do not perceive. And when it is said to them, "Believe as other men believe," they say, "Shall we believe as fools believe?" Are not they themselves the fools? and yet they do not know. And when they meet those who believe, they say, "We do believe;" but when they go aside with their devils, they say, "We are with you; we were but mocking!" God shall mock at them and let them go on in their rebellion, blindly wandering on.[2]

[1] Palmer's translation, Part I., pp. 100–102.
[2] Ibid., pp. 2, 3.

The following, from the same Sura, is a specimen of the manner in which Mohammed garbles and presents incidents of Israelitish history:

Dost thou not look at the crowd of the children of Israel after Moses' time, when they said to a prophet of theirs, "Raise up for us a king, and we will fight in God's way?" He said, "Will ye perhaps, if it be written down for you to fight, refuse to fight?" They said, "And why should we not fight in God's way, now that we are dispossessed of our homes and sons?" But when it was written down for them to fight they turned back, save a few of them, and God knows who are evil doers. Then their prophet said to them, "Verily, God has raised up for you Talut as a king;" they said, "How can the kingdom be his over us; we have more right to the kingdom than he, for he has not an amplitude of wealth?" He said, "Verily, God has chosen him over you, and has provided him with an extent of knowledge and of form. God gives the kingdom unto whom he will; God comprehends and knows."

Then said to them their prophet, "The sign of his kingdom is that there shall come to you the ark with the shechinah in it from your Lord, and the relics of what the family of Moses and the family of Aaron left; the angels shall bear it." In that is surely a sign to you if ye believe.

Whatever opinion we may form of the Koran, or of Islam, it must be conceded that the man, who, like Mohammed, in one generation organized a race of savage tribes into a united people, founded an empire which for more than a thousand years has covered a territory as extensive as that of Rome in her proudest days, and established a religion which to-day numbers over a hundred million adherents, must have been an extraordinary character, and his life and works must be worthy of careful philosophic study. But it will also be conceded, by all competent to judge, that, as a volume of sacred literature, the Koran is very deficient in those elements of independence and originality which are noticeable in the sacred books of the other great religions of the world. The strict Mohammedans regard every syllable of the Koran as of a directly divine origin. "The divine revelation," observes Muir, "was the cornerstone of Islam. The recital of a passage formed an essential part of every celebration of public worship; and its private perusal and repetition was enforced as a duty and a privilege, fraught with the richest religious merit. This is the universal voice of early tradition, and may be gathered from the revelation itself. The Koran was accordingly committed to memory more or less by every adherent of Islam, and the extent to which it could be recited was reckoned one of the chief distinctions of nobility in the early Moslem empire. The custom of

Arabia favoured the task. Passionately fond of poetry, yet possessed of but limited means and skill in committing to writing the effusions of their bards, the Arabs had long been habituated to imprint them on the living tablets of their hearts. The recollective faculty was thus cultivated to the highest pitch; and it was applied with all the ardour of an awakened Arab spirit to the Koran. Several of Mohammed's followers, according to early tradition, could, during his lifetime, repeat with scrupulous accuracy the entire revelation."[1]

THE EDDAS.

Two ancient collections of Scandinavian poems and legends,

General character of the two Eddas. known as the Elder and the Younger Edda, embody the mythology of the Teutonic tribes which settled in early times in the sea-girt lands of Denmark, Sweden, and Norway. From these tribes migrated also the ancient colonists of Iceland. To these old Norsemen the Eddas hold a position corresponding to that of the Vedas among the ancient Hindus, and the Avesta among the Persians.

In the old Norse language the word Edda means ancestress, or great-grandmother. Probably the poems and traditions so named were long perpetuated orally by the venerable mothers, who repeated them to their children and children's children at the blazing firesides of those northern homes. The Elder Edda, often called the Poetic Edda, consists of thirty-nine poems, and would nearly equal in size the books of Psalms and Proverbs combined. The Younger or Prose Edda is a collection of the myths of the Scandinavian deities, and furnishes to some extent a commentary on the older Edda, from the songs of which it quotes frequently. These interesting works were quite unknown to the learned world until the latter part of the seventeenth century. But it appears that the poems of the older Edda were collected about the beginning of the twelfth century by Saemund Sigfusson, an Icelandic priest, who, after pursuing classical and theological studies in the universities of France and Germany, returned to Iceland and settled in a village at the foot of Mount Hecla. Whether he collected these poems from oral tradition, or from runic manuscripts or inscriptions, is uncertain. A copy of this Edda on vellum, believed to date from the fourteenth century, was found in Iceland by Bishop Sveinsson in 1643, and was subsequently published under the title of The Edda of Saemund the Learned.[2] The prose Edda is ascribed to the celebrated Ice-

---

[1] The Life of Mahomet, vol. i. Introduction, p. 5. London, 1861.
[2] Edda Saemundar hins Froda, Copenhagen. 3 vols. 1787–1828. The third volume contains the Lexicon Mythologicum of Finn Magnusson.

landic historian, Snorri Sturlason (born 1178), who probably collected its several parts from oral tradition and other sources. The first copy known to Europeans was found by Jonsson in 1628, and the first complete edition was published by Rask, at Stockholm, in 1818.[1]

The first, and perhaps oldest, poem of the Elder Edda is entitled the Völuspa, that is, the Song of the Prophetess. It narrates in poetic form the creation of the universe The Völuspa. and of man, the origin of evil, and how death entered into the world. It speaks of a future destruction and renovation of the universe, and of the abodes of bliss and woe. The prophetess thus begins her song:

> 1. All noble souls, yield me devout attention,
> Ye high and low of Heimdall's race,[2]
> I will All Father's works make known,
> The oldest sayings which I call to mind.
>
> 2. Of giants eight was I first born,
> They reared me up from ancient times;
> Nine worlds I know, nine limbs I know
> Of that strong trunk within the earth.[3]
>
> 3. In that far age when Ymir[4] lived,
> There was no sand, nor sea, nor saline wave;
> Earth there was not, nor lofty heaven,
> A yawning deep, but verdure none,
>
> 4. Until Bör's sons the spheres upheaved,
> And they the mighty Midgard[5] formed.

[1] An English translation of the Poetic Edda was published by Benjamin Thorpe (Two parts, London, 1866), but is now out of print. Comp. Icelandic Poetry, or the Edda of Saemund translated into English verse by A. S. Cottle (Bristol, 1797). Many fragments of the lays are given in Anderson's Norse Mythology (Chicago, 1880). An English translation of the Prose Edda is given in Blackwell's edition of Mallet's Northern Antiquities (Bohn's Antiquarian Library). A new translation by R. B. Anderson has been published at Chicago (1880). A very complete and convenient German translation of both Eddas, with explanations by Karl Simrock, has passed through many editions (seventh improved edition, Stuttgart, 1878).

[2] Heimdall, according to the old Norse mythology, was the father and founder of the different classes of men, nobles, churls, and thralls.

[3] Referring to the great mundane ash-tree where the gods assemble every day in council. This tree strikes its roots through all worlds, and is thus described in the nineteenth verse of the Völuspa:

> An ash I know named Yggdrasil,
> A lofty tree wet with white mist,
> Thence comes the dew which in the valleys falls;
> Ever green it stands o'er the Urdar-fount.

[4] Ymir was the progenitor of the giants, and out of his body the world was created.

[5] The Prose Edda explains that the earth is round without, and encircled by the ocean, the outward shores of which were assigned to the race of giants. But around

The southern sun shone on the cliffs
And green the ground became with plants.

5. The southern sun, the moon's companion,
Held with right hand the steeds of heaven.
The sun knew not where she[1] might set,
The moon knew not what power he[1] had,
The stars knew not where they might dwell.

6. Then went the Powers to judgment seats,
The gods most holy held a council,
To night and new moon gave they names,
They named the morning and the midday,
And evening, to arrange the times.[2]

Another very interesting poem is the Grimnis-mal, or Lay of Grimner, in which we find a description of the twelve habitations of heavenly deities, by which some scholars understand the twelve signs of the zodiac. The sixth poem is called the Hava-mal, or Sublime Lay. It is an ethical poem, embodying a considerable collection of ancient Norse proverbs. The following passages, from Bishop Percy's prose translation, are specimens:

1. Consider and examine well all your doors before you venture to stir abroad: for he is exposed to continual danger, whose enemies lie in ambush concealed in his court.

3. To the guest, who enters your dwelling with frozen knees, give the warmth of your fire: he who hath travelled over the mountains hath need of food, and well-dried garments.

4. Offer water to him who sits down at your table; for he hath occasion to cleanse his hands: and entertain him honourably and kindly, if you would win from him friendly words and a grateful return.

5. He who travelleth hath need of wisdom. One may do at home whatsoever one will; but he who is ignorant of good manners will only draw contempt upon himself, when he comes to sit down with men well instructed.

7. He who goes to a feast, where he is not expected, either speaks with a lowly voice, or is silent; he listens with his ears, and is attentive with his eyes; by this he acquires knowledge and wisdom.

8. Happy he, who draws upon himself the applause and benevolence of men! for whatever depends upon the will of others, is hazardous and uncertain.

a portion of the inland Odin, Vile, and Ve, the sons of Bör, raised a bulwark against turbulent giants, and to the portion of the earth which it encircled they gave the name of Midgard. For this structure, it is said, they used the eyebrows of Ymir, of his flesh they formed the land, of his sweat and blood the seas, of his bones the mountains, of his hair the trees, of his brains the clouds, and of his skull the vault of heaven. See Mallet, Northern Antiquities, pp. 98, 405. Anderson, Norse Mythology, p. 175.

[1] In the Norse language, sun is feminine and moon is masculine.

[2] Translated from Simrock's German version of the Völuspa.

10. A man can carry with him no better provision for his journey than the strength of understanding. In a foreign country this will be of more use to him than treasures; and will introduce him to the table of strangers.

12–13. A man cannot carry a worse custom with him to a banquet than that of drinking too much; the more the drunkard swallows, the less is his wisdom, till he loses his reason. The bird of oblivion sings before those who inebriate themselves, and steals away their souls.[1]

We add a single extract from the Prose Edda, the account of the formation of the first human pair:

One day, as the sons of Bör were walking along the sea-beach they found two stems of wood, out of which they shaped a man and a woman. The first (Odin) infused into them life and spirit; the second (Vile) endowed them with reason and the power of motion; the third (Ve) gave them speech and features, hearing and vision. The man they called Ask, and the woman, Embla. From these two descend the whole human race, whose assigned dwelling was within Midgard. Then the sons of Bör built in the middle of the universe the city called Asgard, where dwell the gods and their kindred, and from that abode work out so many wondrous things, both on the earth and in the heavens above it. There is in that city a place called Hlidskjalf, and when Odin is seated there on his lofty throne he sees over the whole world, discerns all the actions of men, and comprehends whatever he contemplates. His wife is Frigga, the daughter of Fjörgyn, and they and their offspring form the race that we call the Æsir, a race that dwells in Asgard the old, and the regions around it, and that we know to be entirely divine. Wherefore Odin may justly be called All-Father, for he is verily the father of all, of gods as well as of men, and to his power all things owe their existence. Earth is his daughter and his wife, and with her he had his first-born son, Asa-Thor, who is endowed with strength and valour, and therefore quelleth he everything that hath life.[2]

In all the voluminous literature of the Greeks and the Romans we find no single work or collection of writings analogous to the above-named sacred books.[3] It would not be difficult to compile from Greek and Roman poets and philosophers a body of sacred literature which would compare favourably with that of any of the Gentile nations. But such a compilation would have, as a volume, no recognized authority or national significance. The books we have described, like our own Bible, have had a historical development, and a distinct place in the religious culture of great nations.

---

[1] See the whole poem as translated by Thorpe in Anderson's Norse Mythology, pp. 130–155, and the mysterious Runic section on pp. 254–259.

[2] Blackwell's translation, in Mallet, Northern Antiquities, pp. 405, 406.

[3] Whatever may have been the nature and contents of the old Sibylline Books, which were kept in the Temple of Jupiter Capitolinus at Rome, they perished long ago, and their real character and use are now purely matters of conjecture.

The Koran, the Avesta, the Pitakas, and the Chinese classics embody the precepts and laws which have been a rule of faith to millions. The vedic hymns and the Egyptian ritual have directed the devotions of countless generations of earnest worshippers. They are, therefore, to be accounted sacred books, and are invaluable for the study of history and of comparative theology.[1]

In forming a proper estimate of these bibles of the nations, we must take each one as a whole. In the brief citations we have given above, the reader can only learn the general tone and spirit of the best portions of the several books. The larger part of all of them is filled with either untrustworthy legends, or grotesque fancies and vague speculations. They abound in polytheistic superstitions, incomprehensible metaphysics, and mythological tales. But, doubtless, back of all this mass of accumulated song and superstition and legend, there was once a foundation of comparatively pure worship and belief. Even Mohammed, whose life and works stand out in the light of reliable history, appears to have been, at the beginning of his career, an earnest seeker after truth and a zealous reformer. But afterward the pride of power and numerous victories warped his moral integrity, and later portions of the Koran are apologies for his crimes. It is difficult to see what logical connexion the superstitions of modern Taoism have with the teachings of Laotzse. In fact, the original documents and ideas of most of the great religions of the East appear to have become lost in the midst of the accretions of later times. Especially is this true of Brahmanism and Buddhism. Who can now certainly declare what were the very words of Buddha? The Tripitaka is an uncertain guide. It is much as if the apocryphal gospels, the legends of anchorites and monks and mystics, and the dreams of the schoolmen, were all strung together, and intermingled with the words and works of Jesus. Roman Catholicism is itself a gross corruption and caricature of the religion of Jesus Christ; and were it the sole representative of the Gospel in the world to-day it would be a striking analogue of Buddhism. Could we go back to the true historical starting point of the great religions, we would, perhaps, find them all, in one form and another,

(marginal note) These books must be studied as a whole.

[1] The Holy Scriptures of the Sikhs, a politico-religious sect of India, constitute a volume full of interest, and equal in size to the Old Testament. It is commonly known as the Granth. But it is a late work, compiled about A. D. 1500, and has no national or historical value to entitle it to a place among the bibles of the nations. It has been translated into English, and published at the expense of the British Government for India. See The Adi Granth, or the Holy Scriptures of the Sikhs, translated from the original Gurmukhi, with Introductory Essays, by Dr. Ernest Thrumpp. Lond., 1877.

connected with some great patriarchal Jethro, or Melchizedek, whose name and genealogy are now alike lost to mankind.

It will not do to take up the various bibles of the world, and, having selected choice extracts from them all, compare such selections alone with similar extracts from the Christian and Jewish Scriptures. These latter, we doubt not, can furnish more exquisite passages than all the others combined. But such comparison of choice excerpts is no real test. Each bible must be taken as an organic whole, and viewed in its historical and national relations. Then will it be seen, as one crowning glory of the Scriptures of the Old and New Testaments, that they are the carefully preserved productions of some sixteen centuries, self-verifying in their historical relations, and completed and divinely sanctioned by the Founder of Christianity and his apostles in the most critical and cultivated age of the Roman Empire. All attempts to resolve these sacred books into myths and legends have proved signal failures. The Hebrew people were notably a peculiar people, and their national history stands out in the clear light of trustworthy testimony. They were placed, geographically, in the very center of the great historic empires of Egypt, Asia, and Europe; and the accuracy of their sacred records is confirmed by the records of these empires. Most notable is the fact, moreover, that the languages in which the several parts of the sacred canon were written ceased to be living tongues about the time when those several parts obtained canonical authority; and thereby these sacred books were crystallized into imperishable form, and have become historical and linguistic monuments of their own genuineness. We are, furthermore, confident in the assertion that the Holy Scriptures are not only singularly free from the superstitions and follies that abound in the sacred books of other nations, but also that they contain in substance the inculcation of every excellence and virtue to be found in all the others. Thus in their entirety they are incomparably superior to all other sacred books.[1]

But, taken in parts, the Bible will still maintain a marvellous superiority. Where, in all other literature, will be found a moral code comparable, for substance and historical presentation, with the Sinaitic decalogue? Where else is there such a golden sum-

(margin note: Notable superiority of the Old and New Testament Scriptures.)

---

[1] "It cannot be too strongly stated," says Max Müller, "that the chief, and in many cases the only, interest of the Sacred Books of the East is historical; that much in them is extremely childish, tedious, if not repulsive; and that no one but the historian will be able to understand the important lessons which they teach." Sacred Books of the East, vol. i, p. xliii.

mary of all law and revelation as the first and second commandments of the Saviour? The religious lessons of the Bible are set in a historical background of national life and personal experience; and largely in biographical sketches true to all the phases of human character.[1] Let the diligent student go patiently and carefully through all rival scriptures; let him memorize the noblest vedic hymns, and study the Tripitaka with all the enthusiasm of an Edwin Arnold; let him search the Confucian classics, and the Tau-teh-king of Laotsze, and the sacred books of Persia, Assyria, and Babylon; let him devoutly peruse Egyptian ritual, Moslem Koran, and Scandinavian Eddas; he yet will find in the Psalms of David a beauty and purity infinitely superior to any thing in the Vedas; in the gospels of Jesus a glory and splendour eclipsing the boasted "Light of Asia;" and in the laws of Moses and the Proverbs of Solomon lessons of moral and political wisdom far in advance of any thing that Laotsze and Confucius offer. By such study and comparisons it will be seen, as not before, how, as a body of laws, history, poetry, prophecy, and religious records, the Bible is most emphatically the Book of books, and, above all other books combined, "profitable for doctrine, for reproof, for correction, for instruction in righteousness." Such study will dissipate the notion that Christianity is equivalent to general goodness, and that the Bible is an accident of human history; for it will be seen that the Gospel system essentially excludes all other religions, and evinces a divine right to supersede them all. The written records of other faiths are of the earth and earthy; the Bible is a heavenly gift, in language and history wonderfully prepared, and accompanied by manifold evidences of being the revelation of God. To devotees of other religions the Christian may truly say, in the words of the Lord Jesus (John iv, 22): "Ye worship what ye know not, we worship what we know, for the salvation is from the Jews."

[1] Tayler Lewis observes: "Every other assumed revelation has been addressed to but one phase of humanity. They have been adapted to one age, to one people, or one peculiar style of human thought. Their books have never assumed a cosmical character, or been capable of any catholic expansion. They could never be accommodated to other ages, or acclimated to other parts of the world. They are indigenous plants that can never grow out of the zone that gave them birth. Zoroaster never made a disciple beyond Persia, or its immediate neighborhood; Confucius is wholly Chinese, as Socrates is wholly Greek." The Divine Human in the Scripture, p. 133. New York, 1859.

CHAPTER III.

LANGUAGES OF THE BIBLE.

A THOROUGH acquaintance with the genius and grammatical structure of the original languages of the Bible is essentially the basis of all sound interpretation. A translation, however faithful, is itself an interpretation, and cannot be safely made a substitute for original and independent investigation. As an introduction, therefore, to Biblical Hermeneutics, it is of the first importance that we have a knowledge of those ancient tongues in which the sacred oracles were written. It is important, also, that we make ourselves familiar with the general principles of linguistic science, the growth of families of languages, and the historical position, as well as the most marked characteristics, of the sacred tongues.

Acquaintance with the original languages of Scripture the basis of all sound interpretation.

ORIGIN AND GROWTH OF LANGUAGES.

The origin of human speech has been a fruitful theme of speculation and controversy. One's theory on the subject is likely to be governed by his theory of the origin of man. If we adopt the theory of evolution, according to which man has been gradually developed, by some process of natural selection, from lower forms of animal life, we will very naturally conclude that language is a human invention, constructed by slow degrees to meet the necessities and conditions of life. If, on the other hand, we hold that man was first introduced on earth by a miraculous creation, and was made at the beginning a perfect specimen of his kind, we will very naturally conclude that the beginnings of human language were of supernatural origin.

Origin of language.

Several theories have been advanced to show that language may have had a human origin. According to one theory, maintained by several eminent philologists, such as K. W. L. Heyse, H. Steinthal, and Max Müller, man was originally endowed with a creative faculty which spontaneously gave a name to each distinct conception as it first thrilled through his brain. There was originally such a sympathy between soul and body, and such a dependence of the one upon the other, that every object,

Various theories.

which in any way affected the senses, produced a corresponding The Automatic echo in the soul, and found automatic expression Theory. through the vocal organs. As gold, tin, wood, and stone have each a different ring or sound when struck, so the different sensations and perceptions of man's soul rang out articulate sounds whenever they were impressed by objects from without or intuitions from within. This may properly be called the automatic theory of the origin of speech. Others adopt a theory The Onomato- which may be called onomatopoetic. It traces the poetic Theory. origin of words to an imitation of natural sounds. Animals, according to this theory, would receive names corresponding to their natural utterances. The noises caused by the winds and waters would suggest names for these objects of nature, The Interjec- and in this way a few simple words would come to tional Theory. form the germs of the first language. Then, again, there is the interjectional theory, which seeks for the radical elements of language in the sudden ejaculations of excited passion or desire.

Against all these theories strong arguments may be urged. In-Objections to terjections and onomatopoetic words are in every lanthese theories. guage comparatively few, and can in no proper sense be regarded as the radical elements of speech. "Language begins where interjections end." The two theories last named will account for the origin of many words in all languages, but not for the origin of language itself. The automatic theory assumes too materialistic and mechanical a notion of language-making to command general acceptance. It has been nicknamed the *ding-dong* theory, for it resolves the first men into bells, mechanically ringing forth vocal sounds, and, as Whitney has humorously added, like other bells they rang by the tongue. But Müller, on the other hand, rejects both the other theories, and stigmatizes the onomatopoetic as the *bow-wow* theory, and the interjectional as the *poohpooh* theory. Thus the most eminent philologists reject and spurn each other's theories.

Whitney has argued that, since nineteen-twentieths of our speech is manifestly of human origin, it is but reasonable to suppose that the other twentieth originated in the same way.[1] But such an argument cannot be allowed, for it is precisely with this unknown twentieth that all the difficulty lies. Nor is it really so much the twentieth as the one thousandth part. We can readily trace the causes and methods by which languages have been multiplied and changed, but how the first man began to speak—not merely utter

---

[1] Language and the Study of Language, p. 400.

articulate sounds, but frame sentences and communicate ideas—is quite another question. Necessity may have compelled him to make clothing, build houses, and fabricate implements of art; but in all such cases he somewhere found the raw material at hand. He did not originate the clay and the trees and the stones. But the origin of human language seems, from the nature of the case, to involve the creation of the material as well as the putting it in form.

If we believe that man was originally created upright, with all his natural faculties complete, a most obvious corollary Origin probably is, that language was directly imparted to him by his supernatural. Creator. He learned his first mode of speech from God, or from angelic beings, whom God commissioned to instruct him. Perhaps the original creation involved with it a power in the first man to speak spontaneously. He named whatever he would name as intuitively as the bird builds its nest, and as naturally as the first bud put forth its inflorescence; but, unlike bird and bud, his original power for speaking was a conscious capability of the soul, and not, as the automatic theory assumes, a peculiarity of the vocal organs. Language is not an accident of human nature; else might it utterly perish like other arts and inventions of man. It is an essential element of man's being, and one which ever distinguishes him from the brute. Nor is it ingenuous or honourable in linguists to ignore the statements of Scripture on this subject. The account of Adam naming the creatures brought to him (Gen. ii, 19) is manifestly one illustration of his first use of language. Perfect and vigorous from the start, his faculty of language, as a native law, spontaneously gave names to the objects presented to his gaze. This exercise seems not to have taken place until after he had held intercourse with God (verses 16, 17), but the whole account of his creation and primitive state implies that his power of speech, and its first exercise, were among the mysterious facts of his supernatural origin.

The confusion of tongues, narrated in the eleventh chapter of Genesis, may be an important factor in accounting for The confusion the great multitude and diversity of human languages. of tongues at The plain import of that narrative is, that, by a direct Babel. judgment-stroke of the Almighty, the consciousness of men became confused, and their speech discordant. And this confusion of speech is set forth as the occasion, not the result, of their being scattered abroad over all the earth. Whatever language had been used before that event, it probably went out of existence then or became greatly modified, and any attempt now to determine absolutely the original language of mankind, would be as great a folly as the building of the tower of Babel.[1]

Formation and growth of new languages.

But modern philological research has contributed greatly to our knowledge of the changes, growth, and classification of the languages of men. We, who read and speak the English language of to-day, know that it is very different from the English language of three hundred years ago. We go back to the time of Chaucer, and find what seems almost another language. Go back to the Norman Conquest, and it requires as much study to understand the Anglo-Saxon of that period as to understand German or French. The reason of these changes is traceable to the introduction of new words, new customs, and new ideas by the Norman Conquest and the stern measures of William the Conqueror. A new civilization was introduced by him into England, and, since his day, constant changes have been going on by reason of commerce with other peoples and the manifold researches and pursuits of men. New inventions have, within one hundred years, introduced more than a thousand new words into our language.

Then, also, local changes occur, and the common people of one section of a country acquire a different dialect from those of another section. In Great Britain different dialects distinguish the people of different localities, and yet they all speak English, and can readily understand one another. In the United States we have modes of speech peculiar to New England, others peculiar to the South, and others to the West. But think of a community or colony migrating to a distant region and becoming utterly shut off from their fatherland. New scenes and pursuits in course of time obliterate much of the language of their former life. Their children know little or nothing of the old country. Each new generation adds new words and customs, until they come to use virtually a different language. Many old words will be retained, but they are pronounced differently, and are combined in new forms of expression, until we can scarcely trace their etymology. Under such circumstances it would require but a few generations to bring into existence a new language. The English language has more than eighty thousand words; but Shakspeare uses only fifteen thousand, and Milton less than ten thousand. How small a part of the language, then, would be necessary to a band of unlearned emigrants settling in a new country. The American Indians have a language for

[1] A prevalent opinion among Jews and Christians has been that the original language was Hebrew. This opinion is due mainly to a feeling of reverence for that sacred tongue.

every tribe, and with no literature, or schools, or civil government, their languages are constantly changing, and in some places with marvellous rapidity.

Thus we may see how the dispersion and separation of peoples and tribes originate new languages. "If the tribes of men," says Whitney, "are of different parentage, their languages could not be expected to be more unlike than they are; while, on the other hand, if all mankind are of one blood, their tongues need not be more alike than we actually find them to be." [1]

From our own nation and standpoint we take a hasty glance back over the history of some five thousand years, and notice some of the great families of languages as they have been traced and classified by modern comparative philology. Our English is only one of a vast group of tongues which bear unmistakable marks of a common origin. We trace it back to the Anglo-Saxon of a thousand years ago. We find it akin to the German, Dutch, Swedish, Danish, Icelandic, Russian, and Polish, and each of these, like the English, has a history of changes peculiar to itself. All these form but one family of languages, and all their differences are to be explained by migration, diversity of interests, habits, customs, pursuits, natural scenery, climate, religion, and other like causes. Manifestly, all these nations were anciently one people. But this whole group, called the Germanic, is but one branch of a greater and more extended family. The Italian, French, Spanish, and Portuguese form another branch, and are easily traced back to the Latin, the classic language of the old Roman Empire. The Greek, again, is but an older sister of the Latin, and its superior literature, its wealth of forms and harmony, has placed it first among the so-called "learned tongues." Passing eastward we discover many traces of the same family likeness in the Armenian, the Persian, and the Zend, and also in the Pali, the Prakrit, and other tongues of India. All these are found closely related to the ancient Sanskrit, the language of the Vedas, an older sister, though seeming like a mother, of the rest. All these languages are traceable to a common origin, and form one great family, which is appropriately called the Indo-European.

Another family, less marked in affinity, is scattered over Northern and Central Europe and Asia, and contains the languages of the Laplanders, the Finns, the Hungarians, and the Turks in Europe. Scholars differ as to the more appropriate name for this family, calling it either Scythian, Turanian, or

Families of languages.

Indo-European family.

Scythian.

[1] Language and the Study of Language, p. 394.

Altaic. Still different from these are the languages of China and Japan, and the numberless dialects of the uncivilized tribes of America, of Africa, and of the islands of the Pacific.

Different from all the above, and forming a well-defined and The Semitic closely related family, is that known as the Semitic, so group. called from Noah's famous son, from whom the Chaldee, the Hebrew, and Arabian races are believed to have sprung.[1] Here belong the Hebrew, the Punic or Phœnician, the Syriac and Chaldee, the cuneiform of many of the Assyrian and Babylonian monuments, the Arabic and the Ethiopic. These languages, as a group, are remarkable for the comparatively large number of stem-words, or roots, common to them all. The nations which used them were confined in geographical territory mainly to Western Asia, spreading from the Euphrates and Tigris on the east to the Mediterranean and the borders of Egypt on the west. Phœnician enterprise and commerce carried the Punic language westward into some of the islands of the Mediterranean, and along the Ethiopic. Carthaginian coast; and the Ethiopic spread into Egypt and Abyssinia. The Ethiopic, or Geëz, is an offshoot of the Arabic, and is closely akin to the Himyaritic and the Amharic, which latter is now the most widely spoken dialect Arabic. of Abyssinia. The Arabic is still a living language spoken by millions of people in Western Asia, and contains vast libraries of poetry and philosophy, history and fable, Punic. science and religion The Phœnician language has almost entirely perished, a few inscriptions and fragments only remaining. The cuneiform inscriptions of the Assyrian Assyrian. and Babylonian monuments have, in recent years, been yielding to scholarly research, and are found to contain many important annals and proclamations of ancient kings, and also works of science and of art. The language of many of the monuments is found to be Semitic, and its further decipherment and study will doubtless shed much light upon the history and civilization of the ancient empires of Nineveh and Babylon.

The Syriac and Chaldee are two dialects of what is properly called the Aramaic language. This language prevailed among the

[1] The name Semitic is not an exact designation, for, according to Genesis x, only two of Shem's sons, Arphaxad and Aram, begat nations which are known to have used this speech, while three of his sons, Elam, Asshur, and Lud, were the progenitors of nations which, perhaps, used other languages. On the other hand, two of the sons of Ham—Cush and Canaan—were fathers of Semitic-speaking peoples. Hupfeld has proposed the name "Hither-Asiatic," and Renan "Syro-Arabic," but these names have not commanded any general following, and the name Semitic has now become so fixed in usage that it will, probably, not be displaced by any other.

peoples about Damascus, and thence eastward as far as Babylon. The Chaldee is represented in several chapters of the Books of Ezra and Daniel, and also in the Jewish Tar- Aramaic. gums or paraphrases of the Old Testament. It prevailed in Babylon at the time of the Jewish exile, and was there appropriated by the Jewish people, with whom it was vernacular in Palestine in the time of our Lord. The Samaritan is an offshoot of this language, though mixed with many foreign elements. The Syriac dialect appears to have been a western outgrowth and development of the Chaldee, and it is sometimes called the western Aramaic, as distinguished from the eastern Aramaic, or Chaldæan. At the beginning of the Christian era it prevailed through all the region north and east of Palestine, known as Syria or Aram, and its existing literature is principally Christian. Its oldest monument of note is the Peshito version of the Scriptures, which is usually referred to the second century; but its most flourishing period extended from the fourth to the ninth century. It is still the sacred language of the scattered Christian communities of Syria, and by some of them is still spoken, though in a very corrupt form.

Central and pre-eminent among all these Semitic tongues is the ancient Hebrew, which embodies the magnificent liter- Hebrew. ature of one of the oldest and most important nations of the earth. The great father of this nation was Abram, who migrated from the land of the Chaldæans, crossed the Euphrates, and entered Canaan with the assurance that the land should be given to him and his posterity. How closely his dialect at that time resembled the language of the Canaanites we have no means of knowing, but that he and his family abandoned their own dialect, and adopted that of the Canaanites, is in the highest degree improbable. The Hebrews and the Canaanites appear to have used substantially the same dialect. During the centuries of the Hebrews' residence in Egypt, and the forty years in the peninsula of Sinai, the Hebrew language acquired a form and character which thereafter underwent no essential change until after the time of the Babylonian exile—a period of more than a thousand years.[1]

Having thus glanced over the scattered nations and languages of men, we are enabled to mark the relative national and historical position of the Hebrew tongue. Central among the great nations of the earth; placed in the midst of the great highway of intercourse between the world-powers of the East and the West, the Hebrew people may be Geographical and historical position of the Hebrew.

[1] Comp. Gesenius, Geschichte der heb. Sprache und Schrift. Lpz., 1815.

shown to have had, in many ways, a providential mission to all
nations. Having traced the spread and outgrowth of the principal
families of languages, and noticed the principles and methods by
which new languages and dialects are formed, we are prepared to
investigate more intelligently the special character and genius of
the so-called sacred tongues.

CHAPTER IV.

THE HEBREW LANGUAGE.

THE Hebrew language takes its name from the Hebrew nation,
whose immortal literature it preserves. The word first appears in
Genesis xiv, 13, where Abram is called "the Hebrew." In Gen.
xxxix, 14, 17, Joseph, the great-grandson of Abraham, is so called,
and he himself speaks (chap. xl, 15) of Canaan as "the land of the
Hebrews."[1] Thenceforth the name is frequently applied to the
Derivation of descendants of Jacob. Two different derivations of the
the name He- name have been proposed, between which it is difficult
brew.   to decide. One makes it an appellative noun from עֵבֶר,
beyond; applied to Abram because he came from beyond the Euphrates. Thus the name would follow the analogy of such words
as Transylvania, Transalpine, Transatlantic. But such a designation would scarcely be applied to one who came from beyond the
river rather than to those who continued beyond, and there is no
evidence that the Trans-Euphrateans were ever so designated.
Nevertheless, this derivation is maintained by many distinguished
scholars, and there is no insuperable objection to it. Another, and,
philologically, more natural derivation, is that which makes the
word a patronymic from עֵבֶר, Eber, the great-grandson of Shem,
and ancestor of Abraham. Thus in Gen. xiv, 13, where the name
first occurs, Abram is called הָעִבְרִי, the Eberite, or Hebrew, in contrast with Mamre, הָאֱמֹרִי, the Amorite. This is in thorough analogy with the regular form of Hebrew patronymics, and has in its

---

[1] "This name is never in Scripture applied to the Israelites except when the speaker
is a foreigner (Gen. xxxix, 14, 17; xli, 12; Exod. i, 15; ii, 6; 1 Sam. iv, 6, 9, etc.),
or when Israelites speak of themselves to one of another nation (Gen. xl, 15; Exod.
i, 19; Jonah i, 9, etc.), or when they are contrasted with other peoples (Gen. xliii, 32;
Exod. i, 3, 7, 15; Deut. xv, 12; 1 Sam. xiii, 3, 7)." See Kitto, Cyc. of Bib. Literature, article Hebrew.

favour the peculiar statement of Gen. x, 21, that Shem was the "father of all the sons of Eber." This manifestly gives to Eber a notable prominence among the descendants of Shem, and may, for divers reasons now unknown, have given to Abraham, and to his descendants through Jacob, the name of Eberites, or Hebrews. Accordingly, while either of these derivations is possible, that which makes it a patronymic from Eber seems to be least open to objection, and best supported by linguistic usage and analogy.[1]

The Hebrew language, preserved in the books of the Old Testament, may therefore be regarded as the national speech of the Eberites, of whom the descendants of Abraham, Isaac, and Jacob became the most distinguished representatives. In the later times of the Hebrew monarchy it was called *Judaic* (יְהוּדִית, 2 Kings xviii, 26), because the kingdom of Judah had then become the great representative of the Hebrew race. When Abram, the Hebrew, (Gen. xiv, 13) entered the land of Canaan, he probably found his ancestral language already spoken there, for the Canaanites had migrated thither before him (Gen. xii, 6). It is notable that in all the intercourse of Abram, Isaac, and Jacob with the Canaanitish tribes, no allusion is ever made to any differences in their language, and the proper names among the Canaanites are traceable to Hebrew roots. One hundred and seventy years after the migration of Abram, his grandson Jacob used a form of speech different from that of his uncle Laban the Syrian (Gen. xxxi, 47), and it is not improbable that Laban's dialect had undergone more changes than that of the sons of Abram.[2]

[1] Is it not possible that Eber may have been the last great Semitic patriarch living at the time of the confusion of tongues (see Gen. x, 25), and that he and his family may have retained more nearly than any others the primitive language of mankind, and transmitted it through Peleg, Reu, Serug, and Nahor, to the generations of Terah (comp. Gen. xi, 17–27)? This supposition is not necessarily invalidated by the fact that Aramæans, Cushites, and Canaanites used the same Semitic speech, for these tribes may, at an early date, have appropriated the language of the Eberites.

[2] It is commonly asserted that Abram used the Chaldee language when he first entered Canaan, but there gradually lost its use, and adopted the speech of his heathen neighbours. This supposition, however, is without any solid foundation. The fact incidentally mentioned in Gen. xxxi, 47, is no valid evidence in the case. It merely shows that Laban and Jacob used different dialects, and leaves the question entirely open whether it were Jacob's or Laban's dialect which had most changed subsequently to the migration from Ur of the Chaldees (Gen. xi, 31). Abram's separateness from other tribes favours the idea that his language and that of his children Isaac and Jacob would be less likely to undergo change than that of Laban, whose idolatrous use of Teraphim (Gen. xxxi, 19, 30) indicates in him a cleaving to heathenish practices. The language of the Chaldees at the period of Terah's removal may have resembled the Hebrew much more closely than the later Aramaic. The question is not

When a person with whom the English or any other Indo-European language is vernacular, comes for the first time to investigate
Peculiarities of the Hebrew tongue.
Semitic modes of speech, he finds that he is entering into a new and strange world of thought. In some things he meets the exact reverse of all with which he has become familiar in his own language. The written page reads from right to left; the volume from the end toward the beginning; every letter is a consonant, and represents some object of sense corresponding to the meaning of its name.

The Hebrew alphabet consists of twenty-two letters, and the
The letters.
written characters now in use, commonly called the square letters, are found in the oldest existing manuscripts of the Bible. But these characters are probably not older than the beginning of the Christian era, inasmuch as the Asmonean coins do not use them, but employ an alphabet closely resembling that of the Phœnician coins and inscriptions.[1] The oldest monuments of Hebrew writing are some coins of the Maccabæan prince Simon (about B. C. 140), a number of gems containing names, and probably used for seals, and the famous inscription of Mesha, king of Moab (about B. C. 900), recently discovered among the ruins of the ancient Dibon on the east of the Jordan. The names of the letters are all significant, and their original form was, without doubt, designed to resemble the object denoted by the name. Thus the name of the first letter, *aleph*, א, means an ox, and it is believed that some resemblance of an ox's head may be discerned in the old Phœnician form of this letter ( ). The third letter, *gimel*, ג, means a camel, and in its ancient Phœnician ( ) and Ethiopic ( ) forms, somewhat resembles the head and neck of the camel. According to Gesenius, the earliest form ( ) represented the camel's hump. The name of the letter *daleth*, ד, means a door, and the ancient form △, or ◁, (Greek Δ), resembles the door of a tent.[2]

whether the Canaanites adopted Abram's language after his migration, as Bleek assumes (Introd., vol. i, p. 66), but whether Abram and his father's house, the Eberites, may not have spoken, at the time of their westward migration, substantially the same language as that of the Canaanites. How long the Canaanites had been in the land before Abram came is uncertain (comp. Gen. x, 18; xii, 6), but perhaps not long enough to have undergone notable changes in their speech.

[1] The square character is spoken of in the Talmud as the Assyrian writing, and is said to have been brought from the East by Ezra when he returned from the Babylonian exile; but this tradition, for the reasons given above, is not entitled to credit.

[2] See the whole alphabet similarly exhibited in Smith's Dict. of the Bible, under article Writing. See also the Ancient Semitic Alphabets as exhibited in Gesenius' Hebrew Grammar, and the Ancient Alphabets as given at the end of Webster's Unabridged Dictionary.

These forms, moreover, are probably abbreviations and modifications of still more ancient ones, which, like the hieroglyphics of Egypt, were real pictures or outlines of visible things.[1]

Among the letters, the four gutturals א, ה, ח, and ע have a notable prominence, and give distinction to the conjugation of many verbs. Incapable of being doubled, they greatly affect the vowel system, and the first two (א and ה) represent scarcely audible breathings in the throat, and are frequently altogether quiescent. The two letters *waw* (ו, commonly called *vav*) and *yodh* (י) are also frequently quiescent, and may be called the two vowel letters of the ancient Hebrew. They seem, as a rule, to have been employed only when the sounds which they represent were long. With the exception of these two letters the ancient written Hebrew seems to have had no vowel signs. The same combination of letters might signify several different things, according to the pronunciation received. The indefiniteness of such a mode of writing compares very unfavourably with the ample supply of vowel letters in the Indo-European tongues, and nothing but a familiar acquaintance with the usage of the language as a living tongue could supply this defect.[2]

Gutturals.

The Masoretic system of vowel signs, or points, is a comparatively modern invention, prepared to meet a real necessity when the Hebrew had ceased to be a living language. "Of the date of this punctuation of the Old Testament text," observes Gesenius, "we have no historical account; but a comparison of historical facts warrants the conclusion that the present vowel system was not completed till the seventh century after Christ; and that it was done by Jewish scholars, well versed in the language, who, it is highly probable, copied the example of the Syriac, and perhaps also of the Arabic, grammarians. This vowel system has, probably, for its basis the pronunciation of the Jews of Palestine; and its consistency, as well as the analogy of the kindred languages, furnishes strong proof of its correctness, at least as a whole. We may, however, assume that it exhibits not so much the pronunciation of common life as the formal style, which, in the seventh century after Christ, was sanctioned by tradition and custom in reading the Scriptures in the schools and synagogues. Its authors laboured with great care to represent by signs the minute grada-

Masoretic vowel system.

---

[1] Comp. Böttcher, Ausführliches Lehrbuch der hebräischen Sprache, vol. i, pp. 65, 66.

[2] "A Semitic root," says Bopp, "is unpronounceable, because, in giving it vowels, an advance is made to a special grammatical form, and it then no longer possesses the simple peculiarity of a root raised above all grammar." Comparative Grammar, vol. i, p. 108; Eng. Trans., p. 98.

tions of the vowel sounds, marking even half vowels and help-ing sounds, spontaneously adopted in all languages, yet seldom expressed in writing." [1]

The ancient Hebrew writing being, accordingly, expressed al-together by consonants, the vowel sounds were quite subordinate to them, and formed no conspicuous element of the language. Words and names are exhibited by consonants, to which alone significations may be traced, but relations of thought, modifications of the sense of words, and grammatical inflection, were denoted by vowel sounds.

One of the most marked features of the language is the tri-

The three-let- literal root of all its verbs. This peculiarity is a fun-
ter root. damental characteristic of all the Semitic tongues. No satisfactory reason for its existence, or account of its origin, has yet been produced, though a vast amount of study and research has been expended on the subject. Some have maintained that this triplicity of radical consonants is the result of a philological and historical development. Indications of this are found in mon-osyllabic nouns (like אב, אם, דם, הר, יד), and verbs which double one of their letters (לבב, סבב, שתת), and also in those verbs in which one of the consonants is so weak and servile as to suggest that, origi-nally, it was no radical element of the word (דון or דין, טוב, פוח). Hence the doctrine of a primitive system of two-letter roots has been advanced and defended with great learning and ingenuity. But no satisfactory results have come from these efforts, and the theory of two-letter roots has not obtained a general following among philologists. Why may not these primitive roots of the language have been formed of three letters as well as two? The uniformity and universality of the verbal root of three letters argue that this is an original and fundamental characteristic of Semitic speech.

A most important and interesting feature of the language is the
Conjugations manner in which the different conjugations or voices of
of the verb. the verb are formed. The third person singular of the perfect (or past) tense is the ground form from which all model changes take their departure.[2] These changes consist in varying the vowels, doubling the middle letter of the root, and adding certain formative letters or syllables. In some rare forms there is a repetition or reduplication of one or two of the radical

---

[1] Davies' Gesenius' Hebrew Grammar (Mitchell's Edition), pp. 32, 33. Andover, 1880.

The simple participial form קֹטֵל, or the imperative קְטֹל, may perhaps present equal claim to be the basal form of the Hebrew verb. Comp. Weir, in Kitto's Journal of Sacred Literature for Oct., 1849, pp. 309, 310.

consonants. Since the time of the great Hebraist Danz (about A.D. 1700) the verb קָטַל, *katal*, has been used as a grammatical paradigm to illustrate the various conjugations of the Hebrew verb, and though grammarians have differed somewhat in the number and arrangement of the conjugations, common usage adheres to the following general outline:

Simple.

| Kal,[1] | קָטַל, | *Katal,* | he killed. |
| Niphal, | נִקְטַל, | *Niktal,* | he was killed. |

Intensive.

| Piël, | קִטֵּל, | *Kittel,* | he massacred. |
| Pual, | קֻטַּל, | *Kuttal,* | he was massacred. |

Causative.

| Hiphil, | הִקְטִיל, | *Hiktil,* | he caused to kill. |
| Hophal, | הָקְטַל, | *Hoktal,* | he was caused to kill. |

Reflexive.

Hithpaël, הִתְקַטֵּל, *Hithkattel,* he killed himself.

From the above it will be noticed that the simple, the intensive, and the causative forms have each a corresponding passive. The reflexive, from its very nature, would not be expected to have a corresponding passive, and yet a few rare instances occur of a Hothpaal or Huthpaal form (הֻטַּמְּאָה, *to be made unclean,* Deut. xxiv, 4; הֻדַּשְׁנָה, *to be smeared over with fat,* Isa. xxxiv, 6). It should be noticed in the paradigm how the idea of activity seems to attach to the *a* sound, while the *e, o,* and *u* sounds are used in forms which express passiveness. The doubling of roots expresses intensity, and the prefixing of letters denotes some form of reflexive action.

---

[1] The origin of the terms *Kal, Niphal, Piël,* etc., is thus stated by Nordheimer: "The first investigators of the language, who were Jews, wrote in Hebrew, and accordingly employed Hebrew expressions for the designation of grammatical phenomena. To denote the first or simple species they used the word קַל, *Kal, light, simple ;* a term which modern grammarians have found it convenient to retain. And to represent the remaining species they took the modifications of the verb פָּעַל, *to do, to make,* which itself supplies the name for this part of speech. Thus, instead of a term derived from the signification of that form of the verb which receives the prefix נ, such as the word *passive,* they employed, as a sort of grammatical formula, the corresponding modification of the verb פָּעַל, which is נִפְעַל, *Niphal,* and so on of the rest."—*Critical Grammar of the Hebrew Language,* vol. i, p. 97.

But it must not be understood that there are always exact corre-
pondence and uniformity in the significations of these several
Import of the forms. The Niphal is very generally the passive of
conjugations. Kal, and the older Hebrew grammarians were wont to
regard it as strictly so; but, like the Greek middle voice, it is used
also to express reflexive and reciprocal action. So also the Piël conjugation is used to express not only intensity of action, but repetition and frequency, and sometimes it has a causative signification.
There are also other forms, so rare and exceptional as not to be
classed along with the conjugations of the usual paradigm, but
which represent peculiar shades of meaning not otherwise ex-
pressible. Such forms are the so-called Pilel (קִטְלֵל), Pealal (קְטַלְטַל),
Tiphel (תִּקְטֵל), and other forms peculiar to certain irregular verbs.
In the Arabic language there are fifteen such different conjugations of the verb, though in that language, as in the Hebrew, few
verbs are used in all their possible forms.

The tense-system of the Hebrew verb is very unlike that of the
Tenses or time- Indo-European languages. Some scholars have gone so
forms of the far as to deny that the Hebrew language has any ver-
Hebrew verb. bal forms which can properly be designated tenses.
Sir W. Martin observes that the forms of the Hebrew verb commonly called preterite and future, or perfect and imperfect, "are
not tenses in the proper sense; i. e., the notion of time as past,
present, or future, is not inherent in the form. They note only
actions or conditions, and the persons of whom such actions or
conditions are predicated. They predicate a certain state of a certain subject, and no more. The time to which the action or condition, expressed by the form, belongs in each case, is to be gathered
from the context. The present time is understood if none other is
suggested by the context. The difference between the two forms
is not, then, any difference in time, but a difference in the way of
conceiving the action or condition. The forms then may be accurately described as *moods* indicating modes of thought rather than
as tenses. These moods, taken in connexion with indications of
time supplied by the context, and so having their generality limited and restricted, become equivalent to our tenses. Viewed as
moods, they differ from each other much in the same way as *becoming* from *being*, as *motion* from *rest*, as *progress* from *completion*." [1] Similarly Wright remarks concerning the tenses of the
Arabic verb: "The temporal forms of the Arabic verb are but two
in number, the one expressing a *finished* act, one that is done and

[1] Inquiries concerning the Structure of the Semitic Languages. Part i, p. 11.
London, 1876.

completed in relation to other acts (the perfect); the other an *un-finished* act, one that is just commencing or in progress (the imperfect)." He adds: "We have discarded the names *Preterite* and *Future*, by which these forms are still often designated, especially in our Hebrew and Syriac grammars, because they do not accurately correspond to the ideas inherent in them. A Semitic perfect or imperfect has, in and of itself, no reference to the temporal relations of the speaker (thinker or writer), and of other actions which are brought into juxtaposition with it. It is precisely these relations which determine in what sphere of time (past, present, or future) a Semitic perfect or imperfect lies, and by which of our tenses it is to be expressed." [1]

The Indo-European tongues have distinct verbal forms to express an action of the past as either continuing (imperfect, as, *I was writing*), or completed definitely (pluperfect, *I had written*), or indefinitely (aorist, *I wrote*). They also have forms for expressing action as continuing in the present (as *I am writing*), and as completed in the present (perfect, *I have written*), and other forms for expressing future action in a like twofold way (*I will write*, and *I will have written*). But the less systematic and more emotional Semitic mind seems to have conceived the temporal relations of subject and predicate in a somewhat ideal way. In whatever position or point of view a speaker or writer took his stand, he seems to have viewed all things as having some subjective relation to that standpoint. Time with him was an ever-continuing series of moments (רְגָעִים, *winks* of the eye). The past was ever running into the future, and the future ever losing itself in the past. The future tense-form which he used may have actually referred to events of the remote past, but to him it was an ideal future, taking its departure from some anterior event either expressed or understood.[2] It is a characteristic of the Hebrew writers to throw themselves into the midst of the scenes or events which they describe,

Unlike Indo-European tense forms.

Ideal and relative past and future.

---

[1] Grammar of the Arabic Language, from the German of Caspari, vol. i, pp. 53. 54. Second Edition, London, 1874. Compare the similar views of Ewald, Ausführliches Lehrbuch der heb. Sprache, §§ 135, 136, pp. 348–358 (Gottingen, 1870), and Driver, On the Use of the Tenses in Hebrew, Oxford, 1874. Ewald's doctrine of the Hebrew Tenses was controverted by Prof. M. Stuart in the Biblical Repository for Jan., 1838, pp. 146–173, and Driver's treatise is reviewed by A. Müller in the Zeitschrift für luth. Theologie. 1877, i, p. 198.

[2] Murphy suggests that the two tense-forms of the Hebrew verb be designated respectively as the *anterior* and *posterior*. See his article on the Hebrew Tenses, in Kitto's Journal of Sacred Literature for Jan., 1850 (pp. 194–202), and comp. Weir on the same subject in the same Journal for Oct., 1849. Weir observes (p. 317):

and this consideration largely accounts for the subjective and ideal way in which the two tense-forms (קָטַל and יִקְטֹל) are employed. Thus, at the beginning of Genesis (i, 1), we have first the definite statement, "In the beginning God created (בָּרָא) the heavens and the land." This statement serves as a heading to the narrative that follows. Having taken that beginning as a historical stand-point, the writer next describes the condition of things at that beginning, still using the past tense-form: "And the land was (הָיְתָה) waste and empty, and darkness upon the face of the deep, and the Spirit of God brooding (מְרַחֶפֶת, feminine participle, *kept brooding*) upon the face of the waters." Such was the state of things in the midst of which the narrator took his ideal stand; and from that starting point he proceeds to relate the succession of events. His next verb is in the future or imperfect tense-form: "And God will say, Let there be light;" or as we would more familiarly say, *then says God* (וַיֹּאמֶר אֱלֹהִים), that is, God then, or next, proceeded to say, etc. The tense-thought here is that the divine fiat, "Let there be light," was consequent upon the period and condition of darkness which was upon the deep. A succession of thought and a progress of time are thus indicated, a mode of conception peculiar to the Semitic mind, but not naturally transferable to our language.

The past or perfect tense-form is also used when speaking of

The past tense form for future events conceived of as complete. things to be certainly realized in the future. In such cases the event of the future is conceived as somehow completed; it has become a foregone conclusion and settled purpose of the Divine mind. Thus, for example, in Gen. xvii, 20: "As for Ishmael, I have heard thee (שְׁמַעְתִּיךָ, this hearing was actually past); behold, I have blessed him (בֵּרַכְתִּי), and I have made him fruitful (הִפְרֵיתִי), and I have multiplied him (הִרְבֵּיתִי) exceedingly." All this was to be realized in the future, but it is here presented to the mind as something already finished. It was fixed in the Divine purpose, and from an ideal standpoint in the future it was viewed as something past. Then it is immediately added: "Twelve princes shall he beget (יוֹלִיד, here the indefinite future is both assumed and expressed), and I have given him (נְתַתִּיו) for a great nation." This last verb again assumes an ideal

"The Hebrew writers, instead of keeping constantly in view the period *at* which they wrote, and employing a variety of tenses to describe the different shades of past, present, and future time, accomplished the same object by keeping their own times quite out of view, and regarding as *their present* the period not *at* which, but *of* which, they wrote." He accordingly takes the קָטַל form (commonly called past or perfect) to denote the present, not, however, excluding the idea of a past action or condition continuing on into the present.

past, a something seen in the mind as complete after Ishmael shall have begotten twelve princes.

The past and future import of the two tense-forms, as standing opposed to each other in the indication of time, is apparent in such passages as, "Before them there have been (הָיָה) no such locusts as they, and after them there shall not be (יִהְיֶה) such" (Exod. x, 14). "As I was (הָיִיתִי) with Moses, I will be (אֶהְיֶה) with thee" (Josh. i, 5). "Yea, I have spoken (דִּבַּרְתִּי), also I will bring to pass (אֲבִיאֶנָּה); I have formed a purpose (יָצַרְתִּי), also I will perform it" (Isa. xlvi, 11). But in view of the fact, set forth by the best grammarians, that the past tense is used for the perfect, the pluperfect, the present, and the future, and the future tense is used for the present and the past,[1] these different tense-forms of the Hebrew language are to be understood, not as corresponding to the more fully developed tense-system of Indo-European tongues, but as exhibiting a peculiarity of the Semitic mind, which was wont to view the temporal relation of events in the vivid ideal way explained above. Both the past and future forms of the verb are often best translated into English by the present tense. The past form often indicates a past action which is conceived of as continuing into the present, and having become habitual. "The ox knows (יָדַע) his owner, and the ass the crib of his master" (Isa. i, 3). Observe also, in Psa. i, 1: "Happy the man who walks not (לֹא הָלַךְ, has ceased from walking) in the counsel of wicked ones, and in the way of sinners does not stand, and in the seat of scorners does not sit." Here it is not difficult to apprehend, in the tense-form used, an ideal of the past, but it is scarcely practicable, except by undesirable circumlocution, to transfer the conception into simple idiomatic English. The future form is often used to express the vivid Semitic conception of a past action, or series of actions, as continuing, or as succeeding one another. Thus, in 1 Sam. xxvi, 17, 18, we may express the Hebrew futures by the English present: "And Saul knows the voice of David, and he says, Is this thy voice, my son David? And says David, My voice, my lord, O king. And he says, Why is this—my lord pursuing after his servant?"

In the inflexion[2] of Hebrew nouns there is no neuter gender.

The two tenses have a past and future import.

---

[1] See Gesenius, Heb. Gram., §§ 126, 127, and Nordheimer, Crit. Gram. of the Hebrew Language, vol. ii, pp. 161–174.

[2] "A regular *inflexion* of the noun by cases does not exist in Hebrew. . . . The connexion of the noun with the feminine, with the dual and plural terminations, with suffixes, and with another noun following in the genitive, produces numberless changes in its form, which is all that is meant by the *inflexion* of nouns in Hebrew. Even

All objects of nature, inanimate things, and abstract ideas are viewed
The gender of as instinct with life, and spoken of as either masculine
nouns. or feminine. Mountains, rivers, seas, being objects
of majesty and representing strength, are usually masculine. And
they are often pictured before the fancy as consciously exulting
and moving with exuberance of life. Thus the mountains watch
with a jealous eye (רצד, Psa. lxviii, 16), they rejoice together (Psa.
xcviii, 8), and break forth into song (Isa. xliv, 23), and even leap
and dance like rams (Psa. cxiv, 4, 6). The rushing torrents lift up
their voice and clap their hands (Psa. xciii, 3; xcviii, 8), and the
sea beholds, and flies (Psa. cxiv, 3). The words for city, land, locality, and the like, are feminine, being thought of as mothers of
those who dwell therein. The smaller and dependent towns were
called daughters of the principal city (Num. xxi, 25; Josh. xvii, 11).
The names of things without life are generally feminine, probably
from being regarded as weak and helpless. Abstract ideas are also
usually represented as feminine. We are not able to understand,
in all instances, why this or that word came to be used in its particular gender, but this whole habit of thought and language had
its origin in an intense lively intuition of nature.

The use of the plural number in Hebrew seems often to denote
Use of the not so much a plurality of individuals as fulness, vast-
plural. ness, majesty, or completeness of endowments. Thus
the first word of the first Psalm, which we commonly render as an
adjective—"Blessed is the man," etc.—is a noun in the plural number (אַשְׁרֵי); literally, *the blessedness of the man.* We bring out its
real force when we take it as an exclamation: *O the blessednesses of
the man,* etc.! The idea may be either the manifoldness and multiplicity of blessedness, or the completeness and greatness of blessedness. The word for *life* is often plural, as in Gen. ii, 7, "breathed
into his nostrils the breath of *lives*" (חַיִּים); verse 9 has "tree of
lives," and chap. vii, 22, "breath of the spirit of *lives.*" Here the
meaning cannot be, as some have suggested, twofold life—animal
and spiritual, for the plural is used alike of the life of tree, animal,
and man. It seems rather to denote fulness and completeness of
life. So the words for *water* (מַיִם) and *heaven* (שָׁמַיִם) are always
used in the plural, probably from the idea of vastness or majesty.
This is also the best explanation of the plural form of the name of
God (אֱלֹהִים); what the old grammarians called *the plural of excellency,* expressing the dignity and manifold power of the Creator of
all things.

for the *comparative* and *superlative,* the Hebrew has no appropriate forms, and these
relations must be expressed by circumlocution." Gesenius, Heb. Grammar, § 79, 2.

The foregoing statement of the philological and grammatical peculiarities of the Hebrew language may serve to show that it is a most ancient and primitive type of human speech, and admirably adapted to express vivid conceptions and strong emotion.

Hebrew a primitive type of human speech.

Every letter, as well as every word, represents some visible or material object, and the studious observer may pass among its written monuments as through a picture gallery, and feel that the images of life are all around him.

Keeping in mind what has been said, we proceed to show the simplicity of structure, and the emotional expressiveness of this sacred language, and its consequent fitness to embody and preserve the ancient oracles of God.

Opening almost anywhere in the narrative portions of the Old Testament, we find abundant evidence of the simplicity of Hebrew syntax. The sentences are ordinarily short and vividly expressive.

Simplicity of structure.

The so-called compound sentences rarely involve any trouble or obscurity, being usually only two or more short sentences, whose relation to each other is most direct and simple. There are no involved constructions and long-drawn periods. The first chapter of Genesis may be taken as a specimen of prose narrative, the most simple and natural in its construction of any composition known to literature. Whatever may be the difficulties in its exposition, its grammatical structure is simple and intelligible. The following verse from the beginning of the second chapter of 2 Samuel may be taken as a very fine example of lively narrative:

And it came to pass after this, that David inquires of Jehovah, saying, Shall I go up into one of the cities of Judah? And says Jehovah to him, Go up. And says David, Whither shall I go up? And he says, To Hebron.

Or take the following, from 1 Kings xix, 19–21:

And he goes from there, and he finds Elisha, the son of Shaphat, and he ploughing, twelve yoke before him, and he with the twelfth: and Elijah passes over unto him, and throws his mantle unto him. And he leaves the oxen, and he runs after Elijah, and says, I will kiss, now, my father and my mother, and I will go after thee. And he says to him, Go, Return, for what have I done to thee? And he returns from after him, and he takes the yoke of the oxen and he slaughters him, and with the instruments of the oxen he boiled them, the flesh; and he gives to the people, and they eat, and he arises, and he goes after Elijah, and he serves him.

In these translations we have used the present tense where the Hebrew has the future, as best conveying the spirit of the narrative. The writer views the whole scene, and depicts the several parts as they follow one after the other. Those several acts are relatively future from the point of time he ideally occupies, and his successive sentences are short, rapid, and life-like in their arrangement. Hundreds of similar specimens might be adduced, taken almost at random from the Hebrew scriptures.

In very many of the most simple sentences, the subject and pred-
Omission of icate are placed together without any connective par-
copula.   ticle or copula. Thus, 1 Kings i, 1, "The king David (was) old;" 1 Kings xviii, 21, "If Jehovah (be) the God;" Prov. xx, 1, "A mocker (is) wine; raging (is) strong drink." This omission in prose narrative may often be supplied to advantage in translation, being required by the idiom of another language to complete the sense, and maintain grammatical accuracy. But the omission gives strength and beauty to many passages, as, for instance, the following, Psa. lxvi, 3: "How fearful thy doings!" The attempt of the Authorized Version to supply here what was supposed to be necessary greatly weakens the sentiment: "How terrible *art thou in* thy works." So again in Psa. xc, 2, "From everlasting to everlasting thou, God!" Again, in verse 4, "A thousand years in thy eyes, as yesterday." It may, in fact, be said that the italic words supplied in the Authorized Version detract from the force and spirit of the original in more instances than they supply any essential need.

In the order of words in a sentence, subject or predicate may be
Order of sub- placed first, according as it is designed to give emphasis
ject and predi- to the one or the other. Very frequently the sentence
cate.   opens with a verb, and, according to Gesenius, every finite verb contains in all cases its subject already in itself under the form of a personal pronoun, which is necessarily connected with the verbal form.[1] Thus, Gen. ii, 1, "And they were finished, the heavens, and the land, and all their host." When two or more verbs are construed with a single subject, the first is usually placed before the noun, and the others follow, as so many distinct statements. Thus, Gen. vii, 18, "And they prevailed, the waters, and they increased exceedingly upon the land; and she went, the ark, upon the face of the waters."

In the Hebrew language there is a comparative lack of adjectives. As a substitute, nouns expressive of quality,   Adjectives.
material, or character, are used as genitives after the
nouns to be qualified. Thus, instead of *golden crown*, we have *crown of gold;* instead of *holy mountain*, we have *mountain of holiness*. For *eloquent man* (Exod. iv, 10) the Hebrew is *man of*

---

[1] Hebrew Grammar, § 144, 2.

words. The knowing or intelligent man is called *a man of knowledge* (Prov. xxiv, 5). This Hebraic usage appears often in the New Testament Greek. In accordance with this usage the adjectives proper almost invariably follow the nouns which they qualify. Thus *a wise man, the great river*, would be expressed in Hebrew, *a man wise, river the great.* The primitive conception, lying at the basis of this usage, would seem to be that of an additional word designed to modify the one just uttered. More fully, then, the above examples would be: *a man—a wise one ; the river—the great one.* But when the adjective is used as an emphatic predicate, it usually stands first in the sentence, as, "Good and just is Jehovah" (Psa. xxv, 8).

There is no formal comparison of adjectives in Hebrew. The comparative degree is indicated by a use of the preposition *from* (מִן) prefixed to the word with which the comparison is made. Thus: "The serpent was crafty *from* every beast of the field" (Gen. iii, 1); that is, *more crafty;* his cunning distinguished him from other beasts. The superlative is expressed by means of the article, or a suffix, or some peculiar form of expression which indicates the highest degree. Thus, *the youngest* is *the little one* (הַקָּטֹן, Gen. xlii, 13). The most abject slave is *a servant of servants* (Gen. ix, 25); the holiest place is the *holy of holies ;* the most excellent song is שִׁיר הַשִּׁירִים, *the song of songs.*[1]

Methods of comparison.

The Hebrew particles, namely, adverbs, prepositions, conjunctions, and interjections, are among the most delicate and interesting parts of the language. In order to a keen and discriminating insight into the spirit and bearing of numerous passages, it is necessary to master the force and usage of these little words. Usually the grammars and lexicons supply all the essential information, but it is only by intimate familiarity with the language that we come to appreciate their delicate and varying shades of meaning.

Particles.

---

[1] Nordheimer (Heb. Grammar, vol. ii, p. 60) designates as "the absolute superlative" those striking Hebraic expressions in which a noun is construed with one of the divine names. Thus, we have *wrestlings of God* (Gen. xxx, 8), a *mountain of God* (Psa. lxviii, 15), *mountains of God* (*El*, Psa. xxxvi, 6), *cedars of God* (Psa. lxxx, 10), *trees of Jehovah* (civ, 16), and *sleep of Jehovah* (1 Sam. xxvi, 12). But these genitives are not to be understood as designating, adjectively, a degree of excellence or of intensity. Rachel would vividly portray her wrestlings with her sister Leah as wrestlings which she had carried on with God himself. By the mountains of God (or of El) the psalmist means God's mountains, mountains which God brought forth (comp. Psa. xc, 3). So, too, the cedars of God and the trees of Jehovah are trees which are regarded as the workmanship of God. The sleep of Jehovah (1 Sam. xxvi, 12) was a slumber which Jehovah caused to fall upon Saul and his attendants.

HEBREW POETRY.

Much of the Old Testament is composed in a style and form of language far above that of simple prose. The his- torical books abound in spirited addresses, odes, lyrics, psalms, and fragments of song. The books of Job, Psalms, Proverbs, Ecclesiastes, and Song of Solomon, are highly poetical, and the prophetical books (נביאים אחרונים, *later prophets* of Hebrew Canon) are mainly of the same order. Nearly one half of the Old Testament is written in this poetic style. But the poetry of the Hebrews has peculiarities as marked and distinct from that of other nations as the language itself is different from other families of languages. Its metre is not that of syllables, but of sentences and sentiments. Properly speaking, Hebrew poetry knows nothing of metrical feet and versification analogous to the poet- ical forms of the Indo-European tongues. The learned and ingenious attempts of some scholars to construct a system of Hebrew metres are now generally regarded as failures. There are discernible an elevated style, a harmony and parallelism of sen- tences, a sonorous flow of graphic words, an artificial arrangement of clauses, repetitions, transpositions, and rhetorical antitheses, which are the inmost life of poetry. But the form is nowhere that of syllabic metre.[1] Some scholars have supposed that, since the Hebrew became a dead language, the ancient pronunciation is so utterly lost that it is therefore impossible now to discover or re- store its ancient metres. But this, at best, is a doubtful hypoth- esis, and has all probabilities against it. There is every reason to believe that the Masoretic pronunciation now in use is in the main correct, and substantially the same as that of the ancient Hebrews.

Old Testament largely poeti- cal.

Not metrical in structure.

---

[1] On the subject of Hebrew poetry, see Lowth, Sacred Poetry of the Hebrews, in Latin, with notes of Michaelis, Rosenmüller, and others (Oxford, 1828), and English Translation, edited by Stowe (Andover, 1829), and the Preliminary Dissertation to his Isaiah; Bellermann, Versuch über die Metrik der Hebräer (Berlin, 1813); Saalschutz, Form der hebräischen Poesie nebst einer Abhandlung über die Musik der Hebräer (Konigsb., 1825), and the same author's Form und Geist der hebräischen Poesie (1853); Ewald, Die poetischen Bücher des alten Bundes, vol. i, Translated by Nichol- son in Kitto's Journal of Sacred Literature for Jan. and April, 1848; Herder, Spirit of Hebrew Poetry, English Translation, in two vols., by James Marsh (Burlington, Vt., 1833); Isaac Taylor, The Spirit of Hebrew Poetry (Phila., 1873); De Wette, In- troduction to his Commentar über die Psalmen, pp. 32–63. Most of the more impor- tant works upon the Psalms, and the Biblical Cyclopædias, contain valuable disserta- tions on Hebrew Poetry and Parallelism.

The distinguishing feature of Hebrew poetry is now generally
acknowledged to be the parallelism of members. This
would be a very natural form for such short and vivid
sentences as characterize Hebrew syntax. Let the soul
be filled with deep emotion; let burning passions move the heart,
and sparkle in the eye, and speak loudly in the voice, and the simple
sentences of Hebrew prose would spontaneously take poetic form.
In illustration of this we may instance the exciting controversy of
Jacob and Laban in Gen. xxxi. The whole chapter is like a passage from an ancient epic; but when we read the speeches of Laban
and Jacob we seem to feel the wild throbbings of their human passions. The speeches are not cast in the artificial harmony of parallelism which appears in the poetical books; but we shall best observe their force by presenting them in the following form. After
seven days' hot pursuit, Laban overtakes Jacob in Mount Gilead,
and assails him thus:

> What hast thou done?
> And thou hast stolen my heart,
> And hast carried off my daughters
> As captives of the sword.
> Why didst thou hide thyself to flee?
> And thou hast stolen me,
> And thou didst not inform me,
> And I would have sent thee away with joy,
> And with songs, with timbrel and with harp.
> And thou didst not permit me to kiss my sons and my daughters!
> Now hast thou played the fool—to do!
> It is to the God of my hand
> To do with you an evil.
> But the God of your father
> Yesternight said to me, saying:
> Guard thyself from speaking with Jacob from good to evil.
> And now, going thou hast gone;
> For longing thou hast longed for the house of thy father.
> Why hast thou stolen my gods? Verses 26–30.

After the goods have been searched, and no gods found, "Jacob
was wroth, and chode with Laban," and uttered his pent-up emotion in the following style:

> What my trespass,
> What my sin,
> That thou hast been burning after me?
> For thou hast been feeling all my vessels;
> What hast thou found of all the vessels of thy house?

Place here —
Before my brethren and thy brethren,
And let them decide between us two.
This twenty year I with thee;
Thy ewes and thy goats have not been bereft,
And the rams of thy flock have I not eaten.
The torn I brought not to thee;
I atoned for it.
Of my hand didst thou demand it,
Stolen by day,
Or stolen by night.
I have been —
In the day heat devoured me,
And cold in the night,
And my sleep fled from my eyes.
This to me twenty year in thy house.
I served thee fourteen year for two of thy daughters,
And six years for thy flock;
And thou hast changed my wages ten parts.
Unless the God of my father,
The God of Abraham and the fear of Isaac, were for me,—
That now empty thou hadst sent me away.
The affliction and the labour of my hands
God has seen,
And he was judging yesternight. Verses 36–42.

This may not be poetry, in the strict sense; but it is certainly not the language of common prose. The rapidity of movement, the emotion, the broken lines, and the abrupt transitions, serve to show how a language of such peculiar structure as the Hebrew might early and naturally develop a poetic form, whose distinguishing feature would be a harmony of successive sentences, or some artificial concord or contrast of different sentiments, rather than syllabic versification. Untrammeled by metric limitations, the Hebrew poet enjoyed a peculiar freedom, and could utter the moving sentiments of passion in a great variety of forms.

We cannot too strongly emphasize the fact that some structural Form essential form is essential to all poetry. The elements of poetry to poetry. are invention, inspiration, and expressive form. But all possible genius for invention, and all the inspiration of most fervent passion, would go for nothing without some suitable mould in which to set them forth. When the creations of genius and inspiration have taken a monumental form in language, that form becomes an essential part of the whole. Hence the impossibility of translating the poetry of Homer, or Virgil, or David, into English prose, or the prose of any other language, and at the same time preserving the power and spirit of the original.

Bayard Taylor's translation of Goethe's Faust is a masterpiece in this, that it is a remarkably successful attempt to transfer from one language to another not merely the thoughts, the sentiment, and the exact meaning of the author, but also the form and rhythm. Mr. Taylor argues very Bayard Taylor on form in poetry. forcibly, and we think truly, that "the value of form in a poetical work is the first question to be considered. Poetry," he observes, "is not simply a fashion of expression; it is the form of expression absolutely required by a certain class of ideas. Poetry, indeed, may be distinguished from prose by the single circumstance that it is the utterance of whatever in man cannot be perfectly uttered in any other than a rhythmical form. It is useless to say that the naked meaning is independent of the form. On the contrary, the form contributes essentially to the fulness of the meaning. In poetry which endures through its own inherent vitality, there is no forced union of these two elements. They are as intimately blended, and with the same mysterious beauty, as the sexes in the ancient Hermaphroditus. To attempt to represent poetry in prose is very much like attempting to translate music into speech."[1]

How impossible to translate perfectly into any other form the following passage from Milton:

> Now storming fury rose,
> And clamour such as heard in Heaven till now
> Was never; arms on armour clashing brayed
> Horrible discord, and the maddening wheels
> Of brazen chariots raged; dire was the noise
> Of conflict; overhead the dismal hiss
> Of fiery darts in flaming volleys flew,
> And flying vaulted either host with fire.
> So under fiery cope together rushed
> Both battles main, with ruinous assault
> And inextinguishable rage. All Heaven
> Resounded, and had earth been then, all earth
> Had to her centre shook. What wonder? when
> Millions of fierce encountering angels fought
> On either side, the least of whom could wield
> These elements, and arm him with the force
> Of all their regions.[2]

The very form of this passage, as it stands before the reader's eye, contributes not a little to the emotions produced by it in the

---

[1] Preface to Translation of Goethe's Faust.
[2] Paradise Lost, Book vi, lines 207–223.

soul of a man of taste. Change the order of the words, or attempt
to state their naked meaning in prose, and the very ideas will seem
to vanish. The grandeur and beauty of the passage are due as
much to the rhythm, the emphatic collocation of words, the expressiveness of the form in which the whole is placed before us, as to
the sublime conceptions they embody. But if so much is due to
the form of poetic writing, much must be lost from any noble poem
when transferred to another language shorn of these elements of
power. The least we can do is to make prominent in our translations the measured forms of the original. So far as it may be done
without too great violence to the idioms of our own tongue, we
should preserve the same order of words, emphatic forms of statement, and abrupt transitions. In these respects Hebrew poetry is
Hebrew spirit probably more capable of exact translation than that of
and form may any other language. For there is no rhyme, no metric
be largely pre-
served in trans- scale, to be translated. Two things it is essential to
lation. preserve—the spirit and the form, and both of these
are of such a nature as to make it possible to reproduce them to a
great extent in almost any other language.[1]

[1] No man, perhaps, has shown a greater power to present in English the real spirit
of Hebrew poetry than Tayler Lewis. The following version of Job iv, 12–21, while
not exactly following the Hebrew collocation of the words, and giving to some words
a meaning scarcely sustained by Hebrew usage, does, nevertheless, bring out the spirit
and force of the original in a most impressive way:

> To me, at times, there steals a warning word;
> Mine ear its whisper seems to catch.
> In troubled thoughts from spectres of the night,
> When falls on men the vision-seeing trance,—
> And fear has come, and trembling dread,
> And made my every bone to thrill with awe,—
> 'Tis then before me stirs a breathing form;
> O'er all my flesh it makes the hair rise up.
> It stands; no face distinct can I discern:
> An outline is before mine eyes;
> Deep silence! then a voice I hear:
> Is mortal man more just than God?
> Is boasting man more pure than he who made him?
> In his own servants, lo, he trusteth not,
> Even on his angels doth he charge defect.
> Much more to them who dwell in homes of clay,
> With their foundation laid in dust,
> And crumbled like the moth
> From morn till night they're stricken down;
> Without regard they perish utterly.
> Their cord of life, is it not torn away?
> They die—still lacking wisdom.

See the notes on this rhythmical version, in which Lewis defends the accuracy of
his translation, in Lange's Commentary on Job, pp. 59, 60. See also Lewis' articles
on The Emotional Element in Hebrew Translation, in the Methodist Quarterly Review,
for Jan., 1862, Jan. and July, 1863; and Jan., 1864.

While the spirit and emotionality of Hebrew poetry are aue to a combination of various elements, the parallelism of sentences is a most marked feature of its outward form. This it becomes us now to exhibit more fully, for a scientific interpretation of the poetical portions of the Old Testament requires that the parallelism be not ignored. Joseph Addison Alexander, indeed, animadverts upon Bishop Lowth's "supposed discovery of rhythm or measure in the Hebrew prophets," and condemns his theory as unsound and in bad taste.[1] But his strictures seem to proceed on the assumption that the theory of parallelism involves the idea of metrical versification analogous to the prosody of other languages. Aside from such an assumption they have no relevancy or force. For it is indisputable that the large portions of the Hebrew scriptures, commonly regarded as poetical, are as capable of arrangement in well-defined parallelisms as the variety of Greek metres are capable of being reduced to system and rules.

Structural form of Hebrew parallelism.

The short and vivid sentences which we have seen to be peculiar to Hebrew speech, would lead, by a very natural process, to the formation of parallelisms in poetry. The desire to present a subject most impressively would lead to repetition, and the tautology would show itself in slightly varying forms of one and the same thought. Thus the following, from Prov. i, 24–27:

The process of forming parallelisms natural in Hebrew.

> Because I have called, and ye refuse;
> I have stretched out my hand, and no one attending;
> And ye refuse all my counsel,
> And my correction ye have not desired;
> Also I in your calamity will laugh;
> I will mock at the coming of your terror;
> At the coming—as a roaring tempest—of your terror;
> And your calamity as a sweeping whirlwind shall come on;
> At the coming upon you of distress and anguish.

Other thoughts would be more forcibly expressed by setting them in contrast with something of an opposite nature. Hence such parallelisms as the following:

> They have kneeled down and fallen;
> But we have arisen and straightened ourselves up. Psa. xx, 9.
>
> The memory of the righteous (is) for a blessing,
> But the name of the wicked shall be rotten.
> The wise of heart will take commands,
> But a prating fool shall be thrown down. Prov. x, 7, 8.

[1] See the Introduction to his Commentary on The Earlier Prophecies of Isaiah, pp. 48, 49. New York, 1846.

Such simple distichs would readily develop into more complex examples of parallelism, and we find among the Hebrew poems a great
variety of forms in which the sacred writers sought to set forth
their burning thoughts. The more common and regular forms of
Hebrew parallelism are classified by Lowth under three general
heads, which he denominates Synonymous, Antithetic, and Syn
thetic. These, again, may be subdivided, according as the lines
form simple couplets or triplets, or have measured correspondence
in sentiment and length, or are unequal, and broken by sudden bursts
of passion, or by some impressive refrain.

1. Synonymous Parallelism.

Here we place passages in which the different lines or members
present the same thought in a slightly altered manner of expression. To this class belong the couplets of Prov. i, 24–27 cited
above, where it will be seen there is a constant repetition of thought
under a variety of words. Three kinds of synonymous parallels
may be specified:

a) **Identical,** when the different members are composed of the
same, or nearly the same, words:

> Thou wert snared in the sayings of thy mouth;
> Thou wert taken in the sayings of thy mouth. **Prov. vi, 2.**
> They lifted up, the floods, O Jehovah;
> They lifted up, the floods, their voice;
> They lift up, the floods, their dashing. **Psa. xciii, 3.**
> It shall devour the parts of his skin,
> It shall devour his parts, the first-born of death. **Job xviii, 13.**
> For in a night is spoiled Ar, Moab, cut off.
> For in a night is spoiled Kir, Moab, cut off. **Isa. xv, 1**

b) **Similar,** when the sentiment is substantially the same, but
language and figures are different:

> For he on seas has founded it,
> And on floods will he establish it. **Psa. xxiv, 2.**
> Brays the wild ass over the tender grass?
> Or lows the ox over his provender? **Job vi, 5.**

c) **Inverted,** when there is an inversion or transposition of words
or sentences so as to change the order of thought:

> The heavens are telling the glory of God,
> And the work of his hands declares the expanse. **Psa. xix, 2.**
> They did not keep the covenant of God,
> And in his law they refused to walk. **Psa. lxxviii, 10.**

For unto me is he lovingly joined, and I will deliver him;
I will exalt him, for he has known my name. Psa. xci, 14.

Strengthen ye the weak hands,
And the feeble knees confirm. Isa. xxxv, 3.

2. Antithetic Parallelism.

Under this head come all passages in which there is a contrast or opposition of thought presented in the different sentences. This kind of parallelism abounds in the Book of Proverbs especially, for it is peculiarly adapted to express maxims of proverbial wisdom. There are two forms of antithetic parallelism:

a) **Simple,** when the contrast is presented in a single distich of simple sentences:

Righteousness will exalt a nation,
But the disgrace of peoples is sin. Prov. xiv, 34.

The tongue of wise men makes knowledge good,
But the mouth of fools pours out folly. Prov. xv, 2.

For a moment in his anger:
Lifetimes in his favour.
In the evening abideth weeping;
And at morning, a shout of joy. Psa. xxx, 5. (6.)

b) **Compound,** when there are two or more sentences in each member of the antithesis:

The ox has known his owner,
And the ass the crib of his lord;
Israel has not known,—
My people have not shown themselves discerning. Isa. i, 3.

If ye be willing, and have heard,
The good of the land shall ye eat;
But if ye refuse, and have rebelled,
A sword shall eat—
For the mouth of Jehovah has spoken. Isa. i, 19, 20.

In a little moment I forsook thee,
But in great mercies I will gather thee.
In the raging of wrath I hid my face a moment from thee;
But with everlasting kindness have I had mercy on thee.

Isa. liv, 7, 8.

3. Synthetic Parallelism.

Synthetic or Constructive Parallelism consists, according to Lowth's definition, "only in the similar form of construction, in which word does not answer to word, and sentence to sentence, as equivalent or opposite; but there is a correspondence and equality between different propositions in respect to the shape and turn of the whole sentence and of the constructive parts; such as noun answering to noun, verb to verb, member to member, negative to negative, interrogative to interrogative."[1] Two kinds of synthetic parallels may be noticed:

a) **Correspondent**, when there is a designed and formal correspondency between related sentences, as in the following example from Psa. xxvii, 1, where the first line corresponds with the third, and the second with the fourth:

> Jehovah, my light and my salvation,
> Of whom shall I be afraid?
> Jehovah, fortress of my life,
> Of whom shall I stand in terror?

This same style of correspondence is noticeable in the following compound antithetic parallelism:

> They shall be ashamed and blush together,
> Who are rejoicing in my harm;
> They shall be clothed with shame and disgrace,
> Who magnify themselves over me.
> They shall shout and rejoice,
> Who delight in my righteousness,
> And they shall say continually—be magnified, Jehovah,
> Who delight in the peace of his servant. Psa. xxxv, 26, 27.

b) **Cumulative**, when there is a climax of sentiment running through the successive parallels, or when there is a constant variation of words and thought by means of the simple accumulation of images or ideas:

> Happy the man who has not walked in the counsel of wicked ones,
> And in the way of sinners has not stood,
> And in the seat of scorners has not sat down;
> But in the law of Jehovah is his delight;
> And in his law will he meditate day and night. Psa. i, 1, 2.

> Seek ye Jehovah while he may be found,
> Call upon him while he is near by;
> Let the wicked forsake his way,
> And the man of iniquity his thoughts;
> And let him return to Jehovah, and he will have mercy on him,
> And to our God, for he will be abundant to pardon. Isa. lv, 6, 7.

> For the fig-tree shall not blossom,
> And no produce in the vines;
> Deceived has the work of the olive,
> And fields have not wrought food;

---

[1] Lowth's Isaiah, Preliminary Dissertation, p. 21. London, 1779.

> Cut off from the fold was the flock,
> And no cattle in the stalls;
> But I—in Jehovah will I exult;
> I will rejoice in the God of my salvation. Hab. iii, 17.

But aside from these more regular forms of parallelism, there are numerous peculiarities in Hebrew poetry which are not to be classified under any rules or theories of prosody. The rapt flights of the ancient bards ignored such trammels, and, by abrupt turns of thought, broken and unequal lines, and sudden ejaculations of prayer or emotion, they produced a great variety of expressive forms of sentiment. Take, for illustration, the two following extracts from Jacob's dying psalm—the blessings of Judah and Joseph—and note the variety of expression, the sharp transitions, the profound emotion, and the boldness and abundance of metaphor:

> Judah, thou! Thy brothers shall praise thee;
> Thy hand in the neck of thy foes!
> They shall bow down to thee, the sons of thy father.
> Whelp of a lion is Judah.
> From the prey, O my son, thou hast gone up!
> He bent low;
> He lay down as a lion,
> And as a lioness;
> Who will rouse him up?
> There shall not depart a sceptre from Judah,
> And a ruler from between his feet,
> Until he shall come—Shiloh—
> And to him shall be gathered peoples.
> Fastening to the vine his foal,
> And to the choice vine the son of his ass,
> He has washed in the wine his garment,
> And in the blood of grapes his clothes.
> Dark the eyes from wine,
> And white the teeth from milk. Gen. xlix, 8–12.

> Son of a fruit tree is Joseph,
> Son of a fruit tree over a fountain;
> Daughters climbing over a wall.
> And they imbittered him,
> And they shot,
> And they hated him,—
> The lords of the bow.
> Yet remained in strength his bow,
> And firm were the arms of his hands,
> From the hands of the Mighty One of Jacob;
> From the name of the Shepherd, the Stone of Israel;

From the God of thy father, and he will help thee;
And the Almighty, and he will bless thee;
Blessings of the heavens above,
Blessings of the deep lying down below,
Blessings of breasts and womb.
The blessings of thy father have been mighty,
Above the blessings of the enduring mountains,
The desire of the everlasting hills.
Let them be to the head of Joseph
And to the crown of the devoted of his brothers. Gen. xlix, 22–26.

In the later period of the language we find a number of artificial
Alphabetical poems, in which the several lines or verses begin with
poems. the letters of the Hebrew alphabet in their regular
order. Thus, in Psalms cxi and cxii, the lines or half verses are
arranged alphabetically. In Psalms xxv, xxxiv, cxlv, Prov. xxxi,
10–31, and Lam. i and ii, each separate verse begins with a new
letter in regular order. In Psa. xxxvii, with some slight exceptions,
every alternate verse begins with a new letter. In Psa. cxix and
Lam. iii, a series of verses, each beginning with the same letter, is
grouped into strophes or stanzas, and the strophes follow one another in alphabetical order. Such artificiality evinces a later period
in the life of the language, when the poetical spirit, becoming less
creative and more mechanical, contrives a new feature of external
form to arrest attention and assist the memory.

We find also in the Old Testament several noticeable instances
Hebrew rhymes. of rhyme. The following, in Samson's answer to
the men of Timnath (Judges xiv, 18), was probably
designed

לוּלֵא חֲרַשְׁתֶּם בְּעֶגְלָתִי
לֹא מְצָאתֶם חִידָתִי

If ye had not plowed with my heifer,
Ye had not found out my riddle.

The following are perhaps only accidental:

מַלְכֵי תַרְשִׁישׁ וְאִיִּים מִנְחָה יָשִׁיבוּ
מַלְכֵי שְׁבָא וּסְבָא אֶשְׁכָּר יַקְרִיבוּ

Kings of Tarshish and of isles a gift shall return,
Kings of Sheba and Seba a presen. ball bring. Psa. lxxii, 10.

כִּסְדֹם הָיִינוּ
לַעֲמֹרָה דָּמִינוּ

As Sodom had we been,
To Gomorrah had we been like. Isa. i, 9.

בְּגוֹי חָנֵף אֲשַׁלְּחֶנּוּ
וְעַל־עַם עֶבְרָתִי אֲצַוֶּנּוּ

In a nation profane will I send him,
And upon a people of my wrath will I command him. Isa. x, 6.[1]

But aside from all artificial forms, the Hebrew language, in its words, idiomatic phrases, vivid concepts, and pictorial power, has a remarkable simplicity and beauty. To the emotional Hebrew every thing was full of life, and the manner of the most ordinary action attracted his attention. Sentences full of pathos, sublime exclamations, and profound suggestions often found expression in his common talk. How often the word *behold* (הִנֵּה) occurs in simple narrative! How the very process and order of action are pictured in the following passages: " Jacob lifted up his feet, and went to the land of the sons of the east" (Gen. xxix, 1). "He lifted up his voice, and wept. . . . Laban heard the hearing about Jacob, the son of his brother, and he ran to meet him, and embraced him, and kissed him, and brought him to his house" (verses 11, 13). "Jacob lifted up his eyes, and looked, and, behold! Esau was coming" (Gen. xxxiii, 1). How intensely vivid the picture of Sisera's death, wrought by the hand of Jael:

Vividness of Hebrew words and phrases.

> Her hand to the tent-pin she sent forth,
> And her right hand to the hammer of the workmen;
> And she hammered Sisera, she crushed his head;
> And she smote through and transfixed his temples.
> Between her feet he sunk down; he fell; he lay;
> Between her feet he sunk down, he fell;
> Where he sunk down, there he fell slain. Judges v, 26, 27.

There are, again, many passages where a notable ellipsis enhances the impression: "And now, lest he send forth his hand, and take also from the tree of life, and eat, and live forever—and sent him forth Jehovah God from the garden of Eden" (Gen. iii, 22). "And now, if thou wilt forgive their sin— and if not, wipe me, I pray, from thy book which thou hast written." "Return, O Jehovah—how long!" (Psa. xc, 13.) The attempt of our translators to supply the ellipsis in Psa. xix, 3, 4, perverts the real meaning: " *There is* no speech nor language *where* their voice is not heard." The simple Hebrew is much more impressive:

Ellipsis.

[1] Comp. also Isa. i, 25, where three rhymes appear in one verse; and Isa. i, 29; xliv, 3; xlix, 10; liii, 6; Job vi, 9; Psa. xlv, 8; Prov. vi, 1.

No saying, and no words;—
Not heard—their voice;
In all the land went forth their line,
And in the end of the world their utterances.

That is, the heavens have no audible language or voice such as mortal man is wont to speak; nevertheless, they have been stretched as a measuring line over all the surface of the earth, and, though voiceless, they have sermons for thoughtful souls in every part of the habitable world.

Such elliptical modes of expression would be very natural in a
Hebrew speech naturally elliptical. language which has no vowels in its alphabet. A written document, containing only consonants, and capable
of a variety of meanings according as it was pronounced or understood, must necessarily leave much to the imagination of the reader. The simple but emotional speaker will often convey his meaning as much by signs, gestures, and peculiar intonations of voice, as by his words; and this very habit of leaving much for the common sense and imagination of the reader to supply seems to have impressed itself upon the written language of the sensitive Hebrew. He took it for granted that his hearers and readers would understand much that he did not literally say. In this, however, he was at times mistaken. Like Moses, when he smote the Egyptian, "he supposed that his brethren would understand that God by his hand would give deliverance to them; but they did not understand" (Acts vii, 25). So sacred writers of the Old Testament, as well as of the New, left on record things difficult to understand (δυσνόητα, 2 Peter iii, 16), and hence the variety of meanings attached to certain parts of Scripture.

In direct addresses almost every object of nature, and even abstract ideas, are appealed to as if instinct with living
Emotionality of direct address. consciousness: "Spring up, O well; sing ye to her" (Num. xxi, 17). "Sing, O heavens; and rejoice, O land; break forth the mountains into song!" (Isa. xlix, 13). "Awake, awake, put on strength, O arm of Jehovah! as the days of old, the generations of eternities" (Isa. li, 9). "Awake, awake, put on thy strength, O Zion, put on the garments of thy beauty, O Jerusalem, city of holiness!" (Isa. lii, 1). "Open, O Lebanon, thy doors, and fire shall eat into thy cedars! Howl, O cypress, for the cedar has fallen, which mighty ones did spoil! Howl, oaks of Bashan, for down has gone the inaccessible forest!" (Zech. xi, 1, 2). "O sword, awake against my friend; and against the man of my companionship!" (Zech. xiii, 7).

We should also note the anthropomorphisms and anthropopathisms of the Old Testament. They are but the vivid Old Testament anthropomorphism. concepts which impressed the emotional Hebrew mind, and are in perfect keeping with the spirit of the language. What an affecting conception of the personal God in Gen. vi, 5, 6: "And Jehovah saw that great was the wickedness of men in the land, and every imagination of the thoughts of his heart—only evil all the day. And it repented Jehovah that he made men in the land, and it pained him to his heart." Also in the following: "And there was the bow in the cloud, and I looked at it to remember the covenant eternal between God and every living soul in all flesh, which is upon the land" (Gen. ix, 16). "Jehovah went down to see the city and the tower, which the sons of men were building" (Gen. xi, 5). Moses' song (Exod. xv) extols Jehovah as "a man of war" (verse 3). He calls the strong east wind (xiv, 21), by which the waters of the Red Sea were heaped up, "the wind of thy nose" (verse 8), using thus the metaphor of an enraged animal breathing fury from his distended nostrils. In Hezekiah's prayer (2 Kings xix, 16) we have this form of petition: "Stretch out, O Jehovah, thy ear, and hear; open, O Jehovah, thy eyes, and see." David says (1 Chron. xvii, 25): "For thou, O my God, didst uncover the ear of thy servant—to build for him a house; therefore found thy servant to pray to thy face." Observe the suggestive force of the words here used. David receives the revelation of God from the prophet Nathan as a confidential communication; as if a bosom friend had stolen up to him, removed the locks of hair that covered his ear, and whispered there a secret word of wondrous promise which, at that time, no one else might hear. Then it seemed to the enraptured king that *because* God had thus found him, and *uncovered his ear, therefore* he had come *to find* how to pray to God's face.[1]

We have already seen how many influences combine, in the history of a language, to modify and change its forms and introduce new dialects, which may again be developed into new lan-

---

[1] "Why talk of anthropopathism," says Tayler Lewis, "as if there were some special absurdity covered by this sounding term, when any revelation conceivable must be anthropopathic? If made subjectively—as some claim it should be made, if made at all—that is, to all men directly, through thoughts and feelings inwardly excited in each human soul without any use of language, still it must be anthropopathic. There is no escape from it. Whatever comes in this way to man must take the measure of man. . . . The thoughts and feelings thus aroused would still be human, and partake of the human finity and imperfection. In their highest state they will be but shadows of the infinite, figures of ineffable truths."—The Divine Human in the Scriptures, p. 43.

guages.[1] But a most remarkable fact of the Hebrew language is **Remarkable** that, for more than a thousand years, it suffered no ma-**uniformity of** **the Hebrew** terial change. The Hebrew of the latest books of the **language.** Old Testament is essentially the same as that of the oldest documents. Traces of change and decay may, indeed, be discovered in the books of Ezekiel, Chronicles, Ezra, and Nehemiah; but they consist mainly of a few peculiar modes of expression, and the introduction of various words of a foreign cast. Contact with other nations would naturally introduce some new forms of speech. Especially did Aramaic words and forms work their way into the Hebrew books. But this infusion of new words wrought no essential changes in the structure of the language, and many forms which are commonly called Chaldaisms are found in the oldest books. The fact is, the Hebrew and Aramaic tongues abode side by side for ages. The monumental stone heap which Jacob and Laban set up in Mount Gilead, Jacob called *Galeed;* but Laban, the Syrian, called it *Jegar-sahadutha*—an Aramaic name of the same meaning as Galeed (Gen. xxxi, 47). More frequent intercourse with Syrians and Chaldæans in later times would naturally leave its traces in corresponding fulness on the language of the Hebrews.

Three periods may be distinguished in the Old Testament litera-**Three periods** ture, and may appropriately be called, respectively, the **of Hebrew lit-** *earlier,* the *middle,* and the *later.* The first extended from **erature.** the time of Moses to that of Samuel, the second from David to Hezekiah, and the third from the latter years of the kingdom of Judah until a few generations after the return from the Babylonian exile.[2] But granting all the evidences of decline and change that can be fairly established, it still remains indisputable that the Hebrew language continued remarkably uniform, and in essentially the same stage of development, from the age of Moses

---

[1] Compare above, pp. 72, 73.

[2] Gesenius declares for two periods, the first extending from the time of Moses to the Babylonian exile; the second from the exile to the time of the Maccabees. These periods he calls the *golden* and the *silver* age. See his Geshichte der hebräischen Sprache und Schrift. Lpz., 1815. Böttcher follows Gesenius in.deciding for two periods—the period of rise and bloom (B.C. 1500–600), and the period of decline and fall (B.C. 600–165). Each of these periods he subdivided into three epochs. See his Ausführliches Lehrbuch der hebräischen Sprache, Einleitung, pp. 21, 22. Renan distinguishes three periods, the archaic, the classic, and the Chaldaic. See his Histoire générale des Langues Sémitiques, p. 116. Paris, 1863. Comp. Ewald, Ausführliches Lehrbuch, p. 23, and Keil's, Bleek's and De Wette's Introductions to the Old Testament. See also the articles on the Hebrew Language in Hertzog, Real-encyclopädie, the Encyclopædia Britannica, and the various biblical dictionaries.

to that of Malachi. It never changed so much as even to approach what might be called another dialect. In spite of migrations, conquest, invasions, revolutions, secession, and exile, the Hebrew language, in which the five books of the Torah were cast, retained its sacred mould. Chaldaisms are found in Genesis, and archaisms in Zechariah and Malachi.

Happily, there is little room for dispute as to the approximate dates of most of the books of the Old Testament. A large amount of controversy has turned upon the books of Job and Ecclesiastes, and it is a singular fact that, while some have strenuously contended that Job belongs to the Solomonic period, and Ecclesiastes to a post-exilian date, other critics, equally competent and acute, maintain the Solomonic authorship of Ecclesiastes, and attribute the book of Job to Moses. This fact shows how uncertain and misleading are the attempts to ascertain the age of a Hebrew writer solely from his language. Many words and forms, *Difference of diction no controlling evidence of date or authorship.* which are often alleged as Aramaisms, may be attributed, rather, to the style and diction of an author. Isaiah, Hosea, Amos, Micah, and Nahum, though nearly contemporary, vary greatly in their style, and each of them uses words and forms of expression not elsewhere found; and yet they all wrote in the same general prophetic strain. How many more and how much greater differences, then, are reasonably to be expected between them and writers of another period, whose subject-matter is widely different! The same author may use a very different diction in two different works, treating on different themes, and written twenty years apart. If Moses wrote the book of Job—especially if he wrote it during the forty years of his shepherd life in Arabia—we certainly would not expect such a highly wrought poem to resemble the historical book of Genesis, even though we assume that Genesis and Job were written by him about the same time. If Solomon composed the book of Ecclesiastes in his old age, there is no sufficient reason to assume that his style and language in that work must closely resemble the Proverbs and Canticles written nearly forty years previously.

Such, then, are the principal features of that language in which the ancient oracles of God were embodied, and in which they are preserved to us unto this day. Its *Hebrew a language peculiarly adapted to embody God's ancient word.* letters are a picture gallery; its words, roots, and grammatical forms are intimately blended with profoundest and divinest thoughts. It may well be called, emphatically, the *sacred tongue.* It appears in full development in its earliest written monuments, as if it had been crystallized into

imperishable form by the marvels of the exodus and the fires of
Sinai. The divine calling of Israel, and their national separateness
from all other peoples, served largely to preserve it from any considerable change. It retained every essential element of its
structure until the canon of the Old Testament was complete, and
then it ceased to be a living language. But, though dead, it does
not cease to speak. It seems, rather, to have arisen, and to flourish
in another and immortal life. When it ceased to be a spoken language, behold, it was already petrified in records more enduring
than the granite tables on which the ten commandments were
written by the finger of God. As the ancient cities, buried under
the ashes of Vesuvius, now speak from the tomb of ages, and reveal the life and customs of the old Roman world, so the pictorial
and emotional language of the Hebrew Scriptures transports us
into the very heart and spirit of that olden time when God talked
familiarly with men. Like the holy land, in which this language
Hebrew lan- lived more than a thousand years, it abounds in imagery
guage like the that is apt to strike the imagination or affect the senses.
Hebrews' land. It is, in some respects, a reflexion of Canaan itself.
It has a strength and permanency like the mountains about Jerusalem (Psa. cxxv, 2). It can whisper melodious tones for ode and
psalm and elegy, soft and gentle as the voice of the turtle-dove
(Cant. ii, 12), or the gliding waters of Shiloh (Isa. viii, 6). It
can excite emotions of terror like the rushing floods of the ancient Kishon, which swept whole armies away (Judges v, 21), or
like the thunder and earthquake which opened the beds of the sea,
and revealed the foundations of the world (2 Sam. xxii, 16). It
has landscape paintings as beautiful as the wild flower of Sharon
(Cant. ii, 1), charming as the splendour and excellency of Carmel,
and awe-inspiring as the glory of Lebanon (Isa. xxxv, 2). Through
it all there breathes a spirit of holiness as impressive and solemn as
if proceeding from the mysterious darkness in which Jehovah came
down on Mount Sinai (Exod. xix, 18), or from the veiled Holy of
Holies on the Mount Zion which he loved (Psa. lxxviii, 68). Surely this language was admirably adapted to enshrine the law and
the testimony of God. It is like the wonderful bush which Moses
saw at Horeb; behold! it burns continually, but is not consumed.
And when the devout student comes within the spell of its spirit
and power, he may hear the sound of a voice, exclaiming: "Pull
off thy sandals from thy feet, for the place whereon thou standest
is holy ground" (Exod. iii, 5).

CHAPTER V.

THE CHALDEE LANGUAGE.

A SMALL portion of the Old Testament is written in what is commonly called the biblical Chaldee.[1] In Dan. ii, 4, Ezra iv, 7, 2 Kings xviii, 26, and Isa. xxxvi, 11, it is called *Aramaic*, אֲרָמִית, a word which is translated in the English Version, after the Septuagint, Vulgate, and Luther, "the Syrian tongue." This language became early prevalent in all the region known as אֲרָם, *Aram*, the Syria of the Greeks and Romans, and in course of time branched out into two very similar dialects known as the Eastern and Western Aramaic. These dialects differ chiefly in vocalization, and each maintains an individuality of

Eastern and Western Aramaic.

its own, but lexically and grammatically they are in all essential characteristics most intimately related to each other. The Western Aramaic is now commonly called Syriac; the Eastern, Chaldee. This latter name has not usually been satisfactory to the learned, some preferring the name Babylonian, others Babylonian-Semitic. But the name of Chaldee language, as applied to the Eastern Aramaic, has acquired too great currency to be now set aside. It is universally admitted that this language was in common use among the Babylonians at the time

Chaldee a proper name for the biblical Aramaic.

of the Jewish exile, and the Babylonians are almost always called Chaldeans (Hebrew, כַּשְׂדִים, *Chasdim*) in the Bible.[2] Mention is made in Dan. i, 4, of "the tongue of the Chaldeans," and there appears no sufficient reason to believe that this was any other than the common language of Chaldea at the time.[3] It was sufficiently different from the Jews' language (comp. 2 Kings xviii, 26) to

---

[1] The Chaldee portions are Jer. x, 11, Dan. ii, 4–vii, 28, and Ezra iv, 8–vi, 18, and vii, 12–26.

[2] Compare especially 2 Kings xxiv, 2; xxv, 4, 5, 10, 13, etc.; Isa. xiii, 19; xliii, 14; xlvii, 1; Jer. xxi, 4, 9; xxxii, 4, 5, 24, etc.; xxxvii, 5, 8, 9; l, 1, 8, 10, 13, etc.; Ezek. i, 3, 12, 13; Hab. i, 6.

[3] Most recent critics (see especially Stuart, Keil, and Zöckler, *in loco*) hold that the לְשׁוֹן כַּשְׂדִים, *tongue of the Chasdim* (Dan. i, 4) was the learned language of the priests and wise men, and the court language of the empire, as distinguished from the *Aramaic*, the language of the common people. They urge that in Dan. ii, 2, 4, 5, 10; iv, 7; v, 7, 11, the *Chasdim* are a special and predominant class among the wise men of Babylon, and represent an ancient tribe or people of non-Semitic speech. But it is also a fact that Daniel applies the word *Chasdim* to the inhabitants of Babylonia

make it an object to instruct the young men who were to be trained
for the royal service in its written and spoken (סְפַר וּלְשׁוֹן, Dan. i, 4)
forms. During the seventy years of their exile the Jewish people
largely lost the use of their ancestral language, and appropriated
this Chaldean dialect. When they returned to rebuild their holy
city and temple, they required to have the language of their
sacred books explained to them (Neh. viii, 8). They never again
recovered the use of the Hebrew as a vernacular, but continued
to use the Chaldean dialect until Jerusalem was taken by the
Romans.

When Abram migrated from Ur of the Chaldeans, the differences between the Semitic tongues were doubtless fewer and less
noticeable than in the days of Ezra or of Daniel.[1] After the time

Hebrew inter-
course with Ar-
amaic.

of David, when intercourse between the Israelites and
the Syrians of Damascus became more frequent, Aramaisms would naturally work their way into the Hebrew
language of Palestine. The Chaldee verse in Jer. x, 11 is believed by many to be a gloss, interpolated in the time of the exile,
or very soon afterward,[2] but the language and style of Jeremiah
show many evidences of Aramaic influence. At the time of his
prophesying the Chaldeans were overrunning Palestine (Jer. xxxiv),
and he survived the destruction of Jerusalem, and was carried
down into Egypt (Jer. xxxix, xl). The language of Ezekiel's
prophecies evinces the growing power of Aramean speech over
the Hebrew mind, and "the manifold anomalies and corruptions in
his writings betray the decline and approaching ruin of the Hebrew
language, and remind us that the prophet's home is in a foreign
land."[3]

(Dan. v, 30 ; ix, 1), and in all the other books of the Old Testament this is its common
meaning. It is further urged that the use of the word Aramaic (ארמית) in Dan.
ii, 4, implies that these learned Chasdim addressed the king in the common language
of the empire, and not the learned tongue of the priesthood and the court. This,
however, is by no means clear. Why may not "the tongue of the Chaldees" be also
called Aramaic? This was the common name used by Hebrew writers for the language of Chaldea, and it was every way natural for the author of Dan. ii, 4, to use
the word אֲרָמִית, as Ezra does (in Ezra iv, 7), although he had already spoken of the
same language (in i, 4) as the Chaldee tongue. If, as these critics say, the tongue of
the Chasdim was the court language of Nebuchadnezzar and his dynasty, this tongue,
by all means, should have been used before the king. No satisfactory reason is given
for their using any other. See Bleek, Introduction to the Old Testament, vol. i, pp.
47, 48. English Translation by Venables, Lond., 1875.

[1] Compare page 77, above.

[2] So Houbigant, Venema, Dathe, Blayney, Doederlein, Rosenmüller, Maurer, Ewald,
Graf, Henderson, and Naegelsbach.

[3] Keil, Introduction to Old Testament, vol. i, p. 356.

Daniel, who received an early and thorough training in the
tongue of the Chaldeans, is the first biblical writer who
formally employs this dialect in sacred composition.
After having narrated in Hebrew the successful training of himself and his three companions, he passes, in the second
chapter, to an account of Nebuchadnezzar's dream, and from verse
4, where the Chaldeans begin their address to the king: "O king,
forever live!" the language changes to Aramaic. This being the
very language in which all the conversation of the court was carried on, its use here gives to Daniel's narrative a life-like reality,
and is a monumental evidence of the genuineness and authenticity
of the record. Only a writer of Daniel's time and position, and
bilinguous as he, would have written thus. Nebuchadnezzar's
dream was a God-given vision of world-empire, and of its final
overthrow by the power and kingdom of God; and the dream and
its interpretation were written down in a language then common
alike to the people of God and to the mightiest empire of the
world. The succeeding narratives of the golden image and the deliverance of Daniel's three companions from the burning furnace
(chap. iii), Nebuchadnezzar's proclamation (chap. iv), Belshazzar's
feast and sudden overthrow (chap. v), and Daniel's deliverance
from the lion's den (chap. vi), were also recorded in the language
of the empire, for they were written for the world to know.
Finally, Daniel's great vision of world-empire and its overthrow
(chap. vii), is also recorded in Chaldee, for it was only a repetition
under other symbols and in fuller form of the prophecy embodied
in Nebuchadnezzar's dream (chap. ii). This prophecy was for the
whole world rather than for any special purpose of the Jewish people; but when, in the eighth chapter, the prophet passes to visions
of more special import for his own people, he resumes the Hebrew.

The other writer of biblical Chaldee is Ezra, the learned priest
and scribe, who flourished about a century after Daniel.
He went up from Babylon to Jerusalem, in company
with a large number of the exiles, during the reign of the Persian
king Artaxerxes Longimanus (B. C. 457). Familiar from youth
with the Chaldee dialect of Babylon, he also by diligent study
made himself familiar with the sacred literature of his nation, that
he might be able to instruct the people of his age in the law of
Jehovah (Ezra vii, 1–10). The great mass of these returning exiles
had lost the use of their ancestral language,[1] and now spoke the

The Chaldee passages of Daniel.

The Chaldee of Ezra.

---

[1] It is not to be supposed, however, that all the exiles lost the use of Hebrew.
Many of the better classes preserved it, and the use of it in the books of Ezra, Nehemiah, Haggai, Zechariah, and Malachi implies that it was yet familiar to many.

common language of the Chaldeans among whom they had sojourned more than seventy years. In connexion with other Levites and with Nehemiah, Ezra was wont to assemble the people, and read and explain to them the book of the law of Moses (Neh. viii, 1-8). The agreement of ancient traditions in associating Ezra with the Great Synagogue, and the formation of the Old Testament Canon, may authorize us to believe that, in connexion with Nehemiah and other leading Jews of his time, he did collect and arrange the books of the Jewish Canon in substantially the form in which we now possess them. He lived at a time when such a work could best be done, and he had facilities for it which no later age possessed. Ezra was unquestionably one of the greatest men of Israel, and his mighty influence over the people is attested by the numerous traditions which still linger about his name.

Such being the historical position and character of this writer, we can readily understand the bilingual character of the book which bears his name. When, at chapter iv, 8, he has occasion to insert the letter of the Samaritans to Artaxerxes (Smerdis), which is emphatically said to have been written and translated into Aramaic, he naturally gives it in the language in which he found it written— a language perfectly familiar to himself and his people. For the same reason he continues his narrative in the Aramaic language as far as chap. vi, 18; for this part of his book is principally devoted to foreign and international affairs, and contains copies of letters to and from Artaxerxes and Darius.[1] So, also, the copy of Artaxerxes' letter and decree, in chap. vii, 12-26, is inserted without note or comment in this Aramaic language. Such a peculiar use of two languages, or dialects, was perfectly in keeping with the age and circumstances of Ezra, who was equally familiar with both tongues; but it could scarcely be explicable in a writer of any other age or nation. Ezra had no sufficient reason to translate these Aramaic documents, which he found ready for his use. Rather, we may say, he was divinely inspired and overruled to preserve them in just the form in which he found them. Their subject-matter, like the Aramaic portions of Daniel, had special lessons for the Gentile world, and it was well for them to be published and made immortal in the language of that nation with whose name the exile of the Hebrews was to be forever associated.

[1] It is probable that the whole Chaldee section, from chap. iv, 8 to vi, 18, is an older document, written by a contemporary of Zerubbabel, for in chap. v, 4, the writer uses the first person, as if he were a participant in the matters described. Ezra appropriated this document, containing an authentic history of the troubles attending the rebuilding of the temple, just as he did the document of names and numbers in chap. ii.

This Chaldean language, being, like the Hebrew, only a dialectical outgrowth of the original Semitic speech, is, in its genius, idioms, and general structure, substantially the same as Hebrew. Among its chief peculiarities are (1) the use of nouns in the emphatic state. This usage does away with the article, so that where the Hebrew would have הַמֶּלֶךְ, hammelek, *the king*, the Chaldee has מַלְכָּא, *malka*. (2) The termination of the masculine plural of nouns in ‐ִין where the Hebrew has ‐ִים. (3) The use of the relative דִי (shortened prefix דְּ) in the various senses in which the Hebrew employs אֲשֶׁר, and also as a sign of the genitive case. (4) A pleonastic use of the suffix pronouns; as "unto *him*, unto Artaxerxes, the king (Ezra iv, 11); "the name of *him*, of God" (Dan. ii, 20). (5) There are three ordinary conjugations of the verb, the Peal, Paël, and Aphel, corresponding substantially with the Kal, Piël, and Hiphil in Hebrew,[1] and each of these has a passive or reflexive mode, formed by prefixing the syllable אֶת, thus:

Grammatical peculiarities of the Chaldee.

Simple.		Intensive.		Causative.	
Peal,	קְטַל	Paël,	קַטֵּל	Aphel,	אַקְטֵל
Ithpeal,	אִתְקְטֵל	Ithpaal,	אֶתְקַטַּל	Ittaphal,	אִתְּקְטַל

In Chaldee, as in Hebrew, there are also several rare and peculiar conjugations, and the biblical Chaldee makes use of the conjugations Hiphil and Hophal, and in other instances uses ה instead of א. We also find in Chaldee imperatives in the passive form, and a distinct masculine and feminine termination (וּ‐ and א‐) for the third person plural of the past tense. The participle is also used for the finite verb, and is construed with nouns and pronouns far more frequently than in Hebrew. In its lexical forms the Chaldee is specially noticeable in its use of the letters ד instead of ז, ת and ט instead of שׁ, and ע instead of צ.

In the few Aramean chapters of our Bible we can scarcely expect to find a very full illustration of all the peculiarities of this language. In its general spirit and form we trace, however, a tendency to depart from the suggestive brevity of expression which we notice in the ancient Hebrew, and to leave less to the imagination and understanding of the reader. There is less of animation and freshness of thought, and more of effort to set forth facts and ideas with fulness and precision. Nevertheless, we occasionally meet with passages of peculiar force and emotion. Notice the peculiar pleonastic structure and style of the following verse, which we translate literally from Dan. iii, 8: "All because of this, in it,

---

[1] Comp. the Hebrew paradigm above, page 81.

the time, approached men, Chaldeans, and devoured the pieces of them, of the Jews." The expression, *devoured their pieces*, is metaphorical, denoting the rabid fury of the Chaldeans in accusing the Jews, as if, like ravenous beasts, they would tear them into bits, and devour them. In the twenty-fifth verse of the same chapter, mark the mingled excitement and awe of Nebuchadnezzar's words: "Ha! I see men, four, unbound, walking in the midst of the fire, and hurt there is not in them, and the aspect of him, of the fourth, is like to a son of the gods!" Some passages naturally fall into parallelisms, as the following, from Nebuchadnezzar's proclamation (Dan. iv, 10–14):

> I was looking, and behold, a tree in the midst of the land,
> And the height of it was great;
> Greatly increased became the tree, and mighty,
> And the height of it was reaching to the heavens,
> And the sight of it to the end of all the land.
> Its foliage was beautiful, and its fruit abundant,
> And there was food in it for all.
> Under it the beast of the field found shade,
> And in its branches dwelt the birds of heaven,
> And from it all flesh was fed.
> I was looking, in the visions of my head, upon my bed,
> And behold, a watcher, even a holy one,
> And from the heavens he descended;
> He called aloud, and thus he spoke:
> Cut down the tree, and lop off its branches,
> Remove its foliage, and scatter its fruit,
> Let the beast run away from under it,
> And the birds from its branches.

The current language of such a world-empire as that of Babylon would naturally appropriate many foreign words. It should, therefore, occasion no surprise to find Median, Persian, and Greek words in Chaldee writings belonging to the era of Nebuchadnezzar.[1] This Chaldean dialect, adopted by the Jews during their exile, was retained by them after their return to their fatherland. The prophecies of Haggai, Zechariah, and Malachi, and the books of Ezra and Nehemiah were written in Hebrew, for they were to have a place among the sacred books,[2] but the com-

Foreign words.

---

[1] See Rawlinson on the Persian words in Ezra, and also the Excursus on Persian words in Daniel, in the Speaker's Commentary, vol. iii, p. 421 and vol. vi, p. 246.

[2] The Hebrew did not altogether go out of use until long after the return from the Babylonian exile. It was used by such men as Haggai, Ezra, and other prophets, priests, and scribes of the law. Keil thinks the later prophets studied to imitate the style of the oldest Hebrew, and therefore used archaisms from the Pentateuch.

mon language of the people was this Babylonian-Aramaic, which maintained itself in Palestine during the periods of Persian, Greek, and Roman dominion. It is called *Judaic* (יְהוּדִית) in Neh. xiii, 24, and *Hebraistic*, or *the Hebraic dialect*, in the Apocrypha and in the New Testament.[1] The numerous Chaldee words used in the New Testament[2] are also an evidence that it was the common language of Palestine in the time of our Lord.[3] Its most considerable literature is contained in the Targums, the oldest of which were probably written before the beginning of the Christian era.[4]

It is not without historical significance that Ezra and Daniel wrote a portion of the Scriptures in this language of the Chaldees. These chapters abide a monumental witness of Israel's contact with the mighty world-powers. Out of the land Historical and of the Chaldees Abram was called, and in him, it was apologetic val-said that all families and nations of the earth should ue of the Chaldee parts of the be blessed. After fourteen centuries of religious cul-Bible. ture and revelation, his sons, by many thousands, were carried back into the same Chaldean land. Through Daniel in Babylon God made his wonders and power known to the mightiest nations of the world, and Israel's exile in Babylon, like Joseph's life in Egypt, served the double purpose of preserving the chosen people from utter ruin by idolatry, into which they had been fast running in Canaan, and of showing forth to the mightiest nation of the earth the wisdom and power of God. Daniel wrote in the tongue of the Chaldeans the fall of that mighty monarchy, which was symbolized by the golden head of the image (Dan. ii, 32, 38), and the great lion with eagle's wings (vii, 4). Ezra wrote in the same tongue the conflicts of the restored Israel with other heathen powers. These chapters foreshadow a gradual transition to a new era, and led the way to the subsequent appropriation of the Greek language, in which the New Testament Scriptures appear.

[1] Ἑβραϊστί and τῇ Ἑβραΐδι διαλέκτῳ. See Prologue to Ecclesiasticus and John v, 2; xix, 13, 17, 20; Acts xxi, 40; xxii, 2; xxvi, 14.

[2] Such as *Raca* (Matt. v, 22), *Golgotha* (Matt. xxvii, 33), *Talitha cumi* (Mark v, 41), *Corban* (Mark vii, 11), *Ephphatha* (Mark vii, 34), *Rabboni* (Mark x, 51), *Abba* (Mark xiv, 36), *Gabbatha* (John xix, 13), *Aceldama* (Acts i, 19), *Maran atha* (1 Cor. xvi, 22).

[3] See the Essay of Prof. H. F. Pfannkuche, On the prevalence of the Aramæan Language in Palestine in the Age of Christ and the Apostles; translated from the German by E. Robinson, in the Biblical Repository, for April, 1831.

[4] For a convenient account of the character and age of the Targums, see Harman, Introduction to the Study of the Holy Scriptures, pp. 52–55, and the Appendix to Hackett's translation of Winer's Grammar of the Chaldee Language, Andover, 1845. See also the Biblical Cyclopædias under the word Targums.

CHAPTER VI.

THE GREEK LANGUAGE.

THE Greek language belongs to the so-called Indo-European family,
An Indo-European tongue. which extends from the eastern boundary of India to
the western shores of Europe. Midway between these
two extremes, on that Ægean shore "where every sight is beauty,
and every breath a balm," the nation of the Greeks arose and
flourished. In ideals of government, in models of taste, in oratory,
mathematics, architecture, sculpture, history, and philosophy, they
have furnished the masterpieces of the world. In these several departments, Solon, Homer, Demosthenes, Euclid, Phidias, Thucydides, and Plato, are representative and immortal names.

It has long been observed that natural scenery has much to do
with the development of national life, and may give character to
the civilization of a people. We have already called attention to
the fact that Hebrew civilization and literature resemble the varied
Language and scenery of the Holy Land. So may we also trace a
civilization af- relationship between the land of the Greeks, and that
fected by natu-
ral scenery and exquisite literature and versatile life and talent exhib-
climate. ited in their remaining monuments of science and art.
"If we inquire into the causes of this singular excellence," says
W. S. Tyler, "God laid the foundations for it when he laid the
foundations of the earth; when he based the whole country, not,
like England and America, upon coal and iron, but upon Pentelic,
Hymettian, and Parian marble; when he not only built the mountains round about Athens of the finest materials for sculpture
and architecture, but fashioned their towering fronts and gently
sloping summits into the perfect model of a Grecian temple, and
lifted from the midst of the plain the Acropolis and Mars' Hill—fit
pedestals for temples and statues, fit abodes for gods and god-like
men; when he reared to heaven Helicon, Parnassus, and the snow-
capped Olympus, where dwelt the muses and the gods, and poured
down their sides the rivers in which the river-gods had their dwellingplace, and from which the muses derived their origin; when he
diversified the whole country with mountain and valley, with plain
and promontory, with sea and land, with fountain, and river, and
bay, and strait, and island, and isthmus, and peninsula, as no other
country in the world, within the same compass, is diversified, and

thus gave to each district almost every variety of soil, climate, and natural scenery; when he drew the outline of the shores winding and waving, as if for the very purpose of realizing the ideal line of beauty, and spread around them the clear, liquid, laughing waters of the πολυφλοίσβοιο θαλάσσης,[1] and poured over sea and land the pure transparent air and bright sunshine which distinguish Greece in the dry season scarcely less than the rainless Egypt, and canopied the whole with that wonderfully deep and liquid sky, blue down to the very horizon, which is the never-ceasing admiration of foreigners who visit Athens."[2]

The Greeks were first so called by the Latins, who probably obtained their earliest acquaintance with them from one of their northern tribes called the Græci (Γραικοί). Thence the name passed into most of the languages of Europe. But the more proper name of the nation was *Hellenes* (Ἕλληνες), and the entire territory they occupied was called in general *Hellas*. The earliest settlements and history of the Hellenes are veiled in obscurity. The common tradition is, that they were descended from Hellen, the son of Deucalion and Pyrrha, who survived the flood. According to the genealogy of nations given in the tenth chapter of Genesis, we trace them back to Javan, the son of Japheth (Gen. x, 2). The name *Javan* (יָוָן) is the Hebrew equivalent of *Ion* (Ἴων), the traditional ancestor of the Ionians, with whom the Phœnicians and the Semitic peoples would naturally identify the entire Hellenic race.[3]

The ancient Hellenes early branched off into numerous tribes, known as the Dorians, Æolians, Achæans, and Ionians, and, according to that linguistic law which we have noticed above,[4] these scattered tribes soon became distinguished by differences of dialect. Not only may we now discover the principal dialects, viz., the Doric, Æolic, Ionic, and Attic,[5] and trace different periods in the development of these, such as old, middle, and new; but less noticeable differences may be also traced, as the more or less divergent speech of the Thessalonians, Bœotians, Laconians, and Sicilians. Passing by the confused legends of the

---

[1] "Many-sounding sea," Homer, Iliad, i, 34.

[2] Oration at Andover Theological Seminary on Athens, or Æsthetic Culture and the Art of Expression, published in Bibliotheca Sacra, Jan., 1863.

[3] See Smith, Dictionary of the Bible, article Javan.

[4] See page 72.

[5] See, on these several dialects, the second and improved edition of Kühner, Ausführliche Grammatik der griechischen Sprache, Einleitung, pp. 7–37. Hannover, 1869–70.

earliest migrations, and the history and peculiarities of the Doric and Æolic dialects, we may well believe that the Ionians having crossed the Ægean Sea from Athens, settled on the western coast of Asia Minor, and took the lead of all the Greek tribes in the development of literature and art. The most ancient monuments of their literature are the poems of Homer and Hesiod. But it would scarcely be proper to assume that the language of these poems was the common language of the people. As poets, they would be likely to appropriate many archaic and unusual forms. Hence the Greek language, as exhibited in these most ancient works, is called the Epic. A later form of Ionic speech is seen in the few fragments of lyric poetry attributed to Archilochus, Callinus, and Mimnermus. To a still later period belongs the well-known Ionic prose writer and historian, Herodotus. These writings represent, respectively, the old, the middle, and the new Ionic Greek. This dialect is believed to represent more nearly than others the ancient Hellenic language. Its early and important literature would naturally give it a permanency, but, after their first remarkable activity, the Ionians declined.

Ionic Greek.

Meanwhile Athens, the mother city of the Ionians, began to rise in power and fame, and gradually acquired supremacy among the Grecian cities. The Attic capital became the centre of intellectual activity. Thither repaired Hellenic youths from all the tribes to study models of elegance and taste, and the Attic dialect became, by degrees, the language of the educated classes throughout the states of Greece. But in the Attic, as in the Ionic, we may note three periods, the old, the middle, and the new. The old Attic differed but little from the Ionic, for the Ionians were originally inhabitants of Attica. In this dialect the distinguished Athenian lawgiver, Solon, wrote his laws and poems, several fragments of which are still extant. The middle Attic represents the language in the golden period of its elegance and glory. Its classic monuments are the historical works of Thucydides and Xenophon, the orations of Isocrates and Lysias, the philosophical dialogues of Plato, and the dramatic poetry of Æschylus, Sophocles, Euripides, and Aristophanes. The new Attic is usually dated from Demosthenes and Æschines, whose orations are regarded as models of eloquence. But after the Macedonian conquest (B.C. 338) the Attic dialect suffered a gradual decay. The language of the Macedonians, though genuine Greek, was probably never reduced to writing by the natives; but the ascendency of these ruder northerners, and their subversion of the independence of Athens, had the necessary tendency to

Attic culture.

Decay of Attic elegance.

corrupt the classic speech of Attica. A fusion of dialects ensued. Alexander the Great, trained by the philosopher Aristotle, who used the Attic, must have become early familiar with that dialect and its literature, and his mighty conquests spread this language over all Western Asia, and into Egypt. The breaking up and intermingling of rival states and communities, and the founding of Greek colonies in many parts of this vast territory, led to numerous departures from the classic forms of Attic speech. Nevertheless, the Attic dialect remained the basis and controlling factor of this later Greek. This widespread language of the Macedonian Empire, from its appropriation of words and forms from various sources, and from its general use, received the name of the common dialect (ἡ κοινὴ διάλεκτος). The successors of Alexander maintained and spread its use into all the principal towns and cities. On the reduction of Corinth to a Roman province (B. C. 146) this Greek language and literature extended westward, and every educated Roman became familiar with it. At the beginning of the Christian era, this common dialect was written, read, and spoken from Spain on the west to the borders of India on the east, and from Sarmatia on the north to Ethiopia in the south. "If any one imagines," says Cicero, "that a less amount of glory is to be derived from Greek than from Latin verses, he greatly errs, for Greek writings are read in almost all regions, while the Latin are confined within their own limits, which are narrow enough."[1] One of the fragments of Epictetus declares that "in Rome the women hold Plato's Republic in their hands."[2] "What do the Greek cities desire," asks Seneca, "in the midst of barbarian countries? What means the Macedonian speech among Indians and Persians?"[3] It is obvious, therefore, how the common language of the widespread Macedonian Empire would naturally gather something from almost every quarter. The later Greek had no longer a variety of dialects, in the older sense, but blended many of those ancient local peculiarities, and adopted not a few foreign idioms. Yet, in some places, old forms would maintain themselves more or less fully. Atticisms would prevail at Athens, and Doric forms in the districts where the old Doric had formerly prevailed.

The principal literary centres of this later Attic or common dialect were Athens, Antioch, and Alexandria. The last-named city, founded by Alexander himself, whose keen foresight perceived that a city occupying this site must certainly

The later Attic or common dialect.

Literary centres.

---

[1] Oratio pro A. Licinio Archia, sec. 23.   [2] Epict., Frag. 53.
[3] L. Annæus Seneca, De consolatione ad Helviam matrem, vii.

command the commerce between the East and the West, became, under Ptolemy Soter, renowned for literature and science. This enterprising ruler founded the famous Alexandrian Library, and collected for it the accessible literature of all nations. Thither he Alexandrian invited philosophers and learned men from all lands, culture. and the new city became rapidly filled with the representatives of all schools of philosophy and the devotees of all religions. Among all these the Greek was the common language of intercourse, and was sometimes called the Macedonian, but more commonly the Alexandrine, dialect.

Meantime the Jews had become largely scattered throughout the Macedonian Empire, and, dwelling in numerous cities where the Greek was generally spoken, they adopted it as their common language. But Alexandria especially contained Alexandrian large numbers of Jews.[1] The liberal policy of the first Jews. two Ptolemies (Soter and Philadelphus) invited them thither, and their commercial tastes and tact found there peculiar attractions. According to well-known tradition, the Septuagint version of the Old Testament was made by the direction of one of these kings. Internal evidence, however, shows that this version was made at different times and by different persons during the three centuries preceding the Christian era. As the Jewish exiles at Babylon lost by degrees the use of Hebrew, and adopted the tongue of the Chaldeans, so the Jews of the dispersion, living in Greek cities, adopted the Greek, and required to have their Scriptures translated into the same language. These Greek-speaking Jews Hellenists. were called Hellenists, and since the beginning of the seventeenth century it has been customary to call the later Greek dialect, as used by Jews, the Hellenistic Greek. On the common language of these Greek-speaking Israelites, or Hellenists, the use of the Septuagint version of the Old Testament would necessarily exert a moulding influence. The speech of all Hellenists, whether of Alexandria, or Tarsus, or Antioch, or Corinth, would acquire a certain peculiarity of style, a kind of ethnic tinge. The Greek translators of the Old Testament transferred many Hebrew idioms into their version, and found it necessary to employ Greek words to express ideas entirely new and foreign to the Greek mind. Hebraic forms of speech would thus become common among the Hellenists, and differentiate them from other Greek-speaking peoples.

[1] According to Philo (Treatise against Flaccus, sections vi and viii) they numbered a million of men in all Egypt, and constituted about two fifths of the entire population of Alexandria.

When Christianity introduced a new life and religion into the world, its sacred books were all written by Jews or Jewish proselytes, who used the later Hebraic or Hellenistic Greek. These writers found it necessary again to use this language for the setting forth of ideas and truths which had never before been clothed in any human language. *Christian ideas as influencing Greek speech.* New significations thus became attached to old words, and new forms of speech were coined to express the concepts of the Gospel. Accordingly, the New Testament language and diction have, necessarily, peculiarities of their own.

There is, happily, no occasion now to repeat or continue the old controversy between the Purists and the Hebraists touching the character of the New Testament Greek. The Purists, in claiming for it all the classic purity and elegance of the ancient Greek, seem to have been actuated by the *Controversy between the Purists and the Hebraists.* same principle as those who contended for the inspiration of the Hebrew vowel-points. To them it seemed also a disparagement of the holy books to say that they were written in a corrupted dialect, or one less pure and perfect than any Grecian models. On the other hand, some of the Hebraists went to the extreme of charging barbarisms and manifold inaccuracies upon the language of the New Testament writers. Comparative philology, and more thorough linguistic research, have rendered the old controversies obsolete, and it is now seen, in the light of history and of the science of language, how and why the Hellenistic Greek of the New Testament differs from the older classic tongue.[1]

[1] So early as the latter part of the sixteenth century, Beza (De dono Linguae, etc., on Acts x, 46) acknowledged the Hebraisms of the New Testament, but extolled them as being "of such a nature that in no other idiom could expressions be so happily formed; nay, in some cases not even formed at all" in an adequate manner. He considered them as "gems with which [the apostles] had adorned their writings." The famous Robert Stephens (Pref. to his N. Test., 1576) declared strongly against those, "qui in his scriptis [sacris] inculta omnia et horrida esse putant;" and he laboured not only to show that the New Testament contains many of the elegancies of the true Grecian style, but that even its Hebraisms give inimitable strength and energy to its diction. Thus far, then, Hebraism was not denied but vindicated; and it was only against allowing an excess of it, and against alleged incorrectnesses and barbarisms, that Beza and Stephens contended.

Sebastian Pfochen (Diatribe de Ling. Graec. N. Test. puritate, 1629) first laboured in earnest to show that all the expressions employed in the New Testament are found in good classic Greek authors. In 1658, Erasmus Schmidt vindicated the same ground. But before this, J. Junge, rector at Hamburg, published (in 1637, 1639) his opinion in favour of the *purity* (not the classic elegance) of the New Testament diction; which opinion was vindicated by Jac. Grosse, pastor in the same city, in a series of five essays published in 1640 and several successive years. The last four of these were directed against the attacks of opponents, i. e., of advocates for the Hellenistic diction

The sources from which we are to learn the peculiarities of the later Greek are the writers of the Alexandrine and Roman periods of Greek literature, but more especially the grammarians, scholiasts, and lexicographers, who have expressly treated of the differences between Attic elegance and the corruptions of the later Greek. But the great monuments of the Hellenistic Greek are the Septuagint version of the Old Testament, the apocryphal books, and the scriptures of the New Testament. The writings of Philo Judæus, Josephus, the Apostolical Fathers, and sundry writers of the later Roman period, have also a value in this connexion; but the New Testament itself must furnish the principal illustrations for the purpose of the biblical interpreter. It is of the first importance for us to remember that the New Testament writers learned their Greek not from books, but from the language of common life. There is no sufficient reason for believing that any of the Evangelists or Apostles were extensively familiar with Greek literature; not even Paul, who, indeed, quotes from Greek writers (Acts xvii, 28; Titus i, 12),

Sources of information and study.

of the New Testament; viz., against Dan. Wulfer's Innocentia Hellenist. vindicata (1640), and an essay of the like nature by J. Musæus of Jena (1641, 1642).

Independently of this particular contest, D. Heinsius (in 1643) declared himself in favour of Hellenism; as also Thos. Gataker (1648), who avowedly wrote in opposition to Pfochen, with much learning, but rather an excessive leaning to Hebraism. Joh. Vorstius (1658, 1665) wrote a book on Hebraisms, which is still common. On some excesses in this book Horace Vitringa made some brief but pithy remarks. Somewhat earlier than these last writings, J. E. Boecler (1641) published remarks, in which he took a kind of middle way between the two parties; as did J. Olearius (1668), and J. Leusden about the same time. It was about this time, also, that the majority of critical writers began to acknowledge a Hebrew element in the New Testament diction, which, however, they did not regard as constituting *barbarism*, but only as giving an oriental hue to the diction. M. Solanus, in an able essay directed against the tract of Pfochen, vindicated this position. J. H. Michaelis (1707), and A. Blackwall (Sacred Classics, 1727), did not venture to deny the Hebraisms of the New Testament, but aimed principally to show that these did not detract from the qualities of a good and elegant style; so that, in this respect, the New Testament writers were not inferior to the classical ones. The work of the latter abounds with so many excellent remarks, that it is worthy of attention from every critical reader, even of the present time.

In 1722, Siegm. Georgi, in his Vindiciae, etc., and in 1733 in his Hierocriticus Sacer, vindicated anew the old views of 'the Purists; but without changing the tide of opinion. The same design J. C. Schwartz had in view in his Comm. crit. et philol. in Ling. Graec. (1636); who was followed, in 1752, by E. Palairet (Observ. philol. crit. in N. Test.), the last, I believe, of all the Purists.

Most of the earlier dissertations above named, with some others, were published together in a volume by J. Rhenferd, entitled Dissertationum philol. theol. de Stylo N. Test. Syntagma, 1702; and the later ones by T. H. Van den Honert, in his Syntagma Dissertatt. de Stylo N. Test. Graeco, 1703. Stuart, Grammar of the New Testament Dialect, pp. 8, 9. Andover, 1841.

for such passages as he cites were of a kind that would naturally be current among the people.

Planck, in his valuable Dissertation on the true nature and character of the Greek Style of the New Testament,[1] classifies its chief peculiarities and characteristics under eight heads, which, in the main, we follow, though drawing our illustrations from many other sources. *Peculiarities and characteristics of Hellenistic Greek.*

1. Words adopted into the Greek language from foreign sources. Here belong the Aramaic words already noticed; such as *Abba, Ephphatha, Corban, Aceldama;* names of Roman coins; as *δηνάριον*, Latin *denarius;* *κοδράντης*, a *farthing*, from the Latin *quadrans;* *πραιτώριον*, Latin *prætorium* (John xviii, 28); *φελόνης*, written also *φαιλόνης, φελώνης*, and *φαιλώνης* (2 Tim. iv, 13,) corrupt form of *φαινόλης*, from the Latin *pœnula*, a *cloak.* *Foreign words.*

2. Words peculiar in their orthography·and pronunciation. The New Testament writers did not follow any common standard of orthography. Peter, John, Paul, and James *Peculiar orthography.* had each his peculiar method of spelling certain words, and probably transcribers of their manuscripts used still a different method, according to the custom of later times. In this respect the most ancient manuscripts exhibit variations. Alexandrian copies differ in orthography from those of Constantinople, and the writers or transcribers seem in many instances to have been governed by a preference for certain dialectic forms; as *ἀετός, eagle* (Matt. xxiv, 28), an Attic form for *αἰετός; ὕαλος, glass* (Rev. xxi, 18), instead of *ὕελος; ἵλεως, merciful* (Heb. viii, 12), instead of *ἵλαος.* Doric orthography is seen in *πιάζω*, to *arrest* (John vii, 30), instead of *πιέζω;* *κλίβανος, oven* (Luke xii, 28), instead of *κρίβανος;* Ionic, in *βαθμός, grade* or *degree* (1 Tim. iii, 13), for *βασμός; πρηνʹ͵͵, headlong* (Acts i, 18), for *πρανής.*

3. Peculiarities in the flexion of nouns and verbs. The form *Ἀπολλώ* is used for the accusative (Acts xix, 1), and the genitive (1 Cor. i, 12); the accusative *ὑγιῆ, sound, whole* (John v, 11, 15; Titus ii, 8), instead of the more *Flexion of nouns and verbs.* usual form *ὑγιᾶ; ἀφίενται*, or *ἀφέωνται, are forgiven* (Matt. ix, 2, 5; Luke v, 20; 1 John ii, 12), is used instead of *ἀφεῖνται; κάθου, sit thou* (Matt. xxii, 44; James ii, 3), instead of *κάθησο*, and *κάθῃ, thou sittest* (Acts xxiii, 3), instead of *κάθησαι.* We have also

---

[1] Commentatio de vera Natura atque Indole Orationis Graecæ Novi Testamenti, by Henry Planck, Prof. in the University of Göttingen. This very important essay was first published in 1810, and was afterward republished in Rosenmüller's Commentationes Theologicæ, 1825. It was translated into English by E. Robinson, and published in the American Biblical Repository, Andover, Oct., 1831.

the termination αν for ασι, as ἔγνωκαν for ἐγνώκασι, *they have known* (John xvii, 7), and the insertion of the syllable σα in the third person plural of some words, as ἐδολιοῦσαν for ἐδολιοῦν, *they deceived* (Rom. iii, 13).[1]

4. The heterogeneous use of nouns.   Thus σκότος, *darkness* is
Heterogeneous
nouns. used in the masculine and neuter genders; λιμός, *famine*, and βάτος, *bramble*, in masculine and feminine. We have the neuter plural in τὰ δεσμά, *the bands* (Luke viii, 29), and the masculine plural τοὺς δεσμούς (Phil. i, 13), and ἔλεος, *mercy*, which is used as masculine by all classic Greek writers, is used as neuter in the Septuagint and in the New Testament.   Compare Luke i, 50, 58; Rom. ix, 23; Jude 21, and (Septuagint) Gen. xix, 19; Num. xi, 15.

5. Peculiar forms of words, which passed down from ancient
New or peculiar
forms of words. dialects into the common language, or else were coined anew according to some previous analogy.   Of this class we have (1) among NOUNS: ἀλέκτωρ, a *cock*, a Doric or poetic form for ἀλεκτρυών, σκοτία, *darkness* (Matt. x, 27; John vi, 17), for σκότος; οἰκοδομή, *building* (1 Cor. iii, 9; xiv, 5; Eph. ii, 21), for οἰκοδόμημα; μετοικεσία, *exile* (Matt. i, 11), for μετοικία, or μετοίκησις; μαθήτρια, a *female disciple* (Acts ix, 36), for μαθητρίς; κατάλυμα, a *lodging place* (Luke ii, 7), for καταγώγιον; αἴτημα, a *request* (Phil. iv, 6), for αἴτησις; and many other nouns ending in μα, for which the more classic language used the endings η, εια, and σις.   (2) Among VERBS we find a tendency to prefer the ending οω, as ἀνακαινόω, to *renew* (2 Cor. iv, 16; Col. iii, 10), instead of ἀνακαινίζω; κραταιόω, to *become strong* (Luke i, 80; ii, 40; Eph. iii, 16), instead of κρατύνω; σαρόω, to *sweep* (Luke xv, 8), instead of σαίρω; δεκατόω to *tithe* (Heb. vii, 6, 9), instead of δεκατεύω.   Other Hellenistic forms are ὀρθρίζω, to *do* anything *early in the morning* (Luke xxi, 38), instead of ὀρθρεύω; ἀλήθω, to *grind* (Matt. xxiv, 41), instead of ἀλέω; νήθω, to *spin* (Matt. vi, 28), instead of νέω.   (3) Among ADJECTIVES we have ἀπείραστος, *not temptable* (James i, 13) for ἀπείρατος; καθημερινός, *daily* (Acts vi, 1), for καθημέριος ; ὀρθρινός, *early* (Luke xxiv, 22, and Text. Rec. of Rev. xxii, 16), for ὄρθριος ; and (4) among ADVERBS, ἐξάπινα, *suddenly* (Mark ix, 8), for ἐξαπίνης; πανοικί, *with all one's house* (Acts xvi, 34), for πανοικίᾳ, or πανοικησίᾳ.

6. Words either peculiar to the ancient dialects, or altogether
Old dialects
and new words. new.   Of the former class are ἔκτρωμα, an *abortion* (1 Cor. xv, 8), an Ionic word, for which the Attics used ἄμβλωμα, or ἐξάμβλωμα; and γογγύζω, to *murmur* (John vii, 32),

---

[1] See many other rare forms in Winer's Grammar, §§ 13, 14.

and γογγυσμός, *murmuring* (John vii, 12; Acts vi, 1), Ionic words for which the Attics employed τονθρύζω and τονθρυσμός. New words were coined to express things which were unknown to the ancient Greeks, and peculiar to the Jews or the New Testament writers; as ἀνθρωπάρεσκος, a *man-pleaser* (Eph. vi, 6; Col. iii, 22), ἀλλοτριοεπίσκοπος, an *overseer of other people's matters* (1 Peter iv, 15), ἀρχισυνάγωγος, *ruler of the synagogue* (Mark v, 35), εἰδωλολατρεία, *idol-worship* (1 Cor. x, 14; Gal. v, 20), δωδεκάφυλον, the *people of the twelve tribes* (Acts xxvi, 7). Compare also the lexicons on δυναμόω, and ἐνδυναμόω, to *strengthen*, and βεβηλόω, to *profane*.

7. A notable feature of the New Testament dialect consists in the new significations given to words. To trace such New significa- changes and modifications of meaning, and unfold the tions given to development of biblical ideas, is the most difficult and words. delicate task of the New Testament lexicographer. He must do more than treat the varying forms of words; he must expound the history of thought, and thus become, in the fullest sense, an exegete.[1]

An instance of a word acquiring a new signification may be seen in εὐαγγέλιον, used in the ancient classic authors in the sense of *reward for good news* given to the messenger; in Isocrates and Xenophon it is used of *sacrifice for a good message ;* and still later it came to signify *the good message itself.* Thence it acquired in the New Testament the special sense of *the good news of salvation* in Jesus Christ. So, too, the word παρακαλέω was used in the ancient Greek as meaning *to call to,* to call unto an assembly, or to invite to an entertainment. But in the New Testament we find it used for *begging, comforting,* and *exhorting.* The word εἰρήνη, *peace, quiet,* as contrasted with war and commotion, easily came to be used of *peace of mind,* tranquillity. Then, in the Septuagint and New Testament it took up and embodied the idea of *well-being, welfare,* as represented in the Hebrew שָׁלוֹם, and in connection with χάρις and ἔλεος, *grace* and *mercy,* as in the salutation of the apostolical epistles, denotes the blessed state of soul-rest obtained by remission of sin through Jesus Christ. So *peace with God,* in Rom. v, 1, is the new and happy relationship between God and man obtained through faith in the atonement of Christ.[2]

[1] No modern writer has done a greater service in this department than Dr. Hermann Cremer, whose Biblico-Theological Lexicon of New Testament Greek is a rare monument of learning and critical research, and indispensable to the hermeneutics of the Christian Scriptures. For extensive illustration of New Testament words in their depth and fulness of meaning, see this Lexicon on the words βαπτίζω, ὄνομα, οὐρανός, πίστις, ἅγιος, μετανοέω, κόσμος, ταπεινός, ἀγαπάω, and ἀγάπη.

[2] A like development or modification of meaning may be traced in the words ἀποκρίνω, ἀναπίπτω, ἀνάκειμαι, εὐχαριστέω, πτῶμα, etc.

"It would have been impossible," observes Bleek,[1] "to give expression to all the religious conceptions and Christian ideas of the New Testament, had the writers strictly confined themselves to the words and phrases in use among the Greeks, and with the significations usually attached to them. These Christian ideas were quite unknown to the Greeks, and they had never formed phrases suitable to give expression to them. On the other hand, most of these ideas and conceptions already existed in germ in the Old Testament, and were more or less familiar to the Jews by means of appropriate designations. Hence they would be best expressed for Greek-speaking Jews in the words by which they had been rendered in the Septuagint. These expressions would naturally be chosen and spread by those teachers who were of Jewish extraction and education, and would, of course, be adopted generally to denote Christian ideas. Many of these expressions had been ordinary Greek words, whose meanings had been made fuller and higher when applied among the Jews to religious subjects, and which retained these meanings when adopted by the Christian Church, or were again modified and further elevated, just as the ideas and conceptions of the Old Testament revelation were modified and elevated by Christianity. Hence it frequently came to pass, that when a Greek word in its ordinary signification corresponded with a Hebrew or Aramean word, the derived and developed meanings attaching to the latter would be transferred to the former, and the Greek word would be used in the higher sense of the Hebrew or Aramean word, although this meaning had before been unknown to Greek usage."[2]

8. It remains for us to notice more especially the Hebraisms of the New Testament language, that transfer of Hebrew idioms and forms of expression into Greek, which Attic purity and taste would at once pronounce corruptions or barbarisms. Winer has shown that most of the older writers on this subject have included in their list of Hebraisms many expressions which are not unknown to the Greek prose writers, or are the common property of many languages. He distinguishes two kinds of Hebraisms in the New Testament, the *perfect* and the *imperfect*. Perfect Hebraisms include those words, phrases, and constructions which are strictly peculiar to the Hebrew or Aramean, and were transferred directly thence into the Hellenistic idiom. Imperfect Hebraisms are all those words, phrases, and constructions, which, though found in

Hebraisms.

[1] Introduction to the New Testament. Eng. translation, by Urwick; pp. 72, 73.

[2] See abundant illustration of this in such words as Χριστός, *Christ*; πνεῦμα, *spirit*; λόγος, *word*; σωτηρία, *salvation*; ἀπώλεια, *destruction*; κλητός, *called*; ἐκκλησία, *church*; δικαιοσύνη, *righteousness*.

Greek prose writers, have been in all probability introduced directly from the Hebrew.[1]

(a) Not only were Hebrew or Aramaic words literally adopted into the New Testament Greek (like 'Αββᾶ, Ar. אַבָּא, Words. *Father*, Mark xiv, 36, Rom. viii, 15; ὡσαννά, Heb. הוֹשִׁיעָה־נָּא, *Hosanna, save now*, John xii, 13; Σατᾶν, Heb. שָׂטָן, *Satan*, 2 Cor. xii, 7; σίκερα, Heb. שֵׁכָר, *strong drink*, Luke i, 15), but Greek words were made to represent distinctively Hebrew conceptions; as ῥῆμα, *word*, in the broad and indefinite sense of the Heb. דָּבָר, *thing, matter, affair*. So in Luke ii, 15: τὸ ῥῆμα τοῦτο τὸ γεγονός, *this thing that has come to pass*. The Greek word σπλάγχνα, *bowels*, takes, in the New Testament, the sense of *tender affection, sympathy;* from the common usage of the Heb. רַחֲמִים. Hence the verbal form σπλαγχνίζομαι, *to have compassion.*

(b) Then there are numerous forms of expression which are traceable directly to the Hebrew; as ζητεῖν τὴν ψυχήν, Forms of ex-
pression. Heb. בִּקֵּשׁ אֶת־נֶפֶשׁ, *to seek the life* of any one (Matt. ii, 20; Rom. xi, 3); λαμβάνειν πρόσωπον, Heb. נָשָׂא פָנִים, *to accept the person*, that is, *to lift his face*, or show partiality (Luke xx, 21; Gal. ii, 6); τίθεσθαι ἐν τῇ καρδίᾳ, Heb. שׂוּם בְּלֵב, *to place* or *lay up in the heart* (Luke i, 66; xxi, 14; Acts v, 4); στόμα μαχαίρας, Heb. פִּי־חֶרֶב, *mouth of the sword* (Luke xxi, 24; Heb. xi, 34); καὶ ἐγένετο very frequently for וַיְהִי, *and it came to pass.*

(c) The New Testament Greek has also appropriated sundry grammatical constructions peculiar to the Hebrew. (1) Many Grammatical
constructions. verbs are followed by prepositions governing the accusative or dative, where, in classic Greek, the verbs alone govern without a preposition. Compare the New Testament use of the words προσκυνέω, *to worship;* φεύγω, *to flee;* ὁμολογέω, *to confess.* (2) The particle εἰ is used in expressing a negative oath after the form of the Hebrew אִם, *if*. "I swore in my wrath if they shall enter into my rest" (Heb. iii, 11). That is, they shall not enter. Compare Mark viii, 12. (3) The verb προστίθημι is used, like the Hebrew יָסַף, with another verb, to denote additional action: "He *added to send another servant*" (Luke xx, 11). "He added (i. e., proceeded) to take Peter also" (Acts xii, 3). (4) An imitation of the Hebrew infinitive absolute is apparent in Luke xxii, 15: ἐπιθυμίᾳ ἐπεθύμησα, "with desire I desired to eat this passover." That is, I longingly, or earnestly, desired. John iii, 29: χαρᾷ χαίρει, "with joy he rejoices;" he greatly rejoices. Acts iv, 17: ἀπειλῇ ἀπειλησώμεθα, "with threatening let us threaten them." (5) In Rev. vii, 2 we note the pleonastic use of the pronoun in imitation of a well-

---

[1] See Winer, Grammar of the Idiom of the New Testament, § 3.

known use of the Heb. אֲשֶׁר: οἷς ἐδόθη αὐτοῖς, "*to whom* it was given *to them.* Compare also the adverbial relative in Rev. xii, 14: ὅπου τρέφεται ἐκεῖ, "*where* she is nourished *there,*"=Heb. אֲשֶׁר ... שָׁם. (6) The Hebrew use of nouns in the genitive as substitutes for the kindred adjective is very common: as, λόγοι τῆς χάριτος, *words of grace,* for *gracious words* (Luke iv, 22); σκεῦος ἐκλογῆς, *vessel of choice,* for *chosen vessel* (Acts ix, 15); "the power of his might," for his mighty power (Eph. i, 19); *steward of unrighteousness* and *Mammon of unrighteousness* (Luke xvi, 8, 9), for *unrighteous steward* and *unrighteous Mammon;* and *judge of unrighteousness* (Luke xviii, 6), for *unrighteous judge.* Sometimes these genitive forms yield a profound significance, as in Eph. i, 18: "The riches of the glory of his inheritance in the saints," where it would take much from the force of the expression to say, "His rich and glorious inheritance," or "His gloriously rich inheritance."

The New Testament Greek has also some peculiarities of syntax, of which, however, it is unnecessary here to treat. The Hellenistic writers naturally preferred short sentences, after the manner of the Hebrew. But every student will observe the differences of style among the New Testament writers. The Pauline epistles exhibit a more involved and polemic style than any other portions of the Christian Scriptures. But these differ noticeably among themselves. The Thessalonian epistles have a natural and easy flow, but the prophetic portions, especially 2 Thess. ii, have peculiarities of their own. In the Epistles to the Romans and Galatians we notice the marked argumentative style as contrasted with the more familiar tone and didactic straightforwardness of the pastoral epistles. The Corinthian epistles have an air of freedom and authority which is not so apparent in Ephesians, Philippians, and Colossians, the epistles of Paul's imprisonment. The Epistle to the Hebrews is written in a purer Greek, and has a beauty and flow of style quite in advance of the epistles acknowledged to be Pauline. The Epistle of James is noted for the exceptional purity and elegance of its language, and Luke, "the beloved physician," who was probably not a Jew by birth (Col. iv, 11, comp. verse 14), writes a more classic Greek than any other of the evangelists. The Gospel and Epistles of John have numerous peculiarities of diction; simple and childlike forms of expressing most elevated and profound spiritual conceptions; but the Apocalypse is the most Hebraistic in thought and language of all the New Testament books.[1]

Varieties of style in New Testament writers.

[1] On the linguistic peculiarities of the different New Testament writers, comp. Immer, Hermeneutics of the New Testament, pp. 132–144.

It will not be difficult for any one to perceive that Hellenistic writers, familiar with the prophetic language of the Old Testament, would be likely to transfer its bold and vivid imagery into their Greek, especially when they themselves were writing prophecy. When Isaiah portrays the coming doom of Babylon, he sees all nature in convulsion. "Behold, the day of Jehovah comes, cruel, and wrath, and burning of anger. . . . For the stars of the heavens and their constellations shall not shed forth their light; dark has the sun become in his going forth, and the moon will not cause her light to shine" (Isa. xiii, 9, 10). Compare also chap. xxiv, 19-23; xxxiv, 1-10; Nahum i, 3-6. The celebrated passage in Rom. viii, 19-23 is truly Hebraic in the vividness of its metaphorical conceptions. The whole creation is represented as groaning, hoping, willing, and looking eagerly for the revelation (ἀποκάλυψιν) of the sons of God. We need not wonder, therefore, that in such prophetic passages as the twenty-fourth of Matthew, and the Apocalypse of John, we have the spirit and imagery of the Old Testament predictions reproduced, and the language of the Greeks employed in forms and symbols such as it had never previously used. The Hebrew spirit of prophecy was thus inbreathed into Grecian speech.

If there may be seen any divine purpose, or any special significance, in the use of the Hebrew and Chaldee tongues to embody the Old Testament revelation, there was also a reason for clothing the Christian revelation in the language of the Greeks. The Law and the Prophets were *Greek the most suitable language for the Christian Scriptures.* designed especially for the sons of Abraham, a chosen and peculiar people; but the New Testament revelation was for the world. The miracle of tongues on the day of Pentecost was prophetic, indicating that the new WORD, then first speaking publicly to the world, would make itself heard in all the living languages of men. Parthians and Medes and Elamites, and those that inhabited Mesopotamia, Judea, and Cappadocia, Pontus and Asia, Phrygia and Pamphylia, Egypt and the parts of Libya about Cyrene, and strangers of Rome, both Jews and proselytes, Cretes and Arabians (Acts ii, 9-11) heard with amazement that first preaching of the Gospel, for they heard them speaking "every one in his own dialect" (εἰς ἕκαστος τῇ ἰδίᾳ διαλέκτῳ, ver. 6.) These were all devout Hellenists, then sojourning in Jerusalem (ver. 5); and in all the provinces of the empire from which they came Greek was the common dialect. Besides their own vernacular, these Hellenists understood and spoke the language of the Greeks. What more fitting, then, than that the new Gospel should embody its written records in this most nearly perfect and universal language of that age?

"The Jews require signs" (σημεῖα), observes the most erudite
writer of the New Testament, "but the Greeks seek for wisdom"
(σοφίαν, 1 Cor. i, 22). As if to meet these proclivities, the Old
Testament has been set forth in a hieroglyphic language of the
early world, in which every letter is a sign or picture of something
visible; while the New Testament is written in the historic language of æsthetic culture and philosophy. The tongue of the
versatile Hellenes was peculiarly suited to express and preserve for
all nations the Gospel of the power and wisdom of God. (1 Cor.
i, 24), which was destined to overthrow Judaism, and confound the
boasted wisdom of the world.

We may well believe, then, that the use of Hebrew, Chaldee,
and Greek, as the original languages of the Scriptures, was no mere
accident of history, but a particular providence, grounded in
highest wisdom. The fact that they have all ceased to be living
languages since the inspired records they embody came to be
recognized as a sacred trust, is truly significant. The means
of ascertaining and illustrating the sense of these records are
ample; and the divine oracles thus abide, sanctified and set apart
in well-known forms of speech which can never again be disturbed
by linguistic changes or the revolutions of empire. The Hebrew,
like the temple at Jerusalem, will be studied as a wonder of the
world. The temple's great and costly stones, its unique architecture, and divine plan and purpose—in all essentials a copy of the
pattern shown to Moses in the mount of God (Exod. xxv, 40)—
held notable analogy with the unique and expressive forms of Hebrew speech, in which words stand forth as sacred symbols, and
grammatical constructions are made to suggest profoundest conceptions of the holiness of God and the redemption of mankind. The
Chaldee chapters of Daniel and Ezra are like the monumental
slabs from the ruined palaces of Babylonian and Persian kings—
imperishable witnesses that God once spoke to those mighty nations, and, when they were in highest power and pomp, and Israel
in exile and humiliation, foretold their utter ruin, and the certain
triumph of truth and righteousness in the kingdom of the God of
heaven. The Greek language, like the famous Parthenon at
Athens, breathes a marvellous expressiveness, and abounds in models of beauty. But in its Hellenistic style and New Testament
form we admire the divine wisdom, the deep philosophy, and the
practical judgment, which appropriated the common dialect of a
world-wide civilization, and consecrated its potent formulas of
thought to preserve and perpetuate the Gospel.

CHAPTER VII.

TEXTUAL CRITICISM.

BIBLICAL CRITICISM is a term which has often been applied to the critical treatment of nearly all topics that come under the head of Biblical Introduction, such as questions of the date and authorship of the sacred books, and also of interpretation itself. This use of the term is more definitely known as the Higher Criticism. The other and more proper sense is that which restricts it to the critical labours which aim to restore the original texts of the Bible. This usage of the word is often called the Lower Criticism. It treats the forms and order in which the books of the Bible have been arranged, the history, condition, and relative value of the ancient manuscript copies, and the different printed editions of the original texts. It collates and compares ancient manuscripts, versions, and quotations, and lays down rules and principles by which to detect corruptions and determine the genuine reading.

Higher and lower criticism.

It frequently occurs that the interpretation of a passage of Scripture is so far involved in a question of textual criticism that the critical treatment of the text is essential to the exposition. Especially is this true in the case of texts so doubtful that the ablest critics differ in judgment as to the genuine reading. An exegete who proceeds with the explanation of such a doubtful passage, utterly ignoring or indifferent to the uncertainty of the text itself, exhibits himself as an untrustworthy guide. The competent interpreter of Scripture is supposed to be thoroughly versed in the history and principles of textual criticism, and it is proper that in this Introduction to Biblical Hermeneutics we devote a brief chapter to this subject. Our space and the purpose of this volume will allow us only to present the leading principles and canons.[1]

The interpreter needs also to be a competent textual critic.

[1] On the subject of Textual Criticism see Davidson, Biblical Criticism (2 vols., Edinburgh, 1852), and Revision of the Hebrew Text of the Old Testament (London, 1855); Strack, Prolegomena Critica in Vet. Testamentum Hebraicum (Lps., 1873); F. H. Scrivener, Plain Introduction to the Criticism of the New Testament (Second Ed., Cambridge, 1874); Horne, Introduction to the Holy Scriptures, vol. ii, pp. 1–112 (Ayre & Tregelles' Ed., 4 vols., Lond., 1862); Tregelles, Account of the Printed Text of the

In all ancient writings which have come down to us in a great Causes of various readings. number and variety of manuscripts, we find a multitude of various readings. These have arisen mainly through the carelessness of transcribers: but, in some instances, perhaps, through design. Copyists accidentally confounded similar words, and sometimes transposed, repeated, or omitted letters and words. Some of the ancient manuscripts contained marginal notes, and in' copying from these the glosses were incorporated in the text. Sometimes the text was purposely amended by a scribe, who thought he could improve it. A difficult or obscure word was exchanged for an easy one. A rough passage was made smooth, and sometimes a difficult clause or sentence was entirely omitted. Sometimes dogmatic and party purposes led to the wilful corruption of the text. Thus originated the famous interpolation of the three witnesses in 1 John v, 7. Sometimes the manuscripts used in translation were themselves imperfect, and so errors would be likely to multiply in proportion to the number of manuscripts.

The sources from which the genuine readings are to be determined Sources and means of Textual Criticism. are mainly ancient manuscripts, ancient versions, and scriptural quotations found in the works of ancient writers. Parallel passages and critical conjecture may also be resorted to where other helps are doubtful. The received text of the Old Testament is commonly called the Masoretic, from the system of vowel points and the critical notes appended to it by the so-called Masoretes, or Jewish critics. After the destruction of Jerusalem by the Romans, and the consequent dispersion of the Jews, many learned rabbins continued the cultivation of their national literature. A celebrated school was founded by them at Tiberias, on the coast of the Sea of Galilee, and continued until the sixth century. The learned critics of this school compiled a collection of the critical and grammatical observations of the great teachers, and called it the Masorah. A most important part of their work was the preparation of the Keris (קְרִי, *to be read*, as distinguished from the כְּתִיב, *that which is written;* i. e., the written text), or marginal readings, which these critics probably gathered from manuscripts or tradition, and preferred to the reading of the received text of their day. So scrupulously careful were the Masoretes of every word and letter of the sacred text, that they attempted no changes in it, but wrote in the margin that which in their judgment should be read. All the ancient copies used by these

Greek New Testament (Lond., 1854). See also the introductions to the critical editions of the Greek Testament by Lachmann, Tischendorf, Tregelles, Alford, and Westcott and Hort.

critics seem to have perished, and the later manuscripts, hundreds of which have been collated by Kennicott and De Rossi, have little value for the emendation of the Old Testament text. Hence little has been attempted in this line within the last hundred years. The ancient versions and critical conjecture are the principal means of revising the Hebrew text, and such means are always to be used with the greatest caution.[1]

For the criticism of the New Testament text we have more abundant materials. There are, first, the uncial manuscripts, written in Greek capitals, and without any separation of words. This was the most ancient form of writing, and prevailed until the tenth century. Next we have the cursive manuscripts, existing in the form of writing which came into use in the latter part of the ninth century, and soon afterward became the common style. The three most ancient and valuable uncials are the so-called Sinaitic, the Alexandrian, and the Vatican, usually designated, respectively, א, A, and B. Several of the cursive manuscripts are of great value, having evidently been copied from very ancient exemplars. Next to these ancient manuscripts are the early versions of the New Testament, especially the Latin and the Syriac, the oldest of which belong, probably, to the second century. The quotations from the New Testament, found in the writings of the early Church Fathers, are also often of great value in determining the original text. These different sources of evidence have to be classified, their relative value critically estimated, and reliable rules and principles agreed upon for their use. In order to appreciate properly that vast amount of labour which has in recent years restored to us an approximately pure and trustworthy text of the Greek Testament, one needs to make himself familiar with the lives and works of the great critics Mill, Bentley, Bengel, Wetstein, Griesbach, Lachmann, Tischendorf, and Tregelles.

The principal Canons of Textual Criticism now generally accepted are divisible into two classes, external and internal, and may be stated as follows:

EXTERNAL.

The canons of external evidence are concerned with the character, age, and value of manuscripts, and the principles and rules by which we are to compare and estimate the relative weight of earlier and later copies, and of versions and quotations.

---

[1] A critical edition of the Masoretic text of the several books of the Old Testament is now in course of publication at Leipsic, under the editorial care of S. Baer and Fr. Delitzsch. It furnishes much valuable material for the critical study of the Hebrew text.

1. A reading which is supported by the combined testimony of the most ancient manuscripts, the earliest versions, and patristic quotations, is generally, without doubt, the genuine reading of the original autograph.

This rule is so self-evident that it needs no comment; and it is an interesting and important fact that so great a part of the New Testament rests upon evidence so decisive. Though the whole number of various readings is more than a hundred thousand, by far the greater part of them consist merely of differences of spelling, and other slight variations chiefly due to the peculiar habits of the different scribes. The doubtful readings which essentially affect the sense are comparatively few, and those which involve questions of important doctrine are less than a score.[1]

2. The authority and value of manuscript readings consist not in the number of manuscripts in which a given reading is found, but in the age, character, and country of the manuscripts.

Though, in some instances, we may suppose a cursive manuscript has been copied directly from an uncial more ancient than any that now exist, yet, as a rule, the uncials are older and more authoritative than the cursives. They are, therefore, more likely to represent the oldest readings. Respecting the age and value of ancient manuscripts, we owe great deference to the judgment of experienced critics. The opinion of men who, like Tischendorf and Tregelles, have devoted a lifetime to conscientious study and collation of manuscripts, deservedly carries great weight. The eye must be practiced to note the ancient forms of letters, and the various methods of writing, abbreviation, and correction.

3. When the external evidence is conflicting and of nearly equal weight, special importance should be attached to the correspondency between widely separated witnesses.

The concurrence of two ancient manuscripts, one belonging to the East and the other to the West, would have more weight than the agreement of many manuscripts which contain evidence of

---

[1] The proportion of words virtually accepted on all hands as raised above doubt is very great—not less, on a rough computation, than seven eighths of the whole. The remaining eighth, therefore, formed in great part by changes of order and other comparative trivialities, constitutes the whole area of criticism. . . . We find that, setting aside differences of orthography, the words in our opinion still subject to doubt only make up about one sixtieth of the whole New Testament. In this second estimate the proportion of comparatively trivial variations is beyond measure larger than the former; so that the amount of what can in any sense be called substantial variation is but a small fraction of the whole residuary variation, and can hardly form more than a thousandth part of the entire text. Westcott and Hort, The New Testament in the original Greek. Introduction, p. 2. New York, 1882.

having been copied directly from one another. The concurrence of the Peshito, the Vulgate, and the Ethiopic versions is of great weight in determining a doubtful reading. A quotation appearing in the same form in the writings of Origen, Jerome, and Irenæus would thereby acquire an authority tantamount to that of so many of the most ancient and valuable manuscripts.

4. Great discrimination is necessary in the use of the different classes of external evidence.

The reading found in one of the most ancient manuscripts is usually to be preferred to that of any one of the ancient versions. But there may be considerations of time or place which would render the reading of a version more weighty than that of a single manuscript. The authority of versions, also, would be greater in the case of omissions or additions than in the matter of verbal niceties. Patristic testimony, as observed above, depends for much of its value on the place and circumstances of the writer. The manner and purpose of a quotation may also affect its worth as a witness to an ancient reading.

INTERNAL.

It may often happen that the external evidence is so conflicting, and yet so evenly balanced, that it is impossible from that source alone to form any judgment. In such cases we resort to internal or subjective considerations, which, in many instances, afford the means of forming a reasonable and reliable conclusion. But this kind of evidence and critical conjecture are generally to be used with the greatest caution, and only when the critic is obliged to resort to such means from want of better evidence.

1. That reading which accords with a writer's peculiar style, with the context and the nature of the subject, and which makes a good sense, is to be preferred to one which lacks these internal supports.

This, as a general rule, must commend itself to every one's judgment. But particular applications of it may vary. There can be no reasonable doubt that the true reading in John xiii, 24, is τίς ἐστιν, *who is it?* The reading τίς ἂν εἴη, *who might it be?* though sustained by several ancient authorities, is especially to be rejected because John never uses the optative mood. The placing of ἐξελθόντες after αὐτοῦ in the *textus receptus* of Matt. xii, 14, is most probably an error of some ancient copyist, and the reading ἐξελθόντες δὲ οἱ Φαρισαῖοι συμβούλιον ἔλαβον κατ' αὐτοῦ (supported by א, B, C, and D, and adopted by Lachmann, Tischendorf, Westcott and Hort), is to be preferred because in similar constructions

Matthew uniformly places the participle before its noun. Compare i, 24; ii, 3; iv, 12; viii, 10, 14, 18; ix, 4, 8, 9, 11, 19; xii, 25. 2. The shorter reading is to be preferred to the longer.

Transcribers were much more prone to add than to omit, and in the obscurer passages their tendency was to incorporate marginal glosses into the text, or even to venture upon an explanation of their own. The words μὴ κατὰ σάρκα περιπατοῦσιν, ἀλλὰ κατὰ πνεῦμα, *who walk not according to flesh, but according to Spirit*, in the *textus receptus* of Rom. viii, 1, are wanting in most of the ancient authorities, and are doubtless an ancient gloss introduced from verse 4 of the same chapter, where they appear in their true connection. So, too, the words, "Verily I say unto you, it shall be more tolerable for Sodom and Gomorrah in the day of judgment than for that city," found in the Alexandrian Codex at Mark vi, 11, was probably added by some ancient scribe from memory of Matt. x, 15, where the reading is "land of Sodom and Gomorrah." According to this rule, when the evidences in favour of the insertion or omission of a word, clause, or sentence are about equally divided, it is safer to omit than to insert.

3. The more difficult and obscure reading is to be preferred to the plainer and easier one.

This rule of course applies especially to those passages where there is reason to believe the transcriber was tempted to soften or simplify the language, or explain an apparent difficulty. The word ἐλεημοσύνη, *alms*, was anciently substituted for the harsher Hebraistic word δικαιοσύνη, *righteousness*, in Matt. vi, 1. The insertion of the word εἰκῇ, *without cause*, in Matt. v, 22, seems, in view of the strong external evidence against it, to have been introduced to soften the sentiment. Alford puts it in brackets, and says: "I have not ventured wholly to exclude it, the authorities being so divided, and internal evidence being equally indecisive. Griesbach and Meyer hold it to have been expunged from motives of moral rigourism; De Wette, to have been inserted to soften the apparent rigour of the precept. The latter seems to me the more probable." Lachmann, Tischendorf, Westcott and Hort omit the word, and Tregelles marks it as extremely doubtful.

Under this head we would also place the well-known rule of Griesbach: "That reading is to be preferred which presents a sentiment apparently false, but which upon more careful examination is found to be true."[1] A notable example is seen in 1 Cor. xi, 29,

---

[1] Præferatur aliis lectis, cui sensus subest apparenter quidem falsus, qui vero re penitius examinata verus esse deprehenditur. Griesbach, Novum Testamentum Græce (2 vols., London, 1809), vol. i, Prolegomena, p. lxvi.

where the majority of ancient authorities have inserted the word
ἀναξίως, *unworthily*, which appears in verse 27 in all copies. Four
of the most important uncial manuscripts, however (A, B, C¦ ℵ¹), and
several cursives and versions omit the word. Its insertion from
verse 27 appears to have arisen from misapprehending the exact
force of μή in the clause μὴ διακρίνων τὸ σῶμα, which is here equivalent to *when not*, or *if not*, and therefore different from the stronger and more simple negative οὐ. The apparently unqualified statement: "He that eats and drinks, eats and drinks judgment unto
himself," seemed to convey a false statement, and to remove the
difficulty ἀναξίως was inserted. The whole passage becomes clear
by a correct rendering of the qualifying clause, *if not discerning
the body*. More difficult is it to decide between the two readings
πρῶτος and ὕστερος, in Matt. xxi, 31 ; πρῶτος is sustained by the
greatest number of ancient authorities, and is suited to the context.
But ὕστερος is found in two of the most important manuscripts
(B and D), and is the more difficult reading. It is easier to see
how πρῶτος may have become substituted for ὕστερος than the reverse. Hence Lachmann, Tregelles, Westcott and Hort adopt the
reading ὕστερος; but Tischendorf and Alford read πρῶτος. From
this last example it will be seen what great caution is necessary in
the application of this rule, and also how a final decision may not
be possible in the case.[1]

Under this canon it may also be added that, in parallel passages,
verbal differences are generally considered preferable to exact verbal conformity, inasmuch as transcribers are apt to harmonize such
differences where they attract attention.

4. That reading is to be preferred from which all the others
may be seen to have been naturally or readily derived.

"That is to say," says Gardiner, "when there are different readings which have each of them important evidence in its favour, the
one from which the others could have been easily derived is more
likely to be true than one from which they could not have been."[2]
Under this rule it is claimed that ὅς is the genuine reading in the

---

[1] "When no certainty is attainable," says Tregelles, "it will be well for the case to
be left as doubtful. . . . A critical text of the Greek New Testament, with no indications of doubt, or of the inequality of the evidence, is never satisfactory to a scholar.
It gives no impression of the ability of the editor to discriminate accurately as to the
value of evidence; and it seems to place on a level, as to authority, readings which
are unquestionably certain, and those which have been accepted as *perhaps* the best
attested."—Horne, Introduction (Ed. Ayre and Tregelles), vol. iv, p. 344.

[2] The Principles of Textual Criticism, with a List of all the Known Greek Uncials,
in Bibliotheca Sacra for April, 1875. Also published as an Appendix to the Greek
Harmony of the Four Gospels by the same author.

much-disputed text of 1 Tim. iii, 16. For a long time the Alexandrian and Ephraem Syrus manuscripts (A and C) were said to give the reading ϑεός (written in uncials ΘC), but recent and thorough examination by the most competent critics has discovered that the transverse line in the Θ, and the sign of contraction, are the work of a later hand. The Codex Sinaiticus has been tampered with in this place by several later hands; the latest of all, according to Tischendorf, altered the manuscript about the twelfth century, but so carefully as not to deface the more ancient reading. The Clermont manuscript (D), as is now conceded, originally read ὅ, but a later hand changed the reading to ΘC. This change was done by erasing enough of the O to leave C, and then, as this letter stood at the beginning of the line, Θ was easily placed before it. The reading ὅ may have arisen in the attempt of an ancient scribe to correct what seemed to be a grammatical inaccuracy, and write the relative ὅ to conform with the gender of μυστήριον. Or, a Latin scribe may have so corrected the reading as to make it conform to *quod*, which appears as the reading of the old Latin version. If we suppose the original reading to have been ΘC, it is difficult to explain how the readings OC and O should appear in the most ancient manuscripts; but, as shown above, it is not difficult to show how the word OC may have been changed into ΘC or O.

He who carefully studies and applies the above rules of textual criticism will observe that they are principles rather than rules. They must not be applied mechanically, as if mere majorities of witnesses decided any thing. A great number and variety of considerations must enter into the formation of a sound critical judgment, and every element of evidence must be carefully weighed. "The point aimed at," says Tregelles, "is a moral certainty, or a moral probability. To arrive at this we must use the evidence that is attainable; the truest principles must be borne in mind which teach the proper estimation of such evidence; and also the judgment must be exercised, so as to be accustomed to draw the moral conclusions applicable to the subject. It is thus that some critics possess that critical tact by which they have been distinguished; they form a sound conclusion without apparently going through any elaborate process of reasoning. And this leads others to imagine that criticism is a kind of intuitive faculty, although the conclusions have really resulted from quickness in perceiving *what* the evidence is, and a well-exercised judgment in applying known principles to the evidence so

These canons are principles rather than rules.

----

[1] See an extensive and careful examination of the various readings of 1 Tim. iii, 16, in the Bibliotheca Sacra for January, 1865, pp. 1–50.

apprehended." And the same consummate critic adds, in another place: "He who rightly studies the principles and facts of the textual criticism of the New Testament, will find that he has acquired information not on one subject merely, but also on almost all of those that relate to the transmission of Scripture from the days of the apostles; he will have obtained that kind of instruction which will impart both a breadth and a definiteness to all his biblical studies; he will be led into a kind of unconscious connection with the writers of Scripture and their works." [1]

CHAPTER VIII.

THE DIVINE INSPIRATION OF THE SCRIPTURES.

OUR appreciation of the Holy Scriptures will necessarily be influenced by our views of their claims as divinely inspired. Critical and exegetical study will be more or less serious and painstaking as the student feels a deep conviction that he is handling the very word of God.

There is an inspiration in all great works of genius. Those masterpieces of oratory, which, burning from the impassioned souls of Demosthenes and Cicero, aroused Athenian and Roman audiences, are to this day full of moving power. The poems of Homer and the oracles of Socrates reveal the inspiration of genius. Passages in Shakspeare, Milton, and Byron exhibit a power of expression and a perfection of form which will ever charm the minds of men. Who will deny Toplady's "Rock of Ages" and Charles Wesley's "Wrestling Jacob" a notable degree of divine inspiration? But the great body of believers in the Holy Scriptures have ever felt that the inspiration of the Bible is something far higher and more divine than the rapture of human genius.

Inspiration of genius.

The inspiration of genius is from within, that of the Holy Spirit from without. The one is begotten of the human soul, the other is by revelation from the supernatural and divine. The biblical writers themselves assume to write by a supernatural authority; they speak as men who have seen the visions of the Almighty, have heard the voice of the revealer of secrets, and are moved by the power of the Holy Spirit. It may

Scripture inspiration higher.

[1] S. P. Tregelles, Introduction to the Textual Criticism and Study of the New Testament, in Horne's Introduction (ed. Ayre and Tregelles), vol. iv, pp. 343, 401.

be safely asserted that, in some sense, the sacred writers were used mechanically; they were often employed as the media of words and symbols which they could not comprehend. They were inspired dynamically, for they were actuated by a supernatural force and wisdom which supervised their work, and directed them so as to secure the very purpose of the Almighty. In their inspiration there was a verbal element, for God is represented as speaking by "the mouth of all his prophets." "Behold," he says to Jeremiah (i, 9), "I have put my words in thy mouth." Paul claims to set forth the saving truth of God "not in words taught by human wisdom, but in those taught by the Spirit" (1 Cor. ii, 13). Every devout Christian will acknowledge that this inspiration was plenary, inasmuch as it has furnished in all-sufficient fulness a revelation of the mind and will of God. But when we attempt to say where the divine element in Scripture ends, or where the human begins, we involve ourselves in mysteries which no man is able to solve.

According to the evangelical faith, maintained by the Christian Church in all ages, there exist in the sacred records two elements, a divine and a human. In this respect there is a noteworthy analogy between the personal, incarnate word, and the written word. As, in studying the person and character of Christ, we most naturally begin with the human side, observing that which is tangible to sense, so it will be well for us to examine, first, the human lineaments of the written word of God.

It is evident that a considerable portion of the Bible is a narrative of facts which any ordinary mind might have gathered and put in written form. Such, for example, is the history of the rise, power, glory, decline, and fall of the kingdom of Israel, as contained in the Books of Samuel, Kings, and Chronicles. Many parts of these books appear to have been compiled directly from pre-existing documents.[1] The Book of Nehemiah is an autobiography, and that of Esther a lively sketch of court-life in the Persian Empire. In the preface to his gospel, Luke professes to set forth an orderly arrangement of facts fully believed among the earliest Christians, reported by eye-witnesses, and accurately traced by himself from the very first. The Acts of the Apostles, by the same author, is a simple narrative of the beginnings of the Christian Church. In these books especially, but in others also, there appears no necessity or occasion for claiming an extraordinary assistance for the writers. Many a writer, for whom no such claim was ever made, has traced and recorded facts

Divine and human in the Scriptures.

Human element seen in the narration of facts.

[1] Compare 1 Kings xi, 41; xiv, 29; xv, 31; 1 Chron. xxix, 29; 2 Chron. xxxii, 32, etc.

in human history with a painstaking care and accuracy as great as the biblical narratives evince.

The human element is also noticeable in the style and diction of the sacred writers. No one can fail to observe how widely Isaiah differs in style from Jeremiah, Matthew from John, and Paul from James. The distinct individuality of each author is conspicuous, and there is no reason to suppose that any of these writers were hindered in the freest exercise of their natural faculties, or in the normal use of their peculiar modes of thought and expression. We should explain the marked difference of style in the prayers of Daniel (chap. ix, 4–19) and Habakkuk (chap. iii), the song of Moses (Exod. xv, 1–19), and the *Magnificat* of Mary (Luke i, 46–55), as we explain the differences between Milton's "Hymn of the Nativity" and Pope's "Messiah," or between an exquisite passage of Addison and an oration of Daniel Webster.

Seen also in style and diction.

Other human lineaments are observable in the subject-matter, where expression is given to the writer's personal affection for individuals, or to his sense of want and weakness. The whole catalogue of personal greetings in the sixteenth chapter of Romans is an illustration of this; also the tender familiarity of Paul with his Thessalonian converts, and the personal reminiscences of his first acquaintance (ii, 1), his departure (ii, 17, 18), and his being "left in Athens alone" (iii, 1). The human element is conspicuous in his defence of his apostleship in the first two chapters of Galatians, in his remembrance of the Philippians' kindness (Phil. iv, 15–18), in his messages to the Ephesians by Tychicus (Eph. vi, 21), and his desire for the books, parchments, and cloak left at Troas (2 Tim. iv, 13). He exhibits, also, some doubt and hesitation as to whether, at Corinth, he baptized any others besides Crispus, Gaius, and the household of Stephanas (1 Cor. i, 14, 16), and in his Second Epistle to the Corinthians he writes: "In lack of wisdom I speak" (2 Cor. xi, 21); "as one beside himself I say it" (ver. 23); "I am become a fool; ye compelled me" (xii, 11).

Seen in subject-matter.

To the above instances we may also add the varying forms of statement under which the same thing is reported to us by different writers. Observe the numerous verbal differences in the parable of the sower as reported by Matthew (xiii, 4–9), Mark (iv, 3–9), and Luke (viii, 5–8); or in the parable of the mustard seed (Matt. xiii, 31, 32; Mark iv, 30–32; Luke xiii, 18, 19), and in numerous other sayings of our Lord. Compare, especially, the different forms of the Lord's Prayer (Matt. vi, 9–13; Luke xi, 2–4), and of the language used in instituting the Lord's Sup-

Seen in varying forms of statement.

per (Matt. xxvi, 26–29; Mark xiv, 22–24; Luke xxii, 19, 20; 1 Cor. xi, 23–25). The only rational and truly satisfactory way of explaining such verbal discrepancies is to hold (what seems so apparent and natural) that the writers freely reported, each in his own independent way, the substance of what the Lord had said. The Lord had probably spoken in Aramaic, but his words are reported in Greek. So, perhaps, no one of the evangelists has given us the exact form of the title on the cross; but each one records its substance and purport in a different form of words (Matt. xxvii, 37; Mark xv, 26; Luke xxiii, 38; John xix, 19). In all these varying reports there is no error, no real discrepancy; but simply that variety of human expression which is common to all the languages of men.

But, along with the human element in the Scriptures, there are Evidences of also the claim and the evidence of a divine inspiration. divine element. Paul says: "All Scripture is God-breathed" (θεόπ-νευστος, 2 Tim. iii, 16), and Peter writes: "For not by the will of man was prophecy ever brought, but, borne along by the Holy Spirit, men spoke from God" (2 Peter i, 21). Here is a most important assertion. He declares in the verse preceding that "no prophecy of Scripture comes of its own interpretation," or springs out of the human understanding.[1] The Scripture prophecies are no products of human invention or ingenuity, for the men who Peter's declar- wrote them "spoke from God," as they were impelled ation. or carried along (φερόμενοι) by the divine power. In his first epistle the same apostle tells how the prophets diligently sought and searched (ἐξεζήτησαν καὶ ἐξηραύνησαν) concerning salvation, "searching into what time or what manner of time the Spirit of Christ in them was signifying when he testified beforehand the sufferings pertaining to Christ and the glories after them; to whom it was revealed that not to themselves, but to you they were ministering that which is now announced to you through those who preached you the gospel by the Holy Spirit sent from heaven" (1 Peter i, 11, 12). We should observe the following four things here affirmed: (1) the prophets were actuated by the Spirit of Christ; (2) they did not fully comprehend the time-limits of their own oracles; (3) they were given to understand that their words would minister help to after times; (4) the first preachers of the

---

[1] The reference is, as Lumby observes, "to prophecy as it was uttered by those who first gave it forth. It did not arise from the private interpretation of the prophets. The words of the prophets of old were no mere human exposition, no endeavour on man's part to point to a solution of the difficulties which beset men's minds in this life. The prophets were moved by a Spirit beyond themselves, and spake things deeper than they themselves understood."—Speaker's Commentary in loco.

gospel were also actuated by the same Holy Spirit, and their messages had heavenly origin and authority.

The Old Testament abounds in assertions of the divine origin of its lessons and revelations. A large proportion of the Pentateuch is professedly Jehovah's revelation of him- *Old Testament claims.* self to the patriarchs, or his express word of commandment to Moses and to Israel. The Decalogue is said to have been uttered by God's own voice out of the midst of his theophany of fire and cloud on Horeb (Exod. xix, 9; xx, 1, 19; Deut. v, 4, 22), and afterward written by "the finger of God," and delivered to Moses on tablets of stone (Exod. xxxi, 18). The prophets continually announce their messages as the word of Jehovah, and make frequent use of the formulas, "Hear the word of Jehovah," and "Thus saith Jehovah." Jesus recognized this same divine inspiration and authority in the Psalms; it was David speaking "in the *Jesus' words.* Spirit" (Matt. xxii, 43). And when he sent forth his disciples, and foretold their persecutions, he comforted them with these words: "When they deliver you up, take no thought how or what ye shall speak; for it shall be given you in that hour what ye shall speak. For it is not ye that speak, but the spirit of your Father that speaks in you" (Matt. x, 19, 20). If such divine power directed these founders of Christianity when they spoke before their enemies, much more may we believe that the Scriptures written by them were inspired by God. For they had also the promise: "The Comforter, the Holy Spirit, whom the Father will send in my name, he will teach you all things, and bring to your remembrance all things which I said to you." "He will guide you into all the truth; for he will not speak from himself, but whatever he hears he will speak, and he will tell you the things to come. He will glorify me; because he will receive of mine, and will tell you. All things whatever the Father has are mine; therefore I said that of mine he receives, and will tell you" (John xiv, 26; xvi, 13–15). How they subsequently *remembered* the Lord's words is told in Luke xxiv, 8; John ii, 22; xii, 16; and Acts xi, 16; and the authority with which they spoke may be seen in Paul's words to the Thessalonians: "When ye received the word of God heard from us, ye received not the word of men, but, as it is in truth, the word of God" (1 Thess. ii, 13).

In citing these declarations of the Scriptures, we assume, of course, the divine origin of Christianity, and the authenticity and truthfulness of the Old and New Testaments. Our argument is not with the unbeliever and *Credibility of the Scriptures here assumed.* the sceptic, but with those who accept both Testaments as in some sense the word of God; and our inquiry is concerned merely with the nature and extent of their inspiration. This question must not be judged and decided *a priori*. We need to look at facts of the history, contents, and scope of the several parts, as well as explicit declarations, of the Bible. With these constantly in mind, and disregarding all special theories, we may be helped by the following considerations :

I. God, from the beginning, planned to furnish for mankind such a written testimony of his works, judgments, and will, as would always be "profitable for teaching, for reproof, for correction, for instruction in righteousness." The grand purpose of all is, "that the man of God may be perfect, thoroughly furnished unto all good works" (2 Tim. iii, 16, 17). To fill out such a plan and purpose required thousands of years. The record was to embody a revelation of the creation of man, and of God's gracious dealings and righteous judgments through the lapse of ages. It was to be a record of prophecy and its fulfilment, of miracle, and promise, and comfort. Truth and righteousness were to be exhibited in the concrete by an ample record of the experiences of holy men. Accordingly God spoke in many parts and in many ways to the fathers by the prophets (Heb. i, 1), and, at last, by the incarnation and ministry of Jesus Christ, and by the apostles, completed the providential record of religious truth and enlightenment. Thus the Bible is pre-eminently God's book, a body of writings providentially prepared by divine wisdom for the religious instruction of mankind.

The whole Bible God's book for man.

II. As regards the varied contents of this God-given book, it is well, with many recent writers,[1] to distinguish between revelation and inspiration. The subject-matter of many parts of the Scriptures is of such a character as to lie beyond the unaided powers of the human mind to discover. Such portions must have been communicated in some supernatural way, and were, therefore, from the nature of the case, a divine revelation. Inspiration, on the other hand, was the divine influence and supervision under which the sacred writers made a record of what came to their knowledge either by revelation or otherwise. "Revelation and inspiration," says Lee, "are to be distinguished by the sources from which they proceed, revelation being the peculiar function of the eternal Word; inspiration the result of the agency

Subject-matter revealed or inspired.

[1] See, especially, Lee, on the Inspiration of Holy Scripture, Lectures i, iv, and v, and E. P. Barrow's articles on Revelation and Inspiration, in the Bibliotheca Sacra for Oct., 1867, April, 1868, Jan. and July, 1869, Jan., July, and Oct., 1870, Oct., 1871, Jan., July, and Oct., 1872, and April, 1873.

of the Holy Spirit. Their difference is specific, and not merely one of degree, a point which is amply confirmed by the consideration that either of these divine influences may be exerted without calling the other into action. The patriarchs received revelations, but they were not inspired to record them; the writer of the Acts of the Apostles was inspired for his task, but we are not told that he ever enjoyed a revelation."[1]

It is easy to see that the narrative of creation could have been furnished only in some supernatural way, for no human eye observed it. The visions and dreams of patriarchs and prophets were modes of receiving divine communications (Num. xii, 6). Balaam was so controlled by a supernatural force that he could utter no word or will of his own (Num. xxii, 38; xxiii, 26; xxiv, 13). The ten commandments were uttered by the voice (Exod. xx, 1, 19) and written by the finger of God (Exod. xxxi, 18). Large portions of the prophecies are expressly declared to be Jehovah's oracles, and foretell the things to come. The words of the Lord Jesus must be accepted by every devout Christian as of absolute authority. But, on the other hand, as we have shown above, large portions of the Scripture are records of matters which the writers could have ascertained without supernatural aid. Yet we are told that ALL SCRIPTURE is inspired by God. The final question, then, is reduced to the nature and degree of the inspiration.

III. On this point we affirm the proposition, that a particular divine providence secured the composition of the Scriptures in the language and form in which we possess them. Moses at the beginning of the sacred volume, *Inspiration a particular divine providence.* and John at its close, were commanded to WRITE. The divine revelations of which we have spoken would have been comparatively useless unless divine Providence had secured an accurate and faithful record of them to be transmitted through the ages. For the preparation of such a record holy men were inspired of God. Many revelations may have been given which are not recorded, as well as many facts and experiences which would have been profitable for religious instruction. But the Divine Wisdom guided the human agents in selecting such facts and reporting such truths as would best accomplish the purpose of God in providing a written revelation for the world. We see no good reason for denying that the divine guidance extended to all parts and forms of the record. God secured the composition of the Pentateuch in just the form and style in which we have it. He secured the writing of the Book of Job for the great religious lessons it embodies. Half of it

[1] Inspiration of Holy Scripture, Lecture i, p. 42.

may be composed of the erroneous notions of self-conceited and
mistaken men; but it must be studied as a whole, and its several
parts, as bearing on the one great problem of human suffering,
will then appear as a most beautiful and impressive form of setting
forth certain lessons of divine providence and judgment. The
genealogies of Chronicles, Ezra, and other books, are similarly,
parts of a whole, and links in the history of Israel. So the historical books, the Prophets, the Psalms, the Gospels, and the Epistles
subserve a manifold divine purpose. God has provided that these
books, and no others, should be written and preserved through the
ages as divinely authoritative for instruction in righteousness, and
to this end he called, actuated, energized, and supervised the holy
men who wrote them.

The notion that the Almighty Spirit absolutely controlled the
Divine inspi- sacred writers, so as to select for them the very words
ration affects they employed, is repugnant to the thoughtful mind.
language and
style.   There is no evidence, within or without the record, of
any such mechanical operation. But we conceive that the language
and style of a writer may be mightily affected by divine influences
brought to bear upon his soul. Such influences would produce important effects in his thoughts and his words. To affirm, with
some, that God supplied the thoughts or ideas of Scripture, but left
the writers perfectly free in their choice of words, tends to confuse the subject, for it appears that the inspired penmen were as
free and independent in searching for facts and arranging them in
orderly narrative as they were in the choice of words. (Luke i, 3.)
It seems better, therefore, to understand that, by the inspiring impulse from God, all the faculties of the human agent were mightily
quickened, and, as a consequence, his thoughts, his emotions, his
style, and even his words, were affected. In this sense only we
affirm the doctrine of verbal inspiration. We have seen above,
that *form* and *style* are often essential elements of an organic whole,
and to attempt to give the sentiment, without the form, of some
compositions, is to rob them of their very substance and life.[2]

[1] See on pages 92–94.

[2] Tayler Lewis remarks that "the very words, the very figures outwardly used, yea,
the etymological metaphors contained in the words, be they ever so interior, are all inspired. They are not merely general effects, in which sense all human utterances, and
even all physical manifestations, may be said to be inspired, but the specially designed
products of *emotions* supernaturally inbreathed, these becoming outward in *thoughts*,
and these, again, having their ultimate outward forms in *words* and *figures* as truly
designed in the workings of this chain, and thus as truly inspired, as the thoughts of
which these words are the express image, and the inspired emotions in which both
thoughts and images had their birth." And yet he repudiates "that extreme view of

Four different kinds or degrees of inspiration are thus specified by an English author: "By the inspiration of *suggestion* is meant such communications of the Holy Spirit as suggested and dictated every part of the truths delivered. Four degrees of inspiration suggested. The inspiration of *direction* is meant of such assistance as left the writers to describe the matter revealed in their own way, directing only the mind in the exercise of its powers. The inspiration of *elevation* added a greater strength and vigour to the efforts of the mind than the writers could have otherwise attained. The inspiration of *superintendency* was that watchful care which preserved generally from any thing being put down derogatory to the revelation with which it was connected."[1] But, if God directly suggests, directs, elevates, and superintends in any or all of these ways, how can we consistently maintain that he was concerned merely with the substance and not the form? Is it unworthy of the God who observes the fall of every sparrow, and numbers all the hairs of our heads (Matt. x, 29, 30), to care for the words and forms in which his oracles are given to the world?

But while the particular words and style are essential elements of some parts of Scripture, it should be observed that there are many facts and ideas which may be expressed in a variety of forms. Thus, Jesus might have said: "A certain man, in going from Jerusalem to Jericho, fell among thieves;" or, "There was a man who went on a journey from Jerusalem down to Jericho, and robbers fell upon him by the way;" or, "In passing from Jerusalem down to Jericho a certain traveller was assaulted by a band of robbers." We might thus vary the form and words of the statement in a score of ways, and yet preserve substantially the same idea. But even in such matters of little or no apparent moment, why deny that the supervising Spirit aided in the selection of the particular language used by the sacred writers? Facts may be expressed by a variety of words and forms.

It is possible to make some of the grandest truths appear ludicrous by resolving them, through an artful analysis, into a multitude of frivolous details. It might be asked, Did the Almighty and Eternal God move the muscles of Matthew's arm and fingers, cause his heart to beat with Fallacious trifling with details.

verbal inspiration which regards the sacred penmen as mere amanuenses, writing words and painting figures dictated to them by a power and an intelligence acting in a manner wholly extraneous to the laws of their own spirits, except so far as those laws are merely physical or mechanical." The Divine Human in the Scriptures, pp. 27–30.

[1] Bishop Daniel Wilson, on The Evidences of Christianity, vol. i, p. 508. Lond., 1828.

emotion, and his eyes to glow, as he took up his pen and scratched
upon the parchment before him? Did he move him to spell Δαυΐδ,
or Δαβίδ; to write οὕτω, or οὕτως; εἶπε, or εἶπεν; διὰ τί, or διάτι;
εἴ γε, or εἴγε? Did he furnish him with black ink or red ink, papyrus or parchment, a writing desk or the floor of a room? We
may thus trifle also with the minutiæ of divine Providence, but,
after all our quibbling, we must either admit that the omniscient
Spirit was cognizant of all these details, or else say what particular
things escaped his oversight and care. The argument which maintains the inspiration of the thoughts, but not the words, of Scripture, logically denies any particular providence in the form and
style of God's written word, and leaves the whole subject vague
and visionary.

The opinion that divine inspiration is incompatible with the free
action and varied style of the sacred writers seems to grow out of a
false psychology. Amid the complex sensations, perceptions and activities of the human soul there is room for the normal action of both
divine and human forces. The intellect and the affections may be
thoroughly subject to supernatural power, while the will remains free
in its self-conscious action. The divine inspiration of the sacred
writers no more interfered, necessarily, with their personal freedom than the calling and anointing of Cyrus (Isa. xlv, i) interfered
No conflict be-   with the conscious freedom and action of that mon-
tween the di-   arch. Moses and Paul wrote with as much freedom
vine and hu-
man.   as Cæsar and Bacon; but Moses and Paul were, in a
high and holy sense, chosen ministers to write a portion of the
Bible, and that holy calling and work put them in a position as
superior to Cæsar, and Bacon, as the Pentateuch and the Epistles
are superior to the Gallic Wars and the Novum Organum. The
wisdom and power of God secured, without any violation of individual freedom, the writing of the Holy Scriptures in their original form, and preserved the writers from vital error. So the
Eternal Word was made flesh (John i, 14), but the divine nature
in the person of Christ did not set aside or nullify the perfect
human nature and freedom of the man Christ Jesus. This union
of the divine and human, whether in the incarnate word or in
the written word, is a great mystery, which no human mind can
fathom or explain. But as regards the inspiration of prophets
and apostles, we may affirm with Delitzsch: "The divine thoughts
take their way to the Ego of the prophet through his nature.
They clothe themselves in popular human language, according to
the prophet's individual manner of thinking and speaking, and
they present themselves in a form manifoldly limited, according

to the existing circumstances and the horizon of contemporary history."

"It is inadmissible," he adds, "to distinguish between real and verbal inspiration (*inspiratio realis et verbalis*). Sub- Delitzsch's stance and form are both the effect of one divine act. view. As the soul came into existence when God breathed the spirit into man, so come into existence words of divine nature and human form when God breathes thoughts into man. . . . The act of inspiration should, and must, be represented as an organic vital interworking of the divine and human factor, without thereby jeopardizing the infallibility of the revealed truth written in the Scripture, and the faithfulness of the fundamental history of redemption contained therein for all times. . . . Scripture is no book fallen from heaven; its origination is just as much human as divine. He who is offended at this sins against the Holy Spirit, whose condescension into humanity (by no means Docetic) he ought rather to admire and praise."[1]

The fact that different writers vary in recording what purports to be particular sayings is often urged as an argument Verbal variations not a valid argument against divine inspiration. The words of Jesus at the Last Supper, and the title on the cross, are cited as against divine examples. But under all this argument is the tacit inspiration. assumption that each of the writers is aiming to give the *ipsissima verba*, whereas, in fact, no one of them has given the original words. The *ipsissima verba* were Aramaic,[2] not Greek; each New Testament writer furnishes his own free and independent version of them, and all report correctly the essential sentiment of our Lord. Who is competent to say that these very differences were not desired and directed by the Almighty Spirit? Matthew was inspired to write the words, "Take; eat" (xxvi, 26); Mark to omit the word *eat* (xiv, 22) ; Luke to omit both these words, and write, "This is my body which for you is given" (xxii, 19); and Paul to say, "This my body is, which is for you" (1 Cor. xi, 24). The denial of a divine purpose in these verbal differences seems to involve a distrust of a particular divine providence in the peculiar style and form of the Scriptures of God. If we are not able always to see a reason for such verbal differences, neither are we competent to say that there was, and could have been, no reason, and no care for them in the divine mind.

[1] Biblical Psychology, part v, section 5. Comp. Elliott, A Treatise on the Inspiration of the Holy Scriptures, p. 257. Edinburgh, 1877.

[2] The very words of our Lord are, doubtless, given in such instances as *Talitha cumi* (Mark v, 41), *Ephphatha* (vii, 34), *Rabboni* (John xx, 16).

The thousands of various readings in the ancient manuscripts, and the impossibility of deciding, in all cases, what is the true original text, are construed into an argument against verbal inspiration. If God took pains to influence the writers in the choice of words and forms of thought, why has he not been careful to secure every word from corruption and change? This question, however, assumes that God may never create a thing without miraculously preserving it intact forever, a proposition which we see no good reason to affirm. It was probably no more necessary to preserve all the words ever given by inspiration of God than to record all the things which Jesus did (John xxi, 15); and we, therefore, deny that the existing various readings afford any valid evidence that the original autographs were not verbally inspired. We may add that the denial of verbal inspiration logically diminishes one's devout interest and zeal in the critical study of the Scriptures. It takes away notable motives for anxiety to ascertain the exact words of the original text, for if those words were not divinely inspired we would naturally attach less importance to them.[1]

But the vast majority of readers of the Bible know nothing of the original texts, and are dependent upon a translation; of what benefit, it is asked, is verbal inspiration to such readers? But is not every such dependent reader anxious to have the most faithful translation possible? Why such care? Why have hundreds of devout scholars combined to produce an accurate and trustworthy version for the English-speaking world? Does it not all spring from a feeling that the original is divine, and the ultimate source of all appeal? How irrelevant and fallacious is it, then, to talk of versions? The question of inspiration is concerned solely with the original texts. Moreover, if there was a divine plan and purpose in having the Scriptures written in Hebrew, and Chaldee, and Greek,[2] the divine providence would be likely to have cared for every jot and tittle of the same.

As for alleged discrepancies, contradictions, and errors of the

The side notes in the margin read: "Various readings no valid argument against the verbal inspiration of the originals."

[1] "This theory," says Gilbert Haven, "cuts the nerves of minute study for the harmonizing of the Word. It is as fatal to sound scholarship as to sound doctrine. That scholars and theologians advocate it is no proof of its real effects. They bring with them to their investigation, not their theory, but the old, the divine feeling of its entire and perfect sacredness. They worship at its shrine, they seek to know its full meaning, its intended and real, if hidden, harmony. They are orthodox in spite of their outer creed, by the inward culture of the soul in the elder and superior truth." Methodist Quarterly Review for 1867, p. 848. See also Haven's two subsequent articles in the same Review for 1868.

[2] See above, pp. 106, 128.

Bible, we deny that any real errors can be shown.[1] But our doctrine of divine inspiration is compatible with incorrect spelling, involved rhetoric, imperfect grammar, and inelegant language. The earthen vessels remain earthen though filled with divine treasure. Confusion of thought and obscurity of statement are no valid argument against the inspiration of the Word. As some of God's purposes may sometimes be most effectually carried out by weak or ignorant men, so the apparent defects, alleged of some portions of the Scriptures, may have been divinely permitted among the definite purposes of grace.[2] A prophecy or an epistle written "not with excellency of speech or of wisdom "—" not with persuasive words of man's wisdom "—may, nevertheless, contain a wisdom and excellence "not of this world, nor of the rulers of this world, who come to nought" (1 Cor. ii, 1, 4, 6). Faultless grammar and absolute accuracy of statement were not essential to the best mode of setting forth all the lessons of redemption. No more was it essential that the New Testament should be written in the classic elegance and purity of ancient Attic Greek. The notion that divine inspiration is incompatible with obscurity of style and grammatical inaccuracy springs from an *a priori* judgment that God must needs have given his infallible word in some absolutely perfect or supernatural form. But such a judgment has no foundation in nature or in grace. God gave not his word in the tongues of angels, but of men. " God chose the foolish things of the world that he might put the wise to shame; and God chose the weak things of the world that he might put to shame the things which are strong; and the base things of the world, and the things which are despised, did God choose, and the things which are not, that he might bring to nought things that are; that no flesh should glory before God" (1 Cor. i, 27–29). How futile, then, are all *a priori* human judgments of the form in which God's oracles should be cast?

In the seventh chapter of Acts we have the celebrated address of the proto-martyr Stephen. His face glowing like the face of an angel, and his impassioned soul full of the Holy Spirit, he utters a rapid sketch of Israelitish his-

Margin notes: Inaccurate grammar and obscurity of style no valid objection.

Stephen's address in Acts vii.

---

[1] We devote a chapter, in the subsequent part of this work, to alleged discrepancies, and cannot enlarge upon them here. But comp. the article, Discrepancy and Inspiration not Incompatible, Journal of Sacred Literature for April, 1854, pp. 71–110.

[2] How often has the personal Christian experience of an illiterate convert, uttered in broken speech and stammering voice, but glowing with the ardour of deep convictions, proved more mighty to awaken sinful men, and lead them to repentance, than the most finished sermons of many an eloquent preacher!

tory. In verse 16 he speaks of the tomb at Shechem "which Abraham bought for a sum of money of the sons of Emmor, of Shechem." Here is, apparently, a confusion of thought, but one which could do no possible harm, and did not hinder the speech from cutting the hearers to the heart (verse 54). It seems to us improbable that Stephen should have made such a blunder;[1] but there is no evidence that the text is corrupt; and who knows but the Holy Spirit allowed him in his fervid eloquence to fall into this confusion of facts in order to exhibit how irresistible plenary inspiration is not conditioned "in the wisdom of men, but in the power of God" (1 Cor. ii, 5)?

We have no room to discuss the manifold collateral questions connected with this theme, but have briefly presented the main points, which show both the divine and the human in the written Word. We adopt no technical theory, but indicate how all is divine, and all is human. For "ALL SCRIPTURE is God-breathed." "Given by the divine mind," says Tayler Lewis, "these holy books must have in them a depth and fulness of meaning that the human intellect can never exhaust. If they are holy books, if they are *Sacræ Scripturæ*, as even the neologist conventionally styles them, then can there be thrown away upon them no amount of study, provided that study is ever chastened by a sanctified, truth-loving spirit that rejoices more in the simplest teaching, and in the simplest method of teaching from God, than in the most lauded discoveries of any mere human science. Is it in truth the word of God—is it really God speaking to us? Then the feeling and the conclusion which it necessitates are no hyperboles. We cannot go too far in our reverence, or in our expectation of knowledge surpassing in kind, if not in extent. The wisdom of the earth, of the seas, of the treasures hidden in the rocks and all deep places of the subterranean world, or of the stars afar off, brings us not so nigh the central truth of the heavens, the very mind and thought of God, as one parable of Christ, or one of those grand prophetic figures through which the light of the infinite idea is converged, while, at the same time, its intensity is shaded for the tender human vision."[2]

---

[1] It is not at all impossible that a purchase similar to that recorded of Jacob (Gen. xxxiii, 19) had been made long previously by Abram when he first arrived at Shechem, and found the Canaanite already in that land (Gen. xii, 6). An aboriginal Hamor had probably already founded the city of Shechem, and was known as its father (comp. Judg. ix, 28).

[2] The Divine Human in the Scriptures, pp. 25, 26.

CHAPTER IX.

QUALIFICATIONS OF AN INTERPRETER.

IN order to be a capable [1] and correct interpreter of the Holy Scriptures, one needs a variety of qualifications, both natural and acquired. For though a large proportion of the sacred volume is sufficiently simple for the child to understand, and the common people and the unlearned may find on every page much that is profitable for instruction in righteousness, there is also much that requires, for its proper apprehension and exposition, the noblest powers of intellect and the most ample learning. The several qualifications of a competent interpreter may be classified as Intellectual, Educational, and Spiritual. The first are largely native to the soul; the second are acquired by study and research; the third may be regarded both as native and acquired.

INTELLECTUAL QUALIFICATIONS.

First of all, the interpreter of Scripture, and, indeed, of any other book, should have a sound, well-balanced mind. For dulness of apprehension, defective judgment, and an extravagant fancy will pervert one's reason, and lead to many vain and foolish notions. The faculties of the mind are capable of discipline, and may be trained to a very high degree of perfection; but some men inherit peculiar tendencies of intellect. Some are gifted with rare powers of imagination, but are utterly wanting in the critical faculty. A lifetime of discipline will scarcely restrain their exuberant fancy. Others are naturally given to form hasty judgments, and will rush to the wildest extremes. In others, peculiar tastes and passions warp the judgment, and some seem to be constitutionally destitute of common sense. Any and all such mental defects disqualify one for the interpretation of the word of God.

Defective mental powers disqualify.

A ready perception is specially requisite in the interpreter. He must have the power to grasp the thought of his author, and take in at a glance its full force and bearing. With such ready perception there must be united a breadth of view and clearness of understanding which will be quick to catch, not only the import of words and phrases, but also the drift of the

Quick and clear perception.

[1] Comp. the import of ἱκανοί, ἱκανότης, and ἱκάνωσεν in 2 Cor. iii, 5, 6.

argument. Thus, for example, in attempting to explain the Epistle
to the Galatians, a quick perception will note the apologetic tone
of the first two chapters, the bold earnestness of Paul in asserting
the divine authority of his apostleship, and the far-reaching consequences of his claim. It will also note how forcibly the personal
incidents referred to in Paul's life and ministry enter into his argument. It will keenly appreciate the impassioned appeal to the
"foolish Galatians" at the beginning of chapter third, and the natural transition from thence to the doctrine of Justification. The
variety of argument and illustration in the third and fourth chapters, and the hortatory application and practical counsels of the two
concluding chapters will also be clearly discerned; and then the
unity, scope, and directness of the whole Epistle will lie pictured
before the mind's eye as a perfect whole, to be appreciated more
and more fully as additional attention and study are given to min-
uter details.

The great exegetes have been noted for acuteness of intellect, a
Acuteness of critical sharpness to discern at once the connexion of
intellect. thought, and the association of ideas. This qualification is of great importance to every interpreter. He must be quick
to see what a passage does not teach, as well as to comprehend its
real import. His critical acumen should be associated with a masterly power of analysis, in order that he may clearly discern all the
parts and relations of a given whole. Bengel and De Wette, in
their works on the New Testament, excel in this particular. They
evince an intellectual sagacity, which is to be regarded as a special
gift, an inborn endowment, rather than a result of scientific culture.

The strong intellect will not be destitute of imaginative power.
Imagination Many things in narrative description must be left to be
needed, but supplied, and many of the finest passages of Holy Writ
must be con-
trolled. cannot be appreciated by an unimaginative mind. The
true interpreter must often transport himself into the past, and
picture in his soul the scenes of ancient time. He must have an intuition of nature and of human life by which to put himself in the
place of the biblical writers and see and feel as they did. But it
has usually happened that men of powerful imagination have been
unsafe expositors. An exuberant fancy is apt to run away with
the judgment, and introduce conjecture and speculation in place of
valid exegesis. The chastened and disciplined imagination will associate with itself the power of conception and of abstract thought,
and be able to construct, if called for, working hypotheses to be
used in illustration or in argument. Sometimes it may be expedient to form a concept, or adopt a theory, merely for the purpose

of pursuing some special line of discussion ; and every expositor should be competent for this when needed.

But, above all things, an interpreter of Scripture needs a sound and sober judgment. His mind must be competent to   Sober judg-analyze, examine, and compare. He must not allow   ment. himself to be influenced by hidden meanings, and spiritualizing processes, and plausible conjectures. He must weigh reasons for and against a given interpretation; he must judge whether his principles are tenable and self-consistent; he must often balance probabilities, and reach conclusions with the greatest caution. Such a discriminating judgment may be trained and strengthened, and no pains should be spared to render it a safe and reliable habit of the mind.

Correctness and delicacy of taste will be the result of a discriminating judgment. The interpreter of the inspired vol-   Correct and delicate taste. ume will find the need of this qualification in discerning   icate taste. the manifold beauties and excellences scattered in rich profusion through its pages. But his taste, as well as his judgment, must be trained to discern between the true and the false ideals. Many a modern whim of shallow refinement is offended with the straightforward honesty and simplicity of the ancient world. Prurient sensitiveness often blushes before expressions in the Scriptures which are as far as possible removed from impurity. Correct taste in such cases will pronounce according to the real spirit of the writer and his age.

The use of reason in the interpretation of Scripture is everywhere to be assumed. The Bible comes to us in the   Use of reason. forms of human language, and appeals to our reason and judgment; it invites investigation, and condemns a blind credulity. It is to be interpreted as we interpret any other volume, by a rigid application of the same laws of language, and the same grammatical analysis. Even in passages which may be said to lie beyond the province of reason, in the realm of supernatural revelation, it is still competent for the rational judgment to say whether, indeed, the revelation be supernatural. In matters beyond its range of vision, reason may, by valid argument, explain its own incompetency, and by analogy and manifold suggestion show that there are many things beyond its province which are nevertheless true and righteous altogether, and to be accepted without dispute. Reason itself may thus become efficient in strengthening faith in the unseen and eternal.

But it behooves the expounder of God's word to see that all his principles and processes of reasoning are sound and self-consistent.

He must not commit himself to false premises; he must abstain from confusing dilemmas; he must especially refrain from rushing to unwarranted conclusions. Nor must he ever take for granted things which are doubtful, or open to serious question. All such logical fallacies will necessarily vitiate his expositions, and make him a dangerous guide. The right use of reason in biblical exposi tion is seen in the cautious procedure, the sound principles adopted, the valid and conclusive argumentation, the sober sense displayed, and the honest integrity and self-consistency everywhere maintained. Such exercise of reason will always commend itself to the godly conscience and the pure heart.

In addition to the above-mentioned qualifications, the interpreter should be "apt to teach" (διδακτικός, 2 Tim. ii, 24).
Apt to teach. He must not only be able to understand the Scriptures, but also to set forth in clear and lively form to others what he himself comprehends. Without such aptness in teaching, all his other gifts and qualities will avail little or nothing. Accordingly, the interpreter should cultivate a clear and simple style, and study to bring out the truth and force of the inspired oracles so that others will readily understand.

Educational Qualifications.

The professional interpreter of Scripture needs more than a well-balanced mind, discreet sense, and acuteness of intellect. He needs stores of information in the broad and varied fields of history, science, and philosophy. By many liberal studies will his faculties become disciplined and strong for practical use; and extensive and accurate knowledge will furnish and fit him to be the teacher of others. The biblical interpreter should be minutely acquainted with
Geography. the geography of Palestine and the adjacent regions. In order to be properly versed in this, he will need to understand the physical character of the world outside of Bible lands. For, though the sacred writers may have known nothing of countries foreign to Asia, Africa, and Europe, the modern student will find an advantage in having information, as full as possible, of the entire surface of the globe. With such geographical knowledge
History. he should also unite a familiar acquaintance with universal history. The records of many peoples, both ancient and modern, will often be of value in testing the accuracy of the sacred writers, and illustrating their excellence and worth. What a vast amount of light have ancient authors, and the deciphered inscriptions of Egypt, Assyria, Babylon, and Persia, shed upon the narratives of the Bible!

The science of chronology is also indispensable to the proper interpretation of the Scriptures. The succession of events, the division of the ages into great eras, the scope of genealogical tables, and the fixing of dates, are important, and call for patient study and laborious care. Nor can the interpreter dispense with the study of antiquities, the habits, customs, and arts of the ancients. He should inquire into the antiquities of all the ancient nations and races of whom any records remain, for the customs of other nations may often throw light upon those of the Hebrews. The study of politics, including international law and the various theories and systems of civil government, will add greatly to the other accomplishments of the exegete, and enable him the better to appreciate the Mosaic legislation, and the great principles of civil government set forth in the New Testament. Many a passage, also, can be illustrated and made more impressive by a thorough knowledge of natural science. Geology, mineralogy, and astronomy, are incidentally touched by statements or allusions of the sacred writers, and whatever the knowledge of the ancients on these subjects, the modern interpreter ought to be familiar with what modern science has demonstrated. The same may be said of the history and systems of speculative thought, the various schools of philosophy and psychology. Many of these philosophical discussions have become involved in theological dogma, and have led to peculiar principles and methods of interpretation, and, to cope fairly with them, the professional exegete should be familiar with all their subtleties. We have already seen how all-important to the interpreter is a profound and accurate knowledge of the sacred tongues. No one can be a master in biblical exposition without such knowledge. To a thorough acquaintance with Hebrew, Chaldee, and Greek, he should add some proficiency in the science of comparative philology. Especially will a knowledge of Syriac, Arabic, and other Semitic languages help one to understand the Hebrew and the Chaldee, and acquaintance with Sanskrit and Latin and other Indo-European tongues will deepen and enlarge one's knowledge of the Greek. To all these acquirements the interpreter of God's word should add a familiar acquaintance with general literature. The great productions of human genius, the world-renowned epics, the classics of all the great nations, and the bibles of all religions, will be of value in estimating the oracles of God.

It is not denied that there have been able and excellent expositors who were wanting in many of these literary qualifications. But he who excels as a master can regard no literary attainments as superfluous; and, in maintaining and defending against scepticism and infidelity the faith once delivered to the saints, the Christian apologist and exegete will find all these qualifications indispensable.

SPIRITUAL QUALIFICATIONS.

Intellectual qualities, though capable of development and discipline, are to be regarded as natural endowments; educational or literary acquirements are to be had only by diligent and faithful study; but those qualifications of an interpreter which we call spiritual are to be regarded as partly a gift, and partly acquired by personal effort and proper discipline. Under this head we place all moral and religious qualities, dispositions, and attainments. The spirit is that higher moral nature which especially distinguishes man from the brute, and renders him capable of knowing and loving God. To meet the wants of this spiritual nature the Bible is admirably adapted; but the perverse heart and carnal mind may refuse to entertain the thoughts of God. "The natural man," says Paul, "does not receive the things of the Spirit of God, for they are a folly to him, and he is not able to know, because they are spiritually discerned" (1 Cor. ii, 14).

Partly a gift, partly acquired.

First of all, the true interpreter needs a disposition to seek and know the truth. No man can properly enter upon the study and exposition of what purports to be the revelation of God while his heart is influenced by any prejudice against it, or hesitates for a moment to accept what commends itself to his conscience and his judgment. There must be a sincere desire and purpose to attain the truth, and cordially accept it when attained. Such a disposition of heart, which may be more or less strong in early childhood, is then easily encouraged and developed, or as easily perverted. Early prejudices and the natural tendency of the human soul to run after that which is evil, rapidly beget habits and dispositions unfriendly to godliness. "For the carnal mind is enmity against God" (Rom. viii, 7), and readily cleaves to that which seems to remove moral obligation. "Every one that does evil hates the light, and comes not to the light lest his deeds should be reproved" (John iii, 20). A soul thus perverted is incompetent to love and search the Scriptures.

Desire to know the truth.

A pure desire to know the truth is enhanced by a tender affection for whatever is morally ennobling. The writings of John abound in passages of tender feeling, and suggest

Tender affection.

how deep natures like his possess an intuition of godliness. Their
souls yearn for the pure and the good, and they exult to find it all
in God. Such tender affection is the seat of all pure love, whether
of God or of man. The characteristic utterance of such a soul is:
"Beloved, let us love one another; because love is of God, and
every one that loves has been begotten of God, and knows God.
. . . God is love; and he that abides in love abides in God, and God
in him" (1 John iv, 7, 16).

The love of the truth should be fervent and glowing, so as to beget in the soul an enthusiasm for the word of God. Enthusiasm for
The mind that truly appreciates the Homeric poems the word.
must imbibe the spirit of Homer. The same is true of him who
delights in the magnificent periods of Demosthenes, the easy numbers and burning thoughts of Shakspeare, or the lofty verse of Milton. What fellowship with such lofty natures can he have whose
soul never kindles with enthusiasm in the study of their works?
So the profound and able exegete is he whose spirit God has
touched, and whose soul is enlivened by the revelations of heaven.

Such hallowed fervour should be chastened and controlled by a
true reverence. "The fear of Jehovah is the begin- Reverence for
ning of knowledge" (Prov. i, 7). There must be the God.
devout frame of mind, as well as the pure desire to know the
truth. "God is a Spirit; and they that worship him must worship
him in spirit and in truth" (John iv, 24). Therefore, they who
would attain the true knowledge of God must possess the reverent, truth-loving spirit; and, having attained this, God will seek
them (John iv, 23) and reveal himself to them as he does not unto
the world. Compare Matt. xi, 25; xvi, 17.

Finally, the expounder of the Holy Scriptures needs to have living fellowship and communion with the Holy Spirit. Communion
Inasmuch as "all Scripture is God-breathed" (2 Tim. with the Holy
iii, 16), and the sacred writers spoke from God as they Spirit.
were moved by the Holy Spirit (2 Peter i, 21), the interpreter of
Scripture must be a partaker of the same Holy Spirit. He must,
by a profound experience of the soul, attain the saving knowledge
of Christ, and in proportion to the depth and fulness of that experience he will know the life and peace of the "mind of the Spirit"
(Rom. viii, 6). "We speak God's wisdom in a mystery," says
Paul (1 Cor. ii, 7-11), the hidden spiritual wisdom of a divinely
illuminated heart, which none of the princes of this world have
known, but (as it is in substance written in Isa. lxiv, 4) a wisdom
relating to "what things (ἅ) eye did not see, and ear did not hear,
and into man's heart did not enter—whatever things (ὅσα) God

prepared for them that love him; for [1] to us God revealed them through the Spirit; for the Spirit searches all things, even the depths of God. For who of men knows the things of the man except the spirit of the man which is in him? So also the things of God no one knows except the Spirit of God." He, then, who would know and explain to others "the mysteries of the kingdom of heaven " (Matt. xiii, 11) must enter into blessed communion and fellowship with the Holy One. He should never cease to pray (Eph. i, 17, 18) "that the God of our Lord Jesus Christ, the Father of glory, would give him the spirit of wisdom and of revelation in the full knowledge (ἐπίγνωσις) of him, the eyes of his heart being enlightened for the purpose of knowing what is the hope of his calling, what the riches of the glory of his inheritance in the saints, and what the exceeding greatness of his power toward us who believe."

[1] We follow here the reading of Westcott and Hort, who receive γάρ into the text. This reading has the strong support of Codex B, and would have been quite liable to be changed to the more numerously supported reading δέ by reason of a failure to apprehend the somewhat involved connection of thought. The γάρ gives the reason *why we speak* God's mysterious wisdom, *for to us God revealed it* through the Spirit.

PART SECOND.

PRINCIPLES OF BIBLICAL HERMENEUTICS.

We count it no gentleness or fair dealing, in a man of power, to require strict and punctual obedience, and yet give out his commands ambiguously. We should think he had a plot upon us. Certainly such commands were no commands, but snares. The very essence of truth is plainness and brightness; the darkness and ignorance are our own. The wisdom of God created understanding, fit and proportionable to truth, the object and end of it, as the eye to the thing visible. If our understanding have a film of ignorance over it, or be blear with gazing on other false glisterings, what is that to truth? If we will but purge with sovereign eye-salve that intellectual ray which God hath planted in us, then we would believe the Scriptures protesting their own plainness and perspicuity, calling to them to be instructed, not only the wise and the learned, but the simple, the poor, the babes; foretelling an extraordinary effusion of God's Spirit upon every age and sect, attributing to all men and requiring from them the ability of searching, trying, examining all things, and by the Spirit discerning that which is good.—MILTON.

PRINCIPLES

OF

BIBLICAL HERMENEUTICS.

CHAPTER I.

PRELIMINARY.

THE Principles of Biblical Hermeneutics are those governing laws and methods of procedure by which the interpreter determines the meaning of the Holy Scriptures. These principles are of the nature of comprehensive and fundamental doctrines. They become to the practical exegete so many maxims, postulates, and settled rules. He is supposed to hold them in the mind as axioms, and to apply them in all his expositions with uniform consistency.[1]

Hermeneutical principles defined.

The importance of establishing sound and trustworthy principles of biblical exposition is universally conceded. For it is evident that a false principle in his method will necessarily vitiate the entire exegetical process of an interpreter. When we find that in the explanation of certain parts of the Scriptures no two interpreters out of a whole class agree, we have great reason to presume at once that some fatal error lurks in their principles of interpretation. We cannot believe that the sacred writers desired to be misunderstood. They did not write with a purpose to confuse and mislead their readers. Nor is it reasonable to suppose that the Scripture, given by divine inspiration, is of the nature of a puzzle designed to exercise the ingenuity of critics. It was given to make men wise unto salvation, and in great part it is so direct and simple in its teachings that a little child can understand its meaning. But the Bible contains some riddles and dark sayings, and many revelations in the form of types, symbols, parables, allegories, visions, and dreams, and the interpre-

Importance of sound principles.

---

[1] "The perfect understanding of a discourse," says Schleiermacher, "is a work of art, and involves the need of an art-doctrine, which we designate by the term Hermeneutics. Such an art-doctrine has existence only in so far as the precepts admitted form a system resting upon principles which are immediately evident from the nature of thought and language."—Outline of the Study of Theology," p. 142. Edinb., 1850.

tation of these has exercised the most gifted minds. Many different and often contradictory methods of exposition have been adopted, and some enthusiasts have gone to the extreme of affirming that there are manifold meanings and :"mountains of sense" in every line of Scripture. Under the spell of some such fascination many have been strangely misled, and have set forth as expositions of the Scriptures their own futile fancies.[1]

Sound hermeneutical principles are, therefore, elements of safety True method and satisfaction in the study of God's written word. of determining But how are such principles to be ascertained and es-sound princi-ples. tablished? How may we determine what is true and what is false in the various methods of exposition? We must go to the Scriptures themselves, and search them in all their parts and forms. We must seek to ascertain the principles which the sacred writers followed. Naked propositions, or formulated rules of interpretation, will be of little or no worth unless supported and illustrated by self-verifying examples. It is worthy of note that the Scriptures furnish repeated examples of the formal interpretation of dreams, visions, types, symbols, and parables. In such examples we are especially to seek our fundamental and controlling laws of exposition. Unless we find clear warrant for it in the word itself, we should never allow that any one passage or sentiment of divine revelation has more than one true import. The Holy Scripture is no Delphic oracle to bewilder and mislead the human heart by utterances of double meaning. God's written word, taken as a whole, and allowed to speak for itself, will be found to be its own best interpreter.

The process of observing the laws of thought and language, as Ennobling ten-exhibited in the Holy Scriptures, is an ennobling study. dency of her-meneutical It affords an edifying intercourse with eminent and study. choice spirits of the past, and compels us for the time to lose sight of temporary interests, and to become absorbed with the thoughts and feelings of other ages. He who forms the habit of studying not only the divine thoughts of revelation, but also the principles and methods according to which those thoughts have been expressed, will acquire a moral and intellectual culture worthy of the noblest ambition.

[1] Lange suggestively remarks: "As the sun in the earthly heavens has to break through many cloudy media, so also does the divine word of Holy Scripture through the confusion of every kind which arises from the soil of earthly intuition and representation." Grundriss der biblischen Hermeneutik, p. 77.

CHAPTER II.

DIFFERENT METHODS OF INTERPRETATION.

IN proceding to ascertain the principles of a valid and self-consistent Scripture exegesis, we do well to know beforehand something of the diverse methods and systems of interpretation which have been followed by others. A brief survey of these will be a help both in avoiding false principles and in apprehending the true.

The allegorical method of interpretation obtained an early prominence among the Jews of Alexandria. Its origin is usually attributed to the mingling of Greek philosophy and the biblical conceptions of God. Many of the theophanies and anthropomorphisms of the Old Testament were repugnant to the philosophic mind, and hence the effort to discover behind the outer form an inner substance of truth. The biblical narratives were often treated like the Greek myths, and explained as either a historical or an enigmatical embodiment of moral and religious lessons. The most distinguished representative of Jewish allegorical interpretation was Philo of Alexandria, and an example of his allegorizing many be seen in the following remarks on the rivers of Eden (Gen. ii, 10–14):

In these words Moses intends to sketch out the particular virtues. And they, also, are four in number, prudence, temperance, courage, and justice. Now the greatest river, from which the four branches flow off, is generic virtue, which we have already called goodness; and the four branches are the same number of virtues. Generic virtue, therefore, derives its beginning from Eden, which is the wisdom of God; which rejoices, and exults, and triumphs, being delighted at and honoured on account of nothing else, except its Father, God. And the four particular virtues are branches from the generic virtue, which, like a river, waters all the good actions of each with an abundant stream of benefits.[1]

Similar allegorizing abounds in the early Christian fathers. Thus, Clement of Alexandria, commenting on the Mosaic prohibition of eating the swine, the hawk, the eagle, and the raven, observes: "The sow is the emblem of voluptuous and unclean lust of food. . . . The eagle indicates robbery, the hawk injustice, and the raven greed." On Exod. xv, 1, "Jehovah has triumphed gloriously; the horse and his rider has he thrown into the sea," Clement remarks:

[1] The Allegories of the Sacred Laws, book i, 19 (Bohn's edition).

The many-limbed and brutal affection, lust, with the rider mounted, who gives the reins to pleasures, he casts into the sea—throwing them away into the disorders of the world. Thus, also, Plato, in his book on the soul [Timæus], says that the charioteer and the horse that ran off—(the irrational part, which is divided into two, into anger and concupiscence)—fall down; and so the myth intimates that it was through the licentiousness of the steeds that Phaëthon was thrown out.[1]

The allegorical method of interpretation is based upon a profound reverence for the Scriptures, and a desire to exhibit their manifold depths of wisdom. But it will be noticed at once that its habit is to disregard the common signification of words, and give wing to all manner of fanciful speculation. It does not draw out the legitimate meaning of an author's language, but foists into it whatever the whim or fancy of an interpreter may desire. As a system, therefore, it puts itself beyond all well-defined principles and laws.

Closely allied to the allegorical interpretation is the Mystical,[2] Mystical interpretation. according to which manifold depths and shades of meaning are sought in every word of Scripture. The allegorical interpreters have, accordingly, very naturally run into much that is to be classed with mystical theorizing. Clement of Alexandria maintained that the laws of Moses contain a fourfold significance, the natural, the mystical, the moral, and the prophetical. Origen held that, as man's nature consists of body, soul, and spirit, so the Scriptures have a corresponding threefold sense, the bodily (σωματικός), or literal, the psychical (ψυχικός), or moral, and the spiritual (πνευματικός), which latter he further distinguishes as allegorical, tropological, and anagogical. In the early part of the ninth century the learned Rhabanus Maurus recommended four methods of exposition, the historical, the allegorical, the anagogical, and the tropological. He observes:

By these the mother Wisdom feeds the sons of her adoption. Upon youth and those of tender age she bestows drink, in the milk of history; on such as have made proficiency in faith, food, in the bread of allegory; to the good, such as strenuously labour in good works, she gives a satisfying portion in the savoury nourishment of tropology. To those, in fine, who have raised themselves above the common level of humanity by a contempt of earthly things, and have advanced to the highest by heavenly desires, she gives the sober intoxication of theoretic contemplation in the wine of anagogy. . . . History, which narrates examples of perfect men,

[1] Miscellanies, book v, chap. viii.
[2] According to Ernesti, the mystical interpretation differs from the allegorical, as among the Greeks θεωρία differs from ἀλληγορία. Institutes, chap. ix, 3.

excites the reader to imitate their sanctity; allegory excites him to know the truth in the revelation of faith; tropology encourages him to the love of virtue by improving the morals; and anagogy promotes the longing after eternal happiness by revealing everlasting joys. . . . Since then, it appears that these four modes of understanding the Holy Scriptures unveil all the secret things in them, we should consider when they are to be understood according to one of them only, when according to two, when according to three, and when according to all the four together.[1]

Among the mystical interpreters we may also place the celebrated Emanuel Swedenborg, who maintains a three-fold sense of Scripture, according to what he calls "the Science of Correspondencies." As there are three heavens, a lowest, a middle, and a highest, so there are three senses of the Word, the natural or literal, the spiritual, and the celestial. He says: *Swedenborgian interpretation.*

The Word in the letter is like a casket, where lie in order precious stones, pearls, and diadems; and when a man esteems the Word holy, and reads it for the sake of the uses of life, the thoughts of his mind are, comparatively, like one who holds such a cabinet in his hand, and sends it heavenward; and it is opened in its ascent, and the precious things therein come to the angels, who are deeply delighted with seeing and examining them. This delight of the angels is communicated to the man, and makes consociation, and also a communication of perceptions.[2]

He explains the commandment "Thou shalt not kill" (Exod. xx, 13), first, in its natural sense, as forbidding murder and also the cherishing of hatred and revenge; secondly, in the spiritual sense, as forbidding "to act the devil and destroy a man's soul;" and thirdly, in the celestial or heavenly sense, the angels understand killing to signify hating the Lord and the Word.

Somewhat allied to the mystical is that Pietistic mode of exposition, according to which the interpreter claims to be guided by an "inward light," received as "an unction from the Holy One" (1 John ii, 20). The rules of grammar and the common meaning and usage of words are discarded, and the internal Light of the Spirit is held to be the abiding and infallible Revealer. Some of the later Pietists of Germany, and the Quakers of England and America have been especially given to this mode of handling the Scriptures.[3] It is certainly to be supposed that *Pietistic interpretation.*

---

[1] From Maurus, Allegoriae in Universam Sacram Scripturam, as given in Davidson, Hermeneutics, pp. 165, 166.

[2] The True Christian Religion, chap. iv, 6.

[3] From pietistic extravagance we of course except such men as Spener and A. H. Francke, the great leaders of what is known as Pietism in Germany. The noble practical character of their work and teaching saved them from the excesses into which most of those run who are commonly called Pietists. "The principal efforts of the

this holy inward light would never contradict itself, or guide its followers into different expositions of the same scripture. But the divergent and irreconcilable interpretations prevalent among the adherents of this system show that the "inward light" is untrustworthy. Like the allegorical and mystical systems of interpretation, Pietism concedes the sanctity of the Scriptures, and seeks in them the lessons of eternal life; but as to principles and rules of exegesis it is more lawless and irrational. The Allegorist professes to follow certain analogies and correspondencies, but the Quaker-Pietist is a law unto himself, and his own subjective feeling or fancy is the end of controversy. He sets himself up as a new oracle, and while assuming to follow the written word of God, puts forth his own *dictum* as a further revelation. Such a procedure, of course, can never commend itself to the common sense and the rational judgment.

A method of exposition, which owes its distinction to the celebrated J. S. Semler, the father of the destructive school of German Accommoda- Rationalism, is known as the Accommodation Theory. tion Theory. According to this theory the Scripture teachings respecting miracles, vicarious and expiatory sacrifice, the resurrection, eternal judgment, and the existence of angels and demons, are to be regarded as an accommodation to the superstitious notions, prejudices, and ignorance of the times. The supernatural was thus set aside. Semler became possessed with the idea that we must distinguish between religion and theology, and between personal piety and the public teaching of the Church. He rejected the doctrine of the Divine inspiration of the Scriptures, and argued that, as the Old Testament was written for the Jews, whose religious notions were narrow and faulty, we cannot accept its teachings as a general rule of faith. Matthew's Gospel, he held, was intended for Jews outside of Palestine, and John's Gospel for Christians who had more or less of Grecian culture. Paul at first adapted himself to Jewish modes of thought with the hope of winning over many of his countrymen to Christianity, but failing in this, he turned to the Gentiles, and became pre-eminent in holding up Christianity as the religion for all men. The different books of Scripture were, accordingly, designed to serve only a temporary

---

Pietists," says Immer, "were directed toward the edificatory application of Scripture, as may be seen from Francke's Manuductio ad Lectionem Scripturae Sacrae. This predominance of effort at edification soon degenerated into indifference to science, and at last into proud contempt of it. Mystical and typological trifling arose; chiliastic phantasies found great acceptance; the Scriptures were not so much explained as overwhelmed with pious reflections." Hermeneutics, p. 46.

purpose, and many of their statements may be summarily set aside as untrue.

The fatal objection to this method of interpretation is that it necessarily impugns the veracity and honour of the sacred writers, and of the Son of God himself. It represents them as conniving at the errors and ignorance of men, and confirming them and the readers of the Scriptures in such ignorance and error. If such a principle be admitted into our expositions of the Bible, we at once lose our moorings, and drift out upon an open sea of conjecture and uncertainty.

A passing notice should also be taken of what is commonly called the Moral Interpretation, and which owes its origin to Moral Interpretation of Kant. the celebrated philosopher of Königsberg, Immanuel Kant. The prominence given to the pure reason, and the idealism maintained in his metaphysical system, naturally led to the practice of making the Scriptures bend to the preconceived demands of reason. For, although the whole Scripture be given by inspiration of God, it has for its practical value and purpose the moral improvement of man. Hence, if the literal and historical sense of a given passage yield no profitable moral lesson, such as commends itself to the practical reason, we are at liberty to set it aside, and attach to the words such a meaning as is compatible with the religion of reason. It is maintained that such expositions are not to be charged with insincerity, inasmuch as they are not to be set forth as the meaning strictly intended by the sacred writers, but only as a meaning which the writers may possibly have intended.[1] The only real value of the Scriptures is to illustrate and confirm the religion of reason.

It is easy to see that such a system of interpretation, which professedly ignores the grammatical and historical sense of the Bible, can have no reliable or self-consistent rules. Like the mystical and allegorical methods, it leaves every thing subject to the peculiar faith or fancy of the interpreter.

So open to criticism and objection are all the above-mentioned methods of interpretation, that we need not be surprised to find them offset by other extremes. Of all rationalistic theories the

---

[1] See Kant, Religion innerhalb der Grenzen der blossen Vernunft, p. 161. This "was the work of his old age, and at all periods of his life he seems to have been at least as deficient in religious sentiment as in emotional imagination, which is allied to it. . . . It treats the revelations of Scripture in regard to the fall of man, to his redemption, and to his restoration, as a moral allegory, the data of which are supplied by the consciousness of depravity, and of dereliction from the strict principles of duty. It is Strauss in the germ." M'Clintock and Strong's Cyclopædia, article Kant.

Naturalistic is the most violent and radical. A rigid application
Naturalistic In- of this theory is exhibited in Paulus' Commentary on
terpretation.   the New Testament,[1] in which it is maintained that the
biblical critic should always distinguish between what is fact and
what is mere opinion. He accepts the historical truth of the Gospel
narratives, but holds that the mode of accounting for them is a matter of opinion. He rejects all supernatural agency in human affairs,
and explains the miracles of Jesus either as acts of kindness, or exhibitions of medical skill, or illustrations of personal sagacity and
tact, recorded in a manner peculiar to the age and opinions of the
different writers. Jesus' walking on the sea was really a walking on
the shore; but the boat was all the time so near the shore, that when
Peter jumped into the sea Jesus could reach and rescue him from the
shore. The excitement was so great, and the impression on the disciples so deep, that it seemed to them as if Jesus had miraculously
walked on the sea, and come to their help. The apparent miracle of
making five loaves feed five thousand people was done simply by the
example, which Jesus bade his disciples set, of distributing of their
own little store to those immediately about them. This example was
promptly followed by other companies, and it was found that there
was more than sufficient food for all. Lazarus did not really die, but
fell into a swoon, and was supposed to be dead. But Jesus suspected
the real state of the case, and coming to the tomb at the opportune
moment, happily found that his suspicions were correct; and his wisdom and power in the case made a profound and lasting impression.

The style of exposition, however, was soon seen to set at naught
the rational laws of human speech, and to undermine the credibility
of all ancient history. It exposed the sacred books to all manner
of ridicule and satire, and only for a little time awakened any considerable interest.

The Naturalistic method of interpretation was followed by the
The Mythical Mythical. Its most distinguished representative was
Theory.   David Friedrich Strauss, whose Life of Jesus (Das Leben
Jesu), first published in 1835, created a profound sensation in the
Christian world. The Mythical theory, as developed and rigidly
carried out by Strauss, was a logical and self-consistent application
to biblical exposition of the Hegelian (pantheistic) doctrine that the
idea of God and of the absolute is neither shot forth miraculously,
nor revealed in the individual, but developed in the consciousness
of humanity. According to Strauss, the Messianic idea was gradually developed in the expectations and yearnings of the Jewish

[1] Philologisch-kritischer und historischer Commentar über das neue Testament.
4 vols. 1800–1804.

nation, and at the time Jesus appeared it was ripening into full maturity. The Christ was to spring from the line of David, be born at Bethlehem, be a prophet like Moses, and speak words of infallible wisdom. His age should be full of signs and wonders. The eyes of the blind should be opened, the ears of the deaf should be unstopped, and the tongue of the dumb should sing. Amid these hopes and expectations Jesus arose, an Israelite of remarkable beauty and force of character, who, by his personal excellence and wise discourse, made an overwhelming impression upon his immediate friends and followers. After his decease, his disciples not only yielded to the conviction that he must have risen from the dead, but began at once to associate with him all their Messianic ideals. Their argument was: "Such and such things must have pertained to the Christ; Jesus was the Christ; therefore such and such things happened to him."[1] The visit of the wise men from the East was suggested by Balaam's prophecy of the "star out of Jacob" (Num. xxiv, 17). The flight of the holy family into Egypt was worked up out of Moses' flight into Midian; and the slaughter of the infants of Bethlehem out of Pharaoh's order to destroy every male among the infant Israelites of Egypt. The miraculous feeding of the five thousand with a few loaves of bread was appropriated from the Old Testament story of the manna. The transfiguration in the high mountain apart was drawn from the accounts of Moses and Elijah in the mount of God. In short, Christ did not institute the Christian Church, and send forth his gospel, as narrated in the New Testament; rather, the Christ of the Gospels was the mythical creation of the early Church. Adoring enthusiasts clothed the memory of the man Jesus with all that could enhance his name and character as the Messiah of the world. But what is fact and what is fiction must be determined by critical analysis. Sometimes it may be impossible to draw the dividing line.

Among the criteria by which we are to distinguish the mythical, Strauss instances the following: A narrative is not his- Strauss' criteria of myths. torical (1) when its statements are irreconcilable with the known and universal laws which govern the course of events; (2) when it is inconsistent with itself or with other accounts of the same thing; (3) when the actors converse in poetry or elevated discourse unsuitable to their training and situation; (4) when the essential substance and groundwork of a reported occurrence is either inconceivable in itself, or is in striking harmony with some Messianic idea of the Jews of that age.[2]

[1] See Life of Jesus, Introduction, § 14.
[2] Ibid., Introduction, § 16.

We need not here enter upon a detailed exposure of the fallacies of this mythical theory. It is sufficient to observe, on the four critical rules enumerated above, that the first dogmatically denies the possibility of miracles; the second (especially as used by Strauss) virtually assumes, that when two accounts disagree, both must be false! the third is worthless until it is clearly shown what is suitable or unsuitable in each given case; and the fourth, when reduced to the last analysis, will be found to be simply an appeal to one's subjective notions. To these considerations we add that the Gospel portraiture of Jesus is notably unlike the prevalent Jewish conception of the Messiah at that time. It. is too perfect and marvellous to have been the product of any human fancy. Myths arise only in unhistoric ages, and a long time after the persons or events they represent, whereas Jesus lived and wrought his wonderful works in a most critical period of Greek and Roman civilization. Furthermore, the New Testament writings were published too soon after the actual appearance of Jesus to embody such a mythical development as Strauss assumes. While attempting to show how the Church spontaneously originated the Christ of the gospels, this whole theory fails to show any sufficient cause or explanation of the origin of the Church and of Christianity itself. The mythical interpretation, after half a century of learned labours, has notably failed to commend itself to the judgment of Christian scholars, and has few advocates at the present time.

The four last-named methods of interpretation may all be designated as Rationalistic; but under this name we may also place some other methods which agree with the naturalistic, the mythical, the moral, and the accommodation theories, in denying the supernatural element in the Bible. The peculiar methods by which F. C. Baur, Renan, Schenkel, and other rationalistic critics have attempted to portray the life of Jesus, and to account for the origin of the Gospels, the Acts, and the Epistles, often involve correspondingly peculiar principles of interpretation. All these writers, however, proceed with assumptions which virtually beg the questions at issue between the naturalist and the supernaturalist. But they all conspicuously differ among themselves. Baur rejects the mythical theory of Strauss, and finds the origin of many of the New Testament writings in the Petrine and Pauline factions of the early Church. These factions arose over the question of abolishing the Old Testament ceremonial and the rite of circumcision. The Acts of the Apostles is regarded as the monument of a pacification between these rival parties, effected in the early part of the second century. The book is treated as largely a fiction, in which the author, a disciple of Paul, represents Peter as the first to preach the Gospel to the Gentiles, and exhibits Paul as conforming to divers Jewish customs, thus securing a reconciliation between the Pauline and Petrine Christians.[1] Renan, on the other hand, maintains a legendary theory of the origin of the gospels, and attributes the miracles of Jesus, like the marvels of mediæval saints, partly to the blind adoration and enthusiasm of his followers, and partly to pious fraud. Schenkel essays to make the life and character of Christ intelligible by stripping it of the divine and the miraculous, and presenting him as a mere man.

Against all these rationalistic theories it is obvious to remark that they exclude and destroy each other. Strauss exploded the naturalistic method of Paulus, and Baur shows that the mythical theory of Strauss is untenable. Renan pronounces against the theories of Baur, and exposes the glaring fallacy of making the Petrine and Pauline factions account for the origin of the New Testament books, and the books account for the factions. Renan's own methods of criticism appear to be utterly lawless, and his light and captious remarks have led many of his readers to feel that he is destitute of any serious or sacred convictions, and that he would readily make use of furtive means to gain his end. He is continually foisting into the Scriptures meanings of his own, and making the writers say what was probably never in their thoughts. He assumes, for instance, as a teaching of Jesus, that the rich man was sent to Hades because he was rich, and Lazarus was glorified because he was a pauper. Many of his interpretations are based upon the most unwarrantable assumptions, and are unworthy of any serious attempt at refutation. The logical issue lies far back of his exegesis, in the fundamental questions of a personal God and an overruling providence.

Sceptical and rationalistic assaults upon the Scriptures have called out a method of interpretation which may be called Apologetic. It assumes to defend at all hazards the authenticity, genuineness, and credibility of every document incorporated in the sacred canon, and its standpoint and methods are so akin to that of the Dogmatic exposition of the Bible, that we present the two together. The objectionable feature of these methods is that they virtually set out with the ostensible purpose of maintaining a preconceived hypothesis. The hypothesis may be right, but the procedure is always liable to mislead. It

Apologetic and Dogmatic methods.

---

[1] Several notions of the Tübingen critical school, represented by Baur, may be found in substance among the teachings of Semler, the author of this destructive species of criticism.

presents the constant temptation to *find* desired meanings in words, and ignore the scope and general purpose of the writer. There are cases where it is well to assume a hypothesis, and use it as a means of investigation; but in all such cases the hypothesis is only assumed tentatively, not affirmed dogmatically. In the exposition of the Bible, apology and dogma have a legitimate place. The true apology defends the sacred books against an unreasonable and captious criticism, and presents their claims to be regarded as the revelation of God. But this can be done only by pursuing rational methods, and by the use of a convincing logic. So also the Scriptures are profitable for dogma, but the dogma must be shown to be a legitimate teaching of the Scripture, not a traditional idea attached to the Scripture. The extermination of the Canaanites, the immolation of Jephthah's daughter, the polygamy of the Old Testament saints, and their complicity with slavery, are capable of rational explanation, and, in that sense, of a valid apology. The true apologist will not attempt to justify the cruelties of the ancient wars, or hold that Israel had a legal right to Canaan; he will not seek to evade the obvious import of language, and maintain that Jephthah's daughter was not offered at all, but became a Jewish nun; nor will he find it necessary to defend the Old Testament practice of polygamy, or of slavery. He will let facts and statements stand in their own light, but guard against false inferences and rash conclusions. So also the doctrines of the Trinity, the divinity of Christ, the personality of the Holy Spirit, the vicarious atonement, justification, regeneration, sanctification, and the resurrection, have a firm foundation in the Scriptures; but how unscientific and objectionable many of the methods by which these and other doctrines have been maintained! When a theologian assumes the standpoint of an ecclesiastical creed, and thence proceeds, with a polemic air, to search for single texts of Scripture favourable to himself or unfavourable to his opponent, he is more than likely to overdo the matter. His creed may be as true as the Bible itself; but his method is reprehensible. Witness the disputes of Luther and Zwingle over the matter of consubstantiation. Read the polemic literature of the Antinomian, the Calvinistic, and the Sacramentarian controversies. The whole Bible is ransacked and treated as if it were an atomical collection of dogmatic proof-texts. How hard is it, even at this day, for the polemic divine to concede the spuriousness of 1 John v, 7. It should be remembered that no apology is sound, and no doctrine sure, which rests upon uncritical methods, or proceeds upon dogmatical assumptions. Such procedures are not exposition, but imposition.

In distinction from all the above-mentioned methods of interpretation, we may name the Grammatico-Historical as the method which most fully commends itself to the judgment and conscience of Christian scholars. Its fundamental principle is to gather from the Scriptures themselves the precise meaning which the writers intended to convey. It applies to the sacred books the same principles, the same grammatical process and exercise of common sense and reason, which we apply to other books. The grammatico-historical exegete, furnished with suitable qualifications, intellectual, educational, and moral,[1] will accept the claims of the Bible without prejudice or adverse prepossession, and, with no ambition to prove them true or false, will investigate the language and import of each book with fearless independence. He will master the language of the writer, the particular dialect which he used, and his peculiar style and manner of expression. He will inquire into the circumstances under which he wrote, the manners and customs of his age, and the purpose or object which he had in view. He has a right to assume that no sensible author will be knowingly inconsistent with himself, or seek 'to bewilder and mislead his readers.

Grammatico-Historical Interpretation.

"Nearly all the treatises on hermeneutics," says Moses Stuart, "since the days of Ernesti, have laid it down as a maxim which cannot be controverted, that the Bible is to be interpreted in the same manner, that is, by the same principles, as all other books. Writers are not wanting, previously to the period in which Ernesti lived, who have maintained the same thing; but we may also find some who have assailed the position before us, and laboured to show that it is nothing less than a species of profaneness to treat the sacred books as we do the classic authors with respect to their interpretation. Is this allegation well grounded? Is there any good reason to object to the principle of interpretation now in question? In order to answer, let us direct our attention to the nature and source of what are now called principles or laws of interpretation: Whence did they originate? Are they the artificial production of high-wrought skill, of laboured research, of profound and extensive learning? Did they spring from the subtleties of nice distinctions, from the philosophical and metaphysical efforts of the schools? Are they the product of exalted and dazzling genius, sparks of celestial fire, which none but a favoured few can emit? No; nothing of all this. The principles of interpretation, as to their substantial and essential elements, are no invention of man, no product of his effort and learned skill;

The Bible to be interpreted like other books.

[1] Compare pp. 151-158 on the Qualifications of an Interpreter.

nay, they can scarcely be said with truth to have been discovered by him. They are coeval with our nature. Ever since man was created and endowed with the powers of speech, and made a *communicative*, social being, he has had occasion to practice upon the principles of interpretation, and has actually done so. From the first moment that one human being addressed another by the use of language down to the present hour, the essential laws of interpretation became, and have continued to be, a practical matter. The person addressed has always been an *interpreter* in every instance where he has heard and understood what was addressed to him. All the human race, therefore, are, and ever have been, interpreters. It is a law of their rational, intelligent, communicative nature. Just as truly as one human being was formed so as to address another in language, just so truly that other was formed to interpret and understand what is said.

"I venture to advance a step farther and to aver that all men are, and ever have been, in reality, good and true interpreters of each other's language. Has any part of our race, in full possession of the human faculties, ever failed to understand what others said to them, and to understand it truly? or to make themselves understood by others, when they have in their communications kept within the circle of their own knowledge? Surely none. Interpretation, then, in its basis or fundamental principles, is a native art, if I may so speak. It is coeval with the power of uttering words. It is, of course, a universal art; it is common to all nations, barbarous as well as civilized. One cannot commit a more palpable error in relation to this subject than to suppose that the art of interpretation is . . . in itself wholly dependent on acquired skill for the discovery and development of its principles. Acquired skill has indeed helped to an orderly exhibition and arrangement of its principles; but this is all. The materials were all in existence before skill attempted to develop them. . . . An interpreter, well skilled in his art, will glory in it, that it is an art which has its foundation in the laws of our intellectual and rational nature, and is coeval and connate with this nature." [1]

So far, indeed, as the Bible may differ from other books in its supernatural revelations, its symbols and peculiar claims, it may require some corresponding principles of exposition; but none, we believe, which require us to turn aside from the propositions here affirmed.

---

[1] "Are the same principles of interpretation to be applied to the Scriptures as to other books?" Article by Prof. M. Stuart in the American Biblical Repository for Jan., 1832, pp. 124–126. See also Hahn, On the Grammatico-Historical Interpretation of the Scriptures, in the same Repository for Jan., 1831.

CHAPTER III.

THE PRIMARY MEANING OF WORDS.

IN a previous chapter of this work[1] we showed how new languages originate; how they become modified and changed; how new dialects arise, and how, at length, a national form of speech may go out of use and become known as a dead language. Attention to these facts makes it apparent that any given language is an accumulation and aggregate of words which a nation or community of people use for the interchange and expression of their thoughts. "Language," says Whitney, "has, in fact, no existence save in the minds and mouths of those who use it; it is made up of separate articulated signs of thought, each of which is attached by a mental association to the idea it represents, is uttered by voluntary effort, and has its value and currency only by the agreement of speakers and hearers."[2]

Words practically the elements of language.

To understand, therefore, the language of a speaker or writer, it is necessary, first of all, to know the meaning of his words. The interpreter, especially, needs to keep in mind the difference, so frequently apparent, between the primitive signification of a word and that which it subsequently obtains. We first naturally inquire after the original meaning of a word, or what is commonly called its etymology. Next we examine the *usus loquendi*, or actual meaning which it bears in common usage; and then we are prepared to understand the occasion and import of synonymes, and how a language becomes enriched by them.

Etymology, usus loquendi, and synonymes.

Whatever may be the common meaning of a word, as used by a particular people or age, it often represents a history. Language has been significantly characterized as fossil poetry, fossil history, fossil ethics, fossil philosophy. "This means," says Trench, "that just as in some fossil, curious and beautiful shapes of vegetable or animal life, the graceful fern, or the finely vertebrated lizard, extinct, it may be, for thousands of years, are permanently bound up with the stone, and rescued from that perishing which would have otherwise been theirs, so in words are

Manifold value of etymology.

[1] Part I, chap. iii, pp. 72, 73.
[2] Language and the Study of Language, p. 35.

beautiful thoughts and images, the imagination and feeling of past ages, of men whose very names have perished, preserved and made safe forever."[1] Benjamin W. Dwight declares etymology to be "fossil poetry, philosophy, and history combined. In the treasured words of the past, the very spirits of elder days look out upon us, as from so many crystalline spheres, with friendly recognition. We see in them the light of their eyes; we feel in them the warmth of their hearts. They are relics, they are tokens, and almost break into life again at our touch. The etymologist unites in himself the characteristics of the traveller, roaming through strange and far-off climes; the philosopher, prying into the causes and sequences of things; the antiquary, filling his cabinet with ancient curiosities and wonders; the historiographer, gathering up the records of by-gone men and ages; and the artist, studying the beautiful designs in word-architecture furnished him by various nations."

Take, for example, that frequently occurring New Testament word ἐκκλησία, commonly rendered *church*. Compounded of ἐκ, *out of*, and καλεῖν, to *call*, or *summon*, it was first used of an assembly of the citizens of a Greek community, summoned together by a crier, for the transaction of business pertaining to the public welfare. The preposition ἐκ indicates that it was no motley crowd,[2] no mass-meeting of nondescripts, but a select company gathered *out from* the common mass; it was an assembly of free citizens, possessed of well-understood legal rights and powers. The verb καλεῖν denotes that the assembly was legally *called* (compare the ἐν τῇ ἐννόμῳ ἐκκλησίᾳ of Acts xix, 39), summoned for the purpose of deliberating in lawful conclave. Whether the etymological connexion between the Hebrew קָהָל and the Greek καλεῖν be vital or merely accidental, the Septuagint translators generally render קָהָל by ἐκκλησία, and thus by an obvious process, ἐκκλησία came to represent among the Hellenists the Old Testament conception of "the congregation of the people of Israel," as usually denoted by the Hebrew word קָהָל. Hence it was natural for Stephen to speak of the congregation of Israel, which Moses led out of Egypt, as "the ἐκκλησία in the wilderness" (Acts vii, 38), and equally natural for the word to become the common designation of the Christian community of converts from Judaism and the world. Into this New Testament sense of the word, it was also important that the full force of ἐκ and καλεῖν (κλῆσις, κλητός) should continue.

---

[1] The Study of Words. Introductory Lecture, p. 12. New York, 1861.

[2] Article on The Science of Etymology, in Bibliotheca Sacra, April, 1858, p. 438.

[3] Compare the *confused assembly*, ἡ ἐκκλησία συνκεχυμένη, composed of *the multitude*, ὁ ὄχλος, in Acts xix, 32, 33, 40.

As the old Greek assembly was called by a public herald (κῆρυξ), so "the Church of God (or of the Lord), which he purchased with his own blood" (Acts xx, 28), is the congregation of those who are "called to be saints" (κλητοὶ ἁγίοι, Rom. i, 7), "called out of darkness into his marvellous light" (1 Pet. ii, 9), called "unto his kingdom and glory" (1 Thess. ii, 12), and called by the voice of an authorized herald or preacher (Rom. x, 14, 15; 1 Tim. ii, 7).[1] With this fundamental idea the church may denote either the small assembly in a private house (Rom. xvi, 5; Philemon 2), the Christian congregations of particular towns and cities (1 Cor. i, 2; 1 Thess. i, 1), or the Church universal (Eph. i, 22; iii, 21). But a new idea is added when our Lord says, "I will build my Church" (Matt. xvi, 18). Here the company of the saints (κλητοὶ ἁγίοι) is conceived of as a house, a stately edifice; and it was peculiarly fitting that Peter, the disciple to whom these words were addressed, should afterward write to the general Church, and designate it not only as "a chosen generation, a royal priesthood, a holy nation," but also as "a spiritual house," builded of living stones (1 Pet. ii, 5, 9). Paul also uses the same grand image, and speaks of the household of God as "having been built upon the foundation of the apostles and prophets, Jesus Christ himself being the chief corner stone, in whom all the building, fitly framed together, grows unto a living temple in the Lord" (Eph. ii, 20, 21). And then again, to this image of a building (comp. 1 Cor. iii, 9) he also adds that of a living human body of which Christ is the head, defining the whole as "his body, the fulness (πλήρωμα) of him who fills all things in all" (Eph. i, 23). Comp. also Rom. xii, 5; 1 Cor. xii, 12–28; and Col. i, 18.

Observe also the forms and derivatives of the Hebrew כָּפַר, *to cover.* The primary meaning is to *cover over*, so as to hide from view. The ark was thus covered or overlaid with a covering of some material like pitch (Gen. vi, 14). Then it came to be used of a flower or shrub, with the resin or powder of which oriental females are said to have covered and stained their finger nails (Cant. i, 14). Again we find it applied to villages or hamlets (1 Sam. vi, 18; 1 Chron. xxvii, 25), apparently, as Gesenius suggests, because such places were regarded as a covering or shelter to the inhabitants. The verb is also used of the abolishing or setting aside of a covenant (Isa. xxviii, 18). But the deeper meaning of the word is that of covering, or hiding sin, and thus making an atonement. Thus Jacob thought to *cover* his brother Esau with a present (Gen. xxxii, 20). His words are, literally, "I will cover his face with the present which goes before

כָּפַר, the covering of atonement.

---

[1] A similar interesting history attaches to the words κῆρυξ and κηρύσσω.

me, and afterward I will see his face; perhaps he will lift up my face." Feeling that he had sorely wronged his brother, he would now fain cover his face with such a princely gift that Esau would no more behold those wrongs of the past. His old offences being thus hidden, he hopes to be permitted to see his brother's face in peace; and perhaps even Esau will condescend to lift up his face—raise from the dust the face of the prostrate and penitent Jacob. The transition was easy from this use of the verb to that of *making an atonement*, a meaning which it constantly conveys in the books of the law (Lev. xvii, 11). And hence the use of the noun כֹּפֶר in the sense of *ransom, satisfaction* (Exod. xxx, 12), and the plural כִּפֻּרִים, *atonements* (Exod. xxx, 10; Lev. xxiii, 27, 28). Hence, also, that word of profound significance, כַּפֹּרֶת, *capporeth*, the *mercy-seat*, the lid or cover of the ark which contained the tables of the law (Exod. xxv, 17–22)—the symbol of mercy covering wrath.

Additional interest is given to the study of words by the science of comparative philology. In tracing a word through a whole family of languages, we note not only the variety of forms it may have taken, but the different usage and shades of meaning it acquired among different peoples. The Hebrew words אָב, *father*, and בֵּן, *son*, are traceable through all the Semitic tongues, and maintain their common signification in all. The Greek word for *heart*, καρδία, appears also in the Sanskrit *hrid*, Latin *cor*, Italian *cuore*, Spanish *corazon*, Portuguese, *coraçam*, French *cœur*, and English *core*. Some words, especially verbs, acquire new meanings as they pass from one language to another. Hence the meaning which a word bears in Arabic or Syriac may not be the meaning it was designed to convey in Hebrew. Thus the Hebrew word עָמַד is frequently used in the Old Testament in the sense *to stand*, to *be firm*, to *stand up;* and this general idea can be traced in the corresponding word and its derivatives in the Arabic, Ethiopic (to *erect a column*, to *establish*), Chaldee (to *rise up*), Samaritan and Talmudic; but in the Syriac it is the word commonly used for *baptism*. Some say this was because the candidate stood while he was baptized; others, that the idea associated with baptism was that of *confirming* or *establishing* in the faith; while others believe that the Syriac word is to be traced to a different root. Whatever be the true explanation, it is easy to see that the same word may have different meanings in cognate languages, and, therefore, a signification which appears in Arabic or Syriac may be very remote from that which the word holds in the Hebrew. Hence great caution is necessary in tracing etymologies.

It is well known that, in all languages, the origin of many words has become utterly lost. The wonder, indeed, Rare words,
and ἅπαξ λεγ-
όμενα. is that we are able to trace the etymology of such a large proportion. The extensive literature of the Greek language enables the New Testament interpreter to ascertain without much difficulty the roots and usage of most of the words with which he has to deal. But the Old Testament Scriptures embody substantially all the remains of the Hebrew language, and when we meet with a word which occurs but once in the entire literature extant, we may often be puzzled to know the exact meaning which it was intended to convey. In such cases help from cognate tongues is particularly important. The word סֻלָּם, in Gen. xxviii, 12, occurs nowhere else in Hebrew. The root appears to be סָלַל, to *cast up*, to *raise;* and from the same root comes the word מְסִלָּה, used of public *highways* (Judg. xx, 32; Isa. xl, 3; lxii, 10), the *paths* of locusts (Joel ii, 8), the *courses* of the stars (Judg. v, 20), and *terraces* or *stairways* to the temple (2 Chron. ix, 11). The Arabic word *sullum* confirms the sense of *stairway* or *ladder*, and leaves no reasonable doubt as to the meaning of *sullam* in Gen. xxviii, 12. Jacob saw, in his dream, an elevated ladder or stairway reaching from the earth to the heavens. In determining the sense of such ἅπαξ λεγόμενα, or words occurring but once, we have to be guided by the context, by analogy of kindred roots, if any appear in the language, by ancient versions of the word in other languages, and by whatever traces of the word may be found in cognate tongues.

One of the most noted of New Testament ἅπαξ λεγόμενα is the word ἐπιούσιον in the Lord's prayer, Matt. vi, 11; Luke Ἐπιούσιος. xi, 3. It occurs nowhere else in Greek literature. Two derivations have been urged, one from ἐπί and ἰέναι, or the participle of ἔπειμι, to *go toward* or *approach;* according to which the meaning would be, "give us our *coming* bread," that is, bread for the coming day; to-morrow's bread. This is etymologically possible, and, on the ground of analogy, has much in its favour. But this meaning does not accord with σήμερον, *this day*, occurring in the same verse, nor with our Lord's teaching in verse 34 of the same chapter. The other derivation is from ἐπί and οὐσία, *existence, subsistence* (from εἰμί, *to be*), and means that which is necessary for existence, "our essential bread." This latter seems by far the more appropriate meaning.

Another difficult word is πιστικός, used only in Mark xiv, 3, and John xii, 3, to describe the nard (νάρδος) with which Πιστικός. Mary anointed the feet of Jesus. It is found in manuscripts of several Greek authors (Plato, Gorgias, 455 a.; Aristotle,

Rhet. i, 2) apparently as a false reading for πειστικός, *persuasive;* but this signification would have no relevancy to nard. Scaliger proposed the meaning *pounded nard,* deriving πιστικός from πτίσσω, to *pound,* a possible derivation, but unsupported by any thing analogous. Some think the word may be a proper adjective denoting the place from which the nard came; i. e., *Pistic nard.* The Vulgate of John xii, 3, has *nardi pistici.* This use of the word, however, is altogether uncertain. The Vulgate of Mark xiv, 3, has *spicati,* as denoting the spikes or ears of the nard plant; hence the word *spikenard.* But there is no good ground for accepting this interpretation. Many derive the word from πίνω (or πιπίσκω), to *drink,* and understand *drinkable* or *liquid* nard, and urge that several ancient writers affirm that certain anointing oils were used for drinking. If such were the meaning here, however, the word should refer to the ointment (μύρον), not the nard. The explanation best suited to the context, and not without warrant in Greek usage, makes the word equivalent to πιστός, *faithful, trustworthy;* applied to a material object it would naturally signify *genuine, pure,* that on which one can rely.

In determining the meaning of compound words we may usually resort to the lexical and grammatical analogy of lan- Compound guages. The signification of a compound expression is words. generally apparent from the import of the different terms of which it is compounded. Thus, the word εἰρηνοποιοί, used in Matt. v, 9, is at once seen to be composed of εἰρήνη, *peace,* and ποιέω, to *make,* and signifies *those who make* (work or establish) *peace.* The meaning, says Meyer, is "not the *peaceful* (εἰρηνικοί, James iii, 17 ; 2 Macc. v, 25; or εἰρηνεύοντες, Sirach vi, 7), a meaning which does not appear even in Pollux, i, 41, 152 (Augustine thinks of the *moral inner harmony;* De Wette, of the inclination of the contemporaries of Jesus to war and tumult; Bleek reminds us of Jewish party hatred); but *the founders of peace* (Xen. Hist. Gr., vi, 3, 4; Plut. Mor., p. 279 B.; comp. Col. i, 20; Prov. x, 10), who as such minister to God's good pleasure, who is the God of peace (Rom. xvi, 20; 2 Cor. xiii, 11), as Christ himself was the highest founder of peace (Luke ii, 14; John xvi, 33; Eph. ii, 14)."[1] Similarly we judge of the meaning of ἐθελοθρησκεία in Col. ii, 23, compounded of ἐθέλω and θρησκεία, and signifying *will worship, self-chosen worship;* πολύσπλαγχνος, *very compassionate* (James v, 11); συναυξάνομαι, to *grow together with* (Matt. xiii, 30); τροποφορέω, to *bear as a nourisher* (Acts xiii, 18), and many other compounds, which, like the above, occur but once in the New Testament.

[1] Critical and Exegetical Hand-book to the Gospel of Matthew, in loco.

CHAPTER IV.

THE USUS LOQUENDI.

Some words have a variety of significations, and hence, whatever their primitive meaning, we are obliged to gather from the context, and from familiarity with the usage of the language, the particular sense which they bear in a given passage of Scripture. Many a word in common use has lost its original meaning. The meaning of How few of those who daily use the word *sincere* are words becomes aware that it was originally applied to pure honey, from changed. which all wax was purged. Composed of the Latin words *sine*, without, and *cera*, wax, it appears to have been first used of honey strained or separated from the wax-like comb. The word *cunning* no longer means knowledge, or honourable skill, but is generally used in a bad sense, as implying artful trickery. The verb *let* has come to mean the very opposite of what it once did, namely to *hinder;* and *prevent.* which was formerly used in the sense of *going before,* so as to prepare the way or assist one, now means to intercept or obstruct. Hence the importance of attending to what is commonly called the *usus loquendi,* or current usage of words as employed by a particular writer, or prevalent in a particular age. It often happens, also, that a writer uses a common word in some special and peculiar sense, and then his own definitions must be taken, or the context and scope must be consulted, in order to determine the precise meaning intended.

There are many ways by which the *usus loquendi* of a writer may be ascertained. The first and simplest is when he Writer often himself defines the terms he uses. Thus the word defines his own ἄρτιος, *perfect, complete,* occurring only in 2 Tim. iii, 17, terms. is defined by what immediately follows: "That the man of God may be perfect, thoroughly furnished unto every good work." That is, he is made perfect or complete in this, that he is thoroughly furnished and fitted, by the varied uses of the inspired Scripture, to go forward unto the accomplishment of every good work. We also find the word τέλειοι, commonly rendered *perfect,* defined in Heb. v, 14, as those "who by practice have the senses trained unto a discrimination of good and of evil." They are, accordingly, the mature and experienced Christians as distinguished from *babes, νήπιοι.*

Compare verse 13, and 1 Cor. ii, 6. So also, in Rom. ii, 28, 29, the apostle defines the genuine Jew and genuine circumcision as follows: "For he is not a Jew, who·is one outwardly (ἐν τῷ φανερῷ); nor is that circumcision, which is outward in the flesh: but he is a Jew, who is one inwardly (ἐν τῷ κρυπτῷ); and circumcision is that of the heart, in the spirit, not in the letter; whose praise is not of men, but of God."

But the immediate context, no less than the writer's own defini-
Immediate context. tions, generally serves to exhibit any peculiar usage of words. Thus, πνεῦμα, *wind, spirit,* is used in the New Testament to denote the wind (John iii, 8), the vital breath (Rev. xi, 11), the natural disposition or temper of mind (Luke ix, 55; Gal. vi, 1), the life principle or immortal nature of man (John vi, 63), the perfected spirit of a saint in the heavenly life (Heb. xii, 23), the unclean spirits of demons (Matt. x, 1; Luke iv, 36), and the Holy Spirit of God (John iv, 24; Matt. xxviii, 19; Rom. viii, 9–11). It needs but a simple attention to the context, in any of these passages, to determine the particular sense in which the word is used. In John iii, 8, we note the two different meanings of πνεῦμα in one and the same verse. "The wind (τὸ πνεῦμα) blows where it will, and the sound of it thou hearest; but thou knowest not whence it comes and whither it goes; so is every one who is born of the Spirit" (ἐκ τοῦ πνεύματος). Bengel holds, indeed, that we should here render πνεῦμα in both instances by spirit, and he urges that the divine Spirit, and not the wind, has a *will* and a *voice.*[1] But the great body of interpreters maintain the common version. Nicodemus was curi·us and perplexed to know the *how* (πῶς, verses 4 and 9) of the Holy Spirit's workings, and as the Almighty of old spoke to Job out of the whirlwind, and appealed to the manifold mysteries of nature in vindication of his ways, so here the Son of God appeals to the mystery in the motion of the wind. ("Wouldst thou know the whence and whither of the Spirit, and yet thou knowest not the origin and the end of the common wind? Wherefore dost thou not marvel concerning the air which breathes around thee, and of which thou livest?"[2] "Our Lord," says Alford, "might have chosen any of the mysteries of nature to illustrate the point. He takes that one which is above others symbolic of the action of the Spirit, and which in both languages, that in which he spoke, as well as that in which his speech is reported, is expressed by the same word. So that the words as they stand apply themselves at once to the Spirit and his working, without any figure."[3]

---

[1] Gnomon of the New Testament, in loco.

[2] Comp. Stier, Words of the Lord Jesus, in loco.   [3] Greek Testament, in loco.

The word στοιχεῖον, used in classical Greek for the upright post of a sundial, then for an elementary sound in language (from letters standing in rows), came to be used almost solely in the plural, τὰ στοιχεῖα, in the sense of *elements* or *rudiments*. In 2 Pet. iii, 10 it evidently denotes the elements of nature, the component parts of the physical universe; but in Gal. iv, 3, 9, as the immediate context shows, it denotes the ceremonials of Judaism, considered as elementary object lessons, adapted to the capacity of children. In this sense the word may also denote the ceremonial elements in the religious cultus of the heathen world (compare verse 8).[1] The enlightened Christian should grow out of these, and pass beyond them, for otherwise they trammel, and become a system of bondage. Compare also the use of the word in Col. ii, 8, 20 and Heb. v, 12.

In connexion with the immediate context, the nature of the subject may also determine the usage of a word. Thus, in 2 Cor. v, 1, 2, the reference of the words οἰκία, *house*, σκῆνος, *tabernacle*, οἰκοδομή, *building*, and οἰκητήριον, *habitation*, to the body as a covering of the soul hardly admits of question. The whole passage (verses 1–4) reads literally thus: "For we know that if our house of the tabernacle upon earth were dissolved, a building from God we have, a house not made with hands, eternal, in the heavens. For also in this we groan, yearning to be clothed upon with our habitation which is from heaven, since indeed also (εἴγε᾽ καί) being clothed we shall not be found naked. For, indeed, we who are in the tabernacle groan, being burdened, in that we would not be unclothed, but clothed upon, to the end that that which is mortal may be swallowed up by the life." Hodge holds that the "building from God" is heaven itself, and argues that in John xiv, 2, heaven is compared to a house of many mansions; in Luke xvi, 9, to a habitation; and in Heb. xi, 10, and Rev. xxi, 10, to a city of dwellings.[2] But the scripture in question is too explicit, and the nature of the subject too limited, to allow other scriptures, like those cited, to determine its meaning. No one doubts that the phrase, "our house of the tabernacle upon earth," refers to the human body, which is liable to dissolution. It is compared to a tent, or tabernacle (σκῆνος), and also to a vesture, thus presenting us with a double metaphor. "The word tent," says Stanley, "lent itself to this imagery, from being used in later Greek writers for the human body, especially in medical writers, who seem to have been led to adopt the word from the *skin*-materials

Nature of the subject.

2 Cor. v, 1–4.

---

[1] Comp. Lightfoot's Commentary on Galatians iv, 11.
[2] Commentary on Second Corinthians, in loco.

of which tents were composed. The explanation of this abrupt transition from the figure of a house or tent to that of a garment, may be found in the image, familiar to the apostle, both from his occupations and his birthplace, of the tent of Cilician haircloth, which might almost equally suggest the idea of a habitation and of a vesture. Compare the same union of metaphors in Psa. civ, 2, ' Who coverest thyself with light as with a garment; who stretchest out the heavens like a curtain' (of a tent)."[1]

The main subject, then, is the present body considered as an earthly house, a tabernacle upon earth. In it we groan; in it we are under burden; in it we endure "the momentary lightness of our affliction " (τὸ παραυτίκα ἐλαφρὸν τῆς θλίψεως), which is mentioned in chapter iv, 17, and which is there set in contrast with an " eternal weight of glory " (αἰώνιον βάρος δόξης). To this earthly house, heaven itself, whether considered as the house of many mansions (John xiv, 2) or the city of God (Rev. xxi, 10), affords no true antithesis. The true antithesis is the heavenly body, the vesture of immortality, which is from God. For the opposite of *our house* is the *building from God;* the one may be *dissolved,* the other is *eternal;* the one is *upon earth* (ἐπίγειος), the other is (not heaven itself, but) *in the heavens.* The true parallel to the entire passage before us is 1 Cor. xv, 47–54, where the earthly and the heavenly bodies are contrasted, and it is said (ver. 53) " this corruptible must be clothed with incorruption, and this mortal must be clothed with immortality."

The above example also illustrates how antithesis, contrast, or Contrast or op- opposition, may serve to determine the meaning of position.   words. A further instance may be cited from Rom. viii, 5–8. In verse 4 the apostle has introduced the antithetic expressions κατὰ σάρκα, and κατὰ πνεῦμα, *according to the flesh* and *according to the spirit.* He then proceeds to define, as by contrast, the two characters. " For they who are according to the flesh the things of the flesh do mind (φρονοῦσιν, *think of, care for*), but they, according to the spirit, the things of the spirit. For the mind of the flesh is death, but the mind of the spirit life and peace. Because the mind of the flesh is enmity toward God, for to the law of God it does not submit itself, for it is not able; and they who are in the flesh are not able to please God." The spirit, throughout this passage, is to be understood of the Holy Spirit: "the Spirit of life in Christ Jesus," mentioned in verse 2, which delivers the sinner "from the law of sin and of death." The being *according to the flesh,* and the being *in the flesh,* are to be understood of

[1] Commentary on St. Paul's Epistles to the Corinthians, in loco.

unregenerate and unsanctified human life, conditioned and controlled by carnal principles and motives. This Scripture, and more that might be cited, indicates, by detailed opposition and contrast, the essential and eternal antagonism between sinful carnality and redeemed spirituality in human life and character.

The *usus loquendi* of many words may be seen in the parallelisms of Hebrew poetry. Whether the parallelism be synonymous or antithetic,[1] it may serve to exhibit in an unmistakable way the general import of the terms employed. Take, for example, the following passage from the eighteenth Psalm, verses 6–15 (Heb. 7–16): Hebrew paral lelisms.

6   In my distress I call Jehovah,
    And to my God I cry;
    He hears from his sanctuary my voice,
    And my cry before him comes into his ears.

7   Then shakes and quakes the land,
    And the foundations of the mountains tremble,
    And they shake themselves, for he was angry.

8   There went up a smoke in his nostril,
    And fire from his mouth devours;
    Hot coals glowed from him.

9   And he bows the heavens and comes down,
    And a dense gloom under his feet;

10 And he rides upon a cherub, and flies,
    And soars upon the wings of the wind.

11 He sets darkness his covering,
    His pavilion round about him,
    A darkness of waters, thick clouds of the skies.

12 From the brightness before him his thick clouds passed away,
    Hail, and hot coals of fire.

13 Then Jehovah thunders in the heavens,
    And the Most High gives forth his voice,
    Hail, and hot coals of fire.

14 And he sends forth his arrows and scatters them,
    And lightnings he shot, and puts them in commotion.

15 And the beds of the waters are seen,
    And the foundations of the world are uncovered,
    From thy rebuke, O Jehovah!
    From the breath of the wind of thy nostril.

It requires but little attention here to observe how such words as *call, cry, he hears my voice,* and *my cry comes into his ears* (verse 6), mutually explain and illustrate one another. The same may be said of the words *shakes, quakes, tremble,* and *shake themselves,* in

---

[1] On Hebrew Parallelisms, see pp. 95–98.

verse 7; *smoke, fire,* and *coals* in verse 8; *rides, flies,* and *soars* in verse 10; *arrows* and *lightnings, scatters* and *puts in commotion,* in verse 14; and so to some extent of the varied expressions of nearly every verse.

Here, too, may be seen how subject and predicate serve to ex-

Subject, predicate, and adjuncts. plain one another. Thus, in verse 8, above, *smoke goes up, fire devours, hot coals glow.* So in Matt. v, 13: "if the salt become tasteless," the sense of the verb μωρανθῇ, *become tasteless,* is determined by the subject ἅλας, *salt.* But in Rom. i, 22, the import of this same verb is *to become foolish,* as the whole sentence shows: "Professing to be wise, they become foolish," i. e., made fools of themselves. The word is used in a similar signification in 1 Cor. i, 20: "Did not God make foolish the wisdom of the world?" The extent to which qualifying words, as adjectives and adverbs, serve to limit or define the meaning is too apparent to call for special illustration.

A further and most important method of ascertaining the *usus*

Comparison of parallel passages. *loquendi* is an extensive and careful comparison of similar or parallel passages of Scripture. When a writer has treated a given subject in different parts of his writings, or when different writers have treated the same subject, it is both justice to the writers, and important in interpretation, to collate and compare all that is written. The obscure or doubtful passages are to be explained by what is plain and simple. A subject may be only incidentally noticed in one place, but be treated with extensive fulness in another. Thus, in Rom. xiii, 12, we have the exhortation, "Let us put on the armour of light," set forth merely in contrast with "cast off the works of darkness;" but if we inquire into the meaning of this "armour of light," how much more fully and forcibly does it impress us when we compare the detailed description given in Ephesians vi, 13–17: "Take up the whole armour of God. . . . Stand, therefore, having girded your loins with truth, and having put on the breastplate of righteousness, and having shod your feet with the preparation of the gospel of peace; withal taking up the shield of faith wherewith ye shall be able to quench all the fiery darts of the evil òne. And take the helmet of salvation, and the sword of the Spirit, which is the word of God." Compare also 1 Thess. v, 8.

The meaning of the word אָנֻשׁ (compare the Greek νόσος) in Jer. xvii, 9, must be determined by ascertaining its use in other passages. The common version translates it "desperately wicked," but usage does not sustain this meaning. The primary sense of the word appears to be *incurably sick,* or *diseased.* It is used in

2 Sam. xii, 15, to describe the condition of David's child when smitten of the Lord so that it *became very sick* (אָנַשׁ). It is used in reference to the lamentable idolatry of the kingdom of Israel (Micah i, 9), where the common version renders, "Her wound is *incurable*," and gives in the margin, "She is grievously sick of her wounds." The same signification appears also in Job xxxiv, 6: "My wound (חֵץ, wound caused by an arrow) is incurable." In Isa. xvii, 11, we have the thought of "incurable pain," and in Jer. xv, 18, we read, "Wherefore has my pain been enduring, and my stroke incurable?" Compare also Jer. xxx, 12, 15. In Jer. xvii, 16, the prophet uses this word to characterize the day of grievous calamity as *a day of mortal sickness* (יוֹם אָנֻשׁ). In the ninth verse, therefore, of the same chapter, where the deceitful heart is characterized by this word, which everywhere else maintains its original sense of a *diseased and incurable condition*, we should also adhere to the main idea made manifest by all these parallels: "Deceitful is the heart above every thing; and *incurably diseased* is it; who knows it?[1]

The *usus loquendi* of common words is, of course, to be ascertained by the manner and the connection in which General and they are generally used. We feel at once the incon- familiar usage. gruity of saying, "Adriansz or Lippersheim discovered the telescope, and Harvey invented the circulation of the blood." We know from familiar usage that *discover* applies to the finding out or uncovering of that which was in existence before, but was hidden from our view or knowledge, while the word *invent* is applicable to the contriving and constructing of something which had no actual existence before. Thus, the astronomer invents a telescope, and by its aid discovers the motions of the stars. The passage in 1 Cor. xiv, 34, 35, has been wrested to mean something else than the prohibition of women's speaking in the public assemblies of churches. Some have assumed that the words *churches* and *church* in these verses are to be understood of the business meetings of the Christians, in which it was not proper for the women to take part. But the entire context shows that the apostle has especially in mind the worshipping assembly. Others have sought in the word λαλεῖν a peculiar sense, and, finding that it bears in classic Greek writers the meaning of *babble, prattle*, they have strangely taught that Paul means to say: "Let your women keep silence in the churches; for it is not permitted them to *babble*. . . . For it is a shame for a woman to *babble* in church!" A slight examination shows that in this same chapter the word λαλεῖν, *to speak*, occurs

[1] On the importance of comparing parallel passages, see further in Chapter viii.

more than twenty times, and in no instance is there any necessity or reason to understand it in other than its ordinary sense of *discoursing, speaking.* Who, for instance, would accuse Paul of saying, "I thank God, I *babble* with tongues more than ye all" (verse 18); or "let two or three of the prophets *babble,* and the others judge" (verse 29)? Hence appears the necessity, in interpretation, of observing the general usage rather than the etymology of words.

In ascertaining the meaning of rare words, ἅπαξ λεγόμενα, or words which occur but once, and words of doubtful import, the ancient versions of Scripture furnish an important aid. For, as Davidson well observes, "An interpreter cannot arrive at the right meaning of every part of the Bible by the Bible itself. Many portions are dark and ambiguous. Even in discovering the correct sense, no less than in defending the truth, other means are needed. Numerous passages will be absolutely unintelligible without such helps as lie out of the Scriptures. The usages of the Hebrew and Hebrew-Greek languages cannot be fully known by their existing remains.[1]

In the elucidation of difficult words and phrases the Septuagint translation of the Old Testament holds the first rank among the ancient versions. It antedates all existing Hebrew manuscripts; and parts of it, especially the Pentateuch, belong, without much doubt, to the third century before the Christian era. Philo and Josephus appear to have made more use of it than they did of the Hebrew original; the Hellenistic Jews used it in their synagogues, and the New Testament writers frequently quote from it. Being made by Jewish scholars, it serves to show how before the time of Christ the Jews interpreted their Scriptures. Next in importance to the Septuagint is the Vulgate, or Latin Version, largely prepared in its present form by St. Jerome, who derived much knowledge and assistance from the Jews of his time. After these we place the Peshito-Syriac Version, the Targums, or Chaldee Paraphrases of the Old Testament, especially that of Onkelos on the Pentateuch, and Jonathan Ben Uzziel on the Prophets, and the Greek versions of Aquila, Symmachus, and Theodotion.[2] The other ancient versions, such as the Arabic, Coptic, Æthiopic, Armenian, and Gothic, are of less value, and, in determining the meaning of rare words, cannot be relied on as having any considerable weight or authority.

[1] Hermeneutics, page 616.
[2] On the history and character of all these ancient versions, see Harman's, Keil's, or Bleek's "Introduction;" also the various biblical dictionaries and cyclopædias.

A study and comparison of these ancient versions will show that they often differ very widely. In many instances it is easy to see, in the light of modern researches, that the old translators fell into grave errors, and were often at a loss to determine the meaning of rare and doubtful words. When the context, parallel passages, and several of the versions agree in giving the same signification to a word, that signification may generally be relied upon as the true one. But when the word is an ἅπαξ λεγόμενον, and the passage has no parallel, and the versions vary, great caution is necessary lest we allow too much authority to one or more versions, which, after all, may have been only conjectural.

The following examples will illustrate the use, and the interest attaching to the study, of the ancient versions. In the Authorized English Version of Gen. i, 2, the words תֹהוּ וָבֹהוּ are translated, *without form and void.* The Targum of Onkelos has צְדֵיָא וְרֵיקָנְיָא, *waste and empty;* the Vulgate: *inanis et vacua, empty and void;* Aquila: κένωμα καὶ οὐδέν, *emptiness and nothing.* Thus, all these versions substantially agree, and the meaning of the Hebrew words is now allowed to be *desolation and emptiness.* The Syriac merely repeats the Hebrew words, but the Septuagint reads ἀόρατος καὶ ἀκατασκεύαστος, *invisible and unformed,* and cannot be allowed to set aside the meaning presented in all the other versions.

In Gen. xlix, 6, the Septuagint gives the more correct translation of עִקְּרוּ שׁוֹר, *they houghed an ox,* ἐνευροκόπησαν ταῦρον; but the Chaldee, Syriac, Vulgate, Aquila, and Symmachus read, like the Authorized Version, *they digged down a wall.* Here, however, the authority of versions is outweighed by the fact that, in all other passages where the Piel of this word occurs, it means to *hamstring* or *hough* an animal. Compare Josh. xi, 6, 9; 2 Sam. viii, 4; 1 Chron. xviii, 4. Where the *usus loquendi* can thus be determined from the language itself, it has more weight than the testimony of many versions.

The versions also differ in the rendering of עַצֶּבֶת in Psa. xvi, 4. This word elsewhere (Job ix, 28; Psa. cxlvii, 3; Prov. x, 10; xv, 13) always means *sorrow;* but the form עָצָב means *idols,* and the Chaldee, Symmachus, and Theodotion so render עַצֶּבֶת in Psa. xvi, 4: *they multiply their idols,* or *many are their idols.* But the Septuagint, Vulgate, Syriac, Arabic, Ethiopic, and Aquila, render the word *sorrows,* and this meaning is best sustained by the usage of the language.

In Cant. ii, 12, עֵת הַזָּמִיר is rendered by the Septuagint καιρὸς τῆς τομῆς, *time of the cutting;* Symmachus, *time of the pruning* (κλαδεύσεως); so also the Vulgate, *tempus putationis*. Most modern interpreters, however, discard these ancient versions here, and understand the words to mean, *the time of song is come;* not merely or particularly *the singing of birds*, as the English version, but all the glad songs of springtime, in which shepherds and husbandmen alike rejoice. In this interpretation they are governed by the consideration that זָמִיר and זְמִירוֹת signify *song* and *songs* in 2 Sam. xxiii, 1; Job xxxv, 10; Psa. xcv, 2; cxix, 54; Isa. xxiv, 16; xxv, 5, and that when "the blossoms have been seen in the land" the pruning time is altogether past.

In Isa. lii, 13 all the ancient versions except the Chaldee render the word יַשְׂכִּיל in the sense of *acting wisely*. This fact gives great weight to that interpretation of the word, and it ought not to be set aside by the testimony of one version, and by the opinion, which is open to question, that יַשְׂכִּיל is in some passages equivalent to הִצְלִיחַ, to *prosper*.

From the above examples it may be seen what judgment and caution are necessary in the use of the ancient versions of the Bible. In fact, no specific rules can safely be laid down to govern us in the use of them. Sometimes the etymology of a word, or the context, or a parallel passage may have more weight than all the versions combined; while in other instances the reverse may be true. Where the versions are conflicting, the context and the analogy of the language must generally be allowed to take the precedence.

In ascertaining the meaning of many Greek words the ancient Glossaries and scholia. glossaries of Hesychius, Suidas, Photius, and others are useful; but as they treat very few of the obscure words of the New Testament, they are of comparatively little value to the biblical interpreter. Scholia, or brief critical notes on portions of the New Testament, extracted chiefly from the writings of the Greek Fathers, such as Origen and Chrysostom, occasionally serve a good purpose,[1] but they have been superseded by the more thorough and scholarly researches of modern times, and the results of this research are embodied in the leading critical commentaries and biblical lexicons of the present day. The Rabbinical commentaries of Aben-Ezra, Jarchi, Kimchi, and Tanchum are often found serviceable in the exposition of the Old Testament.

---

[1] The commentaries of Theodoret and Theophylact are largely composed of extracts from Chrysostom. To the same class belong the commentaries of Euthymius, Zigabenus, Œcumenius, Andreas, and Arethas. The Catenae of the Greek Fathers by Procopius, Olympiodorus, and Nicephorus treat several books of the Old Testament. The celebrated Catena Aurea of Thomas Aquinas covers the Four Gospels, and was translated and published at Oxford in 1845 bv J. H. Newman.

CHAPTER V.

SYNONYMES.

WORDS, being the conventional signs and representatives of ideas, are changeable in both form and meaning by reason of the changes constantly taking place in human society. In process of time the same word will be applied to a variety of uses, and come to have a variety of meanings. Thus, the name *board*, another form of the word *broad*, was originally applied to a piece of timber, hewed or sawed so as to form a wide, thin plank. *Some words have many meanings.* It was also applied to a table on which food was placed, and it became common to speak of gathering around the festive *board*. Thence it came by a natural process to be applied to the food which was placed upon the table, and men were said to work or pay for their *board*. By a similar association the word was also applied to a body of men who were wont to gather around a table to transact business, and hence we have *board* of trustees, *board* of commissioners. The word is also used for the deck of a vessel; hence the terms *on board*, *overboard*, and some other less common nautical expressions. Thus it often happens, that the original meaning of a word falls into disuse, and is forgotten, while later meanings become current, and find a multitude and variety of applications. But while a single word may thus come to have many meanings, it also happens that a number of different words are used to designate the same, or nearly the same, thing. By such a multiplication of terms a language becomes greatly enriched, and capable of expressing more minutely the different shades and aspects of any particular idea. Thus in English we have the words *wonder, surprise, admiration, astonishment*, and *amazement*, all conveying the same general thought, but distinguishable by different shades of meaning. *Several words of like meaning.* The same is true of the words *axiom, maxim, aphorism, apothegm, adage, proverb, byword, saying*, and *saw*. Such words are called synonymes, and they abound in all cultivated languages. The biblical interpreter needs discernment and skill to determine the nice distinctions and shades of meaning attaching to Hebrew and Greek synonymes. Often the exact point and pith of a passage will be missed by failing to make the proper discrimination between synonymous expressions. There are, for instance, eleven different Hebrew words used in the Old Testament for *kindling a fire*, or *setting on fire*,[1] and seven Greek words used in the New Testament for *prayer;*[2] and yet a careful study of these several terms will show that they all vary somewhat in signification, and serve to set forth so many different shades of thought or meaning.

We take, for illustration, the different Hebrew words which are used to convey the general idea of *killing*, or *putting to death*. The verb קָטַל occurs but three times in the Hebrew Scriptures, and means in every case to kill by putting an end to one's existence. The three instances are the following: Job xiii, 15, "If he *kill* me," or "Lo, let him kill me;" and Job xxiv, 14, "At light will the murderer rise up; he will *kill* the poor and needy;" and Psa. cxxxix, 19, "Thou wilt *kill* the wicked, O God." The primary idea of the word, according to Gesenius, is that of *cutting;* hence cutting off; making an end of by destruction. So the noun קֶטֶל is used in Obadiah 9 in connexion with כָּרַת, *cut off*—"shall be cut off by *slaughter;*" i. e., by a general destruction. In the Chaldee chapters of Daniel the verb קָטַל is used in a variety of forms seven times, but it seems to retain in every instance essentially the same meaning as the Hebrew verb. The simple fact of the *killing* or *cutting* off is stated without any necessary implication as to the method or occasion of the act.

Hebrew words for putting to death.

קָטַל

The word more commonly used to denote *putting to death* is (the Hiphil, Hophal, and some of the rarer forms of) מוּת, *to die*. The grammatical structure of the language enables us at once to perceive that the primary idea in the use of this word is that of *causing to die*. Thus, in Josh. x, 26 and xi, 17, it is used to denote the result of violent smiting (נָכָה): "Joshua smote them and *caused them to die;*" "All their kings he took, and he smote them and *caused them to die*." Compare 1 Sam. xvii, 50; xxii, 18; 2 Sam. xviii, 15; 2 Kings xv, 10, 14. In short, the distinguishing idea of this word, as used for *killing*, is that of putting to death, or causing to die, by some violent and deadly measure. In this sense the word is used in the Old Testament Scriptures over two hundred times. The prominent thought in קָטַל is merely that of *cutting off;* getting one out of the way; while in הֵמִית and הוּמַת the idea of *death*, as the result of some fatal means and procedure, is more noticeable. The murderer or the assassin *kills* (קָטַל) his victim or enemy; the warrior, the ruler, and the Lord himself, *causes to die*, or *puts to death* (הֵמִית) whom he will, and he

הֵמִית
הוּמַת

---

[1] Namely: שָׂרַף, קָטַר, קָדַח, נָשַׁק, לָהַט, יָקַד, יָצַת, חָרָה, דָּלַק, בָּעַר, אוּר.

[2] Εὐχή, προσευχή, δέησις, ἔντευξις, εὐχαριστία, αἴτημα, and ἱκετηρία.

performs the act by some certain means (specified or unspecified), which will accomplish the desired result. The latter word is accordingly used of public executions, the slaughter involved in war, and the putting to death for the maintenance of some principle, or the attainment of some ulterior end. It is never used to express the idea of murder; but God himself says: "I put to death" (Deut. xxxii, 39). Compare 1 Sam. ii, 6; 2 Kings v, 7; Hosea ix, 16.

Another word for *killing* is הָרַג. Unlike הֵמִית, it may be used for private homicide, or murder (Gen. iv, 8; xxvii, 41), or assassination (2 Chron. xxiv, 25; 2 Kings x, 9), or general slaughter and massacre (Judges viii, 17; Esther ix, 15). The slaying it denotes may be done by the sword (1 Kings ii, 32), or by a stone (Judges ix, 54), or a spear (2 Sam. xxiii, 21), or by the word of Jehovah (Hos. vi, 5), or even by grief, or a viper's tongue (Job v, 2; xx, 16). But the characterizing idea of the word, as distinguished from הֵמִית and קָטַל, seems to be that of *wholesale* or *vengeful slaughter*. Thus Jehovah *slew* all the firstborn of Egypt (Exod. xiii, 15), but the slaughter was a vengeful judgment-stroke, a plague. Thus Simeon and Levi *slew* the men of Shechem, and that slaughter was a cruel and vindictive massacre (Gen. xxxiv, 26; xlix, 6). This word is used of the slaughter of Jehovah's prophets by Jezebel, and of the prophets of Baal by Elijah (1 Kings xix, 1, 10), and in this sense generally, whether the numbers slain be few or many. Compare Judges viii, 17, 21; Esther ix, 6, 10, 12; Ezek. ix, 6. In Isa. xxii, 13 the word is used of the slaughter of oxen, but the context shows that the slaughter contemplated was on a large scale, at a time of feasting and revelry. So, again, in Psa. lxxviii, 47, we read: "He *slays* with hail their vines," but the passage is poetical, and the thought is that of a sweeping destruction, by which vines and trees, as well as other things that suffered in the plagues of Egypt, were, so to speak, slaughtered.

רָצַח has the primary signification of *crushing*, a violent breaking in pieces, and is generally used to denote the *act of murder* or *manslaughter* in any degree. This is the word used in the commandment, "Thou shalt not *commit murder*" (Exod. xx, 13; Deut. v, 17); less properly translated, "Thou shalt not *kill*," for often to kill is not necessarily to murder. In Num. xxxv the participial form of the word is used over a dozen times to denote the *manslayer*, who flees to a city of refuge, and twice (verses 27, 30) the verb is used to denote the execution of such manslayer by the avenger of blood.

The word טָבַח is used for the *slaying of animals*, especially in
טֶבַח preparation for a feast. It corresponds more nearly with
the word *butcher*. Thus, when Joseph's brethren came,
bringing Benjamin with them, Joseph commanded the ruler of his
house to bring the men to the house, and *kill a killing* (טְבֹחַ טֶבַח,
Gen. xliii, 16). Compare 1 Sam. xxv, 11; Prov. ix, 2. When the
word is applied to the slaughter of men it is always with the idea
that they are slaughtered or butchered like so many animals (Psa.
xxxvii, 14; Jer. li, 40; Lam. ii, 21; Ezek. xxi, 10, (15).

A kindred word is זָבַח, used of the *sacrificing of animals for offer-*
זֶבַח *ings*. It is thus ever associated with the idea of *im-*
molation, and the derivative noun זֶבַח means a *sacrificial
offering* to God. "This verb," says Gesenius, "is not used of the
priests as slaughtering victims in sacrifice, but of private persons
offering sacrifices at their own cost." Compare Gen. xxxi, 54; Exod.
viii, 29, (25); 1 Sam. xi, 15; 2 Chron. vii. 4; xxxiii, 17; Ezek. xx,
28; Hos. xiii, 2; Jon. i, 16.

Another word, constantly used in connection with the killing of
שָׁחַט animals for sacrifice, is שָׁחַט; but it differs from זֶבַח
especially in this, that the latter emphasizes rather 'the
idea of *sacrifice*, while שָׁחַט points more directly to the *slaughter* of
the victim. Hence זֶבַח is often used intransitively, in the sense
of *offering sacrifice*, without specifying the object sacrificed; but
שָׁחַט is always transitive, and connected with the object slain.
This latter word is often applied to the slaying of persons (Gen.
xxii, 10; 1 Kings xviii, 40; 2 Kings x, 7, 14; Isa. lvii, 5; Ezek.
xvi, 21), but in a sacrificial sense, as the immediate context shows.
Judg. xii, 6, would seem to be an exception, but the probable
thought there is that the Ephraimites who could not pronounce the
"Shibboleth" were slain as so many human sacrifices.

Thus each of these seven Hebrew words, all of which involve the
idea of *killing* or *slaughter*, has its own distinct shade of meaning
and manner of usage.

The Hebrew language has twelve different words to express the
Hebrew words idea of *sin*. First, there is the verb חָטָא, which, like
for Sin. the Greek ἁμαρτάνω, means, primarily, *to miss* a mark,
and is so used (in Hiphil) in Judg. xx, 16, where mention is made
of seven hundred left handed Benjamites who could sling stones
חָטָא "to the hair, and not *miss*." In Prov. viii, 36, it is contrasted with מָצָא, to *find* (verse 35): "They that *find*
me, find life; . . . and he that *misses* me wrongs his soul." Compare also Prov. xix, 2: "He that hastens with his feet *misses* ;"
that is, makes a misstep; gets off the track. The exact meaning

in Job v, 24, is more doubtful: "Thou shalt visit thy pasture (or habitation), and shalt not *miss*." The sense, according to most interpreters, is: Thou shalt miss nothing; in visiting thy pasture and thy flocks thou shalt find nothing gone; no sheep or cattle missing. It is easy to see how the idea of making a misstep, or missing a mark, passed over into the moral idea of missing some divinely appointed mark; hence *failure, error, shortcoming,* an action that has miscarried. Accordingly, the noun חֵטְא means *fault, error, sin.* It is interesting to note how the Piel, or intensive form of the verb חָטָא, conveys the idea of *making an offering for sin* (compare Lev. vi, 26, (19); ix, 15), or *cleansing* by some ceremonial of atonement (Exod. xxix, 36; Lev. xiv, 52); as if the thought of bearing the penalty of sin, and making it appear loathsome and damnable, were to be made conspicuous by an intense effort to purge away its guilt and shame. Hence arose the common usage of the noun חַטָּאת in the sense of *sin offering.*

We should next compare the words עָוֹן, עָוֶל, and אָוֶן. The first is from the root עָוָה, to *twist*, to *make crooked*, to *distort*, and signifies *moral perversity.* In the English version it is commonly translated *iniquity.* It indicates the inherent badness of a perverted soul, and in Psa. xxxii, 5, we have the expression: Thou hast taken away the *iniquity* (עֲוֹן) of my *sin*" (חַטָּאתִי). Closely cognate with עָוֹן is עָוֶל, from the root עָוַל, to *turn away*, to *distort*, and would seem to differ from it in usage by being applied rather to *outward action* than to *inner character;* עָוֹן indicates specially what a sinner *is*, עָוֶל, what he *does.* The primary sense of אָוֶן, on the other hand, is *emptiness*, or *nothingness.* It is used of idolatry (1 Sam. xv, 23; Isa. xli, 29; lxvi, 3; Hos. x, 5, 8; Zech. x, 2), and in the English version is occasionally translated *vanity* (Job xv, 35; Psa. x, 7; Prov. xxii, 8). It denotes wickedness, or sin, as something that has no enduring reality or value. It is a false, vain appearance; a deceitful shadow, destitute of stability. So, then, in these three words we have suggested to us bad character, bad action, and the emptiness of sinful pursuits.

The word which especially denotes *evil*, or that which is essentially *bad*, is רַע, with its cognate רֹע and רָעָה, all from the root רָעַע, to *break, shatter, crush, crumble.* It indicates a character or quality which, for all useful or valuable purposes, is utterly *broken* and *ruined.* Thus the noun רֹע, in Gen. xli, 19, denotes the utter *badness* of the seven famine-smitten heifers of Pharaoh's dream, and is frequently used of the wickedness of wrong action (Deut. xxviii, 20; Psa. xxviii, 4; Isa. i, 16; Jer. xxiii, 2; xliv, 22; Hos. ix, 15). The words רַע and רָעָה, besides being frequently

employed in the same sense (compare Gen. vi, 5; viii, 21; 1 Kings
ii, 44; Jer. vii, 12, 24; Zech. i, 4; Mal. ii, 17), are also used to denote the *evil* or *harm* which one may do to another (Psa. xv, 3;
xxi, 11; xxxv, 4; lxxi, 13). In all the uses of this word the idea of
a *ruin* or a *breach* is in some way traceable. The wickedness of
one's heart is in the moral *wreck* or *ruin* it discloses. The evil of a
sinner's wicked action is a *breach* of moral order.

Another aspect of sinfulness is brought out in the word מָעַל and

מַעַל   its noun מַעַל. It is usually translated *trespass*, but the
fundamental thought is *treachery*, some covert and
faithless action. Thus it is used of the unfaithfulness of an adulterous woman toward her husband (Num. v, 12), of the taking
strange wives (Ezra x, 2, 10), of the offense of Achan (Josh. vii, 1;
xxii, 20; 1 Chron. ii, 7), and generally of unfaithfulness toward
God (Deut. xxxii, 51; Josh. xxii, 16; 2 Chron. xxix, 6; Ezek. xx,
27; xxxix, 23). By this word any transgression is depicted as a
plotting of treachery, or an exhibition of unfaithfulness to some
holy covenant or bond.

By a transposition of the first two letters of מעל we have the

עָמָל   word עָמָל, which is used of the exhaustive *toils* of mortal life and their attendant *sorrow* and *misery*. In Num.
xxiii, 21, and Isa. x, 1, it is coupled in parallelism with אָוֶן, *emptiness, vanity*, and may be regarded as the accompaniment of the
vain pursuits of men. It is that *labour*, which, in the book of Ecclesiastes, where the word occurs thirty-four times, is shown both to
begin and end in "vanity and vexation of spirit;" a striving after
the wind (Eccles. i, 14; ii, 11, 17, 19).

The word עָבַר, to *cross over*, like the Greek παραβαίνω, is often

עָבַר   used metaphorically of *passing over the line of moral
obligation*, or going aside from it. Hence it corresponds closely with the word *transgress*. In Josh. vii, 11, 15; Judg.
ii, 20; 2 Kings xviii, 12; Hos. vi, 7; viii, 1, it is used of transgressing
a covenant; in Deut. xxvi, 13, of a commandment; in 1 Sam. xv, 24,
of the word (lit., *mouth*) of Jehovah; and in Isa. xxiv, 5, of the law.
Thus words of counsel and warning, covenants, commandments,
laws, may be *crossed over, passed by, walked away from;* and this
is the peculiar aspect of human perversity which is designated by
the word עָבַר, to *transgress*.

The two words פֶּשַׁע and רֶשַׁע may be best considered together.

פֶּשַׁע and רֶשַׁע   The former conveys the idea of *revolt, rebellion ;* the
latter *disturbance, tumultuous rage*. The former word
is used, in 1 Kings xii, 19, of Israel's revolt from the house of David; and in 2 Kings i, 1; iii, 7; viii, 20, 22; 2 Chron. xxi, 10, of the

rebellions of Moab, Edom, and Libnah; and the noun פֶּשַׁע, which is usually rendered *transgression*, should always be understood as a fault or trespass considered as a revolt or an apostasy from some bond of allegiance. Hence it is an aggravated form of sin, and in Job xxxiv, 37, we find the significant expression: "He adds upon his sin rebellion." The primary thought in רָשַׁע may be seen from Isa. lvii, 20, where it is said: "The wicked (הָרְשָׁעִים) are like the troubled (נִגְרָשׁ, *tossed, agitated*) sea; for rest it cannot, and its waters will cast up (יִגְרְשׁוּ, *toss about*) mud and mire." So also in Job xxxiv, 29, the Hiphil of the verb רָשַׁע is put in contrast with the Hiphil of שָׁקַט, to *rest*, to *be quiet:* "Let him *give rest*, and who will *give trouble?*" The wicked man is one who is ever troubled and troubling. His counsels (Psa. i, 1), his plots (Psa. xxxvii, 12), his dishonesty and robberies (Psa. xxxvii, 21; cxix, 61), and manifold iniquities (Prov. v, 22), are a source of confusion and disturbance in the moral world, and that continually.

It remains to notice briefly the word אָשַׁם, the primary idea of which seems to be that of guilt or blame involved in *committing a trespass through ignorance or negligence*, and שָׁנָה (שָׁנָא, שָׁגַג), with which it is frequently associated. The two words appear together in Lev. iv, 13: "If the whole congregation of Israel *err through ignorance* (יִשְׁגּוּ), and the matter be hidden from the eyes of the assembly, and they have done with one from all the commandments of Jehovah what should not have been done, and *have become guilty*" (אָשֵׁמוּ). Compare verses 22, 27, and chapter v, 2, 3, 4, 17, 19. Hence it was natural that the noun אָשָׁם should become the common word for the *trespass offering* which was required of those who contracted guilt by negligence or error. For the passages just cited, and their contexts, show that any violation or infringement of a divine commandment, whether committed knowingly or not, involved one in fault, and the guilt, contracted unconsciously, required for its expiation a trespass offering as soon as the sin became known. Accordingly, it will be seen that שָׁנָה, and its derivatives, point to *errors* committed through ignorance (Job vi, 24; Num. xv, 27), while אָשָׁם denotes rather the guiltiness contracted by such errors, and felt and acknowledged when the sin becomes known.

A study of the divine names used in the Hebrew Scriptures is exceedingly interesting and suggestive. They are *Adonai, El, Elah, Elim, Eloah, Elion, Elohim, Shaddai, Jah*, and *Jehovah*. All these may be treated as synonymes, and yet each divine name has its peculiar concept and its corresponding usage.

Divine names.

The synonymes of the New Testament furnish an equally interesting and profitable field of study. Many words appear to be
used interchangeably, and yet a careful examination will usually
show that each conveys its own distinct idea. Take, for instance,
Καινός and the two Greek words for *new*, καινός and νέος. Both
νέος. are applied to the *new man* (comp. Eph. ii, 15; Col.
iii, 10), the *new covenant* (Heb. ix, 15; xii, 24), and *new wine* (Matt.
ix, 17; xxvi, 29); but a wider comparison shows that καινός denotes
what is new in *quality* or *kind*, in opposition to something that has
already existed and been known, used, and worn out; while νέος
denotes what is new in *time*, what has not long existed, but is
young and *fresh*. Both words occur in Matt. ix, 17: "They put
new (νέον) wine into new (καινούς) skins." The new wine is here
conceived as fresh, or recently made; the skins as never used before. The skin bottles may have been old or new as to age, but
in order to preserve wine just made, they must not have been put
to that use before. But the wine referred to in Matt. xxvi, 29, is
to be thought of rather as a *new kind of wine:* "I will not drink
henceforth of this fruit of the vine until that day when I drink it
with you new (καινόν, new in a higher sense and quality), in the
kingdom of my Father." So also Joseph's tomb, in which our
Lord's body was laid, was called a new one (καινός, Matt. xxvii, 60;
John xix, 41), not in the sense that it had recently been hewn from
the rock, but because no one had ever been laid in it before. The
new (καινή) commandment of John xiii, 34 is the law of love,
which, proceeding from Christ, has a new aspect and scope; a depth
and beauty and fulness which it had not before. But when John
wrote his epistles of brotherly love it had become "an old commandment" (1 John ii, 7), long familiar, even "the word which ye heard
from the beginning." But then he (verse 8) adds: "Again, a new
commandment (ἐντολὴν καινήν) I write to you, which thing is true
in him and in you; because the darkness is passing away and the
true light is already shining." The passing away of the old darkness
and the growing intensity of the true light, according to proper
Christian experience, continually develop and bring out new glories
in the old commandment. This thing (ὅ), namely, the fact that
the old commandment is also new, is seen to be true both in Christ
and in the believer; because in the latter the darkness keeps passing away, and in the former the true light shines more and more.

In like manner the *tongues* mentioned in Mark xvi, 17 are called
καίναι, because they would be new to the world, "other tongues"
(Acts ii, 4), unlike any thing in the way of speaking which had been
known before. So, too, the new name, new Jerusalem, new song,

new heaven and new earth (Rev. ii, 17; iii, 12; v, 9; xiv, 3; xxi, 1), to designate which καινός is used, are the renewed, ennobled, and glorious apocalyptic aspects of the things of the kingdom of God. The word νέος is used nine times in the Synoptic Gospels of wine recently made. In 1 Cor. v, 7, it is applied to the new lump of leaven, as that which has been recently prepared. It is used of the new man in Col. iii, 10, where the putting on the new man is spoken of as *a work recently accomplished;* whereas καινός is used in Eph. ii, 15, denoting rather the *character of the work accomplished.* So the new covenant may be conceived of as new, or recent (Heb. xii, 24), in opposition to that long ago given at Sinai, while it may also be designated as new in the sense of being different from the old (Matt. xxvi, 28; 2 Cor. iii, 6), which is worn out with age, and ready to vanish away (Heb. viii, 13). Let it be noted, also, that "newness of life" and "newness of spirit" (Rom. vi, 4; vii, 6), are expressed by καινότης; but *youth* is denoted by νεότης (Matt. xix 20; Mark x, 20; Luke xviii, 21; Acts xxvi, 4; 1 Tim. iv, 12).

The two words for *life,* βίος and ζωή, are easily distinguishable as used in the New Testament. Βίος denotes the pres- Βίος and ζωή. ent human life considered especially with reference to modes and conditions of existence. It nowhere means *lifetime,* or *period of life;* for the true text of 1 Pet. iv, 3, which was supposed to convey this meaning, omits the word. It commonly denotes the *means of living;* that on which one depends as a means of support- ing life. Thus the poor widow cast into the treasury her whole *living* (βίον, Mark xii, 44). Another woman spent all her *living* on physicians (Luke viii, 14). The same meaning appears in Luke xv, 12, 30; xxi, 4. In Luke viii, 14 and 1 John iii, 17 it denotes, rather, life as conditioned by riches, pleasures, and abundance. In 1 Tim. ii, 2; 2 Tim. ii, 4; 1 John ii, 16 it conveys the idea of the manner and style in which one spends his life; and so, in all its uses, βίος has reference solely to the life of man as lived in this world. Ζωή, on the other hand, is the antithesis of *death* (θάνατος), and while used occasionally in the New Testament in the sense of physical existence (Acts xvii, 25; 1 Cor. iii, 22; xv, 19; Phil. i, 20; James iv, 14), is defined by Cremer as "the kind of existence pos- sessed by individualized being, to be explained as *self-governing existence,* which God *is,* and man *has* or *is said to have,* and which, on its part, is supreme over all the rest of creation."[1] Tholuck

---

[1] Biblico-Theological Lexicon of the New Testament, p. 272. Cremer goes on to show how from the sense of *physical existence* the word is also used to denote a perfect and abiding antithesis to death (Heb. vii, 16), a positive freedom from death (Acts ii, 28; 2 Cor. v, 4), and the sum of the divine promises under the Gospel, "belonging

observes: "The words ζωή and θάνατος (*death*), along with the cognate verbs, although appearing in very various applications, are most clearly explained when we suppose the following views to have lain at the basis of them. God is the *life eternal* (ζωὴ αἰώνιος, 1 John v, 20), or the *light*, (φῶς, 1 John i, 5; James i, 7). Beings made in the image of God have true life only in fellowship with him. Wherever this life is absent there is *death*. Accordingly the idea of ζωή comprehends *holiness* and *bliss*, that of θάνατος sin and *misery*. Now as both the ζωή and the θάνατος manifest themselves in different degrees, sometimes under different aspects, the words acquire a variety of significations. The highest grade of the ζωή is the life which the redeemed live with the Saviour in the glorious kingdom of heaven. Viewed on this side, ζωή denotes continued existence after death, communion with God, and blessedness, of which each is implied in the other."[1]

In Jesus' conversation with Simon Peter at the sea of Tiberias Aγαπάω and (John xxi, 15–17), we have four sets of synonymes. φιλέω. First, the words ἀγαπάω and φιλέω, for which we have no two corresponding English words. The former, as opposed to the latter, denotes a *devout reverential love*, grounded in reason and admiration. Φιλέω, on the other hand, denotes the love of a warm personal affection, a *tender emotional love of the heart.* "The first expresses," says Trench, "a more reasoning attachment, of choice and selection (*diligere = deligere*), from seeing in the object upon whom it is bestowed that which is worthy of regard; or else from a sense that such was fit and due toward the person so regarded, as being a benefactor, or the like; while the second, without being necessarily an unreasoning attachment, does yet oftentimes give less account of itself to itself; is more instinctive, is more of the feelings, implies more passion."[2] The range of φιλέω, according to Cremer, is wider than that of ἀγαπάω, but ἀγαπάω stands high above φιλέω on account of its moral import. It involves the moral affection of conscious, deliberate will, and may therefore be depended on in moments of trial. But φιλέω, involving the love of natural inclination and impulse, may be variable.[3] Observe, then,

to those to whom the future is sure, already in possession of all who are partakers of the New Testament salvation, 'that leadeth unto life,' and who already in this life begin life eternal." (Matt. vii, 14; Tit. i, 2; 2 Tim. i, 1; Acts xi, 18; xiii, 48). He further observes, that in the writings of Paul "ζωή is the substance of Gospel preaching, the final aim of faith (1 Tim. i, 16);" in the writings of John it "is the subject matter and aim of divine revelation." Comp. John v, 39; 1 John v, 20; etc.

[1] Commentary on Romans v, 12.
[2] Synonymes of the New Testament, sub verbo.
[3] Comp. Biblico-Theological Lexicon, pp. 11, 12.

the use of these words in the passage before us. "Jesus says to Simon Peter, Simon, son of Jonah, dost thou devoutly love (ἀγαπᾷς) me more than these? He says to him, Yea, Lord, thou knowest (οἶδας, *seest*) that I tenderly love (φιλῶ) thee." In his second question our Lord, in tender regard for Simon, omits the words *more than these*, and simply asks: "Dost thou devoutly love (ἀγαπᾷς) me?" To this Simon answers precisely as before, not venturing to assume so lofty a love as ἀγαπάω implies. In his third question (verse 17) our Lord uses Simon's word, thus approaching nearer to the heart and emotion of the disciple: "Simon, son of Jonah, dost thou tenderly love (φιλεῖς) me?" The change of word, as well as his asking for the third time, filled Peter with grief (ἐλυπήθη), and he replied with great emotion: "O Lord, all things thou knowest (οἶδας, seest, dost perceive), thou dost surely know (γινώσκεις, art fully cog- Οἶδα and γινnizant of the fact, hast full assurance by personal νώσκω.

knowledge) that I tenderly love (φιλῶ) thee." The distinction between οἶδα (from εἴδω, to *see*, to *perceive*) and γινώσκω (to obtain and have knowledge of) is very subtle, and the words appear to be often used interchangeably. According to Cremer, "there is merely the difference that γινώσκειν implies an active relation, to wit, a self-reference of the knower to the object of his knowledge; whereas, in the case of εἰδέναι, the object has simply come within the sphere of perception, within the knower's circle of vision."[1] As used by Peter the two words differ, in that γινώσκω expresses a deeper and more positive knowledge than οἶδα.

According to many ancient authorities we have in this passage three different words to denote lambs and sheep. In verse 15 the word is ἀρνία, *lambs*, in verse 16 πρόβατα, *sheep*, and in Ἀρνία, πρόβαverse 17 προβάτια, *sheeplings*, or *choice sheep*. The dif- τα, and προference and distinct import of these several words it is βάτια.

not difficult to understand. The *lambs* are those of tender age; the young of the flock. The *sheep* are the full-grown and strong. The *sheeplings*, προβάτια, are the choice full-grown sheep, those which deserve peculiar tenderness and care, with special reference, perhaps, to the milch-ewes of the flock. Compare Isa. xl, 11. Then, in connexion with these different words for sheep we have also the synonymes βόσκω and ποιμαίνω, to denote the various Βόσκω and cares and work of the shepherd. Βόσκω means to *feed*, ποιμαίνω.

and is used especially of a shepherd providing his flock with pasture, leading them to the field, and furnishing them with food. Ποιμαίνω is a word of wider significance, and involves the whole office and work of a shepherd. It comes more nearly to our word

[1] Biblico-Theological Lexicon, p. 230.

tend, and includes the ideas of feeding, folding, governing, guiding, guarding, and whatever a good shepherd is expected to do for his flock. Βόσκω denotes the more special and tender care, the giving of nourishment, and is appropriately used when speaking of lambs. Ποιμαίνω is more general and comprehensive, and means to rule as well as to feed. Hence appear the depth and fulness of the three-fold commandment: "Feed my lambs," "Tend my sheep," "Feed my choice sheep." The lambs and the choice sheep need special nourishment; all the sheep need the shepherd's faithful care. It is well to note, that, on the occasion of the first miraculous draught of fishes, at this same sea of Galilee (Luke v, 1–10), Jesus sounded the depths of Simon Peter's soul (verse 8), awakened him to an awful sense of sin, and then told him that he should thereafter catch men (verse 10). Now, after this second like miracle, at the same sea, and with another probing of his heart, he indicates to him that there is something more for him to do than to catch men. He must know how to care for them after they have been caught. He must be a shepherd of the Lord's sheep as well as a fisher of men, and he must learn to imitate the manifold care of the Great Shepherd of Israel, of whom Isaiah wrote (Isa. xl, 11): "As a shepherd he will feed his flock (עֵדֶר); in his arms he will gather the lambs (טְלָאִים), and in his bosom bear; the milch-ewes (עָלוֹת) he will gently lead."

The synonymes of the Hebrew and Greek Scriptures have been as yet but slightly and imperfectly treated.[1] They afford the biblical scholar a broad and most interesting field of study. It is a spiritual as well as an intellectual discipline to discriminate sharply between synonymous terms of Holy Writ, and trace the diverging lines of thought, and the far-reaching suggestions which often arise therefrom. The foregoing pages will have made it apparent that the exact import and the discriminative usage of words are all-important to the biblical interpreter. Without an accurate knowledge of the meaning of his words, no one can properly either understand or explain the language of any author.

---

[1] The only works of note on the subject are, Girdlestone, Synonymes of the Old Testament, London, 1871; and Trench, Synonymes of the New Testament, originally published in two small volumes, and subsequently in one; Ninth Edition, London, 1880. The work of Tittmann, De Synonymis in Novo Testamento, translated and published in two volumes of the Edinburgh Biblical Cabinet, is now of no great value. Cremer's Biblico-Theological Lexicon of the New Testament contains a very excellent treatment of a number of the New Testament synonymes; and Wilson's Syntax and Synonymes of the Greek Testament (London, 1864) is well worthy of consultation.

CHAPTER VI.

THE GRAMMATICO-HISTORICAL SENSE.

HAVING become familiar with the meaning of words, and thoroughly versed in the principles and methods by which their signification and usage are ascertained, we are prepared to investigate the grammatico-historical sense. This phrase is believed to have originated with Karl A. G. Keil, whose treatise on Historical Interpretation and Text-Book of New Testament Hermeneutics [1] furnished an important contribution to the science of interpretation. We have already defined the grammatico-historical method of interpretation as distinguished from the allegorical, mystical, naturalistic, mythical, and other methods, [2] which have more or less prevailed. The grammatico-historical sense of a writer is such an interpretation of his language as is required by the laws of grammar and the facts of history. Sometimes we speak of the literal sense, by which we mean the most simple, direct, and ordinary meaning of phrases and sentences. By this term we usually denote a meaning opposed to the figurative or metaphorical. The grammatical sense is essentially the same as the literal, the one expression being derived from the Greek, the other from the Latin. But in English usage the word grammatical is applied rather to the arrangement and construction of words and sentences. By the historical sense we designate, rather, that meaning of an author's words which is required by historical considerations. It demands that we consider carefully the time of the author, and the circumstances under which he wrote.

Grammatico-historical sense defined.

"Grammatical and historical interpretation, when rightly understood," says Davidson, "are synonymous. The special laws of grammar, agreeably to which the sacred writers employed language, were the result of their peculiar circumstances; and history alone throws us back into these circumstances. A new language was not made for the authors of Scripture; they conformed to the current language of the country and time. Their compositions would not have been otherwise intelligible. They

Davidson's statement.

---

[1] De historica librorum sacrorum interpretatione ejusque necessitate. Lps., 1788. Lehrbuch der Hermeneutik des N. T. nach Grundsätzen der grammatisch-historischen Interpretation. Lpz., 1810. A Latin translation, by Emmerling, appeared in 1811.

[2] Compare above, pp. 173, 174.

took up the *usus loquendi* as they found it, modifying it, as is quite natural, by the relations internal and external amid which they thought and wrote." The same writer also observes: " The grammatico-historical sense is made out by the application of grammatical and historical considerations. The great object to be ascertained is the *usus loquendi*, embracing the laws or principles of universal grammar which form the basis of every language. These are nothing but the logic of the mind, comprising the modes in which ideas are formed, combined, and associated, agreeably to the original susceptibilities of the intellectual constitution. They are the physiology of the human mind as exemplified practically by every individual. General grammar is wont to be occupied, however, with the usage of the best writers; whereas the laws of language as observed by the writers of Scripture should be mainly attended to by the sacred interpreter, even though the philosophical grammarian may not admit them all to be correct. It is the *usus loquendi* of the inspired authors which forms the subject of the grammatical principles recognized and followed by the expositor. The grammar he adopts is deduced from the use of the language employed in the Bible. This may not be conformed to the practice of the best writers; it may not be philosophically just;·but he must not, therefore, pronounce it erroneous. The modes of expression used by each writer—the utterances of his mental associations, constitute his *usus loquendi*. These form his grammatical principles; and the interpreter takes them as his own in the business of exegesis. Hence, too, there arises a special as well as a universal grammar. Now we attain to a knowledge of the peculiar *usus loquendi* in the way of historical investigation. The religious, moral, and psychological ideas, under whose influence a language has been formed and moulded; all the objects with which the writers were conversant, and the relations in which they were placed, are traced out *historically*. The costume of the ideas in the minds of the biblical authors originated from the character of the times, country, place, and education, under which they acted. Hence, in order to ascertain their peculiar *usus loquendi*, we should know all those institutions and influences whereby it was formed or affected." [1]

The general principles and methods by which we ascertain the *usus loquendi* of single terms, or words, have been presented in the preceding chapter. Substantially the same principles are to serve us as we proceed to investigate the grammatico-historical sense. We must attend to the

General principles and methods.

[1] Davidson, Sacred Hermeneutics, pp. 225, 226.

definitions and construction which an author puts upon his own terms, and never suppose that he intends to contradict himself or puzzle his readers. The context and connection of thought are also to be studied in order to apprehend the general subject, scope, and purpose of the writer. But especially is it necessary to ascertain the correct grammatical construction of sentences. Subject and predicate and subordinate clauses must be closely analyzed, and the whole document, book, or epistle, should be viewed, as far as possible, from the author's historical standpoint.

A fundamental principle in grammatico-historical exposition is that words and sentences can have but one significa- *Words and sentences but one* tion in one and the same connection. The moment we *meaning in one* neglect this principle we drift out upon a sea of un- *place.* certainty and conjecture. It is commonly assumed by the universal sense of mankind that unless one designedly put forth a riddle, he will so speak as to convey his meaning as clearly as possible to others. Hence that meaning of a sentence which most readily suggests itself to a reader or hearer, is, in general, to be received as the true meaning, and that alone. Take, for example, the account of Daniel and his three companions, as given in the first chapter of the Book of Daniel. The simplest child readily grasps the meaning. There can be no doubt as to the general import of the words throughout the chapter, and that the writer intended to inform his readers in a particular way how God honoured those young men because of their abstemiousness, and because of their refusal to defile themselves with the meats and drinks which the king had appointed for them. The same may be said of the lives of the patriarchs as recorded in the Book of Genesis, and, indeed, of any of the historical narratives of the Bible. They are to be accepted as a trustworthy record of facts.

This principle holds with equal force in the narratives of miraculous events. For the miracles of the Bible are re- *Miracles to be* corded as facts, actual occurrences, witnessed by few or *literally understood.* by many as the case might be, and the writers give no intimation that their statements involve any thing but plain literal truth. Thus, in Josh. v, 13–vi, 5, a man appears to Joshua, holding a sword in his hand, announcing himself as "a prince of the host of Jehovah" (verse 14), and giving directions for the capture of Jericho. This may, possibly, have occurred in a dream or a waking vision; but such a supposition is not in strictest accord with the statements. For it would involve the supposition that Joshua dreamed that he fell on his face, and took off his shoes from his feet, as well as looked and listened. Revelations from Jehovah were wont to come through visions and dreams (Num. xii, 6), but the simplest exposition of this passage is that the angel of Jehovah openly appeared to Joshua, and the occurrences were all outward and actual, rather than by vision or dream.

The simple but mournful narrative of the offering up of Jeph- **Jephthah's** thah's daughter (Judg. xi, 30–40) has been perverted to **daughter a** mean that Jephthah devoted his daughter to perpetual **burnt-offering.** virginity—an exposition that arose from the *a priori* assumption that a judge of Israel must have known that human sacrifices were an abomination to Jehovah. But no one presumes to question that he vowed to offer as a burnt-offering that which came forth from the doors of his house to meet him (verse 31). Jephthah could scarcely have thought of a cow, or a sheep, or goat, as coming out of his house to meet him. Still less could he have contemplated a dog, or any unclean animal. The awful solemnity and tremendous force of his vow appear, rather, in the thought that he contemplated no common offering, but a victim to be taken from among the inmates of his house. But he then little thought that of all his household—servants, young men, and maidens—his daughter and only child would be the first to meet him. Hence his anguish, as indicated in verse 35. But she accepted her fate with a sublime heroism. She asked two months of life in which to bewail her virginity, for that was to her the one only thing that darkened her thoughts of death. To die unwedded and childless was the sting of death to a Hebrew woman, and especially one who was as a princess in Israel. Take away that bitter thought, and with Jephthah's daughter it were a sublime and enviable thing to "die for God, her country, and her sire."

The notion that, previously to her being devoted to a life of virginity and seclusion, she desired two months to mourn over such a fate, appears exceedingly improbable, if not absurd. For, as Cappellus well observes, "If she desired or felt obliged to bewail her virginity, it were especially suitable to bewail that when shut up in the monastery; previously to her being shut up it would have been more suitable, with youthful friends and associates, to have spent those two months joyfully and pleasantly, since afterward there would remain to her a time for weeping more than sufficiently long."[1] The sacred writer declares (verse 39) that, after the two months, Jephthah did to his daughter the vow *which he had vowed* —not something else which he had not vowed. He records, not as the manner in which he did his vow, but as the most thrilling knell that in the ears of her father and companions sounded over that

[1] Critici Sacri, tom. ii, p. 2076.

daughter's funeral pile, and sent its lingering echo into the later times, that "she knew no man." [1]

The narratives of the resurrection of Jesus admit of no rational explanation aside from that simple grammatico-histori- Jesus' resur-
cal sense in which the Christian Church has ever under- rection a literal
stood them. The naturalistic and mythical theories, historical fact.
when applied to this miracle of miracles, utterly break down. The alleged discrepancies between the several evangelists, instead of disproving the truthfulness of their accounts, become, on closer inspection, confirmatory evidences of the accuracy and trustworthiness of all their statements. If the New Testament narratives are deserving of any credit at all, the following facts are evident (1) Jesus foretold his death and resurrection, but his disciples were slow to comprehend him, and did not fully accept his statements. (2) Immediately after the crucifixion the disciples were smitten with deep dejection and fear; but after the third day they all claimed to have seen the Lord, and they gave minute details of several of his appearances. (3) They affirm that they saw him ascend into the heavens, and soon afterward are found preaching "Jesus and the resurrection" in the streets of Jerusalem and in all Palestine and the regions beyond. (4) Many years afterward Paul declared these facts, and affirmed that Jesus appeared at one time to above five hundred brethren, of whom the greater part were still alive (1 Cor. xv, 6). He affirmed, that, if Christ had not been raised from the dead, the preaching of the Gospel and the faith of the Church were

---

[1] We gain nothing by attempting to evade the obvious import of any of the biblical narratives. On the treatment of this account of Jephthah's daughter Stanley observes: "As far back as we can trace the sentiment of those who read the passage, in Jonathan the Targumist, and Josephus, and through the whole of the first eleven centuries of Christendom, the story was taken in its literal sense as describing the death of the maiden, although the attention of the Church was, as usual, diverted to distant allegorical meanings. Then, it is said, from a polemical bias of Kimchi, arose the interpretation that she was not killed, but immured in celibacy. From the Jewish theology this spread to the Christian. By this time the notion had sprung up that every act recorded in the Old Testament was to be defended according to the standard of Christian morality ; and, accordingly, the process began of violently wresting the words of Scripture to meet the preconceived fancies of later ages. In this way entered the hypothesis of Jephthah's daughter having been devoted as a nun; contrary to the plain meaning of the text, contrary to the highest authorities of the Church, contrary to all the usages of the old dispensation. In modern times a more careful study of the Bible has brought us back to the original sense. And with it returns the deep pathos of the original story, and the lesson which it reads of the heroism of the father and daughter, to be admired and loved, in the midst of the fierce superstitions across which it plays like a sunbeam on a stormy sea."—Lectures on the History of the Jewish Church. First Series, p. 397.

but an empty thing, based upon a gigantic falsehood. This conclusion follows irresistibly from the above-named facts. We must either accept the statements of the evangelists, in their plain and obvious import, or else meet the inevitable alternative that they knowingly put forth a falsehood (a concerted testimony which was essentially a lie before God), and went preaching it in all the world, ready to seal their testimony by tortures and death. This latter alternative involves too great a strain upon our reason to be accepted for a moment, especially when the unique and straightforward Gospel narratives furnish such a clear and adequate historical basis for the marvellous rise and power of Christianity in the world.

Winer's Grammar of the New Testament, and the modern critical commentaries on the whole or on parts of the New Testament—such as those of Meyer, De Wette, Alford, Ellicott, and Godet—have served largely to place the interpretation of the Christian Scriptures on a sound grammatico-historical basis, and a constant use of these great works is all-important to the biblical scholar. He must, by repeated grammatical praxis, make himself familiar with the peculiarities of the New Testament dialect. The significance of the presence or the absence of the article has often much to do with the meaning of a passage. "In the language of living intercourse," says Winer, "it is utterly impossible that the article should be omitted where it is decidedly necessary, or employed where it is not demanded. Ὄρος can never denote THE *mountain*, nor τὸ ὄρος A *mountain*."[1] The position of words and clauses, and peculiarities of grammatical structure, may often serve to emphasize important thoughts and statements. The special usage of the genitive, the dative, or the accusative case, or of the active, middle, or passive voice, often conveys a notable significance. The same is also true of conjunctions, adverbs, and prepositions. These serve to indicate peculiar shades of meaning, and delicate and suggestive relations of words and sentences, without a nice apprehension of which the real sense of a passage may be lost to the reader. The authorized version often obscures an important passage of the New Testament by a mistranslation of the aorist tense. Take, as a single example, 2 Cor. v, 14: "For the love of Christ constraineth us; because we thus judge, that if one died for all, then were all dead." The *if* is now allowed to be an error in the text and should be omitted. The verse should then be translated: "For the love of Christ constrains us, having judged this, that one died for all; therefore the all died." The first verb, *constrains* (συνέχει), is in the present

Grammatical accuracy to be looked for in the Scriptures.

Greek tenses.

[1] New Testament Grammar, p. 115. Andover, 1874.

tense, and denotes the then present experience of the apostle at the time of his writing: The love of Christ (Christ's love for men) now constrains us ("holds us in bounds"—Meyer); and this is the ever-present and abiding experience of all like the apostle. *Having judged* (κρίναντας) is the aorist participle, and points to a definite judgment which he had formed at some past time—probably at, or soon after, his conversion. The statement that one *died* (ἀπέθανεν, aorist singular) for all, points to that great historic event which, above every other, exhibited the love of Christ for men. Ἄρα οἱ πάντες ἀπέθανον, *therefore the all died*—"the all," who meet the condition specified in the next verse, and "live unto him who for their sakes died and rose again," are conceived as having died with Christ. They were crucified with Christ, united with him by the likeness of his death (Rom. vi, 5, 6).[1] Compare also Col. iii, 3: "For ye died (not ye are dead), and your life is hidden (κέκρυπται, *has become hidden*) with Christ in God." That is, ye died at the time ye became united with Christ by faith, and as a consequence of that death ye now have a spiritual life in Christ.

"With regard to the tenses of the verb," says Winer, "New Testament grammarians and expositors have been guilty of the greatest mistakes. In general, the tenses are employed in the New Testament exactly in the same manner as in Greek authors. The aorist marks simply the past (merely occurrence at some former time—viewed, too, as momentary), and is the tense employed in narration; the imperfect and pluperfect always have reference to secondary events connected in respect to time with the principal event (as relative tenses); the perfect brings the past into connexion with the present, representing an action in reference to the present as concluded. No one of these tenses, strictly and properly taken, can stand for another, as commentators often would have us believe. But where such an interchange appears to take place, either it is merely apparent, and a sufficient reason (especially a rhetorical one) can be discovered why this and no other tense has been used, or it is to be set down to the account of a certain inaccuracy peculiar to the language of the people, which did not conceive and express relations of time with entire precision."[2]

----

[1] When Christ died the redeeming death for all, all died, in respect of their fleshly life, with him; this *objective* matter of fact which Paul here affirms has its *subjective* realization in the faith of the individuals, through which they have *entered into* that death-fellowship with Christ *given* through his death for all, so that they have now, by means of baptism, become buried with him (Col. ii, 12).—Meyer, in loco.

[2] New Testament Grammar, p. 264. Comp. Buttmann's Grammar of the New Testament Greek; Thayer's Translation, pp. 194–206. Andover, 1873.

The grammatical sense is to be always sought by a careful study and application of the well-established principles and rules of the language. A close attention to the meaning and relations of words, a care to note the course of thought, and to allow each case, mood, tense, and the position of each word, to contribute its part to the general whole, and a caution lest we assign to words and phrases a scope and conception foreign to the *usus loquendi* of the language —these are rules, which, if faithfully observed, will always serve to bring out the real import of any written document.

CHAPTER VII.

CONTEXT, SCOPE, AND PLAN.

THE grammatico-historical sense is further developed by a study of the context and scope of an author's work. The word *context*, as the etymology intimates (Latin, *con*, together, and *textus*, woven), denotes something that is woven together, and, applied to a written document, it means the connexion of thought supposed to run through every passage which constitutes by itself a whole. By some writers it is called *the connexion.* The immediate context is that which immediately precedes or follows a given word or sentence. The remote context is that which is less closely connected, and may embrace a whole paragraph or section. The scope, on the other hand, is the end or purpose which the writer has in view. Every author is supposed to have some object in writing, and that object will be either formally stated in some part of his work, or else apparent from the general course of thought. The plan of a work is the arrangement of its several parts; the order of thought which the writer pursues.

Context, Scope, and Plan defined.

The context, scope, and plan of a writing should, therefore, be studied together; and, logically, perhaps, the scope should be first ascertained. For the meaning of particular parts of a book may be fully apprehended only when we have mastered the general purpose and design of the whole. The plan of a book, moreover, is most intimately related to its scope. The one cannot be fully apprehended without some knowledge of the other. Even where the scope is formally announced, an analysis of the plan will serve to make it more clear. A writer who has a well-defined plan in his mind will be likely to keep to that plan, and make all his narratives and particular arguments bear upon the main subject.

The scope of several of the books of Scripture is formally stated by the writers. Most of the prophets of the Old Test- Scope of many ament state the occasion and purpose of their oracles books formally at the beginning of their books, and at the beginning of announced. particular sections. The purpose of the Book of Proverbs is announced in verses 1–6 of the first chapter. The subject of Ecclesiastes is indicated at the beginning, in the words "Vanity of vanities." The design of John's Gospel is formally stated at the close of the twentieth chapter: "These things are written that ye may believe that Jesus is the Christ, the Son of God; and that believing ye may have life in his name." The special purpose and occasion of the Epistle of Jude are given in verses 3 and 4: "Beloved, while giving all diligence to write to you of our common salvation, I found (or had) necessity to write to you exhorting to contend earnestly for the faith once for all delivered to the saints. For there crept in stealthily certain men, who of old were forewritten unto this judgment, ungodly, turning the grace of our God into lasciviousness, and denying the only Master, and our Lord Jesus Christ." The purport of this is, that while Jude was diligently planning and preparing to write a treatise or epistle on the common salvation, the circumstances stated in verse 4 led him to break off from that purpose for the time, and write to exhort them to contend earnestly for the faith once for all (ἅπαξ, *only once;* "no other faith will be given."—Bengel) delivered to the saints.

The scope of some books must be ascertained by a diligent examination of their contents. Thus, for example, the Plan and Scope Book of Genesis is found to consist of ten sections, of Genesis seen each beginning with the heading, "These are the gen- in its contents. erations," etc. This tenfold history of generations is preceded and introduced by the record of creation in chapter i, 1–ii, 3. The plan of the author appears, therefore, to be, first of all to record the miraculous creation of the heavens and the land, and then the developments (evolutions) in human history that followed that creation. Accordingly, the first developments of human life and history are called "the generations of the heavens and the land" (chap. ii, 4). The historical standpoint of the writer is "the day" from which the generations (תּוֹלְדוֹת, *growths*) start, the day when man was formed of the dust of the ground and the breath of life from the heavens. So the first man is conceived as the product of the land and the heavens by the word of God, and the word בָּרָא, *create*, does not occur in this whole section. "The day" of chapter ii, 4, which most interpreters understand of the whole creative week, we take rather to be the *terminus a quo* of generations, the day from which, according to verse 5, all the Edenic growths began; the day when the whole face of the ground was watered, when the garden of Eden was planted, and the first human pair were brought together. It was the sixth day of the creative week, "the day that Jehovah God made (עשה, in the sense of *effected*, *did*, *accomplished*, brought to completion) land and heavens." Adam was the "son of God" (Luke iii, 38), and the day of his creation was the point of time when Jehovah Elohim first revealed himself in history as one with the Creator. In chapter i, which records the beginning of the heavens and the land, only Elohim is named, the God in whom, as the plural form of the name denotes, centre all fulness and manifoldness of divine powers. But at chapter ii, 4, where the record of generations begins, we first meet with the name Jehovah, the personal Revealer, who enters into covenant with his creatures, and places man under moral law. Creation, so to speak, began with the pluripotent God—Elohim; its completion in the formation of man, and in subsequent developments, was wrought by Jehovah, the God of revelation, of law, and of love. Having traced the generations of the heavens and the land through Adam down to Seth (iv, 25, 26), the writer next records the outgrowths of that line in what he calls "the book of the generations of Adam" (v, 1). This book is no history of Adam's origin, for that was incorporated in the generations of the heavens and the land, but of Adam's posterity through Seth down to the time of the flood. Next follow "the generations of Noah (vi, 9), then those of his sons Shem, Ham, and Japheth (x, 1), then those of Shem through Arphaxad to Terah (xi, 10–26), and then, in regular order, the generations of Terah (xi, 27, under which the whole history of Abraham is placed), Ishmael (xxv, 12), Isaac (xxv, 19), Esau (xxxvi, 1), and Jacob (xxxvii, 2). Hence the great design of the book was evidently to place on record the beginning and the earliest developments of human life and history. Keeping in mind this scope and structure of the book, we see its unity, and also find each section and subdivision sustaining a logical fitness and relation to the whole. Thus, too, the import of not a few passages becomes more clear and forcible.

A very cursory examination of the Book of Exodus shows us Plan and Scope of Exodus. that its great purpose is to record the history of the Exodus from Egypt and the legislation at Mt. Sinai, and it is readily divisible into two parts (1) chaps. i–xviii; (2) xix–xl; corresponding to these two great events. But a closer examination and analysis reveal many beautiful and suggestive relations of the different sections. First, we have a vivid narrative of *the bondage of Israel* (chaps. i–xi). It is sharply outlined in chapter i, enhanced by the account of Moses' early life and exile (chaps. ii–iv), and shown in its intense persistence by the account of Pharaoh's hardness of heart, and the consequent plagues which smote the land of Egypt (chaps. v–xi). Second, we have the *redemption of Israel* (chaps. xii–xv, 21). This is first typified by the Passover (chaps. xii–xiii, 16), realized in the marvels and triumphs of the march out of Egypt, and the passage of the Red Sea (xiii, 17–xiv, 31), and celebrated in the triumphal song of Moses (xv, 1–21). Then, third, we have *the consecration of Israel* (xv, 22–xl) set forth in seven sections. (1) The march from the Red Sea to Rephidim (xv, 22–xvii, 7), depicting the first free activities of the people after their redemption, and their need of special Divine compassion and help. (2) Attitude of the heathen toward Israel in the cases of hostile Amalek and friendly Jethro (xvii, 8–xviii). (3) The giving of the Law at Sinai (xix–xxiv). (4) The tabernacle planned (xxv–xxvii). (5) The Aaronic priesthood and sundry sacred services ordained (xxviii–xxxi). (6) The backslidings of the people punished, and renewal of the covenant and laws (xxxii–xxxiv). (7) The tabernacle constructed, reared, and filled with the glory of Jehovah (xxxv–xl).

These different sections of Exodus are not designated by special headings, like those of Genesis, but are easily distinguished as so many subsidary portions of one whole, to which each contributes its share, and in the light of which each is seen to have peculiar significance.

Many have taken in hand to set forth in order the course of thought in the Epistle to the Romans. There can be no doubt, to those who have closely studied this epistle, that, after his opening salutation and personal address, the apostle announces his great theme in verse 16 of the first chapter. It is *the Gospel considered as the power of God unto salvation to every believer, to the Jew first, and also to the Greek.* This is not formally announced as the thesis, but it manifestly expresses, in a happy personal way, the scope of the entire epistle. "It had for its end," says Alford, "the settlement, on the broad principles of God's truth and love, of the mutual relations and union in Christ of God's ancient people and the recently engrafted world. What wonder, then, if it be found to contain an exposition of man's unworthiness and God's redeeming love, such as not even Holy Scripture itself elsewhere furnishes?" [1]

In the development of his plan the apostle first spreads out before

_{Subject and Plan of the Epistle to the Romans.}

[1] Greek Testament; Prolegomena to Romans.

us an appalling portraiture of the heathen world, and adds, that
even the Jew, with all his advantage of God's revelation, is under
the same condemnation; for by the law the whole world is involved
in sin, and exposed to the righteous judgment of God. This is the
first division (i, 18–iii, 20). The second, which extends to the close
of the eighth chapter, and ends with a magnificent expression of
Christian confidence and hope, discusses and illustrates the proposition stated at its beginning: "Now, apart from law, a righteousness of God has been manifested, being witnessed by the law and
the prophets, even a righteousness of God through faith of Jesus
Christ unto all them that believe" (iii, 21). Under this head we
find unfolded the doctrine of justification by faith, and the progressive glorification of the new man through sanctification of the
Spirit. Then follows the apostle's vindication of the righteousness
of God in casting off the Jews and calling the Gentiles (chaps.
ix–xi), an argument that exhibits throughout a yearning for Israel's salvation, and closes with an outburst of wondering emotion over the "depth of riches and wisdom and knowledge of God,"
and a doxology (xi, 33–36). The concluding chapters (xii–xvi) consist of a practical application of the great lessons of the epistle in
exhortations, counsels, and precepts for the Church, and numerous
salutations and references to personal Christian friends.

It will be found that a proper attention to this general plan and
scope of the Epistle will greatly help to the understanding of its
smaller sections.

Having ascertained the general scope and plan of a book of
Scripture, we are more fully prepared to trace the context and bear-
Context of par-   ings of its particular parts. The context, as we have
ticular passages.   observed, may be near or remote, according as we seek
its immediate or more distant connexion with the particular word
or passage in hand. It may run through a few verses or a whole
section. The last twenty-six chapters of Isaiah exhibit a marked
unity of thought and style, but they are capable of several subdivisions. The celebrated Messianic prophecy in chapters lii, 13–liii, 12,
is a complete whole in itself, but most unhappily torn asunder by
the division of chapters. But, though forming a clearly defined
section by themselves, these fifteen verses must not be severed from
their context, or treated as if they had no vital connexion with
what precedes and what follows after. Alexander justly condemns
"the radical error of supposing that the book is susceptible of distribution into detached and independent parts." [1] It has its divisions more or less clearly defined, but they cling to each other,

[1] Later Prophecies of Isaiah, p. 247. New York, 1847.

and are interwoven with each other, and form a living whole. It
is beautifully observed by Nägelsbach, that "chapters xlix–lvii are
like a wreath of glorious flowers intertwined with black ribbon; or
like a song of triumph, through whose muffled tone there courses
the melody of a dirge, yet so that gradually the mournful chords
merge into the melody of the song of triumph. And at the same
time the discourse of the prophet is arranged with so much art that
the mourning ribbon ties into a great bow exactly in the middle.
For chapter liii forms the middle of the entire prophetic cycle of
chapters xl–lxvi." [1]

The immediate connexion with what precedes may be thus seen:
In lii, 1–12, the future salvation of Israel is glowingly depicted as
a restoration more glorious than that from the bondage of Egypt
or from Assyrian exile. Jerusalem awakes and rises from the dust
of ruin; the captive is released from fetters; the feet of fleet messengers speed with good tidings, and the watchmen take up the
glad report, and sound the cry of redemption. And then (verse 11)
an exhortation is sounded to depart from all pollution and bondage,
and the sublime exodus is contrasted (verse 12) with the hasty
flight from Egypt, but with the assurance that, as of old, Jehovah
would still be as the pillar of cloud and fire before them and behind
them. At this our passage begins, and the thought naturally turns
to the great Leader of this spiritual exodus—a greater than Moses,
even though that ancient servant of Jehovah was faithful in all his
house (Num. xii, 7). Our prophet proceeds to delineate Him whose
sufferings and sorrows for the transgressions of his people far transcended those of Moses, and whose final triumph through the fruit
of the travail of his soul shall be also infinitely greater.

The much-disputed passage in Matt. xi, 12 can be properly explained only by special regard to the context. Literally Matt. xi, 12 ex-
translated, the verse reads: "From the days of John plained in the
the Baptist until now, the kingdom of the heavens text.
suffers violence (βιάζεται), and violent ones are seizing upon it."
There are seven different ways in which this passage has been
explained.

1. The violence here mentioned is explained by one class of interpreters as a *hostile violence*—the kingdom is violently persecuted
by its enemies, and violent persecutors seize on it as by storm.
The words themselves would not unnaturally bear such a meaning, but we find nothing in the context to harmonize with a reference to hostile forces, or violent persecution.

2. Fritzsche translates βιάζεται by *magna vi praedicatur* (is

[1] Commentary on Isaiah, lii, 13, in Lange's Biblework.

proclaimed with great power); but this is contrary to the meaning of the word, and utterly without warrant.

3. The most common interpretation is that which takes βιάζεται in a good sense, and explains it of the eager and anxious struggles of many to enter into the new kingdom of God. This view, however, is open to the twofold objection, that it does not allow the word βιάζεται its proper significance, and it has no relevancy to the context. It could scarcely be said of the blind, the lame, the lepers, the deaf, the dead, and the poor, mentioned in verse 5, that they took the kingdom by violence, for whatever violence was exerted in their case proceeded not from them but from Christ.

4. According to Lange "the expression is metaphorical, denoting the violent bursting forth of the kingdom of heaven, as the kernel of the ancient theocracy, through the husk of the Old Testament. John and Christ are themselves the violent who take it by force— the former, as commencing the assault; the latter, as completing the conquest. Accordingly, this is a figurative description of the great era which had then commenced."[1] So far as this exposition might describe an era which began with John, it would certainly have relevancy to the immediate context; but no such era of a *violent* bursting forth of the kingdom of heaven had as yet opened. The kingdom of God was not yet come; it was only at hand. Besides, the making of both John and Christ the violent ones, in the sense of breaking open the husk of the Old Testament to let the kingdom of the heavens out, is a far-fetched and most improbable idea.

5. Others take βιάζεται in a middle sense: the kingdom of heaven violently breaks in—forcibly introduces itself, or thrusts itself forward in spite of all opposition. This usage of the word may be allowed; but the interpretation it offers is open to the same objection as that of Lange just given. It cannot be shown that there was any such violent breaking in of the kingdom of God from the days of John the Baptist to the time when Jesus spoke these words. Besides, it is difficult, on this view, to explain satisfactorily the βιασταί, *violent ones*, mentioned immediately afterward.

6. Stier combines a good and a bad sense in the use of βιάζεται: "The word has here no more and no less than its active sense, which passes into the middle. The kingdom of heaven proclaims itself *loudly and openly, breaking in with violence;* the poor are compelled (Luke xiv, 23) to enter it; those who oppose it are *constrained to take offence.* In short, all things proceed urgently with it; it goes with mighty movement and impulse; it works effectually

[1] Commentary, in loco.

upon all spirits on both sides and on all sides. . . . Its constraining power does violence to all; but it excites, at the same time, in the case of many, obstinate opposition. He who will not submit to it, must be offended and resist; and he, too, who yields to it, must press and struggle through this offence. Thus the kingdom of heaven *does* and *suffers* violence, *both* in its twofold influence."[1] Hence, according to Stier, the *violent ones* are either good or bad, since both classes are compelled to take some part in the general struggle, either for or against. This exposition, however, is without sufficient warrant in the history of the time, "from the days of John the Baptist until now," and it puts too many shades of meaning on the word βιασταί. Besides, this view also has no clear relevancy to the context.

7. We believe the true view will be attained only by giving each word its natural meaning, and keeping attention strictly to the context. The common meaning of βιάζω is to *take something by force*, to *carry by storm*, as a besieged city or fortress; and it here refers most naturally to the violent and hasty efforts to seize upon the kingdom of God which had been conspicuous since the beginning of the ministry of John. For this view seems to be demanded by the context. John had heard, in his prison, about the works of Christ, and, anxious and impatient for the glorious manifestation of the Messiah, sent two of his disciples to put the dubious question, "Art thou he that is coming, or look we for another?" (Matt. xi, 2, 3). Jesus' answer (verses 4–6) was merely a statement of his mighty works, and of the preaching of the Gospel to the poor—Old Testament prophetic evidence that the days of the Messiah were at hand—and the tacit rebuke: "Blessed is he whosoever shall not be offended (σκανδαλισθῇ *find occasion of stumbling*) in me," was evidently meant for John's impatience. When John's disciples went away Jesus at once proceeded to speak of John's character and standing before the multitudes: When ye all flocked to the wilderness to hear John preach, did ye expect to find a wavering reed, or a finely dressed courtier? Or did ye expect, rather, to see a prophet? Yes, he exclaims, much more than a prophet. For he was the Messiah's messenger, himself prophesied of in the Scriptures (Mal. iii, 1). He was greater than all the prophets who were before him; for he stood upon the very verge of the Messianic era and introduced the Christ. But, with all his greatness, he misunderstands the kingdom of heaven; and from his days until now the kingdom of heaven suffers violence from many who, like him, think it may be forced into manifestation. That king-

[1] Words of the Lord Jesus, in loco.

dom comes according to an ordered progress. First, the prophets
and the law until John—the Elijah foretold in Mal. iv, 5. John
was but the forerunner of Christ, preparing his way, and Christ's
manifestation in the flesh was not his coming in his kingdom.
Herein, we think, expositors have generally misapprehended our
Lord's doctrine. Thus Nast: "The Lord speaks of the absolutely
certain and momentous fact that the kingdom of heaven has come,
proclaims its presence, and sends forth its invitations in tones not
to be misunderstood (verse 15)."[1] We believe, on the contrary, that
this is a grave misunderstanding of our Lord's words. He neither
says, nor necessarily implies, that his kingdom *has come*. John's
preaching and Christ's preaching alike declared the kingdom to be
at hand, and not fully come. Compare Matt. iii, 2 and iv, 17. But
from the beginning of this gospel men had been over anxious to
have the kingdom itself appear, and in this sense it was suffering
violence, both by an inward impatience and zeal, such as John himself had just now exhibited, and by an open and outward clamour,
such as was exhibited by those who would fain have taken Jesus
by force and made him king (John vi, 15). This same kind of violence is to be understood in the parallel passage in Luke xvi, 16.
The preaching of "the Gospel of the kingdom" was the occasion of
a violence of attitude regarding it. Every man would fain enter
violently into it.

The word βιάζεται, accordingly, denotes not altogether a hostile
violence, nor yet, on the other hand, a commendable zeal; but it
may combine in a measure both of these conceptions. Stier finely
says: "In a case where exegesis perseveringly disputes which of
the two views of a passage capable of two senses is correct, it is
generally found that both are one in a third deeper meaning, and
that the disputants in both cases have both right and wrong in their
argument."[2] The word in question may combine both the good and
the bad senses of violence: not, however, in the manner in which
Stier explains, as above, but as depicting the violent zeal of those
who would hurry the kingdom of God into a premature manifestation. Such a zeal might be laudable in its general aim, but very
mistaken in its spirit and plan, and therefore deserving of rebuke.

The context of Gal. v, 4, must be studied in order to apprehend
Gal. v, 4, to be the force and scope of the words: "Ye are fallen away
explained by from grace." The apostle is contrasting justification
immediate con-
text. by faith in Christ with justification by an observance
of the law, and he argues that these two are opposites, so that one

---

[1] English Commentary on Matthew, in loco.
[2] Words of the Lord Jesus, on Matt. xi, 12.

necessarily excludes the other. He who receives circumcision as a means of justification (verse 2) virtually excludes Christ, whose gospel calls for no such work. If one seeks justification in a law of works, he binds himself to keep the whole law (verse 3); for then not circumcision only, but the whole law, must be minutely observed. Then, with a marked emphasis and force of words, he adds: "Ye were severed from Christ, whoever of you are being (assuming to be) justified in law, ye fell away from grace." Ye cut yourselves off from the system of grace (τῆς χάριτος). The word *grace*, then, is here to be understood not as a gracious attainment of personal experience, but as the gospel system of salvation. From this system they apostatized who sought justification in law.

It will be obvious from the above that the connexion of thought in any given passage may depend on a variety of considerations. It may be a *historical* connexion, in that facts or events recorded are connected in a chronological sequence. It may be *historico-dogmatic*, in that a doctrinal discourse is connected with some historic fact *The connexion may be historical, historico-dogmatic, logical, or psychological.* or circumstance. It may be a *logical* connexion, in that the thoughts or arguments are presented in logical order; or it may be *psychological*, because dependent on some association of ideas. This latter often occasions a sudden breaking off from a line of thought, and may serve to explain some of the parenthetical passages and instances of *anacoluthon* so frequent in the writings of Paul.

Too much stress cannot well be laid upon the importance of closely studying the context, scope, and plan. Many a passage of Scripture will not be understood at all without the help afforded by the context; for many a sen- *Importance of studying the context, scope, and plan.* tence derives all its point and force from the connexion in which it stands. So, again, a whole section may depend, for its proper exposition, upon our understanding the scope and plan of the writer's argument. How futile would be a proof text drawn from the Book of Job unless, along with the citation, it were observed whether it were an utterance of Job himself, or of one of his three friends, or of Elihu, or of the Almighty! Even Job's celebrated utterance in chapter xix, 25-27, should be viewed in reference to the scope of the whole book, as well as to his intense anguish and emotion at that particular stage of the controversy.[1]

[1] Some religious teachers are fond of employing scriptural texts simply as mottoes, with little or no regard to their true connexion. Thus they too often adapt them to their use by imparting to them a factitious sense foreign to their proper scope and meaning. The seeming gain in all such cases is more than counterbalanced by the loss and danger that attend the practice. It encourages the habit of interpreting

"In considering the connexion of parts in a section," says Davidson, "and the amount of meaning they express, acuteness and critical tact are much needed. We may be
able to tell the significations of single terms, and yet be
utterly inadequate to unfold a continuous argument. A capacity
for verbal analysis does not impart the talent of expounding an
entire paragraph. Ability to discover the proper causes, the natural sequence, the pertinency of expressions to the subject discussed, and the delicate distinctions of thought which characterize
particular kinds of composition, is distinct from the habit of carefully tracing out the various senses of separate terms. It is a
higher faculty; not the child of diligence, but rather of original,
intellectual ability. Attention may sharpen and improve, but cannot create it. All men are not endowed with equal acuteness, nor
fitted to detect the latent links of associated ideas by their outward
symbols. They cannot alike discern the idiosyncrasies of various
writers as exhibited in their composition. But the verbal philologist is not necessarily incapacitated by converse with separate signs
of ideas from unfolding the mutual bearings of an entire paragraph.
Imbued with a philosophic spirit, he may successfully trace the
connexion subsisting between the various parts of a book, while he
notes the commencement of new topics, the propriety of their position, the interweaving of argumentation, interruptions and digressions, and all the characteristic peculiarities exhibited in a particular
composition. In this he may be mightily assisted by a just perception of those particles which have been designated ἔπεα πτερό-
εντα [winged words], not less than by sympathy with the spirit of
the author whom he seeks to understand. By placing himself as
much as possible in the circumstances of the writer, and contemplating from the same elevation the important phenomena to
which his rapt mind was directed, he will be in a favourable position for understanding the parts and proportions of a connected
discourse."[1]

(margin note: Critical tact and ability needed.)

Scripture in an arbitrary and fanciful way, and thus furnishes the teachers of error
with their most effective weapon. The practice cannot be defended on any plea of
necessity. The plain words of Scripture, legitimately interpreted according to their
proper scope and context, contain a fulness and comprehensiveness of meaning sufficient for the wants of all men in all circumstances. That piety alone is robust and
healthful which is fed, not by the fancies and speculations of the preacher who practically puts his own genius above the word of God, but by the pure doctrines and precepts of the Bible, unfolded in their true connexion and meaning. Barrows, Introduction to the Study of the Bible, p. 455.

[1] Sacred Hermeneutics, p. 240.

CHAPTER VIII.

COMPARISON OF PARALLEL PASSAGES.

THERE are portions of Scripture in the exposition of which we are not to look for help in the context or scope. The Book of Proverbs, for example, is composed of numerous separate aphorisms, many of which have no necessary connection with each other. *Some parts of Scripture without logical connection with each other.* The book itself is divisible into several collections of proverbs; and separate sections, like that concerning the evil woman in chapter vii, and the words of wisdom in chapters viii and ix, have a unity and completeness in themselves, through which a connected train of thought is discernible. But many of the proverbs are manifestly without connexion with what precedes or follows. Thus the twentieth and twenty-first chapters of Proverbs may be studied ever so closely, and no essential connexion of thought appears to hold any two of the verses together. The same will be found true of other portions of this book, which from its very nature is a collection of apothegms, each one of which may stand by itself as a concise expression of aphoristic wisdom. Several parts of the Book of Ecclesiastes consist of proverbs, soliloquies, and exhortations, which appear to have no vital relation to each other. Such, especially, are to be found in chapters v–x. Accordingly, while the scope and general subject-matter of the entire book are easily discerned, many eminent critics have despaired of finding in it any definite plan or logical arrangement. The Gospels, also, contain some passages which it is impossible to explain as having any essential connexion with either that which precedes or follows.

On such isolated texts, as also on those not so isolated, a comparison of parallel passages of Scripture often throws much light. For words, phrases, and historical or doctrinal statements, which in one place are difficult to understand, are often *Value of parallel passages.* set forth in clear light by the additional statements with which they stand connected elsewhere. Thus, as shown above (pp. 215–218), the comparatively isolated passage in Luke xvi, 16, is much more clear and comprehensive when studied in the light of its context in Matt. xi, 12. Without the help of parallel passages, some words and statements of the Scripture would scarcely be intelligible. As we ascertain the *usus loquendi* of words from a wide collation of passages in which they occur, so the sense of an entire passage may be elucidated by a comparison with its parallel in another place. " The employment of parallel passages," says Immer, "must go hand in hand with attention to the connexion. The mere explanation according to the connexion often fails to secure the certainty that is desired, at least in cases where the linguistic usage under consideration and the analogous thought cannot at the same time be otherwise established."[1]

"In comparing parallels," says Davidson, "it is proper to observe a certain order. In the first place we should seek for parallels in the writings of the same author, as the same peculiarities of conception and modes of expression are liable to return in different works proceeding from one person. There is a certain configuration of mind which manifests itself in the productions of one man. Each writer is distinguished by a style more or less his own; by characteristics which would serve to identify him with the emanations of his intellect, even were his name withheld. Hence the reasonableness of expecting parallel passages in the writings of one author to throw most light upon each other."[2]

But we should also remember that the Scriptures of the Old and New Testaments are a world by themselves. Although written at sundry times, and devoted to many different themes, taken altogether they constitute a self-interpreting book. The old rule, therefore, that "Scripture must be interpreted by Scripture," is a most important principle of sacred hermeneutics. But we must avoid the danger of overstepping in this matter. Some have gone too far in trying to make Daniel explain the Revelation of John, and it is equally possible to distort a passage in Kings or in Chronicles by attempting to make it parallel with some statement of Paul. In general we may expect to find the most valuable parallels in books of the same class. Historical passages will be likely to be paralleled with historical, prophetic with prophetic, poetic with poetic, and argumentative and hortatory with those of like character. Hosea and Amos will be likely to have more in common than Genesis and Proverbs; Matthew and Luke will be expected to be more alike than Matthew and one of the Epistles of Paul, and Paul's Epistles naturally exhibit many parallels both of thought and language.

The Bible a self-interpreting book.

Nor should we overlook the fact that almost all we know of the history of the Jewish people is embodied in the Bible. The apocryphal books of the Old Testament and the works of Josephus are the principal outside sources. These different books may, then, be

[1] Hermeneutics of the New Testament, p. 159.   [2] Hermeneutics, p. 251.

fairly expected to interpret themselves. Their spirit and purpose, their modes of thought and expression, their doctrinal teachings, and, to some extent, their general subject-matter, would be naturally expected to have a self-conformity. When, upon examination, we find that this is the case, we shall the more fully appreciate the importance of comparing all parallel portions and reading them in each other's light.

Parallel passages have been commonly divided into two classes, *verbal* and *real*, according as that which constitutes the parallel consists in words or in like subject-matter. Parallels verbal and real. Where the same word occurs in similar connexion, or in reference to the same general subject, the parallel is called verbal. The use of such parallel passages has been shown above in determining the meaning of words.[1] Real parallels are those similar passages in which the likeness or identity consists, not in words or phrases, but in facts, subjects, sentiments, or doctrines. Parallels of this kind are sometimes subdivided into historic and didactic, according as the subject-matter consists of historical events or matters of doctrine. But all these divisions are, perhaps, needless refinements. The careful expositor will consult all parallel passages, whether they be verbal, historical, or doctrinal; but in actual interpretation he will find little occasion to discriminate formally between these different classes.

The great thing to determine, in every case, is whether the passages adduced are really parallel. A verbal parallel may be as real as one that embodies many corresponding sentiments, for a single word is often decisive of a Parallels must have a real correspondency. doctrine or a fact. On the other hand, there may be a likeness of sentiment without any real parallelism. Proverbs xxii, 2, and xxix, 13, are usually taken as parallels, but a close inspection will show that though there is a marked similarity of sentiment, there is no essential identity or real parallelism. The first passage is: "Rich and poor meet together; maker of all of them is Jehovah." We need not assume that this *meeting together* is in the grave (Conant) or in the *conflicts* (כְּמִּשְׁי) of life in a hostile sense. The second passage, properly rendered, is: "The poor and the man of oppressions meet together; an enlightener of the eyes of both of them is Jehovah." Here the *man of oppressions* is not necessarily a rich man; nor is *enlightener of the eyes* an equivalent of *maker* in xxii, 2. Hence, all that can be properly said of these two passages is, that they are similar in sentiment, but not strictly parallel or identical in sense.

[1] See above, pages 186, 187.

A careful comparison of the parables of the talents (Matt. xxv, 14–30) and of the pounds (Luke xix, 11–27) will show that they have much in common, together with not a few things that are different. They were spoken at different times, in different places, and to different hearers. The parable of the talents deals only with the servants of the lord who went into a far country; that of the pounds deals also with his citizens and enemies who would not have him reign over them. Yet the great lesson of the necessity of diligent activity for the Lord in his absence is the same in both parables.

A comparison of parallel passages is necessary in order to determine the sense of the word *hate* in Luke xiv, 26 : "If any one comes unto me, and hates not his father, and mother, and wife, and children, and brothers, and sisters, and even his own life besides, he cannot be my disciple." This statement appears at first to contravene the fifth commandment of the decalogue, and also to involve other unreasonable demands. It seems to stand opposed to the Gospel doctrine of love. But, turning to Matt. x, 37, we find the statement in a milder form, and woven in a context which serves to disclose its full force and bearing. There the statement is: "He that loveth father or mother more than me is not worthy of me; and he that loveth son or daughter more than me is not worthy of me." The immediate context of this verse (verses 34–39), a characteristic passage of our Lord's more ardent utterances, sets its meaning in a clear light. "Do not think," he says, verse 34, "that I came to send peace on the earth; I came not to send peace but a sword." He sees a world lying in wickedness, and exhibiting all forms of opposition to his messages of truth. With such a world he can make no compromise, and have no peace without, first, a bitter conflict. Such conflict he, therefore, purposely invites. He will conquer a peace, or else have none at all. "The telic style of expression is not only rhetorical, indicating that the result is unavoidable, but what Jesus expresses is a purpose—not the final design of his coming, but an intermediate purpose—in seeing clearly presented to his view the reciprocally hostile excitement as a necessary transition, which he therefore, in keeping with his destiny as Messiah, must be sent first of all to bring forth." [1] Before his final purpose is accomplished he sees what bitter strifes must come; but the grand result will be well worth all the intermediate woes. Therefore he will call father, mother, child, although it cause many household divisions; and so he adds, as explaining how he will send

The word hate illustrated by parallel passages.

Matt. x, 34–39.

[1] Meyer, Critical and Exegetical Commentary, in loco.

a sword rather than peace: "For I came to set a man at variance against his father, and the daughter against her mother, and the daughter-in-law against her mother-in-law; and a man's foes shall be they of his own household." When this state of things shall come to pass, how many will be called upon to decide whether they will cleave to Christ, or to an unchristian father? Micah's words (vii, 6) will then be true. Son will oppose father, daughter will rise up against mother, and if one remains true to the Lord Christ, he will have to forsake his own household and kin. He cannot be a true disciple and love his parents or children more than Christ. Hence he must needs set them aside, forsake them, love them less, and even oppose them, assuming toward them the hostile attitude of an enemy for Christ's sake. The import of *hate*, in Luke xiv, 26, is accordingly made clear.

This peculiar meaning of the word is further confirmed by its use in Matt. vi, 24: "No man can serve two masters: for either he will hate the one, and love the other; or else he will hold to the one, and despise the other. Ye cannot serve God and Mammon." Two masters, so opposite in nature as God and Mammon, cannot be loved and served at one and the same time. The love of the one necessarily excludes the love of the other, and neither will be served with a divided heart. In the case of such essential opposites, a lack of love for one amounts to a disloyal enmity— the root of all hatred. Another parallel, illustrative of this impressive teaching, is to be found in Deut. xiii, 6–11, where it is enjoined that, if brother, son, daughter, wife, or friend entice one to idolatry, he shall not only not consent, but he shall not have pity on the seducer, and shall take measures to have him publicly punished as an enemy of God and his people. Hence we derive the lesson that one who opposes our love and loyalty to God or Christ is the worst possible enemy. Compare also John xii, 25; Rom. ix, 13; Mal. i, 2, 3; Deut. xxi, 15.

The true interpretation of Jesus' words to Peter, in Matt. xvi, 18, will be fully apprehended only by a comparison and careful study of all the parallel texts. Jesus says to Peter, "Thou art Peter (πέτρος), and upon this *petra* (or *rock*, ἐπὶ ταύτῃ τῇ πέτρᾳ), will I build my Church, and the gates of Hades shall not prevail against her." How is it possible from this passage alone to decide whether the rock (πέτρα) refers to Christ (as Augustine and Wordsworth), or to Peter's confession (Luther and many Protestant divines), or to Peter himself? It is noticeable that in the parallel passages of Mark (viii, 27–30) and Luke (ix, 18–21) these words of Christ to Peter do not occur. The immediate context presents us with Simon Peter, as the spokesman and representative of the disciples, answering Jesus' question with the bold and confident confession, "Thou art the Christ, the Son of the living God." Jesus was evidently moved by the fervid words of Peter, and said to him, "Blessed art thou, Simon Bar-jona, for flesh and blood revealed it not to thee, but my Father who is in the heavens." Whatever knowledge and convictions of Jesus' messiahship and divinity the disciples had attained before, this noble confession of Peter possessed the newness and glory of a special revelation. It was not the offspring of "flesh and blood," that is, not of natural human birth or origin, but the spontaneous outburst of a divine inspiration from heaven. Peter was for the moment caught up by the Spirit of God, and, in the glowing fervour of such inspiration, spoke the very word of the Father. He was accordingly pronounced the blessed (μακάριος) or happy one.

Turning now to the narrative of Simon's introduction to the Saviour (John i, 41–43), we compare the first mention of the name Peter. He was led into the presence of Jesus by his own brother Andrew, and Jesus, gazing on him, said, "Thou art Simon, the son of Jonah; thou shalt be called Cephas, which is interpreted Peter" (πέτρος). Thus, at the beginning, he tells him what he *is* and what he *shall be*. A doubtful character at that time was Simon, the son of Jonah; irritable, impetuous, unstable, irresolute; but Jesus saw a coming hour when he would become the bold, strong, abiding, memorable stone (Peter), the typical and representative confessor of the Christ. Reverting again to the passage in Matthew, it is easy to see that, through his inspired confession of the Christ, the Son of the living God, Simon has attained the ideal foreseen and foretold by his Lord. He has now become *Peter* indeed; now "thou *art* Peter," not "shalt be called Peter." Accordingly, we cannot avoid the conviction that the manifest play on the words *petros* and *petra* (in Matt. xvi, 18,) has a designed and important significance, and also an allusion to the first bestowal of the name on Simon (John i, 43); as if the Lord had said: Remember, Simon, the significant name I gave thee at our first meeting. Then I said, *Thou shalt be called Peter;* now I say unto thee, *Thou art Peter.*

But there is doubtless a designed significance in the change from *petros* to *petra*, in Matt. xvi, 18. It is altogether probable that there was a corresponding change in the Aramaic words used by our Lord on this occasion. He may, perhaps, have said: "Thou art *Keph* (כֵּיף or כֵּיפָת), and upon this *kepha* (כֵּיפָא) I will build my Church." What, then, is meant by the πέτρα, *petra*, on which Christ builds his Church? In answering this question we inquire what other scriptures say about the building of the Church, and in Eph. ii, 20–22 we find it written that Christian believers constitute "the household of God, having been built upon the foundation of the apostles and prophets, Christ Jesus himself being the chief cornerstone; in whom all the building, fitly framed together, grows unto a holy temple in the Lord; in whom ye also are builded together for a habitation of God in the Spirit." Having made the natural and easy transition from the figure of a household to that of the structure in which the household dwells, the apostle speaks of the latter as "built upon the foundation of the apostles and prophets." The *prophets* here intended are doubtless the New Testament prophets referred to in chapters iii, 5 and iv, 11. *Ephesians ii, 20–22 compared.*

The foundation OF the apostles and prophets has been explained (1) as a genitive of *apposition*—the foundation which is constituted of apostles and prophets; that is, the apostles and prophets are themselves the foundation (so Chrysostom, Olshausen, De Wette, and many others); (2) as a genitive of the *originating cause*—the foundation laid by the apostles (Calvin, Koppe, Harless, Meyer, Eadie, Ellicott); (3) as a genitive of *possession*—the apostles and prophets' foundation, that is, the foundation upon which they as well as all other believers are builded (Beza, Bucer, Alford). We believe that in the breadth and fulness of the apostle's conception, there is room for all these thoughts, and a wider comparison of Scripture corroborates this view. In Gal. ii, 9, James, Cephas, and John are spoken of as *pillars* (στῦλοι), foundation-pillars, or columnar supports of the Church. In the apocalyptic vision of the New Jerusalem, which is "the bride, the wife of the Lamb" (Rev. xxi, 9), it is said that "the wall of the city has twelve foundations, and upon them twelve names of the twelve apostles of the Lamb" (Rev. xxi, 14). Here it is evident that the apostles are conceived as foundation-stones, forming the substructure of the Church; and with this conception "the foundation of the apostles and prophets" (Eph. ii, 20) may be taken as genitive of apposition. But in 1 Cor. iii, 10, the apostle speaks of himself as a wise architect, laying a foundation (θεμέλιον ἔθηκα, *a foundation I laid*). Immediately after (verse 11) he says: "Other foundation can no one lay than that which is laid, which is Jesus Christ." This foundation Paul himself laid when he founded the Church of Corinth, and first made known there the Lord Jesus Christ. Having once laid this foundation, no man could lay another, although he *Foundation of the apostles and prophets.* *Rev. xxi, 14.* *1 Cor. iii, 10.*

might build thereupon. Paul himself could not have laid another had some one else been first to lay this foundation in Corinth (compare Rom. xv, 20). How he laid this foundation he tells in chap. ii, 1-5, especially when he says (verse 2) "I determined not to know any thing among you except Jesus Christ, and him crucified." So then, in this sense, Ephesians ii, 20 may be taken as genitive of the originating cause—the foundation which the apostles laid. At the same time we need not overlook or ignore the fact presented in 1 Cor. iii, 11, that Jesus is himself the foundation, that is, Jesus Christ—including his person, work, and doctrine—is the great fact on which the Church is builded, and without which there could be no redemption. Hence the Church itself, according to 1 Tim. iii, 15, is the "pillar and basis (ἑδραίωμα) of the truth." Accordingly we hold that the expression "foundation of the apostles and prophets" (Eph. ii, 20) has a fulness of meaning which may include all these thoughts. The apostles were themselves incorporated in this foundation, and made pillars or foundation stones; they, too, were instrumental in laying this foundation and building upon it; and having laid it in Christ, and working solely through Christ, without whom they could do nothing, Jesus Christ himself, as preached by them, was also conceived as the underlying basis and foundation of all (1 Cor. iii, 11).

Another Scripture, in 1 Peter ii, 4, 5, should also be collated here, for it was written by the apostle to whom the words of Matt. xvi, 18, were addressed, and seems to have been with him a thought that lingered like a precious memory in the soul: "To whom (i. e., the gracious Lord just mentioned) approaching, a living stone, by men indeed disallowed, but before God chosen, precious, do ye also yourselves, as living stones, be built up a spiritual house." Here the Lord is himself presented as the elect and precious corner-stone (comp. verse 6), and at the same time Christian believers are also represented as living stones, built into the same spiritual temple.

1 Peter ii, 4, 5, compared.

Coming back now to the text in Matt. xvi, 18, which Schaff pronounces "one of the profoundest and most far-reaching prophetical, but, at the same time, one of the most controverted, sayings of the Saviour,"[1] we are furnished, by the above collation of cognate Scriptures, with the means of apprehending its true import and significance. Filled with a divine inspiration, Peter confessed his Lord Christ, to the glory of God the Father (compare 1 John iv, 15, and Rom. x, 9), and in that blessed attainment and confession he be-

---

[1] Lange's Commentary on Matthew, translated and annotated by Phillip Schaff, p. 293. New York, 1864. Compare also Meyer, Alford, and Nast, in loco.

came the representative or ideal Christian confessor. In view of this, Jesus says to him: Now thou art Peter; thou art become a living stone, the type and representative of the multitude of living stones upon which I will build my Church. The change from the masculine πέτρος to the feminine πέτρα fittingly indicates that it is not so much on Peter, the man, the single and separate individual, as on Peter considered as the confessor, the type and representative of all other Christian confessors, who are to be "builded together for a habitation of God in the Spirit" (Eph. ii, 22).

In the light of all these Scriptures we may see the impropriety and irrelevancy of what has been the prevailing Prot- *Error of the common Protestant interpretation of πέτρα.* estant interpretation, namely, making the πέτρα, *rock,* to be Peter's confession. "Every building," says Nast, "must have foundation stones. What is the foundation of the Christian Church *on the part of man?* Is it not—what Peter exhibited—a faith wrought in the heart by the Holy Ghost, and a confession with the mouth that Jesus is the Christ, the Son of the living God? But this believing with the heart and confessing with the mouth is something personal; it cannot be separated from the living personality that believes and confesses. The Church consists of living men, and its foundation cannot be a mere abstract truth or doctrine apart from the living personality in which it is embodied. This is in accordance with the whole New Testament language, in which not doctrines or confessions, but men, are uniformly called pillars or foundations of the spiritual building." [1]

It is well known how large a portion of the three synoptic Gospels consists of parallel narratives of the words and works of

[1] Commentary on the Gospels of Matthew and Mark, in loco. To the Roman Catholic interpretation, which explains these words as investing Peter and his successors with a permanent primacy at Rome, Schaff opposes the following insuperable objections: (1) It obliterates the distinction between *petros* and *petra ;* (2) it is inconsistent with the true nature of the architectural figure: the foundation of a building is one and abiding, and not constantly renewed and changed; (3) it confounds priority of time with permanent superiority of rank ; (4) it confounds the apostolate, which, strictly speaking, is not transferable, but confined to the original personal disciples of Christ and inspired organs of the Holy Spirit, with the post-apostolic episcopate; (5) it involves an injustice to the other apostles, who, as a body, are expressly called the foundation or foundation-stones of the Church; (6) it contradicts the whole spirit of Peter's epistles, which is strongly antihierarchical, and disclaims any superiority over his 'fellow-presbyters;' (7) finally, it rests on gratuitous assumptions which can never be proven either exegetically or historically, viz., the transferability of Peter's primacy, and its actual transfer upon the bishop, not of Jerusalem, nor of Antioch (where Peter certainly was), but of Rome exclusively." See Lange's Matthew, in loco, page 297.

Jesus. St. Paul's account of the appearances of Jesus after the resurrection (xv, 4–7), and of the institution of the Lord's Supper (xi, 23–26), are well worthy of comparison with the several Gospel narratives.[1] The Epistles of Paul to the Romans and to the Galatians, being each so largely devoted to the doctrine of righteousness through faith, should be studied together, for they have many parallels which help to illustrate each other. Not a few parallel passages of the Ephesian and Colossian Epistles throw light upon each other. The second and third chapters of 2 Peter should be studied and expounded in connexion with the Epistle of Jude. The genealogies of Genesis, Chronicles, and Matthew and Luke, should be compared, as also large sections of the books of Samuel, Kings, Chronicles, Ezra, and Nehemiah. We have in the Acts of the Apostles three separate accounts of Paul's conversion (chaps. ix, xxii, and xxvi), and all these illustrate and supplement each other. The many passages of the Old Testament which are quoted or referred to in the New, are also parallels; but they are so specific in their nature as to call for special treatment in a future chapter.

Large portions of Scripture parallel.

[1] More than common discretion must be exercised by the interpreter of the New Testament with regard to the parallel passages in the Gospels, particularly in the synoptical Gospels. With respect to the latter chiefly, they often relate the same thing, sometimes they communicate the same conversation or saying of Jesus, but not in the same words. We have here, then, different accounts of the same occurrence or thing. But now the interpreter has no right to conclude from one evangelist to another without any limitation, and e. g. to explain and supplement the words of the Saviour, as recorded by one narrator, out of the account of another. For, in any difference in the accounts, the question is, *what* Jesus actually said. We must commence there, by making a distinction between what was actually said and what is communicated concerning it; and with this last the interpreter has to deal. For instance, according to Matt. vi, 11, Jesus taught them to pray in the "Lord's Prayer:" Give us "this day" our daily bread; according to Luke xi, 3: Give us "day by day," etc. Now we have no right to say: therefore, this day — day by day. In the same prayer Matthew has it: "as we forgive," etc. (thus, standard); Luke: "for we also forgive," etc. (thus, reason for hearing the prayer). Now we may not say that the one is equal to the other. In like manner, also, we may not explain 1 Cor. xiv and Acts ii, 4–13 out of each other, and so confound them with each other. In the latter passage there is indeed mention of other (strange) languages (ἕτεραι γλῶσσαι), in the former, on the contrary, not a word is said of "other" languages, but of tongues (γλῶσσαι); and in Acts ii the context of the narrative compels us quite as much to think of strange languages, as the context in 1 Cor. xiv decidedly forbids it.— Doedes, Manual of Hermeneutics, pp. 100, 101.

CHAPTER IX.

THE HISTORICAL STANDPOINT.

It is of the first importance, in interpreting a written document, to ascertain who the author was, and to determine the time, the place, and the circumstances of his writing. The interpreter should, therefore, endeavour to take himself from the present, and to transport himself into the historical position of his author, look through his eyes, note his surroundings, feel with his heart, and catch his emotion. Herein we note the import of the term grammatico-*historical* interpretation. We are not only to grasp the grammatical import of words and sentences, but also to feel the force and bearing of the historical circumstances which may in any way have affected the writer. Hence, too, it will be seen how intimately connected may be the object or design of a writing and the occasion which prompted its composition. The individuality of the writer, his local surroundings, his wants and desires, his relation to those for whom he wrote, his nationality and theirs, the character of the times when he wrote—all these matters are of the first importance to a thorough interpretation of the several books of Scripture.

A knowledge of geography, history, chronology, and antiquities, has already been mentioned as an essential qualification of the biblical interpreter.[1] Especially should he have a clear conception of the order of events connected with the whole course of sacred history, such as the contemporaneous history, so far as it may be known, of the great nations and tribes of patriarchal times; the great world-powers of Egypt, Assyria, Babylon, and Persia, with which the Israelites at various times came in contact; the Macedonian Empire, with its later Ptolemaic and Seleucidaic branches, from which the Jewish people suffered many woes, and the subsequent conquest and dominion of the Romans. The exegete should be able to take his standpoint anywhere along this line of history wherever he may find the age of his author, and thence vividly grasp the outlying circumstances. He should seek a familiarity with the customs, life, spirit, ideas, and pursuits of these different times and different tribes and

Importance of the historical standpoint.

Extensive historical knowledge necessary.

---

[1] See above, pp. 154, 156.

nations, so as to distinguish readily what belonged to one and what to another. By such knowledge he will be able not only to transport himself into any given age, but also to avoid confounding the ideas of one age or race with those of another.

It is not an easy task for one to disengage himself from the liv-
To transfer one- ing present, and thus transport himself into a past age.
self vividly in-
to the remote As we advance in general knowledge, and attain a
past not easy. higher civilization, we unconsciously grow out of old habits and ideas. We lose the spirit of the olden times, and become filled with the broader generalization and more scientific procedures of modern thought. The immensity of the universe, the vast accumulations of human study and research, the influence of great civil and ecclesiastical institutions, and the power of traditional sentiment and opinions, govern and shape our modes of thought to an extent we hardly know. To tear oneself away from these, and go back in spirit to the age of Moses, or David, or Isaiah, or Ezra, or of Matthew and Paul, and assume the historic standpoint of any of those writers, so as to see and feel as they did—this surely is no easy task. Yet, if we truly catch the spirit and feel the living force of the ancient oracles of God, we need to apprehend them somewhat as they first thrilled the hearts of those for whom they were immediately given.

Not a few devout readers of the Bible are so impressed with ex-
Undue exalta- alted ideas of the glory and sanctity of the ancient
tion of biblical
saints to be worthies, that they are liable to take the record of their
avoided. lives in an unnatural light. To some it is difficult to believe that Moses and Paul were not acquainted with the events of modern times. The wisdom of Solomon, they imagine, must have comprehended all that man can know. Isaiah and Daniel must have discerned all future events as clearly as if they had already occurred. The writers of the New Testament must have known what a history and an influence their lifework would possess in after ages. To such minds the names of Abraham, Jacob, Joshua, Jephthah, and Samson, are so associated with holy thoughts and supernatural revelations that they half forget that they were men of like passions with ourselves. Such an undue exaltation of the sanctity of the biblical saints will be likely to interfere with a true historical exposition. The divine call and inspiration of prophets and apostles did not nullify or set aside their natural human powers, and the biblical interpreter should not allow his vision to be so dazzled by the glory of their divine mission as to make him blind to facts of their history. Abraham's cunning and deceit, conspicuous also in Isaac and Jacob, Moses'

hasty passions, and the barbarous brutality of most of the judges and kings of Israel, are not to be explained away. They are facts which the interpreter must fully recognize; and the more fully and vividly all such facts are realized and set in their true light and bearing, the more accurately shall we apprehend the real import of the Scriptures.

In the exposition of the Psalms, one of the first things to inquire after is the personal standpoint of the author. "The historical occasions of the Psalms," says Hibbard, "have ever been regarded, by judicious commentators, as important aids to their interpretation, and the full exhibition of their beauty and power. In the explanation of a work on exact science, or of a metaphysical essay, no importance is attached to the external circumstances and place of the author at the time of writing. In such a case the work has no relation to passing events, but to the abstract and essential relations of things. Very different is the language of poetry, and indeed of almost all such books as the sacred Scriptures are, which were at first addressed to a particular people, or to particular individuals, for their moral benefit, and much of them occupied with the personal experiences of their authors. Here occasion, contact with outward things, the influence of external circumstances and of passing events, play a conspicuous part in giving mould and fashion to the thoughts and feelings of the writer, scope and design to his subject, and meaning and pertinency to his words. It may be said of the Hebrew poets, as of those of all other nations, that the interpretation of their poetry is less dependent on verbal criticism than on sympathy with the feelings of the author, knowledge of his circumstances, and attention to the scope and drift of his utterances. You must place yourself in his condition, adopt his sentiments, and be floated onward with the current of his feelings, soothed by his consolations, or agitated by the storm of his emotions."[1]

Historical occasions of the Psalms.

Of many of the Psalms it is impossible now to determine the historical standpoint; but not a few of them are so clear in their allusions as to leave no reasonable doubt as to the occasion on which they were composed. There is, for example, no good reason for doubting the genuineness of the inscription to the third psalm, which refers the composition to David when he fled from the face of his son Absalom. "From verse 5 we gather," says Perowne, "that the psalm is a morning hymn. With returning day there comes back on the monarch's heart the recollection of

[1] The Psalms, Chronologically Arranged, with Historical Introductions, General Introduction, page 12. New York, 1856.

the enemies who threaten him—a nation up in arms against him, his own son heading the rebellion, his wisest and most trusted counsellor in the ranks of his foes (2 Sam. xv–xvii). Never, not even when hounded by Saul, had he found his position one of greater danger. The odds were overwhelmingly against him. This is a fact which he does not attempt to hide from himself: 'How *many* are mine enemies;' '*many* rise up against me;' '*many* say to my soul;' '*ten thousands* of the people have set themselves against me' (verses 1, 2, 6). Meanwhile, where are his friends, his army, his counsellors? Not a word of allusion to any of them in the psalm. Yet he is not crushed; he is not desponding. Enemies may be thick as the leaves of the forest, and earthly friends may be few, or uncertain, or far off. But there is one Friend who cannot fail him, and to him David turns with a confidence and affection which lift him above all his fears. Never had he been more sensible of the reality and preciousness of the divine protection. If he was surrounded by his enemies, Jehovah was his shield. If Shimei and his crew turned his glory into shame, Jehovah was his glory. If they sought to revile and degrade him, Jehovah was the lifter-up of his head. Nor did the mere fact of distance from Jerusalem separate between him and his God. He had sent back the ark and the priests, for he would not endanger their safety, and he did not trust in them as a charm, and he knew that Jehovah could still hear him from 'his holy mountain' (verse 4), could still lift up the light of his countenance upon him, and put gladness in his heart (Psa. iv, 6, 7). Sustained by Jehovah, he had laid him down and slept in safety; trusting in the same mighty protection he would lie down again to rest. Enemies might taunt him, (verse 2), and friends might fail him, but the victory was Jehovah's, and he could break the teeth of the ungodly" (vii, 8).[1]

The historical standpoint of a writer is so often intimately connected with his situation at the date of writing, that both the time and the place of the composition should be considered together. The locality of the incidents recorded should also be closely studied and pictured before the mind. It adds much to one's knowledge and appreciation of biblical history to visit the lands trodden by patriarchs, prophets, and apostles. Seeing Palestine is, indeed, a fifth gospel. A personal visit to Beer-sheba, Hebron, Jerusalem, Joppa, Nazareth, and the Sea of Galilee, affords a realistic sense of sacred narratives connected with these places such as cannot otherwise be had. The

Consider the place as well as the time of the composition.

---

[1] The Book of Psalms, New Translation, with Introductions and Notes. Introduction to Psalm iii. Andover, 1876.

decalogue and the laws of Moses become more awful and impressive when read upon Mount Sinai, and the Lord's agony in the garden thrills the soul with deeper emotion when meditated in the Kedron valley, beneath the old trees at the foot of the Mount of Olives.

What a vividness and reality appear in the Epistles of Paul when we study them in connexion with the account of his apostolic journeys and labours, and the physical and political features of the countries through which he passed! Setting out from Antioch on his second missionary tour, accompanied by Silas, he passed through Syria and Cilicia, visiting, doubtless, his early home at Tarsus (Acts xv, 40, 41). Thence he passed over the vast mountain-barrier on the north of Cilicia, and, after visiting Derbe and Lystra, where he attached Timothy to him as a companion in travel, he went through the region of Phrygia and Galatia, where, notwithstanding his physical infirmity, he was received as an angel of God (Gal. iv, 13). Passing westward, and having been forbidden to preach in the western parts of Asia Minor (Acts xvi, 6), he came with his companions to Troas. "The district of Troas," observes Howson, "extending from Mt. Ida to the plain, watered by the Simois and the Scamander, was the scene of the Trojan War; and it was due to the poetry of Homer that the ancient name of Priam's kingdom should be retained. This shore had been visited on many memorable occasions by the great men of this world. Xerxes passed this way when he undertook to conquer Greece. Julius Cæsar was here after the battle of Pharsalia. But, above all, we associate this spot with a European conqueror of Asia, and an Asiatic conqueror of Europe, with Alexander of Macedon and Paul of Tarsus. For here it was that the enthusiasm of Alexander was kindled at the tomb of Achilles by the memory of his heroic ancestors; here he girded on his armour, and from this goal he started to overthrow the august dynasties of the East. And now the great apostle rests in his triumphal progress upon the same poetic shore; here he is armed by heavenly visitants with the weapons of a warfare that is not carnal, and hence he is sent forth to subdue all the powers of the West, and bring the civilization of the world into captivity to the obedience of Christ."[1]

After the vision and the Macedonian call received at this place, he sailed from Troas and came to Neapolis, and thence to Philippi, the scene of many memorable events (Acts xvi, 12–40), and thence on through Amphipolis, Apollonia, Thessalonica, and Berea, to

Journeys and Epistles of Paul.

[1] Conybeare and Howson, Life and Epistles of St. Paul, vol. i, page 280. **Fourth American Edition.** New York, 1855.

Athens. There Paul waited, alone (comp. 1 Thess. iii, 1), for his companions, but failed not meanwhile to preach the Gospel to the inquisitive Athenians, "standing in the midst of the Areopagus" (Acts xvii, 22). After this he passed on to Corinth, and founded there the Church to which he subsequently addressed two of his most important epistles. From Corinth, soon after his arrival, he sent his first epistle to the Thessalonians. From this standpoint how lifelike and real are all the personal allusions and reminiscences of this his first epistle! But that letter, in its vivid allusions to the near coming of the Lord, awakened great excitement among the Thessalonians, and only a few months afterward we find him writing his second epistle to them to allay this trouble of their minds, and to assure them that that day is not so near but that several important events must first come to pass (2 Thess. ii, 1–8). A grouping of all these facts and suggestions adds vastly to one's interest in the study of Paul's epistles.

Without pursuing further the course of the apostles life and labours, enough has been said to show what light and interest a knowledge of the time and place of writing gives to the Epistles of Paul. The situation and condition of the churches and persons addressed in his epistles should also be carefully sought out. His subsequent epistles, especially those to the Corinthians, and those of his imprisonment, would be shorn of half their interest and value but for the knowledge we elsewhere obtain of the persons, incidents, and places to which references are made. What a tender charm hangs about the Epistle to the Philippians from our knowledge of the apostle's first experiences in that Roman colony, his subsequent visits there, and the thought that he is writing from his imprisonment in Rome, and making frequent mention of his bonds (Phil. i, 7, 13, 14), and of their former kindnesses toward him (iv, 15–18).[1]

Thorough inquiries into the narratives of Scripture have evinced

Such inquiries silence infidel cavils.

the minute accuracy of the sacred writers, and silenced many cavils of infidelity. The treatise of James Smith on the Voyage and Shipwreck of St. Paul[2] furnishes an unanswerable argument for the authenticity of the Acts of the Apostles. The author's practical experience as a sailor, his residence at Malta, his familiar intercourse with the seamen of the Levant, and his study of the ships of the ancients, qualified him

---

[1] Stanley's History of the Jewish Church, Farrar's and Geikie's works on the Life of Christ, and Farrar's, Conybeare and Howson's, and Lewin's Life and Epistles of St. Paul, are especially rich in illustrations of the subject of this chapter.

[2] Third Edition. London, 1866.

pre-eminently to expound the last two chapters of the Acts. His volume is a monument of painstaking research, and throws more light upon the narrative of Paul's voyage from Cæsarea to Rome than all that had been written previously on that subject.[1]

The great importance of ascertaining the historical standpoint of an author is notably illustrated by the controversy over the date of the Apocalypse of John. If that pro- phetical book was written before the destruction of Jerusalem, a number of its particular allusions must most naturally be understood as referring to that city and its fall. If, however, it was written at the end of the reign of Domitian (about A. D. 96), as many have believed, another system of interpretation is necessary to explain the historical allusions.

The historical standpoint of the Apocalypse.

Taking, first, the external evidence touching the date of the Apocalypse, it seems to us that no impartial mind can fail to see that it preponderates in favor of the later date. But when we scrutinize the character and extent of this evidence, it seems equally clear that no very great stress can safely be laid upon it. For it all turns upon the single testimony of Irenæus, who wrote, according to the best authorities, about one hundred years after the death of John, and who says that in boyhood he had seen and conversed with Polycarp, and heard him speak of his familiar intercourse with John.[2] This fact would, of course, make his testimony of peculiar value, but, at the same time, it should be borne in mind that at an early age he removed to

External testimony hangs on Irenæus.

---

[1] The following passage from Lewin is a noteworthy illustration of the value of personal research in refuting captious objections to the historical accuracy of the Bible. " It is objected to the account of the viper fastening upon Paul's hand," says Lewin, " that there is no wood in Malta, except at Bosquetta, and that there are no vipers in Malta. How, then, it is said, could the apostle have collected the sticks, and how could a viper have fastened upon his hand? But when I visited the Bay of St. Paul, in 1851, by sea, I observed trees growing in the vicinity, and there were also fig-trees growing among the rocks at the water's edge where the vessel was wrecked. But there is a better explanation still. When I was at Malta in 1853, I went with two companions to the Bay of St. Paul by land, and this was at the same season of the year as when the wreck occurred. We now noticed on the shore, just opposite the scene of the wreck, eight or nine stacks of small faggots, and in the nearest stack I counted twenty-five bundles. They consisted of a kind of thorny heather, and had evidently been cut for firewood. As we strolled about, my companions, whom I had quitted to make an observation, put up a viper, or a reptile having the appearance of one, which escaped into the bundle of sticks. It may not have been poisonous, but was like an adder, and was quite different from the common snake; one of my fellow-travellers was quite familiar with the difference between snakes and adders, and could not well be mistaken."—The Life and Epistles of St. Paul, vol. ii, page 208.

[2] Eusebius, Ecclesiastical History, book v, chap. xx.

the remote West, and became bishop of Lyons, in France, far from
the associations of his early life. It would, therefore, have been no
strange thing if he had somewhat confounded names and dates.
His testimony is as follows: "We therefore do not run the risk of
pronouncing positively concerning the name of the Antichrist [hid-
den in the number 666, Rev. xiii, 18], for if it were necessary to
have his name distinctly announced at the present time, it would
doubtless have been announced by him who saw the Apocalypse;
for it is not a great while ago that it [or he] was seen (οὐδὲ γὰρ πρὸ
πολλοῦ χρόνου ἑωράθη), but almost in our own generation, toward
the end of Domitian's reign."[1] Here it should be noted that the
subject of the verb ἑωράθη, *was seen*, is ambiguous, and may be
either *it*, referring to the Apocalypse, or *he*, referring to John himself. But allowing it to refer to the Apocalypse, we have then this
testimony to the later date.

But what external testimony have we besides? Only Eusebius,
who lived and wrote a hundred years after Irenæus, and who expressly quotes Irenæus as his authority.[2] He also quotes Clement
of Alexandria as saying that "after the tyrant was dead" John
returned from the isle of Patmos to Ephesus.[3] But it nowhere
appears that Clement indicated who the tyrant was, or that he believed him to have been Domitian. It is Eusebius who puts that
meaning in his words, and it is matter of notoriety that Eusebius
himself, after quoting various opinions, leaves the question of the
authorship of the Apocalypse in doubt.[4] Origen's testimony is also
adduced, but he merely says that John was condemned by "the
king of the Romans," not intimating at all who that king was, but
calling attention to the fact that John himself did not name his
persecutor. All other testimonies on the subject are later than
these, and consequently of little or no value. If Eusebius was dependent on Irenæus for his information, it is not likely that later
writers drew from any other source. But that the voice of antiquity was not altogether uniform on this subject may be inferred
from the fact that an ancient fragment of a Latin document, probably as old as Irenæus' writings, mentions Paul as following the
order of his predecessor John in writing to seven churches. The
value of this ancient fragment is its evidence of a current notion
that John's Apocalypse was written before the decease of Paul.
Epiphanius dates John's banishment in the reign of Claudius Cæsar,
and the superscription to the Syriac version of the Apocalypse

---

[1] Adversus Haereses, v, 30.
[2] See Eccles. History, book iii, 18 and v, 8.   [3] Ibid., book iii, 23.
[4] See especially Alford's Prolegomena to the Revelation.

places it in the reign of Nero.[1] No one would lay great stress upon any of these later statements, but putting them all together, and letting the naked facts stand apart, shorn of all the artful colourings of partisan writers, we find the external evidence of John's writing the Apocalypse at the close of Domitian's reign resting on the sole testimony of Irenæus, who wrote a hundred years after that date, and whose words admit of two different meanings.

One clear and explicit testimony, when not opposed by other evidence, would be allowed by all fair critics to control the argument; but not so when many other considerations tend to weaken it. It would seem much easier to account for the confusion of tradition on the date of John's banishment than to explain away the definite references of the Apocalypse itself to the temple, the court, and the city as still standing when the book was written. All tradition substantially agrees, that John's last years of labour were spent among the churches of Western Asia, and it is very possible that he was banished to the isle of Patmos during the reign of Domitian. That banishment may have occurred long after John had gone to the same island for another reason, and later writers, misapprehending the apostle's words, might have easily confounded the two events.

John's own testimony is that he "was in the island which is called Patmos on account of the word of God (διὰ τὸν John's own λόγον τοῦ θεοῦ) and the testimony of Jesus" (Rev. i, 9). testimony. Alford says, though he does not adopt this meaning, that "in St. Paul's usage, διά would here signify *for the sake of;* that is, for the purpose of receiving; so that the apostle would have gone to Patmos [not as an exile, but] by special revelation in order to receive this Apocalypse. Again, keeping to this meaning of διά, these words may mean that he visited Patmos in pursuance of, for the purposes of, his ordinary apostolic employment, which might well be designated by these substantives."[2] This proper and all-suffi-

---

[1] See Stuart, Commentary on the Apocalypse, vol. i, pp. 265–269.

[2] Greek Testament, in loco. See also De Wette, in loco. Alford's "three objections" appear to us without force; for (1) the mention of *tribulation* and *patience* in this verse by no means requires us to understand that he was then suffering from banishment. (2) The parallels (chap. vi, 9; xx, 4) which he cites to determine the use of διά are offset by its use in ii, 3; iv, 11; xii, 11; xiii, 14; xviii, 10, 15, in all which places, as also in vi, 9 and xx, 4, it is to be understood as setting forth the *ground* or *reason* of what is stated. This meaning holds alike, whether we believe that John went to Patmos *freely* or as an exile, *on account* of the word of God. Comp. Winer, N. T. Grammar, § 49, on διά. (3) The traditional banishment of John to Patmos may have occurred, as we have shown above, long after he had first gone there on account of the testimony of Jesus.

cient explanation of his words allows us to suppose that John received the Revelation in Patmos, whither he had gone, either by some special divine call, or in pursuance of his apostolic labours. The tradition, therefore, of his exile under Domitian may be true, and at the same time not affect the question of the date of the Apocalypse.[1]

Turning now to inquire what internal evidence may be found touching the historical standpoint of the writer, observe: (1) That no critic of any note has ever claimed that the later date is required by any internal evidence. (2) On the contrary, if John the apostle is the author, the comparatively rough Hebraic style of the language unquestionably argues for it an earlier date than his Gospel or Epistles. For, special pleading aside, it must on all rational grounds be conceded, that a Hebrew, in the supposed condition of John, would, after years of intercourse and labour in the churches of Asia, acquire by degrees a purer Greek style. (3) The address "to the seven churches which are in Asia" (i, 4, 11), implies that, at this time, there were only seven churches in that Asia where Paul was once forbidden by the Spirit to speak the word (Acts xvi, 6, 7). Macdonald says, "An earthquake, in the ninth year of Nero's reign, overwhelmed both Laodicea and Colossæ (Pliny, Hist. Nat., v, 41), and the church at the latter place does not appear to have been restored. As the two places were in close proximity, what remained of the church at Colossæ probably became identified with the one at Laodicea. The churches at Tralles and Magnesia could not have been established until a considerable time after the Apocalypse was written. Those who contend for the later date, when there must have been a greater number of churches than seven in the region designated by the apostle, fail to give any sufficient reason for his mentioning no more. That they mystically or symbolically represent others is surely not such a reason."[2] (4) The prominence in which persecution from the Jews is set forth in the Epistles to the seven churches also argues an early date. After the fall of Jerusalem, Christian persecution and troubles came almost altogether from pagan sources, and Jewish opposition and Judaizing heretics became of little note.

Internal evidence of date. Six points.

[1] Any one who will compare the rapidity of Paul's movements on his missionary journeys, and note how he addressed epistles to some of his churches (e. g., Thessalonians) a few months after his first visitation, will have no difficulty in understanding how John could have visited all the seven churches of Asia, and also have gone thence to Patmos and received the Revelation, within a year after departing from Jerusalem. But John, like Paul, probably wrote to churches he had not visited.

[2] The Life and Writings of John, p. 155.

(5) A most weighty argument for the early date appears in the mention of the temple, court, and city in chapter xi, 1-3. These references and the further designation, in verse 8, of that city "which spiritually is called Sodom and Egypt, where also their Lord was crucified," obviously imply that the Jewish temple, court, and city were yet standing. To plead that these familiar appellatives are not real, but only mystical allusions, is to assume the very point in question. The most simple reference should stand unless convincing reasons to the contrary be shown. When the writer proceeds to characterize the city by a proper symbolical name, he calls it Sodom and Egypt, and is careful to tell us that it is so called *spiritually* (πνευματικῶς), but, as if to prevent any possibility of misunderstanding his reference, he adds that it is the place where the Lord was crucified.

(6) Finally, what should especially impress every reader is the emphatic statement, placed in the very title of the book, and repeated in one form and another again and again, that this is a revelation of "things which must shortly (ἐν τάχει) come to pass," and the time of which is near at hand (ἐγγύς, Rev. i, 1, 3; xxii, 6, 7, 10, 12, 20). If the seer, writing a few years before the terrible catastrophe, had the destruction of Jerusalem and its attendant woes before him, all these expressions have a force and definiteness which every interpreter must recognize.[1] But if the things contem-

[1] The trend of modern criticism is unmistakably toward the adoption of the early date of the Apocalypse, and yet the best scholars differ. Elliott, Hengstenberg, Lange, Alford, and Whedon contend strongly that the testimony of Irenæus and the ancient tradition ought to control the question; while, on the other hand, Lücke, Neander, De Wette, Ewald, Bleek, Auberlen, Hilgenfeld, Düsterdieck, Stuart, Macdonald, Davidson, J. B. Lightfoot, Glasgow, Farrar, Westcott, Cowles, and Schaff maintain that the book, according to its own internal evidence, must have been written before the destruction of Jerusalem. The last-named scholar, in the new edition of his Church History (vol. i, pp. 834-837), revokes his acceptance of the Domitian date which he affirmed thirty years ago, and now maintains that internal evidence for an earlier date outweighs the external tradition. Writers on both sides of this question have probably been too much influenced by some theory of the seven kings in chap. xvii, 10 (see below, p. 481), and have placed the composition much later than valid evidence warrants. Glasgow (The Apoc. Trans. and Expounded, pp. 9-38) adduces proof not easy to be set aside that the Revelation was written before any of the Epistles, probably somewhere between A. D. 50 and 54. Is it not supposable that one reason why Paul was forbidden to preach the word in Western Asia (Acts xvi, 6) was that John was either already there, or about to enter? The prevalent opinion that the First Epistle of John was written after the fall of Jerusalem rests on no certain evidence. To assume, from the writer's use of the term "little children," that he was very far advanced in years, is futile. John was probably no older than Paul, but some time before the fall of Jerusalem the latter was wont to speak of himself as "Paul the aged." Philem. 9.

plated were in the distant future, these simple words of time must be subjected to the most violent and unnatural treatment in order to make the statements of the writer compatible with the exposition.

A consideration of these evidences, external and internal, of the date of the Apocalypse, shows what delicacy and dis-crimination are requisite in an interpreter in order to determine the historical standpoint of such a prophet-ical book. As far as possible, all systems of prophetical interpreta-tion should be held in abeyance until that question is determined; but it may become necessary, in view of the conflicting evidences of the date and the difficulties of the book itself, to withhold all judgment as to the historical standpoint of the writer until we have tried the different methods of interpretation, and have thus had opportunity to judge which exposition affords the best solution of the difficulties.

Great delicacy and discrimina-tion essential.

The controversy over the date of Daniel's prophecies springs mainly from the miraculous narratives recorded in the first part of the book, and from the rationalistic assumption that neither mir-acles nor such detailed prediction of future events as the visions and dreams involve are consistent with scientific histor-ical criticism. The question is one that belongs more properly to the department of Biblical Introduction; but it is evident that the determining of the date of the prophecies is essential to their interpretation, and if it be admitted that they were written after the events which they assume to foretell, the credibility of the book is necessarily destroyed, and any scientific exposition of it must thence proceed as if dealing with a forgery or a pious fraud. The same may be said of that criticism which places the composition of the Pentateuch long after the days of Moses. Such a hypothesis forces the interpreter who adopts it to give an unnatural meaning to all those words and acts which are attributed to Moses, and which assume the historical standpoint of the great Lawgiver of Israel. The various rationalistic theories of interpreta-tion, which ignore or deny the supernatural, and proceed on the assumption that any of the sacred writers feign a historical stand-point which they did not really occupy, are continually changing, and lead only to confusion.

Questions of historical criti-cism involved.

This, then, is to be held as a canon of interpretation, that all due regard must be had to the person and circumstances of the author, the time and place of his writing, and the occasion and reasons which led him to write. Nor must we omit similar inquiry into the character, conditions, and history of those for whom the book was written, and of those also of whom the book makes mention.

CHAPTER X.

FIGURATIVE LANGUAGE.

THOSE portions of the Holy Scriptures which are written in figurative language call for special care in their interpretation. *Tropes many* When a word is employed in another than its primary *and various.* meaning, or applied to some object different from that to which it is appropriated in common usage, it is called a trope.[1] The necessities and purposes of human speech require the frequent use of words in such a tropical sense. We have already seen, under the head of the *usus loquendi* of words, how many terms come to have a variety of meanings. Some words lose their primary signification altogether, and are employed only in a secondary or acquired sense. Most words in every language have been used or are capable of being used in this way. And very many words have so long and so constantly maintained a figurative sense that their primary meaning has become obsolete and forgotten. How few remember that the word *law* denotes *that which is laid;* or that the common expressions *right* and *wrong*, which have almost exclusively a moral import, originally signified straight and crooked. Other words are so commonly used in a twofold sense that we immediately note when they are employed literally and when figuratively. When James, Cephas, and John are called *pillars* of the Church (Gal. ii, 9), we see at once that the word *pillars* is a metaphor. And when the Church itself is said to be "built upon the foundation of the apostles and prophets" (Eph. ii, 20), we know that a figure, the image of a house or temple, is meant to be depicted before the mind.

The origin of figures of speech has been generally attributed to the poverty of languages in their earliest stages. *Origin and ne-* The scarcity of words required the use of one and the *cessity of figur-* same word in a variety of meanings. "No language," *ative language.* says Blair, " is so copious as to have a separate word for every separate idea. Men naturally sought to abridge this labour of multiplying words *ad infinitum ;* and, in order to lay less burden on their memories, made one word, which they had already appropriated to a certain idea or object, stand also for some other idea or object

[1] From the Greek τροπός, a *turn* or change of language ; that is, a word turned from its primary usage to another meaning.

between which and the primary one they found or fancied some relation." [1]

But it is not solely in the scarcity of words that we are to find the origin of figurative language. The natural operations of the human mind prompt men to trace analogies and make comparisons. Pleasing emotions are excited and the imagination is gratified by the use of metaphors and similes. Were we to suppose a language sufficiently copious in words to express all possible conceptions, the human mind would still require us to compare and contrast our concepts, and such a procedure would soon necessitate a variety of figures of speech. So much of our knowledge is acquired through the senses, that all our abstract ideas and our spiritual language have a material basis. "It is not too much to say," observes Max Müller, "that the whole dictionary of ancient religion is made up of metaphors. With us these metaphors are all forgotten. We speak of spirit without thinking of breath, of heaven without thinking of sky, of pardon without thinking of a release, of revelation without thinking of a veil. But in ancient language every one of these words, nay, every word that does not refer to sensuous objects, is still in a chrysalis stage, half material and half spiritual, and rising and falling in its character according; to the capacities of speakers and hearers." [2]

And more than this. May we not safely affirm that the analogies Figures of traceable between the natural and spiritual worlds are speech suggest parts of a divine harmony which it is the noblest men- divine harmo- tal exercise to discover and unfold? In his chapter, nies. "On Teaching by Parables," Trench has the following profound observations: "It is not merely that these analogies assist to make the truth intelligible, or, if intelligible before, present it more vividly to the mind, which is all that some will allow them. Their power lies deeper than this, in the harmony unconsciously felt by all men, and by deeper minds continually recognized and plainly perceived, between the natural and spiritual worlds, so that analogies from the first are felt to be something more than illustrations, happily but yet arbitrarily chosen. They are arguments, and may be alleged as witnesses; the world of nature being throughout a witness for the world of spirit, proceeding from the same hand, growing out of the same root, and being constituted for that very end. All lovers of truth readily acknowledge these mysterious harmonies, and the force of arguments derived from them. To them the things on earth are copies of the things in heaven. They

[1] Rhetoric, Lecture xiv, On the Origin and Nature of Figurative Language.
[2] Science of Religion, p. 118.

know that the earthly tabernacle is made after the pattern of things
seen in the mount (Exod. xxv, 40; 1 Chron. xxviii, 11, 12); and the
question suggested by the angel in Milton is often forced upon
their meditations—

> 'What if earth
> Be but the shadow of heaven and things therein
> Each to other like, more than on earth is thought?'

For it is a great misunderstanding of the matter to think of these
as happily, but yet arbitrarily, chosen illustrations, taken with a
skilful selection from the great stock and storehouse of unappro-
priated images; from whence it would have been possible that the
same skill might have selected others as good or nearly as good.
Rather they belong to one another, the type and the thing typified,
by an inward necessity; they were linked together long before by
the law of a secret affinity. It is not a happy accident which has
yielded so wondrous an analogy as that of husband and wife to set
forth the mystery of Christ's relation to his elect Church. There
is far more in it than this: the earthly relation is indeed but a lower form of the heavenly, on which it rests, and of which it is the
utterance. When Christ spoke to Nicodemus of a new birth, it
was not merely because birth into this natural world was the most
suitable figure that could be found for the expression of that spiritual act which, without any power of our own, is accomplished
upon us when we are brought into God's kingdom; but all the circumstances of this natural birth had been pre-ordained to bear the
burden of so great a mystery. The Lord is king, not borrowing
this title from the kings of the earth, but having lent his own title
to them—and not the name only, but so ordering, that all true rule
and government upon earth, with its righteous laws, its stable ordinances, its punishment and its grace, its majesty and its terror,
should tell of Him and of his kingdom which ruleth over all—so
that "kingdom of God" is not in fact a figurative expression, but
most literal: it is rather the earthly kingdoms and the earthly kings
that are figures and shadows of the true. And as in the world of
man and human relations, so also is it in the world of nature. The
untended soil which yields thorns and briers as its natural harvest is
a permanent type and enduring parable of man's heart, which has
been submitted to the same curse, and, without a watchful spiritual
husbandry, will as surely put forth *its* briers and *its* thorns. The
weeds that *will* mingle during the time of growth with the corn,
and yet are separated from it at the last, tell ever one and the same
tale of the present admixture and future sundering of the righteous

and the wicked. The decaying of the insignificant, unsightly seed
in the earth, and the rising up out of that decay and death of the
graceful stalk and the fruitful ear, contain evermore the prophecy
of the final resurrection, even as this is itself in its kind a resurrection—the same process at a lower stage—the same power putting
itself forth upon meaner things. . . . And thus, besides his revelation in words, God has another and an elder, and one indeed without which it is inconceivable how that other could be made, for
from this it appropriates all its signs of communication. This entire moral and visible world from first to last, with its kings and its
subjects, its parents and its children, its sun and its moon, its sowing and its harvest, its light and its darkness, its sleeping and its
waking, its birth and its death, is from beginning to end a mighty
parable, a great teaching of supersensuous truth, a help at once to
our faith and to our understanding." [1]

The principal sources of the figurative language of the Bible are
Sources of scrip- the physical features of the Holy Land, the habits and
tural imagery. customs of its ancient tribes, and the forms of Israelitish worship. All these sources should, accordingly, be closely
studied in order to the interpretation of the figurative portions of
the Scriptures. As we traced a Divine Providence in the use of
Hebrew, Chaldee, and Greek as the languages of God's inspired
revelation, and as we believe that the progeny of Abraham through
Jacob were the divinely chosen people to receive and guard the
oracles of God, so may we also believe that the Land of Promise
was an essential element in the process of developing and perfecting the rhetorical form of the sacred records. "It is neither fiction
nor extravagance," says Thomson, "to call this land a microcosm—
a little world in itself, embracing every thing which in the thought
of the Creator would be needed in developing this language of the
kingdom of heaven. Nor is it easy to see how the end sought
could have been reached at all without just such a land, furnished
and fitted up, as this was, by the overruling providence of God.
All were needed—mountain and valley, hill and plain, lake and
river, sea and sky, summer and winter, seedtime and harvest, trees,
shrubs, and flowers, beasts and birds, men and women, tribes and
nations, governments and religions false and true, and other things
innumerable; none of which could be spare¹. Think, if you can,
of a Bible with all these left out, or others essentially different substituted in their place—a Bible without patriarch or pilgrimage,
with no bondage in Egypt, or deliverance therefrom, no Red Sea,
no Sinai with its miracles, no wilderness of wandering with all the

[1] Notes on the Parables, pp. 18–21.

included scenes and associated incidents; without a Jordan with a Canaan over against it, or a Dead Sea with Sodom beneath it; no Moriah with its temple, no Zion with palaces, nor Hinnom below, with the fire and the worm that never die. Whence could have come our divine songs and psalms, if the sacred poets had lived in a land without mountain or valley, where were no plains covered over with corn, no fields clothed with green, no hills planted with the olive, the fig, and the vine? All are needed, and all do good service, from the oaks of Bashan and the cedars of Lebanon to the hyssop that springeth out of the wall. The tiny mustard-seed has its moral, and lilies their lessons. Thorns and thistles utter admonitions, and revive sad memories. The sheep and the fold, the shepherd and his dog, the ass and his owner, the ox and his goad, the camel and his burden, the horse with neck clothed with thunder; lions that roar, wolves that raven, foxes that destroy, harts panting for water brooks, and roes feeding among lilies, doves in their windows, sparrows on the housetop, storks in the heavens, eagles hasting to their prey; things great and small; the busy bee improving each shining hour, and the careful ant laying up store in harvest—nothing too large to serve, too small to aid. These are merely random specimens out of a world of rich materials; but we must not forget that they are all found in this land where the dialect of God's spiritual kingdom was to be taught and spoken." [1]

It is scarcely necessary, and, indeed, quite impracticable, to lay down specific rules for determining when language is used figuratively and when literally. It is an old and oft-repeated hermeneutical principle that words should be understood in their literal sense unless such literal interpretation involves a manifest contradiction or absurdity. It should be observed, however, that this principle, when reduced to practice, becomes simply an appeal to every man's rational judgment. And what to one seems very absurd and improbable may be to another altogether simple and self-consistent. Some expositors have claimed to see necessity for departing from the literal sense where others saw none, and it seems impossible to establish any fixed rule that will govern in all cases. Reference must be had to the general character and style of the particular book, to the plan and purpose of the author, and to the context and scope of the particular passage in question. Especially should strict regard be had to the usage

Specific rules unnecessary and impracticable.

[1] The Physical Basis of our Spiritual Language; by W. M. Thomson, in the Bibliotheca Sacra for January, 1872. Compare the same author's articles on The Natural Basis of our Spiritual Language in the same periodical for Jan., 1873; Jan., 1874; Jan., 1875; July, 1876; and Jan., 1877.

of the sacred writers, as determined by a thorough collation and comparison of all parallel passages. The same general principles, by which we ascertain the grammatico-historical sense, apply also to the interpretation of figurative language, and it should never be forgotten that the figurative portions of the Bible are as certain and truthful as the most prosaic chapters. Metaphors, allegories, parables, and symbols are divinely chosen forms of setting forth the oracles of God, and we must not suppose their meaning to be so vague and uncertain as to be past finding out. In the main, we believe the figurative parts of the Scriptures are not so difficult to understand as many have imagined. By a careful and judicious discrimination the interpreter should aim to determine the character and purport of each particular trope, and explain it in harmony with the common laws of language, and the author's context, scope, and plan.

Figures of speech have been distributed into two great classes, figures of words and figures of thought. The distinction is an easy one in that a figure of words is one in which the image or resemblance is confined to a single word, whereas a figure of thought may require for its expression a great many words and sentences. Metaphor and metonomy are figures of words, in which the comparison is reduced to a single expression, as when, characterizing Herod, Jesus said, "Go and say to that *fox*" (Luke xiii, 32). In Psalm xviii, 2, we find seven figures of words crowded into a single verse: "Jehovah, my rock (סַלְעִי), and my fortress, and my deliverer; my God, my rock (צוּרִי)—I will seek refuge in him;—my shield and horn of my salvation, my height." Figures of thought, on the other hand, are seen in similes, allegories, and parables, where no single word will suffice to convey the idea intended, but an entire passage or section must be taken together. But this classification of figures will be of little value in the study of the figurative language of the Scriptures.

All figures of speech are founded upon some resemblance or relation which different objects bear to one another, and it often happens, in rapid and brilliant style, that a cause is put for its effect, or an effect for its cause; or the name of a subject is used when only some adjunct or associated circumstance is intended. This figure of speech is called Metonymy, from the Greek μετά, denoting *change*, and ὄνομα, a *name*. Such change and substitution of one name for another give language a force and impressiveness not otherwise attainable. Thus, Job is represented as saying, "My *arrow* is incurable" (Job xxxiv, 6); where by *arrow* is evidently meant a wound caused by an arrow, and allusion is made to chapter vi, 4, where the bitter afflictions of Job are represented as caused by the arrows of the Almighty. So again in Luke xvi, 29 and xxiv, 27, *Moses* and *the prophets* are used for the writings of which they were the authors. The name of a patriarch is sometimes used when his posterity is intended (Gen. ix, 27, Amos vii, 9). In Gen. xlv, 21; Num. iii, 16; Deut. xvii, 6, the word *mouth* is used for *saying* or *commandment* which issues from one's mouth. "According to the *mouth* (order or command) of Pharaoh." "According to the *mouth* (word) of Jehovah." "At the *mouth* (word, testimony) of two witnesses or three witnesses shall the dying one (הַמֵּת, the one appointed to die, or worthy of death,) be put to death." The words *lip* and *tongue* are used in a similar way in Prov. xii, 19, and frequently. "The *lip* of truth shall be established forever; but only for a moment [Heb. until I shall wink] the *tongue* of falsehood." Comp. Prov. xvii, 7; xxv, 15. In Ezekiel xxiii, 29, "They shall take away all thy labour, and leave thee naked," the word *labour* is used instead of earnings or results of labour. All such cases of metonymy—and examples might be multiplied indefinitely—are commonly classified under the head of Metonymy of cause and effect. To this same class belong also such passages as Exod. vii, 19, where, instead of vessels, the names of the materials of which they were made are used: "Stretch out thy hand over the waters of Egypt . . . and there shall be blood in all the land of Egypt, both in wood and in stone;" that is, in wooden vessels and stone reservoirs.

Another use of this figure occurs where some adjunct, associated idea, or circumstance is put for the main subject, and *vice versa*. Thus, in Lev. xix, 32, שֵׂיבָה, *gray hair, hoariness,* is used for a person of advanced age: "Thou shalt rise up before the hoary head." Comp. Gen. xlii, 38: "Ye will bring down my gray hairs in sorrow to the grave." When Moses commands the elders of Israel to take a lamb according to their families and "kill the passover" (Exod. xii, 21), he evidently uses the word *passover* for the paschal lamb. In Hosea i, 2, it is written: "The land has grievously committed whoredom." Here the word *land* is used by metonymy for the Israelitish people dwelling in the land. So also, in Matt. iii, 5, Jerusalem and Judea are put for the people that inhabited those places: "Then went out unto him Jerusalem and all Judea and all the region round about the Jordan." The metonymy of the subject for its adjunct is also seen in passages where the container is put for the thing contained, as, "Thou preparest a table before me in the presence of my enemies" (Psa. xxiii, 5). "Blessed shall be thy basket, and thy kneading trough"

Metonymy of subject and adjunct.

(Deut. xxviii, 5). "Ye cannot drink the cup of the Lord and the cup of demons, ye cannot partake of the table of the Lord and of the table of demons" (1 Cor. x, 21). Here *table, basket, kneading-trough*, and *cup* are used for that which they contained, or for which they were used. The following examples illustrate how the abstract is used for the concrete: "He shall justify the circumcision by faith, and the uncircumcision through faith" (Rom. iii, 30). Here the word *circumcision* designates the Jews, and *uncircumcision* the Gentiles. In Rom. xi, 7, the word *election* is used for the aggregate of those who composed the "remnant according to the election of grace" (verse 5), the elect portion of Israel. And Paul tells the Ephesians (v, 8) with great force of language: "Ye were once darkness, but now light in the Lord."

There is another use of this figure which may be called metonymy Metonymy of of the sign and the thing signified. Thus Isa. xxii, 22: sign and thing "I will put the key of the house of David upon his signified. shoulder, and he shall open, and no one shutting, and he shall shut, and no one opening." Here *key* is used as the sign of control over the house, of power to open or close the doors whenever one pleases; and the putting the key *upon the shoulder* denotes that the power, symbolized by the key, will be a heavy burden on him who exercises it. Compare Matt. xvi, 19. So again *diadem* and *crown* are used in Ezek. xxi, 26, for regal dignity and power, and *sceptre* in Gen. xlix, 10, and Zech. x, 11, for kingly dominion. In Isaiah's glowing picture of the Messianic era (ii, 4) he describes the utter cessation of national strife and warfare by the significant words, "They shall beat their swords into ploughshares, and their spears into pruninghooks." In Ezek. vii, 27, we have an example of the use of the thing signified for the sign: "The prince shall be clothed with desolation;" that is, arrayed in the garments or signs of desolation.

Another kind of trope, quite similar in character to metonymy, is Synecdoche. that by which the whole is put for a part, or a part for Synecdoche. the whole; a genus for a species, or a species for a genus; the singular for the plural, and the plural for the singular. This is called Synecdoche, from the Greek συν, *with*, and ἐκδέχομαι, *to receive from*, which conveys the general idea of receiving and associating one thing along with another. Thus "all the world" is used in Luke ii, 1, for the Roman Empire; and in Matt. xii, 40, three days and three nights are used for only part of that time. The soul is often named when the whole man or person is intended; as, "We were in all in the ship two hundred threescore and sixteen souls (Acts xxvii, 37). The singular of *day* is used by synecdoche for days or period in such passages as Eccles. xii, 3: "In the day when the keepers of the house tremble." The singular of *stork, turtle, crane,* and *swallow* is used in Jer. viii, 7, as the representative of the whole class to which each belongs. Jephthah is said to have been "buried in the cities of Gilead" (Judg. xii, 7), where, of course, only one of those cities is intended. In Psa. xlvi, 9, the Lord is represented as "causing wars to cease unto the extremity of the land; bow he will shiver, and cut in pieces spear; war chariots he will burn in the fire." Here, by specifying *bow, spear,* and *chariots,* the Psalmist doubtless designed to represent Jehovah's triumph as an utter destruction of all implements of war. In Deut. xxxii, 41, the flashing gleam of the sword is put for its edge: "If I sharpen the lightning of my sword, and my hand lay hold on judgment."

We have called attention, in the earlier part of this work, to the tendency of the Hebrew mind to form and express vivid conceptions of the external world.[1] Inanimate Personification. objects were spoken of as if instinct with life. And this tendency is noticeable in all languages, and occasions the figure of speech called Personification.[2] It is so common a feature of language that it often occurs in the most ordinary conversation; but it is more especially suited to the language of imagination and passion, and appears most frequently in the poetical parts of Scripture. The statement in Num. xvi, 32, that "the earth opened her mouth and swallowed" Korah and his associates, is an instance of personification, the like of which often occurs in prose narration. More striking is the language of Matt. vi, 34: "Be not therefore anxious for the morrow, for the morrow will be anxious for itself." Here the morrow itself is pictured before us as a living person, pressed by care and anxiety. But the more forcible instances of personification are found in such passages as Psa. cxiv, 3, 4: "The sea saw and fled; the Jordan was turned backward. The mountains leaped like rams; hills like the sons of the flock." Or, again, in Hab. iii, 10: "Mountains saw thee, they writhe; a flood of waters passed over; the deep gave his voice; on high his hands he lifted." Here mountains, hills, rivers, and sea, are introduced as things of life. They are assumed to have self-conscious powers of thought, feeling, and locomotion, and yet it is all the emotional language of imagination and poetic fervour.

---

[1] See above, pp. 86, 102.

[2] The more technical name is *Prosopopœia,* from the Greek πρόσωπον, *face,* or *person,* and ποιέω, to *make;* and, accordingly, means to give personal form or character to an object. *Prosopopœia* is held by some to be a term of more extensive application than personification.

Apostrophe is a figure closely allied to personification. The
name is derived from the Greek ἀπό, *from*, and στρέφω,
to turn, and denotes especially the turning of a speaker
away from his immediate hearers, and addressing an absent and
imaginary person or thing. When the address is to an inanimate
object, the figures of personification and apostrophe combine in one
and the same passage. So, in connexion with the passage above
cited from Psa. cxiv. After personifying the sea, the Jordan, and
the mountains, the psalmist suddenly turns in direct address to
them, and says: "What is the matter with thee, O thou sea, that
thou fleest? Thou Jordan, that thou art turning backward? Ye
mountains, that ye leap like rams; ye hills, like the sons of the
flock?" The following apostrophe is peculiarly impressive by the
force of its imagery. "O, Sword of Jehovah! How long wilt
thou not be quiet? Gather thyself to thy sheath; be at rest and
be dumb" (Jer. xlvii, 6). But apostrophe proper is an address to
some absent person either living or dead; as when David laments
for the dead Absalom (2 Sam. xviii, 33), and, as if the departed
soul were present to hear, exclaims: "My son Absalom! my son,
my son Absalom! Would that I had died in thy stead, O Absalom, my son, my son!" The apostrophe to the fallen king of
Babylon, in Isa. xiv, 9–20, is one of the boldest and sublimest examples of the kind in any language. Similar instances of bold and
impassioned address abound in the Hebrew prophets, and, as we
have seen, the oriental mind was notably given to express thoughts
and feelings in this emotional style.

Interrogatory forms of expression are often the strongest possible
way of enunciating important truths. As when it is
written in Heb. i, 14, concerning the angels: "Are they
not all ministering spirits sent forth into service for the sake of
those who are to inherit salvation?" Here the doctrine of the
ministry of angels in such a noble service is by implication assumed as an undisputed belief. The interrogatories in Rom. viii,
33–35, afford a most impressive style of setting forth the triumph
of believers in the blessed provisions of redemption: "Who shall
bring charge against God's elect ones? Shall God who justifies?
Who is he that is condemning? Is it Christ Jesus that died, but,
rather, that was raised from the dead, who is at the right hand of
God, who also intercedes for us? Who shall separate us from the
love of Christ? Shall tribulation, or anguish, or persecution, or
famine, or nakedness, or peril, or sword? Even as it is written,
For thy sake we are killed all the day; we were accounted as sheep
of slaughter. But in all these things we more than conquer through

him that loved us."[1] Very frequent and conspicuous also are the interrogatory forms of speech in the Book of Job. "Knowest thou this of old, from the placing of Adam on the earth, that the triumph of the wicked is short, and the joy of the profane for a moment?" (xx, 4). "The secret of Eloah canst thou find? Or canst thou find out Shaddai to perfection?" (xi, 7). Jehovah's answer out of the whirlwind (chaps. xxxviii–xli) is very largely in this form.

Hyperbole is a rhetorical figure which consists in exaggeration, or magnifying an object beyond reality. It has its natural origin in the tendency of youthful and imaginative *Hyperbole.* minds to portray facts in the liveliest colours. An ardent imagination would very naturally describe the appearance of the many camps of the Midianites and Amalekites as in Judg. vii, 12: "Lying in the valley like grasshoppers for multitude; and as to their camels, no number, like the sand which is upon the shore of the sea for multitude." So the emotion of David prompts him to speak of Saul and Jonathan as swifter than eagles and stronger than lions (2 Sam. i, 23). Other scriptural examples of this figure are the following: "All night I make my bed to swim; with my tears I dissolve my couch" (Psa. vi, 6). "Would that my head were waters and my eyes a fountain of tears; and I would weep day and night the slain of the daughter of my people" (Jer. ix, 1). "There are also many other things which Jesus did, which things, if written every one, I suppose that the world itself would not contain the books that should be written" (John xxi, 25). Such exaggerated expressions, when not overdone, or occurring too frequently, strike the attention and make an agreeable impression on the mind.

Another peculiar form of speech, deserving a passing notice here, is irony, by which a speaker or writer says the very opposite of what he intends. Elijah's language to *Irony.* the Baal worshippers (1 Kings xviii, 27) is an example of most effective irony. Another example is Job xii, 1: "True it is that ye are the people, and with you wisdom will die!" In 1 Cor. iv, 8, Paul indulges in the following ironical vein: "Already ye are filled; already ye are become rich; without us ye have reigned; and I would indeed that ye did reign, that we also might reign with you." On this passage Meyer remarks: "The discourse, already in

---

[1] The interrogative construction of this passage given above is maintained by many of the best interpreters and critics, ancient and modern (as Augustine, Ambrosiaster, Koppe, Reiche, Köllner, Olshausen, De Wette, Griesbach, Lachmann, Alford, Webster, and Jowett), and seems to us, on the whole, the most simple and satisfactory. But see other constructions advocated in Meyer and Lange.

verse 7, roused to a lively pitch, becomes now bitterly ironical, heaping stroke on stroke, even as the proud Corinthians, with their partisan conduct, needed an admonition (*νουθεσία*, ver. 14) to teach them humility." The designation of the thirty pieces of silver, in Zech. xi, 13, as "a glorious price," is an example of sarcasm. Words of derision and scorn, like those of the soldiers in Matt. xxvii, 30: "Hail, King of the Jews!" and those of the chief priests and scribes in Mark xv, 32: "Let the Christ, the King of Israel, now come down from the cross, that we may see and believe," are not proper examples of irony, but of malignant mockery.

CHAPTER XI.

SIMILE AND METAPHOR.

SIMILE.

WHEN a formal comparison is made between two different objects, Simile defined so as to impress the mind with some resemblance or and illustrated. likeness, the figure is called a simile. A beautiful example is found in Isa. lv, 10, 11: "For as the rain and the snow come down from the heavens, and thither do not return, but water the land, and cause it to bear and to sprout, and it gives seed to the sower and bread to the eater: so shall my word be which goes forth out of my mouth; it shall not return to me empty, but do that which I desired, and be successful in what I sent it." The apt and varied allusions of this passage set forth the beneficial efficacy of God's word in a most impressive style. "The images chosen," observes Delitzsch, "are rich with allusions. As snow and rain are the mediate cause of growth, and thus also of the enjoyment of what is harvested, so also by the word of God the ground and soil of the human heart is softened, refreshed, and made fertile and vegetative, and this word gives the prophet, who is like the sower, the seed which he scatters, and it brings with it bread that nourishes the soul; for every word that proceeds from the mouth of God is bread" (Deut. viii, 3).[1] Another illustration of the word of God appears in Jer. xxiii, 29: "Is not my word even as the fire, saith Jehovah, and as a hammer that breaks a rock in pieces?" Here are portrayed the fury and force of the divine word against false

[1] Biblical Commentary on Isaiah, in loco

prophets. It is a word of judgment that burns and smites the sinful offender unto utter ruin, and the intensity of its power is enhanced by the double simile.

The tendency of the Hebrew writers to crowd several similes together is noticeable, and this may be in part accounted for by the nature of Hebrew parallelism. Thus in Isa. i, 8: "The daughter of Zion is left as a booth in a vineyard; as a night-lodge in a field of cucumbers; as a city besieged." And again in verse 30: "Ye shall be as an oak withering in foliage, and as a garden to which there is no water." And in xxix, 8: "It shall be as when the hungry dreams, and lo, he is eating, and he awakes, and his soul is empty; and as when the thirsty dreams, and lo, he is drinking, and he awakes, and lo, he is faint, and his soul is eagerly longing: so shall be the multitude of all the nations that are warring against Mount Zion." But though the figures are thus multiplied, they have a natural affinity, and are not open to the charge of being mixed or confused.

Crowding of similes together.

Similes are of frequent occurrence in the Scriptures, and being designed to illustrate an author's meaning, they involve no difficulties of interpretation. When the Psalmist says: "I am like a pelican of the wilderness; I have become as an owl of desert places; I watch and am become as a solitary sparrow on a roof" (Psa. cii, 6), he conveys a vivid picture of his utter loneliness. An image of gracefulness and beauty is presented by the language of Cant. ii, 9: "My beloved is like a roe, or a young fawn." Compare verse 16, and chapter iv, 1–5. Ezekiel (xxxii, 2) compares Pharaoh to a young lion of the nations, and a dragon (crocodile) in the seas. It is said in Matt. xvii, 2, that when Jesus became transfigured "his face did shine as the sun, and his garments became white as the light." In Matt. xxviii, 3, it is said of the angel who rolled the stone from the sepulchre, that "his appearance was as lightning, and his raiment white as snow." In Rom. xii, 4, the apostle illustrates the unity of the Church and the diversity of its individual ministers by the following comparison: "Even as in one body we have many members, and all the members have not the same work: so we, who are many, are one body in Christ, and severally members one of another." Compare also 1 Cor. xii, 12. In all these and other instances the comparison is self-interpreting, and the main thought is intensified by the imagery.

Similes self-interpreting.

A fine example of simile is that at the close of the sermon on the mount (Matt. vii, 24–27): "Every one therefore who hears these words of mine, and does them, shall be likened unto a wise man, who built his house upon the rock." Whether we here take the ὁμοιωθήσεται, *shall be likened,* as a prediction of what will take place in the final judgment—I will then make him like; show as a matter of fact that he is like (Tholuck, Meyer), or as simply the predicate of formal comparison (the future tense merely contemplating future cases as they shall arise), the similitude is in either case the same. We have on the one hand the figure of a house based upon the immovable rock, which neither storm nor flood can shake; on the other of a house based upon the shifting sand, and unable to resist the violence of winds and floods. The similitude, thus formally developed, becomes, in fact, a parable, and the mention of *rains, floods,* and *winds* implies that the house is to be tested at *roof, foundation,* and *sides*—top, bottom, and middle. But we should not, like the mystics, seek to find some special and distinct form of temptation in these three words. The grand similitude sets forth impressively the certain future of those who hear and obey the words of Jesus, and also of those who hear and refuse to obey. Compare with this similitude the allegory in Ezek. xiii, 11–15.

Blair traces the pleasure we take in comparisons of this kind to three different sources. "First, from the pleasure which nature has annexed to that act of the mind by which we compare two objects together, trace resemblances among those that are different, and differences among those that resemble each other; a pleasure, the final cause of which is to prompt us to remark and observe, and thereby to make us advance in useful knowledge. This operation of the mind is naturally and universally agreeable, as appears from the delight which even children have in comparing things together, as soon as they are capable of attending to the objects that surround them. Secondly, the pleasure of comparison arises from the illustration which the simile employed gives to the principal object; from the clearer view of it which it presents, or the stronger impression of it which it stamps upon the mind. And, thirdly, it arises from the introduction of a new, and commonly a splendid object, associated to the principal one of which we treat; and from the agreeable picture which that object presents to the fancy; new scenes being thereby brought into view, which, without the assistance of this figure, we could not have enjoyed."[1]

Pleasures afforded by simile.

There is, common to all languages, a class of illustrations, which might be appropriately called assumed comparisons. They are not, strictly speaking, either similes, or metaphors, or parables, or allegories, and yet they include some elements of them all. A fact or figure is introduced for

Assumed comparisons or illustrations.

[1] Lectures on Rhetoric, lecture xvii.

the sake of illustration, and yet no formal words of comparison are used. But the reader or hearer perceives at once that a comparison is assumed. Sometimes such assumed comparisons follow a regular simile. In 2 Tim. ii, 3, we read: "Partake thou in hardship as a good soldier of Christ Jesus." But immediately after these words, and keeping the figure thus introduced in his mind, the apostle adds: "No one on service as a soldier entangles himself with the affairs of life; in order that he may please him who enlisted him as a soldier." Here is no figure of speech, but the plain statement of a fact fully recognized in military service. But following the simile of verse 3, it is evidently intended as a further illustration, and Timothy is left to make his own application of it. And then follow two other illustrations, which it is also assumed the reader will apply for himself. "And if also any one contend as an athlete, he is not crowned if he did not lawfully contend. The labouring husbandman must first partake of the fruits." These are plain, literal statements, but a comparison is tacitly assumed, and Timothy could not fail to make the proper application. The true minister's close devotion to his proper work, his cordial submission, and conformity to lawful authority and order, and his laborious activity, are the points especially emphasized by these respective illustrations. So, again, in verses 20 and 21 of the same chapter: "In a great house there are not only vessels golden and silver, but also wooden and earthen ones, and some Literal statement, but implied comparison. unto honour and some unto dishonour." Here is a simple statement of facts intended for an illustration, but not presented as a simile. It is suggested by the metaphor in the preceding verse, in which the Lord's own chosen, the pure who confess his name, are represented as the firm foundation laid by God, a beautifully inscribed substructure, which, however, is to be gradually builded upon until the edifice becomes complete.[1] Its real character and purport are as if the apostle had said: "And now, for illustration, consider how, in a great house," etc. What he says of this house is, in itself, no figure, but a literal statement of what was commonly found in any extensive building; but in verse 21 he makes his own application thus: "If, therefore, any one purify himself from these (persons like the troublesome errorists, as the babblers, Hymenæus, etc., verses 16, 17, considered as vessels unto dishonour), he shall be as a vessel unto honour, sanctified, useful to the Master, unto every good work prepared."

A similar example of extended illustration appears in Matt. vii, 15-20: "Beware of the false prophets who come to you in sheep's

[1] Compare what is said on Peter, the living stone, pp. 226-229.

clothing, but inwardly they are ravenous wolves." Here is a bold, strong metaphor, obliging us to think of the false teacher as a wolf covered over and concealed from outward view by the skin of a sheep. But the next verse introduces another figure entirely: "From their fruits ye will know them;" and then to make the figure plainer, our Lord asks: "Do they gather grapes from thorns, or figs from thistles?" The question demands a negative answer, and is itself an emphatic way of making such answer. Thereupon he proceeds, using the formula of comparison: "So every good tree produces good fruit, and the bad tree produces bad fruit;" and then, dropping formal comparison, he adds: "A good tree cannot bring forth bad fruit, nor can a bad tree produce good fruit. Every tree that does not produce good fruit is cut down and cast into fire. Therefore (in view of these well-known facts, adduced as illustrations, I repeat the statement made a moment ago, verse 16), from their fruits ye will know them." It will be shown in a subsequent chapter how all true parables are essentially similes, but all similes are not parables. The examples of assumed comparison, given above, though distinguished from both simile and parable proper, contain essential elements of both.

METAPHOR.

Metaphor is an implied comparison, and is of much more frequent occurrence in all languages than simile. It differs from the latter in being a briefer and more pungent form of expression, and in turning words from their literal meaning to a new and striking use. The passage in Hos. xiii, 8: "I will devour them like a lion," is a simile or formal comparison; but Gen. xlix, 9: "A lion's whelp is Judah," is a metaphor. We may compare something to the savage strength and rapacity of a lion, or the swift flight of an eagle, or the brightness of the sun, or the beauty of a rose, and in each case we use the words in their literal sense. But when we say, Judah is a lion, Jonathan was an eagle, Jehovah is a sun, my beloved one is a rose, we perceive at once that the words lion, eagle, etc., are not used literally, but only some notable quality or characteristic of these creatures is intended. Hence metaphor, as the name denotes (Greek, μεταφέρω, to *carry over*, to *transfer*), is that figure of speech in which the sense of one word is transferred to another. This process of using words in new constructions is constantly going on, and, as we have seen in former chapters, the tropical sense of many words becomes at length the only one in use. Every language is, therefore, to a great extent, a dictionary of faded metaphors.

Metaphor defined and illustrated.

The sources from which scriptural metaphors are drawn are to be looked for chiefly in the natural scenery of the lands of the Bible, the customs and antiquities of the Orient, and the ritual worship of the Hebrews.[1] In Jer. ii, 13, we have two very expressive metaphors: "My people have committed two evils: they have forsaken me, a fountain of living waters, to hew for themselves cisterns, broken cisterns, that can hold no water." A fountain of living waters, especially in such a land as Palestine, is of inestimable worth; far more valuable than any artificial well or cistern, that can at best only catch and hold rain water, and is liable to become broken and lose its contents. What insane folly for a man to forsake a living fountain to hew for himself an uncertain cistern! The ingratitude and apostasy of Israel are strikingly characterized by the first figure, and their self-sufficiency by the second. *Examples of metaphor drawn from natural scenery.*

In Job ix, 6, a violent earthquake is represented as Jehovah "causing the land to move from her place, and making her columns tremble." The whole land affected by the earthquake shock is conceived as a building, heaved out of place, and all her pillars or columnar supports trembling and tottering to their fall. In chapter xxvi, 8, the holding of the rain in the heavens is pictured as God "binding up the waters in his dark cloud (עָב), and the cloud (עָנָן, cloud-covering) is not rent under them." The clouds are conceived as a great sheet or bag, strong enough to hold the immense weight of waters. In Deut. xxxii, 40, Jehovah is represented as saying: "For I will lift up to heaven my hand, and say, living am I forever." Here the allusion is to the ancient custom of lifting up the hand to heaven in the act of making a solemn oath. In verse 42 we have these further images: "I will make my arrows drunk with blood, and my sword shall devour flesh." By these metaphors arrows are personified as living things, intoxicated with drinking the blood of Jehovah's slaughtered foes, and the sword, as a ravenous beast of prey, devouring their flesh. Many similar examples exhibit at one and the same time the Old Testament anthropomorphisms,[2] together with personification and metaphor. *Ancient customs.*

The following strong metaphors have their basis in well-known habits of animals: "Issachar is an ass of bone, lying down between the double fold" (Gen. xlix, 14). He loves rest, like a beast of burden, especially like the strong, bony ass, that seeks repose between the sheepfolds. "Naphtali is a hind sent forth, the giver of sayings of beauty" (Gen. *Metaphorical allusions to the habits of animals.*

xlix, 21). The allusion here is specially to the elegance and beauty of the hind, bounding away gracefully in his freedom, and denotes in the tribe of Naphtali a taste for sayings of beauty, such as elegant songs and proverbs. As the neighbouring tribe of Zebulon produced ready writers (Judges v, 14), so, probably, Naphtali became noted for elegant speakers. "Benjamin is a wolf; he shall rend" (Gen. xlix, 27). This metaphor fitingly portrays the furious, warlike character of the Benjamites, from whom sprang an Ehud and a Saul. In Zech. vii, 11, mention is made of those who "refused to hearken, and gave a refractory shoulder," that is, acted like a refractory heifer or ox that shakes the shoulder and refuses to accept the yoke. Comp. Neh. ix, 29 and Hos. iv, 16. In Num. xxiv, 21, it is said of the Kenites, "Enduring is thy dwelling-place, and set in the rock thy nest." The secure dwellings of this tribe in the high fastnesses of the rocky hills are conceived as the nest of the eagle in the towering rock. Comp. Job xxxix, 27; Jer. xlix, 16; Obad. 4; Hab. ii, 9.

The following metaphors are based upon practices appertaining to the worship and ritual of the Hebrews. "I will wash my palms in innocency, I will go round about thy altar, O Jehovah" (Psa. xxvi, 6). Here the allusion is to the practice of the priests who were required to wash their hands before coming near the altar to minister (Exod. xxx, 20). The psalmist expresses his purpose to conform thoroughly to Jehovah's will; he would, so to speak, offer his burnt-offerings, even as the priest who goes about the altar on which his sacrifice is to be offered; and in doing so, he would be careful to conform to every requirement. In Psa. li, 7, "Purify me with hyssop, and I shall become clean," the allusion is to the ceremonial forms of purifying the leper (Lev. xiv, 6, 7) and his house (verse 51), and the person who had been defiled by contact with a dead body (Num. xix, 18, 19). So also the well-known usages of the passover, the sacrifice of the lamb, the careful removal of all leaven, and the use of unleavened bread, lie at the basis of the following metaphorical language: "Purge out the old leaven, that ye may be a new lump, even as ye are unleavened; for our passover also has been sacrificed, even Christ; wherefore, let us keep the feast, not with old leaven, nor with the leaven of malice and wickedness, but with the unleavened loaves of sincerity and truth" (1 Cor. v, 7, 8). Here the metaphors are continued until they make an allegory.

Sometimes a writer or speaker, after having used a striking metaphor goes on to elaborate its imagery, and, by so doing, constructs an allegory; sometimes he introduces a number and variety of images together, or, at other times, laying all figure aside, he proceeds with plain and simple language. Thus, in the Sermon on the Mount, Jesus says: "Ye are the salt of the earth" (Matt. v, 13). It is not difficult to grasp at once the comparison here implied. "The earth, the living world of men, is like a piece of meat, which would putrefy but that the grace of the Gospel of God, like salt, arrests the decay and purifies and preserves it."[1] But the Lord proceeds, adhering closely to the imagery of salt and its power, and develops his figure into a brief allegory: "But if the salt have lost its savour, wherewith shall it be salted?" Here is a most significant query. "The apostles, and in their degree all Christians," says Whedon, "are the substance and body of that salt. They are the substance to which the saltness inheres. But if the living body to which this gracious saltness inheres doth lose this quality, wherewith shall the quality be restored? The *it* refers to the solid salt which has lost its saltness or savour. What, alas! shall ever resalt that savourless salt? The Christian is the solid salt, and the grace of God is his saltness; that grace is the very salt of the salt. This solid salt is intended to salt the world with; but, alas! who shall salt the salt?"[2] But immediately after this elaborated figure, another and different metaphor is introduced, and carried forward with still greater detail. "Ye are the light of the world. A city set on a mountain cannot be hid; nor do they light a lamp and put it under the modius, but on the stand, and it shines for all that are in the house. Even so let your light shine" (Matt. v, 14–16). Here a variety of images is presented to the mind; a light, a city on a mountain, a lamp, a lampstand, and a Roman modius or peck measure. But through all these varying images runs the main figure of a light designed to send its rays afar, and illumine all within its range. A metaphor thus extended always becomes, strictly speaking, an allegory. In Matt. vii, 7, we have three metaphors introduced in a single verse. "Ask and it shall be given you; seek and ye shall find; knock and it shall be opened unto you." First, we have the image of a suppliant, making a request before a superior; next, of one who is in search for some goodly pearl or treasure (comp. Matt. xiii, 45, 46); and, finally, of one who is knocking at a door for admission. The three figures are so well related that they produce no confusion, but rather serve to strengthen one another. So Paul uses with good effect a twofold metaphor in Eph. iii, 18, where he prays "that Christ may dwell in your hearts through faith, being *rooted* and *grounded* in love." Here is the figure of a tree striking its roots

Elaborated and mixed metaphors.

---

[1] Whedon, Commentary, in loco.   [2] Ibid.

into the soil, and of a building based upon a deep and strong foundation.[1] But these figures are accompanied both before and after with a style of language of the most simple and practical character, and not designed to elaborate or even adhere to the imagery suggested by the metaphors.

Sometimes the salient point of allusion in a metaphor may be a matter of doubt or uncertainty. The opening words of Deborah's song (Judg. v, 2) have long puzzled translators and exegetes. The English version, following substantially the Syriac and Arabic, renders the Hebrew בִּפְרֹעַ פְּרָעוֹת בְּיִשְׂרָאֵל, "for the avenging of Israel." The Septuagint (Alex. Codex) has, "for the leading of the leaders," but seems to have been governed by the resemblance of the word פְּרָעוֹת to the official name of Egyptian monarchs פַּרְעֹה, Pharaoh. Neither of these translations has any certain support in Hebrew usage. The noun פֶּרַע occurs in the singular but twice (Num. vi, 5; Ezek. xliv, 20), and in both places means *a lock of hair*. The plural form of the word, פרעות, occurs only here and in Deut. xxxii, 42, and in both places would seem to mean, most legitimately, *locks of hair*, or *flowing locks*. And why should it be thought to mean any thing else? So far from being incongruous, it best suits the imagery of the immediate context in Deut. xxxii, 42. Jehovah there says: "I will make my arrows drunk with blood (Heb. מִדָּם, *from blood*), and my sword shall devour flesh—with the blood (or, from the blood) of slain and of captives, from the head of hairy locks of the enemy"—that is, from the blood of the hairy heads of the enemies. And so at the beginning of Deborah's song we may understand a bold metaphor,

Uncertain metaphorical allusions.

---

[1] Meyer observes: "Paul, in the vivacity of his imagination, conceives to himself the congregation of his readers as a *plant* (comp. Matt. xiii, 3), perhaps a *tree* (Matt. vii, 17), and at the same time as a *building*." Critical Com. on Ephesians, in loco. "The perfect participles," says Braune, "denote a state in which Paul's readers are and continue to be, which is the presupposition in order that they may be able to know. . . . They mark that a profoundly penetrating life (ἐῤῥιζωμένοι) and a well grounded, permanent character (τεθεμελιωμένοι) are necessary. The double figure strengthens the notion of the relation to love; this latter (ἐν ἀγάπῃ) is made prominent by being placed first. *In* marks *love* as the soil *in* which they are rooted, and as the foundation *on* which they are grounded. This implies moreover that it is not their own love which is referred to, but one which corresponds with the soil afforded to the tree, the foundation given to the house; and this would undoubtedly be, in accordance with the context, the love of Christ, were not all closer definition wanting, even the article. Accordingly, this substantive rendered general by the absence of the article corresponds with the verbal idea: in loving, i. e., in that love, which is first God's in Christ, and then that of men who became Christians, who are rooted in him and grounded on him through faith." Commentary on Ephesians (Lange's Biblework), in loco.

"In the loosing of locks in Israel;" for the primary meaning of the verb פָּרַע is everywhere that of *letting something loose*, and when used of locks of hair would naturally denote the loosing of the hair from all artificial coverings and restraint, and leaving it to wave wildly, as was done in the case of a Nazarite. The metaphor of the passage would thus be an allusion to the unrestrained growth of the locks of those who took upon themselves the vows of a Nazarite. And this view of the passage is corroborated by the next line of the parallelism, "In the free self-offering of the people." The people had, so to speak, by this act of consecration, made themselves free-will offerings. Nothing, therefore, could be more striking and impressive than these metaphorical allusions at the opening of this hymn:

> In [1] the loosing of locks in Israel,
> In the free self-offering of the people,
> Praise Jehovah!

In Psa. xlv, 1, "My heart boils up with a goodly word," it is difficult to determine whether the allusion is to an overflowing fountain, or to a boiling pot. The primary idea, according to Gesenius, lies in the noise of water boiling or bubbling, and as the word רָחַשׁ occurs nowhere else, but its derivative, מַרְחֶשֶׁת, denotes in Lev. ii, 7; vii, 9, a pot or vessel used both for boiling and frying, it is perhaps safer to say that the allusion in the metaphor of Psa. xlv, i, is to a boiling pot. The heart of the Psalmist was hot with a holy fervour, and, like the boiling oil of the vessel in which the meat-offering was prepared, it seethed and bubbled in the rapture of exulting song.

The exact point of the allusion in the words, "buried with him through baptism into death" (Rom. vi, 4), and "buried with him in baptism" (Col. ii, 12), has been disputed. The advocates of immersion insist that there is an allusion to the mode in which the rite of water baptism was performed, and most interpreters have acknowledged that such an allusion is in the word. The immersion of the candidate was thought of as a burial in the water. But the context in both passages goes to show that the great thought of the apostle was that of the believer's *death unto sin.* Thus, in Romans, "Are ye ignorant that as many

Buried with Christ through baptism into death.

---

[1] The preposition בְּ, *in*, points out the condition of the people in which they conquered and sang. The song is the people's consecration hymn, and praises God for the prosperous and successful issue with which he has crowned their vows. Cassel's Commentary on Judges (Lange's Biblework), in loco. Comp. Whedon's Old Testament Commentary, in loco.

of us as were baptized into Christ Jesus were baptized into his death? We were buried therefore with him through baptism into death. . . . We have become united with the likeness of his death (ver. 5). . . . Our old man was crucified with him (ver. 6). . . . We died with Christ (ver. 8). . . . Even so consider ye yourselves to be dead unto sin, but alive unto God in Christ Jesus" (ver. 11). Now, while the word *buried with* (συνθάπτω) would naturally accord with the idea of an immersion into water, the main thought is the *deadness unto sin*, attained through a union with Christ in *the likeness of his death*. The imagery does not depend on the mode of Christ's execution or of his burial, much less on the manner in which baptism was administered, but on *the similitude of his death* (τῷ ὁμοιώματι τοῦ θανάτου αὐτοῦ, ver. 5) considered as an accomplished fact. The baptism is *into death*, not into water; and whether the outward rite were performed by sprinkling, or pouring, or immersion, it would have been equally true in either case, that they were "buried with him through the baptism into the death." Or he might have said, "We were crucified with him through baptism into death;" and then as now it would have been the end accomplished, the death, not the mode of the baptism, which is made prominent. In the briefer form of expression in Col. ii, 12, it is written, simply, "having been buried with him in baptism." Here, however, the context shows that the leading thought is the same as in Rom. vi, 3–11. The burial *in baptism* (ἐν τῷ βαπτίσματι, in the matter of baptism) figured "the putting off of the body of the flesh;" that is, the utter stripping off and casting aside the old carnal nature. The burial is not to be thought of as a mode of putting a corpse in a grave or sepulchre, but as indicating that the body of sin is truly dead. Having thus clearly defined the real point of the allusion it need not be denied or disputed that the figure also may include, incidentally, a reference to the practice of immersion. But, as Eadie observes, "Whatever may be otherwise said in favour of immersion, it is plain that here the burial is wholly ideal. Believers are buried in baptism, but even in immersion they do not go through a process having any resemblance to the burial and resurrection of Christ."[1] To maintain from such a metaphorical allusion, where the process and mode of burial are not in point at all, that a burial into, and a resurrection from, water, are essential to valid baptism, would seem like an extravagance of dogmatism.

---

[1] Commentary on the Greek Text of Colossians, in loco.

CHAPTER XII.

FABLES, RIDDLES, AND ENIGMAS.

PASSING now from the more common figures of speech, we come to those peculiar tropical methods of conveying ideas and impressing truths, which hold a special prominence in the Holy Scriptures. These are known as fables, rid- More prominent scriptural tropes.
dles, enigmas, allegories, parables, proverbs, types, and symbols. In order to appreciate and properly interpret these special forms of thought, a clear understanding of the more common rhetorical figures treated in the previous chapters is altogether necessary. For the parable will be found to correspond with the simile, the allegory with the metaphor, and other analogies will be traceable in other figures. A scientific analysis and treatment of these more prominent tropes of Scripture will require us to distinguish and discriminate between some things which in popular speech are frequently confounded. Even in the Scripture itself the proverb, the parable, and the allegory are not formally distinguished. In the Old Testament the word מָשָׁל is applied alike to the proverbs of Solomon (Prov. i, 1; x, 1; xxv, 1), the oracles of Balaam (Num. xxiii, 7; xxiv, 8), the addresses of Job (Job xxvii, 1; xxix, 1), the taunting speech against the King of Babylon (in Isa. xiv, 4, ff.), and other prophecies (Micah ii, 4; Hab. ii, 6). In the New Testament the word παραβολή, parable, is applied not only to what are admitted on all hands to be parables proper, but also to proverb (Luke iv, 23), and symbol (Heb. ix, 9), and type (Heb. xi, 19). John does not use the word παραβολή at all, but calls the allegory of the good shepherd in chap. x, 6, a παροιμία, which word Peter uses in the sense of a proverb or byword (2 Peter ii, 22). The word allegory occurs but once (Gal. iv, 24), and then in verbal form (ἀλληγορούμενα) to denote the allegorizing process by which certain Old Testament facts might be made to typify Gospel truths.

Lowest of these special figures, in dignity and aim, is the fable. It consists essentially in this, that individuals of the brute creation, and of animate and inanimate nature, are Characteristics of the fable.
introduced into the imagery as if possessed with reason and speech, and are represented as acting and talking contrary to the laws of their being. There is a conspicuous element of unreality about the

whole machinery of fables, and yet the moral intended to be set forth is usually so manifest that no difficulty is felt in understanding it.

The oldest fable of which we have any trace is that of Jotham, recorded in Judg. ix, 7-20. The trees are represented as going forth to choose and anoint a king. They invite the olive, the fig-tree, and the vine to come and reign over them, but these all decline, and urge that their own natural purpose and products require all their care. Then the trees invite the bramble, which does not refuse, but, in biting irony, insists that all the trees shall come and take refuge under its shadow! Let the olive-tree, and the fig-tree, and the vine come under the protecting shade of the briar! But if not, it is significantly added, "Let fire go forth from the bramble and devour the cedars of Lebanon." The miserable, worthless bramble, utterly unfit to shade even the smallest shrub, might, nevertheless, well serve to kindle a fire that would quickly devour the noblest of trees. So Jotham, in giving an immediate application of his fable, predicts that the weak and worthless Abimelech, whom the men of Shechem had been so fast to make king over them, would prove an accursed torch to burn their noblest leaders. All this imagery of trees walking and talking is at once seen to be purely fanciful. It has no foundation in fact, and yet it presents a vivid and impressive picture of the political follies of mankind in accepting the leadership of such worthless characters as Abimelech.

Another fable, quite similar to that of Jotham, is found in 2 Kings xiv, 9, where Jehoash, the King of Israel, answers the warlike challenge of Amaziah, King of Judah, by the following short and pungent apologue: "The thornbush which is in Lebanon sent to the cedar which is in Lebanon, saying, Give thy daughter to my son for a wife; and there passed over a beast of the field which was in Lebanon, and trampled down the thornbush." This fable embodies a most contemptuous response to Amaziah, intimating that his pride of heart and self-conceit were moving him to attempt things far beyond his proper sphere. The beast trampling down the thornbush intimates that a passing incident, which could have no effect on a cedar of Lebanon, might easily destroy the briar. Jehoash does not proudly boast that he himself will come forth, and by his military forces crush Amaziah; but suggests that a passing judgment, an incidental circumstance, would be sufficient for that purpose, and it were therefore better for the presumptuous King of Judah to remain at home in his proper place.

Jotham's fable.

Jehoash's fable.

The apologues of Jotham and Jehoash are the only proper fables that appear in the Bible. In the interpretation of these we should guard against pressing the imagery too far. We are not to suppose that every word and allusion has some special meaning. In the apologue of Jehoash *Fabulous imagery not to be pressed too far in the interpretation.* we are not to say that the thornbush was Amaziah, and the cedar Jehoash, and the wild beast the warriors of the latter; and yet, by the contrast between the cedar and the thornbush, the king of Israel would, doubtless, impress his contempt for Amaziah upon the latter's mind, and thus seek to humiliate his pride. Neither are we to suppose that Amaziah had asked Jehoash to give his daughter in marriage to his son; nor that "Israel might properly be regarded as Jehoash's daughter, and Judah as Amaziah's son" (Thenius), as if Amaziah had formally demanded, as Josephus states, (*Ant.* ix, 9, 2), a union of the two kingdoms. Nor in the fable of Jotham are we, like some of the ancient interpreters, to understand by the olive, the fig-tree, and the vine, the three great judges that had preceded Abimelech, viz., Othniel, Deborah, and Gideon, nor seek for hidden meanings and thrusts in such words as *anoint, reign over us,* and *shadow.* We should always keep in mind that it is one distinguishing feature of fables that they are not exact parallels of those things to which they are designed to be applied. They are based on imaginary actions of irrational creatures, or inanimate things, and can therefore never be true to actual life.

We should also note how completely the spirit and aim of the fable accords with irony, sarcasm, and ridicule. Hence its special adaptation to expose the follies and vices of men. "It is essentially of the earth," says Trench, "and never lifts itself above the earth. It never has a higher aim than to inculcate maxims of prudential morality, industry, caution, foresight; and these it will sometimes recommend even at the expense of the higher self-forgetting virtues. The fable just reaches that pitch of morality which the world will understand and approve."[1] But this able and excellent writer goes, as we think, too far when he says that the fable has no proper place in the Scripture, "and, in the nature of things, could have none, for the purpose of Scripture excludes it." The fables noticed above are a part of the Scripture which is received as God-inspired (2 Tim. iii, 16); and though it is not God that speaks through them, but men occupying an earthly standpoint, that fact does not make good the assertion that such fables have no true place in Scripture. For the teachings of Scripture move in the

[1] Notes on the Parables, p. 10.

realm of earthly life and human thought as well as in a higher and holier element, and sarcasm and caustic rebukes find a place on the sacred page. The record of Adam's naming the beasts and fowls that were brought to him in Eden (Gen. ii, 19) suggests that their qualities and habits impressed his mind with significant analogies. Many of the most useful proverbs are abbreviated fables (Prov. vi, 6; xxx, 15, 25–28). Though the fable moves in the earthly element of prudential morality, even that element may be pervaded and taken possession of by the divine wisdom.[1]

The riddle differs from the fable in being designed to puzzle and Characteristics perplex the hearer. It is purposely obscure in order to of the riddle. test the sharpness and penetration of those who attempt to solve it. The Hebrew word for riddle (חִידָה) is from a root which means to *twist*, or tie a knot, and is used of any dark and intricate saying, which requires peculiar skill and insight to unravel. The queen of Sheba made a journey to Solomon's court to test him with riddles (1 Kings x, 1). It is declared, at the beginning of the Book of the Proverbs, that it is the part of true wisdom "to understand a proverb and an enigma (מְלִיצָה); words of the wise and their riddles" (Prov. i, 6). The psalmist says, "I will incline my ear to a proverb; I will open on a harp my riddle" (Psa. xlix, 4). "I will open my mouth in a proverb; I will pour forth riddles of old" (lxxviii, 2). Riddles, therefore, dark sayings, enigmas, which conceal thought, and, at the same time, incite the inquiring mind to search for their hidden meanings, have a place in the Scripture.

Samson's celebrated riddle is in the form of a Hebrew couplet (Judges xiv, 14):

> Out of the eater came forth food,
> And out of strength came forth sweetness.

The clue to this riddle is furnished in the incidents related in Samson's riddle. verses 8 and 9. Out of the carcass of a devouring beast came the food of which both Samson and his parents had eaten; and out of that which had been the embodiment of strength, came forth the sweet honey, which the bees had deposited therein. But Samson's companions, and even his parents, were not acquainted with these facts. Their ignorance, however,

---

[1] The profound significance of Jotham's fable is declared by Cassel to be inexhaustible. "Its truth is of perpetual recurrence. More than once was Israel in the position of the Shechemites; then, especially, when he whose kingdom is not of this world, refused to be a king. Then, too, Herod and Pilate became friends. The thornbush seemed to be king when it encircled the head of the Crucified. But Israel experienced what is here denounced: a fire went forth and consumed city and people, temple and fortress." Cassel's Commentary on Judges (Lange's Biblework), in loco.

is no ground for saying that therefore Samson's riddle was no proper riddle at all. "The ingenuity of the riddle," says Cassel, "consists precisely in this, that the ambiguity both of its language and contents can be turned in every direction, and thus conceals the answer. It is like a knot whose right end cannot be found. . . . Samson's problem distinguishes itself only by its peculiar ingenuity. It is short and simple, and its words are used in their natural signification. It is so clear as to be obscure. It is not properly liable to the objection that it refers to an historical act which no one could know. The act was one which was common in that country. Its turning point, with reference to the riddle was, not that it was an incident of Samson's personal history, but that its occurrence in general was not impossible."[1]

A notable example of riddle in the New Testament is that of the mystic number of the beast propounded in Rev. xiii, 18. The number of "Here is wisdom. Let him that has understanding the beast. reckon the number of the beast, for it is a man's number; and his number is six hundred sixty-six." Another very ancient reading, but probably the error of a copyist, makes the number six hundred and fourteen. This riddle has perplexed critics and interpreters through all the ages since the Apocalypse was written.[2] The number of a man would most naturally mean the numerical value of the letters which compose some man's name, and the two names which have found most favour in the solution of this problem are the Greek Λατεινος, and the Hebrew נרון קסר. Either of these names makes up the required number, and one or the other will be adopted according to one's interpretation of the symbolical beast in question.

Some of the sayings of the wise in the Book of Proverbs seem to have been made purposely obscure. Who shall decide the real meaning of Prov. xxvi, 10? The English ver- Dark proverbs. sion renders: "The great God that formed all things both rewardeth the fool, and rewardeth transgressors." But the margin gives us an alternative reading: "A great man grieveth all, and he hireth the fool, he hireth also transgressors." Others translate: "As the archer that woundeth every one, so is he that hireth the fool, and he that hireth the passer-by." Others: "An arrow that woundeth every one is he who hireth a fool and he who hireth vagrants." Others: "A master forms all things himself, but he that hires a fool is as he that hires vagrants." And the Hebrew words of the

[1] Commentary on Judges, in loco.
[2] For the various conjectures see the leading Commentaries on the passage, especially Stuart, Elliott, and Düsterdieck.

original are susceptible of still other renderings. A proverb couched in words susceptible of so many different meanings may well be called a riddle or "dark saying." It was probably designed to puzzle, and the variety of meanings attaching to its words was a reason with the author for choosing just those words.

One of the "dark sayings of old" is the poetic fragment ascribed to Lamech (Gen. iv, 23, 24), which may be closely rendered thus:

> Adah and Zillah, hear my voice;
> Wives of Lamech, listen to my saying;
> For a man have I slain for my wound,
> And a child for my bruise.
> For sevenfold avenged should Cain be,
> And Lamech seventy and seven.

The obscurity attaching to this song arises probably from our ignorance of the circumstances which called it forth. Some have Lamech's song. supposed that Lamech was smitten with remorse over the murder of a young man, and these words are his lamentation. Others suppose he had killed a man in self-defense, or in retaliation for wounds received. Others make the song a triumphant exultation over Tubal-cain's invention of brass and iron weapons, and, translating the verb as a future "I will slay," regard the utterance as a pompous threat. Verse 24 is then understood as a blasphemous boast that he could now avenge his own wrongs ten times more thoroughly than God would avenge the slaying of Cain.[1] Possibly the whole song was originally intended as a riddle, and was as perplexing to Lamech's wives as to modern expositors.

It would be well to make a formal distinction between the riddle Riddle and enigma should be distinguished. and the enigma, and apply the former term to such intricate sayings as deal essentially with earthly things, and are especially designed to exercise human ingenuity and shrewdness. Such were Samson's riddle, and the puzzling questions put to Solomon by the Queen of Sheba, the number of the beast, and proverbs like that noticed above (Prov. xxvi, 10). Enigmas, on the other hand, would be the more fitting name for those mystic utterances which serve both to conceal and enhance some deep and sacred thought. But the words have been so long used interchangeably of both classes of dark sayings that we can scarcely expect to change from such indiscriminate usage.

The word *enigma* (αἴνιγμα) occurs but once (1 Cor. xiii, 12) in the New Testament, but in the Septuagint it is employed as the Greek equivalent of the Hebrew חִידָה. In 1 Cor. xiii, 12, it is used to

---

[1] For a full synopsis of the various interpretations of this song, see M'Clintock and Strong's Cyclopædia, article Lamech.

indicate the dim and imperfect manner in which in this life we apprehend heavenly and eternal things: "For we see now through a mirror in enigma." Most expositors take the words *in enigma* adverbially, in the sense of *darkly, dimly, in an enigmatical way.* "But αἴνιγμα," says Meyer, "is a dark *saying,* and the idea of the *saying* should as little be lost here as in Num. xii, 8. Luther renders rightly: *in a dark word;* which, however, should be explained more precisely as *by means of an enigmatic word,* whereby is meant the word of the Gospel revelation, which capacitates for the *seeing* (βλέπειν) in question, however imperfect it be, and is its medium to us. It is αἴνιγμα, inasmuch as it affords to us no full clearness of light upon God's decrees, ways of salvation, etc., but keeps its contents sometimes in greater, sometimes in a less, degree (Rom. xi, 33; 1 Cor. ii, 9) concealed, bound up in images, similitudes, types, and the like forms of human limitation and human speech, and consequently is for us of a mysterious and enigmatic nature, standing in need of a future λύσις (solution), and vouchsafing πίστις (faith), indeed, but not εἶδος (appearance, 2 Cor. v, 7)."[1]

There is an enigmatical element in our Lord's discourse with Nicodemus, John iii, 1–13. The profound lesson contained in the words of verse 3: "Except a man be born from above he cannot see the kingdom of God," perplexed and confounded the Jewish ruler. *Enigmatical element in Jesus' words to Nicodemus.* Deep in his heart the Lord, who "knew what was in man" (ii, 25), discerned his spiritual need. His thoughts were too much upon the outward, the visible, the fleshly. The miracles of Jesus had made a deep impression, and he would inquire of the great wonder-worker as of a divinely commissioned *teacher.* Jesus stops all his compliments, and surprises him with a mysterious word, which seems equivalent to saying: Do not now talk about my works, or of whence I came; turn your thoughts upon your inner self. What you need is not *new knowledge,* but *new life;* and that life can be had only by another *birth.* And when Nicodemus uttered his surprise and wonder, he was rebuked by the reflection, "Art thou the teacher of Israel, and knowest not these things?" (ver. 10). Had not the psalmist prayed, "Create in me a clean heart, O God?" (Psa. li, 10). Had not the law and the prophets spoken of a divine circumcision of the heart? (Deut. xxx, 6; Jer. iv, 4; Ezek. xi, 19). Why then should such a man as Nicodemus express surprise at these deep sayings of the Lord? Simply because his heart-life and spiritual discernment were unable then to apprehend "the things of the Spirit of God" (1 Cor. ii, 14). They were as a riddle to him.

[1] Meyer on Corinthians, in loco.

The same style of enigmatical discourse appears in Jesus' sayings in the synagogue at Capernaum (John vi, 53–59); also in his first words to the woman of Samaria (John iv, 10–15), and in his response to the disciples when they returned and "wondered that he was talking with a woman," and asked him to eat of the food they had procured (John iv, 32–38). His reply, in this last case, was, "I have food to eat which ye do not know." They misunderstood him, as did Nicodemus and the Samaritan woman. "What wonder," says Augustine, "if that woman did not understand water? Behold, the disciples do not yet understand food." [1] They wondered whether any one had brought him something to eat during their absence, and then Jesus spoke more plainly: "My food is that (ἵνα, indicating conscious aim and purpose) I shall do the will of him that sent me, and shall complete his work." His success with the Samaritan woman was to him better food than any bodily sustenance, for it elevated his soul into the holy conviction and assurance that he should successfully accomplish the whole of that work for which he came into the world. And then he proceeds, adhering still to the tone and style of intermingled enigma and allegory: "Do not ye say that there is yet a four-month, and the harvest comes? Behold, I say unto you, Lift up your eyes and look on the fields, that they are white unto harvest. Already [2] he that reaps is receiving reward and gathering fruit into (εἰς, as into a garner) life eternal, that he who sows and he who reaps may rejoice together." The winning of that one Samaritan convert opens to Jesus' prophetic soul the great Gospel harvest of the near future, and he speaks of it as already at hand. Whether we regard the saying, "There is yet a four-month, and the harvest comes," as a proverb (Lightfoot, Tholuck, Lücke, De Wette, Stier), equivalent to, There is a space of four months between seedtime and harvest, or understand that the neighbouring grain fields were just sown, or just now green with the young tender grain (Meyer and many), and over them many Samaritans appeared coming to him (ver. 30), the great thought is still the same, and emphasizes the actual joy of Jesus in that hour of ingathering. Sower and reaper were together there and then, but the disciples could scarcely take in the full import of Jesus' glowing words. "The disciples saw no harvest field; they said and they thought assuredly, There must be at least four months yet! But the Lord sets before them a mystery

---

[1] In Joannis Evangelium Tractatus xv, 31.

[2] Most of the oldest and best manuscript authorities omit καί after ἤδη, and many of the best critics join ἤδη with what follows. So Schulz, Tischendorf, Godet, and Westcott and Hort.

and an enigma, and thereby would teach them to lift up aright the eyes of their faith. *Behold, I say unto you, I have now been sowing the word, and already behold a sudden harvest upspringing and ready. Should not this be my meat and my joy? O ye, my reapers, rejoice together with me, the sower, and forget ye also to eat!*"[1]

The words of Jesus in Luke xxii, 36, are an enigma. As he was about to go out to Gethsemane he discerned that the hour of peril was at hand. He reminded his disciples of the time when he sent them forth without purse, wallet, or shoes (Luke ix, 1–6), and drew from them the acknowledgement that they had then lacked nothing. "But now," said he, "he that has a purse, let him take it, and likewise a wallet; and he that has not, let him sell his mantle, and buy a sword." He would impress them with the feeling that the time of fearful conflict and exposure was now imminent. They must expect to be assailed, and should be prepared for all righteous self-defense. They would see times when a sword would be worth more to them than a mantle. But our Lord, evidently, did not mean that they should, literally, arm themselves with the weapons of a carnal warfare, and use the sword to propagate his cause (Matt. xxvi, 52; John xviii, 36). He would significantly warn them of the coming bitter conflict and opposition they must meet. The world would be against them, and assail them in many a hostile form, and they should therefore prepare for self-defense and manly encounter. It is not the sword of the Spirit (Eph. vi, 17) of which the Lord here speaks, but the sword as the symbol of that warlike heroism, that bold and fearless confession, and that inflexible purpose to maintain the truth, which would soon be a duty and a necessity on the part of the disciples in order to defend their faith. But the disciples misunderstood these enigmatical words, and spoke of two swords which they had with them! Jesus paused not to explain, and broke off that conversation "in the tone of one who is conscious that others would not yet understand him, and who, therefore, holds further speech unprofitable."[2] His laconic answer, *it is enough,* was "a gentle turning aside of further discussion, with a touch of sorrowful irony. More than your two swords ye need not!"[3]

Enigma of the sword in Luke xxii, 36.

A similar enigma appears in John xxi, 18, where Jesus says to Simon Peter: "When thou wast young thou girdedst thyself, and walkedst whither thou wouldest; but when thou shalt be old another shall gird thee and carry thee

Enigmatical words to Peter, John xxi, 18.

---

[1] Stier, Words of Jesus, in loco. (Lange's Biblework), in loco.

[2] Van Oosterzee's Commentary on Luke

[3] Meyer, in loco.

whither thou wouldest not." The writer immediately adds that Jesus thereby signified (σημαίνων) "by what death he should glorify God." But it is scarcely probable that Peter then fully comprehended the saying. Comp. also John ii, 19.

The prophetic picture of the two eagles in Ezek. xvii, 2–10, is a mixture of enigma (חִידָה) and fable (מָשָׁל). It is fabulous so far as it represents the eagles as acting with human intelligence and will, but, aside from this, its imagery belongs rather to the sphere of prophetic symbols. Altogether, it is an enigma of high prophetic character, a "dark saying," in which the real meaning is concealed behind typical images. In its interpretation we need to take the whole chapter together, and we observe that it has three distinct parts: (1) The enigma (verses 1–10); (2) its interpretation (11–21); (3) a Messianic prophecy based upon the foregoing imagery (22–24). The great eagle represents the king of Babylon, Nebuchadnezzar. The "great wings, with long pinions, full of feathers of many colours" (ver. 3), altogether furnish a striking figure of majesty, rapidity of movement, and splendour of regal power. Most expositors explain the great wings as denoting the wide dominion of this eagle; the long pinions as the extent and energy of his military power; the fulness of feathers to the multitude of subjects; and the many colours to the diversity of their nations, languages, and customs. But the tracing of such special allusions in the natural appendages of the eagle is of doubtful worth, and should not be made prominent. It is better to understand in a more general way the strength, rapidity, and glory of Nebuchadnezzar. Lebanon is mentioned because of its being the natural home of the cedar, but it here represents Jerusalem (ver. 12), which was the home and seat of the royal seed of Judah. The leafy crown and topmost shoots of the cedar are the king and princes of Judah whom Nebuchadnezzar carried away to Babylon (2 Kings xxiv, 14, 15). Babylon is here called, enigmatically, "a land of Canaan," because its commerce and its diplomacy had made it "a city of merchants." Its self-seeking spirit of policy and trade made it a land of Canaan (Eng. Ver., "traffic").

And now the figure changes. The eagle "took of the seed of the land," of the same land where the cedar grew, "and put it in a field of seed" (ver. 5) where it had every chance to grow. Nay, he took it upon many waters as one would plant a willow; that is, with the care and foresight that one would exercise in setting a willow in a well-watered soil in which alone it can flourish. But this "seed of the land" was not the seed of a willow, but of a vine, and it "sprouted and became a spreading vine of low stature;"

and it was the plan of the eagle that this lowly vine should "turn its branches toward him, and its roots under him" (ver. 6). The "seed of the land" (ver. 5) was the royal seed of the kingdom of Judah (ver. 13), Zedekiah, whom Nebuchadnezzar made king in Jerusalem after the capture of Jehoiachin (2 Kings xxiv, 17). The other great eagle was the king of Egypt, less mighty and glorious than the other. Toward this second eagle the vine turned her roots and sent forth her branches (ver. 7). The impotent but rebellious Zedekiah "sent his messengers to Egypt" for horses and people to help him against Nebuchadnezzar (ver. 15). But it was all in vain. He who broke his covenant and despised his oath (ver. 18) could not prosper; it required no great arm or many people to uproot and destroy such a feeble vine. The eagle of Egypt was powerless to help, and the Chaldæan forces, like a destructive east wind (ver. 10), utterly withered it away. All this is brought out forcibly in the solemn words of the "oracle of the Lord Jehovah," verses 16–21.

Thus far the imagery has been a mixture of fable and symbol,[1] but with verse 22 the prophet enters a higher plane of prophecy. The eagles drop out of view entirely, and Jehovah himself takes from the leafy crown of the high cedar a tender shoot (comp. Isa. xi, 1; liii, 2) and plants it upon the lofty mountain of Israel, where it becomes a glorious cedar to shelter and shade "every bird of every wing." This is a noble prophecy of the Messiah, springing from the stock of Judah, and developing from the holy "mountain of the house of Jehovah" (Micah iv, 1, 2) a kingdom of marvellous growth and of gracious protection to all who may seek its shelter. We should note especially how the Messianic prophecy here leaves the realm of fable and takes on the style of allegory and parable. Comp. Matt. xiii, 31, 32.

---

[1] Schröder observes that the mixed figure here used by Ezekiel goes far beyond mere popular illustration, and must not "be explained away from the æsthetic standpoint, as merely another rhetorical garb for the thought. As in the parable the emblematic form preponderates over the thought, so also here. What the prophet is to say to Israel is said by the whole of that mighty array of figurative expression, for which the animal and vegetable worlds furnish the figures. But the eagle does what eagles otherwise never do; and what is planted as a willow grows as a vine; and the vine is represented as falling in love with the other eagle. The contradictory character of such a representation, and the fact that in the difficulties to be solved (ver. 9, sq.) the comparison comes to a stand, and the closing Messianic portion in which the whole culminates, convert the parable into a riddle. A trace of irony and the moral tendency, such as belong to the fable, are not wanting." Commentary on Ezekiel (in Lange's Biblework), in loco.

CHAPTER XIII.

INTERPRETATION OF PARABLES.

AMONG the figurative forms of scriptural speech the parable has a
Pre-eminence notable pre-eminence. We find a number of examples
of parabolic in the Old Testament, and the esteem in which this
teaching. mode of teaching was held by the ancient Jews is apparent from the following words of the son of Sirach:

> He who gives his soul and exercises his mind in the law of the
> Most High
> Will seek out the wisdom of the ancients,
> And will be occupied with prophecies.
> He will observe the utterances of men of fame,
> And will enter with them into the twists (στροφαῖς) of parables.
> He will seek out the hidden things of proverbs,
> And busy himself with the enigmas of parables.[1]

Parables are especially worthy of our study, inasmuch as they were
the chosen methods by which our Lord set forth many revelations
of his heavenly kingdom. They were also employed by the great
rabbis who were contemporary with Jesus, and they frequently appear in the Talmud and other Jewish books. Among all the oriental peoples they appear to have been a favourite form of conveying
moral instruction, and find a place in the literature of most nations.
The word *parable* is derived from the Greek verb παραβάλλω, to
The parable de- *throw* or *place by the side of*, and carries the idea of
fined. placing one thing by the side of another for the purpose of comparison. The word has been somewhat vaguely used,
as we have seen above,[2] to represent the Hebrew מָשָׁל, and to designate proverbs, types, and symbols (as in Luke iv, 23; Heb. ix, 9;
xi, 19). But, strictly speaking, the parable belongs to a style of
figurative speech which constitutes a class of its own. It is essentially a comparison, or simile, and yet all similes are not parables.
The simile may appropriate a comparison from any kind or class of
objects, whether real or imaginary. The parable is limited in its
range, and confined to that which is real. Its imagery always embodies a narrative which is true to the facts and experiences of human life. It makes no use, like the fable, of talking birds and

---

[1] Ecclesiasticus xxxix, 1–3.　　　　　[2] See above on p. 265.

beasts, or of trees in council. Like the riddle and enigma, it may serve to conceal a truth from those who have not spiritual penetration to perceive it under its figurative form; but its narrative style, and the formal comparison always announced or assumed, differentiate it clearly from all classes of knotty sayings which are designed mainly to puzzle and confuse. The parable, when once understood, unfolds and illustrates the mysteries of the kingdom of heaven. The enigma may embody profound truths, and make much use of metaphor, but it never, like the parable, forms a narrative, or assumes to make a formal comparison. The parable and the allegory come nearer together, so that, indeed, parables have been defined as "historical allegories;" [1] but they differ from each other in substantially the same way as simile differs from metaphor. (The parable is essentially a formal comparison, and requires its interpreter to go beyond its own narrative to bring in its meaning; the allegory is an extended metaphor, and contains its interpretation within itself. The parable, therefore, stands apart by itself as a mode and style of figurative speech. It moves in an element of sober earnestness, never transgressing in its imagery the limits of probability, or of what might be actual fact. It may tacitly take up within itself essential elements of enigma, type, symbol, and allegory, but it differs from them all, and in its own chosen sphere of real, every-day life, is peculiarly adapted to body forth special teachings of Him who is "the *Verax*, no less than the *Verus*, and the *Veritas*." [2]

The general design of parables, as of all other kinds of figurative language, is to embellish and set forth ideas and moral General use of truths in attractive and impressive forms. Many a parables. moral lesson, if spoken in naked, literal style, is soon forgotten; but, clothed in parabolic dress, it arouses attention, and fastens itself in the memory. Many rebukes and pungent warnings may be couched

---

[1] Davidson's Hermeneutics, p. 311.

[2] Trench on the Miracles, p. 127. This eminent divine, whose work on the parables is one of the best of its kind, traces to considerable extent the differences between the parable, the fable, the myth, the proverb, and the allegory, and sums up as follows: "The parable differs from the fable, moving as it does in a spiritual world, and never transgressing the actual order of things natural; from the mythus, there being in the latter an unconscious blending of the deeper meaning with the outward symbol, the two remaining separate and separable in the parable; from the proverb, inasmuch as it is longer carried out, and not merely accidentally and occasionally, but necessarily figurative; from the allegory, comparing as it does one thing *with* another, at the same time preserving them apart as an inner and an outer, not transferring, as does the allegory, the proprieties, and qualities, and relations of one *to* the other."—Notes on the Parables, pp. 15, 16. New York, 1857.

in a parable, and thereby give less offence, and yet work better effects than open plainness of speech could do. Nathan's parable (in 2 Sam. xii, 1–4) prepared the heart of David to receive with profit the keen reproof he was about to administer. Some of our Lord's most pointed parables against the Jews—parables which they perceived were directed against themselves—embodied reproof, rebuke, and warning, and yet by their form and drapery, they served to shield him from open violence (Matt. xxi, 45; Mark xii, 12; Luke xx, 19). It is easy, also, to see that a parable may enshrine a profound truth or mystery which the hearers may not at first apprehend, but which, because of its striking or memorable form, abides more firmly in the mind, and so abiding, yields at length its deep and precious meaning.[1]

The special reason and purpose of the parables of Jesus are stated Special reason in Matt. xiii, 10–17. Up to that point in his ministry and purpose of Jesus appears not to have spoken in parables. "The the parables of Jesus. words of grace ($\lambda\delta\gamma\iota\alpha\ \tau\tilde{\eta}\varsigma\ \chi\acute{\alpha}\rho\iota\tau o\varsigma$) which proceeded from his mouth" (Luke iv, 22) in the synagogue, by the seashore, and on the mount, were direct, simple, and plain. He used simile and metaphor in the sermon on the mount, and elsewhere. In the synagogue at Nazareth he quoted a familiar proverb and called it a parable (Luke iv, 23). His words had power and authority, unlike those of the scribes, and the people were astonished at his teaching. But there came a time when he notably changed his style. His simple precepts were often met with derision and scorn, and among the multitudes there were always some who were anxious to pervert his sayings. When multitudes gathered by the sea of Galilee to hear him, "and he spoke to them many things in parables" (Matt. xiii, 3), his disciples quickly observed the change and asked him, "Why in parables dost thou speak to them?" Our Lord's answer is remarkable for its blended use of metaphor, proverb, and enigma, so combined and connected with a prophecy of Isaiah (vi, 9, 10), that it becomes in itself one of the profoundest of his discourses.

Because to you it is given to know the mysteries of the kingdom of the heavens, but to them it is not given. For whosoever has, to him shall be given and he shall superabound ; but whosoever has not, even what he has

---

[1] Trench writes of our Lord's parables : "His words laid up in the memory were to many that heard them like the money of another country, unavailable, it might be, for present use, of which they knew not the value, but which yet was ready in their hand when they reached that land and were naturalized in it. When the Spirit came and brought all things to their remembrance, then he filled all the outlines of truth which they before possessed with its substance, quickened all its forms with the power and spirit of life."—Notes on the Parables, p. 28.

shall be taken away from him. Therefore I speak to them in parables; because seeing they do not see, and hearing they do not hear, nor understand. And with them is fulfilled the prophecy of Isaiah, which says, By hearing ye shall hear and in no wise understand; and seeing ye shall see and in no wise perceive; for thick became the heart of this people, and they heard heavily with their ears, and their eyes they closed, lest haply they should perceive with their eyes, and with their ears hear, and with the heart understand, and should turn again, and I should heal them. Matt. xiii, 11–15.

The great thought in this answer seems to be that the Lord had a twofold purpose in the use of parables, namely, both to reveal and to conceal great truths.[1] There was, first, that inner circle of followers who received his word with joy, and who, like those who shared in the secret counsels of other kingdoms, were gifted to know the mysteries of the Messianic reign,[2] long hidden, but now about to be made known (comp. Rom. xi, 25 ; xvi, 25 ; Col. i, 26). These should realize the truth of the proverb, "Whosoever has to him shall be given," etc. This proverb expresses in an enigmatical way a most weighty and wonderful law of experience in the things of God. He who is gifted with a desire to know God, and to appropriate rightly the provisions of his grace, shall increase in wisdom and knowledge more and more by the manifold revelations of divine truth. But the man of opposite character, who has heart, soul, and mind wherewith to love God, but is unwilling to use his powers in earnest search for the truth, shall lose even what he seems to have.[3] His powers will become weak and worthless by inactivity, and like the slothful servant in the parable of the talents,[4] he will lose that which should have been his glory.

Parables both reveal and conceal truth.

[1] The ἵνα in the parallel passages of Mark iv, 12 and Luke viii, 10 shows that our Lord teaches in these words the *final end* and *purpose* of his parables, not merely their results. The quotation from Isaiah evinces the same thing.

[2] "The kingdom of heaven," says Stier, "is itself a mystery for the natural earthly understanding, and, like earthly kingdoms, it has its *state secrets*, which cannot and ought not to be cast before every one. When, on a frank and friendly approach being made, no feeling of loyalty shows itself, but rather a threatening of rebellion, then it is wise and reasonable to draw a veil, which, however, is willingly removed whenever any faithful one wishes to join himself more nearly to the king."—Words of the Lord Jesus, in loco.

[3] So Luke (viii, 18) expresses the thought: Καὶ ὃ δοκεῖ ἔχειν. On which Stier remarks: "For every ἔχων (one having) who does not keep (κατέχει) is only a δοκῶν ἔχειν (one seeming to have) in a manifold sense. It is an imaginary having, the nothingness of which is to be made manifest by a so-called taking, which yet properly takes nothing from him. It is a having which has become lost through his unfaithfulness (2 John 8)."

[4] Of whom the same proverb is used again, and more fully illustrated, Matt. xxv, 28, 29. Comp. also John xv, 2.

And so the use of parables, in our Lord's teaching, became a test
Parables a test of character. With those disposed to know and accept
of character. the truth the words of a parable served to arouse attention and to excite inquiry. If they did not at first apprehend the
meaning, they would come, like the disciples to the Master (Matt.
xiii, 36; Mark iv, 10), and inquire of him, assured that all who
asked, searched, or knocked (Matt. vii, 7) at the door of Divine
Wisdom should certainly obtain their desire. Even those who at
first are dull of apprehension may be attracted and captivated by
the outer form of the parable, and by honest inquiry come to master
the laws of interpretation until they "know all parables" (Mark
iv, 13). But the perverse and fleshly mind shows its real character
by making no inquiry and evincing no desire to understand the
mysteries of the kingdom of God. Such a mind treats those mysteries as a species of folly (1 Cor. i, 18).

The parables of the Bible are remarkable for their beauty, vari-
Superior beauty ety, conciseness, and fulness of meaning. There is a
and appropriate- noticeable appropriateness in the parables of Jesus,
ness of Scripture
parables. and their adaptation to the time and place of their
first utterance. The parable of the sower was spoken by the seaside (Matt. xiii, 1, 2), whence might have been seen, at no great
distance off, a sower actually engaged in sowing his seed. The
parable of the dragnet in the same chapter (verses 47–50) may
have been occasioned by the sight of such a net close by. The
parable of the nobleman going into a far country to receive for
himself a kingdom (Luke xix, 12) was probably suggested by the
case of Archelaus, who made a journey from Judea to Rome to
plead his right to the kingdom of Herod his father.[1] As Jesus had
just passed through Jericho and was approaching Jerusalem, perhaps the sight of the royal palace which Archelaus had recently
rebuilt at Jericho[2] suggested the allusion. Even the literal narrative of some of the parables is in the highest degree beautiful and
impressive. The parable of the Good Samaritan (Luke x, 30–37)
was probably based on fact. The road from Jerusalem to Jericho
was notably infested by robbers, and yet, leading as it did from
Perea to the holy city, it would be frequented by priests and Levites passing to and fro. The coldness and neglect of the ministers
of the law, and the tender compassion of the Samaritan, are full of
interest and rich in suggestions. The narrative of the Prodigal
Son has been called "the pearl and crown of all the parables of
Scripture," and "a gospel in a gospel."[3] We never tire of its literal

---

[1] Josephus, Ant., xvii, 9, 1 ff. 11, 4.   [2] Ibid., xvii, 11, 13.
[3] Comp. Trench on the Parables, p. 316.

statements, for they are as full of naturalness and beauty as they are of lessons of sin and redemption.

The parable is commonly assumed to have three parts, (1) the occasion and scope, (2) the similitude, in the form of a real narrative, and (3) the moral and religious lessons. These three parts are called by Salmeron, Glassius, and others, the *root* or *basis* (radix), the *bark* or *covering* (cortex), and the *marrow* (medulla) or inner substance and core.[1] The last two are often called, respectively, the protasis and the apodosis. The main thing in the construction of a parable is its similitude, or literal narrative, for this always appears, and constitutes the parable as a figure of speech. The occasion and scope, as well as the internal sense, are not always expressed. In most cases, in fact, the apodosis, or inner sense, is left for the hearer to find out for himself, and sometimes the occasion and scope are difficult to determine. But our Lord himself has given us two examples of interpreting parables;[2] and frequently the scope and application of the parable are formally stated in the context, so that, with but few exceptions, the parables of Scripture are not difficult to explain.[3]

Three essential elements of a parable.

As every parable essentially involves the three elements named above, the hermeneutical principles which should guide us in understanding all parables are mainly three. First, we should determine the historical occasion and aim of the parable; secondly, we should make an accurate analysis

Three principal Rules for interpreting parables.

[1] Salmeron, De Parabolis Domini nostri, tr. iii, p. 15. Glassius, Philologia Sacra (Lips. 1725) lib. ii, pars i, tr. ii, sect. 5. Horne (Introduction, ed. Ayre and Treg., vol. ii, p. 346) adopts the same division, and calls the three parts, respectively, the *root* or *scope*, the *sensible similitude*, and the *explanation* or *mystical* sense. Davidson (Hermeneutics, p. 311) says: "In the parable as in the allegory three things demand attention: (1) The thing to be illustrated; (2) the example illustrating; (3) the *tertium comparationis*, or the similitude existing between them."

[2] Namely, in the interpretation of the parables of the sower (Matt. xiii, 18–23) and of the tares of the field (Matt. xiii, 36–43). Trench observes, "that when our Lord himself interpreted the two first which he delivered, it is more than probable that he intended to furnish us with a key for the interpretation of all. These explanations, therefore, are most important, not merely for their own sakes, but as laying down the principles and canons of interpretation to be applied throughout."—Notes on the Parables, p. 36.

[3] Trench (Parables, p. 32) beautifully observes: "The parables, fair in their outward form, are yet fairer within—apples of gold in network of silver: each one of them like a casket, itself of exquisite workmanship, but in which jewels yet richer than itself are laid up; or as fruit, which, however lovely to look upon, is yet more delectable still in its inner sweetness. To find the golden key for this casket, at the touch of which it shall reveal its treasures; to open this fruit, so that nothing of its hidden kernel shall be missed or lost, has naturally been regarded ever as a matter of high concern."

of the subject matter, and observe the nature and properties of the things employed as imagery in the similitude; and thirdly, we should interpret the several parts with strict reference to the general scope and design of the whole, so as to preserve a harmony of proportions, maintain the unity of all the parts, and make prominent the great central truth.[1] These principles can become of practical value only by actual use and illustration in the interpretation of a variety of parables.

As our Lord has left us a formal explanation of what were probably the first two parables he uttered, we do well, first of all, to note the principles of interpretation as they appear illustrated in his examples. In the parable of the sower we find it easy to conceive the position and surroundings of Jesus when he opened his parabolic discourse. He had gone out to the seaside and sat down there, but when the multitudes crowded around him, "he entered into a boat and sat; and all the multitude stood on the beach" (Matt. xiii, 2). How natural and appropriate for him then and there to think of the various ˙dispositions and characters of those before him. How like so many kinds of soil were their hearts. How was his preaching "the word of the kingdom" (verse 19) like a sowing of seed, suggested perhaps by the sight of a sower, or of a sown field, on the neighbouring coast.[2] Nay, how was his coming into the world like a going forth to sow.

Principles illustrated in the parable of the Sower.

Passing now to notice the similitude itself, we observe that our Lord attached significance to the seed sown, the wayside and the birds, the rocky places, the thorns, and the good ground. Each of these parts has a relevancy to the whole. In that one field where the sower scattered his grain there were all these kinds of soil, and the nature and properties of seed and soil are in perfect keeping with the results of that sowing as stated in the parable. The soil is in every case a human heart. The birds represent the evil one,[3] who is ever opposed to the work of the sower, and watches to snatch away that which is sown in the heart, "that they may not

---

[1] One may compare the entire parable with a circle, of which the middle point is the spiritual truth or doctrine, and of which the radii are the several circumstances of the narration; so long as one has not placed himself in the centre, neither the circle itself appears in its perfect shape, nor will the beautiful unity with which the radii converge to a single point be perceived, but this is all observed so soon as the eye looks forth from the centre. Even so in the parable, if we have recognized its middle point, its main doctrine, in full light, then will the proportion and right signification of all particular circumstances be clear unto us, and we shall lay stress upon them only so far as the main truth is thereby more vividly set forth.—Lisco, Die Parabeln Jesu, p. 22. Fairbairn's Translation (Edinburgh Bib. Cabinet), p. 29.

[2] See Stanley, Sinai and Palestine, p. 418.   [3] Mark says Satan; Luke, the devil.

believe and be saved" (Luke viii, 12). He who hears the Word and understands not—on whom the heavenly truth makes no impression —may well be likened to a trodden pathway. "He has brought himself to it; he has exposed his heart as a common road to every evil influence of the world till it has become hard as a pavement— till he has laid waste the very soil in which the word of God should have taken root; and he has not submitted it to the ploughshare of the law, which would have broken it; which, if he had suffered it to do the work which God appointed it to do, would have gone before, preparing that soil to receive the seed of the Gospel." [1] With equal force and propriety the rocky places, the thorns, and the good ground represent so many varieties of hearers of the Word. The application of the parable, closing with the significant words, "he that has ears let him hear" (verse 8), might be safely left to the minds and consciences of the multitudes who heard it. Among those multitudes were doubtless many representatives of all the classes designated.

The parable of the tares of the field had the same historical occasion as that of the sower, and is an important supplement to it. In the interpretation of the foregoing parable the sower was not made prominent. The seed was declared to be "the word of the kingdom," [2] and its character and worth are variously indicated, but no explanation was given of the sower. In this second parable the sower is prominently set forth as the Son of man, the sower of good seed; and the work of his great enemy, the devil, is presented with equal prominence. But we are not to suppose that this parable takes up and carries with it all the imagery and implications of the one preceding. Other considerations are introduced under other imagery. But in seeking the occasion and connexion of all the parables recorded in Matt. xiii, we should note how one grows out of the other as by a logical sequence. Three of them were spoken privately to the disciples, but the whole seven were appropriate for the seaside; for those of the mustard-seed, the treasure hid in a field, and the dragnet, no less than the sower and the tares of the field, may have been suggested to Jesus by the scenes around him, and those of the leaven and the merchantman seeking pearls were but counterparts, respectively, of the mustard-seed and the hid treasure. Stier's suggestion, also, is worthy of note, that the parable of the tares corresponds with the first kind of soil mentioned in the parable of the sower, and helps to answer the question, Whence and how that

Parable of the Tares and its interpretation.

---

[1] Trench, Notes on the Parables, p. 61.
[2] In Luke viii, 11, it is written: "The seed is the word of God."

soil had come to serve so well the purpose of the devil. The parable of the mustard-plant, whose growth was so great, stands in notable contrast with the second kind of soil in which there was no real growth at all. The parable of the leaven suggests the opposite of the heart overgrown with worldliness, namely, a heart permeated and purified by the inner workings of grace, while the fifth and sixth parables—those of the treasure and the pearl of great price—represent the various experiences of the good heart (represented by the good ground) in apprehending and appropriating the precious things of the Word of the kingdom. The seventh parable, that of the dragnet, appropriately concludes all with the doctrine of the separating judgment which shall take place "in the end of the age" (verse 49). Such an inner relation and connexion we do well to trace, and the suggestions thereby afforded may be especially valuable for homiletical purposes. They serve for instruction, but they should not be insisted on as essential to a correct interpretation of the several parables.

In the interpretation of the second parable Jesus gives special
Things interpreted and things unnoticed in Jesus' exposition. significance to the sower, the field, the good seed, the tares, the enemy, the harvest, and the reapers; also the final burning of the tares and the garnering of the wheat. But we should observe that he does *not* attach a meaning to the men who slept, nor to the sleeping, nor to the springing up of the blades of wheat, and their yielding fruit, nor to the servants of the householder and the questions they asked. These are but incidental parts of the parable, and necessary to a happy filling up of its narrative. An attempt to show a special meaning in them all would tend to obscure and confuse the main lessons. So, if we would know how to interpret all parables, we should notice what our Lord omitted as well as what he emphasized in those expositions which are given us as models; and we should not be anxious to find a hidden meaning in every word and allusion.

At the same time we need not deny that these two parables con-
We may notice some things which Jesus had no need to note. tained some other lessons which Jesus did not bring out in his interpretation. There was no need for him to state the occasion of his parables, or what suggested the imagery to his mind, or the inner logical connexion which they sustained to one another. These things might be safely left to every scribe who should become a disciple to the kingdom of heaven (Matt. xiii, 52). In his explanation of the first parable, Jesus sufficiently indicated that particular words and allusions, like the *having no root* (τὸ μὴ ἔχειν ῥίζαν, Matt. xiii, 6), and *choked*

(ἀπέπνιξαν, ver. 7; comp. συνπνίγει in ver. 22) may suggest important thoughts; and so the incidental words of the second parable, "lest haply while gathering up the tares ye root up the wheat with them" (verse 29), though not afterward referred to in the explanation, may also furnish lessons worthy of our consideration. So, too, it may serve a useful purpose, in interpretation, to show the fitness and beauty of any particular image or allusion. We would not expect our Lord to call the attention of his hearers to such things, but his well-disciplined disciples should not fail to note the propriety and suggestiveness of comparing the word of God to good seed, and the children of the evil one to tares.[1] The trodden path, the rocky places, and the thorny ground, have peculiar fitness to represent the several states of heart denoted thereby. Even the incidental remark "while men slept" (Matt. xiii, 25) is a suggestive hint that the enemy wrought his malicious work in darkness and secrecy, when no one would be likely to be present and interrupt him; but it would break the unity of the parable to interpret these words, as some have done, of the sleep of sin (Calovius), or the dull slowness of man's spiritual development and human weakness generally (Lange), or the careless negligence of religious teachers (Chrysostom).

It is also to be admitted that some incidental words, not designed to be made prominent in the interpretation, may, nevertheless, deserve attention and comment. Not a little pleasure and much instruction may be derived from the incidental parts of some parables. The hundredfold, sixtyfold, and thirtyfold increase, mentioned in the parable of the sower, and in its interpretation, may be profitably compared with making the five talents increase to ten talents, and the two to four (in Matt. xxv, 16–22), and also with the increase in the parable of the pounds (Luke xix, 16–19). The peculiar expressions, "he that was sown by the wayside," "he that was sown upon the rocky places," are not, as Alford truly observes, "a confusion of similitudes—no primary and secondary interpretation of σπόρος [seed],—but the deep truth both of nature and of grace. The seed sown, springing up in the earth, becomes the plant, and bears the fruit, or fails of bearing it; it is, therefore, the representative, when sown, of the individuals of whom the discourse is."[2] Especially do we notice that the seed which, in the first parable, is said to be "the word of God" (Luke viii, 11), is defined in the second as "the

Suggestive words and allusions deserve Attention and Comment.

---

[1] Greek ζιζάνια, darnel, which is said to resemble wheat in its earlier stages of growth, but shows its real character more clearly at the harvest time.

[2] Greek Testament, in loco.

children of the kingdom " (Matt. xiii, 38). A different stage of progress is tacitly assumed, and we think of the word of God as having
developed in the good heart in which it was cast until it has taken
up that heart within itself and made it a new creation.[1]

From the above examples we may derive the general principles
which are to be observed in the interpretation of
parables. No specific rules can be formed that will
apply to every case, and show what parts of a parable
are designed to be significant, and what parts are mere
drapery and form. Sound sense and delicate discrimination are to be cultivated and matured by a protracted study of all
the parables, and by careful collation and comparison. Our Lord's
examples of interpretation show that most of the details of his parables have a meaning; and yet there are incidental words and allusions which are not to be pressed into significance. We should,
therfore, study to avoid, on the one side, the extreme of ingenuity
which searches for hidden meanings in every word, and, on the
other, the disposition to pass over many details as mere rhetorical
figures. In general it may be said that most of the details in a
parable have a meaning, and those which have no special significance in the interpretation, serve, nevertheless, to enhance the force
and beauty of the rest. Such parts, as Boyle observes, "are like
the feathers which wing our arrows, which, though they pierce not
like the head, but seem slight things, and of a different matter from
the rest, are yet requisite to make the shaft to pierce, and do both
convey it to and penetrate the mark."[2] We may also add, with
Trench, that "it is tolerable evidence that we have found the right
interpretation of a parable if it leave none of the main circumstances unexplained. A false interpretation will inevitably betray
itself, since it will invariably paralyze and render nugatory some
important member of an entire account. If we have the right key
in our hand, not merely some of the words, but all, will have their
corresponding parts, and, moreover, the key will turn without
grating or overmuch forcing; and if we have the right interpretation it will scarcely need to be defended and made plausible with
great appliance of learning, to be propped up by remote allusions
to rabbinical or profane literature, or by illustrations drawn from
the recesses of antiquity."[3]

The prophet Isaiah, in chap. v, 1–6, sings of his Beloved Friend,

Not specific rules, but sound sense and discriminating judgment must guide the interpreter.

---

[1] " Our life," says Lange, " becomes identified with the spiritual seed, and principles
assume, so to speak, a bodily shape in individuals." Commentary on Matthew, in loco.

[2] Quoted by Trench, Notes on the Parables, p. 34.

[3] Notes on the Parables, p. 39.

and his Friend's own song touching his vineyard, and in verse 7 declares that

> The vineyard of Jehovah of hosts is the house of Israel,
> And the man of Judah is the plant of his delight;
> And he waited for justice, and behold bloodshed,
> For righteousness, and behold a cry.

This short explanation gives the main purpose of the parable. No special meaning is put on the digging, the gathering out of the stones, the tower, and the winevat. Our Lord appropriates the imagery of this passage in his parable of the wicked husbandmen (Matt. xxi, 33-44). But to understand, in either parable, that the tower represents Jerusalem (Grotius), or the temple (Bengel), that the winevat is the altar (Chrysostom), or the prophetic institution (Irenæus), that the gathering out of the stones denotes the expulsion of the Canaanites from the Holy Land, together with the stone idols (Grotius), is to go upon doubtful ground, and introduce that which will confuse rather than elucidate. These several particulars are rather to be taken together as denoting the complete provision which Jehovah made for the security, culture, and prosperity of his people. "What is there to do more for my vineyard," he asks, "that I have not done in it?" He had spared no pains or outlay, and yet, when the time of grape harvest came, his vineyard brought forth wild grapes. What would seem to have been so full of hope and promise yielded only disappointment and chagrin. The grapes he expected were truth and righteousness; those which he found were bloodshed and oppression. He announces, accordingly, his purpose to destroy that vineyard, and make it an utter desolation, a threat fearfully fulfilled in the subsequent history of Israel and the Holy Land.

Isaiah's parable of the Vineyard.

Such is the substance of the interpretation of Isaiah's parable, but the language in which it is clothed has many beautiful strokes and delicate allusions which are worthy of attention.[1] Our Lord's parable of the wicked husbandmen, which is based upon its imagery, may be profitably noticed in connexion with it. It is

---

[1] Such, for instance, is the "very fertile hill" in which this vineyard was planted; literally, *in a horn, a son of oil,* or *fatness;* metaphor for a horn-shaped hill of rich soil, and used in allusion to the land of promise (comp. Deut. viii, 7-9). There is also an ironical play on the Hebrew words for *justice* and *bloodshed, righteousness* and *cry* in the last two lines of verse 7: "He looked for מִשְׁפָּט, *mishpat,* and behold מִשְׂפָּח, *mispach,* for צְדָקָה, *tzdhakah,* and behold צְעָקָה, *tzgnakah.*" Contrast also the jubilant opening in which the prophet essays to sing his well-beloved's song with the change of person in verse 3 and the sad tone of disappointment which follows.

recorded by Matthew (xxi, 33–44), Mark (xii, 1–12), and Luke (xx, 9–18), and, though spoken in the ears of "the people" (Luke xx, 9), the chief priests, the scribes, and the Pharisees understood that it was directed against them (Matt. xxi, 45; Luke xx, 19). Parable of the The context also informs us (in Matt. xxi, 43) that the Wicked Hus- vineyard represents "the kingdom of God." In Isaiah's bandmen. parable the whole house of Israel is at fault, and is threatened with utter destruction. Here the fault is with the husbandmen to whom the vineyard was leased, and whose wickedness appears most flagrant; and here, accordingly, the threat is not to destroy the vineyard, but the husbandmen. The great questions, then, in the interpretation of our Lord's parable, are: (1) What is meant by the vineyard? (2) Who are the husbandmen, servants, and son? (3) What events are contemplated in the destruction of the husbandmen and the giving of the vineyard to others? These questions are not hard to answer: (1) The vineyard in Isaiah is the Israelitish people, considered not merely as the Old Testament Church, but also as the chosen nation established in the land of Canaan. Here it is the more spiritual idea of the kingdom of God considered as an inheritance of divine grace and truth to be so apprehended and utilized unto the honour and glory of God as that husbandmen, servants, and Son may be joint heirs and partakers of its benefits. (2) The husbandmen are the divinely commissioned leaders and teachers of the people, whose business and duty it was to guide and instruct those committed to their care in the true knowledge and love of God. They were the chief priests and scribes who heard this parable, and knew that it was spoken against them. The servants, as distinguished from the husbandmen, are to be understood of the prophets, who *were sent* as special messengers of God, and whose mission was usually to the leaders of the people.[1] But they had been mocked, despised, and maltreated in many ways (2 Chron. xxxvi, 16); Jeremiah was shut up in prison (Jer. xxxii, 3), and Zechariah was stoned (2 Chron. xxiv, 21; comp. Matt. xxiii, 34–37, and Acts vii, 52). The one son, the beloved, is, of course, the Son of man, who "came unto his own, and they that were his own received him not" (John i, 11). (3) The destruction of the wicked husbandmen was accomplished in the utter overthrow and miserable ruin of the Jewish leaders in the fall of Jerusalem. Then the avenging of "all the righteous blood" of the prophets came upon that generation (Matt. xxiii, 35, 36), and then, too, the

---

[1] Servants are the extraordinary ministers of God, husbandmen the ordinary. The former are almost always badly received by the latter, who take ill the interruption of their own quiet possession.—Bengel, Gnomon, in loco.

vineyard of the kingdom of God, repaired and restored as the New
Testament Church, was transferred to the Gentiles.

There are many minor lessons and suggestive hints in the language of this parable, but they should not, in an expo- Minor points
sition, be elevated into such prominence as to confuse not to be made
these leading thoughts. Here, as in Isaiah, we should prominent.
not seek special meanings in the hedge, winepress, and tower, nor
should we make a great matter of what particular fruits the owner
had reason to expect, nor attempt to identify each one of the servants sent with some particular prophet or messenger mentioned in
Jewish history. Still less should we think of finding special meanings in forms of expression used by one of the evangelists and not
by another. Some of these minor points may be rich in suggestions and abundantly worthy of comment, but in view of the over-
straining which they have too frequently received at the hands of
expositors we need the constant caution that at most they are incidental rather than important.

Two other parables of our Lord illustrate the casting off of the
Jews and the calling of the Gentiles. They are the Comparison of
marriage of the King's Son (Matt. xxii, 2-14), and the analogous par-
great supper (Luke xiv, 16-24). The former is recorded ables.
only by Matthew, and follows immediately after that of the wicked
husbandmen. The latter is recorded only by Luke. Some of the
rationalistic critics have argued that these are but different versions
of the same discourse, but a careful analysis will show that, while
they have marked analogies, they have also numerous points of
difference. And it is an aid to the interpretation of such analogous
parables to study them together and mark their diverging lines of
thought. The parable of the marriage of the King's Son, as compared with that of the wicked husbandmen, exhibits an advance in
thought as notable as that observed in the parable of the tares as
compared with that of the sower. Trench here observes "how the
Lord is revealing himself in ever clearer light as the central person
of the kingdom, giving here a far plainer hint than there of the
nobility of his descent. There he was indeed the son, the only and
beloved one, of the householder; but here his race is royal, and he
appears himself at once as the King and the King's Son (Psa. lxxii, 1).
This appearance of the householder as the King announces that
the sphere in which this parable moves is the New Parable of Mar-
Testament dispensation—is the kingdom which was an- riage of King's
                                                        Son and Wicked
nounced before, but was only actually present with the Husbandmen
coming of the King. The last was a parable of the compared.
Old Testament history; even Christ himself appears there as

'the last and greatest of the line of its prophets and teachers than as
the founder of a new kingdom. In that, a parable of the law, God
appears demanding something from men ; in this, a parable of
grace, God appears more as giving something to them. There he
is displeased that his demands are not complied with, here that his
goodness is not accepted; there he requires, here he imparts. And
thus, as we so often find, the two mutually complete one another;
this taking up the matter where the other left it." [1] The great
purpose in both parables was to make conspicuous the shameful
character and conduct of those who were under great obligation to
show all possible respect and loyalty. The conduct of the husbandmen was atrocious in the extreme; but it may be said that a
claim of rent was demanded of them, and there was some supposable motive to treat the messengers of the owner of the vineyard
with disrespect. Not so, however, with those bidden to the royal
marriage feast. That guests, honoured by an invitation from the
king to attend the marriage of his son, should have treated such invitation with wilful refusal and contempt, and even have gone to
the extreme of abusing the royal servants who came to bid them to
the marriage, and of putting some to death, seems hardly conceivable. But this very feature which seems so improbable in itself is
a prominent part of the parable, and designed to set in the most
odious light the conduct of those chief priests and Pharisees who
were treating the Son of God with open contempt, and would fain
have put him to death. Such ingratitude and disloyalty deserved
no less a punishment than the sending forth of armies to destroy
the murderers and to burn their city (verse 7).

When now we compare the parable of the marriage of the king's
Parables of Mar- son with that of the great supper (Luke xiv, 16) we
riage of King's find they both agree (1) in having a festival as the
Son and Great basis of their imagery, (2) in that invitations were sent
Supper com-
pared. to persons already bidden, (3) in the disrespect shown
by those bidden, and (4) the calling in of the poor and neglected
from the streets and highways. But they differ in the following
particulars: The parable of the great supper was spoken at an
earlier period of our Lord's ministry, when the opposition of chief
priests, scribes, and Pharisees was as yet not violent. It was
uttered in the house of a Pharisee whither he had been invited to
eat bread (verses 1, 12), and where there appeared in his presence
a dropsical man, whose malady he healed. Thereupon he addressed
a parable to those who were bidden, counselling them not to recline
on the chief seat at table unless invited there (verses 7–11). He

[1] Notes on the Parables, p. 180.

also uttered a proverbial injunction to the Pharisee who had invited him to make a feast for the poor and the maimed rather than kinsmen and rich friends (verses 12-14); and then he added the parable of the great supper. But the parable of the marriage of the king's son was uttered at a later period, and in the temple, when no Pharisee would have invited him to his table, and when the hatred of chief priests and scribes had become so bitter that it gave occasion for ominous and fearful words, such as that parable contained. We note further that, in the earlier parable, the occasion was a great supper (δεῖπνον), in the latter a wedding (γάμος). In the one, the person making the feast is simply "a certain man" (Luke xiv, 16), in the other he is a king. In the one the guests all make excuse, in the other they treat the royal invitation with contempt and violence. In the one those who were bidden are simply denounced with the statement that none of them shall taste of the supper; in the other the king's armies are sent forth to destroy the murderers of his servants and to burn their city. In the earlier parable there are two sendings forth to call in guests, first from the streets and lanes of the city, and next from the highways and hedges—intimating first the going unto the lost sheep of the house of Israel (Matt. x, 6; xv, 24), and afterward to the Gentiles (Acts xiii, 46); in the latter only one outgoing call is indicated, and that one subsequent to the destruction of the murderers and their city. In that later prophetic moment Jesus contemplated the ingathering of the Gentiles. Then to the later parable is added the incident of the guest who appeared without the wedding garment (Matt. xxii, 11–14), which Strauss characteristically conjectures to be the fragment of another parable which Matthew by mistake attached to this, because of its referring to a feast.[1] But with a purer and profounder insight Trench sees in these few added words "a wonderful example of the love and wisdom which marked the teaching of our Lord. For how fitting was it in a discourse which set forth how sinners of every degree were invited to a fellowship in the blessings of the Gospel, that they should be reminded likewise, that for the lasting enjoyment of these, they must put off their former conversation—a most needful caution, lest any should abuse the grace of God, and forget that while as regarded the past they were freely called, they were yet now called unto holiness."[2]

The parable of the barren fig-tree (Luke xiii, 6–9) had its special application in the cutting off of Israel, but it is not necessarily limited to that one event. It has lessons of universal application, illustrating the forbearance and longsuffering

The barren Fig-tree.

[1] Life of Jesus, § 78. [2] Notes on the Parables, pp. 179, 180.

of God, as also the certainty of destructive judgment upon every one
who not only produces no good fruit, but "also cumbers the ground"
(καὶ τὴν γῆν καταργεῖ). Its historical occasion appears from the
preceding context, (verses 1–5), but the logical connexion is not so
apparent. It is to be traced, however, to the character of those in-
formants who told him of Pilate's outrage on the Galileans. For
the twice-repeated warning, "Except ye repent ye shall all likewise
perish" (verses 3 and 5), implies that the persons addressed were
sinners deserving fearful penalty. They were probably from Jerusalem, and representatives of the Pharisaic party who had little
respect for the Galileans, and perhaps intended their tidings to be
a sort of gibe against Jesus and his Galilean followers.

The means for understanding the occasion and import of Nathan's
Old Testament parable (2 Sam. xii, 1–4) are abundantly furnished in
parables. the context. The same is true of the parable of the
wise woman of Tekoah (2 Sam. xiv, 4–7), and that of the wounded
prophet in 1 Kings xx, 38–40. The narrative, in Eccles. ix, 14, 15,
of the little city besieged by a great king, but delivered by the wisdom of a poor wise man, has been regarded by some as an actual
history. Those who date the Book of Ecclesiastes under the
Persian domination think that allusion is made to the delivery of
Athens by Themistocles, when that city was besieged by Xerxes,
the great king of Persia. Others have suggested the deliverance
of Potidæa (Herod., viii, 128), or Tripolis (Diodor., xvi, 41). Hitzig
even refers it to the little seaport Dora besieged by Antiochus the
Great (Polybius, v, 66). But in none of these last three cases is it
known that the deliverance was effected by a poor wise man; and
as for Athens, it could hardly have been called a little city, with
few men in it, nor could the brilliant leader of the Greeks be properly called "a poor wise man." It is far better to take the narrative as a parable, which may or may not have had its basis in some
real incident of the kind, but which was designed to illustrate the
great value of wisdom. The author makes his own application in
verse 16: "Then said I, Better is wisdom than strength; yet the
wisdom of the poor is despised, and his words—none of them are
heard." That is, such is the general rule. A case of exceptional
extremity, like the siege referred to, may for a moment exhibit the
value of wisdom, and its superiority over strength and weapons of
war; but the lesson is soon forgotten, and the masses of men give
no heed to the words of the poor, whatever their wisdom and worth.
The two verses that follow (17 and 18) are an additional comment
upon the lesson taught in the parable, and put its real meaning beyond all reasonable doubt. But it is a misuse of the parable, and a

pressing of its import beyond legitimate bounds, to say, with Hengstenberg: "The poor man with his delivering wisdom is an image of Israel. . . . Israel would have proved a salt to the heathen world if ear had only been given to the voice of wisdom dwelling in his midst." [1] Still more unsound is the spiritualizing process by which the besieged city is made to represent "the life of the individual: the great king who lays siege to it is death and the judgment of the Lord." [2]

All the parables of our Lord are contained in the first three Gospels. Those of the door, the good shepherd, and the vine, recorded by John, are not parables proper, but allegories. In most instances we find in the immediate context a clue to the correct interpretation. Thus the parable of the unmerciful servant (Matt. xviii, 23–34) has its occasion stated in verses 21 and 22, and its application in verse 35. The parable of the rich man who planned to pull down his barns and build greater in order to treasure up all the increase of his fields (Luke xii, 16–20), is readily seen from the context to have been uttered as a warning against covetousness. The parable of the importunate friend at midnight (Luke xi, 5–8) is but a part of a discourse on prayer. The parables of the unjust judge and the importunate widow, and of the Pharisee and the publican at prayer (Luke xviii, 1–14), have their purpose stated by the evangelist who records them. The parable of the good Samaritan (Luke x, 30–37) was called forth by the question of the lawyer, who desired to justify himself, and asked, "Who is my neighbour?"

All Jesus' parables in the Synoptic Gospels.

The parable of the labourers in the vineyard (Matt. xx, 1–16), although its occasion and application are given in the context, has been regarded as difficult of interpretation. It was occasioned by the mercenary spirit of Peter's question (in chap. xix, 27), "What then shall we have?" and its principal aim is evidently to rebuke and condemn that spirit. But the difficulties of interpreters have arisen chiefly from giving undue prominence to the minor points of the parable, as the penny a day, and the different hours at which the labourers were hired. Stier insists that the penny ($\delta\eta\nu\alpha\varrho\iota\upsilon\nu$), or day's wages ($\mu\iota\sigma\vartheta\delta\varsigma$), is the principal question and main feature of the parable. Others make the several hours mentioned represent different periods of life at which men are called into the kingdom of God, as childhood, youth, manhood, and old age. Others have supposed that the Jews were denoted by those first hired, and the Gentiles by those who were

Parable of the Labourers in the Vineyard.

---

[1] Commentary on Ecclesiastes, in loco.
[2] Wangemann, as quoted by Delitzsch, in loco.

called last. Origen held that the different hours represented the different epochs of human history, as the time before the flood, from Abraham to Moses, from Moses to Christ, etc. But all this tends to divert the mind from the great thought in the purpose of the parable, namely, to condemn the mercenary spirit, and indicate that the rewards of heaven are matters of grace and not of debt. And we should make very emphatic the observation of Bengel, that the parable is not so much a prediction as a warning.[1] The fundamental fallacy of those exegetes who make the penny the most prominent point, is their tacit assumption that the narrative Mistakes of in- of the parable is designed to portray a murmuring and terpreters. fault finding which will actually take place at the last day. Unless we assume this, according to Stier, "no reality would correspond with the principal point of the figurative narration."[2] Accordingly, the ὕπαγε, *go thy way* (verse 14), is understood, like the πορεύεσθε, *depart* (of Matt. xxv, 41), as an angry rejection and banishment from God; and the ἆρον τὸ σόν, *take thine own*, "can mean nothing else than what, at another stage, Abraham says to the rich man (Luke xvi, 25): What thou hast contracted for, with that thou art discharged; but now, away from my service and from all further intercourse with me!"[3] So also Luther says that "the murmuring labourers go away with their penny and are damned." But the word ὑπάγω has been already twice used in this parable (verses 4 and 7) in the sense of going away into the vineyard to work, and it seems altogether too violent a change to put on it here the sense of going into damnation. Still less supposable is such a sense of the word when addressed to those who had filled an honourable contract, laboured faithfully in the vineyard, and "borne the burden of the day and the burning heat" (verse 12).

Let us now carefully apply the three principles of interpretation enunciated above[4] to the exposition of this intricate parable. First, Occasion and the historical occasion and scope. Jesus had said to the scope. young man who had great possessions: "If thou wouldst be perfect, go (ὕπαγε), sell thy possessions and give to the poor, and thou shalt have treasure in heaven; and come, follow me" (Matt. xix, 21). The young man went away sorrowful, for he had many goods (κτήματα πολλά), and Jesus thereupon spoke of the difficulty of a rich man entering into the kingdom of heaven (verses 23–26). "Then answered Peter and said to him, Lo, we forsook all things and followed thee: what then shall we have?" Τί ἄρα ἔσται ἡμῖν; *what then shall be to us?*—that is, in the way of compensation and

---

[1] Non est praedictio sed admonitia. Gnomon, in loco.
[2] Words of the Lord Jesus, in loco.   [3] Ibid.   [4] See above, pp. 281, 282.

reward. What shall be our ϑησαυρὸς ἐν οὐρανοῖς, *treasure in heaven?* This question, not reprehensible in itself, breathed a bad spirit of overweening confidence and self-esteem, by its evident comparison with the young man: We have done all that you demand of him; we forsook our all; what treasure shall be ours in heaven? Jesus did not at once rebuke what was bad in the question, but, first, graciously responded to what was good in it. These disciples, who did truly leave all and follow him, shall not go without blissful reward. "Verily, I say unto you that ye, who followed me, in the regeneration, when the Son of man shall sit upon the throne of his glory, ye also shall sit upon twelve thrones, judging the twelve tribes of Israel." This was, virtually, making to them a promise and pledge of what they should have in the future, but he adds: "And every one who forsook houses, or brothers, or sisters, or father, or mother, or children, or lands for my name's sake, shall receive manifold more,[1] and shall inherit life eternal." Here is a common inheritance and blessing promised to all who meet the conditions named. But in addition to this great reward, which is common alike to all, there will be distinctions and differences; and so it is immediately added: "But many first will be last and last first." And from this last statement the parable immediately proceeds: "For (γάρ) the kingdom of heaven is like," etc. This connexion Stier recognizes: "Because Peter has inquired after reward and compensation, Christ says, first of all, what is contained in verses 28, 29; but because he has asked with a culpable eagerness for reward, the parable concerning the first and the last follows with its earnest warning and rebuke."[2] But to say, in the face of such a connexion and context, that the reward contemplated in the penny has no reference to eternal life, but is to be understood solely of temporal good which may lead to damnation, is virtually to ignore and defy the context, and bring in a strange and foreign thought. The scope of the parable is no doubt to admonish Peter and the rest against the mercenary spirit and self-conceit apparent in his question, but it concludes, as Meyer observes, "and that very appropriately, with language which no doubt allows the apostles to contemplate the prospect of receiving rewards of a peculiarly distinguished character (xix, 28), but does not warrant the absolute certainty of it, nor does it recognize the existence of any thing like so-called valid claims."[3]

[1] Πολλαπλασίονα is the reading of two most ancient codices, B and L, a number of versions, as Syriac and Sahidic, and is adopted by Lachmann, Alford, Tischendorf, Tregelles, and Westcott and Hort. Comp. Luke xviii, 30.

[2] Words of the Lord Jesus, in loco.   [3] Commentary on Matt. xx, 16.

Having ascertained the historical occasion and scope, the next step is to analyze the subject matter, and note what appears to **Prominent** have special prominence. It will hardly be disputed **points in the** that the particular agreement of the householder with **parables.** the labourers hired early in the morning is one point too prominent to be ignored in the exposition. Noticeable also is the fact that the second class (hired at the third hour) go to work without any special bargain, and rely on the word " whatsoever is right I will give you." So also with those called at the sixth and ninth hours. But those called at the eleventh hour received (according to the true text of verse 7) no special promise at all, and nothing is said to them about reward. They had been waiting and seem to have been anxious for a call to work, and were idle because no one had hired them, but as soon as an order came they went off to their labour, not stopping so much as to speak or hear about wages. In all this it does not appear that the different hours have any special significance; but we are rather to note the *spirit and disposition* of the different labourers, particularly the first and the last hired. In the account of the settlement at the close of the day, only these last and the first are mentioned with any degree of prominence. The last are the first rewarded, and with such marks of favour that the self-conceit and mercenary spirit of those who, in the early morning, had made a special bargain for a 'penny a day, are shown in words of fault finding, and elicit the rebuke of the householder and the declaration of his absolute right to do what he will with his own.

If now we interpret these several parts with strict reference to **The parable** the occasion and scope of the parable, we must think **primarily an** of the apostles as those for whom its admonition **admonition for** **the disciples.** was first of all intended. What was wrong in the spirit of Peter's question called for timely rebuke and admonition. Jesus gives him and the others assurance that no man who becomes his disciple shall fail of glorious reward; and, somewhat after the style of the agreement with the labourers first hired, he bargains with the twelve, and agrees that every one of them shall have a throne. But, he adds (for such is the simplest application of the proverb, "Many first shall be last," etc.): Do not imagine, in vain self-conceit, that, because you were the first to leave all and follow me, you therefore must needs be honoured more than others who may hereafter enter my service. That is not the noblest spirit which asks, *What shall I have?* It is better to ask, *What shall I do?* He who follows Christ, and makes all manner of sacrifices for his sake, confident that it will be well, is nobler than he who lingers to make a bargain. Nay, he who goes into the Lord's vineyard asking no questions, and not even waiting to talk about the wages, is nobler and better still. His spirit and labour, though it continue but as an hour, may have qualities so beautiful and rare as to lead Him, whose heavenly rewards are gifts of grace, and not payments of debts, to place him on a more conspicuous throne than that which any one of the apostles may attain. The murmuring, and the response which it draws from the householder, are not to be taken as a prophecy of what may be expected to take place at the final judgment, but rather as a suggestive hint and warning for Peter and the rest to examine the spirit in which they followed Jesus.

If this be the real import of the parable, how misleading are those ˙expositions which would make the penny a day the most prominent point. How unnecessary and irrelevant to regard the words of the householder (in verses 13–16) as equivalent to the final sentence of damnation, or to attach special significance to the standing idle. How unimportant the different hours at which the labourers were hired, or the question whether the householder be God or Christ. The interpretation which aims to maintain the unity of the whole narrative, and make prominent the great central truth, will see in this parable a tender admonition and a suggestive warning against the wrong spirit evinced in Peter's words.[1]

The parable of the unjust steward (Luke xvi, 1–13) has been regarded, as above all others, a *crux interpretum*. It appears to have no such historical or logical connexion with what precedes as will serve in any material way to help in its interpretation. It follows immediately after the three parables of the lost sheep, the lost drachma, and the prodigal son, which were addressed to the Pharisees and the scribes who murmured because Jesus received sinners and ate with them (chap. xv, 2). Having uttered those parables for their special benefit, he spoke one "also to the disciples" (καὶ πρὸς τοὺς μαθητάς, xvi, 1). These disciples are probably to be understood of that wider circle which included others besides the twelve (compare Luke x, 1), and among them were doubtless many publicans like Matthew and Zacchæus, who needed the special lesson here enjoined. That lesson is now quite generally acknowledged to be a *wise and prudent use of this world's goods*. For the sagacity, shrewd foresight, and care to

Parable of the Unjust Steward.

---

[1] The words, "For many are called, but few chosen," which appear in some ancient codices (C, D, N), at the close of verse 16, are wanting in the oldest and best manuscripts (אֹ, B, L, Z), and are rejected by the best textual critics (Tischendorf, Tregelles, Westcott and Hort). We have, therefore, taken no notice of them above.

shift for himself, which the steward evinced in his hasty action with his lord's debtors (φρονίμως ἐποίησεν, ver. 8), are emphatically the *tertium comparationis*, and are said to have been applauded (ἐπήνεσεν) even by his master.

The parable first of all demands that we apprehend correctly the literal import of its narrative, and avoid the reading or imagining in it any thing that is not really there. Thus, for example, it is said the steward was accused of wasting the rich man's goods, and it is nowhere intimated that this accusation was a slander. We have, therefore, no right (as Köster) to assume that it was. Neither is there any warrant for saying (as Van Oosterzee and others) that the steward had been guilty of exacting excessive and exorbitant claims of his lord's debtors, remitting only what was equitable to his lord, and wasting the rest on himself; and that his haste to have them write down their bills to a lower amount was simply, on his part, an act of justice toward them and an effort to repair his former wrongs. If such had been the fact he would not have wasted his lord's goods (τὰ ὑπάρχοντα αὐτοῦ), but those of the debtors. Nor is there any ground to assume that the steward made restitution from his own funds (Brauns), or, that his lord, after commending his prudence, retained him in his service (Baumgarten-Crusius). All this is putting into the narrative of our Lord what he did not see fit to put there.

Unauthorized additions to the parable.

We are to notice, further, that Jesus himself applies the parable to the disciples by his words of counsel and exhortation in verse 9, and makes additional comments on it in verses 10–13. These comments of the author of the parable are to be carefully studied as containing the best clue to his meaning. The main lesson is given in verse 9, where the disciples are urged to imitate the prudence and wisdom of the unjust steward in making to themselves friends out of unrighteous mammon (ἐκ τοῦ, κ. τ. λ., *from* the resources and opportunities afforded by the wealth, or the worldly goods, in their control). The steward exhibited in his shrewd plan the quick sagacity of a child of the world, and knew well how to ingratiate himself with the men of his own kind and generation. In this respect it is said the children of this age are wiser than the children of the light;[1] therefore, our Lord would say,

Jesus' own application.

---

[1] The latter part of verse 8 is, literally, " Because the sons of this age are wiser than the sons of the light in reference to their own generation." Not *in their generation*, as Authorized Version, but εἰς τὴν γενεὰν τὴν ἑαυτῶν, *for their generation, as regards*, or *in relation to*, their own generation. " The whole body of the children of the world —a category of like-minded men—is described as a *generation*, a clan of connexions, and how appropriately, since they appear precisely as υἱοί, *sons*."—Meyer. " The ready accomplices in the steward's fraud showed themselves to be men of the same

emulate and imitate them in this particular. Similarly, on another occasion, he had enjoined upon his disciples, when they were sent forth into the hostile world, to be wise as serpents and harmless as doves (Matt. x, 16).

So far all is tolerably clear and certain, but when we inquire Who is the rich man (in verse 1), and who are the friends who receive into the eternal tabernacles (verse 9), we find great diversity of opinion among the best interpreters. Usually the rich man has been understood of God, as the possessor of all things, who uses us as his stewards of whatever goods are entrusted to our care. Olshausen, on the other hand, takes the rich man to be the devil, considered as the prince of this world. Meyer explains the rich man as Mammon, and urges that verses 9 and 13 especially require this view. It will be seen that the adoption of either one of these views will materially effect our exegesis of the whole parable. Here, then, especially, we need to make a most careful use of the second and third hermeneutical rules afore mentioned, and observe the nature and properties of the things employed as imagery, and interpret them with strict reference to the great central thought and to the general scope and design of the whole. Our choice would seem to lie between the common view and that of Meyer; for Olshausen's explanation, so far as it differs essentially from Meyer's, has nothing in the text to make it even plausible; and the other views (as of Schleiermacher, who makes the rich man represent the Romans, and Grossmann, who understands the Roman emperor) have still less in their favour. The common exposition, which takes the rich man to be God, may be accepted and maintained without serious difficulty. The details of the parable are then to be explained as incidental, designed merely to exhibit the shrewdness of the unjust steward, and no other analogies are to be pressed. The disciples are urged to be discreet and faithful to God in their use of the unrighteous mammon, and thereby secure the friendship of God, Christ, angels, and their fellow men,[1] who may

---

generation as he was—they were all of one race, children of the ungodly world."— Trench. There is no sufficient reason to supply the thought, or refer the phrase, *their own generation*, to the *sons of light* (as De Wette, Olshausen, Trench, and many). If that were the thought another construction could easily have been adopted to express it clearly. As it stands, it means that the children of light do not, in general, in relation to themselves or others evince the prudence and sagacity which the children of the world know so well how to use in their relations to their own race of worldlings.

[1] Some, however, who adopt this exposition in general, will not allow that God or the angels are to be understood by the *friends*, inasmuch as such reference would not accord strictly with the analogy of the parable.

all be thereby disposed to receive them, when the goods of this world fail, into the eternal habitations.

But the interpretation which makes the rich man to be Mammon, The rich man gives a special point and force to several noticeable to be under- remarks of Jesus, maintains a self-consistency within stood as Mammon. itself, and also enforces the same great central thought as truly as the other exposition. It contemplates the disciples as about to be put out of the stewardship of Mammon, and admonishes them to consider how the world loves its own, and knows how to calculate and plan wisely (φρονίμως) for personal and selfish ends. Such shrewdness as that displayed by the unjust steward calls forth the applause of even Mammon himself, who is defrauded by the act. But, Jesus says, "Ye cannot serve God and Mammon." Ye must, in the nature of things, be unfaithful to the one or the other. If ye are true and faithful to the unrighteous lord Mammon, ye cannot be sons of the light and friends of God. If, on the other hand, ye are unfaithful to Mammon, he and all his adherents will accuse you, and ye will be put out of his service. What will ye do? If ye would secure a place in the kingdom of God, if ye would make friends now, while the goods of unrighteous Mammon are at your control—friends to receive and welcome you to the eternal dwellings of light—ye must imitate the prudent foresight of the unjust steward, and be unfaithful to Mammon in order to be faithful servants of God.[1]

The scope and purport of the parable, as evidenced by the com-
Geikie's com- ments of Jesus (in verses 9–13), is thus set forth by
ment. Geikie: "By becoming my disciples you have identi-
fied yourselves with the interest of another master than Mammon, the god of this world—whom you have hitherto served—and have before you another course and aim in life. You will be represented to your former master as no longer faithful to him, for my service is so utterly opposed to that of Mammon, that, if faithful to me, you cannot be faithful to him, and he will, in consequence, assured-ly take your stewardship of this world's goods away from you— that is, sink you in poverty, as I have often said. I counsel you, therefore, so to use the goods of Mammon—the wordly means still at your command—that by a truly worthy distribution of them to

---

[1] Meyer remarks: "This circumstance, that Jesus sets before his disciples the pru-dence of a *dishonest* proceeding as an example, would not have been the occasion of such unspeakable misrepresentations and such unrighteous judgments if the princi-ple, *Ye cannot serve God and Mammon,* (verse 13), had been kept in view, and it had been considered accordingly that even the disciples, in fact, by beneficent application of their property, must have acted unfaithfully toward Mammon in order to be faith-ful toward their contrasted master, toward God."—Commentary, in loco.

your needy brethren—and my disciples are mostly poor—you may make friends for yourselves, who, if they die before you, will welcome you to everlasting habitations in heaven, when you pass thither, at death. Fit yourselves, by labours of love and deeds of true charity, as my followers, to become fellow citizens of the heavenly mansions with those whose wants you have relieved while they were still in life. If you be faithful thus, in the use of your possessions on earth, you will be deemed worthy by God to be entrusted with infinitely greater riches hereafter. . . . Be assured that if you do not use your earthly riches faithfully for God, by dispensing them as I have told you, you will never enter my heavenly kingdom at all. You will have shown that you are servants of Mammon, and not the servants of God; for it is impossible for any man to serve two masters." [1]

There is a deep inner connexion between the parable of the unjust steward and that of the rich man and Lazarus, narrated in the same chapter (Luke xvi, 19–31). A wise faithfulness toward God in the use of the mammon of unrighteousness will make friends to receive us into eternal mansions. But he who allows himself, like the rich man, to become the pampered, luxury-loving man of the world—so true and faithful to the interests of Mammon that he himself becomes an impersonation and representative of the god of riches—will in the world to come lift up his eyes in torments, and learn there, too late, how he might have made the angels and Abraham and Lazarus friends to receive him to the banquets of the paradise of God.

It is interesting and profitable to study the relation of the parables to each other, where there is a manifest logical connexion. This we noticed in the seven parables recorded in Matt. xiii. It is more conspicuous in Luke xv, where the joy over the recovery of that which was lost is enhanced by the climax: (1) a lost sheep, and one of a hundred; (2) a lost drachma, and one out of ten; (3) a lost child, and one out of two. The parables of the ten virgins and the talents in Matt. xxv, enjoin, (1) the duty of *watching* for the coming of the Lord, and (2) the duty of *working* for him in his absence. But we have not space to trace the details. The principles and methods of interpreting parables, as illustrated in the foregoing pages, will be found sufficient guides to the interpretation of all the scriptural parables.

[1] Geikie, **Life of Christ**, chap. liii.

CHAPTER XIV.

INTERPRETATION OF ALLEGORIES.

An allegory is usually defined as an extended metaphor. It bears
Allegory to be the same relation to the parable which the metaphor does
distinguished to the simile. In a parable there is either some formal
from Parable. comparison introduced, as "The kingdom of heaven is
like a grain of mustard seed," or else the imagery is so presented
as to be kept distinct from the thing signified, and to require an
explanation outside of itself, as in the case of the parable of the
sower (Matt. xiii, 3, ff.). The allegory contains its interpretation
within itself, and the thing signified is identified with the image;
as "I am the true vine, and my Father is the husbandman" (John
xv, 1); "Ye are the salt of the earth" (Matt. v, 13). The allegory
is a figurative use and application of some supposable fact or history, whereas the parable is itself such a supposable fact or history.
The parable uses words in their literal sense, and its narrative never
transgresses the limits of what might have been actual fact. The
allegory is continually using words in a metaphorical sense, and
its narrative, however supposable in itself, is manifestly fictitious.
Hence the meaning of the name, from the Greek ἄλλος, *other*, and
αγορεύω, to *speak*, to *proclaim;* that is, to say another thing from
that which is meant, or, so to speak, that another sense is expressed
than that which the words convey. It is a discourse in which the
main subject is represented by some other subject to which it has a
resemblance.[1]

Some have objected to calling an allegory a continued metaphor.[2]
Allegory is a Who shall say, they ask, where the one ends and the
continued Met- other begins? But the very definition should answer
aphor. this question. When the metaphor is confined to a
single word or sentence it is improper to call it an allegory; just
as it is improper to call a proverb a parable, although many a proverb is a condensed parable, and is sometimes loosely called so in
the Scriptures (Matt. xv, 14, 15). But when it is extended into a

---

[1] "The allegory," says Cremer, "is a mode of exposition which does not, like the
parable, hide and clothe the sense in order to give a clear idea of it; on the contrary,
it clothes the sense in order to hide it."—Biblico-Theol. Lex. N. Test., p. 96.

[2] See Davidson's Hermeneutics, p. 306, and Horne's Introduction, vol. ii, p. 338.

narrative, and its imagery is drawn out in many details and analogies, yet so as to accord with the one leading figure, it would be improper to call it a metaphor. It is also affirmed by Davidson that in a metaphor there is only one meaning, while the allegory has two meanings, a literal and a figurative.[1] It will be seen, however, on careful examination, that this statement is misleading. Except in the case of the mystic allegory of Gal. iv, 21–31, it will be found that the allegory, like the metaphor, has but one meaning. Take for example the following from Psalm lxxx, 8–15:

8 A vine from Egypt thou hast torn away;
  Thou hast cast out the heathen, and planted it;
9 Thou didst clear away before it,
  And it rooted its roots,
  And it filled the land.
10 Covered were the mountains with its shade,
  And its branches are cedars of God.
11 It sent out its boughs unto the sea,
  And unto the river its tender shoots.
12 Wherefore hast thou broken down its walls,
  And have plucked it all that pass over the road?
13 Swine from the forest are laying it waste,
  And creatures of the field are feeding on it.
14 O God of hosts, return now,
  Look from heaven, and behold,
  And visit this vine;
15 And protect what thy right hand has planted,
  And upon the son thou madest strong for thyself.

Surely no one would understand this allegory in a literal sense. No one supposes for a moment that God literally took a vine out of Egypt, or that it had an actual growth elsewhere as here described. The language throughout is metaphorical, but being thus continued under one leading figure of a vine, the whole passage becomes an allegory. The casting out of the heathen (verse 8) is a momentary departure from the figure, but it serves as a clue to the meaning of all the rest, and after verse 15 the writer leaves the figure entirely, but makes it clear that he identifies himself and Israel with the

---

[1] Hermeneutics, p. 306. This writer also says: "The metaphor always asserts or imagines that one object is another. Thus, 'Judah is a lion's whelp' (Gen. xlix, 9); 'I am the vine' (John xv, 1). On the contrary, allegory never affirms that one thing is another, which is in truth an absurdity." But the very passage he quotes from John xv, 1, as a metaphor, is also part of an allegory, which is continued through six verses, showing that allegory as well as metaphor may affirm that one thing is another. The literal meaning of the word *allegory*, as shown above, is the affirming one thing for another.

vine. The same imagery is given in the form of a parable in Isa. v, 1–6, and the distinction between the two is seen in this, that the meaning of the parable is given separately at the close (verse 7), but the meaning of the allegory is implied in the metaphorical use of its words.

Having carefully distinguished between the parable and the allegory, and shown that the allegory is essentially an extended metaphor, we need no separate and special rules for the interpretation of the allegorical portions of the Scriptures. The same general principles that apply to the interpretation of metaphors and parables will apply to allegories. The great error to be guarded against is the effort to find minute analogies and hidden meanings in all the details of the imagery. Hence, as in the case of parables, we should first determine the main thought intended by the figure, and then interpret the minor points with constant reference to it. The context, the occasion, the circumstances, the application, and often the accompanying explanation, are, in each case, such as to leave little doubt of the import of any of the allegories of the Bible. The following passage from Prov. v, 15–18 serves to exhibit what a variety of interpretations may attach to a single allegory:

Same hermeneutical principles apply to Allegory as to Parable.

15 Drink waters from thine own cistern,
   And streams from the midst of thine own well.
16 Shall thy fountains spread abroad
   Brooks of water in the streets?
17 Let them be for thee, by thyself,
   And not for strangers with thee.
18 Let thy spring be blest,
   And have joy of the wife of thy youth.

Our first inquiry should be as to the main purpose of the allegory. A clue to this is furnished in the words "wife of thy youth" in verse 18, from which we might infer, if we had nothing else to guide us, that by the cistern, well, etc., mentioned before, this wife is to be understood. But others have understood the well to mean the word of God as given in the Law (Jerome, Rashi), others true wisdom (C. B. Michaelis), others one's own possessions in goods and estate (Junius, Cornelius à Lapide). In view of this variety of opinions, we need something more than the single allusion to the wife of one's youth in order to determine the application of the allegory. But when we further observe that the entire preceding part of the chapter is a warning against the strange woman, and the subsequent part continues in the same vein, it becomes very evident that the allegory of verses

Main purpose of the allegory to be first sought.

15–18 is designed to enjoin and extol connubial fidelity and love, as against illicit intercourse. This is made more certain by the language of verse 19, immediately following, in which the figure changes, and the youthful wife is called "a lovely hind and a graceful roe," which metaphor serves as an elegant transition to further warning against the evil woman. The great majority of interpreters, therefore, ancient and modern, have adopted this view. Hence we observe the importance of consulting the context in order to determine the main purpose of an allegory.

But having determined the main point we proceed to particulars, and first inquire what fitness there is in comparing a wife to a fountain of waters. Umbreit answers: "The wife is appropriately compared with a fountain, not merely inasmuch as offspring are born of her, but also because she satisfies the desire of the man. In connexion with this we must call to mind, in order to feel the full power of the figure, how in antiquity, and especially in the East, the possession of a spring was regarded as a great and even sacred thing."[1] This being accepted, we next observe that there are five different Hebrew words here used for a water source, which we have translated respectively by *cistern, well, fountain, brook,* and *spring.* Any attempt to find in each of these words a special metaphorical allusion would be pressing particulars too far, and would lead to confusion and folly. Familiarity with the usages of Hebrew parallelism[2] will show that these different but synonymous terms are used for the sake of variety and rhetorical effect, and are not to be pressed in the interpretation. The meaning of the first couplet (verse 15), therefore, is: Be content with the waters that are thine own; find thy delight and satisfaction in them, and go not abroad to meddle with the wells and cisterns of other people. That is, as the context has shown, be satisfied and happy with thy own lawful wife, as with a precious living fountain of thine own possession, and go not in the way of the strange woman.

Particular allusions to be studied in the light of main purpose.

Verse 16 has been translated variously; (1) affirmatively: "thy fountains shall spread abroad;" (2) imperatively: "let thy fountains spread abroad;" (3) interrogatively, as in our version above. Some, without any authority, have inserted the negative particle, and rendered, "thy fountains shall *not* be spread abroad" (Ewald, Bertheau, Stuart). This bold effort to amend the text was evidently prompted by the feeling that the affirmative and imperative renderings (1 and 2 above) made the author contradict himself. For he has just said, Drink of thine own well, and in verse 17 he

[1] Commentar über die Sprüche, in loco.   [2] Compare above, pp. 95–99.

adds, Let thy fountains be for thyself alone, and not for strangers also. How could he then say that these fountains should spread and become rivulets in the streets? Many of the older interpreters, taking the sentence affirmatively or imperatively, understood the fountains spreading abroad and becoming brooks in the streets as indicating a numerous progeny that should go forth and be honoured in public life. Comp. Num. xxiv, 7; Psa. lxviii, 26; Isa. xlviii, 1; li, 1. But this conception of the passage would seriously confuse the figure, break its unity, and be impossible to harmonize naturally with verse 17. All this difficulty is avoided by adopting the interrogative form of translation: "Shall thy fountains spread abroad, (and become) brooks of water in the streets?" Wouldst thou have thy wife go abroad as a public harlot? Nay, (but as verse 17 adds) let her be for thyself alone, and not for strangers with thee. In these last two verses (16 and 17), however, some give the thought a more general turn, as: "Shall the fountains at which thou drinkest be such as are common to all in the street?" But it gives greater unity to the entire allegory to keep in mind the one particular wife definitely referred to at the close (verse 18), and suppose the question to imply that as one would not have his own wife become a harlot of the street, so he should keep himself only unto her as one that drinks of his own well.

The allegory of old age, in Eccles. xii, 3–7, under the figure of a
Allegory of old house about to fall in ruins, has been variously inter-
age in Eccles. preted. Some of the fathers (Gregory Thaumaturgus,
xii, 3-7. Cyril of Jerusalem) understood the whole passage as referring to the day of judgment as connected with the end of the world. Accordingly, "the day" of verse 3 would be "the great and terrible day of the Lord" (Joel ii, 31; comp. Matt. xxiv, 29). Other expositors (Umbreit, Elster, Ginsburg) regard the passage as describing the approach of death under the figure of a fearful tempest which strikes the inmates of a noble mansion with consternation and terror. But the great majority of expositors, ancient and modern, have understood the passage as an allegorical description of old age. And this view, we may safely say, is favoured and even required by the immediate context and by the imagery itself. But we lose much of its point and force by understanding it of old age generally. It is not a truthful portraiture of the peaceful, serene, honoured, and "good old age" so much extolled in the Old Testament. It is not the picture presented to the mind in Prov. xvi, 31: "A crown of glory is the hoary head; in the way of righteousness will it be found;" nor that of Psa. xcii, 12–14, where it is declared that the righteous shall flourish like the palm, and grow great like

the Lebanon cedars; "they shall still bear fruit in hoary age; fresh and green shall they be." Comp. also Isa. xl, 30, 31. It remains for us, then, with Tayler Lewis, to understand that "the picture here given is the old age of the sensualist. This appears, too, from the connexion. It is the 'evil time,' the 'day of darkness' that has come upon the youth who was warned in the language above, made so much more impressive by its tone of forecasting irony. It is the dreary old age of the young man who *would* 'go on in every way of his heart and after every sight of his eyes,' who did not 'keep remorse from his soul nor evils from his flesh,' and now all these things are come upon him, with no such alleviations as often accompany the decline of life. Such also might be the inference from the words with which the verse begins: 'Remember thy Creator *while* the evil days come not.' It expresses this and more. There is a negative prohibitory force in the עַד אֲשֶׁר לֹא: So remember Him that the evil days come not—implying a warning that such coming will be a consequence of the neglect. Piety in youth will prevent such a realizing of this sad picture; it will not keep off old age, but it will make it cheerful and tolerable instead of the utter ruin that is here depicted." [1]

It is the old age of the sensualist.

Passing now to the particular figures used, we should exercise the greatest caution and care, for some of the allusions seem almost to be enigmatical. Barely to name the different interpretations of the several parts of this allegory would require many pages.[2] But the most judicious and careful interpreters are agreed that the "keepers of the house" (verse 3) are the arms and hands, which serve for protection and defence, but in decrepit age become feeble and tremulous. The "strong men" are the legs, which, when they lose their muscular vigour, become bowed and crooked in supporting their wearisome load. "The grinders," or rather *grinding maids* (טֹחֲנוֹת fem. plural in allusion to the fact that grinding with hand mills was usually performed by women), are the teeth, which in age become few and cease to perform their work. "Those that behold in the windows" are the eyes, which become dim with years. Beyond this point the interpretations become much more various and subtle. "The doors into the street" (verse 4) are generally explained of the mouth, the two lips of which are conceived of as double doors (Heb. דְּלָתַיִם), or a door consisting of two sides or leaves. But it would seem better to understand these double doors of the two ears, which become

Doubtful allusions.

[1] American edition of Lange's Commentary on Ecclesiastes, pp. 152, 153.
[2] See Poole's Synopsis, in loco.

shut up or closed to outer sounds. So Hengstenberg explains it, and is followed by Tayler Lewis, who observes: "The old sensualist, who had lived so much *abroad* and so little at home, is shut in at last. With no propriety could the mouth be called the *street door*, through which the master of the house goes abroad. . . . It is rather the door to the interior, the cellar door, that leads down to the stored or consumed provision, the stomach."[1] The "sound of the grinding" is by many referred to the noise of the teeth in masticating food; but this would be a return to what has been sufficiently noticed in verse 3. Better to understand this sound of the mill as equivalent to "the most familiar household sounds," as the sound of the mill really was. The thought then connects naturally with what precedes and follows; the ears are so shut up, the hearing has become so dull, that the most familiar sounds are but faintly heard,[2] "and," he adds, "it rises to the sound of the sparrow;" that is, as most recent critics explain, the "sound of the grinding" rises to that of a sparrow's shrill cry, and yet this old man's organs of hearing are so dull that he scarcely hears it. Others explain this last clause of the wakefulness of the old man: "he rises up at the voice of the sparrow." Thus rendered, we need not, as many, understand it of rising or waking up early in the morning (in which case the Hebrew word עוּר rather than קוּם should have been used), but of restlessness. Though dull of hearing, he will, nevertheless, at times start and rise up at the sound of a sparrow's shrill note. "The daughters of song" may be understood of the women singers (chap. ii, 8) who once ministered to his hilarity, but whose songs can now no longer charm him, and they are therefore humbled. But it is, perhaps, better to understand the voice itself, the various tones of which become low and feeble (comp. the use of שָׁחַח in Isa. xxix, 4).

As we pass to verse 5 we note the peculiar nature of allegory to interweave its interpretation with its imagery. The figure of a house is for the time abandoned, and we read: "Also from a height they are afraid, and terrors are in the way, and the almond disgusts, and the locust becomes heavy, and the caperberry fails to produce effect; for going is the

The allegory blends its meaning with its imagery.

---

[1] Lange's Commentary on Ecclesiastes (Am. ed.), p. 155.
[2] There was hardly any part of the day or night when this work was not going on with its ceaseless noise. It was, indeed, a sign that the senses were failing in their office when this familiar, yet very peculiar, sound of the grinding had ceased to arrest the attention, or had become low and obscure—

When the hum of the mill is faintly heard,
And the daughters of song are still.—Ibid., p. 156.

man to his everlasting house, and round about in the street pass the mourners." That is, looking down from that which is high, the tottering old man quickly becomes dizzy and is afraid; terrors seem to be continually in his path (comp. Prov. xxii, 13; xxvi, 13); the almond is no longer pleasant to his taste, but, on the contrary, disgusts;[1] and the locust, once with him perhaps a dainty article of food (Lev. xi, 22; Matt. iii, 4; Mark i, 6), becomes heavy and nauseating in his stomach, and the caperberry no longer serves its purpose of stimulating appetite.

In verse 6 we meet again with other figures which have a natural association with the lordly mansion. The end of life is represented as a removing (רחק) or sundering of the silver cord and a breaking of the golden lampbowl. The idea is that of a golden lamp suspended by a silver cord in the palatial hall, and suddenly the bowl of the lamp is dashed to pieces by the breaking of the cord. The pitcher at the fountain and the wheel at the cistern are similar metaphors referring to the abundant machinery for drawing water which would be connected with the mansion of a sumptuous Dives. These at last give out, and the whole furniture and machinery of life fall into sudden ruin. The explaining of the silver cord as the spinal marrow, and the golden bowl as the brain, and the fountain and cistern as the right and left ventricles of the heart, seems too far fetched to be safe or satisfactory. Such minute and ramified explanations of particular figures are always likely to be overdone, and generally confuse rather than illustrate the main idea which the author had in mind. The words of verse 7 show that the metaphors of verse 6 refer to the utter breaking down of the functions and processes of life. The pampered old body falls a pitiable ruin, in view of which Koheleth repeats his cry of "vanity of vanities."

In the interpretation of an allegory so rich in suggestions as the above, the great hermeneutical principles to be carefully adhered to are, first, to grasp the one great idea of the whole passage, and, second, to avoid the Hermeneutical principles to be observed.

---

[1] יְנָאץ, Hiphil of נָאץ, and meaning to *cause disgust*, or *is despised*. The old versions and most interpreters render *shall flourish*, deriving the form from נוץ, and understand the silvery hair of the old man as resembling the almond-tree, which blossoms in winter, and its flowers, which at first are roseate in colour, become white like snowflakes before they fall off. But, aside from this doubtful derivation of the form יְנָאץ (Stuart affirms that "ינאץ for ינץ has no parallel in Hebrew orthography"), the immediate connexion is against the introduction of such an image as the silvery hair of age in this place. The hoary head can only be thought of as a crown of glory—a beautiful sight; but to introduce it between the mention of the old man's fears and terrors on the one side, and the disturbing locust on the other, would make a most unhappy confusion of images.

temptation of seeking manifold meanings in the particular figures. By the minute search for some special significance in every allusion the mind becomes wearied and overcrowded with the particular illustrations, so as to be likely to miss entirely the great thought which should be kept mainly in view.

The work of the false prophets in Israel, and the ruin of both it

Ruin of false prophets allegorized in Ezek. xiii, 10-15. and them, are set forth allegorically in Ezek. xiii, 10-15. The people are represented as building a wall, and the prophets as plastering it over with תָּפֵל, a sort of *coating* or whitewash (comp. Matt. xxiii, 27; Acts xxiii, 3), designed to cover the worthless material of which the wall is built, and also to hide its unsafe construction. Ewald observes that this word (תָּפֵל) denotes elsewhere what is absurd intellectually, what is inconsistent with itself; here the mortar which does not hold together, clay without straw, or dry clay.' The meaning of these figures is very clear. The people built up vain hopes, and the false prophets covered them over with deceitful words and promises; they "saw vanity and divined a lie" (verses 7 and 9). The ruin of wall and plastering and plasterers is announced by Jehovah's oracle as fearfully effected by an overwhelming rain of judgment; the rain is accompanied by falling hailstones and a violent rushing tempest; all these together hurl wall and plastering to the ground, expose the false foundations, and utterly destroy the lying prophets in the general ruin. Here we have, in the form of an allegory, or extended metaphor, the same image, substantially, which our Lord puts in the form of a simile at the close of the sermon on the mount (Matt. vii, 26, 27).[2]

The much-disputed passage in 1 Cor. iii, 10-15, is an allegory.

Allegory of wise and unwise masterbuilding. In the preceding context Paul represents himself and Apollos as the ministers through whom the Corinthians had believed. "I planted, Apollos watered; but God gave the increase" (ver. 6). He shows his appreciation of the honour and responsibility of such ministry by saying (ver. 9): "For we (apostles and ministers like Paul and Apollos)

---

[1] Die Propheten des Alten Bundes, vol. ii, p. 399. Göttingen, 1868.

[2] The prophecies of Ezekiel abound in allegory. Chapter xvi contains an allegorical history of Israel, representing, by way of narrative, prophecy, and promise, the past, present, and future relations of God and the chosen people, and maintaining throughout the general figure of the marriage relation. Under like imagery, in chapter xxiii, the prophet depicts the idolatries of Samaria and Jerusalem. Compare also the similitudes of the vine wood and the vine in chapters xv and xix, 10-14, and the allegory of the lioness and her whelps in xix, 1-9. The allegorical history of Assyria, in chapter xxxi, may also be profitably compared and contrasted with the enigmatical fable of chapter xvii.

are God's fellow workers," and then he adds: "God's tilled field (*γεώργιον*, in allusion to, and in harmony with, the *planting* and watering mentioned above), God's building, are ye." Then dropping the former figure, and taking up that of a building (*οἰκοδομή*), he proceeds:

According to the grace of God which was given unto me, as a wise architect, I laid a foundation, and another is building thereon. But let each man take heed how he builds thereon. For other foundation can no man lay than the one laid, which is Jesus Christ. But if any one builds on the foundation gold, silver, precious stones, wood, hay, stubble; each man's work shall be made manifest, for the day will make it known, because in fire it is revealed, and each man's work, of what sort it is, the fire itself will prove. If any one's work shall endure which he built thereon, he shall receive reward. If any one's work shall be burned, he shall suffer loss, but he himself shall be saved, yet so as through fire.

The greatest trouble in explaining this passage has been to determine what is meant by the "gold, silver, precious stones, wood, hay, stubble," in verse 12. According to the majority of commentators these materials denote *doctrines* supposed to be taught in the Church.[1] Many others, however, understand *the character of the persons* brought into the Church.[2] But the most discerning among those who understand *doctrines*, do not deny that the doctrines are such as interpenetrate and mould character and life; and those who understand *persons* are as ready to admit that the personal character of those referred to would be influenced and developed by the doctrines of their ministers. Probably in this, as in some other Scripture, where so many devout and critical minds have differed, the real exposition is to be found in a blending of both views. The Church, considered as God's building, is a frequent figure with Paul (comp. Eph. ii, 20–22; Col. ii, 7; also 1 Peter ii, 5), and in every case it is the Christian believer who is conceived as builded into the structure. So here Paul says to the Corinthians, "Ye are God's building," and it comports fully with this figure to understand that the material of which this building is to be constructed consists of persons who accept Christ in faith. The Church is builded of persons, not of doctrines, but the persons are not brought to such use without doctrine. As in the case of Peter,

Are the materials persons or doctrines.

Both views allowable.

[1] So Clemens Alexandrinus, Ambrosiaster, Lyra, Cajetan, Erasmus, Luther, Beza, Calvin, Piscator, Grotius, Estius, Calovius, Lightfoot, Stolz, Rosenmüller, Flatt, Heidenreich, Neander, De Wette, Ewald, Meyer, Hodge, Alford, and Kling.

[2] So, substantially, Origen, Chrysostom, Photius, Theodoret, Theophylact, Augustine, Jerome, Billroth, Bengel, Pott, and Stanley.

the stone (Matt. xvi, 18), the true material of which the abiding Church is built, is not the doctrine of Christ, or the confession of Christ put forth by Peter, nor yet Peter considered as an individual man (Πέτρος), but both of these combined in *Peter confessing*—a believer inspired of God and confessing Christ as the Son of the living God—thus making one new man, the ideal and representative confessor (πέτρα),[1] so the material here contemplated consists of persons made and fashioned into various character through the instrumentality of different ministers. These ministers are admonished that they may work into God's building "wood, hay, stubble," worthless and perishable stuff, as well as "gold, silver, precious stones." The material may be largely made what it is by the doctrines taught, and other influences brought to bear on converts by the minister who is to build them into the house of God, but is it not clear that in such case the doctrines taught are the tools of the workman rather than the material of which he builds? Nevertheless, this process of building (ἐποικοδομεῖ) on the foundation already laid, like the work of Apollos in watering that which was planted by Paul (ver. 6), is to be thought of *chiefly in reference to the responsibility of the ministers* of the Gospel. The great caution is: "Let each man (whether Apollos or Cephas, or any other minister) take heed how he builds thereon " (ver. 10). Let him take heed to the doctrine he preaches, the morality he inculcates, the discipline he maintains, and, indeed, to every influence he exerts, which goes in any way to mould and fashion the life and character of those who are builded into the Church. The gold, silver, and precious stones, according to Alford, "refer to the *matter* of the minister's teaching, primarily, and by inference to those whom that teaching penetrates and builds up in Christ, who should be the living stones of the temple."[2] So also Meyer: "The various specimens of building materials, set side by side in vivid asyndeton, denote the various *matters of doctrine* propounded by teachers and brought into connexion with faith in Christ, in order to develop and complete the Christian training of the Church."[3] These statements contain essential truth, but they are, as we conceive, misleading, in so far as they exalt matters of doctrine alone. We are rather to think of the whole administration and work of the minister in making converts and influencing their character and life. The materials are rather the Church members, but considered primarily as made, or allowed to remain what they are by the agency of the minister who builds the Church.

[1] See on this subject above, pp. 228, 229.   [2] Greek Testament, in loco.
[3] Critical Commentary on Corinthians, in loco.

The great thoughts in the passage, then, would be as follows: On the foundation of Jesus Christ, ministers, as fellow workers with God, are engaged in building up God's house. But let each man take heed how he builds. On that foundation may be erected an edifice of sound and enduring substance, as if it were built of gold, silver, and precious stones (as, for instance, costly marbles); the kind of Christians thus "builded together for a habitation of God in the Spirit" (Eph. ii, 20) will constitute a noble and enduring structure, and his work will stand the fiery test of the last day. But on that same foundation a careless and unfaithful workman may build with unsafe material; he may tolerate and even foster jealousy, and strife (ver. 3), and pride (iv, 18); he may keep fornicators in the Church without sorrow or compunction (v, 1, 2); he may allow brother to go to law against brother (vi, 1), and permit drunken persons to come to the Lord's Supper (xi, 21)—all these, as well as heretics in doctrine (xv, 12),[1] may be taken up and used as materials for building God's house. In writing to the Corinthians the apostle had all these classes of persons in mind, and saw how they were becoming incorporated into that Church of his own planting. But he adds: The day of the Lord's judgment will bring every thing to light, and put to the test every man's work. The fiery revelation will disclose what sort of work each one has been doing, and he that has builded wisely and soundly will obtain a glorious reward; but he that has brought, or sought to keep, the wood, hay, stubble, in the Church —he who has not rebuked jealousy, nor put down strife, nor excommunicated fornicators, nor faithfully administered the discipline of the Church—shall see his life-work all consumed, and he himself shall barely escape with his life, as one that is saved by being hastened through the fire of the burning building. His labour will all have been in vain, though he assumed to build on Christ, and did in fact minister in the holy place of his temple.

It is to be especially kept in mind that this allegory is intended to serve rather as a *warning* than to be understood as a *prophecy*. As the parable of the labourers in the vineyard (Matt. xix, 27–xx, 16) is spoken against Peter's mercenary spirit, and thus serves as a warning and rebuke rather than as a prophecy of what will actually take place in the judgment, so here Paul warns those who are fellow labourers with God to take heed how they build, lest they involve both themselves and others in irreparable loss. We are not to understand the wood,

The passage paraphrased.

The allegory a warning rather than a prophecy.

---

[1] In his parable of the tares and the wheat (Matt. xiii, 24–30, 37–43) Jesus himself taught that the good and the evil would be mixed together in the Church.

hay, stubble, as the profane and ungodly, who have no faith in Christ. Nor do these words denote false, anti-Christian doctrines. They denote rather the character and life-work of those who are rooted and grounded in Christ, but whose personal character and work are of little or no worth in the Church. All such persons, as well as the ministers who helped to make them such, will suffer irreparable loss in the day of the Lord Jesus, although they themselves may be saved. And this consideration obviates the objection made by some that if the *work* which shall be burned (ver. 15) are the *persons* brought into the Church, it is not to be supposed that the ministers who brought them in shall be saved. The final destiny of the persons affected by this work is, no doubt, necessarily involved in the fearful issue, but for their ruin the careless minister may not have been solely responsible. He may be saved, yet so as through fire, and they be lost. In chapter v, 5, Paul enjoins the severest discipline of the vile fornicator "in order that the spirit might be saved in the day of the Lord." But a failure to administer such discipline would not necessarily have involved the final ruin of those commissioned to administer it; they would "suffer loss," and their final salvation would be "as through fire." So, on the other hand, the work which the wise architect builds on the true foundation (ver. 14), and which endures, is not so much the final salvation and eternal life of those whom he brought into the Church and trained there as the general character and results of his labour in thus bringing them in and training them.

We thus seek the true solution of this allegory in carefully distinguishing between the *materials* put into the building and the *work* of the builders, and, at the same time, note the essential blending of the two. The wise builder will so teach, train, and discipline the church in which he labours as to secure excellent and permanent results. The unwise will work in bad material, and have no regard for the judgment which will test the work of all. In thus building, whether wisely or unwisely, the *persons* brought into the church and the ministerial *labour* by which they are taught and disciplined have a most intimate relation; and hence the essential truth in both the expositions of the allegory which have been so widely maintained.

Another of Paul's allegories occurs in 1 Cor. v, 6–8. Its imagery Allegory of is based upon the well-known custom of the Jews of re-1 Cor. v, 6–8. moving all leaven from their houses at the beginning of the passover week,[1] and allowing no leaven to be found there during

[1] The allusion may have been suggested by the time of the year when the epistle was written, apparently (chap. xvi, 8) a short time before Pentecost, and, therefore,

the seven days of the feast (Exod. xii, 15–20; xiii, 7). It also assumes the knowledge of the working of leaven, and its nature to communicate its properties of sourness to the whole kneaded mass. Jesus had used leaven as a symbol of pharisaic hypocrisy (Matt. xvi, 6, 12; Mark viii, 15; Luke xii, 1), and the power of a little leaven to leaven the whole lump had become a proverb (Gal. v, 9; comp. 1 Cor. xv, 33). All this Paul constructs into the following allegory:

Know ye not that a little leaven leavens the whole lump? Purge out the old leaven, that ye may be a new lump, even as ye are unleavened. For our passover, also, has been sacrificed, even Christ; wherefore let us keep the feast, not with old leaven, nor with the leaven of malice and wickedness, but with the unleavened loaves of sincerity and truth.

The particular import and application of this allegory are to be found in the context. The apostle has in mind the case of the incestuous person who was tolerated in the church at Corinth, and whose foul example would be likely to contaminate the whole Church. He enjoins his immediate expulsion, and expresses amazement that they showed no humiliation and grief in having such a stain upon their character as a church, but seemed rather to be puffed up with self-conceit and pride. "Not goodly," not seemly or beautiful (οὐ καλόν), he says, "is your *Paraphrase of* glorying" (καύχημα, ground of glorying). Sadly out of *the passage.* place your exultation and boast of being a Christian church with such a reproach and abuse in your midst. Know ye not the common proverb of the working of leaven? The toleration of such impurity and scandal in the Christian society will soon corrupt the whole body. Purge out, then, the old leaven. Cast off and put utterly away the old corrupt life and habits of heathenism. You know the customs of the passover. "You know how, when the lamb is killed, every particle of leaven is removed from every household; every morsel of food eaten, every drop drunk in that feast, is taken in its natural state. This is the true figure of your condition. You are the chosen people, delivered from bondage; you are called to begin a new life, you have had the lamb slain for you in the person of Christ. Whatever, therefore, in you corresponds to the literal leaven, must be utterly cast out; the perpetual passover to which we are called must be celebrated, like theirs, uncontaminated by any corrupting influence."[1]

with the scenes of the passover, either present or recent, in his thoughts.—Stanley on the Epistles to the Corinthians, in loco.

[1] Stanley on Corinthians, in loco.

In such an allegory care should be taken to give the right mean-
The more im- ing to the more important allusions. The *old leaven* in
portant allu- verse 7 is not to be explained as referring directly to
sions. the incestuous person mentioned in the context. It has
a wider import, and denotes, undoubtedly, all corrupt habits and immoral practices of the old heathen life, of which this case of incest
was but one notorious specimen. The leaven in the Corinthian
church was not so much the person of this particular offender, as
the corrupting influence of his example, a residuum of the old unregenerate state. So "the leaven of the Pharisees" was not the persons, but the doctrine and example of the Pharisees. Furthermore,
the words "even as ye are unleavened" are not to be taken literally
(as Rosenmüller, Wieseler, and Conybeare), as if meaning "even
as ye are now celebrating the feast of unleavened bread." Such a
mixing of literal and allegorical significations together is not to be
assumed unless necessary. If such had been the apostle's design
he would scarcely have used the word *unleavened* (ἄζυμοι) of persons abstaining from leavened bread. Nor is it supposable that
the whole Corinthian church, or any considerable portion of them,
observed the Jewish passover. And even if Paul had been observing this feast at Ephesus at the time he wrote this epistle (chap.
xvi, 8), it would have been some time past when the epistle reached
Corinth, so that the allusion would have lost all its pertinency and
effect. But Paul here uses *unleavened* figuratively of the Corinthians considered as a "new lump;" for so the words used immediately before and after imply.

The vivid allegory of the Christian armour and conflict, in Eph.
Allegory of the vi, 11–17, furnishes its own interpretation, and is espe-
Christian ar- cially notable in the particular explanations of the dif-
mour. ferent parts of the armour. It appropriates the figure
used in Isa. lix, 17 (comp. also Rom. xiii, 12; 1 Thess. v, 8), and
elaborates it in great detail. Its several parts make up τὴν πανο-
πλίαν τοῦ Θεοῦ, "the whole armour (panoply) of God," the entire
outfit of weapons, offensive and defensive, which is supplied by
God. The enumeration of the several parts shows that the apostle
has in mind the panoply of a heavy-armed soldier, with which the
dwellers in all provinces of the Roman Empire must have been sufficiently familiar. The conflict (ἡ πάλη, a life and death struggle)
is not against blood and flesh (weak, fallible men, comp. Gal. i, 16),
but against the organized spiritual forces of the kingdom of darkness, and hence the necessity of taking on the entire armour of
God, which alone can meet the exigencies of such a wrestling. The
six pieces of armour here named, which include girdle and sandals,

are sufficiently explained by the writer himself, and ought not, in interpretation, to be pressed into all possible details of comparison which corresponding portions of ancient armour might be made to suggest. Here, as in Isa. lix, 17, *righteousness* is represented as a breastplate, but in 1 Thess. v, 8, *faith and love* are thus depicted. Here the helmet is *salvation*—a present consciousness of salvation in Christ as an actual possession—but in 1 Thess. v, 8 it is the *hope of salvation.* Each allusion must be carefully studied in the light of its own context, and not be too widely referred. For the same figure may be used at different times for different purposes.[1]

The complex allegory of the door of the sheep and of the good shepherd, in John x, 1-16, is in the main simple and self- Allegory of interpreting. But as it involves the twofold comparison John x, 1-16. of Christ as the door and the good shepherd, and has other allusions of diverse character, its interpretation requires particular care, lest the main figures become confused, and non-essential points be made too prominent. The passage should be divided into two parts, and it should be noted that the first five verses are a pure allegory, containing no explanation within itself. It is observed, in verse 6, that the allegory (παροιμία) was not understood by those to whom it was addressed. Thereupon Jesus proceeded (verses 7–16) not only to explain it, but also to expand it by the addition of other images. He makes it emphatic that he himself is "the door of the sheep," but adds further on that he is the good shepherd, ready to give his life for the sheep, and thus distinguished from the hireling who forsakes the flock and flees in the hour of danger.

The allegory stands in vital relation to the history of the blind man who was cast out of the synagogue by the Phari- Occasion and sees, but graciously received by Jesus. The occasion and scope of the scope of the whole passage cannot be clearly apprehended allegory. without keeping this connexion constantly in mind. Jesus first

[1] Meyer appropriately observes: "The figurative mode of regarding a subject can by no means, with a mind so many-sided, rich, and versatile as that of St. Paul, be so stereotyped that the very same thing which he has here viewed under the figure of the protecting breastplate, must have presented itself another time under this very same figure. Thus, for example, there appears to him, as an offering well pleasing to God, at one time Christ (Eph. v, 2), at another the gifts of love received (Phil. iv, 18), at another time the bodies of Christians (Rom. xii, 1); under the figure of the seed-corn, at one time the body becoming buried (1 Cor. xv, 36), at another time the moral conduct (Gal. vi, 7); under the figure of the leaven, once moral corruption (1 Cor. v, 6), another time doctrinal corruption (Gal. v, 9); under the figure of clothing which is put on, once the new man (Eph. iv, 24), another time Christ (Gal. iii, 27), at another time the body (2 Cor. v, 3), and other similar instances."—Critical Commentary on Ephesians, in loco.

contrasts himself, as the door of the sheep, with those who acted rather the part of thieves and robbers of the flock. Then, when the Pharisees fail to understand him, he partly explains his meaning, and goes on to contrast himself, as the good shepherd, with those who had no genuine care for the sheep committed to their charge, but, at the coming of the wolf, would leave them and flee. At verse 17 he drops the figure, and speaks of his willingness to lay down his life, and of his power to take it again. Thus the whole passage should be studied in the light of that pharisaical opposition to Christ which showed itself to be selfish and self-seeking, and ready to do violence when met with opposition. These pharisaical Jews, who assumed to hold the doors of the synagogue, and had agreed to thrust out any that confessed Jesus as the Christ (chap. ix, 22), were no better than thieves and robbers of God's flock. Against these the allegory was aimed.

Keeping in view this occasion and scope of the allegory, we next Import of par- inquire into the meaning of its principal allusions. ticular parts. "The fold of the sheep" is the Church of God's people, who are here represented as his sheep. Christ himself is the door, as he emphatically affirms (verses 7, 9), and every true shepherd, teacher, and guide of God's people should recognize him as the only way and means of entering into the fold. Shepherd and sheep alike should enter through this door. "He that enters in through the door is a shepherd [1] of the sheep" (ver. 2); not a thief, nor a robber, nor a stranger (ver. 5). He is well known to all who have any charge of the fold, and his voice is familiar to the sheep. A stranger's voice, on the contrary, is a cause of alarm and flight.[2] Such, indeed, were the action and words of those Jewish officials toward the man who had received his sight. He perceived in their words and manner that which was strange and alien to the truth of God (see chap. ix, 30–33).

So far all seems clear, but we should be less positive in finding other special meanings. The porter, or doorkeeper ($\vartheta\nu\rho\omega\rho\acute{o}\varsigma$, ver. 3), has been explained variously, as denoting God (Calvin, Bengel, Tholuck), or the Holy Spirit (Theodoret, Stier, Alford, Lange), or even Christ (Cyril, Augustine), or Moses (Chrysostom), or John Baptist, (Godet). But it is better not to give the word any such

---

[1] Not *the shepherd*, as the English version renders ποιμήν here. This has led to a mixture of figures by supposing Christ to be referred to. In this first simple allegory Christ is only the *door ;* further on, where the figure is explained, and then enlarged, he appears also as the good shepherd (verses 11, 14).

[2] For a description of the habits and customs of oriental shepherds, see especially, Thomson, The Land and the Book, vol. i, p. 301. New York, 1858.

remarkable prominence in the interpretation. The porter is rather
an inferior servant of the shepherd. He opens the door to him
when he comes, and is supposed to obey his orders. We should,
therefore, treat this word as an incidental feature of the allegory,
legitimate and essential to the figure, but not to be pressed into any
special significance. The distinction made by some between "the
sheep" and "his own sheep" in verse 3, by supposing that several
flocks were accustomed to occupy one fold, and the sheep of each
particular flock, which had a separate shepherd, are to be understood by "his own sheep," may be allowed, but ought not to be
urged. It is as well to understand the calling his own sheep by
name as simply a special allusion to the eastern custom of giving
particular names to favourite sheep. But we may with propriety
understand the *leading them out* (ἐξάγει αὐτά, ver. 3), and *putting
forth all his own* (τὰ ἴδια πάντα ἐκβάλῃ, ver. 4), as an intimation of
the exodus of God's elect and faithful ones from the fold of the old
Testament theocracy. This view is maintained by Lange and Godet,
and is suggested and warranted by the words of Jesus in verses
14–16.

The language of Jesus in defining his allegory and expanding its
imagery (verses 7–16) is in some points enigmatical. Jesus' explana-
For he would not make things too plain to those who, tion somewhat
like the Pharisees, assumed to see and know so much enigmatical.
(comp. chap. ix, 39–41), and he uses the strong words, which seem
to be purposely obscure: "All as many as came before me are
thieves and robbers" (ver. 8). He would prompt special inquiry
and concern as to what might be meant by *coming before him*, a
procedure so wrong that he likens it to the stealth of a thief and
the rapacity of a robber. Most natural is it to understand the *coming before me*, in verse 8, as corresponding with the *climbing up
some other way*, in verse 1, and meaning an entrance into the fold
other than through the door. But it is manifestly aimed at those
who, like these Pharisees, by their action and attitude, assumed to
be lords of the theocracy, and used both deceit and violence to accomplish their own will. Hence it would seem but proper to
give the words *before me* (πρὸ ἐμοῦ, ver. 8) a somewhat broad and
general significance, and not press them, as many do, into the one
sole idea of a *precedence in time*. The preposition πρό is often used
of place, as *before* the doors, *before* the gate, *before* the city (comp.
Acts v, 23; xii, 6, 14; xiv, 13) and may here combine with the
temporal reference of ἦλθον, *came*, the further idea of position in
front of the door. These Pharisees *came* as teachers and guides of
the people, and in such conduct as that of casting out the man born

blind, they placed themselves *in front of the true door,* shutting up
the kingdom of heaven against men, and neither entering them·
selves nor allowing others to enter through that door (comp. Matt.
xxiii, 13). All this Jesus may have intended by the enigmatical
came before me. Accordingly, the various explanations, as "instead
of me," "without regard to me," "passing by me," and "pressing
before me," have all a measure of correctness. The expression is
to be interpreted, as Lange urges, with special reference to the
figure of the door. "The meaning is, All who *came before the door*
(πρὸ τῆς θύρας ἦλθον). With the idea of passing by the door this
other is connected: the setting of themselves up for the door; that is,
all who came claiming rule over the conscience as spiritual lords.
The time of their coming is indicated to be already past by the
ἦλθον, not however by the πρό, forasmuch as the positive πρό does
not coincide with the temporal one. . . . At the same time emphasis is given to the ἦλθον. They came as though the Messiah had
come; there was no room left for him. It is not necessary that we
should confine our thought to those who were false Messiahs in the
stricter sense of the term, since the majority of these did not appear until after Christ. Every hierarch prior to Christ was pseudo-
Messianic in proportion as he was anti-Christian; and to covet rule
over the conscience of men is pseudo-Christian. Be it further observed that the thieves and robbers, who climb over the wall, appear in this verse with the assumption of a higher power. They
stand no longer in their naked selfishness, they lay claim to positive importance, and that not merely as shepherds, but as the door
itself. Thus the hierarchs had just been attempting to exercise
rule over the man who was born blind." [1]

The import of the other allusions and statements of this passage
is sufficiently clear, but in a thorough and elaborate treatment of
the whole subject the student should compare the similar allegories
which are found in Jer. xxiii, 1-4; Exek. xxxiv; Zech. xi, 4-17;
and also the twenty-third Psalm. So also the allegory of the vine
and its branches, John xv, 1-10 [2]—an allegory like that of the door
and the shepherd peculiar to John—may be profitably compared

---

[1] Lange's Commentary on John, in loco.

[2] According to Lange (on John xv, 1) "Jesus' discourse concerning the vine is
neither an allegory nor a parable, but a parabolic discourse, and that a symbolical
one." But this is an over-refinement, and withal, misleading. The figures of some
allegories may be construed as symbols, and allegory and parable may have much in
common. But this figure of the vine, illustrating the vital and organic union between
Christ and believers, has every essential quality of the allegory, and contains its own
interpretation within itself.

and contrasted with the psalmist's allegory of the vine (Psa. lxxx, 8–15) which we have already noticed.

The allegorizing process by which Paul, in Gal. iv, 21–31, makes Hagar and Sarah illustrate two covenants, is an excep-   Paul's allegory
tional New Testament instance of developing a mysti-   in Gal. iv, 21-
cal meaning from facts of Old Testament history. Paul   31, peculiar and
exceptional.
elsewhere (Rom. vii, 1–6) illustrates the believer's release from the law, and union with Christ, by means of the law of marriage, according to which a woman, upon the death of her husband, is discharged from (κατήργηται) the law which bound her to him alone, and is at liberty to become united to another man. In 2 Cor. iii, 13–16, he contrasts the open boldness (παρρησία) of the Gospel preaching with the veil which Moses put on his face purposely to conceal for the time the transitory character of the Old Testament ministration which then appeared so glorious, but was, nevertheless, destined to pass away like the glory of his own God-lit face. He also, in the same passage, makes the veil a symbol of the incapacity of Israel's heart to apprehend the Lord Christ. The passage of the Red Sea, and the rock in the desert from which the water flowed, are recognized as types of spiritual things (1 Cor. x, 1–4; comp. 1 Peter iii, 21). But all these illustrations from the Old Testament differ essentially from the allegory of the two covenants. Paul himself, by the manner and style in which he introduces it, evidently feels that his argument is exceptional and peculiar, and being addressed especially to those who boasted of their attachment to the law, it has the nature of an *argumentum ad hominem.* "At the conclusion of the theoretical portion of his epistle," says Meyer, "Paul adds a quite peculiar antinomistic disquisition—a learned rabbinico-allegorical argument derived from the law itself—calculated to annihilate the influence of the pseudo-apostles with their own weapons, and to root them out of their own ground."[1]

We observe that the apostle, first of all, states the historical facts, as written in the Book of Genesis, namely, that Abra-   Historical facts
ham was the father of two sons, one by the bond wom-   accepted as lit-
an, the other by the free woman;—the son of the bond-   erally true.
maid was born κατὰ σάρκα, *according to flesh*, i. e., according to the ordinary course of nature, but the son of the free woman was born through promise, and, as the Scripture shows (Gen. xvii, 19; xviii, 10–14), by miraculous interposition. He further on brings in the rabbinical tradition founded on Gen. xxi, 9, that Ishmael persecuted (ἐδίωκε, ver. 29) Isaac, perhaps having in mind also some subsequent aggressions of the Ishmaelites upon Israel, and then adds the words.

[1] Critical Commentary on Galatians, in loco.

of Sarah, as written in Gen. xxi, 10, adapting them somewhat freely
to his purpose. It is evident from all this that Paul recognizes the
grammatico-historical truthfulness of the Old Testament narrative.
But, he says, all these historical facts are capable of being allegorized: *ἅτινά ἐστιν ἀλληγορούμενα, which things are allegorical ;* or as
Ellicott well expresses it: " All which things, viewed in their most
general light, are allegorical." [1] He proceeds to allegorize the facts
referred to, making the two women represent the two covenants,
the Sinaitic (Jewish) and the Christian, and showing in detail how
one thing answers to, or *ranks with (συστοιχεῖ)* another, and also
wherein the two covenants stand opposed. We may represent the
correspondences of his allegory as follows:

a	{ 1 Hagar, bondmaid, =Old Covenant, συστοιχεῖ,	The present Jerusalem.
	{ 2 Sarah, free woman,=New Covenant,	"	Jerusalem above, our mother.
b	{ 3 Ishmael, child of flesh,	"	Those in bondage to the law.
	{ 4 Isaac, child of promise,	"	We, Christian brethren (ver. 28).
c	{ 5 Ishmael persecuted Isaac,	".	So now legalists pers. Christians.
	{ 6 Scripture says: Cast out bondmaid and son, "	{ I say, (ver. 31 ; v, 1): Be not en- tangled in yoke of bondage.

The above tabulation exhibits at a glance six points of similitude
(on a line with the figures 1, 2, 3, etc.), and three sets of things contrasted (as linked by the braces *a, b, c*). The general import of the
apostle's language is clear and simple, and this allegorizing process
served most aptly both to illustrate the relations and contrasts of
the Law and the Gospel, and also to confound and silence the Judaizing legalists, against whom Paul was writing.

Here arises the important hermeneutical question, What inference
are we to draw from this example of an inspired apostle
allegorizing the facts of sacred history? Was it a fruit
of his rabbinical education, and a sanction of that allegorical method of interpretation which was prevalent,
especially among Jewish-Alexandrian writers, at that time?

*What authori-
ty attaches to
Paul's exam-
ple of allegor-
izing?*

That Paul in this passage treats historical facts of the Old Testament as capable of being used allegorically is a simple matter of
fact. That he was familiar with the allegorical methods of expounding the Scriptures current in his day is scarcely to be doubted.
That his own rabbinical training had some influence on him, and
coloured his methods of argument and illustration, there seems no
valid reason to deny. It is further evident that in his allegorical
use of Hagar and Sarah he employs an exceptional and peculiar
method of dealing with his Judaizing opponents, and, so far as the
passage is an argument, it is essentially an *argumentum ad hominem.*

[1] Commentary on Galatians, in loco.

But it is not merely an argument of that kind, as if it could have no worth or force with any other parties. It is assumed to have an interest and value as illustrating certain relations of the Law and the Gospel.[1] But its position, connexion, and use in this epistle to the Galatians gives no sufficient warrant for such allegorical methods in general. Schmoller remarks: "Paul to be sure allegorizes here, for he says so himself. But with the very fact of his saying this himself, the gravity of the hermeneutical difficulty disappears. He *means* therefore to give an allegory, not an exposition; he does not proceed as an exegete, and does not mean to say (after the manner of the allegorizing exegetes) that only what he now says is the true sense of the narrative."[2] Herein especially consists the great difference between Paul's example and that of nearly all the allegorists. He concedes and assumes the historical truthfulness of the Old Testament narrative, but makes an allegorical use of it for a special and exceptional purpose.[3]

[1] According to Jowett, "it is neither an argument nor an illustration, but an interpretation of the Old Testament Scripture after the manner of the age in which he lived; that is, after the manner of the Jewish and Christian Alexandrian writers. Whatever difference there is between him and them, or between Philo and the Christian fathers, as interpreters of Scripture, is not one of kind, but of degree. The Christian writers lay aside many of the extravagances of Philo; St. Paul is free also from their extravagances, employing only casually, and exceptionally, and when reasoning with those 'who desire to be under the law,' what they use habitually and unsparingly, so as to overlay, and in some cases to destroy the original sense. Instead of seeking to draw subtle distinctions between the method of St. Paul and that of his age, probably of the school in which he was brought up, it is better to observe that the noble spirit of the apostle shines through the 'elements of the law' in which he clothes his meaning."—The Epistles of St. Paul to the Thessalonians, Galatians, etc., with Critical Notes and Dissertations, vol. i, p. 285. London, 1855.

[2] Commentary on Galatians (Lange's Biblework), in loco.

[3] J. B. Lightfoot compares and contrasts Philo's allegory of Hagar and Sarah, and shows how the two move in different realms of thought, and yet have points of resemblance as well as points of difference. He shows how, "with Philo, the allegory is the whole substance of his teaching; with St. Paul it is but an accessory." He furnishes also, on the general subject, the following judicious and sensible remarks: "We need not fear to allow that St. Paul's mode of teaching here is coloured by his early education.in the rabbinical schools. It were as unreasonable to stake the apostle's inspiration on the turn of a metaphor or the character of an illustration or the form of an argument, as on purity of diction. No one now thinks of maintaining that the language of the inspired writers reaches the classical standard of correctness and elegance, though at one time it was held almost a heresy to deny this. 'A treasure contained in earthen vessels,' 'strength made perfect in weakness,' 'rudeness in speech, yet not in knowledge,'—such is the far nobler conception.of inspired teaching which we may gather from the apostle's own language. And this language we should do well to bear in mind."—St. Paul's Epistle to the Galatians, Greek Text, Notes, etc., p. 370. Andover, 1881.

Hence we may say, in general, that as certain other Old Testament characters and events are acknowledged by Paul to have a typical significance (see Rom. ix, 14; 1 Cor. x, 5), so he allows a like significance to the points specified in the history of Hagar and Sarah. But he never for a moment loses sight of the historical basis, or permits his allegorizing to displace it. And in the same general way it may be allowable for us to allegorize portions of the Scripture, providing the facts are capable of typical significance, and are never ignored and displaced by the allegorizing process. Biblical characters and events may thus be used for homiletical purposes, and serve for "instruction in righteousness;" but the special and exceptional character of such handling of Scripture must, as in Paul's example, be explicitly acknowledged. The apostle's solitary instance is a sufficient admonition that such expositions are to be indulged in most sparingly.

Paul's method of allegorizing allowable.

The allegorical interpretation of the Book of Canticles, adopted by all the older Jewish expositors and the great majority of Christian divines, is not to be lightly cast aside. Where such a unanimity has so long prevailed, there is at least the presumption that it is rooted in some element of truth. The methods of procedure adopted by individual exegetes may all be open to objection, while, at the same time, they may embody principles in themselves essentially correct.

Interpretation of Canticles.

The allegorists agree in making the pure love and tender relations of Solomon and Shulamith represent the relations of God and his people. But when they come to details they differ most widely, each writer finding in particular passages mystic or historical allusions, which, in turn, are disregarded or denied by others. In fact, it can scarcely be said that any two allegorizing minds have ever agreed throughout in the details of their exposition. The Jewish Targum, which takes the bridegroom to be the Lord of the world, and the bride the congregation of Israel, explains the whole song as a picture of Israel's history, from the exodus until the final redemption and restoration of the nation to the mountain of Jerusalem.[1] Aben-Ezra makes the song an allegorico-prophetic history of Israel from Abraham onward. Origen and the Christian allegorists generally make Christ the bridegroom and his Church the bride. Some, however, explain all the allusions of the loving intercourse between Christ and the individual believer, while others treat the whole song as a sort of apocalypse, or prophetic picture of the history of the Church in all ages. Ambrose, in a sermon on the

Allegorical methods.

_____
[1] An English translation of the Targum of Canticles is given in Adam Clarke's Commentary, at the end of his notes on Solomon's Song.

perpetual virginity of the virgin Mary, represents Shulamith as identical with Mary, the mother of God. But these are only some of the more general types or outlines of exposition pursued by the allegorists. Besides such leading differences there is an endless and most confusing mass of special expositions. It is assumed that every word must be explained in a mystic sense. The Targum, for example, in chap. ii, 4, understands the bringing into the house of wine as the Lord bringing Israel to the school of Mount Sinai to learn the law from Moses. Aben-Ezra explains the coming of the beloved, leaping over the mountains (chap. ii, 8), as Jehovah descending upon Sinai and shaking the whole mountain by his thunder. The Christian allegorists also find in every word and allusion of the song some illustration of the "great mystery" of which Paul speaks in Eph. v, 31–33, and some have carried the matter into wild extravagance. Thus Epiphanius makes the eighty concubines (vi, 8) prefigure eighty heresies of Christendom; the winter (ii, 11) denotes the sufferings of Christ, and the voice of the turtle-dove (ii, 12) is the preaching of Paul. Hengstenberg makes the hair of the bride, which is compared to a flock of goats that leap playfully from Mount Gilead (iv, 1), signify the mass of the nations converted to the Church, and Cocceius discovered in other allusions the strifes of Guelphs and Ghibellines, the struggles of the Reformation, and even particular events like the capture of the elector of Saxony at Mühlberg! And so the interpretation of this book has been carried to the same extreme as that of John's Apocalypse.

Against the allegorical interpretation of Canticles we may urge three considerations. First, the notable disagreement of its advocates, as indicated above, and the constant tendency of their expositions to run into irrational extremes. These facts warrant the inference that some fatal error lies in that method of procedure. Secondly, the allegorists, as a rule, deny that the song has any literal basis. The persons and objects described are mere figures of the Lord and his people, and of the manifold relations between them. This position throws the whole exposition into the realm of fancy, and explains how, as a matter of fact, each interpreter becomes a law unto himself. Having no basis in reality, the purely allegorical interpretation has not been able to fix upon any historical standpoint, or adopt any common principles. Thirdly, the song contains no intimation that it is an allegory. It certainly does not, like the other allegories of Scripture, contain its exposition within itself. Herein, as we have shown above, the allegory differs from the parable, and to

Objections to the allegorical method.

be self-consistent in allegorizing the song of songs we should either
adopt Paul's method with the history of Sarah and Hagar, and, allowing a literal historical basis, say: All these things may be allegorized; or else we should call the song a parable, and, as in the
parable of the prodigal son, affirm that its imagery is true to fact
and nature and capable of literal explanation, but that it serves
more especially to set forth the mystic relation that exists between
God and his people.

Following, therefore, the analogy of Scripture we may more appropriately designate the Canticles as a dramatic parable. It may or may not have had a literal historical
occasion, as the marriage of Solomon with Pharaoh's
daughter (1 Kings iii, 1), or, as many think, with some beautiful
shepherd-maiden of Northern Palestine (comp. chap. iv, 8). In
either case the imagery and form of the composition are poetic and
dramatic, and, as in the book of Job, we are not to suppose a literal
narrative of persons actually addressing one another in such perfect
and ornamental style. Solomon is a well-known historical person,
and also, in Scripture, a typical character. Shulamith may have been
one of his wives. But the song of songs is a parable, and its leading
actors are, as in all parables, typical of others besides themselves.
The parable depicts in a most charming style the highest ideal of
pure connubial love, and "we cannot but believe that the writer
of this divine song recognized the symbolical character of that love,
which he has here embellished. . . . The typical character of Solomon's own reign was well understood by himself, as appears from
Psalm lxxii. That the Lord's relation to his people was conceived
of as a marriage from the time of the covenant at Sinai, is shown by
repeated expressions which imply it in the law of Moses. That, under
these circumstances, the marriage of the king of Israel should carry
the thought up by a ready and spontaneous association to the cov-
enant-relation of the King *par excellence* to the people whom he had
espoused to himself, is surely no extravagant supposition, even if the
analogous instance of Psalm xlv did not remove it from the region
of conjecture to that of established fact. The mystical use made of
marriage so frequently in the subsequent scriptures, with evident
and even verbal allusion to this song, and the constant interpretation of both the Synagogue and the Church, show the naturalness of
the symbol, and enhance the probability that the writer himself saw
what the great body of his readers have found in his production."[1]

Canticles a dramatic Par-able.

[1] Prof. W. H. Green, in American edition of Lange's O. T. Commentary, Introduction, pp. 24, 25. This learned exegete adopts, along with Zöckler, Delitzsch, and
some others, what he calls the typical method of interpreting the Canticles. "I am

Accepting, then, the view that the song is of parabolic import, we should avoid the extravagances of those allegorists who find a spiritual significance in every word and metaphor. We should, first of all, study to ascertain the literal sense of every passage. First the natural, afterward that which is spiritual. The assumption of many that the literal sense involves absurdities and revolting images is a grave error. Such writers seem to forget that " the work is an oriental poem, and the diction should therefore not be taken as prose. It is the offspring of a luxuriant imagination tinged with the voluptuousness characteristic of the eastern mind. There love is warm and passionate even while pure. It deals in colours and images which seem extravagant to the colder ideas of the West." [1]

Having apprehended the literal sense, we should proceed, as in a parable, to define the general scope and plan of the entire song. But remembering that the whole is poetry of the most highly ornamented character, the particular descriptions of persons, scenes, and events must not be supposed to have in every detail a spiritual or mystic significance. The mention of spikenard, myrrh, and cypress flowers (chap. i, 12–14), yields an intensified thought of fragrance, and indicates the mutual attractiveness of the lovers, and their desire and care to please one another; and from this general idea it is not difficult to infer similar relations between the Lord and his chosen ones. But an attempt to find special meanings in the spikenard, and myrrh, and cypress flower, as if each allusion pointed to some distinct feature of the economy of grace, would lead to certain failure in the exegesis. The carping critics who have found fault with the descriptions of the bodies of Solomon and Shulamith, and condemned them as revolting to a chaste imagination, too readily ignore the fact that from the historical standpoint of the ancient writer these were the noblest ideals of the perfect human form, which, according to the psalmist (Psa. cxxxix, 14), is "fearfully and wonderfully made." The highly wrought eulogy of the person of the beloved (chap. v, 10–16) gives a vivid idea of his surpassing beauty and perfection, and, like John's glowing vision of the Son of man in the midst of the seven golden candlesticks (Rev. i, 13–16), may well depict the glorious person of the Lord. But the description must be taken as a whole, and not torn into pieces by an effort to

not sure," he says, " but the absence of the name of God, and of any distinctive religious expressions throughout the song, is thus to be accounted for—that the writer, conscious of the parabolic character of what he is describing, felt that there would be an incongruity in mingling the symbol with the thing symbolized."

[1] Davidson, Introduction to the Old Testament, vol. ii, p. 404.

find some separate attribute or doctrine of the Divine Person in head, hair, eyes, etc. The same principle must be maintained in explaining the description of the charmingly beautiful and perfect form of Shulamith in chap. vii, 2–6. The allegorical interpreters have been guilty of the most extravagant folly in spiritualizing every part of that portraiture of womanly beauty. But, taken as a whole, it may appropriately set forth, in type, the perfection and beauty of " a glorious Church, not having spot, or wrinkle, or any such thing " (Eph. v, 27).

CHAPTER XV.

PROVERBS AND GNOMIC POETRY.

THE Old Testament Book of Proverbs has been appropriately called an Anthology of Hebrew gnomes.[1] Its general form is poetic, and follows the usual methods of Hebrew parallelism. The simpler proverbs are in the form of distichs, and consist of synonymous, antithetic and synthetic parallelisms, as has been explained in a previous part of this work.[2] But there are many involved passages and obscure allusions, and the book contains riddles, enigmas, or dark sayings (מְלִיצָה, חִידָה), as well as proverbs (מָשָׁל). Many a proverb is also a condensed parable; some consist of metaphors, some of similes, and some are extended into allegories. In the interpretation of all scriptural proverbs it is important, therefore, to distinguish between their substance and their form.

Proverbs defined and described.

The Hebrew word for *proverb* (מָשָׁל) is derived from the verb מָשַׁל, which signifies to *liken* or *compare*. The same verb means also to *rule*, or *have dominion*, and some have sought to trace a logical connexion between the two significations; but, more probably, as Gesenius suggests, two distinct and independent radicals have coalesced under this one form. The proverb proper will generally be found, in its ultimate analysis, to be a comparison or similitude. Thus, the saying, which became a proverb (מָשָׁל) in Israel, "Is Saul also among the prophets?" arose from his prophesying after the manner of the prophets with whom he came in contact (1 Sam. x, 10–12). The proverb used by Jesus in the synagogue of Nazareth,

[1] Bruch's Weisheitslehre der Hebräer, p. 104. Strasburg, 1851.
[2] See above, pp. 95–99.

"Physician, heal thyself," is a condensed parable, as, indeed, it is there called (Luke iv, 23), and it would be no difficult task to enlarge it into a parabolic narrative. Herein also we may see how proverbs and parables came to be designated by the same word. The word παροιμία, *adage, byword,* expresses more nearly the later idea commonly associated with the Hebrew מָשָׁל, and stands as its representative in the Septuagint. In the New Testament it is used in the sense of adage, or common byword, in 2 Peter ii, 22, but in John's Gospel it denotes more especially an enigmatical discourse (John x, 6; xvi, 15, 29).[1]

Proverbs proper are therefore to be understood as short, pithy sayings, in which a wise counsel, a moral lesson, or a suggestive experience, is expressed in memorable form. Such sayings are often called *gnomic* because of their pointed and sententious form and force. "The earliest ethical and practical wisdom of most ancient nations," observes Conant, "found expression in short, pithy, and pointed sayings. These embodied, in few words, the suggestions of common experience, or of individual reflection and observation. Acute observers and thinkers, accustomed to generalize the facts of experience, and to reason from first principles, were fond of clothing their results in striking apophthegms, conveying some instruction or witty reflection, some moral or religious truth, a maxim of worldly prudence or policy, or a practical rule of life. These were expressed in terms aptly chosen to awaken attention, or inquiry, and reflection, and in a form that fixed them indelibly in the memory. They thus became elements of the national and popular thought, as inseparable from the mental habits of the people as the power of perception itself."[1]   "Proverbs," says another, "are characteristic of a comparatively early stage in the mental growth of most nations. Men find in the outer world analogies to their own experience, and are helped by them to generalize and formulate what they have observed. A single startling or humorous fact fixes itself in their minds as the type to which all like facts may be referred, as when men used the proverb, 'Is Saul also among the prophets?' The mere result of an induction to which other instances may be referred fixes itself in their minds with the charm of a discovery, as in 'the proverb of the ancients, Wickedness proceedeth from the wicked' (1 Sam. xxiv, 13). . . . Such proverbs are found in the history of all nations, generally in their earlier stages. For the most part there is no record of

Called Gnomic because of pointed sentiment.

---

[1] Comp. above, p. 265.

[2] The Book of Proverbs, with Hebrew text, King James' Version, and Revised Version, etc. For the American Bible Union. Introduction, p. 3. New York, 1872.

their birth. No one knows their author. They find acceptance among men, not as resting upon the authority of a reverend name, but from their inherent truth, or semblance of truth." [1]

The biblical proverbs are not confined to the book which bears **Rules for the** that title. The Book of Ecclesiastes contains many a **interpretation** gnomic sentence. Proverbs appear also in almost every **of proverbs.** part of the Scriptures, and, from the definition and origin of proverbs, as given above, it will be readily seen that much care and discrimination may be often required for their proper exposition. In such exposition the following observations will be found of practical value and importance.

1. As proverbs may consist of simile, metaphor, parable, or alle- **Discrimination** gory, the interpreter should, first of all, determine to **of form and** which of these classes of figures, if to any, the proverb **figure.** properly belongs. We have seen above that Prov. v, 15–18, is an allegory. In Prov. i, 20; viii, 1; ix, 1, wisdom is personified. Eccles. ix, 13–18, is a combination of parable and proverb, the parable serving to illustrate the proverb. Some proverbial similes are of the nature of a conundrum, requiring us to pause and study awhile before we catch the point of comparison. The same is true of some proverbial expressions in which the comparison is not formally stated, but implied. Thus, in Prov. xxvi, 8, "As binding a stone in a sling, so is he that gives honour to a fool." Here is a formal comparison, the point of which is not at first apparent, but it soon dawns on the mind as we reflect that the binding fast of a stone in a sling would of itself be a piece of folly. The next verse is enigmatical: "A thornbush (חוֹחַ) goes up in a drunkard's hand, and a proverb in the mouth of fools." The distich implies a comparison between the thornbush in the drunkard's hand and a proverb in the mouth of fools. But what is the point of comparison? The passage is obscure by reason of the uncertainty attaching to the word חוֹחַ, which may mean *thorn, thornbush,* or *thistle.* The authorized English version reads: "As a thorn goeth up into the hand of a drunkard, so is a parable in the mouth of fools." Stuart renders: "As a thornbush which is elevated [riseth up, Zöckler] in the hand of a drunkard, so is a proverb in the mouth of a fool," and he explains as follows: "As a drunken man, who holds a high thornbush in his hand, will be very apt to injure others or himself, so a fool's words will injure himself or others." [2] But Conant translates and explains the passage thus: "A thorn comes up

---

[1] Prof. Plumptre in the Speaker's Commentary on Proverbs (Am. ed.). Introduction, p. 514.

[2] Commentary on Proverbs, in loco.

into the drunkard's hand, so is a proverb in the mouth of fools. . . .
The drunkard's hand, as he gropes around, blindly grasping at
whatever comes in his way, is pierced by a thorn. So fares the
fool when he awkwardly attempts to apply some sharp saying of
the wise." The enigmatical character of the next verse we have
already noticed (p. 269). It is evident, therefore, from this variety
in the nature and style of proverbs, that the interpreter should be
able to determine the exact character of each proverbial passage
which he essays to explain.

2. Great critical and practical sagacity is also necessary both to
determine the character of a proverb and to apprehend Critical and
its scope and bearing. Many proverbs are literal state- practical sagac-
ments of fact, the results of observation and experience; ity.
as, " A child is known by his doings, whether pure and whether
right his deed" (Prov. xx, 11). Many are simple precepts and
maxims of a virtuous life, or warnings against sin, which any one
can understand, as, "Trust in Jehovah with all thy heart, and upon
thine own understanding do not rely " (Prov. iii, 5). " In the path of
the wicked come thou not, and proceed not in the way of the evil "
(Prov. iv, 14). But there are other proverbs that seem to defy all
critical sharpness and ingenuity, as, "To eat much honey is not
good, and to search out their glory is glory" (Prov. xxv, 27). The
last clause has been a puzzle to all exegetes. Some, as the Authorized Version, carry over the negative particle from the preceding
sentence, and so make the author say the precise opposite of what
he does say. Others reject the *usus loquendi* of the verb חָקַר, to
search out, and, appealing to the corresponding Arabic root, make
the word mean to *despise:* "To despise their glory is glory."
Others take the word כָּבוֹד, *glory*, in its radical sense of *weight:* "To
search into weighty matters is itself a weight; i. e., men soon become satiated with it as with honey " (Plumptre). Zöckler renders:
"To search out the difficult bringeth difficulty; " Stuart: "Searching after one's own glory is burdensome." Others suggest an emendation of the text. Amid such a diversity of possible constructions
the sagacious critic will be slow to venture a positive judgment.
He will consider how many such obscure sayings have arisen from
events now utterly forgotten. Their whole point and force may
have depended originally upon some incident like that of Saul
prophesying, or upon some provincial idiom. So, again, the mysterious word עֲלוּקָה, in Prov. xxx, 15, translated *horseleech* in all the
ancient versions, and *vampire* by many modern exegetes, gives an
uncertainty to every exposition. Possibly here the text is corrupt,
and we may take the word Alukah as a proper name, like Agur in

verse 1, and Lemuel in chap. xxxi, 1. Then we would supply something, as, "Words of Alukah," or, "Words which one spoke to Alukah." It will, at least, be granted that among so many proverbs as have been preserved to us in the Scriptures, several of which were manifestly designed to puzzle, there are probably some which can now be only conjecturally explained.

3. Wherever the context lends any help to the exposition of a Context and proverb great deference is to be paid to it, and it is to parallelism. be noted that in the Book of Proverbs, as in the other Scriptures, the immediate context is, for the most part, a very safe guide to the meaning of each particular passage. So, also, the poetic parallelisms, in which this book is written, help greatly in the exposition. The synonymous and the antithetic parallelisms, especially, are adapted, by way of the analogies and contrasts they furnish, to suggest their own meaning from within themselves. Thus Prov. xi, 25: "The soul of blessing (liberal soul that is a blessing to others) shall become fat (enriched), and he that waters shall also himself be watered." Here the second member of the parallelism is a metaphorical illustration of the somewhat enigmatical sentiment of the first. So, again, in the antithetic parallelism of Prov. xii, 24, each member is metaphorical, and the sense of each is made clearer by the contrast: "The hand of the diligent shall bear rule, but the slothful shall be under tribute."

4. But there are passages in the Book of Proverbs where the context affords no certain or satisfactory help. There are Common sense and sound judg- passages that seem at first self-contradictory, and we ment. are obliged to pause awhile to judge whether the language be literal or figurative. "There is," says Stuart, "scarcely any book which calls upon us so often to apply the golden mean between literality on the one hand and flimsy and diffuse generality on the other."[1] Especially must common sense and sound judgment be appealed to where other helps are not at hand. These are, in all doubtful cases, to be our last resort to guard us against construing all proverbs as universal propositions. Prov. xvi, 7, expresses a great truth: "When Jehovah delights in the ways of a man he makes even his enemies to be at peace with him." But there have been many exceptions to this statement, and many cases to which it could apply only with considerable modification. Such, to some extent, have been all cases of persecution for righteousness' sake. So, too, with verse 13 of the same chapter: "Delight of kings are lips of righteousness, and him that speaks right things he will love." The annals of human history show that this has not

[1] Commentary on Proverbs. Introduction, p. 128.

always be_n. true; and yet the most impious kings understand the value of uprig.'t counsellors. Prov. xxvi, 4 and 5, are contradictory in form and statement, but, for reasons there given, both are at once seen to be true: "Answer not a fool according to his folly, lest thou also be like unto him. Answer a fool according to his folly, lest he become wise in his own eyes." A man's good sense and judgment must decide how to answer in any particular case. Prov. vi, 30, 31, has been supposed to involve an absurdity: "They do not despise a thief when he steals to satisfy his soul when he is hungry; but if found he shall restore sevenfold, the whole substance of his house shall he give." Theft is theft in any case, but if a man is so impoverished as to steal to satisfy hunger, wherewithal, it is asked, can he be made to restore sevenfold? Whence all that substance of his house? The absurdities here alleged arise from a lack of knowledge of Hebrew sentiment and law. To begin with, the passage is proverbial, and must be taken subject to proverbial limitations. Then the context must be kept in view, in which the writer is aiming to show the exceeding wickedness of adultery. No one shall be innocent, he argues, (ver. 29), who touches his neighbor's wife. A man who steals to satisfy the cravings of hunger is not despised, for the palliating circumstances are duly considered; nevertheless. if discovered, even he is subject to the full penalty of the law (comp. Exod. xxii, 1–4). The *sevenfold* is, doubtless, to be taken idiomatically. His entire property shall be given up, if necessary, to make due restitution. All this of a thief under the circumstances named. But an adulterer shall find even a worse judgment—blows, and shame, and reproach that may not be wiped away (verses 32–35). As for the supposed absurdity of compelling a man who has nothing to restore sevenfold, it arises from an absurdly literal interpretation of the proverb. The sense evidently is, that whatever the circumstances of the theft, if the thief be found, he shall certainly be punished as the case may demand. A man might own estates and yet steal to satisfy his hunger; or, if he owned no property, he could be sold (Exod. xxii, 3) for perhaps more than seven times the value of what he had stolen. So, also, in Eccles. x, 2, it is at once evident that the language is not to be taken literally, but metaphorically: "The heart of a wise man is on his right, but the heart of a fool on his left." The exact meaning of the proverb, however, is obscure. *Heart* is probably to be taken for the judgment or understanding, and the sentiment is that a wise man has his understanding always at ready and vigorous command, while the opposite is the case with the fool.

CHAPTER XVI.

INTERPRETATION OF TYPES.

TYPES and symbols constitute a class of figures distinct from all
those which we have treated in the foregoing chapters;
but they are not, properly speaking, figures of speech.
They resemble each other in being sensible representations of moral and religious truth, and may be defined, in general,
as figures of thought in which material objects are made to convey
vivid spiritual conceptions to the mind. Crabb defines types and
symbols as different species of the emblem, and observes: "The
type is that species of emblem by which one object is made to
represent another mystically; it is, therefore, only employed in
religious matters, particularly in relation to the coming, the office,
and the death of our Saviour; in this manner the offering of Isaac
is considered as a type of our Saviour's offering himself as an
atoning sacrifice. The *symbol* is that species of emblem which is
converted into a constituted sign among men; thus the olive and
laurel are the symbols of peace, and have been recognized as such
among barbarous as well as enlightened nations."[1]   The symbols
of Scripture, however, rise far above the conventional signs in
common use among men, and are employed, especially in the apocalyptic portions of the Bible, to set forth those revelations, given
in visions or dreams, which could find no suitable expression in
mere words.

Types and Symbols defined and distinguished.

Types and symbols may, therefore, be said to agree in their general character as emblems, but they differ noticeably in
special method and design. Adam, in his representative character and relation to the human race, was a
type of Christ (Rom. v, 14). The rainbow is a symbol of the covenanted mercy and faithfulness of God (Gen. ix, 13–16; Ezek. i, 28;
Rev. iv, 3; comp. Isa. liv, 8–10), and the bread and wine in the
sacrament of the Lord's Supper are symbols of the body and blood
of Christ. There are also typical events like the passage of the
Red Sea (1 Cor. x, 1–11), and symbolico-typical actions like Ahi-
jah's rending his new garment as a sign of the rupture of the kingdom of Solomon (1 Kings xi, 29–31). In instances like the latter

Examples of types and symbols.

[1] English Synonymes, p. 531. New York, 1859.

certain essential elements of both type and symbol become blended in one and the same example. The Scriptures also furnish us with examples of symbolical metals, names, numbers, and colours.

Certain analogies may be traced between types and symbols, and several figures of speech. Symbols, being always **Analogy be-** based upon some points of resemblance between them- **tween types** selves and the things to be symbolized, correspond **and symbols,** **and certain fig-** somewhat closely with metonymy of the adjunct, or **ures of speech.** metonymy of the sign and the thing signified (comp. above, pp. 249, 250). Then there are analogies between the simile, the parable, and the type, on the one hand, and between the metaphor, the allegory, and the symbol, on the other. Similes, parables, and types have this in common, that a formal comparison is made or assumed between different persons and events, and the language is employed in its literal sense; but in metaphor, allegory, and symbol, the characteristic feature is that one thing is said or seen, and another is intended. If we say "Israel is like a barren fig-tree," the sentence is a simile. In Luke xiii, 6–9, the same image is expanded into a narrative, in the parable of the fruitless fig-tree. But our Lord's miracle of cursing the leafy but fruitless fig-tree (Mark xi, 13, 14) was a symbolico-typical action, foreshadowing the approaching doom of the Jewish nation. If, however, we say "Judah is an olive-tree," we have a metaphor; one thing is said to be another. But in Jer. xi, 16, 17, this metaphor is extended into an allegory, and in Zech. iv, 3, two olive-trees are symbols of Zerubbabel and Joshua," the two anointed ones (Hebrew, sons of oil) who stand by the Lord of all the earth " (ver. 14). At the same time it is to be observed that as the metaphor differs from the simile in being an implied rather than a formal comparison, and as the allegory differs from the parable in a similar way— saying one thing and meaning another—so the symbol differs from the type in being a suggestive *sign* rather than an *image* of that which it is intended to represent. The interpretation of a type requires us to show some formal analogy between two persons, objects, or events; that of a symbol requires us rather to point out the particular qualities, marks, features, or signs by means of which one object, real or ideal, indicates and illustrates another. Melchizedek is a type, not a symbol, of Christ, and Heb. vii furnishes a formal statement of the typical analogies. But the seven golden candlesticks (Rev. i, 12) are a symbol, not a type, of the seven churches of Asia. The comparison, however, is implied, not expressed, and it is left to the interpreter to unfold it, and show the points of resemblance.

Besides these formal distinctions between types and symbols there is the more radical and fundamental difference that while a symbol may represent a thing either past, present, or future, a type Natural distinction between types and symbols. is essentially a prefiguring of something future from itself. In the technical and theological sense a type is a figure or adumbration of that which is to come. It is a person, institution, office, action, or event, by means of which some truth of the Gospel was divinely foreshadowed under the Old Testament dispensations. Whatever was thus prefigured is called the antitype.[1] A symbol, on the other hand, has in itself no essential reference to *time*. It is designed rather to represent some *character, office,* or *quality,* as when a *horn* denotes either strength or a king in whom strength is impersonated (Dan. vii, 24; viii, 21). The origin of symbols has been supposed to be connected with the history of hieroglyphics.[2]

"The word *type,*" observes Muenscher, "is employed not only Essential characteristics of the type. in theology, but in philosophy, medicine, and other sciences and arts. In all these departments of knowledge the radical idea is the same, while its specific meaning varies with the subject to which it is applied. Resemblance of some kind, real or supposed, lies at the foundation in every case. In the science of theology it properly signifies *the preordained representative relation which certain persons, events, and institutions of the Old Testament bear to corresponding persons, events, and institutions in the New.*"[3] Accordingly the type is always something real, not a fictitious or ideal symbol. And, further, it is no ordinary fact or incident of history, but one of exalted dignity and worth—one divinely ordained by the omniscient Ruler to be a foreshadowing of the good things which he purposed in the fulness of time to bring to pass through the mediation of Jesus Christ.[4] Three things are,

[1] It should be observed, however, that this word (ἀντίτυπον), as used in the New Testament (Heb. ix, 24; 1 Peter iii, 21), is not equivalent to the technical sense of *antitype,* or *counterpart,* as now used in theological literature. It has the more general meaning of *image* or *likeness.*

[2] Comp. Warburton, Divine Legation of Moses, book iv, sect. iv.

[3] Types and the Typical Interpretation of Scripture. Article in the American Biblical Repository for January, 1841, p. 97.

[4] In the New Testament the word τύπος, *type,* is applied variously, but always with the fundamental idea of a *figure* or real *form.* In John xx, 25, it is used of the print of the nails in the Saviour's hands—visible marks which identified him as the crucified. In Acts vii, 43, it denotes idolatrous images, and in verse 44, and Heb. viii, 5, the pattern or model after which the tabernacle was made. In Acts xxiii, 25, it denotes the form or style of a letter, and in Rom. vi, 17, a form of doctrine. Comp. ὑποτύπωσις in 2 Tim. i, 13. In Phil. iii, 17; 1 Thess. i, 7; 2 Thess. iii, 9; 1 Tim. iv, 12; Titus ii, 7; 1 Peter v, 3, the word is used in the sense of an *example*

accordingly, essential to make one person or event the type of
another.

1. There must be some notable point of resemblance or analogy
between the two. They may, in many respects, be to- Likeness and
tally dissimilar. In fact it is as essential that there be unlikeness.
points of dissimilarity as that there be some notable analogy, otherwise we should have identity where only a resemblance is designed.
Adam, for instance, is made a type of Christ, but only in his headship of the race, as the first representative of humanity; and in
Rom. v, 14–20, and 1 Cor. xv, 45–49, the apostle notes more points
of unlikeness than of agreement between the two. Moreover, we
always expect to find in the antitype something higher and nobler
than in the type, for "much greater honour than the house has he
who built it" (Heb. iii, 3).

2. There must be evidence that the type was designed and appointed by God to represent the thing typified. This Divinely ap-
proposition is maintained with great unanimity by the pointed.
best writers on scriptural typology. "To constitute one thing the
type of another," says Bishop Marsh, "something more is wanted
than mere resemblance. The former must not only resemble the
latter, but must have been designed to resemble the latter. It
must have been so designed in its original institution. It must
have been designed as something preparatory to the latter. The
type as well as the antitype must have been pre-ordained, and they
must have been pre-ordained as constituent parts of the same general scheme of divine providence."[1] "It is essential to a type,"
says Van Mildert, "in the scriptural adaptation of the term, that
there should be competent evidence of the divine intention in the
correspondence between it and the antitype—a matter not to be
left to the imagination of the expositor to discover, but resting on

or pattern of Christian character and conduct. But the more technical theological
sense of the word appears in Rom. v, 14, where Adam is called a "type of him who
was to come." On this passage Meyer remarks: "The type is always something historical (a person, thing, saying) which is destined, in accordance with the divine plan
to prefigure something corresponding to it in the future—in the connected scheme of
sacred historical teleology, which is to be discerned from the standpoint of the antitype." The word is used in the same sense in 1 Cor. x, 6: "These things (the experiences of the fathers, verses 1–5) became types of us." That is, says Meyer, they
were "historical transactions of the Old Testament, guided and shaped by God, and
designed by him, figuratively, to represent the corresponding relation and experience
on the part of Christians." In verse 11 of the same chapter we have the word τυπι-
κῶς, typically, or, after the manner of type; and it here bears essentially the same
sense as verse 6. "These things came to pass typically with them; and it was
written for our admonition upon whom the ends of the ages are come."

[1] Lectures on Sacred Criticism and Interpretation, p. 371. Lond., 1838.

some solid proof from Scripture itself."[1] But we should guard
against the extreme position of some writers who declare that nothing in the Old Testament is to be regarded as typical but what the
New Testament affirms to be so. We admit a divine purpose in
every real type, but it does not therefore follow that every such
purpose must be formally affirmed in the Scriptures.

3. The type must prefigure something in the future. It must
Foreshadowing serve in the divine economy as a shadow of things to
of the future. come (Col. ii, 17; Heb. x, 1). Hence it is that sacred
typology constitutes a specific form of prophetic revelation. The
Old Testament dispensations were preparatory to the New, and
contained many things in germ which could fully blossom only
in the light of the Gospel of Jesus. So the law was a schoolmaster to bring men to Christ (Gal. iii, 24). Old Testament characters, offices, institutions, and events were prophetic adumbrations
of corresponding realities in the Church and kingdom of Christ.

The principal types of the Old Testament may be distributed into
five different classes, as follows:

1. Typical Persons. It is to be noted, however, that persons are
typical, not as persons, but because of some character or relation
which they sustain in the history of redemption. Adam was a type
Typical Per- of Christ because of his representative character as the
sons. first man, and federal head of the race (Rom. v, 14).
"As through the disobedience of the one man the many were made
sinners, so also through the obedience of the one the many shall be
made righteous." (Rom. v, 19). "The first man Adam became a
living soul; the last Adam a life-giving spirit" (1 Cor. xv, 45).
Enoch may be regarded as a type of Christ, in that, by his saintly
life and translation he brought life and immortality to light to the
antediluvian world. Elijah the Tishbite was made, in the same
way, a type of the ascending Lord, and these two were also types
of God's power and purpose to change his living saints, "in a moment, in the twinkling of an eye, at the last trump" (1 Cor. xv, 52).
In the spirit and power of his prophetic ministry Elijah was also a
type of John the Baptist. Abraham's faith in God's word, and
consequent justification (Gen. xv, 6), while yet in uncircumcision
(Rom. iv, 10), made him a type of all believers who are justified by
faith "apart from works of law" (Rom. iii, 28). His offering of
Isaac, at a later date (Gen. xxii), made him a type of working faith,
showing how "a man is justified by works and not by faith only"
(James ii, 24). Typical relations may also be traced in Melchizedek,
Joseph, Moses, Joshua, David, Solomon, and Zerubbabel.

---

[1] Bampton Lectures for 1814, p. 239.

2. Typical Institutions. The sacrificing of lambs and other animals, the blood of which was appointed to make atone- Typical Institutions. ment for the souls of men (Lev. xvii, 11), was typical of the offering of Christ, who, "as a lamb without blemish and without spot" (1 Pet. i, 19), was "once offered to bear the sins of many" (Heb. ix, 28). The sabbath is a type of the believer's everlasting. rest (Heb. iv, 9). The provision of cities of refuge, into which the manslayer might escape (Num. xxxv, 9-34), was typical of the provisions of the Gospel by which the sinner may be saved from death. The Old Testament passover was typical of the New Testament eucharist, and the feast of tabernacles a foreshadowing of the universal thanksgiving of the Church of the latter day (comp. Zech. xiv, 16). The Old Testament theocracy itself was a type and shadow of the more glorious New Testament kingdom of God.

3. Typical Offices. Every holy prophet of the Old Testament, by being the medium of divine revelation, and a mes- Typical Offices. senger sent forth from God, was a type of Christ. It was in the office of prophet that Moses was a type of Jesus (Deut. xviii, 15). The priests, and especially the high priest, in the performance of their priestly duties, were types of Him who through his own blood entered into the holy place once for all, and thereby obtained eternal redemption (Heb. iv, 14; ix, 12). Christ is also, as king, the antitype of Melchizedek, who was king of righteousness and king of peace (Heb. vii, 2), and of David and Solomon, and of every other of whom Jehovah might say, "I have set my king upon my holy hill of Zion" (Psa. ii, 6). So the Lord Christ unites in himself the offices of prophet, priest, and king, and fulfills the types of former dispensations.

4. Typical Events. Under this head we may name the flood, the exodus from Egypt, the sojourn in the wilderness, the Typical Events. giving of manna, the supply of water from the rock, the lifting up of the brazen serpent, the conquest of Canaan, and the restoration from the Babylonish captivity. It is such events and experiences as these, according to Paul (1 Cor. x, 11), which "came to pass typically with them; and it was written for our admonition upon whom the ends of the ages are come."

5. Typical Actions. These partake so largely of the nature of symbols that we may appropriately designate them as Typical Actions. symbolico-typical, and treat them in a chapter by themselves. So far as they were prophetic of things to come they were types, and belong essentially to what we have defined as typical events; so far as they were signs (ninx, σημεῖα), suggestive of lessons of present or permanent value, they were symbols. The symbol

may be a mere outward visible sign; the type always requires the presence and action of an intelligent agent. So it should be noted that typical characters, institutions, offices, or events are such by bringing in the activity or service of some intelligent agent. The brazen serpent, considered merely as a sign—an object to look to—was rather a symbol than a type; but the personal agency of Moses in lifting up the serpent on a pole, and the looking upon it on the part of the bitten Israelites, places the whole transaction properly in the class of typical events; for as such it was mainly a foreshadowing of things to come. The miracle of the fleece, in Judges vi, 36–40, was not so much a type as a symbolical sign, an extraordinary miraculous token, and our Lord cites the case of Jonah, who was three days and three nights in the whale, not only as a prophetic type of his burial and resurrection, but also as a symbolical "sign" for that "evil and adulterous generation" (Matt. xii, 39). The symbolico-typical actions of the prophets are: Isaiah's walking naked and barefoot for three years (Isa. xx, 2–4); Jeremiah taking and hiding his girdle by the Euphrates (Jer. xiii, 1–11); his going to the potter's house and observing the work wrought there (xviii, 1–6); his breaking the potter's bottle in the valley of Hinnom (xix); his putting a yoke upon his neck for a sign to the nations (xxvii, 1–14; comp. xxviii, 10–17); and his hiding the stones in the brick-kiln (xliii, 8–13); Ezekiel's portraiture upon a brick of the siege of Jerusalem, and his lying upon his side for many days (Ezek. iv); his cutting off his hair and beard, and destroying it in different parcels (v); his removing the baggage, and eating and drinking with trembling (xii, 3–20); his sighing (xxi, 6, 7); and his peculiar action on the death of his wife (xxiv, 15–27); Hosea's marrying "a wife of whoredoms and children of whoredoms" (Hos. i), and his buying an adulteress (iii); and Zechariah's making crowns of silver and gold for the head of Joshua (Zech. vi, 9–15).

The hermeneutical principles to be used in the interpretation of types are essentially the same as those used in the interpretation of parables and allegories. Nevertheless, in view of the peculiar nature and purpose of the scriptural types, we should be careful in the application of the following principles:

Hermeneutical principles to be observed.

1. The real point of resemblance between type and antitype should, first of all, be clearly apprehended, and all far-fetched and recondite analogies should be as carefully avoided. It often requires the exercise of a very sober discrimination to determine the proper application of this rule.

All real correspondences to be noted.

Every real correspondence should be noted. Thus, the lifting up of the brazen serpent, narrated in Num. xxi, 4–9, is one of the most notable types of the Old Testament, and was explained by Jesus himself as a prefiguration of his being lifted up upon the cross (John iii, 14, 15). Three points of analogy are clearly traceable: (1) As the brazen serpent was lifted up upon a pole, so Christ upon the cross. (2) As the serpent of brass was made, by divine order, in the likeness of the fiery serpents, so Christ was made in the likeness of sinful flesh (Rom. viii, 3) a curse for us (Gal. iii, 13). (3) As the offending Israelites, bitten and ready to die, looked unto the serpent of brass and lived, so sinful men, poisoned by the old serpent, the devil, and ready to perish, look by faith to the crucified Christ, and are made alive for evermore. Other incidental analogies involved in one or another of these three may be allowed, but should be used with caution. Thus, Bengel says: "As that serpent was one without venom placed over against venomous serpents, so the man Christ, a man without sin, against the old serpent."[1] This thought may be incidentally included in analogy (2) above. Lange's observation, however, seems too far-fetched and mystical: "The fiery serpents in the wilderness were primarily the form of a divine punishment, presented in a form elsewhere denoting sin. The elevated serpent-standard was thus the type of punishment lifted in the phantom of sin, and transformed into a means of salvation. This is the nature of the cross. The look at the cross is a look at the curse-laden One, who is not a sinner, but a divine token of evil and penalty, and of the suffering of [a substitute for] penalty which is holy, and therefore transformed into deliverance."[2] Such incidental analogies, as long as they adhere consistently to the main points, may be allowed, especially in homiletical discourse. But to find in the brass—a metal inferior to gold or silver—a type of the outward meanness of the Saviour's appearance; or to suppose that it was cast in a mould, not wrought by hand, and thus typified the divine conception of Christ's human nature; or to imagine that it was fashioned in the shape of a cross to depict more exactly the form in which Christ was to suffer— these, and all like suppositions, are far-fetched, misleading, and to be rejected.

In Hebrews vii the priesthood of Christ is illustrated and enhanced by typical analogies in the character and position of Melchizedek. Four points of resemblance are there set forth. (1) Melchizedek was both king and priest; so Christ. (2) His timelessness—being without recorded parentage, genealogy,

The brazen serpent.

Melchizedek and Christ.

[1] Gnomon, on John iii, 14.　　　[2] Commentary on John, in loco.

or death—is a figure of the perpetuity of Christ's priesthood. (3) Melchizedek's superiority over Abraham and over the Levitical priests is made to suggest the exalted dignity of Christ. (4) Melchizedek's priesthood was not, like the Levitical, constituted by formal legal enactment, but was without succession and without tribe or race limitations; so Christ, an independent and universal priest, abides forever, having an unchangeable priesthood. Much more is said in the chapter by way of contrasting Christ with the Levitical priests, and the manifest design of the writer is to set forth in a most impressive way the great dignity and unchangeable perpetuity of the priesthood of the Son of God. But interpreters have gone wild over the mysterious character of Melchizedek, yielding to all manner of speculation, first, in attempting to answer the question "Who was Melchizedek?" and second, in tracing all imaginable analogies. Whedon observes sensibly and aptly: "Our opinion is, that Melchizedek was nobody but himself; himself as simply narrated in Gen. xiv, 18–20; in which narrative both David, in Psa. cx, and our author after him, find every point they specify in making him a king-priest, typical of the king-priesthood of Christ. Yet it is not in the person of Melchizedek alone, but in the grouping, also, of circumstances around and in his person, that the inspired imagination of the psalmist finds the shadowing points. Melchizedek, in Genesis, suddenly appears upon the historic stage, without antecedents or consequents. He is a king-priest not of Judaism, but of Gentilism universally. He appears an unlineal priest, without father, mother, or pedigree. He is preceded and succeeded by an everlasting silence, so as to present neither beginning nor end of life. And he is, as an historic picture, forever there, divinely suspended, the very image of a perpetual king-priest. It is thus not in his actual unknown reality, but in the Scripture *presentation*, that the group of shadowings appears. It is by optical truth only, not by corporeal facts, that he becomes a picture, and with his surroundings a tableau, into which the psalmist first reads the conception of an adumbration of the eternal priesthood of the Messiah; and all our author does is to develop the particulars which are in mass presupposed by the psalmist."

2. The points of difference and of contrast between type and antitype should also be noted by the interpreter. The type from its very nature must be inferior to the antitype, for we cannot expect the shadow to equal the substance. "For," says Fairbairn, "as the typical is divine truth on a lower stage, exhibited by means of outward relations and

Notable differences and contrasts to be observed.

¹ Commentary on New Testament, in loco.

terrestrial interests, so, when making the transition from this to the antitypical, we must expect the truth to appear on a loftier stage, and, if we may so speak, with a more heavenly aspect. What in the one bore immediate respect to the bodily life, must in the other be found to bear immediate respect to the spiritual life. While in the one it is seen and temporal objects that ostensibly present themselves, their proper counterpart in the other is the unseen and eternal —there, the outward, the present, the worldly; here, the inward, the future, the heavenly." [1]

The New Testament writers dilate upon these differences between type and antitype. In Heb. iii, 1–6, Moses, considered Moses and as the faithful apostle and servant of God, is repre- Christ. sented as a type of Christ, and this typical aspect of his character is based upon the remark in Num. xii, 7, that Moses was faithful in all the house of God. This is the great point of analogy, but the writer immediately goes on to say that Jesus is "worthy of more glory than Moses," and instances two points of superiority: (1) Moses was but a part of the house itself in which he served, but Jesus is entitled to far greater glory, inasmuch as he may be regarded as the builder of the house, and much greater honour than the house has he who built or established it. Further (2), Moses was faithful in the house as a minister (ver. 5), but Christ as a son over the house. Still more extensively does this writer enlarge upon the superiority of Christ, the great High Priest, as compared with the Levitical priests after the order of Aaron.

In Rom. v, 14, Adam is declared to be "a type of Him who was to come," and the whole of the celebrated passage, Adam and verses 12–21, is an elaboration of a typical analogy Christ. which has force only as it involves ideas and consequences of the most opposite character. The great thought of the passage is this: As through the trespass of the one man Adam a condemning judgment, involving death, passed upon all men, so through the righteousness of the one man, Jesus Christ, the free gift of saving grace, involving justification unto life, came unto all men. But in verses 15–17 the apostle makes prominent several points of distinction in which the free gift is "not as the trespass." First, it differs *quantitively*. The trespass involved the one irreversible sentence of death to the many, the free gift abounded with manifold provisions of grace to the same many (τοὺς πολλούς). It differs also *numerically* in the matter of trespasses; for the condemnation followed one act of transgression, but the free gift provides for justification from many trespasses. Moreover, the free gift differs

[1] The Typology of Scripture, vol. i, p. 131. Philadelphia, 1867.

qualitatively in its glorious results. By the trespass of Adam "death reigned"—acquired domination over all men, even over those who sinned not after the likeness of the transgression of Adam; but through the one man, Jesus Christ, they who receive the abundance of his saving grace will themselves reign in eternal life.

3. The Old Testament types are susceptible of complete interpre-

Old Testament types apprehended only by the Gospel. tation only by the light of the Gospel. It has too often been hastily assumed that the ancient prophets and holy men were possessed of a full knowledge of the mysteries of Christ, and vividly apprehended the profound signifi-cance of all sacred types and symbols. That they at times had some idea that certain acts and institutions foreshadowed better things to come may be admitted, but according to Heb. ix, 7–12, the meaning of the holiest mysteries of the ancient worship was not manifest while the outward tabernacle was yet standing. And not only did the ancient worshippers fail to understand those mys-teries, but the mysteries themselves—the forms of worship, "the meats, and drinks, and divers washings, ordinances of flesh, imposed until a time of rectification" (διορθώσεως, *straightening up*),[1] were unable to make the worshippers perfect. In short, the entire Mo-saic cultus was, in its nature and purpose, preparatory and peda-gogic (Gal. iii, 25), and any interpreter who assumes that the ancients apprehended clearly what the Gospel reveals in the Old Testament types, will be likely to run into extravagance, and in-volve himself in untenable conclusions.

We may appropriately add the following words of Cave: "Hav-ing apprehended that the divine revelation to the human race had been made at successive times and by successive stages, the doc-trine of types gave utterance to the further apprehension that these revelations were not incongruous and disconnected, but by numer-ous links, subtle in their location, and by concords prearranged, were inseparably interwoven. To the belief that holy men had spoken things beyond the limits of human thought, the doctrine of types superadded or testified to the addition of the belief that these holy men were moved by one Spirit, their utterances having mysterious interconnexions with each other, this explaining that, and that completing this. . . . It is this community of system, this fundamental resemblance under different forms, which the doctrine of types aids us to apprehend. Nor, when once the conception of the historical development of the Scriptures has been seized, is it

---

[1] That is, says Alford, "when all these things would be better arranged, the sub stance put where the shadow was before, the sufficient grace where the insufficient type." Greek Testament on Heb. ix, 10.

any longer difficult to fix the precise significance of the type. Type and antitype convey exactly the same truth, but under forms appropriate to different stages of development." [1]

It remains for us to inquire into the validity of the principle, maintained by many writers, that only those persons and things are to be regarded as typical which are expressly declared to be such in the New Testament. A leading authority for this view is Bishop Marsh, who says: "There is no other rule by which we can distinguish a real from a pretended type, than that of Scripture itself. There is no other possible means by which we can know that a previous design and a preordained connexion existed. Whatever persons or things, therefore, recorded in the Old Testament, were especially declared by Christ, or by his apostles, to have been designed as prefigurations of persons and things relating to the New Testament, such persons and things so recorded in the former are types of the persons or things with which they are compared in the latter. But if we assert that a person or thing was designed to prefigure another person or thing, where no such prefiguration has been declared by divine authority, we make an assertion for which we neither have nor can have the slightest foundation. And even when comparisons are instituted in the New Testament between antecedent and subsequent persons and things, we must be careful to distinguish the examples, where a comparison is instituted merely for the sake of *illustration*, from the examples where such a *connexion* is declared as exists in the relation of a type to its antitype." [2]

This principle, however, is altogether too restrictive for an adequate exposition of the Old Testament types. We should, indeed, look to the Scriptures themselves for general principles and guidance, but not with the expectation that every type, designed to prefigure Gospel truths, must be formally announced as such. We might with equal reason demand that every parable and every prophecy of Scripture must have inspired and authoritative exposition. Such a rigid rule of interpretation could scarcely have been adopted by so many excellent divines except under the pressure of the opposite extreme, which found hidden meanings and typical lessons in almost every fact of Scripture. The persons and events which are expressly declared by the sacred

Limitation of types.

Bishop Marsh's dictum.

Marsh's rule too narrow.

[1] The Scriptural Doctrine of Sacrifice, p. 157. Edinb., 1877.
[2] Lectures on Sacred Criticism and Interpretation, p. 373. This extreme view is, in substance, affirmed by Macknight, Ernesti, Conybeare, Van Mildert, Horne, Nares, Chevalier, Stuart, Stowe, and Muenscher.

writers to be typical are rather to be taken as specimens and examples for the interpretation of all types. For it will hardly be deemed reasonable or satisfactory to affirm that Moses and Jonah were typical characters and deny such character to Samuel and Elisha. The miraculous passage of the Jordan may have as profound a typical significance as that of the Red Sea, and the sweetened waters of the desert as that of the smitten rock in Horeb. Our Lord rebuked the two disciples for having a heart so dull and slow to believe in all things which the prophets spoke (Luke xxiv, 25), clearly implying the duty of seeking to apprehend the sense of all the prophetic Scriptures. A similar reproof is administered to the Hebrews (Heb. v, 10–14) for their incapacity to understand the typical character of Melchizedek, "thus placing it beyond a doubt," says Fairbairn, "that it is both the duty and the privilege of the Church, with that measure of the Spirit's grace which it is the part even of private Christians to possess, to search into the types of ancient Scripture and come to a correct understanding of them. To deny this is plainly to withhold an important privilege from the Church of Christ, to dissuade from it is to encourage the neglect of an incumbent duty." [1]

A better principle.

Such Old Testament persons and events as are cited for typical lessons should always, however, possess some notably exceptional importance. Some have taken Abel, as a keeper of sheep, to be a type of Christ the great Shepherd. But a score of others might as well be instanced, and the analogy is, therefore, too common to be exalted into the dignity of a prefiguring type. So, also, as we have said, every prophet, priest, and king of the Old Testament, considering merely their offices, were types of Christ; but it would be improper to cite every one, of whom we have any recorded history, as a type. Only exceptional characters, such as Moses, Aaron, and David, are to be so used. Each case must be determined on its own merits by the good sense and sound judgment of the interpreter; and his exegetical discernment must be disciplined by a thorough study of such characters as are acknowledged on all hands to be scriptural types.

---

[1] Typology, vol. i, page 29. See this subject more amply discussed by this writer in connexion with the passage above quoted (pp. 26–32) where he ably shows that the writers belonging to the school of Marsh "drop a golden principle for the sake of avoiding a few lawless aberrations." He observes that their system of procedure "sets such narrow limits to our inquiries that we cannot, indeed, wander far into the regions of extravagance. But in the very prescription of these limits it wrongfully withholds from us the key of knowledge, and shuts us up to evils scarcely less to be deprecated than those it seeks to correct."

CHAPTER XVII.

INTERPRETATION OF SYMBOLS.

BIBLICAL SYMBOLISM is, in many respects, one of the most difficult subjects with which the interpreter of divine revelation Difficulties of has to deal. Spiritual truths, prophetic oracles, and the subject. things unseen and eternal, have been represented enigmatically in sacred symbols, and it appears to have been the pleasure of the Great Author of divine revelation that many of the deepest mysteries of providence and grace should be thus enshrined. And, because of its mystic and enigmatic character, this whole subject of symbolism demands of the interpreter a sober and discriminating judgment, a most delicate taste, a thorough collation and comparison of Scripture symbols, and a rational and self-consistent procedure in their explanation.

The proper and logical method of investigating the principles of symbolization is first to collate a sufficient number and Principles of variety of the biblical symbols, especially such as are procedure. accompanied by an authoritative solution. And it is all-important that we do not admit into such a collation any objects which are not veritable symbols, for such a fundamental fallacy would necessarily vitiate our whole subsequent procedure. Having brought together in one field of view a goodly number of unquestionable examples, our next step is to mark carefully the principles and methods exhibited in the exposition of those symbols which are accompanied by a solution. As, in the interpretation of parables, we make the expositions of our Lord a main guide to the understanding of all parables, so from the solution of symbols furnished by the sacred writers we should, as far as possible, learn the principles by which all symbols are to be interpreted.

It is scarcely to be disputed that the cherubim and flaming sword placed at the east of Eden (Gen. iii, 24), the burn- Classification of ing bush at Horeb (Exod. iii, 2), and the pillars of symbols. cloud and fire which went before the Israelites (Exod. xiii, 21) were of symbolical import. In a scientific classification of symbols these are, perhaps, sufficiently exceptional to be placed by themselves, and designated as miraculously signal. Other symbols are appropriately named material, because they consist of material objects, as the blood offered in expiatory sacrifices, the bread and wine of the Eucharist, and the tabernacle and temple with their apartments and furniture. But by far the more numerous symbols are the visional, including all such as were seen in the dreams and visions of the prophets. Under one or the other of these three heads we may bring all the biblical symbols, and any attempt at a more minute classification would, at this stage of our investigation, be unnecessary and inexpedient.[1]

As the visional symbols are the most numerous and common, and many of them have special explanations, we begin with these, and take the simplest and less important first. In Jer. i, 11, the prophet is represented as seeing "a rod of an almond tree," which is at once explained as a symbol of the active vigilance with which Jehovah would attend to the performance of his word. The key to the explanation is found in the Hebrew name of the almond tree, שָׁקֵד, which Gesenius defines as "the waker, so called as being the earliest of all trees to awake from the sleep of winter."[2] In verse 12 the Lord appropriates this word in its verbal form, and says: "For I am watching (שֹׁקֵד) over my word to perform it."

The Almond Rod.

[1] Winthrop, in his Essay on the Characteristics and Laws of Prophetic Symbols (2d ed., New York, 1854, pp. 16–19), adopting substantially the theory of Mr. D. N. Lord (Theological and Literary Journal for April, 1851, p. 668), divides what he regards as the biblical symbols into five classes, as follows: (1) Living conscious agents, as God, the Son of man, the Lamb, angels, men, souls (Rev. vi, 9), beasts, monster animals, and insects; (2) dead bodies, as the slain witnesses in Rev. xi; (3) natural unconscious agents or objects, as the earth, sun, moon, stars, and waters; (4) artificial objects, as candlesticks, sword, cities, books, diadems, and white robes; (5) acts, effects, characteristics, conditions, and relations of agents and objects, as speaking, fighting, and colour. But a large proportion of the agents and objects he enumerates are not symbols. He makes God and Christ, disembodied souls, risen saints, and living men, symbols of themselves! Other objects named, as acts, effects, colours, and relations, are symbolical only as they form part of a composite image, and should be rather designated as symbolical *attributes*, and not erected into independent symbols. E. R. Craven, the American editor of Lange on the Revelation (pp. 145, 146), adopts the first four classes of Lord and Winthrop, and then propounds a further classification based upon the relations of symbols to the ultimate objects symbolized. He finds five orders, which he designates (1) immediate-similar, (2) immediate-ideal, (3) mediate-individual, (4) classical, and (5) aberrant. But he falls into the error of Lord and Winthrop, of making an object symbolize itself. His immediate-similar, and at least some of his immediate-symbols, cannot, for this reason, be accepted as symbols until proven to be such by valid evidence. Such proof we do not find that he has attempted to produce.

[2] Heb. Lex., sub verbo. Pliny (Hist. Nat., xvi, 25) observes that the almond blossoms first of all trees in the month of January, and matures its fruit in March. Nägelsbach (Com. on Jeremiah, in loco) remarks: "What the cock is among domestic animals, the almond is among trees."

A seething pot (סִיר נָפוּחַ, *a pot blown upon*, i. e., by fire) appeared to the prophet with "its face from the face of the north" (Jer. i, 13), that is, its front and opening were turned toward the prophet at Jerusalem, as if a furious fire were pouring its blaze upon its northern side, and was likely to overturn it and drive its boiling hot waters southward "upon all the cities of Judah" (ver. 15). This is explained in the immediate context as the irruption of "all the families of the kingdoms of the north" upon the inhabitants of Judah and Jerusalem. "The swelling waters of a flood are the usual symbol of any overwhelming calamity (Psa. lxix, 1, 2), and especially of a hostile invasion (Isa. viii, 7, 8); but this is a flood of scalding waters whose very touch is death." [1] Here, also, in the inspired exposition of the vision, appears a play upon Hebrew words. Jehovah says, in verse 14, "From the north shall be opened (תִּפָּתַח) the evil upon all the inhabitants of the land." There is a designed assonance between נָפוּחַ in verse 13 and תִּפָּתַח in verse 14.

The symbol of the good and bad figs, in Jer. xxiv, is accompanied by an ample exposition. The prophet saw "two baskets of figs set before the temple of Jehovah" (ver. 1), as if they had been placed there as offerings to the Lord. The good figs were pronounced very good, and the bad figs were very bad, and, for that reason, not fit to be eaten (ver. 3). The good figs represent, according to the Lord's own showing, the better classes of the Jewish people, who were to be taken for a godly discipline to the land of the Chaldæans, and in due time brought back again. The bad figs represent Zedekiah and the miserable remnant that were left with him in the land of Judah, but were soon cut off or driven away.

Very similar is Amos' vision of "a basket of summer fruit" (Amos viii, 1), that is, early-ripe fruit (קַיִץ; comp. 2 Sam. xvi, 1, and Isa. xvi, 9) ready to be gathered. It was a symbol of the end (קֵץ) about to come upon Israel. As in the symbols of the almond rod and the seething pot, there is here also a paronomasia of the Hebrew words for *ripe fruit* and *end, quayts* and *qets*. The people are *ripe* for judgment, and Jehovah will bring the matter to an early *end;* and, as if the end had come, it is written (ver. 3): "And the songs of the temple have wailed in that day, saith the Lord Jehovah. Vast the corpse! In every place he has cast it forth. Hush!"

The resurrection of dry bones, in Ezek. xxxvii, 1–14, is explained of the restoration of Israel to their own land. The vision is not a parable (Jerome), but a composite visional symbol of life from the dead.

[1] R. Payne Smith, in Speaker's Commentary, in loco.

The dry bones are expressly declared to be "the whole house of Israel" (ver. 11), and are represented as saying: "Our bones are dried,
and our hope is perished." These bones were not encased in sepulchres, or buried in the ground, but were seen in great numbers "on the surface of the valley" (ver. 2). So the exiled Israelites were scattered among the nations, and the lands of their exile were their graves. But the prophecy now comes from Jehovah (ver. 12): "Behold, I open your graves and bring you up out of your graves, O my people!" In verse 14 it is added: "I will put my Spirit in you, and ye shall live, and I will cause you to rest on your own ground, and ye shall know that I, Jehovah, have spoken and accomplished, saith Jehovah." To all outward appearances Israel was politically and spiritually ruined, and the promised restoration was, in reality, as life from the dead.

The Resurrection of dry Bones.

In the opening vision of the Apocalypse, John saw the likeness of the Son of man in the midst of seven golden candlesticks, and was told that the candlesticks were symbols of the seven churches of Asia. And there is no question but that the golden candlestick with its seven lamps seen by the prophet Zechariah (chap. iv, 2), and the seven-branched candlestick of the Mosaic tabernacle (Exod. xxv, 31–40), were of like symbolical import. These all denote the Church or people of God considered as the light of the world (comp. Matt. v, 14; Phil. ii, 15; Eph. v, 8).

The golden Candlestick.

In Zechariah's vision (Zech. iv) there appeared two olive trees, one at the right and the other at the left of the golden candlestick, and through two of their branches they poured the golden oil out of themselves. The composite symbol was "a word of Jehovah to Zerubbabel, saying, Not in might and not in power, but in my Spirit, saith Jehovah of hosts" (ver. 6); and the two olive trees denoted "the two anointed ones (Hebrew, sons of oil) who stand by the Lord of all the land" (ver. 14). These two anointed ones are spoken of as if well known, and needing no further designation. The vision had special comfort and encouragement for Zerubbabel. At that time of trouble, when the supremacy of Persia seemed so absolute that Israel might well despair of regaining any of its ancient glory, and might be overawed by an undue estimate of national and military power, the lesson is given that the people of God need not aspire after that sort of prowess. God's people are set to be the light of the world, and their glory is to be seen not in worldly might and pomp, but in the Spirit of Jehovah of hosts. And this Spirit, as contrasted with the might of the world, is to be understood, not solely as the sanctifying grace of God in the heart, but as the divine wisdom and

The two Olive Trees.

power of the Almighty, by which he ever carries to completion the great purposes of his will. The mountains of difficulty which confronted this great leader of God's people should become a plain (ver. 7); his hands had laid the foundation of the house of God (which itself was a symbol of the Church), and he has the assurance that he shall complete it, and in the triumph of his labour even the eyes of Jehovah shall rejoice (ver. 10). "Joshua, the high priest standing before the angel of Jehovah" (chap. iii, 1) has already received special comfort and encouragement from the vision and prophecy of the previous chapter, and these two, Joshua and Zerubbabel, are evidently "the two anointed ones" denoted by the olive trees. These were raised up in the providence of God and prepared and consecrated to be the ministers of his grace to the people in that perilous time.[1] There is no propriety in making these trees represent, as some do, the Church and the State; for, if the candlestick represents the Church, it would be incongruous to make one of the olive trees represent the same thing. For the same reason we must reject the view of Kliefoth and Wright, who make the olive trees denote Jews and Gentiles as jointly aiding and sustaining the light of truth, for this also confounds candlestick and olive trees. There is, further, no warrant for making these trees symbolize the regal and priestly offices or orders, for the Scripture furnishes no valid evidence that those *offices* and *orders* as such were ever designed to be media of communicating the grace and power of God to the Church. The office of priest was established, not as a means of communicating divine grace to the people, but rather to offer the people's gifts and sacrifices for sins to God (Heb. v, 1), and the office of king certainly had no such function as that of these olive trees. Neither was Zerubbabel in any proper sense a king. Individual priests and kings were, indeed, a means of blessing to Israel, but an equal or greater number were a curse rather than a blessing. Joshua and Zerubbabel were the chosen and anointed agents for building the second temple, and they fully meet the requirements of the symbol.[2]

[1] "The two sons of oil," says Keil, "can only be the two media, anointed with oil, through whom the spiritual and gracious gifts of God were conveyed to the Church of the Lord, namely, the existing representatives of the priesthood and the regal government, who were at that time Joshua, the high priest, and the prince Zerubbabel. These stand by the Lord of the whole earth as the divinely appointed instruments through whom the Lord causes his Spirit to flow into his congregation."—Commentary on the Minor Prophets, in loco.

[2] Cowles observes: "I prefer to apply the phrase, *the two anointed ones*, to the two orders, kings and priests, rather than to the two individuals then filling those offices, Zerubbabel and Joshua, because this provision for oil through these conducting tubes

The mention of "the two olive trees and the two candlesticks,
standing before the Lord of the earth," in Rev. xi, 4, is
merely a metaphorical allusion to these symbols in
Zechariah, and serves to enhance the dignity of the two witnesses
whom the writer is describing. But with John they are not symbols, and were not seen as such in his vision. And this fact should
make us distrust all those expositions which make the two witnesses
represent offices and orders in the Church, or two lines of witnesses,
or the Law and the Gospel, or two different Christian bodies, as
the Waldenses and Albigenses. If the olive trees in Zechariah represent individuals, the allusion in Rev. xi, 4 would most properly
designate the two witnesses as individuals also, and the whole description of their work, power, death, resurrection, and ascension to
heaven, most readily harmonizes with this view. The singularity of
their position is also denoted by calling them "the two candlesticks,"
as well as the two olive trees. They were not only God's two
anointed ones, but the two sole light holders which he had remaining in that doomed city "where their Lord was crucified" (ver. 8).

The symbols employed in the Book of Daniel are, happily, so
fully explained that there need be no serious doubt as to the import
of most of them. The great image of Nebuchadnezzar's
dream (chap ii, 31–35) was a symbol of a succession of
world-powers. The head of gold denoted Nebuchadnezzar himself, as the mighty head and representative of the Babylonian monarchy (vers. 37, 38). The other parts of the image,
composed of other metals, symbolized kingdoms that were subsequently to arise. The legs of iron denoted a fourth kingdom of
great strength, "forasmuch as iron breaks in pieces and crushes
every thing" (ver. 40). The feet and toes, part of iron and part of
clay, indicated the mingled strength and weakness of this kingdom
in its later period (vers. 41–43). The stone that smote the image,
and became a great mountain filling the whole land, was a prophetic
symbol of the kingdom of the God of heaven (vers. 44, 45).[1]

The allusion in Rev. xi, 4.

The composite Image of Daniel ii.

---

was not transient, limited to the lifetime of these two men, but permanent—to continue as long as God should give them kings and priests, and, especially, because
permanence was a cardinal idea in the symbol."—Notes on the Minor Prophets, in
loco. Here are several unwarranted and fallacious assumptions. There is nothing
in the symbol that represents enduring permanence; Zerubbabel, though of royal ancestry, was not a king, but, like Nehemiah, of later times, was merely a temporary
governor, and a subject of the Persian Empire. And no king, in any worthy sense
of the name, ever reigned in Israel after the exile.

[1] Nebuchadnezzar's dream of the great tree, in Dan. iv, is so fully and minutely explained there, that we need only make this reference to it, and leave the reader to examine the details for himself.

The four great beasts, in Dan. vii, 1–8, are said to represent four kings that should arise out of the earth (ver. 17). The fourth beast is also defined, in verse 23, as a fourth The four Beasts of Daniel vii. kingdom, from which we infer that a wild beast may symbolize either a king or a kingdom. So in the image, the king Nebuchadnezzar was the head of gold (chap. ii, 38), and also the representative of his kingdom. The ten horns of the fourth beast are ten kings (ver. 24), but from a comparison of Dan. viii, 8, 22, and Rev. xvii, 11, 12, it appears that horns may also symbolize either kings or kingdoms. In any such image of a wild beast with horns, the beast would properly represent the kingdom or world-power, and the horn or horns some particular king or kings in whom the exercise of the power of the kingdom centered itself. So a horn may represent either a king or kingdom, but always with this implied distinction. No explanation is given of the wings and the heads of the beasts, nor of other noticeable features of the vision, but we can hardly doubt that they also had some symbolical import. The vision of the ram and the he-goat, in chap. viii, contains no symbols essentially different, for the ram is explained as the kings of Media and Persia, the goat as the king of Greece, and the great horn as the first king (vers. 20, 21).

Most of the symbols employed by Zechariah are accompanied by a partial explanation, but so vague and general as to Symbols in Zechariah. leave much room for conjecture. The riders on various coloured horses, indefinite in number, are said to be "those whom Jehovah sent forth to walk up and down in the land" (Zech. i, 10), and they are represented as saying to the angel of Jehovah: "We have walked up and down in the land, and behold, all the land is sitting and resting" (ver. 11). Whether they traversed the land together in a body, or separately and successively; and whether their mission was merely one of inspection, or for the purpose of bringing the land to the quiet condition reported, are points left undecided by the language of the sacred writer. Any one of these suppositions is possible; and our opinion on the subject should be formed by a careful study of the historical standpoint of the prophet, and the analogy of other similar visions and symbols.

The four horns (Zech. i, 18, 19 in Eng. Ver., Sept., and Vulg., but chap. ii, 1, 2 in Heb. text), described in the next vis- The four Horns and four Smiths. ion are explained as "the horns which scattered Judah, Israel, and Jerusalem." Horns here, as in the visions of Daniel, doubtless represent kings or kingdoms, but whether these four horns belonged to one beast or more is not stated. Many interpreters understand by the four horns the four kingdoms predicted by Daniel; but against this view is the consideration that these four horns *have wrought* their work of violence (זֵרוּ, *have scattered,* or *did scatter*), but a part of the kingdoms foretold by Daniel were future from the historical standpoint of Zechariah. Others understand four distinct world-powers, as Assyria, Babylon, Egypt, and Persia, while others understand the number four as a symbolical number, having a very general reference to the four points of the compass, and denoting enemies from all quarters. Either of the last two suppositions may be held, but the last named, in the absence of any thing more specific in the language of the prophet, is the safer hypothesis. The four smiths or "carpenters" (vers. 20, 21), which are evidently the providential agencies raised up to awe and cast out the powerful enemies and scatterers of God's people, may denote either human or divine instrumentalities, or an interworking of both.

The flying roll (Zech. v, 1-4) was a symbol of Jehovah's curse *The flying Roll and the Ephah.* upon thieves and false swearers. Its dimensions, twenty cubits by ten, exactly the size of the porch of the temple (1 Kings vi, 3), might naturally intimate that the judgment denoted must begin at the house of the Lord (Ezek. ix, 6; 1 Pet. iv, 17). In immediate connexion with this vision the prophet saw also an ephah going forth (ver. 6), an uplifted talent of lead,[1] and a woman sitting in the midst of the ephah. The woman was declared to be a symbol of "wickedness" (ver. 8). But what sort of wickedness? The ephah and the stone of lead, naturally suggestive of *measure* and *weight*, would indicate the wickedness of unrighteous traffic— the sin denounced by Amos (viii, 5) of "making the ephah small and the shekel great, and falsifying the balances by deceit." This symbol of wickedness is here presented as a woman who had an empty measure for her throne, and a weight of lead for a sign. But her punishment and confusion are brought about by the

---

[1] Very many expositors understand כִּכַּר עֹפֶרֶת to mean a *circle* or *cover of lead;* but, as Wright well observes, "if the ephah had a cover of lead, that cover would scarcely have been termed *the stone of lead,* or leaden stone (ver. 8). The rendering *leaden cover* obscures the real sense of the vision. The Hebrew word rendered *talent* does, indeed, literally mean a *circle,* and the expression *a circle of bread* is used to denote a round loaf (Exod. xxix, 23; 1 Sam. ii, 36). The word is not found in the signification of a *cover,* though that is a possible signification. It is constantly used in the sense of a fixed weight by which gold, silver, and other things were weighed and measured, and is naturally spoken of in such a meaning here in connexion with the ephah, as the latter was the usual measure of capacity. The talent was the standard measure of quantity, and the weight was made of lead as the most common heavy metal, and was used in all commercial transactions for weighing out money."—Bampton Lectures on Zechariah, pp. 111, 112.

instruments of her sin (comp. Matt. vii, 2). She is cast into the ephah, and the leaden weight is cast like a stone upon her mouth. She is not, however, destroyed, but transported to a distant land, and this is effected by two other women, apparently her aiders and abettors in wickedness, who had wings like the wings of a stork, and who were therefore quick and powerful enough to rescue the one woman from immediate doom, and carry her off and establish her in another land. Thus the children of this world are wise toward their own kind (Luke xvi, 8). This distant land is called the land of Shinar (ver. 11), perhaps for the reason that it was the land where wickedness first developed itself after the flood (Gen. xi, 2).

The four chariots, probably war chariots, which this same prophet saw going forth from between the two mountains of brass, and drawn by different coloured horses (Zech. vi, 1–8), are but another and fuller form of presenting the facts symbolized in the vision of the horsemen in chap. i, 8–11. The import of the mountains of brass is undefined. The chariots and horses "are the four winds [1] of the heavens, going forth from standing before the Lord of all the land" (ver. 5). The black horses were said to go forth to the land of the north, the white behind them (perhaps meaning to regions behind or beyond them, אֶל־אַחֲרֵיהֶם), and the speckled (בְּרֻדִּים, spotted) to the land of the south. Whither the red horses went is not stated, unless we suppose (as is very probable) that the word אֲמֻצִּים, strong, in ver. 7, (rendered bay in Eng. Ver.), is a copyist's blunder for אֲדֻמִּים, red. These, it is said, "sought to go forth to walk up and down in the land" (ver. 7), and were permitted to have their way, and it is added that those that went to the land of the north "have caused my spirit to rest (in judgment) in the land of the north."

The four Chariots.

There can be no doubt that these warlike symbols denoted certain agencies of divine judgment. They were, like the winds of the heavens, the messengers and ministers of the divine will (comp. Psa. civ, 4; Jer. xlix, 36), and it is to be noted that the horsemen of chap. i, 8–11, and these chariots, respectively, open and close the series of Zechariah's symbolic visions. No more specific explanation of their meaning than that furnished above is given in the Scripture. Perhaps, in distinguishing the import of the several symbols, we might reasonably suppose that the warlike riders on horses denoted so many military chieftains and conquerors (as for example Shalmaneser, Nebuchadnezzar, Pharaoh Necho, and Cyrus),

[1] The word רוּחוֹת, winds, does not anywhere appear to be used in the plural in the sense of spirits, or personal beings; but these four chariots correspond with the mystic wheels of Ezek. i, 15–21; x, 9–13.

and the more impersonal vision of the chariots and horses as conquering world-powers, and having regard to the military forces of a kingdom rather than any individual conqueror; as when, in Isa. x, 5, Assyria (not Assyrian as Eng. Ver.) is a rod of God's anger.

The foregoing examples of symbols, more or less fully explained, should have great weight with us in determining the general principles of biblical symbolism. We note that the names of all these symbols are to be taken literally. Trees, figs, bones, candlesticks, olive trees, beasts, horns, horses, riders, and chariots, are all simple and natural designations of what the prophets saw. But, while the words are to be understood literally, they are symbols of something else. As, in metonymy, one thing is put for another, or, as in allegory, one thing is said and another is intended, so a symbol always denotes something other than itself. Ezekiel saw a resurrection of dry bones, but it meant the restoration of Israel from the lands of their exile. Daniel saw a great horn upon the head of a he-goat, but it represented the mighty Grecian conqueror, Alexander the Great. But, though one thing is said and another is intended in the use of symbols, there is always traceable a resemblance, more or less detailed, between the symbol and the thing symbolized. In some cases, as that of the almond rod (Jer. i, 11), the analogy is suggested by the name. A candlestick represents the Church or people of God by holding a light where it may shine for all in the house (Matt. v, 15), even as God's people are to occupy a position in the visible Church, and let their light so shine that others may see their good works. The correspondences between the beasts in Daniel and the powers they represented are in some points quite detailed. In view of these several facts, therefore, we accept the following as three fundamental principles of symbolism: (1) The names of symbols are to be understood literally; (2) the symbols always denote something essentially different from themselves; and (3) some resemblance, more or less minute, is traceable between the symbol and the thing symbolized.

The foregoing Examples authorize—

Three fundamental Principles.

The great question with the interpreter of symbols should, therefore, be, What are the probable points of resemblance between this sign and the thing which it is intended to represent? And one would suppose it to be obvious to every thoughtful mind that in answering this question no minute and rigid set of rules, as supposably applicable to all symbols, can be expected. For there is an air of enigma and mystery about all emblems, and the examples adduced above show that while in some the points of resemblance are many and minute, in others they are

No minute set of rules applicable to all symbols.

slight and incidental. In general it may be said that in answering
the above question the interpreter must have strict regard (1) to
the historical standpoint of the writer or prophet, (2) to the scope
and context, and (3) to the analogy and import of similar symbols
and figures elsewhere used. That is, doubtless, the true interpretation of every symbol which most fully satisfies these several conditions, and which attempts to press no point of supposable resemblance beyond what is clearly warranted by fact, reason, and
analogy.

For the interpretation of prophetic symbols Fairbairn enunciates
two very important principles: (1) "The image must *Fairbairn's*
be contemplated in its broader and commoner aspects, *statement of*
as it would naturally present itself to the view of per- *Principles.*
sons generally acquainted with the works and ways of God, not as
connected with any smaller incidents or recondite uses known only
to the few. . . . (2) The other condition with which the use and
interpretation of symbols must be associated is that of a consistent
and uniform manner of applying them; not shifting from the symbolical to the literal without any apparent indication of a change
in the original; or from one aspect of the symbolical to another
essentially different, but adhering to a regular and harmonious
treatment of the objects introduced into the representation. Without such a consistence and regularity in the employment of symbols
there could be no certainty in the interpretations put upon them,
all would become arbitrary and doubtful." [1]

The hermeneutical principles derived from the foregoing examination of the visional symbols of Scripture are equally *Same Princi-*
applicable to the interpretation of material symbols, *ples apply to*
such as the tabernacle, the ark of the covenant, the *bols.*
mercy-seat, the sacrificial offerings and ceremonial washings required by the law, the water of baptism and the bread and wine in
the Lord's supper. For, as far as they set forth any spiritual fact or
thought, their imagery is of essentially the same general character.[2]

---

[1] Fairbairn on Prophecy, pp. 150, 151. The writer goes on to show how current
systems of apocalyptic interpretation violate both of these principles.

[2] Bähr enunciates the following hermeneutical principles and rules for the explanation of symbols: (1) The meaning of a symbol is to be determined first of all by an
accurate knowledge of its nature. (2) The symbols of the Mosaic cultus can have, in
general, only such meaning as accords with the religious ideas and truths of Mosaism,
and with its clearly expressed and acknowledged principles. (3) The import of each
separate symbol is to be sought, in the first place, from its name. (4) Each individual
symbol has, in general, but one signification. (5) However different the connexion in
which it may occur, each individual symbol has always the same fundamental meaning. (6) In every symbol, whether it be object or action, the main idea to be symbol-

The symbolical import of the shedding of blood in sacrificial
worship is shown in Lev. xvii, 11, where it is stated,
as the reason for the prohibition of eating blood, that
"the soul of the flesh is in the blood, and I have given it to you
upon the altar to make expiation for your souls, for the blood makes
expiation in the soul." The exact sense of the last clause is somewhat obscure. The phrase בַּנֶּפֶשׁ, *in the soul*, is rendered in the
common version, after the Septuagint, Vulgate, and Luther, *for
the soul;* but the verb כִּפֶּר is never elsewhere construed with בְּ, referring to that *for which* expiation is made. It is better, therefore, to translate as Keil does: "For the blood, it expiates *by virtue
of* the soul." The preposition בְּ thus denotes the means by which
the atonement is accomplished. "It was not the blood as such,"
says Keil, "but the blood as the vehicle of the soul, which possessed expiatory virtue, because the animal soul was offered to God
upon the altar as a substitute for the human soul."[1] Delitzsch renders: "For the blood, by means of the soul, is an atonement."
That is, as he observes, "the blood atones by the means, or by the
power, of the soul which is in it. The life of the sinner has specially incurred the punitive wrath of Jehovah, but he accepts for it
the substituted life of the sacrificial beast, the blood of which is
shed and brought before him, whereupon he pardons the sinner.
The prohibition of eating the blood is thus doubly established: the
blood has the soul in itself, and it is, in consequence of a gracious
arrangement of God, the means of atonement for the souls of men,
in virtue of the soul contained in it. The one reason lies in the
nature of the blood, and the other in its destination to a holy purpose, which, even apart from the other reason, withdraws it from a
common use: it is that which contains the soul, and God suffers it
to be brought to his altar as an atonement for human souls. It
atones not by indwelling power, which the blood of beasts has not,
except, perchance, as given by God for this purpose—given, namely, with a view to the fulness of the times foreseen from eternity,
when that blood is to flow for humanity which atones, because a
soul united to the eternal Spirit (comp. Heb. ix, 14) has place therein, and because it is exactly of such value that it is able to screen
the whole of humanity."[2]

Nothing pertaining to the Mosaic worship is more evident than

---

ized must be carefully distinguished from that which necessarily serves only for its
appropriate exhibition, and has, therefore, only a secondary purpose. See his Symbolik des mosaischen Cultus, pp. 89–93. Second ed. Heidelberg, 1874.

[1] Commentary on Leviticus xvii, 11.

[2] Biblical Psychology, p. 283. See the whole section on soul and blood, part iv, sec. 11.

the fact that " apart from shedding of blood (αἱματεκχυσία, *pouring out of blood*, Heb. ix, 22) there is no remission." This No Remission without blood-shedding. solemn pouring out of blood was the offering of a living soul, for the warm life blood was conceived as the element in which the soul subsisted, or with which it was in some mysterious way identified (comp. Deut. xii, 23). When poured out at the altar it symbolized the surrender of a life which had been forfeited by sin, and the worshipper who made the sacrifice thereby acknowledged before God his death-deserving guilt. " The rite of expiatory sacrifice," says Fairbairn, " was, in its own nature, a symbolical transaction embodying a threefold idea; first, that the worshipper, having been guilty of sin, had forfeited his life to God; then, that the life so forfeited must be surrendered to divine justice; and, finally, that being surrendered in the way appointed, it was given back to him again by God, or he became re-established as a justified person in the divine favour and fellowship." [1]

The symbolism and typology of the Mosaic tabernacle are recognized in the ninth chapter of the Epistle to the He- Symbolism of the Tabernacle. brews, from which it appears that specific objects, as the candlestick, the showbread, and the ark, had a symbolical meaning, and that the various ordinances of the worship were shadows of good things to come. But the particular import of the various symbols, and of the tabernacle as a whole, is left for the interpreter to gather from the various Scripture passages which bear upon the subject. It must be ascertained, like the import of all other symbols not formally expounded in the Scriptures, from the particular names or designations used, and from such allusions by the sacred writers as will serve either for suggestion or illustration.

The words by which the tabernacle is designated serve as a clue to the great idea embodied in its complex symbolism. Names of the Tabernacle. The principal name is מִשְׁכָּן, *dwelling*, but אֹהֶל, *tent*, usually connected with some distinguishing epithet, is also frequently used, and is applied to the tabernacle in the books of Exodus, Leviticus, and Numbers more than one hundred and fifty times. In Exod. xxiii, 19 ; xxxiv, 26, it is called בֵּית יְהוָה, *house of Jehovah*, and in 1 Sam. i, 9 ; iii, 3, הֵיכַל יְהוָה, *temple of Jehovah*. But a fuller indication of the import of these names is found in the compound

[1] Typology, vol. i, p. 54. On the symbolism and typology of the Old Testament sacrifices, see Kurtz, Der alttestamentliche Opfercultus (Mitau, 1862); English translation, Sacrificial Worship of the Old Testament (Edinb., 1863); Cave, The Scriptural Doctrine of Sacrifice (Edinb., 1877); Keil, Die Opfer des alten Bundes nach ihrer symbolischen und typischen Bedeuting (in Luth. Zeitschrift for 1856 and 1857).

expressions אֹהֶל מוֹעֵד, *tent of meeting*, אֹהֶל הָעֵדוּת, *tent of the testimony*, and מִשְׁכַּן הָעֵדוּת, *dwelling of the testimony*. The testimony is a term applied emphatically to the law of the two tables (Exod. xxv, 16, 21; xxxi, 18), and designated the authoritative declaration of God, upon the basis of which he made a covenant with Israel (Exod. xxxiv, 27; Deut. iv, 13). Hence these tables were called tables of the covenant (Deut. ix, 9) as well as tables of the testimony. As the representatives of God's most holy testimony against sin they occupied the most secret and sacred place of his tabernacle (Exod. xxv, 16). All these designations of the tabernacle serve to indicate its great design as a symbol of Jehovah's meeting and dwelling with his people. One passage which, above all others, elaborates this thought, is Exod. xxix, 42–46: "It shall be a continual burnt offering throughout your generations, at the door of the tent of meeting (אֹהֶל־מוֹעֵד) before Jehovah, where I will meet (אִוָּעֵד) you, to speak unto thee there. And I will meet (נֹעַדְתִּי) there the sons of Israel, and he (i. e., Israel) shall be sanctified in my glory. And I will sanctify the tent of meeting (אֹהֶל־מוֹעֵד) and the altar, and Aaron and his sons will I sanctify to act as priests for me. And I will dwell (שָׁכַנְתִּי) in the midst of the sons of Israel, and I will be God to them, and they shall know that I am Jehovah their God, who brought them out of the land of Egypt, that I might dwell (לְשָׁכְנִי) in their midst—I, Jehovah, their God."

The tabernacle, therefore, is not to be thought of as a symbol of things external and visible,[1] not even of heaven itself considered merely as a *place*, but of the meeting and dwelling together of God and his people both in time and eternity. The ordinances of Tabernacle worship may be expected to denote the way in which symbolizes a Jehovah condescends to meet with man, and enables divine - human man to approach nigh unto him—a meeting and fellow-Relation rather ship by which the true Israel become sanctified in the than a place. divine glory (Exod. xxix, 43). The divine-human relationship realized in the kingdom of heaven is attained in Christ when God comes

---

[1] A full statement of the various opinions of the symbolical import of the tabernacle would require more space than this work allows, and would tend, perhaps, only to confuse. Our purpose is to direct the student to the right method of ascertaining the meaning of the principal symbols, and leave him to pursue the details for himself. For a condensed statement of opinions on the subject, see especially Leyrer, article Stiftshütte, in Herzog's Real-Encyclopädie (Stuttgardt ed., 1855–66). See also Bähr, Symbolik des mosaischen Cultus (Heidelb., 2 vols., 1837–39; revised ed., vol. i, 1874); Bähr, Der salomonische Temple (Karlsr., 1848); Friedrich, Symbolik der mosaischen Stiftshütte (Lpz., 1841); Simpson, Typical Character of the Tabernacle (Edinb., 1852); Keil, Biblischen Archaeologie, pp. 124–129 (Frankf., 1875); Atwater, History and Significance of the Sacred Tabernacle of the Hebrews (New York, 1875).

unto man and makes his abode (μονήν) with him (John xiv, 23), so
that the man dwells in God and God in him (1 John iv, 16). This
is the glorious indwelling contemplated in the prayer of Jesus that
all believers " may be one, as thou, Father, art in me, and I in thee,
that they also may be in us, that the world may believe that thou
didst send me. And the glory which thou hast given me I have
given them, that they may be one, even as we are one, I in
them and thou in me, that they may be perfected into one " (John
xvii, 21–23). Of this blessed relationship the tabernacle is a significant symbol, and being also a shadow of the good things to come,
it was a type of the New Testament Church or kingdom of God,
that spiritual house, built of living stones (1 Pet. ii, 5) which is a
habitation of God in the spirit (Eph. ii, 22).

The two apartments of the מִשְׁכָּן (dwelling, or tabernacle proper),
the holy place and the most holy, would naturally rep-   The two Apart-
resent the twofold relation, the human and the divine.   ments.
The Holy of Holies, being Jehovah's special dwellingplace, would
appropriately contain the symbols of his testimony and relation to
his people; the holy place, with ministering priest, incense altar,
table of showbread and candlestick, expressed the relation of the
true worshippers toward God. The two places, separated only by
the veil, denoted, therefore, on the one hand, what God is in his
condescending grace toward his people, and on the other, what his
redeemed people—the salt of the earth and the light of the world—
are toward him. It was meet that the divine and human should
thus be made distinct.[1]

As the Holy of Holies in the temple was a perfect cube (1 Kings
vi, 20), so was it doubtless in the tabernacle. The·   The Most Holy
length and breadth and height of it being equal, like   place and its
the heavenly Jerusalem (Rev. xxi, 16), its form was a   Symbols.
symbol of perfection. Here was placed the ark, the depository of

---

[1] However near God may come to his creatures, and however close the fellowship to
which he admits them, there still must be something to mark his incomparable greatness and glory. Even in the sanctuary above, where all is stainless purity, the ministering spirits are represented as veiling their faces with their wings before the manifested glory of Godhead; and how much more should sinful men on the earth be alive
to his awful majesty, and feel unworthy to stand amid the splendours of his throne?
If, therefore, he should so far condescend as to pitch among them a tent for his dwelling, we might certainly have expected that it would consist of two apartments—one
which he would reserve for his own peculiar residence, and another to which they
should have free access, who, as his familiars, were to be permitted to dwell with him
in his house. For in this way alone could the two grand ideas of the glorious majesty
of God, which raises him infinitely above his people, and yet of his covenant nearness
to them, be reconciled and imaged together.—Fairbairn, Typology, vol. ii, p. 249.

the two tables of testimony. This testimony was Jehovah's declaration from the thick darkness (עֲרָפֶל) of the mount on which he
descended in smoke and fire, and would remain a monumental witness of his wrath against sin. The ark or chest, made of the most
durable wood, and overlaid within and without with gold, was a
becoming shrine in which to preserve inviolate the sacred tables of
divine testimony. The most holy God is jealous (קַנָּא, comp. Exod.
xx, 5) for the honour of his law. Over the ark, and thus covering
the testimony, was placed the capporeth (כַּפֹּרֶת), or mercyseat
(Exod. xxv, 21; xxvi, 34), to be sprinkled with blood on the great
day of atonement (Lev. xvi, 11–17). This was a most significant
symbol of mercy covering wrath. Made of fine gold, and having
its dimensions the same as the length and breadth of the ark (Exod.
xxv, 17), it fittingly represented that glorious provision of Infinite
Wisdom and Love by which, in virtue of the precious blood of
Christ, and in complete harmony with the righteousness of God,
atonement is made for the guilty but penitent transgressor. The
Septuagint translates כַּפֹּרֶת, capporeth, by ἱλαστήριον, which word
Paul uses in Rom. iii, 25, where he speaks of the "righteousness of
God through faith of Jesus Christ," and "the redemption (ἀπολύ-
τρωσις) which is in Christ Jesus, whom God set forth an expiatory
covering (ἱλαστήριον), through faith in his blood," etc. The divine
provision for the covering of sin is the deepest mystery of the kingdom of grace. "It must be noticed," says Cremer, "that according to Exod. xxv, 22, and Lev. xvi, 2, the Capporeth is the central
seat of the saving presence and gracious revelation of God; so that
it need not surprise that Christ is designated ἱλαστήριον, as he can
be so designated when we consider that he, as high priest and sacrifice at the same time, comes ἐν τῷ ἰδίῳ αἵματι (in his own blood),
and not as the high priest of the Old Testament, ἐν αἵματι ἀλλοτρίῳ
(with blood not his own) which he must discharge himself of by
sprinkling on the Capporeth. The Capporeth was so far the principal part of the Holy of Holies, that the latter is even termed 'the
house of the capporeth' (1 Chron. xxviii, 11)."[1]

The two cherubim, placed at the ends of the mercyseat, and
spreading their wings over it, were objects too prominent to be without significance. In Eden the cherubim
appear with the flaming sword to watch (שְׁמֹר) the way of the tree
of life (Gen. iii, 24). In Ezek. i, 5–14 they appear as "living creatures" (חַיּוֹת), their composite form is described, and they are represented as moving the mystic wheels of divine providence and
judgment (vers. 15–21). Over their heads was enthroned "the

The Cherubim.

---

[1] Biblico-Theological Lexicon, p. 306.

appearance of the likeness of the glory of Jehovah" (vers. 26–28).
In Rev. iv, 6–8 they appear also as living creatures (ζῷα) "in the
midst of the throne, and round about the throne." Whatever the
various import of these figures, we note that they everywhere appear in most intimate relation to the glory of God. May we not
believe that they were symbols of the ultimate glory of redeemed
humanity, conveying at the same time profound suggestions of the
immanent presence and intense activity of God in all creature life,
by which (presence and activity) all that was lost in Eden shall be
restored to heavenly places in Christ, and man, redeemed and filled
with the Spirit, shall again have power over the tree of life, which is
in the midst of the paradise of God (comp. Rev. ii, 7 and xxii, 14)?
Though of composite form, and representing the highest kinds of
creature life on earth (Ezek. i, 10; Rev. iv, 7), these ideal beings
had preeminently the likeness of a man (Exek. i, 5). Jehovah is
the God of the living, and has about the throne of his glory the
highest symbols of life. Both at the gate of paradise and in the
Holy of Holies these cherubim were signs and pledges that in the
ages to come, having made peace through the blood of the cross,
God would reconcile all things unto himself, whether things upon
the earth or things in the heavens (Col. i, 20), and sanctify them in
his glory (Exod. xxix, 43).[1] Then the redeemed "shall reign in
life" (ἐν ζωῇ βασιλεύσουσιν) through Jesus Christ (Rom. v, 17.)

The pot of manna, Aaron's rod that blossomed, and the book of
the law, were subsequently deposited by the ark (Exod. xvi, 33, 34;
Num. xvii, 10; Deut. xxxi, 26). These were evidently regarded as
so many additional testimonies of God, similar in character to the

---

[1] "The cherubim," says Fairbairn, "were in their very nature and design artificial
forms of being—uniting in their composite structure the distinctive features of the
highest kinds of creaturely existence on earth—man's first and chiefly. They were
set up for representations to the eye of faith of earth's living creaturehood, and more
especially of its rational and immortal, though fallen head, with reference to the better
hopes and destiny in prospect. From the very first they gave promise of a restored
condition to the fallen, and by the use afterward made of them the light became
clearer and more distinct. By their designations, the positions assigned them, the actions from time to time ascribed to them, as well as their own peculiar structure, it
was intimated that the good in prospect should be secured, not at the expense of, but
in perfect consistence with, the claims of God's righteousness—that restoration to the
holiness must precede restoration to the blessedness of life; and that only by being
made capable of dwelling beside the presence of the only Wise and Good could man
hope to have his portion of felicity recovered. But all this, they further betokened,
it was in God's purpose to have accomplished; and so to do it, as, at the same time,
to raise humanity to a higher than its original destination—in its standing nearer to
God, and greatly ennobled in its powers of life and capacities of working."—Typology,
vol. i, pp. 202, 203. Comp. also vol. ii, p. 271.

two tables placed within the ark, and they were accordingly enshrined in immediate contiguity with them.

As the Holy of Holies symbolized Jehovah's relations to his people, and intimated what he is to them and what he purposes to do for them; and as its symbols of mercy covering wrath showed how and on what terms he condescends to meet and dwell with men; so, The Holy Place on the other hand, the holy place, with its golden altar and its symbols. of incense, table of showbread, golden candlestick, and ministering priests, represented the relations of the true Israel toward God. The priests who officiated in this holy place acted not for themselves alone; they were the representatives of all Israel, and their service was the service of all the tribes, whose peculiar relation to God, so long as they obeyed his voice and kept his covenant, was that of "a kingdom of priests and a holy nation" (Exod. xix, 5, 6; comp. 1 Pet. ii, 5, 9; Rev. i, 6; v, 10). As the officiating priest stood in the holy place, facing the Holy of Holies, The Table of he had on his right the table of showbread, on his left Showbread. the candlestick, and immediately before him the altar of incense (Exod. xl, 22–27). The twelve cakes of showbread kept continually on the table symbolized the twelve tribes of Israel continually presented as a living sacrifice before God (Lev. xxiv, 5–9). "The laying out of these loaves," says Keil, "assumed the form of a bloodless sacrifice, in which the congregation brought the fruit of its life and labour before the face of the Lord, and presented itself to its God as a nation diligent in sanctification to good works. If the showbread was a *minchah*, or meat offering, and even a most holy one, which only the priests were allowed to eat in the holy place, it must naturally have been unleavened, as the unanimous testimony of Jewish tradition affirms it to have been."[1]

The golden candlestick, with its seven lamps, placed opposite the The golden table, was another symbol of Israel considered as the Candlestick. Church of the living God. As the showbread represented the relation of Israel to God as a holy and acceptable offering, the candlestick represented what this same Israel would do for God as causing the light of the Spirit in them to shine forth. To all thus exalted may it well be said: "Ye were once darkness, but now light in the Lord; walk as children of light (for the fruit of the light is in all goodness, and righteousness, and truth), proving what is well pleasing unto the Lord" (Eph. v, 8–10).

But the highest continual devotion of Israel to God is represented at the golden altar of incense, which stood immediately before the

---

[1] Biblical Commentary on Lev. xxiv, 6. Comp. Paul's language in 1 Cor. v, 7, and pp. 315, 316 above.

veil and in front of the mercyseat (Exod. xxx, 6). The offering
of incense was an expressive symbol of the prayers of The Altar of In-
the saints (Psa. cxli, 2; Rev. v, 8; viii, 3, 4), and the cense.
whole multitude of the people were wont to pray without at the
hour of the incense-offering (Luke i, 10). Jehovah was pleased to
"inhabit the praises of Israel" (Psa. xxii, 3), for all that his people
may be and do in their consecrated relation to him expresses itself
in their prayers before his altar and mercyseat.   "But it ought
ever to be considered," says Fairbairn, "what kind of devotions it
is that rise with such acceptance to the sanctuary above. That the
altar of incense stood before the Lord, under his immediate eye,
intimates that the adorations and prayers he regards must be no
formal service in which the lip rather than the heart is employed;
but a felt approach to the presence of the living God, and a real
transaction between the soul and him. That this altar, from its
very position, stood in a close relation to the mercyseat or propitia-
tory, on the one hand, and by its character and the live coals that
ever burned in its golden vials, stood in an equally close relation to
the altar of burnt offering, on the other, tells us, that all acceptable
prayer must have its foundation in the manifested grace of a redeeming God, and draw its breath of life, in a manner, from that
work of propitiation, which he has in his own person accomplished
for the sinful.   And since it was ordained that a 'perpetual incense
before the Lord' should be ever ascending from the altar—since
injunctions so strict were given for having the earthly sanctuary
made peculiarly and constantly to bear the character of a house of
prayer, most culpably deaf must we be to the voice of instruction
that issues from it if we do not hear enforced, on all who belong to
the spiritual temple of an elect church, such a lesson as this—Pray
without ceasing; the spirit of devotion is the very element of your
being; your beginning and ending are alike here; all, from first to
last, must be sanctified by prayer; and, if this be neglected, neither
can you fitly be named a house of God, nor have you any ground
to expect the blessing of heaven on your means of grace and works
of welldoing." [1]

We need not linger in detail upon the symbolism of the court of
the tabernacle, with its altar of burnt offerings and its Great Altar and
laver of brass. There could be no approach to God, on Laver in the
the part of sinful men, no possible meeting or dwelling court.
with him, except by the offerings made at the great altar in front
of the sacred tent. All that belongs to the symbolism of sacrificial
blood centred in this altar, where the daily offerings of Israel were

[1] Typology, vol. ii, pp. 287, 288.

made. No priest might pass into the tabernacle until sprinkled with blood from that altar (Exod. xxix, 21), and the live coals used for the burning of incense before Jehovah were taken from the same place (Lev. xvi, 12). Nor might the priest, on penalty of death, minister at the altar or enter the tabernacle without first washing at the laver (Exod. xxx, 20, 21). So the great altar continually proclaimed that without the shedding of blood there is no remission, and the priestly ablutions denoted that without the washing of regeneration no man might enter the kingdom of God (comp. Psa. xxiv, 3, 4; John iii, 5; Heb. x, 19–22). All those blessed relations, which were symbolized in the holy place, are possible only because of the reconciliation effected at the altar of sacrifice without. Having there obtained remission of sins, the true Israel, as represented in the priests, draw near before God in forms of holy consecration and service.

The profound symbolism of the tabernacle is further seen in connexion with the offerings of the great day of atonement. Once a year the high priest entered the Holy of Holies to make atonement for himself and Israel, but in connexion with his work on that day all parts of the tabernacle are brought into notice. Having washed his flesh in water, and put on the hallowed linen garments, he first offered the burnt offering on the great altar to make atonement for himself and his house (Lev. xvi, 2–6). Then taking a censer of live coals from the altar he offered incense upon the fire before the Lord, so that the cloud covered the mercyseat, and, taking the blood of a bullock and a goat, he passed within the veil and sprinkled the mercyseat seven times with the blood of each (Lev. xvi, 12–16). All this, we are told in the Epistle to the Hebrews, prefigured the work of Christ for us: "Christ having come a high priest of the good things to come, through the greater and more perfect tabernacle not made with hands, that is, not of this creation [not material, tangible, or local], nor through the blood of goats and calves, but through his own blood entered in once for all into the holy places (τὰ ἅγια, plural, and indefinitely intimating more than places merely), having obtained eternal redemption. . . . For Christ entered not into holy (places) made with hands, patterns of the true, but into the heaven itself, now to appear in the presence of God for us" (Heb. ix, 11, 12, 24). The believer is, ac-

Symbolico-typical suggestions of the High Priest's action on the day of Atonement.

---

[1] "The holy place," says Kurtz, "represented that stage in the history of salvation in which the great fact of vicarious suffering for the sins of the world lies in the past, and all that is needed is the personal appropriation of the atoning virtue of the blood which has been shed."—Sacrificial Worship of the Old Testament, p. 315. Edinb., 1863.

cordingly, exhorted to enter with confidence into the holy places by the blood of Jesus, and to draw near with a true heart in full assurance of faith (Heb. x, 19, 22). Whither our high priest has gone we may also go, and the position of the cherubim over the mercyseat and in the garden of Eden suggests the final glorification of all the sons of God. This is the profound and suggestive teaching of Paul in Eph. i, 15; ii, 10, where he speaks of "the riches of the glory of his inheritance in the saints," and "that energy of the strength of his might which he wrought in Christ, when he raised him from the dead and made him sit at his right hand in the heavenly" (ἐν τοῖς ἐπουρανίοις, not heavenly places merely, but heavenly associations, fellowships, powers, glories), and then goes on to say that God, in like manner, quickens those who were dead in trespasses and sins, makes them alive with Christ, raises them up and makes them sit together "in the heavenly—in Christ Jesus" (ἐν τοῖς ἐπουρανίοις, i. e., in the same heavenly regions, associations, and glories into which Christ himself has gone). Thus we see the fullest revelation of the means by which, and the extent to which, Israel shall be sanctified in Jehovah's glory (Exod. xxix, 43).[1] Then, in the highest and holiest sense, will "the tabernacle of God be with men, and he will tabernacle with them, and they shall be his people, and God himself shall be with them" (Rev. xxi, 3). In the heavenly glory there will be no place for temple, or any local shrine and symbol, "for the Lord, the God, the Almighty, is its temple, and the Lamb" (Rev. xxi, 22).

The graduated sanctity of the several parts of the tabernacle is very noticeable. In front was the court, into which any Israelite who was ceremonially clean might enter; next was the holy place, into which none but the consecrated priests might go to perform the work of their office, and,

The graduated sanctity of the holy places.

---

[1] The profound expression, in Exod. xxix, 43, may well be compared with that of Jesus, in John xvii, 24, which, according to the best-authenticated text, reads: "Father, that which thou hast given me (ὃ δέδωκάς μοι), I will that where I am they also (κἀκεῖνοι) may be with me, that they may behold my glory which thou hast given me, for thou didst love me before the foundation of the world." The pleonastic construction here seems to have a designed significance. The whole body of the redeemed is first conceived as a unit; it is Christ's inheritance, regarded as the Father's gift to him. It is the same as the πᾶν ὃ δέδωκέν μοι, all that which he has given me, in John vi, 39. But as the thought turns to the individual beholding (comp. "I shall see for myself," etc., Job xix, 27) on the part of the redeemed the plural (κἀκεῖνοι) is resumed. Thus Alford: "The neuter has a peculiar solemnity, uniting the whole Church together as one gift of the Father to the Son. Then the κἀκεῖνοι resolves it into the great multitude whom no man can number, and comes home to the heart of every individual believer with inexpressibly sweet assurance of an eternity with Christ."—Greek Test., in loco.

especially, to offer incense. Beyond this, veiled in thick darkness, was the Holy of Holies, into which only the high priest entered, and he but once a year. This graduated sanctity of the holy places was fitted to inculcate and impress the lesson of the absolute holiness of God, whose special presence was manifested in the innermost sanctuary. The several apartments were also adapted to show the gradual and progressive stages of divine revelation. The outer court suggests the early patriarchal period, when, under the open sky, the devout fathers of families and nations, like Noah, Melchizedek, and Abraham, worshipped the God of heaven.[1] The holy place represents the period of Mosaism, that intermediate stage of revelation and law, when many a type and symbol foreshadowed the better things to come, and the exceptional entrance of the high priest once a year within the veil signified that "the way of the holies was not yet made manifest" (Heb. ix, 8). The Holy of Holies represents the Messianic æon, when the Christian believer, having boldness to enter into the holiest by the blood of Jesus (Heb. x, 19), is conceived to "have come to Mount Zion, and to the city of the living God, the heavenly Jerusalem, and to myriads of angels, to the whole assembly and Church of the firstborn who are enrolled in heaven, and to God, the judge of all, and to spirits of just men made perfect, and to Jesus, mediator of the new covenant, and to the blood of sprinkling that speaks better than that of Abel" (Heb. xii, 22–24).

The symbolism of the tabernacle furnishes much of the imagery used in the records of subsequent revelations, and is, therefore, worthy of the most careful study.[2] But in this, as in other forms of expressing divine thoughts in figure, we should avoid attempting to find meanings in every minute object and allusion. Our best security is to keep closely to the analogy of biblical symbols and imagery as seen in a full collation of pertinent examples.[3]

[1] For a somewhat different conception of the import of the holy places, as representing periods of revelation, see Atwater, Sacred Tabernacle of the Hebrews, pp. 269–271.

[2] Such passages as Psa. xxvii, 5 ; xxxi, 20 ; xci, 1, are best explained by understanding an allusion to the Holy of Holies. The symbolico-typical portraiture of the Messianic kingdom, in the closing chapters of Ezekiel and John, is largely based upon the symbolism of the tabernacle. See further on pp. 491, 492.

[3] Valuable hints for the study of biblical symbolism may be found in works on general symbology, such as Nork's Etymologisch-symbolisch-mythologisches Worterbuch (four vols., Stuttgart, 1843–1845), and Wemyss, Clavis Symbolica (Edinb. Bib. Cabinet, 1835). See also Mills, Sacred Symbology (Edinb., 1853), Dudley, Naology, etc. (London, 1846), Thompson, Symbols of Christendom (London, 1867).

CHAPTER XVIII.

SYMBOLICO-TYPICAL ACTIONS.

In receiving his divine commission as a prophet, Ezekiel saw a roll of a book spread out before him, on both sides of which were written many doleful things. He was *Visional actions.* commanded to eat the book, and he obeyed, and found that which seemed so full of lamentation and woe to be sweet as honey in his mouth (Ezek. ii, 8–iii, 3). The same thing is, in substance, repeated in the Apocalypse of John (x, 2, 8–11), and it is there expressly added that the book which was sweet as honey in his mouth became bitter in his stomach. These transactions manifestly took place in vision. The prophet was lifted into a divine trance or ecstacy, in which it seemed to him that he saw, heard, obeyed, and experienced the effects which he describes. It was a symbolical transaction, performed subjectively in a state of prophetic ecstacy. It was an impressive method of fastening upon his soul the conviction of his prophetic mission, and its import was not difficult to apprehend. The book contained the bitter judgments to be uttered against "the house of Israel," and the prophet was commanded to cause his stomach to eat it and to fill his bowels with it (iii, 3); that is, he must make the prophetic word, as it were, a part of himself, receive it into his innermost being (ver. 10), and there digest it. And though it may be often bitter to his inner sense, the process of prophetic obedience yields a sweet experience to the doer.[1] "It is infinitely sweet and lovely," says Hengstenberg, "to be the organ and spokesman of the Most High."[2]

But in the fourth and fifth chapters of Ezekiel we are introduced to a series of four symbolico-typical actions in which *Symbolico-typical acts of Ezek. iv and v.* the prophet appears not as the *seer*, but the *doer*. First he is commanded to take a brick[3] and engrave upon it a portraiture of Jerusalem in a state of siege. He is also to set

---

[1] What Ezekiel and John did in vision Jeremiah describes in other and more simple style. Comp. Jer. xv, 16.

[2] Commentary on Ezekiel, in loco.

[3] לבנה, *a white brick*, so called, according to Gesenius, from the white chalky clay of which certain bricks were made. In the valley of the Euphrates Ezekiel's eyes had, doubtless, become familiar with bricks and stone slabs covered with images and inscriptions.

up an iron pan between it and himself, and direct his face against it, as if he were the besieging party, and had erected an iron wall between himself and the doomed city. This, it was declared, would be "a sign to the house of Israel" (Ezek. iv, 1-3). Evidently, therefore, the sign was intended to be outward, actual, and visible, for how could these things, if imagined only in the prophet's soul, be made a sign to Israel? In the next place he is to lie upon his left side three hundred and ninety days, and then upon his right side forty days, thus symbolically bearing the guilt of Israel and Judah four hundred and thirty days, each day of his prostration denoting a year of Israel's abject condition. During this time he must keep his face turned toward the siege of Jerusalem, and his arm made bare (comp. Isa. lii, 10), and God lays bands upon him that he shall not turn from one side to another (Ezek. iv, 4-8). As the days of this prostration are symbolical of years, so it would seem the number four hundred and thirty is appropriated from the term of Israel's sojourn in Egypt (Exod. xii, 40), the last forty years of which, when Moses was in exile, were the most oppressive of all. This number would, from its dark associations, become naturally symbolical of a period of humiliation and exile; not, however, necessarily denoting a chronological period of just so many years. Still further, the prophet is directed to prepare for himself The prophet's food of divers grains and vegetables, some desirable food. and some undesirable, and put them in one vessel, as if it were necessary to use any and all kinds of available food, and one vessel would suffice for all. His food and drink are to be weighed out and measured, and in such small rations as to denote the most pinching destitution. He is also commanded to bake his barley cakes with human excrement, to denote how Israel would eat their defiled bread among the heathen; but in view of his loathing at the thought of food thus prepared, he is permitted to substitute the excrement of cattle for that of man. All this was designed to symbolize the misery and anguish which should come upon Israel (verses 9-17). A fourth sign follows in chapter v, 1-4, and is accompanied (verses 5-17) by a divine interpretation. The prophet is directed to shave off his hair and beard with a sharp sword, and weigh and divide the numberless hairs in three parts. One third he is to burn in the midst of the city (i. e., the city portrayed on the brick), another third he is to smite with the sword, and another he is to scatter to the wind. These three acts are explained as prophetic symbols of a threefold judgment impending over Jerusalem, one part of whose inhabitants shall perish by pestilence and famine, another by the slaughter of war, and a third by dispersion among the nations, whither also the perils of the sword shall follow them.

Many able expositors insist that these symbolical actions of the prophet took place only in vision, as the eating of the The actions outward and actual. roll in chapter ii, 8. And yet they are all obliged to acknowledge that the language used is such as to make a different impression on the mind of a reader. Certain it is that the eating of the roll is described as a vision: "I saw, and behold a hand stretched out unto me, and behold in it a roll of a book" (Ezek. ii, 9). No such language is used in connexion with the transactions of chapters iv and v, but the prophet is the *doer*, and his actions are to serve as a *sign* to the house of Israel.

Five reasons have been urged to show that these actions could not have been outward and actual: (1) The spectacle of Five objections considered. such a miniature siege would only have provoked among the Israelites who saw it a sense of the ludicrous. But even if this were true, it would by no means disprove that the acts were, nevertheless, actually done, for many of the noblest oracles of prophecy were ridiculed and scoffed at by the rebellious house of Israel. The assertion, however, is purely a subjective fancy of modern interpreters. It is like the untenable notion of those allegorical expounders of Canticles, who presume to say that a literal interpretation of some parts of the song is monstrous and revolting, but, at the same time, allegorically descriptive of the holiest things! If these symbolic actions of Ezekiel, literally performed, would have been childish and ludicrous, would not any conceivable communication of them to Israel as a sign have been equally ludicrous? As long as the actions were possible and practicable, and were calculated to make a notable impression, there is no objection to their literal occurrence which may not be urged with equal force against their ideal occurrence.

But it is urged (2) that lying motionless on one side for three hundred and ninety days was a physical impossibility. The prostration not without intermissions. The prophet's language, however, sufficiently intimates that his prostration was not absolutely continuous during the whole twenty-four hours of each of the days. He prepared his own food and drink, weighed and measured it, and, we may suppose, that as a Jewish fast of many days allowed eating at night while requiring abstinence by day, so Ezekiel's long prostration had many incidental reliefs. The prohibition of turning from one side to another required, at most, only that during the longer period he must not lie at all on his right side, and during the last forty days he must not lie at all on his left. (3) Fairbairn declares that it would have been a moral impossibility to eat bread composed of such abominable materials, since it would have involved a violation of the Mosaic law.[1] But it cannot be shown that the law anywhere prohibits the materials which Ezekiel was ordered to prepare for his food; and, even if it did, it would not follow that Ezekiel might not thus symbolically exhibit the penal judgments that were to visit Israel, when fathers should even eat their own sons, and sons their fathers (chap. v, 10).

Another objection (4) is that between the dates given at Ezek. i, 1, 2, and viii, 1, there could not have been four hun- *The Dates no valid objection.* dred and thirty days for these symbolical actions to really take place. But between the fifth day of the fourth month of the fifth year of Jehoiachin's captivity (chap. i, 1, 2) and the fifth day of the sixth month of the sixth year (chap. viii, 1) there intervened one year and two months, or four hundred and twenty-seven days, a period not only sufficiently approximate to meet all the necessity of the case, but so closely approximate as to be in itself an evidence of the real performance of these actions. And all this might be said after subtracting from the period the seven days mentioned in chapter iii, 15. But the visions of chapters viii, xi may have taken place while Ezekiel yet remained lying on his side. We are not to suppose that his body was literally transported to Jerusalem, for he expressly states that it was done "in visions of God" (chap. viii, 3). His *sitting* in his house, with the elders of Judah before him (viii, 1), does not necessarily define either his or their posture, and the word יָשַׁב is commonly used in the sense of *abiding* or *staying.* The long prostration and symbolical acts of this priest-prophet would naturally attract the elders of Judah to his house, and cause them to linger long in his presence; and all this time his arm was made bare, and he prophesied against Jerusalem (iv, 7). There was nothing in his posture or surroundings to hinder his receiving, during that signal year and two months, many an additional word and vision of Jehovah. (5) It has been further objected that it was literally impossible for him to burn the third part of his hair "in the midst of the city" (chap. v, 2). But the city here referred to is to be understood of the miniature city engraved on the brick, which consideration at once obviates the objection.

---

[1] Commentary on Ezekiel, p. 48. Fairbairn's references to Deut. xiv, 3; xxiii, 12–14, and xiii, 1–5, are pointless in this argument, for those passages have no necessary bearing on this subject, inasmuch as Ezekiel was excused from using human ordure. Nor was a mixture of various kinds of food a transgression, as Hitzig imagines, of the law of Lev. xix, 19; Deut. xxii, 9.

There appears, therefore, no sufficient reason to deny that Ezekiel's symbolic actions, described in chapters iv and v, were outwardly performed. Nor is it difficult to conceive the impression which these performances must naturally have made upon the house of Israel—especially upon the elders. After his first overwhelming vision (see chap. i, 28), and the hearing of his divine commission, he went to certain captives who dwelt along the Chebar, and sat down among them in mute astonishment (מַשְׁמִים) for seven days (chap. iii, 15). Then Jehovah's word came to him again, and he went forth into the plain, and there again beheld the glory of the cherubim (ver. 23), and received the command to go and shut himself up within his house, and perform the symbolical actions which we have examined. And no more impressive or signal prophecies could have been given than these symbolic deeds. Not to have done the things commanded would have been to withhold from the house of Israel the signs of judgment which he was commissioned to exhibit. The fourfold symbol denoted, (1) the coming siege of Jerusalem, (2) the exile and consequent prostration of Israel and Judah (comp. Isa. l, 11; Amos v, 2), which should be like another Egyptian bondage, (3) the destitution and humiliation of this sad period, and, (4) finally, the threefold judgment with which the siege should end, namely, pestilence and famine, the sword, and dispersion among the nations.

No valid argument against their outward performance.

Other symbolical actions of this prophet are his removal of his baggage through the broken wall (chap. xii, 3–8), and his eating his bread with quaking, and drinking water with trembling and anxiety (xii, 18), his deep and bitter sighing (xxi, 6; Heb. xxi, 11), and his strange deportment on the death of his wife (xxiv, 16–18). But the symbol of the boiling caldron in chap. xxiv, 3–12, is expressly presented as an *uttered parable,* or symbolical discourse, and the imagery is, accordingly, ideal, and not to be understood of an outward action. The symbolical actions of Isaiah (xx, 2–4) and Jeremiah (xiii, 11; xviii, 1–6; xix, 1–2; xxvii, 1–14, and xliii, 8–13) are, like those of Ezekiel, amply explained in their immediate context.

Other symbolical actions.

Of all the symbolical actions of the prophets the most difficult and disputed example is that of Hosea taking unto himself "a woman of whoredoms and children of whoredoms" (Hosea i, 2), and his loving "a woman beloved of a friend, and an adulteress" (Hosea iii, 1). The great question is: Are these transactions to be understood as mere visional symbols, or as real events in the outward life of the prophet? No one will venture to deny that the language of Hosea most

Hosea's Marriage.

naturally implies that the events were outward and real. He plainly says that Jehovah commanded him to go and marry an
adulterous woman, and that he obeyed. He gives the
name of the woman and the name of her father, and
says that she conceived and bore him a son, whom he named Jezreel,
and subsequently she bore him a daughter and another son, to whom
he also gave significant names as God directed him. There is no
intimation whatever that these events were merely visions of the
soul, or that they were to be published to Israel as a purely parabolic discourse. If the account of any symbolical action on record
is so explicit and positive as to require a literal interpretation, this
surely is one, for its terms are clear, its language is simple, and its
general import not difficult to comprehend.

*Language im-
plies outward
reality.*

Whence, then, the difficulties which expositors have felt in its interpretation? It is mainly in the supposition that
such a marriage, commanded by God and effected by
a holy prophet, was a moral impossibility. A part of
the difficulty has also arisen from a misapprehension
of the meaning of certain allusions, and the scope of the entire passage. Upon these misapprehensions false assumptions have been
based, and false interpretations have naturally followed. Thus, it
has been assumed that the three children of the prophet, Jezreel,
Lo-ruhamah, and Lo-ammi, were themselves the "children of whoredoms" whom the prophet was to take, and that the prophet's wife
herself continued her dissolute life after her marriage with him. Of
all this there is nothing in the text. The most simple and natural
meaning of "a woman of whoredoms and children of whoredoms"
(chap. i, 2) is a woman who is a notable harlot, and who, as such, has
begotten children who also follow her lewd practices. If it had
been otherwise, and the prophet had been directed to take a pure
virgin, the language of our text would have been utterly out of
place. For how could Hosea know how and where to select a virgin who would, after her marriage with him, become a harlot?
That the prophet's wife continued her lewd practices after her
marriage with him is nowhere intimated.

*Supposed impos-
sibility based
on Misapprehen-
sion of Scope and
Import.*

The straightforward, literal statement that the prophet "went
and took Gomer, the daughter of Diblaim, and she conceived and
bare him a son" (ver. 3), is the furthest possible from describing
something which occurred only in idea. The sophism of Hengstenberg, that these things took place "actually, but not outwardly,"[1]

---

[1] Christology of the Old Testament, English translation (Edinb., 1863), vol. i, p.
185. Hengstenberg's whole discussion of this subject, which assumes to be very full
and thorough, is a notable exhibition of exegetical dogmatism.

is too glaring to be for a moment entertained. If the things here narrated had no outward reality in the prophet's life, it is an abuse of language to say they actually occurred. All attempts to explain the names Gomer and Diblaim symbolically are manifest failures, and Schmoller is candid enough to admit that "we cannot say that, in themselves, they necessarily demand such an explanation."[1] Gomer may indeed denote *completion*, but no parallel usage justifies the meaning of "completed whoredom," which most English expositors adopt from Aben Ezra and Jerome. The verb גָּמַר means either to come to an end in the sense of *ceasing to exist* (Psa. vii, 10; xii, 2; lxxvii, 9), or to *complete*, or bring to perfection, in a good sense (Psa. lvii, 3; cxxxviii, 8; comp. the Chaldee גְּמַר in Ezra vii, 12). Gesenius and Fürst (Heb. Lex.) suggest the meaning of *coals, heat*, or fireglow. The name of Diblaim is also too uncertain to warrant a symbolical interpretation. If we allow its identity with דְּבֵלִים, *fig cakes*, the explanation, "completed whoredom, the daughter of two fig cakes," is sufficiently awkward and far-fetched to discredit the whole interpretation.

Hengstenberg is also guilty of the bold and remarkable assertion that "there exists a multitude of symbolical actions, in regard to which it is undeniable and universally admitted (!) that they took place internally only."[2] He does not deign to inform us what they are, and we may with equal propriety, therefore, affirm that there is not a single instance of a vision, or of a symbolical action, that took place only internally, but that there is in the context something which clearly indicates its visional character. Jeremiah's taking the wine cup of Jehovah's fury and presenting it to the nations (Jer. xxv, 15–33) is not a parallel case, but is metaphorical, as the expression "cup of the wine of this fury" (ver. 15) abundantly shows. This is confirmed by its causal connexion (כִּי, *for*) with verse 14, and by the whole tone and spirit of the passage, which is highly figurative; see, especially, verses 27–31. The same is true of Zech. xi, 4–14, where the prophet by inspiration identifies himself with the Lord, and describes no vision, or internal transaction, but a highly figurative account of the relations of the Lord and Israel. The breaking of the staves, Beauty and Bands, was the Lord's doing, and not that of the prophet. Much more scientific and trustworthy is the procedure of Cowles, who collates all the Old Testament examples bearing on this point, and exhibits "a clear line of distinction drawn between

Marginalia: Gomer and Diblaim not symbolical names. Hengstenberg's unwarrantable assertion.

[1] Commentary on Hosea (Lange's Biblework), in loco.
[2] Christology, vol. i, p. 186.

the things seen and shown in vision only, and those which were done in outward life for symbolic or other purposes. These distinctions," he observes, " lie not mainly—indeed scarcely at all—in the nature of the things as convenient to be done, or as impossible, but in the very *form* of the statements. In other words, the Lord has been specially careful to leave us in no doubt as to what was actually *done* by his prophets on the one hand, and what was only *seen* by them in vision on the other." [1]

The prophet Hosea was not commanded to go and rehearse a parable before the people, nor to relate what occurred to him in vision, but to perform certain actions. The time necessary for his marriage, and the birth of the three children of Gomer, need have been no greater than that in which Isaiah was required to walk naked and barefoot for a sign (Isa. xx, 3). The names of the three children are symbolical of certain purposes and plans of God in his dealings with the house of Israel, but there is no hint that these children were at all given to licentiousness. Their names point to coming judgments, as did the name of Isaiah's son (Isa. viii, 3), but those symbolical names are no disparagement of the character of the persons who bore them. As long as Gomer was no man's lawful wife, her marriage to Hosea, even though she had become noted as a harlot, and had thus begotten "children of whoredoms," involved no breach of law. The law governing a priest's marriage (Lev. xxi, 7–15), and which even prohibited his marrying a widow, did not apply to a prophet more than to any other man in Israel. That a prophet should marry a harlot, and take her children with her, was indeed surprising, and calculated to excite wonder and astonishment; but to excite such wonder, and deeply impress it on the popular heart, was the very purpose of the whole transaction. We cannot conceive how the actions here recorded could have been made signs and wonders in Israel (comp. Isa. viii, 18), or have been at all impressive, if they were known to have never occurred. In that case they would have been either ridiculed as a silly fancy, or denounced as an utter falsehood. Their real occurrence, however, would have been a sign and a wonder too striking to be trifled with; but it is not probable that when the people of the whole land had grievously committed whoredom away from Jehovah (chap. i, 2) their moral sense would have been so shocked at these actions of a prophet as many modern critics imagine.

The main purport and scope of the passage may be indicated as follows: Hosea is commanded to marry a harlot " because the land

The facts as stated not insupposable.

[1] Notes on the Minor Prophets. Dissertation i, p. 413. New York, 1866.

has grievously committed whoredom away from Jehovah." The adulterous woman would thus represent idolatrous Israel, whose sins are so frequently set forth under this figure. Scope of passage indicated. No particular historical period is indicated, none need be assumed. All question here as to when Jehovah was married to Israel, or what Israel was before, and what after such marriage, only tends to confuse and obscure the main purport of this Scripture, into which a consideration of such questions does not enter. The marriage of the prophet to a harlot was a striking symbol of Jehovah's relation to a people to whom it would be supposed he would have utter aversion. Yet of that people, so guilty of spiritual adultery, will Jehovah beget a holy seed, and the three symbolical names, Jezreel, Lo-ruhamah, and Lo-ammi, denote the severe measures, stated in the passage itself, by which the redemption of Israel must be accomplished. Jezreel may have a double reference, one local, taken from the well-known valley of this name where Jehu wrought his bloody deeds (2 Kings x, 1-7); the other etymological (as the word denotes "God sows," or, "God will sow"), and indicating that the very judgments by which the kingdom of the house of Israel was overthrown were a sowing of the seed from which should spring a regenerated nation. The names Lo-ruhamah and Lo-ammi symbolize other forms of judgment. The symbolical Names. By his unpitying chastisements (Lo-ruhamah) and the utter rejection of them as a people (Lo-ammi) will he secure the redemption of that vast multitude mentioned in verses 10, 11, and chapter ii, 1 (Heb. ii, 1-3), whose glory and triumph will give new significance to the "day of Jezreel," and change the name of Lo-ruhamah to Ruhamah (compassionated), and Lo-ammi to Ammi (my people). This view fully harmonizes with the language of chapter ii, 22, 23, and gives a unity and definiteness to the whole of the first two chapters of Hosea. The oracle of chapter ii, is, accordingly, to be understood as Jehovah's appeal to Israel. It is addressed to the "children of whoredoms," who are called on to plead with their mother (ii, 2; Heb. ii, 4). It consists of complaint, threatening, and promises, and from verse 14 on to the end of the chapter (Heb., verses 16-25) indicates the process by which Jehovah will woo and marry that mother of profligate children, making for her "the valley of Achor as a door of hope" (ver. 15),[1] and thereby

---

[1] Achor (עָכוֹר) means *troubler*, or *troubling*, and is here used in allusion to the events recorded in Josh. vii, 24-26. In the valley of Achor, Achan was punished for his crimes, and the ban was thereby removed from Israel. "Through the name *Achor* this valley became a memorial how the Lord restores his favour to the Church after the expiation of the guilt by the punishment of the transgressor. And this divine

accomplishing her redemption. To emphasize this most wonderful prophecy and promise the marriage of Hosea and Gomer served as a most impressive sign.

The third chapter of Hosea records another symbolical action of Hosea, chap. iii, this prophet, by which it is shown, in another form, another Symbol-ical act with how Jehovah would reform and regenerate the chil-similar purport. dren of Israel. Who this adulterous woman beloved by a friend (ver. 1) was, we are not told, and conjectures are idle. The supposition of many, that she was identical with Gomer, has no valid foundation, and has many considerations against it. If Gomer were intended, she would hardly be designated merely as "a woman beloved of a friend," nor would the prophet be likely to have pur-chased her (ver. 2) without some further explanation. In the long life and ministry of Hosea (comp. chap. i, 1) there was room for several events of this kind, and we most naturally assume that in the meantime his former wife, Gomer, had died. In the very brief record here made there was no space for such details. Hosea's loving this woman, buying her according to oriental custom, and placing her apart for many days, are explained as a symbol of Israel's exile and dispersion until the appointed time of restitution should come. All that is here said about Israel's remaining many days without king, sacrifices, and images was amply fulfilled during the Assyrian exile. No traces of idolatry or spiritual whoredom re-mained in Israel or Judah after the restoration which took place under Cyrus and his successors. The reason why so many exposi-tors have supposed that this chapter refers to another and later exile arises from failure to note the habit of prophetic discourse to Repetition of repeat the same things under different symbols. This symbols. error has misled many into the notion that the adul-terous woman of chapter ii, must be identified with the Gomer of chapter i. As in the prophecies of Daniel we find the composite image of chapter ii, and the four beasts of chapter vii, only different symbols of the same events, and the vision of the ram and he-goat, in chapter viii, going over a part of the same ground again, so here we should understand that Hosea, at different periods of his life, depicted by entirely different symbolic actions different phases of

mode of procedure will be repeated in all its essential characteristics. The Lord will make the valley of troubling a door of hope; that is, he will so expiate the sins of his Church and cover them with his grace, that the covenant of fellowship with him will no more be rent asunder by them; or he will so display his grace to the sinners that compassion will manifest itself even in wrath, and through judgment and mercy the pardoned sinners will be more and more firmly and inwardly united to him."—Keil on Hosea, in loco.

the same great facts. Similar repetition abounds in Ezekiel, Zechariah, and the Apocalypse of John.

These actions of Hosea, then, according to all sound laws of grammatico-historical interpretation, are to be understood as having actually occurred in the life of the prophet, and are to bo classed along with other actions which we have termed symbolico-typical. Such actions, as we have observed before, combine essential elements of both symbol and type, and serve to illustrate at once the kinship and the difference between them. Serving as signs and visible images of unseen facts or truths, they are symbolical; but being at the same time representative actions of an intelligent agent, actually and outwardly performed, and pointing especially to things to come, they are typical. Hence the propriety of designating them by the compound name symbolico-typical. And it is worthy of note that every instance of such actions is accompanied by an explanation of its import, more or less detailed.

The miracles of our Lord may not improperly be spoken of as symbolico-typical. They were σημεῖα καὶ τέρατα, signs and wonders, and they all, without exception, have a moral and spiritual significance. The cleansing of the leper symbolized the power of Christ to heal the sinner, and so all his miracles of love and mercy bear the character of redemptive acts, and are typically prophetical of what he is evermore doing in his reign of grace. The stilling of the tempest, the walking on the sea, and the opening of the eyes of the blind furnish suggestive lessons of divine grace and power, as some of the noblest hymns of the Church attest. The miracle of the water made wine, says Trench, "may be taken as the sign and symbol of all which Christ is evermore doing in the world, ennobling all that he touches, making saints out of sinners, angels out of men, and in the end heaven out of earth, a new paradise of God out of the old wilderness of the world."[1] Hengstenberg observes that Jesus' triumphal entry into Jerusalem, as predicted in Zech. ix, 10, "was a symbolical action, the design and purport of which were to assert his royal dignity, and to set forth in a living picture the true nature of his person and kingdom, in opposition to the false notions of both friends and foes. Apart, therefore, from the prophecy, the entry had its own peculiar meaning, as, in fact, was the case with every act of Christ and every event of his life."[2]

Our Lord's miracles symbolical.

---

[1] Notes on the Miracles of our Lord, p. 98. New York, 1858.
[2] Christology of the Old Testament, vol. iii, p. 375. Edinb., 1863.

CHAPTER XIX.

SYMBOLIC NUMBERS, NAMES, AND COLOURS.

EVERY observant reader of the Bible has had his attention arrested at times by what seemed a mystical or symbolical use of numbers. The numbers three, four, seven, ten, and twelve, especially, have a significance worthy of most careful study. Certain well-known proper names, as Egypt, Assyria, and Babylon, are also used in a mystic sense, and the colours red, black, and white are understood to be so associated with the ideas respectively of bloodshed, evil, and purity as to have become emblematic of those ideas. The only Process of as- valid method of ascertaining the symbolical meaning certaining Sym- and usage of such numbers, names, and colours in the bolism of Num- bers, etc. Scriptures, is by an ample collation and study of the passages where they occur. The hermeneutical process is therefore essentially the same as that by which we ascertain the *usus loquendi* of words, and the province of hermeneutics is, not to furnish an elaborate discussion of the subject, but to exhibit the principles and methods by which such a discussion should be carried out.[1]

SYMBOLICAL NUMBERS.

The number one, as being the first, the startingpoint, the parent, and source of all numbers, the representative of unity, might naturally be supposed to possess some mystical significance, and yet there appears no evidence that it is ever used in any such sense in the Scriptures. It has a notable emphasis in that watchword of Israelitish faith, "Hear, O Israel, Jehovah our God is ONE JEHOVAH" (Deut. vi, 4; comp. Mark xii, 29, 32; 1 Cor. viii, 4), but neither here nor elsewhere is the number used in any other than its literal

---

[1] On the symbolism of numbers see Bähr, Symbolik des mosaischen Cultus, vol. i, (1874), pp. 185–282 ; Kurtz, Ueber die symbolische Dignität der Zahlen an der Stiftshütte, in the Studien und Kritiken for 1844, pp. 315–370 ; Lämmert, Zur Revision der biblischen Zahlensymbolik, in the Jahrbücher für deutsche Theologie for 1864, pp. 1–49 ; and Engelhardt, Einiges über symbolische Zahlen, in the same periodical for 1866, pp. 301–332 ; Kliefoth, Die Zahlensymbolik der heiligen Schrift, in Dieckhoff und Kliefoth's Theologische Zeitschrift for 1862, pp. 1–89, 341–453, and 509–623 ; Stuart's Excursus (appropriating largely from Bähr) on the Symbolical Use of Numbers in the Apocalypse, in his Commentary on the Apocalypse, vol. ii, pp. 409–434 ; White, Symbolical Numbers of Scripture (Edinb., 1868).

sense. The number three, however, is employed in such relations as to suggest that it is especially the number of divine full- The number ness in unity. Bähr seems altogether too fanciful when Three. he says : " It lies in the very nature of the number three, that is, in its relation to the two preceding numbers one and two, that it forms in the progression of numbers the first conclusion (Abschluss); for the one is first made a number by being followed by the two, but the two as such represents separation, difference, contrast, and this becomes cancelled by the number three, so that three is in fact the first finished, true, and complete unity." [1] But he goes on to say that every true unity comprises a trinity, and instances the familiar triads, beginning, middle, and end; past, present, and future; under, midst, and upper; and he cites from many heathen sources to show the mystic significance that everywhere attached to the number three. He also cites from the Scripture such triads as the three men who appeared to Abraham (Gen. xviii, 2), the three forefathers of the children of Israel, Abraham, Isaac, and Jacob (Exod. iii, 6), the three sons of Noah, by whom the postdiluvian world was peopled (Gen. ix, 19), the three constituent parts of the universe, heaven, earth, and sea (Exod. xx, 11; Psa. cxlvi, 6), the cedar wood, scarlet, and hyssop, used in the ceremonial purification (Lev. xiv, 6; Num. xix, 6), the threefold cord that is not quickly broken (Eccl. iv, 12), and other less noticeable examples. More important and conspicuous, however, as exhibiting a sacredness .in the number three, are those texts which associate it immediately with the divine name. These are the thrice-repeated benediction of Num. vi, 24–26, or threefold *putting the name* of Jehovah (ver. 27) upon the children of Israel; the threefold name in the formula of baptism (Matt. xxviii, 19), and the apostolic benediction (2 Cor. xiii, 14); and the *trisagion* of Isa. vi, 3, and Rev. iv, 8, accompanied in the latter passage by the three divine titles, Lord, God, and Almighty, and the additional words "who was, and who is, and who is to come." From all this it would appear, as Stuart [2] has observed, "that the doctrine of a Trinity in the Godhead lies much deeper than the New-Platonic philosophy, to which so many have been accustomed to refer it. An original impression of the character in question plainly overspread all the ancient oriental world . . . That many philosophistic and superstitious conceits have been mixed with it, in process of time, proves nothing against the general fact as stated. And this being admitted, we cease to think it strange that such distinction and significancy have been given in the Scriptures to the number three."

---

[1] Symbolik des mosaischen Cultus, p. 205.
[2] Commentary on Apocalypse, vol. ii, pp. 419, 420.

If its peculiar usage in connexion with the divine Name gives mystical significance to the number three, and entitles it to be called "the number of God," the use of the number four in the Scriptures would in like manner entitle it to be called "the number of the world," or of the visible creation. Thus we have the four winds of heaven (Jer. xlix, 36; Ezek. xxxvii, 9; Dan. vii, 2; viii, 8; Zech. ii, 6; vi, 5; Matt. xxiv, 31; Mark xiii, 27; Rev. vii, 1), the four corners or extremities of the earth (Isa. xi, 12; Ezek. vii, 2; Rev. vii, 1; xx, 8), corresponding, doubtless, with the four points of the compass, east, west, north, and south (1 Chron. ix, 24; Psa. cvii, 3; Luke xiii, 29), and the four seasons. Noticeable also are the four living creatures in Ezek. i, 5, each with four faces, four wings, four hands, and connected with four wheels; and in Zechariah the four horns (i, 18), the four smiths (i, 20), and the four chariots (vi, 1).

The number seven, being the sum of four and three, may naturally be supposed to symbolize some mystical union of God with the world, and accordingly, may be called the sacred number of the covenant between God and his creation. The hebdomad, or period of seven days, is so essentially associated with the record of creation (Gen. ii, 2, 3; Exod. xx, 8–11), that from the beginning a sevenfold division of time was recognized among the ancient nations. In the Scripture it is peculiarly a ritual number. In establishing his covenant with Abraham God ordained that seven days must pass after the birth of a child, and then, upon the eighth day, he must be circumcised (Gen. xvii, 12; comp. Lev. xii, 2, 3). The passover feast continued seven days (Exod. xii, 15). The feast of Pentecost was held seven weeks after the day of the wave offering (Lev. xxiii, 15). The feast of trumpets occurred in the seventh month (Lev. xxiii, 24), and seven times seven years brought round the year of jubilee (Lev. xxv, 8). The blood of the sin offering was sprinkled seven times before the Lord (Lev. iv, 6). The ceremonial cleansing of the leper required that he be sprinkled seven times with blood and seven times with oil, that he tarry abroad outside of his tent seven days (Lev. xiv. 7, 8; xvi, 27), and that his house also be sprinkled seven times (Lev. xiv, 51). Contact with a dead body and other kinds of ceremonial uncleanness required a purification of seven days (Num. xix, 11; Lev. xv, 13, 24). And so the idea of covenant relations and obligations seems to be associated with this sacred number. Jehovah confirmed his word to Joshua and Israel, when for seven days seven priests with seven trumpets compassed Jericho, and on the seventh day compassed the city seven times (Josh. vi, 13–15). The golden candlestick had seven

lamps (Exod. xxxviii, 23). The seven churches, seven stars, seven
seals, seven trumpets, seven thunders, and seven last plagues of the
Apocalypse are of similar mystical significance.

The number ten completes the list of primary numbers, and is
made the basis of all further numeration. Hence, it is   Ten.
naturally regarded as the number of rounded fulness
or completeness. The Hebrew word for ten, עֶשֶׂר, is believed to
favour this idea. Gesenius (Lex.) traces it to a root which conveys
the idea of *conjunction*, and observes that "etymologists agree in
deriving this form from the conjunction of the ten fingers." Fürst
adopts the same fundamental idea, and defines the word as if 'it
were expressive of "*union*, association; hence *multitude, heap, multiplicity*" (Heb. Lex). And this general idea is sustained by the
usage of the number. Thus the Decalogue, the totality and substance of the whole Torah, or Law, is spoken of as *the ten words*
Exod. xxxiv, 28; Deut. iv, 13; x, 4); ten elders constitute an ancient Israelitish court (Ruth iv, 2); ten princes represent the tribes
of Israel (Josh. xxii, 14); ten virgins go forth to meet the bridegroom (Matt. xxv, 1). And, in a more general way, ten times is
equivalent to many times (Gen. xxxi, 7, 41; Job xix, 3), ten wom-
en means many women (Lev. xxvi, 26), ten sons many sons (1 Sam.
i, 8), ten mighty ones are many mighty ones (Eccles. vii, 19), and
the ten horns of Dan. vii, 7, 24; Rev. xii, 3; xiii, 1; xvii, 12, may
fittingly symbolize many kings.[1]

The symbolical use of the number twelve in Scripture appears
to have fundamental allusion to the twelve tribes of   Twelve.
Israel. Thus Moses erects "twelve pillars according
to the twelve tribes of Israel" (Exod. xxiv, 4), and there were
twelve stones in the breastplate of the high priest (Exod. xxviii, 21),
twelve cakes of showbread (Lev. xxiv, 5), twelve bullocks, twelve
rams, twelve lambs, and twelve kids for offerings of dedication
(Num. vii, 87), and many other like instances. In the New Testament we have the twelve apostles, twelve times twelve thousand
are sealed out of the tribes of Israel, twelve thousand from each
tribe (Rev. vii, 4–8), and the New Jerusalem has twelve gates,
bearing the names of the twelve tribes, and guarded by twelve angels (Rev. xxi, 12), and its wall has twelve foundations, bearing
the twelve names of the apostles (xxi, 14). Twelve, then, may
properly be called the mystical number of God's chosen people.

It is thus by collation and comparison of the peculiar uses of these
numbers that we can arrive at any safe conclusion as to their

[1] Compare Wemyss, Clavis Symbolica, under the word Ten, and Bähr, Symbolik,
vol. i, pp. 223, 224.

symbolical import.   But allowing that they have such import as the
Symbolical does foregoing examples indicate, we must not suppose that
not always ex-
clude literal they thereby necessarily lose their literal and proper
sense.   meaning.   The number ten, as shown above, and some
few instances of the number seven (Psa. xii, 6; lxxix, 12; Prov.
xxvi, 16; Isa. iv, 4; Dan. iv, 16), authorize us to say that they are
used sometimes indefinitely in the sense of *many*.   But when, for
example, it is written that seven priests, with seven trumpets, compassed Jericho on the seventh day seven times (Josh. vi, 13–15), we
understand the statements in their literal sense.   These things
were done just so many times, but the symbolism of the sevens
suggests that in this signal overthrow of Jericho God was confirming his covenant and promises to give into the hand of his chosen
people their enemies and the land they occupied (comp. Exod.
xxiii, 31; Josh. ii, 9, 24; vi, 2).   And so the sounding of the seven
trumpets of the Apocalypse completed the mystery of God as declared to his prophets (Rev. x, 7), so that when the seventh angel
sounded great voices in heaven said: "The kingdom of the world
is become that of our Lord and of his Christ, and he shall reign
forever and ever" (Rev. xii, 15).

The "time and times and dividing (or half) of a time" (Dan. vii,
Time, times, 25; xii, 7; Rev. xii, 13) is commonly and with reason
and half a time. believed to stand for three years and a half, a time denoting a year.   A comparison of verses 6 and 12 of Rev. xii shows
this period to be the same as twelve hundred and sixty days, or exactly three and a half years, reckoning three hundred and sixty
days to a year.   But as this number is in every case used to
denote a period of woe and disaster to the Church or people of
God (Rev. xi, 2), we may regard it as symbolical.   It is a divided
seven (comp. Dan. ix, 27) as if suggesting the thought of a broken
covenant, an interrupted sacrifice, a triumph of the enemy of God.

The twelve hundred and sixty days are also equivalent to forty-
Forty-two two months (Rev. xi, 2, 3; xiii, 5), reckoning thirty
months.   days to a month, and, thus used, it is probably to be
regarded, not as an exact designation of just so many days, but as
a round number readily reckoned and remembered, and approximating the exact length of the period denoted with sufficient nearness.   In Dan. viii, 14 we have the peculiar expression "two thousand and three hundred evening mornings," which some explain as
meaning so many days, in allusion to Gen. i, 5, where evening and
morning constitute one day.   Others, however, understand so many
morning and evening sacrifices, which would require half the number of days (eleven hundred and fifty).   Perhaps, however, the

word אֲלָפִים, *two thousand*, should be pointed אֶלֶף, *one thousand*, then we would have thirteen hundred days of evening and morning. This closely approximates the twelve hundred and ninety days of Dan. xii, 11, which, when compared with the thirteen hundred and thirty-five days mentioned in the next verse, seems rather to show that in the peculiarly exact designations of time here recorded we have not mystical or symbolical numbers, but literal designations of the length of important periods.

The number forty designates in so many places the duration of a penal judgment, either forty days or forty years, that it may be regarded as symbolic of a period of judg- Forty. ment. The forty days of the flood (Gen. vii, 4, 12, 17), the forty years of Israel's wandering in the wilderness (Num. xiv, 34), the forty stripes with which a convicted criminal was to be beaten (Deut. xxv, 3), the forty years of Egypt's desolation (Ezek. xxix, 11, 12), and the forty days and nights during which Moses, Elijah, and Jesus fasted (Exod. xxiv, 28; 1 Kings xix, 8; Matt. iv, 2), all favour this idea. But there is no reason to suppose that in all these cases the number forty is not also used in its proper and literal sense. The symbolism, if any, arises from the association of the number with a period of punishment or trial.

The number seventy is also noticeable as being that of the totality of Jacob's sons (Gen. xlvi, 27; Exod. i, 5; Deut. x, 22) and of the elders of Israel (Exod. xxiv, 1, 9; Seventy. Num. xi, 24); the Jews were doomed to seventy years of Babylonian exile (Jer. xxv, 11, 12; Dan. ix, 2); seventy weeks distinguish one of Daniel's most important prophecies (Dan. ix, 24), and our Lord appointed seventy other disciples besides the twelve (Luke x, 1). Auberlen observes: "The number seventy is ten multiplied by seven; the human is here moulded and fixed by the divine. For this reason the seventy years of exile are a symbolical sign of the time during which the power of the world would, according to God's will, triumph over Israel, during which it would execute the divine judgments on God's people." [1]

We have already seen (p. 370), in discussing the symbolical actions of Ezekiel, that the four hundred-and thirty days Prophetic des- of his prostration formed a symbolical period in allu- ignations of sion to the four hundred and thirty (390+40) years of the Egyptian bondage (Exod. xii, 40). Like the number forty, as shown above, it was associated with a period of discipline and sorrow. Each day of the prophet's prostration represented a year of Israel's humiliation and judgment (Ezek. iv, 6), as the forty days

[1] The Prophecies of Daniel and the Revelation, Eng. Trans., p. 134. Edinb., 1856.

during which the spies searched the land of Canaan were typical of the years of Israel's wandering and wasting in the wilderness (Num. xiv, 33, 34).

Here it is in place to examine the so-called "year-day theory" of prophetic interpretation, so prevalent among modern expositors.[1] Upon the statement of the two passages just cited from Numbers and Ezekiel, and also upon supposed necessities of apocalyptic interpretation, a large number of modern writers on prophecy have advanced the theory that the word *day*, or *days*, is to be understood in prophetic designations of time as denoting years. This theory has been applied especially to the "time, times, and dividing of a time" in Dan. vii, 25, xii, 7, and Rev. xii, 14; the twelve hundred and sixty days of Rev. xi, 3; xii, 6; and also by many to the two thousand three hundred days of Dan. viii, 14, and the twelve hundred and ninety and thirteen hundred and thirty-five days of Dan. xii, 11, 12. The forty and two months of Rev. xi, 2, and xiii, 5, are, according to this theory, to be multiplied by thirty (42×30=1260), and then the result in days is to be understood as so many years. After the like manner, the time, times, and a half, are first understood as three years and a half, and then the years are multiplied by three hundred and sixty, a round number for the days of a year, and the result (1260) is understood as designating, not so many days, but so many years.

If this is a correct theory of interpreting the designations of prophetic time, it is obvious that it is a most important one. It is necessarily so farreaching in its practical results as fundamentally to affect one's whole plan and process of exposition. Such a theory, surely, ought to be supported by the most convincing and incontrovertible reasons. And yet, upon the most careful examination, we do not find that it has any sufficient warrant in the Scripture, and the expositions of its advocates are not of a character likely to commend it to the critical mind. Against it we urge the five following considerations:

The year-day theory.

A theory so far reaching and fundamental should have most valid support.

1. This theory derives no valid support from the passages in Numbers and Ezekiel already referred to. In Num. xiv, 33, 34, Jehovah's word to Israel simply states that they must suffer for their iniquities forty years, "in the

Has no support in Num. xiv and Ezek. iv.

---

[1] See on this subject Stuart's article on the Designation of Time in the Apocalypse in the American Biblical Repository for Jan., 1835. Also a reply to the same by Dr. Allen in the same periodical for July, 1840. Compare also Cowles' Dissertation on the subject at the end of his Commentary on Daniel. Elliott's laboured argument on this subject (Horæ Apocalypticæ, vol. iii, pp. 260–298) is mainly a series of presumptions.

number of the days which ye searched the land, forty days, a day for the year, a day for the year." There is no possibility of misunderstanding this. The spies were absent forty days searching the land of Canaan (Num. xiii, 25), and when they returned they brought back a bad report of the country, and spread disaffection, murmuring, and rebellion through the whole congregation of Israel (xiv, 2–4). Thereupon the divine sentence of judgment was pronounced upon that generation, and they were condemned to "graze (רֹעִים, *pasture, feed*) in the wilderness forty years" (xiv, 33). Here then is certainly no ground on which to base the universal proposition that, in prophetic designations of time, a day means a year. The passage is exceptional and explicit, and the words are used in a strictly literal sense; the days evidently mean days, and the years mean years. The same is true in every particular of the days and years mentioned in Ezek. iv, 5, 6. The days of his prostration were literal days, and they were typical of years, as is explicitly stated. But to derive from this symbolico-typical action of Ezekiel a hermeneutical principle or law of universal application, namely, that days in prophecy mean years, would be a most unwarrantable procedure.

2. If the two passages now noticed were expressive of a universal law, we certainly would expect to find it sustained and capable of illustration by examples of fulfilled prophecy. But examples bearing on this point are overwhelmingly against the theory in question. God's word to Noah was: "Yet seven days, I will cause it to rain upon the land forty days and forty nights" (Gen. vii, 4). Did any one ever imagine these days were symbolical of years? Or will it be pretended that the mention of nights along with days removes the prophecy from the category of those scriptures which have a mystical import? God's word to Abraham was that his seed should be afflicted in a foreign land four hundred years (Gen. xv, 13). Must we multiply these years by three hundred and sixty to know the real time intended? Isaiah prophesied that Ephraim should be broken within threescore and five years (Isa. vii, 8); but who ever dreamed that this must be resolved into days in order to find the period of Ephraim's fall? Was it ever sagely believed that the three years of Moab's glory, referred to in Isa. xvi, 14, must be multiplied by three hundred and sixty in order to find the import of what Jehovah had spoken concerning it? Was it by such mathematical calculation as this that Daniel "understood in the books the number of the years, which was a word of Jehovah to Jeremiah (comp. Jer. xxv, 12) the prophet, to complete as to the desolations of Jerusalem seventy

Not sustained by Prophetic Analogy.

years" (Dan. ix, 2)? Or is it supposable that the seventy years of
Jeremiah's prophecy were ever intended to be manipulated by such
calculations? In short, this theory breaks down utterly when an
appeal is taken to the analogy of prophetic scriptures. If the time,
times, and a half of Dan. vii, 25 means three and a half years multiplied by three hundred and sixty, that is, twelve hundred and
sixty years, then the seven times of Dan. iv, 16, 32, should mean
seven times three hundred and sixty, or two thousand five hundred and twenty years. Or if in one prophecy of the future,
twelve hundred and sixty days must, without any accompanying
qualification, or any statement to that effect in the context, be understood as denoting so many years, then the advocates of such a
theory must show pertinent and valid reason why the forty days of
Jonah's prophecy against Nineveh (Jon. iii, 4) are not to be also
understood as denoting forty years.

3. The year-day theory is thought to have support in Daniel's
prophecy of the *seventy weeks* (Dan. ix, 24-27). But
that prophecy says not a word about days or years, but
seventy *heptads*, or *sevens* (שָׁבֻעִים). The position and
gender of the word indicate its peculiar significance. It nowhere
else occurs in the masculine except in Dan. x, 2, 3, where it is expressly defined as denoting *heptads of days* (שָׁבֻעִים יָמִים). Unaccom-
panied by any such limiting word, and standing in such an emphatic
position at the beginning of ver. 24, we have reason to infer at once
that it involves some mystical import. When, now, we observe
that it is a Messianic oracle, granted to Daniel when his mind was
full of meditations upon Jeremiah's prophecy of the seventy years
of Jewish exile (ver. 2), and in answer to his ardent supplications,
we most naturally understand the seventy heptads as heptads of
years. But this admission furnishes slender support to such a
sweeping theory as would logically bring all prophetic designations
of time to the principle that days mean years.

*Daniel's proph-
ecy of the sev-
enty weeks not
parallel.*

4. It has been argued that in such passages as Judg. xvii, 10;
1 Sam. ii, 19; 2 Chron. xxi, 19, and Isa. xxxii, 10, the
word *days* is used to denote *years*, and "if this word
be sometimes thus used in Scripture in places not prophetic, why should it not be thus employed in prophetic passages?"[1]
But a critical examination of those passages will show that the word
for *days* is not really used in the sense of years. In Judg. xvii, 10,
Micah says to the Levite: "Dwell with me, and be to me for a
father and a priest, and I will give thee ten (pieces) of silver *for*

*Days nowhere
properly mean
Years.*

[1] See Allen's article "On the Designations of Time in Daniel and John," in The
American Biblical Repository, for July, 1840, p. 39.

the days" (לַיָּמִים), that is, for the days that he should dwell with him as a priest. In 1 Sam. ii, 19, it is said that Samuel's mother made him a little robe, and brought it up to him *from days to days* in her going up along with her husband to offer the sacrifice *of the days*." Here the reference is to the particular days of going up to the tabernacle to worship and sacrifice, and the exact sense is not brought out by the common version, "year by year" or "yearly." They may have gone up several times during the year at the days of the great national feasts. And this appears from a comparison of 1 Sam. i, 3 and 7, where, in the first place, it is said that Elkanah went up *from days to days*, and in ver. 7, "so he did *year by year.*" That is, he went up three times a year according to the law (Exod. xxiii, 14-17) "from days to days," as the well-known national feastdays came round; and his wife generally accompanied him. 2 Chron. xxi, 19 is literally: "And it came to pass at days from days (i. e., after several days), and about the time of the going out (expiration) of the end, at two days, his bowels went out," etc.[1] Similarly, Isa. xxxii, 10: "Days above a year shall ye be troubled," etc. That is, more than a year shall ye be troubled.[2] The most that can be said of such a use of the word days, is, that it is used indefinitely in a proverbial and idiomatic way; but such a usage by no means justifies the broad proposition that a day means a year.

5. The advocates of the year-day theory rest their strongest argument, however, upon the necessity of such a theory for what they regard the true explanation of certain proph- Disproved by ecies. They affirm that the three times and a half of repeated Failures in interpretation. Dan. vii, 25, and the twelve hundred and sixty days of Rev. xii, 6, and their parallels, are incapable of a literal interpretation. And so, carrying the predictions both of Daniel and John down into the history of modern Europe for explanation, most of these writers understand the twelve hundred and sixty year-days as designating the period of the Roman Papacy. Mr. William Miller, famous in the last generation for the sensation he produced, and the large following he had, adopted a scheme of interpreting not only the twelve hundred and sixty days, but also the twelve hundred and ninety, and the thirteen hundred and thirty-five (of Dan. xii, 11, 12), so that he ascertained and published with great assurance that the coming of Christ would take place in October, 1843. We have lived to see his theories thoroughly exploded, and yet there have not been wanting others who have adopted his hermeneutical principles, and named A. D. 1866 and

[1] See Keil and Bertheau on Chronicles, in loco.
[2] See Alexander on Isaiah, in loco.

A. D. 1870 as "the time of the end." A theory which is so destitute of scriptural analogy and support as we have seen above, and presumes to rest on such a slender showing of divine authority, is on those grounds alone to be suspected; but when it has again and again proved to be false and misleading in its application, we may safely reject it, as furnishing no valid principle or rule in a true science of hermeneutics.[1] Those who have supposed it to be necessary for the exposition of apocalyptic prophecies, should begin to feel that their systems of interpretation are in error.

The duration of the thousand years, or the millenial reign, mentioned in Rev. xx, 2–7, has been variously estimated. Most of those who advocate the year-day theory have singularly agreed to understand this thousand years literally. With them days mean years, and times mean years, to be resolved into three hundred and sixty days each, but the thousand years of the Apocalypse are literally and exactly a thousand years! Many, however, understand this number as denoting an indefinitely long period, and some have not scrupled to apply to it the theory of a day for a year, and multiplying by three hundred and sixty, estimate the length of the millenium at three hundred and sixty thousand years. But in this case we have no analogy, no real parallel, in other parts of scripture. Allen himself candidly admits that "there is nothing in the customary use of the phrase *a thousand*, in other places, which will determine its import in the Book of Revelation. The probability of its being used there definitely or indefinitely must be determined by examining the place itself, and from the nature of the case."[2] This is a very safe and proper rule, and it may well be added that, as we have found the number ten to symbolize the general idea of *fulness, totality, completeness*, so not improbably the number one thousand may stand as the symbolic number of manifold fulness, the rounded æon of Messianic triumph, (ὁ αἰὼν μέλλων), during which he shall abolish all rule and all authority and power, and put all his enemies under his feet (1 Cor. xv, 24, 25), and bring in the fulness (τὸ πλήρωμα) of both Jews and Gentiles (Rom. xi, 12, 25).

The thousand years of Rev. xx.

---

[1] It may be said that Bengel's long-ago exploded theory of explaining apocalyptic designations of time is worthy of as much credence as this more popular year-day theory. In his Erklärten Offenbarung Johannis (1740) he takes the mystic number 666 (Rev. xiii, 18) for his startingpoint, and dividing it by 42 months, he makes a prophetic month equal 15⅞ years. His prophetic days were of corresponding length, amounting to about half a year, and his scheme fixed the end of all things in A. D. 1836. In favour of Bengel it may be said that he started with a number which is propounded as a riddle, which is more than we can say in favour of these other theorists.

[2] American Biblical Repository, July, 1840, p. 47.

Symbolical Names.

A symbolical use of proper names is apparent in such passages as Rev. xi, 8, where the great city, in which the bodies of Sodom and the slain witnesses were exposed, and "where also their Egypt. Lord was crucified," is called, spiritually,[1] Sodom and Egypt. Evidently this wicked city, whether we understand Jerusalem or Rome, is so designated because its moral corruptions and bitter persecuting spirit were like those of Sodom and Egypt, both famous in Jewish history for these ungodly qualities. In a similar way Isaiah likens Judah and Jerusalem to Sodom and Gomorrah (Isa. i, 9, 10). Compare also Jer. xxiii, 14. In Ezek. xvi, 44–59, the abominations of Jerusalem are made to appear loathsome by comparison and contrast with Samaria on one side and Sodom on the other.

In like manner "Babylon the great," is evidently a symbolical name in Rev. xiv, 8; xvi, 19; xvii, 5; xviii, 2, etc. Babylon and Whether the name is used to denote the same city as Jerusalem. that called Sodom and Egypt, in chapter xi, 8, or some other city, its mystical designation is to be explained, like that of Sodom and Egypt, as arising from Jewish historical associations with Babylon, the great city of the exile. That city could, in Jewish thought, be associated only with oppression and woe, and their antipathy to it as a persecuting power is well expressed in Psa. cxxxvii. The opposite of Babylon, the Harlot, in the Apocalypse, is Jerusalem, the Bride (Rev. xxi, 9, 10). So, too, in the psalm just referred to, the opposite of Babylon, with its rivers and willows, was Jerusalem and Mount Zion. And the careful student will note that, as one of the seven angels said to the prophet, "Come hither," and then "carried him away in spirit into a wilderness" and showed him the mystic Babylon, the Harlot (Rev. xvii, 1–3), so also one of the same class of angels addressed him with like words, and then "carried him away in spirit into a mountain great and high," and showed him the holy Jerusalem, the Bride (chap. xxi, 9, 10). And if the Bride denotes the true Church of the people and saints of the Most High, doubtless the Harlot represents the false and apostate Church, historically guilty of the blood of saints and martyrs. Which great city best represents that harlot—Rome, which truly has been a bitter persecutor, or Jerusalem, so often called a harlot by the prophets, and charged by Jesus himself as guilty of "all the righteous blood poured out upon the land, from the blood of Abel, the righteous,

---

[1] Πνευματικῶς, i. e., by a mental discernment intensified and exalted by a divine inspiration which enables one to see things according to their real and spiritual nature.

unto the blood of Zachariah, son of Barachiah" (Matt. xxiii, 35)—
where also their Lord and ours was crucified—each expositor will
determine for himself.

The name of Egypt is used symbolically in Hos. viii, 13, where
Ephraim is sentenced, on account of sin, to "return to
Egypt." The name had become proverbial as the land
of bondage (Exod. xx, 2), and Moses had threatened such a return
in his warnings and admonitions addressed to Israel (Deut. xxviii,
68). In Hos. ix, 3, this return to Egypt is, by the Hebrew poetic
parallelism of the passage, made equivalent to eating unclean
things in the land of Asshur. Hence the Assyrian exile is viewed
as another Egyptian bondage.

Return to Egypt.

The names of David and Elijah are used after the same symbolical manner to designate, prophetically, the prince
Messiah and the prophet John the Baptist. In Ezek.
xxxiv, 23, 24, Jehovah declares that he will set his servant
David for a shepherd over his people, and for a prince among
them. Here, assuredly, the language cannot be taken literally,
and no one will contend that the historical David is to appear
again in fulfilment of this prediction. Compare Ezek. xxxvii, 24;
Jer. xxx, 9; Hos. iii, 5. So, too, the prophecy of the coming of
Elijah in Mal. iv, 5, was fulfilled in John the Baptist (Matt. xi, 14;
xvii, 10-13).

David and Elijah.

The name Ariel is used in Isa. xxix, 1, 2, 7, as a symbolical designation of Jerusalem, but its mystical import is quite
uncertain. The word, according to Gesenius,[1] may denote either *lion of God*, or *altar of God;* but whether it should be
understood as denoting the city of lion-like heroes, or of invincible
strength, or as the city of the altar place, it is impossible to determine. Fuerst thinks (Heb. Lex.), in view of Isa. xxxi, 9, "where
Jerusalem is celebrated as a sacred hearth of the everlasting fire, it
is more advisable to choose this signification."

Ariel.

A hostile, oppressive world-power is designated in Isa. xxvii, 1,
as "Leviathan, a flying serpent, Leviathan, a crooked
serpent . . . a dragon which is in the sea." Some
think three different hostile powers are meant, but the repetition of
the name Leviathan, and the poetic parallelism of the passage, are
against that view. Egypt, Assyria, Babylon. Media, Persia, and
Rome have all been suggested as the hostile power intended. It
is, perhaps, best to understand it generically as a symbolic name for
any and every godless world-power that sets itself up as an opposer
and oppressor of the people of God.

Leviathan, the serpent.

[1] Commentar über den Jesaia, in loco.

SYMBOLISM OF COLOURS.

The setting of the rainbow in the cloud for a covenant sign between God and the land, that no flood of waters should Rainbow and tabernacle colours. again destroy all flesh (Gen. ix, 8–17) would naturally associate the prominent colours of that bow with ideas of heavenly grace. In the construction of the tabernacle four colours are prominent, *blue, purple, scarlet,* and *white* (Exod. xxv, 4; xxvi, 1, 31; xxxv, 6, etc.), and the blending of these in the coverings and appurtenances of that symbolic structure probably served not only for the sake of beauty and variety, but also to suggest thoughts of heavenly excellence and glory. The exact colours, tints, or shades denoted by the Hebrew words translated *blue, purple,* and *scarlet* (תְּכֵלֶת, אַרְגָּמָן, and תּוֹלַעַת שָׁנִי), it is hardly possible now to determine with absolute certainty,[1] but probably the common version is sufficiently correct.

The import of these several colours is to be gathered from the associations in which they appear. Blue, as the colour Import of colours to be inferred from their association. of the heaven, reflected in the sea, would naturally suggest that which is heavenly, holy, and divine. Hence it was appropriate that the robe of the ephod was made wholly of blue (Exod. xxviii, 31; xxxix, 22), and the breastplate was connected with it by blue cords (ver. 28). It was also by a blue cord or ribbon that the golden plate inscribed Blue. "Holiness to Jehovah" was attached to the high priest's mitre (ver. 31). The loops of the tabernacle curtains were of this colour (Exod. xxvi, 4), and the children of Israel were commanded to place blue ribbons as badges upon the borders of their garments (Num. xv, 37–41) as if to remind them that they were children of the heavenly King, and were under the responsibility of having received from him commandments and revelations. Hence, too, it was appropriate that a blue cloth was spread over the holiest things of the tabernacle when they were arranged for journeying forward (Num. iv, 6, 7, 11, 12).

Purple and scarlet, so often mentioned in connexion with the dress of kings, have very naturally been regarded as Purple and Scarlet. symbolical of royalty and majesty (Judg. viii, 26; Esther

[1] See Bähr's section on the Beschaffenheit der Farben in his chapter on Die Farben und Bildwerke der Cultus-Stätte, Symbolik, vol. i (new ed.), pp. 331–337. See also Atwater, Sacred Tabernacle of the Hebrews, pp. 209–224, and the various biblical dictionaries and cyclopædias, under the word *Colours.* Josephus' explanation of the import of these colours (Ant., iii, 7, sec. 7) is more fanciful than authoritative or satisfactory.

viii, 15; Dan. v, 7; Nah. ii, 3). Both these colours, along with
blue, appeared upon the curtains of the tabernacle (Exod. xxvi, 1)
and upon the veil that separated the holy place from the most holy
(Exod. xxvi, 31). A scarlet cloth covered the holy vessels which
were placed upon the table of showbread, and a purple cloth the
altar of burnt offerings (Num. iv, 8, 13).

White is, pre-eminently, the colour of purity and righteousness.
The Hebrew word for *fine linen*, or *byssus* (שֵׁשׁ), of
which the covering and veil and curtains of the tabernacle were partly made (Exod. xxvi, 1, 31, 36) is from a root which
signifies *whiteness*, or *to be white*. It was also largely used in the
vestments of the high priest (Exod. xxviii, 5, 6, 8, 15, 39). Of
kindred signification is the Hebrew word בּוּץ, *white linen*, in which
the Levitical singers were arrayed (2 Chron. v, 12). With these
white garments of the priests and Levites (comp. Psa. cxxxii, 9)
we naturally associate the raiment "white as the light" in which
the transfigured Christ appeared (Matt. xvii, 2; Mark ix, 3), the
apparel of the angels (Matt. xxviii, 3; John xx, 12; Acts i, 10), the
white robes of the glorified (Rev. vii, 9), and the fine linen bright
and pure, symbolic of "the righteous acts of the saints" (Rev. xix,
8), which is the ornamental vesture of the wife of the Lamb. Also,
as characterizing the horses of victorious warriors (Zech. i, 8; vi,
3; Rev. vi, 2; xix, 11), and the throne of judgment (Rev. xx, 11),
white may represent victorious royalty and power.

Black, as being the opposite of white, would easily become associated with that which is evil, as mourning (Jer. xiv, 2),
pestilence, and famine (Rev. vi, 5, 6). Red is naturally
associated with war and bloodshed, as the armour of the armed
warrior is suggestive of tumult and garments rolled in blood (Isa.
ix, 5; Nah. ii, 3). But in any attempt to explain the symbolism
of a particular colour the interpreter should guard against pressing
the matter to an unwarranted extreme. The most prudent and
learned exegetes have reasonably doubted whether the different
colours of the horses seen in Zechariah's first vision (Zech. i, 8)
should be construed as having each a definite symbolical significance. The several colours of the curtains of the tabernacle appear to have been somewhat promiscuously blended together
(Exod. xxvi, 1, 31), and when thus used they served probably
for beauty and adornment rather than for separate and specific
symbolical import. Only as an interpreter is able to show from
parallel usage, analogy and inherent propriety, that a given colour
is used symbolically, will his exposition be entitled to command
assent.

The same thing, substantially, may be said of the symbolical import of metals. No specific significance should be sought in each separate metal or precious stone, for any attempt to point out such significancy is apt to run into various freaks of fancy.[1] But the pure gold with which the ark, mercy seat, cherubim, altar of incense, table, and candlestick, were either overlaid or entirely constructed (Exod. xxv), might very appropriately symbolize the light and splendour of God as he dwells in his holy temple. The altar of burntofferings was overlaid with brass or copper (Exod. xxvii, 2), an inferior metal. The pillars of the court were also made of this material (Exod. xxvii, 10). The sockets of the tabernacle boards, and the hooks and joinings of the pillars, were of silver (Exod. xxvi, 19; xxvii, 10). Outside of any attempt to trace a mystic meaning in each of these metals, it may be enough to say, in general, that gold, as being the more costly, would appropriately be used in constructing the holiest things of the inner sanctuary. Brass would, accordingly, be more appropriate for the things of the outer court, and silver, intermediate between the two, would naturally serve, to some extent, in both. The great image of Nebuchadnezzar's dream combined gold, silver, brass, iron, and clay (Dan. ii, 32, 33). The power, strength, and glory of the Babylonian monarchy, as represented in the regal splendour of the king, Nebuchadnezzar, was represented by the golden head (verses 37 and 38). The silver denoted an inferior kingdom. The iron denoted, especially, the strength of the fourth kingdom, "inasmuch as iron breaks in pieces and crushes everything" (ver. 40). So the different metals used in the construction of the tabernacle were expressive of the relative sanctity of its different parts. The twelve precious stones in the high priest's breastplate, bearing the names of the twelve tribes of Israel (Exod. xxviii, 15-21), and the twelve foundations of Jerusalem the golden (Rev. xxi, 14), may symbolize God's own elect as his precious jewels; but an effort to tell which tribe, or which apostle, was designated by each particular jewel, would lead the interpreter into unauthorized speculations, more likely to bewilder and confuse than to furnish any valuable lesson.

Symbolical import of the precious Metals and Jewels.

[1] See the third chapter of Bähr's Symbolik (vol. i, New ed.) on Das Baumaterial der Cultus-Stätte, pp. 283–330, in which not a little of valuable suggestion is presented along with much that is too fanciful to be safely accepted. See also Atwater, Sacred Tabernacle of the Hebrews, pp. 225–232.

CHAPTER XX.

DREAMS AND PROPHETIC ECSTACY.

IN an intelligent exposition of the prophetic portions of Holy Scrip-
Methods of di- ture, the methods and forms by which God communi-
vine revelation. cated supernatural revelations to men become questions
of fundamental importance. Dreams, night visions, and states of
spiritual ecstacy are mentioned as forms and conditions under which
men received such revelations. In Num. xii, 6, it is written: "If
there be a prophet among you, I, Jehovah, will make myself known
to him in the vision; in the dream will I speak within him."[1] The
open and visible manner in which Jehovah revealed himself to Moses is then (verses 7, 8) contrasted with ordinary visions, showing
that Moses was honoured above all prophets in the intimacy of his
communion with God. The *appearance* (תְּמֻנָה, *form, semblance,*
ver. 8) of Jehovah which Moses was permitted to behold was some
thing far above what other holy seers beheld (comp. Deut. xxxiv,
12). This appearance "was not the essential nature of God, his
unveiled glory, for this no mortal man can see (Exod. xxxiii, 18),
but a form which manifested the invisible God to the eye of man
in a clearly discernible mode, and which was essentially different,
not only from the visional sight of God in the form of a man
(Ezek. i, 26; Dan. vii, 9, 13), but also from the appearances of God
in the outward world of the senses in the person and form of the
angel of Jehovah, and stood in the same relation to these two forms
of revelation, so far as directness and clearness were concerned, as
the sight of a person in a dream to that of the actual figure of the
person himself. God talked with Moses without figure, in the
clear distinctness of a spiritual communication, whereas to the
prophets he only revealed himself through the medium of ecstacy
or dream."[2]

The dream is noticeably prominent among the earlier forms of
The Dreams of receiving divine revelations, but becomes less frequent
Scripture. at a later period. The most remarkable instances of
dreams recorded in the Scriptures are those of Abimelech (Gen. xx,

---

[1] בֹּו, *within him,* not *unto him,* as the common version. "*In him,*" says Keil, "inasmuch as a revelation in a dream fell within the inner sphere of the soul life."—
Commentary on the Pentateuch, in loco. Compare Job xxxiii, 14–17.

[2] Keil's Commentary on Num. xii, 8.

3–7), Jacob at Bethel (xxviii, 12), Laban in Mt. Gilead (xxxi, 24), Joseph respecting the sheaves and the luminaries (xxxvii, 5–10), the butler and the baker (xl, 5–19), Pharaoh (xli, 1–32), the Midianite (Judg. vii, 13–15), Solomon (1 Kings iii, 5; ix, 2), Nebuchadnezzar (Dan. ii and iv), Daniel (Dan. vii, 1), Joseph (Matt. i, 20; ii, 13, 19), and the Magi from the East (Matt. ii, 12). The "night vision" appears to have been of essentially the same nature as the dream (comp. Dan. ii, 19; vii, 1; Acts xvi, 9; xviii, 9; xxvii, 23).

It is manifest that in man's interior nature there exist powers and latent possibilities which only extraordinary occa- Dreams evince sions or peculiar conditions serve to display. And these latent powers facts it becomes the interpreter to note. These latent of the soul. powers are occasionally seen in cases of disordered mental action and insanity. The phenomena of somnambulism and clairvoyance also exhibit the same. And ordinary dreams, considered as abnormal operations of the perceptive faculties uncontrolled by the judgment and the will, are often of a striking and impressive character. The dreams of Joseph, of the butler and baker, and of the Midianite, are not represented as divine or supernatural revelations. Innumerable instances equally striking have occurred to other men. But at the same time, all such impressive dreams bring out into partial manifestation latent potencies of the human soul which may well have served in the communication of divine revelations to men. "The deep of man's internal nature," observes Delitzsch, "into which in sleep he sinks back, conceals far more than is manifest to himself. It has been a fundamental error of most psychologists hitherto to make the soul extend only so far as its consciousness extends; it embraces, as is now always acknowledged, a far greater abundance of powers and relations than can commonly appear in its consciousness. To this abundance pertains, moreover, the faculty of foreboding, that leads and warns a man without conscious motive, and anticipates the future—a faculty which, in the state of sleep, wherein the outer senses are fettered, is frequently unbound, and looms in the remoteness of the future." [1]

The profound and far-reaching significance of some prophetic dreams may be seen in that of Jacob at Bethel (Gen. Jacob's dream xxviii, 10–22). This son of Isaac was guilty of grave at Bethel. wrongs, but in his quiet and thoughful soul there was a hiding of power, a susceptibility for divine things, a spiritual insight and longing that made him a fitter person than Esau to lead in the development of the chosen nation. He appears to have passed the

---

[1] Biblical Psychology, English translation (Edinb., 1879). p. 330. See his whole section on Sleeping, Waking, and Dreaming, from which the above extract is taken.

night in the open field near the ancient town of Luz (ver. 19). Before darkness covered him he, doubtless, like Abraham in that same place long before (Gen. xiii, 14), looked northward, and southward, and eastward, and westward, and saw afar the hills and mountains towering up like a stairway into heaven, and this view may have been, in part, a psychological preparation for his dream. For, falling asleep, he beheld a ladder or stairway (סֻלָּם), perhaps a gigantic staircase composed of piles of mountains placed one upon another so as to look like a wondrous highway of passage to the skies. The main points of his dream fall under four BEHOLDS, three of vision—"behold, a ladder," "behold, angels of God," " behold, Jehovah " (verses 12, 13)—and one of promise—"behold, I am with thee " (ver. 15). These words imply an intense impressiveness in the whole revelation. It was a night vision by means of which the great future of Jacob and his seed was set forth in symbol and in promise. For Jacob at the bottom of the ladder, Jehovah at the top, and angels ascending and descending, form altogether a complex symbol full of profound suggestions. It indicated at least four things: (1) There is a way opened between earth and heaven by which spirits may ascend to God. (2) The ministry of angels. (3) The mystery of the incarnation: for the ladder was a symbol of the Son of man, the way (ἡ ὁδός, John xiv, 4, 6; Heb. ix, 8) into the holiest heaven, the Mediator upon whom, as the sole ground and basis of all possibility of grace, the angels of God ascend and descend to minister to the heirs of salvation (John i, 52). In that mystery of grace Jehovah himself reaches down as from the top of the ladder, and lays hold upon this son of Abraham and all his spiritual seed, and lifts them up to heaven. (4) The promise, in connexion with the vision (verses 13–15), emphasized the wonderful providence of God, who stood (ver. 13) gazing down upon this lonely, helpless man, and making gracious provision for him and his posterity.

We need not assume that Jacob understood the far-reaching import of that dream, but it led him to make a holy vow, and, doubtless, it was often afterward the subject of his quiet meditations. It could not fail to impress him with the conviction that he was a special object of Jehovah's care, and of the ministry of angels.

It is noticeable that the record of the prophetic dreams of the Interpretation heathen, as, for example, those of Pharaoh and his but- of dreams. ler and baker, of the Midianite, and of Nebuchadnezzar, are accompanied by an ample explanation. We observe also that the dreams of Joseph and of Pharaoh were double, or repeated under different forms. Joseph's first dream was a vision of sheaves in the harvest field; his second, of the sun, moon, and eleven stars (Gen. xxxvii, 5–11). They both conveyed the same prognostication, and were so far understood by his brethren and his father as to excite the envy of the former and draw the serious attention of the latter. Joseph explains the two dreams of Pharaoh as one (Gen. xli, 25), and declared that the repetition of the dream to Pharaoh twice was because the word was established from God, and God was hastening to accomplish it (ver. 32). Here is a hint for the interpretation of other dreams and visions. Daniel's dream-vision of the four beasts out of the sea (Dan. vii) is, in substance, a repetition of Nebuchadnezzar's dream of the great image, and the visions of the eighth and eleventh chapters, go partly over the same ground again. God thus repeats his revelations under various forms, and thereby denotes their certainty as the determinate purposes of his will. Many visions of the Apocalypse are also, apparently, symbols of the same events, or else move so largely over the same field as to warrant the belief that they, too, are repetitions, under different forms, of things that were shortly to come to pass, and the certainty of which was fixed in the purposes of God.

Repetition of dreams and visions.

But dreams, we observed, were rather the earlier and lower forms of divine revelation. A higher form was that of prophetic ecstasy, in which the spirit of the seer became possessed of the Spirit of God, and, while yet retaining its human consciousness, and susceptible of human emotion, was rapt away into visions of the Almighty and made cognizant of words and things which no mortal could naturally perceive. In 2 Sam. vii, 4–17, we have the record of "a word of Jehovah" that came to Nathan in a night vision (see ver. 17) and was communicated to David. It contained the prophecy and promise that his kingdom and throne should be established forever. It was for David an impressive oracle, and he "went and sat down before Jehovah" (ver. 18), and wondered and worshipped. Such wonder and worship were probably, at that or some other time, a means of inducing the psychological condition and spiritual ecstasy in which the second psalm was composed. David becomes a seer and prophet. "The Spirit of Jehovah spoke within him, and his word was upon his tongue" (2 Sam. xxiii, 2). He is lifted into visional ecstasy, in which the substance of Nathan's prophecy takes a new and higher form, transcending all earthly royalty and power. He sees Jehovah enthroning his Anointed (מְשִׁיחוֹ, *his Messiah*) upon Zion, the mountain of his holiness (Psa. ii, 2, 6). The nations rage against him, and struggle to cast off his authority, but they are

Prophetic ecstasy or visional trance.

utterly discomfited by him who "sitteth in the heavens," and to
whom the nations are given for an inheritance. Thus, the second
psalm is seen to be no mere historical ode, composed upon the regal
inauguration of David or Solomon, or any other earthly prince.
A greater than either David or Solomon arose in the psalmist's
vision. For he is clearly styled the Messiah, the Son of Jehovah;
the kings and judges of the earth are counselled to kiss him, that
they may not perish, and all who put their trust in him are
pronounced blessed. And it is only as the interpreter attains a
vivid apprehension of the power of such ecstasy that he can
properly perceive or explain the import of any Messianic prophecy.

Another illustration of the prophetical ecstasy may be seen in
Ezekiel's Rapture. Ezekiel's statements. At the beginning of his prophecies he uses four different expressions to indicate the
form and power in which he received revelations (Ezek. i, 1, 3).
The heavens were opened, visions of God were seen, the word of
Jehovah came with great force,[1] and the hand of Jehovah was laid
upon him. Allowing for whatever of the poetical element these
expressions contain, it remains evident that the prophet experienced
a mighty interworking of human and superhuman powers. The
visions of God caused him to fall upon his face (ver. 28), and, anon,
the Spirit lifted him up upon his feet (chap. ii, 1, 2). At another
time the form of a hand reached forth and took him by a lock of
his head, and transported him in the visions of God to Jerusalem
(Ezek. viii, 3). From this it would appear that for a mortal man
to receive consciously a revelation from the Infinite Spirit two
things are essential. The human spirit must become divinely exalted, or rapt away from its ordinary life and operations, and the
Divine Spirit must so take possession of its energies, and quicken
them into supersensual perception, that they become temporary
organs of the Infinite. The whole process is manifestly a divine-
human, or theandric operation. And yet, through it all, the human
spirit retains its normal consciousness and knows the vision is
divine.

The same things appear also in the visions of Daniel. He be-
Other examples holds the prophetic symbols, he hears the words of the
of Ecstasy. angel interpreter Gabriel, and he too falls upon his
face, overwhelmed with the deep sleep that stupifies the active
powers of the mind, and puts him in full possession of the revealing angel (Dan. viii, 17, 18). The touch of the angel lifts him into
the ecstasy in which he sees and hears the heavenly word. This

---

[1] Heb. הָיֹה הָיָה, *coming came*, the Hebrew idiomatic way of giving emphasis to a
thought by repeating the verb, and using its absolute infinitive form.

peculiar form of prophetic ecstasy appears to have differed from the "dream and visions of his head upon his bed" (Dan. vii, 1), in that this latter seized him during the slumbers of the night, whereas the other came upon him during his waking consciousness, and probably while in the act of prayer (comp. chap. ix, 21). The ecstasy which came upon Peter on the housetop came in connexion with his praying and a sense of great hunger (Acts x, 9, 10). The act of prayer was a spiritual preparation, and the hunger furnished a physical and psychical condition, by means of which the form of the vision and the command to slay and eat became the more impressive. Paul's similar ecstasy in the temple at Jerusalem was preceded by prayer (Acts xxii, 17). and his experience of these "visions and revelations of God," narrated in 2 Cor. xii, 1–4, was in such a transcendent rapture of soul that he knew not whether he were in the body or out of the body. That is, he knew not whether his whole person had been rapt away in visions of God, like Ezekiel (viii, 3), or whether merely the spirit had been elevated into visional ecstasy. His consciousness in this matter seems to have been overcome by the excessive greatness ($\dot{\upsilon}\pi\epsilon\rho\beta o\lambda\dot{\eta}$) of the revelations (ver. 7). And probably had Ezekiel been called upon to say whether his rapture to Jerusalem were in the body or out of the body, he would have answered as uncertainly as Paul.

The prophetic ecstasy, of which the above are notable examples, was evidently a spiritual sight seeing,[1] a supernatural illumination, in which the natural eye was either closed (comp. Num. xxiv, 3, 4) or suspended from its ordinary functions, and the inner senses vividly grasped the scene that was presented, or the divine word which was revealed. We need not refine so far as, with Delitzsch, to classify this divine ecstasy into three forms, as mystic, prophetic, and charismatic. All ecstasy is mystic, and charismatic ecstasy may have been prophetic; but we may still, with him, define prophetic ecstasy as consisting essentially in this, that the human spirit is seized and compassed by the Divine Spirit, which searcheth all things, even the deep things of God, and seized with such uplifting energy that, being averted from its ordinary conditions of limitation in the body, it becomes altogether a seeing eye, a hearing ear, a perceiving sense, that takes most vivid cognizance of things in time or eternity, according as they are presented by the power and wisdom of God.[2]

The grandest form of prophetic ecstasy is that in which the vision

---

[1] For this reason the Old Testament prophet is often called the *seer* (רָאָה and חָזָה). He was a *beholder* of visions from the Almighty.

[2] Comp. Delitzsch, Biblical Psychology, p. 421.

(חֵן) and word (דָּבָר) of Jehovah appear to have become so absorbed by the prophet's heaven-lit soul that he himself personates the Holy One, and speaks in Jehovah's name. So we understand the later chapters of Isaiah, where the person of the prophet sinks comparatively out of sight, and Jehovah announces himself as the speaker. So, too, Zechariah announces the word of Jehovah touching "the flock of slaughter" Zech. xi, 4), but as he proceeds with the divine oracle, he seems to lose the consciousness of his own distinct personality, and to speak in the name and person of his Lord (vers. 10–14).[1]

The prophet lost in God.

A later and mysterious manifestation of spiritual ecstasy appears in the New Testament glossolaly, or gift of speaking with tongues. Among the signs to follow those who should believe through the apostles' preaching, a speaking with "new[2] tongues" was specified (Mark xvi, 17); and the disciples were commanded by Jesus to tarry in the city of Jerusalem until they were clothed with power from on high (Luke xxiv, 49). On the day of Pentecost "there came suddenly from heaven a sound as of a rushing mighty wind, and it filled all the house where they were sitting, and there appeared unto them self-distributing (διαμεριζόμεναι) tongues as of fire, and it sat upon each one of them, and they were all filled with the Holy Spirit, and they began to speak with other tongues as the Spirit gave them utterance" (Acts ii, 3, 4). A like display was manifest at the conversion of Cornelius (Acts x, 46), and when, after their baptism, Paul laid his hands upon the twelve disciples of John the Baptist whom he found at Ephesus (Acts xix, 6). But the most extensive treatment of the subject is found in 1 Cor. xiv, with which are to be compared also the incidental references in chaps. xii, 10, 28, and xiii, 1. From this Corinthian epistle it appears, (1) that it was a supernatural gift, a divine χάρισμα, that marked with a measure of novelty the first outgoings of the Gospel of Christ. (2) There were different kinds (γένη, sorts, classes, 1 Cor. xii, 10) of tongues. (3) The speaking with tongues was a speaking unto God rather than man (xiv, 2) and an utterance of mysteries, which edified the subjective spirit of the

Glossolaly, or speaking with tongues.

---

[1] "The prophet himself sometimes speaks from God," observes Delitzsch, "sometimes God himself speaks from the prophet; sometimes the divine Ego asserts itself with a supreme power that absorbs all other, sometimes the human in the entire fulness of sanctified humanity; but in both cases it is the personality of the prophet, in the totality of its pneumatico-psychical powers, which becomes the more active or passive organ of God."—Biblical Psychology, p. 421.

[2] The word καιναῖς, new, is omitted by several of the chief MS. authorities for the close of Mark's Gospel. In Westcott and Hort's edition of the Greek Testament the word is placed in the margin, but omitted from the text.

speaker (ver. 4), but was unintelligible to the common understanding (νοῦς, ver. 14). (4) The speaking with tongues took the form of worship, and manifested itself in prayer, singing, and thanksgiving (vers. 14-16). (5) Though edifying to the speaker, it did not tend to edify the Church unless one gifted with the interpretation of tongues, either the speaker himself or another, explained what was uttered. (6) It was a sign to the unbeliever, accompanied probably with such evidences of the supernatural as, at first, to impress the hearer with a sense of awe, but calculated on the whole to lead such as had no sympathy with the Gospel to say that these speakers were either mad or filled with wine (ver. 23; comp. Acts ii, 13). (7) It was a gift for which one might thank God (ver. 18), and not to be forbidden in the Church (ver. 39), but was to be coveted less than other charisms, and, especially, less than the gift of prophesying unto the edifying of the Church (vers. 1, 5, 19); for "greater is he who prophesies than he who speaks with tongues, except he interpret."

Such is substantially what Paul says of this remarkable gift. On the day of Pentecost it took the form of appropriating the various dialects of the hearers, so as to fill them all with amazement and wonder (Acts ii, 5-12). This, how- ever, appears to have been an exceptional manifestation, perhaps a miraculous exhibition, for a symbolic purpose, of all the *kinds* of tongues (comp. 1 Cor. xii, 10), which on other occasions were separate and individually distinct. Certainly the speaking with tongues in the Corinthian church was accompanied by no such effect upon the hearers as on the day of Pentecost. The once prevalent notion that this glossolaly was a supernatural gift, by which the first preachers of the Gospel were enabled to proclaim the word of life in the various languages of foreign nations, has little in its favour. There is no intimation, outside of the miracle of Pentecost, that this gift ever served such a purpose. And that miracle, whatever its real nature, seems rather like a symbolical sign, signifying that the confusion of tongues, which came as a curse at Babel, should be counteracted and abolished by the Gospel of the new life, then just breaking in heavenly charismatic power upon the world.[1] That evangelic word was destined to become potent in all the languages of men, and by the living voice of preachers, and through the written volume, utter its heavenly messages to the nations, until all should know the Lord.

The Pentecostal Glossolaly symbolical.

---

[1] Poena linguarum dispersit homines (Gen. xi); donum linguarum dispersos in unam populum collegit (The punishment of tongues scattered men abroad; the gift of tongues gathered the dispersed into one people).—Grotius, Annotations on Acts, ii, 8.

The exact nature of the New Testament glossolaly it is probably now impossible to define. It may have been, in some instances, a soul-ecstasy, in which men worshipped strangely, and lost control of a part of their faculties. Something like this was experienced by Saul when he met the band of prophets (1 Sam. x, 9-12), and when, at a later time, he prophesied before Samuel, and fell down under the power of the Spirit of God (1 Sam. xix, 23, 24). At other times it may have been a condition of receiving visions and revelations of God, as when Paul was caught up to paradise, "and heard unspeakable words, which it is not lawful for a man to utter " (2 Cor. xii, 4). Possibly in that heavenly rapture this apostle received his conception of "the tongues of the angels" (1 Cor. xiii, 1).[1] But whatever its real nature, it was essentially an ecstatic speaking of mysteries (1 Cor. xiv, 2), involving such a divine communion with God as lifted the spirit of the rapt believer into the realm of the unseen and eternal, and produced in him an awe-inspiring sense of supernatural exaltation.[2]

Glossolaly a mysterious power.

[1] According to Stanley, the gift of tongues "was a trance or ecstasy, which, in moments of great religious fervour, especially at the moment of conversion, seized the early believers; and this fervour vented itself in expressions of thanksgiving, in fragments of psalmody or hymnody and prayer, which to the speaker himself conveyed an irresistible sense of communion with God, and to the bystander an impression of some extraordinary manifestation of power, but not necessarily any instruction or teaching, and sometimes even having the appearance of wild excitement, like that of madness or intoxication. It was the most emphatic sign to each individual believer that a power mightier than his own was come into the world; and in those who, like the Apostle Paul, possessed this gift in a high degree, 'speaking with tongues more than they all,' it would, when combined with the other more remarkable gifts which he possessed, form a fitting mood for the reception of ' God's secrets ' ($\mu\nu\sigma\tau\dot{\eta}\rho\iota\alpha$), and of 'unspeakable words, which it is not lawful for man to utter,' 'being caught into the third heaven,' and into ' Paradise.' And thus the nearest written example of this gift is that exhibited in the abrupt style and the strange visions of the Apocalypse, in which, almost in the words of St. Paul, the prophet is described as being 'in the Spirit on the Lord's day,' and 'hearing a voice as of a trumpet,' and seeing ' a door open in heaven,' and 'a throne set in heaven,' and 'the New Jerusalem,' ' the river of life,' and 'the tree of life.'"—Epistles of St. Paul to the Corinthians, pp. 246, 247. London, 1876.

[2] See Rossteuscher, Gabe der Sprachen (Marb., 1850); Hilgenfeld, Glossolalie in der alten Kirche (Lpz., 1850); Neander, Planting and Training, of the Christian Church (New ed., New York, 1864), Book I, chap. i; Schaff, Hist. of the Christian Church (New ed., New York, 1882), vol. i, pp. 230-242; Stanley, St. Paul's Epistles to the Corinthians, Introductory Dissertation to chap. xiv; Kling on the Corinthians (in Lange's Biblework), pp. 282-301, Amer. ed., translated and enlarged by Dr. Poor; Keim, article Zungenreden, in Herzog's Real-Encyclopädie (vol. xviii, ed. Gotha, 1864); Plumptre's article on the Gift of Tongues in Smith's Dictionary of the Bible.

CHAPTER XXI.

PROPHECY AND ITS INTERPRETATION.

A THOROUGH interpretation of the prophetic portions of the holy Scripture is largely dependent upon a mastery of the principles and laws of figurative language, and of types and symbols. It requires also some acquaintance with the nature of vision-seeing ecstacy and dreams. The foregoing chapters have, therefore, been a necessary preparation for an intelligent study of those more abstruse writings, which have continuously exercised the most gifted minds of the Church, and yet have been most variously interpreted.

Inspired oracles, forecasting the future, wrought out with every variety of figurative speech, and often embodied in type and symbol, are interspersed throughout the entire Scriptures, and constitute a uniting bond between the Old Testament and the New. The first great prophecy was uttered in Paradise, where man originally sinned and first felt the need of a Redeemer. It was repeated in many forms and portions as years and centuries passed. The Christ of God, the mighty Prophet, Priest, and King, was its loftiest theme; but it also dealt so copiously with all man's relations to God and to the world, with human hopes and fears, with civil governments and national responsibilities, with divine laws and purposes, that its written records are a, textbook of divine counsel for all time.[1]

Magnitude and scope of Scripture Prophecy.

Prophesying, according to the Scriptures, is not primarily a prediction of future events. The Hebrew word for prophet, נָבִיא,

---

[1] The subjects of prophecy varied. Whilst it was all directed to one general design, in the evidence and support of religion, there was a diversity in the administration of the Spirit in respect of that design. In Paradise, it gave the first hope of a Redeemer. After the deluge, it established the peace of the natural world. In Abraham it founded the double covenant of Canaan and the Gospel. In the age of the law, it spoke of the second prophet, and foreshadowed, in types, the Christian doctrine, but foretold most largely the future fate of the selected people, who were placed under that preparatory dispensation. In the time of David it revealed the Gospel kingdom, with the promise of the temporal. In the days of the later prophets it presignified the changes of the Mosaic covenant, embraced the history of the chief pagan kingdoms, and completed the annunciation of the Messiah and his work of redemption. After the captivity, it gave a last and more urgent information of the approaching advent of the Gospel.—Davison, Discourses on Prophecy, pp. 355, 356. Oxford, 1834.

signifies one who speaks under the pressure of a divine fervour,[1]
Prophecy not and the prophet is especially to be regarded as one who
merely predic- bears a divine message, and acts as the spokesman of
tion, but utter-
ance of God's the Almighty. Aaron was divinely appointed as the
truth. spokesman of Moses, to repeat God's word from his
mouth (Exod. iv, 16), and thereby was Moses made as God to
Pharaoh, and Aaron served as his prophet (נָבִיא, Exod. vii, 1).
Hence the prophet is the announcer of a divine message, and that
message may refer to the past, the present, or the future. It may
be a revelation, a warning, a rebuke, an exhortation, a promise, or
a prediction. The bearer of such a message is appropriately called
a "man of God" (1 Kings xiii, 1; 2 Kings iv, 7, 9), and a "man of
the Spirit" (Hos. ix, 7). It is important also to observe that a very
large proportion of the Old Testament prophetical books consists
of warning, expostulation, and rebuke; and there are intimations
of many unwritten prophecies of this character. "The prophets,"
says Fairbairn, "were in a peculiar sense the spiritual watchmen of
Judah and Israel, the representatives of divine truth and holiness,
whose part it was to keep a wakeful and jealous eye upon the manners of the times, to detect and reprove the symptoms of defection
which appeared, and by every means in their power foster and encourage the spirit of real godliness. And such pre-eminently was
Elijah, who is therefore taken in the Scripture as the type of the
whole prophetical order in the earlier stages of its development; a
man of heroic energy of action rather than of prolific thought and
elevating discourse. The words he spoke were few, but they were
words spoken as from the secret place of thunder, and seemed more
like decrees issuing from the presence of the Eternal than the utterances of one of like passions with those whom he addressed."[2]

[1] Gesenius derives the word from the root נָבָא, equivalent to נָבַע, to *boil forth;* to
gush out; to *flow,* as a fountain. Hence the idea of one upon whom the vision-seeing
ecstacy falls; or of one who is borne along and carried aloft by a supernatural inspiration (ὑπὸ πνεύματος ἁγίου φερόμενοι; 2 Pet. i, 21). "Hebrew prophecy, like the
Hebrew people, stands without parallel in the history of the world. Other nations
have had their oracles, diviners, augurs, soothsayers, necromancers. The Hebrews
alone have possessed prophets and a prophetic literature. It is useless, therefore, to
go to the manticism of the heathen to get light as to the nature of Hebrew prophecy.
To follow the rabbis of the twelfth and thirteenth centuries is just as vain. The
only reliable sources of information on the subject are the Scriptures of the Old and
New Testaments."—M'Call, in Aids to Faith, p. 97. On the distinction between the
prophet (נָבִיא) and the seer (רֹאֶה, and חֹזֶה) see Smith, Prophecy a Preparation for
Christ (Bampton Lectures), pp. 68–86. Boston, 1870.

[2] Prophecy, viewed in respect to its Distinctive Nature, Special Functions, and
Proper Interpretation, p. 37. N. Y., 1866. Philippi (Commentary on Romans xii, 6)
observes that "the New Testament idea of the prophetic office is essentially identical

It is principally those portions of the prophetic Scriptures which forecast the future that call for special hermeneutics. *Only prophecies of the future call for special hermeneutics.* Being exceptional in their character, they demand exceptional study and care in interpretation. Other prophecies, consisting mainly of rebuke, expostulation, or warning, are so readily apprehended by the common mind as to need no extended explanation. Avoiding, on the one side, the extreme literalistic error that the biblical predictions are "history written beforehand," and on the other, the rationalistic notions that they are either happy guesses of the probable outcome of impending events, or else a peculiar portraiture of them after they had taken place (*vaticinium post eventum*), we accept these predictions as divine oracles of events that were subsequently to come to pass, but so expressed in figure and symbol as to demand great care on the part of him who would understand and interpret them. When we deny that prophecy is a history of events before they come to pass, we mean to say that prophecy is in no proper sense history. *History and prediction should not be confused.* History is the record of what has already occurred; prediction is a foretelling of what is to come, and nearly always in some form of statement or revelation that takes it outside of the line of literal narrative. There are cases, indeed, where the prediction is a specific declaration of incidents of the simplest character; as when Samuel foretold to Saul the particular events that would befall him on his return to Gibeah (1 Sam. x, 3–6); but it is misleading to call even such predictions a *history* of future events, for it is a confusion of the proper usage of words. There is an element of mystery about all predictions, and those of greatest moment in the Scriptures are clothed in a symbolic drapery.[1]

with that of the Old Testament. Prophets are men who, inspired by the Spirit of God, and impelled to theopneustic discourse, partly remove the veil from the future (Rev. i, 3; xxii, 7, 10; John xi, 51; Acts xi, 27, 28; xxi, 10, 11. Comp. 1 Pet. i, 10)—partly make known concealed facts of the present, either in discovering the secret counsel and will of God (Luke i, 67; Acts xiii, 1; Eph. iii, 5), or in disclosing the hidden thoughts of man (1 Cor. xiv, 24, 25), and dragging into light his unknown deeds (Matt. xxvi, 68; Mark xiv, 65; Luke xxii, 64; John iv, 19)—partly dispense to their hearers instruction, comfort, exhortation, in animated, powerfully impassioned language, going far beyond the wonted limits of the capacity for teaching, which, although spiritual, still confines itself within the forms of reason (Matt. vii, 28, 29; Luke xxiv, 19; John vii, 40; Acts xv, 32; 1 Cor. xiv, 3, 4, 31)."

[1] Fairbairn has an able chapter on "The place of prophecy in history, and the organic connexion of the one with the other" (Prophecy, pp. 33–53). He traces the beginning and growth of prophecy in the sacred history, showing how "it appears somewhat like a river, small in its beginnings, and though still proceeding, yet often losing itself for ages under ground, then bursting forth anew with increased volume, and at last rising into a swollen stream—greatest by far when it has come within

In order to a proper interpretation of prophecy three things are to be particularly studied, (1) the organic relations and inter-dependence of the principal predictions on record; (2) the usage and import of figures and symbols; and (3) analysis and comparison of similar prophecies, especially such as have been divinely interpreted, and such as have been clearly fulfilled.

Fundamental principles.

1. ORGANIC RELATIONS OF PROPHECY.

In studying the general structure and organic relations of the great prophecies, it will be seen that they are first presented in broad and bold outline, and subsequently expanded in their minor details. Thus the first great prophecy on record (Gen. iii, 15) is a brief but far-reaching announcement of the long conflict between good and evil, as these opposing principles, with all their forces, connect themselves with the Promised Seed of the woman on the one side, and the old serpent, the devil, on the other. It may be said that all other prophecies of the Christ and the kingdom of God are comprehended in the *protevangelium* as in a germ. From this point onward through the Scripture revelations the successive prophecies sustain a noticeably progressive character. Varying ideas of the Promised Seed appear in the prophecy of Noah (Gen. ix, 26, 27), and the repeated promises to Abraham (Gen. xii, 3; xvii, 2–8; xviii, 18). These Messianic predictions became more definite as they were repeatedly confirmed to Isaac, to Jacob, to Judah, and to the house of David. They constitute the noblest psalms and the grandest portions of the Greater and the Lesser Prophets. Taken separately, these different predictions are of a fragmentary character; each prophet

Progressive character of Messianic prophecy.

prospect of its termination" (p. 33). He observes further (p. 43): "Prophecy, therefore, being from the very first inseparably linked with the plan of grace unfolded in Scripture, is, at the same time, the necessary concomitant of sacred history. The two mutually act and react on each other. Prophecy gives birth to the history; the history, in turn, as it moves onward to its destined completion, at once fulfils prophecies already given, and calls forth further revelations. And so far from possessing the character of an excrescence, or existing merely as an anomaly in the procedure of God toward men, prophecy cannot even be rightly understood unless viewed in the relation to the order of the divine dispensations, and its actual place in history. . . . However closely related the two are to each other, they still have their own distinctive characteristics and, through these, their respective ends to serve. History is the *occasion* of prophecy, but not its *measure ;* for prophecy rises above history, borne aloft by wings which carry it far above the present, and which it derives, not from the past occurrences of which history takes cognizance, but from Him to whom the future and the past are alike known. It is the communication of so much of his own supernatural light as he sees fit to let down upon the dark movements of history, to show whither they are conducting."

knew or caught glimpses of the Messianic future only in part, and he prophesied in part (1 Cor. xiii, 9); but when the Christ himself appeared, and fulfilled the prophecies, then all these fragmentary parts were seen to form a glorious harmony.[1]

The oracle of Balaam touching Moab, Edom, Amalek, the Kenites, Asshur, and the power from the side of Chittim (Num. xxiv, 17-24), is the prophetic germ of many later oracles against these and similar enemies of the chosen people. *Repetitions of oracles against heathen powers.* Amos long after takes up the prophetic word, and speaks more fully against Damascus, Gaza, Tyre, Edom, Ammon, and Moab, and does not except even Judah and Israel (Amos i and ii). Compare also Isaiah's burden-prophecies (משא) against Babylon, Moab, Damascus, Ethiopia, Egypt, Media, Edom, Arabia, and Tyre (Isa. xiii-xxiii), in which we observe the minatory sentence uttered against these heathen powers in great detail. And as Balaam noticed the affliction of Eber, (i. e., Israel) in connexion with his last-named hostile power from Chittim (Num. xxiv, 24), so Isaiah introduces the "burden of the valley of vision" (Isa. xxii, 1) just before announcing the overthrow of Tyre (Isa. xxiii, 1). Jeremiah devotes chapters xlvi to li to the announcement of judgments upon Egypt, Philistia, Moab, Ammon, Edom, Damascus, Kedar, Hazor, Elam, and Babylon, and amid these utterances of coming wrath are intimations of Israel's dispersion and sorrow (comp. chap. l, 17-20, 33; li, 5, 6, 45). Compare also Ezekiel's seven oracles against Ammon, Moab, Edom, Philistia, Tyre, Sidon and Egypt (Ezek. xxv to xxxii).

In noticeable analogy with the repetition of similar prophecies by different prophets, is the repetition of the same prophecy by one and the same prophet.

The vision of the four great beasts, in Dan. vii, is essentially a repetition of the vision of the great image in chapter ii. The same four great world-powers are denoted in these prophecies; but, as has often been observed, the imagery *Daniel's two great prophecies (chaps. ii and vii) compared.* is varied according to the relative standpoint of the king and the prophet. "As presented to the view of Nebuchadnezzar, the worldly power was seen only in its *external* aspect, under the form of a colossal image possessing the likeness of a man, and in its more

---

[1] On the Messianic prophecies see J. Pye Smith, Scripture Testimony to the Messiah, 3 vols. (Lond., 1829); Hengstenberg, Christology of the Old Testament, 4 vols. (Eng. trans. by Meyer, Edinb., 1863); Tholuck, Die Propheten und ihre Weissagungen, pp. 146-189 (Gotha, 1860); Leathes, Witness of the Old Testament to Christ (Boyle Lectures for 1868); Riehm, Messianic Prophecy (Eng. trans., Edinb., 1876); Gloag, The Messianic Prophecies, pp. 98-208 (Baird Lecture, Edinb., 1879).

conspicuous parts composed of the shining and precious metals; while the divine kingdom appeared in the meaner aspect of a stone, without ornament or beauty, with nothing, indeed, to distinguish it but its resistless energy and perpetual duration. Daniel's visions, on the other hand, direct the eye into the *interior* of things, strip the earthly kingdoms of their false glory by exhibiting them under the aspects of wild beasts and nameless monsters (such as are everywhere to be seen in the grotesque sculptures and painted entablatures of Babylon), and reserve the *human* form, in conformity with its divine, original, and true idea, to stand as the representative of the kingdom of God, which is composed of the saints of the Most High, and holds the truth that is destined to prevail over all error and ungodliness of men." [1]

So, again, the impressive vision of the ram and the he-goat, in Dan. viii, is but a repetition from another standpoint (Shushan, in Elam, a chief seat of the Medo-Persian monarchy) of the previous vision of the third and fourth beasts. Differences in detail appear according to the analogy of all such repeated prophecies, but these minor differences should not be allowed to obscure and obliterate the great fundamental analogies. Few expositors of any note have doubted that the little horn of Dan. viii, 9, denoted Antiochus Epiphanes, the bitter persecutor of the Jews, who "spoiled the temple, and put a stop to the constant practice of offering a daily sacrifice of expiation for three years and six months." [2] The first and most natural presumption is that the little horn of chap. vii, 8, denotes the same impious and violent persecutor. The fact that one prophecy delineates the impiety and violence of this enemy more fully than another is no evidence that two different persons are intended. Otherwise the still fuller delineation of this monster of iniquity, given in chap. xi, must on this sole ground be referred to yet another person. The statements that the little horn of chap. vii, 8 came up between the ten horns, and rooted up three of them, and that of chap. viii, 9 came out from one of the four horns of the he-goat, can have no force in disproving the identity of the little horns in both passages unless it is assumed that the four horns of chap. viii, 8 are identical with the ten horns of chap. vii, 7 —an assumption which no one will allow. These are but the minor variations called for by the different positions occupied by the prophet in the different visions. If we understand the ten horns of chap. vii, 7 as a round number denoting the kings more fully

The little horn of Dan. vii, 8, and viii, 9, the same power under different prophetic aspects.

---

[1] Fairbairn on Prophecy, p. 122.
[2] Josephus, Wars, i, 1. Comp. Ant., xii, 5, 4, and 1 Maccabees i.

described in chap. xi, and the four conspicuous horns of chap. viii, 8 as the four notable successors of Alexander, the harmony of the two visions will be readily apparent. From one point of view the great horn (Alexander) was succeeded by ten horns, and also a lit- tle horn more notable in some respects than any of the ten; from another standpoint the great horn was seen to be followed by four notable horns (the famous Diadochoi), from the stump of one of which (Seleucus) came forth Antiochus Epiphanes. Only a failure to note the repetition of prophecies under various forms, and from different points of view, occasions the trouble which some have found in identifying prophecies of essentially the same great events.[1]

According to the principle here illustrated the still more minute prophecy of the later period of the Græco-Macedonian Empire, in Dan. xi, is seen to travel over much of the same field as those of chapters vii and viii. In the same manner we should naturally presume that the seven vials of the seven last plagues in Rev. xvi are intended to correspond with the seven woe-trumpets of chapters viii–xi. The striking resemblances between the two are such as to force a conviction that the terrible woes

Other prophetic repetitions.

---

[1] Pusey's discussion of this subject (Lectures on Daniel, Oxford, 1868) is an illustration of the dogmatic way in which a writer may magnify and mystify the merely formal and structural differences of visions. He affirms (p. 91): "The four-horned he-goat cannot agree with the fourth empire, whose division into ten is marked by the ten horns of the terrible beast and the ten toes of the image. Nor can the heavy ram, with its two horns, be identified with the superhuman swiftness of the four-headed leopard." But, according to Pusey, the two-horned ram of chap. viii, 3, 4, corre-sponds with the bear of chap. vii, 5, and the he-goat corresponds with the four-winged and four-headed leopard of chap. vii, 6. If, then, a ram with two horns "pushing westward, and northward, and southward, etc." (viii, 4), agrees with a bear having no horns at all, and, so far from pushing in any direction, is merely "raised up on one side ready to use the arm in which its chief strength lies," and "lifts itself up heav-ily, in contrast with the winged rapidity of the Chaldean conquests" (Pusey, p. 72), and holds three ribs in its teeth—with what consistency can it be claimed that the differences in the descriptions of the little horns of chaps. vii and viii must be fun-damental? Pusey has no difficulty in harmonizing a he-goat having one notable horn, and then four horns in its place, and one little horn branching out of one of the four, with a leopard having four wings and four heads; but he pronounces it impossible for a goat which at one stage has one horn, and at another four, to agree with a ter-rible beast which at one period had ten horns! It is, forsooth, easy to harmonize an animal having one horn and four horns, with an animal having four heads and four wings, and no horns at all; but impossible to believe that a goat having one horn, and afterward four horns, can agree with a beast having ten horns! Such incon-sistency cannot be based upon sound hermeneutical principles. See Zöckler on Dan-iel in loco, translated and annotated by Strong in the American edition of Lange's Biblework.

denoted by the trumpets are substantially identical with the plagues denoted by the vials of wrath. A contrary opinion would make the case a remarkable exception to the analogy of prophecy, and should not be accepted without the most convincing reasons.

2. FIGURATIVE AND SYMBOLICAL STYLE OF PROPHECY.

The fact already observed, that the word of prophecy was received by visions and dreams, and in a state of ecstacy, accounts largely for the further fact that so great a portion of the prophetic Scriptures is set forth in figurative language and in symbol.[1] This important fact is too often overlooked in prophetic interpretation, and hence has arisen the misleading doctrine that prophecy is "history written beforehand." Accepting such an idea, one is prone to press the literal meaning of all passages which may, by any possibility, admit of such a construction; and hence the endless controversies and vagaries in the exposition of the prophetical Scriptures. But observe for a moment the style and diction of the great predictions. The first one on record announces a standing enmity between the serpent and the woman and their progeny; and, addressing the serpent, God says: "He shall bruise thy head, and thou shalt bruise his heel" (Gen. iii, 15). There have not been wanting literalists who have applied the prophecy to the enmity between men and serpents, and who declare that it is fulfilled whenever a serpent bites a man, or whenever a man crushes a serpent's head. But such an interpretation of the passage has never been able to command any general acceptance. Its deeper import respecting the children of light and the children of darkness, and

[margin note: Imagery the most natural form of expressing revelations obtained by visions and dreams.]

---

[1] The fundamental reason of the figurative style, which is so prominent a characteristic of prophecy, must be sought in the mode of revelation by vision. In the higher species of prophecy, which was connected with no ecstatic elevation on the part of the writer, but with his ordinary frame of mind; that, namely, of which the most eminent examples are to be found in Moses and Christ; the language employed does not, in general, differ from the style of ordinary discourse. But prophecy, in the more special and peculiar sense, having been not only framed on purpose to veil while it announced the future, but also communicated in vision to the prophets, must have largely consisted of figurative representations; for, as in vision it is the imaginative faculty that is more immediately called into play, images were necessary to make on it the fitting impressions, and these impressions could only be conveyed to others by means of figurative representations. Hence the two, prophetic visions and figurative representations, are coupled together by the prophet Hosea (xii, 10) as the proper correlatives of each other: "I have also spoken by the prophets, and I have multiplied visions and used similitudes by the ministry of the prophets."—Fairbairn on Prophecy, p. 147.

their respective heads (Messiah and Satan), has been universally recognized by the best interpreters. "It is a sign and witness," says Fairbairn, " set up at the very threshold of the prophetic ^{Fairbairn on} territory, showing how much prophecy, in the general ^{Gen. iii, 15.} form of its announcements, might be expected to take its hue and aspect from the occasion and circumstances that gave rise to it; how it would serve itself of things seen and present as a symbolical cover under which to exhibit a perspective of things which were to be hereafter; and how, even when there might be a certain fulfilment of what was written according to the letter, the terms of the prediction might yet be such as to make it evident that something of a higher kind was required properly to verify its meaning. Such plainly was the case with respect to the prediction at the fall; and in proof that it must be so read and understood, some of the later intimations of prophecy, which are founded upon the address to the serpent, vary the precise form of the representation which they give of the ultimate termination of the conflict. Thus Isaiah, when descanting on the peace and blessedness of Messiah's kingdom, tells us not of the serpent's head being bruised, but of his power to hurt being destroyed; of dust being his meat, and of the child playing upon his hole (chapters xi, 8, 9; lxv, 25). It is the same truth again that appears at the close of the Apocalypse under the still different form of chaining the old serpent, and casting him into the bottomless pit, that he might not deceive the nations any more (Rev. xx, 2, 3); his power to deceive in the one case corresponding to his liberty to bruise the heel in the other, and his being chained and imprisoned in the bottomless pit to the threatened bruising of his head." [1]

In like manner we note that Jacob's dying prophecy (Gen. xlix) is written in the highest style of poetic fervour and of ^{Poetic form} figurative speech. All the events of the patriarch's life ^{and style of many prophe-} and the storied fulness of the future moved his soul, ^{cies.} and gave emotion to his words. The oracles of Balaam and the songs of Moses are of the same high order. The Messianic psalms abound with simile and metaphor, drawn from the heavens, the earth, and the seas. The prophetical books are mostly written in the forms and spirit of Hebrew poetry, and, in predictions of notable events, the language often rises to forms of statement, which, to an occidental critic, might seem a hyperbolical extravagance. Take, for example, the following "burden of Babylon" which Isaiah saw (חָזָה), and note the excessive emotion and the boldness of figures (Isa. xiii, 2–13):

[1] Fairbairn on Prophecy, p. 102.

2   On a mountain bare set up a signal;
    Lift up a voice to them; wave a hand,
    And they shall enter gates of nobles.

3   Also I have called my mighty ones for my anger—
    Those that exult proudly in my glory.

4   Voice of a multitude in the mountains, as of much people;
    Voice of a tumult of kingdoms of nations assembled,
    Jehovah of hosts mustering a host of battle;

5   Coming from a land afar,
    From the end of the heavens—
    Jehovah and the instruments of his fury,
    To lay waste all the land.

6   Howl ye! For near is the day of Jehovah;
    As a destruction from Shaddai shall it come.

7   Therefore shall all hands become slack,
    And every heart of man shall melt.

8   And they shall be in trepidation;
    Writhings and throes shall seize them;
    As the travailing woman shall they twist in pain.
    Each at his neighbour they shall look astonished,
    Their faces, faces of flames.

9   Behold, the day of Jehovah comes;
    Cruel—and wrath, and burning of anger,
    To make the land a desolation,
    And her sinners will be destroyed out of her.

10 For the stars of the heavens and their constellations
    Shall not shed forth their light;
    Dark has the sun become in his going forth,
    And the moon will not cause her light to shine.

11 And I will visit upon the world evil,
    And upon the wicked their iniquity.
    And I will cause the arrogance of the proud to cease,
    And the haughtiness of the lawless I bring low.

12 I will make men rarer than refined gold,
    And mankind than the gold of Ophir.

13 Therefore I will make heaven tremble,
    And the land shall shake from her place,
    In the overflowing wrath of Jehovah of hosts,
    And in the day of the burning of his anger.

It has never been questioned by the best interpreters that the above passage refers to the overthrow of Babylon by the Medes. The heading of the chapter, and the specific statements that follow (verses 17, 19), put this beyond all doubt. And yet it is done, according to the prophet, by Jehovah, who musters his host of mighty heroes from the end of the heavens, causes a tumultuous noise of kingdoms of nations, fills human

Refers to the fall of Babylon.

hearts with trembling, and despair, and throes of agony, shakes heaven and earth, and blots out sun, and moon, and stars. This fearful judgment of Babylon is called "the day of Jehovah," "the day of the burning of his anger." Standing in the forefront of Isaiah's oracles against the heathen world-powers, it is a classic passage of the kind, and its style and imagery would naturally be followed by other prophets when announcing similar judgments.[1]

Such highly emotional and figurative passages are common to all the prophetic writers, but in the so-called apocalyptic prophets we note a peculiar prominence of symbolism. In its earlier and yet undeveloped form it first strikes our attention in the Book of Joel, which may be called the oldest apocalypse. Prominence of symbols in the apocalyptic books. But its fuller development appears among the later prophets, Daniel, Ezekiel, and Zechariah, and its perfected structure in the New Testament Apocalypse of John. In the exposition, therefore, of this class of prophecies it is of the first importance to apply with judgment and skill the hermeneutical principles of biblical symbolism. This process requires, especially, three things: (1) That we be able clearly to discriminate and determine what are symbols and what are not; (2) that the symbols be contemplated in their broad and striking aspects rather than their incidental points of resemblance; and (3) that they be amply compared as to their general import and usage, so that a uniform and self-consistent method be followed in their interpretation. Three hermeneutical principles to be observed. A failure to observe the first of these will lead to endless confusion of the symbolical and the literal. A failure in the second tends to magnify minute and unimportant points to the obscuring of the greater lessons, and to the misapprehension, ofttimes, of the scope and import of the whole. Not a few interpreters have put great stress upon the import of the ten toes of Nebuchadnezzar's image (Dan. ii, 41, 42), and have searched to find ten kings to correspond; whereas, from aught that appears to the contrary, the image may have had twelve toes, like the giant of Gath

---

[1] "Such passages," says Fairbairn, "are not to be regarded simply as highly wrought descriptions in the peculiar style of oriental poetry, possessing but a slender foundation of nature to rest upon. On the contrary they have their correspondence in the literature of all nations, and their justification in the natural workings of the human mind; we mean its workings when under circumstances which tend to bring the faculty of imagination into vigorous play, much as it was acted on with the prophets when, in ecstacy, they received divine revelations. For it is the characteristic of this faculty when possessed in great strength, and operated upon by stirring events such as mighty revolutions and distressing calamities, that it fuses every object by its intense radiation, and brings them into harmony with its own prevailing passion or feeling."—Prophecy, p. 158.

(2 Sam. xxi, 20). A care to observe the third rule will enable one to note the differences as well as the likeness of similar symbols, and save him from the error of supposing that the same symbol, when employed by two different writers, must denote the same power, person, or event.

3. ANALYSIS AND COMPARISON OF SIMILAR PROPHECIES.

Not only are the same, or like figures and symbols, employed by different prophets, but also many whole prophecies are so like one another in their general form and import as to require of the interpreter a minute comparison. Thus only can he distinguish things which are alike and things which differ.

First we observe numerous instances in which one prophet appears to quote from another. Isa. ii, 1–4 is almost identical with Micah iv, 1–3, and it has been a problem of critics to determine whether Isaiah quoted from Micah, or Micah from Isaiah, or both of them from an older prophet now unknown. Jeremiah's prophecy against Edom (xlix, 7–22) is appropriated largely from Obadiah. The Epistle of Jude and the second chapter of Peter's Second Epistle furnish a similar analogy. A comparison of the oracles against the heathen nations by Balaam, Amos, Isaiah, Jeremiah, and Ezekiel, as already indicated, shows many verbal parallels. From all which it appears that these sacred writers freely appropriated forms of expression from each other as from a common treasure house.[1] The word of God, once uttered by an inspired man, became the common property of the chosen people, and was used by them as times and occasions served.

The twofold presentation of prophetic revelations, both of visions and of dreams, demands particular attention. It is first brought to our attention in the dreams of Joseph and of Pharaoh, and as we have seen above (pp. 398, 399), the double dream was, in its significance, but one, and the repetition under different symbols was the divine method of intensifying the impression, and indicating the certainty of the things revealed. "As to the doubling of the dream to Pharaoh twice, it is because the word (הַדָּבָר, this particular revelation) from God is established, and God is hastening to accomplish it" (Gen. xli, 32). A principle of prophetic interpretation so explicitly enunciated in the earliest records of divine revelation deserves to be made

Side notes: Verbal analogies. Twofold presentation of prophetic revelations.

---

[1] "Such verbal repetitions," says Hengstenberg, "must not be, by any means, considered as unintentional reminiscences. They served to exhibit that the prophets acknowledged one another as the organs of the Holy Spirit." — Christology, vol. i, p. 291.

prominent.[1] It serves as a key to the explanation of many of the most difficult questions involved in the apocalyptic Scriptures. We shall have occasion to illustrate this principle more fully in treating the visions of Daniel and John.

It is important, furthermore, to study the analogies of imagery in the apocalyptic portions of prophecy. Isaiah's vis- Analogies of ion of the Seraphim (Isa. vi, 1–8), Ezekiel's vision of imagery. the Living Creatures (Ezek. i and x), and John's vision of the throne in heaven (Rev. iv), have manifest relations to one another which no interpreter can fail to observe. The scope and bearing of each can, however, be apprehended only as we study them from the standpoint of each individual prophet. Daniel's vision of the four beasts out of the sea (Dan. vii) furnishes the imagery by which John depicts his one beast out of the sea (Rev. xiii, 1–2), and we note that the one beast of the latter, being a nameless monster, combines also the other main features (leopard, bear, lion) of the four beasts of the former. John's second beast out of the earth, with two horns like a lamb (Rev. xiii, 11), combines much of the imagery of both the ram and the he-goat of Daniel (viii, 1–12). Zechariah's vision of the four chariots, drawn by different coloured horses (vi, 1–7), forms the basis of the symbolism of the first four seals (Rev. vi, 1–8), and John's glowing picture of the New Jerusalem, the new heavens and the new land (xxi, xxii), is a manifest counterpart of the closing chapters of Ezekiel. The most noticeable difference, perhaps, is that Ezekiel has a long and minute description of a temple and its service (xl–xliv), while no temple appears in the vision of John, but rather the city itself becomes all temple, nay, a Holy of Holies, being filled with the glory of God and of the Lamb (Rev. xxi, 3, 22, 23).

It will be evident from the above-mentioned analogies that no proper interpretation of any one of these similar prophecies Similar imagcan be given without a clear analysis and careful compar- ery applied to different subison of all. We are not to assume, however, that by the jects. use of the same or similar imagery one prophet must needs refer to the same subject as the other. The two olive trees of Rev. xi, 4 are not necessarily the same as those of Zech. iv, 3, 14. The beasts of John's Apocalypse are not necessarily identical with those of Daniel. John's vision of the new heaven, and the new land, and the golden city, is doubtless a fuller revelation of redeemed Israel than Ezekiel's corresponding vision. But one of these visions cannot be fully expounded without the other, and each should

[1] For many valuable suggestions on what he calls the "Double Allegory," see Cochran, The Revelation of John its Own Interpreter, New York, 1860.

be subjected to a minute analysis, and studied from its own historical or visional standpoint.

From these considerations it will be also seen that, while duly General summary. appreciating the peculiarities of prophecy, we neverthe-less must employ in its interpretation essentially the same great principles as in the interpretation of other ancient writings. First, we should ascertain the historical position of the prophet; next the scope and plan of his book; then the usage and import of his words and symbols; and, finally, ample and discriminating comparison of the parallel Scriptures should be made.

CHAPTER XXII.

DANIEL'S VISION OF THE FOUR EMPIRES.

ALL interpreters agree that the empires or world-powers denoted by Principles il-lustrated by Daniel's double revelation of empires. the various parts of the great image in Dan. ii, 31–45, and by the four beasts from the sea (Dan. vii), are the same. The prophecy is repeated under different symbols, but the interpretation is one. This double revelation, then, will be of special value in illustrating the hermeneutical principles already enunciated. But in no portion of Scripture do we need to exercise greater discrimination and care. These prophecies, in their details, have been variously understood, and the most able and accomplished exegetes have differed widely in their explanations. All dogmatism of tone and method should therefore be excluded, and we should endeavour to place ourselves in the very position of the prophet, and study with minute attention his language and his symbols. Where such wide differences of opinion have prevailed we cannot for a moment allow any *a priori* assumptions of what ought to be found in these prophecies, or of what ought not to be found there.[1] All such assumptions are fatal to

---

[1] The Roman Empire, the papacy, the Mohammedans, the Goths and Vandals, the French Revolution, the Crimean War, the United States of America, and our late civil war between the North and the South, have all been assumed to have such an importance in the history of humanity and of the Gospel that we should expect to find some notice of them somewhere in the prophets of the Bible. Daniel and the Revelation of John, abounding as they do in vision and symbol, have been searched more than other prophecies with such an expectation. We find even Barnes writing as follows: "The Roman Empire was in itself too important, and performed too important an agency in preparing the world for the kingdom of the Redeemer, to be omitted in such an enumeration."—Notes on Dan. ii, 40, p. 147. On the same principle we

sound interpretation. The prophet should be permitted, as far as possible, to explain himself; and the interpreter should not be so full of ideas drawn from profane history, or from remote ages and peoples, as to desire to find in Daniel what is not manifestly there. Especially when it is a notable fact that profane history knows nothing of Belshazzar,[1] or of Darius the Mede, should we be cautious how far we allow our interpretation of other parts of Daniel to be controlled by such history.

Three different interpretations of Daniel's vision of the four world-powers have long prevailed. According to the first and oldest of these, the fourth kingdom is the Roman Empire; another identifies it with the mixed dominion of Alexander's successors, and a third makes it include Alexander and his successors.[2] Those who adopt this last view regard the Median rule of Darius at Babylon (Dan. v, 31) as a distinct dynasty. The four kingdoms, according to these several expositions, may be seen in the following outline:

Three different interpretations.

1st.	2d.	3d.
1. Babylonian.	1. Babylonian.	1. Babylonian.
2. Medo-Persian.	2. Medo-Persian.	2. Median.
3. Græco-Macedonian.	3. Alexander.	3. Persian.
4. Roman.	4. Alexander's successors.	4. Græco-Macedonian.

Any one of these views will suffice to bring out the great ethical and religious lessons of the prophecy. No doctrine, therefore, is affected,

might insist that the Chinese Empire, with its great dynasties, and countless millions of people, and also those of India and Japan, should also have some kind of notice. We have no right to assume in advance what Daniel's vision or Nebuchadnezzar's dream should contain.

[1] This fact greatly puzzled all expositors until an inscription discovered on a cylinder at Mugheir showed that a *Bel-shar-uzur* was associated with his father as co-regent at Babylon. See Rawlinson, Ancient Monarchies, vol. iii, p. 70. New York, 1871.

[2] The first of these views is ably defended by Barnes, Pusey, and Keil, and is the one held, probably, by most evangelical divines. The second has its ablest advocates in Bertholdt, Stuart, and Cowles. The third is maintained by Eichhorn, Lengerke, Maurer, Bleek, De Wette, Hilgenfeld, Kranichfeld, Delitzsch, and Westcott. It is quite possible that the prevalence among English expositors of the first theory is largely, if not mainly, due to the fact that the arguments in its favour have been scattered broadcast by the popular commentaries, and the able expositions of the other theories have been quite generally inaccessible to English readers. Many have accepted the current exposition because they never had a better one clearly set before them. It is almost amusing to hear some of the advocates of the Roman theory saying, with Luther: "In this interpretation and opinion all the world are agreed, and history and fact abundantly establish it" (see Keil, p. 245). Desprez is equally interesting when he says: "The almost unanimous opinion of modern criticism is in favour of a separate Median kingdom, distinct from the united Medo-Persian Empire under Cyrus."—Daniel and John, p. 50.

whichever interpretation we adopt. The question at issue is purely one of exegetical accuracy and self-consistency: Which view best satisfies all the conditions of prophet, language, and symbol?

Great stress has been laid by the advocates of the Roman theory upon three considerations: (1) First they urge that Rome was too important to be left out of sight in such a vision of world-empire. "The Roman kingdom," says Keil, "was the first universal monarchy in the full sense. Along with the three earlier world-kingdoms, the nations of the world-historical future remained still unsubdued." [1] But such presumptions cannot properly be allowed to weigh at all. It matters not in the least how great Rome was, or how important a place it occupies in universal history. The sole question with the interpreter of Daniel must be, What world-powers, great or small, fell within his circle of prophetic vision? This presumption in favour of Rome is more than offset by the consideration that geographically and politically that later empire had its seat and centre of influence far aside from the territory of the Asiatic kingdoms. But the Græco-Macedonian Empire, in all its relations to Israel, and, indeed, in its principal component elements, was an Asiatic, not a European, world-power. The prophet, moreover, makes repeated allusion to kings of Greece (יָוָן, *Javan*), but never mentions Rome.

Argument in favour of the Roman theory.

(2) It is further argued that the strong and terrible character of the fourth kingdom is best fulfilled in Rome. No previous dominion, it is said, was of such an iron nature, breaking all things in pieces. [2] Here again we must insist that the question is not so much whether the imagery fits Rome, but whether it may not also appropriately depict some other kingdom. The description of iron strength and violence is, no doubt, appropriate to Rome, but for any one to aver that the conquests and rule of Alexander and his successors did not "break in pieces and bruise" (Dan. ii, 40), and trample with terrible violence the kingdoms of many nations, is to exhibit a marvellous obtuseness in reading the facts of history. The Græco-Macedonian power broke up the older civilizations, and trampled in pieces the various elements of the Asiatic

Iron strength and violence.

---

[1] Biblical Commentary on Daniel, p. 267. English translation. Edinburgh, 1872.

[2] "Neither the monarchy of Alexander," says Keil (p. 252), "nor the Javanic world-kingdom accords with the iron nature of the fourth kingdom, represented by the legs of iron, breaking all things in pieces, nor with the internal division of this kingdom, represented by the feet consisting partly of iron and partly of clay, nor finally with the ten toes formed of iron and clay mixed." Such an assertion from a commentator usually so guarded and trustworthy inclines one to believe that its author was here labouring under the blinding effects of a foregone conclusion.

monarchies more completely than had ever been done before. Rome never had any such triumph in the Orient, and, indeed, no great Asiatic world-power, comparable for magnitude and power with that of Alexander, ever succeeded his. If now we keep in mind this utter overthrow and destruction of the older dynasties by Alexander, and then observe what seems especially to have affected Daniel, namely, the wrath and violence of the "little horn," and note how, in different forms, this bitter and relentless persecutor is made prominent in this book (chapters viii and xi), we may safely say that the conquests of Alexander, and the blasphemous fury of Antiochus Epiphanes, in his violence against the chosen people, amply fulfilled the prophecies of the fourth kingdom.

(3) It is also claimed that the Roman theory is favoured by the statement, in chap. ii, 44, that the kingdom of God should be set up "in the days of those kings." For the Roman Empire, it is urged, ruled Palestine when Christ appeared, and all the other great monarchies had passed away. But on what ground can it be quietly assumed that "these kings" are Roman kings? If we say that they are kings denoted by the toes of the image, inasmuch as the stone smote the image on the feet (ii, 34), we involve ourselves in serious confusion. The Christ appeared when Rome was in the meridian of her power and glory. It was three hundred years later when the empire was divided, and much later still when broken in pieces and made to pass away. But the stone smote not the legs of iron, but the feet, which were partly of iron and partly of clay (ii, 33, 34). When, therefore, it is argued that the Græco-Macedonian power had fallen before the Christ was born, it may on the other hand be replied with greater force that a much longer time elapsed after the coming of Christ before the power of Rome was broken in pieces.

Evidently, therefore, no satisfactory conclusion can be reached as long as we allow ourselves to be governed by subjective notions of the import of minor features of the symbols, or by assumptions of what the prophet ought to have seen. The advocates of the Roman theory are continually laying stress upon the supposed import of the *two* arms, and *two* legs, and *ten* toes of the image; whereas these are merely the natural parts of a human image, and necessary to complete a coherent outline. The prophet lays no stress upon them in his exposition, and it is nowhere said that the image had *ten* toes. We must appeal to a closer view of the prophet's historical standpoint and his outlying field of vision; and especially should we study his visions in the

Subjective presumptions must be set aside.

light of his own explanations and historical statements, rather than from the narratives of the Greek historians.

Applying principles already sufficiently emphasized, we first attend to Daniel's historical position. At his first vision Nebuchadnezzar was reigning in great splendour (Dan. ii, 37, 38). At his second, Belshazzar occupied the throne of Babylon (vii, 1). This monarch, unknown to the Greek historians, fills an important place in the Book of Daniel. He was slain in the night on which Babylon was taken, and the kingdom passed into the hand of Darius the Mede (v, 30, 31). Whatever we may think or say, Daniel recognizes Darius as the representative of a new dynasty upon the throne of Babylon (ix, 1). The prophet held a high position in his government (vi, 2, 3), and during his reign was miraculously delivered from the den of lions. Darius the Mede was a monarch with authority to issue prolamations "to all people, nations, and languages that dwelt in all the land" (vi, 25). From Daniel's point of view, therefore, the Median domination of Babylon was no such insignificant thing as many expositors, looking more to profane history than to the Bible itself, are wont to pronounce it. Isaiah had foretold that Babylon should fall by the power of the Medes (Isa. xiii, 17; xxi, 2), and Jeremiah had repeated the prophecy (Jer. li, 11, 28). Daniel lived to see the kingdom pass into the hands of Cyrus the Persian, and in the third year of his reign received the minute revelation of chapters x and xi touching the kings of Persia and of Greece. Already, in the reign of Belshazzar, had he received specific revelations of the kings of Greece who were to succeed the kings of Media and Persia (viii, 1, 21). But no mention of any world-power later than Greece is to be found in the Book of Daniel. The prophetic standpoint of chap. viii is Shushan, the throne-centre of the Medo-Persian dominion, and long after the Medes had ceased to hold precedence in the kingdom. All these things, bearing on the historical position of this prophet, are to be constantly kept in view.

Daniel's historical standpoint.

Prominence of the Medes in Scripture.

Having vividly apprehended the historical standpoint of the writer, we should next take up the prophecies which he has himself most clearly explained, and reason from what is clear to what is not clear. In the explanation of the great image (ii, 36–45), and of the four beasts (vii, 17–27), we find no mention of any of the world-powers by name, except Babylon under Nebuchadnezzar (ii, 38). But the description and explanation of the fourth beast, in vii, 17–27, correspond so fully with those of the he-goat in chap. viii as scarcely to leave any rea-

The varied but parallel descriptions.

sonable ground to doubt that they are but varied portraitures of the same great world-power, and that power is declared in the latter chapter to be the Grecian (viii, 21). In chap. xi, 3 the Grecian power is again taken up, its partly strong and partly brittle character (comp. Dan. ii, 42) is exhibited, together with the attempts of the rival kings to strengthen themselves by intermarriage (comp. ii, 43 and xi, 6), and also the conflicts of these kings, especially those between the Ptolemies and the Seleucids. At verse 21 is introduced the "vile person" (נִבְזֶה, despised or despicable one), and the description through the rest of the chapter of his deceit and cunning, his violence and his sacrilegious impiety, is but a more fully detailed picture of the king denoted by the little horn of chapters vii and viii. As the repetition of Joseph's and Pharaoh's dreams served to impress them the more intensely, and to show that the things were established by God (Gen. xli, 32), so the repetition of these prophetic visions under different forms and imagery served to emphasize their truth and certainty. There appears to be no good ground to doubt that the little horn of chap. viii, and the vile person of chap. xi, 21, denoted Antiochus Epiphanes. We have shown above (pp. 410, 411) that the reasons commonly alleged to prove that the little horn of chap. viii denotes a different person from the little horn of chap. vii are superficial and nugatory. It follows, therefore, that the fourth kingdom described in chapters ii, 40 ff., vii, 23 ff., is the same as the Grecian kingdom symbolized by the he-goat in chap. viii. The repetitions and varied descriptions of this tremendous power are in perfect accord with other analogies of the style and structure of apocalyptic prophecy.

If we have applied our principles fairly thus far, it now follows that we must find the four kingdoms of Daniel between Nebuchadnezzar and Alexander the Great, including these two monarchs. Reasoning and searching from *The prophet should be allowed to explain himself.* Daniel's position, and by the light of his own interpretations, we are obliged to adopt the third view named above, according to which the four kingdoms are, respectively, the Babylonian, the Median, the Persian, and the Græco-Macedonian. We have been able to find but two real arguments against this view, namely, (1) the assumption that the Median rule of Babylon was too insignificant to be thus mentioned, and (2) the statement of chap. viii, 20 that the ram denoted the kings of Media and Persia. The first argument should have no force with those who allow Daniel to explain himself. He clearly recognizes Darius the Mede as the successor of Belshazzar on the throne of Babylon (v, 31). This Darius was "the son of Ahasuerus of the seed of the Medes" (ix, 1), and though he reigned but two years, that reign was, from the prophet's standpoint, as truly a new world-power at Babylon as if he had reigned fifty years. Whatever his relation to Cyrus the Persian, he set a hundred and twenty princes over his kingdom (vi, 1), and assumed to issue decrees for "all people, nations, and languages" (vi, 25, 26). Most writers have seemed strangely unwilling to allow Daniel's statements as much weight as those of the Greek historians, who are notably confused and unsatisfactory in their accounts of Cyrus and of his relations to the Medes.

The other argument, namely, that in chap. viii, 20, the two-horned ram denotes "the kings of Media and Persia," is very properly supposed to show that Daniel himself recognised Medes and Persians as constituting one monarchy. But this argument is set aside by the fact that the position of the prophet in chap. viii is Shushan (ver. 2), the royal residence and capital of the later Medo-Persian monarchy (Neh. i, 1; Esther i, 2). The standpoint of the vision is manifestly in the last period of the Persian rule, and long after the Median power at Babylon had ceased to exist. The Book of Esther, written during this later period, uses the expression "Persia and Media" (Esther i, 3, 14, 18, 19), thus implying that Persia then held the supremacy. The facts, then, according to Daniel, are that a Median world-power succeeded the Babylonian; but that, under Cyrus the Persian, it subsequently lost its earlier precedence, and Media became thoroughly consolidated with Persia into the one great empire known in other history as the Medo-Persian.

The prophet's point of view in Dan. viii.

With this view all the prophecies of Daniel readily harmonize. According to chap. ii, 39, the second kingdom was inferior to that of Nebuchadnezzar, and in vii, 5, it is represented by a bear raised up on oné side, and holding three ribs between his teeth. It has no prominence in the interpretation given by the prophet, and nothing could more fitly symbolize the Median rule at Babylon than the image of a bear, sluggish, grasping, and devouring what it has, but getting nothing more than its three ribs, though loudly called on to "arise and devour much flesh." No ingenuity of critics has ever been able to make these representations of the second kingdom tally with the facts of the Medo-Persian monarchy. Except in golden splendour this latter was in no sense inferior to the Babylonian,[1] for its dominion was

Inner harmony of all the visions to be sought.

---

[1] Calvin, Auberlen, and others think the Medo-Persian was inferior *in moral condition* to the Babylonian. But surely the Persian monotheism was far higher in point of moral and religious worth than the polytheism of Babylon. Keil and others find the inferiority of the Medo-Persian monarchy in its *want of inner unity*, the combina-

every way broader and mightier. It was well represented by the fleet leopard with the four wings and four heads which, like the third kingdom of brass, acquired wide dominion over all the earth (comp. ii, 39, and vii, 6), but not by the sluggish, half-reclining bear, which merely grasped and held the ribs put in its mouth, but seemed indisposed to arise and seek more prey.

Those interpreters who adopt the second view above named, and, distinguishing between Alexander and his successors, make these latter constitute the fourth kingdom, have *The Diadochoi theory.* brought most weighty and controlling arguments against the first or Roman theory,[1] showing that chronologically, geographically, politically, and in relation to the Jewish people, the Roman Empire is excluded from the range of Daniel's prophecies. "The Roman Empire," says Cowles, "came into no important relations to the Jews until the Christian era, and never disturbed their repose effectually until A. D. 70. . . . Rome never was Asiatic, never was oriental; never, therefore, was a legitimate successor of the first three of these great empires. . . . Rome had the seat of her power and the masses of her population in another and remote part of the world."[2]

But this second theory is unable to show any sufficient reason for dividing the dominion of Alexander and his successors into two distinct monarchies. According to every proper analogy and implication, the fourth beast with its ten horns and one little horn of chap. vii, and the he-goat with its one great horn and its four succeeding ones, *Dominion of Alexander and his successors not two different world-powers.* and the little horn out of one of these—as presented in chap. viii, 8, 9, 21-23—all represent but one world-power. From Daniel's point of vision these could not be separated, as the Median domination at Babylon was separated from the Chaldæan on the one side, and the later Medo-Persian on the other. It would be an unwarrantable confusion of symbols to make the horns of a beast represent a different kingdom from that denoted by the beast itself. The two horns of the Medo-Persian ram are not to be so understood, for the Median and Persian elements are, according to chap. viii, 20, symbolized by the whole body, not exclusively by the horns of the ram, and the vision of the prophet is from a standpoint where the Median tion of Medes and Persians being an element of weakness. But, from all that appears in history, this combination of two great peoples was an element of might and majesty rather than of weakness or of inferiority.

[1] See Stuart's "Excursus on the Fourth Beast" in his Commentary on Daniel, pp. 205-210. Cowles' Notes on Daniel, pp. 354-371, and Zöckler on Daniel ii and vii in Lange's Biblework, translated and annotated by Strong.

[2] Notes on Daniel vii, 28, p. 355.

and Persian powers have become fully consolidated into one great empire. If, in chap. viii, 8, 9, we regard the goat and his first horn as denoting one world-power, and the four succeeding horns another and distinct world-power, analogy requires that we should also make the ten horns of the fourth beast (vii, 7, 8, 24) denote a kingdom different from the beast itself. Then, again, what a confusion of symbols would be introduced in these parallel visions if we make a leopard with four wings and four heads in one vision (vii, 6) correspond with the one horn of a he-goat in another, and the terrible fourth beast of chap. vii, 7, horns and all, correspond merely with the horns of the goat!

From every point of view, therefore, we are driven by our hermeneutical principles to hold that view of Daniel's four symbolic beasts which makes them represent, respectively, the Babylonian, the Median, the Medo-Persian, and the Grecian domination of Western Asia. But the "Ancient of days" (vii, 9–12) brought them into judgment, and took away their dominion before he enthroned the Son of man in his everlasting kingdom. The penal judgment is represented as a great assize, the books are opened, and countless thousands attend the bidding of the Judge. The blasphemous beast is slain, his body is destroyed and given to burning flames, and his dominion is rent from him, and consumed by a gradual destruction (verses 10, 11, 26).

Conclusion.

We have dwelt the longer on these prophecies because their proper interpretation is of fundamental importance in illustrating the principles by which we are to explain other apocalyptic visions. It must be evident that a book of prophecy should be studied as a whole, so that if there be any marked correlation of its several parts, or any system or principles of interpretation deducible from comparison and analogy, they may be duly noted. The minor points should then be studied in the light of the whole revelation. It has been generally conceded that Daniel's prophecies and the Apocalypse of John have notable analogies, and may be profitably studied in connexion with each other. The same may be said of large portions of Ezekiel and Zechariah. But we must not therefore assume that these different prophets, by the use of like symbols, all treat the same subjects, and that the riders on different coloured horses in Zechariah, and the beasts in Daniel, denote the same things as the corresponding symbols in John. Like symbols must represent like things, but not necessarily the same things.

Each book of prophecy to be studied as a whole.

CHAPTER XXIII.

OLD TESTAMENT APOCALYPTICS.

APOCALYPTICS is a theological term of recent origin employed in biblical literature to designate a class of prophetic writings which refer to impending or future judgments, and the final triumph and glory of the Messianic king- *Biblical apoc-alyptics de-fined.* dom. Biblical apocalyptics is defined by Lücke as "the sum total (Inbegriff) of the eschatological revelations of the Old and the New Testament."[1] To this class we assign the oracles of Joel, large portions of Daniel, Ezekiel, and Zechariah, our Lord's eschatological discourse in Matt. xxiv, and its parallels in Mark and Luke, Paul's doctrine of the Parousia in the Thessalonian epistles, and in 1 Cor. xv, and the Apocalypse of John. The great theme of all these apocalyptic Scriptures is the holy kingdom of God in its conflict with the godless and persecuting powers of the world—a conflict in which the ultimate triumph of righteousness is assured.[2]

"The name apocalyptic," says Auberlen, "signifies that the divine communication and revelation are more prominent in the prophet than the human mediation and receptivity, for ἀποκάλυψις (revelation) signifies a divine, προφητεία (prophecy) a human activity. . . . The two expressions are used as two distinct species of one and the same genus, according as the objective revelation or the subjective inspiration is more prominent. Thus St. Paul distinguishes them

[1] Versuch einer vollständigen Einleitung in die Offenbarung des Johannes, p. 25. Second ed., Bonn, 1852. See his whole chapter entitled Erörterung des Begriffs oder Theorie der Apokalyptik, pp. 17-39; and compare Hilgenfeld, Die jüdische Apokalyptik, Einleitung, pp. 1-16 (Jena, 1857); Düsterdieck, Kritisch-exegetisches Handbuch über die Offenbarung Johannis, pp. 35-46 (Göttingen, 1877); Lange, The Revelation of John, pp. 1-6. American ed., New York, 1874.

[2] The amount of apocryphal apocalyptical literature still extant is very large, and may be divided into Jewish and Christian apocalyptics. Comp. Lücke, pp. 223-230. Much of it may be properly called Jewish-Christian; but, altogether, it is of little value in the elucidation of scriptural prophecy, which holds an incomparable elevation above it. Lücke and Stuart devote a considerable part of their works on the Apocalypse to an account of these pseudepigraphal books. Hilgenfeld (Jüdische Apokalyptik, pp. 5-8) disregards entirely the distinction between canonical and apocryphal apocalyptics, and treats the books of Daniel, Enoch, Pseudo-Ezra, and the Sibylline Oracles as a precursory history (Vorgeschichte) of Christianity. But most, if not all, of the apocryphal Apocalypses (at least in their present form) are posterior to the Christian Scriptures.

in 1 Cor. xiv, 6: 'either by revelation or by prophecy. . . . In prophecy the Spirit of God, who inspires the human organ of revelation, finds his immediate expression in words; in the Apocalypse human language disappears, for the reason given by the apostle (2 Cor. xii, 4): he 'heard unspeakable words which it is not lawful for a man to utter.' A new element appears here which corresponds to the subjective element of seeing, the vision. The prophet's eye is opened to look into the unseen world; he has intercourse with angels; and as he thus beholds the unseen, he beholds also the future, which appears to him embodied in plastic symbolic shapes as in a dream, only that these images are not the children of his own fancy, but the product of divine revelation adapting itself essentially to our human horizon." [1]

Same hermeneutical principles. Although apocalyptics may thus be distinguished from other prophetic Scriptures, the same hermeneutical principles are applicable to them all. We have already examined most of the apocalyptic portions of Daniel and Zechariah; it remains for us to show the application of the principles we have enunciated to other eschatological prophecies, especially those of the New Testament. We find the same formal elements, [2] the same wealth of figure and symbol, and a constant reference to the great day of the Lord in the words of Joel, the visions of Ezekiel, the twenty-fourth of Matthew, the Epistles to the Thessalonians, the Book of Revelation, and in other less noticeable Scriptures.

THE REVELATION OF JOEL.

Joel the oldest formal Apocalypse. A scientific treatise on biblical apocalyptics should begin with an analysis of the Book of Joel. "If Joel and other prophets had been secular writers," says Meyrick, "we should say that with Joel originated that apocalyptic literature which culminated in the Book of Revelation. Being what they are, we say that it pleased God first to reveal to Joel that which he, in a similar, though not in the same, form afterward revealed to his other prophets respecting the end of the world and the occurrences which were to precede it. The glorious prospect of a future blessedness became the inheritance of the Jewish people from the time of Joel onward, and with it the terrors of the day of judgment. The prophetic form which the idea takes in Joel and his successors is that of a universal reign of righteousness, peace and happiness,

[1] The Prophecies of Daniel and the Revelation of St. John viewed in their mutual Relation, pp. 80, 83, 84. Edinb., 1856.

[2] See Lange, on the Formal Elements of Apocalyptics, in his Introduction to the Revelation of John, American edition, pp. 14–41.

under the visible headship of Jehovah, the centre of whose kingdom would be the earthly Jerusalem. This glorious period is to be inaugurated by a terrible 'day of the Lord' (itself ushered in by signs and wonders in the universe) wherein, the Jewish exiles having been restored, a judgment will be pronounced by Jehovah in solemn assize upon all the heathen; and the foes of Jehovah and of his people Israel will be exterminated. Our Lord, divesting the idea, which is permanent, of the form, which is transitory, declares to us that the 'day of the Lord' shall come, ushered in by the signs and wonders described by the prophet; that he, the Son of man, shall sit upon the throne of his glory; that, his elect having been gathered from all quarters, he shall give solemn judgment upon all nations collected before him; and that those who are his foes, and the foes of his elect, will be dismissed into everlasting punishment, while the righteous are admitted to the inheritance of the kingdom prepared for them from the foundation of the world (Matt. xxiv–xxv). St. John, in like manner, in his final apocalyptic visions, sees Joel's vision spiritualized—the gathering of the heathen, the day of judgment, the destruction of the wicked, and the creation of the new Jerusalem, in which God's people shall dwell forever around the throne of God and of the Lamb. . . . The dearest hopes and the most awful fears which encourage and restrain the human race at the present day were revealed by God to the prophet Joel, and from his time onward became the inheritance of his Church."[1]

These formal elements of the chief apocalyptic prophecies should receive our careful attention as they appear in Joel. Analysis of Joel's prophecy. His prophecy is arranged in two leading divisions. The first part consists of a twofold revelation of judgment, each revelation being accompanied by words of divine counsel and promise (chapters i, 1–ii, 27); the second part goes over a portion of the same field again, but delineates more clearly the blessings and triumph which shall accompany the day of Jehovah (chapters ii, 28–iii, 21; Hebrew text, chapters iii and iv). These two parts may be properly entitled: (1) *Jehovah's impending judgments;* (2) *Jehovah's coming triumph and glory.* The first may again be subdivided into four sections, the second into three, as follows:

1. Chap. i, 1–12. After the manner of Moses, in Exod. x, 1–6, Joel is commissioned to announce a fourfold plague of locusts. What one swarm leaves behind them another devours (ver. 4), until

[1] Speaker's Commentary, vol. vi, pp. 494, 495. Merx, also, though singularly misapprehending the historical standpoint of the prophet Joel, recognizes the eschatological and apocalyptic character of his prophecies. See his Die Prophetie des Joel und ihre Ausleger, pp. 62–78. Halle, 1879.

all vegetation is destroyed, and the whole land is left in mourning.
This fourfold scourge, as a beginning of sorrows in the impending
day of Jehovah, should be compared with the four riders on different coloured horses, and the four horns of Zech. i, 8, 18, the four
war chariots of Zech. vi, 1–8, the wars, famines, pestilences, and
earthquakes of Matt. xxiv, 7; Luke xxi, 10, 11, and the four horses
of Rev. vi, 1–8. It is thus. a habit of apocalyptics to represent
punitive judgments in a fourfold manner.

2. Chap. i, 13–20. After the manner of Jehoshaphat, when the
combined forces of Moab, Ammon, and Seir were marching against
him (2 Chron. xx, 1–13), the prophet calls upon the priests to
lament, and proclaim a fast, and gather the people in solemn assembly to bewail the awful day that is coming as a destruction from
Shaddai. Under this head other features of the calamity are incidentally mentioned, as the distress of beast, cattle, and flock, and
the ravages of fire·(verses 18–20).

3. Chap. ii, 1–11. In this section the prophet proclaims the day
of Jehovah in still more fearful aspects. Under the blended imagery of darkness, devouring fire, numberless locusts, and rushing
armies (all which are represented in a plague of locusts),[1] the earth
and the heavens are shaken, and sun, moon, and stars withhold
their light.

4. Chap. ii, 12–27. The second portrayal of the great and terrible day is in turn followed by another call to penitence, fasting,
and prayer, and also the promise of deliverance and glorious recompense. So the double proclamation of judgment has for each
announcement a corresponding word of counsel and hope.

The second part of the prophecy is distinguished by the words,
"And it shall come to pass afterward" (וְהָיָה אַחֲרֵי־כֵן), a formula which

---

[1] An eyewitness of a plague of locusts, which visited Palestine in 1866, says:
"From early morning till near sunset the locusts passéd over the city in countless
hosts, as though all the swarms in the world were let loose, and the whirl of their
wings was as the sound of chariots. At times they appeared in the air like some
great snowdrift, obscuring the sun, and casting a shadow upon the earth. Men stood
in the streets and looked up, and their faces gathered blackness. At intervals those
which were tired or hungry descended on the little gardens in the city, and in an incredibly short time all that was green disappeared. They ran up the walls, they
sought out every blade of grass or weed growing between the stones, and after eating to satiety, they gathered in their ranks along the ground, or on the tops of the
houses. It is no marvel that as Pharaoh looked at them he called them 'this death'
(Exod. x, 17). . . . One locust has been found near Bethlehem measuring more than
five inches in length. It is covered with a hard shell, and has a tail like a scorpion."
—Journal of Sacred Literature for 1866, p. 89. . Compare the same Journal for
1865, pp. 235–237.

may be regarded as equivalent to בְּאַחֲרִית הַיָּמִים, *in the end of the days,*
or, in the last days.

1. Chap. ii, 28–32 (Hebrew text, chap. iii). In accordance with
the prayer of Moses (Num. xi, 29), Jehovah promises a great out-
pouring of his Spirit upon all the people, so that all will become
prophets. This token of grace is followed by wonders in heaven
and earth (מוֹפְתִים, *prodigious signs,* like the plagues of Egypt):

> And I will give wonders in the heavens and in the land,
> Blood, and fire, and columns of smoke;
> The sun shall be turned to darkness,
> And the moon to blood,
> Before the coming of the day of Jehovah—
> The great and the terrible.
> And it shall come to pass that all who call upon the name
>   of Jehovah shall be saved.
> For in Mount Zion and in Jerusalem shall be deliverance,
> As Jehovah has said,
> And in the remnant whom Jehovah calls.

2. Chap. iii, 1–17 (Heb. iv, 1–17). The great day of Jehovah will
issue in a judgment of all nations (comp. Matt. xxv, 31–46). Like
the combined armies of Moab, Ammon, and Seir, which came against
Judah and Jerusalem in the time of Jehoshaphat, the hostile nations
shall be brought down into "a valley of Jehoshaphat" (verses 2,
12), and there be recompensed according as they had recompensed
Jehovah and his people (comp. Matt. xxv, 41–46).

> Multitudes, multitudes in the valley of judgment!
> For near is the day of Jehovah,
> In the valley of judgment (ver. 14).

Jehovah, who dwells in Zion, will make that valley—a valley of
judgment to his enemies—like another valley of blessing to his
people. Comp. 2 Chron. xx, 20–26.

3. Chap. iii, 18–21 (Heb. iv, 18–21). The judgment of the nations shall be followed by a perpetual peace and glory like the
composure and rest which God gave the realm of Jehoshaphat
(2 Chron. xx, 30). The figures of great plenty, the flowing waters,
the fountain proceeding from the house of Jehovah, Judah and
Jerusalem abiding forever, and "Jehovah dwelling in Zion," are
in substance equivalent to the closing chapters of Ezekiel and John.

Thus this oldest Apocalypse virtually assumes a sevenfold structure, and repeats its revelations in various forms. The first four
sections refer to a day of Jehovah near at hand, an impending

judgment, of which the locust scourge had, perhaps, already ap-
Joel's prophecy peared as the beginning of sorrows; the last three stand
a generic Apoc- out in the more distant future (afterward = the last
alypse. days, Acts ii, 17). The allusions of the book to events
of the reign of Jehoshaphat have led most critics to believe that
Joel prophesied soon after the days of that monarch, but beyond
those allusions this ancient prophet is unknown. The absence of any
thing to determine his historical standpoint, and the far-reaching
import of his words, render his oracles a kind of generic prophecy
capable of manifold applications.

EZEKIEL'S VISIONS.

The numerous parallels between the Book of Ezekiel and the
Peculiarities of Revelation of John have arrested the attention of all
Ezekiel. readers.[1] But the number and extent of Ezekiel's prophecies carry him over a broader field than that of any other apocalyptic seer, so that he combines vision, symbolico-typical action,
parable, allegory, and formal prophesying. "Ezekiel's style of
prophetic representation," says Keil, "has many peculiarities. In
the first place the clothing of symbol and allegory prevails in him
to a greater degree than in all the other prophets; and his symbolism and allegory are not confined to general outlines and pictures,
but elaborated in the minutest details, so as to present figures of a
boldness surpassing reality, and ideal representations, which produce an impression of imposing grandeur and exuberant fulness.[2]

Ezekiel's prophecies, like Joel's, may be divided into two parts:
Analysis of the first (chapters i-xxxii) announcing Jehovah's judg-
Ezekiel's proph- ments upon Israel and the heathen nations; the second
ecies. (chapters xxxiii-xlviii) announcing the restoration and
final glorification of Israel. The first part, however, is not without
gracious words of promise (xi, 13-20; xvii, 22-24), and the second
contains the fearful judgment of God (xxxvii, xxxviii) after the manner of the judgment of all nations described in the second part of
Joel (iii, 2-14). The first part of Ezekiel may be subdivided into
seven sections, the second part into three, as follows:

1. Chapters i-iii, 14. The opening vision is threefold, consist-
The opening ing of the living creatures, the wheels, and the throne
vision. of Jehovah. The symbolic parts of this vision embody
the substance of all the subsequent prophecies. The fourfold wheel,
like the horsemen, the horns, the smiths, and the chariots in Zech.

[1] See a list of parallels between Ezekiel, Daniel, Zechariah, and John in the Speaker's Commentary on Ezekiel, pp. 12-16.

[2] Biblical Commentary on the Prophecies of Ezekiel, vol. i, p. 9. Edinb., 1876.

i, 10, 19, 21; vi, 5, and the four horses and their riders in Rev. vi, 2–8, represent the potent agencies of divine judgment. Whether these go forth against rebellious Israel or against the heathen, they move at the will and command of the cherubim. So in Rev. vi, the symbols of conquest, bloodshed, famine, and aggravated mortality proceed on their solemn mission only as the cherubim say Come. Here is a profound intimation that all things work together for good to them who love God, and who are, accordingly, predestined to be conformed to the image of his Son, and to be sanctified in his glory (Rom. viii, 28–30; comp. Exod. xxix, 43). For if the cherubim are prophetic symbols of redeemed and glorified humanity (see above, p. 363) this vision suggests that every agency of providence or judgment in all the world moves with a foreseen (προέγνω, Rom. viii, 29; xi, 2; comp. 1 Peter i, 1, 2) vital relation to the ultimate glory of God's elect. The vision was followed by the divine call and commission of the prophet.

2. Chapters iii, 15–vii describe the further commission of the prophet, and contain his first series of symbolico-typical and oracular announcements of the approaching woes and desolation of Jerusalem.

3. Chapters viii–xi. The prophet is carried in vision to Jerusalem, and there beholds a fourfold picture of the idolatrous abominations which constituted Judah's guilt and shame. This vision was followed by that of the seven angels, six of whom were commanded to go through the city and smite all who had not the mark of God upon their foreheads (comp. Rev. vii, 3; ix, 4, and the seven trumpet angels of Rev. viii, 2). One of the angels takes fire from between the wheels under the cherubim, and scatters it over the city (comp. Rev. viii, 5), after which the cherubim depart from the temple and the city, and with it that series of visions ends (xi, 24):

4. Chapters xii–xix belong to the cycle of prophecies which are dated in the sixth year (viii, 1), but the standpoint of the prophet is changed, and he appears among the captives in Chaldæa, and by symbolico-typical action, allegory, parable, lamentation, and various expostulation and warning he exhibits the sins of Israel, and shows that rebellion against God is sure to bring misery and destruction upon the transgressors.

5. Chapters xx–xxiii contain the prophecies of the seventh year, and repeat in other words and figures the catalogue of Israel's sins. "The same subject is continued," says Fairbairn, "though, as the time of judgment had approached nearer, there is an increased keenness and severity in the prophet's tone; he sits, as it were, in judgment upon the people, brings out in full form the divine

indictment against them, and with awful distinctness and frequent reiteration announces both their consummate guilt and its appropriate judgment." [1]

6. Chap. xxiv bears the date of the memorable day on which Nebuchadnezzar commenced the siege of Jerusalem, and under the figure of a boiling pot depicts the fearful ruin that was then about to fall upon the city. In the evening of that day the prophet's wife, the desire of his eyes, was removed by death, and he was commanded not to mourn or weep, that he might be a sign to Israel of a grief too deep for tears (comp. Jer. xvi, 4-6).

7. Chapters xxv-xxxii are a series of seven oracles [2] against so many different heathen nations, namely, (1) the Ammonites, (2) Moab, (3) Edom, (4) the Philistines, (5) Tyre, (6) Sidon, and (7) Egypt. "These seven nations," observes Currey, "are all mentioned by Jeremiah (xxv, 15-32) as bidden to drink of the cup of the fury of the Lord; for five of them (Egypt and Philistia being excepted) Jeremiah was to make bonds and yokes (Jer. xxvii, 3). In prophesying against foreign nations the more recent prophets often adopt the language of those who preceded them." [3]

The second part of Ezekiel's prophecies is full of consolation and hope for the house of Israel. As in the opening vision, the dark cloud out of the north had a circle of brightness about it (i, 4), and the fiery human likeness of the glory of Jehovah was encompassed by the appearance of a rainbow (i, 28), so the punitive judgments of God, if not themselves blessings in disguise, are compassed with radiations of divine mercy, and are the agencies of holy love which either chastens to reform, or punishes with death to secure the final peace and glory of Messiah's kingdom.

1. Chapters xxxiii-xxxvii abound in consolation and hope for the

Prophecies of chosen people. After the renewal of the prophet's restoration. charge, which occurred on the day in which he heard of the fall of Jerusalem (xxxiii, 21), the word of Jehovah through him announces the restoration of Israel in six different forms. (1) As an offset to the work of the unfaithful shepherds who had caused the flock to be scattered abroad, Jehovah, like a good shepherd, will seek his scattered sheep, and lead them into rich pastures

---

[1] Ezekiel and the Book of his Prophecy, p. 14. Edinburgh, 1855.

[2] These oracles against the seven nations are, perhaps, sufficiently distinct to be regarded as a leading section by themselves. In that case we should subdivide the first half of Ezekiel's prophecies into two leading parts, the first (chapters i-xxiv) against idolatrous Israel, consisting of six subdivisions as above, the second (chapters xxv-xxxii) against the heathen, and consisting of seven subdivisions.

[3] Speaker's Commentary on Ezekiel, p. 106.

upon the mountains of Israel (chap. xxxiv). (2) As an ouset to the
evils Israel suffered from the surrounding nations, the doom of
Edom is foretold as a specimen of the manner in which Jehovah
will avenge his people on their heartless enemies (chap. xxxv).
(3) As an offset to the prophecy against the mountains of Israel, in
chap. vi, 1–7, there now comes a promise to restore and beautify all
that was laid waste (xxxvi, 1–15). (4) Thereupon follows the pledge
of multiplied blessings to be showered upon the restored house of
Israel (xxxvi, 16–38), and the section closes with the two symbolical signs (5) of the resurrection of dry bones (xxxvii, 1–14), and
(6) of the two rods of wood (עץ) which represented the divided
kingdoms of Israel and Judah (xxxvii, 15–28).   These symbols
declared that Israel's restoration should be as life from the dead,
and should result in their becoming one nation again upon the
mountains of Israel.

2. Chapters xxxviii and xxxix contain the great apocalyptic pic-
The battle of ture of the last conflict of the world with God. This
Gog.   section has four subdivisions: (1) The gathering of the
army of Gog and their march against Israel (xxxviii, 1–13); (2) His
fearful overthrow by the power of God (verses 14–23); (3) Another
portraiture of the utter destruction of all the multitudes of Gog
xxxix, 1–16); (4) The issue of this final victory in the sanctification and glory of the house of Israel (verses 17–29).   On this mysterious prophecy Currey appropriately remarks: " We must bear in
mind that Ezekiel is not predicting the invasion of an actual army,
but the advance of evil under that figure.   So he declares the overthrow of evil by the figure of a host routed and slain, and the consequent purification of a land partially overrun and disturbed.   It
is the manner of Ezekiel to dwell upon the details of the figurative
acts which he portrays, bringing them before the mind as vivid
pictures, and employing, so to speak, the strongest colouring.   This
has led some so to rest on the picture as to forget that it is a figure.
Thus they have searched history to find out some campaign in the
land of Israel, some overthrow of invaders, on which to fix this
prophecy, and have assigned localities to the burial place, and even
thought to discover the spot to which belongs the appellation
Hamon-Gog.   But in truth the details are set forth in order to
carry out the allegory, and their very extravagance, so to speak,
points out that we have but the shadow of a great spiritual reality which man can only faintly represent and feebly grasp in a
figure." [1]

(3) Chapters xl–xlviii contain an elaborate vision of the kingdom

Speaker's Commentary on Ezekiel, p. 158.

of God, and is the Old Testament counterpart of the new heaven
and new land portrayed in Rev. xxi and xxii. Ezekiel
is carried in the visions of God to a very high mountain in the land of Israel (xl, 2; comp. Rev. xxi, 10) and
sees a new temple, new ordinances of worship, a river of waters of
life, new land and new tribal divisions, and a new city named JE-
HOVAH-SHAMMAH. The minuteness of detail is characteristic of
Ezekiel, and no one would so naturally have portrayed the Messianic times under the imagery of a glorified Judaism as a prophet
who was himself a priest. From his historical standpoint, as an
exile by the rivers of Babylon, smitten with grief as he remembered
Zion, and the ruined city and temple, and the desolated land of
Canaan (comp. Psa. cxxxvii), no ideal of restoration and glory could
be more attractive and pleasing than that of a perfect temple, a
continual service, a holy priesthood, a restored city, and a land completely occupied and watered by a never-failing river that would
make the deserts blossom as the rose.

The new temple, land, and city.

Three different interpretations of these closing chapters of Ezekiel have been maintained. (1) The first regards this
description of the temple as a model of the temple of
Solomon which was destroyed by the Chaldæans. The
advocates of this view suppose that the prophet designed this pattern to serve in the rebuilding of the house of God after the return
of the Jews from their exile. (2) Another class of interpreters hold
that this whole passage is a literal prophecy of the final restoration
of the Jews. At the second coming of Christ all Israel will be gathered out from among the nations, become established in their ancient land of promise, rebuild their temple after this glorious model,
and dwell in tribal divisions according to the literal statements of
this prophecy. (3) That exposition which has been maintained
probably by the majority of evangelical divines may be called the
figurative or symbolico-typical. The vision is a Levitico-prophetic
picture of the New Testament Church or kingdom of God. Its
general import is thus set forth by Keil: "The tribes of Israel
which receive Canaan for a perpetual possession are not the Jewish
people converted to Christ, but the Israel of God, i. e., the people
of God of the new covenant gathered from among both Jews and
Gentiles; and that Canaan in which they are to dwell is not the
earthly Canaan or Palestine between the Jordan and the Mediterranean Sea, but the New Testament Canaan, the territory of the
kingdom of God, whose boundaries reach from sea to sea, and from
the river to the ends of the earth. And the temple upon a very
high mountain in the midst of this Canaan in which the Lord is

Interpretation of the closing vision of Eze-kiel.

enthroned, and causes the river of the water of life to flow down from his throne over his kingdom, so that the earth produces the tree of life with leaves as medicine for men, and the Dead Sea is filled with fishes and living creatures, is a figurative representation and type of the gracious presence of the Lord in his Church, which is realized, in the present period of the earthly development of the kingdom of heaven, in the form of the Christian Church, in a spiritual and invisible manner, in the indwelling of the Father and the Son through the Holy Spirit in the hearts of believers, and in a spiritual and invisible operation in the Church, but which will eventually manifest itself when our Lord shall appear in the glory of the Father to translate his Church into the kingdom of glory in such a manner that we shall see the Almighty God and the Lamb with the eyes of our glorified body, and worship before his throne." [1]

This symbolico-typical interpretation recognizes a harmony of Ezekiel's method and style with other apocalyptic representations of the kingdom of heaven, and finds in this fact a strong argument in its favour. The measurements recorded, the ideal character of the tribe divisions, and especially the river of healing waters flowing from the threshold of the temple into the eastern sea, are insuperable difficulties in the way of any literal exposition of the vision. The modern chiliastic notion of a future return of the Jews to Palestine, and a revival of the Old Testament sacrificial worship, is opposed to the entire genius and spirit of the Gospel dispensation. [2]

The illustrations now given of the artistic structure of Old Testament apocalyptics should be kept in mind and utilized in the study of the eschatological portions of the New Testament. The habit of repeating prophetic pictures, *Artistic structure of apocalyptics to be noted.* like Pharaoh's dreams and Daniel's visions, under various forms, the abundance of imagery, and the highly metaphorical style of predictions of falling empires, should be particularly studied. A failure to observe these formal elements has been one chief cause of the numerous conflicting expositions of this class of Scriptures. That certainly would be an untrustworthy method which, in the interpretation of the New Testament, insists on the literal import of language which, in the Old Testament, is authoritatively shown to be figurative.

---

[1] Biblical Commentary on the Prophecies of Ezekiel, vol. ii, p. 425. Edinb., 1876.

[2] For extended arguments in favour of the symbolico-typical, and against the literal, interpretation of Ezek. xl–xlviii, see the commentaries on this prophet by Fairbairn, Schroeder, Cowles, and Currey.

CHAPTER XXIV.

THE GOSPEL APOCALYPSE.

OUR Lord's eschatological discourse in Matt. xxiv (and the parallel passages of Mark and Luke) may be appropriately called the apocalypse of the Gospels.[1] It was uttered in connexion with his terrible denunciation of Jerusalem, the murderess of prophets (Matt. xxiii, 34–39). The disciples were awestruck by his words, and as he took his departure from the temple they called his attention to the magnificent buildings and great stones; but this only drew from him the further remark: "Days will come, in which there shall not be left stone upon stone here, which shall not be thrown down" (Luke xxi, 6). He passed out of the city, and sat down upon the Mount of Olives opposite the temple, when four of the disciples (Peter, James, John, and Andrew) asked him privately (Mark xiii, 3, 4): "Tell us when these things shall be, and what the sign when these things are all about to be accomplished?" Luke (xxi, 7) records their inquiry in nearly the same words, but according to Matthew (xxiv, 3) they asked: "Tell us when these things shall be, and what is the sign of thy coming (τῆς σῆς παρουσίας) and of the completion of the age" (συντελείας τοῦ αἰῶνος)? Let it be noted, then, that our Lord's apocalyptic sermon on the Mount of Olives was in answer to this question of his disciples, and with explicit reference to the overthrow of the temple and the fall of Jerusalem.

But although the occasion and scope of this discourse are so clearly defined, and our Lord himself declared emphatically, in answer to the disciples' question, "This generation shall not pass away until all these things be accomplished" (Matt. xxiv, 34; Mark xiii, 30; Luke xxi, 32; comp. Matt. xvi, 28; Mark ix, 1; Luke ix, 27), a large number of expositors insist that even now, after a lapse of nearly two thousand years, the prophecy

Occasion of Jesus' apocalyptic discourse.

Various opinions.

---

[1] This designation is justified by the subject matter of the discourse, and its formal reference to his coming and the end of the age. But it lacks some of the formal elements of biblical apocalyptics, and for the obvious reason that it became this Teacher and Prophet from heaven to speak unlike those who received their revelations by vision or dream. So far, however, as he uses the tone and style of apocalyptic prophecy, we should interpret his language by the same hermeneutical principles which we apply to other revelations.

remains in great part unfulfilled. It is quite generally admitted that Matt. xxiv, 1–28 refers to the fall of Jerusalem, but the language of verses 29–31 is supposed to be incompatible with that event, and to refer to a future literal coming of Christ in the clouds of heaven. Some, however, find the transition from the destruction of Jerusalem to the end of the world at verse 35 (E. J. Meyer), others at verse 36 (Doddridge), others at verse 43 (Kuinoel), while others find it in chap. xxv, 14 (Eichhorn), and others in chap. xxv, 31 (Wetstein).[1] Another class of interpreters (Stier, Alford) apply the theory of a double sense to the whole chapter, and teach that our Lord referred primarily to the destruction of Jerusalem, but only as to a type of the end of the world and the final judgment. "Two parallel interpretations," says Alford, "run through the former part as far as verse 28, the destruction of Jerusalem and the final judgment being both enwrapped in the words, but the former, in this part of the chapter, predominating. From verse 28, the lesser subject begins to be swallowed up by the greater, and our Lord's second coming is the predominant theme, with, however, certain hints thrown back as it were at the event which was immediately in question; till, in the latter part of the chapter, and the whole of the next, the second advent, and at last the final judgment ensuing on it, are the subjects."[2]

Lange's outline of this sublime prophecy of our Lord is as follows: "In harmony with apocalyptical style, he exhibited the judgments of his coming in a series of cycles, each of which depicts the whole futurity, but in such a manner that with every new cycle the scene seems to approximate to and more closely resemble the final catastrophe. Thus, the first cycle delineates the whole course of the world down to the end, in its general characteristics (chap. xxiv, 4–14). The second gives the signs of the approaching destruction of Jerusalem, and paints this destruction itself as a sign and a commencement of the judgment of the world, which from that day onward proceeds in silent and suppressed days of judgment down to the last (vers. 15–28). The

Lange's analysis of chapters xxiv and xxv.

[1] The position taken by some that it was one great purpose of Jesus, in answering his disciples' question, to warn them against confounding Jerusalem's destruction with the end of the world can scarcely be made out of a strict interpretation of our Lord's words. He clearly warned them against deceivers and false Christs who would appear before the end. But we can find no word or sentence which appears designed to impress any one with the idea that the destruction in question and the parousia would be far separate as to time. The one, it is said, will immediately follow the other, and all will take place before that generation shall pass away.

[2] Greek Testament on Matt. xxiv, 1, 2.

third describes the sudden end of the world, and the judgment
which ensues (vers. 29–44).[1] Then follows a series of parables and
similitudes, in which the Lord paints the judgment itself, which
unfolds itself in an organic succession of several acts. In the last
act Christ reveals his universal judicial majesty. Chap. xxiv, 45–51,
exhibits the judgment upon the servants of Christ, or the clergy.
Chap. xxv, 1–13, (the wise and foolish virgins) exhibits the judgment upon the Church, or the people. Then follows the judgment
upon individual members of the Church (14–30). Finally, verses
31–46 introduce the universal judgment of the world."[2]

In view of the various opinions of this important prophecy one
may well approach the investigation of it with great reserve. All
dogmatic assumptions and prepossessions should be set aside, and
the entire passage should be studied with strict regard to the context, scope, and plan.

The prophecy, as we have seen, was uttered in reply to the
question of the disciples, as given in Matt. xxiv, 3,
Mark xiii, 4, and Luke xxi, 7. The form of the question as stated by Matthew has apparently a threefold implication,
touching, respectively, the time of those things, the sign of the
parousia, and the end of the age (see above, p. 438). But is this
sufficient to warrant an expectation of finding in our Lord's answer
a triple division, each referring to a different event, or authorizing
a threefold meaning in his words? Or if we regard the question as
twofold, is it of a nature to authorize the theory of a double sense,
or of two parallel interpretations enwrapped in one and the same
passage? Much more reasonable, we submit, is the supposition
that, when the disciples made their inquiry, they had no clearly
defined outline of the future in their minds. "They obviously had
not," says Robinson, "at the time, any definite and distinct notions
of that terrible overthrow and subversion of the Jewish people
which was so soon to take place. They were also equally ignorant
in respect to the awful events which are to be the accompaniments
of the day of judgment and the end of the world. We cannot suppose nor admit that the inquiry, as Matthew puts it, suggested to

The question of the disciples. (marginal note)

[1] According to Nast we may "take what is said of the coming of Christ, in verses
29–36, figuratively, and understand by it a judicial visitation of nominal Christendom
by Christ, in order to destroy all ungodly institutions and principles in Church and
State, of which (providential) visitation the overthrow of the Jewish polity was but a
type, and which itself is, in turn, the full type of the final and total overthrow of all
powers of darkness on the great day of judgment."—Commentary on Matthew and
Mark, p. 538. Cincinnati, 1864. This writer's entire discussion of Matt. xxiv, is
worthy of study for its helpful suggestions.

[2] Commentary on the Gospel of Matthew (Amer. ed., 1864), p. 418.

their minds the same ideas, nor events of the same character, as the same language, taken by itself, would now suggest to us under the full light of a completed revelation."[1] Any assumptions, therefore, built upon the threefold form of the disciples' question, will be liable to mislead.

It is also important that, in this and other Scriptures which speak of the συντέλεια τοῦ αἰῶνος, *consummation*, or *comple-* The end of the *tion of the age*, we disabuse our minds of the mislead- age. ing impression begotten by the common translation, "end of the world." A misinterpretation of this phrase is the root of many false assumptions. "It is not surprising that mere English readers of the New Testament should suppose that this phrase really means the destruction of the material earth; but such an error ought not to receive countenance from men of learning. The true signification of *aἰών* is not *world*, but *age*. Like its Latin equivalent *aevum*, it refers to a period of time. The 'end of the age' means the close of the epoch or age—that is, the Jewish age or dispensation which was drawing nigh, as our Lord frequently intimated. All those passages which speak of 'the end,' 'the end of the age,' or 'the ends of the ages,' refer to the same consummation, and always as nigh at hand. In 1 Cor. x, 11, St. Paul says, 'The ends of the ages have stretched out to us;' implying that he regarded himself and his readers as living near the conclusion of an æon, or age. So, in the Epistle to the Hebrews, we find the remarkable expression, 'Now, once, close upon the end of the ages, hath he appeared to put away sin by the sacrifice of himself' (Heb. ix, 26); clearly showing that the writer regarded the incarnation of Christ as taking place near the end of the æon, or dispensational period. To suppose that he meant that it was close upon the end of the *world*, or the destruction of the material globe, would be to make him write false history as well as bad grammar. It would not be true in fact; for the world has already lasted longer since the incarnation than the whole duration of the Mosaic economy, from the exodus to the destruction of the temple. It is futile, therefore, to say that the 'end of the age' may mean a lengthened period,

---

[1] Bibliotheca Sacra of 1843, p. 533. "The disciples assume, as a matter of course," says Meyer, "that immediately after the destruction in question the Lord will appear, in accordance with what is said xxiii, 39, for the purpose of setting up his kingdom, and that with this the current (pre-Messianic) era of the world's history will come to an end. Consequently they wish to know, in the second place (for there are only two questions, not three, as Grotius and Ebrard suppose), what is to be the sign which, after the destruction of the temple, is to precede this second coming and the end of the world, that by it they may be able to recognize the approach of those events."— Critical Commentary on Matthew xxiv, 3.

extending from the incarnation to our times, and even far beyond them. That would be an æon, and not the close of an æon. The æon of which our Lord was speaking was about to close in a great catastrophe; and a catastrophe is not a protracted process, but a definitive and culminating act."[1]

A study of the contents and scope of Matt. xxiv–xxv will be **Analysis of the Gospel Apocalypse.** greatly aided by a discriminating analytical outline of the subject-matter. Lange's "series of cycles" given above (pp. 439, 440) is suggestive, and designates the more noticeable points of transition in the course of the prophecy. It also recognizes its apocalyptical character. But the notion that "each cycle depicts the whole futurity" is without warrant in the language of our Lord. The following is a condensed summary of the principal statements:

I.

1 There will be false Christs and a great apostasy, verses 4, 5.
2 There will be wars, rumours of wars, famines, and earthquakes, 6, 7.
3 You will suffer persecution and martyrdom, 9.
4 Great offences, betrayals, and feuds, 10.
5 Many false prophets, great wickedness, and apostasy, 11, 12.
6 The Gospel will be preached in all the world, 13, 14.
7 Then comes the end, 14.

II.

1 The abomination of desolation, 15.
2 The flight to the mountains, 16–20.
3 The great tribulation, 21, 22.
4 Warnings against false Christs and false prophets, 23–26.
5 The parousia like the lightning-flash, 27.
6 Eagles will gather on the carcass, 28.

III.

1 Darkening and shaking of sun, moon, and stars immediately after the great tribulation, 29.
2 The sign of the Son of man in the clouds, 30.
3 The sending forth of trumpet angels and gathering of the elect, 31.

IV.

1 The similitude of the fig-tree, 32, 33.
2 All these things within this generation, 34.
3 Infallible certainty of Jesus' words, 35.

---

[1] The Parousia. A Critical Inquiry into the New Testament Doctrine of our Lord's Second Coming, pp. 58, 59. Lond., 1878. Meyer says, "The τοῦ αἰῶνος (the age), with the article, but not further defined, is to be understood as referring to the existing, the then current, age of the world, i. e., to the αἰὼν οὗτος (this age), which is brought to a close (συντέλεια) with the second coming, inasmuch as, with this latter event, the αἰὼν μέλλων (coming age) begins."—Commentary on Matthew xxiv, 3.

4 The day and hour unknown, verse 36.
5 It will be as the flood in Noah's days, 37–39.
6 Sudden separations, 40–41.
7 Admonition to watch, 42–51.

The twenty-fifth chapter readily falls into three parts, (1) the parable of the ten virgins (verses 1–13), (2) the parable of the talents (14–30), and (3) the prophecy of eternal judgment (31–46). The entire discourse, as given in Matthew, thus manifests a sevenfold structure, and a comparison of these several parts with our analysis of the words of Joel (see above, pp. 429–431) will disclose many noticeable analogies.

The principles of grammatico-historical interpretation require our close attention to the specific time-limitations of this prophecy. The entire discourse appears to have grown out of Jesus' declaration: "The days will come in which there shall not be left stone upon stone here which shall not be thrown down" (Luke xxi, 6; comp. Matt. xxiv, 2; Mark xiii, 2). These words, especially, occasioned the disciples' question: "When shall these things be?" The whole prophecy purports to be an answer to that question, and no affirmation in it is more emphatic than the words: "Verily I say unto you, This generation shall not pass away till all these things be accomplished" (Matt. xxiv, 34; Mark xiii, 30; Luke xxi, 32). On what valid hermeneutical principles, then, can it be fairly claimed that this discourse of Jesus comprehends all futurity? Why should we look for the revelations of far distant ages and millenniums of human history in a prophecy expressly limited to the generation[1] in which it was uttered?

It will be answered that the statements of Matt. xxiv, 14, and Luke xxi, 24, and the style of language used in Matt. xxiv, 29–31,

A sevenfold structure.

Time-limitations of this prophecy.

[1] The significations which, apparently under the pressure of an assumed exegetical necessity, have been put upon the words ἡ γενεὰ αὔτη, _this generation_, may well seem absurd to the unbiassed critic. To put upon them such meanings as "the human race" (Jerome), or "the Jewish race" (Clarke, Dorner, Auberlen), or "the race of Christian believers" (Chrysostom, Lange), may reasonably be condemned as a reading whatever suits our purpose into the words of Scripture. The evident meaning of the word is seen in such texts as Matt. i, 17; xvii, 17; Acts xiv, 16; xv, 21 (by-gone generations, generations of old), and nothing in New Testament exegesis is capable of more convincing proof than that γενεά is the Greek equivalent of our word _generation;_ i. e., the mass or great body of people living at one period—the period of average lifetime. Even if it be allowed that in such passages as Matt. xi, 16, or Luke xvi, 8, the thought of a particular race or class of people is implied, it is beyond doubt that in those same passages the persons referred to are conceived as contemporaries.

and xxv, 31–46, are incompatible with the time-limitations designated above.   A careful study of these passages, however, in the
light of other apocalyptic Scriptures, will serve to show that they
do not warrant the dogmatic construction which many interpreters
have put upon them.[1]

1. The preaching of the Gospel of the kingdom "in the whole
Import of Matt. world for a testimony unto all the nations" (Matt.
xxiv, 14.   xxiv, 14) must precede the end, and therefore, it is
argued, the end here contemplated must be in the far future, after
all nations have been evangelized.   But a comparison of Luke ii, 1,
shows that all this same world (οἰκουμένη) was enrolled by a decree
of Cæsar.   In Col. i, 6, 23, the Gospel is said to be " bearing fruit
in all the world" (ἐν παντὶ τῷ κόσμῳ), and to be "preached in all
creation under the heaven."   The Gospel, therefore, uttered its
testimony to all the nations of this same world before the ruin of
the temple and the end of the Jewish æon.

---

[1] Godet (Commentary on Luke xxi, 5–7) affirms that Matt. xxiv is a confused mixture of at least two distinct discourses of Jesus, and, he argues, "Jesus could not
affirm here what he elsewhere declares that he did not know" (Mark xiii, 32).   In
this statement Godet, like many others, makes no distinction between a *day* and an
hour, and the period of a *generation*.   Might one not have assurance that momentous
events would take place within a generation (i. e., forty or fifty years) and yet not
know the day or the hour?   Moreover, the hypothesis of a confused report of Jesus'
words involves a loose doctrine of inspiration, and virtually makes it the work of the
exegete to correct the mistakes of the apostles.   Godet proceeds: "While he announces the destruction of Jerusalem as an event to be witnessed by the contemporary generation, he speaks of the parousia as one which is possibly yet very remote.   Consider the expression *days will come* (Luke xvii, 22) [but why assume that
these days must be very remote?   The full import of the words would be satisfied if
the days came within ten years], and the parable of the widow, the meaning of
which is that God will seem to the Church an unjust judge, who, *for a protracted
time*, refuses to hear her [but the time need not be protracted forty years to seem
very long to those who cry day and night—much less need it be protracted thousands
of years!], so that during this time of waiting the faith of many shall give way
(Luke xviii, 1–8) [but was it not possible for the faith of many to give way during
that generation as well as in any subsequent generation?].   The Master is to
return; but, perhaps, it will not be till the *second* or the *third watch*, or even *till
the morning*, that he will come (Mark xiii, 35; Luke xii, 38) [and, forsooth, no second, third, or fourth watch of any day or night within forty years after these words
were spoken, could fulfil this saying!].   The great distance at which the capital
lies (Luke xix, 12) can signify nothing else than the considerable space of time
which will elapse between the departure of Jesus and his return."   But one generation would seem to be time enough for this; few noblemen would expect a longer
period for such a work!   Far less time would probably be necessary for the Son of
man to go through the clouds to the Ancient of days and receive from him a kingdom
(Dan. vii, 13, 14), and return to supplant Judaism and her rule by a more spiritual
dominion.

2. The statement in Luke xxi, 24, that "Jerusalem shall be trodden down by Gentiles until the times of the Gentiles Import of Luke
be fulfilled," is supposed to involve events which did xxi, 24.
not take place in that generation. The "times of the Gentiles"
(καιροὶ ἐθνῶν) are assumed to be the times and opportunities of
grace afforded to the Gentiles under the Gospel. But to understand the words in this sense would be, as Van Oosterzee observes,
to interpolate a thought entirely foreign to the context.[1] "The
times of the Gentiles," says Bengel, "are the times allotted to the
Gentiles to tread down the city;" but there is nothing in the passage or context to authorize his further remark that "these times
shall be ended when the Gentiles' conversion shall be fully con-
summated,"[2] and that the treading down by Romans, Persians, Sara-
cens, Franks, and Turks is to be understood. These καιροί are
manifestly times of judgment upon Jerusalem, not times of salvation to the Gentiles. The most natural and obvious parallel is Rev.
xi, 2, where the outer court of the temple is said to be "given to
the Gentiles," by whom the holy city shall be trodden down forty-
two months, a period equivalent to the "time and times and half a
time" of Rev. xii, 14, and of Dan. vii, 25; xii, 7. This is a symbolical period of judgment (see above, p. 384), but does not denote ages and generations. It is three and a half—a divided
seven, a short but signal period of woe. The "times of the Gentiles," therefore, are the three and a half times (approximating
three and a half years) during which the Gentile armies besieged
and trampled down Jerusalem.[3]

3. The language of Matt. xxiv, 29-31, has probably been the
principal reason for believing that this prophecy must Import of Matt.
refer to other events than the destruction of Jerusalem xxiv, 29-31.
and the end of the Jewish dispensation. Pressing the literal sense
of the words, many interpreters have asked: When was the sun
thus darkened and the heavens shaken? Who ever saw the Son
of man thus coming in the clouds, or heard the loud-sounding
trumpet of his angels? Or when did he thus gather his elect from

---

[1] Commentary on Luke (Lange's Biblework), in loco.

[2] Gnomon of the New Testament on Luke xxi, 24. These "times of the Gentiles"
must not be confounded with the "fulness of the Gentiles" in Rom. xi, 25.

[3] Meyer explains the passage "till the times of the Gentiles be fulfilled," as meaning "till the time that the periods which are appointed to the Gentiles for the completion of divine judgments (not the *period of grace* for the Gentiles, as Ebrard foists
into the passage) shall have run out. Comp. Rev. xi, 2. Such times of the Gentiles
are ended in the case in question by the parousia (verses 25-27) which is to occur
during the lifetime of the hearers (ver. 28); hence those καιροί are in no way to be
regarded as of longer duration."—Critical Commentary, in loco.

one end of heaven to the other? If all this is figurative, where shall we find a literal description of the final day?

To all which it may be answered: There is no valid reason for Analogous presuming in advance that we should anywhere find a prophecies. literal description of the last judgment. On the contrary there is the analogy of prophecy, and especially of apocalyptic prophecy, to show that great catastrophes of divine judgment are foretold mainly in figure and by symbol. The language of Matt. xxiv, 29, is manifestly appropriated from such Scriptures as Joel ii, 10, 31; Ezek. xxxii, 7, and Isa. xiii, 10.[1] Our Lord made use of the prophetical style familiar to every well-read Jew,[2] but the extreme literalism maintained by modern Chiliasts would utterly destroy any rational exposition of such a passage as Isa. xxxiv, 4, 5:

> All the hosts of the heavens shall be melted,
> And the heavens shall be rolled together as the scroll,
> And all their host shall fall,
> As falls a leaf from the vine,
> And as a fallen fig from the fig-tree.
> For my sword shall be sated in the heavens;
> Behold upon Edom it shall come down,
> And upon the people of my curse, for judgment.

When the leading Old Testament prophet makes use of such language in foretelling the desolation of Edom, with what reason or propriety can we insist on the literal import of such passages as Matt. xxiv, 29, and 2 Peter iii, 10.

The language of Matt. xxiv, 30, concerning "the Son of man com-Language of ing in the clouds of the heaven with power and much Matt. xxiv, 30. glory," is taken from Daniel's night vision (Dan. vii, 13) in which he saw the Son of man coming to the Ancient of days and receiving from him dominion, and glory, and a kingdom. That vision was a part of the composite symbol of world-empire, and signified that "the kingdom, and dominion, and the greatness of the kingdom under the whole heaven, shall be given to the people of the saints of the Most High, whose kingdom is an everlasting

---

[1] See the whole passage, Isa. xiii, 2–13, as translated on page 414 above, and used to portray a great national catastrophe, the fall of Babylon.

[2] "There have been many interpreters," says Planck, "who knew nothing at all of the local and temporary meaning of certain phrases and expressions in the Bible; to whom, in fact, it never once occurred that the early Jews could have attached other ideas to certain forms of speech than those which the literal sense of the terms expressed."—Introduction to Sacred Philology and Interpretation, p. 146. Edinb. (Bib. Cab.), 1834.

kingdom, and all dominions shall serve and obey him" (Dan. vii, 27). The kingdom received from the Ancient of days is no other than the kingdom symbolized by the stone cut out of the mountain, in chap. ii, 34, 35, which "became a great mountain and filled all the land." This is the kingdom of Messiah, which the Chiliasts believe to be yet future, but which is more generally believed to be the Gospel dispensation, a kingdom not of this world, and not inaugurated with phenomenal splendour visible to mortal eyes. Like the stone cut out of the mountain, and the mustard seed, it is small and comparatively unimportant at its beginning, but it grows so as to fill the earth. This kingdom, according to Jesus' own testimony (Luke xvii, 20), "comes not with observation;" that is, says Meyer, "the coming of the Messiah's kingdom is not so conditioned that this coming could be *observed* as a visible development, or that it could be said, in consequence of such observation, that here or there is the kingdom."[1] It may safely be affirmed, therefore, that this language concerning the coming of the Son of man in the clouds means no more on the lips of Jesus than in the writings of Daniel. It denotes in both places a sublime and glorious reality, the grandest event in human history, but not a visible display in the heavens of such a nature as to be a matter of scenic observation. The Son of man came in heavenly power to supplant Judaism by a better covenant, and to make the kingdoms of the world his own, and that parousia dates from the fall of Judaism and its temple. The mourning of "all the tribes of the land" (not all the nations of the globe) was coincident with the desolation of Zion, and our Lord appropriately foretold it in language taken from Zech. xii, 11, 12.

The sending forth of the angels, and the gathering of the elect, described in Matt. xxiv, 31, whatever its exact mean- Import of Matt. ing, does not necessarily depict a scenic procedure vis- xxiv, 31. ible to human eyes.[2] If understood literally, it may, nevertheless, be only a verbal revelation of what took place in such a supernatural manner as that no man might behold it and remain alive. It is said in verses 40 and 41 that at the parousia "two men shall be

[1] Critical Commentary on Luke, in loco.

[2] This verse has been understood, figuratively, of the sending forth of the messengers of the Gospel to gather unto Christ an elect Church in place of the outcast Israel. In that sense it was a procedure which followed the parousia and still continues. So Lightfoot: "When Jerusalem shall be reduced to ashes, and this impious race shall have been cut off and rejected, then the Son of man will send forth his ministers with the Gospel trumpet, and they shall gather his elect among the Gentiles from the four corners of heaven; so that God will not be left without a Church, although his ancient people be rejected and disowned."—Horæ Hebraicæ on Matt. xxiv, 31. This explanation, however, will be accepted by very few.

in the field; one is taken and one is left; two women shall be grinding at the mill; one is taken and one is left." In such a miraculous rapture of living saints (comp. 1 Thess. iv, 16, 17; 1 Cor. xv, 51, 52) the person left may not have been permitted to see the one taken. It was a special favour to Elisha that he was enabled to behold Elijah when the latter was caught up into heaven (2 Kings ii, 9–12). A similar favour enabled Elisha's servant to see the mountain full of horses and chariots of fire (2 Kings vi, 17). Those heavenly forces were truly present to execute Jehovah's judgment, though invisible to the eyes of men. At the resurrection of Jesus "many bodies of the saints who had fallen asleep were raised, and coming forth out of the tombs, they entered into the holy city, and appeared unto many" (Matt. xxvii, 52, 53). But that wonderful event was not made a phenomenon visible to the world. So, there appears no sufficient reason for denying that at the judgment of Jerusalem many other bodies of the saints which slept arose, and many living saints were miraculously translated. Hence we may not dogmatically conclude that any of the statements of Matt. xxiv, 29–31 are inconsistent with the time-limits which Jesus so positively set to this eschatological prophecy.

Whatever the events described in these verses, they are said to follow "immediately after the tribulation of those days" (ver. 29). That tribulation is conceded to be the unparalleled sufferings referred to in verses 21 and 22 which were occasioned by the siege of Jerusalem. Josephus observes that, in his judgment, the misfortunes of all men from the beginning of time were comparatively of less magnitude than those of the Jews in this fearful war.[1] It is notable that great efforts have been made by a number of expositors to escape the force and bearing of the word εὐθέως, *immediately*. Some try to explain it as equivalent with *suddenly*, but this scarcely helps the case, for thus, says Desprez, "Matthew is taken to mean, ' When the tribulation of the days in which Jerusalem shall be destroyed shall have passed away, then, after some indefinite interval, which may amount to myriads of years, all of a sudden the great consummation will fall like a thunderbolt upon mankind.' To this the reply is—(1) that the interpretation is ungrammatical, and that if this be the meaning of the words translated "immediately" (εὐθέως δέ), any words may be made to mean any thing; (2) that the parallel passage in Mark (xiii, 24) states distinctly that the signs of the final consummation shall be seen in the very days which follow the former tribulation; and (3) that Jesus himself is described as saying that every thing

Import of εὐθέως, immediately.

[1] Wars of the Jews, Preface, 4.

should be accomplished within the limits of the existing generation."[1]

We are driven, then, by every sound principle of hermeneutics, to conclude that Matt. xxiv, 29–31, must be included within the time-limits of the discourse of which it forms an essential part, and cannot be legitimately applied to events far separate from the final catastrophe of the Jewish state.[2]

4. The description of the judgment of all nations in Matt. xxv, 31–46 is expressly associated with the coming of the Son of man in his glory. It is connected with the preceding discourse by the particle δέ, and is, there-fore, not to be regarded as a distinct and independent prophecy. Its tropical character, however, is apparent from its use of the terms sheep and goats, and the scenic portraiture of the separation and the judgment; but its doctrine manifestly involves the eternal destinies of the righteous and the wicked.

The judgment of all nations, Matt. xxv, 31–46.

The apparent difficulty of connecting this picture of judgment and eternal destiny with the ruin of Jerusalem will be obviated by a more careful attention to the scriptural doctrine of divine judgment. We miss the full scrip-tural idea of judgment (מִשְׁפָּט, שָׁפַט, κρίνω, κρίσις) when we conceive of it as confined to one last day, one formal rehearsal of every act of human history before a tribunal in the heavens, at which the in-dividuals of all nations and ages shall be simultaneously assembled. So far as this conception involves the fundamental idea that every individual shall be brought into judgment before God, and that the

Scriptural doctrine of Judgment.

---

[1] Daniel and John, p. 241. London, 1878. Whedon explains the *immediately* by borrowing Luke xxi, 24 as a context. Assuming that the "times of the Gentiles" are "the period of the more exclusive Gentile churchdom," he supposes that, subsequent to that period, the millennial ages will terminate in the "tribulation of those days," immediately after which the final judgment will take place. All these suppositions are based upon the assumption "that we may be allowed to supply from one evangelist the omissions by another of important passages, and allow the parts so supplied to modify the meaning of the context which they supplement."—Commentary on Matthew, p. 277. Facts or statements in one gospel may, indeed, help us to understand facts and statements in another, but to appropriate a *context* from another book is scarcely allowable to an interpreter.

[2] The statement that "that day and hour" is unknown to any but the Father (Matt. xxiv, 36; Mark xiii, 32; comp. Acts i, 7; 1 Thess. v, 1, 2; 2 Peter iii, 10) is not in the least inconsistent with the assurance that a.l will take place within a generation. To pretend otherwise would be to accuse Jesus of solemn trifling, for it would involve the absurd proposition: Verily I say unto you, This generation shall not pass away till all these things be accomplished; nevertheless, that day and hour may be two thousand years in the future. See the strictures on Godet's comment, footnote to page 444.

issue of such judgment will be according to character and deeds, it is warranted not only by numerous particular texts, but also by the whole drift of Scripture teaching concerning the character of God and his governmental relation to men. The mediatorial reign of Christ may appropriately culminate in such a final κρίσις, and this is the common belief of the Church. But nothing could be more unscriptural than the notion that the judgment of nations and of individuals is limited to one last day. It is a continual process, running through the Messianic era, and a necessary part of the administration of the King of kings. Nations are continually undergoing signal judgment,[1] and the eternal destinies of individuals are being determined every day. And this is essentially the order of Christ's reign. He is enthroned at the right hand of God, and must reign till he has overthrown all rival authority and power, and has put all his enemies under his feet. One of the notable features of the Messiah's reign is that the Father commits all judgment unto the Son (John v, 22); he "gave him authority to execute judgment, because he is the Son of man" (ver. 27). That is, he is the Son of man described in the visions of Daniel who came with the clouds of heaven and received of the Ancient of days a kingdom and dominion over all nations (Dan. vii, 9–14). His regal office and authority constitute him judge and ruler of all, and Matt. xxv, 31–46 is a vivid picture not merely of what will take place at the end of time, but of what the Christ continually does from the time of his session upon the throne of his glory until he shall have delivered up the kingdom to the Father (1 Cor. xv, 24).

The judgment scene of Matt. xxv, 31–46, is, therefore, to be understood of a divine procedure which has its formal inauguration at the beginning of Messiah's reign, and goes on with the progress of the Messianic age. Accordingly it contains nothing inconsistent with the time limitation of the prophecy of which it forms a part.

According to all these accounts the parousia of the Son of man was to be coincident with the appalling catastrophe of Jerusalem and the Jewish polity. As the Mosaic polity was instituted at Sinai when Jehovah came down upon the mountain amid fire and smoke and earthquake and the sound of a trumpet (Exod. xix, 16–20), so that polity

The Parousia coincident with the fall of the Jewish polity and the end of that age.

---

[1] Hence the profound and far-reaching significance of that prophetic utterance of Joel (see above, p. 431) which stands as a generic prophecy of divine judgment, and has a thousandfold application in the history of men and nations:

> Multitudes, multitudes in the valley of judgment!
> For near is the day of Jehovah,
> In the valley of judgment.

was made to cease, and its æon came to an end when the Son of man, Jehovah-Christ, came in terrible judgment to execute vengeance upon his enemies.[1] Then was fulfilled the prophecy of Joel:

I will give wonders in the heavens and in the land
Blood, and fire, and columns of smoke;
The sun shall be turned to darkness,
And the moon to blood,
Before the coming of the day of Jehovah,
The great and the terrible. (Joel ii, 30, 31.)

There is not wanting evidence that the destruction of Jerusalem was accompanied by many awe-inspiring portents, signs, and supernatural agencies co-operating with the armies of men. Josephus describes a marvellous prodigy that appeared in the heavens on this wise: "I suppose the account of it would seem to be a fable were it not related by those that saw it, and were not the events that followed it of so considerable a nature as to deserve such signals; for, before sun-setting, chariots and troops of soldiers in their armour were seen running about among the clouds and surrounding of cities."[2] *Visible signs of judgment.* He also relates how a star resembling a sword hung over the city, and a comet appeared, and a great light one night shone about the altar and the temple for half an hour. There were also quakings and strange noises. Such portents amply fulfilled the "terrors and great signs from heaven" of which Luke speaks (xxi, 11). But who can say what other sights appeared at the final moment of the catastrophe? The parousia was like the lightning flash (Matt. xxiv, 27), not abiding for days like the Glory on Sinai (Exod. xxiv, 16). "The sight of the glory of Jehovah was like devouring fire on the top of the mountain to the eyes of the sons of Israel" (Exod. xxiv, 17); and that glory was a real presence, a veritable parousia, for "Jehovah came down upon Mount Sinai" (Exod. xix, 20). And yet in that Sinaitic parousia the Israelites saw no form or shape (תְּמוּנָה) of the divine Person (Deut. iv, 15). Whether those who saw the SIGN of the Son of man which appeared in heaven

---

[1] Chiliastic writers, in claiming that the word παρουσία, *coming*, or *presence*, always means a personal presence, appear to assume that there can be no personal coming or presence of the Lord unless it be literally visible to human eyes. This would exclude the personal presence of God and of angels from the divine government of the world. Will it be pretended that there was no personal coming or presence of Jehovah at the destruction of Sodom and Gomorrah? Comp. Gen. xviii, 21; xix, 24, 25. But the Scriptures give no intimation of any visible appearance of the holy One to the inhabitants of the doomed cities. And so again and again has God come in terrible judgment upon wicked men and nations without any visible display of his person—a sight which no man may behold and live (Exod. xxxiii, 20).

[2] Wars, vi, 5, 3. Comp. Tacitus, Annals, xiv, 12, 22; xv, 22, 47; xvi, 13.

immediately after the tribulation of those days (Matt. xxiv, 29, 30) saw the person and form of the Son of man himself, or only some symbol of his presence, must remain a mystery.' In either case his coming at that time was a real, particular, personal, and momentous coming, to consummate an old dispensation and inaugurate a new one. It was truly a shaking of earth and heaven for the purpose of removing that which was ready to pass away, and of instituting "a kingdom which cannot be shaken" (Heb. xii, 26–28).

This view of the parousia of Christ harmonizes with all his utterances of its nearness. He had before this said: "There are some of them standing here who shall not taste of death until they see the Son of man coming in his kingdom" (Matt. xvi, 28). Compare the no less decisive statements in Mark ix, 1, and Luke ix, 27. These declarations, probably often repeated, made a deep impression on the disciples, and led them to look in their own day for "the blessed hope and appearing of the glory of the great God and of our Saviour Jesus Christ" (Titus ii, 13). We should bear in mind that all the books of the New Testament, except the Gospel of John, were written before the destruction of Jerusalem, and they all witness the current vivid expectation of a speedy coming of the Lord.

On the fulfilment of the prophecies of Matt. xxiv the author of "The Parousia" makes the following observations: "It is possible to believe in the fulfilment of predictions which take effect in the visible order of things, because we have historical evidence of that fulfilment; but how can we be expected to believe in fulfilments which are said to have taken place in the region of the spiritual and invisible when we have no witnesses to depose to the facts? We can implicitly believe in the accomplishment of all that was predicted respecting the horrors of the siege of Jerusalem, the burning of the temple, and the demolition of the city, because we have the testimony of Josephus to the facts; but how can we believe in a coming of the Son of man, in a resurrection of the dead, in an act of judgment, when we have nothing but the word of prophecy to rely upon, and no Josephus to vouch for the historical accuracy of the facts?

---

[1] "The sign of the Son of man" may mean the ruin of the Jewish temple, considered as a sign or token that the old æon thereby is ended, and the new Messianic æon is begun. "The sign of the prophet Jonah" (Matt. xii, 39; xvi, 4) was no miraculous phenomenon in the heavens. The analogy between Christ and Jonah for three days and three nights (Matt. xii, 40) may be compared with John ii, 19–21 as suggesting that "the temple of his body," which was raised up in three days, was a prophetic sign that upon the ruin of Judaism and its temple there would rise that nobler "spiritual house" (1 Peter ii, 5), "which is his body, the fulness of him who filleth all in all" (Eph. i, 23).

"To this it can only be said in reply that the demand for human testimony to events in the region of the unseen is not altogether reasonable. If we receive them at all it must be on the word of Him who declared that *all* these things would assuredly take place before that generation passed away. But, after all, is the demand upon our faith in this matter so very excessive? A large portion of these predictions we know to have been literally and punctually fulfilled; we recognise in that accomplishment a remarkable proof of the truth of the word of God and the superhuman prescience that foresaw and foretold the future. Could any thing have been less probable at the time when our Lord delivered his prophetic discourse than the total destruction of the temple, the razing of the city, and the ruin of the nation in the lifetime of the existing generation? What can be more minute and particular than the signs of the end enumerated by our Lord? What can be more precise and literal than the fulfilment of them?

"But the part which confessedly has been fulfilled, and which is vouched for by uninspired history, is inseparably bound up with another portion which is not so vouched for. Nothing but a violent disruption can detach the one part of this prophecy from the other. It is one from beginning to end—a complete whole. The finest instrument cannot draw a line separating one portion which relates to that generation from another portion which relates to a different and distant period. Every part of it rests on the same foundation, and the whole is so linked and concatenated that all must stand or fall together. We are justified, therefore, in holding that the exact accomplishment of so much of the prophecy as comes within the cognizance of the senses, and is capable of being vouched for by human testimony, is a presumption and guarantee in favour of the exact fulfilment of that portion which lies within the region of the invisible and spiritual, and which cannot, in the nature of things, be attested by human evidence. This is not credulity, but reasonable faith, such as men fearlessly exercise in all their worldly transactions.

"We conclude, therefore, that all the parts of our Lord's prediction refer to the same period and the same event; that the whole prophecy is one and indivisible, resting upon the same foundation of divine authority. Further, that all that was cognizable by the human senses is proved to have been fulfilled, and, therefore, we are not cnly warranted, but bound to assume the fulfilment of the remainder as not only credible, but certain." [1]

[1] The Parousia, pp. 547, 548.

CHAPTER XXV.

THE PAULINE ESCHATOLOGY.

IN exhibiting the chief points of the Pauline doctrine of the parousia and the resurrection and taking away of saints, we pass over numerous incidental allusions, scattered here and there throughout the several epistles, and take first the classic passage in 1 Thess. iv, 13–17. The following is a literal and accurate translation:

(13) But we would not have you to be ignorant, brethren, concerning those who are falling asleep; that ye sorrow not, even as the rest, who have no hope. (14) For if we believe that Jesus died and rose again, so also will God through Jesus bring with him those who fell asleep. (15) For this we say to you in a word of the Lord, that we, the living who remain unto the coming of the Lord, shall not precede those who fell asleep; (16) because the Lord himself shall descend from heaven with a shout, with voice of archangel and with trump of God, and the dead in Christ shall rise first; (17) then we, the living who remain, shall together with them be caught away in clouds to meet the Lord in the air; and so shall we ever be with the Lord.

It seems hardly possible to mistake the import of these words. "Most modern expositors," says Ellicott, "seem rightly to coincide *The Thessalon-* in the opinion that in the infant church of Thessalonica *ian anxiety.* there had prevailed, apparently from the very first, a feverish anxiety about the state of those who had departed, and about the time and circumstances of the Lord's coming. They seem especially to have feared that those of their brethren who had fallen on sleep before the expected advent of the Lord would not participate in its blessings and glories. Thus their apprehensions did not so much relate to the resurrection generally, as to the share which the departed were to have in the coming of the Lord." [1]

As little open to question are the four following propositions: *Four things in* (1) The Lord will come from heaven with signal ac- *the Pauline* companiments. (2) The dead in Christ shall rise first. *doctrine.* (3) The living saints shall be caught up to meet the Lord. (4) Those thus glorified shall ever be with the Lord. But while all agree that these four doctrines are clear and explicit beyond controversy, there has been wide difference of opinion as to

[1] Commentary on St. Paul's Epistles to the Thessalonians, in loco.

the time and order of these sublime events. According to one class of interpreters, all these events are to take place at the end of time, or at the close of the Messianic era. The "we" is generic, and does not therefore imply an expectation of the parousia and a resur rection within the lifetime of that generation. The pre-millennialists, on the other hand, maintain the doctrine of two resurrections, and hold that the dead in Christ, and no others, will be raised at the coming of the Lord, but the rest of the dead, according to Rev. xx, 5, will be raised at the end of the millennium. The most learned and pious interpreters, whom the whole Church delights to honour, are found divided in opinion and taking opposite sides in this great controversy.

The main question, which logically controls all others in the case, is whether the words, "we, the living, who remain unto We, who re-the coming of the Lord" (ver. 15, comp. ver. 17 and main alive. 1 Cor. xv, 51, 52) imply an expectation that Paul and his contemporaries might live to witness the parousia. That they do imply such an expectation is the judgment of many of the best interpreters, and, perhaps, it may be said that, were it not for certain dogmatic prepossessions, no one would ever have formed a contrary opinion. "From the construction of these words," says Lünemann, "it undoubtedly follows that Paul reckoned himself with those who would survive till the commencement of the advent, as indeed the same expectation is also expressed in 1 Cor. xv, 51."[1] "Beyond question," says Alford, "he himself expected to be alive, together with the majority of those to whom he was writing, at the Lord's coming. For we cannot for a moment accept the evasion of Theodoret (cf. also Chrysostom and the majority of ancient commentators, down to Bengel, and even some of the best of the moderns, warped by their subjectivities): 'he speaks not of his own person, but of the men who would be living at that time;' nor the ungrammatical rendering of Turretin and Pelt, 'we, if we live and remain;' nor the idea of Œcumenius, that *the living* are the *souls, those fallen asleep* the *bodies;* but must take the words in their only plain grammatical meaning, that *the living who remain* are a class distinguished from *those fallen asleep*, by being yet in the flesh when Christ comes, in which class, by prefixing *we*, he includes his readers and himself."[2]

On the other hand, one of the most guarded and able expressions of the opposite opinion is that of Ellicott: "The deduction from these words, that St. Paul himself expected to be alive, must fairly

---

[1] Commentary on Thessalonians (Meyer's Crit. Handbook), in loco.
[2] Greek Testament, in loco.

be pronounced more than doubtful. Without giving any undue latitude to ἡμεῖς, *we*, or to περιλειπόμενοι, *those remaining*, it seems just and correct to say that περιλειπόμενοι is simply and purely present, and that St. Paul is to be understood as classing himself with those who are *being left* on earth (comp. Acts ii, 47), without being conceived to imply that he had any precise or definite expectations as to his own case. At the time of writing these words he was one of the *living* and *remaining*, and as such he distinguishes himself and them from the *fallen asleep*, and naturally identifies himself with the class to which he then belonged. It does not seem improper to admit that, in their ignorance of the day of the Lord (Mark xiii, 32), the apostles might have imagined that he who was coming would come speedily, but it does seem over hasty to ascribe to inspired men *definite* expectations, since proved to be unfounded, when the context, calmly weighed and accurately interpreted, supplies no certain elements for such extreme deductions."[1]

Ellicott's conservative judgment.

These expressions of judgment may be taken as specimens of the best that can be said on either side of the question. It is worthy of note that writers of the one class exhibit a settled assurance of following the most obvious import of the apostle's language, whilst those of the opposite class manifestly feel that the language does not favour their view, and they accordingly either plead the ignorance of the apostle, or else give his words an unnatural meaning.

The two opinions compared.

Putting aside all special pleading and dogmatic bias, it seems hardly doubtful that the language of the apostle implies an expectation that many of his generation would remain alive until the coming of the Lord. No one can fairly claim that Paul's language implies that both himself and all those to whom he wrote would be living at that hour, for what he says about them that "are falling asleep" (ver. 13) implies the contrary. So also his words in 1 Cor. xv, 51, "we all shall not sleep," are virtually equivalent to "some of us will sleep." He intimates that he himself rather expected to die (1 Cor. xv, 31, 32), and, later on, this expectation became a positive conviction (Phil. iii, 7–11; 2 Tim. iv, 6–8). But these facts and considerations do not militate against the opinion that his language in the passage in question clearly implies the doctrine of the speedy coming of the Lord, and that many, if not most, of his contemporaries would live until that glorious event. Ellicott is quite correct in saying that these words do not necessarily imply that "Paul himself expected

The words imply an expectation of a speedy coming of the Lord.

[1] Commentary on 1 Thess. iv, 15.

to be alive," and Lünemann and Alford are altogether too positive in their language on this point. It is unnecessary and uncalled for to maintain that Paul here expresses any "definite expectations" *about himself, personally* (or of any other individual), as if he might not fall asleep before the parousia. "He was one of the *living* and *remaining*," as Ellicott says, "and naturally identifies himself with the class to which he then belonged," but when one argues that his language does not imply that any of that class then living would remain alive until the Lord came, he will probably have the unbiassed judgment of the best critics against him. This is virtually confessed by Ellicott himself, when he adds: "It does not seem improper to admit that in their ignorance of the day of the Lord (Mark xiii, 32) the apostles 'might have imagined that he who was coming would come speedily.'"

How, then, are we to understand the language of the apostle? Shall we put upon his words an unnatural construction, ␣The exegetical or say, as not a few eminent expositors affirm, that Paul ␣dilemma. was mistaken in his expectations? Here is a dilemma, and it has been commonly assumed that we are shut up to the one or the other of these two positions. Calvin and Cornelius à Lapide, while assuming that the apostle knew the day of the Lord was in the far future, hold that he represented it as imminent in order to promote watchfulness in believers. Few, however, will accept such a theory, for it virtually makes the apostle guilty of a pious fraud. Nor is it consistent with sound views of divine inspiration to believe that the inspired writers were mistaken in their expectations of an event so important in Christian doctrine as this. The plea so often made, that they recognize the uncertainty of the day and hour of the parousia, is futile, inasmuch as all they say on this point is perfectly consistent with a speedy coming of that day. Paul, in this immediate context (1 Thess. v, 1–10), speaks of the uncertainty of "the times and the seasons." He admonishes the Thessalonians that the day comes "as a thief in the night" (as if referring to the words of the Lord himself in Matt. xxiv, 42–44), and then adds: "But ye, brethren, are not in darkness that that day should overtake you as a thief." Were these words meant for the Thessalonians, or for brethren of a far distant age? Or can they mean: Brethren, ye are in no danger of having that day overtake you as a thief, for it will not come until untold centuries after ye have all fallen asleep?

If it be held that the apostles were mistaken in ex-␣Apostles' doc-pecting the parousia in their own day, it may be main-␣trine based on tained with equal and indeed greater show of reason ␣Jesus' most emphatic statements.␣that our Lord himself was responsible for their error.

No words of theirs are more specific or emphatic than the assuring declarations of Jesus that some of those who heard him speak should not taste of death till they beheld the Son of man coming in his kingdom (Matt. xvi, 28), and that generation should not pass away till all these things were fulfilled (Matt. xxiv, 34). We reject, therefore, the idea that the apostles were in error on a subject on which their Lord had been so explicit in his teachings. Nor can we accept the other alternative of the dilemma, above stated, and construe the language of Paul so as to make it harmonize with the supposition that he did not expect himself or any of his contemporaries to remain alive until the coming of the Lord.

Is there no other way to understand the words of Paul? Does not the doctrine of our Lord, as we have traced it in the Gospel Apocalypse, warrant us in believing that all these sublime events occurred at that momentous crisis of the ages when Judaism and her temple fell a hopeless ruin? Why should it be thought a thing incredible that God should then have raised many of them that slept in death? Why assume that the rapture of living saints must needs be visible to all mortal eyes? The parousia, according to the Scriptures, was to take place at the end of an age, and not to involve the cessation of the human race on earth. Our Lord most plainly declared that then some should be taken and some should be left (Matt. xxiv, 40, 41), and as we have already shown (see above, p. 448), there is no sufficient reason for assuming that such a rapture of living saints must have been visible to those who were left.[1] The ascension of our Lord into heaven was witnessed by no great multitude.

All occurred in Paul's generation.

---

[1] "It is strange," says a recent writer, "that so great incredulity should exist respecting the plain sense of our Lord's declarations on this subject. Fulfilled or unfulfilled right or wrong, there is no ambiguity or uncertainty in his language. It may be said that we have no evidence of such facts having occurred as are here described—the Lord descending with a shout, the sounding of the trumpet, the raising of the sleeping dead, the rapture of the living saints. True; but is it certain that these are facts cognizable by the senses? Is their place in the region of the material and the visible? As we have already said, we know and are sure that a very large portion of the events predicted by our Lord, and expected by his apostles, did actually come to pass at that very crisis called "the end of the age." There is no difference of opinion concerning the destruction of the temple, the overthrow of the city, the unparalleled slaughter of the people, the extinction of the nationality, the end of the legal dispensation. But the parousia is inseparably linked with the destruction of Jerusalem; and, in like manner, the resurrection of the dead, and the judgment of the "wicked generation," with the parousia. They are different parts of one great catastrophe; different scenes in one great drama. We accept the facts verified by the historian *on the word of man ;* is it for Christians to hesitate to accept the facts which are vouched *by the word of the Lord?* "—The Parousia, pp. 168, 169.

But it is said Paul wrote his Second Epistle to the Thessalonians to counteract the wrong impressions of the first, and to show that the day of the Lord would not come until many and great events had first taken place. All this is conceded, ^{2 Thess. ii, 1-10.} and yet nothing can be found in this second epistle which legitimately implies either that the parousia would not be in that generation, or that any statement of the former epistle was incorrect or misleading. The most that can be made of the apostle's language is that the parousia was not so immediately present, or at hand, that they should suddenly become excited, give up their usual occupations, and refuse to work. The great passage of this epistle bearing on the subject reads as follows (2 Thess. ii, 1-10):

(1) But we beseech you, brethren, concerning the coming of our Lord Jesus Christ, and our gathering together unto him, (2) that ye be not quickly shaken from your mind, nor yet be troubled either by spirit, or by word, or by epistle as from us, as that the day of the Lord is just now at hand (ἐνέστηκεν [1]). (3) Let no one deceive you in any way, for (it will not come) except there come the apostasy (ἡ ἀποστασία) first, and there be revealed the man of sin,[2] the son of perdition, (4) who opposes and exalts himself against all that is called God, or an object of worship, so that he sits down in the temple of God, exhibiting himself that he is God. (5) Do ye not remember that being yet with you I told you these things? (6) And now what hinders ye know, for the purpose of his being revealed in his own time. (7) For the mystery of lawlessness is already working only until he who now hinders be taken out of the way. (8) And then shall be revealed the lawless one, whom the Lord Jesus shall take off [3] by the breath of his mouth, and bring to naught by the manifestation of his coming: (9) of whom the coming is according to the working of Satan with all power and signs and wonders of falsehood, (10) and with all deceit of unrighteousness for them that perish, because they received not the love of the truth that they might be saved.

Two things, according to this Scripture, must take place before the coming of the Lord: first, the apostasy, some notable falling

---

[1] "The verb ἐνέστηκεν," says Ellicott, "is somewhat stronger than ἐφέστηκεν (2 Tim. iv, 6), and seems to mark not only the nearness, but the actual presence and commencement of the day of the Lord."—Commentary on Thessalonians, in loco. Ellicott translates it by "is now commencing," or "is already come;" Lünemann: "as if the day of the Lord is already present, or is even on the point of commencing;" Alford says: "These Thessalonians imagined it to be already come, and, accordingly, were deserting their pursuits in life, and falling into other irregularities, as if the day of grace were closed."—Greek Testament, in loco.

[2] Tischendorf, Tregelles, Gebhardt, Westcott and Hort, following codices ℵ and B, read ὁ ἄνθρωπος τῆς ἀνομίας, the man of lawlessness.

[3] Tischendorf, Tregelles, Alford, Gebhardt, Westcott and Hort read ἀνελεῖ, will take off suddenly, will seize away. Others read ἀναλώσει, will consume.

away from God and the true religion; and, secondly, the revela-
The apostasy an event of that generation. tion of a monster of wickedness who would be the embodiment of lawlessness and impiety. As for the apos-
tasy, why should any one imagine it to be other than that
going astray of many, of which the Lord spoke repeatedly in his
eschatological sermon (Matt. xxiv, 5, 11, 12, 24). He foretold how
the love of many would wax cold; false Christs and false prophets
would arise, and faith in the true Messiah would be painfully deficient at the coming of the Son of man (Luke xviii, 8). Such apostasy became notably apparent before that generation passed away
(1 Tim. iv, 1–3; 2 Tim. iii, 1–9; 1 John ii, 18, 19).

But who is "the man of sin, the son of perdition," to be revealed
The man of sin. before the parousia? The language by which he is described is evidently appropriated from Daniel where
that prophet delineates the character of Antiochus Epiphanes, symbolized in "the little horn" of chap. vii, 8, and viii, 9–12.[1] Antiochus was recognized in Jewish history as a typical incarnation of
cruelty, blasphemy, and lawlessness. He sought to "wear out the
saints of the Most High" (Dan. vii, 25). "He exalted and magnified himself above every god, and against the God of gods
would he utter wonderful things" (Dan. xi, 36).

Does history inform us of any such monster of lawlessness before
Nero a revela- tion of Anti- Christ. the close of the Jewish æon? Most assuredly. In
Nero, the son of the dissolute Agrippina, who succeeded
Claudius on the throne of the Cæsars, we find every
feature of this dark picture verified. The power and vigilance of
Claudius hindered the manifestation of this son of perdition [2] until
he was poisoned by his infamous wife, the mother of Nero, and
thus taken out of the way. Paul might well have told the Thessalonians of these things while he was yet with them, and common
prudence dictated that he should not write more explicitly upon the
subject. He had told them before, and now admonishes them
again, that the coming lawless one would be like another Antiochus
the sinful.[3] He would usurp the place of God, and exhibit himself

[1] Comp. Dan. vii, 24–26; viii, 23–25; xi, 21, 36–38, and our exposition on pp. 410,
411, above.

[2] Bengel observes (Gnomon, in loco): "The ancients thought that Claudius himself
was this check; for hence, as it appears, it happened that they considered Nero,
Claudius' successor, to be the man of sin." Grotius, Le Clerc, Wetstein, Whitby, and
others, hold that this prophecy of the man of sin was fulfilled before the destruction
of Jerusalem, which event they also regard as coincident with the parousia.

[3] Compare the expression, "the words of the sinful man" (ἀνδρὸς ἁμαρτωλοῦ), in
1 Macc. ii, 62, where the allusion is to Antiochus, of whom chap. i speaks so largely.
"The day of Christ does not come," says Bengel, "unless Daniel's prediction concern-

as an object of worship.[1] According to the working of Satan himself, of whom he seemed the veriest incarnation, he made use of all the "power and signs and wonders of falsehood" which imperial authority could command to accomplish his purposes of wickedness and cruelty, until he was finally cut off under circumstances of terrible judgment.[2]

Many have thought that the language of the apostle is too highly wrought to be applied to the taking off of Nero. With what propriety, it is asked, can he be said to have fallen by the breath of the Lord Jesus and by the appearance of his coming? The question springs from the same assumption of literalism as when it is asked, concerning Matt. xxiv, 29–31, When were the heavens shaken, and the Son of man seen on the clouds sending forth his angels with the sound of a trumpet? The apostle, like his Lord, simply appropriates the language and style of prophecy. According to Daniel, Antiochus, the beast represented by the little horn, "was slain, and his body was destroyed and given 'to the burning flame" (Dan. vii, 11). So, too, when the impious Herod allowed himself to be honoured as a god, "immediately an angel of the Lord smote him," and he became eaten of worms (Acts xii, 22, 23).[3] The execution of providential judgments may be often wrought by unseen messengers of God, and, in the case of Herod, where human eyes saw nothing but the ravages of foul disease, there was at the same time the potent ministrations of a destroying angel (comp. Exod. xii, 23; 2 Sam. xxiv, 16). The visible effects of divine judgment were terribly manifest both in the taking off of Nero and in the unparalleled miseries of the destruction of Jerusalem. Verily the righteous blood of unnumbered martyrs was visited upon that generation (Matt. xxiii, 35, 36), and where the inquiring and observant historian made record of appalling tribulation and woes, the inspired apostle beheld a "revelation of the Lord Jesus from heaven

The language not unsuitable to the death of Nero.

ing Antiochus be so fulfilled (in the man of sin) that it shall even better suit the man of sin who corresponds to Antiochus, and is worse than he."—Gnomon on 2 Thess. ii, 4.

[1] It is well known that the persecuting emperors sought to compel Christians to worship their images. The following words of Howson are worthy of note: "The image of the emperor was at that time the object of religious reverence; the emperor was a deity on earth (Dis æqua potestas, Juv. iv, 71); and the worship paid to him was a real worship (see Merivale's Life of Augustus, p. 159). It is a striking thought that in those times (setting aside effete forms of religion) the only two genuine worships in the civilized world were the worship of a Tiberius or a Claudius, on the one hand, and the worship of Christ on the other."—Conybeare and Howson's Life and Epistles of St. Paul, vol. i, p. 56. New York, 1855.

[2] On the miserable end of Nero's life, see Merivale, History of the Romans under the Empire, chap. lv.

[3] Compare the description of the awful death of Antiochus in 2 Macc. ix.

with the angels of his power in flaming fire, rendering vengeance to them that know not God and to them that obey not the Gospel" (2 Thess. i, 7, 8).

The momentous events, therefore, of which Paul wrote in both of his epistles to the Thessalonians, and the language in which he portrayed them, are in harmony with what occurred in that generation; and the exposition, which we have briefly outlined, accords with the most natural and obvious import of the prophecy. "But the question may be asked, Why should the revelation of Nero in his true character be a matter of such concern to the apostle and the Christians of Thessalonica? The answer is not far to seek. It was the ferocity of this lawless monster that first let loose all the power of Rome to crush and destroy the Christian name. It was by him that torrents of innocent blood were to be shed, and the most exquisite tortures inflicted upon unoffending Christians. It was before his sanguinary tribunal that St. Paul was yet to stand and plead for his life, and from his lips that the sentence was to come that doomed him to a violent death. It was under Nero, and by his orders, that the final Jewish war was commenced, and that darkest chapter in the annals of Israel was opened which terminated in the siege and capture of Jerusalem, the destruction of the temple, and the extinction of the national polity. This was the consummation predicted by our Lord as the 'end of the age,' and 'the coming of his kingdom.' The revelation of the man of sin, therefore, as antecedent to the parousia, was a matter that deeply concerned every Christian disciple." [1]

Nero's relations to Judaism and Christianity.

Additional features of the Pauline eschatology are seen in 1 Cor. xv, 20–28:

(20) But now has Christ been raised from the dead, the firstfruits of them who have fallen asleep. (21) For since through a man death (came), also through a man the resurrection of the dead. (22) For as in Adam all die, so also in Christ shall all be made alive. (23) But each in his own order (τάγματι, company, division, as of an army): Christ the firstfruits, then they who are the Christ's at his coming; (24) afterward the end, when he gives over the kingdom to the God and Father, when he shall have abolished all rule and all authority and power; (25) for he must reign until he has put all the enemies under his feet. (26) As the last enemy, death shall be abolished; (27) for (as it was written in Psa. viii, 6) all things he put under his feet. But when he says that all things are put under, it is evident that there is an exception of him who put all things under him. (28) But when he shall have put all things under him, then also shall the Son himself become subject to him (the Father) who put all things under him (the Son) that God may be all things in all.

[1] The Parousia, p. 187.

What especially demands our attention here is the doctrine of successive resurrections, of which the resurrection of Christ himself—a fact already past when the apostle wrote—is the first in rank and order, and the firstfruits and pledge of the rest.[1] All the dead shall be raised, according to Paul, but they will come forth by successive companies; Christ first of all, for "he is the beginning, the firstborn from the dead, that he might be in all things himself pre-eminent" (Col. i, 18). Then, at the parousia, they who are Christ's shall be made alive. How comprehensive this division (τάγμα) may be is quite uncertain. "Those of the Christ" (οἱ τοῦ Χριστοῦ, *the* [confessors] *of the Christ*) need not in this connexion mean more than those who are in some special sense related to the kingdom and glory of Christ. We naturally think of "those who are beheaded for the testimony of Jesus, and for the word of God," who "have part in the first resurrection," described in Rev. xx, 4–6. There appears no sufficient warrant for making this company include all the righteous dead who fall asleep before the parousia. The language employed in both these passages denotes at most only a select portion of the dead, and does not designate the character of all the rest of the dead who are not made alive at that time. "Those of the Christ" are not necessarily *all those* who are, or have been, in any way brought into saving relations with Christ. "Afterward (εἶτα, not τότε) the end." What end? The words which follow show that the end of the Messianic reign is meant. It is the end (τέλος) which will come when Christ delivers over the kingdom to the Father, having put down all his enemies, the last of whom to be abolished is death. Manifestly, then, it is the close of the Messianic æon, and after the millennium of Rev. xx, 4, for how could they reign with Christ after he had given over the kingdom to the God and Father?

According to Paul, therefore, a resurrection of "those of the Christ" takes place at the parousia. This accords with 1 Thess. iv, 16, 17; comp. 1 Cor. xv, 52. But at the end of the Messianic reign all the rest of the dead will be made alive, for, ultimately, the resurrection will be co-extensive with the race of Adam; "for as in Adam all die, so also in Christ shall all be made alive." There is nothing, however, in this part of the apostle's writings to indicate how long an interval may separate the several acts or stages

---

[1] "Paul regards the resurrection of all," says Meyer, "including Christ himself, as one great connected process, only taking place in several acts, so that thus by far the greater part indeed belongs to the future, but, in order not simply to the completeness of the whole, but at the same time for the sure guarantee of what was to come, the ἀπαρχή (firstfruits) also may not be left unmentioned."

of the resurrection. It may be longer or shorter as the Scriptures may elsewhere intimate and the intervening events may require. The language of the apostle in Phil. iii, 10, 11 implies the doctrine of a partial and special resurrection. He speaks of his ambition and longing to know Christ, "and the power of his resurrection, and fellowship of his sufferings, becoming conformed to his death, if by any means I may attain unto the resurrection from the dead" (εἰς τὴν ἐξανάστασιν τὴν ἐκ νεκρῶν). Why should Paul express such an anxiety to attain what was inevitable? If all must needs rise at some far future period, at the same moment of time, this language is manifestly inappropriate; but if a resurrection of martyrs and distinguished confessors of Christ was to take place at the parousia, within that generation, the words have a pertinency and force which all must feel.[1]

Phil. iii, 10, 11.

The same thought is suggested in the words of Jesus, Luke xx, 35: "Those who are reckoned worthy to attain (τυχεῖν, comp. Heb. xi, 35) that age, and the resurrection from the dead, neither marry nor are given in marriage." These, it is said in verse 36, "being sons of the resurrection, are sons of God." Meyer here remarks: "The context shows that Jesus has in view only those who are to be raised, apart from those who are still living here, at the parousia."[2] Godet in like manner says: "The resurrection *from the dead* is very evidently, in this place, not the resurrection of the dead in general. What is referred to is a special privilege granted only to the faithful who shall be accounted worthy" (comp. xiv, 14, and Phil. iii, 11).[3]

Luke xx, 35.

Notice also in this connexion the language of John v, 24–29:

(24) Verily, verily, I say unto you, he who hears my word, and believes him who sent me, has life eternal, and into judgment comes not, but has passed from death unto life. (25) Verily, verily, I say unto you, the hour is coming, and now is, when the dead shall hear the voice of the Son of God, and they who hear shall live. (26) For as the Father has life in himself, so also he gave to the Son to have life in himself; (27) and he gave

---

[1] "To grant a particular resurrection," says Mede, "before the general, is against no article of faith, for the Gospel tells us that at our Saviour's resurrection the graves were opened, and many bodies of the saints which slept arose and went into the holy city, and appeared unto many (Matt. xxvii, 52, 53). Neither was the number of them a small number, if we may credit the fathers or the most ancient records of Christian tradition. . . . Cyril of Jerusalem, Chrysostom, and others suppose this resurrection to have been common to all the saints that died before our Saviour. Howsoever it be, it holds no unfit proportion with this supposed of the martyrs. And how it doth more impeach any article of our faith to think that may be true of martyrs which we believe of patriarchs, I yet see not.—Works, p. 604. London, 1672.

[2] Critical Commentary, in loco.   [3] Commentary on the Gospel of Luke, in loco.

him authority to execute judgment, because he is Son of man. (28) Marvel not at this; for the hour is coming in which all who are in the tombs shall hear his voice (29) and come forth, those who did good unto a resurrection of life, those who wrought evil unto a resurrection of judgment.

It is common to understand verses 24–27 of a spiritual resurrection. This view, however, involves a needless tautology, John v, 24-29. and fails to exhibit the noticeable progress of thought in the passage. A spiritual resurrection is set forth in verse 24, and is explicitly defined as a passing from death unto life. But verse 25, adds with emphasis another and distinct idea. It speaks of an "hour," both present and yet coming, when the dead (οἱ νεκροί) shall hear the voice of the Son of God, and they who hear (impliedly a select number) shall live. This hearing the voice (verse 25, comp. verse 28) of the Son of God is not the same as hearing his word (verse 24). Therefore, with Olshausen and others, we understand the spiritual resurrection, which is so clearly set forth in verse 24, traced onward in verses 25–27 to a higher glorification in the making alive of the mortal bodies of saints through the. indwelling Spirit (Rom. viii, 11), and the power of God (Matt. xxii, 29). The resurrection of the righteous, at whatever hour it takes place, rests upon the 'fact that they have heard the word of Christ, believed in him that sent him, and thereby laid hold on eternal life. Thus only may any man come to "know the power of his resurrection" (Phil. iii, 10). "The hour is coming, and now is," should be explained by the analogy of 1 John ii, 18, "It is the last hour." It is a Johannean form of expression, and denotes the closing period of the pre-Messianic æon. The miracles of resurrection, like that of Jairus' daughter, the son of the widow of Nain, and Lazarus, exhibited Jesus at that "hour" as "the resurrection and the life" (John xi, 25). The many saints who arose with him (Matt. xxvii, 52, 53) furnish a further illustration of his word, and the power of his resurrection, and his authority to "make alive whom he will." The resurrection of the confessors of the Christ at his coming (1 Cor. xv, 23; 1 Thess. iv, 16) would then mark the ultimate consummation of that "hour." Verses 28 and 29 proceed to designate, as all admit, the resurrection of the rest of the dead, which would take place at a coming hour, which was not then present or near at hand.

Paul's doctrine of the parousia, and of distinct and successive resurrections, may therefore be seen to rest upon the authority of the teachings of Jesus, and is in essential harmony with the eschatology of the gospels.

CHAPTER XXVI

THE APOCALYPSE OF JOHN.

No portion of the Holy Scriptures has been the subject of so much controversy and of so many varying interpretations as the Apoca-
Systems of in- lypse of John. The principal systems of exposition
terpretation. may, however, be reduced to three, which are commonly known as the Preterist, the Continuous-Historical, and the Futurist. The Preterists hold that the larger part of the prophecy of this book was fulfilled in the overthrow of Jerusalem and pagan Rome. The Continuous-Historical school of interpreters find most of those prophecies fulfilled in the history of the Roman Empire and of modern Europe. The Futurists maintain that the book relates mainly to events which are yet to come, and which must be literally fulfilled at the end of the world. Any attempt to discuss these systems in detail, and examine their numerous divergent methods, as carried out by individual expositors, would require a very large volume. Our plan is simply to seek the historical position of the writer, and trace the scope and plan of his book in the light of the hermeneutical principles already set forth. Especially are we to regard the analogy of the apocalyptic scriptures and the general principles of biblical symbolism.

The writer addresses the book of his prophecy to the churches
Historical of seven well-known cities of western Asia, and ex-
standpoint. pressly declares in the opening verses that his revela-
tion is of "things which must shortly come to pass." At the close (chap. xxii, 12, 20) the Alpha and the Omega, who himself testifies all these things, and manifestly aims to make the thought of their imminence emphatic, says: "Behold, I come quickly;" "Yea, I come quickly." The prophet, moreover, is admonished not to seal "the words of the prophecy of this book, for the time is near at hand" (xxii, 10). Surely, if words have any meaning, and thoughts are capable of emphatic statement, the events contemplated were impending in the near future at the time this book was written.[1] The

---

[1] The plea of Alford and others that the ἐν τάχει, *shortly*, of this book is "a measure by which, not our judgment of its contents, but our estimate of worldly events and their duration, should be corrected," and that the word "confessedly contains, among other periods, a period of a thousand years" (Greek Testament, Proleg. to Rev., chap. viii, §§ 4, 10), is a singular proposition. He might as well have said that

import of all these expressions is in noticeable harmony with our Lord's repeated declaration: "This generation shall not pass away until all these things be accomplished." But when John wrote the things contemplated were much nearer at hand than when Jesus addressed his disciples on the Mount of Olives.[1]

After the manner of other apocalypses this book is divisible into two principal parts, which may be appropriately desig- Plan of the nated, (1) *The Revelation of Christ, the Lamb* (chaps. Apocalypse. i-xi), and (2) *The Revelation of the Bride, the Wife of the Lamb* (chaps. xii-xxii). These two parts, after the manner of Daniel's repeated visions, traverse the same field of view, and each terminates in the fall of a great city, and the establishment of the kingdom of God. But each of these parts is divisible again into smaller sections, the first into three, the second into seven. The whole will be apparent in the following outline:

I. Revelation of the Lamb.

1. In the Epistles to the Seven Churches, i-iii.
2. By the Opening of the Seven Seals, iv-vii.
3. By the Sounding of the Seven Trumpets, viii-xi.

II. Revelation of the Bride.

1. Vision of the Woman and the Dragon, xii.
2. Vision of the Two Beasts, xiii.
3. Vision of the Mount Zion, xiv.
4. Vision of the Seven Last Plagues, xv, xvi.
5. Vision of the Mystic Babylon, xvii, xviii.
6. Vision of Parousia, Millennium, and Judgment, xix, xx
7. Vision of the New Jerusalem, xxi, xxii.

It should be observed that John's Apocalypse is, in its artificial arrangement and finish, the most perfect of all the prophecies. Its

it confessedly contains the " for ever and ever " of chap. xxii, 5. Manifestly the thou sand years of chap. xx, 2, like the ages of ages in chaps. xi, 15 and xxii, 5, is a statement that runs far beyond the great catastrophes of the book, and is too exceptional in its nature to be included among the things which were to come to pass quickly.

[1] On the early date of the Apocalypse see Glasgow, The Apocalypse Translated and Expounded, pp. 9-54 (Edinb., 1872); Farrar, The Early Days of Christianity, chap. xxvii (Lond., 1882); and Schaff's new edition of his History of the Christian Church, pp. 834-836. We have already discussed at some length the time of this prophecy (see pp. 237-242), and have shown good reasons for believing that it was written before the destruction of Jerusalem and the temple. The preponderance of the best modern criticism is in favour of this view. If now, in harmony with such date, we find the structure and import of the book, as studied in the light of biblical apocalyptics, a self-consistent whole, and meeting signal fulfilment in the ruin of Judaism and the rise of Christianity, the interpretation itself becomes a controlling argument in favour of the early date.

outline and the correlation of its several parts evince that its ima-
Artificial form gery was most carefully chosen, and yet there is scarcely
of the Apoca- a figure or symbol that is not appropriated from the
lypse. Old Testament. The books of Daniel, Ezekiel, and
Zechariah are especially made use of. The number seven is notably prominent—as seven spirits, seven churches, seven seals, seven
trumpets, seven heads, seven eyes, seven horns, seven plagues. The
numbers three, four, ten, and twelve are also used in a significant
way,[1] and where symbolical numbers are so frequently used we
should at least hesitate about insisting on the literal import of any
particular number. Constant reference, therefore, should be had, in
the interpretation of this book, to the analogous prophecies of the
Old Testament.

Immediately after the opening statements, and the salutation and
The great Theme doxology of verses 4–6, the great theme of the book is
of the book. announced in this truly Hebraic and emotional style:
"Behold he is coming with the clouds, and every eye shall see him,[2]
and they who pierced him, and all the tribes of the land,[3] shall wail
over him" (chap. i, 7). Let it be particularly noted that these words
are appropriated substantially from our Lord's discourse (Matt.
xxiv, 30): "Then shall appear the sign of the Son of man in heav-
en, and then shall all the tribes of the land wail, and they shall see
the Son of man coming on the clouds of heaven with power and
much glory." The words "they who pierced him" are from Zech.
xii, 10, and should here be understood not so much of the soldiers

---

[1] See Stuart on the "Numerosity of the Apocalypse" in his Commentary, vol. i, pp.
130–149. Comp. Trench, Com. on the Epistles to the Seven Churches of Asia, pp.
83–91.

[2] To press the literal import of the words "every eye shall see him," and insist that
at the parousia Christ must literally appear on a cloud, and be visible to every person
on the habitable globe, involves manifest absurdities. The statement of the angels in
Acts i, 11, is that the Lord would come again in like manner as the disciples beheld him
going into heaven; but that ascension, like the appearance of the angels, was visible
to only a chosen few. That he personally came again in that generation, and was seen
by multitudes, and by those who were guilty of his blood, we accept upon the testimony
of the Scriptures. But no person or phenomenon in the clouds of heaven could be
visible, at one and the same time, to all the inhabitants of the earth; and no one pretends that the Son of man is to pass through the clouds and make the circuit of the
globe so as to appear literally to every eye. The words of Rev. i, 7, are, therefore, to
be understood in general harmony with both the temporal and geographical limitations
of the prophecy.

[3] The common English Version, "all kindreds of the earth," appears to have misled
not only many common readers, but even learned commentators. No Hellenist of our
Lord's day would have understood πᾶσαι αἱ φυλαὶ τῆς γῆς as equivalent to all nations
of the habitable globe. The phrase is traceable to Zech. xii, 12, where all the families of the land of Judah are represented as mourning.

who nailed him to the cross, and pierced his side, as of the Jews, upon whom Peter charged the crime (Acts ii, 23, 36; v, 30), and who had cried, "His blood be upon us and upon our children" (Matt. xxvii, 25). To these Jesus himself had said: "Hereafter ye shall see the Son of man sitting at the right hand of power, and coming on the clouds of heaven" (Matt. xxvi, 64).

Having announced his great theme, the writer proceeds to record his vision of the Alpha and the Omega, the first and Words to the Seven Churches. the last—an expression taken from Isa. xli, 4; xliv, 6; xlviii, 12. The description of the Son of man is mainly in the language by which Daniel describes the Ancient of days (Dan. vii, 9) and the Son of man (x, 5, 6), but it also appropriates expressions from other prophets (Isa. xi, 4; xlix, 2; Ezek. i, 26, 28; xliii, 2). The seven golden candlesticks remind us of Zechariah's one golden candlestick with its seven lamps (Zech. iv, 2). The meaning of the symbols is given by the Lord himself, and the whole forms an impressive introduction to the seven epistles. These epistles, though written in a most regular and artificial form, are full of individual allusions, and show that there was much persecution of the faithful, and that a momentous crisis was at hand. The various characteristics of the seven Churches may be typical of varying phases of church life and character for subsequent ages, but they are nevertheless distinct portraitures of then existing facts. The mention of Nicolaitans (ii, 6), the faithful martyr Antipas (ii, 13), and the mischievous prophetess Jezebel (ii, 20), is evidence that the epistles deal with actual persons and events, though the names employed are probably symbolical. The warnings, counsels, and encouragements given to these Churches correspond in substance with those our Lord gave to his disciples in Matt. xxiv. He warned them against false prophets, told them they should have tribulation, and some would be put to death, and the love of many would wax cold, but that he who endured to the end should be saved. It is not to be supposed that in this remoteness of time we can feel the force of the personal allusions of these epistles as well as those to whom they were first addressed.

The prophecy of the seven seals is opened by a glorious vision of the throne of God (chap. iv), and its symbols are The Seven Seals. taken from the corresponding visions of Isa. vi, 1–4, and Ezek. i, 4–28. Then appears in the right hand of Him who sat on the throne a book close sealed with seven seals (v, i). The Lion of Judah, the Root of David, is the only one who can open that book, and he is revealed as "a Lamb standing as though it had been slain, having seven horns and seven eyes." His position was "in

the midst of the throne" (v, 6). The eyes and horns, symbols of
the perfection of wisdom and power, the appearance of a slain
lamb, expressive of the whole mystery of redemption, and the position in the throne,[1] as suggestive of heavenly authority—all serve
to extol the Christ as the great Revealer of divine mysteries. The
first four seals correspond virtually with the symbols of Zech. vi,
2, 3, and denote dispensations of conquest, bloodshed, famine, and
aggravated slaughter or mortality.[2] These rapidly successive and
commingling judgments correspond strikingly with our Lord's prediction of wars and rumours of wars, falling by the edge of the
sword, famines, pestilences, terrors, days of vengeance, and unheard
of horrors. The pages of Josephus, descriptive of the unparalleled
woes which culminated in the utter ruin of Jerusalem, furnish an
ample commentary on these symbols and on the words of our Lord.
Why should we ignore the statements of the Jewish historian, and
search in the pages of Gibbon, or in the annals of modern Europe,
to find the fulfilment of prophecies which were so signally fulfilled
before the end of the Jewish age?

The fifth seal is a martyr-scene—the blood of souls crying from
The Martyr- under the altar where they had been slain for the Word
Scene.   of God (vi, 9, 10). This corresponds with the Lord's
announcement that his followers should be put to death (Matt.
xxiv, 9; Luke xxi, 16). The white robes and the comfort given to
the martyrs answer to Jesus' pledge that in their patience they
should win their souls (Luke xxi, 19), and that "whosoever shall lose
his life for my sake and the Gospel's shall save it" (Mark viii, 35).
But these souls wait only for "a little time" (ver. 11), even as Jesus
declared that all the martyr-blood shed from the time of Abel
should be visited in vengeance upon that generation, even upon Jerusalem the murderess of prophets (Matt. xxiii, 34–38). And then,
to show how quickly the retribution comes, like the "immediately
The Sixth Seal. after the tribulation" of Matt. xxiv, 29, the sixth seal
               is opened, and exhibits the terrors of the end (verses
12–17). We need not linger to show how the symbols of this seal
correspond with the language of Jesus and other prophets when
describing the great and terrible day of the Lord. But we should
note that before this judgment falls the elect of God are sealed,

[1] In chap. xxii, 1, it is called "the throne of God *and of the Lamb*." The throne
belonged to the Lamb as well as to God. Comp. chap. iii, 21.

[2] To understand the rider on the white horse as a symbol of Christ, as many do,
and the others as symbols of war, famine, etc., involves the interpretation in manifest
confusion of imagery. If the first rider denote a person, so should the others; but,
according to the analogy of corresponding prophecies, we have here a fourfold symbol
of impending judgments. Comp. above, pp. 429, 430.

and there appear two companies, the elect of the twelve tribes (the Jewish-Christian Church—the circumcision), and an innumerable company out of all nations and tongues (the Gentile Church—the uncircumcision) who had washed their robes and made them white in the blood of the Lamb (chap. vii). This is the apocalyptic counterpart of Jesus' words: "He shall send forth his angels with a great trumpet-sound, and they shall gather his elect from the four winds, from one end of heaven to the other" (Matt. xxiv, 31).

The opening of the sixth seal brought us to the very verge of doom, and we might naturally suppose that the seventh The seven would usher in the ultimate consummation. But it Trumpets. issues in the vision of the seven trumpets, which traverses a part of the same field again, and awfully portrays the signs, wonders, and horrors indicated by the symbols of the sixth seal. These trumpet woes we understand to be a highly wrought picture of the fearful sights and great signs from heaven of which Jesus spoke, the abomination of desolation, Jerusalem compassed with armies, and "signs in the sun and moon and stars; and upon the land distress of nations in perplexity for the roaring of the sea and the billows; men fainting for fear and for expectation of the things coming on the world" (Luke xxi, 25, 26).[1] Accordingly, the first four trumpet-woes fall, respectively, on the land, the sea, the rivers and fountains of water, and the lights of heaven, and their imagery is appropriated from the account of the plagues of Egypt, and from other parts of the Old Testament. These plagues do not ruin everything, but, like Ezekiel's symbols (Ezek. v, 2), each destroys a third.

The last three trumpets are signals of direr woes (viii, 13). The tormenting locusts from the abyss, introduced by the The plague fifth trumpet, assume the form of a moving army, after from the abyss. the manner of Joel's description (Joel ii, 1–11), and are permitted to torment those men who have not the seal of God upon them. They may appropriately denote the unclean spirits of demons, which were permitted to come forth in those days of vengeance and possess and torment the men who had given themselves over to

---

[1] "The descriptions are of a kind," says Bleek, "that cannot be meant literally, since they cannot be shaped into intuitive ideas. But it is also inadmissible to refer them to single political events and catastrophes happening upon the earth, either at the time of the writing, so that the seer must have had them already before his eyes, or occurring later, so that these visions were fulfilled in them. Rather should we view the contents of these visions as a general poetical representation of the great revolutions of nature connected with the appearing of the Lord. or preceding it, in which Old Testament images, taken particularly from the narrative of the Egyptian plagues, lie at the foundation, and particulars should not be especially urged"—Lectures on the Apocalypse, p. 228. Lond., 1874.

all wickedness. Describing the excessive impiety of the Jewish leaders, Josephus remarks: "No age ever bred a generation more fruitful in wickedness than this was from the beginning of the world." "I suppose that had the Romans made any longer delay in coming against these villains the city would either have been swallowed up by the ground opening upon them, or been over-whelmed by water, or else been destroyed by such thunder as the country of Sodom perished by; for it had brought forth a genera- tion of men much more atheistical than were those that suffered such punishments; for by their madness it was that all the people came to be destroyed."[1] Was not some fact like this before the mind of our Lord when he spoke of the unclean spirit that took seven others more wicked than himself, and returned and entered the house from which he had been cast out? "So shall it be," said he, "with this wicked generation" (Matt. xii, 43-45).[2]

The sixth trumpet is the signal for unloosing the armies restrained The armies of "at the great river Euphrates" (ix, 14). All proper Euphrates. names of this book appear to be symbolical. So we understand Sodom and Egypt (xi, 8), Michael (xii, 7), Zion (xiv, 1), Har-Magedon (xvi,16), Babylon (xvii, 5), and New Jerusalem (xxi, 2). It would be contrary to all these analogies to understand the name Euphrates (in ix,. 14, and xvi, 12) in a literal sense. In chap. xvii, 1 the mystic Babylon is represented as sitting upon many waters, and these waters are explained in verse 15 as symbolizing peoples and multitudes and nations and tongues.[3] What more natural explana- tion of this symbol, then, than to understand it of the multitudinous armies, which in their appointed time came with their prowess and terror, compassed the Jewish capital about, and pressed the siege with unrelenting fury to the bitter end? The Roman army was composed of soldiers from many nations, and fitly corresponds with the abomination of desolation spoken of in our Lord's discourse (Matt. xxiv, 15). "When ye see Jerusalem compassed with armies, then know that her desolation is at hand" (Luke xxi, 20).

At this momentous point in the revelation, and when we might

[1] Whiston's Josephus; Wars, book v, chapters x, 5, and xiii, 6.

[2] The star fallen from heaven, to whom is given the key of the pit of the abyss, can scarcely denote any other than the Satan whom Jesus saw falling like lightning from heaven (Luke x, 18), and the names Abaddon and Apollyon are but symbolic names of Satan, the prince or chief of the demons. It should be noticed also that in chap. xviii, 2 the fallen Babylon is described as having "become a habitation of de- mons, and a hold of every unclean spirit, and a hold of every unclean and hateful bird."

[3] That Euphrates is here to be taken as a symbolical name is ably shown by Fair- bairn, Prophecy, etc., pp. 410, 411, and Appendix M.

naturally expect the seventh trumpet to sound, there is a pause, and lo, " another strong angel, coming down from the heav- The mighty en, arrayed with *a cloud, and the rainbow upon his Angel arrayed with cloud and head, and his face as the sun, and his feet as pillars of rainbow. fire " (x, 1). The attributes of this angel, and their correspondence with the sublime description of the Son of man in chap. i, 13–16, point him out as no other than the Lord himself,[1] and his lion-like cry, and the accompanying voices of the seven thunders, remind us of Paul's prophecy that "the Lord himself shall descend from heaven with a shout, with voice of archangel, and with trump of God " (1 Thess. iv, 16). This is no other than "the Son of man coming in the clouds of heaven with power and great glory," which Jesus himself foretold as destined to come to pass in that generation (Matt. xxiv, 30–34). His glorious appearance seems like a prelude to the sound of the last trumpet, but the delay is not to defer the catastrophe, but to furnish an opportunity to say that with the voice of the seventh angel the mystery of God is to be finished (verses 6 and 7). The prophet also takes a book from the angel's hand and eats it (8–11) after the manner of Ezekiel (ii, 9–iii, 3), and is told that he shall " prophesy again over many peoples and nations and tongues and kings." For John survived that terrible catastrophe, and lived long after to make known the testimony of God. It was more than a suggestion that that disciple should tarry till the coming of the Lord (comp. John xxi, 21–24). The measurement of the temple, altar, and worshippers (xi, 1), and the treading under foot of the holy city forty-two months (three years and a half=a time, times, and a half a time), signify that the whole will be given over to desolation. This, again, corresponds with our Lord's words (Luke xxi, 24): "Jerusalem shall be trodden down of the Gentiles until the times of the Gentiles be fulfilled." Judging from the analogy of the language of Daniel, the "times of the

---

[1] It is in accord with the habit of repetition common to apocalyptic prophecies that the Son of man should appear in this book under various forms. First the glorious Christophany of chap. i, then as the Lamb with seven horns and seven eyes (v, 6), then as the mighty, rainbow-encircled Angel of this passage (x, 1), then as Michael (xii, 7), and again as a Lamb (xiv, 1), and as the Son of man on a cloud (xiv, 14), then as the rider on the white horse (xix, 11), and finally as the Judge sitting on a great white throne (xx, 11). Thus the Apocalypse of Jesus Christ fittingly reveals him in manifold aspects of his character and glory. So, also, on the other hand, the arch-enemy, or antichrist, appears under various forms of manifestation, as Abaddon, or Apollyon, the angel of the abyss (ix, 11), the great red dragon (xii, 3), the beast out of the sea and out of the land (xiii, 1, 11), the scarlet-coloured beast on which the harlot is sitting (xvii, 3), the beast out of the abyss (xvii, 8; comp. xi, 7), and even the mystic Babylon considered as a habitation of devils (xviii, 2).

Gentiles" ($\kappa\alpha\iota\rho o\iota$; comp. Luke xxi, 24, with the Septuagint and Theodotion of Dan. vii, 25; xi, 7) are the "time, times, and half a time" during which the destructive siege was to continue, and the city be trodden without and within. During these same times the two witnesses prophesy within the doomed city. Who these witnesses were we cannot now tell, for history has left no more record of them than of Antipas, the faithful witness of Pergamum (chap. ii, 13).[1]

With this revelation, which stands as an episode between the sixth and seventh trumpets, we are the more fully prepared to feel The last trum- the tremendous significance of the last trumpet. In that pet. lingering hour of the sixth trumpet—an awful pause before the final blast—"There was a great earthquake, and the tenth part of the city fell." It would not be difficult to cite from the pages of Josephus an almost literal fulfilment of these words.[2] The imagery has allusion to the trumpet signaled fall of Jericho.

[1] The allusion to Zech. iv, as shown above (p. 352), may suggest that these were two notable persons who alone remained in the city after the other Christians had fled. These thus became the sole representatives there of the Christian Church. The author of the Parousia gives several plausible reasons for supposing that they were none other than James and Peter—the apostles of the circumcision, who abode in Jerusalem to the last. See the Parousia, pp. 430-444.

[2] See Josephus, Wars, book iv, chap. iv, 5, and chap. v, 1. If any one would see the fanciful and arbitrary hermeneutical methods into which some of the continuous-historical interpreters of the Revelation unconsciously involve themselves, let him note the following from Faber: "The great city (mystic Babylon) is said to comprehend ten different parts, or streets, which answer to the ten horns of the first apocalyptic wild beast, and which denote the ten kingdoms of the divided Roman Empire; for, since one tenth part of the great city is thrown down by an earthquake at the close of the second woe, such language necessarily implies a division into ten parts. The same great city is viewed also under two different aspects, according to its wider and its narrower extent. As a literal city may, at one time, comprehend within its walls a much larger tract of land than it does at another, whence a district which was formerly within it may be subsequently without it; so the allegorical great city is variously spoken of, according as in point of geography it is variously contemplated. On this principle the platform of the ten streets, though it constituted the whole city when viewed in reference to the ecclesiastical authority exercised from its palace or centre, constituted but a part of it when viewed in reference to the wide dominions of the Roman Cæsars; and on the same principle, any province which lies beyond the geographical limits of the ten streets may be truly described as being either within or without the city. In this same manner, accordingly, we find the province of Judea spoken of. Our Lord is said to have been crucified *within* the great city because he was crucified in the province of Judea, at that time within the limits of the Roman Empire [so was Britain! Surely a remarkable way of telling *where* the Lord was crucified]; yet is that identical province described as being without the great city (Rev. xi, 8; xiv, 20), because it lies without the platform of the ten streets which constitute the proper Western Empire, or Latin Patriarchate."— The Sacred Calendar of Prophecy (3 vols., Lond., 1828), vol. i, pp. 31, 32. Comp. other specimens in Farrar, The Early Days of Christianity, pp. 434, 435.

Next and "quickly" (xi, 14) the last trumpet sounds, and great voices in the heaven say "The kingdom of the world is become our Lord's and his Christ's, and he shall reign unto the ages of the ages" (ver. 15). The old æon has passed, the new one has begun, and the heavenly host shout a pæan of triumph. The blood of the souls that cried from under the altar (vi, 10) is now avenged, and those prophets and saints receive their reward (xi, 18). The old temple disappears, and the temple of God which is in heaven opens, and reveals the long-lost ark of the covenant (ver. 19), henceforth accessible to all who are washed in the blood of the Lamb.

The second part of the Apocalypse (chaps. xii–xxii) is not a chronological sequel to the first, but travels over the same ground again. The two parts have a relation to each other somewhat like the dream of the great image and the vision of the four beasts in the Book of Daniel. They cover the same field of vision, but view things under different aspects. The first part exhibits the terrible vengeance of the Lamb upon his enemies, as if contemplating everything from the idea of the king "who sent forth his armies and destroyed those murderers, and burned their city" (Matt. xxii, 7). The second part presents a vivid outline of the struggling Church passing her first crisis, and rising through persecution and danger to triumph and glory. The same great struggles and the same fearful catastrophe appear in each part, though under different symbols.

The second part of the Apocalypse a repetition of the first under other symbols.

By the woman, in chap. xii, 1, we understand the apostolic Church; the man-child (ver. 5) represents her children, the adherents and faithful devotees of the Gospel. The imagery is taken from Isa. lxvi, 7, 8. These are the children of "the Jerusalem which is above," and which Paul calls "our mother" (Gal. iv, 26). The statement that this child was to rule all nations with a rod of iron, and be caught up to the throne of God, has led many to suppose that Christ is designated. But the language of the promise to the church of Thyatira (chap. ii, 26, 27), and the vision of the martyrs who live and reign with Christ a thousand years (chap. xx, 4–6), show that Christ's faithful martyrs, whose blood was the seed of the Church, are associated with him in the authority and administration of his Messianic rule. The dragon is the old serpent, the devil, and his standing ready to devour the child as soon as born is an image appropriated from Pharaoh's attitude toward the infant Israelites (Exod. i, 16). Michael and his angels are but symbolic names of Christ and his apostles. The war in heaven was fought in the same element where the woman appeared, and the casting out of demons by Christ and his apostles

The Woman and the Dragon.

was the reality to which these symbols point (comp. Luke x, 18; John xii, 31). The soul-conflicts of the Christian are of like character.[1] The flight of the woman into the wilderness was the scattering of the Church by reason of bitter persecutions (comp. Acts viii, 1), but especially that flight of the church in Judea which Jesus authorized when his disciples should see the signs of the end (Matt. xxiv, 16; Luke xxi, 21).

Being cast down from the heavenly places, the dragon stood upon the sand of the sea, and next revealed himself in a wild beast, which is seen coming up out of the sea (xiii, 1). He combines various features of a leopard, a bear, and a lion, the first three beasts of Daniel's vision (Dan. vii, 4, 6), and the power which the dragon gives him imparts to him all the malignity, blasphemy, and persecuting violence which characterized Daniel's fourth beast at the appearance of the little horn. This beast we understand to be the Roman Empire, especially as represented in Nero, under whom the Jewish war began, and by whom the woman's seed, the saints (comp. xii, 17, and xiii, 7), were most bitterly persecuted. He was the veriest incarnation of wickedness, a signal revelation of antichrist, and corresponds in every essential feature with the man of sin, the son of perdition, of whom Paul wrote to the Thessalonians (2 Thess. ii, 3–10).[2] At the same time another beast is seen coming up out of the land (xiii, 11), having two horns like a lamb. But he is only the satellite, the *alter ego* and representative of the first beast, and exercises his authority. This second beast is a proper symbol of the Roman government of Judea by procurators, and if we seek for the meaning of the two horns, we may find it in the two procurators specially noted for their tyranny and oppression, Albinus and Gessius Florus.[3] It is a well known fact that the Christians of this period were required to worship the image of the emperor or die, and the procurators were the emperor's agents to enforce this measure.[4] Thus the second beast

The Beasts from the sea and from the land.

---

[1] Paul fully recognized the spiritual and demoniacal character of the Christian's struggle when he wrote: "Our wrestling is not against blood and flesh, but against the principalities, against the powers, against the world-rulers of this darkness, against the spiritual hosts of wickedness in the heavenly places" (Eph. vi, 12). Such conflict was a war in heaven.

[2] See above, pp. 460–462.

[3] See Josephus, Ant., book xx, chap. ix, 1, and chap. xi, 1. Wars, book ii, chaps. xiv and xv.

[4] Alford, after quoting in evidence from Pliny's letter to Trajan, observes: "If it be said, as an objection to this, that it is not an image of the emperor, but of the beast itself, which is spoken of, the answer is very simple, that as the seer himself in chap. xvii, 11 does not hesitate to identify one of the *seven kings* with the beast itself, so

is appropriately called "the false prophet" (chaps. xvi, 13; xix, 20), for his great work was to turn men to a blasphemous idolatry. The mystic number of the beast (xiii, 18) would then be represented both by the Greek Λατεινος, and the Hebrew נרון קסר, the numerical value of each being 666. For the beast was both the *Latin* kingdom, and its representative and head, *Nero Cæsar*.

The vision of Mount Zion in chap. xiv is a glorious contrast to the preceding revelations of antichrist. It presents the heavenly side of this period of persecution and trial, Vision of Mount Zion. and sets it forth in seven exhibitions: (1) First is seen the Lamb on Mount Zion (the heavenly Zion), and with him are the thousands of his redeemed Israel in great glory (verses 1–5). These are no other than the woman's seed who have been caught up to the throne of God (xii, 5), but are now seen from another point of view. (2) Next follows the vision of the flying angel bearing eternal good tidings to every nation (verses 6, 7). This is done in spite of the dragon and his agents. While the dragon, wielding the forces of empire, seeks to annihilate the Church of God, the true children of the heavenly Jerusalem are caught up to be with Christ in glory; but the Gospel is still preached in all the world, accompanied by warning and promise. Thus the saints triumph "on account of the blood of the Lamb, and on account of the word of their testimony" (chap. xii, 11). (3) Then an angel, as by anticipation, announces the fall of Babylon the great (ver. 8), and is followed (4) by another who warns men against the worship of the beast and his image (verses 9–12). (5) Then a voice from heaven pronounces them blessed who die in the Lord *from henceforth* (ver. 13); as if from that eventful epoch the dead in Christ should enter at once into a rest

---

we may fairly assume that the image of the beast for the time being would be the image of the reigning emperor."—Greek Test. on Rev. xiii, 15. It is strange that learned critics will turn, with an air of contempt, away from an explanation of the "image of the beast" so natural and simple as that given above, and find satisfaction in such fancies as that this image denotes the images of saints set up in papal churches (Faber); or the pope considered as the idol of the Roman Church (Newton, Daubuz); or the temporal power of the pope, and the patrimony granted by Pepin in A. D. 754 (Glasgow); or the papal kingdom or hierarchy which the priesthood established (Lord); or the empire of Charlemagne, regarded as the image of the old heathen Roman Empire (Mede); or the pope's decretals (Osiander); or the Inquisition (Vitringa); or the papal General Councils of Western Europe (Elliott). Writers so full of visions of modern Europe and the fortunes of the papacy that they quickly discern apocalyptic epochs in such events as the battle of Sadowa, July 3, 1866, the pope's bull of July, 1868, the insurrection in Spain under Prim, and the revolution in France consequent upon the battle of Sedan, 1870, can scarcely be expected to view any prophecy from the historical standpoint of the sacred writer. Comp. Elliott, Horæ Apocalypticæ, 5th ed., Lond., 1872; Preface and Postscript.

which the dead of the previous æon could not know. (6) **The sixth**
scene is that of the Son of-man represented as wearing a golden
crown, holding a sharp sickle in his hand, and attended by an angel
(verses 14–16); and with these soon appears another angel having a
sharp sickle, and the land was reaped, and the winepress, trodden
without the city, spread rivers of blood that seemed to deluge all
the land. This is but another picture of the same great catastrophe,
seen from another point of view.

The vision of the seven vials (φιάλας, *bowls*) full of the wrath of
The seven last God, which are also called the seven last plagues (chap-
Plagues. ters xv, xvi), is but another symbolization of the seven
trumpet-woes (of chapters viii–xi), with which they minutely correspond. The duplicate vision of these terrible judgments (one judgment of sevenfold fury, comp. Dan. iii, 19) is analogous to other repetitions of the same subject under different imagery (see above, pp.
409–411, and 416, 417). This double vision of wrath, like the double
dream of Pharaoh, served to show that these things were established by the Almighty, and that he would shortly bring them to
pass (Gen. xl, 32).[1]

The vision of Babylon the great (chapters xvii, xviii) is a highly
Vision of the wrought apocalyptic picture of the apostate Church of
mystic Baby- the old covenant (comp. above, p. 391). The then exist-
lon. ing Jerusalem, in bondage with her children (Gal. iv, 25),
is portrayed as a harlot, and the language and imagery are appropriated largely from Ezekiel's allegory of the same city (Ezek. xvi;
comp. Ezek. xxiv).[2] It is that murderess of prophets against whom
Jesus uttered the terrible words of Matt. xxiii, 34–36. From 'the
beginning of the Roman Empire Jerusalem sought and maintained
a heathenish complicity with the Cæsars, and the empire became,
politically, her dependence and support. There was constant strife
among ambitious rulers to obtain the so-called "kingdom of Judea."
Jerusalem was the chief city of that province, and is, therefore,
properly said to "reign over the kings (not of the *earth*, and not
over *emperors* and *monarchs* of the *world*), but of the land " (chap.

---

[1] "The repetition of the vision of judgment in various forms," says Farrar, "is one
of the recognized Hebrew methods of expressing their certainty. The same general
calamities are indicated by diverse symbols." He cites from the ancient Commentary
of Victorinus the statement that the seven vials are but another symbol of the same
judgments as those denoted by the trumpets, and adds: "There is fair reason to suppose that Victorinus derived this valuable and by no means obvious principle of interpretation from early, and perhaps from apostolic, tradition."—The Early Days of
Christianity, chap. xxviii, p. 450. London, 1882.

[2] Comp. Isa. i, 21: "How has the once faithful city become a harlot!" Comp. also
Jer. ii, 2, 20; iii, 3–6; iv, 30; xiii, 27.

xvii, 18). It is the same land (γῆ), the tribes of which mourn over the coming of the Son of man (chap. i, 7).[1] We, accordingly, take the mystic Babylon to be identical with the great city which, in chap. xi, 8, is called Sodom and Egypt, where the Lord was crucified.[2]

The explanation of the mystery of the woman and the beast, given in chap. xvii, 7–18, has puzzled all interpreters. It is noticeably a composite explanation, and avowedly applies partly to the woman and partly to the beast which carries her. The mystery requires for its solution "the mind which hath wisdom" (ver. 9), and it may have had a meaning and force for John's contemporaries which we of a long subsequent age cannot so easily feel. "The beast which was, and is not, and is about to come up out of the abyss, and to go away into destruction" (ver. 8), is an expression of cautious reserve, which is notably like Paul's guarded language about the man of sin (2 Thess. ii, 5–7). The beast with seven heads and ten horns is usually identified with the wild beast from the sea (chap. xiii, 1), and may be understood of Rome and her allied and tributary princes who took part in the war against Judea and Jerusalem. The great harlot city, whose

Mystery of woman and beast.

---

[1] "The kings of the land," who. in Psa. ii, 2, set themselves against Jehovah and his Christ, are declared by the Apostle Peter to be such kings as Herod and Pontius Pilate (Acts iv, 27). These, he declares, "were gathered together with Gentiles and peoples of Israel." Josephus says: "The city of Jerusalem is situated in the very middle (of the land), on which account some have called that city the navel of the country. Nor indeed is Judea destitute of such delights as come by the sea, since its maritime places extend as far as Ptolemais. It was parted into eleven portions, of which the royal city Jerusalem was supreme, and presided over all the neighbouring country as the head does over the body."—Wars of the Jews, book iii, iii, 5.

[2] It deserves notice that there is a title which, in the Apocalypse, is applied to one particular city *par excellence*. It is the title "that great city" [ἡ πόλις ἡ μεγάλη]. It is clear that it is always the same city which is so designated, unless another be expressly specified. Now, the city in which the witnesses are slain is expressly called by this title, "that great city;" and the names Sodom and Egypt are applied to it; and it is furthermore particularly identified as the city "where also our Lord was crucified" (chap. xi, 8). There can be no reasonable doubt that this refers to ancient Jerusalem. If, then, "the great city" of chap. xi, 8, means ancient Jerusalem, it follows that "the great city" of chap. xiv, 8, styled also Babylon, and " the great city" of chap. xvi, 19. must equally signify Jerusalem. By parity of reasoning, "that great city" [ἡ πόλις ἡ μεγάλη] in chap. xvii, 18, and elsewhere, must refer also to Jerusalem. It is a mere assumption to say, as Dean Alford does, that Jerusalem is never called by this name. There is no unfitness, but the contrary, in such a distinctive title being applied to Jerusalem. It was to an Israelite the royal city, by far the greatest in the land, the only city which could properly be so designated; and it ought never to be forgotten that the visions of the Apocalypse are to be regarded from a Jewish point of view.—The Parousia, pp. 486, 487.

holy temple had been made a place of merchandise and a den of thieves (Matt. xxi, 13; John ii, 15), was carried for a hundred years by Rome, and at last hated and destroyed by the very kings with whom she had maintained her heathenish traffic. Jerusalem's relation to Rome and her tributary princes was well voiced in that Jewish appeal to Pilate: "If thou release this man, thou·art not Cæsar's friend. . . . We have no king but Cæsar" (John xix, 12, 15).

But while the relations of Jerusalem and Rome are thus outlined, The beast from the beast "which was, and is not, and shall come" the abyss. (πάρεσται, *shall be present*, ver. 8), may symbolize a deeper mystery. He is not a combination of the lion, the leopard, and the bear, nor does he "come up out of the sea" like the beast of chap. xiii, 1, but he is a "scarlet-coloured beast,", and "comes up out of the abyss." May he not, therefore, be more properly regarded as a special manifestation of the "great red dragon" of chap. xii, 3? The seven heads and ten horns of the dragon indicate seats of power and regal and princely agents through whom the kingly "angel of the abyss" (chap. ix, 11) accomplishes his satanic purposes. We need not, therefore, look to the seven hills of Rome,[1] or to ten particular kings, for the solution of the mystery of the scarlet-coloured beast. The language of the angel interpreter, even when ostensibly explaining the mystery, is manifestly enigmatical. Just as when, in chap. xiii, 18, he that has understanding is called upon to "count the number of the beast," so here the clue to the mystery of the seven heads and ten horns is itself a riddle. "The seven heads are seven mountains on which the woman is sitting" (ver. 9). This may indeed refer literally to seven mountains, either of Jerusalem or Rome, for both these cities covered seven heights; but it is as likely to refer, enigmatically, to manifold political supports or alliances, considered as so many seats of power or consolidated kingdoms, and called seven because of covenanted arrangements.[2] The words which follow

---

[1] The seven mountains on which the woman sitteth (ver. 9) may be the mountains of Jerusalem as well as the seven hills of Rome. There were Zion, Moriah, Acra. and Bezetha, and the three fortified heights, Millo, Ophel, and the rock, seventy-five feet high, on which the Castle of Antonia was built. See Edersheim, The Temple, pp. 11, 13. Boston, 1881 The notion that the *septem colles* of Latin writers were familiar to John and his Greek and Hebrew readers, and, necessarily to be understood here, is as fanciful as that the eagles of Matt. xxiv, 28, are the Roman eagles.' The number seven, in this allusion to the mountains, need not be pressed into fuller significance than the seven horns and seven eyes of- the Lamb in chap. v, 6, where no one insists on a literal significance of the number seven.

[2] "The mountains," says Glasgow, "are, like other terms, to be understood

should be rendered: "And seven kings there are," not necessarily, as commonly translated, "*they* are seven kings," that is, the mountains represent seven kings. We are not satisfied with any solution of the riddle of these seven kings which we have yet seen, and will not presume to add another to the legion of guesses which have been put forth.[1] But we venture to suggest that the beast "which was, and is not, and shall come," may be understood primarily of Satan himself, under his different and successive manifestations, in the persons of bitter persecutors of the Church. It was the beast from the abyss by whom the two witnesses were slain (chap. xi, 7; comp. chap. xx, 7). Cast out by the death of one imperial persecutor he goes into the abyss (comp. Luke viii, 31), and, anon, comes up again out of the abyss, and appropriates the blasphemy and forces and diadems of the empire to make war upon the Lamb and his faithful followers. As the Elijah, who was to come before the great and notable day of Jehovah (Mal. iv, 5), appeared in the person of John the Baptist (Matt. xi, 14), and was so called because he represented the spirit and power of Elijah (Luke i, 17), so the beast "which was, and is not, is himself also an eighth,[2] and

symbolically. If the woman is not literal, why should the mountains be so thought? And to call the woman a literal city, built on seven hills, is equally gratuitous, whether a Protestant says it of Rome or a Romanist of Constantinople."—The Apocalypse Translated and Expounded, p. 439.

[1] The explanations of the seven kings may be divided into three classes: I. Those which regard them as so many different historical phases of world-power, as (1) Egypt, (2) Assyria, (3) Babylon, (4) Persia, (5) Greece, (6) Rome, (7) Germanic-Sclavonic Empire (Auberlen); or (1) Babylonian, (2) Medo-Persian, (3) Greek, (4) Syrian, (5) Egyptian, (6) Roman, (7) German Empire (Wordsworth). II. Those which make them represent so many different classes of rulers, as (1) kings, (2) consuls, (3) decemvirs, (4) military tribunes, (5) dictators, (6) emperors, (7) popes (Vitringa); or (1) kings, (2) consuls, (3) dictators, (4) decemvirs, (5) military tribunes, (6) the wreath-crowned (στέφανος) emperors, (7) the diadem (διάδημα) emperors (Elliott). III. Those which understand seven individual kings, as the first seven Cæsars, (1) Julius, (2) Augustus, (3) Tiberius, (4) Caligula, (5) Claudius, (6) Nero, (7) Galba (Stuart). Others begin the seven with Augustus; Grotius begins with Claudius; Düsterdieck throws out of the number the three usurpers, Galba, Otho, and Vitellius, and makes the seventh head Vespasian. Züllig understands the seven kings to be (1) Herod the Great, (2) Archelaus, (3) Philip, (4) Antipas, (5) Agrippa, (6) Herod of Chalcis, (7) Agrippa II., considered as antitypes of the seven Edomite kings mentioned in Gen. xxxvi, 33-38. The author of The Parousia (Lond., 1878) identifies them with the seven procurators of Judea, (1) Cuspius Fadus, (2) Tiberius Alexander, (3) Ventidius Cumanus, (4) Antonius Felix, (5) Porcius Festus, (6) Albinus, (7) Gessius Florus. The above by no means exhausts the various explanations. Surely he who would presume to determine an important question of apocalyptic interpretation upon any theory of the seven kings builds upon a very uncertain foundation.

[2] According to Gebhardt "the eighth king is identical with the beast (comp. Cowles on the Revelation, in loco), whose seven heads are seven kings. As individual

is of the seven [of the same spirit and power], and goes away into destruction " (ver. 11). It is not at all impossible that the wide-spread rumour that Nero was to appear again grew out of a misap-prehension of this riddle, just as some modern interpreters still insist (see Alford on Matt. xi, 14) that the real Elijah is yet liter-ally to come. The early Chiliasts, like their modern followers, often insisted on the literal interpretation even of riddles.

The fall of Babylon the great is portrayed in glowing colours in chap. xviii, 1–xix, 10, and the language and imagery are appropriated almost wholly from the Old Testa-ment prophetic pictures of the fall of ancient Babylon and Tyre.[1] The vision is fourfold: First (1) an angel proclaims the

Fall of the mystic Baby-lon.

forms of world-power appear to the seer to culminate and unite in an empire which he calls *the beast*, so he sees again the particular stages of the development of this empire, the individual rulers of the same culminate in one prince, which he also de-scribes as *the beast*. As the leopard, the bear, and the lion are contained in the beast, so are the seven heads of the beast contained in the one head. We may say that as he sees in an individual king the nature of a definite empire, uniting in itself all ear-lier empires, personified, so also he sees unfolded in this empire the nature of that individual king: this king is to him the empire in person; this empire is to him the king in the form of a kingdom. It is also evidently much easier in the one place to think of an individual king, and in the other of an empire, and it is therefore ever to be maintained that the seer so thought; the empire of which this is the king, the king whose is the empire."—The Doctrine of the Apocalypse, English translation, p. 221. Edinb., 1878.

[1] How notably strange it is that learned exegetes, who can see striking fulfilments of this prophecy in comparatively unimportant events of the politics and feuds of modern Europe and the papacy, are forgetful of such events as the following, which is only one of many similar pictures of woe given us by the Jewish historian. De-scribing the destruction of the temple, Josephus says: " While the holy house was on fire everything was plundered that came to hand, and ten thousand of those that were caught were slain; nor was there a commiseration of any age, or any reverence of gravity; but children and old men, and profane persons and priests, were all slain in the same manner; so that this war went round all sorts of men, and brought them to destruction, and as well those that made supplication for their lives as those that de-fended themselves by fighting. The flame was also carried a long way, and made an echo together with the groans of those that were slain; and because this hill was high, and the works at the temple were very great, one would have thought the whole city had been on fire. Nor can one imagine anything either greater or more terrible than this noise; for there was at once a shout of the Roman legions, who were march-ing all together, and a sad clamour of the seditious, who were now surrounded with fire and sword. The people also that were left above were beaten back upon the enemy, and under a great consternation, and made sad moans at the calamity they were under; the multitude also that was in the city joined in this outcry with those that were upon the hill; and, besides, many of those that were worn away by the famine, and their mouths almost closed, when they saw the fire of the holy house, they exerted their utmost strength, and brake out into groans and outcries again : Perea did also return the echo, as well as the mountains round about [the city], and

awful ruin (xviii, 1–3). He repeats the words already used in chap.
xiv, 8, but which were used of old by Isaiah (xxi, 9) and Jeremiah
(li, 8) in foretelling the ruin of the Chaldæan capital. (2) Then another heavenly voice is heard, like the words of Jesus in Matt.
xxiv, 16, and like the prophetic word which long before had called the chos-
en people to "flee out of the midst of Babylon, and deliver every man
his soul " (Jer. li, 6; comp. l, 8; Isa. xlviii, 20; Zech. ii, 6, 7), and
this call is followed by a woeful dirge over the sudden ruin of the
great city (xviii, 4–20). This oracle of doom should be closely
compared with that of Isaiah and Jeremiah over ancient Babylon
(Isa. xiii, 19–22; Jer. l, li), and that of Ezekiel over the fall of
Tyre (Ezek. xxvi–xxviii). (3) The violence of the catastrophe is
next illustrated by the symbol of a mighty angel hurling a mill-
stone into the sea, and the consequent cessation of all her former
activity and noise (xviii, 21–24). (4) After these things there is
heard a pæan of victory in the heavens—notable contrast to the
voice of the harpers and minstrels of the fallen Babylon, and all
the servants of God are admonished to prepare for the marriage
supper of the Lamb.

After the fall of the great Babylon there follows a sevenfold
vision of the coming and kingdom of the Christ (chap. The Parousia
xix, 11–xxi, 8). As, in Matt. xxiv, 29, "immediately and Kingdom
after the tribulation of those days " the sign of the Son of the Son of
man.
of man appears in heaven, so, immediately after the horrors of the
woe-smitten city, the seer of Patmos beholds the heaven opened,
and the glorious King of kings and Lord of lords comes forth to
judge the nations and avenge his own elect. This great apocalyptic picture contains: (1) The parousia of the Son of man in his
glory (xix, 11–16). (2) The destruction of the beast and the false
prophet with all their impious forces (verses 17–21). This overthrow is portrayed in noticeable harmony with that of the lawless
one in 2 Thess. ii, 8, " whom the Lord Jesus shall take off with the
breath of his mouth, and bring to naught with the manifestation of
his coming; " and the beastly agents of Satan, like those of Daniel's
visions (Dan. vii, 11), are given to the burning flame. (3) The destruction of these beasts, to whom the dragon gave his power and

augmented the force of the entire noise. Yet was the misery itself more terrible
than this disorder; for one would have thought that the hill itself, on which the temple stood, was seething hot, as full of fire on every part of it, that the blood was
larger in quantity than the fire, and those that were slain more in number than those
that slew them; for the ground did nowhere appear visible for the dead bodies that
lay on it; but the soldiers went over heaps of these bodies as they ran upon such as
fled from them."—Wars of the Jews, book vi, chap. v, 1.

authority (chap. xiii, 2, 11, 12), is appropriately followed by the binding and imprisonment of the old dragon himself (chap. xx, 1–3). The symbols employed to set forth all these triumphs are surely not to be understood literally of a warfare carried on with carnal weapons (comp. 2 Cor. x, 4; Eph. vi, 11–17), but they vividly express momentous facts forever to be associated with the consummation of that age, and crisis of ages, when Judaism fell, and Christianity opened upon the world.   From that period onward no well-authenticated instance of demoniacal possession can be shown.[1]

The Millennium. With that shutting up of Satan the millennium begins, a long indefinite period, as the symbolical number most naturally suggests (see above, p. 390), but a period of ample fulness for the universal diffusion and triumph of the Gospel (verses 4–6). "The first resurrection" takes place at the beginning of this period, and is chiefly conspicuous as a resurrection of martyrs; a bliss of which not all the dead appear to have been "accounted worthy" (καταξιωθέντες, Luke xx, 35), but which Paul was anxious to attain (Phil. iii, 11).   For it is written, "Blessed and holy is he who has a part in the first resurrection; over these the second death has no authority," for of such Jesus said, "neither can they die any more" (Luke xx, 36).   Moreover, they sit upon thrones, and judgment is given to them (comp. Dan. vii, 22; Matt. xix, 28; Luke xxii, 28–30; 1 Cor. vi, 2), and they are made "priests of God and of Christ, and reign with him the thousand years." The language of verse 4, however, intimates that others besides the martyrs may sit upon thrones and exercise judgment with the Christ (comp. chap. ii, 26, 27; iii, 21).

Of other things which may occur during the millennium no mention is here made, and yet all manner of fancies have been built upon this brief passage of the Apocalypse.
The Chiliastic interpretation.
The Chiliasts assume that this millennium is to be a visible reign of Christ and his saints upon the earth, and with this reign they associate a most literal conception of other prophecies.   The following, from Justin Martyr, is one of the earliest expressions of this view: "I, and others," he says, "who are right-minded Christians on all points, are assured that there will be a resurrection of the

---

[1] "We conclude," says the author of The Parousia, "that at the end of the age a marked and decisive check was given to the power of Satan; which check is symbolically represented in the Apocalypse by the chaining and imprisoning of the dragon in the abyss.   It does not follow from this that error and evil were banished from the earth.   It is enough to show that this was, as Schlegel says, 'the decisive crisis between ancient and modern times,' and that the introduction of Christianity 'has changed and regenerated, not only government and science, but the whole system of human life.'"—Parousia, p. 518.

dead, and a thousand years in Jerusalem, which will then be built, adorned, and enlarged, as the prophets Ezekiel and Isaiah and others declare. . . . And, further, there was a certain man with us whose name was John, one of the apostles of Christ, who prophesied, by a revelation that was made to him, that those who believed in our Christ would dwell a thousand years in Jerusalem; and that thereafter the general and, in short, the eternal resurrection and judgment of all men would likewise take place."[1] This Ebionite conception, having gained an early prominence, has infected apocalyptic interpretation with a disturbing leaven even until now, and there is little hope of a better exegesis until all dogmatic notions are set aside and we fearlessly accept what the Scripture says, and no more.

The old Chiliastic ideas of a restoration of all Israel at Jerusalem, and of Christ and his glorified saints literally sitting Chiliastic interpretation without sufficient warrant. on thrones and reigning in visible material glory on the earth, are without warrant in this Scripture. Nothing is here said about Jerusalem, or the Jews, or the Gentiles. An indefinite number sit upon thrones and receive judgment. Among them those who had been beheaded for the testimony of Jesus have a most conspicuous place, and thus they receive the reward promised in chap. vi, 9–11. These now live and reign with Christ, not on the earth, but where the throne of his kingdom is, namely, in the heavens. This accords with Paul's words in 2 Tim. ii, 11: "If we died with him (i. e., by martyrdom; comp. Phil. iii, 10) we shall also live with him; if we endure suffering we shall also reign with him." A resurrection of martyrs, to take place at the beginning of the millennial era, is evidently taught in Rev. xx, 4–6, and is also in harmony with the Pauline eschatology as we have already shown (see above, p. 463). "I do not see," says Stuart, "how we can, on the ground of exegesis, fairly avoid the conclusion that John has taught in the passage before us that there will be a resurrection of the martyr-saints at the commencement of the period after Satan shall have been shut up in the dungeon of the great abyss."[2]

---

[1] Dialogue with Trypho, lxxx, lxxxi. "The Book of Revelation," says Hagenbach, "in its twentieth chapter, gave currency to the idea of a millennial kingdom, together with that of a second resurrection; and the imagination of those who dwelt fondly upon sensuous impressions delineated these millennial hopes in the most glowing terms. This was the case, not only with the Judaizing Ebionites and Cerinthus, but also with several orthodox fathers, such as Papias, Justin, Irenæus, and Tertullian."— History of Doctrines, Translated by Smith, vol. i, p. 213. New York, 1861.

[2] Commentary on the Apocalypse, vol. ii, p. 476. Similarly Alford: "No legitimate treatment of this text will extort from it what is known as the spiritual interpretation now in fashion. If, in a passage where two resurrections are mentioned, where

(5) At the end of the millennial period there is to be a loosing of
The last defeat Satan, a rising of hostile forces, symbolized by Gog and
of Satan, and Magog (comp. Ezek. xxxviii, xxxix), and a fearful
the last judg-
ment. catastrophe, resulting in the final and everlasting overthrow of the devil—the culmination of the prophecy of Gen. iii, 15.
This last conflict, belonging to a distant future, is rapidly passed
over by the seer, and its details are not made known (verses 7–10).
(6) The last great judgment is next portrayed (verses 11–15), and
may well be regarded as the culmination and completion of that
continual judgment (depicted in Matt. xxv, 31–46) which began
with the parousia and continues until the Son of man delivers over
the kingdom to the Father (1 Cor. xv, 24). (7) The last picture in
this wonderful apocalyptical series is that of the new heavens and
new land, and the descent of the heavenly Jerusalem (xxi, 1–8). It
corresponds with Matt. xxv, 34, where the king says to those on his
right hand: "Come, ye blessed of my Father, inherit the kingdom
prepared for you from the foundation of the world." As there the
glory of the righteous is put in striking contrast with the curse
and doom of the wicked, and, it is finally said, "These shall go
away into eternal punishment" (Matt. xxv, 46), so here, after the
glory of the redeemed is outlined, it is added, as the issue of an
eternal judgment: "But as for the fearful, and unbelieving, and
abominable, and murderers, and fornicators, and sorcerers, and idol-
aters, and all liars, their part is in the lake that burns with fire and
brimstone (comp. 'the eternal fire, prepared for the devil and his
angels,' Matt. xxv, 41), which is the second death."

It should be noticed how this last sevenfold apocalyptic vision

certain *souls lived* at the first, and *the rest of the dead lived* only at the end of a specified period after the first—if in such a passage the first resurrection may be understood to mean *spiritual* rising with Christ, while the second means *literal* rising from
the grave; then there is an end of all significance in language, and Scripture is wiped
out as a definite testimony to any thing."—Greek Testament, in loco. This argument
holds equally good against all theories of the "first resurrection," which allow that
the first is figurative and the other literal. Brown's nine famous arguments against
the literal, and in favour of a figurative explanation of the first resurrection (Christ's
Second Coming, pp. 231-258. New York, 1866), are all aimed against the sensuous
Chiliastic notion that it is the simultaneous resurrection of *all* the righteous dead—a
view which we repudiate as unscriptural. But Brown himself fairly overthrows the
notion of Scott and others that John saw a resurrection of *souls*, and not of *bodies*.
"This is to mistake what the apostle saw in the vision. He did not see a *resurrection
of souls*. He saw 'the souls of them that were slain;' that is, he had a vision of the
martyrs themselves in the state of the dead—after they were dead, and just before
their resurrection. Then he saw them rise: 'They lived'—not their souls, but *themselves*. All figurative resurrections in Scripture are couched in the language of literal
ones; and why should this be any exception?"—Christ's Second Coming, p. 229.

(chap. xix, 11–xxi, 8) covers the entire field of biblical eschatology. The whole is rapidly sketched, for details would have transcended the purpose of "the prophecy of this book" (xxii, 10), which was to make known things which were shortly to come to pass (chap. i, 1–3). But like the last section of our Lord's discourse (Matt. xxv, 31–46), which introduces things running far beyond the time-limits of that prophecy, but which were to commence "when the Son of man should come in his glory;" so this sevenfold vision begins with the parousia (chap. xix, 11), and sketches in brief outline the mighty triumphs and eternal issues of the Messiah's reign.[1]

These visions introduce what transcends the time-limits of the book.

We understand that the millennium of Rev. xx, 1–6, is now in progress. It dates from the consummation of the Jewish age. It is a round definite number used symbolically for an indefinite æon. It is the period of the Messianic reign, and the kingdom of the heavens, like the mustard seed and the leaven (Matt. xiii, 31–33), is passing through its gradual development. It may require a million years. The impatient Chiliast will not be satisfied with this slow Messianic order, and refuses to see that the powers of darkness have been repressed, and the progress of human civilization has been more marked since the end of that age than ever before. But others see and know that since the dawn of Christianity, idolatry has been well nigh abolished, and every element of righteousness and truth has been gaining prominence and control in the laws of nations.[2] It is not in accord

The Millennium is the Gospel dispensation.

---

[1] Lange suggestively but somewhat fancifully observes: "The entire æon is to be conceived of as an æon of separations and eliminations in an ethical and a cosmical sense, separations and eliminations such as are necessary to make manifest and to complete the ideal regulations of life. Of judgments of damnation between the judgment upon Antichrist and the judgment upon Satan there can be no question; the reference can be only to a critical government and management preparatory to the final consummation. The whole æon is a crisis which occasions the visible appearance of the heaven on earth. The whole æon is the great last day. We may even conceive of the mutiny which finally breaks out as a result of these preparations, for a sort of protest on the part of the wicked was hinted at by Christ in his eschatological discourse (Matt. xxv, 44), and the most essential element in the curse of hell is the continuance of revolt, the gnashing of teeth."—Commentary on the Revelation of John, p. 350. American edition. New York, 1874.

[2] Pope represents the Catholic faith and interpretation as "content, to understand figuratively the glowing representations of the ancient prophecies as applying to the present Christian Church. It takes the Apocalypse as a book of symbols, which does not give consecutive history, but continually reverts to the beginning, and exhibits in varying visions the same one great final truth. Satan was bound or *cast out* when our Saviour ascended; he has never since been the god and seducer of the nations as he was before, and as he will for a season be permitted to be again. The saints,

with either history or prophecy to believe that the Gospel of the
kingdom of Christ will have for its historical period an æon shorter
than that required for its preparation in the typical dispensations
which preceded it. It is not probable that God would take four
thousand years of type and shadow to prepare the world for two
thousand years of light. We should not expect the earlier part of
the Messianic millennium to be without any darkness, and there is
nothing in the Scriptures to warrant the idea that it is to be a period
of uniform and unclouded blessedness and glory.

There remains for our notice but one more great apocalyptic
picture, the vision of the New Jerusalem. As in chap.
xvi, 19, under the seventh and last plague, the fall of
the great Babylon (old Jerusalem) was briefly outlined,
and then, in chap. xvii–xix, 10, another and more detailed portraiture of that "mother of the harlots and of the abominations of the
land" was added, going over many of the same things again, so
here, having given under the last series of visions a short but vivid
picture of the heavenly Jerusalem (xxi, 1–8), the apocalyptist, following his artistic style and habit of repetition, tells how one of the
same seven angels (comp. xvii, 1–4, and xxi, 9–11) took him to a lofty
mountain, and gave him a fuller vision of the Bride, the wife of the
Lamb. This wife of the Lamb is no other than the woman of chap.
xii, 1, but she is here revealed at a later stage of her history, after
the dragon has been shut up in the abyss. After the land has been
cleared of dragon, beast, and false prophet, the seed of the woman
who fled into the wilderness, the seed caught up to the throne of
God, are conceived as "coming down out of heaven from God,"
and all things are made new. The language and symbols used are
appropriated mainly from Isaiah lxv, 17–lvi, 24, and the closing
chapters of Ezekiel. The great thought is: Babylon, the bloody
harlot, has fallen, and New Jerusalem, the glorious Bride, appears.

As the closing chapters of Ezekiel have been variously understood (see above, pp. 436, 437), so this vision of the
New Jerusalem, which is evidently modelled after the
pattern of that older Apocalypse, has been explained in different

The vision of the New Jeru- salem.

Meaning of the New Jerusalem.

martyrs, and others—the martyrs pre-eminently—now rule with Christ: *and hath made
us a kingdom* (Rev. i, 6), they themselves sing; *and they reign upon earth* (Rev. v, 10)..
The apostles, and all saints, have part in the first resurrection, and in the present
regeneration reign with Jesus, though the future regeneration shall be yet more abundant. The unanimous strain of prophecy concerning the glory of the Messiah's kingdom is to be interpreted as partly fulfilled in the spiritual reign of Christ in this
world, which is not yet fully manifested as it will be; and partly as the earthly figure
of a heavenly reality hereafter."—Compendium of Christian Theology, vol. iii, pp.
400, 401. N. Y., 1881.

ways. (1) According to one class of interpreters, the future restoration of the Jews to Palestine, and the rebuilding of Jerusalem on a magnificent scale, are here predicted.[1] (2) According to others, the new heaven, new land, and new Jerusalem are but a symbolic recapitulation of the visions of chap. xx, for the purpose of fuller detail, and are to be understood as synchronizing with the period of the thousand years. (3) But most interpreters regard the prophecy as post-millennial, and descriptive of the final heavenly state of the glorified saints of God. Rejecting the first of the above named views (which represents the sensuous Ebionite conception of the kingdom of heaven, and magnifies the letter to the quenching of the spirit of Scripture), we may blend the two other interpretations. Ezekiel's vision, as we have seen (p. 437), symbolized the New Testament Church and kingdom of God; why should not the same conception enter into this parallel prophecy? But as later revelations are wont to embody fuller and more perfect outlines of the provisions of grace, so John's picture of new heaven, new land, and new city is more luminous and far reaching in its indications of what God has prepared for those who love him and keep his commandments.

The words of Haggai ii, 6, 7, are acknowledged by the best interpreters to be a Messianic prophecy: "Yet once—it is Hag. ii, 6, 7, and a little while—and I will shake the heavens, and the Heb. xii, 26-28. land, and the sea, and the desert; and I will shake all the nations, and they shall come to the delight[2] of all the nations, and I will

---

[1] Here properly belongs that exposition of the "new heaven and new earth," which finds in Isa. li, 16; lxv, 17; lxvi, 22; 2 Pet. iii, 10-13; Rev. xx, 11; xxi, 1, a literal prophecy of the destruction of the world by fire, and the creation of a new world in its place. The only question among these interpreters is whether an absolutely new creation is intended, or only a renovation (παλιγγενεσία, regeneration (Matt. xix, 28) of the materials of the old. That these texts may intimate or dimly foreshadow some such ultimate reconstruction of the physical creation, need not be denied, for we know not the possibilities of the future, nor the purposes of God respecting all things which he has created. But the contexts of these several passages do not authorize such a doctrine. Isa. li, 16, refers to the resuscitation of Zion and Jerusalem, and is clearly metaphorical. The same is true of Isa. lxv, 17, and lxvi, 22, for the context in all these places confines the reference to Jerusalem and the people of God, and sets forth the same great prophetic conception of the Messianic future as the closing chapters of Ezekiel. The language of 2 Pet. iii, 10, 12, is taken mainly from Isa. xxx, 4, and is limited to the parousia, like the language of Matt. xxiv, 29. Then the Lord made "not only the land but also the heaven" to tremble (Heb. xii, 26), and removed the things that were shaken in order to establish a kingdom which cannot be moved (Heb. xii, 27, 28).

[2] This most simple construction of the Hebrew has been strangely ignored by a supposed necessity of making חֶמְדַּת, delight, or desire, the subject of the verb בָּאוּ,

fill this house with glory." This prophecy is quoted and explained, in Heb. xii, 26–28, as the removal of an earth and heaven which shall give place to an "immovable kingdom." Is there any reason for believing this immovable kingdom to be other than that of which the Lord spoke in Matt. xvi, 28: "There are some standing here who shall not taste of death, till they see the Son of man coming in his kingdom"? The greatest "glory of that latter house," of which Haggai (ii, 7, 9) spoke, was attained when the Lord Christ entered and taught within its courts; but the destruction of the second temple, and the shaking of "the heaven and the land" which it represented, prepared the way for the nobler temple of "his body, the fulness of him who fills all things in all" (Eph. i, 23). Of this body Christ is the head, the husband, and Saviour (Eph. v, 23), having loved her and given himself for her, "that he might sanctify her, having purified her by the laver of water in the word, that he himself might present to himself in glorious beauty the Church, not having spot or wrinkle, or any such thing" (Eph. v, 26, 27).[1] This glorious Church is manifestly the same as the Bride, the wife of the Lamb, the holy city, New Jerusalem. It was necessary that the Old Testament visible Church should be shaken and fall and pass away, for its glory had departed; but in its place comes forth "the whole assembly and church of the firstborn who are enrolled in heaven" (Heb. xii, 23).

If, furthermore, we allow the author of the Epistle to the Hebrews to guide us to a right understanding of the New Jerusalem, we will observe that the communion and fellowship of New Testament saints are apprehended as heaven begun on earth. It is altogether probable that this epistle was

Allusion of Heb. xii, 22, 23.

---

come. But בָּאוּ is plural, and has naturally for its subject the nations (גּוֹיִם) just mentioned. So in Isa. xxxv, 10, "The ransomed of Jehovah shall return, and come to Zion, with shouting and everlasting joy upon their heads." When we read further, in Isa. lxv, 18, as explanatory of the new heavens and new land (ver. 17), "Behold, I create Jerusalem a rejoicing, and her people a joy," we will find therein the surest explanation of the חֶמְדַּת, delight, of Hag. ii, 7. The New Jerusalem, the New Testament Church and kingdom of God, is the delight and desire of the nations, which, according to Rev. xxi, 24, walk by the light of it.

[1] "The union of Christ," says Meyer, "with his Church, at the parousia, in order to confer upon it Messianic blessedness, is conceived of by Paul (as also by Christ himself, Matt. xxv, 1; comp. Rev. xix, 7; see also John iii, 29) under the figure of the bringing home of a bride, wherein Christ appears as the bridegroom, and sets forth the bride, i. e., his Church, as a spotless virgin (the bodily purity is a representative of the ethical) before himself, after he has already in this age cleansed it by the bath of baptism, and sanctified it through his word."—Critical Com. on Ephesians, in loco.

written after the Book of Revelation,[1] and direct allusions to it are apparent in the following passage: "Ye are come ($\pi\rho o\sigma\epsilon\lambda\eta\lambda\acute{v}\vartheta a\tau\epsilon$, ye have already come) unto Mount Zion, and unto the city of the living God, the heavenly Jerusalem." The Christian believer, when his life becomes hidden with Christ in God, has already entered into a communion and fellowship that never ceases.[2] His name is enrolled in heaven. He dwells in God and God in him, and all subsequent glorification in time and in eternity is but a continuous and growing realization of the blessedness of the Church and Kingdom of God.

In the vision of the New Jerusalem we have the last New Testament revelation of the spiritual and heavenly blessedness and glory of which the Mosaic tabernacle was a material symbol. The "dwelling of the testimony" (מִשְׁכַּן הָעֵדוּת, Exod. xxxviii, 21) and its various vessels and services were "copies of the things in the heavens" (Heb. ix, 23), and Christ has entered into the holy places "through the greater and more perfect tabernacle" (Heb. ix, 11), thereby making it possible for all true believers to enter "with boldness into the entrance way of the holies" (Heb. x, 19). This entrance into the holy places and fellowships is realized only as "we draw near with a true heart, in full assurance of faith, having our hearts sprinkled from an evil conscience, and the body washed with pure water" (Heb. x, 22), and such spiritual access is possible to us now. The Alpha and the Omega, accordingly, says: "Blessed are they who wash their robes, that they may have the authority over the tree of life, and by the gates may enter into the city" (Rev. xxii, 14). This city is represented as a perfect cube in form (Rev. xxi, 16), and may therefore be regarded as the heavenly Holy of Holies, into the entrance way ($\epsilon\check{i}\sigma o\delta o\nu$) of which we may now approach. All this accords with the voice from the throne, which said: "Behold the tabernacle of God is with men, and he will tabernacle with them, and they shall be his people, and God himself shall be with them" (Rev. xxi, 3). Herein we discern the true antitype of the ancient tabernacle and temple, and hence it is that this holy city

New Jerusalem the heavenly outline of what the tabernacle symbolized.

---

[1] Comp. the "innumerable company of angels" (Heb. xii, 22) with Rev. v, 11; and the "assembly and church enrolled in heaven" with Rev. xiii, 8; xxi, 27; and "spirits of just men made perfect" with Rev. vii, 13-17. References and allusions as direct and explicit as these, made by any of the early Fathers to books of the New Testament, would be regarded by all critics as indisputable evidence of the pre-existence of such books. Comp. Cowles, The Revelation of John, p. 22; Glasgow, The Apocalypse, Translated and Expounded, pp. 29, 30.

[2] Comp. Riehm, Messianic Prophecy, pp. 164-166. Edinb., 1876.

admits of no temple, and no light of sun and moon, for the Lord
God, the Almighty, and the Lamb are its light and its temple
(Rev. xxi, 22, 23). Moreover, no cherubim appear within this Holy
of Holies, for these former symbols of redeemed humanity are now
supplanted by the innumerable company of Adam's race, from
whom the curse (κατάθεμα, Rev. xxii, 3) has been removed, and
who take their places about the throne of God and of the Lamb,
act as his servants there, behold his face, and have his name upon
their foreheads (Rev. xxii, 3, 4).[1]

The New Jerusalem, then, is the apocalyptic portraiture of the
New Testament Church and Kingdom of God. Its symbolism exhibits the heavenly nature of the communion and fellowship of God
and his people, which is entered here by faith, but which opens
into unspeakable fulness of glory through ages of ages.

There is room for differences of opinion in the interpretation of
particular passages and symbols in all the apocalyptic Scriptures.
But attention to their general harmonies, and a careful study of
the scope and outline of each prophecy as a whole, will go far to
save us from the hopeless confusion and contradiction into which
many by neglecting this method have fallen.

We are now prepared to note the unity and harmony of New
Summary of Testament apocalyptics. There is no contradiction be-
New Testa- tween the teachings of Jesus, the Epistles of Paul, and
ment Apoca- the Apocalypse of John, touching the end of the age
lyptics and Es- and the coming of the Lord. They all agree that the
chatology.
end was near at hand, and that the Lord would come in his kingdom before that generation should pass away. It is further evident that the coming of Christ is pre-millennial, for it is the formal
assumption of the dominion and power and judgment which he will
exercise until he has put all enemies under his feet. The modern
Chiliasts have done the Church an excellent service in calling attention to this great fact. But their error is in making that coming yet
future, whereas Jesus affirmed that it would take place before some
of those who heard him speak should taste of death. The post-
millenarians, on the other hand, err in confounding the parousia
with the mysteries of that final hour when Christ shall give over
the kingdom to the Father, and God shall be all in all. Between
these two events the Messianic æon intervenes. Its beginning was
like the little mustard-seed, or like the stone cut out of the mountain without hands, but it grows, and rolls on, and will increase until
it becomes a great mountain and fills all the earth. Its history and

---

[1] Compare the exposition of the symbolism of the tabernacle and its services on
pp. 359-368, above.

triumphs are still mainly in the future, and centuries will probably elapse before it reaches fulness of development. When the Christ shall have put down all other enemies he will finally abolish death. At that hour "all who are in the tombs shall hear his voice, and shall come forth; those who did good unto a resurrection of life, and those who wrought evil unto a resurrection of damnation" (John v, 28). This resurrection is associated with the last judgment (Rev. xx, 12–15). The final manifestation of the Christ, when he shall have completed the work of redemption, and delivers over the kingdom to the Father, is left by the sacred writers in too great mystery for us to affirm definitely any thing concerning it.

CHAPTER XXVII.

NO DOUBLE SENSE IN PROPHECY.

THE hermeneutical principles which we have now set forth necessarily exclude the doctrine that the prophecies of Scripture contain an occult or double sense. It has been alleged by some that as these oracles are heavenly and divine we should expect to find in them manifold meanings. They must needs differ from other books. Hence has arisen not only the doctrine of a double sense, but of a threefold and fourfold sense, and the rabbis went so far as to insist that there are "mountains of sense in every word of Scripture." We may readily admit that the Scriptures are capable of manifold practical *applications;* otherwise they would not be so useful for doctrine, correction, and instruction in righteousness (2 Tim. iii, 16). But the moment we admit the principle that portions of Scripture contain an occult or double sense we introduce an element of uncertainty in the sacred volume, and unsettle all scientific interpretation. "If the Scripture has more than one meaning," says Dr. Owen, "it has no meaning at all." "I hold," says Ryle, "that the words of Scripture were intended to have one definite sense, and that our first object should be to discover that sense, and adhere rigidly to it. . . . To say that words *do* mean a thing merely because they *can* be tortured into meaning it is a most dishonourable and dangerous way of handling Scripture."[1] "This scheme of interpretation," says Stuart, "forsakes and sets aside the common

Theory of a double sense unsettles all sound interpretation.

[1] Expository Thoughts on St. Luke, vol. i, p. 388.

laws of language. The Bible excepted, in no book, treatise, epistle, discourse, or conversation, ever written, published, or addressed
by any one man to his fellow beings (unless in the way of sport,
or with an intention to deceive), can a double sense be found. There
are, indeed, charades, enigmas, phrases with a *double entente*, and
the like, perhaps, in all languages; there have been abundance of
heathen oracles which were susceptible of two interpretations; but
even among all these there never has been, and there never was a
design that there should be, .but one sense or meaning in reality.
Ambiguity of language may be, and has been, designedly resorted
to in order to mislead the reader or hearer, or in order to conceal
the ignorance of soothsayers, or to provide for their credit amid
future exigencies; but this is quite foreign to the matter of a serious and *bona fide* double meaning of words. Nor can we for a moment, without violating the dignity and sacredness of the Scriptures,
suppose that the inspired writers are to be compared to the authors
of riddles, conundrums, enigmas, and ambiguous heathen oracles." [1]

Some writers have confused this subject by connecting it with
Typology and
double sense of
language not
to be con-
founded. the doctrine of type and antitype. As many persons
and events of the Old Testament were types of greater
ones to come, so the language respecting them is supposed to be capable of a double sense. The second
Psalm has been supposed to refer both to David and Christ, and
Isa. vii, 14–16, to a child born of a virgin who lived in the time of
the prophet, and also to the Messiah. Psalms xlv and lxxii have
been supposed to have a double reference to Solomon and Christ, and
the prophecy against Edom in Isa. xxxiv, 5–10, to comprehend also
the general judgment of the last day. [2] But it should be seen that
in the case of types the language of the Scripture has no double
sense. The types themselves are such because they prefigure
things to come, and this fact must be kept distinct from the question of the sense of language used in any particular passage. We
have shown above (pp. 399, 400) that the language of Psa. ii is not
applicable to David or Solomon, or any other earthly ruler. The
same may be said of Psalms xlv and lxxii. Isa. vii, 14 was fulfilled
in the birth of Jesus Christ (Matt. i, 22), and no expositor has ever
been able to prove a previous fulfilment. [3] The oracle against Edom

---

[1] Hints on the Interpretation of Prophecy, p. 14. Andover, 1842.

[2] See Davidson's Hermeneutics, pp. 49, 50. Woodhouse on the Apocalypse, pp.
172–174. Horne, Introduction, vol. ii, pp. 404–408.

[3] It is not impossible, however, that such an event occurred in the days of Ahaz,
and served, in its way, as a type of the birth of Jesus from the Virgin Mary. But
upon this supposition the language of the passage would have no double sense, and

(Isa. xxxiv, 5-10), like that against Babylon (Isa. xii), is clothed in the highly wrought language of apocalyptic prophecy, and gives no warrant to the theory of a double sense. The twenty-fourth of Matthew, so commonly relied on to support this theory, has been already shown to furnish no valid evidence of either an occult or a double sense.

Some plausibility is given to the theory by adducing the suggestive fulness of some parts of the prophetic Scrip- The suggestive fulness of Scripture no proof of a double sense. tures. Such fulness is readily admitted, and ever to be extolled. The first prophecy is a good example. The enmity between the seed of the woman and that of the serpent (Gen. iii, 15) has been exhibited in a thousand forms. The precious words of promise to God's people find more or less fulfilment in every individual experience. But these facts do not sustain the theory of a double sense. The sense in every case is direct and simple; the applications and illustrations are many. Such facts give no authority for us to go into apocalyptic prophecies with the expectation of finding two or more meanings in each specific statement, and then to declare: This verse refers to an event long past, this to something yet future; this had a partial fulfilment in the ruin of Babylon, or Edom, but it awaits a grander fulfilment in the future. The judgment of Babylon, or Nineveh, or Jerusalem, may, indeed, be a type of every other similar judgment, and is a warning to all nations and ages; but this is very different from saying that the language in which that judgment was predicted was fulfilled only partially when Babylon, or Nineveh, or Jerusalem fell, and is yet awaiting its complete fulfilment.

We have already seen that the Bible has its riddles, enigmas, and dark sayings, but whenever they are given the context clearly advises us of the fact. To assume, in the absence of any hint, that we have an enigma, and in the face of explicit statements to the contrary, that any specific prophecy has a double sense, a primary and a secondary meaning, a near and a remote fulfilment, must necessarily introduce an element of uncertainty and confusion into biblical interpretation.

The same may be said about explicit designations of time. When a writer says that an event will shortly and speedily come No misleading designations of time in prophecy. to pass, or is about to take place, it is contrary to all propriety to declare that his statements allow us to believe the event is in the far future. It is a reprehensible abuse of language to say that the words *immediately*, or *near at hand*, mean

its fulfilment in the birth of Jesus would be like the fulfilment of Hosea xi, 1 in the return of the child Jesus out of Egypt.

ages hence, or *after a long time.* Such a treatment of the language
of Scripture is even worse than the theory of a double sense. And
yet interpreters have appealed to 2 Peter iii, 8 as furnishing inspired authority to disregard designations of time in prophecy.
"Let not this one thing be hid from you, beloved, that one day
with the Lord is as a thousand years, and a thousand years as one
day." This statement, it is urged, is made with direct reference to
the time of the Lord's coming, and illustrates the arithmetic of
God, in which *soon*, *quickly*, and similar terms may denote ages.
A careful attention to this passage, however, will show that it
teaches no such strange doctrine as this.

The language in question is a poetical citation from Psa. xc, 4,
A thousand and is adduced to show that the lapse of time does not
years as one invalidate the promises of God. Whatever he has
day.   pledged will come to pass, however men may think
or talk about his tardiness. Days and years and ages do not affect
him. From everlasting to everlasting he is God (Psa. xc, 2).
But this is very different from saying that when the everlasting
God promises something *shortly*, and declares that it is *close at
hand*, he may mean that it is a thousand years in the future.
Whatever he has promised indefinitely he may take a thousand
years or more to fulfil; but what he affirms to be at the door let no
man declare to be far away. "It is surely unnecessary," says a
recent writer, "to repudiate in the strongest manner such a non-
natural method of interpreting the language of Scripture. It is
worse than ungrammatical and unreasonable, it is immoral. It is
to suggest that God has two weights and two measures in his dealings with men, and that in his mode of reckoning there is an ambiguity and variableness which makes it impossible to tell what
manner of time the Spirit of Christ in the prophets may signify.
It seems to imply that a day may not mean a day, nor a thousand
years a thousand years, but that either may mean the other. If
this were so, there could be no interpretation of prophecy possible;
it would be deprived of all precision, and even of all credibility;
for it is manifest that if there could be such ambiguity and uncertainty in respect to *time*, there might be no less ambiguity and uncertainty in respect to every thing else. . . . Faithfulness is one
of the attributes most frequently ascribed to the covenant-keeping
God, and the divine *faithfulness* is that which the apostle in this
very passage affirms. To the taunt of the scoffers who impugn the
faithfulness of God, and ask, 'Where is the promise of his coming?' he answers, 'the Lord is not slack concerning his promises as
some men count slackness.' Long or short, a day or an age, does

not affect his faithfulness. He keepeth truth forever. But the apostle does not say that when the Lord promises a thing for *to-day* he may not fulfil his promise for a thousand years: *that would be slackness;* that would be a breach of promise. He does not say that because God is infinite and everlasting, therefore he reckons with a different arithmetic from ours, or speaks to us in a double sense, or uses two different weights and measures in his dealings with mankind. The very reverse is the truth." [1]

As an illustration of the fallacious and confusing theory of a double sense, especially when applied to prophetic des- *Fallacies of* ignations of time, witness tue following from Bengel. *Bengel's theory of prophet-* Commenting on the words, "Immediately after the *ic perspective.* tribulation of those days," in Matt. xxiv, 29, he says: "You will say it is a great leap from the destruction of Jerusalem to the end of the world which is subjoined to it *immediately.* I reply, a prophecy resembles a landscape painting which represents distinctly the houses, paths, and bridges in the foreground, but brings together, into a narrow space, most widely severed valleys and mountains in the distance. Such a view should they who study prophecy have of the future to which the prophecy refers. And the eyes of the disciples, who in their question had connected the end of the temple with that of the world, are left somewhat in the dark (for it was not yet time to know, ver. 36); hence they afterward, with entire harmony, imitated the Lord's language, and declared that the end was at hand. By advancing, however, both the prophecy and the prospect continually reveal a further and still further distance. In this manner also we ought to interpret, not the clear by the obscure, but the obscure by the clear, and to revere in its dark sayings the divine wisdom which sees all things always, but does not reveal all things at once. Afterward it was revealed that antichrist should come before the end of the world; and again Paul joined these two things closely, until the Apocalypse placed even millenniums between. On such passages there rests, as St. Anthony used to call it, a *prophetical cloudlet.* It was not yet time to reveal the whole series of future events from the destruction of Jerusalem to the end of the world." [2]

Here, we may say, are almost as many fallacies, or misleading statements, as there are sentences. The figure of a land- *As many falla-* scape painting with its principles of perspective is a *cies as sen-* favourite illustration with those expositors who advo- *tences.*

[1] The Parousia, pp. 221-223.
[2] Gnomon of the New Testament, in loco. Lewis and Vincent's translation. Philadelphia, 1860.

eate the theory of a double sense, and some, who reject such theory, employ this figure to illustrate the uncertainty of prophetic designations of time. But it is a great error to apply this illustration to *specific* designations of time. Where no particular time is indicated, or where time-limitations are kept out of view, the figure may be allowed, and is, indeed, a happy illustration. But when the Lord says that certain events are to follow *immediately after* certain other events, let no interpreter presume to say that millenniums may come between. This is not "to interpret the obscure by the clear," but to obscure the clear by a misleading fancy. To say that "the eyes of the disciples were left in the dark," and that they afterward, "imitating the Lord's language, declared that the end was at hand," is virtually equivalent to saying that Jesus misled them, and that they went forth and perpetuated the error! The notion that any portion of Scripture "reveals the whole series of events from the destruction of Jerusalem to the end of the world," is a fancy of modern interpreters, who would all do well, like the pious Bengel, to confess that over their forced method of explaining the statements of Christ and the apostles there truly rests an obscuring "prophetical cloudlet."

There are, indeed, manifold applications of certain prophecies Practical applications of prophecy may be many. which may be called generic, and some events of modern history may illustrate them, and, in a broad sense, fulfil them as truly as the events to which they had original reference. In the days of John many antichrists had appeared (1 John ii, 18; comp. Matt. xxiv, 5, 24), and the demoniacal attributes of Paul's "man of sin" (2 Thess. ii, 3-8) may appear again and again in monsters of lawlessness and crime. Antiochus and Nero are definite typical illustrations in whom great prophecies were specifically fulfilled, but other similar impersonations of wickedness may also have revealed the beast from the abyss, which was, and then, after disappearing for a time, appeared again, and then again went into perdition (Rev. xvii, 8). But such allowable applications of prophecy are not to be confounded with grammaticohistorical interpretation. When Satan shall be loosed out of his prison after the millennium (Rev. xx, 7) he may, indeed, reveal himself in some man of sin more fearful and more lawless far than any Antiochus or Nero of the past.

It may, in truth, be said that a large proportion of the confusion and errors of biblical expositors has arisen from mistaken notions of the Bible itself.[1] No such confusion and diversity of views ap-

---

[1] This thought is made prominent in Hofman's valuable work, Biblische Hermeneutik. Nordlingen, 1880.

pear in the interpretation of other books. A strained and unnatural theory of divine inspiration has, doubtless, led many into the habit of assuming that somehow the Scriptures must be explained differently from other compositions. Hence, also, the assumption that in prophetic revelations God has furnished us with a detailed historical Mistaken notions of the Bible itself the cause of much false exposition. outline of particular occurrences ages in advance, so that we may properly expect to find such events as the rise of Islam, the Wars of the Roses, and the French Revolution recorded in the prophetical books. This assumption is often found attaching itself to the theory of a double or triple sense. The interpretation of the Apocalypse of John has especially suffered from this singular error. There is such a charm in the fancy that we have a New Testament prophecy of the events of all coming time—a graphic outline of the history of the Church and the world until the final judgment— that not a few have yielded to the delusion that we may reasonably search this mystic book for any character or event which we deem important in the history of human civilization.[1]

We must set aside these false assumptions touching the Bible itself, and the character and purport of its prophecies. A rational investigation of the scope and analogies of the great prophecies gives no support to such extravagant fancies as that "the whole Apocalypse of John, from chapter iv to the end, is but a development of Daniel's imperfect tense."[2] The Holy Scriptures have lessons for all time. God's specific revelation to one individual, age, or nation will be found to have a practical value for all men. We need no specific predictions of Napoleon, or of the Waldenses, or of the martyrdom of John Huss, or of the massacre of St. Bartholomew to confirm the faith of the Church, or to convince the infidel; else, doubtless, we should have had them in a form capable of producing conviction. It cannot be shown that such predictions would have accomplished any worthy purpose not already met by fulfilled prophecies with their practical lessons of universal application.

[1] A friend of the writer once observed: It always seemed strange to me that Babylon, and Persia, and Greece, and Rome, and European states should be noticed in the prophecies, and yet no mention of the United States of America. He, accordingly, set himself to work to find something on the subject, and by and by discovered the great North American Republic in the fifth kingdom of Daniel—the stone cut out of the mountain without hands. Further research in the same line soon enabled him to see that the "war in heaven" between Michael and the dragon (Rev. xii, 7) was a specific prophecy of the late civil war between the Northern and Southern States, which resulted in the abolition of American slavery.

[2] Pre-Millennial Essays of the Prophetic Conference, p. 326. New York, 1879.

CHAPTER XXVIII.

SCRIPTURE QUOTATIONS IN THE SCRIPTURES.

IN comparing Scripture with Scripture, and tracing the parallel and analogous passages of the several sacred writers, the interpreter continually meets with quotations, more or less exact, made by one writer from another. These quotations may be distributed into **Four classes of quotations.** four classes: (1) Old Testament parallel passages and quotations made by the later writers from the earlier books; (2) New Testament quotations from the Old Testament; (3) New Testament quotations from New Testament sources; and (4) quotations from apocryphal writings and oral tradition. The verbal variations of many of these citations, the formulas and methods of quotation, and the illustrations they furnish of the purposes and uses of the Holy Scriptures, are all matters of great importance to the biblical exegete.

As examples of each of these classes of citations we mention, **Examples of Scripture quotations and parallels.** first, genealogical tables, as Gen. xi, 10–26, compared with 1 Chron. i, 17–27, and Gen. xlvi compared with Num. xxvi. Psa. xviii is substantially identical with 2 Sam. xxii. The same is true of 2 Kings xviii–xx and Isa. xxxvi–xxxix, 2 Kings xxiv, xxv, and Jer. lii. Large portions of the Books of Samuel and Kings are appropriated in the Books of Chronicles, and there are numerous textual parallels like Psa. xlii, 7, and Jonah ii, 3. The New Testament quotations from the Old Testament are manifold in character and form. In most cases they are taken *verbatim*, or nearly so, from the Septuagint version; in some instances they are a translation of the Hebrew text, more accurate than that of the Septuagint (Matt. ii, 15, compared with Heb. and Sept. of Hos. xi, 1; Matt. viii, 17, comp. Isa. liii, 4). Some of the quotations differ notably both from the Hebrew and the Septuagint, while others were apparently constructed by a use of both sources. Sometimes several passages of the Old Testament are blended together, as in 2 Cor. vi, 16–18, where use is made of Exod. xxix, 45; Lev. xxvi, 12; Isa. lii, 11; Jer. xxxi, 1, 9, 33; xxxii, 38; Ezek. xi, 20; xxxvi, 28; xxxvii, 27; Zech. viii, 8. Sometimes the Old Testament passage is merely paraphrased, or the general sentiment or substance is given, while in other cases it is merely referred to or hinted at (comp. Prov. xviii, 4; Isa. xii, 3; xliv, 3, with John vii, 38. Isa. lx, 1-3, with Eph. v, 14. Hos. xiv, 2, with Heb. xiii, 15).[1] In the New Testament it is evident that the many parallel portions of the Gospels must have been derived from some common source, either oral or written, or both. In Acts xx, 35, Paul quotes a saying of the Lord which is to be found nowhere else. Peter evinces a knowledge of the epistles of Paul (2 Pet. iii, 15, 16), and in the second chapter of his second epistle appropriates much from the Epistle of Jude. Finally, the quotations from apocry- phal and other sources, and allusions to them, both in the Old Testament and in the New, are quite numerous.

Apocryphal and traditional sources.

Thus, in the Old Testament we have "The Book of the Wars of the Lord" (Num. xxi, 14), "The Book of Jasher" (Josh. x, 13), "The Book of the Acts of Solomon" (1 Kings xi, 41), "The Book of Shemaiah" (2 Chron. xii, 15), and numerous others quoted or referred to. Jude quotes apparently from the pseudepigraphal Book of Enoch, and also makes allusion to traditions of the fall of the angels, and the dispute of Michael and the devil over the body of Moses (Jude 6, 9, 14). St. Paul calls the magicians, who opposed Moses, Jannes and·Jambres (2 Tim. iii, 8), names which had probably been transmitted by oral tradition. Many such traditions found their way into the Targums, the Talmud, and the apocryphal and pseudepigraphal Jewish literature. Quotations from such books and allusions to such traditions give them no canonical authority. An apostle or any one else, addressing those who were familiar with such traditions, might appropriately refer to them for homiletical purposes, without thereby designing to assume or declare their verity. Similarly Paul quotes from the Greek poets Aratus, Menander, and Epimenides (Acts xvii, 28; 1 Cor. xv, 33; Titus i, 12).

The great number of parallel passages, both in the Old Testament and in the New, is evidence of a harmony and organic relation of Scripture with Scripture of a most notable kind. Once written, the oracles of God became the public and private treasure of his people. Any passage that would serve a useful purpose was used by prophet

---

[1] See Drusius, Parallela Sacra, etc., in vol. viii of the Critici Sacri, pp. 1261-1325; Davidson, Sacred Hermeneutics, chap. xi; Gough, New Testament Quotations Collated with the Old Testament (Lond., 1853); Horne's Introduction (Ayers and Tregelles' Ed.), vol. ii, pp. 113-207; and especially Turpie, The Old Testament in the New; A Contribution to Biblical Criticism and Interpretation. Lond., 1868. This last-named work conveniently classifies and tabulates the Old Testament quotations in the New Testament according to their agreement with, or variation from, both the Hebrew text and the Septuagint version. Comp. also Scott, Principles of New Testament Quotation established and applied to Biblical Science (Edinb., 1875), and Boehl, Die alttestamentlichen Citate im neuen Testament. Wien, 1878.

or apostle as part of a common heritage. With this understanding, there is little in the matter or style of the Scripture quotations in the Scriptures to give any trouble to the interpreter.

Only the O. T. quotations in the N.T. call for special hermeneutical treatment. The comparison of parallel passages is, as we have seen (pp. 221–230), a great help in exposition, and some passages become clear and forcible only when read in the light of their parallels. The alleged discrepancies between these different Scriptures will be noticed in a separate chapter; it is only the Old Testament citations in the New Testament which call for special treatment here. These, as we have said, are so manifold in character and form that we should examine (1) the sources of quotation, (2) the formulas and methods of quotation, and (3) the purposes of the several quotations.

I. It is now generally conceded that the sources from which the *Sources of N.T. quotation.* New Testament writers quote are the Hebrew text of the Old Testament, and the Septuagint translation of it. Formerly it was maintained by some that the Septuagint only was used; others, feeling that such a position was disparaging to the Hebrew Scriptures, maintained as strenuously that the apostles and evangelists must have always cited from the Hebrew, and though the quotations were in the exact words of the Septuagint, it was thought that two translators might have used the same language. But calmer study has made all such discussions obsolete. It is well known that the Septuagint version was in current use among the Hellenistic Jews. The New Testament writers follow it in some passages where it differs widely from the Hebrew. A critical comparison of all the New Testament citations from the Old shows beyond a question that in the great majority of cases the Septuagint rather than the Hebrew text was the source from which the writers quoted.[1]

But it is noticeable that the New Testament writers do not uniformly follow either source. The Septuagint version *No uniform method of quotation.* of Mal. iii, 1, is an accurate translation of the Hebrew, but Matthew, Mark, and Luke agree literally in a rendering which is noticeably different.[2] In short, it is impossible to discover any rule that will account for all the variations between the citations and the Hebrew and Septuagint texts. Sometimes the

---

[1] See Horne's Introduction, vol. ii, pp. 114–178, where the Hebrew, the Septuagint version, and the New Testament citation of all the Old Testament quotations in the New, are given in the original texts, arranged in parallel columns, and each accompanied by an English version.

[2] Matt. xi, 10; Mark i, 10; Luke vii, 27. Matthew inserts ἐγώ, and Mark omits ἔμπροσθέν σου.

variation is merely a change of person, number, or tense; sometimes it consists of a transposition of words; sometimes in the omission or addition of words and phrases. In many cases only the general sense is given, and often the citation is but an allusion or reference, not a formal quotation at all. In view of all these facts it seems best to understand that the sacred writers followed no uniform method in quoting the older Scriptures. They were familiar both with the Hebrew text and the Septuagint. But textual accuracy had no special weight with them. From childhood the contents of the sacred writings had been publicly and privately made known to them (2 Tim. iii, 15), and they were wont to cite them in familiar discourse without any attempt at verbal accuracy. With them as with us an inaccurate quotation might become common and current on the lips of the people, and, while known by many to differ from the ancient text, was nevertheless sufficiently correct for all practical purposes. How few of us now recite the Lord's prayer accurately? So, doubtless, the inspired writers made use of Scripture, in many instances, without care to conform the quotation with the exact letter of the Hebrew text, or of the common Septuagint version. They quoted probably in most cases from memory, and the Holy Spirit preserved them from any vital error (John xiv, 26). The idea that divine inspiration must necessitate verbal uniformity among the sacred writers is an unnecessary and untenable assumption.[1] Variety marked both the portions and manner of the successive revelations of God (Heb. i, 1).

II. The introductory formulas by which quotations from the Old Testament are adduced are many and various, and have been thought by some to be a sort of index or key to the particular purpose of each citation. But we find different formulas used by different writers to introduce one and the

Inaccurate quotations may become current.

Formulas and methods of quotation.

---

[1] "In examining cited passages, we perceive," says Davidson, "that every mode of quotation has been employed, from the exactest to the most loose, from the strictest verbal method to the widest paraphrase. But in no case is violence done to the meaning of the original. A sentiment expressed in one connexion in the Old Testament is frequently in the New interwoven with another train of argument; but this is allowable and natural. . . . Let it be remembered, then, that the sacred writers were not bound in all cases to cite the very words of the originals; it was usually sufficient for them to exhibit the sense perspicuously. The same meaning may be conveyed by different terms. It is unreasonable to expect that the apostles should scrupulously abide by the precise words of the passage they quote. . . . In every instance we suppose them to have been directed by the superintending Spirit, who infallibly kept them from error, and guided them in selecting the most appropriate terms where their own judgments would have failed."—Sacred Hermeneutics, pp. 469, 470.

same passage, so that we cannot suppose that in all cases the formula used will direct us to the special purpose of the quotation. The more usual formulas are, "It is written," "Thus it is written," "According as it is written," "The Scripture says," "It was said," "According as it is said;" but many other forms are used. The same formulas are used by the Rabbinical writers,[1] and there is every reason to believe that they exhibit a common usage of our Lord's time. There was no division of chapters and verses to facilitate reference. Occasionally the place of a citation is indicated, as in Mark xii, 26; Acts xiii, 33; and Rom. xi, 2; but more frequently Moses, the Law, Isaiah, Jeremiah, or some other prophet is

[1] The following list exhibits in parallel columns the resemblance between the New Testament and Rabbinical formulas:

New Testament.	Rabbinical.
καθὼς γέγραπται, οὕτω γέγραπται, γέγραπται, γεγραμμένον ἐστί, κατὰ τὸ γέγραμμένον.	כדכתיב, דכתיב, וכתיב.
καθὼς εἴρηται, κατὰ τὸ εἰρημένον.	שנאמר
ἐρρέθη.	איתמר.
ἐρρέθη τοῖς ἀρχαίοις.	קדמאין אמרו, זקנים (ראשונים) אמרו etc.
λέγει ἡ γραφή, εἶπε ἡ γραφή.	אמר קרא, or אמר הכתוב.
τί γὰρ λέγει ἡ γραφή; τί οὖν ἐστι τὸ γεγραμμένον; πῶς γέγραπται; οὐκ ἐστι γεγραμμένον;	מי כתיב, מאי דכתיב, etc.
διὸ λέγει.	מעלה עליו הכתוב.
διότε περιέχει ἐν τῇ γραφῇ.	הכתיב, or מקרא מסייעו.
βλέπετε τὸ εἰρημένον.	ראה מה כתיב.
πῶς ἀναγινώσκεις;	מאי קראת.
προϊδοῦσα ἐδ ἡ γραφή.	מה ראה הכתוב, etc.
καὶ πάλιν λέγει, καὶ πάλιν, πάλιν γέγραπται, καὶ ἐν τούτῳ πάλιν, καὶ ἐν τούτῳ λέγει, καὶ πάλιν ἐτέρα γραφὴ λέγειν.	כתיב הכא וכתיב התם, כתיב וכתיב, אומר ועוד, שנאמרוכתיב בהריה, etc.
ὁ λόγος γεγραμμένος ἐν τῷ νόμῳ αὐτῶν.	דבר תורה, or כתוב בתורה.
ὁ νόμος ἔλεγεν.	התורה אמרה.
αὐτὸς γὰρ Δαβὶδ εἶπεν.	כן אמר דוד.
ἵνα πληρωθῇ ἡ γραφή, or τὸ ῥηθὲν διὰ τοῦ προφήτου.	לקיים מה שנאמר.
ἐπληρώθη ἡ γραφή.	זה קיים מה שכתיב.

"It is impossible," says Davidson, from whom the above list is taken, "for any unprejudiced reader to observe the coincidence between the New Testament and Rabbinical formulas just given without believing that the one class was influenced and modified by the other. When we recollect that the writers were Jews, and that their modes of conception and speech were essentially Jewish, we are led to expect in their compositions a large assimilation to current phraseology."—Sacred Hermeneutics, pp. 449, 450. Many other examples are given by Surenhusius, ספר המשוה, sive Βίβλος Καταλλαγῆς, pp. 1–36; and by Döpke, Hermeneutik, pp. 60–69.

mentioned as writing or saying what is quoted. It is assumed that the persons addressed were so familiar with the holy writings that they needed no more specific reference.

"Besides the quotations introduced by these formulas there are a considerable number scattered through the writings of the apostles which are inserted in the train of their own remarks without any announcement whatever of their being cited from others. To the cursory reader the passages thus quoted appear to form a part of the apostle's own words, and it is only by intimate acquaintance with the Old Testament Scriptures, and a careful comparison of these with those of the New Testament, that the fact of their being quotations can be detected. In the common version every trace of quotation is in many of these passages lost, from the circumstance that the writer has closely followed the Septuagint, while our version of the Old Testament is made from the Hebrew. Thus, for instance, in 2 Cor. viii, 21,· Paul says, προνοοῦμεν γὰρ καλὰ οὐ μόνον ἐνώπιον Κυρίου, ἀλλὰ καὶ ἐνώπιον ἀνθρώπων, which, with a change in the mood of the verb, is a citation of the Septuagint version of Prov. iii, 4. Hardly any trace of this, however, appears in the common version, where the one passage reads, "Providing for honest things not only in the sight of the Lord, but also in the sight of men;" and the other, "So shalt thou find favour and good understanding in the sight of God and man." So, also, in 1 Peter iv, 18, the apostle quotes word for word from the Septuagint version of Prov. xi, 31, the clause εἰ ὁ δίκαιος μόλις σώζεται, ὁ ἀσεβὴς καὶ ἁμαρτωλὸς ποῦ φανεῖται; a quotation which we should in vain endeavour to trace in the common version of the Proverbs, where the passage in question is rendered "Behold, the righteous shall be recompensed in the earth; much more the wicked and the sinner." Such quotations evidently show how much the minds of the New Testament writers were imbued with the sentiments and expressions of the Old Testament as exhibited in the Alexandrine version." [1]

There is one formula peculiar to Matthew and John which deserves more than a passing notice. It first occurs in Matt. i, 22: "*All this has come to pass in order. that what was spoken by the Lord through the prophet might be fulfilled.*" This is its fullest form; elsewhere it is only ἵνα πληρωθῇ, *in order that it might be fulfilled* (Matt. ii, 15; iv, 14; xxi, 4; John xii, 38; xiii, 18; xv, 25; xvii, 12; xviii, 9, 32; xix, 24, 36), but in John's Gospel these words vary in their connexion, as, "in order that the word of Isaiah might be fulfilled;" "in order that the Scripture might be fulfilled;" "in order that the word of Jesus

The formula ἵνα πληρωθῇ.

---

[1] Alexander, in Kitto's New Cyclopædia of Biblical Literature, article Quotations.

might be fulfilled." Sometimes it is written ὅπως πληρωθῇ (Matt. ii, 23; viii, 17; xii, 17), and occasionally τότε ἐπληρώθη, *then was fulfilled.* The great question with interpreters has been to determine the force of the conjunction ἵνα (and ὅπως) in these formulas. Is it *telic*, that is, expressive of *final cause, purpose*, or *design ;* or is it *ecbatic*, denoting merely the *outcome* or *result* of something? If telic, it should be translated *in order that ;* if ecbatic, it should be rendered *so that.*

Bengel, commenting on the words ἵνα πληωθῇ in Matt. i, 22, ob-
Views of Bengel and Meyer.
serves: "Wherever this phrase occurs we are bound to recognise the authority of the evangelists, and (however dull our own perception may be) to believe that the event they mention does not merely chance to correspond with some ancient form of speech, but was one which had been predicted, and which the divine truth was pledged to bring to pass at the commencement of the new dispensation."[1] Meyer, commenting on the same passage, observes: "ἵνα is never ecbatic, *so that*, but always telic, *in order that ;* it presupposes here that what was done stood in the connexion of purpose with the Old Testament declaration, and consequently in the connexion of the divine necessity as an actual fact by which the prophecy was destined to be fulfilled. The divine decree, expressed in the latter, must be accomplished, and to that end *this*, namely, which is related from verse 18 onward, *came to pass*, and that, according to the whole of its contents (ὅλον)."

This view of the telic force of ἵνα, especially in the words ἵνα
The telic force of ἵνα generally to be maintained.
πληρωθῇ in connexion with prophetic statements, is maintained by many of the most eminent critics and scholars, as Fritzsche, De Wette, Olshausen, Alford, and Winer. Others, as Tittmann, Stuart, and Robinson, contend for the ecbatic use of ἵνα in this phrase as well as in many other passages.[2] The question can be determined only by a critical examination of the passages where the alleged ecbatic use of the particle occurs. In most of these cases we believe the ordinary telic sense of ἵνα has been misapprehended by a superficial view of the real import of the passage. Thus Tittmann cites Mark xi, 25, as a clear instance of the ecbatic use of ἵνα: "Whenever ye stand praying, forgive, if ye have aught against any one, in order that your Father also who is in the heavens may forgive you your trespasses."

[1] Gnomon of the New Testament, in loco.
[2] See Tittmann's essay on the "Use of the particle ἵνα in the New Testament," translated into English with introductory remarks by M. Stuart in the Biblical Repository of Jan., 1835. Also Robinson's Lexicon of the New Testament under the words ἵνα and ὅπως.

According to Tittmann, "the Saviour could not inculcate on his disciples the mere prudential duty of forgiving others *in order that* they themselves might obtain forgiveness, which would be quite foreign to real integrity and purity of mind; but he wished them to consider that if they cherished an implacable spirit they could have no grounds to hope for pardon from God; so that if they themselves were not ready to forgive it was impossible that they should obtain forgiveness."[1] But this reasoning would exclude everywhere the telic force of *Ἵνα*. According to the writer's own admission, the forgiving of others is an indispensable condition of pardon; why not then regard this condition, as well as any other, in the light of a means to an end? Is it possible to believe that obtaining forgiveness from God is an object and aim at all inconsistent with "real integrity and purity of mind?" Much more soundly does Meyer give the real thought of the passage: "To the exhortation to confidence in prayer Jesus links on another principal requisite of being heard—namely, the necessity of forgiving in order to obtain forgiveness."[2] The forgiving is presented as an indispensable means to an end.

It need not, however, be denied that in some passages the ecbatic rendering of *Ἵνα* may bring out more clearly the sense of the author. The particle may be allowed some measure of its native telic import, and yet the final cause or end may be conceived of as an accomplished result or attainment rather than an objective ideal necessary to be reached.[3] The ecbatic sense of *Ἵνα* need not in all cases be denied.

Ellicott's position may be accepted as every way sound and satisfactory: "The uses of *Ἵνα* in the New Testament appear to be three: (1) *Final*, or indicative of the *end*, *purpose*, or *object* of the action —the primary and principal meaning, and never to be given up except on the most distinct counter arguments. (2) *Sub-final*, occasionally, especially after verbs of entreaty (not of command), the subject of the prayer being blended with, and even in some cases obscuring, the *purpose* of making it. (3) *Eventual*, or indicative of result, apparently in a few cases, and due, perhaps, more to what is called 'Hebrew teleology' (i. e., the reverential aspect under which the Jews regarded prophecy and its fulfilment) than grammatical depravation."[4]

---

[1] Biblical Repository for Jan., 1835, p. 105.

[2] Critical Commentary on Mark xi, 25.

[3] Comp. Winer's New Testament Grammar (English translation, Andover, 1874), pp. 457–461, and Buttmann's Grammar of the New Testament Greek (English translation, Andover, 1873), pp. 235–241.

[4] Critical and Grammatical Commentary on Ephesians i, 17.

But when the words *ἵνα πληρωθῇ* are used in connexion with the
fulfilment of prophecy we should not hesitate to accept
the telic force of *ἵνα*. The Scriptures themselves recognise a sort of divine necessity for the fulfilment of all
that predicted or typified the Christ. As it was necessary (*ἔδει*)
for the Christ to suffer (Luke xxiv, 26), so "it was necessary that
all things which were written in the law of Moses, and the Prophets,
and the Psalms concerning him should be fulfilled" (Luke xxiv, 44;
comp. the *ἔδει πληρωθῆναι* of Acts i, 16). The objection that it is
absurd to suppose all these things were done merely to fulfil a
prophecy is based upon a misconception and misrepresentation of the
evangelist. The statement that this particular divine purpose was
served does not imply that no other divine purpose was accom
plished. "All these things did transpire," says Whedon, "in order,
among other purposes, to the fulfilment of that prophecy, inasmuch
as the fulfilment of that prophecy was at the same time the accomplishment of the Incarnation of the Redeemer, and the verification
of the divine prediction. Nor is there any predestinarian fatalism
in all this. God predicts what he foresees that men will freely do;
and then men do freely in turn fulfil what God predicts, and so unconsciously act in order to verify God's veracity. Moreover there
is no fatalism in supposing that God has high plans which he does
with infinite wisdom carry out through the free, unnecessitated,
though foreseen wills of men. Such is his inconceivable wisdom
that he can so place free agents in a free system of probation that
which ever way they freely turn they will but further his great
generic plans and verify his foreknowledge. So that it may, in a
right sense, be true that all these things are done by free agents *in
order to* so desirable an end as to fulfil the divine foresight." [1]

Marginal note: ἵνα telic in formulas of prophetic citation.

The passage in Matt. ii, 15, has been thought by many to be a
certain instance of the ecbatic usage of *ἵνα*. It is there
written that Joseph arose and took the child Jesus and
his mother by night and withdrew into Egypt, and was
there until the death of Herod, "in order that (*ἵνα πληρωθῇ*) it
might be fulfilled which was spoken by the Lord through the
prophet, saying, Out of Egypt I called my son." The quotation is
a literal translation of the Hebrew of Hos xi, 1, and the reference
of the prophet is to Israel. The whole verse of Hos. xi, 1, reads
thus: "For a child was Israel, and I loved him, and out of Egypt I
called my son." Here some would see a double sense of prophecy,
and others an Old Testament text accommodated to a New Testament use. But the true interpretation of this quotation will recog-

Marginal note: Hosea xi, 1, as cited in Matt. ii, 15.

[1] Commentary on Matthew i, 22.

nise the typical character of Israel as "God's firstborn," a familiar thought of the Old Testament Scripture. Thus, in Exod. iv, 22, Jehovah is represented as saying: "My son, my firstborn, is Israel." And again in Jer. xxxi, 9; "For I have been to Israel for a father, and Ephraim is my firstborn." Compare also Isa. xlix, 3. Recognising this typical character of Israel as God's firstborn son, the evangelist readily perceived that the ancient exodus of Israel out of Egypt was a type of this event in the life of the Son of God while he was yet a child. Among the other purposes (and there were doubtless many) that were served by this going down into Egypt, and exodus therefrom, was the fulfilment of the prophecy of Hosea. This fulfilment of typical events, as we have shown above (p. 494), does not authorize the doctrine of a double sense in the language of prophecy. The words of Hosea xi, 1, have but one meaning, and announce in poetic form a fact of Israel's ancient history. That fact was a type which was fulfilled in the event recorded in Matt. ii, but the language used by the prophet had no previous fulfilment. It was not a prediction at all, but an allusion to an event which occured six hundred years before Hosea was born.[1]

III. It remains to notice the purposes for which any of the sacred writers quoted or referred to the more ancient Scriptures. Attention to this point will be an important aid in enabling us to understand and appreciate the various uses of the holy writings. *Purposes of Scripture quotation.*

1. The citation of many ancient prophecies was manifestly for the purpose of showing and putting on record their fulfilment. This is true of all the prophecies which are introduced with the formula *ἵνα πληρωθῇ, in order that it might be fulfilled.* And the same thought is implied in the context of quotations introduced by

___

[1] Lange (Commentary on Matthew ii, 15) has the following: "As the flight and the return had really taken place, the evangelist, whose attention was always directed to the fulfilment of prophecy, might very properly call attention to the fact that even this prediction of Hosea had been fulfilled. And, in truth, viewed not as a verbal but as a typical prophecy, this prediction was fulfilled by this flight into Egypt. Israel of old was called out of Egypt as the son of God, inasmuch as Israel was identified with the Son of God. But now the Son of God himself was called out of Egypt, who came out of Israel, as the kernel from the husk. When the Lord called Israel out of Egypt, it was with special reference to his Son; that is, in view of the high spiritual place which Israel was destined to occupy. In connexion with this it is also important to bear in mind the historical influence of Egypt on the world at large. Ancient Greek civilization—nay, in a certain sense, the imperial power of Rome itself —sprung from Egypt; in Egypt the science of Christian theology originated; from Egypt proceeded the last universal Conqueror; out of Egypt came the typical son of God to found the theocracy; and thence also the true Son of God to complete the theocracy."

other formulas. These facts exhibit the interdependence and organic connexion of the entire body of Holy Scripture. It is a divinely constructed whole, and the essential relations of its several parts must never be forgotten.

2. Other quotations are made for the purpose of establishing a doctrine. So Paul, in Rom. iii, 9–19, quotes the Scriptures to prove the universal depravity of man; and in Rom. iv, 3, he cites the record of Abraham's belief in God to show that a man is justified by faith rather than works, and that faith is imputed unto him for righteousness. This manner of his using the Old Testament obviously implies that the apostle and his readers regarded it as authoritative in its teachings. What was written therein, or could be confirmed thereby, was final, and must be accepted as the revelation of God.

3. Sometimes the Scripture is quoted for the purpose of confuting and rebuking opponents and unbelievers. Jesus himself appealed to his Jewish opponents on the ground of their regard for the Scriptures, and showed their inconsistency in refusing to receive him of whom the Scriptures so abundantly testified (John v, 39, 40). With those who accepted the Scripture as the word of God such argumentation was of great weight. How effectually Jesus employed it may be seen in his answers to the Sadducees and Pharisees (Matt. xxii, 29–32, 41–46). Compare John x, 34–36.

4. Finally, the Scriptures were cited or referred to in a general way as a book of divine authority, for rhetorical purposes, and for illustration. Its manifold treasures were the heritage of the people of God. Its language would be naturally appropriated to express any thought or idea which a writer or speaker might wish to clothe in sacred and venerable form. Hence the manners, references, allusions, and citations which serve mainly to enhance the force or beauty of a statement, and to illustrate some argument or appeal. "The writings of the Jewish prophets," says Horne, "which abound in fine, descriptions, poetical images, and sublime diction, were the classics of the later Jews; and, in subsequent ages, all their writers affected allusions to them, borrowed their images and descriptions, and very often cited their identical words when recording any event or circumstance that happened in the history of the persons whose lives they were relating, provided it was similar and parallel to one that occurred at the times, and was described in the books, of the ancient prophets."[1]

---

[1] Introduction to the Holy Scriptures, vol. ii, p. 191.

CHAPTER XXIX.

THE FALSE AND THE TRUE ACCOMMODATION.

INASMUCH as many passages of the Old Testament Scripture are appropriated by New Testament writers for the sake of illustration, or by way of special application, it has been held by many that all the Old Testament quotations, even the Messianic prophecies, have been applied in the New Testament in a sense differing more or less widely from their original import. This especially has been a position taken by many rationalists of Germany, and some have gone so far as to teach that our Lord accommodated himself to the prejudices of his age and people. His use of Scripture, they tell us, was of the nature of argument and appeal *ad hominem ;* even his words and acts in regard to unclean spirits of demons, and other matters of belief among the Jews, were a falling in line with the errors and superstitions of the common people.

Such a theory of accommodation should be utterly repudiated by the sober and thoughtful exegete. It virtually teaches that Jesus Christ was a propagator of falsehood. It would convict every New Testament writer of a species of mental and religious delusion. The divine Teacher did, indeed, accommodate his teaching to the capacity of his hearers, as every wise teacher will do; or, rather, he condescended to put himself on the plane of their limited knowledge. He would speak so that men might understand, and believe, and be saved. But in those who had no disposition to search and test his truth he declared that Isaiah's words (Isa. vi, 9, 10) received a new application, and a most significant fulfilment (Matt. xiii, 14, 15). And this was strictly true. Isaiah's words were first spoken to the dull and blinded hearts of the Israel of his own day. Ezekiel repeated them with equal propriety to the Israel of a later generation (Ezek. xii, 2). And our Lord quoted and applied them to the Israel of his time as one of those homiletic Scriptures which are fulfilled again and again in human history when the faculties of spiritual perception become perversely dull to the truths of God. The prophecy in question was not the prediction of a specific event, but a general oracle of God, and of such a nature as to be capable of repeated fulfilments.

Hence such prophecies afford no proof of a double sense. The
sense is in each instance simple· and direct, but the language is
capable of double or manifold applications.

And herein we observe a true sense in which the words of Scripture may be accommodated to particular occasions and
purposes. It is found in the manifold uses and applications of which the words of divine inspiration are capable. This is not, strictly speaking, a manifold *fulfilment* of Scripture, though it may be affirmed that a forcible and legitimate
application of a passage is truly a fulfilment of it. When a given
passage is of such a character as to be susceptible of application to
other circumstances or subjects than those to which it first applied,
such secondary application should not be denied the name of a fulfilment. In such a case we do not say: The first reference was to
an event near at hand, but that primary fulfilment did not exhaust
the meaning; its higher fulfilment is to be seen in a future event.
Much truth may attach to such a statement, but it is liable to mislead one, and to foster the idea of a hidden sense, a mystic meaning, a so-called hyponoia (ὑπόνοια). Thus the psalmist says: "I
will open my mouth in a parable; I will utter dark sayings of old"
(Psa. lxxviii, 2). This is quoted by Matthew (xiii, 35), the first
sentence according to the Septuagint, the second a free rendering
of the Hebrew, but following strictly neither the Hebrew nor the
Septuagint. The evangelist affirms that Jesus made use of parables
in order that these words might be fulfilled. And we are not at
liberty to deny that this was one real purpose of Jesus in the use of
parables. The words of the psalmist prophet herein found a new
and higher application, but in no different sense than that in which
they were first used.

The language of Jer. xxxi, 15, is quoted by Matthew (ii, 17, 18)
as being fulfilled in the weeping and lamentation occasioned by Herod's slaughter of the infants of Bethlehem. In the highest strain of poetical conception the
prophet Jeremiah sets forth the grief of Israel's woes and exile. It
seems to him as if the affectionate Rachel—the mother of the house
of Joseph, Ephraim and Manasseh (Gen. xxx, 24; xli, 51, 52), and
the mother of Benjamin (Gen. xxxv, 16–18), might be heard weeping and wailing at Ramah over the loss of her children. The
prophet mentions Ephraim (Jer. xxxi, 18, 20) as the chief tribe and
representative of all Israel. The tender mother's agony is over a
wider woe than the exile of Judah only. It takes in Ephraim's
overthrow and captivity as well. And Rachel, rather than Leah, is
named because of her great desire for children (Gen. xxx, 1), and

*The true idea
of accommoda-
tion.*

*Jer. xxxi, 15, as
cited in Matt.
ii, 17, 18.*

the touching and melancholy circumstances of her death (Gen. xxxv, 18). The weeping is represented as heard at Ramah, perhaps for various reasons. That city occupied a conspicuous eminence [1] in the tribe-territory of Benjamin, whence the lamentation might be conceived as sounding far and wide through all the coasts of Benjamin and Judah.[2] Ramah was the home of Hannah (the mother of Samuel, 1 Sam. i, 19, 20), whose motherly yearning was so much like that of Rachel.[3] It was at Ramah also where the Jewish exiles were gathered before their deportation to Babylon (Jer. xl, 1). The heart of Rachel, in the prophet's view, was large enough to feel and lament the woes of all the sons of Jacob. All this comes up to the evangelist when he pens the slaughter of the children of the coasts of Bethlehem (Matt. ii, 16). It seems to him as if the motherly heart of Rachel cried from the tomb again, and this later sorrow was but a repetition of that of the exile, the former sorrow being a type of the latter. And this was a fulfilment of that poetic prophecy, although it is not said that this sorrow of Bethlehem came to pass *in order to fulfil* the words of Jeremiah. By a true and legitimate accommodation the words of the prophet were appropriated by the evangelist as enhancing his record of that bitter woe. "By keeping in mind," says Davidson, "the close relation of type and antitype, whether the former be a person, as David, or an event, as the birth of a child, we shall not stumble at the manner in which certain quotations in the New Testament are introduced, nor have recourse to other modes of explanation which seem to be objectionable. We do not adopt, with some, the hypothesis of a double sense, to which there are weighty objections. Neither do we conceive that the principle of accommodation, in its mildest form, comes up to the truth. The passages containing typical prophecies have always a direct reference to facts or things in the history of the persons or people obviously spoken of in the context. But these facts or circumstances were typical of spiritual transactions in the history of the Saviour and his kingdom."[4]

[1] Robinson's Biblical Researches, vol. i, p. 576.

[2] Comp. Keil, Commentary on Jeremiah xxxi, 15.

[3] "The prophet goes back in spirit," says Nägelsbach, "to the time when the inhabitants of the kingdom of the ten tribes were led away to Assyria into captivity. . . . The mother of the ruling tribe appears thus as the personification of the kingdom ruled by it. The spirit of Rachel is the genius of the kingdom of the ten tribes whom the prophet represented by a bold poetical figure as rising from her tomb by night and bewailing the misery of her children."—Commentary on Jeremiah xxxi, 15.

[4] Sacred Hermeneutics, p. 488.

CHAPTER XXX.

ALLEGED DISCREPANCIES OF THE SCRIPTURES.

In comparing the Scriptures of the Old and New Testaments, and also in examining the statements of the different writers of either Testament, the reader's attention is occasionally arrested by what appear to be contradictions. Sometimes different passages of the same book present some noticeable inconsistency, but more frequently the statements made by different writers exhibit discrepancies which some critics have been hasty to pronounce irreconcilable. These discrepancies are found in the genealogical tables, and in various numerical, historical, doctrinal, ethical, and prophetical statements. It is the province of the interpreter of Scripture to examine these with great patience and care; he must not ignore any difficulty, but should be able to explain the apparent inconsistencies, not by dogmatic assertions or denials, but by rational methods of procedure. If he find a discrepancy or a contradiction which he is unable to explain he should not hesitate to acknowledge it. It does not follow that because he is not able to solve the problem it is therefore insoluble. The lack of sufficient data has often effectually baffled the efforts of the most able and accomplished exegetes.

General character of the discrepancies.

A large proportion of the discrepancies of the Bible are traceable to one or more of the following causes: The errors of copyists in the manuscripts; the variety of names applied to the same person or place; different methods of reckoning times and seasons; different local and historical standpoints; and the special scope and plan of each particular book. Variations are not contradictions, and many essential variations arise from different methods of arranging a series of particular facts. The peculiarities of oriental thought and speech often involve seeming extravagance of statement and verbal inaccuracies, which are of a nature to provoke the criticism of the less impassioned writers of the West. And it is but just to add that not a few of the alleged contradictions of Scripture exist only in the imagination of sceptical writers, and are to be attributed to the perverse misunderstanding of captious critics.

Causes of the discrepancies.

It is easy to perceive how, in the course of ages, numerous

little errors and discrepancies would be likely to find their way into
the text by reason of the oversight or carelessness of   Discrepancies
arising from
errors of copy-
ists.
transcribers. To this cause we attribute many of the
variations in orthography and in numerical statements.
The habit of expressing numbers by letters, several of which closely
resemble each other, was liable to occasion many discrepancies.
Sometimes the omission of a letter or a word occasions a difficulty
which cannot now be removed. Thus the only proper rendering of
the present Hebrew text of 1 Sam. xiii, 1, is, "Saul was a year old
(Hebrew, son of a year) when he began to reign, and two years he
reigned over Israel." The writer is here evidently following the
custom exhibited in 2 Sam. ii, 10; v, 4; 1 Kings xiv, 21; xxii, 42;
2 Kings viii, 26, of opening his account of a king's reign with a formal statement of his age when he became king, and of the number
of years that he reigned. But the numbers have been lost from
the text, and the omission is older than the Septuagint version
which follows our present corrupt Hebrew text. The following
form may best present the passage with its omissions: "Saul was
—— years old when he began to reign, and he reigned —— and
two years over Israel." These omissions can now be supplied only
by conjecture. It is evident that Saul was more than a year old
when he began to reign, and that he reigned more than two years.
According to Acts xiii, 21, and Josephus (Ant., vi, 14, 9) he reigned
forty years, but this may include the seven years and a half assumed to have passed between the death of Saul and that of Ishbosheth (2 Sam. ii, 11). Ishbosheth, however, is said to have reigned
but two years (2 Sam. ii, 10). The language of Paul and Josephus
more likely expresses a current Jewish tradition which was not exact.

A comparison of genealogical tables often exhibits discrepancies
in names and numbers. But the transcription and repe-   Discrepancies
in genealogi-
cal tables.
tition of such records through a long period of time,
and by many different scribes, would naturally expose
them to numerous variations. A comparison of the family record
of Jacob and his sons, the seventy souls that came into Egypt
(Gen. xlvi), with that of the census of these families in the time of
Moses (Num. xxvi) will serve to illustrate the peculiarities of Hebrew genealogies. We give these lists, on the adjoining page, in
parallel columns, and also select from the lists in 1 Chron. ii–viii
the corresponding names, so far as they appear there, that the
reader may see at a glance the variations in orthography. For
convenience of reference we place the corresponding names opposite each other; but the student should note the variations in the
order of names as they appear in these different lists. The list

in Genesis is arranged according to the wives and concubines of Jacob. The first thirty-three include Jacob and the sons and daughter of Leah; the next sixteen are the sons of Zilpah; the next fourteen are the sons of Rachel; and the remaining seven are the sons of Bilhah. It is a manifest purpose to make the list number "seventy souls." In Num. xxvi the order of names follows no apparent plan.[1]

Jacob's family record.

Leah's Sons—33.

	Gen. xlvi.	Num. xxvi.	1 Chron. ii-viii.
1.	**JACOB.**		
2.	**REUBEN**	**REUBEN**	**REUBEN.**
3.	Hanoch	Hanoch	Hanoch.
4.	Phallua	Phallua	Phallua.
		(Descendants.)	
5.	Hezron	Hezron	Hezron.
6.	Carmi	Carmi	Carmi.
7.	**SIMEON**	**SIMEON**	**SIMEON.**
8.	Jemuel	* Nemuel	* Nemuel.
9.	Jamin	Jamin	Jamin.
10.	Ohad	——	——
11.	Jachin	Jachin	* Jarib.
12.	Zohar	* Zerah	* Zerah.
13.	Shaul	Shaul	Shaul.
14.	**LEVI**	**LEVI**	**LEVI.**
15.	Gershon	Gershon	* Gershom.
		(Descendants.)	
16.	Kohath	Kohath	Kohath.
17.	Merari	Merari	Merari.
		(Descendants.)	
18.	**JUDAH**	**JUDAH**	**JUDAH.**
19.	Er. **Hezron**	Er. **Hezron**	Er. **Hezron**
20.	Onan. **Hamul**	Onan. **Hamul**	Onan. **Hamul.**
21.	Shelah	Shelah	Shelah.
22.	Pherez	Pherez	Pherez.
23.	Zerah	Zerah	Zerah.
24.	**ISSACHAR**	**ISSACHAR**	**ISSACHAR.**
25.	Tola	Tola	Tola.
26.	Phuvah	Phuvah	* Phuah.
27.	Job	* Jashub	* Jashib.
28.	Shimron	Shimron	Shimron.
29.	**ZEBULUN**	**ZEBULUN**	**ZEBULUN.**
30.	Sered	Sered	No genealogy recorded.
31.	Elon	Elon	
32.	Jahleel	Jahleel	
33.	Dinah	——	

[1] The names of the tribes, or tribe-fathers, are frequently written, but in no two places do they stand in the same order. Comp. Gen. xxix, 32 – xxx, 24; xlix; Exod. i, 1–5; Num. i, 5–15 and 20–47; xiii, 1–16; xxxiv, 17–28; Deut. xxxiii

	Gen. xlvi.	Num. xxvi.	1 Chron. ii-viii.
34.	GAD	GAD	GAD.
35.	Ziphion	* Zephon	
36.	Haggi	Haggi	
37.	Shuni	Shuni	
38.	Ezbon	* Ozni	
39.	Eri	Eri	
40.	Arodi	* Arod	
41.	Areli	Areli	
42.	ASHER	ASHER	ASHER.
43.	Jimnah	Jimnah	Jimnah.
44.	Jishvah	——	Jishvah.
45.	Jishvi	Jishvi	Jishvi.
46.	Beriah	Beriah	Beriah.
47.	Serah	Serah	Serah.
48.	**Heber**	**Heber**	**Heber.**
49.	**Malchiel**	**Malchiel**	**Malchiel.**
50.	JOSEPH	JOSEPH	JOSEPH.
51.	Manasseh	Manasseh	Manasseh.
		(Descendants.)	
52.	Ephraim	Ephraim	Ephraim.
		(Descendants.)	
53.	BENJAMIN	BENJAMIN	BENJAMIN.
54.	Bela	Bela	Bela.
55.	Becher	——	..(Comp. Heb. text of 1 Chron. viii, 1.)
56.	Ashbel	Ashbel	Ashbel.
57.	Gera	——	**Gera.**
58.	Naaman	**Naaman**	**Naaman.**
59.	Ehi	* Ahiram	* Aharah.
60.	Rosh	——	——
61.	Muppim	Sheshupham	**Shephuphan.**
62.	Huppim	* Hupham	——
63.	Ard	**Ard**	* **Addar.**
64.	DAN	DAN	DAN.
65.	Hushim	* Shuham	——
66.	NAPHTALI	NAPHTALI	NAPHTALI.
67.	Jahzeel	Jahzeel	* Jahzieel.
68.	Guni	Guni	Guni.
69.	Jezer	Jezer	Jezer.
70.	Shillem	Shillem	* Shallum.

Left margin labels:

ZILPAH'S SONS—16. (rows 34–49)

No genealogy, but see 1 Chronicles v, 11–17. (rows 35–41)

RACHEL'S SONS—14. (rows 50–63)

BILHAH'S SONS—7. (rows 64–70)

* The asterisk is designed to call attention to several variations in orthography; the small capitals designate the tribe-fathers; names in black letter are supposed to levirate substitutions of grandchildren; and the word (descendants) stands in place of names given in the Scripture record, but for want of room not printed above.

In studying these lists of names, it is important to attend to the historical position and purpose of each writer. The Historical standpoint. list of Gen. xlvi was probably prepared in Egypt, some time after the migration of Jacob and his family thither. It was probably prepared, in the form in which it there stands, by the sanction of Jacob himself.¹ The aged and chastened patriarch went down into Egypt with the divine assurance that God would make him a great nation, and bring him up again (Gen. xlvi, 3, 4). Great interest therefore would attach to his family register, as it was made out under his own direction. But at the time of the census of Num. xxvi, whilst the names of the heads of families are all carefully preserved, they have become differently arranged, and other names have become prominent. Numerous later descendants have become historically conspicuous, and are accordingly added under the proper family heads. The tables given in 1 Chron. i–ii show much more extensive additions and changes. The peculiar differences between the lists show that one has not been copied from the other; nor were both taken from a common source. They were evidently prepared independently, each from a different standpoint, and for a definite purpose.

We should notice also the peculiar Hebrew methods of thought and expression as exhibited in the ancient list of Gen. xlvi. In verses 8 and 15 Jacob is included among his own sons, and the immortal thirty-three, which includes the father and one daughter, and two great-grandsons (Hezron and Hamul) probably not yet born when Jacob moved into Egypt, are desig-

Hebrew style and usage.

---

¹ The following suggestive observations of Dr. Mahan, in his little work entitled "The Spiritual Point of View; An Answer to Bishop Colenso" (New York, 1863, pp. 57, 58), illustrate how many considerations and circumstances may have naturally influenced in the preparation of this genealogy. "Jacob's family list, whether written in any way or merely committed to memory, contained before he went into Egypt precisely *seventy* souls; though *four* of these, namely, his two wives and two of the sons of Judah, were souls of the departed. Thus, arithmetically, and in a matter-of-fact way, Jacob had *sixty-six* in his company when he first settled in Egypt; but religiously, or, as some might say, poetically—in the spirit of the little maid of Wordsworth's ballad, who insisted so strenuously 'we are seven'—he might still count them seventy. To this fact may be added the following probabilities: When Jacob arrived in Egypt he probably gave to his list the title or heading which it still bears, namely, *The names of the children of Israel which came with him into Egypt.* And it is likely enough that he did this without troubling himself to erase, either from the tablets or his memory, the names of the dear departed souls whom the kind-hearted and faithful patriarch still regarded as 'of his company.' At a later date, however, he may have revised his list. Affectionate heads of families are apt to do such things. Their family list is the solace of their old age; and they turn it over and over as fondly as a miser counts over his hoarded money. The patriarch, then, turning his list over in this way, and counting his seventy souls which the Lord had given him, and reluctant to erase his four departed souls, availed himself of the first opportunity to substitute for them four new souls—among his great-grandchildren—whom the Lord had granted him *in their place.* Thus the names of the grandchildren of Judah and Asher may easily have come in. No other names were added, because no others were needed."

nated as "all the souls of his sons and his daughters." Similar usage appears in Exod. i, 5, where it is said that "all the souls that came out of the loins of Jacob were seventy souls."[1] The writer has in mind the memorable "seventy" that came into Egypt (comp. Deut. x, 22). In Gen. xlvi, 27, the two sons of Joseph, who are expressly said to have been "born to him in Egypt," are reckoned among the seventy who "came into Egypt." It is a carping and captious criticism which fastens upon peculiarities of Hebrew *usus loquendi* like these, and pronounces them "remarkable contradictions, involving such plain impossibilities that they cannot be regarded as true narratives of actual historical matters of fact."[2]

The probable reason for reckoning Hezron and Hamul (verse 12) among the seventy was that they were adopted by Judah in the places of the deceased Er and Onan, who died in the land of Canaan. This appears from the fact that in the later registers of Num. xxvi and 1 Chron. ii they appear as permanent heads of families in Judah. Heber and Malchiel, grandsons of Asher (ver. 17), are also reckoned among the seventy, and probably for the reason that they, were born before the migration into Egypt. They also appear in the later lists as heads of families in Israel.

In the list of Gen. xlvi, 21, the names of Naaman and Ard appear among the sons of Benjamin, but in Num. xxvi, 40, they appear as sons of Bela. The most probable explanation of this discrepancy is that the Naaman and Ard, mentioned in Gen. xlvi, 21, died in Egypt without issue, and two of their brother Bela's sons were named after them, and substituted in their place to perpetuate intact the families of Benjamin. In 1 Chron. viii many other names appear among the sons of Benjamin and Bela, but whether Nohah and Rapha were substituted for families that had become extinct, or are other names for some of the same persons who appear in the list of Gen. xlvi, it is now impossible to

Substitution of names.

---

[1] In the mention of *seventy-five souls*, Acts vii, 14, Stephen simply follows the reading of the Septuagint.

[2] Bishop Colenso on the Pentateuch and the Book of Joshua (New York, 1863), p. 60. This remarkable critic quotes Gen. xlvi, 12, and then observes: "It appears to me to be certain that the writer here means to say that Hezron and Hamul were *born in the land of Canaan*." But it is absolutely certain that that is one particular thing which the writer *does not say*. Again, after quoting Exod. i, 1, 5, and Deut. x, 22, he observes: "I assume that it is absolutely undeniable that the narrative of the Exodus distinctly involves the statement, that the sixty-six persons 'out of the loins of Jacob,' mentioned in Gen. xlvi. and no others (!), went down with him into Egypt." Mark the words "*and no others*," although Jacob's sons' wives are expressly mentioned in Gen. xlvi, 26. Such a critic would appear to be utterly incapable of grasping the spirit and style of the Hebrew writers.

determine. Ashbel is mentioned as second in Chronicles, but in
Gen. xlvi he stands third.[1] Gera, the fourth name in the list in
Genesis, appears twice in 1 Chron. viii, 3, 5, among the sons of Bela.
Such variations evince the independence of the different lists, and
yet they are of a nature to confirm rather than discredit the genuineness of the several genealogies. Each list had its own distinct
history and purpose.

It was in accordance with the Hebrew spirit and custom to frame
a register of honoured names so as to have them produce a definite
and suggestive number. So Matthew's genealogy of our Lord is
arranged into three groups of fourteen names each (Matt. i, 17),
and yet this could be done only by the omission of several important names.[2] While the compiler might, by another process equally
correct, have made the list of Gen. xlvi number sixty-nine by omit-
ting Jacob, or have made it exceed seventy by adding the names
of the wives of Jacob's sons, he doubtless purposely arranged it so
as to make it number seventy souls. The number of the descendants of Noah, as given in the genealogical table of Gen. x, amounts
to seventy. This habit of using fixed numbers, being a help to
memory, may have originated in the necessities of oral tradition.
The seventy elders of Israel were probably chosen with some reference to the families that sprung from these seventy souls of
Jacob's household, and Jesus' sending out of seventy disciples
(Luke x, 1) is evidence that his mind was influenced by the mystic
significance of the number seventy.

It is well known that intermarriages between the tribes, and
Legal and lin- questions of legal right to an inheritance, affected a
eal genealogies person's genealogical status. Thus, in Num. xxxii, 40,
often differ.
41, it is said that Moses gave the land of Gilead to
Machir, the son of Manasseh, "and Jair, the *son of Manasseh*, went
and seized their hamlets, and called them Havoth-jair " (comp.
1 Kings iv, 13). This inheritance, therefore, belonged to the tribe
of Manasseh; but a comparison of 1 Chron. ii, 21, 22, shows that by
lineal descent Jair belonged to the tribe of Judah, and is so reckoned by the chronicler, who also gives the facts which explain the
whole case. He informs us that Hezron, the son of Pharez, the son
of Judah, married the daughter of Machir, the son of Manasseh,

---

[1] Perhaps for וּבְכֶר, *and Becher*, in Gen. xlvi, 21, we should read בְּכֹרוֹ, *his firstborn*.

[2] "According to the evangelist," says Upham, " the time-cycles of the Hebrews
(and if so, the time-cycles of the world) had relations to the coming of the Lord. He
points out that the life of the Hebrews unrolled in three time-harmonies, one ending
in triumph, one in mourning; and thus may intimate that in the end of the third the
notes of the two former blend."—Thoughts on the Holy Gospels, p. 199.

and by her became the father of Segub, who was the father of Jair. If now Jair would make out his legal claim to the inheritance in Gilead he would show how he was a descendant of Machir, the son of Manasseh; but if his paternal lineage were inquired after, it would be as easily traceable to Hezron, the son of Judah.

Considerations of this kind will go far to solve the difficulties which have so greatly perplexed critics in the two diverse genealogies of Jesus, as given in Matt. i, 1–17, and Luke iii, 23–38. At this late day the particular facts are wanting which would put in clear light the discrepancies of these lists of our Lord's ancestry, and can only be supplied by such reasons and probable suppositions as are warranted by a careful collation of genealogies, and well-known facts of Jewish custom in reckoning legal succession and lineal descent. The hypothesis, quite prevalent and popular since the time of the Reformation, that Matthew gives the genealogy of Joseph, and Luke that of Mary, is justly set aside by a majority of the best critics as incompatible with the words of both evangelists, who alike claim to give the genealogy of Joseph.[1] The right to "the throne of David his father" (Luke i, 32) must, according to all Jewish precedent, ideas, and usage, be based upon *a legal ground of succession*, as of an inheritance; and therefore his genealogy must be traced backward from Joseph the legal husband of Mary. And it is clear, outside of these genealogies, that Joseph was of the royal house of David. Thus, the angel addressed him: "Joseph, son of David, do not fear to take Mary thy wife" (Matt. i, 20). He went to Bethlehem, the city of David, to enroll himself with Mary, "because he was of the house and family of David" (Luke ii, 45). It is, however, not at all improbable that Mary also was of the house and family of David,[2] a near relative — cousin perhaps — of Joseph, and thus the natural succession of Jesus to the throne of David would, according

The two diverse genealogies of Jesus.

---

[1] Many critics read Luke iii, 23, as if it implied that Mary's rather than Joseph's genealogy is given. Thus: ὢν υἱός, ὡς ἐνομίζετο, Ἰωσήφ, τοῦ Ἡλεί: "Being the son, as was supposed, of Joseph (but in fact of Mary), of Eli," etc. This, however, is manifestly interpolating a most important statement into the words of the evangelist, a statement too important for him to have omitted had he intended such a thought. See Meyer, in loco.

[2] Fairbairn observes that the marriage of cousins "perfectly accords with Jewish practice. . . . It was the constant aim of the Jews to make inheritance and blood-relationship, as far as possible, go together."—Hermeneutical Manual, p. 222. Upham similarly remarks: "Royal blood intermarries with royal blood. When Victoria was betrothed to Albert every one knew that Albert was a prince, and every one would know that the betrothed of a Czarowitz, or of a Prince of Wales, was a princess. The family of King David, obscure people for centuries, must have married below their rank, or have intermarried among themselves. That they did the latter is so

to Jewish ideas, be most remarkably complete. Certain it is that our Lord's descent from David was never questioned in the earliest times. He allowed himself to be called the Son of David (Matt. ix, 27; xv, 22), and no one of his adversaries denied this important claim. He was "of the seed of David," according to Paul's Gospel (2 Tim. ii, 8; comp. Rom. i, 3; Acts xiii, 22, 23), and the Epistle to the Hebrews says: "It is evident (πρόδηλον, conspicuously manifest) that our Lord has sprung from Judah" (Heb. vii, 14).

The Emperor Julian attacked these genealogies on the ground Jerome and of their discrepancies, and Jerome, in replying to him, Africanus on observes that if Julian had been more familiar with the Lord's gene- alogy. Jewish modes of speech he might have seen that one evangelist gives the *natural* and the other the *legal* pedigree of Joseph.[1] Essentially the same method of reconciling these dis- crepancies was advanced long previously by Africanus, who writes as follows: "It was customary in Israel to calculate the names of the generations either according to nature or according to the law; according to nature by the succession of legitimate offspring; ac- cording to law when another raised children to the name of a brother who had died childless. For as the hope of a resurrection was not yet clearly given, they imitated the promise which was to take place by a kind of mortal resurrection, with a view to perpet- uate the name of the person who had died. Since then there are some of those who are inserted in this genealogical table that suc- ceed each other in the natural order of fa her and son, some again that were born of others and were ascribed to others by name, both the real and reputed fathers have been recorded. Thus neither of the Gospels has made a false statement, whether calculating in the order of nature or according to law. For the families descended from Solomon, and those from Nathan, were so intermingled by substitutions in the place of those who had died childless, by second marriages, and the raising up of seed, that the same persons are justly considered as in one respect belonging to one of these, and in another respect belonging to others. Hence it is that, both of these accounts being true, they come down to Joseph, with considerable intricacy, it is true, but with great accuracy."[2]

probable, from the tendency of Jewish families to keep together, and from the usage of royal families, that it may be held for certain that when St. Matthew stated that Joseph, a prince of the house of David, married Mary, he plainly told his countrymen (and, if he thought of others, he thought that through them all would know) that the betrothed of this prince was a princess of the house of David."—Thoughts on the Holy Gospels, p. 204.

[1] Jerome on Matt. i.

[2] Quoted by Eusebius, Eccl. Hist. (Bohn's ed.), book i, chap. vii.

These general considerations furnish the basis on which several different methods of harmonizing the genealogies are possible. In the absence of certain information no hypothesis can well claim absolute certainty. The theory of Africanus is that Jacob and Heli were brothers by the same mother. Heli died childless, and Jacob married his widow, and by her begat Joseph, the husband of Mary (Matt. i, 16), and yet, according to levirate law, Joseph was also of Heli (Luke iii, 23).[1] According to this theory Matthew records the natural, and Luke the legal, line of descent. Grotius, on the other hand, maintains that Matthew's table gives the legal succession, inasmuch as he recounts those who obtained the kingdom (which was the right of the firstborn) without the admixture of a private name.[2] He observes further that, according to Matt. i, 12, Jechonias begat Salathiel, but according to Luke iii, 27, Salathiel was the son of Neri. Now, according to Jer. xxii, 30 (comp. xxxvi, 30), Jechonias was sentenced to become childless. In that case the right to the throne of David would devolve upon the next nearest heir, which was probably Salathiel, the son of Neri, whose direct lineage Luke traces up to Nathan, another son of David (Luke iii, 27–31). This theory is most fully developed by Hervey, who maintains "that Salathiel, of the house of Nathan, became heir to David's throne on the failure of Solomon's line in Jechonias, and that as such he and his descendants were transferred as 'sons of Jeconiah' to the royal genealogical table, according to the principle of the Jewish law laid down in Num. xxvii, 8–11. The two genealogies then coincide for two, or rather four, generations [Salathiel, Zorobabel (= Rhesa), Joana (= Hananiah, 1 Chron. iii, 19), Juda (= Abiud of Matt. i, 13, and Hodaiah of 1 Chron. iii, 24)]. There then occur six names in Matthew which are not found in Luke; and then once more the two genealogies coincide in the name of Matthan, or Matthat (Matt. i, 15; Luke iii, 24), to whom two different sons, Jacob and Heli, are assigned, but one and the same grandson and heir, Joseph, the husband of Mary. The simple and obvious explanation of this is, on the same principle as before, that Joseph was descended from Joseph, a younger son of Abiud (the Juda of Luke iii, 26), but that on the failure of the line of Abiud's eldest son in Eleazar (Matt. i, 15), Joseph's grandfather, Matthan, became the heir; that Matthan had two sons, Jacob and Heli; that Jacob had no son, and consequently that Joseph, the son of his younger brother Heli, became heir to his uncle, and to the throne of David. . . . Mary, the

No hypothesis should claim absolute certainty.

[1] Eusebius, Eccl. Hist., book i, chap. vii.
[2] See his Annotations on Matt. i, 16, and Poole, Synopsis Criticorum, in loco.

mother of Jesus, was, in all probability, the daughter of Jacob,
and first cousin to Joseph, her husband. So that in point of *fact*,
though not of *form*, both the genealogies are as much hers as her
husband's." [1]

The biblical genealogies may appear to the modern reader like
Genealogies not a useless part of Scripture, and lists of places, many
useless.   of them now utterly unknown, like that of Israel's
places of encampment (Num. xxxiii), and the cities allotted to the
different tribes (e. g., Josh. xv, 20–62), have been pronounced by
sceptics as incompatible with lofty ideas of a written revelation of
God. But such notions spring from a stilted and mechanical conception of what the revelation ought to be. These apparently dry
and tiresome lists of names are among the most irrefragable evidences of the historical verity of the Scripture records. If to our
modern thought they seem of no practical worth, we should not
forget that to the ancient Hebrew they were of the first importance
as documents of ancestral history and legal rights. The most uncritical and absurd of all sceptical fancies would be the notion that
these lists have been fabricated for a purpose. One might as well
maintain that the fossil remains of extinct animals have been set in
the rocks for the purpose of deception. The superficial utilitarian
may indeed pronounce both the fossils and the genealogies alike
worthless; but the profounder student of the earth and of man will
recognise in them invaluable indexes of history. These genealogies
are like the rough stones in the lower foundation of a building.
Some of the stones are out of sight in the subsoil; others have become nicked and bruised, and some displaced and lost in the lapse
of centuries, but they were all in some way essential to the origin,
rise, stability, and usefulness of the noble superstructure.

[1] A. C. Hervey, article on Genealogy of Jesus Christ in Smith's Bible Dictionary.
For fuller details and discussion of the same theory see the same author's volume entitled Genealogies of our Lord (Cambridge, 1853). Dr. Holmes attempts (article Gen.
of Jesus Christ in Kitto's New Cyclopædia of Biblical Literature) to controvert
Hervey's positions and arguments, but we think entirely without success. The same
may be said of Meyer's note at the end of Luke iii. The fact is that while no one
should affirm that Hervey's hypothesis is perfectly certain (for in the absence of sufficient data no theory is entitled to such a claim) no one can prove that it is not correct. All that can well be asked for in the case is a hypothesis which will exhibit
how both genealogies may be true, and that which holds Matthew's to be the legal
(royal) line and Luke's the natural seems on the whole to be most entitled to credit.
On the minor discrepancies and difficulties of these genealogies see the works named
above, the several Bible dictionaries and commentaries, and W. H. Mill's discussion of
the genealogies in his Observations on the attempted Application of Pantheistic Principles to the Theory and Historical Criticism of the Gospel. Cambridge, 2d edition,
1855.

The greater number of the numerical discrepancies of the Bible are probably due to the mistakes of copyists. The an- Numerical discient custom of using letters for numbers, and the great crepancies. similarity of some of the letters, will account for such differences as that of 2 Sam. viii, 4, compared with 1 Chron. xviii, 4, where final Nun (ן), which stands for 700, might easily be confounded with Zayin with two dots over it (ז֔) which was used to denote 7000. According to 1 Kings vii, 15, the two brazen pillars were each eighteen cubits high; in 2 Chron. iii, 15, it is written: "He made before the house two pillars thirty and five cubits long." Some have thought that, as in Kings, the *height* (קוֹמָה) of each pillar is given, and in Chronicles the *length* (אֹרֶךְ) of the two pillars, we should understand the latter passage as giving the length of the two pillars together. They may have been cast in one piece, and afterward cut into two pillars, each being, in round numbers, eighteen cubits. The more probable supposition, however, is that the discrepancy arose by confounding יח = 18, with לה = 35.

The two lists of exiles who returned with Zerubbabel (Ezra ii, 1–70, and Neh. vii, 6–73) exhibit numerous discrepan- Lists of returncies as well as many coincidences, and it is remarkable ing exiles in Ezra and Nehethat the numbers in Ezra's list amount to 29,818, and miah. in Nehemiah's to 31,089, and yet, according to both lists, the entire congregation numbered 42,360 (Ezra ii, 64; Neh. vii, 66). The probability is that neither list is intended as a perfect enumeration of all the families that returned from exile, but only of such families of Judah and Benjamin as could show an authentic genealogy of their father's house, while the 42,360 includes many persons and families belonging to other tribes who in their exile had lost all certain record of their genealogy, but were nevertheless true descendants of some of the ancient tribes. It is also noticeable that Ezra's list mentions 494 persons not recognised in Nehemiah's list, and Nehemiah's list mentions 1,765 not recognised in Ezra's; but if we add the surplus of Ezra to the sum of Nehemiah (494 + 31,089 = 31,583) we have the same result as by adding Nehemiah's surplus to the sum of Ezra's numbers (1,765 + 29,818 = 31,583). Hence it may be reasonably believed that 31,583 was the sum of all that could show their father's house; that the two lists were drawn up independently of each other; and that both are defective, though one supplies the defects of the other.

As an instance of doctrinal and ethical inconsistency Doctrinal and between the Old and New Testaments we may cite the ethical discrepancies. Hebrew law of retaliation as treated by our Lord. In Exod. xxi, 23–25, it is commanded that in cases of assault and strife resulting in the injury of persons, "thou shalt give life for life, eye for eye, tooth for tooth, hand for hand, foot for foot, burning for burning, wound for wound, stripe for stripe" (comp. Lev. xxiv, 20; Deut. xix, 21). But Jesus says: "Do not resist the evil man; but whosoever smites thee upon thy right cheek turn to him the other also" (Matt. v, 39). A proper explanation of these contradictory Scriptures will also answer for many other passages of like spirit and import. The true explanation is to be had by a careful consideration of the historical standpoint of each speaker, and the particular end or purpose which each had in view. We are not to assume that the Mosaic legislation was without divine sanction, and that by the words "it was said to the ancients" (Matt. v, 21) Jesus meant to cast a reflection on the source or authority of the old law, as if to set himself against Moses. What was said to them of old was well said, but it needed modifying at a later age and under a new dispensation. Moreover, Moses was legislating for a peculiar nation at a distinctive crisis, and enunciating the rights and methods of a civil jurisprudence. The old law of retaliation was grounded essentially in truth and justice. In the maintenance of law and order in any body politic personal assault and wilful wrong demand penal satisfaction, and this self-evident truth the Gospel does not ignore or set aside. It recognises the civil magistrate as a minister of God ordained to punish the evildoer (Rom. xiii, 1–5; 1 Peter ii, 14).

Supposed conflict between the Law and the Gospel.

But in the sermon on the mount Jesus is urging the principle of Christian tenderness and love as it should prevail in the personal intercourse of men as individuals. The great principle of Christian action should be: Let not bitterness and hatred toward any man possess your soul. The spirit of law, national honour, and right logically led to the general motto, "Thou shalt love thy neighbour and hate thy enemy" (Matt. v, 43). Jesus would bring about a better age, a kindlier feeling among men, a higher and nobler civilization. To effect this he issues a new commandment designed, first of all, to operate in a man's private relations with his fellow man: "Love your enemies, and pray for them that persecute you" (Matt. v, 44). Here our Lord is evidently not putting forth a maxim or method of civil jurisprudence, but a principle of individual conduct. He shows us, as Alford observes, "the condition to which a Christian community should *tend*, and to further which every private Christian's own endeavours should be directed. It is quite beside the purpose for the world to say that these precepts of our Lord are too highly pitched for humanity, and so to find an excuse for violating them. If we were disciples of his in the true sense, these precepts would, in their spirit, as indicative of frames of mind, be strictly observed; and, as far as we are disciples, we shall attain to such observance." [1]

That Jesus, by these precepts of personal conduct in the ordinary affairs of life, did not intend to forbid the censure and punishment of evildoers, is evident from his own conduct. When struck by one of the officers in the presence of the high priest, our Lord remonstrated against the flagrant abuse (John xviii, 22, 23). When Paul was similarly smitten by command of the high priest (Acts xxiii, 3), the apostle indignantly cried out: "God will smite thee, thou whited wall!" The same apostle sets forth the true Christian doctrine on all these points in Rom. xii, 18–xiii, 6: "If it be possible, as much as lieth in you, be at peace with all men." Here he more than intimates the improbability of being at peace with all, and then, assuming that one suffers personal assault and injury, he adds: "Avenge not yourselves, beloved, but give place to the wrath" (of God). That is, let the divine wrath take its own course. and do not attempt to anticipate it, or stand in its way by retaliation and personal revenge. And then he quotes from the old law (Deut. xxxii, 35) where "it is written, To me belongeth vengeance; I will recompense, saith the Lord." God will bring his wrath (ὀργῇ) to bear upon the offender in due time, and will requite the wrong. And then follows another quotation from the Old Testament (Prov. xxv, 21, 22): "If thine enemy hunger, feed him; if he thirst, give him drink; for by doing this thou wilt heap coals of fire upon his head." Thereupon he sums up the whole thought by saying: "Be not overcome by the evil (which has been committed against thee), but overcome the evil in the good" (in the element and life of that all-conquering goodness which will be exhibited by this course of conduct). But so far is the apostle from teaching that crimes and offences are never to be avenged that he proceeds immediately to show that God has ordained the civil power as an agency and instrument for this very end. Is it asked what course the wrath of God takes when he recompenses vengeance upon evildoers? Doubtless his methods of judgment are manifold, but the apostle shows us, in the immediate context, one of the established methods by which God has arranged to punish the impious offender, namely, through "the higher powers" (Rom. xiii, 1). Rulers are designed to be a terror to evildoers. The civil magistrate "does not vainly bear the sword; for he is God's minister, an avenger for wrath (ἔκδικος εἰς ὀργήν, a divinely ordained avenging agent for the purpose of

Civil rights maintained by Jesus and Paul.

---

[1] Greek Testament on Matt. v, 38.

executing the wrath, ἡ ὀργή, mentioned above in xii, 19) to him that doeth the evil" (Rom. xiii, 4). Let no man, therefore, presume to say that the spirit and precepts of the New Testament are at war with those of the Old. In both Testaments the principles of brotherly love and of doing good for evil are inculcated, as well as the duty of maintaining human rights and civil order.

Some persons have strangely assumed that the prohibition of *The avenging* murder (Exod. xx, 13) in the Decalogue is inconsistent *of blood.* with the taking of human life in any form. This fallacy arises from a failure to distinguish between individual relations and the demands of public and administrative justice. The right and justice of capital punishment are affirmed in the most ancient legislation (Gen. ix, 6). The law of Moses, which makes so prominent the prohibition of murder, forbids the taking of any satisfaction for the life of a murderer. He that wickedly takes the life of a man must pay the penalty with his own life, or the very land will be defiled (Num. xxxv, 31–34). Ancient law and custom, recognized in the books of Moses, gave the nearest kinsman of the murdered man the right of avenging this crime. The practice, however, was liable to grave abuses, and Moses took measures to restrict them by providing cities of refuge. But the necessity of punishing the guilty criminal is everywhere recognised, and the Gospel of Jesus nowhere assumes to set it aside. The methods of penalty may change in the course of ages, and sins which called for capital punishment among the ancient Hebrews may demand no such severity of treatment under the Gospel dispensation. But it may be gravely doubted whether the "higher powers" can bear the sword to any excellent purpose if they be denied the right to recompense the crime of murder with capital punishment.[1]

A prominent example of supposed inconsistency of doctrine in *Difference be-* the New Testament is found in the different methods of *tween Paul and* presenting the subject of justification in the epistles of *James on Justi-* *fication.* Paul and of James. Paul's teaching is thus expressed in Gal. ii, 15, 16: "We Jews by nature, and not sinners from the

---

[1] Meyer observes that Rom. xiii, 4, compared with Acts xxv, 11, "proves that the abolition of the *right* of capital punishment deprives the magistracy of a power which is not merely given to it in the Old Testament, but is also decisively confirmed in the New Testament, and which it (herein lies the sacred limitation and responsibility of this power) possesses as God's minister; on which account its application is to be upheld as a principle with reference to those cases in law, where the actual satisfaction of the divine Nemesis absolutely demands it, while, at the same time, the right of pardon is still to be kept open for all concrete cases. The character of being unchristian, of barbarism, etc., does not adhere to the *right itself*, but to its *abuse* in legislation and practice."—Critical Commentary on Rom. xiii, 4.

Gentiles, but knowing that a man is not justified by the works of the law (ἐξ ἔργων νόμου, *from works of law*, i. e., as a source of merit, ground of procedure in the given case, and so the reason and cause of the justification) save through faith of Jesus Christ, even we believed in (εἰς, *into*, in allusion to the definite fact of *entering into* vital union with Christ at conversion) Christ Jesus, that we might be justified by faith of Christ, and not by works of law; because by works of law shall no flesh be justified." Substantially the same statement is made in Rom. iii, 20, 28, and in Rom. iv the doctrine is illustrated by the case of Abraham, who "believed God and it was reckoned unto him for righteousness" (ver. 3). On the other hand James insists on being "doers of the word" (Jas. i, 22–25). He extols practical godliness, the fulfilling of "the royal law according to the Scripture" (ii, 8), and declares that "faith, if it have not works, is dead by itself" (ii, 17). He also illustrates by the case of Abraham "when he offered Isaac his son upon the altar," and argues "that the faith wrought with his works, and by the works the faith was perfected, and the Scripture was fulfilled which says: Abraham believed God and it was reckoned unto him for righteousness, and he was called God's Friend. Ye see," he concludes, "that by works (ἐξ ἔργων) a man is justified, and not by faith only" (ii, 21–24).

The solution of this apparent opposition is to be had by a study of the personal religious experience of each writer, and their different modes of thought and fields of operation in the early Christian Church. We must also observe the peculiar *Method of solution.* sense in which each one uses the terms *faith, works,* and *justification,* for these words have each been used in all periods of the Church to express a number of quite distinct though kindred ideas.

We should first remember that Paul was led to Christ by a sudden and marvellous conversion. The conviction of sin, the smitings of soul when he found that he had been persecuting the Lord Jesus, the falling of the scales *Different personal experiences of Paul and James.* from his eyes, and his consequent keen and vivid perception of the free grace of the Gospel realized through faith in Christ Jesus—all this would necessarily enter into his ideal of the justification of a sinner. He sees that neither Jew nor Gentile can enter into saving relations with Christ except through such a faith. Then his mission and ministry led him pre-eminently to combat legal Judaism, and he became "the apostle of the Gentiles." James, on the other hand, had been more gradually indoctrinated in Gospel life. His conception of Christianity was that of the consummation and perfection of the old covenant. His mission and ministry led him mainly, if not altogether, to labour among those of the circumcision (Gal. ii, 9). He was wont to view all Christian doctrine in the light of Old Testament Scripturè, which thereby became to him "the implanted word" (i, 21), "a perfect law, the (law) of liberty" (ver. 25), "a royal law" (ii, 8). And we must also bear in mind, as Neander observes, "that James in his peculiar position had not, like Paul, to vindicate an independent and unshackled ministration of the Gospel among the Gentiles in opposition to the pretensions of Jewish legal righteousness; but that he felt himself compelled to press the practical consequences and requirements of the Christian faith on those in whom that faith had been blended with the errors of carnal Judaism, and to tear away the supports of their false confidence."[1]

Such different experiences and fields of action would naturally
Different modes of apprehending and expressing great truths.
develop in these ministers of Jesus Christ correspondingly different styles of thought and teaching. But when, with these facts in view, we analyze their respective teachings, we find nothing that is really contradictory. They simply set before us different aspects of the same great truths of God. Paul's teaching in the passages quoted above has reference to *faith* in its first operation; the confidence with which a sinner, conscious of guilt and condemnation, throws himself upon the free grace of God in Jesus Christ, and thus obtains pardon and peace with God. James, on the other hand, treats of faith rather as the abiding principle of a godly life, with works of piety flowing from it as waters from a living spring. Paul cites the case of Abraham while he is yet in uncircumcision, and before he had received that seal of the righteousness of faith (Rom. iv, 10, 11); but James reverts to the later time when he offered up Isaac, and by that act of fidelity to God's word had his faith perfected (Jas. ii, 21). The term *works* is also used with different shades of meaning. Paul has in mind the *works of the law* with reference to the idea of a legal righteousness; James evidently has in view works of practical piety, like visiting the fatherless and widows in their affliction (i, 27), and ministering to the wants of the needy (ii, 15, 16). Justification, accordingly, is viewed by Paul as a judicial act involving the remission of sins, reconciliation with God, and restoration to the divine favour; but with James it is rather the maintenance of such a state of favour with God, a continued approval in the sight of God and man. All this will appear the more clearly when we note that James addresses his Jewish brethren of the dispersion, who

[1] Planting and Training of the Christian Church. English Translation, by Ryland, p. 499. New York, 1865.

were exposed to divers temptations and trials (i, 1–4), and were in danger of reposing in a dead antinomian Pharisaism; but Paul is discussing, as a learned theologian, the doctrine of salvation, as it originates in the counsels of God, and is developed in the history of God's dealings with the whole race of Adam.

Moreover, it should be observed that James does not deny the necessity and efficacy of faith, nor does Paul ignore the importance of good works. What James opposes is the mischievous doctrine of faith apart from works. He **Different aim of Paul and James.** condemns the man who says he has faith, and yet exhibits a life and conduct inconsistent with the faith of our Lord Jesus Christ. Such faith, he declares, is dead in itself (ii, 14–17). Justification is by faith, but not by faith only (ver. 24). It evidences itself by works of piety and love. Paul, on the other hand, opposes the idea of a legal righteousness. He condemns the vain conceit that a man can merit God's favour by a perfect keeping of law, and shows that the law serves its highest purpose when it discloses to a man "the knowledge of sin" (Rom. iii, 20) and makes sin itself appear "exceedingly sinful" (vii, 7–13). But Paul is as far from denying the necessity of good works as evidences of a believer's faith in Christ, as James is from denying the necessity of faith in Christ in order to obtain the remission of sin. In Gal. v, 6, he speaks of "faith working through love," and in 1 Cor. xiii, 2, he affirms that though one have all faith, so as to remove mountains, but have not love, he is nothing. Evidently both these apostles are in harmony with Jesus, who comprehends the essential relations of faith and works when he says: "Either make the tree good and its fruit good; or make the tree corrupt and its fruit corrupt; for the tree is known by its fruit" (Matt. xii, 33).

These differences between Paul and James illustrate the individual freedom of the sacred writers in their enunciation of divine truth. Each maintains his own peculiarities of thought and style. Each receives and communicates his word of revelation and knowledge of the mystery of **Individual freedom of different writers.** Christ according to the conditions of life, experience, and action under which he has been trained. All these facts are to be taken into consideration when we compare and contrast the teachings of Scripture which are apparently diverse. It will be found that these variations constitute one manifold and self-evidencing revelation of the only true God.

The general principles of exegesis set forth above will suffice for the explanation of all other doctrinal and ethical inconsistencies which have been alleged as existing in the Bible. Strict regard to the standpoint of the speaker or writer, the occasion, scope, and plan, together with a critical analysis of the details, will usually show that there exists no real contradiction. But when men bring forward hyperbolical expressions peculiar to oriental speech, or instances of Hebraic anthropomorphism, and press them into an assumed literal significance, they simply create the difficulties over which they stumble. Doctrinal and ethical inconsistencies, developed by such a process, are all dissipated by attention to the nature of the scriptural language and a rational interpretation of the same.

Mr. Haley, in his comprehensive and valuable work on the Discrepancies of the Bible,[1] observes that these discrepancies are not without a value. They may well be believed to contemplate the following ends: (1) They stimulate intellectual effort, awaken curiosity and inquiry, and thus lead to a closer and more extensive study of the sacred volume. (2) They illustrate the analogy between the Bible and nature. As the earth and heavens exhibit marvellous harmony in the midst of great variety and discord, so in the Scriptures there exists a notable harmony behind all the seeming discrepancies. (3) They prove that there was no collusion among the sacred writers, for their differences are such as would never have been introduced by their design.[2] (4) They also show the value of the spirit as above the letter of the word of God, and (5) serve as a test of moral character. To the captious spirit, predisposed to find and magnify difficulties in the divine revelation, the biblical discrepancies will be great stumblingblocks, and occasions of disobedience and cavil. But to the serious inquirer, who desires to " know the mysteries of the kingdom of heaven" (Matt. xiii, 11), a faithful study of these discrepancies will disclose hidden harmonies and undesigned coincidences which will convince him that these multiform Scriptures are truly the word of God.

Value of biblical discrepancies.

[1] An Examination of the Alleged Discrepancies of the Bible, pp. 30–40. Andover, 1874.

[2] " These discrepancies," observes Wordsworth, " being such as they are found to be, are of inestimable value. They show that there has been no collusion among our witnesses, and that our manuscript copies of the Gospels, about five hundred in number, and brought to us from all parts of the world, have not been mutilated or interpolated with any sinister design ; they have not been tampered with by any religious sect for the sake of propagating any private opinion as the word of God. These discrepancies are, in fact, evidences of the purity and integrity of the sacred text."— The New Testament in the original Greek, with Notes and Introductions. Preface to the Four Gospels, p xxii. Lond., 1859.

CHAPTER XXXI.

ALLEGED CONTRADICTIONS OF SCIENCE.

It has been alleged that the statements of Scripture and the results of scientific research are in numerous instances opposed to one another. The charge appears to have begotten in some devout minds a suspicion and fear that scientific research in the realm of nature is essentially hostile to religion. On the other hand, there are those who seem to labour under a conviction that the doctrine of a supernatural revelation, and a life nourished by faith in a personal God, are inimical to the scientific investigation of the laws and processes of nature and of life. Others, again, have affirmed that the Bible was not given to teach us natural science; that its great purpose is to teach morals and religion, to instruct us in righteousness; and that, therefore, we need not be disturbed if we do occasionally find its statements in conflict with discoveries in science. Others have attempted various methods of "reconciling" science and the Bible, and these have generally acted on the supposition that the results of scientific discovery necessitate a new interpretation of the Scripture records, or call for new principles of interpretation. The new discoveries, they say, do not conflict with the ancient revelation; they only conflict with the old interpretation of the revelation. We must change our hermeneutical methods, and adapt them to the revelations of science. How for the thousandth time have we heard the story of Galileo and the Inquisition.

We may well pause in the presence of these grave allegations and issues, and consider a few self-evident propositions. It is not to be supposed that any fact of nature or history can be in conflict with the express declarations of the omniscient God. If there be an apparent conflict it must be that there is some mistake or misunderstanding about the fact or about the revelation. For it may be either that the fact alleged is not as stated, or that the revelation has been misapprehended. If the alleged fact is clear beyond all question, and yet stands in certain conflict with a statement of divine revelation, it would furnish valid ground for believing that that which purported to be a revelation of God was spurious. Truths of whatever kind can never be in real conflict with each other. And it is unworthy of a

Christian believer to be disturbed with a fear that any well-established fact or law of nature can harm the interests of true religion. We may welcome light and knowledge from whatever source, confident that the truth of God must and will stand all possible investigation and trial. Hasty natures, however, indulging in pride of intellect, or given to following the dictum of honoured masters, may fall into grievous error in either of two ways: They may shut their eyes to facts, and hold to a delusion in spite of evidence; or they may become the obsequious victims of "science falsely so called." That certainly is a false science which is built upon inferences, assumptions, and theories, and yet presumes to dogmatize as if its hypotheses were facts. And that is a system of hermeneutics equally false and misleading which is so flexible, under the pressure of new discoveries, as to yield to the putting of any number of new meanings upon an old and common word. The interests of science and religion alike require that we do no violence to the facts of the one, or the written records of the other.

The principal points on which Science and the Bible have been thought to be in conflict may be briefly considered under three heads: (1) The record of miracles, (2) Descriptions of physical phenomena, and (3) The origin of the world and of man. A brief discussion of these will show how large a proportion of the alleged contradictions are based upon needless assumptions.

1. The Record of Miracles.

With those atheistic and pantheistic writers who deny the existence of a personal God the idea of a miracle is, of course, a monstrosity. The very possibility of miracles is by them denied, and they, accordingly, reject a volume which teems from beginning to end with accounts of supernatural events. The deist also finds in the record of these miracles what he regards as inconsistent with the constancy of nature's methods. The unchangeable Deity, he affirms, will never violate his own laws. There is a uniform order in the whole round and course of nature; the action and reaction of the forces of the universe are permanent and sure, and it is contrary to experience and observation to suppose that these abiding universal laws were ever violated and set at naught by their divine Author. Such a supposition, it is imagined, involves the idea that God allows his own laws to be violated and dishonoured; or that he perceives defects in his works which he would fain now remedy by arbitrary interposition. There is no doubt but the popular mind has been greatly affected and

Assumed impossibility of miracles.

disposed to scepticism by these and similar teachings touching the supposed impossibility of miracles.[1]

With the atheist and the pantheist the believer in a supernatural divine revelation can have no ground in common. The denial of a personal God, the creator and ruler of the world, is at war with the profoundest intuitions of the human soul. It essentially gives the lie to the most sacred convictions of the noblest minds, and makes a mockery of all religious worship. All moral distinctions, all sense of guilt, all workings of conscience, all yearnings of the heart after the living God, are but so many forms and phases of delusion. With atheist or pantheist, therefore, it would be folly to dispute on the subject of miracles. *No common ground between Atheist, Pantheist, and Christian.*

But the deist cannot consistently deny the possibility of miracles. He accepts the doctrine of a Supreme Ruler, the creator and upholder of the universe, and any rational conception of primordial creation involves all the essentials of a stupendous miracle. On what rational grounds, then, can he assume or assert that the Supreme Creator will no more interpose to check, or change, or modify for particular ends, the laws and forces of the natural world? It will be found, we think, that the common objections to miracles grow out of false definitions of the miraculous, and baseless assumptions as to what constitutes the order of nature. In order to place the whole subject in its proper light three considerations are especially important: *Deist cannot consistently deny possibility of miracles.*

1. Miracles are themselves parts of a divine order. So far from being violations or transgressions of nature's laws they are striking manifestations of the majesty and power of him who is the Supreme Author of law and harmony. No interposition or interference of God with the order of nature is without reason and design. An intelligent will, accompanied by adequate power, may change the course of a river in order to save or to subvert a city, but the introduction of such efficient causes is no violation of law. The arresting of disease, the stilling of a tempest, the opening of the eyes of the blind, require only the presence and action of adequate wisdom and power. No miracle *Miracles parts of a divine order.*

---

[1] "There are those," says Fisher, "who find it hard to believe in a miracle because the word is associated in their minds with the notion of a capricious act, or of a make-shift to meet an unexpected emergency. They conceive of a miracle not as an event planned and fitting into an established order, but as done in obedience to a sudden prompting, as a kind of desperate expedient to prevent the consequences of a previous neglect or want of forecast. Such an act, they properly feel, cannot be attributed to God."—Supernatural Origin of Christianity, p. 471.

ever took place without a cause. Indeed, "the law of nature's constancy is subordinate to the higher law of change."[1] Before we can pronounce any miracle on record a violation of law we must be competent to say that divine wisdom had no purpose to serve by the working of such miracle. "The need of miracles," observes Fisher, "is not founded on the existence of any defect in nature. The system of nature is good, and is worthy of God. It is fitted, in itself considered, to disclose the attributes of the Creator, and to call forth feelings of adoration in the human mind. The defect is not in nature. But the mind of man is darkened so that this primal revelation is obscurely discerned; his character, moreover, is corrupted beyond the power of self-recovery in consequence of his apostasy from God. Now, if God shall mercifully approach with new light and new help, why shall he not verify to man the fact of his presence by supernatural manifestations of his power and goodness? In this case nature is used as an instrument for an ulterior moral end. The miracle is not to remedy an imperfection in nature, but is, like the revelation which it serves to attest, a product of the condescension of God. He condescends to address evidence to the senses, or to the understanding through the senses, in order to open a way for the conveyance of the highest spiritual blessing to mankind. Material nature, be it remembered, does not include the end of existence in itself. It is a subordinate member of a vaster system, and has only an instrumental value."[2]

2. It is important to observe, further, that God's revelation to men was gradually given. It was communicated in many parts and modes (Heb. i, 1), and its historic unfolding and development were in accordance with a well-defined plan and order.[3] "We have to contemplate," says Fisher, "the striking peculiarity of this great historic movement, which embraces the unfolding, through successive stages or epochs, of a religion distinct in its spirit as well as in its renovating power from all other religions known among men. And we have to connect with this view a survey of its subsequent diffusion and leavening influence in human society. Comparing this religion with the native characteristics of the people among whom it appeared, and from whose hands the priceless treasure was at length delivered to mankind, we are to

God's revelation involves the plan and order of a great historical movement of which miracles are a part.

---

[1] See this proposition ably maintained and illustrated by Prof. Edward Hitchcock in the Bibliotheca Sacra for July, 1863, pp. 489–561.

[2] Supernatural Origin of Christianity, p. 502.

[3] See on this subject the propositions and arguments of Walker, Philosophy of the Plan of Salvation, chapters iii–x. Boston, 1855.

ask ourselves if this religion, so pure and salutary, so enduring and influential, so strong as to survive temporary eclipse, and withstand through a long succession of ages, before the full light appeared, an adversary as powerful as human barbarism and corruption, can be the product of man's invention. And whatever reason there is for rejecting this supposition as irrational is so much argument for the Christian miracles. . . . Miracles appear especially at the signal epochs in the progress of the gradually developing system of religion. . . . In connexion with Moses, who marks an era in the communication of the true religion; then, after a long interval, in connexion with the prophets, who introduce an era not less peculiar and momentous; and then, after a long suspension of miraculous manifestation, in conjunction with the final and crowning epoch of revelation, with the ministry of Christ and the founding of the Church, the supernatural is seen to break into the course of history. There is an impressive analogy between the spiritual creation or renewal of humanity, and the physical creation, where successive eras are inaugurated by the exertion of supernatural agency in the introduction of new species, and after each epoch history is remanded, as it were, to its natural course in pursuance of an established order. Miracle would seem to be the natural expression and verification of an opening era in the spiritual enlightenment of mankind, when new forces are introduced by the great Author of light and life, and a new development sets in." [2]

3. Another and highly important consideration is that the miracles of Scripture are worthy of the Author of a divine revelation. They are not prodigies put forth merely to startle and confound the curious mind. The early revelations to the patriarchs by dreams and visions of the night, or by the ministry of angels, have no affinity with the myths

The Scripture miracles worthy of the Author of revelation.

---

[1] Hume's famous argument, that miracles are contrary to experience, and that it is easier to believe that any given testimony is false than that a law of nature was ever violated, has received many answers. Fisher well observes that "the fallacy does not lie in the postulate that a miracle is contrary to experience; for there is a logical propriety in this provisional assumption. But the fallacy lies in the assumption that a miracle is *just as likely to occur in the one place as in the other;* that we may as rationally expect a miracle to be wrought in the matter of testimony, whereby the laws of evidence are miraculously converted into a vehicle for deceiving and misleading mankind, as to suppose a miracle in the physical world like the healing of the blind. Hume's argument is valid only on the hypothesis that God is as ready to exert supernatural power to make truthful men falsify as to perform the miracles of the Gospel. Introduce the fact of a personal God, a moral government, and a wise and benevolent end to be subserved through miraculous interposition, and Hume's reasoning is emptied of all its force."—Supernatural Origin of Christianity, pp. 495, 496.

[2] Supernatural Origin of Christianity, pp. 506–508.

and legends of paganism. The miracles of the Exodus were both an evidence of the divine mission of Moses and a series of judgments upon the idolatrous superstitions of Egypt. Each sign and wonder was in style and character worthy of the God who spoke the decalogue from the quaking mountain. The miracles that attended the ministry of later prophets had a pertinency which shows them to have been grounded in divine and not in human wisdom. But, especially, in the mighty works of the Son of God do we observe a character that harmonizes with the purposes of redemption. The miracles of Jesus are acts of tenderness and love, exhibitions of divine glory and wisdom, and at the same time symbolical tokens of the mysteries of redemption.' Even the miracle of judgment, the cursing of the barren fig-tree, abounds with suggestive lessons of the highest moral value. Trench observes that the pretended prodigies of witchcraft, even if actually performed, were, nevertheless, works which had no worthy significance; [1] "they were not, what each true. miracle is always more or less, *redemptive* acts; in other words, works not merely of power, but of grace, each one an index and a prophecy of the inner work of man's deliverance, which it accompanies and helps forward. But it was pre-eminently thus with the miracles of Christ. Each one of these is in small, and upon one side or another, a partial and transient realization of the great work which he came that, in the end, he might accomplish perfectly and forever. They are all pledges in that they are themselves firstfruits of his power; in each of them the word of salvation is incorporated in an act of salvation. Only when regarded in this light do they appear not merely as illustrious examples of his might, but also as glorious manifestations of his holy love." [2]

The miracles of Scripture, then, are to be regarded as historical facts, and interpreted as other facts of history.

2. DESCRIPTIONS OF PHYSICAL PHENOMENA.

There are found in the Bible descriptions of natural phenomena, allusions to the movement of the heavenly bodies, and narratives

[1] This thought appears in the Recognitions of Clement, where Peter is represented as opposing Simon Magus: "For tell me, I pray you, what is the use of showing statues walking, dogs of brass or stone barking, mountains dancing, of flying through the air, and such like things, which you say that Simon did? But those signs which are of the good One are directed to the advantage of men, as are those which were done by our Lord, who gave sight to the blind and hearing to the deaf, raised up the feeble and the lame, drove away sicknesses and demons, raised the dead, and did other like things."—Recognitions, etc., book iii, chap. 60, English translation, as in Clark's Ante-Nicene Library.

[2] Trench, Notes on the Miracles, p. 31.

of changes effected on the surface of the earth, which have been alleged to be unscientific and inconsistent with facts. The instances usually cited in proof of this charge are descriptions of the sun, moon, and stars, allusions to their apparent movements, the account of the sun and moon standing still, and the deluge of waters which occurred in the days of Noah.

The statement that God made two great luminaries to rule respectively the day and the night, and set them, along with the stars, in the expanse of heaven to give light upon the earth (Gen. i, 16, 17), is supposed to rest upon the now exploded Ptolemaic theory of the universe, according to which the earth is the centre of the whole system, and sun, moon, and stars revolve around it. With this accords the frequent mention of the rising of the sun and the going down of the same (Psa. l, 1). In Psa. xix, 4–6, the sun is poetically conceived as having his tent or dwelling in the heavens, and coming forth out of his chamber in the morning to run a race from one end of the heavens unto the other. The poetical parts of Scripture abound in similar descriptions of things in the earth and the heavens. All such allusions, it has been claimed, betray a false astronomy. *Supposed evidences of a false astronomy.*

This class of objections, alleged as contradictions of science, can scarcely now be regarded as ingenuous. Can anything be more evident than the fact that in descriptions of such phenomena the sacred writers use the language of common life? In spite of all scientific advancement the world still speaks, and probably ever will continue to speak, of the sun's rising and setting. The stars appear to the common observer as so many bright lights set in the vault of heaven. To an observer on the earth the sun and moon are the two great lights of the sky, and the fact is not in the least altered by the discovery that the moon is the earth's satellite, and the earth is a comparatively small planet revolving about the sun. To the human observer the sun is the great luminary; he rises and sets, and rules the day; and this fact remains in spite of the discovery that many of the stars are also luminaries immensely larger than our "king of day." The Bible is written in the common and popular language of men, not in the technical forms of science. And when we read such poetic strains as that which embodies the striking similes of the sun in Psa. xix, 4–6, we no more suppose the author to have been teaching a false astronomy than we would accuse Longfellow of such false science when he writes: *Such expressions merely the language of common life.*

> Silently, one by one, in the infinite meadows of heaven,
> Blossomed the lovely stars.

The standing still of the sun and moon at the command of Joshua
(Josh. x, 12–14) has been supposed to predicate a miracle incredibly stupendous. It was believed to yield
such evidence that the earth was stationary, and that the
sun revolved around it that, when Galileo taught a contrary doctrine, he was charged with formal heresy, and his scientific system
was declared by the Church of Rome to be "expressly contrary to
the Scripture." The literal interpretation of the passage naturally
assumed that the sun stopped short in mid-heaven at the fiat of
Joshua. Afterward, the general acceptance of the Copernican
system led to the supposition that the diurnal motion of the earth
was checked for a time, thus causing the sun to appear to stand
still. Probably no well-informed student of the Scriptures will
now accept either of these views. The two prevalent interpretations of the passage, between which the best expositors are now
divided, may be designated the *optical* and the *poetical*. Those
who adopt the first-named exposition believe that we have here the
record of a miracle, which consisted in a supernatural refraction of
light. They suppose that after the sun had gone down, the light
was miraculously prolonged, and by refraction both sun and moon
appeared for a long time to be stationary above the horizon. This
hypothesis, however, scarcely accords with Joshua's command for
the sun to stand still in Gibeon, and the statement that "the sun
stood still in the midst of the heavens" (Josh. x, 13), not over the
western horizon.

But commentators have been slow to note the fact that the passage in question is professedly a quotation from the
Book of Jasher. That book appears to have been a
compilation of national songs (comp. 2 Sam. i, 18), and
such a quotation should no more be pressed into a literal interpretation than the highly wrought passage from the nineteenth psalm
already noticed. Where the quotation begins and ends is somewhat uncertain,[1] but the whole passage, from verse 12 to verse 15,
has every appearance of an interpolation. As the Book of Jasher
contained David's elegy it could not have been completed before
the time of David; but the Book of Joshua was probably written
long before that date. The song of Joshua's victory, however,

Standing still of the sun and moon. [side note]

The passage a poetical quota-tion. [side note]

---

[1] It is commonly affirmed that the formula of citation must stand at the beginning
or end of the passage cited, and hence some hold that what follows the words, "Is not
this written in the Book of Jasher?" (Josh. x, 13), do not belong to the book referred
to. But this is by no means certain. We may understand the formula of citation to
be thrown in parenthetically in the midst of the passage cited, and such appears to
be the case in this quotation.

may have been written by an eyewitness of the battle, and may have been directly quoted by the author of the Book of Joshua, for such an anthology as the Book of Jasher would be likely to receive additions from time to time, as one national song after another obtained popular currency. Considered therefore as a poetical quotation, the passage is not to be literally understood, and all supposed conflict between its statements and scientific facts is at once set aside. "The standing still of the sun and moon," says Fay, "is no more to be understood literally than that fighting of the stars from their courses (Judges v, 20), or the melting down of the mountains (Isa. xxxiv, 3; Amos ix, 13; Micah i, 4), the rending of the heavens (Psa. xviii, 9), or the skipping of Lebanon (Psa. xxix, 6), or the clapping of hands by the trees in the field (Isa. lv, 12), or the leaping of the mountains and hills (Psa. cxiv, 6). It is the language of poetry which we have here to interpret, and poetry, too, of the most figurative, vehement kind, which honours and celebrates Joshua's confidence in God in the midst of the strife. In this the most positive interpreters (Keil, Kurtz, Hengstenberg), however they may differ as to the particulars, and as to textual criticism, are perfectly at one against a literal interpretation of the passage."[1]

Another point at which science and the Bible have been alleged to be in conflict is the narrative of the Deluge in Gen. vi–viii. The doctrine of a universal flood is beset with insuperable difficulties. The shells and corals found in deposits at the tops of high mountains, and which were once believed to furnish evidence of a universal deluge, are seen upon closer inspection to be results of geologic action older than the age of Noah. They are not scattered over the surface, as would have been the case if they had been carried there by a flood of waters, but deposited deep in the layers of the mountains as well as near the surface. It is to be further observed that the loose scoriæ on the mountains of Auvergne and Languedoc in France must have been disturbed and swept away by a deluge that covered those heights. Yet the dust and cinders of these volcanic craters bear witness that they have remained undisturbed by any flood of waters from a period long anterior to that of the time of Noah.

It may also be reasonably objected to a universal flood that the salt waters of the fountains of the great deep, in overflowing the

Narrative of the Deluge.

[1] Commentary on Joshua in Lange's Biblework. The Speaker's Commentary takes substantially the same view: "Thé whole passage may, and even ought, on critical grounds to be taken as a fragment of unknown date and uncertain authorship, interpolated into the text of the narrative, the continuity of which is broken by the intrusion."—Note at end of Chapter x.

land, must have destroyed, in the course of nearly a year, all fresh-water fish, and plants and seeds of the land, none of which appear to have been taken into the ark. Add to these considerations the inadequacy of any ark constructed by human hands to contain pairs of all cattle, beasts, fowls, and insects now known to exist upon the earth, together with food sufficient to sustain them for a year. The different classes and species of living creatures are known to number hundreds of thousands. They are distributed into groups and provinces, and many of them seem to have been propagated from distinct centres of creation. The animals of the polar regions and those of the tropics could not long live together except by a protracted miracle. "To collect specimens," says Geikie, "of all the species of terrestrial creatures inhabiting the earth, it would be necessary not only to visit each parallel of latitude on both sides of the equator, but to explore the whole extent of each parallel, so as to leave out none of the separate provinces. With all the appliances of modern civilization, and all the labours of explorers in the cause of science throughout every part of the world, the task of ascertaining the extent of the animal kingdom is probably still far from being accomplished. Not a year passes away without witnessing new names added to the list of the zoologist. Surely no one will pretend that what has not yet been achieved by hundreds of labourers during many centuries could have been performed by one of the patriarchs during a few years. It was of course necessary that the animals should be brought alive; but this, owing to their climatal susceptibilities, was in the case of many species impossible, and even with regard to those which might have survived the journey, the difficulties of their transport must have been altogether insuperable." [1]

It should further be added that the flooding of all continents and islands so as to submerge the tops of the highest mountains would increase the earth's diameter by many miles; it would involve inconceivable climatic changes over the whole surface of the globe, add greatly to the force of its attraction, change its orbit round the sun, and disturb the movements of all the other planets. In short, the doctrine of a universal deluge involves a multiplicity of such stupendous miracles that it cannot be accepted except on statements and reasons of the most absolute and imperative character.

But why should we assume or teach that the flood described in Gen. vi–viii was universal? The assumption has arisen from a supposed necessity of understanding such expressions as those in

Marginal note: Insuperable objections to its universality.

[1] Kitto's New Biblical Cyclopedia, article Deluge.

Gen. vi, 13 ; vii, 19, in their widest possible import. In the first passage God says to Noah : "An end of all flesh has come before me," and in the second : "The waters prevailed very exceedingly upon the land, and all the high hills which were under all the heavens were covered." These expressions properly denote universality, but before any interpreter decides their real import he must consider the standpoint of the writer, and the familiar usage of such terms among the ancient orientals. The narrative of the flood is probably the account of an eyewitness. Its vividness of description and minuteness of details contain the strongest evidence that it is such. It was probably a tradition handed down from Shem to his descendants until it was finally incorporated in the Books of Moses. The terms, "all flesh," "all the high hills," and "all the heavens," denote simply all those known to the observer. They are parallel with such expressions as, "This day I begin to put the dread and awe of thee upon the face of the nations under all the heavens" (Deut. ii, 25 ; comp. iv, 19) ; "There is not a nation or kingdom where my lord has not sent to seek thee" (1 Kings xviii, 10). So the allusion, in Job xxxvii, 3, to the thunder and lightning, is essentially confined to a limited area : "Under all the heavens he lets it loose, and his lightning over the borders of the land." A comparison of such passages as Isa. lxvi, 23 ; Jer. xxv, 31, 32 ; and Ezek. xx, 48 ; xxi, 4, shows also that "all flesh" is a familiar Hebraism denoting the great mass of mankind, but not necessarily implying the absolute and universal totality of the human race. The common translation of the Hebrew word אֶרֶץ by our word *earth* is also misleading, and the source of much false exegesis. This word denotes, according to the common *usus loquendi*, a limited territory, a region or country, and may always be properly rendered by our word *land*. The Noachic deluge submerged all the land under all the heavens (or sky) known to the antediluvians. It was in all probability universal to the human race, destroying the entire family of man except Noah and his household. This opinion is corroborated by the traditions of a flood preserved among all existing nations.

The entire territory occupied by the human race up to the time of the deluge need not have been larger than the land of Egypt, or of Canaan ; but if it had been a hundred times larger than either of those countries it would still have been a comparatively small portion of the entire face of the earth. The considerations briefly indicated above have led nearly all recent expositors to abandon the notion of a universal deluge. All conflict with science is, accordingly,

Scripture usage applies universal terms to limited areas.

The Noachic deluge local and limited, but universal as to the human race.

disposed of by these considerations, and no one can justly allege
that the biblical narrative of the flood is contradicted by scientific
discovery until he can prove that no limited section of the earth's
surface has, since man began his existence, been subjected to such
a destructive judgment.

3. The Origin of the World and of Man.

But the great battle-field on which theologians and scientists
have been most in conflict is the Mosaic narrative of
creation. This narrative is supposed to describe the
origin of all things, including matter, life, and mind;
and the modern theories of evolution, and assertions of man's immense antiquity, have seemed to command such an array of evidences that it has become very common to study Genesis with constant deference to these theories and assertions, and even to study
biology and evolution with equal deference to the Book of Genesis.
The highest aim of some writers would seem to be the construction
of an exegesis of Genesis that may at once harmonize with the
statements of the sacred writer and the hypothesis of leading scientists. These writers all assume that the creation described at the
beginning of Genesis must be identical with the primordial construction of the whole material universe, and the origin of all its
living tribes. And this kind of effort at exegesis became noticeable
long before the doctrine of Darwinian evolution attained the prominence and prevalence it now holds. Ever since the researches of
geologists and astronomers disclosed the great antiquity of our
globe, and the immensity of the starry universe, there has been a
ceaseless effort to "reconcile Science and the Bible." In some of
these attempts devout men have seemed to lose all common sense
and reason, and have launched out upon a series of fanciful conjectures by which the revelation of God has been strangely handled.
From some of these attempted reconciliations it appears that good
men may unwittingly trifle with the Scriptures in the name of
science. That, surely, is a most unscientific process which ignores
the *usus loquendi* of the simplest words of a language, gives a
well-known term half a dozen different meanings in a single chapter, and lugs in conjecture and doubtful hypothesis to determine
the meaning of words familiar as our mother tongue.

The Mosaic narrative of creation.

Among the many modern attempts to interpret the Mosaic record there have arisen into prominence three different methods, which we may appropriately designate
the Geological, the Cosmological, and the Idealistic.
According to the first-named method, the six days of creation

Geological method of interpretation.

correspond with six long periods of geological development tracea-ble in the crust of the earth. But more careful and extended re-searches fail to find in the testimony of the rocks an exact or even substantial agreement between the geological epochs and the days of Genesis. Even Hugh Miller, one of the most distinguished ad-vocates of this theory, is obliged to acknowledge that geology has no epochs that correspond with the first, second, and fourth days of the Mosaic narrative. Of these periods he says, "we need expect to find no record in the rocks. The geologist, in his attempts to collate the divine with the geologic record has only three of the six periods of creation to account for—the period of plants, the period of great sea-monsters and creeping things, and the period of cattle and beasts of the earth." [1] But this is well pronounced by a later critic "a very inadmissible assertion. Any one, be he geolo-gist, astronomer, theologian, or philologist, who attempts to explain the Hebrew narrative, is bound to take it with all that belongs to it; and, in truth, if the fourth day really represented an epoch of creative activity, geology would be able to give some account of it." [2] Prof. C. H. Hitchcock seems to admit that geology has prop-erly no period corresponding to the fourth day, but he adopts the notion that the Paleozoic Age of geologists may synchronize with the fourth day of Genesis, and supposes "that the attention of the prophet during this vision was so much occupied with the contem-plations of the astronomical bodies that he overlooked the progress of events upon the earth, none of which were very different from what had been previously perceived." [3] Such a notion could scarce-ly have been entertained except under the pressure of a foregone conclusion that the days of Genesis and the epochs of Geology must somehow be synchronized.

Others, not satisfied with the dubious results of the geological interpretation, have sought a wider and grander mean- The Cosmolog-ing in the first of Genesis by making it a cosmogony. ical theory. They base their exposition, not merely on the results of geological research, but more especially on the nebular hypothesis, and their method of explaining Genesis may be called the Cosmological. We have no fault to find with the nebular hypothesis of the origin of the universe. We see no reason why God may not have brought forth the world in that way as well as in any other imaginable. But we object to the methods of interpretation by which that hypothesis is forced into an exposition of the simple narrative of Genesis. Twisting words out of their natural and established usage,

---

[1] Testimony of the Rocks, p. 159.   [2] Essays and Reviews, p. 269.
[3] Relations of Geology to Theology, Bibliotheca Sacra for July, 1867, p. 444.

and foisting into them the ideas of a later age, is a process essentially at war with all safe and sound interpretation. The ideas may be true, and, in themselves, of the highest scientific value; but the question of the interpreter must be: Are these the ideas intended in this narrative?

Prof. A. H. Guyot's essay on "Cosmogony and the Bible"[1] is regarded as one of the ablest expositions of Genesis from the standpoint of the nebular hypothesis. He considers the days as vast cosmogonic periods, or, as he calls them, "organic phases of creation." But he affirms that in the first chapter of Genesis the word *day* is used *in five different senses!* Who knows, then, but the word *God* may have, in the same chapter, six or seven different meanings—one for every day? He also affirms that the word *earth* means, in the second verse, "the primordial cosmic material out of which God was going to organize the heavens and the earth," and is "an equivalent to matter in general." So it would appear that in the first verse of the Bible *earth* and *heavens* are synonymous terms. "The same reasoning," he adds, "applies to the *waters* of the second verse. The Hebrew word *maïm* does not necessarily mean waters, but applies as well to the fluid atmosphere; it is simply descriptive of the state of cosmic matter comprised in the word earth." And so he proceeds, dogmatically putting meanings to suit his convenience upon the most simple words of the language. Upon such principles and such reasoning we may, doubtless, make the Bible mean anything we please. If words like *day, land, heavens, and waters* may be explained as is done by this writer, can we fairly hope for any settled *principles* of interpretation? The explanations of the biblical narrative itself are treated as of no account. The sacred writer tells us that God called the light day, and the dry land earth. Why, then, should we set aside or ignore the meaning which he puts upon his own words? But if one would be consistent when he insists that earth means cosmical matter, and light means cosmical light, and days mean cosmogonic ages, why should he not also complete the cosmogonic symmetry of the picture with cosmical cattle and cosmical man?

Guyot's essay.

Rorison's idealistic interpretation. Another class of interpreters, not satisfied with either the geological or cosmological exposition of Genesis, have attempted to escape all responsibility for a literal interpretation by resolving the Mosaic narrative into a

---

[1] Cosmogony and the Bible; or, the Biblical Account of Creation in the Light of Modern Science. Printed among the Papers of the Sixth General Conference of the Evangelical Alliance, New York, 1873.

poem, "The Inspired Psalm of Creation." This may be called the Idealistic method of interpretation.[1] "It is enough," says Mr. Rorison, "if the Bible opens with a divinely illuminated survey of creation such as readily *assimilates* the results of that research it was never meant to supersede or forestall." "Respect the parallelism," he urges; "cease to ignore the structure, allow for the mystic significance of the number seven, and all perplexities vanish. The two groups of days are each perfectly regular, when group, in its integrity, is collated with group; neither triad, if it is to exhaust its own aspect of creation, can afford to part with or dislocate any of its members; and the second triad, as a whole, is rightly and of necessity second, as the first is rightly and of necessity first. And yet it is self evident that if, for any reason, we trisect or break up the groups, the true *continuation* of day one is not day two, but day four; of day two, not day three, but day five; of day three, not day four, but day six. And thus the 'days' themselves are transfigured from registers of time into definitives of strophes or stanzas —lamps and landmarks of a creative sequence—a mystic drapery, a parabolic setting—shadowing by the sacred cycle of seven the truths of an ordered progress, a foreknown finality, an achieved perfection, and a divine repose."

Here we are carried out of a narrative of facts and introduced into a realm of fancy. Even days are "transfigured" into some ideal conceptions that no common mind will find it easy to grasp, and the whole array of "lamps and landmarks," "mystic drapery," and "parabolic setting" are acknowledged to be only "shadows" that may "assimilate" the results of scientific research. This writer points out the artistic form of the record, which he calls a poem, and refers also to the similar artistic structure of the Decalogue and the Lord's Prayer; but would he affirm that those inimitable compositions are not to be literally understood? The mere correspondency, so often pointed out, of the work of the first day to that of the fourth, and of the second to the fifth, and of the third to the sixth, does not by any means make the passage a poem; nor does the six times repeated "there was evening and there was morning," constitute any proper Hebrew parallelism. If such artificiality of structure be a reason for regarding the whole as a "mystic drapery," merely indicative "of an ordered progress, a foreknown finality, an achieved perfection, and a divine repose," the genealogy of the fifth chapter may be resolved into a similar "shadowing," for its structure is exceedingly regular,

Fanciful and unsound exegesis.

[1] See especially the essay of the Rev. G. Rorison, entitled the Creative Week, in Replies to Essays and Reviews.

and the record of every name closes with the solemn refrain—"and he died." But every thorough Hebrew scholar knows that in all the Old Testament there is not to be found a more simple, straightforward prose narrative than this first chapter of Genesis. Prof. Strong has well said that it "lacks every element of acknowledged Hebrew poetry. In form it has neither the lyrical prosody of the Psalms, nor the epic structure of Job; neither the dithyrambic march of the prophets, nor the idyllic colloquies of the Canticles, nor even the didactic collocations of the Proverbs and Ecclesiastes. . . . As to sentiment, it lacks that lofty moral tone, that fine play of the imagination, that abrupt change of subject and field, which, even when other criteria fail, serve to indicate the rhapsodies of the Hebrew bards. . . . Even Mr. Rorison fails to point out in its body the requisite artistic constructiveness, or in its spirit the fire of genius essential to all poetic effusions. Almost any descriptive portion of the Old Testament would be found to exceed it in these respects if carefully analyzed. The very next chapter of Genesis is fully as poetical, whether in regard to its topics, its style, or its composition; and thus, by the same loose, unscientific process, we might (as many would fain do) reduce the accounts of Adam's specific formation, of a local Eden, and of the origin of human depravity, to poetic legends. Just criticism forbids such a distortion of prose to accommodate speculative preconception."[1]

Let us now inquire what a simple grammatico-historical interpretation of the Mosaic narrative most obviously indicates. Few, if any, will deny that the entire description is adapted to impress the reader with a feeling that the creation here recorded was sublimely miraculous. We should, then, give strict attention to the primary signification of the terms employed.

---

[1] Cyclopædia of Biblical, Theological, and Ecclesiastical Literature, article Cosmology. At the beginning of his essay Mr. Rorison furnishes us with the following sound and excellent observations: "There is no attaining a satisfactory view of the mutual relations of science and Scripture till men make up their minds to do violence to neither, and to deal faithfully with both. . . . We ought to harbour no hankering after so-called 'reconciliations,' or allow these to warp in the very least our rendering of the record. It is our business to keep our ears open to what the Scripture says, not exercise our ingenuity on what it can be made to say. . . . Those who seek the repose of truth had best banish from the quest of it, in whatever field, the spirit and the methods of sophistry. The geologist, for example, if loyal to his science, will marshal his facts as if there were no Book of Genesis. Even so is it the duty of the interpreter of the Mosaic text to fix [ascertain?] its sense and investigate its structure as though it were susceptible of neither collation nor collision with any science of geology." The marvel is, that having acknowledged such sound principles of interpretation, this writer should have gone on to construct one of the most fanciful expositions to be found in all the literature of the subject in hand.

The words "heavens and earth" are so commonly used among us moderns to denote the astronomic heavens, and the earth considered as a planet or globe, that interpreters have too generally overlooked the fact that, according to the *usus loquendi* of the Hebrew language, שָׁמַיִם and אֶרֶץ mean simply *sky* and *land*. In verse 8 it is said that God called the expanse שָׁמַיִם—*heavens*, and a comparison of other passages, where the word occurs, will show that it commonly and almost universally denotes the ethereal space above us in which the sun, moon, and stars appear to move, from which the rain falls, and through which the birds fly (comp. Gen. i, 14, 15, 17, 20, 26, 28, 30; ii, 19, 20; vi, 7–17; vii, 3–11; viii, 2, etc.). When occasionally used of the abode of God it arises from the natural conception of him as the Most High, who is exalted above the heavens (Psalms lvii, 5–11; cxiii, 4–6). We are further told, in verse 10, that God called the dry ground אֶרֶץ—*land*. This familiar word nowhere denotes the cubic contents of the earth considered as a globe. Such a conception never appears to have entered the Hebrew mind. The word אֶרֶץ occurs over three hundred times in the Book of Genesis alone, and in most of those places cannot have any other meaning than *land*, an area of ground, a region or section of country. Furthermore, the word בָּרָא, to *create*, does not, according to Hebrew *usus loquendi*, signify the original production of the material or substance of that which is brought into being. This is merely the notion of some modern writers. In Gen. i, 21, the word is applied to the bringing forth of creatures which are expressly said to have been produced from the waters, and in verse 27 it is used of man who was formed in part of the dust of the ground (comp. Gen. v, 2). According to both Gesenius and Fürst, the radical signification of בָּרָא is that of *cutting, carving*, and separating. We may, therefore, properly understand it, in Gen. i, 1, as denoting the forming or construction, out of pre-existing material, of the heavens and the land contemplated in the biblical narrative of "the beginning."

The natural meaning of these words, then, should suggest to the interpreter that in the opening chapters of Genesis he is not to look for a universal cosmogony. The heavens and land of these chapters are the visible sky and country where the first human pair were created. The various species of vegetable and animal life which were brought forth on that land, or to multiply in those heavens and waters, were such as were there to serve some interest of man, and he was to have dominion over them. The primeval darkness on the face of the deep need not be supposed to have been other than local and temporary.

"Heavens and Land" in Hebrew usus loquendi.

The first of Genesis not a universal cosmogony.

Dense mists, hiding sun, moon, and stars from view for many days, and shrouding all things in utter gloom, have not unfrequently covered a large portion of the earth's surface (comp. Acts xxvii, 20). The light of the first three days of the biblical narrative appears to have been local and miraculous, like that which was in the dwellings of Israel when dense darkness covered all the rest of Egypt (Exod. x, 23). The setting of the luminaries in the expanse on the fourth day was phenomenal; not a primordial creation, but what was apparent from the land of Eden. What had taken place on any other portion of the terrestrial globe, or what classes of living creatures may have elsewhere existed before or at the time of this beginning of human history, are questions with which the sacred writer was not at all concerned. A region no larger than any one of several islands of Malaysia would have been ample for the history of the whole human race before the flood. That land, however, may have been a portion of one of the existing continents, then for the first time elevated above the waters. The language used would apply equally well to any limited region, whether of a continent, a peninsula, or an island.[1] The simplest and most natural meaning of the narrative is that God at first upheaved such a land from under the waters of the deep, and, subsequently, when all flesh had corrupted its way (Gen. vi, 12), he broke up the fountains of the great deep and submerged that region with all its teeming tribes. At the subsidence of the deluge the ark rested, not again in Eden but on the mountain of Ararat (Gen. viii, 4), from which region the sons of Noah spread abroad. The original Eden may have been obliterated by the flood, but the names of its countries and rivers would very naturally have been transferred to the new land and rivers discovered and occupied by the sons of Noah.

---

[1] John Pye Smith, a generation ago, in his work on The Relation between the Holy Scriptures and some Parts of Geological Science (4th edition, London, 1848), showed by a variety of evidence "that there must have been separate original creations, perhaps at different and respectively distant epochs" (p. 49). He also maintained that a strict interpretation of the language of Genesis required no wider application of its terms than to "the part of our world which God was adapting for the dwelling of man and the animals connected with him. Of the spheroidal figure of the earth it is evident that the Hebrews had not the most distant conception." He understood *the land* of Gen. i to be only "*a portion of the surface of the earth*, adjusted and furnished for most glorious purposes, in which a newly formed creation should be the object of those manifestations of the authority and grace of the Most High, which shall to eternity show forth his perfections above all other methods of their display" (pp. 189, 190). He conceived this portion of the earth "to have been a part of Asia lying between the Caucasian ridge, the Caspian Sea, and Tartary on the north, the Persian and Indian seas on the south, and the high mountain ridges which run at considerable distances on the eastern and the western flank."

It would be manifestly unfair to say that an exposition of Genesis on so limited a scale is but another hypothesis as futile as the Geological, the Cosmological, or the Idealistic. For let it be observed that it rests, as its principal claim for acceptance, upon a strict grammatico-historical interpretation of the language of the sacred writer. *This explanation of Gen. 1 not a hypothetical theory, but a strictly natural interpretation.* Moreover, it accords most perfectly with the scope and plan of the entire Book of Genesis. We have shown above (pp. 211, 212) how the author prefaces his tenfold history of generations with an account of the creation of the land where the first man appeared; and Gen. i, 1, is, properly, the heading of that prefatory narrative, just as each of the ten subsequent sections has its appropriate title. It is incorrect to say, as some have done, that the first chapter is a narrative of the universal creation, and the second chapter an account of Eden and Paradise. A discriminating analysis shows that chapters i–ii, 3, is the narrative of the *beginning,* or *creation* of the heavens and land, and chapters ii, 4–iv, 26, a record of the *generations* (or evolutions) of the same heavens and land, dating from the day when the Edenic growths began.[1]

Setting aside the assumption, therefore, that the first of Genesis is an outline of universal cosmogony, and following the simple grammatico-historical sense of the language, we find a more natural exposition of what has so sadly perplexed the harmonists. All grounds of controversy between science and the Bible are at once removed.[2] The first of Genesis describes a local and limited creation. How large a region it affected, and where that land was situated, are questions that now admit of no answer. It is the record of a sevenfold miracle, projected by a well-defined plan and order through the first week of historic time. It furnishes the lessons of a personal God, the eternal, the all-wise, the omnipotent, and thus stands opposed to polytheism and pantheism. It exhibits God as the Creator, the great First Cause of things. It shows how matter is his creature, and subject to his will, and how life—vegetable, animal, and spiritual — originates with him. It shows an orderly progress from lower to higher, and the correspondency between the work of the two triads of days serves to illustrate the wisdom and the knowledge of God. It may be that the six days of creative procedure here narrated are typical of corresponding ages of cosmical development, and a wider and more complete

---

[1] See further on pp. 567, 568.

[2] That is, the science which allows the possibility of miracles. With that infidel science, which spurns the thought of a miraculous creation, the evangelical interpreter can have no argument on the Mosaic narrative.

induction of facts may yet confirm this supposition. But even if now confirmed, it would not add essentially to the great lessons of order and progress furnished by the literal interpretation of the biblical record. For it does not follow that God must have created or developed each part of the whole universe in the same manner. There were doubtless other beginnings, and there are probably innumerable forms of life and ranks and orders of living creatures in other spheres which no descendant of Adam has ever been able to discover, and which it is no purpose of the Bible to reveal. Let it be once conceded that God literally and miraculously formed the Eden-land and sky, and all that they contained, in the manner described in Genesis, and it necessarily follows *a fortiori* that he also must be the absolute and universal Creator. And if the noble lessons above indicated are taught, as Mr. Rorison thinks, in a grand cosmological poem, whose artistic periods mean anything or everything in general, and nothing in particular, how much more forcibly are they taught in a historical record of literal fact.

Rightly to interpret the Mosaic narrative, therefore, it is necessary to disabuse our minds of the assumption that it is a revelation of the primordial origin of the universe. How and when God originated matter, and what were the first forms and modes of life—whether of plants, insects, reptiles, fish, fowls, beasts, cattle, or angels—it appears not the purpose of revelation to inform us; but this beginning of the Bible does inform us of the miraculous creation of man in the image of God. If to some minds, familiar with cosmological conceptions, it seems to belittle the biblical creation to confine it to a limited portion of the earth, let it be considered whether the plagues of Egypt were belittled by being confined solely to the land of the Nile. Was it no sublime and impressive miracle that when oppressive darkness covered Egypt for three days light filled the dwellings of Israel in the land of Goshen? Does it detract from the life and mighty works of Jesus that they were confined to the little land of Canaan? Was the judgment of the deluge less signal because confined to only a portion of the globe? As a more careful attention to the usage of Hebrew terms has led nearly all modern exegetes to abandon the notion that the Noachic deluge was universal, so we believe a closer study of the Hebrew text of Genesis i and ii will set aside the idea that those chapters were designed to furnish a universal cosmogony. To have prefaced the account of the creation of man with a description of the origin of the entire universe might have been as much out of place as to have introduced the Gospel of Jesus with a history of all the angels of God.

No valid presumption against a limited creation.

CHAPTER XXXII.

HARMONY AND DIVERSITY OF THE GOSPELS.

THE life of Jesus forms a turningpoint in the history of the world. The Old Testament Scriptures show the steady trend of history toward that eventful epoch. The prophets with one voice place the coming of the Christ "in the end of the days" (Gen. xlix, 1; Num. xxiv, 14; Isa. ii, 2; Dan. x, 14), and conceive his advent and reign as the ushering in of a new age. The God of the prophets spoke, in the last days of the old æon, in the person of his incarnate Son, "whom he made heir of all things, through whom also he made the ages" (τοὺς αἰῶνας, the æons, Heb. i, 2). The death and consequent exaltation of Jesus were the crucial hour of the world's history (John xii, 23–33), and from that hour there was a new departure in the course of human affairs. After the Gospel of the Messianic kingdom had been preached in the whole Roman world, for a witness to all the nations of the same (Matt. xxiv, 14), the end of that age came. For it was necessary, before the old economy came to its decisive end, that the new Gospel should first obtain a sure standing in the world. The utter overthrow of the Jewish polity and state, and the awful ruin of that wicked city where the Lord was crucified, marked the consummation of that æon. And from that point onward the triumphs of the cross extend. It is but natural, therefore, that the four gospels, being the authoritative records of the life and words of the Lord Jesus, are esteemed the most precious documents of Christianity.

The life of Jesus a turningpoint in human history.

Each of the four gospels presents us with a life picture of the Lord Jesus, and assumes to tell what he did and what he said. But while narrating many things in common, these four witnesses differ much from one another. How to account for so many differences in the midst of so many coincidences has always been a perplexing study among expositors. In modern times the rationalistic critics have pointed to the apparent discrepancies of the gospels as evidences against their credibility, and these most cherished records of the Church have become the central point of controversy between faith and unbelief. The rationalists all concede that the man Jesus lived and died, but that he rose again from the dead, according to the gospels,

The Gospels the chief ground of conflict between faith and unbelief.

they stoutly deny, and resort to all manner of conjectures to account for the uniform and universal faith of the Church in his resurrection. The common sense of all Christendom logically concludes that if Jesus Christ arose from the dead that miracle at once confirms the credibility of the gospels, and accounts for the marvellous rise, the excellency and present power, of the Christian religion. It proves that its origin was supernatural and divine. But if the miracle of Christ's resurrection be a falsehood, the entire Christian system, which rests upon it, is a stupendous fraud. Well might Paul write: "If Christ has not been raised, vain then is our preaching, vain also your faith, and we are found even false witnesses of God, because we witnessed respecting God that he raised up the Christ" (1 Cor. xv, 14, 15).

Many writers, ancient and modern, have undertaken to construct Attempts at a (so-called) Harmony of the Gospels.[1] They have adopted constructing Gospel Harmonies. various methods of explaining the several discrepancies, and of constructing one harmonious narrative out of the four different accounts of the life of Christ. Eusebius compiled an arrangement of the gospels in ten canons or tables, according as the different events are related by one or more of the evangelists. Thus, under one head he brought those passages that are common to all the gospels; under another those that are found only in one gospel; in three other tables he exhibited those facts which are common to any three of the gospels, and in five others those that are common to any two. At a later period effort was directed more to the combining of the four gospels into one chronological order, and then the great question arose, Which of the evangelists gives us the true order of events? Some maintained that all four gospels give the events of the Lord's life in their true chronological order, and wherever the events are arranged differently by different writers we should understand that the transactions in question occurred more than once. Others strenuously maintained that chronological order is not observed by any of the evangelists, while others were uncertain which particular evangelist is the best chronological guide, some preferring Matthew's arrangement, others Luke's, inasmuch as he professes to set forth things in their true order (καθεξῆς, Luke i, 3). Cartwright follows the arrangement of Mark,

---

[1] The most valuable works on the Harmony of the Gospels are those of J. Macknight (London, 1756), W Newcome, in Greek (Dublin, 1778), and English (1802), G. Townsend (London, 1825), edited by T. W. Coit (Boston, 1837), E. Robinson, in Greek (Boston, 1845), and English (1846), J. Strong, in English (New York, 1852), and Greek (1854), W. Stroud, in Greek (London, 1853), Tischendorf, Synopsis Evangelica (New edition, Leipsic, 1864), F. Gardiner, in Greek and English (Andover, 1871).

and John's Gospel, having comparatively few things in common with the others, is generally believed to present the true chronological order of the matters it records.

The harmonists have furnished many valuable expositions, together with many solutions of the alleged discrepancies of the gospels. But as far as they have attempted to *Use of Harmonies.* combine the four gospels into one continuous narrative, and settle positively the exact chronological order of events, they have rather hindered than helped a satisfactory understanding of these priceless records. Such a process brings these lifelike and independent narratives to a test they were never meant to meet, and assumes a standard of judgment that is both unscientific and unfair. But most of the later harmonists concede that it was no purpose of the evangelists to compose a complete account of the life and works of Jesus, and that all of them record some things without strict regard to the order of time. "The true use of harmonies," says J. A. Alexander, "is threefold: exegetical, historical, and apologetical. By mere juxtaposition, if judicious, the gospels may be made to throw light upon each other's obscure places. By combination—not mechanical, but rational; not textual, but interpretative—harmonies put it in our power not to grind, or melt, or boil four gospels into one, but out of the four, kept apart, yet viewed together, to extract one history for ourselves. And, lastly, by the endless demonstration of the possible solutions of apparent or alleged discrepancies, even where we may not be prepared to choose among them, they reduce the general charge of falsehood or of contradiction, not only *ad absurdum*, but to a palpable impossibility. How *can* four independent narratives be false or contradictory which it is possible to reconcile on so many distinct hypotheses? The art of the most subtle infidelity consists in hiding this convincing argument behind the alleged necessity of either giving a conclusive and exclusive answer to all captious cavils and apparent disagreements, or abandoning our faith in the history as a whole. This most important end of gospel harmonies has been accomplished."[1]

An intelligent and profitable study of the gospels requires attention especially to three things: (1) Their origin; (2) The *Three considerations.* distinct plan and purpose of each gospel, and (3) The marked characteristics of the several gospels. These considerations, leading as they do to a proper understanding of the gospel records, and to the solution of their discrepancies, are really so many hermeneutical principles to be applied in any thorough exposition of these records.

[1] Article on Harmonies of the Gospels in the Princeton Review, vol. xxviii, p. 105.

The most cursory examination of the four gospels must show the Origin of the observant critic that they are not, in any proper sense, Gospels. formal histories. Nor do they assume to be complete biographies. There is, really, nothing like them in the whole range of literature. They manifestly sprung from a common source, and they all agree in recording more or less of the life, words, works, death, and resurrection of Jesus Christ. But whether that common source were written documents or oral traditions has long been a matter of controversy. Some have maintained the existence of an original gospel in Hebrew or Aramaic; others an original gospel in Greek; while others have supposed the earlier written gospel was supplemented by apostolical traditions.[1] But the hypothesis of an oral gospel, embodying the substance of the apostolic preaching, is now very generally held as the principal source of our four gospels. "The hypothesis of an oral gospel," says An original Westcott, "is most consistent with the general habit oral Gospel. of the Jews and the peculiar habit of the apostles; it is supported by the earliest direct testimony, and in some degree implied in the apostolic writings. The result of the examination of the internal character of the gospels is not less favourable to its adoption than the weight of external evidence. The general form of the Gospels points to an oral source. A minute biography, or a series of annals, which are the simplest and most natural forms of writing, are the least natural forms of tradition, and the farthest removed from the evangelical narratives, which consist of striking scenes and discourses, such as must have lived long in the memories of those who witnessed them. Nor are the gospels fashioned only on an oral type; they are fashioned also upon that type which is preserved in the other apostolic writings. The oral gospel, as far as it can be traced in the Acts and the Epistles, centered in the crowning facts of the passion and the resurrection, while the earlier ministry of the Lord was regarded chiefly in relation to its final issue. In a narrative composed on such a plan it is evident that the record of the last stage of Christ's work would be conspicuous for detail and fulness, and that the events chosen to represent the salient features of its earlier course would be combined together without special reference to date or even to sequence. Viewed in the light of its end the whole period was one in essence, undivided

---

[1] For an account of the various theories of the origin of the gospels, see Introductions to the New Testament by Eichhorn, De Wette, Bleek, Davidson, etc., and Marsh's Translation of Michaelis' Introduction to the New Testament, Westcott's Introduction to the Study of the Gospels, pp. 174–216, and the biblical dictionaries and cyclopædias under the word Gospels.

by years or festivals, and the record would be marked not so much by divisions of time as by groups of events. In all these respects the synoptic gospels exactly represent the probable form of the first oral gospel. They seem to have been shaped by the pressure of recurring needs, and not by the deliberate forethought of their authors. In their common features they seem to be that which the earliest history declares they are, the summary of the apostolic preaching, the historic groundwork of the Church." [1]

But granting the earliest form of the gospel narrative to have been oral, that concession is far from determining the particular origin of our present gospels. And it ought to be agreed among discerning critics that, from the nature of the case, in the absence of sufficient evidence, no absolute certainty can be attained. How and when Matthew and Mark wrote, what was the special occasion of their writing, how far they may have used written documents, and what understanding the apostles and evangelists may have had among themselves about writing down the words and works of their Lord, are all questions which admit of no positive answer. It is not the province of a work on hermeneutics to discuss the different theories of the origin of the written gospels, but to define principles of procedure essential to any profitable discussion of the subject. And it is all important to bear in mind that where absolute certainty on a given question is impossible, dogmatic assumptions must be avoided, and considerate attention should be bestowed upon any reasonable suppositions which will help to elucidate the problem. In the absence of external testimony the gospels themselves, and other New Testament books, may be expected to suggest the best indications of the origin and aim of any one of the gospels. It appears that it was regarded as an essential qualification for apostleship to have seen the Lord (Acts i, 21, 22; 1 Cor. ix, 1). And is it not every way reasonable to suppose that the apostles had an understanding among themselves as to what principal facts of the Lord's life should be embodied in their preaching? May it not have been agreed among them that Matthew and John should each write a gospel of the Lord? At one time it was agreed, according to Paul (Gal. ii, 9), that James, Peter, and John should go as apostles to the Jews, and Paul and Barnabas to the Gentiles. The council of the apostles and elders at Jerusalem, described in Acts xv, shows how carefully matters of general interest to the Church were discussed by the great leaders. Is it likely, then, that so important a matter as the publication of authoritative

No absolute certainty as to the particular origin of each Gospel.

Probable suppositions as to their origin.

[1] Introduction to the Gospels, pp. 212, 213, Boston, 1862.

accounts of the Christ would have been neglected by them? **There** was a saying abroad in the Church that John should not die (John xxi, 23). Whatever its precise meaning, it may have been the occasion of his putting off the composition of his gospel until all the rest of the apostles had passed away. The ancient tradition that Mark's Gospel is essentially that of Peter, and Luke's essentially that of Paul, is corroborated by their general character and form. With those who accept the apostolic origin and divine in spiration of the four gospels there is no reasonable ground for denying that these records were put forth by a common understanding of the apostles and elders of the Church, and for the purpose of providing the churches everywhere with an authoritative testimony of the life and works of the Lord Jesus. It appears from Luke's preface (Luke i, 1) that many persons took in hand, at an early day, to publish narratives of the current oral gospel, namely, the things that were looked upon as fully accomplished by God in the person of Jesus, and before the eyes of those who were with him from the first. This fact probably made it expedient that the great events of that gospel should be set forth by apostolic authority, and when at length these four authoritative records went forth to the churches they supplanted all others, and have ever commended themselves to the faith of Christian believers in all lands.

Further suggestions as to the origin of the four gospels will Distinct plan appear as we proceed to inquire into the distinct plan and purpose of and purpose of each. Is it reasonable to suppose that each Gospel. these gospel records were composed and sent forth among the early churches without any definite plan and purpose? Are they merely so many collections of fragmentary traditions thrown together haphazard? When an event recorded by one is omitted by another, are we to suppose that the omission arose from ignorance of the event? To suppose the affirmative of any one of these questions would seem highly absurd, for each of the four gospels contains so many evidences of definite design, and so many inimitable word-pictures, that we cannot believe that any authors, competent for the writing of such books, would have put them forth without orderly arrangement and without special purpose. It is far more probable that each evangelist had a reason for what he omitted as well as for what he recorded.

Irenæus gives the following account of the gospels: "Matthew Tradition of the issued a written gospel among the Hebrews in their early Church. own dialect, while Peter and Paul were preaching at Rome, and laying the foundation of the Church. After their departure, Mark, the disciple and interpreter of Peter, did also hand down to us in writing what had been preached by Peter. Luke also, the companion of Paul, recorded in a book the gospel preached by him. Afterward, John, the disciple of the Lord, who also had leaned upon his breast, did himself publish a gospel during his residence at Ephesus in Asia."[1] With this general statement of Irenæus all ancient history and tradition substantially agree.

A cursory examination of Matthew's Gospel will discover its special adaptation to Jewish readers. The first verse, *Matthew's Gospel adapted to the Jew.* in true Jewish style, declares it to be "The Book of the generation of Jesus Christ, the son of David, the son of Abraham." The great purpose of this gospel throughout is to exhibit Jesus as the Messiah of whom the prophets had spoken, the divine founder of the kingdom of God. Hence he makes more extensive and more elaborate use of Old Testament prophecy than any other of the evangelists. These prominent features of the first gospel are certainly a fair indication of its special purpose.

The ancient tradition that Mark's Gospel is substantially that of Peter,[2] is confirmed by the general style, scope, and plan *Mark's Gospel adapted to the Roman taste.* of the gospel itself. Peter's active and rapid manner would naturally dictate a condensed and pointed gospel. His ministry to such Gentile converts as Cornelius would be likely to show the need of an account of the Lord Jesus especially adapted to that class of minds. Mark's Gospel well meets this ideal. It omits genealogies and long discourses. It has comparatively few citations from Old Testament prophecy. It portrays the life of Jesus as that of a mighty conqueror. It was certainly adapted to meet the tastes of the Roman mind, whose ideals of rapidity, power, and triumph were well expressed in the famous words of Cæsar, "I came, I saw, I conquered."

Luke's Gospel, declared by the voice of the most ancient tradition

---

[1] Against Heresies, book iii, chap. i, 1. That Matthew's Gospel was originally written in Hebrew, or Aramæan, but early put forth in Greek by the hand or under the oversight of Matthew himself, is now the opinion of many of the best biblical scholars. But the arguments *pro* and *con* may be seen in Meyer, Commentary on Matthew, Introduction; Alford, Greek Testament, Prolegomena; Introduction to New Testament by Hug, De Wette, Bleek, Davidson, etc., and Biblical Dictionaries of Smith, Kitto, and M'Clintock and Strong.

[2] Eusebius says that Peter, having established the Gospel among the Romans, "so greatly did the splendour of piety enlighten the minds of his hearers, that it was not sufficient to hear but once, nor to receive the unwritten doctrine of the Gospel of God, but they persevered in every variety of entreaties to solicit Mark, as the companion of Peter, that he should leave them a monument of the doctrines thus orally communicated in writing. Nor did they cease their solicitations until they had prevailed with the man, and thus became the means of that history which is called the Gospel according to Mark."—Eccl. Hist., book ii, chap. xv (Bohn's Ed.).

to be the substance of Paul's preaching,[1] is pre-eminently the gospel of the Gentiles. It deals more than any other gospel with Jesus' words and works for the whole world. Luke alone records the mission of the seventy. He alone records the parable of the Good Samaritan, and that of the Prodigal Son. He narrates the journey and ministry in Peræa, a comparatively heathen land. But while adding many things of this kind, he also sets forth in his own way the main facts recorded in Matthew and Mark.[2] And the three together, because of the general view they give of the same great outline of facts, are called the Synoptic Gospels.

Luke's the Pauline Gospel to the Gentiles.

Not without reason has the Gospel of Luke been believed to have special adaptations to the mind of the Greeks. As a mighty universal conqueror was the grand ideal of a Roman, so the perfection of humanity was the dream of the noblest Grecian intellect. Luke's orderly narrative, with all those delicate traits which none but the "beloved physician" could so well detail, is pre-eminently the gospel of the Son of man, the gospel of universal redemption.[3]

The Gospel of John has manifestly a specific design different from that of the other gospels. Its lofty spiritual tone, its fulness of doctrine, and its profound conceptions of the divinity of the Lord, arrest the attention of all readers. "The Synoptic Gospels," says Westcott, "contain the gospel of the infant Church; that of St. John the gospel of its

John's the spiritual Gospel of the life of faith.

---

[1] Irenæus Against Heresies, iii, 1. Eusebius, Eccl. Hist., book vi, chap. xxv, where Origen is quoted as saying: "The third Gospel is that according to Luke, the gospel commended by Paul, which was written for the converts from the Gentiles."

[2] "The Gospel of St. Paul," says Westcott, "is, in its essential characteristics, the complementary history to that of St. Matthew. The difference between the two may be seen in their opening chapters. The first words of the Hebrew evangelist gave the clue to his whole narrative; and so the first chapter of St. Luke, with its declarations of the blessedness of faith, and the exaltation of the lowly, lead at once to the point from which he contemplated the life of Him who was 'to give light to them that sit in darkness and in the shadow of death.' The perfect manhood of the Saviour, and the consequent mercy and universality of his covenant, is his central subject, rather than the temporal relations or eternal basis of Christianity. In the other gospels we find our King, our Lord, our God; but in St. Luke we see the image of our great High Priest, 'made perfect through suffering, tempted in all points as we are, but without sin,' so that each trait of human feeling and natural love helps us to complete the outline and confirms its truthfulness."—Introduction to the Study of the Gospels, pp. 370–372.

[3] See Da Costa, The Four Witnesses, pp. 185–225, and Prof. D. S. Gregory, Why Four Gospels? pp. 207–276. In both these valuable works the idea that Matthew's is the gospel for the Jew, Mark's for the Roman, Luke's for the Greek, and John's for the Church is elaborated with much detail. Gregory, however, at some points, carries the matter to an undue extreme.

maturity. The first combine to give the wide experience of the many; the last embraces the deep mysteries treasured up by the one. All alike are consciously based on the same great facts; but yet it is possible, in a more limited sense, to describe the first as historical, and the last as ideal; though the history necessarily points to truths which lie beyond all human experience, and the 'ideas' only connect that which was once for all realized on earth with the eternal of which it was the revelation."[1] Clement of Alexandria, as quoted by Eusebius,[2] also observes: "John, last of all, perceiving that what had reference to the body in the gospel of our Saviour was sufficiently detailed, and, being encouraged by his familiar friends, and urged by the Spirit, he wrote a spiritual gospel." John's Gospel is pre-eminently the gospel of the word of God. It deals especially with the mystery of God in Christ, and sets forth the Lord as the life of men and the light of the world. It is a revelation of the life of faith in the Son of God. It was written "that ye may believe that Jesus is the Christ, the Son of God; and that, believing, ye may have life in his name" (John xx, 31).[3]

Keeping in mind the leading idea and aim of each of the four gospels, we may study their several characteristics to advantage. It will often be found that what at first arrests attention as an inconsistency is an evidence of the scrupulous fidelity of the evangelist. What sceptical critics have pronounced unaccountable omissions may be evidences of special design. The vivid portrayal of events, the little incidents true to life, the touches of pathos, the forms of expression which none but eyewitnesses of the events could use, are a mightier proof of the credibility of the gospels than all the alleged discrepancies are of their incredibility. *Characteristics of the several evangelists.*

Considering now, for example, the Gospel of Matthew as designed especially for Jewish readers, how natural for him to announce it as the book of the generation of Jesus Christ, *the son of David, the son of Abraham.* How to his purpose to describe the birth of Jesus, in the days of Herod the *Noticeable characteristics of Matthew.*

---

[1] Introduction to Gospels, p. 254.　　[2] Ecclesiastical History, vi, 14.

[3] Thus Westcott, "The subject which is announced in the opening verses is realized, step by step, in the course of the narrative. The word 'came to his own,' and they 'received him not;' but others 'received him,' and thereby became 'sons of God.' This is the theme which requires for its complete treatment, not a true record of events or teaching, but a view of the working of both on the hearts of men. The ethical element is co-ordinate with the historical; and the end which the evangelist proposes to himself answers to this double current of his gospel. He wrote that men might believe the fact that Jesus is the Christ, the Son of God, and believing—by spiritual fellowship—might have life in his name."—Introduction to Gospels, pp. 276, 277.

king, as one that was *born King of the Jews,* and born in Bethlehem, according to the prophets. How the Sermon on the Mount is presented in one connected whole, as if it were a republication of the ancient law of Sinai in a new and better form. How the series of miracles in the eighth and ninth chapters follows as if designed to evidence the divine power and authority of this new Lawgiver and King. The calling, ordaining, and sending out the twelve disciples (chap. x) was like the election of a new Israel to reclaim the twelve tribes scattered abroad. The seven parables of chap. xiii are a revelation of the mysteries of the kingdom of heaven, the kingdom which he, as the Christ of God, was about to establish. Then follows ample record of the conflict between this King of the Jews and the scribes and Pharisees, who looked for another kind of Messianic kingdom (xiv–xxiii). The great apocalyptic discourse of chaps. xxiv and xxv discloses the end of that age as in the near future, and is in striking analogy with the spirit and forms of Old Testament prophecy. The record of the last supper, the betrayal, the crucifixion, and the resurrection, completes the picture of the great Prophet, Priest, and King. The entire book has thus a unity of purpose and of detail admirably adapted to be the gospel to the Hebrews, and to show to all the thoughtful in Israel that Jesus was indeed the Messiah of whom the prophets had spoken. Moreover, while thus breathing the Hebrew spirit, it has fewer explanations of Jewish customs than the other gospels.

Many have deemed it strange that Matthew says nothing about *Omissions of* the first miracle of Jesus, at Cana, or of the healing at *the earlier Gos-* Capernaum of the nobleman's son, or of the resurrec- *pels not with-* *out a purpose.* tion of Lazarus, facts of such great interest. These notable miracles are omitted in all the synoptic gospels, and some have rushed to the conclusion that they were unknown to Matthew, Mark, and Luke. Much more reasonable is the suggestion of Upham, that in the earlier oral gospel, preached everywhere by the apostles, and represented in substance in the synoptic gospels, it was agreed, as a matter of prudence, to abstain from any mention of living persons who would be exposed to peril by such a publication of their connexion with Jesus. The persecution that arose upon the death of Stephen would naturally seek out the relatives of the hated Nazarene, and any other parties whose testimony mightily confirmed the divine power of Jesus. The evangelists and apostles would not needlessly expose the nobleman or his son, who were probably still living at Capernaum. They would not publish the home of the relatives of the mother of Jesus, where he wrought his first miracle, nor jeopardize the lives of Mary and Martha and their friends at Bethany by sending forth a publication likely to intensify the feeling that was already so violent against them.[1]

The above considerations are sufficient to set aside all arguments against the genuineness and credibility of the gospels, which are based upon omissions which modern critics may deem strange. To the beloved disciple, John, who was expected to outlive the others, it was appropriately left to record the fuller account of Jesus' Judean ministry, and to make mention of persons and events of whom it was inexpedient to write so fully at an earlier time. And a minute study of the peculiar characteristics of Mark, Luke, and John, will show that, both in what they record and in what they omit, each consistently carries out his own individual plan and purpose.[2]

The inner and essential harmony of the gospels is accordingly enhanced by their diversity. These narratives consti- *The harmony of the Gospels enhanced by their diversity.* tute a fourfold witness of the Christ of God. As broad-minded philosophers have discerned in the national characteristics and history of the Jews, the Greeks, and the Romans a providential preparation of the world for the Gospel, so in the gospels themselves may be seen, in turn, a providential record of the world's Redeemer, wonderfully adapted by manifold forms of statement to impress and convince the various minds of men. We

[1] "Bethany," observes Upham, "was one of the suburbs of Jerusalem. The miracle there wrought was the immediate occasion of the arrest and trial of Jesus, though the hatred of the Jews had kindled to the heat of murder before the raising of Lazarus, and even the neighbourhood of the unholy city had become so unsafe that Jesus stayed on the eastern bank of the Jordan. While there Mary and her sister Martha sent this message, 'Lord, he whom thou lovest is sick.' And, when he would go to Bethany, the thoughtful Thomas said, 'Let us go and die with him.' These words disprove the notion that most of the disciples were then away from their Master; his time was too near for that; but they do prove not only the chivalry of St. Thomas, but his sagacity. He judged rightly of the peril of the place and time; for, as soon as the chief priests knew that Jesus was again so near, and heard of what he did at Bethany, they took counsel how they might kill him.

"At that time it was their plan to kill Lazarus also. Only St. John records this, and he does not say how Lazarus escaped. But such was the wealth and rank of the family of Bethany that its love for Jesus greatly enraged the rulers of the Jews; and, as Mary foresaw the Lord's death, she may have seen the danger of Lazarus, and the family have had the power to guard against it. Perhaps they did so because of some intimation from their Lord; all we know is, that the Jews then failed to kill Lazarus. But such was their purpose then; and this purpose would naturally revive in the midst of the provocations that led them to murder St. Stephen."—Thoughts on the Holy Gospels, pp. 170, 171.

[2] See these characteristics elaborated in detail by Da Costa and Gregory in their works named above. Comp. also Westcott's chapter on The Characteristics of the Gospels, in his Introduction to the Study of the Gospels, pp. 217-253.

should not say that Matthew wrote for the Jews only, Mark for the Romans, and Luke for the Greeks. That would imply that when these several nations ceased these gospels would have no further special adaptation. We should rather bear in mind that, so far as the several gospels have the special adaptations named, they have a divinely-ordained fitness to make the person and character of Jesus the more powerfully impressive upon all classes of men. The types of mind and character represented by those great historic races are ever appearing, and require perpetually the manifold testimony of Jesus furnished by the four evangelists. The four are better than one. We need the living picture of the Prince of the house of David as given by Matthew, for it reveals him as the perfecter of the old economy, the fulfiller of the law and the prophets. We need the briefer gospel of the mighty Son of God as given by Mark. Its rapid style and movement affect multitudes more deeply than a gospel so fully imbued with the Old Testament spirit as that of Matthew. "If in the first gospel," observes Ellicott, "we recognise transitions from theocratic glories to meek submissions, in the second we see our Redeemer in one light only, of majesty and power. If in St. Matthew's record we behold now the glorified and now the suffering Messiah, in St. Mark's vivid pages we see only the all-powerful Son of God; the voice we hear is that of the Lion of the tribe of Judah."[1] Luke's gospel, on the other hand, opens before us the broader vision of the Son of man, born, to be sure, under the law, but born of a woman, "a light for revelation of the Gentiles," as well as for the glory of Israel (Luke ii, 32). He appropriately traces the Redeemer's lineage away back beyond David, and beyond Abraham, to Adam, the son of God (Luke iii, 38). This Pauline gospel gives us the living embodiment of the perfect Man, the Friend and Saviour of helpless humanity. Not only does it offer the noblest ideal to the mind of the Greek; it must always have a charm for every Theophilus who has a disposition and desire to know the immovable certainty ($\tau\grave{\eta}\nu$ $\dot{\alpha}\sigma\phi\acute{\alpha}\lambda\epsilon\iota\alpha\nu$, Luke i, 4) of the things of the Gospel. And John's record notably supplements the others. It is pre-eminently the gospel for the Church of God. It is the gospel of the heart of Jesus, and the disciple who leaned upon the Lord's bosom, and imbibed so fully the inspirations of that sacred heart, was the only one of the twelve who could write this inimitable gospel of the Word, the Light, the Way, the Truth, the Resurrection, and the Life.

In view of the marvellous harmonies and the all-embracing scope and purposes of the written gospels of our Lord, how unworthy the

[1] Historical Lectures on the Life of our Lord Jesus Christ, pp. 39, 40, Boston, 1863.

scepticism that fastens upon their little differences of statement (which may be explained by divers reasonable supposi- tions), and magnifies these differences into contradictions with design to disparage the credibility of the evangelists. Why puzzle over the fact that Matthew and Mark relate that the two thieves who were crucified with Jesus reviled him, while Luke says that one reviled him, and was rebuked by the other, who prayed to the Lord, and received the promise of paradise? Is it not supposable that during the three hours of mortal agony on the cross all these things might have occurred? Great variety is noticeable in the different accounts of the appearances of Jesus after the resurrection, but no man has ever been able to show a real discrepancy or contradiction.[1] In the absence of particulars we may not be able to detail the exact order of events, but when it is shown, on a number of hypotheses, that it was possible for all the events to take place, the diversity of statements becomes an undeniable evidence that they all are true.

[1] The following order of events following the resurrection is given by Gardiner: "The resurrection itself occurred at or before the earliest dawn of the first day of the week (Matt. xxviii, 1; Mark xvi, 2; Luke xxiv, 1; John xxi, 1). The women coming to the sepulchre find the stone rolled away and the body gone. They are amazed and perplexed. Mary Magdalene alone runs to tell Peter and John (John xx, 2). The other women remain, enter the tomb, see the angels, are charged by them to announce the resurrection to the disciples, and depart on their errand. Meantime Peter and John run very rapidly (verse 4) to the sepulchre. (A glance at the plan of Jerusalem shows that there were so many different gates by which persons might pass between the city and the sepulchre that they might easily have failed to meet the women on their way). They enter the tomb and are astonished at the orderly arrangement of the grave-clothes, and then return to the city. Mary follows to the tomb, unable quite to keep pace with them, and so falling behind. She remains standing at the entrance after they had gone, and, looking in, sees the angels. Then turning about she sees Jesus himself, and receives his charge for the disciples. This was our Lord's first appearance after his resurrection (Mark xvi, 9). To return to the women who were on their way from the sepulchre to the disciples: They went in haste, yet more slowly than Peter and John. There were many of them, and being in a state of great agitation and alarm (Mark xvi, 8) they appear to have become separated, and to have entered the city by different gates. One party of them, in their astonishment and fear, say nothing to any one (Matt. xxviii, 8); the others run to the disciples and announce all that they had seen, namely, the vision of the angels (Mark xvi, 8; Luke xxiv, 9–11). At this time, before any report had come in of the appearance of our Lord himself, the two disciples set out for Emmaus (Luke xxiv, 13). Soon after Mary Magdalene comes in announcing that she had actually seen the risen Lord (Mark xvi, 10, 11; John xx, 18). While these things are happening the first-mentioned party of the women are stopped on the way by the appearance of the Lord himself, and they also receive a charge to his disciples (Matt. xxviii, 9, 10). Beyond this point there is no difficulty in the narrative.—Harmony of the Gospels in Greek, pp. 253, 254.

CHAPTER XXXIII.

PROGRESS OF DOCTRINE AND ANALOGY OF FAITH.

THE interpreter of the Holy Scriptures must never forget that the *The Holy Scrip-* Bible in its entirety, as now possessed by the Church, *tures a growth.* was no sudden gift from heaven, but the slow and gradual accretion of many centuries. It is made up of many parts, which were produced at many different times. For the first twenty-five centuries of human history, according to the common chronology, the world was without any part of our Bible.[1] Then, in the course of forty years, the Books of Moses appeared. Possibly the Book of Job belongs to that early period. Subsequently such historical collections as the Books of Joshua and Judges were compiled, and in due time other histories, with psalms, proverbs, and the oracles of prophets, were gathered into many separate rolls or volumes, and at length, after the Babylonian captivity, this whole body of sacred literature was combined together, and came to be recognized as a book of divine authority. The different writings of the New Testament all appeared within a period of about half a century but they also furnish the means of tracing the development of life and thought in the early apostolic Church. Our present canonical Scriptures, therefore, are to be recognised as the records of a progressive divine revelation. We recognise the Spirit of God as the presiding and controlling wisdom which shaped these lively oracles. He not only employed holy men in the accomplishment of his purpose (2 Sam. xxiii, 2; Luke i, 70; Acts i, 16; iii, 18; 2 Peter i, 21), but also the ministry of angels (Acts vii, 53; Gal. iii, 19; Heb. ii, 2). A minute divine providence secured the embodiment of the entire revelation in the written forms in which we now possess it. The same God who spoke in the last days in the person of his Son spoke also in the older revelations (Heb. i, 1), and we may search his word in confidence that divine order. and wisdom will be found from the beginning to the end.

The Book of Genesis exhibits, as we have seen (pp. 211, 212), a

---

[1] That is, in its present form. No doubt the narratives of the creation, of the fall, and the flood, were handed down by oral tradition. They may, indeed, long before Moses' time, have existed in written form, and, with the genealogical tables and other fragmentary portions of patriarchal history, have constituted a sort of sacred literature among the descendants of Shem.

series of evolutions, which serve well to illustrate the progress and order of the divine revelation. First comes the account Genesis a series of evolutions and of revelations. of the miraculous beginning, the cutting, forming, and making (בָּרָא and עָשָׂה) of Adam's world (Gen. i, 1–ii, 3). This we have already explained (pp. 549–552) as the supernatural preparation of the heavens and land where the first man appeared. From that geographical and historical beginning we trace a well-defined series of generations (תּוֹלְדֹת). The first series comprises the "generations of the heavens and the land" (ii, 4). The starting-point is "a day of Jehovah God's making land and heavens," when as yet no plant or herb of the new creation had commenced the processes of growth; no rain had yet fallen, no man to work the soil had yet appeared (ver. 5). It is the morning of the sixth day of the creative week. The whole surface of the ground is watered, and the processes of growth begin (ver. 6). Man is formed (יָצַר) from the dust of the soil, and becomes (וַיְהִי) a living soul by the breath of Jehovah God (ver. 7). His formation is, therefore, conceived as a generation or birth out of the heavens and the land by the breath (נִשְׁמָה) of God. Then the woman was produced from the man, another step in the process of these generations (ver. 23; comp. 1 Cor. xi, 8). Then follows the narrative of the fall, showing how the first man was from the earth and earthy (1 Cor. xv, 47), and by disobedience lost his original relation to God. The first generations run to violence and crime, and become more and more earthly until Seth is born, and with him the revelation takes a new departure. "The book of the generations of Adam" (v, 1) is not a record of Adam's origin, but of his posterity in the line of Seth. But again the race deteriorates, and the sons of Seth, so much nobler than the Cainites, and other children of Adam, that they are called the sons of God (vi, 2), intermarry with the fair but ignoble daughters of men, and the land is filled with violence. With Noah, who was just and upright, and walked with God (vi, 9), another series of generations takes its departure, and the flood destroys all the rest of men.

After the flood God establishes a covenant with Noah (ix, 9), and through him foretells the honour that shall come to the From Noah onward. dwellings of Shem (ix, 27). But the tendencies of the sons of Noah still appear to be earthy, and their generations are rapidly sketched (x). Shem's line is traced to Terah (xi, 10–26), with whose son, Abram, the covenant of grace and the promise of unspeakable glory in the after times are set forth in fuller light. The history of Abraham, the friend of God, first exhibits in clear outline the wonderful condescension of Jehovah; he is separated from country and kindred, and disciplined in faith. He receives the covenant of circumcision, and the promise of a seed through whom all nations shall be blessed. Jehovah speaks to him in visions and dreams, and in the person of his angel. Additional revelations come in connexion with Isaac and Ishmael, the generations of Jacob branch out into twelve tribes, and the prophetic blessing of the dying patriarch reveals the outline of their history in after times (Gen. xlix).

It is impossible to trace the record of these ten generations of the Book of Genesis without observing the steady progress of divine revelation. Again and again the history, darkened by the growth of human wickedness, fastens upon a divinely chosen name, and from it takes a new departure. With each new series of generations some new promise is given, or some great purpose of God is brought to light. While the tendency of the race is to grow worse and worse, there appears at the same time the unwavering purpose of the Almighty to choose out and maintain a holy seed. Thus the Book of Genesis is an essential part of the history of redemption.

A progress of Revelation in Genesis.

The centuries of Egyptian bondage are rapidly passed over, but the history of the deliverance from Egypt is detailed with notable fulness. Jehovah's triumph over the gods of Egypt, the establishing of the passover, the journey to Sinai, the giving of the law, the building of the tabernacle, and the entire Mosaic ministry and legislation were the beginnings of a new era. Captious critics, incompetent to grasp the scope and moral grandeur of the Mosaic system, may cavil at some of its enactments, and forget that Moses had to do with a nation of emancipated serfs; but the philosophical historian will ever recognise the Sinaitic legislation as one of the greatest wonders of the world. The Decalogue, sublimely uttered from the mount of God, embodies the substance of all true religion and all sound morality. The construction of the tabernacle, modelled after a divine plan (Exod. xxv, 40), and the order of the Levitical service, most truly symbolize the profoundest conceptions of the curse of sin and the power of God in redemption.

The Mosaic legislation a new era of revelation.

But, aside from the Decalogue and the symbolism of the Mosaic cultus, how full and comprehensive the doctrinal and moral teachings of the last four books of the Pentateuch. The personality, attributes, nd moral perfections of God are set forth in unspeakably superior form to that of any and all other religious systems of the ancient or modern world. The self-existence and eternity of God, his holiness, justice, and mercy, his

Doctrine of God.

wisdom and his providence, are revealed in many ways. How aw-fully sublime and yet how gracious that revelation to Moses in the mount, when "Jehovah descended in the cloud, and stood with him there, and called in the name of Jehovah; and Jehovah passed by before him, and called : Jehovah, Jehovah, God, merciful and gra-cious, long-suffering and abundant in kindness and truth, keeping kindness for thousands, lifting iniquity, and transgression and sin, but in punishing will not let go unpunished, visiting the iniquity of fathers upon children, and upon children of children, upon the third and upon the fourth" (generations). Exod. xxxiv, 5-7.

Such a revelation would necessarily beget the holiest reverence, and at the same time evince that he was worthy of all love. Hence the commandment, "Thou shalt love Jehovah, thy God, with all thy heart and with all thy soul and with all thy might" (Deut. vi, 5). This doctrine of God furnished the basis of a superior ethical code. The true Israelite was required to guard the morals of his neighbour, and love him as himself. He must not yield to feelings of vengeance, nor hold bit-terness in his heart toward any of his brethren (Lev. xix, 17, 18). He must not oppress the poor and the needy, but leave large glean-ings for them in his harvest field (Lev. xix, 10). He must not even allow his neighbour's ox or sheep to go astray, but seek to restore them to him as if they were his own (Deut. xxii, 1-3). Even in taking the young of birds for any proper purpose, he must, in kindness and consideration, spare the mother bird. Surely a code which enacted such humane provisions ought never to have been charged with barbarous severity.[1] Its severest penalties were grounded in the highest expediency,[2] and ample securities were provided against injustice and capricious acts of power. While the governments of all the great nations of that age were despotic and largely barbarous, that of the Mosaic legislation was essentially republican.[3]

The Pentateuch holds the same relation to the subsequent books

Superior ethi-cal and civil code.

[1] See Sewall, Humaneness of the Mosaic Code, Bib. Sacra for 1862, pp. 368-384.

[2] Barrows observes: "The attitude of the Mosaic economy toward the Gentile na-tions was indeed severe, but it was the severity of love and goodwill. It had for its object not their destruction, but a speedier preparation of the way for the advent of Christ, in whom the promise, 'In thy seed shall all the nations of the earth be blessed,' was to find its fulfilment."—Missionary Spirit of the Psalms and Prophets. Bib. Sacra for 1860, p. 459.

[3] See the excellences of the Mosaic legislation elaborately set forth by Michaelis, Commentaries on the Laws of Moses (Eng. Trans. by Smith, 4 vols., Lond., 1814); Warburton, The Divine Legation of Moses; Graves, on the Four Last Books of the Pentateuch (Lond., 1850).

of the Old Testament that the gospels hold to the rest of the New
The Pentateuch Testament. It contains in some form the substance of
fundamental to all the Old Testament revelation, but it intimates in
Old Testament
revelations. many a passage that other revelations will be given.
It assumes that a great and glorious future is awaiting the chosen
nation, and indicates the ways by which the glories may be realized.
At the same time it warns against the possibility of lamentable
failure. The entire system of Mosaic laws, moral, civil, and ceremonial, was wisely adapted to train the Israelitish nation, and
served as a schoolmaster to prepare them and the world for the reception of the Gospel of Christ. So far was Moses from regarding
his work as final in the training of Israel, that he announced by
the word of Jehovah that another prophet should arise, to whom
divine revelations would be given, and whom the people should
obey (Deut. xviii, 15-19). The last words of the great lawgiver
are full of warning, of promise, and of prophecy (Deut. xxix-xxxiii).

After the death of Moses Joshua received his divine commission
Revelation to carry forward the great work of establishing Israel
continued after in the land of promise. Jehovah spoke to him as he
Moses.
did to Moses (Josh. i, 1; iii, 7; iv, 1). He also revealed
himself in the person of his angel (Josh. v, 13), and in all the history of the conquest and settlement of Canaan, Jehovah spoke as
frequently and familiarly with Joshua as he had done with Moses.
In the dark times of the Judges God left himself not without prophetic witness. Revelations came to Deborah and Gideon and
Manoah. At length Samuel arose when prophecy was rare in
Israel (1 Sam. iii, 1), and in his day the schools of the prophets appear (1 Sam. x, 5; xix, 20). When David became king of all Israel,
the promise and prophecy of the Messiah assumed a fuller form.

The word which came to the king through Nathan the prophet
(2 Sam. vii, 4-17) was the germ of the Messianic psalms, and the
Theology of the entire collection of lyrics, which constitutes the Hebrew
Psalter.
psalter, is an invaluable index of the highest religious
thought and feeling of Israel in the times of David and later. The
Messianic hope is enhanced by a variety of conceptions: he is the
anointed King in Zion, declared to be the very Son of Jehovah
(Psa. ii); he is a reigning Lord, who is at the same time a priest forever after the order of Melchizedek (Psa. cx); his majesty and grace
are extolled above all the sons of men (Psa. xlv); but he is also a
sufferer, crying out as if forsaken of God, while his enemies deride
him and cast lots for his vesture (Psa. xxii); he even sinks into the
grave, but exults in hope and confidence that he shall not see corruption (Psa. xvi). The doctrine of God is also set forth in the psalter

in new force and beauty. He is Lord of earth and sea and heavens, ruling on high and beholding all; the almighty Preserver, the omnipresent Spirit, infinitely perfect in every moral excellence; tender, compassionate, long-suffering, marvellous in mercy, and yet terrible in his judgments, fearful in holiness, ever vindicating the truth; he is the absolute and eternal God, the fountain of life and of light. The guardianship of angels (Psa. xxxiv, 7; xci, 11) and the hope of a blissful immortality (xvii, 15) were not wanting in the psalmist's faith. The doctrines of redeeming grace, of pardon from sin, of cleansing from guilt; the hidden life of trust; the personal approach of the worshipper into closest fellowship with God; the joy and gladness of that fellowship, and the probationary discipline of the saints, are doctrines which find manifold expression in the hymn book of the Israelitish people.[1]

The age of Solomon was the golden age of the proverbial philosophy of the Hebrews. The Book of Proverbs repre- The Solomonic sents the Old Testament doctrines of practical wisdom Proverbial Phi- (חָכְמָה), and is the great textbook of biblical ethics. It losophy. brings out in fuller form and in a great variety of precepts the ethical principles embodied in the Mosaic law. It has to do with practical life, and so serves, at the right stage in the progress of the divine revelation, to exalt that human element in which pure religion necessarily finds some of its most beautiful manifestations. "The Book of Proverbs," says Stanley, "is not on a level with the Prophets or the Psalms. It approaches human things and things divine from quite another side. It has even something of a worldly, prudential look, unlike the rest of the Bible. But this is the very reason why its recognition as a sacred book is so useful. It is the philosophy of practical life. It is the sign to us that the Bible does not despise common sense and discretion. It impresses upon us, in the most forcible manner, the value of intelligence and prudence, and of a good education. The whole strength of the Hebrew language, and of the sacred authority of the book, is thrown upon these homely truths. It deals, too, in that refined, discriminating,

---

[1] "This book," says Calvin, "not unreasonably, am I wont to style an anatomy of all parts of the soul, for no one will discover in himself a single feeling whereof the image is not reflected in this mirror. All griefs, sorrows, fears, doubts, hopes, cares, and anxieties—in short, all the tumultuous agitations wherewith the minds of men are wont to be tossed—the Holy Ghost hath here represented to the life. The rest of Scripture contains the commands which God gave to his servants to be delivered unto us. But here the prophets themselves, holding converse with God, inasmuch as they lay bare all their inmost feelings, invite or impel every one of us to self-examination, that of all the infirmities to which we are liable, and all the sins of which we are so full, none may remain hidden."—Commentary on the Psalms, Preface.

careful view of the finer shades of human character, so often overlooked by theologians, but so necessary to any true estimate of human life."[1]

In the great prophets of the Old Testament the depth and spirituality of the Mosaic religion attained their highest expression. We have already outlined the progressive character of the Messianic prophecies, and seen the organic and vital relations of prophecy to the history of the Israelitish people (p. 408). The Messianic hope, first uttered in the garden of Eden (Gen. iii, 15), was a fountain-head from which a gradually increasing stream went forth, receiving constant accessions as prophet after prophet arose commissioned to utter some clearer oracle. In a general way, at least, each new prophet added to the work of his predecessors.[2] The prophecy of Jonah, one of the earliest written, emphasizes Jehovah's compassion upon a great heathen city which repents at his word. It is conspicuously an oracle of hope to the Gentiles. Joel, the ancient apocalyptist, sees in the desolating judgments on the land signs of the coming of Jehovah, and calls upon the people to rend their hearts rather than their garments in evidence of contrite humiliation before God (Joel ii, 12). His visions stretch away to the latter times when the Spirit of Jehovah shall be poured out upon all flesh, and whosoever shall call upon the name of Jehovah shall be saved (ii, 28, 32). Hosea bewails the idolatry of Israel and Judah, but sees great hope for them if they will but offer their lips as sacrificial offerings of prayer and praise (Hos. xiv, 2). The formal ceremonial worship of the nation was fast losing all its deep sacredness, and ceasing to be a means of holy, heartfelt devotion. With such outward unspiritual worship Jehovah could not be pleased, and he says in Amos (v, 21, 22):

(Marginal notes: Old Test. revelation reached its highest spirituality in the great prophets.)

[1] History of the Jewish Church, second series, p. 269. New York, 1869.

[2] R. Payne Smith observes: "Men never do understand anything unless already in their minds they have some kindred ideas, something that leads up to the new thought which they are required to master. Our knowledge grows, but it is by the gradual accumulation of thought upon thought, and by following out ideas already gained to their legitimate conclusions. God followed this rule even in the supernatural knowledge bestowed upon the prophets. It was a growing light, a gradual dawning preparatory to the sunrise, and no flash of lightning, illuminating everything for one moment with ghastly splendour, to be succeeded immediately by a deeper and more oppressive gloom. . . . Carefully, and with prayer, the prophets studied the teaching of their predecessors, and by the use of the light already given were made fit for more light, and to be the spokesmen of Jehovah in teaching ever more clearly to the Church those truths which have regenerated mankind."—Bampton Lectures. Prophecy a Preparation for Christ, pp. 304, 305. Boston, 1870.

I have hated, I have despised your feasts,
And I will not breathe in your assemblies;
For if ye offer me burnt-offerings and your meat-offerings
I will not be delighted,
And a peace-offering of your fatlings I will not regard.
Put away from me the noise of thy songs;
And the music of thy harps I will not hear.
And let judgment be rolled along as the waters,
And righteousness as a perennial stream.

It would thus appear that as idolatry increased, and the ceremonial worship became cold, heartless, and idolatrous, the prophets, as inspired watchmen and teachers, turned the thoughts of the people to those deeper spiritual truths of which the ceremonial cultus furnished only the outer symbols. They yearned for a purer worship, and a more real and vital approach to God. They began to realize, what the New Testament so fully reveals, that the law was only a shadow, not the very likeness, of the good things to come, and that the ritual sacrifices could never perfect the worshippers who depended on them alone (Heb. x, 1). Thus Micah (vi, 6–8):

With what shall I come before Jehovah—
Bend myself to the God of height?
Shall I come before him with burnt-offerings?
With calves, sons of a year?
Will Jehovah be pleased with thousands of rams,
With myriads of streams of oil?
Shall I give my firstborn for my transgression,
Fruit of my body for the sin of my soul?
He has showed thee, O man, what is good;
And what is Jehovah seeking from thee,
But to execute judgment and the love of mercy,
And humbly to walk with thy God?

In the Book of Isaiah the prophetic word reaches a lofty climax. This evangelist among the prophets seems to rise at will above the limitations of time, and to see the past, the present, and the future converge in great historic epochs vital to the interests of the kingdom of God. Although the first thirty-nine chapters deal mainly with the matters of contemporary interest and note, they are filled with glowing visions of Messianic triumph. The first part of the second chapter, apparently borrowed from Micah, portrays the universality and glory of that spiritual dominion which is to supplant Judaism, and go forth from Jerusalem to establish peace among all nations. The Messianic promise again and again finds varied expression (chap. vii, 14;

ix, 1–7; xi, 1–10). Where, in all the pictures of a coming golden age, can be found a more beautiful outline than Isa. xxxv? But in the last twenty-seven chapters Isaiah's prophecies exhibit their highest spirituality. He depicts things in their divine relations, and contemplates the redemption of Israel as from the position of the high and exalted One who dwells in eternity (lvii, 15). His thoughts and ways are loftier than those of men, even as the heavens are higher than the earth (lv, 8, 9). Looking away from the darkening present, and exulting in glowing visions of Messiah's triumph, the prophet often speaks in the name and person of Messiah and his elect, and apprehends the glories of his reign as the creation of a new heavens and a new earth.

The prophecies of Daniel exhibit the increasing light of divine The prophecies revelation which came when Israel, by exile, was brought of Daniel. in contact with the great heathen world-powers. Daniel speaks as one who looks out from the midst of the operations of great empires; and sees a throne higher than that of the kings of Babylon or of Persia, and forces more numerous and mighty than all the armies of the world (Dan. vii, 9, 10). "In him," says R. Payne Smith, "prophecy has a new development; it breaks away from the bonds of Jewish thought, and sets before us the grand onward march of the world's history, and the Christian Church as the centre and end of all history."[1] His visions make prominent a determined END or consummation, when a desolating abomination shall destroy the sanctuary (ix, 26, 27; comp. Matt. xxiv, 15; Mark xiii, 14; Luke xxi, 20):

And many, sleeping in the dust of the ground, shall awake,
These to life eternal,
And those to shame and eternal contempt.
And the wise ones shall shine as the brightness of the firmament,
And those who make many righteous
As the stars for ever and ever (Dan. xii, 2, 3).

In some respects Ezekiel surpasses Daniel in the depth and fulness of his revelations. His vision of the cherubim and Prophecies of Ezekiel. the theophany is set forth in the first chapter of his prophecy with a wealth of suggestive symbols not to be found elsewhere in the Old Testament, and the detailed description of the new temple and land of Israel (chapters xl–xlviii) is an anticipation of John's vision of the new heavens and the new earth (Rev. xxi). Ezekiel's city of Jehovah-Shammah (xlviii, 35) is no other than the New Jerusalem of John. The doctrine of the resurrection, which

[1] Prophecy a Preparation for Christ, p. 238.

in Isaiah (xxvi, 19) is suggested by a striking apostrophe, is expressed in formal statement by Daniel (xii, 2), and assumed as a common belief in the imagery of Ezekiel (xxxvii, 1–14).

After the Babylonian exile we note that Haggai sees in the second temple a glory greater than that of the former Post-exile (Hag. ii, 9). Zechariah combines in his prophetic book prophets. the varied symbolism of Daniel and Ezekiel with the lofty spirituality of Isaiah. And the "burden of Jehovah's word to Israel by the hand of Malachi" (Mal. i, 1), the last of the Old Testament prophets, is a series of rebukes to a false and heartless formalism, and an earnest call to repentance and personal self-consecration.[1]

Passing over the four hundred years of silence between Malachi and the advent of Jesus Christ, we find the two Testa- Prophetic link ments linked by a noticeable prophetic bond. The Old between the Old and New Testament closes with a promise that Elijah the prophet Testaments. shall come before the great day of Jehovah, and the gospel history of the New Testament opens with the ministry of this Elijah who was to come (Luke i, 17; Matt. xi, 14; xvii, 10–13). But John the Baptist, though filled with the spirit and power of Elijah, was merely a forerunner, a herald, a voice (John i, 23), provided in the divine order to prepare the way of the Lord. His ministry was professedly introductory to the Gospel Age, and his constant testimony was that one mightier than himself was about to come, who would baptize with the Holy Ghost and fire (Matt. iii, 11).

The ministry and words of the Lord Jesus, as recorded in the gospels, constitute the substance of all Christian doc- Christ's teach-trines. As the five books of Moses really embody the ings the sub-germs of all subsequent revelation, so in a clearer form stance, but not the final form, the teachings of Jesus embrace every great truth of the of Christian Christian faith. But our Lord himself was explicit in doctrine. declaring that his own teaching must needs be supplemented by the fuller revelations of the Spirit. He taught by parable, by precept, and by example, but he found the hearts of the people and of his own disciples too heavy to apprehend the grand scope and spirituality of his Gospel, and declared that it was expedient for him to

---

[1] R. Payne Smith observes that prophecy "was not withdrawn abruptly. It still lingered in those beautiful psalms of degrees sung by the exiles, and in those prophets who helped in rearing the second house. But at the dispersion it had done its work. The Jews wondered that no prophet more arose. We can see why the gift was withdrawn. The time for teaching had ceased. The Jews were children no longer, but grown men; and, like grown men, they must leave home, and go out into all lands to carry to them the truths which the prophets had taught them."—Prophecy a Preparation for Christ, p. 335.

go away in order that the Spirit of truth might come to guide into all the truth, and to teach all things (John xiv, 25, 26; xvi, 7-15).[1]

The Acts of the Apostles shows that divine revelations were Revelations continued after the ascension of the Lord. On the day continued after of Pentecost the waiting disciples received the gift of the ascension of Jesus. the Holy Spirit, and began to realize as never before the "powers of the coming age" (Heb. vi, 5). Thenceforth they went forth with a heavenly authority to proclaim the newly enunciated truth of God. The angel of the Lord opened the prison doors where the apostles were shut up, and commanded them to continue speaking the words of eternal life (Acts v, 19, 20; comp. xii, 7; xvi, 26). The martyr Stephen saw the heavens opened, and the Son of man standing on the right hand of God (vii, 56). The same Lord Jesus appeared to Saul on his way to Damascus (ix, 17), and also to Ananias, in a vision (ix, 10). Peter was guided into opening the kingdom of God to the Gentiles by a symbolic vision (x, 9-16), and was aided by the ministry of an angel of God (x, 3-7). Special revelations of the Spirit directed Philip and Paul in their journeys (viii, 29, 39; xvi, 7). The great apostle of the Gentiles was repeatedly directed by visions and revelations of God (Acts xvi, 9; xxii, 17-21; comp. 2 Cor. xii, 1-4). Thus it is evident from the Acts of the Apostles that what Jesus *began* to do and teach (Acts i, 1) was carried into completion by those whom he chose to be the authoritative expounders of his word.

The Book of the Acts of the Apostles is a connecting link between the gospels and the epistles. It is essentially a historical introduction to the latter, and without the information it affords, both the The Epistles em- gospels and the epistles would be involved in much body the elabo- obscurity. The epistles preserve for the Church the rated teachings of the apostles. teachings of the apostles, and present them in a form admirably adapted to meet the wants of all classes of readers.[2]

---

[1] This subject is ably presented in Bernard's Bampton Lectures on the Progress of Doctrine in the New Testament. In Lecture iii he lays down and elaborates the following propositions: "First, The teaching of the Lord in the gospels includes the substance of all Christian doctrine, but does not bear the character of finality. Secondly, The teaching of the Lord in the gospels is a visibly progressive course, but on reaching its highest point announces its own incompleteness, and opens another stage of instruction."—P. 79.

[2] "The prophets," writes Bernard, "delivered *oracles to the people*, but the apostles wrote *letters to the brethren*, letters characterized by all that fulness of unreserved explanation, and that play of various feeling, which are proper to that form of intercourse. It is in its nature a more familiar communication, as between those who are, or should be, equals. That character may less obviously force upon us the sense, that the light which is thrown upon all subjects is that of a divine inspiration; but this is

Great principles, enunciated by Jesus, are elaborated and applied to practical life and experience by the apostolic epistles. The Epistles of Paul, including that to the Hebrews, traverse a wide field of Christian doctrine and experience. Their range may be indicated by the following classification: (1) Dogmatical, discussing especially the doctrines of sin and redemption (Romans and Galatians); (2) Christological (Ephesians, Philippians, Colossians, Hebrews); (3) Ecclesiastical, devoted to the order, practice, and life of the Church (Corinthians); (4) Pastoral (Timothy, Titus, Philemon); and (5) Eschatological (Thessalonians). Of course, none of these epistles is devoted exclusively to one particular subject, but each contains more or less of doctrine, reproof, exhortation, and counsels for practical life. The catholic epistles are concerned more exclusively with the practical affairs of the Christian life. Bernard emphasizes the fact that they were written by Peter and John, the two chief apostles, and James and Jude, the brethren of the Lord. "We take knowledge of them that they have been with Jesus, and own the highest authority which association with him can give." But he observes that the united epistles of these representatives of our Lord form only a kind of supplement to the writings of Paul. "Had we been permitted," he adds, "to choose our instructors from among 'the glorious company,' three of these names at least would have been uttered by every tongue; and besides our desire to be taught by their lips, we should, as disciples of St. Paul, have felt a natural anxiety to know whether 'James, Cephas, and John, who seemed to be pillars, added nothing to' (Gal. ii, 6, 9), and took nothing from, the substance of the doctrine which we had received through him. . . . We have words from these very apostles, expressing the mind of their later life, words in which we recognise the mellow tone of age, the settled manner of an old experience, and the long habit of Christian thought." [1]

The Apocalypse of John is, as we have seen (pp. 466–493), a magnificent expansion of the eschatological prophecy of our Lord in Matt. xxiv. It is professedly a further revelation from the Lord Jesus himself (Rev. i, 1). As Paul's Thessalonian Epistles, containing his prophecies of the parousia and the end of the age, were earlier in date than his other

The Apocalypse a fitting conclusion of the New Test. canon.

only the natural effect of the greater fulness of that light; for so the moonbeams fix the eye upon themselves, as they burst through the rifts of rolling clouds, catching the edges of objects and falling on patches of landscape; while, under the settled brightness of the universal and genial day, it is not so much the light that we think of, as the varied scene which it shows."—Progress of Doctrine, p. 156.

[1] Progress of Doctrine, pp. 161, 165.

writings, so John's book of eschatology antedates his gospel. But there is a fitness in having the Book of Revelation close the New Testament canon, even as the Thessalonian Epistles stand in canonical order at the close of Paul's letters to seven different churches.[1] For the Apocalypse reveals the marvellous things of the parousia, and the consummation of that age, when both earth and heavens were shaken, and the former things passed away in order to give place to the Messianic kingdom, which cannot be shaken (Heb. xii, 26–28). No vision could more appropriately close the Christian Canon than the apocalyptic symbol of the heavenly and etérnal kingdom.

This rapid outline of the development and progress of doctrine, traceable in the several books of the Old and New Testament Scriptures, will serve to show that God did not communicate his revelations all at once. The successive portions which he revealed from time to time were adapted to the varying conditions and needs of his people. Sometimes the word was left defective because of the hardness of the people's hearts (Mark x, 5). Sometimes the progress was slow, and interrupted by long periods of spiritual decline; then again it broke forth in new developments of national life. A careful attention to this progressive character of the divine revelation is necessary to a thorough interpretation and efficient use of the Holy Scriptures. It helps to set aside the charges of doctrinal and ethical discrepancies which have been alleged. The notion that the Pauline doctrine of justification is something essentially different from the teachings of Jesus, will have no force when it is seen that the whole Epistle to the Romans is virtually a systematic elaboration of our Lord's words to Nicodemus: "God so loved the world that he gave his only begotten Son, that whosoever believeth on him should not perish, but have eternal life" (John iii, 16). The allegation that the New Testament contradicts the Old is seen to be an error when we discover that the older revelations were necessarily imperfect, and manifestly not designed to set forth all the truth of God. Things which from one standpoint seem to be contradictory, from another are seen to be only separated portions of one grand harmony. The *lex talionis* and the violent procedures of the blood-avenger were grounded in the righteous demands of retributive justice, and were archaic forms of executing law. A higher civilization, based on clearer revelations, adopts other methods of executing penalty, but recognises the same essential principles of right.

Marginal note: Attention to progress of doctrine a help to the interpreter.

---

[1] Comp. Bernard, Progress of Doctrine, p. 169.

The Analogy of Faith.

The foregoing observations prepare the way to a proper apprehension of the "Analogy of Faith" as an aid in expounding the Scriptures. This expression, appropriated from Rom. xii, 6, but used in a different sense from that which the apostle intended,[1] denotes that general harmony of fundamental doctrine which pervades the entire Scriptures. It assumes that the Bible is a self-interpreting book, and what is obscure in one passage may be illuminated by another. No single statement or obscure passage of one book can be allowed to set aside a doctrine which is clearly established by many passages. The obscure texts must be interpreted in the light of those which are plain and positive. "The faith," says Fairbairn, "according to which the sense of particular passages is determined, must be that which rests upon the broad import of some of the most explicit announcements of Scripture, about the meaning of which there can be, with unbiassed minds, no reasonable doubt. And in so far as we must decide between one passage and another, those passages should always be allowed greatest weight in fixing the general principles of the faith in which the subjects belonging to it are not incidentally noticed merely, but formally treated and discussed; for, in such cases, we can have no doubt that the point on which we seek for an authoritative deliverance was distinctly in the eye of the writer."[2]

Progress of doctrine explains the true Analogy of Faith.

---

[1] In Rom. xii, 6, the apostle is speaking of the gifts, χαρίσματα, the spiritual qualifications and aptitudes for Christian activity and usefulness in the Church, "gifts differing according to the grace given" to each individual. Of these varying gifts he specifies several examples, one of which is that of prophesying. Let the one thus gifted, he says, exercise his gift, κατὰ τὴν ἀναλογίαν τῆς πίστεως, *according to the proportion of the faith,* that is, the faith which he individually possesses. This proportion or analogy (ἀναλογία) of one's individual faith is not an external rule or doctrinal standard, the *regula fidei* (as Philippi, Hodge, and others hold), but the measure of faith with which each is endowed. "They are not to depart from the proportional measure which their faith has, neither wishing to exceed it, nor falling short of it, but are to guide themselves by it, and are therefore so to announce and interpret the received revelation, as the peculiar position in respect of faith bestowed on them, according to the strength, fervour, clearness, and other qualities of that faith, suggests—so that the character and mode of their speaking is conformed to the rules and limits, which are implied in the proportion of their individual degree of faith. In the contrary case they fall, in respect of contents and of form, into a mode of prophetic utterance, either excessive and overstrained, or, on the other hand, insufficient and defective, not corresponding to the level of their faith. The same revelation may, in fact—according to the difference in the proportion of faith with which it, objectively given, subjectively connects itself—be very differently expressed and delivered."—Meyer, in loco.

[2] Hermeneutical Manual, p. 128.

We may distinguish two degrees of the analogy of faith. The
Two degrees first and highest is positive, in which the doctrine or
of the analogy revelation is so plainly and positively stated, and sup-
of faith. ported by so many distinct passages, that there can be
no doubt of its meaning and value. Thus the Scriptures teach positively that all men are sinners; that God has provided redemption
for all; that God is omnipotent, omnipresent, omniscient, holy,
righteous, and merciful; that he requires in those who seek his
Positive. grace, repentance, faith, humility, love, and obedience;
that he purposes to save and glorify those who love and
serve him, and to punish those who disobey and hate him. These
and many similar great truths are so positively and repeatedly set
forth in the Holy Scriptures that no one who reads with care can
fail to apprehend them.

The next degree is appropriately called the general analogy of
General. faith. It rests not like the first upon explicit declarations, but upon the obvious scope and import of the
Scripture teachings taken as a whole. Thus, for example, the subject of human slavery is referred to in various ways, both in the
Old Testament and in the New. Some passages have been construed as sanctioning the practice, others as opposing and condemning it. A valid conclusion as to the general import of Scripture on
this subject can be reached only by a broad and thorough investigation of all that bears upon it in the revelation of God. The
Mosaic legislation, which expressly permits the buying of slaves
from foreigners (Lev. xxv, 44, 45), makes the stealing and selling
of a Hebrew a capital crime (Exod. xxi, 16; Deut. xxiv, 7). A
leading feature of the Mosaic system was to distinguish sharply
between the Israelite and the foreigner, always to the prejudice of
the latter. This fact must be kept in mind in discussing any subject of Mosaic ethics. No Hebrew could, without his own consent,
be retained in slavery more than six years (Exod. xxi, 2), and the
year of jubilee might terminate the bondage sooner (Lev. xxv,
40, 54). Paul counsels the Christian slaves to be obedient to their
masters (Eph. vi, 5; Col. iii, 22; 1 Tim. vi, 1, 2), but he sends
back the fugitive, Onesimus, to his master, "no longer a slave, but
more than a slave, a brother beloved" (Philem. 16). He proclaims,
moreover, that under the Gospel "there is neither Jew nor Greek,
there is neither bond nor free, there is no male and female" (Gal.
iii, 28). The putting on of Christ by being baptized into Christ (ver.
27) causes all distinctions of nation (comp. Rom. x, 12), condition,
and even of sex, to be wholly lost sight of and forgotten. When to
these and other similar teachings we add the consideration that the

Old Testament commandment, "Thou shalt love thy neighbour as thyself," dropped somewhat incidentally in the Mosaic legislation (Lev. xix, 18), is called by James "the royal law" (James ii, 8), and is announced by the Lord as a fundamental pillar of the divine revelation (Matt. xxii, 39; Mark xii, 31; Luke x, 27), we can scarcely doubt that the holding of any fellow being in bondage against his will is essentially contrary to the highest ethics. The general analogy of faith is thus made apparent by a broad and careful collation of all that the Scripture says on any given subject.[1]

It is evident that no doctrine which rests upon a single passage of Scripture can belong to fundamental doctrines recognised in the analogy of faith. But it must not be inferred from this that no specific statement of Scripture is authoritative unless it has support in other passages. *Limitations and uses of the analogy of faith.* Nor can we set aside any legitimate inference from a statement of Scripture on the ground that such inference is unsupported by other parallel statements. Unless it be clearly contradicted or excluded by the analogy of faith, or by some other equally explicit statement, one positive declaration of God's word is sufficient to establish either a fact or a doctrine. Hence the analogy of faith as a principle of interpretation is necessarily limited in its application. It is useful in bringing out the relative importance and prominence of different doctrines, and guarding against a one-sided exposition of the sacred oracles. It exhibits the inner unity and harmony of the entire divine revelation. It magnifies the importance of consistency in interpretation. But it cannot govern the interpreter in the exposition of those parts of the Scriptures which are without real parallel, and which stand unopposed by other parts. For it may justly be inferred from the progress of doctrine in the Bible that here and there single revelations of divine truth may have been given in passages where the context furnished no occasion for further development or elaboration.

[1] Celérier (Manuel d'Hermeneutique, pp. 194–196) specifies two inferior degrees of analogy which he defines as *deduced* and *imposed;* but he very properly observes that they are unworthy of the name of analogy of faith; for the one rests upon the logical process by which it is attempted to prove a doctrine, the other upon an assumed authority supposed to inhere in the consensus of the creeds of Christendom. The consensus or analogy of Christian creeds is not without its value, but to use it as a method of interpreting Scripture is to substitute authority in the place of rational principles and rules of hermeneutics. What is believed everywhere, always, and by all (Quod ubique, quod semper, quod ab omnibus creditum est), is, doubtless, worthy of serious consideration, but cannot be admitted as a means of unfolding the sense of any particular portions of the Bible.

CHAPTER XXXIV.

DOCTRINAL AND PRACTICAL USE OF SCRIPTURE.

PAUL, the apostle, declares that all Scripture which is divinely in-
Paul's state- spired is also profitable for teaching, for reproof, for
ment of the correction, for instruction in righteousness (2 Tim. iii,
uses of Scrip-
ture. 16). These various uses of the holy records may be
distinguished as doctrinal and practical. The Christian teacher
appeals to them as authoritative utterances of divine truth, and unfolds their lessons as theoretical and doctrinal statements of what
their divine author would have men believe. Our fifth Article of
Religion (the sixth of the Church of England) says: "The Holy
Scriptures contain all things necessary to salvation; so that whatsoever is not read therein, nor may be proved thereby, is not to be
required of any man that it should be believed as an article of faith,
or be thought requisite or necessary to salvation." The inspired
word, moreover, serves a most important practical purpose by furnishing conviction and reproof (ἔλεγχον, or ἐλεγμόν) for the sinful,
correction (ἐπανόρθωσιν) for the fallen and erring, and instruction
or disciplinary training (παιδείαν) for all who would become sanctified by the truth (comp. John xvii, 17) and perfected in the ways
of righteousness.

The Roman Church, as is well known, denies the right of private
Roman doc- judgment in the interpretation of the Scriptures, and
trine of inter- condemns the exercise of that right as the source of all
pretation by
Church author- heresy and schism. The third article of the creed of
ity. Pope Pius IV., which is one of the most authoritative
expressions of Roman faith, reads as follows: "I admit the Holy
Scriptures, according to that sense which our holy mother Church
has held and does hold, to which it belongs to judge of the true
sense and interpretation of the Scriptures; neither will I ever take
and interpret them otherwise than according to the unanimous consent of the fathers."[1] The Romanist, therefore, finds in the Church
and tradition an authority superior to the inspired, Scripture. But
when we find that the fathers notoriously disagree in the exposition
of important passages, that popes have contradicted one another,
and have condemned and annulled the acts of their predecessors,

[1] Comp. Schaff, The Creeds of Christendom, vol. i, pp. 96–99; vol. ii, p. 207. New
York, 1877.

and that even great councils, like those of Nice (325), Laodicea (360), Constantinople (754), and Trent (1545) have enacted decrees utterly inconsistent with each other,[1] we may safely reject the pretensions of the Romanists, and pronounce them absurd and preposterous.

The Protestant, on the other hand, maintains the right of exercising his own reason and judgment in the study of the *The Protestant* Scriptures. But he humbly acknowledges the fallibility *principle of using one's* of all men, not excepting any of the popes of Rome. *own reason.* He observes that there are portions of the Bible which are difficult to explain; he also observes that no Roman pontiff, whatever his claim of infallibility, has ever made them clear. He is convinced, furthermore, that there are many passages of holy writ on which good and wise men may agree to differ, and some of which no one may be able to interpret. By far the greater portion of the Old and New Testaments is so clear in general import that there is no room for controversy, and those parts which are obscure contain no fundamental truth or doctrine which is not elsewhere set forth in clearer form. Protestants, accordingly, hold it to be not only a right but a duty of all Christians to search the Scriptures, that they may know for themselves the will and commandments of God.[2]

But while the Holy Scriptures contain all essential revelation of divine truth, "so that whatsoever is not read therein, *Statement and* nor may be proved thereby, is not to be required of any *defence of doc-trine to conform* man that it should be believed as an article of faith," *to correct Her-* it is of fundamental importance that all formal state- *meneutics.* ments of biblical doctrine, and the exposition, elaboration, or defence of the same, be made in accordance with correct hermeneutical principles. The systematic expounder of Scripture doctrine is expected to set forth, in clear outline and well-defined terms, such teachings as have certain warrant in the word of God. He must not import into the text of Scripture the ideas of later times, or build upon any words or passages a dogma which they do not legitimately teach. The apologetic and dogmatic methods of interpretation which proceed from the standpoint of a formulated creed, and appeal to all words and sentiments scattered here and there in the

---

[1] See the proof of these statements in Elliott, Delineation of Roman Catholicism, vol. i, pp. 144–147. New York, 1841.

[2] "If a position is demonstrably scriptural," says Dorner, "according to the evangelical doctrine of the Church, it has an essentially ecclesiastical character; it has citizenship and a claim to regard even though it do not enjoy a formal validity; and a position which is demonstrably opposed to Scripture has similarly no claim to acceptance though it be ecclesiastical."—System of Christian Doctrine, vol. i, p. 176. Edinb., 1880.

Scriptures, which may by any possibility lend support to a foregone conclusion, have been condemned already (see above, pp. 171, 172). By such methods many false notions have been urged upon men as matters of faith. But no man has a right to foist into his expositions of Scripture his own dogmatic conceptions, or those of others, and then insist that these are an essential part of divine revelation. Only that which is clearly read therein, or legitimately proved thereby, can be properly held as scriptural doctrine.[1]

We should, however, clearly discriminate between biblical theol-Biblical and ogy, and the historical and systematic development of historical the-ology to be dis-tinguished. Christian doctrine. Many fundamental truths are set forth in fragmentary forms, or by implication, in the Scriptures; but in the subsequent life and thought of the Church, they have been brought out by thorough elaboration, and the formulated statements of individuals and ecclesiastical councils.[2] All the great creeds and confessions of Christendom assume to be in harmony with the written word of God, and manifestly have great historical value; but they contain not a few statements of doctrine which a legitimate interpretation of the Scripture proof-texts appealed to does not authorize. A fundamental principle of Protestantism is that the Scriptures only are the true sources of doctrine. A creed has no authority further than it clearly rests upon what God has spoken by his inspired prophets and apostles. All true Christian doctrine is contained in substance in the canonical Scriptures.[3] But the elaborate study and exposition of subsequent ages

---

[1] "In the domain of Christian doctrine," says Van Oosterzee, "the Scripture is rightly made use of, when it is duly tested, interpreted according to precise rules, employed in explaining, purifying, and developing Church confessions, and is consulted as a guide in individual Christian philosophic investigation of truth."—Christian Dogmatics, vol. i, pp. 220, 221. New York, 1874.

[2] Thus Martensen: "As the archetypal work of the Spirit of Inspiration, the Scriptures include within themselves a world of germs for a continuous development. While every dogmatic system grows old, the Bible remains eternally young, because it does not give us a systematic presentation of truth, but truth in its fulness, involving the possibility of a variety of systems."—Christian Dogmatics, p. 52. Edinb., 1866.

[3] "The history of doctrines," says Hagenbach, "presupposes biblical theology as its basis; just as the general history of the Church presupposes the life of Jesus and the apostolic age."—Text-Book of the History of Doctrines, p. 16. Eng. trans., revised by H. B. Smith, New York, 1861. He observes further (p. 44): "With the incarnation of the Redeemer, and the introduction of Christianity into the world, the materials of the history of doctrines are already fully given in the germ. The object of all further doctrinal statements and definitions is, in the positive point of view, to unfold this germ; in the negative, to guard it against all foreign additions and influences." Similarly Schaff: "In the Protestant system, the authority of symbols, as of all human compositions, is relative and limited. It is not co-ordinate with, but always subordinate

may be presumed to have put some things in clearer light, and the judgments expressed by venerable councils are entitled to great respect and deference.

Most of the great controversies on Christian doctrine have grown out of attempts to define what is left in the Scriptures undefined. The mysteries of the nature of God, the person and work of Jesus Christ, sacrificial atonement in its relations to divine justice, man's depraved nature and the relative possibilities of the human soul with and without the light of the Gospel, the method of regeneration, and the degrees of possible Christian attainment, the resurrection of the dead, and the mode of immortality and eternal judgment—these and kindred subjects are of a nature to invite speculation and vain theorizing, and it was most natural that everything in the Scripture bearing on such points should have been pressed into service. On such mysterious themes it is quite easy for men to become "wise above what is written," and in the historical development of the blended life, thought, and activities of the Church, some things came to be generally accepted as essential Christian doctrine which in fact are without sufficient warrant in the Scriptures.

Human tendency to be wise above what is written.

Inasmuch, then, as the Scriptures are the sole source of revealed doctrine, and were given for the purpose of making known to men the saving truth of God, it is of the utmost importance that we study, by sound hermeneutical methods, to ascertain from them the whole truth, and nothing but the truth. We may best illustrate our meaning by taking several leading doctrines of the Christian faith, and indicating the unsound and untenable methods by which their advocates have sometimes defended them.

True and false methods to ascertain Scripture doctrines.

Nothing is more fundamental in any system of religion than the doctrine of God, and the catholic faith of the early Christian Church, as formulated in the Athanasian Creed, is this:

The catholic doctrine of God.

That we worship one God in Trinity, and Trinity in Unity; neither confounding the Persons, nor dividing the substance. For there is one Person of the Father; another of the Son; and another of the Holy Spirit. But the Godhead of the Father, of the Son, and of the Holy Spirit is all one: the glory equal, the majesty co-eternal. Such as the Father is, such is the

to, the Bible, as the only infallible rule of the Christian faith and practice. The value of creeds depends upon the measure of their agreement with the Scriptures. In the best case a human creed is only an approximate and relatively correct exposition of revealed truth, and may be improved by the progressive knowledge of the Church, while the Bible remains perfect and infallible."—The Creeds of Christendom, vol. i, p. 7.

Son, and such is the Holy Spirit: The Father uncreated, the Son uncreated, and the Holy Spirit uncreated; the Father incomprehensible (*immensus*), the Son incomprehensible, and the Holy Spirit incomprehensible; the Father eternal, the Son eternal, and the Holy Spirit eternal. And yet there are not three Eternals, but one Eternal; as also there are not three uncreated, nor three incomprehensibles, but One uncreated, and One incomprehensible. So likewise the Father is Almighty, the Son Almighty, and the Holy Spirit Almighty; and yet there are not three Almighties, but one Almighty. So the Father is God, the Son is God, and the Holy Spirit is God; and yet there are not three Gods, but one God.

Here is a very succinct and explicit statement of doctrine, and its definitions, so far as quoted above, have obtained all but universal acceptance among evangelical believers. Though commonly ascribed to Athanasius, this symbol of faith, like the Apostles' Creed, is of unknown authorship, and furnishes one of the most remarkable examples of the extraordinary influence which some works of that kind have exerted.

But are the definitions and sharp distinctions set forth in this creed according to the Scriptures? May we read them therein, or prove them thereby? No one pretends that the several clauses, or any of the formal definitions, are taken from the Bible. All such systematic presentations of dogma are foreign to the style of the Scriptures; but this fact is no valid reason for rejecting them, or supposing them to be unscriptural. "A creed," says Schaff, "ought to use language different from that of the Bible. A string of Scripture passages would be no creed at all, as little as it would be a prayer or a hymn. A creed is, as it were, a doctrinal poem written under the inspiration of divine truth. This may be said at least of the œcumenical creeds."[1] Hence a well-constructed creed is supposed to express the sum total of what the Scriptures teach on a given subject, but not necessarily in the language or terms of the sacred writers. Nor are its statements to be supposed to depend on any one or two particular texts or passages of the Bible. It is quite possible that the general judgment of men may legitimately accept as a positive doctrine of Scripture what no one text or passage, taken by itself alone, would be sufficient to authorize. The catholic doctrine of the Trinity is very much of this character. A calm and dispassionate review of ages of controversy over this important dogma will show that, on the one hand, the advocates of the catholic faith have made an unscientific and inconclusive use of many Scripture texts, while, on the other hand, their opponents have been equally unfair in rejecting

Doctrinal symbols not unscriptural.

[1] The Creeds of Christendom, vol. i, p. 7, foot note.

the logical and legitimate conclusion of a cumulative argument which rested on the evidence of many biblical statements, of which they themselves could furnish no sufficient or satisfactory explanation. The argument from each text may be nullified or largely set aside, when taken singly and alone; but a great number and variety of such evidences, taken as a whole, and exhibiting a manifest coherency, may not thus be set aside.

Thus, for example, the plural form of the name of God (אֱלֹהִים) in the Hebrew Scriptures has often been adduced as proof of a plurality of persons in the Godhead. A similar application has been made of the threefold use of the divine name in the priestly blessing (Num. vi, 24–27), and the trisagion in Isa. vi, 3. Even the proverb, "A threefold cord is not quickly broken" (Eccles. iv, 12), has been quoted as a proof-text of the Trinity. Such a use of Scripture will not be likely to advance the interests of truth, or be profitable for doctrine. A repetition of the divine name three or more times is no evidence that the worshipper thereby intends a reference to so many personal distinctions in the divine nature. The plural form אֱלֹהִים may as well designate a multiplicity of divine potentialities in the deity as three personal distinctions, or it may be explained as the plural of majesty and excellency (see p. 86). Such forms of expression are susceptible of too many explanations to be used as valid proof texts of the Trinity.

Plural form of the name of God.

So, again, of the passage in Gen. xix, 24, often quoted in the Trinitarian controversies. "The name Jehovah," says Watson, "if it has not a plural form, has more than one personal application. 'Then the Lord rained upon Sodom and upon Gomorrah brimstone and fire from the Lord out of heaven.' We have here the visible Jehovah who had talked with Abraham raining the storm of vengeance from another Jehovah out of heaven, and who was, therefore, invisible. Thus we have two Jehovahs expressly mentioned, 'the Lord rained from the Lord,' and yet we have it most solemnly asserted in Deut. vi, 4, 'Hear, O Israel, Jehovah our God is one Jehovah.'"[1] Much more natural and simple, however, is the explanation which recognises in this repetition of the name Jehovah a Hebraistic mode of statement. "It is," says Calvin, "an emphatic repetition." Browne remarks: "Aben Ezra, whom perhaps a majority of Christian commentators have followed in this, sees in these words a peculiar 'elegance or grace of language;' 'the Lord rained from the Lord' being a grander and more impressive mode of saying, 'the Lord rained from himself.'

Language of Gen. xix, 24.

[1] Theological Institutes, vol. i, p. 467.

It is a common idiom in Hebrew to repeat the noun instead of using a pronoun." [1]

The theophanies of the Old Testament have also been adduced Angel of Jeho- in maintaining the doctrine of the Trinity. But whatever else may be made of the argument, it furnishes no sound proof that the Godhead consists of a number of distinct persons. The Angel of Jehovah, so mysteriously identified with Jehovah himself (Gen. xvi, 7, 10, 13; xxii, 11, 12, 15, 16), and in whom is the name of Jehovah (Exod. xxiii, 21), is not necessarily a manifestation of one person of the Godhead rather than another, but may be explained as a singular manifestation of Jehovah himself without any idea of personal distinctions in his nature or essence. But while this is admitted on the one hand, it ought not to be denied, on the other, that in the light of New Testament revelations of Christ, as the revealed wisdom and power of God, we may discern in the Old Testament Angel of Jehovah a manifestation of him who in the fulness of time took upon himself the form of a servant, and was made in the likeness of men (Phil. ii, 7). It was, moreover, a part of the theology of the ancient synagogue that this angel was the Shekinah, or manifested power and mediation of God in the world.

A similar disposition may be made of many other proofs of the New Testament Trinity which have been cited from the Old Testament, doctrine of God. but passing into the New Testament we cannot but be impressed with the language used in John i, 18: "No one has ever seen God; God only begotten, who is in the bosom of the Father, he made him known." [2] This remarkable statement leads one to ask, Who is this only begotten God who is in the bosom of the Father, and reveals God, or makes him known? In the first verse of the same chapter he is called the Word (ὁ λόγος), and is said to have been " with the God " (πρὸς τὸν θεόν), and the further statement

---

[1] Speaker's Commentary, in loco.

[2] The more familiar and almost equally well-supported reading, "only begotten Son," conveys essentially the same mysterious and wonderful suggestion. "Both readings," says Hort, "intrinsically are free from objection. The text (God only begotten), though startling at first, simply combines in a single phrase the two attributes of the Logos marked before (θεός, ver. 1, μονογενής, ver. 14). Its sense is 'One who was both θεός and μονογενής.' The substitution of the familiar phrase ὁ μονογενής υἱός for the unique μονογενὴς θεός would be obvious, and μονογενής, by its own primary meaning, directly suggested υἱός. The converse substitution is inexplicable by any ordinary motive likely to affect transcribers. There is no evidence that the reading had any controversial interest in ancient times. And the absence of the article from the more important documents is fatal to the idea that $\overline{\text{ΘC}}$ was an accidental substitution for $\overline{\text{ΥC}}$."—Appendix to Westcott and Hort's Greek Testament, p. 74.

is made that he "was God." Creation is ascribed to him (ver. 3), and he is declared to be the life and the light of men (ver. 4). This Word, it is added in verse 14, "became flesh, and tabernacled among us, and we beheld his glory—glory as of an only begotten from a Father full of grace and truth." It is quite possible that polemic writers may make too much of these wonderful words. What it is to *be with the God*, and also to *be God*, may well be treated as a mystery too deep for the human mind to solve. The Word which became flesh, according to John i, 14, may fairly be understood to be identical with him who, according to Paul in 1 Tim. iii, 16, embodies "the mystery of godliness; he who was manifested in the flesh, justified in the Spirit, seen by angels, preached among the nations, believed on in the world, received up in glory." This can be no other than Jesus Christ, the Son of God and Son of man. When, now, we observe that the apostles were commissioned to "go forth and make disciples of all nations, baptizing them in the name of the Father, and of the Son, and of the Holy Spirit" (Matt. xxviii, 19;) that Paul invokes "the grace of the Lord Jesus Christ, and the love of God, and the communion of the Holy Spirit," to be with all the brethren of the Corinthian church (2 Cor. xiii, 13); and that John invokes grace and peace upon the seven churches of Asia "from Him who is, and who was, and who is to come, and from the seven spirits which are before his throne, and from Jesus Christ, the faithful witness, the firstborn of the dead, and the prince of the kings of the land" (Rev. i, 4, 5), we may with good reason conclude that God, as revealed in the New Testament, consists of Father, Son, and Spirit existing in some myste- Mysterious distinctions in the rious and incomprehensible unity of nature. From divine nature. such a basis the exegete may go on to examine all those texts which indicate in any way the person, nature, and character of Christ: his pre-existence, his divine names and titles, his holy attributes and perfections, his power on earth to forgive sins, and other prerogatives and works ascribed to him, and the command for all men and angels to worship him. The fact that "God is Spirit" (John iv, 24) allows us readily to conceive that the Holy Spirit and God himself are one in substance, and the manner in which our Lord speaks of the Holy Spirit as the Comforter whom he will send (John xv, 26; xvi, 7), and whom the Father will send in his name (xiv, 26), points by every fair construction to a distinction between the Father and the Holy Spirit. Putting all these together we find so many far-reaching and profoundly suggestive declarations concerning these divine persons, that we cannot logically avoid the conclusion enunciated in the creed, that "the Father is God, the Son is God, and the Holy Spirit is God; and yet there are not three Gods, but one God."

But in the systematic elaboration of this argument the theologian should carefully abstain from unauthorized assertions. A theme so full of mystery and of majesty as the nature of God, and his personal revelations in Christ and through the Holy Spirit, admits of no dogmatic tone.

Abstain from unauthorized assertions and disputed readings.

Assertions like the following from Sherlock are no advantage to the interests of truth: "To say they are three divine persons, and not three distinct infinite minds, is both heresy and nonsense. . . . The distinction of persons cannot be more truly and aptly represented than by the distinction between three men; for Father, Son, and Holy Ghost are as really distinct persons as Peter, James, and John."[1] This is being wise above what is written, and is as harmful to valid argument as citing and urging texts where the reading and punctuation are doubtful, or where (as in the case of 1 John v, 7) the evidence of interpolation is overwhelming. No man should assume to *explain* the mysteries of Deity.

The doctrine of atonement in Christ is thus set forth in the Canons of the Synod of Dort: "The death of the Son of God is the only and most perfect sacrifice and satisfaction for sin; is of infinite worth and value, abundantly sufficient to expiate the sins of the whole world."[2] The Westminster Confession of Faith expresses it thus: "The Lord Jesus, by his perfect obedience and sacrifice of himself, which he through the eternal Spirit once offered up unto God, hath fully satisfied the justice of the Father, and purchased not only reconciliation, but an everlasting inheritance in the kingdom of heaven, for all those whom the Father hath given unto him."[3] It is probable that to many evangelical Christians neither of these forms of statement is satisfactory, while yet, at the same time, they would not reject them as unscriptural. They contain several phrases which have been so mixed with dogmatic controversy that many would for that reason decline to use them, and prefer the simple but comprehensive statement of the Gospel: "God so loved the world that he gave the Son, the only begotten, that every one who believes in him should not

Vicarious Atonement.

---

[1] Vindication of the Doctrine of the Trinity, pp. 66, 105. London, 1690. Equally dogmatic, on the other hand, is the declaration of Norton concerning the doctrines of the Trinity and the twofold nature of Christ: "There is not a passage to be found in the Scriptures which can be imagined to affirm either of those doctrines that have been represented as being at the very foundation of Christianity."—Statement of Reasons for not believing the Doctrines of Trinitarians concerning the Nature of God and the Person of Christ, p. 63. Third edition, Boston, 1856.

[2] See Schaff, Creeds of Christendom, vol. iii, p. 586.   [3] Ibid., p. 621.

perish, but have life eternal" (John iii, 16). This Scripture does not say that the Son was given as "a sacrifice and satisfaction for sin," or that the procedure was a "perfect obedience and sacrifice of himself" in order to "fully satisfy the justice of the Father," and "purchase reconciliation for all those whom the Father hath given unto him." But, as Alford well says: "These words, whether spoken in Hebrew or in Greek, seem to carry a reference to the offering of Isaac; and Nicodemus in that case would at once be reminded by them of the love there required, the substitution there made, and the prophecy there uttered to Abraham (Gen. xxii, 18) to which 'every one who believes' so nearly corresponds."[1]

When we proceed to compare with this Scripture its obvious parallels (as Rom. iii, 24–26; v, 6–10; Eph. i, 7; 1 Peter i, 18, 19; iii, 18; 1 John iv, 9), and bring forward in illustration of them the Old Testament idea of sacrifice, and the symbolism of blood (see above, pp. 358, 359), we may construct a systematic exhibition of the doctrine of atonement which no faithful interpreter of the Scriptures can fairly gainsay or resist. It is not a special dogmatic exposition of any single text, or a peculiar stress laid upon isolated words or phrases by which a scriptural doctrine is best set forth, but rather by accumulation of a number and variety of passages bearing on the subject, the meaning and relevancy of each of which are obvious.

The awful doctrine of eternal punishment has been greatly con-fused by mixing with it many notions which are desti- Eternal Pun-tute of valid scriptural proof. The refinements of ishment. torture, delineated in the appalling pictures of Dante's Inferno, should not be taken as guides to help us in understanding the words of Jesus, even though we be told that the Gehenna, "where their worm dieth not, and the fire is not quenched" (Mark ix, 48), and "the outer darkness, where shall be weeping and gnashing of teeth" (Matt. xxv, 30), authorize such horrible portraitures of the final doom of the wicked. The fearful representations of divine judgment and penalty set forth in Scripture need not be interpreted literally in order to enforce the doctrine of the hopeless perdition of the incorrigible sinner, and the exegete, who assumes in his dis-cussion that the literal import of such texts must be held, weakens his own argument. Far more convincing and overwhelming is that mode of teaching which makes no special plea over the ety-mology or usage of some disputed word (even though it be αἰώνιος), but rather holds up to view the uniform and awful indications of hopeless ruin and utter exclusion from the glory of God which the

---

[1] Greek Testament, in loco.

Scriptures continually furnish as a certain fearful expectation of the ungodly. A momentous and eternal truth may be set forth in figure as well as in literal statement, and the force of the Scripture doctrine of the final doom of the wicked lies not more in the terri- Utter absence ble suggestions of positive punishment, tribulation, and of scriptural hope for the anguish, than in the absence of any hope of pardon and wicked. salvation in the future. Vain is the appeal to such a text as Matt. xii, 32: "Whosoever shall speak against the Holy Spirit it shall not be forgiven him, neither in this age nor in that which is to come." Here, say some, is an implication that for other sins and blasphemies there may be forgiveness in the age or world to come. But to this it may at once be answered that such an implication is at best a most uncertain hope, while on the contrary the assertion is most positive that the blasphemy against the Spirit shall never be forgiven. Endless perdition, therefore, awaits such blaspheming sinners, and will the opponents of eternal punishment assume that no one ever has committed, or will commit, the blasphemy here meant? In the parallel passage of Mark (iii, 29) we meet with that profound and fearfully suggestive statement, that "whosoever shall blaspheme against the Holy Spirit has no forgiveness forever, but is guilty of ($\check{\epsilon}\nu o\chi o\varsigma$, is held fast bound by) eternal sin." How futile and delusive, then, to build a hope on the suggestions of such a text, when, for aught the reasoner knows, every wilful sinner, who deliberately rejects the claims of the Gospel and dies impenitent, commits this blasphemy against the Spirit.

Equally delusive would it be to build a hope of future pardon on Preaching to what is written in 1 Peter iii, 18–20, and iv, 6. For if the spirits in we allow the strictest literal construction, and believe prison. that Christ went in spirit and preached to the spirits in prison, we have no intimation as to what he preached, or of the results of that preaching; and the entire statement is confined to those who were disobedient in the days of Noah. There is no intimation that he preached to any other spirits, or that any other such preaching ever took place before, or ever will take place hereafter. Furthermore, if we infer, from 1 Peter iv, 6, that the purpose of this preaching to the dead was that they might be rescued from their prison, and "live according to God in spirit," it is entirely uncertain whether any one of them accepted the offer, and were thus saved. If, however, it be urged that it is altogether presumable that such a preaching of the Gospel by Christ himself would not be without blessed results, and that such grace shown to one class of imprisoned spirits is a fair ground for presuming that like mercy may be extended to many others, if not to all, we have only to answer: All these are presumptions which have too much against them in other parts of Scripture to be made the ground of hope to any wilful sinner, or to allow our laying down any universal proposition touching the unknown future.[1]

We repudiate the notion, often asserted by some, that we may not use the figurative portions of Scripture for the purpose of establishing or maintaining a doctrine. Figures of speech, parables, allegories, types, and symbols are divinely chosen forms by which God has communicated a large part of his written word to men, and these peculiar methods *Doctrine not confined to any one class or portion of the Scriptures.* of communicating thought may teach doctrine as well as any thing else (comp. pp. 247, 248). Our Lord has seen fit to set forth his truth in manifold forms, and it is our duty to recognise that truth whether it appear in metaphor, parable, or symbol. Is there no doctrine taught in such metaphors as (Psa. li, 7) "Purify me with hyssop," or (1 Cor. v, 7) "Christ, our passover, was sacrificed"? Can the doctrine of a new creation in Christ (2 Cor. v, 17; Gal. vi, 15), and the renewing of the Holy Spirit (Titus iii, 5), be more clearly or forcibly set forth than by the figure of the new birth (regeneration) as used by Jesus (John iii, 3-8)? Does the allegory of the vine and its branches (John xv, 1-6) teach no doctrine? Was there no doctrine taught by the lifting up of the serpent in the wilderness, or in the symbolism of blood, or in the pattern and service of the tabernacle? And as to teaching by parables, we may well observe with Trench: "To create a powerful impression language must be recalled, minted, and issued anew, cast into novel forms, as was done by him of whom it is said that without a parable (παραβολή, in its widest sense) spake he nothing to his hearers; that is, he gave no doctrine in the abstract form, no skeletons of truth, but all clothed, as it were, with flesh and blood. He acted himself as he declared to his disciples they must act if they would be scribes instructed unto the kingdom, and able to instruct others (Matt. xiii, 52); he brought forth out of his treasure things new and old; by the help of the old he made intelligible the new; by the aid of the familiar he introduced them to that which was strange; from the known he passed more easily to the unknown. And in his own

---

[1] It scarcely accords with the true spirit of calm theological inquiry to obtrude dogmatical assertions as to any possibilities of grace beyond this life. What may be the future development and opportunities of those who die in infancy, or what may be allowed in another state of being to such as may be supposed never to have had suitable opportunities of accepting salvation in this life, are questions which God alone can answer, and the presumption of those who, in the absence of specific revelation, dogmatize on such themes, is only equalled by the folly of those who would rest their hopes of the future on such unknown and uncertain possibilities.

manner of teaching, and in his instruction to his apostles, he has
given us the secret of all effectual teaching—of all speaking which
shall leave behind it, as was said of one man's eloquence, stings in
the minds and memories of the hearers." [1]

But when we come to study the doctrines of biblical eschatology,
how little do we find that is not set forth in figure or in
symbol? Perhaps the notable confusion of modern
teaching on the subjects of the parousia, resurrection,
and judgment is largely due to a notion that these doctrines must
needs have been revealed in literal form. The doctrine of divine
judgment with its eternal issues is none the less positive and sure
because set forth in the highly wrought and vivid picture of
Matt. xxv, 31–46, or the vision of Rev. xx, 11, 12. "The judgment seat of Christ" (Rom. xiv, 10; 2 Cor. v, 10) is a metaphorical
expression, based on familiar forms of dispensing justice in human
tribunals (comp. Matt. xxvii, 19; Acts xii, 21; xviii, 12, 16; xxv,
6, 10, 17), and the expositor who insists that we must understand
the eternal judgment of Christ only *as executed after the forms of
human courts*, only damages the cause of truth.

Eschatology mostly taught in figurative language.

How, also, has the doctrine of the resurrection become involved
in doubt and confusion by overwise attempts to tell
how the dead are raised up, and *with what body* they
come forth! That the body is raised is the manifest scriptural
teaching. Christ's body was raised, and his resurrection is the
type, representative, and pledge that all will be raised (1 Cor.
xv, 1–22). Many saints who had fallen asleep arose with him, and
it is expressly written that their bodies (σώματα) were raised (Matt.
xxvii, 52). Paul's doctrine clearly is that "he who raised up Christ
Jesus from the dead, shall also make alive your mortal bodies"
(Rom. viii, 11; comp. Phil. iii, 21). He does not entertain the
question, on which so many modern divines have wasted speculation, as, wherein consists identity of body, and may not the dust of
different bodies become mixed, and will all the particles of matter
be restored? But he does employ suggestive illustrations, and by
the figure of the grain of wheat shows that the body which is sown
is "not the body that shall be" (1 Cor. xv, 37). He calls attention
to the varieties of flesh (σάρξ), as of men, beasts, birds, and fishes,
and to the great difference between the glory of heavenly and
earthly bodies, and then says that the human body is sown in corruption, dishonour, and weakness, but raised up in incorruption,
glory, and power (verses 39–45). "It is sown a natural (ψυχικόν)
body; it is raised a spiritual body." The interests of divine truth

The resurrection of the body.

---

[1] Notes on the Parables, p. 27.

have not been helped by dogmatic essays to go beyond the apostle in the explanation or illustration of this mystery.

In the systematic presentation, therefore, of any scriptural doctrine, we are always to make a discriminating use of sound hermeneutical principles. We must not study them in the light of modern systems of divinity, but should aim rather to place ourselves in the position of the sacred writers, and study to obtain the impression their words would naturally have made upon the minds of the first readers.[1] The question should be, not what does the Church say, or what do the ancient fathers and the great councils and the œcumenical creeds say, but what do the Scriptures legitimately teach? Still less should we allow ourselves to be influenced by any presumptions of what the Scriptures *ought* to teach. It is not uncommon for writers and preachers to open a discussion with the remark that in a written revelation like the Bible we might naturally expect to find such or such things. All such presumptions are uncalled for and prejudicial. The assumption that the first chapter of Genesis describes a universal cosmogony, and that the Book of Revelation details all human history, or that of the Church, to the end of time, has been the fruitful source of a vast amount of false exegesis.

Freedom from prepossessions and presumptions.

The teacher of Scripture doctrine should not cite his proof-texts *ad libitum*, or at random, as if any word or sentiment in harmony with his purpose, if only found in the Scriptures, must needs be pertinent. The character of the whole book or epistle, and the context, scope, and plan are often necessary to be taken into consideration before the real bearings of a given text can be clearly apprehended. That doctrine only is theologically sound which rests upon a strict grammatico-historical interpretation of Scripture, and while all divinely inspired Scripture is profitable for doctrine and discipline in righteousness, its inspiration does not require or allow us to interpret it on any

Texts not to be cited ad libitum.

---

[1] In order to be able to explain any one's words to others, one must understand them himself, otherwise he cannot render them intelligible to others. One understands another's words when by means of them he thinks as did the speaker or writer, and as he wished one should think. Thus one explains another's words rightly to others when he enables them to think precisely what the speaker or writer thought or wished to be thought. In the interpretation of any writing, it has not to be inquired what the readers for whom it was destined thought, but what, according to the intention of the writer, they should have thought in reading it. The object of the interpretation is the thoughts of the writer or speaker, in as far as he has expressed them in words for others. This does not take away that it often is of great importance to the interpretation of one or more sayings to inquire how the hearers understood them.—Doedes, Manual of Hermeneutics, pp. 2, 3. Edinb., 1867.

other principles than those which are applicable to uninspired writings. The interpreter is always bound to consider how the subject lay in the mind of the author, and to point out the exact ideas and sentiments intended. It is not for him to show how many meanings the words may possibly bear, nor even how the first readers understood them. The real meaning intended by the author, and that only, is to be set forth.

There is much reason for believing that the habit, quite general since the time of Ernesti, of treating the hermeneutics of the New Testament separately from the Old, has occasioned the misunderstanding of some important doctrines of Holy Writ. The language and style in which certain New Testament teachings are expressed are so manifestly modelled after Old Testament forms of statement, that they cannot be properly explained without a minute and thorough apprehension of the import of the older Scriptures.[1] We cannot, therefore, accept without qualification the following words of Van Oosterzee : "We have no right for a use of these (O. T.) Scriptures, in which we do not take heed to their peculiar character, as distinguished from those of the New Testament. The Old Testament revelation must always be regarded first in relation to Israel, and has only value for our dogmatics in so far as it is confirmed by the gospel of the New. The letter of the Old Testament must thus be tested by the spirit of the New, and whatever therein stands in opposition

New Testament doctrine not clear without the help of the Old.

---

[1] Take for illustration the following passage from one of our most recent and able works on theology. Speaking of the lawless one mentioned in 2 Thess. ii, 8, Pope says : "Prophetical theology has its many hypotheses for the explanation of the symbols of Daniel and the Apocalypse, and the plain words of St. Paul. But there has not yet been found on earth the power or the being to whom all St. Paul's terms are applicable."—Compendium of Chr. Theology, vol. iii. p. 394. The critical student of Daniel's description of the little horn (Dan. vii, 8, 25 ; viii, 9-12, 23-25 ; comp. xi, 36-38), will note that the words of Paul in 2 Thess. ii, 3-10, are no plainer than those of Daniel, from whom they are so evidently copied. And if Daniel's symbols and language were fulfilled, as most of the leading Old Testament exegetes admit, in the lawless Antiochus Epiphanes, how can it be said, in view of the equally lawless and blasphemous Nero, that "there has not yet been found on earth the power or the being to whom all St. Paul's terms are applicable?" We might fill volumes with extracts showing how exegetes and writers on New Testament doctrine assume as a principle not to be questioned that such highly wrought language as Matt. xxiv, 29-31 ; 1 Thess. iv, 16 ; and 2 Pet. iii, 10, 12, taken almost *verbatim* from Old Testament prophecies of judgment on nations and kingdoms which long ago perished, must be literally understood. Too little study of Old Testament ideas of judgment, and apocalyptic language and style, would seem to be the main reason for this one sided exegesis. It will require more than assertion to convince thoughtful men that the figurative language of Isaiah and Daniel, admitted on all hands to be such in those ancient prophets, is to be literally interpreted when used by Jesus or Paul.

to the New has as little binding force for our belief as for our life. A dogma which can be supported only by an appeal to the Old Testament can only maintain its place in Christian dogmatics if it manifestly does not conflict with the letter and spirit of the New, and also stands in close connexion with other propositions derived from the New Testament."[1]

Every distinct portion of Scripture, whether in the Old or the New Testament, must, indeed, be interpreted in harmony with its own peculiar character, and the historical standpoint of each writer must be duly considered. *One and the same spirit in both Testaments.* The Old Testament cannot be truly apprehended without always regarding its relation to Israel, to whom it was first intrusted (Rom. iii, 2). And while it is true that "the letter of the Old Testament must be tested by the spirit of the New," it is equally true that, to understand the spirit and import of the New Testament, we are often dependent on both the letter and spirit of the Old. It may be that no important doctrine of the Old Testament is without confirmation in the Christian Scriptures, but it is also to be remembered that every important doctrine of the New Testament may be found in germ in the Old, and the New Testament writers were all, without exception, Jews or Jewish proselytes, and made use of the Jewish Scriptures as oracles of God.

A correct view of this whole subject is taken when we regard the Hebrew people as of old divinely chosen to hold and teach the principles of true religion. It was not theirs to develop science, philosophy, and art. Other *Confusion of Hebrew and Aryan modes of thought.* races attended more to these. It was not until the mystery of God, enclosed in the Israelitish worship as the bud, blossomed out in the Gospel, and was given to the Aryan world, that a systematic theology began to be developed. These Gentile peoples had long been trying, by reason and from nature, to solve the mysterious problems of the universe, and when the Gospel revelation came to them, it was eagerly seized by many as a clue to the intricate and perplexing secrets of God and the world. But a failure to apprehend the letter and spirit of the Hebrew records of faith led also to a failure to understand some of the doctrines of the Gospel, so that, from the apostolic age until now, there has been a conflict of Gnostic and Ebionitish tendencies in Christian thought. It is only as a correct scientific method enables us to distinguish between the true and the false in each of these tendencies that we shall perceive that the revelations of both Testaments are essentially one and inseparable. There can be, therefore, no complete and thorough hermeneutics of

[1] Christian Dogmatics, vol. i, p. 18. New York, 1874.

New Testament doctrine without a clear insight into the letter and spirit of the Old.

In the practical and homiletical use of the Scriptures we are also to seek first the true grammatico-historical sense. The life of godliness is nourished by the edifying, comforting, and assuring lessons of divine revelation. They serve also, as we have *Practical and* seen, for reproof and correction. But in this more sub-*Homiletical use of Scripture.* jective and practical use of the Bible, words and thoughts may have a wider and more general application than in strict exegesis. Commands and counsels which had their first and only direct reference to those of bygone generations may be equally useful for us. An entire chapter, like that of Rom. xvi, filled with personal salutations for godly men and women now utterly unknown, may furnish many most precious suggestions of brotherly love and holy Christian fellowship. The personal experiences of Abraham, Moses, David, Daniel, and Paul exhibit lights and shades from which every devout reader may gather counsel and admonition. Pious feeling may find in such characters and experiences lessons of permanent worth even where a sound exegesis must disallow the typical character of the person or event. In short, every great event, every notable personage or character, whether good or evil, every account of patient suffering, every triumph of virtue, every example of faith and good works, may serve in some way for instruction in righteousness.[1]

The promises of divine oversight and care, the hopes and pledges *Promises, ad-* set before the holy men of old, and all exhortations to *monitions, and* watchfulness and prayer, may have manifold practical *warnings.* applications to Christians of every age. The same may be said of all the ancient warnings and appeals to escape the coming wrath of God which had primary reference to impending judgments. The carelessness and disobedience of those who lived in the days of Noah are a lively admonition and warning to all men of

---

[1] The Bible constantly presents general principles, absolute commandments, and living examples, but it never applies these principles to human actions as recorded upon its pages. This is left to the enlightened conscience and thoughtful judgment of the reader. It is God's will that we should meditate upon all Scripture, and make ourselves the moral application. The Bible records the pious obedience and simple and singular faith of Noah, but makes no comment upon it; and it relates the story of his shame when overcome by his appetite without a note of warning. Abraham is sometimes called the friend of God, and is styled in Scripture the father of them that believe. His marvellous simplicity of character, and unfaltering trust in God, are fully described in the sacred word, and without note of comment or excuse the stories of his deceit are also written out.—Pierce, The Word of God Opened, p. 77. New York, 1868.

every age who follow worldly things alone, and have no care about their eternal destiny. All the New Testament admonitions to watch and be in constant readiness for the coming of the Lord are capable of a most legitimate practical application to believers now, in reference to the uncertainty of the hour of death. To say, as many modern Chiliasts, that such an application of the admonitions to prepare for the parousia is a perversion of the Scripture teaching, is most futile. The coming of the Lord to a believer at death, in order to transport his redeemed spirit to paradise, is not, to be sure, the parousia which Jesus declared would take place within a generation from his time. But as departure from this life puts an end to probation, and "inasmuch as it is appointed unto men once to die, and after that—judgment" (Heb. ix, 27), every motive which should have led men to prepare and watch for the judgment of the flood, and every exhortation for the contemporaries of Jesus and Paul to watch and be ready for the parousia, serve ever to admonish and warn us and all generations to be prepared for that day and hour when we must pass to eternal judgment of weal or woe. How much more sensible and forcible is this practical exhortation, the point and propriety of which all men must feel, than the visionary appeals of those expositors who would have us believe that we are now, any day and hour, to expect what Jesus said should take place within his own generation!

Pre-millennialists and post-millennialists have fallen into noticeable confusion in attempts to make such commands as "Watch therefore, for ye know not on what day your Lord cometh;" "Therefore, be ye also ready;" "Watch therefore, for ye know not the day nor the hour" (Matt. xxiv, 42, 44; xxv, 13), consistent with two thousand years' delay. Brown, indeed, concedes (Christ's Second Coming, p. 20) that "the death of any individual is, to all practical purposes, the coming of Christ to that soul. It is his summons to appear before the judgment seat of Christ. It is to him the close of time, and the opening of an unchanging eternity, as truly as the second advent will be to mankind at large." "There is a perfect analogy," he adds, "between the two classes of events. . . . Still, it is in the way of analogy alone that texts expressive of the one can or ought to be applied to the other. It can never be warranted, and is often dangerous to make that the primary and proper *interpretation* of a passage which is but a secondary, though it may be a very legitimate, and even irresistible, *application* of it." All this is very correct, but Mr. Brown falls into the error of the Chiliasts themselves when he goes on to argue that all the New Testament admonitions and warnings which imply the nearness of the parousia are consistent with centuries, and even millenniums, of delay. All those warnings and exhortations had, as we have shown above, immediate and primary application and reference to the end of the pre-millennial age (æon), which took place at the fall of the temple and its cultus, and correct *interpretation* finds their primary and only direct reference to that event. But by way of manifest analogy, and in practical and homiletical use, they have a pertinent and impressive lesson to all generations of men. And it detracts from the force and usefulness of these texts to import into them an imaginary significance which they were never intended to bear.

In all our private study of the Scriptures for personal edification

Practical and homiletical use of Scripture to be based on correct interpretation.

we do well to remember that the first and great thing is to lay hold of the real spirit and meaning of the sacred writer. There can be no true application, and no profitable taking to ourselves of any lessons of the Bible, unless we first clearly apprehend their original meaning and reference. To build a moral lesson upon an erroneous interpretation of the language of God's word is a reprehensible procedure. But he who clearly discerns the exact grammatico-historical sense of a passage, is the better qualified to give it any legitimate application which its language and context will allow.

Accordingly, in homiletical discourse, the public teacher is bound to base his applications of the truths and lessons of the divine word upon a correct apprehension of the primary signification of the language which he assumes to expound and enforce. To misinterpret the sacred writer is to discredit any application one may make of his words. But when, on the other hand, the preacher first shows, by a valid interpretation, that he thoroughly comprehends that which is written, his various allowable accommodations of the writer's words will have the greater force, in whatever practical applications he may give them.

PART THIRD.

HISTORY OF BIBLICAL INTERPRETATION.

Next to the Holy Scriptures, which are themselves a history and depository of divine revelation, there is no stronger proof of the continual presence of Christ with his people, no more thorough vindication of Christianity, no richer source of spiritual wisdom and experience, no deeper incentive to virtue and piety, than the History of Christ's kingdom. Every age has a message from God to man, which it is the greatest importance for man to understand. The Epistle to the Hebrews describes, in stirring eloquence, the cloud of witnesses from the Old Dispensation for the encouragement of Christians. Why should not the greater cloud of apostles, evangelists, martyrs, confessors, fathers, reformers, and saints of every age and tongue, since the coming of Christ, be held up for the same purpose?—SCHAFF.

HISTORY

OF

BIBLICAL INTERPRETATION.

CHAPTER I.

ANCIENT JEWISH EXEGESIS.

A KNOWLEDGE of the history of biblical interpretation is of inestimable value to the student of the Holy Scriptures. *Value and importance of history of interpretation.* It serves to guard against errors and exhibits the activity and efforts of the human mind in its search after truth and in relation to noblest themes. It shows what influences have led to the misunderstanding of God's word, and how acute minds, carried away by a misconception of the nature of the Bible, have sought mystic and manifold meanings in its contents. From the first, the Scriptures, like other writings, were liable to be understood in different ways. The Old Testament prophets complained of the slowness of the people to apprehend spiritual things (Isa. vi, 10; Jer. v, 21; Ezek. xii, 2). The apostolical epistles were not always clear to those who first received them (comp. 2 Thess. ii, 2; 2 Pet. iii, 16). When the Old and New Testaments assumed canonical form and authority, and became the subject of devout study and a means of spiritual discipline, they furnished a most inviting field for literary research and theological controversy. On the one hand, there were those who made light of what the prophets had written, attacked the sacred books, and perverted their meaning; on the other, there arose *Origin and variety of interpretations.* apologists and defenders of the holy volume, and among them not a few who searched for hidden treasures, and manifold meanings in every word. Besides assailants and apologists there were also many who, withdrawing from the field of controversy, searched the Scriptures on account of their religious value, and found in them wholesome food for the soul. The public teachers of religion, in oral and written discourses, expounded and applied the oracles of God to the people. Hence, in the course of ages, a great variety of expositions and a vast amount of biblical literature have appeared. The student who acquaints himself with the various methods of exposition, and with the works of the great exegetes of ancient and modern times, is often saved thereby from following new developments of error, and is guarded against the novelties of a restless fancy. He observes how learned men, yielding to subtle speculation and fanciful analogies, have become the founders of schools and systems of interpretation. At the same time be becomes more fully qualified to maintain and defend the faith once delivered to the saints.

It was the distinguishing advantage of the Jewish people that they were entrusted with the oracles of God (Rom. iii, 1, 2). But during the long period between Moses and the Babylonian exile they showed little appreciation of their heavenly treasure. The law was ignored, the prophets were persecuted, the people turned to idolatry, and the penalty of exile and dispersion, foreannounced by Jehovah himself (Deut. xxviii, 63, 64), followed at last with terrible severity. In the land of exile, a descendant of Aaron the high priest, hopeless of Israel's rise by worldly prowess, set his heart upon the devout study of the ancient Scriptures. "Ezra prepared his heart to seek the law of Jehovah and to do it, and to teach in Israel statutes and judgments" (Ezra vii, 10). Possibly the one hundredth and nineteenth psalm was the result of that study, and shows the impression the law made upon that studious priest while yet a young man. A profound appreciation of God's law, such as this psalm evinces, would prompt a man like Ezra to seek the reformation of Israel by calling them to a rigid obedience of the commandments. We may, accordingly, date the beginning of formal exposition of the Scriptures at the time of Ezra. A need was then felt, as not before, of appealing to the oracles of God. The Book of the Law was recognized as fundamental in the records of divine revelation. The noblest Israelite was he who delighted in Jehovah's law, and meditated therein by night and by day (Psa. i, 2; comp. Psa. cxix, 34, 35, 97). The loss of temple, throne, palace, and regal splendour turned the heart of the devout Jew to a more diligent inquiry after the words of Jehovah.

Ezra, accordingly, led a company of exiles back to Jerusalem and instituted numerous reforms. The commandments forbidding intermarriage with the heathen were rigidly enforced, and the legal feasts and fasts were observed. The public instruction of the people, as recorded in Neh. viii, 1–8, was a measure designed to make known the will of Jehovah, and to develop a purer religious sentiment among the people. Thenceforth the office and work of the scribe became important. He was no longer the mere recorder of passing events, the secretary, clerk, or registrar of the king (2 Sam. viii, 17; 1 Kings iv, 3), but the copyist and authorized expounder of the sacred books. Their devotion to the study and interpretation of the law brought to the scribes after a time the title of lawyers (νομικοί). At an early period they became known as a distinct class, and were spoken of as families or guilds (1 Chron. ii, 55). Ezra is to be regarded as a distinguished representative of his class. He was not the only scribe who returned from Babylon (Ezra viii, 16). On the occasion of the public reading of the law he had the assistance of learned Levites, who were able to explain the ancient Scriptures to the people. Constant searching of these holy writings led to the various reforms narrated in the Books of Ezra and Nehemiah.

The great convocations described in Neh. viii, 1–15, were the first sessions of what is known in Jewish tradition as the Great Synagogue. The acts of the Jewish leaders of that time were without doubt greatly embellished in the later traditions, but nothing is more probable than that these eminent reformers arranged the order of the sacred books of their nation, and provided for their systematic reading and exposition. Many motives would have naturally prompted to this. The troubles with the Samaritans, the tendencies to mingle with the heathen, the neglect to provide for the service of the house of God, all required that thorough measures should be taken to imbue the Israelites with the ancient theocratic spirit. Ezra and Nehemiah were too wise and discerning not to perceive that a devout study of the law and the prophets would be a mighty educational means of securing for their people the surest safeguard against the evils to which they were constantly exposed. With the knowledge of the condition and circumstances of the Jews at Jerusalem which the Books of Ezra and Nehemiah furnish, we can scarcely conceive that such farsighted men as these great leaders and their coadjutors—priests, Levites, and scribes (Neh. xiii, 13), men of knowledge and discernment (Neh. x, 28)—would have failed to do substantially all those things which the unanimous voice of tradition ascribes to the men of the Great Synagogue. They reformed abuses, provided for the temple service, and for the public reading and exposition of the law, and these measures imply a collection of the canonical Scriptures as the authoritative basis of the entire procedure.[1]

The office and work of the scribes.

The Great Synagogue.

---

[1] The attempts of some scholars (Alting, Rau, Kuenen) to set aside the traditions of the Great Synagogue as worthless rabbinical fables are scarcely of a character to commend themselves to a candid critic. Fables and foolish legends are probably

The progress of Jewish exegesis from the time of Ezra to the
beginning of the Christian era may be dimly traced in
scattered notices of the learned Jews of that period,
in the pre-Christian apocryphal and pseudepigraphal
literature, in the works of Philo Judæus and Josephus, and in the
Talmud. The rigid measures adopted by Ezra, Nehemiah, and their
associates would seem to have prepared the way for Pharisaism.
The scribes of the period succeeding that of Nehemiah not only
copied the sacred books, and explained their general import, but
took measures to make a hedge about the law. They set a value
on the very letters of the law, and counted their number.[1] They
scrupulously guarded against interpolations and changes, but, at
the same time, they gathered up traditions and constructed an oral
law which in time came to have with them an authority equal to
that of the sacred books. Thus originated the Jewish Halachah
and Hagadah, the legal and homiletic exegesis. "The
Bible," says Stanley, "and the reading of the Bible as
an instrument of instruction, may be said to have been begun on
the sunrise of that day when Ezra unrolled the parchment scroll of
the law. It was a new thought that the divine will could be communicated by a dead literature as well as by a living voice. In the
impassioned welcome with which this thought was received lay the
germs of all the good and evil which were afterward to be developed
out of it; on the one side, the possibility of appeal in each successive age to the primitive, undying document that should rectify the
fluctuations of false tradition and fleeting opinion; on the other
hand, the temptation to pay to the letters of the sacred book a
worship as idolatrous and as profoundly opposed to its spirit as
once had been the veneration paid to the sacred trees or the sacred
stones of the consecrated groves or hills."[2]

Progress of Jewish exegesis after Ezra.

Halachah and Hagadah.

associated with the tradition, as they are with most of the great persons and events of
Jewish history; but to reject the entire tradition as unworthy of belief is going quite
too far. It is too well supported by the necessary implication of Ezra's and Nehemiah's acts to be thus summarily rejected. It would be very uncritical and arbitrary
to reject the statement of 2 Maccabees ii, 13, viz., that Nehemiah founded a library,
and collected the acts of kings and prophets, because the writer elsewhere records
numerous idle legends. In chap. i, 18, the same writer ascribes to Nehemiah what
was done by Zerubbabel and Joshua (comp. Ezra iii–vi), but shall we thence argue
that no such work was done at all?

[1] See Ginsburg, article Scribes, in Kitto's Cyclopædia of Biblical Literature.

[2] Lectures on Hist. of Jewish Church, Third Series, pp. 158, 159. The same writer
further on observes: "There is one traditional saying, ascribed to the Great Synagogue, which must surely have come down from an early stage in the history of the
scribes, and which well illustrates the disease to which, as to a parasitical plant, the
order itself, and all the branches into which it has grown, has been subject. It

This superstitious reverence for the letter of the law, and the disposition of the scribes to fence it around with au- Pharisees and
Sadducees. thoritative oral precepts, most naturally led to the later Pharisaism. But the excessive claims of these ancient scribes produced a reaction, and gave rise to the sect of the Sadducees, who refused to be bound by the traditions of the elders. "The Pharisees," says Josephus, "have delivered to the people a great many observances by succession from their fathers which are not written in the law of Moses, and for that reason it is that the Sadducees reject them, and say that we are to esteem those observances to be obligatory which are in the written word, but are not to observe what are derived from the tradition of our forefathers; and concerning these things it is that great disputes and differences have arisen among them, while the Sadducees are able to persuade none but the rich, and have not the populace obsequious to them; but the Pharisees have the multitude on their side." [1]

The manifold precepts and rules, expositions and traditions, which are commonly known as the Halachah and the Haga- The Midrashim. dah, had their origin in these Pharisaic tendencies of the scribes who succeeded Ezra and his coadjutors. These various expositions constitute the Midrashim, or most ancient Jewish commentary. The Halachic, or legal exegesis, was confined to the Pentateuch, and aimed, by analogy and combination of specific written laws, to deduce precepts and rules on subjects which had not been formally treated in the Mosaic Code. This was, in the main, a reading into the laws of Moses a great variety of things which they could not, by any fair interpretation, be made to teach. The Hagadic exegesis, on the other hand, was extended over the entire Old Testament Scriptures, and was of a more practical and homiletical character. It aimed, by means of memorable sayings of illustrious men, parables, allegories, marvellous legends, witty proverbs, and mystic interpretations of Scripture events, to stimulate the Jewish people to pious activity and obedience. The Midrashim thus became a vast treasury of Hebrew national lore. It

resembles in form the famous mediæval motto for the guidance of conventual ambition, although it is more serious in spirit: 'Be circumspect in judging—make many disciples—make a hedge round the law.' Nothing could be less like the impetuosity, the simplicity, or the openness of Ezra than any of these three precepts. But the one which in each succeeding generation predominated more and more was the last: 'Make a hedge about the law.' To build up elaborate explanations, thorny obstructions, subtle evasions, enormous developments, was the labour of the later Jewish scribes, till the Pentateuch was buried beneath the Mishna, and the Mishna beneath the Gemara."—Jewish Church, Third Series, pp. 165, 166.

[1] Antiquities, book xiii, chap. x, 6. Comp. Wars, book ii, chap. viii.

was developed gradually, by public lectures and homilies, and became more and more comprehensive and complicated as new legends, secret meanings, hidden wisdom, and allegorical expositions were added by one great teacher after another. We have the substance of the Midrashim preserved in the Talmud and the Hagadic literature of the first three centuries of the Christian era.[1]

The character of these ancient Jewish expositions of Scripture *Hagadic hermeneutics.* may be inferred from the kind of hermeneutical principles which were adopted. Among the thirty-two rules of interpretation collected and arranged by Elieser Ben-Jose the following are specimens:

By the superfluous use of the three particles, את, גם, and אף, the Scriptures indicate in a threefold manner that something more is included in the text than the apparent declaration would seem to imply. This rule is illustrated by Gen. xxi, 1, where it is said "Jehovah visited Sarah" (אֶת־שָׂרָה), and the particle אֶת is supposed to show that the Lord also visited other women besides Sarah.

A subject often explains itself while it imparts information on other subjects. Thus, in Jer. xlvi, 22, "Its cry shall go like the serpent," is a statement which serves, besides describing the loud cry of Egypt, to indicate that the serpent set up a great cry when the Lord pronounced his curse against it.

A great and incomprehensible thing is represented by something small, to render it intelligible. Thus, in Deut. xxxii, 2, "My doctrine shall drop as the rain," the great and incomprehensible doctrines of revelation are made comprehensible by comparison with the rain.

Explanations are obtained by reducing the letters of a word to their numerical value, and substituting for it another word or phrase of the same value, or by transposing the letters. Thus, for example, the sum of the letters in the name of Eliezer (אליעזר), Abraham's servant, is equivalent to three hundred and eighteen (318), the number of his trained men (Gen. xiv, 14), and, accordingly, shows that Eliezer alone was worth a host of servants.[2]

---

[1] Ishmael Ben-Elisa's Commentary on Exodus xii–xxiii, called Mechilta (מכלתא), is an allegorical treatment of various Mosaic ceremonies, and is one of the oldest specimens of formal Jewish exposition. Ishmael Ben-Elisa flourished about the close of the first and the beginning of the second century of our era, and was the author of several mystic treatises which are still extant. His Mechilta with a Latin translation is given by Ugolino in the Thesaurus Antiquitatum Sacrarum, vol. xiv, Venice, 1752. A German translation of numerous ancient Midrashim is given by Wünsche, Bibliotheca Rabbinica; eine Sammlung alter Midrashim zum ersten Male ins Deutsche übertragen, Lpz., 1880–1881, 12 thin vols., 8vo.

[2] See all these Halachic and Hagadic rules of interpretation stated and illustrated by Ginsburg, in the article Midrash, in Kitto's Cyclopædia of Biblical Literature, and also in M'Clintock and Strong's Cyclopædia of Biblical, Theological, and Ecclesiastical Literature.

It is easy to see how such hermeneutical principles must necessarily involve the exposition of the Scriptures in utter Mischief and confusion. The study of the ancient Jewish exegesis value of the
Hagadic exe- is, therefore, of little practical value to one who seeks gesis. the true meaning of the oracles of God.[1] But for evidences of ancient Jewish opinions, and for the criticism of the Hebrew text, the comments of the older rabbis may sometimes be of great service. "When it is borne in mind," says Ginsburg, "that the annotators and punctuators of the Hebrew text, and the translators of the ancient versions, were Jews impregnated with the theological opinions of the nation, and who prosecuted their biblical labours in harmony with these opinions and the above-named exegetical rules, the importance of the Halachic and Hagadic exegesis to the criticism of the Hebrew text, and to a right understanding of the Greek, Chaldee, Syriac, and other versions, as well as of the quotations of the Old Testament in the New Testament, can hardly be overrated. If it be true—and few will question the fact—that every successive English version, either preceding or following the Reformation, reflects the peculiar notions about theology, Church government, and politics of each period and every dominant party; and that even the most literal translation of modern days is, in a certain sense, a commentary of the translator; we ought to regard it as natural that the Jews, without intending to deceive, or wilfully to alter the text, should, by the process of the Midrash, introduce or indicate, in their biblical labours, the various opinions to which shifting circumstances give rise."[2]

How far this Hagadic method of interpretation became current, or to what extent it was generally adopted by the great The Septuagint
as a witness to body of Jews in the world before the Christian era, it Hagadic prin- is impossible to tell. That it became quite general is ciples. evident. The plain meaning of the Old Testament, as it would impress itself upon the unsophisticated reader, was probably everywhere allowed. Only the anthropomorphisms and more difficult passages would at first be set aside as not to be understood literally. The Septuagint version is a monumental witness to the manner

---

[1] Surely no exposition of Scripture, however deep its reverence for the letter of God's word, could be safe or useful which proceeded on the principles of Rabbi Akiba, who maintained that every repetition, figure, parallelism, synonyme, word, letter, particle, pleonasm, nay, the very shape of a letter, had a recondite meaning, just as every fibre of a fly's wing or an ant's foot has its peculiar significance. See Ginsburg, Coheleth, translated, with a Commentary, pp. 495, 496, Lond., 1861. For much valuable information on Hagadic exegesis, see the whole of Appendix I, and also the learned Introduction to this Commentary.

[2] Ginsburg, in Kitto's Cyclopædia, article Midrash.

in which the Jews of that age freely admitted fictitious legends and entire apocryphal books among their holy writings. This was a very natural outgrowth of Hagadic principles, and while the Hebrew text was honoured with a superstitious reverence, its translation into a Gentile tongue so far removed it from its original glory that no scruple was felt in lengthening its chronology to a more apparent harmony with Egyptian notions, and incorporating with it books like that of the Son of Sirach and the Wisdom of Solomon, which seemed like a connecting link with Greek philosophy.[1] In like manner the whole body of apocryphal and pseudepigraphal literature of a pre-Christian date serves to illustrate the uncritical looseness of Hagadic principles. For while these ancient books furnish no examples of formal exegesis, they clearly indicate the freedom with which many of the more learned Jews of those days added philosophy, fiction, and highly coloured legend to their acceptance of the genuine ancient Scriptures.

Aristobulus, the priest, who is mentioned in 2 Macc. i, 10, appears to have been the author of a commentary on the Books of Moses. Eusebius speaks of him as "that most distinguished scholar who was one of the Seventy who translated the Holy Scriptures from the Hebrew for Ptolemy Philadelphus and his father, and dedicated his exposition of the law of Moses to the same kings."[2] Fragments of this work have been preserved in Eusebius.[3] But all formal attempts, among the Alexandrian Jews, to expound the Scriptures seem to have sought especially after hidden and mysterious lore. "The allegorical

Aristobulus, the priest and scholar.

---

[1] "The Wisdom of the Son of Sirach," says Stanley, "was followed, at how long an interval we know not, by the Wisdom of Solomon. As the former book was the expression of a sage at Jerusalem, with a tincture of Alexandrian learning, so the latter book was the expression of an Alexandrian sage presenting his Grecian ideas under the forms of Jewish history. We feel with him the oppressive atmosphere of the elaborate Egyptian idolatry (chap. xiii, 2–19; xv, 17–19). We see through his eyes the ships passing along the Mediterranean waters into the Alexandrian harbour (xiv, 1–6). We trace the footprint of Aristotle in the enumeration, word by word, of the four great ethical virtues (viii, 7). We recognise the rhetoric of the Grecian sophists in the Ptolemæan court (v, 9–12; xi, 17, 18); we are present at the luxurious banquets and lax discussions of the neighbouring philosophers of Cyrene (ii, 1–7). But in the midst of this Gentile scenery there is a voice which speaks with the authority of the ancient prophets to this new world. The book is a signal instance of the custom prevalent in the two centuries before the Christian era, both in the Jewish and the Gentile world, of placing modern untried writings under the shelter of some venerable authority."—History of Jewish Church, Third Series, pp. 304, 305.

[2] Ecclesiastical History, book vii, chap. xxxii.

[3] Præparatio Evangelica, vii, 14; viii, 10; xiii, 12. The genuineness of these fragments of Aristobulus has been disputed, but is now quite generally conceded.

explanation," says Gförer, "could come into existence only among
a people possessed of sacred books, and only at a time when the
spokesmen and leaders of that nation had already chosen for their
possession another philosophy than that presented by the literal
meaning of the written revelation." [1]

In the writings of Philo, the philosophical Jew of Alexandria,
we may trace the development of the Halachic and Philo Judæus,
Hagadic hermeneutical principles as they became more the Alexan-
fully shaped and coloured by Hellenic culture.[2] Juda- drian.
ism and Hellenism, so to speak, came into closest contact in this
celebrated metropolis of Egypt, and in their spiritual and intellectual mingling produced what came to be known as Neo-Platonism.
Kingsley maintains that Philo Judæus was the real father and
founder of this eclectic philosophy.[3] The historical importance of
his writings, as a conspicuous fountain-head of allegorical exegesis,
justifies a fuller notice than their intrinsic merits deserve. He was
born about twenty-five years before Christ, and was contemporary
with the principal events of the New Testament history. He was
not improbably an associate or intimate acquaintance of Apollos of
Alexandria, the eloquent Jew who was mighty in the Scriptures
(Acts xviii, 24). He united a deep reverence for the Mosaic revelation with an absorbing fondness for the speculations of Greek
philosophy, and thus became, from the force of circumstances, an
eclectic philosopher.

Philo appears, at times, to assume or allow the literal sense of a
passage, but his great aim is to exhibit the mystic Notions of mys-
depths of significance which lie concealed beneath the tic depths of
sacred words. He would not have it supposed that Scripture.
the divine revelation is of easy apprehension by the common mind,
for such a supposition would have seemed to him like a disparagement of its hidden labyrinths of divine knowledge, to explore which
requires a kind of supernatural vision. The Hellenic philosophy,
with which he was so fascinated, was assumed to be a natural and
necessary part of the laws of Moses. He seems to entertain no
conception of the historical standpoint of his author, and to have
no realistic or historical sense of the truthfulness or accuracy of the
statements of Moses. He seizes upon chance expressions and incidental analogies as matters of great moment, and lugs in farfetched
notions that are utterly foreign to the plain meaning of the text.

[1] Philo und die alexandrinische Theosophie, vol. i, p. 69.
[2] See Ritter, Philo und die Halacha. Eine vergleichende Studie unter steter Be-
rüchsichtigung des Josephus, Lpz., 1879.
[3] Alexandria and Her Schools, p. 79, Cambridge, 1854.

He shows not the least regard for the connexion and scope of a passage, or for the integrity of Scripture as a trustworthy record of facts; nevertheless he treats the law itself as the divinely inspired word of God.

His principal works consist of a series of expository treatises on The works of the books of the Mosaic law. He makes occasional Philo. references to other parts of the Old Testament, and also to a large number of Greek writers, especially the poets and philosophers. His philosophical theories, theological opinions, and especially his doctrine of the Logos, have been the subject of a vast amount of study and disputation. It is still a question whether the Logos of Philo is to be understood as a person, or a personification of the divine reason, or merely a divine attribute. But in a writer so eclectic and so full of mysticism it is quite probable that these several notions are much confused, and that no definite answer can be given. The creation by the word of God, as suggested in the expression, *and God said,* so often repeated in the first chapter of Genesis, was the first indication of the doctrine of the Logos. Another element was added to it by the language used concerning the angel of Jehovah (Exod. xxiii, 20–22). The doctrine of the divine wisdom, as set forth in Job xxviii, 12–28, and Prov. viii and ix, presented it in still another form. The personification of wisdom is still more emphatic in the apocryphal books of the Son of Sirach (Ecclesiasticus, chaps. i and xxiv) and the Wisdom of Solomon (vii, 22–29). The peculiar use of the terms, מֵימְרָא, דִּבּוּרָא (Word), and שְׁכִינָה (Shechinah), instead of, or in addition to, the name of God in the Targums, seems to belong to the same development of thought. Is it strange, then, that with an allegorist and mystic like Philo all the various and vague conjectures that had long floated about these words should have been appropriated, to some extent, and blended further with Platonic ideas?

The following specimens will serve to illustrate Philo's general style and method of interpreting the Scriptures. Speaking of Paradise, and the trees of life and of knowledge, he observes:

These statements appear to me to be dictated by a philosophy which is symbolical rather than strictly accurate. For no trees of life or of knowledge have ever at any previous time appeared upon the earth, nor is it likely that any will appear hereafter. But I rather conceive that Moses was speaking in an allegorical spirit, intending by his Paradise to intimate the dominant character of the soul, which is full of innumerable opinions, as this figurative Paradise was of trees. And by the tree of life he was shadowing out the greatest of the virtues—namely, piety toward the gods, by means of which the soul is made immortal—and by the tree which had the knowledge of good and evil he was intimating that wisdom and moderation by means of which things contrary in their nature to one another are distinguished.[1]

In Gen. ii, 6, where the Hebrew reads, "A mist (אֵד) went up from the land and watered the whole face of the ground," Philo adopts the Septuagint version, which is, "A fountain went up from the land and watered all the face of the land," and comments thus:

He here calls the mind the fountain of the earth, and the sensations he calls the face of the earth, because there is the most suitable place in the whole body for them with reference to their appropriate energies, a place that nature, which foreknows everything, has assigned to them. And the mind waters the sensations like a fountain, sending appropriate streams over each.[2]

He thus comments on the planting of Paradise at the east in Eden (Gen. ii, 8):

Virtue is called a Paradise metaphorically, and the appropriate place for the Paradise is Eden; and this means luxury; and the most appropriate field for virtue is peace and ease and joy, in which real luxury especially consists. Moreover, the plantation of this Paradise is represented in the east; for right reason never sets and is never extinguished, but it is its nature to be always rising. And, as I imagine, the rising sun fills the darkness of the air with light, so also does virtue when it has arisen in the soul irradiate its mist, and dissipate the dense darkness. "And there," says Moses, "he placed the man whom he had formed;" for God being good, and having formed our race for virtue, as his work which was most· akin to himself, places the mind in virtue, evidently in order that it, like a good husband, may cultivate and attend to nothing else except virtue.[3]

Pages might be filled with examples of exegesis like these from any of the treatises of Philo. The excess of mystic and allegorical fancies which this distinguished writer crowds into his expositions is, no doubt, due to a great extent to the peculiar Alexandrian culture and the spirit of eclectic philosophy in the midst of which he was trained. A similar spirit prevailed at that time among all the Jews of the dispersion, and the great feasts which brought them to Jerusalem "from every nation under heaven" (Acts ii, 5) tended to cultivate and strengthen it. Hellenists and Hebrews were terms full of significance (comp. Acts vi, 1). The Jews of Palestine would naturally

The allegorical and Hagadic method pervaded all Judaism.

---

[1] Treatise on the Creation of the World, sec. liv. Yonge's Translation (Bohn's Ecclesiastical Library), vol. i, p. 46.

[2] Treatise On the Allegories of the Sacred Laws, book i, sec. xi. Yonge's Translation, vol. i, p. 59.

[3] Ibid., book i., sec. xiv. Yonge's Translation, vol. i, pp. 63, 64.

maintain their national and religious peculiarities with greater zeal and firmness than the foreign-born, Greek-speaking Jews on whom the Hebraic culture and customs would have an inferior hold. Nevertheless, the tendency to allegorize the Scriptures, and to hedge them in and load them down with legend, proverb, and parable, was common wherever Judaism had planted a synagogue and maintained a rabbi. Philo was not the author of his system of interpretation, nor did it end with him. We trace it in the most ancient Hagadic literature; it was condemned by Christ and by Paul (Matt. xv, 1–10; xxiii, 16–24; Mark vii, 5–13; Col. ii, 8; 1 Tim. i, 4; vi, 20; Titus i, 14), but it prevailed in the rival rabbinical schools of Hillel and Shammai. The oldest collection of Halachic interpretations is said to have been made by the school of Hillel, and the Talmud preserves to us in written form many an illustration of the absurdly trifling points of difference on which those ancient masters disputed.

The best ancient Jewish exegesis is represented in the Targums of Onkelos and Jonathan Ben Uzziel. These are the *The Targums.* Chaldee paraphrases of the Pentateuch and the Prophets. The Targum of Onkelos on the Pentateuch is of great value as a translation. It is in the main a tolerably faithful rendering of the Hebrew, and its occasional explanatory additions are usually worthy of attention and regard. Its deviations from the Hebrew consist for the most part in changes of words and constructions for the purpose of elucidating difficulties, explaining figurative terms, avoiding forms of expression which might savour of heathenism or be offensive to the philosophical mind. He avoids anthropomorphisms, and renders Elohim and Jehovah by the Word (מימרא) of God, the Splendour (יקרא) of God, or the Shechinah of God. The greatest liberty is taken with the poetical passages, where, in some instances, it is impossible to recognise the original. This Targum is believed to belong to the first century of the Christian era.

The Targum of Jonathan Ben Uzziel on the Prophets is much *Jonathan Ben Uzziel.* more free in its paraphrasing the Hebrew text. On Joshua, Judges, Samuel, and Kings it is generally simple, and fairly gives the sense, but on the prophetical books it often runs into Hagadic additions which have no foundation in the Scripture text. It is interwoven with Jewish dogmatical opinions and current traditions of the time.

Still more free in its interpretations is the Targum of the *Other Targums.* Pseudo-Jonathan on the Pentateuch. It is a mixture of loose paraphrase and Halachic and Hagadic legends, and is evidently of much later origin than the Talmud. The so-called

Jerusalem Targum on portions of the Pentateuch is of substantially the same character as that of Pseudo-Jonathan, and has been thought by some to be only a fragmentary recension of it. The Targums on the Hagiographa are of various dates and worth, that on the Proverbs adhering more closely to the original text than any of the others.[1]

The Talmud in its present form is a collection of the comments, opinions, and discussions of generations of Jewish teachers. It is divided into two parts, the Mishna and the Gemara, and embodies the substance of the Halachic and Hagadic comments and traditions which were current at the time of the destruction of Jerusalem, and for hundreds of years thereafter.[2] According to Jewish tradition Moses received at Sinai, in addition to the Pentateuch, an unwritten oral law, and afterward delivered it over to Joshua. Joshua delivered the same to the elders, and they to the prophets, from whom it came into the possession of the men of the Great Synagogue, the last of whom was Simon the Just, who was contemporary with Alexander the Great (B. C. 325). Simon transmitted it to Antigonus of Soco, and so it was passed onward until it came into possession of the schools of Hillel and Shammai. All this is recorded in the Talmudic treatise on the Fathers (פִּרְקֵי אָבוֹת, *Pirke Aboth*). These schools, especially that of Hillel, sifted and preserved these laws, until Rabbi Judah the Holy (about A. D. 200) compiled and codified them in six Sedarim (סְדָרִים, orders, or arrangements), thenceforth known as the Mishna. "Rabbi Judah's great desire," says Polano, "was to create among the people a love for the study of the law, and a familiarity with its beauties and its moral and religious code. He saw that a complete knowledge of the law was limited to a comparatively few, who were dispersed through many countries, and he feared it might in time be entirely forgotten if the interest in its study was allowed to decrease as it had for some time been diminishing. With the aid of the sages and pupils of his college he set diligently to work, and collecting the rules, explanations, and traditions extant since the death of Moses, he inscribed them into six volumes, which he called the Mishna, or Second Law. One hundred and fifty years after the destruction of the second temple the redaction was completed. Many of the laws were already

The Talmud.

Polano on the Mishna.

---

[1] On the Targums, see Smith's Dictionary of the Bible, Kitto's Cyclopædia of Biblical Literature, and McClintock and Strong's Cyclopædia of Biblical, Theological, and Ecclesiastical Literature, article Targum.

[2] For a popular account of the Talmud, see Emanuel Deutsch, in the Quarterly Review (Lond.) of Oct., 1867, and republished among his Literary Remains, N. Y., 1874.

obsolete, even on their first publication. Rome had long before substituted her own penal code for that belonging to the Jewish nationality; the minute injunctions regulating the sacrifices and the temple services had but an ideal value, and many of the other laws applied particularly to Palestine, where but comparatively few of the people remained. Yet the whole was received in Palestine and Babylonia, not merely as a record of the past, but as a holy work, an infallible textbook, a record of laws that, with the restoration of the commonwealth, would come into practice as in time past. All Israel gave thanks for the completion of this great undertaking."[1]

The Mishna, however, did not include all the Midrashim which The formation were current at the time of its compilation. Nor was of the Gemara. the text of the Mishna sufficient to furnish law and counsel for every question of Jewish casuistry. Doubts and differences of opinion led to new discussions, and these later comments and opinions, chiefly those of great teachers at Tiberias, in Palestine, and at Sora, in Babylonia, grew into a vast commentary on the Mishna. These later doctors of the law are known as the Amoraim (or Gemaraim, from גְמַר, to *complete*—supplementers or finishers of the law), and the collection of their comments on the Mishna, accordingly, acquired the name of the Gemara.[2] The Amoraim of Tiberias completed their work about A. D. 350, and, together with the Mishna, this collection is known as the Palestinian or Jerusalem Talmud.[3] The Babylonian Talmud was not

---

[1] Selections from the Talmud; being Specimens of the Contents of that Ancient Book, etc. Translated from the Original, p. 24. Philadelphia, 1876. For a convenient English translation of selections from all the Sedarim of the Talmud, see Barclay, The Talmud. London, 1878. The best edition of the entire Mishna is that of Surenhusius, with a Latin translation. Amsterdam, 1668–1703. 6 vols., fol.

[2] The rabbis of the period, A. D. 180 to A. D. 500, are commonly called the Talmudists. They are divided into two classes, the Tanaim, who compiled the Mishna, and the Amoraim, who formed the Gemara. These Talmudists were preceded by the more ancient scribes, known as the Sopherim, and followed by the Saboraim, or teachers of the Law, after the completion of the Talmud (from A. D. 500 to A. D. 657), and later by the Gaonim, who flourished at Babylon from A. D. 657 to A. D. 1038. See Ginsburg, article Scribes, in Kitto's Cyclopædia of Biblical Literature, and M'Clintock and Strong's Cyclopædia of Biblical, Theological, and Ecclesiastical Literature. See also Bacher, Die Agada der babylonischen Amoräer. Ein Beitrag zur Geschicnte der Agada und zur Einleitung in den babylonischen Talmud. Strassburg, 1878.

[3] The Jerusalem Talmud treats only four of the six Sedarim or orders of the Mishna, the treatise Niddah, and a few fragmentary portions. It was first published at Venice in 1523. Many subsequent editions. A large part of it, with a Latin translation, is published in Ugolino's Thesaurus Antiquitatum Sacrarum, vols. xvii, xviii, xx, xxv, and xxx. See Wünsche, Der jerusalemische Talmud in seiner haggadischen Bestandtheilen, zum ersten Male ins Deutsche übertragen. Zürich, 1880.

completed until about A. D. 550.[1] The language of both Talmuds is a corrupt form of Hebrew, a kind of barbarous mixture of Hebrew and Aramaic, made specially obscure by a liberal use of words from the Arabic, Persian, Coptic, Greek, and Latin tongues. The style is made the more obscure by an abundance of technical terms and abbreviations. It is a most difficult and uninviting task for an English student to attempt to master this storehouse of Jewish thought.

On the general character of the Talmud as a whole Delitzsch remarks: "Those who have not in some degree accomplished the extremely difficult task of reading the work for themselves will hardly be able to form a clear idea of this polynomial colossus. It is a vast debating club, in which there hum confusedly the myriad voices of at least five centuries. As we all know by experience, a law, though very minutely and exactly defined, may yet be susceptible of various interpretations, and question on question is sure to arise when it comes to be applied to the ever-varying circumstances of actual life. Suppose, then, you have about ten thousand legal definitions all relating to Jewish life and classified under different heads, and add to these ten thousand definitions of about five hundred doctors and lawyers, belonging mostly to Palestine or Babylonia, who make these definitions, one after the other, the subject of examination and debate, and who, with hair-splitting acuteness, exhaust not only every possible sense the words will bear, but every possible practical occurrence arising out of them. Suppose that the fine-spun threads of these legal disquisitions frequently lose themselves in digressions, and that, when one has waded through a long tract of this sandy desert, one lights, here and there, on some green oasis consisting of stories and sayings of universal interest. This done, you will have some tolerable idea of this enormous and, in its way, unique code of laws, in comparison with which, in point of comprehensiveness, the law books of all other nations are but lilliputian, and, when compared with the hum of its kaleidoscopic Babel, they resemble, indeed, calm and studious retreats."[2] Nevertheless the Talmud has for twelve hundred years exerted a moulding influence on Jewish thought, and the later rabbinical exposition of the Old Testament Scriptures is deeply imbued with its spirit.

[1] The Babylonian Talmud was first published at Venice, 12 vols. fol., 1520–1523. Many subsequent editions. A Latin translation of three treatises of this Talmud may be found in Ugolino's Thesaurus, vols. xix and xxv.

[2] Jüdisches Handwerkerleben zur Zeit Jesu, p. 35. Erlangen, 1879.

CHAPTER II.

LATER RABBINICAL EXEGESIS.

INASMUCH as all Jewish interpretation of the Old Testament forms
a kind of world by itself, we may, for the sake of unity
of treatment, attend in this place to the later rabbinical methods of exposition which followed upon the
completion of the Talmud, and which still obtain. As
long as the veil, which is upon the heart of Israel (2 Cor. iii, 14–16),
remains unlifted, so that they cannot discern in their ancient oracles the prophecies of the Lord Christ as they have been fulfilled in
Jesus of Nazareth, so long we may not expect to find among Jewish
exegetes a clear and consistent elucidation of the Old Testament.

*Jewish exposi-
tions obscure
because of the
veil on Israel's
heart.*

Although the Talmudists, like the Pharisees of our Lord's time,
have ever been the more numerous and popular party
among the Jews, their methods of teaching were probably never at any one period universally accepted among the scattered tribes. The more rationalistic class, known in antiquity as
the Sadducees, have had their representatives in all later times,
though these later critics have not continued to accept the doctrines
known to have been once held by the Sadducees. One of the oldest sects of the Jewish synagogue was that of the Karaites (קְרָאִים,
readers, or literalists), who rejected the authority of the oral law,
and all the traditions and precepts of Hagadic literature. They
did not, however, refuse to accept from the Talmud, tradition, or
any other source, that which might serve as an exegetical aid to the
understanding of the Scriptures, nor did they ignore the deeper
spiritual sense. They made frequent use of metaphorical modes of
explanation, but studied to be free from the superstitions and follies of the Talmudists. The Karaites exist, at the present day, in
greatest numbers in the Crimean peninsula, and possess an extensive literature on biblical interpretation and other subjects; but
their works are written in Arabic, corrupt Hebrew, Turkish, and
other languages of the East, and are little known to the western
nations.[1]

*The sect of the
Karaites.*

The strict methods of the Karaites had much influence in
restraining the extravagance of the opposite schools, and obtained

[1] See Fürst, Geschichte des Karäerthums (Lpz., 1865), and Rule, History of the
Karaite Jews, London, 1870.

considerable prevalence during the eighth and ninth centuries. The celebrated Rabbi Saadia-Gaon, born in Egypt about A.D. 892, received his early training from an eminent Saadia Hag-Gaon. Karaite teacher, and thereby doubtless acquired a freedom from many of the current rabbinical superstitions of his age. He was among the first of his race to cultivate the science of grammar, and became distinguished as a commentator, theologian, and orator. He did not embrace the Karaite doctrines, but contended for the necessity of tradition, and urged that many precepts of the Mosaic law, as well as numerous Jewish doctrines and historical facts, were dependent on oral tradition. He was the author of an Arabic translation (with annotations) of the Pentateuch,[1] the Book of Job, the Psalms of David, and the prophecy of Isaiah. He also wrote commentaries on the Song of Songs, the Minor Prophets, the Book of Daniel, and other parts of the Old Testament. Contemporary with Saadia was Jeshua Ibn Sadal (about 920), who wrote Ibn Sadal. a commentary on the Pentateuch and Job; his son, Abul Faraj Aaron, also wrote an Arabic commentary on the Pentateuch. Other less noted Jewish scholars wrote similar works about the same period.[2]

One of the most eminent of the Karaite exegetes was Japheth Ben Ali, who flourished at Basra, in Arabia, in the Japheth Ben Ali. latter part of the tenth century. "His gigantic commentaries," says Ginsburg, "must have exercised great influence on the development of biblical exegesis, as may be concluded from the fact that Aben Ezra had them constantly before him when writing his expositions of the Old Testament, and that he quotes them with the greatest respect. The manuscripts of these commentaries, which consist of twenty large volumes, are in Paris and Leyden. The eminent orientalist, Munk, brought, in 1841, from Egypt to the royal library at Paris, eleven volumes, five of which are on Genesis, and many sections of Exodus, Leviticus, and Numbers; two volumes are on the Psalms, one is on Proverbs, and one on the five Megilloth. The commentaries, which are in Arabic, are preceded by the Hebrew text and an Arabic translation."[3]

From the tenth century and onward a more grammatical and thorough exegesis obtained among the learned Jews. The influence of the Karaites, and the studies and disputes of the rabbinical

---

[1] Saadia's Arabic version of the Pentateuch is published in the Paris and London Polyglots.

[2] See Fürst's Contribution to the History of Hebrew Lexicography, prefixed to his Hebrew and Chaldee Lexicon.

[3] Kitto's Cyclopædia of Biblical Literature, article Japheth Ben Ali.

schools at Tiberias in Palestine, and of Sora and Pumbaditha in
Babylonia, all had this necessary effect. "About this
time," says Nordheimer, "occurred the dispute respecting the various readings of the Bible between Aaron
Ben Asher of Tiberias and Jacob Ben Naphtali of Pumbaditha, from which dates the general collection of such readings
and their division into two classes, called, after those who used
them, Oriental and Occidental. From the period when the Jewish
mind ceased to be fettered by the almost despotic power of their
spiritual and secular rulers, other branches of knowledge, as philosophy, philology, and poetry, began to be cultivated among the
rabbis, although long held subordinate to the study of the Talmud,
and considered simply in the light of auxiliaries to the religious
and moral teachings of the synagogue. The attention of the rabbis
and other learned men of the time was, accordingly, directed for
the most part to Talmudic explanations of the Scriptures, and to
polemical treatises in defence of the Mosaic religion against Christianity and Islamism."[1]

*More gram-
matical turn of
Jewish studies
in tenth cen-
tury.*

One of the most distinguished scholars of this period was Rabbi
Solomon Isaac, commonly called Rashi (sometimes erro-
neously Jarchi). He was born at Troyes, in France,
about A. D. 1040, and at an early age became notably proficient in
his acquaintance with the Scriptures and the Talmud. Much of
his life was spent in travel and visiting the different seats of learning in Germany, Italy, Greece, Palestine, Egypt, and Persia. He
wrote commentaries on the entire Old Testament (excepting Job
and Chronicles), and also on a large portion of the Talmud. His
commentaries on the Scriptures are printed in the great rabbinical Bibles, and are regarded by the Jewish people as almost a part
of the Bible itself. His method is to give a simple and literal
explanation of the Hebrew text, but his great devotion to the Talmud led him to attempt a combination of the Halachic and Hagadic
fancies with the literal sense. This course often involved him in
manifest contradictions and inconsistency. His effort to condense
and abbreviate makes his style very obscure, and several Jewish
scholars have written commentaries on his expositions in order to
elucidate some of his perplexing passages.[2]

Rashi.

---

[1] The Rabbis and their Literature; article in the American Biblical Repository for
July, 1841, p. 162.

[2] All Rashi's commentaries, together with several Jewish commentaries upon them,
were translated into Latin by Breithaupt, and accompanied by extensive annotations,
four vols., Gotha, 1710–14. Specimens of Jewish commentary, translated into English, and representing Rashi, Kimchi, Aben Ezra, Saadia, and Maimonides, are given

Rabbi Joshua Ben Jehudah, a famous Karaite commentator, also lived in the eleventh century. His expositions are said Joshua Ben Judah. to cover all the books of the Old Testament, but they exist only in manuscript. He is often quoted by Aben Ezra. He was distinguished as a philosopher and grammarian as well as a learned exegete.

As the Jews became more and more scattered abroad, rabbinical schools and learned teachers arose in different places, The Spanish schools. and not the least noted were those of Spain. During the rule of the Moors in Spain the Jewish population of that country enjoyed great liberties, and many who fled from persecution in other lands found a refuge and protection there. Already the cabalistic philosophy and mysticism, as represented in the books Jezirah and Zohar,[1] had become widespread, and, indeed, Jewish thought had always manifested a tendency to indulge in mystic fancy. But against this tendency, and in favour of a thorough grammatical interpretation, was Aben Ezra of Toledo. We know but little of the facts of his life, save that he Aben Ezra. was born in 1092, travelled extensively, and was regarded as second to none of the great rabbinical scholars of the Middle Ages. His greatest work is a commentary on the Pentateuch which is published in the rabbinical Bibles, and also separately. His hermeneutical principles may be best inferred from the following passage in the preface to his Commentary on Genesis: "Those rabbis who reside among the Arabs take occasion to connect the study of biblical interpretation with that of natural history and metaphysics; but every one who desires to become acquainted with these sciences will do better to study them in books that treat of them alone. Others, as the Karaites, seek to explain all these matters from the Bible, and to establish them upon what is there contained. A third class, the Cabalists, grope in total darkness, thinking to discover symbols in every part of the law; the errors of these men scarcely deserve a serious refutation; although in one respect they are right, viz., in asserting that all laws are to be weighed in the balance of reason—for in every heart is a mind which is a reflection of God's Spirit, and when this is opposed to the literal acceptance

in Turner's useful little volume entitled Biographical Notices of some of the Most Distinguished Jewish Rabbis, and translations of portions of their commentaries. New York, 1847.

[1] See the articles Cabala (or Kabalah), Jezirah, and Zohar, in the Cyclopædias of Herzog, Kitto, and M'Clintock and Strong. See also the Kabbalah; its Doctrines, Development, and Literature; an Essay, by C. D. Ginsburg (London, 1865); and Franck, La Kabbale; ou La Philosophie Religieuse des Hébreux. Paris, 1843.

of the Scripture, a deeper meaning is to be looked for, reason being the messenger between God and man. If, however, the plain interpretation of a passage be not opposed to reason, why should we seek for any other? Notwithstanding, there are phrases which contain both a literal and an allegorical meaning, as, for instance, the terms *circumcision* and *tree of knowledge*. A fourth class explain everything according to the Hagadah without regard to the laws of grammar; but what purpose is served by repeating the often contradictory views that have been already detailed in so many Talmudic writings? Some of these Hagadic explanations have, indeed, a deeper meaning than appears on the surface; but the majority of them are designed merely as an agreeable relaxation for the mind when wearied by the study of the Halachah. A fifth method is that followed by myself: this is, first to determine the grammatical sense of a passage; next to consult the Chaldee version of Onkelos, although this, especially in the poetical portions, often departs from the simple meaning; and for the legislative books of the Bible I call in the aid of tradition."

We note here the strong hold which Talmudic study and Jewish tradition had upon the mind of Aben Ezra, but it is remarkable that he should nevertheless become so free from Hagadic fancies in an age when that style of exegesis extensively prevailed. Despite his occasional allegorizing, and self-amusement in cabalistic trifling, his exegetical works are full of varied learning and valuable suggestions.[1]

Moses Maimonides, often called Rambam, was born at Cordova, A. D. 1135. While yet a youth he became thoroughly instructed by his father in Hebrew and Talmudic literature, and in mathematics and astronomy. When only thirteen years old he was obliged to leave Spain on account of Mohammedan persecution, and went to Accho, Jerusalem, Hebron, and finally settled in Egypt, where, about 1168, he completed his great commentary on the Mishna, and published it with the title of Book of Light. This was written in Arabic, and afterward translated into Hebrew, and has been published in many editions, generally along with the text of the Mishna. His great aim was to harmonize Judaism with science and philosophy, and so great became his influence and authority as a teacher that he was resorted to by Jews from all lands as the great oracle in matters of religion. He subsequently published another work of even greater magnitude than the former, which he called Second Law (Mishna-Torah), or the

^{Moses Maimon-}
^{ides.}

---

[1] See Turner, Biographical Notices of some of the Most Distinguished Rabbis, pp. 31–34. New York, 1847.

Mighty Hand (יד החזקה, *Yad Hachezakah*). It consists of fourteen books (יד=14), and is a cyclopædia of biblical and Jewish literature. Each article furnishes a lucid abstract of the ancient traditional expositions of those who were regarded as the highest authorities in their respective departments. It was like the creation of a new Talmud, and marked the beginning of a new epoch in Judaism. His third great work was entitled Moreh Nebuchim (מורה נבוכים), or Guide of the Perplexed. "This religio-philosophical work," says Ginsburg, "created a new epoch in the philosophy of the Middle Ages. Not only did Mohammedans write commentaries on it, but the Christian schoolmen learned from it how to harmonize the conflicts between religion and philosophy. The great aim of Maimonides—to harmonize in his writings the written and the oral law—obliged him to reject many things in the rabbinic writings which many of his talmudic brethren held inviolably sacred. This involved him in extensive and painful controversies during the rest of his life, and he had the mortification of seeing the Jewish nation divided into two parties; the one fighting with anathemas against him, regarding him as a heretic, and consigning his work to the flames, and the other defending him as an angel, the messenger of a new covenant. In the midst of this conflict the ' Great Luminary ' of the Jewish nation was extinguished Dec. 13, 1204."[1] Notwithstanding all the opposition to some of his views which has here and there been made, there is probably no Jewish name more honoured than that of Maimonides. His works have appeared in many editions and translations, and the Jews have a saying that "from Moses even until Moses there has not arisen one like Moses." He has been honoured with the titles of "the Great Luminary," "the Glory of Israel," and "the Second Moses."[2]

Other Spanish Jews who greatly promoted the interests of Hebrew grammar and philology were Ibn Balaam, of Seville, Salomon Ben Jehuda, of Malaga, and Ibn Giath (Isaac Ben Jehudah), who is said to have written a commentary on Ecclesiastes. But of far

---

[1] Kitto's Cyclopædia of Biblical Literature, article Maimonides. For an account of the editions and translations of Maimonides' works, comp. also M'Clintock and Strong's Cyclopædia, article Maimonides.

[2] "No man since Ezra," says Wise, "had exerted so deep, universal, and lasting an influence on Jews and Judaism as Moses Maimonides. His theologico-philosophical works gained an authority among the progressive thinkers equal to his Mishna-Torah among rabbinical students. All Jewish thinkers up to date—Baruch Spinoza, Moses Mendelssohn, and the writers of the nineteenth century included—are more or less the disciples of Maimonides; so that no Jewish theologico-philosophical book, from and after A. D. 1200, can be picked up in which the ideas of Maimonides form not a prominent part."—The Israelite for Dec. 1, 1871.

greater fame in exegetical literature were the three Kimchis, father
and two sons. Joseph Kimchi, the father of Moses and
David Kimchi, was born in the latter part of the eleventh
century, but was driven from Spain by Mohammedan persecution,
and settled at Narbonne, in France, where he introduced the
thorough methods of scriptural study for which the Spanish Jews
had become justly celebrated. He has been called the Aben Ezra
of Southern France. He wrote commentaries on the Pentateuch
and the Prophets, and on Job and Proverbs. He excelled especially
as a theologian and polemical writer, and was the author of
several treatises against Christianity.

The Kimchis.

Moses Kimchi, the eldest son of the preceding, was the author of
several treatises on grammar, and of commentaries on Proverbs,
Ezra, and Nehemiah, which are printed in the rabbinical Bibles,
and are much esteemed by Jewish scholars. But the most distinguished
of this name was David, son of Joseph and brother of Moses
Kimchi, born at Narbonne about A. D. 1160. He is often called
by the Jews Redak (from the initial letters רדק, Rabbi
David Kimchi). He defended the simple grammatical
method of exposition against the Jewish writers of his time who
adopted Hagadic and cabalistic opinions, and also defended Maimonides
in the disputes which arose over the publication of his Moreh
Nebuchim. He wrote commentaries on the Pentateuch, the earlier
and later prophets, the Psalms, and the Books of Job, Ruth, and
Chronicles, most of which have been published in the rabbinical
Bibles.[1] Christian scholars of his time and long after were greatly
influenced by his writings, and used them freely in the preparation
of their lexical and grammatical works.

Redak.

About A. D. 1201 Bechai, or Bachja Ben Asher, composed a
commentary on the Pentateuch. He aimed, however, to
exhibit a fourfold sense in the Scriptures, the grammatical,
rational, allegorical, and cabalistic.[2]

Bechai.

Ibn Caspi, born in France about 1280, deserves honourable mention
among Jewish scholars and exegetes. He early became
a great admirer of Maimonides, and travelled in
many lands to perfect his studies. He composed commentaries on
Proverbs, the Song of Songs, Ecclesiastes, and several of the
prophets, but only a few portions of his exegetical works have yet
been published. He appears to have discarded the allegorical and

Ibn Caspi.

[1] Latin translations of David Kimchi's commentaries on Isaiah, Joel, Jonah, and the
Psalms have been published at various places, and an English translation of his commentary
on Zechariah and Preface to the Psalms by M'Caul appeared at London, 1837.
[2] Comp. Fürst, Bibliotheca Judaica, vol. i, p. 75.

mystical methods of interpretation current in his day, and to have maintained the simple grammatical import of the Scriptures.[1]

In the latter part of the thirteenth century Jewish biblical exegesis received some valuable contributions from Tanchum Ben Joseph of Jerusalem. He wrote commentaries in Arabic on the entire Old Testament, most of which are said to Tanchum· be still extant in manuscript in the Bodleian Library. Those on Joshua, Judges, Samuel, Kings, and Lamentations have been published, and show that his general method is that of a free and rational interpretation.[2]

Levi Ben Gershon, commonly called Ralbag (also Gershonides), flourished in France at the beginning of the fourteenth century, and published commentaries on nearly all the Ralbag. books of the Old Testament, most of which have been published in the rabbinical Bibles. His habit is first to give an explanation of the words of a section, then set forth the sense according to the context, and finally to make a practical application of the whole.[3]

Ibn Danan, who flourished at Grenada A. D. 1460–1502, acquired distinction by several learned works on the Criticism and Interpretation of the Old Testament. His Commentary Ibn Danan. on Isa. liii is noted for its opposition to the anti-Messianic exposition of that Scripture by Ibn Caspi.

Another famous rabbi of this period was Isaac Abrabanel, born at Lisbon in 1437, and died at Venice in 1508. His work entitled Mashmia Yeshuah (משמיע ישועה, Herald of Sal- Abrabanel. vation) furnishes a complete view of the Jewish doctrine of the Messiah. He was also the author of commentaries on the Pentateuch, the earlier and later Prophets, and on Daniel. He is regarded by later Jewish writers as almost the equal of Maimonides. His exegetical method is in the main sound and useful, and he studies to bring out the primary and literal sense of the Scriptures.[4]

---

[1] Parts of Ibn Caspi's Commentary on Proverbs were published by Werblumer in 1846, and an analysis of his work on Ecclesiastes, and Introduction to Song of Songs is given in Ginsburg's commentaries on these books.

[2] Tanchum's Arabic Commentary on Judges i–xii was published by Schnurrer, Tüb., 1791; chaps. xii–xxi, by Haarbrücker, Halle, 1847; on Samuel and Kings, Lpz., 1844; and on Joshua, Berl., 1862. His Habakkuk was published with a French translation by Munk, in Cahen's Bible (vol. xiii), Paris, 1843.

[3] Excerpts of Ralbag's commentaries on the Pentateuch and the earlier prophets are given in a Jewish-German version in Jekutiel's German version of the Bible, Amsterd., 1676–78, and a Latin translation of his Proverbs was published by Ghigghco, Milan, 1620.

[4] Abrabanel's commentaries have been issued in many editions. A Latin translation of his Commentary on the Pentateuch was published at Hannover, 1710· on the earlier prophets, Lips., 1686; on Isaiah, Frankfurt, 1711.

Among other Jewish writers who contributed to the literature of Urbino and Old Testament exegesis, we find Solomon Ben Abraham Norzi. Urbino, the author of a Lexicon of the Synonymes of the Old Testament, illustrated by quotations from the Bible, the Targums, and the works of the great Hebrew philologists of the preceding ages.[1] Another distinguished name is Salomon Jedidja, commonly called Norzi, an Italian rabbi, born about 1560, whose great work was a critical edition of the Hebrew text of the Bible. For this purpose he made a very extensive collation and use of all the various readings he could find in manuscripts, Midrash, Talmud, and the whole cycle of rabbinical literature. His work remained in manuscript for more than a hundred years, and was published by Basila, in two volumes, Mantua, 1742–44. A second edition appeared at Vienna in 1816.

Ibn Chajim, born at Fez, in Africa, about 1570, wrote a commentary on Joshua, parts of which are published in Frankfurter's great Rabbinical Bible. He also wrote a treatise on Rabbi Ishmael's thirteen rules for interpreting the Scriptures. It was in the sixteenth century, also, that Rabbi Salomon Ben Melech wrote his commentary on the whole Bible, which Bleek describes as "short and condensed, giving almost exclusively grammatical and lexicographical explanations, mostly from Kimchi's writings."[2] About the year 1594, Laniado, an Italian rabbi, became noted by the publication of a commentary on the Pentateuch, which he entitled Delightful Vessel (כלי חמדה). He also wrote commentaries on Joshua, Judges, Samuel, and Kings, which he called Precious Vessel (כלי יקר), excerpts of which are printed in Frankfurter's Rabbinical Bible; also a commentary on Isaiah, entitled Vessel of Pure Gold (כלי פז). His expositions consist chiefly of extracts from Rashi, Aben-Ezra, and Ralbag.[3] Abraham Ben Isaac Laniado, another Italian rabbi, also wrote comments on the Pentateuch, and on several books of the Hagiographa, which still remain in manuscript.

Elias Levita flourished in the earlier part of the sixteenth century, and was one of the most learned Jewish scholars of any age. He wrote numerous works on Hebrew grammar and philology, some of which have an enduring merit. His most celebrated treatise is entitled מָסֹרֶת הַמָּסֹרֶת, Masoreth ham-Masoreth, and is a work of remarkable scholarship, displaying thorough

---

[1] This lexicon was published at Venice in 1548, but is now very rare.

[2] Introduction to the Old Testament, vol. i, pp. 115, 116.

[3] His Pentateuch was published at Venice, 1594; his work on Joshua—Kings, Venice, 1603; and his Isaiah in 1657.

acquaintance with all questions pertaining to the Hebrew text of the Old Testament.[1] It is, says Holmes, " an elaborate treatise on the criticism of the Hebrew Scriptures. Among the many interesting topics discussed in it, the question of the vowel points attracted special notice, owing to the author's assertion of their modern origin. He was the first to give prominence to the opinion which has since been adopted by most of the learned, whether British or foreign, that the Hebrew points were invented about five hundred years after Christ, by the Masoretic doctors of the school of Tiberias, in order to indicate and fix the genuine pronunciation of the sacred language." [2]

We have now traced the course of Jewish biblical exegesis down to the period of the Protestant Reformation. Beyond this point it seems unnecessary to follow it as distinct from the general history of biblical interpretation. *The Reformation a turning point.* Since the time of the Buxtorfs, about the beginning of the seventeenth century, Hebrew and rabbinical learning has not been the sole possession of the Jew. The best Christian exegetes have made free use of accessible Jewish literature, and regard a thorough acquaintance with the Hebrew language as essential to the complete exposition of the Old Testament. On the other hand, the best Jewish expositors no longer allow themselves to be so trammelled by Talmudic lore as to regard the storehouse of ancient Halachah and Hagadah as a great authority. The modern Jewish spirit and its methods of exegesis are well represented in Moses Mendelssohn, who flourished in the latter half of the eight-*Moses Mendelssohn.* eenth century. Intimate with Lessing and Nicolai, and familiar with the ideas of the great philosophers of his time, he nevertheless held to the principles of Maimonides, with whose work, the Moreh Nebuchim, he early became fascinated, maintained his ancestral faith, and acquired the title of both the Jewish Socrates and the Jewish Plato. He published a Hebrew commentary on Ecclesiastes, and an elaborate introduction to the Pentateuch, in which he discussed various topics connected with biblical interpretation. He prepared also a German translation of the Pentateuch, which, with his introduction just named, and with a grammatical and critical commentary in Hebrew, contributed by several Jewish literati, was published at Berlin, 1780–83. He was also the author of a German

---

[1] The best edition is that of C. D. Ginsburg: The Masoreth Ha-Masoreth of Elias Levita, being an Exposition of the Masoretic Notes of the Hebrew Bible; or, the Ancient Critical Apparatus of the Old Testament. In Hebrew, with an English Translation and Critical and Explanatory Notes. Lond., 1867. 8vo.

[2] Kitto's Cyclopædia of Biblical Literature ; article, Elias Levita.

version of the Psalms and of the Song of Songs.[1] "Nothing," says Pick, "could have more powerfully affected the orientalism of his countrymen than these efforts of Mendelssohn for biblical criticism from a modern Platonic standpoint. The new medium of vision brought new insight; critical inquiry took the place of fanaticism; the divergences of Semitic and European thought proved not so irreconcilable after all. Cabalism and other kindred superstitions quietly dropped out of sight; the old dialectical barbarism was extirpated; the Jews who read his Scriptures in the translation attained purity of idiom, and with it the power of appreciating the writings of the great minds of Germany, to whom they had remained strangers. Ere long the best minds of the race became thoroughly associated with the intellectual movement of Germany, content to abandon mystical ambitions and theocratic pretensions, and to find their Canaan in Europe."[2]

It should, however, be observed that the general drift of the most advanced modern Jewish thought is strongly toward rationalism. The leading representatives of this progressive Judaism, as it is often called, are Unitarian in theology, and make their highest appeal to reason and conscience in the exposition of the Scriptures. They reject the doctrine of a Messiah yet to come, and the future restoration of Israel to Palestine, with the revival of sacrificial worship. They discard the evidence of miracles, the doctrine of a resurrection of the body, and allow no authority to the Talmud above any other collection of human opinions. Even the so-called conservative Judaism is not altogether free from the influences of rationalism.

Modern Judaism rationalistic.

It is apparent, from the foregoing sketch of Jewish and rabbinical interpretation, that a vast library of exegetical theology is extant in the published and unpublished writings of that wonderful race to whom the sacred oracles were first entrusted. Much of this literature is, without doubt, of very little value, especially the more ancient expositions. Until the ninth and tenth centuries of our era we find scarcely anything that looks like a considerate grammatical method of interpretation. But in such writers as Rashi, Aben-Ezra, Maimonides, and David Kimchi, prominence is given to the great principles of grammatico-historical interpretation which are generally accepted by all the leading biblical critics and expositors of the present day.

General summary.

---

[1] Mendelssohn's complete works were collected and edited by his grandson, G. B. Mendelssohn, 7 vols. Leipsic, 1843–45.

[2] M'Clintock and Strong's Cyclopædia of Biblical, Theological, and Ecclesiastical Literature, article Mendelssohn.

CHAPTER III.

THE EARLIEST CHRISTIAN EXEGESIS.

WE naturally look to the New Testament for the earliest indications of the spirit and methods of Christian exegesis. The divine Founder of Christianity constantly appealed to the Scriptures of the Old Testament as to a sacred authority, and declared that they bore testimony to himself (John v, 39; comp. Luke xxiv, 27). With equal emphasis did he condemn the current Halachic and Hagadic tradition of the elders, which in some instances nullified the commandments of God (Matt. xv, 1–9; Mark vii, 1–13). He reproved the Sadducees also for not understanding the Scriptures and the power of God (Matt. xxii, 29). The error of the disciples in construing the prophecy of the coming of Elijah (Mal. iv, 5) to mean a literal return of the ancient Tishbite—an error which they had received from the scribes —was exposed by showing that the "spirit and power of Elijah" (Luke i, 17) had reappeared in John the Baptist (Matt. xi, 14; xvii, 10–13). Paul makes mention of his proficiency in Judaism (ἐν τῷ Ἰουδαϊσμῷ), and his excessive zeal for the traditions of his fathers, for which he was noted before his conversion (Gal. i, 13, 14); but after it pleased God to give him the revelation of his grace in Jesus Christ he denounced "Jewish fables and commandments of men who turn away from the truth" (Titus i, 14), and also "foolish questionings and genealogies and strife and fightings (or controversies) about the law" (Titus iii, 9). He counselled Timothy to "turn away from the profane babblings and oppositions of the falsely named knowledge" (τῆς ψευδωνύμου γνώσεως, 1 Tim. vi, 20), and warned the Colossians against the spoiling tendencies of "philosophy and vain deceit, after the tradition of men, after the rudiments of the world, and not after Christ" (Col. ii, 8; comp. 1 Tim. i, 4; iv, 7; 2 Tim. ii, 14–16, 23). In these admonitions and warnings there is a manifest reference to the Jewish Midrashim and the speculative tendencies of that age. It was a time of intense mental activity throughout the Roman world, especially in the more eastern cities where Greek philosophy and oriental mysticism met and blended, as in the case of Philo of Alexandria. The endless genealogies and the falsely named knowledge indicate the beginnings of heretical Gnosticism, already disturbing

Methods of Christian exegesis indicated in the New Testament.

Hagadic methods condemned.

the faith and practice of the Christian Church. From all which it
appears that neither the Hagadic exegesis and ancestral traditions
of the Jews, nor the allegorizing and speculative habit of Hellenists like Philo, received any encouragement from Christ or his apostles. Paul's single instance of allegorizing the history of Hagar
and Sarah was, as we have seen (p. 321), essentially an *argumentum
ad hominem*, professedly put as a special plea to those "who desire to be under law" (Gal. iv, 21). Its exceptional character only
serves to set in stronger light Paul's constant habit elsewhere of
construing the Scriptures according to the simple and natural import of the words.

We have already devoted a chapter to the consideration of the
method in which the sacred writers quote from one another.[1] When the New Testament writers adduce a
passage from the Old Testament they evidently assume that they
are making use of the oracles of God, and nowhere can it be shown
that they put upon the language quoted a farfetched or irrelevant
idea. Thus, for example, Peter, on the day of Pentecost, cites the
latter part of Psalm xvi (8–11) according to the Septuagint, and
then proceeds to comment upon it (Acts ii, 25–31). He shows, from
the obvious import of the language of the psalmist, that it could not
refer to David, but was literally and amply fulfilled in Jesus Christ.
Peter elsewhere speaks of the steadfast prophetic word, which is
like a lamp shining in a dark place, and declares that "no prophecy
of Scripture is of private interpretation" (2 Peter i, 19–21) It is
God's revelation, as the context indicates, and not a private essay
on the part of the prophet who uttered it to set forth something of
his own will. Nothing could be further from Peter's thought than
the notion that the Scripture is a riddle, or that its language may
be used arbitrarily to clothe in attractive guise allegories and speculations which originate in the will of man.

Peter's use of Scripture.

But though the New Testament exhibits in itself the principles
and methods of a sound and trustworthy exegesis, the
widely prevalent Hellenistic habit of allegorizing what
seemed offensive to philosophic taste carried along with
its strong tide many of the Christian writers of the post-apostolic
age. The Church of this early period was too much engaged in
struggles for life to develop an accurate or scientific interpretation
of Scripture. There was great intellectual activity, and the early
forms of heresy which disturbed the Church developed by controversy great strength and subtlety of reasoning. But the tone and
style of the earlier writers were apologetical and polemical rather

Allegorizing tendency of the post-apostolic age.

[1] See above, pp. 500–510.

than exegetical. Harassed by persecution, distracted by occasional factions, and exposed to manifold dangers, the early Christian propagandists had no opportunities to cultivate those habits of careful study which lead to broad generalization and impartial decisions. In the hurry and pressure of exciting times men take readily what first comes to hand, or serves an immediate purpose, and it was very natural that many of the early Christian writers should make use of methods of Scripture interpretation which were widely prevalent at the time.

In the writings of the apostolical fathers we observe a frequent, practical, and, in the main, appropriate, use of Scripture. The Epistle of Clement of Rome contains a great many citations from the Old and New Testaments adduced for the legitimate purpose of strengthening practical counsels and exhortations. A few of his quotations seem ill adapted to his purpose, but that might be said of many later writers whose general principles of exposition are unexceptionable. Rahab's scarlet thread is said to indicate " that redemption should flow through the blood of the Lord to all them that believe and hope in God " (chap. xii). The fable of the phœnix is also cited as a veritable fact to illustrate the doctrine of the resurrection (chap. xxv). But aside from these two things there is little in this Clementine epistle that can fairly be pronounced farfetched or fanciful. The so-called Second Epistle of Clement, though doubtless of much later date, and of different authorship, is also free from fanciful interpretations of Scripture.

The Epistle of Barnabas, which belongs, probably, to the earlier part of the second century, is full of mystic allegorizing much after the style of Philo. It would seem to have been written by some Alexandrian Christian who had read the works of Philo, or who had imbibed the spirit of eclecticism which was so strong in the great metropolis of Egypt. His knowledge of the Scriptures was manifestly very imperfect, and his attempts to spiritualize the statements of the sacred writers sometimes pervert the sense and produce an absurd exposition. He seems everywhere anxious to allegorize or explain away those parts of Scripture which enjoin outward ordinances, or in any way favour Judaism.

The Epistles of Ignatius, the spurious as well as those commonly received as genuine, contain very little which can properly be regarded as exposition of the Scriptures. In the Syriac version, in which three of them exist, and which Cureton and some others regard as the only genuine productions of Ignatius, there is hardly a citation of Scripture to be found. The

shorter Greek recension contains numerous citations from the New
Testament, and a few from the Old, which are adduced for the purpose of enforcing Christian counsel and exhortation. The longer
Greek recension contains more quotations from the Old Testament
and a more abundant use of Scripture generally. The writer appears peculiarly anxious that those to whom he wrote should honour
and obey their bishop and the presbytery. For he says to the Ephesians, " Your justly renowned presbytery, worthy of God, is fitted as
exactly to the bishop as the strings are to the harp." He argues
further that " we ought to receive every one whom the Master of
the house sends to be over his household, as we would do him that
sent him. It is manifest, therefore, that we should look upon the
bishop even as we look upon the Lord himself." [1] He says, in another place, that Jesus Christ was " both the Son of man and Son of
God, to the end that ye obey the bishop and the presbytery with
an undivided mind, breaking one and the same bread, which is the
medicine of immortality, and the antidote to prevent us from
dying." [2] He speaks of " being stones of the temple of the Father,
prepared for the building of God the Father, and drawn up on
high by the instrument (μηχανῆς) of Jesus Christ, which is the
cross, making use of the Holy Spirit as a rope, while your faith
was the means by which you ascended (ἀναγωγεὺς ὑμῶν), and your
love the way which led up to God." [3] He says that Jesus allowed
the ointment to be poured upon his head " that he might breathe
immortality into the Church," [4] and " he was born and baptized
that by his passion he might purify the water." [5] Whoever the author of these Ignatian epistles, he was a fanciful reasoner and an
unsafe interpreter of the Scriptures.

The Epistle to Diognetus and the Shepherd of Hermas, two most
Value of the   interesting documents of early Christianity, usually pub-
Apostolical Fa- lished with the apostolic fathers, contain no specimens
thers.
         of Scripture exegesis, and furnish no special help to
trace the history of interpretation. The few remaining fragments
of the writings of Papias indicate that that ancient father was
somewhat of an expositor. Eusebius describes him as " a man well
skilled in all manner of learning, and well acquainted with the
Scriptures," but much given to following traditions, and " very limited in his comprehension." [6] " The apostolic fathers," says Pressensé,[7] " are to be regarded, not as great writers, but as great

[1] Epistle to the Ephesians, chapters iv and vi.
[2] Ibid., chap. xx.   [3] Ibid., chap. ix.   [4] Ibid., chap. xvii.   [5] Ibid., chap. xviii.
[6] Ecclesiastical History, book iii, chap. xxxix.
[7] The Early Years of Christianity, pp. 216, 217. New York, 1871.

historical characters. They preserved the treasure of evangelical doctrine without themselves fully knowing all it contained. They esteemed it, nevertheless, more highly than their own life, which they were ever ready to lay down at the call of duty. The Christians of this epoch were martyrs in the holiest of causes, and set a sacred seal on the claims of God by their faithfulness to the truth, and on the rights of man by their resistance to all religious tyranny. The apostolic fathers accept the great principles laid down in the previous period by St. Paul and St. John. They never appeal to the ceremonial law in opposition to the law of Christian liberty. But since Judæo-Christianity was not so much a simple fact as the embodiment of a principle and natural tendency of the human heart, we must not be surprised to meet with it again under new forms in the orthodox Church at the commencement of the second century. The divergences of view among these early fathers do not reach positive opposition. There is no collision of hostile parties; no stormy discussion is raised; but there are, nevertheless, very distinct shades of doctrine variously colouring the faith in Christ which is held in common by all. On the one hand we have Pauline doctrine represented by Clement of Rome, Ignatius, and Polycarp. The teaching of Polycarp bears also the distinct impress of the spirit of St. John, whose immediate disciple he was. On the other hand, the idealistic symbolism of the Epistle to the Hebrews is carried to the verge of Gnosticism by the author of the epistle known as that of Barnabas. Lastly, Papias, and the writer of the allegory of the Pastor, revive, if not the views, at least the principles, of Judæo-Christianity." [1]

In the writings of Justin, surnamed the Philosopher and the Martyr, we have the earliest extant apologies of the Christian faith, and the first elaborate attempt to ex- *Justin Martyr.* plain the Old Testament Messianic prophecies as fulfilled in the Christ of the gospels. His two Apologies and his Dialogue with the Jew Trypho were written about the middle of the second century, and abound with citations from the Scriptures (generally from memory). Of many of these citations he gives an exposition, especially texts which in any way foretell or prefigure the Christ. In his discourse with Trypho (chap. ii) he informs us

[1] The latest and most complete edition of the Apostolic Fathers is that of Gebhardt, Harnach, and Zahn, Patrum Apostolicorum Opera, 3 vols. Lps., 1875-77. In grateful acknowledgment of the services of that distinguished scholar they published their work as the third edition of Dressel, whose second edition (Lps., 1863) had been for some time exhausted, and yet in great demand. An excellent English translation by Roberts, Donaldson, and Crombie forms the first volume of the Ante-Nicene Christian Library. Edinb., 1873.

of his studies in the philosophy of the Stoics, the Peripatetics, the Pythagoreans, and the Platonists, and such was his love for philosophical pursuits that he clung with tenacity to some of the teachings of Plato as not essentially different from those of Christ. In his Second Apology he says (chap. xiii): "Each man spoke well in proportion to the share he had of the spermatic word, seeing what was related to it. . . . For all the writers were able to see realities darkly through the sowing of the implanted word that was in them." But in Jesus Christ he finds the sum and substance of all philosophy. "Our doctrines," he says (chap. x), "appear to be greater than all human teaching; because Christ, who appeared for our sakes, became the whole rational being, body and reason and soul. For whatever either lawgivers or philosophers uttered well they elaborated by finding and contemplating some part of the Word. But since they did not know the whole of the Word, which is Christ, they often contradicted themselves." Justin was an enthusiastic lover and fearless defender of Christianity. He was a man of great learning, and delighted to use his knowledge of Greek philosophy to illustrate and enhance the teachings of Scripture. But his expositions are often fanciful, sometimes almost silly. He His fanciful is notably wanting in critical discrimination and judgexpositions. ment, and carries the typical interpretation of the Old Testament to wild extravagance. In a single chapter of the Dialogue with Trypho (chap. cxxxiv) he says:

The marriages of Jacob were types of that which Christ was about to accomplish. For it was not lawful for Jacob to marry two sisters at once. Being deceived in obtaining the younger he again served seven years. Now, Leah is your people and the synagogue, but Rachel is our Church. And for these, and for the servants in both, Christ even now serves. For while Noah gave to the two sons the seed of the third as servants, now, on the other hand, Christ has come to restore both the free sons and the servants among them, conferring the same honour on all of them who keep his commandments. . . . Jacob served Laban for speckled and many-spotted sheep, and Christ served, even to the slavery of the cross, for the various and many-formed races of mankind, acquiring them through the blood and mystery of the cross. Leah was weak-eyed; for the eyes of your souls are excessively weak. Rachel stole the gods of Laban, and has hid them to this day; and we have lost our paternal and material gods. Jacob was hated for all time by his brother; and we now, and our Lord himself, are hated by you and by all men, though we are brothers by nature. Jacob was called Israel; and Israel has been demonstrated to be the Christ, who is, and is called Jesus.[1]

[1] The best edition of the works of Justin is that of Otto, new edition, in 3 vols. Jena, 1847–50. An accurate English translation is given in the second volume of the Ante-Nicene Christian Library. Edinb., 1867.

In the writings of Theophilus of Antioch and Melito of Sardis we discover a more formal and systematic exegesis. Theophilus and Theophilus composed commentaries on the Gospels and Melito. or the Book of Proverbs, in which, according to Neander,[1] we may observe the germ of that exegetical bent for which the Church of Antioch became noted. His apologetical work addressed to Autolycus is of the same general character as the Apologies of Justin Martyr, and contain some fanciful interpretations of Scripture; but he was evidently an earnest student and distinguished expounder of the sacred writings.[2] Melito appears to have been especially proficient in Old Testament literature, and is said by Eusebius[3] to have written on the Passover, on the Prophets, and on the Revelation of John. Only a few fragments of his works are now extant.[4]

But while in the above-named writers we see the dialectic skill and speculative tendencies of the Churches of Asia Minor and Syria, in Irenæus, bishop of Lyons, in France, "the Light of the Western Church," we observe that Christian thought Irenæus. was not inactive, nor without rich products, in the churches of Western Europe. Irenæus passed his youth in Asia Minor, and was a disciple of Polycarp, who had seen and talked with the Apostle John; but his removal to France, where, in the latter part of the second century, he became presbyter, and afterward bishop of the Church at Lyons, has identified him with the Western Church. Dorner pronounces him "the greatest Church teacher of the generation before Clement, and especially worthy of notice, because he combines in himself the different tendencies in the Church, and brings them to a harmonious interpenetration. Well versed in Gnostic and Church literature, fitted by the events of his life to be a bond of union between oriental and occidental Christianity, he had a mild, free, and open feeling for what was true in all the often mutually exclusive parties; and the deeper he penetrated scientifically and practically into the essence of Christianity, with so much firmer a hand could he unite what was cognate and mutually attractive, and eliminate what was abnormal. No one in the second century represents as he does the purity and the fulness of the

[1] General History of the Christian Religion and Church. Torrey's translation, vol. i, p. 674.

[2] The second and third books of his Apology contain large extracts from the first part of Genesis, with comments upon them. See English translation in vol. iii of the Edinburgh Ante-Nicene-Christian Library.

[3] Ecclesiastical History, book iv, chap. xxvi.

[4] The best collection of these fragments is by Routh, Reliquiae Sacrae. Oxford, 1814. Several have been published in the Journal of Sacred Literature, vols. xv, xvi, and xvii.

development within the Church; scarcely any one in the Church of his time is so highly esteemed as he."[1]

The principal work of Irenæus consists of five books, entitled Refutation and Subversion of Knowledge Falsely So-called. The more common title is simply Against Heresies. It is the chief storehouse of our information respecting the Gnostic heresies of that age, especially the Valentinian system. The work is a great polemico-theological treatise, ably defending the doctrines of the Church, and, in the last three books, dealing largely with Scripture exposition. These expositions are sometimes manifestly erroneous, and occasionally farfetched and strange, but on the whole evince a thorough acquaintance with the sacred books, and avoid the most objectionable features of the typical and allegorical interpretations so prevalent at that time. Irenæus' early training, and his devotion to the memory of the apostolic fathers, led him to place overmuch confidence in tradition and the authority of the Church.[2]

It is evident from a careful study of the above-named representatives of the earlier patristic exegesis, that during the second century of our era there was no uniform or settled method of interpreting the Scriptures. Controversy and heresy prevailed even in the midst of bitter persecution. The converts from heathenism who became apologists and defenders of the Christian faith had no acquaintance with the original Hebrew Scriptures, and no occasion or inducement to cultivate a scientific hermeneutics. Jewish exegesis at that time was, as we have seen, utterly destitute of rational and self-consistent method. Ebionism and Gnosticism affected to some extent all Christian thought, and it is not difficult to understand how, under such circumstances, no well-defined principles of Scripture exposition were anywhere recognised or applied. Some of these early fathers exhibit a commendable moderation and judgment in the use of Scripture texts, while others load them with fanciful and even puerile notions of their own.[3]

No settled or uniform hermeneutics in the second century.

[1] History of the Development of the Doctrine of the Person of Christ. Eng. trans., vol. i, p. 303. Edinb., 1861.

[2] The best edition of Irenæus is that of Harvey, S. Irenaei Episcopi Lugdunensis libri quinque adversus Haereses. 2 vols. Cambridge, 1857. Eng. trans. by Roberts and Rambaut in vols. v and ix of the Edinburgh Ante-Nicene Christian Library.

[3] Hence we should exercise great care in making an appeal to the antiquity of an opinion or an interpretation. Modern millenarians are wont to claim that Chiliasm was the universal faith of the early Church. Thus West, in the Pre-Millennial Essays of the Prophetic Conference, p. 332 (New York, 1879): "Chiliasm was the common inheritance of both Jewish and Gentile Christians, and passed from the Jewish Christian to the Gentile Christian Church precisely in the way the Gospel passed. It was

CHAPTER IV.

LATER PATRISTIC EXEGESIS.

THE history of biblical interpretation was notably influenced after the beginning of the third century by the famous schools of Alexandria and Antioch. We have seen how, long before School of Alexandria. the time of Christ, Alexandria had become the home of letters. Thither learned men from all parts of the world resorted for studious inquiry. The Asiatic mystic, the Jewish rabbi, and the Greek and Roman philosopher there came together and interchanged their thoughts. "Born of this heterogeneous union," says Pressensé, "the Alexandrian mind rose above all national divergences; but it also rose above reality, above history, to the cloudy summits of speculation, and it was utterly wanting in the historic sense. Strong in its allegorical method, it sported with facts; and its philosophical theories were at once aspiring and unsubstantial."[1] A school of sacred learning, such as Eusebius says had been established there from ancient times,[2] would of necessity partake largely of the eclectic and speculative spirit of the place, and we do not

fragrant at Antioch as at Jerusalem, at Rome as at Ephesus. History has no consensus more unanimous for any doctrine than is the consensus of the apostolic fathers for the pre-millennial advent of Christ." This sweeping statement is based upon *ex parte* testimony. Hagenbach, on the contrary, avers that in the writings of Clement of Rome, Ignatius, Polycarp, Tatian, Athenagoras, and Theophilus of Antioch no millenarian notions appear. See his History of Doctrines, vol. i, p. 215 (New York, 1861). The fact is that some of these fathers have been quoted in favour of views which their language will not warrant, and while Papias, Justin, Irenæus, and some others are pronounced Chiliasts, an equal or greater number can be cited who give no sanction to such views. The first Chiliasts, moreover, sometimes present their views in connexion with expositions of Scripture which are utterly untenable (as, for example, Irenæus Against Heresies, book v, chaps. xxxii–xxxvi). To assume, from the silence of any of the fathers, that they accepted the Chiliastic views is most absurd, especially in view of what Eusebius says of Papias (Eccl. History, iii, 39): "He says that there would be a certain millennium after the resurrection and a corporeal reign of Christ on this very earth; which things he appears to have imagined, as if they were authorized by the apostolic narrations, not understanding correctly those matters which they propounded mystically in their representations. For he was very limited in his comprehension, as is evident from his discourses. Yet he was the cause why most of the ecclesiastical writers, urging the antiquity of the man, were carried away by a similar opinion; as, for instance, Irenæus, or any other that adopted such sentiments."

[1] Early Years of Christianity, p. 266.   [2] Ecclesiastical History. book v, chap. x.

wonder that the great lights of the Alexandrian Church were notably given to allegorical expositions of the Scriptures.

The first great teacher of the Alexandrian school, whose works
Clemens Alex- have come down to us, is Titus Flavius Clement.   He
andrinus.   was preceded by Pantænus, and perhaps Athenagoras,[1]
and others, who, like Apollos of apostolic times, had profited by
Alexandrian culture, and were "mighty in the Scriptures" (Acts
xviii, 24). Clement was privileged, as he tells us, to travel extensively, and listen to the teachings of various learned men from
Greece, Syria, Palestine, and the East, but he at last found in
Egypt the man who gave him rest. "He, the true, the Sicilian bee,
gathering the spoil of the flowers of the prophetic and apostolic
meadow, engendered in the souls of his hearers a deathless element
of knowledge."[2] The one here referred to is believed to have been
Pantænus, the distinguished Christian philosopher, whom Clement
succeeded as head of the Alexandrian school, and who, according
to Eusebius, commented, both orally and in writing, on the treasures of divine truth.[3] The disciple was worthy of his master, and
his works evince prodigious learning, and could scarcely have been
composed anywhere but within easy access to the famous library of
the Egyptian metropolis. He is said to have written commentaries
on several books of Scripture, but only three great works of his are
still extant, namely, The Exhortation to the Greeks, The Instructor
(or Pædagogue), and The Miscellanies (Stromata). These three
works form a well-related series, and their great aim is to expose
the follies and absurdities of heathenism, and extol the word and
wisdom of God.

But Clement is a fanciful interpreter. Deeply read in the works
Clement a phil- of Philo Judæus, he adopted his allegorical methods.
osophical alle- He was fascinated with heathen philosophy. "The
gorist.   Greek preparatory culture," he says, "with philosophy
itself came down from God to men, not with a definite direction,
but in the way in which showers fall down on the good land, and
on the dunghill, and on the houses." "And by philosophy," he
adds, "I do not mean the Stoic, or the Platonic, or the Epicurean,
or the Aristotelian, but whatever has been well said by each of
these sects which teach righteousness along with a science pervaded
by piety—this eclectic whole I call philosophy."[4] But in the Son
of God, the eternal Word, he recognised and worshipped the sum

---

[1] See Emerson, On the Catechetical School, or Theological Seminary, at Alexandria
in Egypt. American Biblical Repository for Jan., 1834, p. 25.

[2] The Miscellanies (Stromata), book i, chap. i.

[3] Ecclesiastical History, book v, chap. x.   [4] Miscellanies, book i, chap. vii.

and substance of all true philosophy, and he holds that the utmost perfection of the logical faculty is necessary to expound the three-fold sense of the law, the mystic, the moral, and the prophetic.[1] "For many reasons," he argues, "the Scriptures hide the sense. First, that we may become inquisitive, and be ever on the watch for the discovery of the words of salvation. Then it was not suit-able for all to understand, so that they might not receive harm in consequence of taking in another sense the things declared for sal-vation by the Holy Spirit. Wherefore the holy mysteries of the prophecies are veiled in parables."[2]

Clement was succeeded, at Alexandria, by a pupil even greater than himself, a man of the purest character, who, while yet a little child, disclosed a remarkable insight into
Origen.
the depth and fulness of the Scriptures, and later, by his untiring devotion to multifarious studies, his unremitting labours by night and by day, and his indomitable firmness through all temptation and persecution, acquired the name of Man of Adamant (Adamantinus). Notwithstanding his questionable methods of interpretation, and not infrequent errors, Origen was the greatest biblical critic and exegete of the ancient Church. Jerome, who violently opposed some of his views, pronounced him the greatest teacher since the days of the apostles, "a man of immortal genius, who understood logic, geometry, arithmetic, music, grammar, rhetoric, and all the sects of the philosophers, so that he was resorted to by many stu-dents of secular literature whom he received chiefly that he might embrace the opportunity of instructing them in the faith of Christ."[3] He practiced the most rigid asceticism, refused the gifts of admir-ing friends and pupils, and after devoting the day to teaching and

---

[1] Miscellanies, book i, chap. xxviii. He does not deny the natural or literal sense, but often makes use of it, so that he really held to a fourfold sense of Scripture.

[2] Ibid., book vi, chap. xv. The following comment on Gen. xxii, 3, 4, will illus-trate the mystico-allegorical style in which this writer treats the sacred narratives: "Abraham, when he came to the place which God told him of on the third day, looking up, saw the place afar off. For the first day is that which is constituted by the sight of good things; and the second is the soul's best desire; on the third the mind perceives spiritual things, the eyes of the understanding being opened by the Teacher who rose on the third day. The three days may be the mystery of the seal (bap-tism) in which God is really believed. It is, consequently, afar off that he perceives the place. For the reign of God is hard to attain, which Plato calls the reign of ideas, having learned from Moses that it was a place which contained all things uni-versally. But it is seen by Abraham afar off, rightly, because of his being in the realms of generation, and he is forthwith initiated by the angel. Thence says the apostle, 'Now we see through a glass, but then face to face,' by those sole pure and incorporeal applications of the intellect."—Ibid., book v, chap. xi.

[3] Liber de viris illustribus, chap. liv.

pious labours, he was wont to spend the greater part of the night
in the study of the Scriptures, and when he slept he chose the bare
floor for his couch. He even mutilated himself that he might be a
eunuch for the sake of the kingdom of heaven. Such a man would
be likely to fall in with some of the superstitions of his age, and we
do not wonder that he studied Hebrew, not merely for its practical
use in meeting Jewish opponents, but with a notion that it was the
original language of mankind, and was destined to become the universal language. Though rejecting personal gifts, there was one
favour offered him by his admiring friend, Ambrose, whom he had
converted from Gnostic heresy, which he felt not at liberty to decline. This wealthy benefactor furnished Origen with ample means
for the prosecution of his studies and the publication of his works
by placing at his command seven secretaries to write at his dicta-
tion, and as many copyists, skilled in caligraphy, to transcribe fair
copies of what the others hastily took down from the lips of the
master. In this way Origen was enabled to publish a vast number
of works—some say over six thousand—most of which are lost.

The first notable attempt at textual criticism may be traced to
Origen's great work, the Hexapla. His veneration for
the Scriptures led him to ascribe a sort of magical value
to the original text, and he sought to establish it by the widest possible collation and comparison. He arranged in six parallel columns the Hebrew text, a Greek transliteration of the same, the text
of the Septuagint, and the Greek versions of Aquila, Symmachus, and
Theodotion. Some pages, which contained books of which other
Greek versions were extant, were arranged with seven, eight, or
nine columns, according to the number of different versions. On
this immense work, which extended to nearly fifty volumes, he was
engaged for twenty-eight years.[1] He also prepared the Tetrapla,
which presented in four columns the Septuagint, and the versions
of Aquila, Symmachus, and Theodotion.

The exegetical works of Origen comprised brief Scholia on the
more difficult texts, and also extended commentaries
and homilies on most of the Bible, considerable portions of which are still extant. He also composed several apologetical and dogmatical works, the most important of which are the
Treatise against Celsus and the De Principiis. But with all his devotion to the interests of truth, and the enormous magnitude of his

---

[1] The remains of this great work were collected and published in two folio volumes
by Montfaucon, Paris, 1713. Revised edition by Bahrdt, Lpz., 1769–70, 2 vols. 8vo.
It is also published in vols. xv and xvi of Migne's Greek Patrologiæ Cursus Completus,
and in two fine quartos by Field, Oxford, 1875.

labours, he was a mystico-allegorical exegete. He followed in the path of Philo the Jew, and Clement the Christian, and, assuming that many portions of the Scriptures are unreasonable and absurd when taken literally, he maintained a threefold sense, the corporeal, the psychical, and the spiritual.[1] But he protests against being supposed to teach that no history is real, and no law to be literally observed, because some narratives and laws, literally understood, are absurd or impossible. "For," he says, "the passages that are true in their historical sense are much more numerous than those which have a purely spiritual signification."[2]

The wonderful influence of Origen is to be explained mainly by the grandeur of his character, his immense learning, his fortitude under persecution, and the enthusiasm with which he performed everything he took in hand. Driven by persecution from Alexandria, he resorted to Cæsarea, in Palestine, and there established a school which for a time surpassed that of the Egyptian metropolis. The magnetism of his person, and his widespread fame as an expounder of the Scriptures, attracted great multitudes to him. His pernicious habit of explaining the sacred records as the Platonists explained the heathen myths, and his heretical views touching the pre-existence of souls, a new probation after death, and some other doctrines, were so far offset by his pure zeal for God, and his many and great virtues, that he has been quite generally acknowledged as pre-eminently the father of biblical science, and one of the greatest prodigies of learning and industry among men.[3]

Influence of Origen.

[1] " The way, as it appears to us," says Origen, "in which we ought to deal with the Scriptures, and extract from them their meaning, is the following, which has been ascertained from the Scriptures themselves. By Solomon in the Proverbs (chap. xxii, 20, 21) we find some such rule as this enjoined respecting the divine doctrines of Scripture : 'And do thou portray them in a threefold manner, in counsel and knowledge, to answer words of truth to them who propose them to thee' [so Septuagint and Vulgate]. The individual ought, then, to portray the ideas of Holy Scripture in a threefold manner upon his own soul; in order that the sinful man may be edified by the flesh, as it were, of the Scripture, for so we name the obvious sense; while he who has ascended a certain way may be edified by the soul, as it were. The perfect man, again, and he who resembles those spoken of by the apostle when he says, 'we speak wisdom among them that are perfect, but not the wisdom of the world, nor of the rulers of this world, who come to naught, but we speak the wisdom of God in a mystery, the hidden wisdom which God ordained before the ages, unto our glory' (1 Cor. ii, 6, 7), may be edified by the spiritual law, which has a shadow of good things to come. For, as man consists of body and soul and spirit, so in the same way does Scripture, which has been arranged to be given by God for the salvation of men."—De Principiis, book iv, chap. i, 11.

[2] De Principiis, book iv, chap. i, 11.

[3] Origen's works have been printed in many editions. The best is that of the

Origen's name so far eclipsed that of all other teachers of the
Dionysius of Alexandrian school that there are few others who call
Alexandria. for special mention. Dionysius of Alexandria, one of
Origen's pupils, acquired some fame as an interpreter. His work
on the Promises, fragments of which are preserved in Eusebius,[1]
appears to have been written against Nepos, an Egyptian bishop,
who had published a Refutation of the Allegorists, and maintained
therein, by a literal interpretation of John's Apocalypse, the Chiliastic doctrine of a temporal reign of Christ on earth. Dionysius
refers to the fact that some, before his time, had rejected the Book
of Revelation as the work of a Cerinthian heretic, but he accepts it
as the work of an inspired man, though not the Apostle John, the
son of Zebedee. He confesses his inability to understand it, but
regards it as containing a hidden and wonderful meaning. Dionysius wrote also many epistles to leading ecclesiastics of his day, and
commentaries on Ecclesiastes, Luke, and John, fragments of which
are still extant.[2] He appears to have been less given to allegorizing than his distinguished master.

Pierius, who took charge of the school at Alexandria at the death
Pierius, Peter of Dionysius, is said to have given Origen much assist-
Martyr, and ance in his critical labours, and also to have written
Hesychius. twelve books of commentary, and other works, all of
which have perished. Peter Martyr, who was bishop of Alexandria
at the beginning of the fourth century, is described by Eusebius as
a man of wonderful ability as a teacher of the Christian faith, and
distinguished alike for the excellence of his life and his study of
the sacred Scriptures.[3] Hesychius, another Egyptian bishop, who
suffered martyrdom about A. D. 311, is said to have revised the
text of the Septuagint, and to have also published an edition of
the New Testament.

The school of Cæsarea, in Palestine, owed its notoriety to Ori-
School of Cæs- gen, who made that place his home when driven by per-
area. secution from Alexandria. Many young men there
gathered around him, imbibed his enthusiastic devotion to the study
of the Scriptures, and went out from thence to preach and teach in

Benedictines De la Rue, Paris, 1733–59, 4 vols. fol. It is reprinted in Migne's Greek
Patrologiæ Cursus Completus, Paris, 9 vols. English translations of the De Principiis, the Contra Celsum, and several of his epistles are given in vols. x and xxiii of
the Edinburgh Ante-Nicene Christian Library.
[1] See Ecclesiastical History, book vii, chaps. xxiv, xxv.
[2] The extant fragments of Dionysius' works are published in all the large collections
of the Fathers, and an English translation is given in vol. xx of the Edinburgh Ante-
Nicene Christian Library.
[3] Ecclesiastical History, book viii, chap. xiii.; book ix, chap. vi.

various cities of the East. The most distinguished disciple of this school was Gregory, bishop of Neo-Cæsarea, in Pontus, commonly known as Gregory Thaumaturgus. He was the author of a Metaphrase on Ecclesiastes, a work of some merit, which is still extant. His Panegyric on Origen, one of the earliest productions of its kind among Christians, is pronounced by Dupin one of the finest pieces of rhetoric in all antiquity.[1] Later names, which must ever shed lustre on Cæsarea, are those of Pamphilus and Eusebius. The former of these Neander describes as "a man distinguished for his zeal in the cause of piety and science. He founded at Cæsarea an ecclesiastical library, which contributed in no small degree to the furtherance of scientific studies, even in the fourth century. Every friend of science, and in particular every one who was disposed to engage in a thorough study of the Bible, found in him all possible encouragement and support. He exerted himself to multiply, to disseminate, and to correct the copies of the Bible. Many of these copies he distributed as presents, sometimes to women whom he saw much occupied in reading the Scriptures. He founded a theological school in which the study of the sacred writings was made a special object of attention."[2]

Gregory Thaumaturgus.

Pamphilus.

Eusebius of Cæsarea, the devoted friend of Pamphilus, on account of which he is often called Eusebius Pamphilus, is distinguished as the father of Church history rather than as an exegete. His two great apologetical productions, the Præparatio Evangelica and the Demonstratio Evangelica, are also of great value to the Christian scholar. Books iii–x of the last-named work contain comments on the Messianic prophecies, and four books of his allegorical interpretations of these prophecies are extant under the title of Prophetical Eclogues. His Onomasticon is a valuable topographical and alphabetical index of the names of places mentioned in the Scriptures. He wrote commentaries on the Psalms, Proverbs, Canticles, Isaiah, and Daniel, and various dissertations on the gospels. As an interpreter he followed in the main the allegorical method of Origen, for whose writings he had a glowing admiration.[3]

Eusebius of Cæsarea.

---

[1] The extant works of Gregory Thaumaturgus have been published in many editions; the best is probably that of Migne, in vol. x of his Greek Patrologiæ Cursus Completus. English translation in vol. xx of the Edinburgh Ante-Nicene Christian Library.

[2] History of the Christian Religion and Church, Torrey's translation, volume i, p. 721.

[3] The most complete edition of Eusebius' works is that of Migne, Greek Patrologiæ Cursus Completus, vols. xix–xxiv.

The last considerable representative of the Alexandrian school of
theology and exegesis was Cyril, who flourished in the
first half of the fifth century. He was noted as a violent and ambitious man, and too much given to oppose and persecute those who differed from him to be a safe and judicious expositor. Nevertheless, he was a man of extensive learning and of vigorous mind, and is the author of numerous dogmatical and exegetical works which are still extant. His commentaries are upon the Pentateuch, Isaiah, the twelve Minor Prophets, and the Gospels of Luke and John. He does not ignore or reject the historical sense, but is addicted to allegorizing, and illustrates how the Scriptures may be tortured to mean almost anything. He finds the mystery of Christ set forth typically or enigmatically throughout the entire Old Testament, and carries a most extravagant system of allegorizing even into the narratives of the gospels. For example, the five loaves in John vi, 9, are made to represent the five books of Moses, as a comparatively coarse food, and the two fishes denote the finer and more luxurious nourishment of the teachings of Christ.[1]

To Antioch, where the disciples were first called Christians (Acts xi, 26), belongs the honour of introducing a more scientific and profitable system of biblical study. About the beginning of the fourth century there was established at this place a school which opposed to the Alexandrian allegorical exegesis the historico-critical method of interpretation. We have already made note of Ignatius and Theophilus, whose labours and influence gave renown to that Syrian city, but they founded no school, and acquired no great fame as exegetes. In his spirit and method Julius Africanus, of Nicopolis (Emmaus) in Palestine, was a forerunner of the Antiochian school of historical criticism. His brief letter to Origen, still extant, in which he disputes the authenticity of the apocryphal history of Susannah, exhibits him as more than a match for the great Alexandrian scholar. For he displays a critical penetration and judgment, a freedom from ecclesiastical traditions, and an incisive way of stating his views which make his short epistle more weighty and convincing than the elaborate reply of Origen.[2] His letter to Aristides on the genealogies of Matthew and Luke, a part of which is preserved in

Cyril of Alexandria.

The School of Antioch.

Africanus.

---

[1] The most convenient edition of Cyril's works is that of Migne, Greek Patrologiæ Cursus Completus, vols. lxviii–lxxvii. An English translation of his Commentary on Luke, by R. P. Smith, was published at Oxford, 1859.

[2] See Africanus' letter and Origen's reply translated into English in vol. x of the Edinburgh Ante-Nicene Christian Library.

Eusebius (see above, p. 522), is another evidence of his exegetical skill. He was also the author of a valuable chronological work entitled Pentabiblos, from its being arranged in five sections, of which only fragments remain. Some affirm that he wrote a commentary on the New Testament, but this is doubtful.[1]

About A. D. 290 there flourished at Antioch a distinguished presbyter, named Dorotheus, of whom Eusebius says: "He was a man of fine taste in sacred literature, and Dorotheus. was much devoted to the study of the Hebrew language, so that he read the Hebrew Scriptures with great facility. He was also of a very liberal mind, and not unacquainted with the preparatory studies pursued among the Greeks, but in other respects a eunuch by nature, having been such from his birth; so that the emperor, on this account, as if it were a great miracle, received him into his house and family, and honoured him with an appointment over the purple dye establishment of Tyre. Him we have heard in the Church expounding the Scriptures with great judgment."[2] It does not appear that Dorotheus left any writings, but his oral teaching imparted the true critical spirit to those who heard him, and prepared the way for the formal opening of the theological school at Antioch.

The real founder of the school of Antioch was Lucian, who was born at Samosata, in Syria, but in early life removed to Edessa, where he laid the foundation of his thorough Lucian. biblical scholarship under the training of Macarius, an eminent teacher of that place. He afterward removed to Antioch, where he was ordained a presbyter, and acquired great fame as a critical student and expounder of the Holy Scriptures. His stricter methods put a check to the allegorical and mystical interpretations so popular at the time, and which had received great strength and currency by the influence of Origen. Jerome speaks of him as a most eloquent man, so laborious in his critical study of the Scriptures that copies edited by him were long afterward known as Lucianean.[3] He elsewhere says that while Hesychius' edition of the Septuagint was used in Egypt, that of Lucian was preferred by all the Church from Constantinople to Antioch.[4] Unfortunately, none of the works of Lucian, with the exception of a few fragments, have come down to us.

It is worthy of note that Arius and Eusebius of Nicomedia

---

[1] See Lardner, Credibility of the Gospel History, vol. ii, p. 434. London, 1788.
[2] Ecclesiastical History, book vii, chap. xxxii.
[3] De viris illustribus, chap. lxxvii.
[4] Præfatio in Librum Paralipomenon.

received their training in the school of Lucian. The principles
Arian leaders of free grammatical interpretation inculcated by the
sprang from learned presbyter of Antioch encouraged an indepen-
the Antiochian
school.   dent and fearless tendency which was liable to run into
extremes. Neander thoughtfully observes: "In cases where this
direction was not accompanied with a general intuition of biblical
ideas vitalized by Christian experience, and this general intuition
had not made plain the true relation of the particular to the general
in the expressions of holy writ, it might tend, by laying too great
stress on particulars, and giving them undue prominence, to promote narrow views of the truths of faith. This was the case with
Arius, in whom a tendency to narrow conceptions of the understanding, exclusive of the intuitive faculty, predominated."[1]

Lucian suffered martyrdom about A. D. 312, and does not appear
            to have been succeeded by any one of equal ability or
Eustathius.
            fame. But we find the sharp opposition of the Antio-
chian school to that of Origen represented in Eustathius, who became bishop of Antioch in A. D. 325. He was distinguished both
for secular learning and for thorough acquaintance with the Scriptures. He was a voluminous writer, but of all his works only one, a
treatise on the Witch of Endor, is now known to be extant. This
treatise was written against Origen, who maintained that the witch
had really brought up the spirit of the prophet Samuel. Eustathius
opposed this view with great learning and acuteness, and argued
that Samuel did not appear at all, but that the whole transaction
was a work of deception, perpetrated through the agency of Satan.[2]

Eusebius, commonly known as bishop of Emesa, was for some
            time identified with the church and school of Antioch.
Eusebius of
Emesa.   He was descended from a noble family of Edessa, and
from childhood was carefully instructed in the Scriptures and in
Greek literature. He died at Antioch about A. D. 360. According to Jerome he maintained the historical sense of Scripture and
was the author of Homilies on the Gospels, and a commentary on
the Epistle to the Galatians;[3] but only a few fragments of his
writings remain.

More noted and influential than any of the above-named teachers
            at Antioch was Diodorus, who afterward became bishop
Diodorus.
            of Tarsus. Socrates, the Church historian, speaks of him
as president of a monastery, and the author of "many treatises, in

---

[1] History of the Christian Religion and Church, vol. ii, p. 361.

[2] This treatise of Eustathius, and fragments of his and other works, are given in
Migne's Greek Patrologiæ Cursus Completus, vol. xviii, pp. 614–794.

[3] De viris illustribus, chap. xci.

which he limited his expositions to the literal sense of Scripture, without attempting to explain that which was mystical."[1] According to Jerome he was a distinguished presbyter of Antioch, and wrote commentaries and other books, in which he imitated the manner of Eusebius of Emesa, but could not equal him in eloquence because of his ignorance of secular literature.[2] He is said to have written commentaries on all the books of the Old Testament, and upon the four Gospels, the Acts, and the Epistle of John.[3] It appears from numerous brief notices of him in the ancient writers that he was held in the highest esteem, and was chosen by the Council of Constantinople (A. D. 381) to take charge of the administration of the churches of the East, without, however, infringing on the prerogatives of the bishop of Antioch.[4] He set himself firmly against the allegorical method of interpretation, and instilled his principles in the minds of many pupils, some of whom became very famous in the Church. Theodoret says of him: "The wise and courageous Diodorus resembled a large and limpid stream, which furnishes plentiful supplies of water to those who dwell on its banks, and which, at the same time, engulfs adversaries. He despised the advantages of high birth, and underwent the severest exertions in defense of the faith."[5]

The two most distinguished disciples of Diodorus were Theodore of Mopsuestia, and John Chrysostom of Constantinople. Theodore of Both of them studied philosophy and rhetoric in the Mopsuestia. school of the celebrated sophist Libanius, the friend of the Emperor Julian. Theodore was made a presbyter at Antioch, but rapidly acquired reputation, and was made bishop of Mopsuestia in Cilicia, about A. D. 390. His long life and incessant labour as a Christian teacher, the extent of his learning, the vigour and acuteness of his intellect, and the force of his personal character, won for him the title of Master of the Orient. He was a prolific author, and composed commentaries on various books of Scripture, of which only his exposition of the Minor Prophets has been preserved intact until the present time. His commentaries on Philippians, Colossians, and Thessalonians are preserved in a Latin version.[6] He was an

---

[1] Eccl. Hist., book vi, chap. iii.   [2] De viris illustribus, chap. cxix.

[3] So stated by Theodore the Reader, as cited in Suidas' Lexicon (Kuster's ed., vol. i, p. 593. Cambr., 1705), under the name Diodorus. Fragments of the commentaries of Diodorus are given in vol. xxxiii of Migne's Greek Patrologiæ Cursus Completus.

[4] Socrates, Eccl. Hist., book v, chap. viii.

[5] Theodoret, Eccl. Hist., book iv, chap. xxv.

[6] Theodore's Commentary on the Minor Prophets was published by Mai, in vol. vii of his Patrum Nova Bibliotheca (Rome, 1854), and by Wegner (Berol., 1834). Fragments of his other works are given by Fritzsche, Theod. Mops., in N. Test. Comm.

independent critic, and a straightforward, sober, historical interpreter. He had no sympathy with the mystical methods of the
Alexandrian school, and repudiated their extravagant notions of
inspiration; but he went to an opposite extreme of denying the inspiration of many portions of the Scriptures, and furnished rationalistic specimens of exposition quite barren and unsatisfactory.
Nevertheless the Syrian Nestorians regarded him as the greatest of
exegetes. His doctrines on the subjects of Christology and anthro-
pology were severely condemned after his decease, especially because the Nestorians appealed to them as identical with their own.

While Theodore represented the more independent and rationalistic spirit of the Antiochian school, Chrysostom exhib-
Chrysostom. ited its more conservative and practical tendency. The
tender devotion of a pious Christian mother, the rhetorical polish
acquired in the school of Libanius, and the assiduous study of the
Scriptures at the monastery of the learned Diodorus, were all together admirably adapted to develop the profound exegete and the
eloquent preacher of the word of God. "Through a rich inward
experience," says Neander, "he lived into the understanding of the
Holy Scriptures; and a prudent method of interpretation, on logical
and grammatical principles, kept him in the right track in deriving
the spirit from the letter of the sacred volume. His profound and
simple, yet fruitful homiletic method of treating the Scriptures,
show to what extent he was indebted to both, and how, in his case,
both co-operated together."[1]

Chrysostom wrote more than six hundred homilies on the Scriptures. They consist of expository discourses on Genesis, the Psalms,
and most of the New Testament. Those on the Gospel of Matthew
and the Pauline epistles are specially valuable, and such modern
exegetes as Tholuck and Alford have enriched their pages by
numerous quotations from this father. The least valuable of his
expository discourses are those upon the prophets, only a few of
which remain. His ignorance of Hebrew, and his failure to apprehend the spirit of the Old Testament prophets, are apparent. The
homilies on the Psalms, however, though without critical merit,
furnish a rich banquet, for Chrysostom's deep religious experience
brought him into complete sympathy with the psalmist. Although
his credulous nature yielded to many superstitions of his age, and
his pious feeling inclined him to asceticism and the self-mortifica-

(Turici, 1847), and Pitra, Spicil. Solesm. (Par., 1854). See also Sieffert, Theod. Mops.
V. T. sobre interpretandi vindex, (Regiom., 1827), and Kihn, Theod. Mops. und J.
Africanus als Exegeten (Freib., 1880).
[1] History of the Christian Religion and Church, vol. ii, p. 693.

tions of monastic life, John Chrysostom is unquestionably the greatest commentator among the early fathers of the Church. Theodore of Mopsuestia may have been more sharply critical, Origen was more encyclopædic in his learning, and others were more original and profound in apprehending some of the doctrines of the Christian faith, but he surpassed them all in the general good judgment which appears in his expositions, in the richness of his suggestions, and the practical value of what he said or wrote. He is the greatest ornament and noblest representative of the exegetical school of Antioch.[1]

Isidore of Pelusium, who flourished in the early part of the fifth century, was a disciple of Chrysostom. He has left Isidore of Pelusium. numerous epistles, which are largely occupied with interpretations of the Scriptures, and treat nearly all the great theological questions of his time. His method of exposition is like that of Chrysostom, sober, practical, and in the main free from allegorizing. His style of interpretation may appropriately be called historico-theological, and his expositions evince sound judgment, piety, and learning.[2]

In this connexion we should also notice the works of Theodoret, who was trained at the monastery near Antioch, where Theodoret. he abode for twenty years, devoting himself to theological studies. The teachings of Diodorus, Theodore, and Chrysostom, who were identified with this same monastery, exerted great influence over the mind of Theodoret, and he followed substantially their system of biblical interpretation. In his Preface to the Psalms he says: "When I happened upon various commentaries, and found some expositors pursuing allegories with great superabundance, others adapting prophecy to certain histories so as to produce an interpretation accommodated to the Jews rather than to the nurselings of faith, I considered it the part of a wise man to avoid the excess of both, and to connect now with ancient histories whatever things belonged to them." Most of his remaining works are expository, but often mixed with that which is apologetic and controversial.[3] They cover most of the books of the Old Testament, and the epistles of Paul. In treating the historical books his method is to

[1] The best edition of Chrysostom's works is that of Montfaucon, Greek and Latin, 13 vols., Paris, 1718–38. Reprinted 1834–39, and also in Migne's Greek Patrology, vols. xlvii–lxiv. An English translation of many of the Homilies is given in the Oxford Library of the Fathers, 1842–53.

[2] The best edition of Isidore's works is probably that of Migne, Greek Patrologiæ Cursus Completus, vol. lxxviii. Paris, 1860.

[3] Comp. Rosenmüller, Historia Interpretationis Librorum Sacrorum, vol. iv, pp. 35–142.

state and discuss the questions which arise on difficult passages, but on other books his discussions assume the form of a continuous commentary. His learning was not great, and he borrowed much from the homilies of Chrysostom, but the real merits of his biblical expositions, from whatever source he gathered them, are universally acknowledged. Ernesti recommends his commentaries, especially those on the Pauline epistles, as peculiarly adapted to the wants of students who are commencing a course of exegetical study. His comments are usually short, clear, and concise, evince a sober and discriminating judgment, and are to be reckoned among the best specimens of ancient exegesis.[1]

The churches of Syria early developed into two main divisions, Schools of Edes- those of the eastern and the western provinces. As sa and Nisibis. Antioch was the chief center of the western cities, so were Edessa and Nisibis of the more eastern, and when, after the days of Chrysostom and Theodoret, the school of Antioch declined, those chief centres of Christian activity in Mesopotamia became more famous as literary towns and seats of exegetical learning. The appearance of the Syriac version of the New Testament as early as the middle of the second century, and the Diatessaron of Tatian, indicates the interest of the Syrian mind in the study of the Scriptures. Lucian, the founder of the Antiochian school, received his early training in the Scriptures from Macarius of Edessa. The Ignatian epistles appear also to have exerted great influence in Eastern Syria, and they were early translated into the Syriac tongue. "The school of Eastern Syria," says Dorner, "was distinguished by its vivid fancy, by its religious spirit, at once fiery and practical, by fervour, and, in part, depth of thought. It exhibited, also, a tendency to the impassioned style and too gorgeous imagery of the East, to mysticism and asceticism. . . . The Church of Western Syria displayed, at an early period, that sober, judicious, and critical spirit for which it became renowned, and by which it was especially distinguished from the third to the fifth century. The eastern school inclined to theosophy, and thus had a certain affinity with the religious systems which prevailed in the East; the western, on the other hand, took its stand on the firm basis of experience and history. In a word, the contrast between the two divisions of the Syrian Church bore a not inconsiderable resemblance to that which exists between the Lutheran and Reformed Confessions in Germany."[2]

[1] The best edition of Theodoret's works is that of Schulze and Nösselt, 5 vols., Halle, 1769–74. See also Migne's Greek Patrologiæ Cursus Completus, vols. lxxx–lxxxiv.

[2] History of the Development of the Doctrine of the Person of Christ, div. ii, vol. i, p. 29.

One of the greatest fathers of the Syrian Church was Ephraem, commonly called Ephraem Syrus, who flourished at Edessa about A. D. 370. He spent most of his life in Ephraem Syrus. writing and preaching, and was a vigorous opponent of Arianism. His learning and piety were the admiration of his contemporaries, and he was often designated as the prophet of the Syrians. He was a voluminous writer, and has left numerous commentaries, homilies, and poems. Many of his exegetical discourses and polemical and practical homilies are written in poetic form. His commentaries on the historical books of the Old Testament and the Book of Job are extant in Syriac, and those of the Pauline epistles in an Armenian translation. It is doubtful whether he understood or used the Greek language. His method of exposition is mainly that of the allegorists, his style is brilliant and glowing, often running into bombast, and his interpretations are often fanciful, farfetched, and extravagant.[1]

The school of Nisibis maintained itself longer than that of Edessa, and continued until the ninth century. The Canon Barsumas and of Nisibis prescribed a three years' course of exegetical Ibas. study in the Old and New Testaments. Barsumas, who was ejected from the school of Edessa, became bishop of Nisibis in A. D. 435, and founded there the theological seminary which served to maintain and propagate Nestorianism in various countries of the East. The works of Diodorus of Tarsus, and Theodore of Mopsuestia, translated into Syriac by Ibas, contributed much toward the cultivation of biblical and theological study throughout Eastern Syria.

Several eminent fathers of the fourth century, who belong to no particular school of exegesis, but became noted in the Athanasius. dogmatic controversies of the early Church, deserve a passing notice in the history of biblical interpretation. Pre-eminent among these is Athanasius of Alexandria, the father of orthodoxy, and the great defender of the faith against the Arian heresy. His polemic purposes unfitted him for calm and thoughtful exposition, and yet, despite his Alexandrian training, he rarely falls into allegorizing, and his scriptural arguments Epiphanius. generally proceed upon correct principles of interpretation. Epiphanius, the patriarch of heresy hunters, has left some

[1] The best edition of the works of Ephraem Syrus is that of Assemanni in six vols., Rome, 1732–46. Nine of the metrical homilies and thirty-five of the Syriac hymns have been translated into English by Burgess, Select Metrical Hymns and Homilies of Ephraem Syrus, London, 1853. See also Lengerke, De Ephraemi Syri arte hermeneutica, Königsb., 1831.

writings which are especially useful in preserving various opinions of his time. But he was deficient in good judgment, and fell into frequent blunders and self-contradictions. He is said to have been familiar with five languages, Hebrew, Syriac, Egyptian, Greek, and Latin.

Basil the Great has left numerous homilies on various parts of Scripture, which show that he was a man of extensive learning and a sound interpreter. He condemns those who do not accept the obvious sense of what is written, but seek after occult meanings, and make themselves wiser than the Holy Spirit by introducing into the sacred writings fancies and fictions of their own. Gregory of Nyssa, a younger brother of Basil, composed several doctrinal, exegetical, and practical treatises, and pursued essentially the same line of exposition. He was a diffuse writer, and his style is often heavy and wearisome to the reader. Gregory of Nazianzum was one of the most polished writers of the fourth century, and ranks with Basil and Chrysostom, but he is celebrated as the theologian rather than the interpreter.

Basil.

The two Gregories.

Ulphilas, the apostle and bishop of the Goths, was master of the Greek and Hebrew languages, and propagated among his people the love of letters as well as the Gospel of Christ. He constructed a Mœso-Gothic alphabet, and translated into that language the entire Bible except the Books of Kings. Cyril of Jerusalem was the author of eighteen books of sermons entitled Catecheses. These discourses abound with quotations from the Scriptures, and help to illustrate the life and discipline of the Church at Jerusalem during the fourth century.

Ulphilas and Cyril of Jerusalem.

Andreas, bishop of Cæsarea, in Cappadocia, in the latter part of the fifth century wrote a commentary in Greek upon the Book of Revelation. It is somewhat miscellaneous in its character, and claims to make use of what others had written, referring by name to Irenæus, Hippolytus, Methodius, Epiphanius, Gregory of Nazianzum, and Cyril of Alexandria. The writer maintains a threefold sense, the literal, the tropological, and the anagogical or mystical, which last he makes most prominent in his expositions. Arethas, a later bishop of this same place, wrote a still more copious commentary on the Apocalypse, and followed the same style and system of interpretation as Andreas. These works are valuable for their antiquity, but not for intrinsic merit.

Andreas and Arethas.

Before passing to notice the fathers of the Western Church, we should consider for a moment the critical assault made by Porphyry upon the allegorical system of interpretation,

Porphyry.

and his theory of the prophecies of Daniel. In the latter part of the third century this celebrated Neo-Platonic philosopher wrote a work in fifteen books against the Christians. Only a few fragments of this treatise have been preserved, from which it appears that in the first book Porphyry sought to expose the discrepancies of the Bible; in the third book he attacked the allegorical method of exegesis so prevalent at the time, and urged that writings, which must be handled so unhistorically in order to maintain a satisfactory meaning, cannot be worthy of belief. In the twelfth and thirteenth books he attacked the prophetic portions of the Book of Daniel, maintaining that Scriptures purporting to foretell future events with such minuteness of detail must have been written after the events which they portray. He discovered what he regarded as evidence that the writer lived in the reign of Antiochus Epiphanes, and detailed events to a definite period of his reign, beyond which he is vague and uncertain. The critical sharpness of this heathen philosopher is apparent from these few indications of his argument, and it will be seen how his theory of explaining the predictions of Daniel is virtually identical with the rationalistic criticism of the nineteenth century.

The fathers of the Western Church were, as a class, much inferior to those of the Eastern in their expositions of the Scriptures. One chief reason for this fact was their comparative ignorance of the original languages of the Bible. A notable exception is that of Hippolytus, bishop of Portus, at the mouth of the Tiber, near Rome. It is doubtful whether he should be claimed more by the West than the East, for he was a disciple of Irenæus, and a friend and admirer of Origen, and, according to Baronius, a disciple of Clement of Alexandria. Nevertheless, it is quite certain that he spent the greater portion of his life in Rome and its vicinity. His great work, recently discovered, on the Refutation of all Heresies, contains numerous expositions of different passages of Scripture, and shows that he was an extreme allegorist. He appears to have written commentaries on most of the Bible, and numerous fragments remain. His exegetical method is substantially that of Philo, Clement of Alexandria, and Origen, and in some things, if possible, even more extravagant. Nevertheless, his writings are of great value as exhibiting the heresies and disputes of his time, and some of his Scripture expositions are thoughtful and suggestive.[1]

Hippolytus.

[1] The extant works of Hippolytus have been published in many editions, the best of which is, perhaps, that of Lagarde, Lps., 1858. An English translation is given in vols. vi and ix of the Edinburgh Ante-Nicene Christian Library.

Tertullian occupies a conspicuous place among the Latin fathers,
and is the most ancient whose works are now extant. He
flourished at the beginning of the third century, and is
chiefly distinguished for his vigorous and violent writings against
the Gnostics. So far as his works deal with the exposition of
the Scriptures, he belongs to the historico-theological school, and
he lays great stress upon the *regula fidei*, rule of faith, supposed
to have been transmitted from the apostles to all the true
Churches of Christ.[1] He allows allegorical interpretation in the
treatment of prophecies, and in a few cases adopts it where the
passage cannot reasonably admit of any such method of exposition;
but he generally maintains the literal and most obvious sense of
Scripture.[2]

Cyprian, who was bishop of Carthage from A. D. 248 to 258, was
very simple and practical in his expositions of Scripture. He followed the general method of Tertullian,
whom he called the Master, and for whose writings he ever showed
a special fondness. He is pre-eminently famous for his maintain-
ance of the authority of the Church, and prelatical doctrines which
placed the unity of the Church in the episcopate, and involved the
legitimate primacy of the bishop of Rome. Like other fathers
who have left numerous writings, he incidentally treats many passages of the Scriptures, and, like Tertullian, is to be classed with
the historico-theological interpreters.[3]

There is extant, under the name of Victorinus, bishop of Petau
(Petavium in Pannonia), a commentary on the Apocalypse. Victorinus lived near the close of the third century, and, according to Jerome, wrote commentaries on most of the
books of the Old Testament. Besides his work on the Apocalypse
we have also a fragment of his treatise on the Creation of the
World. The writer is exceedingly fanciful in most of his expositions, and spiritualizes after the manner of the allegorists generally.
Here and there an excellent thought is presented, and there are

Tertullian. (marginal)
Cyprian. (marginal)
Victorinus. (marginal)

[1] "It is impossible," says Davidson, "to calculate the mischief which this appeal
to ecclesiastical authority occasioned in after times. The sufficiency of the holy
word was virtually impugned and denied; the overseers of the Church claimed to be
authorized interpreters by virtue of a commission handed down from the apostles;
and doctrines were promulgated, not by the aid of the Scriptures, but by the aid of a
tradition in the Church."—Sacred Hermeneutics, p. 111.

[2] The best edition of Tertullian is that of Oehler, 3 vols., Lps., 1853. English translation in four vols. (vii, xi, xv, and xviii) of the Edinburgh Ante-Nicene Christian
Library.

[3] An English translation of Cyprian's writings is given in vols. viii and xiii of the
Edinburgh Ante-Nicene Christian Library.

some sensible explanations of single passages, but, as a whole, the work is rambling and full of arbitrary conceptions. It is especially interesting as being one of the oldest specimens of continuous commentary.[1]

About the middle of the fourth century flourished Hilary of Poitiers, in France, a man "who was distinguished among the doctrinal writers of the Western Church for a profoundness of intellect and a freedom of spirit peculiarly his own."[2] So forcibly did he maintain the Athanasian faith against its enemies that he was called the Hammer of the Arians. In his doctrinal writings he is often discriminating and able in his use of appropriate proof-texts, but as an exegete he belongs to the school of Origen, whose works had much influence over both his thought and his style, and whose commentary on Job he is said to have translated into Latin. His commentaries on the Psalms and the Gospel of Matthew are modelled after the tone and spirit of the great Alexandrian scholar, and abound with allegorical fancies.[3]

Hilary.

Ambrose, bishop of Milan (A. D. 374–397), was even a more fanciful and lawless allegorizer than either Origen or Hilary. He treats the historical sense as of no account, and extols the hidden mystical meaning of the sacred oracles, some parts of which he affirms have several different significations. He sees in Noah's ark a mystical representation of the human body. The four kings of the East mentioned Gen. xiv, 1, denote the allurements of the flesh and the world; the five kings of the plain of Sodom (ver. 8) are the five senses of the body, and Abraham represents Christ as the conqueror of fleshly appetites. In the narrative of our Lord's entry into Jerusalem the ass which was tied represents mankind as bound in sin, and the loosing of the same is the redemption of Christ. The placing of their garments under Christ showed that the apostles were ready to sacrifice their own works for the honour of preaching the Gospel. The strewing of the branches by the way denotes the cutting off of unfruitful works![4]

Ambrose.

[1] An English translation of Victorinus' Commentary on the Apocalypse, and also of the fragment on the Creation, is given in vol. xviii of the Edinburgh Ante-Nicene Christian Library.

[2] Neander, History of the Christian Religion and Church, vol. ii, p. 396.

[3] Hilary's works have been published in many editions, the best is, perhaps, that of the Benedictines, Paris, 1693, fol.

[4] The writings of Ambrose are more numerous than useful. The best edition is that of the Benedictines in 2 vols., fol., Paris, 1686–90. The exegetical treatises are in the first volume.

In the latter part of the fourth and the earlier part of the fifth
century there flourished, contemporaneously, the greatest biblical scholar, the greatest theologian, and the
most distinguished heretic, of the ancient Western Church. These
were Jerome, Augustine, and Pelagius. Jerome was born at Stri-
don, on the borders of Pannonia, but early in life removed to Rome,
where he diligently prosecuted his studies under the best masters.
He afterward travelled through Gaul, and transcribed Hilary's commentary on the Psalms. About A. D. 372 he visited the East, passing through the most interesting provinces of Asia Minor, and
pausing for a time at Antioch in Syria. Here he was prostrated by
a severe fever, and in a dream received strong condemnation for
his devotion to the heathen classics, which he thereupon vowed to
renounce forever. He betook himself to monastic life, and thought
to crucify his taste for Roman literature by the study of Hebrew.
He afterward visited Constantinople, and pursued his studies, especially in Greek, under Gregory of Nazianzum. Here he translated
Eusebius' Chronicle, and the commentaries of Origen on Jeremiah
and Ezekiel. About A. D. 386 he settled in Bethlehem of Judæa,
and there, in monkish seclusion and assiduous study, spent the rest
of his life. He wrote commentaries upon most of the books of the
Bible, revised the old Latin version, and made a new translation of
the Old Testament from the original Hebrew text. His generation
was not competent to appreciate these literary labours, and not a
few regarded it as an impious presumption to assume that the Septuagint version could be improved by an appeal to the Hebrew.
That seemed like preferring Barabbas to Jesus. Nevertheless, the
Vulgate speedily took rank with the great versions of the Bible,
and became the authorized translation used in the Western Church.
It is more faithful to the Hebrew than the Septuagint, and was
probably made with the help of Origen's Hexapla, which was then
accessible in the library of Cæsarea.

"As a commentator," writes Osgood, " Jerome deserves less honour than as a translator, so hasty his comments generally are, and so frequently consisting of fragments
gathered from previous writers. His merit however is—
and this was by no means a common one in his day—that he generally aims to give the literal sense of the passages in question. He
read apparently all that had been written by the leading interpreters
before him, and then wrote his own commentaries in great haste
without stopping to distinguish his own views from those of the
authorities consulted. He dashed through a thousand lines of the
text in a single day, and went through the Gospel of Matthew in a

fortnight. He sometimes yielded to the allegorical methods of interpretation, and showed frequent traces of the influence of his study of Origen. Yet he seems not to have inclined to this method so much from his own taste as from the habit of his time. And if, of the four doctors of the Church particularized by some writers, to Gregory belongs excellence in tropology, to Ambrose in allegory, to Augustine in anagoge, to Jerome is given the palm in the literal and grammatical sense. . . . Rich and elegant as his style frequently is, he does not appear to have had very good taste as a critic. He had not that delicate appreciation of an author's meaning that enables one to seize hold of the main idea or sentiment, and through this interpret the language and illustrations. He could not reproduce the thoughts of the prophets and poets of the Old Testament in his own mind, and throw himself into their position. Their poetic figures he sometimes treats as logical propositions, and finds grave dogmas in casual illustrations."[1]

In learning and general culture Jerome was much superior to Augustine, but in depth and penetration, in originality of genius and power of thought, Augustine, bishop of Hippo, in Africa, was by far the greatest man of his age. If it be any evidence of greatness for one mind to shape and direct the theological studies and speculations of more than a thousand years, and after all the enlightenment of modern times to maintain his hold upon men of the deepest piety and the highest intellectual power, then must it be conceded that few if any Christian writers of all the ages have equalled Augustine. But of his doctrines and his rank as a theologian it is not in our way to speak. Only as an interpreter of Scripture do we here consider him, and as such we cannot in justice award him a place correspondent with his theological fame. His conceptions of divine truth were comprehensive and profound, but having no knowledge of Hebrew and a very imperfect acquaintance with Greek, he was incapacitated for thorough and independent study of the sacred books. He was dependent on the current faulty Latin version, and not a few of his theological arguments are built upon an erroneous interpretation of the Scripture text. In his work on Christian Doctrine he lays down a number of very sensible rules for the exposition of the Bible, but in

Augustine.

[1] Jerome and his Times; article in the Bibliotheca Sacra for Feb., 1848, pp. 138, 139. The works of Jerome have been published in many forms; best edition, by Vallarsi and Maffei in 11 vols., Verona, 1734-42; reprinted, with some revision, Venice, 1766-71. See also Migne's Latin Patrologiæ Cursus Completus, vols. xxii-xxx, Paris, 1845, 1846. The best treatise on Jerome is that of Zöckler, Hieronymus, sein Leben und Werken aus seinem Schriften dargestellt, Gotha, 1865.

practice he forsakes his own hermeneutical principles, and often
runs into excessive allegorizing. He allows four different kinds of
interpretation, the historical, the ætiological, the analogical, and
the allegorical, but he treats these methods as traditional, and gives
them no extended or uniform application. His commentaries on
Genesis and Job are of little value. His exposition of the Psalms
contains many rich thoughts, together with much that is vague and
mystical. The treatise in four books on the Consensus of the
Evangelists is one of the best of the ancient attempts to construct
a Gospel harmony, but his Evangelical Inquiries (Quaestiones Evan-
gelicae) are full of fanciful interpretation and mystic allegorizing.
His best expositions are of those passages on which his own rich
experience and profound acquaintance with the operations of the
human heart enabled him to comment with surpassing beauty and
great practical force. His exegetical treatises are the least valuable
of his multifarious writings, but through all his works are scattered
many brilliant and precious gems of thought.[1]

Pelagius, supposed to have been a British monk, went to Rome
about the beginning of the fifth century, and there pub-
Pelagius.
lished a commentary on the Epistles of Paul, in which he
set forth the heretical opinions which have ever since been associated with his name. His theological views were shared and earnestly defended by his disciple and friend Coelestius, who accompanied him to Carthage. Pelagius appears to have been a man of
blameless moral character, and of considerable learning and force.
Besides his comments on the Pauline epistles he wrote numerous
treatises which exerted much influence on the theological thinking
of that period. His defective views of the nature of sin and the
work of divine grace in salvation disqualified him both as a profound
exegete and a theologian. But his comments are specimens of brief
and simple exposition, and avoid the habit of allegorizing.[2]

Tichonius, a contemporary of Jerome and Augustine, de-
Tichonius.
serves notice for making perhaps the first formal attempt
to lay down a number of hermeneutical rules for the interpretation

---

[1] Augustine's works have been printed in very many editions, the latest of which is
that of Migne, in fifteen vols. Paris, 1842. More sumptuous is the Benedictine edition, in eleven folio vols. Venice, 1729–35. An English translation of his exposition
of the Psalms and Gospels is given in the Oxford Library of the Fathers, and his
commentary on John, the work on Christian Doctrine, the Enchiridion, and numerous
other treatises are published in Clark's Foreign Theological Library, Edinburgh.

[2] The extant works of Pelagius are usually printed with the writings of Jerome, and
numerous extracts are found in Augustine's controversial treatises; but they have
all suffered more or less mutilation. Comp. Rosenmüller, Historia Interpretationis
Librorum Sacrorum, vol. iii, pp. 503–537.

of the Scriptures. His work is entitled Seven Rules for investigating and discovering the sense of the Scriptures. He propounds his canons as so many keys to unlock, and lamps to illuminate, the secrets of the law; but his rules consist mainly of rambling observations on particular passages of Scripture, and are of very little value.[1]

Vincentius, a monk and priest, who was educated at a cloister in the island of Lerins in Provence, deserves a passing notice on account of his Commonitorium, a work designed to show that Scripture and the tradition of the Catholic Church are both necessary in order to establish the true doctrines of faith. That exposition which is believed everywhere, always, and by all (quod ubique, quod semper, quod ab omnibus creditum est) is the only true one. His treatise is a textbook of ecclesiastico-traditional interpretation, but it is of no value except with those who hold Church tradition and authority above reason and conscience.

Vincent of Lerins.

Cassiodorus, commonly called the Senator, flourished during the first half of the sixth century, and was noted for his devotion to biblical literature. He was the author of a work entitled De Institutione Divinarum Literarum, and also of comments on the Psalms and the apostolical epistles. His expositions are partly in the form of a paraphrase, and usually set forth the literal sense of the Scripture; but they show no great penetration, and are without much interest or value.[2]

Cassiodorus.

Gregory the Great, who became pope of Rome A. D. 595, was a very voluminous writer, and, besides many other works, composed a commentary (called Moralia) on the Book of Job, and homilies on Ezekiel and the Gospels. Although he laid the foundations of the papacy and the Romish mediæval system, he disclaimed the title of universal bishop, and exerted himself to promote the study of the Scriptures among the clergy and the laity. When Bishop Natalis would fain excuse himself from such study on the ground of physical infirmity, Gregory referred him to Rom. xv, 4, and urged that the more we are bowed down with affliction or burdened with the troubles of the times, the more we need the comfort of the Scriptures. But this distinguished prelate was too thoroughly imbued with the superstitions of his age to be a sound interpreter. His learning and critical judgment were notably inferior to his piety and devotion to the Church. As an interpreter he maintains the historical sense, but also the allegorical and the

Gregory the Great.

---

[1] The writings of Tichonius may be found in the sixth volume of the Maxima Bibliotheca Veterum Patrum. Lyons, 1677.

[2] Cassiodorus' works were published by Dom Garet in two vols. fol., Rouen, 1679, and Venice, 1729; also in Migne's Latin Patrologiæ Cursus Completus, vols. lxix–lxxi.

spiritual, or moral. His work on Job is full of mystical allegorizing; his homilies on Ezekiel are of much the same cast, but those on the Gospels are of a more practical character.[1]

As we review the history of patristic exegesis we notice the progress of two opposite tendencies operative from the beginning of the Christian era. The one was a speculative spirit, a habit of allegorizing, begotten of associated Judaism and Platonism; it received a mighty impulse in the Alexandrian school, and has maintained more or less influence even to the present day. The other tendency was of a more practical character. It originated with our Lord and his apostles, who condemned the fanciful speculations and Hagadic traditions of their time, and set the example of a sober and rational interpretation of the Scriptures. It was the distinguishing feature of the school of Antioch, and exhibits some of its best results in the exegetical works of Chrysostom and Theodoret. But this more grammatical and logical method of interpretation attained no complete development among the ancient fathers. The prevalence of superstitions, the blind credulity of the masses, the strong tendencies to asceticism and mysticism, and the defective knowledge of the original languages of the Bible, gave, in the main, an advantage to the allegorists, and rendered a thorough grammatico-historical interpretation impossible.[2] Hence, we are not to look to the ancient fathers for models of exegesis. Their writings contain numerous imperishable gems of thought, and exhibit great intellectual acumen and logical subtlety, but as interpreters of the sacred volume they have been far surpassed by the moderns. Notwithstanding his extravagant allegorizing, Origen will ever be prized for his great learning and remarkable service in biblical criticism, and the works of Chrysostom, Theodoret, and Jerome, despite their frequent errors, will ever hold high rank in biblical literature; but the time is passed when an appeal to the opinions of the early fathers has any considerable weight with men of learning.

General character of patristic exegesis.

---

[1] The best edition of Gregory's works is the Benedictine, in four vols. folio, Paris, 1705. They were also published in seventeen vols. at Venice, 1768–76, and in five vols. in Migne's Latin Patrologiæ Cursus Completus (vols. lxxv–lxxix). An English translation of the Moralia on Job is given in four vols. in the Oxford Library of the Fathers.

[2] The allegorizing tendency could, without much difficulty, accommodate itself wholly to the form of the tradition in the dominant Church, and explain the Bible in conformity therewith. The more unprejudiced, grammatical, and logical interpretation of the Bible would tend, on the other hand, to purge the existing system of Church doctrine of the various foreign elements which had found entrance through the Church tradition, guided as that tradition had been by no clear consciousness of the truth.— Neander, History of the Christian Religion and Church, vol. ii, p. 351.

CHAPTER V.

EXEGESIS OF THE MIDDLE AGES.

DURING the period extending from Gregory the Great to the time of Luther (A. D. 600 to A. D. 1500), the true exegetical spirit could scarcely be expected to maintain itself, or produce works of great merit. The monasteries be- *No great exegetes during this period.* came the principal seats of learning, and the treasures of theological literature gradually found their way to them as to so many asylums. The Scriptures were everywhere regarded as a holy treasure, and many were wont to consult them for oracular responses. If one was about to embark in some dangerous enterprise, he would open the Bible and regard the first words which met his eye as a special revelation to himself.[1] Superstition and ignorance effectually hindered the progress of critical inquiry. Nevertheless, a number of distinguished writers appeared during the Middle Ages who devoted themselves to the study of the sacred books, and have left works in the department of biblical exegesis which deserve attention.

To this period belong the so-called catenists, or compilers of expositions from the more ancient fathers. It was not an *The early Catenists.* age of original research, but of imitation and appropriation of the treasures of the past. Among the earliest of these compilers was Procopius of Gaza, who wrote commentaries on the Pentateuch, Joshua, Judges, Samuel, the Books of Kings, Chronicles, Proverbs, Canticles, and Isaiah.[2] To this class of expositors belong also Andreas and Arethas, already mentioned, and Olympiodorus, who lived in the early part of the sixth century, and wrote comments on Job, Ecclesiastes, and Jeremiah. The more distinguished catenists appeared at a later date.

The Venerable Bede, one of the most eminent fathers of the English Church, flourished about the beginning of the eighth

---

[1] When Clovis was about to make war on the West Goths in Spain he prayed God that he would reveal to him, as he entered the Church of St. Martin, a fortunate issue of the war; and as at that moment the words of Psa. xviii, 40, 41, were chanted, the king regarded this as an infallible oracle by which he was assured of the victory. He, in fact, obtained the victory, which confirmed him in his belief.—Neander, History of the Christian Religion and Church, vol. iii, p. 129.

[2] Given in vol. lxxxvii of Migne's Greek Patrologiæ Cursus Completus, Paris, 1860.

century. He spent his life in the monasteries of Jarrow and Wear-
The Venerable mouth, and made himself familiar with all the learning of
Bede.   his age. His commentaries extend over the entire New
Testament and a large portion of the Old. They are, in substance,
compilations from the works of Augustine, Basil, and Ambrose,
and properly belong to the class called catenæ. Later catenists,
however, placed him among the fathers, and transcribed his comments as if they had been original. His expositions are mainly
allegorical, for he closely followed the methods of those from whom
he took the principal part of his comments.[1]

Bede was the educator of many other Church teachers. During
School of York. the latter part of his life he was surrounded by admir-
ing disciples whom he had inspired with a love for
study. Egbert, archbishop of York, was one of his pupils, and,
after the master's death, he sought to carry forward his work, and
superintended a school at York where biblical studies were cultivated. In this school Flaccus Alcuin received his training, and
learned the Latin, Greek, and Hebrew languages. He afterward
became headmaster of the school, and made it so famous that
Alcuin.   scholars came from distant places to enjoy its advantages. In a journey to Rome about A. D. 780, having
made the acquaintance of Charlemagne, he was retained in the
service of that ruler for the rest of his life. He gave direction to
the studies of the monks in many places, and founded the so-called
Palatine Schools in the houses of the princes, which long rivalled
the cloister establishments. The palace of Charlemagne himself
was turned into an academy in which the family and counsellors of
the king became the devoted pupils of Alcuin. About A. D. 796
he took charge of the abbey of St. Martin of Tours, which he succeeded in making the most famous school of his age. The learning
and attainments of this man were certainly extraordinary for the
time in which he lived. Besides numerous treatises on theology,
philosophy, philology, and rhetoric, and several poems, he compiled
questions and answers on Genesis, an exposition of the penitential
psalms, and a commentary on the Gospel of John. He belongs,
however, to the class of catenists. His questions on Genesis are
taken mainly from Jerome and Gregory, and his comments on John
are avowedly compiled from the works of Augustine, Ambrose,
Gregory, and Bede.[2]

[1] The works of Bede, nearly complete, were published in vols. xc–xcv of Migne's
Latin Patrologiæ Cursus Completus (Paris, 1850), and an edition of his historical and
theological works by Giles, London, 1842, 1843, 12 vols.
[2] Alcuin's works were published at Paris, 1617, in one vol. fol., and at Ratisbon,

Rhabanus Maurus was a disciple of Alcuin at Tours, and afterward became head of the school at Fulda, where his Rhabanus Maurus. fame as a most learned and successful teacher attracted to him many scholars. Among these were not a few of the sons of the nobility. He was afterward made archbishop of Mentz. His commentaries cover all the books of the Bible, and have obtained considerable celebrity. But they are full of mystic allegorizing, and advocate a fourfold sense, namely, the historical, the allegorical, the anagogical, and the tropological (see above, pp. 164, 165). He also is essentially a catenist, and appropriates the larger part of his comments from the Greek and Latin fathers. His writings served to bring into circulation many excellent things from the more ancient times, and to diffuse a warm, practical, Christian spirit.[1]

Haymo, teacher at Fulda, abbot of Hirschfeld, and finally bishop of Halberstadt, was another disciple of Alcuin, and is Haymo. noted for the compilation of Glosses upon the Psalms, Canticles, and the Prophets, and homilies upon the Gospels and Epistles. The Glosses are short annotations of no great value, and were taken mainly from the fathers.[2] "A work, however, which had greater influence than other writings of this kind on the following centuries, not so much on account of its intrinsic contents as on account of the very convenient manner in which it adapted itself to the ordinary theological wants of all such as were not profound scholars, was the short explanatory re- Walafrid Strabo. marks which Walafrid Strabo, abbot of Reichenau, following, for the most, his teacher, Rhabanus Maurus, compiled on the sacred Scriptures, and which formed the common exegetical manual of the Middle Ages known as the Glossa Ordinaria. A man of far greater theological importance, as an expositor of Scripture, was Christian Druthmar, in the ninth century, who had received his education in the French monastery of Corbie. Druthmar. He first gave lectures on the exposition of the New Testament to the young monks in the monasteries of Stavelo and Malmedy, in the diocese of Liege. In this way he was led to write out, as he had been invited to do, an elaborate commentary on the Gospel of Matthew; and it is singular to observe, in an interpreter

1777, in 2 vols. fol. Comp. Rosenmüller, Historia Interpretationis Librorum Sacrorum, vol. v, pp. 109-122.

[1] The works of Rhabanus Maurus were published at Cologne, in 1627, in 6 vols. fol.; also in Migne's Latin Patrologiæ Cursus Completus, vols. cvii-cxii. Comp. Rosenmüller, Historia Interpretationis, vol. v, pp. 123-134.

[2] Haymo's writings are published in vols. cxvi-cxviii of Migne's Latin Patrologiæ Cursus Completus.

of Scripture belonging to these times, the revival of the hermeneutical principles of the Antiochian school, which direction in favour of the grammatical interpretation of the Bible no doubt acquired for him the surname of Grammaticus. He declared himself, in the preface to this commentary, opposed to a onesided, arbitrary, mystical exposition of the Bible, and maintains that the spiritual explanation of Scripture presupposes the exploration of the literal historical sense." [1]

Other distinguished catenists of the ninth century were Claudius, bishop of Turin, sometimes called the first Protestant reformer because of his vigorous opposition to numerous Romish superstitions; Sedulius and Florus Magister, who prepared Collectanea on all the epistles of Paul; Remigius, whose compilations extend over the Psalms and eleven of the Minor Prophets; Smaragdus, who wrote on the Gospels and Epistles; and Paschasius Radbert, who is especially famous for originating the doctrine of transubstantiation. [2]

Catenists of the ninth century.

The tenth century was an age of barbarism and almost universal ignorance, but near its close we meet with the most distinguished of all the catenists, the Byzantine bishop, Œcumenius, whose elaborate commentaries, compiled mainly from Chrysostom, cover all the books of the New Testament. Though taking the expositions of others, and stringing them together without any system or logical order, he occasionally expresses his own independent judgment. Inasmuch as he uses Chrysostom's works as his principal source, his method of interpretation is the literal or grammatical, but he also quotes the comments of the two Gregories, Cyril of Jerusalem, Basil, Isidore, Methodius, Photius, Athanasius, and Theodoret. [3]

Œcumenius.

Among the catenists of the eleventh century Theophylact of Bulgaria is the most celebrated. He wrote commentaries on Hosea, Jonah, Micah, Nahum, Habakkuk, the Gospels, the Acts, and the Epistles. His notes on the prophets are of little value, but those on the New Testament have always been held in high estimation. [4] Although the works of Chrysostom are

Theophylact.

---

[1] Neander, History of Christian Religion and Church, vol. iii, pp. 458, 459. Druthmar's Commentary on Matthew was published at Strasburg, 1514, and also with that on Luke and John in the xvth vol. of the Maxima Bibliotheca Patrum (Lyons, 1627). Strabo's Glossa Ordinaria have been published in many editions. Latest ed. vols. cxiii and cxiv of Migne's Latin Patrology.

[2] The works of most of these catenists may be found in Migne's Latin Patrologiæ Cursus Completus; but some are still in manuscript.

[3] The commentaries of Œcumenius were published in two vols. folio, Paris, 1631.

[4] Comp. Rosenmüller, Hist Interpretationis Librorum Sacrorum, vol. iv, pp. 286–316.

the chief source of his extracts, he occasionally expresses his dissent from his views, and shows more independence than most of the catenists. "The circumstance of the extracts being taken from Chrysostom," says Davidson, "is rather a commendation than otherwise; for thus the time of the student who desires to know the sentiments of the Constantinopolitan archbishop is saved. The interpretations are here exhibited in shorter compass than in the voluminous works of the original author. We would therefore recommend the commentaries of Theophylact to the biblical student. They may be fairly classed with those of Œcumenius. Both follow the grammatical method of exposition; both are founded upon Chrysostom more than any or all of the other fathers. We prefer the simplicity and brevity of Theophylact to the profuseness of Œcumenius." [1]

Other exegetical compilers of the eleventh century are Lanfranc, who wrote glosses on the Pauline epistles, taken mainly from Ambrose and Augustine; and Nicetas, archbishop of Heraclea, in Thrace, the author of a useful commentary on Job, taken mostly from Olympiodorus, but also making free use of many other writers. [2] Mention should also be made of Willeram, abbot of Ebersberg, in Bavaria, who was much devoted to the study of the Scriptures, and composed a double paraphrase of Solomon's Song, one in Latin hexameter verse, another in prose in the language of the ancient Franks.

In the early part of the twelfth century flourished Rupert, abbot of Deutz, probably the most prolific writer of his time, and greatly devoted to the study of the Scriptures. His exegetical works are an abridgment of Gregory's Moralia on Job, and commentaries on the Song of Solomon, Ecclesiastes, the Minor Prophets, the Gospel of John, and the Apocalypse. [3] About this time appeared also Peter Lombard, the noted scholastic divine, who wrote a commentary on the Psalms, and Collectanea on the Pauline epistles, gathered chiefly from the works of Jerome, Ambrose, and Augustine. [4] More valuable are the compilations of Euthymius Zigabenus, a Greek monk of Constantinople, on the Psalms, the Gospels, and the Epistles. They

(margin notes: Lanfranc, Nicetas, and Willeram. Rupert, Peter Lombard, and Euthymius Zigabenus.)

---

[1] Sacred Hermeneutics, p. 170. The finest edition of Theophylact is that published at Venice, 1754–63, 4 vols. fol.

[2] Lanfranc's works were edited by Giles, 2 vols. 8vo, Oxford, 1844, 1845, and Nicetas' Catena on Job appeared in London, 1637.

[3] Rupert's complete works were published at Venice, 1751, 4 vols. fol.

[4] His complete works have been published in many editions; the first, at Nuremberg, 1478.

are taken mostly from the works of Chrysostom, and follow his grammatical method of exposition.[1]

It was in the twelfth century that the Abbot Joachim put forth his Exposition of the Apocalypse, in which he maintains that the divine government of the world is arranged in three great æons, or dispensational periods: the first, extending from the creation until the incarnation of Christ, is the reign of the Father; the second, is the reign of the Son of God, and is denoted by the twelve hundred and sixty days mentioned in Rev. xi, 3; xii, 6, each day representing a year; the third, is the reign of the Holy Spirit, to begin in the year A. D. 1260, during which mankind, having been carnal under the Father, half carnal and half spiritual under the Son, will become altogether spiritual. He also wrote a work on the Harmony of the Old and New Testaments, and there are commentaries bearing his name on most of the Prophets.[2]

Joachim.

Thomas Aquinas, the distinguished theologian known as "the Angelical Doctor," has left among his voluminous writings expositions of Job, the Psalms, Canticles, Isaiah, Jeremiah, and the Gospel of John. More important than any of these, however, is his Catena Aurea on the Four Evangelists and the Epistles of Paul, which presents in an abridged form the comments of Augustine, Bede, Alcuin, Haymo, Rhabanus Maurus, and others. The name of each author from whom he quotes is given at the end of the quotation. His works are marked with numerous subtleties peculiar to the schoolmen, and are of little value in the interpretation of the Scriptures. In Aquinas the scholastic philosophy of the Middle Ages reached its culmination, but exegesis made no real advance.[3] Associated with him in scholastic theology was his contemporary, Bonaventura, called "the Seraphic Doctor." He also wrote expositions of various books of Scripture, as the Psalms, Ecclesiastes, Lamentations of Jeremiah, and portions of the Gospels, but his exegesis abounds with farfetched and worthless speculations, and in some instances assumes a sevenfold sense, the historical, the allegorical, the mystical, the moral, the symbolical, the synecdochical, and the hyperbolical. The first four of these senses are supposed to be indicated by the four feet

Thomas Aquinas.

Bonaventura.

---

[1] His works are given in Migne's Greek Patrologiæ Cursus Completus, vols. cxxx, cxxxi.

[2] His Exposition of the Apocalypse has been often printed, and all his works were published at Venice in 1519–24, and at Cologne in 1577.

[3] The works of Aquinas have been published separately in many editions; best edition of his complete works in 28 vols. 4to. Venice, 1775. An English translation of his Catena Aurea was published at Oxford in 1845.

of the table which the psalmist speaks of as prepared for him in the presence of his enemies (Psa. xxiii, 5), and the whole seven correspond with the seals of the Apocalypse. His comments on the Gospels exhibit much better judgment.[1]

To this same class of extreme mystical interpreters belong the Car- Hugo and Al-
dinal Hugo de St. Caro and Albert, bishop of Ratisbon. bert.
The former of these is chiefly famous for his revision of
the text of the Vulgate, and his concordance of the same, with all the words of this Latin version arranged in alphabetical order. In connexion with this work he divided the Bible into chapters, and also wrote a brief commentary on the whole. This last-named work maintains a fourfold sense, the literal, the allegorical, the moral, and the anagogical.[2] The expository works of Albert, some-times called, on account of his vast erudition, Albert the Great, con-sist of commentaries on the Psalms, Lamentations, the twelve Minor Prophets, the four Gospels, and the Apocalypse. His annotations are full of mystical allegorizing and scholastic speculation.[3]

Nicholas de Lyra flourished at the beginning of the fourteenth century. In addition to the usual studies of his age he Nicholas de
acquired a thorough knowledge of Hebrew, a rare ac- Lyra.
complishment for a Christian, and his great learning and useful writings secured him the friendship of the most illustrious men of his times, and the title of the "plain and useful doctor." His greatest work is entitled Continual Comments, or Brief Annotations on the whole Bible (Postillæ perpetuæ, seu brevia commentaria in universa Biblia), and exhibits a great advance upon most of the exegesis of the Middle Ages. For although he recognises a four-fold sense, as shown in the well-known lines,

> Litera gesta docet, quid credas allegoria,
> Moralis quid agas, quo tendas anagogia,

he gives decided preference to the literal sense, and in his exposi-tions shows comparatively little regard for any other. He frankly acknowledges his indebtedness to the learned Hebrew exegetes,

---

[1] Bonaventura's works were published in 13 vols. 4to. Venice, 1751. His ex-egetical writings are contained in vols. i and ii.

[2] Hugo's Postillæ on the whole Bible were published at Basle in 1487, and his Con-cordance at Avignon in 1786, 2 vols. 4to. The word postilla, which came to be used in mediæval Latin for a running commentary, means literally *that which follows after*, and arose from the habit of delivering homilies or expository remarks immediately af-ter the reading of the text of Scripture. Thus, too, the comments in a written volume, which followed after the text, which was placed first, came to be known as postillæ.

[3] Albert's exegetical writings are published in vols. vii–x of the edition of all his works in 21 vols. fol. Lyons, 1651.

especially Rabbi Solomon Isaac (Rashi), whose sober methods of interpretation he generally followed. The influence his writings had on Luther and other reformers is celebrated in the familiar couplet:

> Si Lyra non lyrasset,
> Lutherus non saltasset.

His comments on the New Testament are less valuable than those on the Old, and follow closely Augustine and Aquinas. He was ignorant of the Greek language, and based his expositions on the text of the Vulgate.[1] But his great Postillæ perpetuæ accomplished much in preparing the way of a more thorough grammatical interpretation of the Bible.[2] His exegetical principles were opposed by Paulus Burgensis, who thought that Lyra had given undue emphasis to the literal sense to the neglect of the other meanings which he allowed. Lyra was in turn defended by Matthias Döring, a Franciscan monk. These polemical treatises contain nothing of value.

Along with Lyra we may appropriately mention John Wycliffe, the first English translator of the Bible, and the "morning star of the Reformation." His translation of the entire Scriptures, including also the Apocrypha, was made from the Vulgate, and is of little or no intrinsic value, having been superseded by more accurate English versions, but its influence at the time of its appearance, and for a long period afterward, was incalculable. It placed the divine Word within reach of multitudes of the common people, and set them thinking for themselves.

John Huss, the illustrious Bohemian reformer, who suffered martyrdom at Constance in 1415, was greatly influenced in his views by the writings of Wycliffe. He wrote an exposition of the Gospels, compiled mostly from the Latin fathers, and a commentary on the Catholic Epistles, and a portion of First Corinthians. He follows the grammatical sense, but aims especially to bring out the doctrinal and moral lessons of the sacred text. John Wessel, whose life extended over the greater part of the fifteenth century, was another precursor of the Reformation, and is worthy of our notice because of his holding up the Scriptures in that dark age as the final appeal in matters of faith. So far as his writings deal with expositions of the Bible he follows the historico-theological method, and maintains the simple and obvious sense of the text. Tradition, how-

---

[1] Comp. Meyer, Geschichte der Schrifterklärung seit der Wiederherstellung der Wissenschaften, vol. i, pp. 109–120.

[2] The best edition of Lyra's Postillæ is that published at Antwerp, 1634, 6 vols. fol.

ever, was not altogether rejected, and he showed great deference to the rule or analogy of faith.

A very different style of interpretation was that maintained by John Charlier Gerson, who co-operated with the Council of Constance in the condemnation and martyrdom of Huss. Gerson, however, laboured earnestly for the reform of the Church, and thereby provoked the enmity of many leading men of his time. He wrote a doctrinal exposition of the Seven Penitential Psalms, and a treatise on the Song of Songs. In other works of his production he advocates the literal sense of Holy Scripture, but insists, like a true papist, that this sense is to be determined, not by the judgment of the individual interpreter, but by the authority of the Church.

Gerson.

Lorenzo (or Laurentius) Valla, an Italian scholar, was one of the most celebrated leaders in the revival of literature, and, as Hase concisely puts it, "first developed the laws of a true Latinity, and was induced by the artistic refinement which it produced decidedly to pronounce the scholastic style absurd, by the philological knowledge it afforded to explain and illustrate the original text of the New Testament, and by the historical criticism it fostered to give judgment against the fables of the hierarchy." [1] He wrote, besides other important works, Annotations on the New Testament, which entitle him to the honour of being the best interpreter of the fifteenth century. He urged the importance of understanding the original language of the New Testament, and showed that the Vulgate text must be amended by the Greek original. He opposed the traditional follies of the Church, refused to allow the scholastic philosophy to control biblical exposition, and adhered closely to the grammatical sense. He was pre-eminently a critic and grammarian, and his system of interpretation may best be designated as philological.[2] He paid little or no attention to the theological and normal teachings of the Bible, and while, doubtless, erring in this extreme, his labours and influence produced a wholesome and much-needed reaction against superstition and mystic scholasticism, and in favour of a grammatical interpretation of the Scriptures.

Laurentius Valla.

With the general revival of learning, and the knowledge of Grecian antiquity which was introduced by Grecian refugees into Southern and Western Europe, and prepared the way for

---

[1] History of the Christian Church, translated by Blumenthal and Wing, p. 327. New York, 1855.

[2] Comp. Meyer, Geschichte der Schrifterkärung seit der Wiederherstellung der Wissenschaften, vol. i, pp. 154–166.

the great Protestant Reformation of the sixteenth century, there
Revival of learn- was a notable breaking away from mediæval super-
ing. and in- stition, and an increasing regard for the study of the
creased study of
the Bible.   Holy Scriptures. The Church of Rome was hostile to
these tendencies. "The opposition of the Church to primitive Christianity," says Hase, "was evinced in the fact that when it perceived the almost universal use of the sacred writings by parties
hostile to it the hierarchy ventured more and more decidedly to
prevent the perusal of the Scriptures in the language of the people,
and to subject every translation to an ecclesiastical censorship.
In spite of all their efforts, however, after the middle of the
fifteenth century, the wishes of the people and the power of the
press prevailed, and fourteen editions of a translation in the high
German, all founded upon the Vulgate, though none were in the
genuine language of the people, are evidence to the extent to which
it was used." [1] The first notable specimen of printing with metal
types was an edition of the Latin Vulgate in two folio volumes
(somewhere between 1450 and 1455). The art of printing became
from that time a most important aid in the diffusion of knowledge.

At the beginning of the sixteenth century, but hardly to be
John Reuchlin.   classed with the great reformers, flourished two celebrated scholars to whom biblical literature is greatly
indebted, Reuchlin and Erasmus. John Reuchlin was recognised
as a leader of the German Humanists, and was particularly famous
for his devotion to the study of Hebrew. He justly deserves the
title of father of Hebrew learning in the Christian Church. He
far surpassed the Jews of his time in the knowledge of their own
language, and published, besides many other works, a treatise on
the Rudiments of Hebrew, another on the Accents and Orthography of the Hebrew Language, and a Grammatical Interpretation
of the Seven Penitential Psalms. He was also acknowledged everywhere as an authority in Latin and Greek, as well as in Hebrew,
and the most learned men of his age sought his instruction and
counsel. His great services in the cause of biblical learning led
men to say of him, "Jerome is born again."

Desiderius Erasmus was by his wit, wisdom, culture, and varied
Erasmus.   erudition the foremost representative, and, one might
say, the embodiment, of Humanism. He and Reuchlin
were called the "Eyes of Germany." Erasmus became early fascinated with the ancient classics, translated several Greek authors
into Latin, and edited numerous editions of their works. He also
edited a number of the Greek and Latin fathers. Without any

[1] History of the Christian Church, p. 332.

such deep religious experience and profound convictions as Luther, and possessed of no such massive intellect as Melanchthon, he was noted rather for versatility of genius and prodigious literary industry. Nevertheless, he was one of the most distinguished precursors of the Reformation, and it was truly said: "Erasmus laid the egg; Luther hatched it." He appears to have turned his attention to biblical studies about the beginning of the sixteenth century, and published in 1505 a new edition of Lorenzo Valla's Remarks on the New Testament. He edited and published in 1516 the first edition of the Greek Testament. It was printed in folio, accompanied with an elegant Latin version, and various readings from several manuscripts, the works of the fathers, and the Vulgate. This first edition was hastily prepared, precipitated rather than edited, as Erasmus himself wrote, in order to bring it out in advance of Cardinal Ximenes' Complutensian Polyglot, which did not appear until 1520. Erasmus afterward wrote and published Annotations on the New Testament, and also Paraphrases on the whole New Testament except the Book of Revelation, which were so highly esteemed in England that it was required of every parish church to possess a copy of the English translation. These publications introduced a new era in biblical learning, and went far toward supplanting the scholasticism of the previous ages by better methods of theological study.[1]

Jacques Lefèvre, born at Etaples (about 1455), and commonly known as Jacobus Faber Stapulensis, can hardly be ranked with the great Reformers, and yet in fact he was Lefèvre. the father of the Reformation in France. He, however, never left the Roman Church, and we may properly notice his work in biblical literature as belonging to the transition period which prepared the way for the triumph of Protestantism. In 1509 he published his Psalterium Quintuplex, or Psalms, in five versions, accompanied with short annotations. He afterward published commentaries on the Psalms, the four Gospels, the Epistles of Paul, and the Catholic Epistles. But his most important work was his French translation of the Bible, which was the basis of the later work of Olivetan. The New Testament part appeared at Paris in 1523, and the Old Testament at Antwerp in 1538.

Belonging to this same transition period, and worthy of a passing notice, we find the Italian, Pico Mirandula (Giovanni Mirandula. Pico della Mirandula), who was learned in Hebrew, Chaldee, and Arabic, as well as Greek and Latin, and wrote an

[1] Erasmus' works have been printed in many forms. The best edition is that of Le Clerc, in 11 vols. folio. Leyden, 1703.

allegorical exposition of Genesis, a work of no value, and a commentary on the Lord's Prayer.

Mention should also be made of Sanctes Pagninus, an Italian Sanctes Pagninus. monk, distinguished for his knowledge of Latin, Greek, Arabic, Chaldee, and Hebrew, especially the last. He published a Hebrew Lexicon, and an Introduction to the Mystical Meanings of Holy Scripture, in which he explained parts of Job, Solomon's Song, and the seventh chapter of First Corinthians in a very fanciful and cabalistic manner. His most useful work, however, is his new Latin version of the Old and New Testaments, the first Latin Bible in which the verses of each chapter were numbered as in the original. This translation is remarkable for its close adherence to the Hebrew idiom. He also composed Institutes of the Hebrew language, and a catena of Greek and Latin writers on the Pentateuch.

The beginning of the sixteenth century was notable for the growing interest taken in the study of the ancient tongues, The first Polyglots. and the publication (at Genoa in 1516) of the Polyglot Psalter of Justinian (Giustiniani), a bishop of Corsica, and the great Complutensian Polyglot, commenced in 1502 under the auspices of Cardinal Ximenes of Toledo, completed in 1517, and published in 1522. The editors of this work were Demetrius Ducas, a Greek by birth, and a teacher in the University of Alcala; Anthony of Nebrissa, a Spanish theologian, professor in the University of Alcala, and author of several valuable works; Stunica, noted for skill in the Hebrew, Greek, and Latin languages; Ferdinand Nonnius, a distinguished orientalist; Alphonsus, a physician of Alcala, Alphonsus Zamora, and Paul Coronel; these last three converted Jews, who were all proficient in Hebrew and in rabbinical learning. Most of these editors of the Complutensian Polyglot were also noted for other works in biblical literature and philology.

The publication of the whole Bible and separate parts of it in Latin, Greek, Hebrew, Chaldee, Arabic, and Syriac prepared the way for the more accurate and scientific exposition of the following centuries. The fetters of ignorance were broken, a widespread love for literature and learning prevailed, and earnest and devout students of the Scriptures began to cultivate a more thorough and useful system of interpretation.

CHAPTER VI.

EXEGESIS OF THE REFORMATION.

WITH the Reformation of the sixteenth century the mind of Germany and of other European states broke away from *The Reformation the morning of a better day.* the ignorance and superstition of the Middle Ages, the Holy Scriptures were appealed to as the written revelation of God, containing all things necessary to salvation, and the doctrine of justification by faith was magnified against priestly absolution and the saving meritoriousness of works. The great commanding mind and leader of this remarkable movement was Martin Luther, who, in October, 1517, published the famous theses which were like the voice of a trumpet sounding forth the beginning of a better day. Five years later he put forth his German translation of the New Testament. This was one of the most valuable services of his life, for it gave to his people the holy oracles in the simple, idiomatic, and racy language of common life, and enabled them to read for themselves the teachings of Christ and *Luther's German Bible.* the apostles. It was followed by successive portions of the Old Testament until, in 1534, the whole Bible was completed and became of incalculable influence in effecting the triumph of Protestantism. The arduous effort of Luther to make his translation of the Bible as accurate as possible went far toward the establishing of sound methods of criticism and exegesis. His helps in this great enterprise consisted of Erasmus' edition of the New Testament, the Septuagint, the Vulgate, a few of the Latin fathers, and an imperfect knowledge of the Hebrew. He also received valuable assistance from Melanchthon, Bugenhagen, Jonas, Cruciger, and several learned rabbis. He spent twelve of the best years of his life upon this monumental work. Portions of the original autograph are still preserved in the royal library of Berlin, and show with what anxious care he sought to make the version as faithful as possible. Sometimes three or four different forms *His exegetical works.* of expression were written down before he determined which one to adopt. Luther's commentary on the Galatians, which has been translated into English, and published in many editions, was characterized by himself as being very "plentiful in words." It is an elaborate treatise adapted for use as public lectures and devotional reading, and is particularly notable for its ample exposition of the doctrine of justification by faith. Luther also prepared notes on Genesis, the Psalms, the Sermon on the Mount, the Gospel of John, and other portions of the New Testament.[1] His knowledge of Hebrew and Greek was limited, and he sometimes mistook the meaning of the sacred writer, but his religious intuitions and deep devotional spirit enabled him generally to apprehend the true sense of Scripture.

Although Luther occupies the foremost place among the reform-
Melanchthon. ers, he was far surpassed in scholarship and learning by Philip Melanchthon, in whom he found an indispensable friend and helper, in temperament and manners the counterpart of himself. Luther may be compared with Paul, whose bold and fearless spirit he admirably represented; Melanchthon exhibited rather the tender and loving spirit of John. Melanchthon appears to have been favoured with every opportunity and means of education which that age afforded. He was regarded as a prodigy of ancient learning, especially skilled in the knowledge of Greek, a pupil of Reuchlin, and a friend of Erasmus, both of whom extolled his remarkable talents and ripe scholarship. His thorough acquaintance with the original languages of the Scriptures, his calm judgment and cautious methods of procedure, qualified him for preeminence in biblical exegesis. He clearly perceived the Hebraic character of the New Testament Greek, and showed the importance of the study of Hebrew even for the exposition of the Christian Scriptures. As an aid in this line of study he published an edition of the Septuagint. Luther listened with delight to his expository lectures on Romans and Corinthians, obtained his manuscript, and sent it without his knowledge to the printer. On its appearance he wrote to his modest friend thus characteristically: "It is I who publish this commentary of yours, and I send yourself to you. If you are not satisfied with yourself you do right; it is enough that you please us. Yours is the fault, if there be any. Why did you not publish them yourself? Why did you let me ask, command, and urge you to publish to no purpose? This is my defence against you. For I am willing to rob you and to bear the name of a thief. I fear not your complaints or accusations."[2]

Melanchthon's exegetical lectures embrace Genesis, the Psalms, Proverbs, Ecclesiastes, Isaiah, Jeremiah, Lamentations, Daniel, Haggai, Zechariah, and Malachi, of the Old Testament; and Matthew,

---

[1] Luther's exegetical works in Latin, edited by Elsperger, Schmid, and Irmischer, were published at Erlangen in 23 vols. 12mo, 1729–44; in German, in vols. xxxiii–lii of his collected works as edited by Irmischer, 1843–53.

[2] Luther's Briefe, Sendschreiben u. Bedenken, ed. De Wette, ii, 238. Comp. ii, 303.

John, Romans, Corinthians, Colossians, Timothy, and Titus, of the New Testament. Luther's German Bible was greatly His exegetical lectures. indebted to the careful revision of Melanchthon, who himself translated the books of Maccabees. Although his quiet, meditative tendencies led him at times into allegorical methods of exegesis, which he found so generally adopted by the fathers, he followed in the main the grammatico-historical method, was careful to trace the connexion and course of thought, and aimed to ascertain the mind of the Spirit in the written word. His celebrated Loci Communes, and his authorship of the Augsburg Confession, entitle him to rank with the greatest theologians of any age or nation.[1]

Similar to Luther and Melanchthon, in their relations to one another, were the great Swiss reformers, Zwingle and Œco- Zwingle. lampadius. Zwingle was inferior to Luther in depth and genius, but his superior in humanistic culture and less mystical in his nature. He wrote scholia on Genesis, Exodus, Isaiah, and Jeremiah, and also on the Gospels. There is yet preserved in the Zurich library his manuscript copy in Greek of the Epistles of Paul, with marginal annotations from Erasmus, Origen, Ambrose, Jerome, and others. He made extensive use of the Greek and Roman classics, with which he was very familiar, forming his style after those ancient models, and bringing them to the illustration of various passages of Scripture.[2]

Œcolampadius was more gentle and meditative than Zwingle, and his scholarship was more varied and thorough. In Œcolampadius. his intellectual habits, love of retirement, and academic tastes he greatly resembled Melanchthon. He studied under Reuchlin, assisted Erasmus in preparing the second edition of his Greek Testament, and became distinguished over all the continent for his vast erudition, and especially for his proficiency in Hebrew and Greek. He was famous as a preacher and expounder of the Holy Scriptures. While professor of biblical literature in the University of Basle his lecture room could not contain the crowds of students and citizens who thronged to hear him. His exegetical works consist mainly of commentaries on Genesis, Job, and all the prophetical books, (3 vols. fol., 1553-8), and are of considerable value.

Contemporary with Zwingle and Œcolampadius was Conrad Pellican, for thirty years professor of Hebrew at Zurich, Pellican. where, in 1527, he published an edition of the Hebrew Bible with the comments of Aben-Ezra and Salamon. He also

---

[1] Melanchthon's works, edited by Bretschneider and Bindseil, form 2: vols. of the Corpus Reformatorum. Halle and Brunswick. 1834-60.

[2] His works were published at Zurich in 8 vols., 1828-42.

published commentaries on all the books of the Old and New Testaments, except Jonah, Zechariah, and the Revelation. His method is to adhere to the literal sense, amend where needed the Vulgate text, and make considerable use of rabbinical authors, with whom he appears to have been quite familiar. His exegetical writings served a useful purpose during the period of the Reformation.

Sebastian Münster identified himself with the Protestant reform-ers, and showed the liveliest sympathy with their prin-ciples, but he kept aloof from all their controversies, and gave himself up to the quiet study of Hebrew and other oriental languages. He published an edition of the Hebrew Bible, with a new Latin version and extensive annotations drawn mainly from the rabbinical commentaries. He was also the author of numerous works on Hebrew and Chaldee grammar, and of expositions of several books of the Old Testament, which have been printed in the Critici Sacri. Isidore Clarius belongs to this same period. His principal work was an amended edition of the Latin Vulgate, accompanied by annotations taken largely from Münster. John Draconites also acquired reputation as a biblical scholar by his Biblia Pentapla, and commentaries on various portions of the Old and New Testaments.

Münster and Clarius.

Of all the exegetes of the period of the Reformation the first place must unquestionably be given to John Calvin, whose learning was ample, whose Latin style surpassed in purity and elegance that of any writer of his time, and whose intellect was at once acute and penetrating, profound and comprehensive. His stern views on predestination are too often offensively prominent, and he at times indulges in harsh words against those who differ from him in opinion. In textual and philological criticism he was not equal to Erasmus, Melanchthon, Œcolampadius, or his intimate friend Beza, and he occasionally falls into notably incorrect interpretations of words and phrases; but as a whole, his commentaries are justly celebrated for clearness, good sense, and masterly apprehension of the meaning and spirit of the sacred writers. With the exception of Judges, Ruth, Kings, Esther, Ezra, Nehemiah, Proverbs, Ecclesiastes, Solomon's Song, and the Apocalypse, his comments, expository lectures, and homilies extend over the whole Bible. In his Preface to the Epistle to the Romans he maintains that the chief excellence of an interpreter is a perspicuous brevity which does not divert the reader's thoughts by long and prolix discussions, but directly lays open the mind of the sacred writer. His commentaries, accordingly, while not altogether free from blemishes, exhibit a happy exegetical tact, a ready grasp of

John Calvin.

the more obvious meaning of words, and an admirable regard to the context, scope, and plan of the author. He seldom quotes from other commentators, and is conspicuously free from mystical, allegorical, and forced methods of exposition. His exegesis breathes everywhere—especially in the Psalms—a most lively religious feeling, indicating that his own personal experience enabled him to penetrate as by intuition into the depths of meaning treasured in the oracles of God. "In the Pauline epistles," says Tholuck, "he merges himself in the spirit of the apostle, and becoming one with him, as every one clearly feels, he deduces everywhere the explanation of that which is particular from that which is general, and is in this respect to be compared with Chrysostom, whose rhetorical education, however, sometimes exerted a bad influence upon him. The whole history of the New Testament becomes in his hand alive and vivid. He lives in every person who comes forward, either speaking or acting, in the wicked as well as in the good; and explains every discourse from the circumstances, and from the soul of him who speaks." [1]

Next to Calvin we may appropriately notice his intimate friend and fellow reformer, Theodore Beza, who early enjoyed the instruction of such masters as Faber (Stapulensis), Budæus, and John Lascaris, and became so distinguished as an apt and brilliant scholar that of one hundred, who with him received the master's degree, he stood first. He lived to the great age of eighty-six, and was the author of many useful works. The principal monument of his exegetical skill is his Latin translation of the New Testament, with full annotations. [2] He was a consummate critic, a man of remarkable quickness and versatility of intellect, and widely distinguished for his profound and varied learning. His comments are unlike those of Calvin in not making prominent the religious element of the sacred writings, but his philological

Theodore Beza.

---

[1] The Merits of Calvin as an Interpreter of the Holy Scriptures. Translated from the German in the Biblical Repository for July, 1832, p. 562. Comp. Gotch on same subject in Kitto's Journal of Sacred Literature for 1849, p. 222. Calvin's works were published in 9 folio vols., Amsterdam, 1671 (best edition). A new edition, edited by Baum, Cunitz, and Reuss, is given in the Corpus Reformatorum, Brunswick, 1863–82 (yet incomplete). Tholuck's edition of his New Testament Commentaries, in 7 vols. 8vo, is a very convenient one. English translation of Calvin's works in 52 vols. 8vo. Edinburgh.

[2] The editio optima of Beza's New Testament was published at Cambridge (1 vol. fol., 1642), and contains his own new translation placed in a column between the Greek text on the one side and the Vulgate on the other. It is accompanied by a copious critical and exegetical commentary by the translator himself, and the commentary of Camerarius is appended to the end of the volume.

learning and constant reference to the Greek and Hebrew texts are more conspicuous.

Other exegetes.

Other distinguished exegetical writers of this period were Bugenhagen, Bucer, Osiander, Camerarius, Fagius, Musculus, Aretius, Castellio, and Bullinger. John Bugenhagen (called also Pomeranus, from his native place) assisted Luther in translating the Scriptures, and wrote annotations on several books of the Old and New Testaments. Luther extolled him as being the first who deserved the name of commentator on the Psalms. Martin Bucer was noted for his refinement, ingenuity, and conciliatory methods. He was one of Luther's coadjutors, and became famous as a preacher and teacher throughout Germany. In 1549 he was invited to England and appointed professor of theology at Cambridge. He was a voluminous author, and, as a biblical expositor, maintained the grammatico-historical sense. Peter Martyr was the author of commentaries on Genesis, Judges, Samuel, Kings, Lamentations, and some of the Pauline epistles. Andreas Osiander wrote a Harmony of the Gospels, in which he maintained that the parallel narratives are not accounts of the same events, but of similar events which followed one another in four different periods. He also published an emended edition of the Latin Vulgate with numerous annotations, and various polemical treatises. Camerarius was the author of a critical commentary on the New Testament, which is published in the Cambridge edition of Beza's New Testament. Fagius, like Bucer, was appointed a professor in Cambridge University, and, at the request of Cranmer, they together planned a critical edition of the entire Scriptures, but their work was cut off by early death. Fagius was especially noted for his Hebrew learning, and was the author of several works on the Hebrew language and literature. Musculus acquired some note as a biblical interpreter, and Aretius wrote a commentary on the Pentateuch and the entire New Testament. Sebastian Castellio (or Castalion) was for a time associated with Calvin at Geneva, but after a few years left that place because of his opposition to the Calvinian doctrine of predestination. He wrote several exegetical treatises, and published complete Latin and French versions of the Bible, which were made the subject of much conflicting criticism. He was more of a critic and philologist than an expositor.[1] Heinrich Bullinger, the friend and ally of Zwingle, and his successor at Zurich, was the author of many expository discourses, which were so highly esteemed in England that Archbishop Whitgift gave order that every clergyman should

[1] Comp. Meyer, Geschichte der Schrifterklarung seit der Wiederherstellung der Wissenschaften, vol. ii, pp. 290–297.

obtain a copy and read one of the sermons every week. Mention should also be made of Carlstadt, Luther's violent and unmanageable fellow reformer, who maintained against him the genuineness of the Epistle of James, and also published a work on the Canonical Scriptures, in which the great Protestant doctrine of the paramount authority of the Bible is ably set forth. John Agricola, the antinomian, acquired considerable fame as an expositor, and published commentaries on the Gospel of Luke and several epistles of Paul, and John Brentius published expository discourses upon all the books of the Old and New Testaments. Strigel, also, the gifted pupil of Melanchthon, is noted for his scholia on the Old Testament, and his Hypomnemata on all the books of the New Testament.

Matthias Flacìus, (often called, from his native country, Illyricus), the projector of the Magdeburg Centuries, was for a Flacius. time professor of Old Testament literature at Wittenberg. He was the author of numerous theological treatises; but especially deserving of notice is his Clavis Scripturæ Sacræ, an important biblical and hermeneutical dictionary. "The work," says Davidson, " is an extraordinary one, whether we consider the time at which it appeared, the copiousness of its materials, the acuteness of mind which it manifests, the learning it contains, or the amazing industry of its author amid the violent restlessness of his turbulent spirit. Succeeding writers have drawn largely from its pages; yet its merits are such as to recommend a thorough perusal even at the present day." [1]

Johannes Piscator flourished in the latter part of the sixteenth century, and was distinguished for his assiduous devotion to biblical and theological studies. He translated the Piscator. entire Bible into German, and also published a commentary on the Old and New Testaments. Another eminent biblical scholar of this period was Junius, who was associated at Heidel- Junius and Tremellius. berg with the converted Jew, Immanuel Tremellius, in preparing a Latin translation of the Old Testament. This important version was published in parts (from 1575 to 1579), and in the course of twenty years passed through twenty editions.[2] The translation follows the original with great closeness, and was for many years the most popular Latin version in use among Protestants. Junius was also the author of commentaries on several Marlorat. books of the Old and New Testaments. Augustine Marloratus deserves honourable mention among the exegetes of this

---

[1] Sacred Hermeneutics, p. 680. Best edition of the Clavis Scripturæ is that of Musæus, Jena, 1674, and Erfurt, 1719.

[2] The best edition is thought to be the seventh, Frankfort, 1624, fol.

period. He composed expositions of various books of Scripture, but his most valuable work is his Catholic Exposition of the New Testament, which contains Erasmus' Latin version, and the comments of several ancient fathers, along with those of Erasmus, Calvin, Bucer, Melanchthon, Zwingle, and others. The object of this work was to exhibit the substantial harmony of the two Protestant parties and their agreement with the ancient Church.

Maldonatus. John Maldonatus, a Spanish Jesuit, acquired great distinction at Paris as an expounder of the Scriptures, and Romanists and Protestants attended his lectures. He was the author of commentaries on the principal books of the Old Testament and on the four Gospels. He maintained the literal sense of Scripture, and also showed great familiarity with the writings of the fathers.

Great attention was given during the sixteenth century to the translation of the Bible into modern languages. Of Translations of the Bible. Luther's German version we have already spoken; also of the work of Lefèvre, whose French version did much to advance the Protestant Reformation, although Lefèvre never left the Roman Church (see above, p. 671). Olivetan, a relative of Calvin, published in 1535 a French translation of the whole Bible, which was subsequently revised by Calvin, Beza, Bertram, and others, and appeared in many successive editions. In 1530 Antonio Bruccioli published an Italian version of the New Testament, and in 1532 an Italian version of the whole Bible. In 1562 an Italian version of the New Testament, by Gallars and Beza, was published at Geneva along with a revised edition of Bruccioli's Old Testament. In 1607 the superior Italian version of Diodati appeared at Geneva. In 1543 the Spanish version of the New Testament by Enzinas was issued at Antwerp. Other Spanish translations made by learned Jews appeared a little later. A translation of the whole Bible into the Helvetian, or German Swiss dialect, made chiefly by Leo Judæ, appeared in parts at Zurich from 1524 to 1529. In 1526 a Belgic or Dutch translation of the Bible was published by Jacob à Liesveldt at Antwerp, and several editions of the Bohemian Bible were printed at Prague from 1549 to 1577. The first edition of the Polish Bible was issued at Cracow in 1561. It was a Catholic publication, but being much indebted to the Protestant Bohemian Bible, it never received the sanction of the pope. Numerous other Polish versions, however, made by Protestants, were published during the century. A Danish translation of the New Testament appeared at Leipsic in 1524, and at Wittemberg in 1558; and a translation of the whole Bible into the Pomeranian tongue, a dialect of Lower Saxony, was printed at Bardi in 1588. During the latter half of this century translations of the whole or parts of the Bible were published in the Icelandic, Finnish, Swedish, and Hungarian languages. In 1525 William Tyndale published his English version of the New Testament at Worms. He also translated the Pentateuch and the Book of Jonah, which appeared subsequently. Coverdale's English version of the whole Bible appeared in 1535, and in 1537 the so-called " Matthew's Bible," edited by the martyr Rogers, who used the unpublished manuscripts of Tyndale. In 1539 the version known as the " Great Bible " was published under the superintendence of Grafton. In 1540 Cranmer's Bible, a mere revision of the Great Bible, was printed in England; in 1560 the " Geneva Bible," the work of English refugees led by William Whittingham, was printed at Geneva; in 1568 appeared the " Bishop's Bible," under the superintendence of Archbishop Parker. All these prepared the way for the Authorized Version, issued in 1611, which has been the standard English version until the present time. In 1582 the Anglo-Rhemish New Testament appeared, and in 1609 and 1610 the so-called Douay Bible, made by English Romanists from the Latin Vulgate.

The interest taken in biblical studies during the sixteenth century is further shown in the Polyglot Bibles, which were published at Antwerp (1568–73) and Nuremberg (1599–1600). The former included the whole of the Complutensian edition of Ximenes (see above, p. 672), and other important texts and philological helps, and was prepared by Arias Montanus, assisted by a number of eminent scholars. Only five hundred copies of this work were printed, and a part of these were lost by the wreck of the vessel which conveyed them to Spain.[1] The Nuremberg Polyglot was due to the enterprise of Elias Hutter, a learned German, and contained the New Testament in twelve languages. He also published considerable portions of the Old Testament in six different languages.

Polyglots.

A careful study of the exegetical writings of the sixteenth century reveals two tendencies which early appeared among the Protestant reformers, and developed gradually during the next two

[1] The honor of projecting this Polyglot is said to belong to Christopher Plantin, who, finding himself inadequate to support the expenses of such an immense undertaking, presented a petition to Philip II., King of Spain, who promised to advance the money necessary for the execution of the work, and to send learned men from Spain to undertake the arrangement and direction of the impression. For this success Plantin was considerably indebted to Cardinal Spinosa, counsellor of Philip II., who approved the plan, and persuaded the sovereign to sanction it.—Townley, Illustrations of Biblical Literature, vol. ii, p. 206. New York, 1842.

centuries, until in modern times the one has run into extreme rationalism, and the other into a narrow and dogmatic
orthodoxy. These tendencies early separated the so-
called Lutheran and Reformed parties. The more rigid
orthodox Lutherans exhibited a proclivity to authoritative forms, and assumed a dogmatic tone and method in their use
of the Scripture. The Reformed theologians showed greater readiness to break away from churchly customs and traditional ideas,
and treat the Scriptures with a respectful, but free, critical spirit.
The two methods were made conspicuous in the dispute between
Luther and Zwingle over the meaning of the words, "This is my
body." Luther and Melanchthon, Zwingle and Œcolampadius, met
at Marburg to reconcile, if possible, their differences. "The theologians sat by a table," writes Fisher, "the Saxons on one side and
the Swiss opposite them. Luther wrote upon the table with chalk
his text—*hoc est meum corpus*—and refused to budge an iota from
the literal sense. But his opponents would not admit the actual
presence of the body of Christ in the sacrament, or that his body is
received by unbelievers. Finally, when it was evident that no
common ground could be reached, Zwingle, with tears in his eyes,
offered the right hand of fraternal fellowship to Luther. But this
Luther refused to take, not willing, says Ranke, to recognise them
as of the same communion. But more was meant by this refusal:
Luther would regard the Swiss as friends, but such was the influence of his dogmatic system over his feelings that he could not
bring himself to regard them as Christian brethren. Luther and
Melanchthon at this time appeared to have supposed that an agreement in every article of belief is the necessary condition of Christian fellowship."[1] The tone and attitude of these men toward one
another on that memorable occasion is a fair index of the relations
of rigid dogmatic exposition on the one hand, and conscientious
rational inquiry on the other. In general exposition no great differences appeared among the early reformers. Luther and Melanchthon represent the dogmatic, Zwingle, Œcolampadius, and Beza the
more grammatico-historical method of scriptural interpretation.
Calvin combined some elements of both, but belonged essentially
to the Reformed party. It was not until two centuries later that a
cold, illiberal, and dogmatic orthodoxy provoked an opposite extreme of lawless rationalism.

Marginal note: Exegetical tendencies of the Lutheran and Reformed parties.

---

[1] History of the Reformation, p. 152. New York, 1873.

CHAPTER VII.

EXEGESIS OF THE SEVENTEENTH CENTURY.

THE spirit of religious inquiry, and the widespread interest in biblical studies, which were created by the Protestant   Progress of bib-
Reformation, continued with unabated vigour in the   lical studies.
seventeenth century. The Scriptures were translated into many
languages, and former translations were carefully revised, critical
and philological pursuits engaged the talents of the most distinguished scholars of Europe, and almost innumerable exegetical
works made their appearance, from the diminutive pocket volume
to the ponderous folio commentaries and polyglots.

Toward the close of the sixteenth century the study of Hebrew
literature was greatly promoted by John Buxtorf, the   Buxtorf.
first notable Protestant rabbinical scholar. He was the
head of a family which for more than a century was distinguished
for attainments in Hebrew learning. The elder Buxtorf published
numerous treatises on Hebrew and Chaldee grammar and lexicography, and his Lexicon Chaldaicum Talmudicum et Rabbinicum
(Basle, 1639) remains to this day the most complete work of its
kind extant. Valentine Schindler prepared about this   Schindler.
time his Lexicon Pentaglotton, in which the cognate
Hebrew, Chaldee, Syriac, Talmudico-Rabbinic, and Arabic words
are alphabetically arranged and defined. The learned Frenchman,
Vatablus, may also be mentioned as having a little be-   Vatablus, De
fore this revived the study of Hebrew among his coun-   Dieu, and Dru-
trymen, and somewhat later Louis De Dieu did a similar   sius.
work at the university of Leyden in the Netherlands. At this
university John Drusius was made professor of oriental languages
in 1577, and distinguished himself by several valuable contributions
to biblical literature, especially by his Annotations upon the New
Testament. The learned philologist, Joseph Scaliger, was also one
of the early professors at Leyden. The labors of these men prepared the way for a more thorough grammatical study of the Old
Testament Scriptures.

It was in the early part of this century (1611), as we have noticed, that the Authorized English Version appeared,   King James'
under the direction of King James, and the forty-seven   Version.
learned men who took part in its execution indicate how many

competent scholars in England were at that time giving themselves to the critical study of the Scriptures. About 1615 Le Jay projected his immense work, the Paris Polyglot. Its publication was begun in 1628 and completed in 1645 in ten imperial folio volumes, containing the entire Bible in seven languages (Hebrew, Samaritan, Chaldee, Greek, Syriac, Latin, and Arabic). It is inconvenient in not presenting all these versions together, but placing them in different volumes. Volumes i–iv contain the Hebrew, Chaldee, Septuagint, and Vulgate texts of the Old Testament; volumes v and vi give the New Testament in Greek, Syriac, Arabic, and Latin; volume vii contains the Hebrew, the Samaritan Pentateuch, and the Samaritan version, with a Latin translation by Morinus (J. Morin), and the Arabic and Syriac Pentateuch; volumes viii–x contain the rest of the Old Testament in Syriac and Arabic. The work is too unwieldy to be of practical value, and its great cost ruined the fortune of Le Jay. It was soon superseded by the London Polyglot of Brian Walton, the first volume of which was issued in 1654, and the sixth and last in 1657. It presents in parallel columns, or on the same page, the Pentateuch in eight languages, the Psalms in seven, Joshua, Judges, Ruth, Samuel, Kings, Chronicles, and the four Gospels in six, the rest of the New Testament and the Book of Esther in five, and the other books of the Old Testament and the Apocrypha (excepting Judith and Maccabees) in four. It was followed in 1669 by the Lexicon Heptaglótton of Castell, a joint lexicon of the Hebrew, Chaldee, Syriac, Samaritan, Ethiopic, and Arabic, and a separate lexicon of the Persian, with short grammars of those tongues (2 vols. folio). The entire work in eight uniform volumes is a magnificent monument of human learning and industry.

Soon after the publication of the London Polyglot appeared that immense collection of critical and exegetical writings known as the Critici Sacri (London, 1660, 9 vols. folio). It was prepared under the editorial supervision of Bishop Pearson, Anthony Scattergood, and Francis Gouldman, and printed by Cornelius Bee. It was republished at Amsterdam, with considerable additions, in 1698–1702, in thirteen folio volumes. This work contains all the annotations of Grotius, Drusius, Münster, Vatablus, Castalio, Clarius, Fagius on the first four chapters of Genesis, and on the Chaldee paraphrase of the Pentateuch, Masius on Joshua, Codurcus on Job, J. Price on the Psalms, Bayne on Proverbs, Forerius on Isaiah, Edward Lively on Hosea, Amos, Obadiah, and Jonah, and Badwell on the Apocrypha. The New Testament part contains a similar range of authors, and the work is enriched by numerous philological dissertations and tracts, such as Louis Cappel on Jephthah's vow, Urstius on the Construction of Noah's ark, and Fagius on the Principal Translations of the Old Testament. This great work, with its supplements, has treasured up and preserved the writings of many critics which would have otherwise been quite inaccessible.

Poole's Synopsis, published in 1669–74, in five folio volumes, is, for substance, an abridgment of the Critici Sacri, although it includes the comments of many other writers, and refers to versions not represented in the larger work. The *Poole's Synopsis.* method of the Synopsis also differs from that of the Critici Sacri in consolidating the various comments on each verse in one continuous paragraph, and designating the several writers by their initials in the margin. This work is convenient in that it presents in a brief space the views of many different expositors. It should be remarked that the London Polyglot, with Castell's Lexicon, the Critici Sacri, and the Synopsis Criticorum, forming in all twenty-two large folios, begun and finished in the space of twenty-one years (1653–74) at the expense of a few English divines and noblemen, constitute a magnificent exegetical library, and will long stand as a monument of English biblical learning and scholarship in the seventeenth century. Matthew Poole, the author of the Synopsis Criticorum, distinguished himself further by his English Annotations upon the whole Bible, a work which he left unfinished, and which was completed after his death by other hands.

Among the learned men who assisted Walton, Castell, and Poole in the preparation of the works above named, was John Lightfoot, pre-eminent for his attainments in Hebrew *Lightfoot.* and rabbinical literature. He was a member of the Westminster Assembly, and opposed with great courage many of the tenets which the Presbyterians were seeking to establish. He afterward occupied several important positions in the Church of England. His principal works are a Chronological Arrangement of the Books of the Old and New Testaments, Gleanings in Exodus, Erubhim, or Miscellaneous Tracts on Sundry Biblical Themes, a Harmony of the Four Gospels, a Commentary on the Acts of the Apostles, Description of the Temple at Jerusalem in the Time of our Saviour, and Horæ Hebraicæ et Talmudicæ, on the Gospels, Acts, Romans, and First Corinthians. In all his works, but especially in the last-named, he draws upon his vast stores of Hebrew and rabbinical learning to illustrate the language of the Bible, and show the connexion between the New Testament and the Jewish Midrashim. Lightfoot's works have been published in Latin and in English, and have ever commanded, and still hold, a deservedly high place in biblical literature.[1]

Another important helper in the preparation of the London Poly- glot, and without whose aid that great work would have wanted much of its perfection, was Edward Po- cock, probably at that time the most accomplished oriental scholar of Europe. One of his earliest labours in biblical literature was the transcription, from a manuscript in the Bodleian library at Ox- ford, of a Syriac version of the Second Epistle of Peter, the Second and Third Epistles of John, and the Epistle of Jude, the only books at that time wanting to complete an edition of the Syriac New Testament. He was too modest to publish it himself, but Vossius obtained his copy and took it to Leyden, where it was printed un- der the care of De Dieu. A residence of six years at Aleppo, in Syria, gave Pocock great advantages in prosecuting oriental studies. On his return to England he was made professor of Arabic at Ox- ford, and, notwithstanding various privations, interruptions, and embarrassments, he continued his favourite literary pursuits through a long lifetime, and left behind him many works of enduring value. He published six prefatory discourses of Maimonides' Commentary on the Mishna, with a Latin translation and notes, under the title of Porta Mosis. He was also the author of commentaries, some- what diffuse and abounding with rabbinical learning, on Hosea, Joel, Micah, and Malachi.

Other English exegetes of note belonging to this century were Henry Hammond, an Arminian divine, and author of a valuable Paraphrase and Annotations on the New Test- ament and on the Psalms and Proverbs; William Pemble, an emi- nent Calvinistic preacher and scholar, who wrote expositions of Ecclesiastes, Zechariah, and many obscure passages of Scripture; Robert Leighton, archbishop of Glasgow, whose Practical Com- mentary on the First Epistle of Peter, and other expository writ- ings, are full of excellent sense; Henry Ainsworth, an early leader of the Independents, and author of useful annotations on several books of the Bible, containing a new translation of the Pentateuch, Psalms, and Canticles. Thomas Gataker was one of the ablest divines of the Westminster Assembly, and one of the principal authors of the Annotations upon all the Books of the Old and New Testaments, which are commonly known as the Westminster Annotations. Gataker's share of this work embraced the Greater

Marginal notes: Edward Po- cock. — Other English exegetes.

---

[1] Lightfoot's works were published at London in 1684 in 2 vols. folio; at Rotterdam, 1686, 2 vols. folio; at Utrecht, in 1699, 3 vols. folio; and at London, 1822–25, 13 vols. 8vo.

Prophets. Among his collaborators were Ley, William Gouge (who also wrote a commentary on Hebrews), Meric Casaubon, Francis Taylor, Edward Reynolds, and John Richardson. William Attersoll, a nonconformist divine, wrote commentaries on Numbers and the Epistle to Philemon. Bythner, a native of Poland, gave instruction in Hebrew at the University of Oxford, and wrote a number of philological treatises, and a grammatical explanation of the Psalms entitled the Lyre of David, an excellent and full Chrestomathy of the entire Hebrew Psalter. Joseph Caryl is known chiefly from his immense work on the Book of Job (12 vols. 4to, and 2 vols. folio). Richard Baxter, chiefly distinguished for his modifications of Calvinism, and pre-eminent as theologian, preacher, and pastor, was author of a Paraphrase of the New Testament. Arthur Jackson wrote valuable Annotations on the Prophecy of Isaiah, and "A Help for the Understanding of the Holy Scriptures" (Camb., 1643, 3 vols. 4to). Thomas Godwin composed a useful treatise on the Civil and Ecclesiastical Rites of the Ancient Hebrews, and several other works illustrative of the Old Testament Scriptures. John Goodwin, the famous English Arminian, wrote, in addition to his numerous theological treatises, an exposition of Romans ix; and Thomas Goodwin, a contemporary Calvinistic divine, wrote on Ephesians and Revelation. Davenant, bishop of Salisbury, one of the English theologians who attended the Synod of Dort, was author of an elaborate exposition (in Latin) of Paul's Epistle to the Colossians, which was afterward translated into English by Allport. Bishop Bull wrote an extensive work, entitled Harmonia Apostolica, to show the agreement between the Epistles of James and Paul, and to explain the peculiar doctrine of each apostle. Here also we should mention the learned James Usher, a laborious student and accomplished biblical scholar, whose Annals of the Old and New Testaments established a chronology of the Bible which has been quite generally adopted until the present time.

The encouragement and patronage which Archbishop Laud gave to biblical and oriental learning deserves a passing notice. Laud. Although he wrote very little himself, he employed the most learned men in foreign countries to purchase valuable Greek and oriental manuscripts; he founded the chair of Arabic at Oxford, which Pocock was the first to fill, and he presented to the university, first and last, more than twelve hundred manuscripts, which he had procured from various places and at vast expense.

Few Englishmen of the seventeenth century are more widely known for their theological writings than John John Owen. Owen, the acknowledged leader of the Congregationalists during

the time of Cromwell, and for some time after the restoration
of Charles II. His most extensive work is an Exposition of the
Epistle to the Hebrews, which has been published in many separate
editions as well as in his collected works. Joseph Mede
distinguished himself in the early part of the century
by his various contributions to biblical literature, especially his
Clavis Apocalyptica, and other writings, both in Latin and English,
on the Revelation of John. Hurd speaks of him as "a sublime
genius, without vanity, interest, or spleen, but with a single un-
mixed love of truth, dedicating his great talents to the study of
the prophetic Scriptures, and unfolding the mysterious prophecies
of the Revelation."[1]

    The famous French scholar, Isaac Casaubon, flourished at the be-
ginning of this century, and deserves our notice for his
critical edition of the Greek Testament, the notes of
which were reprinted in the Critici Sacri. The two brothers
Jacques and Louis Cappel contributed largely to the exegetical
literature of this period by their various observations, disquisitions,
commentaries, and critical notes on the Old and New Testaments.
Many of these were also reprinted in the Critici Sacri. Menochius,
a learned Italian, was the author of brief but valuable annotations
on the whole Bible. Antoine Goddeau, a Roman Catholic bishop,
distinguished himself by a French translation and exposition of the
New Testament and the Psalms. Richard Simon acquired a deserved celebrity by his Critical History of the Old Testament, and
showed a boldness and independence of thought remarkable for a
Roman Catholic. He anticipated modern Rationalism in denying
the Mosaic authorship of the Pentateuch, and attributing its composition to the age of Ezra and the Great Synagogue. The Catholic
theologian Estius also obtained great repute as a biblical scholar by
annotations on the difficult parts of Scripture, and a valuable commentary on the apostolical epistles. Jacob Tirinus, a Jesuit, was
also distinguished as an exegete, and his comments, along with those
of Gagner, Estius, and Menochius, were published by De la Haye
in what was called the Biblia Magna (5 vols. fol., 1643), a work
somewhat after the order of the Critici Sacri. This work was afterward enlarged by the notes of Lyra and others, and issued in
nineteen volumes (Paris, 1660) under the title of Biblia Maxima.
Rivet, a French Protestant, spent his best years in Holland, and
wrote, in addition to many other works, a General Introduction to
the Holy Scriptures, and commentaries on Exodus and Hosea.
Jacques Gaillard became pastor of a Walloon church in Holland

---

[1] Introduction to the Study of the Prophecies, vol. ii, p. 122.

about 1662, and became known as the author of a treatise on the genealogy of Jesus as recorded in Matthew and Luke, and also on Melchizedek as a type of Christ. Samuel Bochart, born at Rouen in 1599, was a man of vast learning, acquainted with Hebrew, Syriac, Chaldee, and Arabic, and author of a Sacred Geography, which obtained for him an invitation to the court of Sweden, where he was greatly honoured. He is better known by his Hierozoicon, or Natural History of the Bible.

The Protestant Reformation found in no European country a more congenial soil than that of the Netherlands. The people were of independent spirit, and noted for their love of freedom, industry, and extensive commerce with foreign countries. The University of Leyden, founded in 1575, became in *Early progress of the Reformation in the Netherlands.* the early part of the seventeenth century the most renowned seat of learning in all Europe, numbering at times nearly two thousand students. In this celebrated university James Arminius became professor of theology in 1603. He had already, in *Arminius.* his published lectures on the ninth chapter of Romans, opposed the views of Calvin and Beza on predestination, and soon after his appointment at Leyden he fell into controversy with one of his fellow professors, Francis Gomar, a strenuous Calvinist. This controversy disturbed for many years the peace of the Reformed Church of the Netherlands, and continued with increased bitterness after the death of Arminius (1609), and led to the holding of the Synod of Dort (1618), at which (the Calvinists being largely in the majority) the opinions of the Arminian Remonstrants were condemned, their ministers were deposed, and many of them banished from the country; and all who embraced Arminian doctrines were excluded from the fellowship of the Church, and their religious assemblies were suppressed by law. The Arminian theology was, however, too deeply grounded in a comprehensive and rational exegesis of the Scriptures to be thus put down. When Arminius entered upon his work at Leyden, he openly set himself against scholastic subtleties and arbitrary assumptions, and maintained that the truth of God could be ascertained only by a thorough study of the Holy Scriptures. He was an adept in the original languages of the Bible, thoroughly versed in the writings of the ancient fathers, a man of profound spiritual insight, and, at the same time, most engaging in his personal demeanor. Neander calls him the "pattern of a conscientious and zealously investigating theologian, who endeavoured to guard himself against all partiality."[1] His exegetical and theological

[1] History of Christian Dogmas, vol. ii, p. 677. Lond., 1858. See the works of Arminius, translated into English by Nicholls and Bagnall, 3 vols. New York, 1843.

writings bear evidence of his great learning, clear judgment, and convincing logic, which his opponents found it difficult to meet.

Uytenbogaert was a distinguished leader of the Arminian Remon-
Other Dutch strants, and a most able and eloquent preacher. He was
divines. noted for casting aside the dry scholastic methods, and basing his discourses directly on the Scriptures. Simon Episcopius was the chief representative of the Arminians at the Synod of Dort, after which he was obliged, with other Remonstrants, to leave Holland. During his absence from the country he published several learned dissertations in defence of Arminianism, and among them an exegetical paraphrase of Rom. viii–xi. In 1626 he returned to his native land, became identified with the Remonstrants' college at Amsterdam, and spent the rest of his life in preaching and literary activity. His contemporaries, both friends and enemies, acknowledged his great abilities and acquaintance with the Scriptures. He was succeeded at Amsterdam by Curcellæus, who was especially devoted to New Testament studies, and published a critical edition of the Greek Testament. A worthy associate of these celebrated divines was Limborch, who edited several of their works, and was the author of the Theologia Christiana, an original and complete system of Arminian doctrine. He also wrote commentaries on the Acts of the Apostles and the Epistles to the Romans and Hebrews, which deserve commendation for their clear and simple method of interpretation.

In connexion with these Dutch divines of the Arminian school
Grotius. we should notice Hugo Grotius, one of the most remarkable men of the seventeenth century, and eminent alike in theology, politics, and general literature. Though suffering the confiscation of his property, imprisonment, and exile, his learning and talents commanded for him the attention of kings and princes, and of the educated men of Europe. Besides learned works in civil jurisprudence, apologetics, and dogmatic theology, he wrote annotations on the Old and New Testaments and the Apocrypha. His exegesis is distinguished for its philological and historical character, and the uniform good sense and good taste displayed. He has been called the forerunner of Ernesti, but he often noticeably fails to grasp the plan and scope of the sacred writers, and to trace the connexion of thought. He lacked the profound religious intuition of Luther and Calvin, and leaned to a rationalistic treatment of Scripture.[1] Abraham Calovius, a contemporary Lutheran theologian,

---

[1] All the theological works of Grotius were published in three folio volumes at London, in 1679. His annotations, with a life of the author, are contained in the first two volumes. They also appear in the Critici Sacri.

published the Biblia Illustrata (4 vols. fol., Dresden, 1719), in
which he embodied the whole of Grotius' annotations, and accompanied them with severe criticisms. He also
violently opposed the teachings of George Calixtus, whose mild and conciliatory methods aimed to settle the disputes between contending parties in the Church.

Calovius.

The names of Heinsius, Vossius, and Spanheim will ever be associated with the cultivation of biblical and philological learning. Heinsius acted as secretary to the Synod of Dort, and is known as the editor of many of the Greek
and Roman classics, and author of twenty books of dissertations on the New Testament. Gerard Jan Vossius and his son Isaac were both eminent as philologists and theologians, but not as great biblical exegetes. The same may be said of Friedrich Spanheim and his two sons, Ezekiel and Friedrich, whose lives and labours together extended over the entire seventeenth century. The great Swiss theologian and scholar, J. H. Hottinger, may be mentioned here as contributing largely to the progress of Semitic and other oriental studies; also Anthony Bynæus, who made great attainments in Hebrew and Syriac, and wrote several exegetical works, and James Alting, professor of Hebrew at Groningen, author of a Syro-Chaldaic grammar, commentaries on most of the books of the Bible, and various theological treatises.

Heinsius, Vossius, Spanheim, Hottinger, etc.

One of the most eminent scholars of the Dutch Reformed Church of the seventeenth century was Voetius, who received his early training at Leyden under Gomar, Arminius, and their colleagues. He was an influential member of the Synod of Dort, and a violent opponent of the Arminians. He also made it a great work of his life to oppose the Cartesian philosophy. But his methods of procedure tended to cultivate a narrow and dogmatic spirit, and his exegesis, accordingly, aimed rather to support and defend a theological system than to ascertain by valid reason the exact meaning of the sacred writers. He was vehemently polemical, and became the acknowledged head and leader of a school of exegesis which assumed to adhere strictly to the literal sense, but, at the same time, regarded all biblical criticism as highly dangerous to the orthodox faith. The Voetians would fain have made the dogmas of the Synod of Dort the authoritative guide to the sense of Scripture, and were restless before an appeal to the original texts of the Bible and independent methods of interpretation.

Voetius.

The great opponent both of scholasticism and of a narrow dogmatical exegesis was John Cocceius, a man of broad and thorough scholarship, an adept in Greek, Hebrew, Chaldee,

Cocceius.

Arabic, and rabbinical literature, and a worthy compeer of such
scholars as Buxtorf, Vossius, and Grotius. He devoted himself chiefly to biblical exposition, publishing commentary after
commentary until he had gone through nearly all the canonical
books.[1] Although his labours revived and encouraged allegorical
and mystical methods of interpretation, it must be conceded that
he exhibited many of the very best qualities of a biblical exegete
and did as much as any man of his time to hold up the Holy Scriptures as the living fountain of all revealed theology, and the only
authoritative rule and standard of faith. He insisted that the Old
and New Testaments must be treated as one organic whole, and
that each passage should be interpreted according to the meaning
of its words, the connexion of thought as traceable through an entire discourse, book, or epistle, and the analogy of faith, or scope
and plan of the one complete revelation of God. He maintained
that Christ is the great subject of divine revelation in the Old Testament as well as in the New, and hence arose the saying that Cocceius found Christ everywhere in the Old Testament, but Grotius
nowhere. It is due, however, to the memory of Cocceius to say
that while he too often pressed the typical import of Old Testament texts to an undue extreme, he acted on the valid principle
that the Hebrew Scriptures contain the germs of the Gospel revelation, and that, according to the express teaching of our Lord (John
v, 39; Luke xxiv, 27), the Old Testament contained many things
concerning himself. The errors into which he fell are less grave
than those of not a few modern critics who exhibit a notable one-
sidedness in failing to see that the written revelation of God is
truly an organic whole, and that the New Testament cannot be
interpreted without the Old, nor the Old without the New. Cocceius' method was not always safe or satisfactory. "His federal
theology," says Immer, "had an influence on his treatment of Scripture in so far as not dogma, but the economy of salvation was his
guiding principle. This might lead to a natural religio-historical,
it might also lead to an artificial typological, treatment. Cocceius
was too much under the influence of his time not to have fallen
into the latter. Yet it was already a great gain that an attempt
was made to give to Scripture, and indeed to the fundamental idea
of Scripture, the supremacy in theology."[2]

John Leusden was professor of Hebrew at Utrecht during nearly
all the latter half of the seventeenth century. His critical and

---

[1] The works of Cocceius were published at Amsterdam, 1676-78, in 8 vols. folio,
and in 1701 in 10 vols. folio.

[2] Hermeneutics of the New Testament, p. 45. Andover, 1877.

exegetical works embrace several editions of the Hebrew and Greek Scriptures, a Hebrew grammar and lexicon, various treatises in the department of biblical introduction, and Latin translations of David Kimchi's commentaries on Jonah, Joel, and Obadiah. He also edited Lightfoot's works in Latin, and Poole's Synopsis. His writings were not only characterized by exact and ample learning, but also adapted to meet practical wants, and are of solid value even at this day. Cornelius à Lapide, the learned Roman Catholic commentator, and professor of Hebrew at Louvain, and afterward at Rome, compiled from the fathers an elaborate exposition of all the books of the Bible except Job and the Psalms. It was published at Antwerp (1681, 10 vols fol.), Venice (1730, 11 vols. fol.), and Lyons (1838, 11 vols. 4to).

Leusden and Cornelius a Lapide.

Biblical scholarship in Germany during the seventeenth century furnished fewer names and works of great celebrity than either Holland or England. Nevertheless, many German exegetes of great merit appeared, some of whom have already been incidentally noticed. The name of Olearius was made famous by eight different persons, members of one family, who contributed in various ways to the advancement of exegetical and theological learning. The most distinguished of these for biblical scholarship was John Olearius, professor of Greek and of theology at the University of Leipsic. He wrote a work on the Elements of Sacred Hermeneutics, another on the style of the New Testament, and also several philological and theological treatises. His son Gottfried wrote a learned analysis of the Epistle to the Hebrews, and Observations on the Gospel of Matthew.

Olearius.

Other distinguished German scholars, who contributed to the progress of biblical learning, were Solomon Glassius and Erasmus Schmidt. The former was educated at Wittenberg and Jena, and became noted for his knowledge of Hebrew and cognate languages. He wrote several useful works, among which were an Exposition of the Gospels and Epistles, and his celebrated Philologia Sacra, a kind of philologico-biblical lexicon of scriptural words and tropes.[1] Schmidt was the author of a very convenient concordance of the Greek Testament, which is still in use, but which has recently been greatly enlarged and improved by Bruder. George Pasor was author of a lexicon and grammar of the New Testament, and Dietrich, a Lutheran

Other German biblical scholars.

---

[1] The best edition of the Philologia Sacra is that of Leipsic, 1725, 4to. The edition of Dathe and Bauer (Lps., 1776–97, 3 vols. 8vo) is interpolated with rationalistic notions

theologian, distinguished himself in the same department by his Philologico-Theological Lexicon•of the New Testament. (Frankf., 1680). Augustus Pfeiffer became noted toward the close of this century for his rare attainments in philology and contributions to biblical literature. His Dubia Vexata is a convenient and useful series of dissertations on the more difficult passages of the Old Testament.[1] Martin Geier wrote a commentary on the Psalms, Proverbs, and Ecclesiastes. Sebastian Schmid was the author of a Latin translation of the Old and New Testaments, and learned commentaries on Genesis, Judges, Ruth, Kings, Job, Ecclesiastes, Isaiah, Jeremiah, and the Minor Prophets; also on Romans, Galatians, Ephesians, Colossians, and Hebrews.

In the latter part of the seventeenth century there appeared many notable indications of a widespread yearning for liberty of thought and of speech. The Baconian and Cartesian systems of philosophy did not a little in preparing the way. The speculations of the celebrated Spinoza gave a mighty impulse to the movement. His famous Tractatus Theologico-Politicus was to the seventeenth century what Strauss' Life of Jesus has been to the nineteenth. "The book marks an epoch," says Farrar, "a new era in the critical and philosophical investigation of religion. Spinoza's ideas are, as it were, the head waters from which flows the current which is afterward parted into separate streams."[2] His speculations anticipated many of the later teachings of rationalism. His philosophy necessarily excluded the reality of any miraculous interference of Deity in the affairs of the world, and he explained prophecy as the combined product of vivid imagination and ardent desire. The writings of Lord Herbert and Hobbes contributed also to the politico-religious theorizing of that age. As early as 1644 Milton published his Areopagitica, or plea for the liberty of unlicensed printing, and a little later Jeremy Taylor produced his work, entitled Liberty of Prophesying, in which he warmly pleaded for freedom of public worship and religious ministrations. Locke's Letters on Toleration advocated entire religious freedom. The irrepressible tendencies to freedom of thought and speech, indicated by such publications, led to virulent controversy and political revolution, but were the means of developing a more thorough investigation of the historical beginnings of Christianity, and a more exact and scientific interpretation of its sacred books.

Progress of free thought.

Spinoza.

---

[1] Third edition with valuable additions, Leipsic, 1692, 4to.
[2] Critical History of Free Thought, p. 112. New York, 1866.

CHAPTER VIII.

EXEGESIS OF THE EIGHTEENTH CENTURY.

THE eighteenth century was notably a period of enlightenment. Biblical criticism and interpretation assumed a more sci- A period of enentific character, penetrating to the historical founda- lightenment. tions of the books of Scripture. It was an age of research, of philosophical investigation, of sceptical and rationalistic assaults upon Christianity, of extensive religious revival, and of political revolution. These exciting and often conflicting movements gave a new and marked impulse to biblical studies. The great exegetical scholars of this period, too numerous to be fully described in these pages, laid the foundations of that exact grammatico-historical interpretation which is yielding its rich and varied products in our own day.

The Cocceian school of exegesis, already described (pp. 691, 692), was ably represented at the beginning of this century by Vitringa. Campegius Vitringa, whose elaborate commentary on Isaiah is one of the most comprehensive, carefully arranged, and exhaustive specimens of biblical exposition which has ever appeared in any age. It has the faults of the Cocceian method, and occasionally runs into mystical and allegorical interpretations. It assumes such a fulness of meaning in the words of prophecy that effort is constantly made to show how much the language of Isaiah may signify. Nevertheless, it exhibits great exegetical ability; it is a storehouse of useful exposition, and has been acknowledged by all succeeding writers as a work of solid and permanent value. Vitringa was also the author of an important work on the Ancient Synagogue, and numerous other treatises on various topics of sacred literature. His son Campegius, known as "the younger," acquired some distinction by a work on Natural Theology and a volume of Sacred Dissertations.

Another distinguished writer of this school was Herman Witsius, who maintained with great learning, and on a scriptural Witsius, Lampe. basis, the Federal theology. He was surpassed, however, as an exegete, by F. A. Lampe, professor of theology at Utrecht and later at Bremen, whose very full commentary on the Gospel of John holds even to this day a high rank among the

learned expositions of that important book. A more voluminous
commentator was the learned Dutch divine, Herman
Venema, professor of theology at Frankener. His life
extended over the greater part of the eighteenth century, and he
wrote extensively upon Genesis, the Psalms (6 vols. 4to), and many
of the prophetical books.

Venema.

John Le Clerc, often called Clericus, was one of the most prolific
exegetical writers of the Netherlands. Though born
and educated at Geneva he became identified with the
Remonstrants, and spent most of his life as professor at the Arminian college of Amsterdam. Besides editing many of the Greek
and Latin classics, a new issue of Cotelerius' Patres Apostolici, the
complete works of Erasmus, and some theological treatises of Peta-
vius and Grotius, he published a French translation of the New
Testament, and a Latin translation of Hammond's Annotations on
the New Testament, with valuable additions of his own. But his
greatest exegetical work was a Latin translation of the Old Testament and commentary on the same (4 vols. fol., Amsterd., 1693–
1731). The translation is faithful, though not as close to the original
Hebrew as others that have been made, and the notes are critical,
abounding in happy and pertinent suggestions, usually clear and discriminating, but at times evincing a notable rationalistic tendency.[1]

Le Clerc.

Albert Schultens, professor of Arabic and Hebrew at Leyden,
was among the first to oppose the notion then prevalent
that Hebrew was the original language of mankind. He
has been called the father of modern Hebrew grammar, and his
labours not only contributed greatly to the advancement of oriental
learning, but also gave a decided impulse to Old Testament philology and exegesis. Besides his various works on Hebrew, Chaldee,
and Syriac grammar, and numerous philological dissertations, he
wrote commentaries on several books of the New Testament, some
of which yet remain in manuscript. His son John Jacob, and his
grandson Heinrich, were also distinguished as oriental scholars.

Schultens.

Unsurpassed by any of these as an orientalist was Reland, professor at Utrecht. He was pre-eminent for his ample
learning, painstaking accuracy, and sound judgment.
His published works are mainly in the field of biblical antiquities,
and among them the most important is his Palestine Illustrated
from Ancient Monuments, which yet remains the standard work on
Palestine before the time of the Crusades, and, so far as it goes,
cannot well be superseded.

Reland.

[1] See Meyer, Geschichte der Schrifterklärung seit der Wiederherstellung der Wissenschaften, vol. iv, pp. 441–446.

Christian Schoettgen is especially known by his Horae Hebraicae et Talmudicae on the New Testament (2 vols. 4to, Dres- Schoettgen, Meuschen.
den, 1733–42). This valuable work follows the plan of
Lightfoot's Horae Hebraicae (see above, p. 685), and aims to sup·
plement or complete it by a similar treatment of the books of the
New Testament not covered by the work of Lightfoot. Schoettgen
was also the author of a volume on the true Messiah, and a Lexicon
of the New Testament. J. G. Meuschen deserves honourable notice
for his work on the New Testament as illustrated from the Talmud
(Coburg, 1724, 4to), and for other miscellaneous contributions to
biblical literature. Surenhusius was also distinguished
for his attainments in Hebrew and rabbinical learning. Surenhusius.
His edition of the Mishna, with a Latin translation and notes, has
not been superseded, and his work on the Old Testament citations
in the New Testament, illustrated by the rabbinical writings, remains without a rival to this day. Leydecker, a theological professor at Utrecht, was famous both for his Leydecker.
proficiency in biblical and rabbinical studies and his opposition to
the systems of Cocceius and Descartes. His most useful contribution to biblical literature was a treatise on the Republic of the
Hebrews, a large folio volume (Amst., 1704), in which the antiquities of the Hebrew people are set forth in connexion with a historical narrative, arranged by epochs, and abounding with evidences
of extensive research in Jewish history and literature. Peter Wes-
seling, another professor at Utrecht, published several works on
Jewish antiquities, and dissertations on various books of Scripture.
J. C. Wolf distinguished himself in the field of Jewish literature
by his celebrated Bibliotheca Hebraea, a storehouse of information
on matters of Jewish antiquity. His Curae Philologicae on the
New Testament also contains a vast mass of sound and useful annotations. Alberti, a Dutch theologian, and Kypke, a German orientalist, wrote valuable works designed to illustrate the language of
the New Testament by means of parallel passages from Greek classic
authors. Augustine Calmet, a learned Benedictine, is known in
all Christendom by his voluminous commentaries on the Old and
New Testaments and his Dictionary of the Bible; and the French
Protestant scholar, Beausobre, acquired great distinction by his
various contributions to dogmatic and biblical theology. Pasquier
Quesnel, the devout French Catholic, is also widely known by his
Moral Reflections on the New Testament.

Noteworthy progress was made during this century in the science
of Textual Criticism. Critical editions of the Hebrew text of the
Old Testament had been published by Münster (1536), Buxtorf

(1619), and Jablonski (1699). In 1705 appeared the excellent edi-
Progress in
Textual Criti-
cism.
　　　tion of Van der Hooght, giving the Masoretic readings
in the margin, and at the end an additional collection
of various readings. J. H. Michaelis published his
edition in 1720. He collated, somewhat inaccurately, twenty-four
printed editions of the Hebrew Bible, and five manuscripts in the
library of Erfurt. Christian Reineccius, a Lutheran divine, published a Hebrew Bible in which he professed to incorporate the
results of a faithful collation of the best codices and editions; but
his work is without critical apparatus or notation. Houbigant, a
Houbigant.
　　　French priest, published in four folio volumes (Paris,
1753, 1754) a new edition, using the text of Van der
Hooght, and proposing in the margin and at the end of each volume numerous corrections. He made use of the Samaritan Pentateuch and various manuscripts accessible in the libraries of Paris.
Although the work was executed with great care, its numerous
conjectural emendations have exposed it to adverse criticism. Ben-
Kennicott.
　　　jamin Kennicott, a learned Englishman, after having published various dissertations on the state of the printed
Hebrew text of the Old Testament, entered upon the preparation
of a critical edition of it, and secured the co-operation of several
foreign scholars. Six hundred and ninety-four manuscripts were
collated, sixteen manuscripts of the Samaritan Pentateuch, and all
the most noted printed editions of the Hebrew Bible. Twenty
years of assiduous labour were given to this enterprise, and the
result was published at Oxford in two folio volumes, the first in
1776, the second in 1780. Although it was a work of herculean
labour and praiseworthy industry, the great number of various
readings furnished are comparatively unimportant, and serve to
show that no great help to the emendation of the Hebrew text can
be expected from a collation of existing manuscripts. An important supplement to Kennicott's work was published at Parma
De Rossi.
　　　(4 vols. 4to, 1784–88) by the Italian orientalist, De Rossi,
who collated anew many of the manuscripts used by
Kennicott, and nearly six hundred others, besides printed editions,
Samaritan manuscripts, and ancient versions. An edition of the
Hebrew Bible, based upon that of Reineccius, and containing the
most important of Kennicott's and De Rossi's various readings, was
published at Leipsic, 1793, by Döderlein and Meisner, and a much
more correct and elegant edition, embodying the best results of
previous collations, was published a little later by Jahn (Vienna,
1806, 4 vols. 8vo).

New Testament textual criticism was greatly promoted during

this period by the labours of Mill and Bentley in England, and Bengel and Wetstein in Germany. John Mill spent thirty years in preparing his edition of the Greek Testament, which was published at Oxford in 1707, only fourteen days before its author's death. Its various readings amount to about thirty thousand, and its prolegomena are of permanent value. In 1720 Richard Bentley, then regius professor of divinity at Cambridge, published his proposals for a new edition of the Greek and Latin Testament, which should abandon the Textus Receptus, and, making use of no authority under nine hundred years old, would "take two thousand errors out of the Pope's Vulgate, and as many out of the Protestant Pope Stephen's." He gave the last chapter of the Apocalypse in Greek and Latin as a specimen.[1] His plan was essentially that which was carried out a century later by Lachmann, and his rare attainments in classical scholarship and extensive preparations for his task would doubtless have produced a most important contribution to biblical literature. But unfortunate controversies into which he became involved frustrated this worthy enterprise, and no other important effort in that line was made again in England until the following century.

John Albert Bengel published in 1734 a critical edition of the Greek Testament together with a critical commentary, in which he enunciated his principles, and set the example of giving the testimonies both for and against the received text. Bengel is better known by his Gnomon of the New Testament, a condensed but remarkably rich and suggestive commentary, which aims, according to the titlepage, to "point out from the natural force of the words the simplicity, depth, harmony, and saving power of the divine thoughts." His principles of interpretation are in the main essentially sound, and his methods of exposition have not been greatly improved upon by any later writers.[2] In his attempt to expound prophecy, however, especially the book of Revelation, he showed defective judgment, and indulged in vain speculations.

In 1751-2 John J. Wetstein published his exceedingly valuable edition of the Greek Testament (Amst., 2 vols. fol.). His judgment as a critic was not of the highest order, but his work is of enduring value for its vast research and collation of

J. Mill.

Bentley.

Bengel.

Wetstein.

---

[1] Proposals for Printing a New Edition of the Greek Testament and St. Hierom's Latin version, with a full Answer to all the Remarks of a late Pamphleteer. Lond., 1721. 4to.

[2] An English translation of the Gnomon was published at Edinburgh, 5 vols., 1857, 1858, and another, much improved by Lewis and Vincent, at Philadelphia, 1860, 1861.

authorities, its abundant citation of Hebrew, Greek, and Latin writers, and its learned prolegomena, so indispensable to every thorough critic. With him originated the custom, now universally current, of designating the uncial manuscripts by the letters of the alphabet, and the cursive by numerals. Other scholars of note who contributed to the advancement of textual criticism were C. F. Matthæi, a professor at Moscow, Alter, a German Jesuit and professor of Greek at Vienna, who published a critical edition of the Greek Testament (1786, 1787), Adler, Birch, Moldenhauer, and Woide, who collated manuscripts and prepared valuable materials for the use of later critics. Matthæi published a valuable edition of the New Testament, Greek and Latin (12 vols., Riga, 1782–88), which was injured by its unfair attacks on Griesbach, but is conceded by later scholars to possess much merit.

John J. Griesbach improved upon all his predecessors in New Testament criticism by arranging his authorities and classifying them according to their age and place of origin. He made much of the families or "recensions" of manuscripts, a principle already recognised by Bengel and Semler, and distributed the families into Alexandrian, Western, and Byzantine. His Greek Testament appeared in parts at Halle and London in 1774–77, and again in 1796–1806 (2 vols. 8vo). It was also printed in other forms. Griesbach was unquestionably a consummate critic, and his work marks an epoch in textual criticism. He was also the author of a critical commentary on the New Testament text, and a work on New Testament hermeneutics.

The labours of these eminent critics met with much opposition, and were naturally looked upon by many with grave suspicion. The tendency of such researches seemed to unsettle the foundations of the faith, and polemic divines of the Voetian school could not be expected to favour or encourage them.

Among the English divines of this century who distinguished themselves by contributions to exegetical literature we should give a prominent place to Symon Patrick, bishop of Ely. The greater part of his life belongs to the seventeenth century. His principal literary work was a paraphrase and commentary on the historical and poetical books of the Old Testament, a learned, but eminently practical and useful, exposition, in which the meaning of the sacred writers is set forth in clear and simple style, adapted to meet the wants of ordinary readers, and at the same time evincing wide and thorough acquaintance with ancient and modern writers. Patrick's commentary was continued after his death by William Lowth, whose exposition of the prophetical books, first published in separate portions, was afterward joined with Whitby's Paraphrase and Commentary on the New Testament, Lowman's Apocalypse, and Arnald's Apocrypha, the whole forming a complete commentary on the Bible, including the Old Testament apocryphal books. William Lowth was a judicious exegete, and his work on the Prophets is one of the best commentaries of its kind. It is not strictly a critical work, but, like the notes of Patrick, exhibits thorough scholarship, and furnishes a clear and useful exposition. Whitby's Commentary on the New Testament first appeared in 1703, and has ever since maintained a high place in exegetical literature. Whitby is noted for his opposition to Mill's useful labours in textual criticism, and he ventured to defend the Textus Receptus as if it were infallible. This effort, like that of Owen against Brian Walton in the previous century, displayed much more zeal than good sense or judgment. *W. Lowth.* *Whitby.*

Robert Lowth, son of William, and bishop of London, won a deserved celebrity by the publication (in 1753) of his Sacred Poetry of the Hebrews, which has been translated into English and issued in many editions. Although the spirit and characteristics of Hebrew poetry had been pointed out by previous writers, Lowth was the first to set them forth in clear and convincing form, and this work marks a new epoch in the treatment of that subject, and has a permanent value. A later and more widely read and useful work of this distinguished prelate was his new translation of Isaiah, with a preliminary dissertation and notes. The design of this work, the author states, "is not only to give an exact and faithful representation of the words and of the sense of the prophet, by adhering closely to the letter of the text, and treading as nearly as may be in his footsteps; but, moreover, to imitate the air and manner of the author, to express the form and fashion of the composition, and to give the English reader some notion of the peculiar turn and cast of the original." This design was very worthily executed, and the work soon obtained a European fame. It was reprinted in many editions, and translated by Koppe into the German language. *Robert Lowth.*

Probably no English commentary has had a wider circulation or is better known than that of Matthew Henry. It is made up of the substance of expository lectures which were delivered by him through a period of many years, prepared by his own hand as far as the Acts of the Apostles, and completed from his manuscripts by a number of ministers. It is not a critical work, and not strictly exegetical; but it is full of practical good sense, *Henry.*

and pithy remarks which often breathe the very spirit of the sacred writers, and always tend to edification. Of a similar spirit and style, but less elaborate, is the Family Expositor of

Doddridge.

Philip Doddridge. His notes and observations display an ardent piety, a love for the truth, and a desire to profit others, but are wanting in philological merit and discriminating judgment. Greater ability and exegetical skill are manifested in the commen-

Dodd.

tary of William Dodd, who made large use of previous writings, both English and foreign. As an exposition of the true sense of the Scriptures its decided merits have always been acknowledged. Adam Clarke pronounced it the best English commentary in existence. Coke's commentary on the Bible is substantially a reprint of the work of Dodd, and published without proper acknowledgment. The well-known and widely circulated commen-

Scott.

tary of Thomas Scott belongs to this same class of practical notes and observations upon the English Bible. It has little or no value in criticism and exegesis, but, like the work of Henry, abounds with pious reflections of a homiletical character. The same may be said of Burkitt's Expository Notes on the New Testament, which has passed through many editions, and is still widely read.

John Gill, an eminent English Baptist, was especially distin-

Gill, Chandler, Pearce.

guished for his rabbinical learning. His exposition of the Old and New Testaments, in nine large octavo volumes, is a monument of industry and research, but is too diffuse to be of practical value, and sometimes runs into spiritualizing processes. Samuel Chandler, a dissenting minister, published a critical history of David, a vindication of Daniel's prophecies, a paraphrase and commentary on Joel, and also on the Epistles to the Galatians and Ephesians. Zachary Pearce wrote a valuable commentary on the Gospels and Acts of the Apostles, and a reply to Woolston's

Macknight.

Discourses on Miracles. James Macknight, a Scotch divine, won distinction as an expositor by his Harmony of the Gospels, and his new translation, paraphrase, and notes on the Epistles. This latter work, though not of the first rank, was the result of thirty years of labour, and is still worthy of attention

Campbell.

and study. George Campbell is also widely known by his valuable translation of the Four Gospels, with preliminary dissertations and critical and explanatory notes. His Dissertation on the Miracles, in reply to Hume, had an extensive

Newcome.

circulation, and was translated into several of the languages of Europe. William Newcome is known chiefly by his Harmony of the Gospels. He also prepared a new version of Ezekiel and the Minor Prophets, with critical notes. His exegetical writings show good judgment, and have met with deserved commendation. Blayney, professor at Oxford, was noted for his knowledge of Hebrew. His princi- **Blayney, Green, and Wells.** pal writings are a dissertation on the Seventy Weeks of Daniel, and a new version of Jeremiah, Lamentations, and Zechariah, with critical and philological notes. William Green was the author of new translations of Isaiah, the Psalms, and other poetical parts of the Old Testament, accompanied with notes. Edward Wells, less widely known than the writers just mentioned, published in the early part of the eighteenth century a revised translation of the New Testament, with a paraphrase and annotations. He was also the author of an exposition of Daniel, and a historical geography of the Old and New Testaments. Samuel Wesley wrote a history of the Old and New Testaments, and a Latin commen- **Wesley.** tary on the Book of Job. John Wesley, his more famous son, prepared and published a volume of Explanatory Notes on the New Testament, which has been widely circulated among his followers, and is recognized as one of the doctrinal standards of Methodism. He gives the Authorized Version, slightly revised, and for many of his short and suggestive comments acknowledges his great indebtedness to Bengel's Gnomon and Doddridge's Family Expositor. His notes on the Old Testament are too meager to be of any considerable value.

The devout and useful cultivation of biblical studies, indicated by such works as those mentioned above, furnish an **English Deism, French Infidelity, and German Rationalism.** interesting evidence of the faith and piety of multitudes at a time when strong sceptical assaults were being made upon the doctrines of revealed religion. It was during this century that English deism reached its highest power and passed into decline. French infidelity followed in its wake, and led to fanaticism and political anarchy; and afterward, at slower pace, the more refined and scholarly rationalism of Germany made its advance, and affected the religious thought of all Protestant Christendom. To trace these currents of religious life and thought, and note the political, philosophical, and dogmatical discussions of this eventful period, falls not within the line of our purpose. And yet to understand the origin of the exact and searching methods of Scripture exegesis which were introduced in the latter part of the eighteenth, and have been carried to still greater perfection in the nineteenth, century, one needs to cast at least a hasty glance over the growth of English deism, French unbelief, and German speculative thought, which unquestionably

provoked and prompted a more thorough study of the Scriptures,
both in Germany and England.

We have already noticed the influence exerted by Spinoza on
Deistical writ- religious thought (p. 694). His views on miracles re-
ers. ceived another form of presentation in Blount's Life of
Apollonius of Tyana, in which the miracles of Christ were made to
suffer disparagement by an invidious comparison with those of the
Pythagorean philosopher. The writings of Toland and Lord
Shaftesbury aim to assert the supremacy of reason, and to ground
morality on expediency and natural right. Collins treated more
directly the interpretation of Scripture, and in his Discourse on the
Grounds and Reasons of the Christian Religion (London, 1724)
maintained that the Jewish expectation of the Messiah arose only
a short time before the birth of Jesus, and that the New Testament
citations of Old Testament Messianic prophecy are merely fanciful
accommodations of the Hebrew books, and at best mystical and
allegorical portraitures of Christian truth. The logic of this work
was to show that Christian evidences drawn from prophecy are
invalid. Woolston's Discourses on the Miracles were another critical assault upon the historical verity of the New Testament, and
it was therein boldly asserted that the narratives of our Lord's
miracles were full of extravagance and unreasonable statements,
but may nevertheless be understood as figurative representations of
spiritual experience. " The history of Jesus, as recorded in the evangelists," says Woolston, " is an emblematical representation of his
spiritual life in the soul of man, and his miracles are figures of his
mysterious operations. The four gospels are in no part a literal
story, but a system of mystical philosophy or theology." [1] Matthew
Tindal laboured to show the essential perfection of natural religion,
and denied both the necessity and the possibility of a supernatural
revelation. These positions, together with much adverse criticism
of the Scripture records, were vigorously maintained in his celebrated work entitled Christianity as Old as the Creation, or the
Gospel a Republication of the Religion of Nature. [2] The works of
Morgan and Chubb follow much in the same line, and in a measure
supplement the arguments of Tindal. The philosophical writings

---

[1] A Discourse on the Miracles of our Saviour, p. 65. Sixth edition. London, 1729.

[2] This was not only the most important work that deism had yet produced, composed with care, and bearing the marks of thoughtful study of the chief contem
porary arguments, Christian as well as deist, but derives an interest from the circum
stance. that it was the book to which more than to any other single work Bishop
Butler's Analogy was designed as the reply. — Farrar, Critical History of Free
Thought, p. 138.

of Bolingbroke and Hume tended likewise to unsettle all faith in divine revelation.

The writings of the English deists were answered by a great number of divines of various scholarship and ability. Anti-deistical Chief among them were Chandler, Sherlock, Butler— writers. whose immortal Analogy must ever stand as one of the grandest monuments of human thought—John Conybeare, Leland, Waterland, and Warburton—whose celebrated work on the Divine Legation of Moses remains to this day an invaluable help to the study of the Pentateuch. In fact no period in the history of Christianity witnessed in so short a space such a number and variety of works on the evidences of revealed religion as that of the rise and decline of English deism.

The relation of English deism to French infidelity is very obvious. The philosophy of Descartes and Spinoza had, French unbe-indeed, prepared the way in France as well as else- lief. where for the progress of sceptical thought, and the sensational philosophy of Locke, modified and adapted to the French mind by Condillac, tended strongly to materialism and unbelief. The acute and witty Voltaire, for three years an exile in England, appropriated such products of the deistical writers as served his purpose, and in a superficial and flippant, but taking, style, disseminated them with most demoralizing effect among the French people. The encyclopædic Diderot, and his immediate associates, the more cultivated and philosophical Rousseau, and, later, the brilliant Volney, contributed their influence to the same destructive movement, and the welcome which Frederick the Great gave to men of this class, making the Prussian court at Berlin a place of refuge for them when persecuted at home, discloses the parental relation of French unbelief to German rationalism. In tracing the rise of the latter, however, we need to go back a little and note the origin and progress of other influences.

A new impulse was given to biblical studies in Germany by the founding of the University of Halle in 1694. This was Spener. due mainly to the influence of Spener, the father of Pietism. The Protestant Churches had fallen into a cold, formal orthodoxy, and the symbols and sacraments took precedence of scriptural knowledge and personal piety. As early as 1675 Spener had urged, in his Pia Desideria, that all Christian doctrine should be sought in a faithful study of the Holy Scriptures rather than in the symbols of the Church, and that the living truths of God's word should be brought home to the hearts of the people. Associated with him at Halle was A. H. Francke, who had previously

become noted at Leipsic by his exegetical lectures. Both these
men were eminent as preachers and abundant in pulpit
ministrations. Francke's exegetical lectures extended
over the books of the Old and New Testaments, and he published
treatises on the interpretation of Scripture, and on methods of theological study. These noble leaders of Pietism maintained that it
is the first duty of the theologian to ascertain the true meaning of
the Scriptures, not from traditional beliefs, but from a critical and
grammatical study of the original texts. "The theological instruction of Francke and his coadjutors in the University of Halle,"
says Hurst, "was very influential. During the first thirty years
of its history six thousand and thirty-four theologians were trained
within its walls, not to speak of the multitudes who received a
thorough academic and religious instruction in the Orphan House.
The Oriental Theological College, established in connexion with the
university, promoted the study of biblical languages, and originated
the first critical edition of the Hebrew Bible." [1]

Francke.

One of the most learned men of Germany was J. H. Michaelis, who
was associated with Francke in establishing the Oriental Theological College of Halle, and was editor of the
critical Hebrew Bible above referred to. He devoted
thirty years of labour to the preparation of this work, and collated
the best printed editions and a number of Hebrew manuscripts.
Along with it was published his Philologico-Exegetical Annotations
on the Hagiography (3 vols. 4to, Halle, 1720). C. B. Michaelis,
nephew of the preceding, was professor at Halle from 1713 to 1764,
during which time he published numerous treatises on Hebrew philology, biblical exegesis, and the various readings of the Greek
Testament. He assisted his uncle in the preparation of his Annotations on the Hagiography. His son, J. D. Michaelis, became
more famous as a theologian and biblical scholar than any other of
this celebrated family. He planned the expedition into the Orient
which was executed by Carsten Niebuhr, and contributed greatly
to our knowledge of the Arabian peninsula. He published grammars of the Hebrew, Chaldee, Syriac, and Arabic languages, and
various other philological treatises, together with valuable works
on history, geography, chronology, and Jewish antiquities. He
wrote an Introduction to the New Testament, and commentaries on
Ecclesiastes and First Maccabees. His greatest and best known
work is his Mosaisches Recht (6 vols., 1770–75), or Commentaries on
the Laws of Moses, of which an English translation has been published by Alexander Smith (4 vols., London, 1814). With all his

The Michaelis family of bibli-cal scholars.

[1] History of Rationalism, p. 97. New York, 1865.

greatness as a scholar and critic he imbibed many of the rationalistic notions of his time, and seems to have been deficient in religious convictions and experience. He was a fair specimen of the incipient neology, and retained the outward forms of orthodoxy, but went not to the extremes of rationalism. John F. and John G. Michaelis, two other members of this family, were also distinguished for their labours in biblical science.

John Lawrence von Mosheim, who was pre-eminent for his contributions to ecclesiastical history, and has been deservedly honoured for placing Church history on a truer Mosheim. scientific basis than it had ever attained before, was also the author of several sound and useful exegetical works. His exposition of First Corinthians and the two Epistles to Timothy, his Sacred Observations (Amst., 1721), and critical treatment of select passages of the New Testament, evince rare powers of criticism. He showed himself a master in nearly every department of theology.

John Benjamin Koppe, professor of theology at Göttingen, published numerous treatises on biblical subjects, and commenced, near the close of this century, a critical edition Koppe. of the New Testament. He lived to publish only two volumes, embracing Romans, Galatians, Ephesians, and Thessalonians. His plan was to furnish a revised Greek text (which agrees closely with that of Griesbach), prolegomena to each book, critical and philological annotations, and excursus on difficult passages. The work was continued on the same plan by Heinrichs and Pott, the former publishing the Acts, Colossians, Timothy, Titus, and Philemon, and the latter the Epistles of Peter and Jude.

Probably the most distinguished name in the history of exegesis in the eighteenth century is that of John Augustus Ernesti, whose Institutio interpretis Novi Testamenti Ernesti. (Lips., 1761), or Principles of New Testament Interpretation, has been accepted as a standard textbook on hermeneutics by four generations of biblical scholars. "He is regarded," says Hagenbach, "as the founder of a new exegetical school, whose principle simply was that the Bible must be rigidly explained according to its own language, and, in this explanation, it must neither be bribed by any external authority of the Church, nor by our own feeling, nor by a sportive and allegorizing fancy—which had frequently been the case with the mystics—nor, finally, by any philosophical system whatever. He here united in the main with Hugo Grotius, who had laid down similar principles in the seventeenth century. Ernesti was a philologian. He had occupied himself just as enthusiastical'y with the ancient classics of Rome and Greece as with the Bible, and claimed that the same exegetical laws should be observed in the one case as in the other. He was perfectly right in this respect; even the Reformers wished the same thing. His error here was, perhaps, in overlooking too much the fact that, in order to perceive the religious truths of the Scriptures, we must not only understand the meaning of a declaration in its relations to language and history, but that we must also spiritually appropriate it by feelingly transposing ourselves to it, and by seeking to understand it from itself. Who will deny that, in order to understand the epistles of the Apostle Paul, we must adopt from the very outset a mode of view different from that which we would employ in order to understand the epistles of Cicero, since the circle of ideas of these two men is very different? Religious writings can be perfectly understood only by an anticipating spirit, which peers through the logical and grammatical web of the thoughts to the depth below. . . . The principle that we must expound the Scriptures like every other book could at least be so misapprehended that it might be placed in the same rank with the other writings of antiquity, and the assistance of the Holy Spirit, which is the only guide to the depths of the Scriptures, be regarded as superfluous. As for Ernesti personally, he was orthodox, like Michaelis and Mosheim. He even defended the Lutheran view of the Lord's Supper. And yet these men, and others of like character, are distinguished from their orthodox predecessors by their insisting upon independence, by struggling for sobriety, and, if you will allow, for dryness also. But, with all this, they were further distinguished from their predecessors by a certain freedom and mildness of judgment which men had not been accustomed to find in theologians. Without any desire or wish on their own part they effected a transition to a new theological method of thought, which soon passed beyond the limits of their own labours." [1]

Ernesti was also the author of a volume of exegetical essays entitled Opuscula philologica-critica (Amst., 1762), and the Neue Theologische Bibliothek (14 volumes), which greatly promoted the interests of theological literature in Germany. The principles so ably set forth by Ernesti were further elaborated toward the

K. A. G. Keil. close of this century by Karl Augustus Keil, whose various contributions to biblical hermeneutics (comp. p. 203) did much to prepare the way for the solid and enduring methods of exegesis which are now generally prevalent in Germany, England, and America. The refined and gifted Herder did much for

[1] History of the Church in the Eighteenth and Nineteenth Centuries, vol. i, pp. 259–261. English translation by Hurst. New York, 1869.

the cause of biblical science by emphasising the human element in
the Scriptures. In his treatise on the Spirit of Hebrew   Herder.
Poetry (Dessau, 1782) he aimed to exhibit the real
beauties, the deep poetical fervour, and glowing oriental imagery
of the Old Testament Scriptures. In other publications he traced
the influence of Parseeism on the biblical writers, expounded the
Apocalypse as having been fulfilled in the destruction of Jerusalem,
and dwelt with peculiar pleasure on the Epistles of James and Jude
as the productions of real brothers of the Lord Jesus. Though influenced by the rationalism prevalent at the court of Weimar,[1] his
labours in the department of biblical literature were far more useful than harmful. It was well to have attention called to the human as well as to the divine elements in the Holy Scriptures.

Contemporaneous with the above-mentioned critics and scholars
were others of a more decided rationalistic bent, and   Wolf and
both the old rigid orthodoxy and the declining Pietism   Lange.
of the period met with opposing tides of thought. The philosophy
of Christian von Wolf, which was but a modification and popular
presentation of the theories of Leibnitz, introduced a disturbing
element at Halle. It found a strong opponent in Joachim Lange,
an intimate friend of Francke, who was also noted for his comments
on most of the books of the Bible. The later Pietists, revolting
from the Wolfian claims for reason, opposed to it a blind emotional
faith, which speedily deteriorated into superstitious mys-   Degenerate
ticism and extravagance. Their capricious methods of   Pietism.
interpretation are represented in the Berleburg Bible, which unites
a running exposition with a new translation, and assumes to set
forth the hidden spiritual sense of the Word. Such mystical trifling
with the natural sense of Scripture could not fail to provoke reaction, which might easily run to an opposite extreme. In 1735 the
Wertheim Bible appeared, the translation and notes of which were
a manifest attempt to interpret the Scriptures according to the principles of the Wolfian philosophy. Baumgarten, a disciple of Wolf,
and his successor at Halle, wrote several critical and exegetical
works, and prepared the way for the rise of German rationalism,

[1] At the end of the last century there was one spot which became the very focus of
intellectual life. The court of Karl August, at Weimar, insignificant in political importance, was great in the history of the human mind. There were gathered most of
the mighty spirits of the golden age of German literature—Herder, Wieland, Goethe,
Schiller, Jean Paul: a constellation of intellect unequalled since the court of Ferrara
in the days of Alphonso. The influence made itself felt in the adjacent university of
Jena, and this little seminary became from that time for about twenty years, until
the foundation of Berlin, the first university in Germany.—Farrar, Critical History of
Free Thought, p. 228.

of which Semler, his pupil, is commonly regarded as more directly the father.

John Solomon Semler was born and reared under the influences of Pietism, but from early childhood showed little inclination to adopt its peculiar dialect and methods. He went to Halle the year before Lange died, and there received many kind attentions from the Pietists; but he declined to follow their counsels, and soon became the favourite scholar of Baumgarten. Early recognising the conflict between his subjective notions and the current dogmas of the Church, he began to distinguish between religion and theology. One's private religion, he fancied, might be largely a matter of personal taste, and should be cultivated as individual feeling and the dictates of reason prompted. In the elaboration of his views he propounded the so-called Accommodation theory of expounding the Scriptures (see above, p. 166), and distinguished between what is local and temporary and what is universal and permanent in the divine revelation. Large portions of the Scriptures, including many entire books, were set aside as of no authority. Observing that Samaritans, Jews, and the Septuagint translators differed in the number of books which they accepted as sacred, he rejected the traditional idea of an inspired canon of Scripture, and made reason and his own judgment the test by which to determine what was and what was not inspired. Much in the Bible was regarded as purely ephemeral, a mere accommodation to the prejudices and barbarism of ancient times. The doctrine of angels and demons was but an accommodation to prevailing errors. Most of these views were set forth in Semler's various publications on biblical interpretation and the free use of the canon, works abounding with sound and excellent observations, but so mixed with pernicious errors that, in other hands, they were made instruments for the destruction of all faith in divine revelation. Semler was not the founder of a school, but his writings gave a mighty impulse to the critical methods of interpretation which were then becoming current. He scattered doubts and set afloat many sceptical notions. "By the critical inquiry into which he was constantly drawn further and further," observes Hagenbach, "he doubted much which had hitherto stood fast and had lately passed as authentic, and threw much overboard which it was afterward believed necessary to gather carefully up again." [1]

Semler's beautiful piety preserved him from the evil effects of his own theories, and he himself was surprised at the use others made of his critical principles. There were

Semler.

Growth of Rationalism.

[1] Hist. of the Church in the Eighteenth and Nineteenth Centuries, vol. i, p. 266.

men in Germany who were thoroughly infected with the leaven of English deism and French infidelity, and they were not slow to appropriate Semler's destructive methods for the propagation of neology and unbelief among the people. Of this class were Edelmann and Bahrdt, whose writings breathed the most offensive spirit of hostility to all accepted Christian doctrine. The Allgemeine Deutsche Bibliothek (Universal German Library), projected and managed by Nicolai (1765–92), served as a most powerful organ for the dissemination of rationalistic opinions. The publication of the Wolfenbüttel Fragments by Lessing (1774–78) contributed still more to the spread of scepticism and infidelity. They extolled the deists, glorified human reason, and treated the miracles of the Bible as a string of incredible myths and legends, which an intelligent age ought to reject. To the same class of publications belonged Teller's Wörterbuch des neuen Testament (Lexicon of the New Testament), which assumed to define the ideas rather than the words of Scripture. Repent, according to this authority, means "to become better;" to convert is "to restore to a righteous disposition;" and atonement signifies "the union of men among themselves in one religion." It was a worthy companion of the Wertheim translation of the Bible.

Thus it appears that at the close of the eighteenth century rationalism was dominant over the leading minds of Germany. Here and there a voice was heard protest- Scholarly form of Rationalism. ing against these innovations in theology, and occasionally a bold writer was suppressed by the civil power. A great diversity of views appeared. "The position of rationalism during the last quarter of the eighteenth century," says Hurst, "was surrounded with circumstances of the most conflicting nature. Had it been advocated by a few more such ribald characters as Bahrdt, its career would soon have been terminated from the mere want of respectability. But had it assumed a more serious phase, and become the protégé of such pious men as Semler was at heart, there would have been no limit to the damage it might inflict upon the cause of Protestantism. And there were indications favourable to either result. However, by some plan of fiendish malice, scepticism received all the support it could ask from the learned, the powerful, and the ambitious. Here and there around the horizon could be seen some rising literary star that, for the hour, excited universal attention. His labour was to impugn the contents of the Scriptures and insinuate against the moral purity of the writers themselves. Another candidate for theological glory appeared, and reproached the style of the inspired record. A third came

vauntingly forward with his geographical discoveries and scientific
data, and raised the accommodation theory so many more stories
higher than Semler had left it, that it almost threatened to fall of
its own weight."[1]

At the close of this century we meet with a name that towers
above most others of his time, and marks an epoch in the
history of philosophical criticism. Immanuel Kant contributed little directly to biblical exegesis, but his philosophical
principles have influenced three generations of biblical critics. His
attempt to construct a system of moral interpretation has been
sufficiently noticed in a previous part of this volume (p. 167). The
relation of his philosophy to religion and the Scriptures is thus
concisely stated by Farrar: "He detected, as he supposed, innate
forms of thought in the mental structure, which form the condition
under which knowledge is possible. When he applied his system
to give a philosophy of ethics and religion, he asserted nobly the
law of duty written in the heart, but identified it with religion.
Religious ideas were regarded as true regulatively, not specula-
tively. Revelation was reunited with reason by being resolved into
the natural religion of the heart. Accordingly, the moral effect of
this philosophy was to expel the French materialism and illuminism,
and to give depth to the moral perceptions: its religious effect was
to strengthen the appeal to reason and the moral judgment as the
test of religious truth; to render miraculous communication of
moral instruction useless, if not absurd; and to reawaken the attempt, which had been laid aside since the Wolfian philosophy, of
endeavoring to find a philosophy of religion. From this time in
German theology we find the existence of the twofold movement:
the critical one, the lawful descendant of Semler, examining the
historic revelation; and the philosophical one, the offshoot of the
system of Kant, seeking for a philosophy of religion."[2]

The development of speculative philosophy through Jacobi, Her-
bart, Fichte, Schelling, and Hegel exerted a profound influence
upon the critical minds of Germany, and affected the exegetical
style and methods of many of the great biblical scholars of the
nineteenth century. The influence of this philosophy has tended
to make the German mind intensely subjective, and has led many
theologians to view both history and doctrines in their relations
to some preconceived principle rather than in their practical bearings on human life.

[1] History of Rationalism, pp. 148, 149. New York, 1865.
[2] Critical History of Free Thought, pp. 229, 230.

CHAPTER IX.

EXEGESIS OF THE NINETEENTH CENTURY.

THE progress of biblical science during the present century has been conspicuous above that of any former period of its history. The century opened rich with the results of previous philological and theological research. The *Marked progress of knowledge.* long-buried treasures of Hebrew and classical literature were made accessible to all scholars. Questions of politics, philosophy, and religion began to be sifted with a freedom and fulness of discussion unknown in Europe before. Political revolutions and the widespread popular demand for liberty of thought and speech prompted to the acquisition of knowledge, and gave encouragement to all educational and literary enterprises. New departments of literature and science were gradually developed; new inventions and improvements on old ones greatly facilitated the means of scientific research; geological investigation, comparative philology, the deciphering of ancient monumental inscriptions, and uncovering of entire libraries of oriental history and literature contemporary with the Hebrew Scriptures; the exploration of Bible lands, the discovery and collation of ancient manuscripts, and the principles and processes of textual criticism have become so many distinct sciences, and are now prosecuted with enthusiasm by the ablest men of Christendom.

At the beginning of the century rationalism had well nigh taken possession of the best minds of Germany. Eichhorn succeeded J. D. Michaelis at the university of Göttingen, and lectured and wrote extensively on oriental literature and the exegesis of the Old and New Testaments. His Introduction to the Scriptures and his commentary on the Apocalypse were remarkable for their bold rationalistic criticism. Explicit statements of the sacred writers were set aside or explained away by the most arbitrary assumptions. The Mosaic history was treated as consisting largely of ancient sagas or legends. Its miraculous narratives were explained as the vivid portrayal of natural events which was alleged to be characteristic of all ancient records of primeval and unhistoric times. A happy accident or a joyous thought was wont to be conceived and spoken of as the appearance or the salutation of an angel. The smoke, fire, and quaking of Mount Sinai (Exod. xix, 18) were merely a fire kindled by Moses himself for the purpose of impressing the people with awe, and the happy coincidence of a terrible thunderstorm. Eichhorn insisted that all ancient history, whether Jewish or pagan, should be treated alike, and that all miraculous elements should be eliminated by rational methods of interpretation. This naturalistic method of expounding the Scriptures was car-

Paulus.

ried out in greater detail and applied with a more rigid consistency to the gospel narratives by Paulus, professor at Jena, and subsequently at Heidelberg. His philologico-critical and historical commentary on the New Testament is one of the most notable attempts on record to explain away every supernatural event narrated in the Christian Scriptures (see above, p. 168). Similar views were advocated about the same period by Henke, Ammon, Wegscheider, and the Swiss rationalist, Schulthess.

About this time, also, the rationalistic criticism of the Pentateuch

Criticism of the Pentateuch.

took a notable turn, and inaugurated a controversy which has continued to the present time. The documentary. hypothesis of the composition of Genesis, propounded as early as 1753 by Astruc, maintained that the book is made up of twelve documents of different authorship, of which the two principal ones are the Elohistic and Jehovistic, conspicuous for the use they make of the divine names. A similar theory, generally known as the fragmentary hypothesis, was set forth with much ability by J. S. Vater in his Commentary on the Pentateuch (Halle, 1802–b). According to this theory the whole Pentateuch consists of a number of fragments loosely strung together. Its nucleus was a collection of laws made in the time of David and Solomon, to which a variety of other fragments was added between the time of Josiah and the Babylonian exile. Essentially the same hypothesis was maintained by Hartmann in his Linguistic Introduction to the Study of the Books of the Old Testament (Rostock, 1818). These older theories were gradually superseded by that commonly called the supplementary hypothesis, which recognises one original fundamental document to which various interpolations and supplements were subsequently added. The most prominent advocates of this theory were Stähelin, Tuch, Lengerke, Von Bohlen, and De Wette.

In connexion with this free handling of the Pentateuch the myth-

Mythical interpretations.

ical interpretation of the biblical narratives gradually developed. The philologist Heyne maintained that the early history of all nations is enwrapped in myths; Semler suggested that the stories of Samson and Esther were myths, and Gabler explained the account of the fall of man in much the same way. The Mosaic narrative of creation was placed on a par with the cosmogonies of the heathen world. In 1820 G. L. Bauer published his Hebrew Mythology of the Old and New Testaments, and argued therein that it is highly inconsistent and unphilosophical to allow the mythical element in the early history of all other nations, and yet deny it in the Hebrew records. Other writers put forth similar views, and by one and another myths were conceived and classified as historical, philosophical, and poetical, according to the manner of their origin and development. But it was the skilful hand of David Friedrich Strauss that gave fullest presentation of the mythical interpretation, and boldly applied it to the gospel history. The work of Strauss. His subjection to the Hegelian philosophy, and the consequent treatment of scriptural narratives in accord with foregone conclusions, are apparent from the following passage at the beginning of his celebrated Life of Jesus: " The divine cannot so have happened (not immediately, not in forms so rude); or, that which has so happened cannot have been divine. And if a reconciliation be sought by means of interpretation, it will be attempted to prove either that the divine did not manifest itself in the manner related, which is to deny the historical validity of the ancient Scriptures; or, that the actual occurrences were not divine, which is to explain away the absolute contents of these books."[1] With this dilemma as a governing principle, the grammatico-historical interpretation of miraculous narratives became essentially impossible, and Strauss proceeded to construct with great learning and ingenuity the mythical interpretation, which we have sufficiently outlined in a former part of this work (pp. 168–170). The publication of Strauss' Leben Jesu (in 1835) produced a most wonderful sensation, and marked a new epoch in biblical and theological criticism. Scarcely a work on the gospel history has since appeared in which there is not some notice taken of its propositions. The replies to it from various divines were almost numberless, and constitute a special department of theological literature.

A few years after the work of Strauss appeared, C. H. Weisse published his Evangelical History, critically and philosophically treated (2 vols., Lpz., 1838). Its method of C. H. Weisse. treating the gospel narratives, while adopting substantially the principles of Strauss, might not improperly be called the idealistic. Persons and events are regarded as symbolical representations of great religious truths. John the Baptist represents the whole body of Jewish prophets in their relations to Christ. The genealogies of Jesus in Matthew and Luke are merely expressive of the outward historical connexion of the old Israelitish monarchy and the Christian

[1] Introduction, § 1.

system of salvation. In short, the whole gospel history is but an ideal representation of the divine process by which God reveals himself subjectively in man through all periods of the world's history, and the person and character of Jesus exhibits this revelation in highest perfection. And yet all this wonderful portraiture of divine truth was the product, as in the mythical theory, of the imagination and loving devotion of the followers of Jesus, upon whom his personal excellence and magnetic power as a healer of diseases had made a profound impression.

This philosophical method of developing history out of the inner religious consciousness of an imaginative and uncritical

Bruno Baur. age was carried out to even a greater extreme by Bruno Baur in his Critique of John's Gospel (1840), and his three volumes on the Synoptic Gospels (1841–42). He boldly denied the existence of Messianic expectations at the time of Jesus' birth, and in the same reckless and arbitrary way assumed to set aside any statements of the gospel history which appeared inconsistent with his speculative theories.

The founder of what is commonly known as the new Tübingen school of theology was F. C. Baur, who, before the

F. C. Baur and the Tübingen School. appearance of Strauss' Life of Jesus, had attacked the authenticity of some of the books of the New Testament. In 1835 he published a treatise on the Pastoral Epistles in which he maintained that Galatians, Corinthians, and Romans were the only genuine productions of the Apostle Paul. In 1845 appeared his work on Paul the Apostle of Jesus Christ, and in 1847 his Critical Examination of the Canonical Gospels. In these and other works of similar character Baur endeavoured to show that the New Testament books were polemical documents written in the interest of different factions of the early Church. He especially assumed to discover in these documents a hostility between the Petrine and Pauline parties. These parties continued their antagonism until the middle of the second century, when the Petrine or Judaic faction yielded some of its rigidity, and by mutual concessions the two parties became united in one catholic Church. Other theologians belonging to the Tübingen school, and agreeing with Baur in his main line of argument, though arriving at conclusions somewhat different from each other, are Edward Zeller, Albert Schwegler, Köstlin, Hilgenfeld, and Volkmar. These writers, following the Hegelian philosophy, disallow any truly miraculous events in the gospel history, regard Christianity as an offshoot of Judaism, and deny the authenticity of all the books of the New Testament except the four Pauline epistles named above.

The rationalistic school of French critics has been led in recent years by such men as Reville, Scherer, Pecaut, Rouge- French critical mont, and Colani. More famous than any of these is school. Ernest Renan, whose Life of Jesus (Paris, 1863) is a brilliant portraiture of the gospel narrative according to naturalistic principles. The man Jesus lived, and did many extraordinary things, but was a most susceptible Jewish enthusiast, who gradually became possessed with the idea that he was to be the chosen Redeemer of Israel. His disciples participated in his magnetic enthusiasm, and, after his death, magnified his work, and constructed out of current legends and their own imagination the marvellous stories which we now find in the gospel records.

Such bold and reckless criticism could not fail to call out earnest and powerful answers, and there have not been want- German Rationalism promoted more thorough investigation. ing, during the progress of the century, men of ample learning and ability to meet the new issues and defend the faith of the Church. The entire rationalistic movement in biblical criticism, from Semler onward, served to develop a more thorough and scientific treatment of the inspired writings than they had ever before received. Scholars of all parties were led to examine afresh the earliest sources of history, and to study with strictest care the original texts of the Bible and all questions bearing on their genuineness and authenticity.

The man who more than any other initiated a reaction against the rationalism current at the beginning of this cen- Schleiermacher. tury was Schleiermacher, one of the first professors of the University of Berlin (1810). And yet Schleiermacher was far from orthodox in his teaching. He was neither strictly evangelical nor rationalistic, but combined in himself elements of both. "Gifted with an acute and penetrating intellect, capable of grappling with the highest problems of philosophy and the minutest details of criticism, he could sympathize with the intellectual movement of the old rationalism; while his fine moral sensibility, the depth and passionateness of his sympathy, the exquisite delicacy of his taste, and the brilliancy of his imagination, were in perfect harmony with the literary and æsthetic revival which was commencing. German to the very soul, he possessed an enthusiastic sympathy with the great literary movements of his age, philosophical, classical, or romantic."[1] His most useful service was to expose the fallacy that religion is attainable by reason, or is any way dependent on culture. He showed that vital piety is a matter of the heart, and consists in the consciousness of God in the soul, and of

[1] Farrar, Critical History of Free Thought, p. 242.

absolute dependence upon him. This doctrine was a potent antidote to the current rationalism which would bring everything in
religion and theology to the test of reason. Schleiermacher's principal works are devoted to dogmatic and practical theology. But
he published a commentary on the Epistles to Timothy (1807), and
lectured on hermeneutics and biblical introduction. In his methods
of interpretation he moved much in the ways of the rationalists.
His doctrine of inspiration was loose, and his view of miracles
doubtful. He treated the Old Testament Scriptures as having no
divine authority, and as being important chiefly because of their
historical relations to Christianity. His disciples, accordingly,
branched off into different schools, and in their attitude toward
evangelical doctrine were negative or positive, or followed a middle
course between the two, and each school could appeal in defence of
its positions to the teachings of the master whom they all honoured.
Schleiermacher founded no school of theology, but he kindled an
influence that affected all schools. "Whether we view him," says
Farrar, "in his own natural gifts and susceptibilities; in the aim of
his life; in his mixture of reason and love, of philosophy and criticism, of enthusiasm and wisdom, of orthodoxy and heresy; or regard the transitory character of his work, the permanence of his
influence, Church history offers no parallel to him since the days
of Origen." [1]

In connexion with Schleiermacher we should also mention the
celebrated Neander, the father of modern Church his-
Neander. tory, whose more profound religious experience and
more evangelical tone of expression went far toward counteracting
the progress of rationalism. When the Prussian government proposed to forbid the introduction of Strauss' Life of Jesus into its
dominion Neander strenuously opposed the measure, and urged
that works of that kind must be met and nullified, not by force,
but by argument. In 1837 he published his Life of Jesus Christ,
which was, to a great extent, a reply to the Tübingen professor.
This work has, from the time of its appearance, held a high place
in exegetical literature. It treats the alleged difficulties of the
gospel narratives with a candour which commands respect and
admiration. Neander's earlier work on the Planting and Training of the Christian Church is also a valuable contribution to
the exposition of the New Testament. He also wrote practical
commentaries on the Epistle to the Philippians, the Epistle of
James, and the First Epistle of John. Most of his works have been
translated into English.

[1] Critical History of Free Thought, pp. 243, 244.

In critical tact and exegetical ability William M. L. De Wette probably stands unsurpassed by any biblical scholar of modern times. His views and critical methods were De Wette. formed under the influence of such theological teachers as Paulus, Gabler, and Griesbach, and are essentially rationalistic. He rejected, however, the naturalistic method of explaining the biblical miracles, and anticipated Strauss in many of the prominent positions of the mythical interpretation; but he showed greater regard for the religious element of Scripture, and never indulged in light and disrespectful insinuations hostile to its divine character and authority. In his Introductions to the Old and New Testaments he subjected the sacred books to the keenest scrutiny, condensing a vast amount of material into small space, and exhibiting in the arrangement and construction of his work the hand of a master. His commentary on the Psalms has ever been esteemed as a model of exegetical taste and judgment, and has been issued in several editions. His new translation of the Bible is conceded by eminent judges to be one of the most finished and accurate versions which has ever been made in any language. His crowning work was his condensed Exegetical Handbook of the New Testament, in which his exquisite taste and remarkable exegetical tact appear in highest perfection. Despite the rationalism everywhere apparent, one cannot but be deeply impressed with the skill and ability of the writer. "One thing, at least," says Stuart, "can be truly said of De Wette as a commentator, especially as he appears in his latest works of interpretation, this is, that he rarely introduces anything but the simple principles of exegesis and philology in order to establish his views of the meaning of Scripture. All creeds and confessions are left out of sight, and the text, the context, and tenor of discourse, and peculiarities of idiom, and matters of antiquity that have respect to various objects, opinions, and circumstances, are ever resorted to as the only reliable guides on which an interpreter can depend. Impartially, for the most part, has he dealt with all these exegetical subsidiaries. And that he brings to the decision of any exegetical question a rare skill in detecting the nicer shades of language, a highly cultivated aesthetical feeling, and great discrimination in judging of the real and logical course of thought, no intelligent reader of him can deny or even doubt."[1]

Gottfried Friedrich Lücke was an intimate friend of De Wette, and shared largely in his theological opinions. He was Lücke. professor of theology at Bonn, and subsequently at Göttingen. Besides numerous valuable articles in various German

[1] Bibliotheca Sacra for 1848, pp. 264, 265.

periodicals he wrote a treatise on New Testament hermeneutics, and an elaborate series of works on the writings of John. He was a most learned and skilful exegete, and worthy of the love and friendship of men like Schleiermacher and De Wette.

Many other exegetes, belonging essentially to the critical and philological school of De Wette, flourished during the first half of our century. Among these the two Rosenmüllers attained much distinction, although in exegetical skill and critical acuteness they were much inferior to De Wette. John G. Rosenmüller was a popular preacher and a theologian of indefatigable literary activity. Among his numerous publications his History of Biblical Interpretation in the Christian Church (5 vols., 1795-1814), and his Scholia on the New Testament, attained a well-deserved celebrity. The former work brings the history of interpretation down to the time of the Reformation; his Scholia are philological and simple, but not of a high order. E. F. C. Rosenmüller, son of the preceding, was distinguished for his attainments in oriental languages, and his Scholia on the Old Testament (23 vols., Lpz., 1788-1835). His proficiency in Semitic philology, extensive knowledge of the Orient, and general good judgment, combined to make him an expositor of no small merit. His larger Scholia make too prolix a work for the ordinary student. A large proportion of it is a compilation of the opinions of others, and too often the reader is at a loss to know what were the views of the author himself. The compendium of this work (6 vols., Lpz., 1828-36), made by Lechner under the supervision of the author, is confined mainly to the explanation of the Scripture text, and is more convenient and useful.

The Rosenmüllers.

Less evangelical in spirit, but more exact in the treatment of grammatical questions, and more independent in its mode of handling the Scriptures, is Maurer's Grammatico-critical Commentary on the Old Testament (4 vols., Lpz., 1835-47). The work abounds throughout with references to the Hebrew grammars of Gesenius and Ewald. The notes on the Pentateuch and the historical books, however, are too brief to be satisfactory, and the author exhibits no proper appreciation of the divine element in the Scriptures. The fourth volume, embracing Job, Ecclesiastes, and Canticles, were written by Augustus Heiligstedt.

Maurer.

A later and more complete critical commentary on the Old Testament, and more closely corresponding to De Wette's New Testament Handbook, is the joint work of Knobel, Thenius, Bertheau, Hirzel, J. Olshausen, and Hitzig, entitled **Kurzgefasstes exegetisches Handbuch zum alten Testament**

Old Test. Exegetical Handbook.

(16 vols., Lpz., 1838–61; several subsequent editions). As is always apparent in such works, the authors vary in merit and ability, but they all exhibit thorough training in grammar and philology, and discuss obscure and difficult words and texts with the greatest critical acumen. Besides his contributions to this Old Testament Handbook, Knobel wrote a commentary on Ecclesiastes (1836), a work on Hebrew Prophecy (2 vols., 1837), and a learned treatise on the genealogical tables of Genesis (1850). Hitzig has also published a critical commentary on the Psalms (revised ed., 2 vols., 1863–65), and a history of Israel (1869), both coldly and extremely rationalistic.

Leonhard Bertholdt, a prominent representative of the same rationalistic school of critics, flourished during the first quarter of the century. His chief productions are a commentary on Daniel (2 vols., Erlangen, 1806–8), and a Historico-critical Introduction to the Canonical and Apocryphal Books of the Old and New Testaments. Cæsar von Lengerke's commentaries on Daniel (Königsb., 1835) and the Psalms (1847) exhibit the same spirit, but in critical and philological matters are worthy of commendation. The exegetical writings of Kuinoel (C. G. Kühnöl) evince notable tact and ability, and consist of new translations (with annotations) of Hosea, the Messianic prophecies, and the Psalms, and commentaries on the historical books of the New Testament (many editions) and the Epistle to the Hebrews (Lpz., 1831). In expounding the miracles Kuinoel inclines to the naturalistic method of Eichhorn and Paulus.

Bertholdt.

Lengerke.

Kuinoel.

Among the great Hebraists, whose labours gave a new impulse to the cause of Old Testament philology, no name stands higher than that of William Gesenius. At the age of twenty-four he became professor of theology at Halle, and in the same year published the first volume of his Hebrew-German Lexicon of the Old Testament (1810). The second volume appeared in 1812. New and revised editions of this work were issued in 1823, 1828, and often subsequently, and a Latin edition, almost a new and independent production, appeared in 1833. But his greatest work in this department was his Thesaurus philologicus criticus Linguae Hebraeae et Chaldaeae Veteris Testamenti, on which he was engaged at the time of his death (1842), and which was completed by his friend and colleague, Roediger. These publications, along with his Hebrew Grammar, which has appeared in numerous editions and translations, opened a new era in the cultivation of Old Testament literature. The Hebrew Lexicon was translated into English by Christopher Leo (Camb., 1825), by J. W. Gibbs (Andover, 1824), and by E. Robinson (Boston, 1836); and English

Gesenius.

translations of the Hebrew Grammar have been made by Stuart, Conant, and Davies. Besides several other works on Hebrew and oriental literature, Gesenius wrote a philological, critical, and historical commentary on Isaiah, with an accompanying translation in German (Lpz., 1821). This commentary is especially valuable for its able philological and archæological discussions. It belongs, however, to the rationalistic school of exegesis. In all his works Gesenius exhibits thorough and accurate scholarship, diligent and painstaking research, and a discriminating use of the ample materials at his command.

Scarcely less distinguished as a Semitic and biblical scholar was Georg Heinrich August Ewald. Born at Göttingen in 1803, he was educated at the gymnasium and university of his native town, and in his twentieth year, on leaving the university, he published his first work, Die Komposition der Genesis kritische untersucht, a treatise which long held a respectable place among critical dissertations on the first book of the Bible. His Arabic and Hebrew grammars, which have been published in larger and smaller forms, and in many editions, gave a new impulse to all studies in that department of oriental research. His translation and exposition of the Poetical Books of the Old Testament, and also of the Old Testament Prophets, evinced a profound acquaintance with the Hebrew language, great critical acumen and power of original investigation, but have never been accepted as either safe in method or sound in exegesis. He also wrote on the Apocalypse (1828), the Synoptic Gospels (1850), the Epistles of Paul (1857), the writings of John (1861), Hebrews and the General Epistles (1870), and a vast number of important articles in various German periodicals. His History of the People of Israel (Geschichte des Volkes Israel, 7 vols.; English translation, 7 vols.) is in many respects his masterpiece. For critical and philological discussions, original research, and numerous suggestions of unquestionable value, this work must long hold a high place among the most important contributions of this century to the study of the Old Testament. But with all evangelical scholars Ewald's arbitrary methods of dislocating and rearranging the sacred books will be regarded as unscientific, violent, and fanciful.

In 1843 Hermann Hupfeld succeeded Gesenius in the University of Halle, and became noted as one of the most learned Hebraists of Europe. His most important contribution to biblical literature is his translation and exposition of the Psalms (4 vols., Gotha, 1855–62), a work of vast learning, enriched with a masterly arrangement and use of exegetical material drawn from ancient and modern commentators both Jewish and Christian. In many passages he opposes the views of Hengstenberg and Ewald. Andreas Hoffmann also deserves mention in connexion with Gesenius, as a Semitic scholar, whose lectures on Hebrew Antiquities and Old Testament exegesis contributed much to the advancement of biblical science.

    Hoffmann.

    The German evangelical school of interpreters includes men of different shades of opinion, from the rigidly orthodox, like those of the old Tübingen school, to divines of a free critical spirit, intent, like Neander, to know and maintain essential truth. G. C. Storr, at the beginning of the century, was the leading representative of what is known as the old Tübingen school. He aimed to check the growth of rationalism by a purely scriptural teaching, but his method was unscientific in that it failed to give due prominence to the organic unity of the Bible, and rested too largely on isolated texts. He published, in connexion with Flatt, an Elementary Course of Biblical Theology (English translation, Andover, 1836), and was author of a commentary on the Hebrews (Tübingen, 1809). The two brothers, John F. and Karl C. Flatt, belong to the same school, and wrote several useful expository treatises. Steudel and C. F. Schmid, later representatives of this school, adopted somewhat freer methods, and are supposed to have been influenced, to some extent, by the views of Schleiermacher.

    The Old Tübingen School.

    Hengstenberg, professor of theology at Berlin, was recognised for almost half a century as one of the staunchest defenders of orthodoxy. His principal exegetical works are Contributions to an Introduction to the Old Testament (3 vols., Berlin, 1831–39), in which he ably defends the genuineness of the Pentateuch, Christology of the Old Testament (an elaborate commentary on the Messianic prophecies), commentaries on the Psalms, Ecclesiastes, Ezekiel, the Gospel and Revelation of John, and disquisitions on the genuineness of Daniel and Isaiah, the history of Balaam, and the Books of Job, Isaiah, and Solomon's Song. He was a man of decided ability and great learning, but often needlessly dogmatic and supercilious in setting forth his views. Most of his works have been translated into English, and are greatly prized by evangelical divines. Closely attached to Hengstenberg, and of the same exegetical school, was Hävernick, whose Introduction to the Old Testament, and commentaries on Daniel and Ezekiel, occupy a high place in biblical literature.

    Hengstenberg.

    Hävernick.

    Frederick Bleek was a pupil of Schleiermacher, De Wette, and Neander, and in 1829 became professor of theology at the University

of Bonn. His elaborate commentary on the Epistle to the Hebrews
Bleek.   (3 vols., Berlin, 1828–40) placed him in the front rank
of biblical exegetes, and in his Contributions to the
Criticism of the Gospels (1846) he showed himself a powerful opponent of the Tübingen rationalists, and ably defended the authenticity of the Gospel of John. His Introductions to the Old and
New Testaments were edited and published after his death by J. F.
Bleek and A. Kamphausen, and rank among the most valuable
works of their kind. Other posthumous publications are his Commentary on the Synoptic Gospels, edited by Holtzman, and Lectures on Revelation, edited by Hossbach (1862). His works on
Biblical Introduction, and his Lectures on the Apocalypse, have
been translated into English.

Other distinguished exegetes of this period were Umbreit, pro-
Umbreit, Ull- fessor at Heidelberg, whose expositions embrace the
mann, etc.   poetical and prophetical books of the Old Testament,
and the Epistle to the Romans; Ullmann, of the same university,
whose work on the Sinlessness of Jesus has become a classic in
apologetical literature; Otto Von Gerlach, whose commentary on
the Old and New Testaments is a popular and practical exposition
consisting of brief annotations, and admirably adapted to the use
of unlearned readers; Usteri, a Swiss divine, whose works on John's
Gospel and Paul's System of Doctrine, and commentary on Galatians, exhibit great keenness of investigation combined with accurate scholarship; Hug, an eminent Roman Catholic theologian,
whose principal contribution to biblical literature is an Introduction
to the New Testament, a work of learning and ability which has
been translated into English and French; Schleusner, whose Lexicon
of the Septuagint Version (5 vols., Lips., 1821) remains without a
rival; Karl F. A. Fritzsche, whose commentaries on Matthew and
Mark, and especially on Paul's Epistle to the Romans (3 vols.,
Halle, 1836–43), are pre-eminent for critical and philological acuteness ; and Baumgarten-Crusius, whose exegetical writings treat
most of the books of the New Testament.

Probably no German theologian of modern times exerted a wider
Tholuck.   influence for good than Tholuck, who was theological
professor at Halle from 1826 to the time of his death
(1877). He was master of many languages, and almost a prodigy
of learning. His exegetical works consist of a practical exposition
of the Psalms, learned and comprehensive commentaries on the
Sermon on the Mount, the Gospel of John, and the Epistles to the
Romans and the Hebrews. They have been translated into English
and widely circulated. His exegesis is marked by a devout regard

for the Holy Scriptures, a profound theological insight, a clear perception of the writer's scope and plan, and a wealth of learned illustration drawn from very wide and varied fields of research. His own deep and beautiful religious experience enabled him, like Chrysostom, to apprehend as by intuition " the mind of the Spirit."

More mystical in tone, but similarly profound and comprehensive in his treatment of Scripture, was Rudolf Stier, familiar Stier. to all evangelical scholars by his admirable exposition of the Words of the Lord Jesus. This work is a minute and exhaustive commentary on all the sayings of Jesus as preserved in the Gospels, and, though notably diffuse, is remarkable for its richness of thought, manifold beauties of expression, and deep devotional spirit. To this he subsequently added the Words of the Angels.[1] He also wrote on Isaiah, Proverbs, the Epistles to the Ephesians and Hebrews, and those of James and Jude. In connexion with Theile he published a very convenient and valuable Polyglot Bible, in which the Old Testament is given in the Hebrew, Septuagint, Vulgate, and Luther's German in parallel columns, and the New Testament in Greek, with the Vulgate, German, and Authorized English versions.

Hermann Olshausen was of much the same spirit and method as Stier. Accepting the Bible as God's word, he aimed to Olshausen. penetrate to the innermost sense, and gather up the divine thoughts of the Spirit. His mystical tendency led him at times too far from the path of sound criticism, but his expositions as a whole are well worthy of the hearty reception and extensive use they have obtained. His great work is a commentary on the New Testament, which he did not live to finish. The exposition of Philippians, the Pastoral Epistles, and Peter, James, and Jude was subsequently completed by Augustus Weisinger, and that of Hebrews and the Epistles and Revelation of John by Ebrard, who has also written an able work on the Gospel History.[2]

M. Baumgarten of the University of Rostock has published a very full work on the Acts of the Apostles, which real- Baumgarten ly forms a history of the Apostolic Church, and opposes and Philippi. with vigour the rationalistic theories of Baur and Zeller of the Tübingen school. It has been translated into English (3 vols.,

---

[1] Stier's Words of the Lord Jesus, translated into English by Pope, has been published in Edinburgh (8 vols., 1855–58), and a revised edition, including the Words of the Angels, by Strong and Smith. New York, 3 vols., 1864.

[2] Olshausen's Commentary and Ebrard's work on Hebrews and the Epistles of John have been published in Clark's Foreign Theol. Library, and, in a revised and improved form, as far as the end of Hebrews, by A. C. Kendrick, 6 vols. New York, 1856–58.

Edinb., 1854), and is a fitting companion of Neander's Planting and Training of the Christian Church. F. A. Philippi, of the same university, is the author of a very able critical and theological Commentary on the Epistle to the Romans, which has also been published in an English translation in Clark's Foreign Theological Library.

The grammatical and philological exposition of the New Testament is greatly indebted to the labours of George Benedict Winer, whose Grammar of the Idioms of the New Testament was first published in 1822, and has passed through many improved editions and translations (best Eng. ed., Andover, 1874). It called attention to the precision of the language of the New Testament writers, checked the lawless treatment of its idiom and diction then widely prevalent, and inaugurated a more thorough and scientific exegesis of the Christian Scriptures. This work has been ably supplemented but not superseded by Alexander Buttmann's Grammar of the New Testament Greek, (Eng. trans. by Thayer, Andover, 1873). Winer also published a grammar of the Biblical and Targumic Chaldee, a Hebrew and Chaldee Lexicon, and a condensed but comprehensive Biblical Dictionary (Realwörterbuch), all which have received deserved commendation.

The Critical and Exegetical Commentary on the New Testament by H. A. W. Meyer is an admirable complement of Winer's New Testament Grammar, and a noble illustration of its principles. The first part of Meyer's work appeared in 1832, and to the completion and perfection of it he devoted his best years and ability, making additions and alterations up to the time of his death (1873). At his invitation the commentary on Thessalonians and Hebrews was prepared by Lünemann (who also edited the seventh edition of Winer's Grammar), that on the Pastoral and Catholic Epistles by Huther, and that on the Apocalypse by Düsterdieck. Among all New Testament exegetes Meyer stands unrivalled. In penetration and critical ability, in philological accuracy and rare exegetical tact, he is scarcely inferior to De Wette, while in fulness of treatment and repeated painstaking revision Meyer's work has great advantage over the more condensed manual of De Wette. It is pre-eminently critical and exegetical, and does not aim at theological and homiletical disquisition. Each chapter is prefaced by a lucid statement of the evidence for and against the various readings of the original text, and the exegesis which follows keeps closely to the grammatical and philological presentation of the sacred writer's thought. In his theory of the origin of the written gospels, and on some other points, Meyer leans toward rationalism, and in spiritual insight he is inferior to Stier; but his tone is always reverent, and he belongs essentially to the evangelical school of interpreters.[1] An English translation of his entire New Testament commentary (except Revelation) has been published by the Clarks of Edinburgh.

Among these later biblical scholars of Germany, Karl Auberlen is well known by his able volume on Daniel and the Revelation (Basel, 1854), which has been also published in an English and a French translation. J. H. Kurtz, professor of theology at Dorpat, is author of an exceedingly valuable contribution to the exposition of the Pentateuch under the title of History of the Old Covenant (Eng. trans. by Edersheim, 3 vols., Phila., 1859). A most excellent and convenient series of commentaries on the Old Testament is that prepared by Karl F. Keil and Franz Delitzsch. The work is eminently critical and exegetical, and deals fully and fairly with all the great questions which the modern higher criticism has raised. The learned authors have long been known as representative exegetes of the evangelical school, and have furnished numerous other contributions to biblical literature besides the commentaries belonging to this series. English translations of most of them have been published in Clark's Foreign Theological Library.

Auberlen and Kurtz.

Keil and Delitzsch.

Another series of commentaries still more comprehensive in its plan is the immense Biblework recently issued under the editorial supervision of J. P. Lange. It aims to be a complete critical, exegetical, and homiletical commentary on the Old and New Testaments. Lange himself contributed to this great work more than any other writer. His principal assistants were J. J. Van Oosterzee, Otto Zöchler, C. B. Moll, W. J. Schroeder, Fay, Bähr, Nägelsbach, Schmoller, Kleinert, Lechler, Kling, Braune, and Fronmüller. The work has been translated into English by Philip Schaff, assisted by a large number of American scholars, and published in a greatly enlarged form in twenty-five octavo volumes, including one on the Apocrypha, by E. C. Bissel (New York, 1864–80). It is by far the most learned and comprehensive commentary

Lange's Biblework.

---

[1] In the preface to the fourth edition of his Commentary on Romans (1865) Meyer wrote: "We older men have seen the day when Dr. Paulus and his devices were in vogue; he died without leaving a disciple behind him. We passed through the tempest raised by Strauss some thirty years ago; and with what a sense of solitariness might its author now celebrate his jubilee! We saw the constellation of Tübingen arise, and, even before Baur departed hence, its lustre had waned. A fresh and firmer basis for the truth which had been assailed, and a more complete apprehension of the truth—these were the blessings which the waves left behind; and so will it be when the present surge has passed away."

on the whole Bible which has appeared in modern times. Schaff has also editorial supervision of a popular commentary on the New Testament, by English and American scholars of various evangelical denominations, several volumes of which have already appeared.

F. Godet, a French biblical scholar and professor of theology at Neuchâtel, has published commentaries on the Gospels of Luke and John and the Epistle to the Romans, which have been translated into English and received everywhere with great favour. His exegesis is perspicuous, fresh, and full of suggestion, but needlessly diffuse. The elaborate work of Luthardt on John's Gospel (Eng. trans., 3 vols., Edinb.) is rigidly orthodox, and treats the difficult questions connected with the fourth gospel in great detail and with ample learning.

Godet and Luthardt.

A large number of excellent and useful commentaries by English writers have appeared during the present century. Next to Matthew Henry's exposition no work of similar scope and magnitude has had a wider circulation or is better known than the commentary of Adam Clarke. It is marked by a number of eccentricities of opinion, but displays a vast amount of learning, and is a monument of the tireless industry of its author. It has especially served a useful purpose among the Methodist ministry and people, by whom it has been chiefly used. Less critical and learned, but more practical, is the commentary of Joseph Benson. It is, however, largely a compilation from Poole's Annotations. Richard Watson's exposition of Matthew, Mark, and other portions of the Scriptures (Lond., 1833), evinces a talent for simple, yet thorough and profound, exegesis superior to that of Clarke and Benson, and remains a noble fragment of his projected exposition of the entire New Testament. Ebenezer Henderson's commentaries on Isaiah, Jeremiah, Ezekiel, and the Minor Prophets have commanded the attention of the learned world, and entitle him to a place among the ablest biblical expositors. Bloomfield's Recensio Synoptica (8 vols., Lond., 1826-28), and Greek Testament with English notes (1829, and often), served a useful purpose in their day, and contain much judicious exposition, but they have been superseded by later and more accurate works of the same class. John Kitto, one of the most eminent biblical scholars of England, greatly promoted the interests of sacred learning by his Pictorial Bible, histories of Palestine, and Cyclopædia of Biblical Literature. The last-named work, which has been issued in a greatly enlarged form under the editorship of W. L. Alexander, gave a new and mighty impulse to biblical studies in England and America. It is scarcely too much to say

Adam Clarke.

Benson and Watson.

Henderson and Bloomfield.

Kitto.

that Smith's Dictionary of the Bible, and M'Clintock and Strong's Cyclopædia of Biblical, Theological, and Ecclesiastical Literature, are the outgrowth and fruitage of the encyclopædic labours in biblical science inaugurated by John Kitto. Kitto also projected and edited for many years the Journal of Sacred Literature, and wrote a very popular series of expository dissertations entitled Daily Bible Illustrations. Thomas Hartwell Horne is widely and favourably known by his Introduction to the Critical $\quad$ Horne. Study and Knowledge of the Holy Scriptures, which has passed through numerous editions, and has been, in the course of years, greatly improved and enlarged, especially by Ayre and Tregelles. It has long commanded in English biblical literature the position of a standard work, and has inspired and cultivated in thousands a taste for critical and exegetical studies. Samuel David- $\quad$ Davidson. son has also added lustre to British scholarship by his treatise on Sacred Hermeneutics and Biblical Criticism, Introductions to the Old and New Testaments, English translation of Fürst's Hebrew and Chaldee Lexicon, and other valuable works. His Introduction to the Old Testament and some of his other writings are notably rationalistic.

Among the more recent English exegetes Henry Alford holds a conspicuous place. His chief work is a critical edition $\quad$ Alford. of the Greek Testament, with a digest of various readings, learned prolegomena, and copious philological and exeget cal notes (5 vols., London, 1851–61). The author was fluctuating and somewhat inconsistent in several parts of his exposition, and successive editions show numerous changes of opinion, but his work as a whole has gathered up in convenient form a large amount of valuable material, and has made judicious use of the labours of German critics as well as those of other exegetes, both ancient and modern. The work has had an extensive circulation, and has met a wide-felt want. Webster and Wilkinson have also published an edition of the Greek Testament with grammatical and exegetical notes. It is less elaborate and learned than Alford's, and is adapted for learners rather than the learned.

The liberal views of Alford on inspiration and some other topics probably had an influence in leading Christopher $\quad$ Wordsworth. Wordsworth to prepare his more strictly orthodox edition of the Greek Testament with notes (4 parts, London, 1856–61). He has also extended his exposition over the whole Bible (6 vols., 1864–72). He exhibits a profound veneration for the Scriptures as the word of God, and furnishes many excellent comments. But his work as a whole is disproportionate, makes much use of the fathers, is often fanciful, and avoids difficulties on which such a work is expected to throw light. Far more profound and satisfactory are the exegetical productions of Trench, whose Notes on the Miracles and Parables of our Lord are models of biblical exposition. He has also written a brief commentary on the second chapter of Matthew, a volume of most valuable exegetical essays entitled Studies in the Gospels, a Commentary on the Epistles to the Seven Churches of Asia, and the best work yet extant on the Synonymes of the New Testament. He combines in his expositions a discriminating use of the fathers, the mediæval exegetes, and later writers, with the best results of the most recent criticism, and touches every point with the hand of a master.

No finer specimens of critical and grammatical commentary exist in the English language than those of Charles J. Ellicott on the Epistles of Paul. His exegesis is based upon a critically revised text (substantially that of Tischendorf), and proceeds with steady and deliberate care to set forth the exact meaning of the apostle according to the most approved methods of grammatico-historical interpretation. No difficulty is evaded or overlooked; no peculiarity of language or construction escapes his notice. "I have in all cases striven," he says, "humbly and reverently to elicit from the words their simple and primary meaning. Where that has seemed at variance with historical or dogmatical deductions—where, in fact, exegesis has seemed to range itself on one side, grammar on the other—I have never failed candidly to state it; where it has confirmed some time-honoured interpretation I have joyfully and emphatically cast my small mite into the great treasury of sacred exegesis, and have felt gladdened at being able to yield some passing support to wiser and better men than myself." [1] This eminent divine has written on all the epistles of Paul except Romans and Corinthians, and is also favourably known from other publications, especially his Hulsean Lectures on the Life of Christ.

Of very much the same order and style are the recent commentaries of J. B. Lightfoot on the Epistles of Paul. They are accompanied, however, with learned introductions and elaborate discussions of various critical and historical questions connected with the several epistles. The writer is a sound and judicious expositor, and has announced his purpose to furnish a complete edition of Paul's epistles on the same plan as those (Galatians, Philippians, Colossians, and Philemon) already published. Professor John Eadie's commentaries on the

Marginal notes: Trench.   Ellicott.   J. B. Lightfoot.   Eadie.

[1] Preface to Galatians, first edition.

Greek text of Ephesians, Colossians, Galatians, and Thessalonians are more detailed in their expositions, and abound in theological and practical disquisition. The writer, however, draws from many sources an interesting and useful mass of illustration. The fathers, the schoolmen, the reformers, the poets, the French and German writers, and the English and Scotch theologians are made to contribute to the explanation and illustration of the apostle's thoughts. Paton J. Gloag has written a critical and exegetical commentary on the Acts of the Apostles (Edinb., 1870), *Gloag.* in which the critical and philological element is less prominent than the purely exegetical. The notes are based on a new translation made from the seventh edition of Tischendorf's Greek text, and aim to bring out fully and clearly the meaning of the sacred writer. The work is worthy of a place by the side of those of Lightfoot and Eadie.

The commentaries of J. G. Murphy on Genesis, Exodus, Leviticus, and the Psalms have elicited universal commendation. They make no great display of learning, but are *Murphy.* lucid, discriminating, and comprehensive, yet sufficiently concise, and adapted to the wants of unlearned readers. James Morison's Critical Exposition of the Third Chapter of Romans, *Morison.* and his commentaries on Matthew and Mark, are comprehensive and elaborate, but often infelicitous in style, and, perhaps, needlessly diffuse. Perowne's work on the Psalms (2 vols., Lond., 1864–68) consists of a new translation, with introductions and notes, and exhibits numerous excellen- *Perowne.* ces. It would be difficult to name another exposition of the Psalter which surpasses this one in its combination of good sense, scholarly finish, sound exegesis, and the admirable arrangement and distribution of its several parts.

Jamieson, Fausset, and Brown are the authors of a critical, experimental, and practical commentary on the whole *Jamieson, Faus-* Bible. The notes are brief, but characterized by good *set, and Brown.* sense, and well adapted to the wants of that numerous class who desire the results of the best criticism and exegesis presented to them in a clear and concise form. Much more comprehensive and complete is the recent commentary suggested and planned by Denison, the Speaker of the House of Commons, and prepared by eminent clergymen of the Church of England under the editorial supervision of F. C. Cook, canon of Exeter. It is *Speaker's Com-* known in England as the Speaker's Commentary, and *mentary.* has been republished in this country under the title of The Bible Commentary. The introductions to the several books, and the special essays on important subjects of biblical science, are of the highest value, while the commentary and critical notes are usually learned and judicious. As in all productions of this class, we notice the inequality of the different writers, but the work, as a whole, is abundantly worthy of the place it was designed to fill, and as a learned and recent English commentary on the whole Bible it has no equal.

Other English exegetes, in learning and ability equal to the best, Other English are A. P. Stanley, whose Lectures on the History of exegetes. the Jewish Church, and commentary on Corinthians, combine ample and accurate learning with great vividness and beauty of statement; Benjamin Jowett, whose critical notes and dissertations on Paul's Epistle to the Thessalonians, Galatians, and Romans, though rationalistic, are pre-eminently scholarly and suggestive; Conybeare and Howson, whose great work on the Life and Epistles of St. Paul furnishes the most graphic portraiture of the history and writings of the Apostle to the Gentiles which has ever appeared in any language; Thomas Lewin, whose magnificent volumes, covering the same field as that of the work last named, is worthy to stand by its side, and, in not a few matters, is its superior. E. B. Elliott's ponderous work on the Apocalypse (4 vols., fifth edition, London, 1862) shows great industry and research, and contains a vast amount of valuable material, but his system of interpretation is not likely to command confidence. Kalisch, a learned Jew, has written an English translation and critical exposition of Genesis, Exodus, and Leviticus. His volumes are a storehouse of learning, and are very helpful to a thorough study of the Pentateuch, but they are leavened with rationalism. His theological notions generally are much less satisfactory than his historical and critical comments. Ginsburg's commentaries on Koheleth (Ecclesiastes) and the Song of Songs are also very full of the products of critical, exegetical, and historical research, and well deserving of the careful study of all biblical scholars.

It must be confessed that American scholars have as yet pro-American exe- duced comparatively little that will endure favourable getes. comparison with the great exegetical works of British and German authors. The copious work of Lange (see p. 727), which has been reproduced in a greatly improved form in this country, has served to demonstrate the ample critical and exegetical ability of American scholarship to rival that of the Old World. Nevertheless that work is essentially German. There are two American names which stand pre-eminent in biblical literature, and have commanded attention both in England and Germany. Moses Stuart and Edward Robinson did more than any other two men to initiate an interest in critical studies and to promote the cultivation of biblical science in their own country. Stuart was made professor of sacred literature at Andover in 1810, and *Moses Stuart.* continued in that position until 1848. During these years he published a grammar of the Hebrew language, based on that of Gesenius, a Hebrew Christomathy, a New Testament grammar, a Critical History and Defence of the Old Testament Canon, and commentaries on Hebrews, Romans, and the Apocalypse. He afterward published commentaries on Daniel, Ecclesiastes, and Proverbs. In all these works he shows the skill of a master, and his commentaries have maintained, up to the present time, a place among the ablest expositions of the books which they treat.

Robinson's contributions to biblical literature were more profound and massive than those of Stuart. In 1825 he *Edward Robinson.* published a translation of Wahl's Clavis Philologica of the New Testament, which was at a later period of his life entirely superseded by his own Greek and English Lexicon of the New Testament (new and revised ed., New York, 1850), a work that has had incalculable influence in directing the studies of theological students and ministers. In 1831 he founded the Biblical Repository, which subsequently became united with the Bibliotheca Sacra, and received some of the best exegetical productions both of himself and Professor Stuart. His translation of Gesenius' Hebrew and Chaldee Lexicon did for promoting the study of Hebrew what his New Testament Lexicon has done for the study of the Greek Testament. His biblical researches in Palestine still remain, after the lapse of more than forty years, an indispensable authority on matters of biblical geography. His translation of Buttmann's Greek Grammar, and his Greek and English Harmonies of the Gospels, are of less note, but very useful in their way. He ranks among the most distinguished biblical scholars of the nineteenth century, and his name is as well known in England and Germany as in his own land.

Joseph Addison Alexander acquired a reputation in Europe as well as in America by his learned and useful commentaries on Isaiah, the Psalms, the Acts, and the Gospels *Alexander.* of Matthew and Mark. For fulness of treatment, and as a thesaurus of the views of the most important expositors, his work on Isaiah is unsurpassed. His scholarship was broad, accurate, and profound, and his exegetical talent commanded the attention of all the great biblical scholars of his time.

Among the other more noted American exegetes we name

Andrews Norton, a Unitarian scholar, and author of a learned and
Other American valuable work on the Genuineness of the Gospels
expositors. (2d ed., 3 vols., 1846); Charles Hodge, whose commentary on Romans (new ed., 1864), notably Calvinistic in its theology, ranks among the ablest expositions of that important epistle;
he has also written on the two Epistles to the Corinthians and on
Ephesians; S. H. Turner, who is widely and favourably known by
his commentaries on Romans, Hebrews, and Ephesians, a critical
work on Genesis, a volume on the interpretation of Prophecy, and
translations of various German exegetical works; and George Bush,
whose Notes on Genesis, Exodus, Leviticus, Numbers, Joshua, and
Judges are judicious and practical, have served a very useful purpose, and have had a wide circulation. Albert Barnes has written
expository notes on all the books of the New Testament, and
also on Job, Isaiah, Daniel, and the Psalms. They have been eminently popular, and have served to meet the great demand for a
clear, full, and simple exposition, based upon the common English
version, and adapted to the wants of Sunday-school teachers and
ordinary readers. Melanchthon W. Jacobus is the author of excellent commentaries on the Gospels, the Acts of the Apostles, and
the Book of Genesis. John J. Owen's Critical, Expository, and
Practical Commentary on Matthew, Mark, and the Acts is a lucid,
thorough, evangelical exposition, and deservedly ranks among the
very best popular commentaries which our country has produced.
Whedon's Commentary on the New Testament (5 vols. 12mo,
1860-80), intended for popular use, is more original and independent in its plan, and more complete for its purpose than any of the
manual expositions just mentioned. Its style is incisive, epigram-
matic, and brilliant; its tone, profoundly evangelical. It deals in a
manly way with all difficulties, and sets numerous important passages in a light and beauty not recognised before by any exegete.
It is judiciously confined to exposition proper, usually seizes the
central thought of the sacred writer, and exhibits it concisely and
impressively. A series of commentaries on the Old Testament,
prepared by different authors and executed on the same plan as
that of Whedon's New Testament, is in preparation, and several
volumes (covering Joshua to Jeremiah) have already been published. Henry Cowles has completed a series of expository notes
on the whole Bible, designed for pastors and people (16 vols.
12mo), which, without any parade of learning, are distinguished by
good sense and brevity, clearness of statement, sound and discriminating judgment, and able treatment of the obscure and difficult
parts of Scripture, on which the ordinary reader needs information.

Hackett's commentary on the original text of the Acts (Boston, 1858), and Conant's work on Genesis, Job, Proverbs, and other books, in connexion with the new translations of the American Bible Union, are more learned and philological than the popular commentaries named above. For critical purposes they are of a high order, and worthy of the many commendations which they have received. The Greek and English Harmonies of the Gospels by James Strong and Frederic Gardiner are the best works of the kind extant, and exhibit accurate scholarship, excellent judgment, and the most painstaking fidelity and care. Nast's English commentary on Matthew and Mark, modelled much after the style of Lange's work on the same books, with an elaborate Introduction to the Gospel Records (Cincinnati, 1864, 8vo), is an exceedingly valuable contribution to biblical literature. The introduction has been published separately. W. G. T. Shedd has recently published a Critical and Doctrinal Commentary on the Epistle to the Romans, which is based upon the Greek text of Lachmann, and is truly an elaborate exegetical and theological discussion of the great questions which centre in this book. Its doctrinal position is that of the Calvinistic confessions, and it is a worthy compeer and complement of Hodge's commentary on the same epistle.

The textual criticism of the New Testament has been carried during the present century to a high degree of perfection. New Test. Textual Criticism. In 1813 G. C. Knapp, author of a translation and exposition of the Psalms, lectures on Christian Theology and other works, published a second edition of his Greek Testament (Halle, 2 vols. 8vo), in which he availed himself of Griesbach's labours, and furnished a work so useful that it rapidly passed Knapp, Schulz, through numerous reprints and editions, and met with and Scholz. general approbation. In 1827 David Schulz supervised a new edition of Griesbach's Greek text of the Four Gospels, which he enriched with numerous additions. J. M. A. Scholz spent twelve years of diligent research in the libraries of Europe and in several monasteries of the East collecting and collating manuscripts and other material for a new critical Greek Testament, which appeared at Leipsic in two quarto volumes (1830–36), and served a useful purpose chiefly because of the large amount of critical materials which it supplied. Lachmann's Critical New Testament Lachmann. (2 vols., 1842–50) was executed on the plan proposed long before by Bentley (see above, p. 699), and ignoring the textus receptus, which had too greatly fettered sound and independent criticism, he aimed, by the exclusive use of the oldest authorities, to reconstruct the text which was current in the fourth century.

The number of his authorities was limited, and his work was at first subjected to very hostile criticism, largely because of a misunderstanding of his plan and purpose; but later critics have almost universally acknowledged the correctness of his principles and the great value of his services.

No textual critic of the century has contributed to this department of biblical science as much as Tischendorf. He
Tischendorf. repeatedly visited the libraries of Europe and the monasteries of the East, made valuable discoveries of ancient critical authorities, edited many of the most important manuscripts, and published in all twenty-four editions of the Greek Testament, four of which (editions of 1841, 1849, 1859, and 1872) mark a definite progress in the acquisition of critical materials. His method is essentially that of Lachmann, but makes use of all authorities which may reasonably be expected to aid in ascertaining the most ancient text. S. P. Tregelles, an English scholar who has pub-
Tregelles. lished several very useful works in biblical criticism and exegesis, is probably best known by his Greek Testament edited from ancient authorities, with the Latin version of Jerome (1857–79). He follows out the principles of Lachmann more rigidly than Tischendorf, and evinces a superior judgment and caution; but his resources were more limited, and his practice in the collation and transcription of manuscripts much less, than that of his German contemporary.[1]

The vast accumulation of documentary evidence made accessible
Westcott and by the manifold labours of preceding generations en-
Hort. abled B. F. Westcott and J. A. Hort, two eminent English critics, to issue in 1881, after more than twenty-five years of conscientious toil, an admirable edition of the Greek Testament, the text of which is based exclusively on ancient authorities. It is considered the maturest product of New Testament criticism, and creates a conviction among scholars best competent to judge that we are in possession of an approximately pure text of the Christian Scriptures. A comparison of the readings in which Tischendorf, Tregelles, and Westcott and Hort vary will best serve to show the degree of perfection which the science of textual criticism has attained. The passages in which there appears any important variation are scarcely a thousandth part of the entire text of the New Testament.

The revised English version of the Scriptures, prepared by the leading biblical scholars of Great Britain and America, is a

---

[1] For a complete list of the printed editions of the Greek Testament, see Reuss, Bibliotheca Novi Testimenti Græci. Brunswick, 1872.

monumental witness of the advanced state of sacred criticism and interpretation at the present time. The New Testament portion, issued in 1881, was received with an eagerness and re- *The revised* printed and sold to an extent unparalleled in all the his- *English ver-* tory of letters. Whatever opinions are held as to the *sion.* rendering of particular texts, or the infelicities of occasional passages, competent judges concede that, as a whole, it worthily exhibits the ripest biblical scholarship of the nineteenth century. The accuracy and thoroughness of that scholarship may be further apprehended by observing that many of the least known and read of modern exegetes are far superior in exact learning and hermeneutical method to any of the fathers or the mediæval writers. We have made no special mention of the works of Billroth, and Hendewerk, and Hahn, and Titmann, and Reuss, of Reiche, and Köllner, *Condition of* and Rückert, and Harless, of Bisping, and Reitmayr, *modern exege-* and Windischmann, and Beet, and scores besides, whose *sis.* varied contributions to biblical exegesis fully rank with many of those described in the foregoing pages. The historical importance of Philo, and Origen, and Chrysostom, and Jerome, and Lyra, makes them much more conspicuous than these later writers, but the intrinsic value of the expositions of Scripture produced by the moderns is immeasurably superior to those of the ancients. Neology and rationalism have indirectly done great service for the cause of biblical science. The researches and suggestions of Semler and Gesenius, the critical acuteness of De Wette and Ewald, and even the works of Strauss, and Baur, and Hilgenfeld, have given an impulse to the scientific study of the Holy Scriptures which has already produced inestimable gain, and which promises even better for the future.

The present condition of biblical interpretation is, therefore, very encouraging. The results of modern travel and *Present outlook* exploration have silenced not a few of the cavils of *and demand.* infidelity, and placed the historical accuracy and trustworthiness of the sacred writers beyond reasonable doubt. The most accomplished scholars of the world are finding in the study and elucidation of the Scriptures a worthy and ennobling field of labour, and are devoting their lives to it with enthusiastic delight. While here and there we meet with some who cling tenaciously to traditional opinions and allegorical methods, or indulge in extravagant notions touching the character of the inspired books, the great body of evangelical expositors are united on the fundamental principles of interpretation. They agree, moreover, that a proper commentary on the Bible, or on any part of it, should clearly set forth the true meaning of the words and the train of thought intended by the sacred writer; it should point out the grammatico-historical sense of every passage, giving careful attention to the context, scope, and plan. Where searching criticism and minute analysis are required we are not to be put off with dogmatic assertion, nor should there be any evasion of difficulties, whether they be textual, geographical, chronological, historical, or doctrinal. A commentary notably full on easy passages, and meagre or superficial on difficult ones, meets with no favour, and such diffuse and ponderous works as Caryl on the Book of Job, and Venema on the Psalms, are intolerable to the modern student. No single commentary is now expected to meet the wants of all classes of readers. Philological and grammatical treatises are demanded by critical scholars; professional divines require elaborate disquisitions on important texts, and the great body of ordinary readers need practical and suggestive expositions. Especially popular and widely used are those commentaries which, without being pedantic or obscure, are both critical and thorough, and furnish the common reader with a concise and clear statement of all difficulties involved in disputed passages, and the best methods of explaining them. What has been written by way of comment on the Holy Scriptures seems truly prodigious, and no lifetime is long enough to make a thorough use of half of it; and yet more is needed, and new and superior works of biblical exposition will be demanded and supplied as one generation succeeds another.

BIBLIOGRAPHY OF HERMENEUTICS.

ACOSTA, JOSEPH.—De vera scripturas interpretandi ratione libri tres. A part of his work entitled De Christo revelato (Rome, 1590, 4to), and published also in the appendix of Menochius' Commentary on the Bible. Paris, 1719, and Venice, 1771.

AIKEN, C. A.—The Citations of the Old Testament in the New. Translated from the German of Tholuck, in Bibliotheca Sacra for July, 1854.

ALBER, J. N.—Institutiones Hermeneuticae Scripturae Novi Testamenti. Pestini, 1818. 3 vols. 8vo.
———— Institutiones Hermeneuticae Scripturae Sacrae Veteris Testamenti. Pestini, 1827. 3 vols. 8vo.

ALEXANDER, ARCHIBALD. —Principle of Design in the Interpretation of Scripture. Biblical Repertory and Princeton Review for July, 1845.
On Schools and Systems of Interpretation, see same Review for April, 1855.

ANGUS, JOSEPH.—The Bible Handbook. An Introduction to the Study of Sacred Scripture. Many English and American editions. Revised with Notes and Index of Scripture texts by F. S. Hoyt. Phila., 1868. 8vo.
Chapters iv–vii of Part First relate to Biblical Hermeneutics.

APTHORP, EAST.—Discourses on Prophecy. London, 1786. 2 vols. 8vo.
The second discourse (vol. i, pp. 49–106) discusses the Canons of Prophecy.

ARIGLER, ALTMAN.—Hermeneutica Biblica generalis usibus academicis accommodata. Vienna, 1813. 8vo. See UNTERKIRCHER.

ARIZZARRA, F. HYACINTHE.—Elementa Sacrae Hermeneuticae, seu Institutiones ad Intelligentiam Sacrarum Scripturarum. Castrinovi Carfagnanae, 1790. 4to.

ARNOLD, THOMAS.—Sermons chiefly on the Interpretation of Scripture. New edition. London, 1878. 8vo.
The last two sermons of the volume are on the Interpretation of Prophecy, and are accompanied with Notes and Appendices.

AST, F.—Grundlinien der Grammatik, Hermeneutik und Kritik. Landshut, 1808. 8vo.

AYRE, JOHN. See HORNE.

BARROWS, E. P.—A new Introduction to the Study of the Bible. Published by Religious Tract Society. London. 8vo.
Part Fourth of this work is devoted to the Principles of Biblical Interpretation, and contains in clear outline and compact form an excellent presentation of the fundamental principles of Hermeneutics.

BAUER, G. L.—Hermeneutica Sacra Veteris Testamenti. Lips., 1797. 8vo.
Published as a new edition of Glassius' Philologia Sacra, but in fact a new work
of no great value.

——— Entwurf einer Hermeneutik des alten und neuen Testaments.
Lpz., 1799. 8vo.
Rationalistic, but full of useful hints.

BAUMGARTEN, S. J.—Unterricht von Auslegung der heiligen Schrift, für
seine Zuhörer ausgefertiget. Halle, 1742. 8vo. Published in an enlarged
form with the title, Ausführlicher Vortrag der biblischen Hermeneutik,
by J. C. Bertram. Halle, 1769. 4to.
A work of considerable value.

BECK, C. D.—Commentationes de interpretatione Veterum Scriptorum.
Lips., 1791. 4to.

——— Monogrammata Hermeneutices librorum Novi Fœderis. Pars
prima, Hermeneutice Novi Testamenti universa. Lips., 1803. 8vo.

BECK, J. T.—Versuch einer pneumatisch-hermeneutischen Entwickelung
des neuen Kapitels im Briefe an die Römer. Stuttgart, 1833. 8vo.
Somewhat mystical, but suggestive.

——— Zur theologischen Auslegung der Schrift. Appended to his Einleitung in das System der christlichen Lehre. Stuttgart, 1838. 8vo.

BECKHAUS, J. H.—Remarks on the Interpretation of the Tropical Language
of the New Testament (vol. ii, Edinburgh Biblical Cabinet). Edinburgh, 1833. 16mo.

BELLARMINE, ROBERT. — De Verbi Dei Interpretatione. Opera, vol. i,
book iii, pp. 159-198. Ingolstadt, 1590. Folio.

BLUNT, J. H.—Key to the Knowledge and Use of the Holy Bible. Lond.,
1873. 8vo. Phila., 1873. 16mo.

BOSANQUET, S. R.—Interpretation; being Rules and Principles assisting to
the Reading and Understanding of the Holy Scriptures. London,
1874. 12mo.

BRETSCHNEIDER, C. G.—Die historische-dogmatische Auslegung des neuen
Testaments, nach ihren Principien, Quellen, und Hülfsmitteln darges-
tellt. Lpz., 1806. 12mo.
Rationalistic, and of no great value.

BROOKS, J. W.—Elements of Prophetical Interpretation. Phila., 1841.
12mo.

BUDDÆUS, J. F.—Isagoge Historico-Theologica ad Theologiam Universam
singulasque ejus Partes. Lips., 1727. 4to.
Pages 1427-1796 are devoted to Exegetical Theology.

CAMPBELL, GEORGE.—Preliminary Dissertations to the Gospels. London,
1789. 4to. New edition in 2 vols. London, 1834. 8vo.
The first volume contains twelve dissertations in which important questions of
New Testament exposition are ably handled.

CARPENTER, WILLIAM.—Popular Lectures on Biblical Criticism and Interpretation. London, 1829. 8vo.

CARPENTER, WILLIAM.—A Popular Introduction to the Study of the Holy Scriptures for the Use of English Readers. London, 1826.
Part First of this work contains a number of very useful directions for reading the Holy Scriptures.

CARPZOV, JOHN B.—Primae lineae Hermeneuticae et Philologiae sacrae cum Veteris tum Novi Testamenti brevibus aphorismis comprehensae in usum lectionum academicarum. Helmstadt, 1790. 8vo.

CELLÉRIER, J. E.—Manuel D'Herméneutique Biblique. Geneva, 1852. 8vo.
An admirably planned, systematic, and ably executed work; one of the best of modern times.

———— Biblical Hermeneutics. Chiefly a Translation of the Manuel D'Herméneutique Biblique, par J. E. Cellérier. By Charles Elliott and William J. Harsha. New York, 1881. 8vo.

CHAMIER, D.—Panstratiae Catholicae, sive controversiarum de religione adversus Pontificios corpus. Geneva, 1626. 4 vols. folio.
The first volume treats biblical interpretation, but polemically.

CHLADENIUS, MARTIN.—Institutiones Exegeticae, regulis et observationibus luculentissimis instructae, largissimisque exemplis illustratae. Wittenberg, 1725. 8vo.

———— Einleitung zur rechtigen Auslegung von Reden und Schriften. Lpz., 1742. 8vo.

CLARK, JAMES A.—Diversity of Interpretation. Article in the Christian Review of 1857, pp. 196-215.

CLAUSEN, H. N. (commonly Klausen).—Hermeneutik des neuen Testaments; aus dem Danischen übersetzt von C. O. Schmidt-Phiseldek. Lpz., 1841. 8vo.
A learned and valuable production, and especially useful for its discriminating history of biblical interpretation.

CLERICUS, (LE CLERC) JOHN.—Dissertatio de optimo genere Interpretum Sacrae Scripturae.
Prefixed to his Commentary on the Old Testament, vol. i, pp. xiv-xxviii. Amsterdam, 1710.

COBET, C. G.—Oratio de arte interpretandi grammatices et critices fundamentis innixa primario philologi officio. Leyden, 1847. 8vo.

COLLYER, DAVID.—The Sacred Interpreter; or, a practical Introduction toward a beneficial Reading and a thorough Understanding of the Holy Bible. Fifth edition. Carlisle, 1796. 2 vols. 8vo, with cuts.
It was first published in 1746, and translated into German by F. E. Rambach (Rostock, 1750, 8vo), but is a work of no great merit.

CONYBEARE, J. J.—The Bampton Lectures for the year 1824, being an Attempt to trace the History and to ascertain the Limits of the secondary and spiritual Interpretation of Scripture. Oxford, 1824. 8vo.

CONYBEARE, W. D.—Elementary Course of Theological Lectures. London, 1836. 12mo.

DANNHAUER, J. C.—Hermeneutica Sacra, sive methodus exponendarum Sacrarum Literarum. Argentor, 1654. 8vo.

DATHE, J. A.—Opuscula ad Crisin et Interpretationem Veteris Testamenti (edited by Rosenmüller). Lips., 1795. See GLASSIUS.

DAVIDSON, SAMUEL.—Sacred Hermeneutics developed and applied, including a History of Biblical Interpretation from the earliest of the Fathers to the Reformation. Edinburgh, 1843. 8vo.
  A learned and very valuable work, but lacks completeness, and is disproportionate in its several parts.

DAVISON, JOHN.—Discourses on Prophecy. Oxford, 1821. 8vo. Fifth edition, 1845.

DE ROSSI, G. B.—Sinopsi della Ermeneutica Sacra. Parma, 1819.

DIESTEL, L.—Geschichte des alten Testaments in der Christlichen Kirche. Jena, 1868. 8vo.

DIXON, JOSEPH.—A General Introduction to the Sacred Scriptures in a series of Dissertations, Critical, Hermeneutical, and Historical. Dublin, 1852. 2 vols. 8vo. Baltimore, 1853. 2 vols. in one, 8vo.
  Dissertation xii, in vol. i, consisting of eight chapters, sets forth succinctly the principles of Roman Catholic Hermeneutics.

DOBIE, DAVID.—A Key to the Bible: Being an Exposition of the History, Axioms, and General Laws of Sacred Interpretation. New York, 1856. 12mo.

DOEDES, J. J.—Manual of Hermeneutics for the Writings of the New Testament. Translated from the Dutch by G. W. Stegmann. Edinburgh, 1867. 12mo.
  Brief, but excellent, and well worthy of repeated study.

DOEPKE, J. C. C.—Hermeneutik der neutestamentlichen Schriftsteller. Lpz., 1829. 8vo.
  Evinces great learning and careful research.

DUKES, L.   See EWALD and DUKES.

EICHSTAEDT.   See MORUS.

ELLICOTT, C. J.—Scripture and its Interpretation. One of the essays in Aids to Faith—Replies to Essays and Reviews. London, 1863. 8vo.

ELSTER, ERNST.—De medii aevi Theologia Exegetica. Göttingen, 1855. 8vo.

EWALD, H.   See EWALD and DUKES.

EWALD and DUKES.—Beiträge zur Geschichte der ältesten Auslegung und Schrifterklärung des alten Testament, 3 vols. 8vo. Stuttgart, 1844.

ERNESTI, JOHN AUGUST.—Institutio Interpretis Novi Testamenti ad usus lectionum. Lips., 1761. 8vo. Fifth edition, edited by Ammon, 1809.
  A great work for its day, almost an epoch-making book, and still useful, though superseded by later treatises.

——— Elements of Biblical Criticism and Interpretation, translated from the Latin of Ernesti, Keil, Beck, and Morus, and accompanied with notes, by Moses Stuart. Andover, 1827. 12mo. This translation was republished, with additional observations, by Henderson. London, 1827.

——— Principles of Biblical Interpretation, translated from the Institutio Interpretis of J. A. Ernesti, by Charles H. Terrot. Edinburgh (Biblical Cabinet), 1843. 2 vols. 12mo.
  Terrot's is the best English translation.

FAIRBAIRN, PATRICK. — Hermeneutical Manual; or, Introduction to the Exegetical Study of the Scriptures of the New Testament. Edinburgh, 1858. 8vo. Phila., 1859.

—— The Typology of Scripture, viewed in connexion with the entire Scheme of the Divine Dispensations. Vol. i, Edinburgh, 1845; vol. ii, 1847. 8vo. Fifth edition, revised and enlarged, Edinb., 1870. New York, 1877.

—— Prophecy, viewed in its distinctive Nature, its special Function, and proper Interpretation. Edinb., 1865. New York, 1866. 8vo. All these productions of Fairbairn are works of enduring value.

FLACIUS, MATTHIAS. — Clavis Scripturae Sacrae, seu de sermone Sacrarum Literarum. Basle, 1567. Folio. Edited by Musæus. Jena, 1674. Lips., 1695. Erfurt, 1719. Copious in material, and executed with great learning and ability for the time when it appeared.

FORBES. See PAREAU.

FRANCKE, A. H. — Manuductio ad lectionem Sacrae Scripturae. Halle, 1693. 8vo. London, 1706.

—— Prælectiones Hermeneuticae ad viam dextre indagandi et exponendi sensum Sacrae Scripturae. Halle, 1717.

—— A Guide to the Reading and Study of the Holy Scriptures. Translated by William Jaques with life of Francke. London, 1813. 8vo. Phila., 1823. 12mo.

FRANKEL, Z. — Ueber den Einfluss der palästinischen Exegese auf den alexandrinische Hermeneutik. Lpz., 1851. 8vo.

FRANZIUS, WOLFGANG. — Tractatus theologicus novus et perspicuus de Interpretatione Sacrarum Scripturarum, etc. Wittenberg, 1619. 4to. Several times reprinted. Sixth ed., 1708. Controversial, and of little worth.

GABLER, J. P. — Entwurf einer Hermeneutik des neuen Testament. Altdorf, 1788. 4to.

GERARD, GILBERT. — Institutes of Biblical Criticism, or Heads of the course of Lectures on that subject, read in the University of Aberdeen. Edinb., 1808. 8vo. Boston, 1823.

GERHARD. JOHN. — Tractatus de legitima Scripturae Sacrae Interpretatione. Jena, 1610. 4to.

GERHAUSER, G. B. — Biblische Hermeneutik. Zweiter Theil: Die Grundsätze der Schriftauslegung. Kempten, 1829. 8vo.

GERMAR, F. H. — Die panharmonische Interpretation der heiligen Schrift. Ein Versuch. Schleswig, 1821. 8vo.

—— Beitrag zur allgemeinen Hermeneutik und zu deren Anwendung auf die theologische. Altona, 1828. 8vo.

—— Die hermeneutischen Mängel der sogenannten grammatisch-historischen. eigentlich aber der Tact-Interpretation. Halle, 1834. 8vo.

—— Kritik·der modernen Exegese, nach den hermeneutischen Maximen eines competenten Philologen. Halle, 1841. 8vo. Suggestive dissertations, still worthy of perusal.

GERSON, JOHN.—Propositiones de sensu literali Sacrae Scripturae. Opera, vol. i. Antwerp, 1706. Folio.

GLAIRE. See JANSSENS.

GLASSIUS. SOLOMON.—Philologiae sacrae, qua totius sacrosanctae Veteris et Novi Testamenti Scripturae tum stylus et literatura, tum sensus et genuinæ Interpretationis ratio expenditur. Jena, 1623. 4to.
> Most correct edition, Frankfort and Hamburg, 1653. 4to. Fullest of the old editions, with Preface by Buddæus, Lips., 1725. New edition, with valuable additions by Dathe and Bauer, Lips., 1776–97. 3 vols. 8vo. A work of considerable value.

GOLDHAGEN, HERMANN.—Introductio in Sacram Scripturam Veteris et Novi Testamenti. Maintz, three parts, 1766-68. 8vo.

GRIESBACH, J. J.—Vorlesungen über die Hermeneutik des neuen Testaments; herausgegeben von J. C. S. Steiner. Nüremberg, 1815. 8vo.

GUENTNER, G. J. B.—Hermeneutica Biblica generalis juxta Principia Catholica. Prague, 1848. Vienna, 1851. 8vo.

HENDERSON, E. See ERNESTI.

HILLER, M.—Syntagma Hermeneutica. Tübingen, 1711. 4to.

HIRSCHFELD, H. S.—Der Geist der talmudischen Auslegung der Bibel. Erster Theil, Halachische Exegese. Berlin, 1840. 8vo.

—— Der Geist der ersten Schrift-auslegungen, oder die hagadische Exegese. Berlin, 1847. 8vo.

HOEPFNER, C. F.—Grundlinien zu einer fruchtbaren Auslegung der heiligen Schrift. Lpz., 1827. 8vo.

HOFMANN, J. CHRISTIAN K., VON.—Biblische Hermeneutik. Nördlingen, 1880. 16mo.
> A new and very valuable contribution to the Science of Biblical Interpretation. It is a posthumous publication, edited by W. Volck.

HORNE, THOMAS HARTWELL.—An Introduction to the Critical Study and Knowledge of the Holy Scriptures. London, 1818. 3 vols. 8vo. Many editions. The second volume of the tenth edition was edited and nearly rewritten by Samuel Davidson: The Text of the Old Testament, with a Treatise on Sacred Interpretation, 1856. Eleventh edition, revised and largely rewritten, by John Ayre and S. P. Tregelles. London, 1860. 4 vols. 8vo. Thirteenth edition, 1872.
> The second volume, revised by Ayre, is devoted to tbe Criticism and Interpretation of Scripture, and is a comprehensive and useful work.

HUETIUS, PETER DANIEL.—De Interpretatione libri duo; quorum prior est, de optimo genere interpretandi: alter, de claris interpretibus. Stadæ, 1680. 16mo.

IMMER, A.—Hermeneutik des neuen Testaments. Wittenberg. 1873. 8vo.

—— Hermeneutics of the New Testament. Translated from the German by A. H. Newman. Andover, 1877. 8vo.
> One of the best hermeneutical treatises of modern times.

IRONS, W. J.—The Bible and its Interpreters. Miracles and Prophecy. Second edition. London, 1869. 8vo.

JACKSON, ARTHUR.—A Help for the Understanding of the Holy Scripture. Camb., 1643. 3 vols. 4to.

JACKSON, THOMAS.—The true Sense of Scripture determinable by Rules of Art. Works xii, 174 (folio edition iii, 895).

JAHN, J.—Enchiridion Hermeneuticae generalis tabularum Veteris et Novi Foederis. Vienna, 1812. 8vo.

  A work of much good sense. See SANDBICHLER and STUART.

JANSSENS, J. HERMANN.—Hermeneutica Sacra, seu Introductio in omnes ac singulos libros sacros Veteris et Novi Foederis. Maintz, 1818. 2 vols. 8vo.

——— Herméneutique Sacrée, ou Introduction à l'Écriture Sainte. Trad. du Lat. par J. J. Pacaud. Paris, 1827. 2 vols. 8vo. New ed., rev. by J. B. Glaire, 1840. Fifth ed., rev. by Sionnet, 1855.

JONES, WILLIAM.—Course of Lectures on the Figurative Language of the Holy Scriptures. London, 1787. 8vo. Second edition, 1789. Also in vol. iv. of his Theological and Miscellaneous Works. London, 1810.

JOWETT, BENJAMIN.—On the Interpretation of Scripture. One of the essays in Essays and Reviews by eminent English Churchmen. London, 1861. 8vo.

KAISER, G. P. C.—Grundriss eines Systems der neutestamentlichen Hermeneutik. Erlangen, 1817. 8vo.

KEIL, KARL A. G.—De historica librorum sacrorum Interpretatione ejusque necessitate. Lips., 1788. 8vo.

——— Ueber die historische Erklärungsart der heiligen Schrift und deren Nothwendigkeit. Aus d. Lat. von C. A. Hempel. Lpz., 1793. 8vo.

——— Lehrbuch der Hermeneutik des neuen Testaments nach Grundsätzen der grammatisch-historischen Interpretation. Lpz., 1810. 8vo.

——— Elementa Hermeneutices Novi Testamenti (Latine reddita a C. A. G. Emmerling). Lips., 1811. 12mo.

  All these treatises display the skill of a master, and emphasize the necessity of strict grammatico-historical interpretation.

KLAUSEN. See CLAUSEN.

KOHLGRUBER, J.—Hermeneutica Biblica generalis. Vienna, 1850. 8vo.

LAMAR, J. S.—The Organon of Scripture; or, the Inductive Method of Biblical Interpretation. Philadelphia, 1860. 12mo.

LANDERER.—Article Hermeneutik in Herzog, Real-Encyklopädie (edition Stuttgart and Hamburg, 1856). Comp. SCHMIDT.

LANGE, JOACHIM.—Hermeneutica Sacra. Halle, 1733. 8vo.

LANGE, J. P.—Grundriss der biblischen Hermeneutik. Heidelb., 1878. 8vo.

  Suggestive, well arranged, compact, and convenient for use.

LEE, SAMUEL.—Six Sermons on the Study of the Holy Scriptures, their Nature, Interpretation, and some of their most Important Doctrines. London, 1830. 8vo.

——— An Inquiry into the Nature, Progress, and End of Prophecy. Cambridge, 1849. 8vo.

LINDANUS, W. D.—De optimo Scripturas interpretandi genere libri iii. Coloniæ, 1558. 16mo.

LITTON, E. A.—Guide to the Study of the Holy Scripture. London, 1860.

LOEHNIS, J. M. A.—Grundzüge der biblischen Hermeneutik und Kritik.
Giessen, 1839. 8vo.

LOESCHER, V. E.—Breviarium Theologiae Exegeticae. Frankfort, 1715. 8vo.

———— Breviarium Theologiae Exegeticae legitimam Scripturae Sacrae
Interpretationem, nec non studii biblici rationem succincte tradens.
Wittenberg, 1719. 8vo.

LOWTH, W.—Directions for the Profitable Reading of the Holy Scriptures;
with some Observations for confirming their Divine Authority, and illustrating their Difficulties. Seventh edition, London, 1799. 12mo.

LUECKE, G. C. F.—Grundriss der neutestamentlichen Hermeneutik und
ihrer Geschichte. Göttingen, 1817. 8vo.

LUTZ, J. L. S.—Biblische Hermeneutik. Pforzheim, 1849. 8vo. Second
ed., edited by Adolf Lutz, 1861.

MACKNIGHT, JAMES.—Concerning the Right Interpretation of the Writings
in which the Revelations of God are contained.
Essay viii, appended to his Translation and Commentary on the Apostolical
Epistles. Many editions.

MAIMONIDES, MOSES (Rambam).—Moreh Nebuchim, or Guide of the Perplexed. Many editions and translations.

MAITLAND, CHARLES.—The Apostles' School of Prophetic Interpretation,
with its History to the present time. London, 1849. 8vo.

MAITLAND, S. R.—Eight Essays on the Mystical Interpretation of Scripture. London, 1852. 8vo.

MARSH, HERBERT.—Lectures on the Criticism and Interpretation of the
Bible. London, 1838 and 1842. 8vo.

MARTIANAY, JEAN.—Traitè methodique, ou maniere d'expliquer l'Écriture
par le secours de trois Syntaxes, la propre, la figurèe, l'harmonique.
Paris, 1704. 12mo.

———— Methode Sacrée pour apprendre et expliquer l'Ecriture Sainte par
l'Écriture même. Paris, 1716. 8vo.

MATTHAEI, G. C. R.—Uebersicht der Fehler der neutestamentlichen Exegese. Göttingen, 1835. 8vo.

MAYER, G.—Institutio interpretis sacri. Vindobonæ, 1789. 8vo.

M'CLELLAND, ALEXANDER.—Manual of Sacred Interpretation, for the Special Benefit of Junior Theological Students; but intended for private
Christians in general. New York, 1842. 12mo.

———— A Brief Treatise on the Canon and Interpretation of the Holy Scriptures. New York, 1850.
This is a second and enlarged edition of the preceding. Another revised edition
appeared in 1860

MEIER, G. F.—Versuch einer allgemeinen Auslegungskunst. Halle, 1756.
8vo.

MEYER, G. W.—Versuch einer Hermeneutik des alten Testaments. Erster
Theil, Lübeck. 1799. 8vo. Zweiter Theil, 1800. 8vo. New edition, 1812.
Rationalistic, but full of excellent thoughts; concise and comprehensive.

MEYER, G. W.—Geschichte der Schrifterklärung seit der Wiederherstellung der Wissenschaften. Göttingen, 1802-9. 5 vols. 8vo.

MEYER, LEWIS.—Philosophia Scripturae Interpres. Eleutheropolis, 1666. 4to. Edited, with preface and various notes, by J. S. Semler. Halle, 1776. 8vo.

MOEGELIN, W.—Die allegorische Bibelauslegung, besonders in der Predigt, historisch und didactisch betrachtet. Nürnberg, 1844. 8vo.

MONSPERGER, J. J.—Institutiones Hermeneuticae sacrae Veteris Testamenti praelectionibus academicis accommodatae. Pars i, Viudobonæ, 1776. 8vo. Pars ii, 1777. 8vo. Second edition, 1784.

MORUS, S. F. N.—Super Hermeneutica Novi Testamenti Acroases Academicae. Edited, with additions, by Eichstädt. Vol. i, Lips., 1797; vol. ii, 1802. 8vo.
> Consists substantially of lectures on Ernesti's Institutes.

MUENSCHER, JOSEPH.—On Types and the Typical Interpretation of Scripture. Article in the American Biblical Repository for Jan., 1841.

—— Manual of Biblical Interpretation. Gambier, Ohio, 1865. 16mo.

NEUBAUER, E. F. See RAMBACH.

NEVIN, J. W.—Sacred Hermeneutics. Article in the Mercersburg Review, for 1878, pp. 5-38.

NEWMAN, A. H. See IMMER.

NICHOLLS, BENJAMIN ELLIOT.—Introduction to the Study of the Scriptures. Published by the American S. S. Union. Phila., 1853. 8vo.
> Originally published by the London Christian Knowledge Society under the title of The Mine Explored.

NOESSELT, J. A.—Exercitationes ad Sacrarum Scriptuarum Interpretationem. Halle. 4 vols. 8vo.

OLEARIUS, J.—Elementa Hermeneuticae Sacrae cum praxi hermen. in quibusdam exemplis. Lips., 1699.

OLSHAUSEN, H.—Ein Wort über tiefern Schriftsinn. Königsberg, 1824. 8vo.

—— Die biblische Schriftauslegung; noch ein Wort über tiefern Schriftsinn. Sendschreiben an Steudel. Hamburg. 1825. 8vo.

OSTERWALD, J. F.—The Necessity and Usefulness of Reading the Holy Scriptures; and the Disposition with which they ought to be read. Translated by J. Moore. London, 1750. 18mo.

OWEN, JOHN.—The Causes, Ways, and Means of understanding the Mind of God as Revealed in his Word. Works, iii, 369.

PAGNINUS, SANCTES.—Isagoge ad Sacras Literas. Isagoge ad mysticos Sacrae Scripturae sensus. Lugduni, 1536. Folio.

PAREAU, J. H.—Institutio Interpretis Veteris Testamenti. Trajecti. 1822. 8vo.

—— Principles of Interpretation of the Old Testament. Translated from the original by Patrick Forbes. Edinburgh (Biblical Cabinet), 1835 1840. 2 vols. 12mo.
> A very excellent and useful treatise.

PAREAU, L. G.—Hermeneutica Codicis Sacri. Gronigen, 1846. 8vo.

PEIRCE, B. K.—The Word of God Opened. Its Inspiration, Canon, and Interpretation considered and illustrated. New York, 1868. 16mo.

PERION, JOACHIM.—Commentarii de optimo genere interpretandi. Paris, 1548.

PFEIFFER, AUGUSTUS.—Hermeneutica Sacra, sive luculenta de legitima Interpretatione Sacrarum Literarum Tractatus. Dresden, 1684. 12mo. Revised and enlarged, with Preface, by S. B. Carpzov (Thesaurus Hermeneuticus). Lips. and Frankf., 1690. 4to.

PFEIFFER, J. E.—Elementa Hermeneuticae Universalis, veterum atque recentiorum et proprias quasdam praeceptiones complexa. Jena, 1743. 8vo.

——— Institutiones Hermeneuticae Sacrae, veterum atque recentiorum et propria quaedam praecepta complexae. Erlangen, 1771. 8vo.

PLANCK, G. J.—Einleitung in die theologischen Wissenschaften. Lpz., 1795. 2 vols. 8vo.

——— Introduction to Sacred Philology and Interpretation. Translated from the German of G. J. Planck, by S. H. Turner. Edinburgh (Biblical Cabinet), 1834. 12mo. New York, 1834.
Worthy of repeated perusal.

RAMBACH, JOHN JAMES.—Institutiones Hermeneuticae Sacrae, variis observationibus copiosissimisque exemplis biblicis illustratae, cum praefatione J. F. Buddei. Jena, 1723. 8vo. Eighth edition, 1764.
Of this work Davidson says: "In the nature and richness of its materials, the perspicuous method in which they are presented, and the judicious use of ancient as well as modern literature, it leaves preceding works far behind."

——— Commentatio Hermeneutica de sensus mystici criteriis ex genuinis principiis deducta, necessariisque cautelis circumscripta. Jena, 1728. 8vo. Second edition, 1741.

——— Erläuterung über seine eigne Institutiones Hermeneuticae Sacrae, darin nicht nur dieses ganze Werk erklärt, imgleichen manches von ihm geändert und verbessert, sondern auch neue hermeneutische Regeln und Anmerkungen hinzugethan, alles aber mit mehr als 1000 erklärten Oertern der Schrift erläutert worden; mit einer Vorrede von der Vortrefflichkeit der rambachischen Hermeneutik, in zwei Theilen ans Licht gestellt yon E. F. Neubauer. Giessen, 1738. 4to. (See also REIERSEN.)

RANOLDER, J.—Hermeneuticae Biblicae generalis Principia rationalia Christiana et Catholica. Lips., 1839. 8vo.

RAETZE, J. G.—Die höchsten Prinzipien der Schrifterklärung. Lpz., 1814. 8vo.

RECKENBERGER, J. L.—Tractatus de studio Sacrae Hermeneuticae, in quo de ejus natura et indole, absoluta in omnibus Theologiae partibus necessitate, impedimentis ac mediis agitur. Jena, 1732. 8vo.
Chiefly based on Rambach.

REICHEL, V.—Introductio in Hermeneuticam Biblicam. Vienna, 1839. 8vo.

REIERSEN, ANDREAS.—Hermeneutica Sacra per Tabulas, seu Tabulae synopticae in Institutiones Hermeneuticae Sacrae earumque liustrationem seu Erläuterung J. J. Rambachii. Lips., 1741. 8vo.

REITMAYER, FRANZ XAVER.—Lehrbuch der biblischen Hermeneutik, herausgegeben von Thalhofer. Kempten. 1874. 8vo.

RIVET, ANDREW.—Isagoge, seu Introductio generalis ad Scripturam Sacram Veteris et Novi Testamenti. Ludg. Batav., 1627. 4to.
Chapters xiv to xxiv of this work are devoted to Hermeneutics.

ROSENMUELLER, J. G.—Historia Interpretationis Librorum Sacrorum in Ecclesia Christiana, ab Apostolorum aetate ad literarum instaurationem. Hildburg, 1795-1814. 5 vols. 12mo.
An excellent review of patristic and mediæval interpretation.

ROSENMUELLER, E. F. K.—Handbuch für die Literatur der biblischen Kritik und Exegese. Göttingen, 1797-1800. 4 vols.

SALMERON, ALPHONSO. — De Scripturae sensu literali et spirituali, etc. Opera, vol. i, pp. 69-369. Coloniæ, 1612. Folio.

SALMOND, C. D. F.—Article Hermeneutiçs in the new edition of the Encyclopædia Britannica.

SANDBICHLER. A.—Darstellung der Regeln einer allgemeinen Auslegungskunst von den Büchern des neuen und alten Bundes, nach Jahn. Salzburg, 1813. 8vo.

SAWYER, LEICESTER A.—The Elements of Biblical Interpretation, or an Exposition of the Laws by which the Scriptures are capable of being correctly interpreted, together with an Analysis of the Rationalistic and Mystic Modes of interpreting them, adapted to common Use, and designed as an Auxiliary to the Critical Study of the Bible. New Haven, 1836. 12mo.

SCHAEFER, J. N.—Ichnographia Hermeneuticae Sacrae. Maintz, 1784. 8vo.

SCHLEIERMACHER, F.—Hermeneutik und Kritik mit besonderer Rücksicht auf das neue Testament. Berlin, 1838. 8vo. (Vol. vii of his Theological Works.)
Masterly in many of its statements, but tinged with speculative philosophy.

SCHMIDT, W.—Article Hermeneutik in new edition of Herzog's Real-Encyklopädie. Lpz., 1880. Comp. LANDERER.

SCHMITTER, A.—Grundlinien der biblischen Hermeneutik. Regensb., 1844. 8vo.

SCHULER, P. H.—Geschichte der populären Schrifterklärung unter den Christen. Tübingen, 1787. 8vo.

SCOTT, J.—Principles of New Testament Quotation established and applied to Biblical Science. Edinburgh, 1875. 12mo.

SEEMILLER, SEBASTIAN.—Institutiones ad Interpretationem Sacrae Scripturae, seu Hermeneutica Sacra. Augsburg, 1779. 8vo.

SEILER, G. F. — Biblische Hermeneutik; oder Grundsätze und Regeln zur Erläuterung der heiligen Schrift des alten und neuen Testaments. Erlangen, 1800. 8vo.

—————— Biblical Hermeneutics, or the Art of Scripture Interpretation. From the German of George Frederic Seiler, with Notes, Strictures, and Supplements from the Dutch of J. Heringa. Translated from the originals, with additional notes and observations, by William Wright. London, 1835. 8vo.
Slightly rationalistic, but on the whole a very comprehensive and useful work.

SEMLER, J. S. — Vorbereitung zur theologischen Hermeneutik. Halle, 1760–69. 4 vols. 8vo.

——— Institutio brevior ad liberalem eruditionem theologicam. Halle, 1765. 8vo. See MEYER, LEWIS.

——— Apparatus ad liberalem Novi Testamenti Interpretationem. Halle, 1767. 8vo.

——— Apparatus ad liberalem Veteris Testamenti Interpretationem. Halle, 1773. 8vo.

——— Neuer Versuch, die gemeinnützige Auslegung und Anwendung des neuen Testaments zu befördern. Halle, 1786. 8vo.
All Semler's works are rich in suggestion, but replete with rationalistic errors, and have exerted a pernicious influence on German exegesis.

SETWIN, J. B.—Hermeneuticae Biblicae Institutiones theoretico-practicae secundum philologiae regulam ad analogiam fidei Ecclesiae Romanae Catholicae in compendium collatae. Vienna, 1872. 8vo.

SIMON, R.—Histoire Critique du Vieux Testament. Amst., new edition, 1685. 4to.

——— A Critical History of the Old Testament. London, 1882. 4to.
English translation of the preceding.

——— Histoire Critique des principaux Commentateurs du Nouveau Testament. Rotterdam, 1693.

SIONNET. See JANSSENS.

SIXT, G. A.—De Interpretatione universa ab Ernestio observata notulis aucta. 1785.

SIXTUS SENENSIS. — Ars interpretandi Scripturas Sacras absolutissima. Forms the third book of his Bibliotheca Sancta. Venice, 1566. Folio. Often reprinted.

SMITH, JOHN PYE.—Principles of Interpretation as applied to the Prophecies of Holy Scripture. London, 1829. Second edition, 1831.

STARK, W.—Beiträge zur Vervollkommung der Hermeneutik, insbesondere des Neuen Testament. Two Parts, Jena, 1817–18.

STAUDLIN, K. F.—De Interpretatione librorum Novi Testamenti historica non unice vera. Göttingen, 1807.

STEGMANN. See DOEDES.

STEIN, K. W.—Ueber den Begriff und den obersten Grundsatz der historischen Interpretation des neuen Testament. Lpz., 1815. 8vo.
An able and suggestive treatise.

STEINER. See GRIESBACH.

STIER, R.—Andeutungen für gläubiges Schriftverständniss im Ganzen und Einzelnen. Königsberg, 1824. 8vo.

STORR, G. C.—Opuscula Academica ad Interpretationem Librorum Sacrorum pertinentia. Tübingen, 1796. 8vo.

——— Essay on the Historical Sense of the New Testament. Translated by J. W. Gibbs. Boston, 1817. 12mo.

STOWE, C. E.—The Right Interpretation of the Holy Scriptures. The Helps and the Hindrances. Bibliotheca Sacra, 1853, pp. 34–62.

STUART, MOSES.—Hints on the Interpretation of Prophecy. Andover, 1842. 12mo.

———— Dissertations on the Importance and best Method of Studying the original Languages of the Bible, by Jahn and others. Translated from the originals, and accompanied with notes. Andover, 1827. 8vo.

These, like all of Professor Stuart's writings, are very worthy of careful perusal.

———— On the Alleged Obscurity of Prophecy. Article in the American Biblical Repository for April, 1832.

———— Translation of Hahn, On the Grammatico-Historical Interpretation of the Scriptures, with additional essay on the same subject, in American Biblical Repository for January, 1831.

————Are the same Principles of Interpretation to be applied to the Scripture as to other books. American Biblical Repository for January, 1832. See also ERNESTI.

SURENHUSIUS, W.—ספר המשוה, sive Βίβλος Καταλλαγῆς, in quo secundum Veterum Theologicorum Hebraeorum formulas allegandi, et modus interpretandi conciliantur loca ex V. in N. T. allegata. Amst., 1713. 4to.

Unsurpassed in the field it occupies.

TELLER. See TURRETIN.
TERROT. See ERNESTI.

THOLUCK, AUGUSTUS.—Beiträge zur Spracherklärung des neuen Testaments. Halle, 1832. 8vo.

———— Hints on the Interpretation of the Old Testament. Translated by R. B. Patton (vol. ii of Edinburgh Biblical Cabinet). Edinb, 1833. 16mo.

———— On the Use of the Old Testament in the New, and especially in the Epistle to the Hebrews. Translated by J. E. Ryland. (Vol. xxxix of the Biblical Cabinet). Edinburgh, 1842. 16mo. See AIKEN.

———— Hermeneutics of the Apostle Paul, with special reference to Gal. iii, 16. (Vol. xxxix Biblical Cabinet).

These last two are Dissertations at the end of Tholuck's Commentary on the Epistle to the Hebrews, and all the above are worthy of careful study.

TOELLNER, J. G.—Grundriss einer erwiesenen Hermeneutik der heiligen Schrift. Züllichau, 1765. 8vo.

Philosophical, learned, and excellent for its day.

TURNER, S. H.—Thoughts on the Origin, Character, and Interpretation of Scriptural Prophecy. New York, 1851. 12mo. See also PLANCK.

TURRETIN, J. A.—De Sacrae Scripturae interpretandae methodo Tractatus bipartitus, in quo falsae multorum interpretum hypotheses refelluntur, veraque interpretandae sacrae Scripturae methodus adstruitur. Dort, 1728. 8vo. Revised and enlarged by G. A. Teller. Frankfort, 1776. 8vo.

TURPIE, DAVID McC.—The Old Testament in the New. A Contribution to Biblical Criticism and Interpretation. London, 1868. 8vo.

UNGER, A. F.—Populäre Hermeneutik, oder Anleitung die Schrift auszulegen für Lehrer des Volkes in Schulen und Kirchen. Lpz., 1845. 8vo.

UNTERKIRCHER, C.—Hermeneutica Biblica generalis. Œniponti, 1834. 8vo.

Arigler's work of the same title adapted to the use of Romanists in Austria.

VAIL, STEPHEN M.—Hermeneutics and Homiletics; or, The Study of the Original Scriptures and Preaching. Articles in Methodist Quarterly Review for 1866, pp. 37–50 and 371–386.

VAN MILDERT, WILLIAM.—An Inquiry into the General Principles of Scripture Interpretation, in eight sermons, preached before the University of Oxford in the year 1814. (Bampton Lectures). Oxford, 1814. 8vo. Third edition, 1831.

VOLCK, W.—Section on Biblical Hermeneutics in Zöckler's Handbuch der theologischen Wissenschaften. Nördlingen, 1883. See HOFMANN.

WEMYSS, THOMAS.—A Key to the Symbolical Language of Scripture, by which numerous Passages are explained and illustrated. Edinb., 1835. 16mo.

WETTSTEIN, J. J.—Libelli ad Crisin atque Interpretationem Novi Testamenti. Halle, 1766. 12mo.

WHITAKER, WILLIAM.—On the Interpretation of Scripture. Cambridge, 1849.

Part of a disputation on Holy Scripture against the papists, especially Bellarmine and Stapleton.

WHITTAKER, JOHN WILLIAM.—An Historical and Critical Enquiry into the Interpretation of the Hebrew Scriptures. London, 1819. 8vo.

WHITBY, DANIEL.—Dissertatio de Sacrarum Scripturarum Interpretatione secundum Patrum Commentarios. Lond., 1714. 8vo.

WILKE, CHRISTIAN G.—Die Hermeneutik des neuen Testamentes systematisch dargestellt. Lpz., 1843. 8vo.

——— Biblische Hermeneutik nach katholischen Grundsätzen in streng systematischen Zusammenhange und unter Berücksichtigung der neuesten approbirten hermeneutischen Lehrbücher. Würzburg, 1853. 8vo.

WILSON, J.—The Scripture's genuine Interpreter asserted; or, a Discourse concerning the right Interpretation of Scripture. Lond., 1678. 8vo.

WINTHROP, EDWARD.—The Premium Essay on the Characteristics and Laws of Prophetic Symbols. Second edition. New York, 1854. 12mo.

WOLLIUS, C.—Hermeneutica Novi Foederis acroamatico-dogmatica certissimis defecatae philosophiae principiis corroborata eximiisque omnium Theologiae Christianae partium usibus inserviens. Lips., 1736. 4to.

Appendix to Blackwall's Auctores Sacri classici defensi et illustrati.

WORDSWORTH, C.—On the Interpretation of Scripture. An essay in Replies to Essays and Reviews. London, 1862. 8vo.

WRIGHT. See SEILER.

WYTTENBACH, DANIEL.—Elementa Hermeneuticae Sacrae, eo quo in scien tiis fieri debet, modo proposita. Marburg, 1760. 8vo.

ZACHARIAE, G. T.—Einleitung in die Auslegungskunst der heiligen Schrift. Göttingen, 1778. 8vo.

ZENKEL, G. P.—Elementa Hermeneuticae Sacrae, methodo naturali concinnata. Jena, 1752. 8vo.

INDEX TO SCRIPTURE TEXTS.

To facilitate reference each page (including foot-notes) is supposed to be divided into three nearly equal sections, designated by the letters a, b, and c. Thus, 125a denotes the upper portion of page 125 ; 125b denotes the middle section ; and 125c the lower part of of the page. The letter n following a number indicates that the passage referred to is in a foot-note. The asterisk (*) designates pages on which the text referred to receives some comment or interpretation.

GENERAL INDEX.

The different sections of the pages are designated as in the preceding Index of Scripture Texts (see page 753). The sign + denotes that the subject referred to is continued beyond the page designated.